Human Resource Management

Visit the *Human Resource Management, fifth edition* Companion Website at **www.pearsoned.co.uk/beardwell** to find valuable **student** learning material including:

- Multiple choice questions for every chapter, with instant feedback
- Questions and exercises with suggested answers for self-directed study
- Links to useful websites to facilitate independent research
- Flashcards of key terms and definitions for reference and revision
- Online glossary

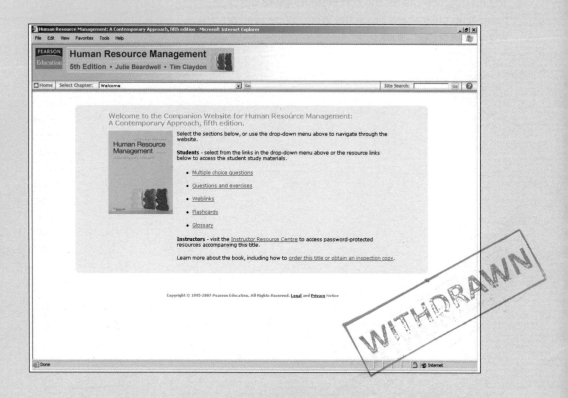

We work with leading authors to develop the strongest educational materials in business, bringing cutting-edge thinking and best learning practice to a global market.

Under a range of well-known imprints, including Financial Times Prentice Hall, we craft high quality print and electronic publications which help readers to understand and apply their content, whether studying or at work.

To find out more about the complete range of our publishing please visit us on the World Wide Web at:
www.pearsoned.co.uk

Fifth Edition

Human Resource Management

A Contemporary Approach

Edited by

Julie Beardwell
Leeds Metropolitan University

Tim Claydon
De Monfort University, Leicester

WITHDRAWN

FT Prentice Hall
FINANCIAL TIMES

An imprint of **Pearson Education**
Harlow, England • London • New York • Boston • San Francisco • Toronto
Sydney • Tokyo • Singapore • Hong Kong • Seoul • Taipei • New Delhi
Cape Town • Madrid • Mexico City • Amsterdam • Munich • Paris • Milan

Pearson Education Limited

Edinburgh Gate
Harlow
Essex CM20 2JE
England

and Associated Companies throughout the world

Visit us on the World Wide Web at:
www.pearsoned.co.uk

First edition published in Great Britain in 1994
Second edition 1997
Third edition 2001
Fourth edition 2004
Fifth edition published 2007

© Longman Group Limited 1994
© Financial Times Professional Limited 1997
© Pearson Education Limited 2001, 2007

ISBN: 978-0-273-70763-9

British Library Cataloguing-in-Publication Data
A catalogue record for this book is available from the British Library

Library of Congress Cataloging-in-Publication Data
A catalog record for this book is available from the Library of Congress

10 9 8 7 6 5 4 3 2 1
11 10 09 08 07

Typeset in 10/12pt Minion by 30
Printed and bound by Graficàs Estella, Bilbao, Spain

The publisher's policy is to use paper manufactured from sustainable forests.

Contents

5 Human resource planning
Julie Beardwell 157

6 Recruitment and selection
Julie Beardwell 189

7 Managing equality and diversity
Mike Noon 225

Part 2 Case study:
Teacher shortages 254

Part 3
DEVELOPING THE HUMAN RESOURCE

8 Learning and development
Audrey Collin 260

9 Human resource development: the organisational and national framework
Mairi Watson 307

Preface

This fifth edition is the first edition of this text that has not been co-edited and contributed to by Len Holden. The book was in many ways Len's brainchild and the fact that the book goes on even though he has relinquished his role is a tribute to the quality of the vision that he and Ian Beardwell shared nearly fifteen years ago. As new co-editors we have tried to ensure that this edition maintains the analytical and critical standard that they set in earlier ones.

HRM is a continually evolving field of practice and study. In its successive editions this book has tried to reflect critically upon new developments as the issues and policies that have become associated with it have multiplied considerably. Previous editions have traced the debates over the role of the HRM specialist within organisations, the role and nature of HRM in relation to organisational change initiatives such as total quality management (TQM), and the strategic role of HRM and its effect on organisational performance. They also addressed the implications for HRM of the emergence of new concepts such as the learning organisation and the knowledge-based organisation and new approaches to employee involvement (EI) and empowerment.

In the last edition we noted how in academic circles the search for a universal HRM paradigm has given way to an emphasis on understanding how HRM operates in diverse situations and what contribution it can make to the effectiveness and profitability of the organisation. Particular attention was paid to concepts such as high performance work systems, the resource-based view of HRM and 'bundles' of HR policies. That edition also examined the operation of HRM across national boundaries, reflecting the growing importance of multinational companies and the globalising trends in the world economy.

This edition continues to explore these themes and to reflect further developments in the field, including changes in employees' legal rights, developments in employee involvement and the implications of the continuing emphasis on the need to raise skills and compete in world markets on the basis of skills and knowledge. We have paid particular attention to the final section dealing with comparative and international HRM in order to address more fully the issues for HRM raised by globalisation. There are new chapters that discuss whether distinctive national patterns of HRM can survive in the face of US-led globalisation, how HRM is developing in the rapidly growing economies of China and India, and the ways in which multinational companies are influencing not only HRM ideas and practice across the globe but also the national and international policy environments within which HRM operates. A single volume cannot encompass the huge area in and around the HRM sphere, and we apologise for any omissions. Nevertheless, we have covered the broad sweep of the HRM field and some aspects in considerable detail.

We would again like to thank our long-standing contributors and those who are making their first appearance in this edition for their hard work and willing cooperation in getting this edition to press. We would also like to thank partners, family members and colleagues for their help and support in the arduous process of academic writing. Finally, we would like to thank our editors at Pearson for their enthusiastic help and encouragement.

Julie Beardwell
Tim Claydon

Guided tour

Chapter 2

Strategic human resource management

Nicky Golding

Objectives

- To indicate the significance of the business context in developing an understanding of the meaning and application of SHRM.
- To analyse the relationship between strategic management and SHRM.
- To examine the different approaches to SHRM including:
  - the best-fit approach to SHRM;
  - the configurational approach to SHRM;
  - the resource based view of SHRM
  - the best-practice approach to SHRM.
- To evaluate the relationship between SHRM and organisational performance.
- To present a number of activities and case studies that will facilitate the reader's understanding of the nature and complexity of the SHRM debate, and enable the reader to apply their knowledge and understanding.

Introduction to strategic human resource management

This chapter charts the development of strategic human resource management. It assumes a certain familiarity with the evolution of HRM, early HRM models and frameworks and their theoretical underpinning as discussed in other chapters and particularly Chapter 1. The aim of this chapter is to provide a challenging and critical analysis of the strategic human resource management literature, so that you will be able to understand the synthesis both within and between strategic human resource management and strategic management in its various forms.

Since the early 1980s when human resource management arrived on the managerial agenda, there has been considerable debate concerning its nature and its value to organisations. From the seminal works emerging from the Chicago school and the matching model of HRM (Fombrun, Tichy and Devanna, 1984) the emphasis has very much concerned its *strategic* role in the organisation. Indeed the now large literature rarely differentiates between human resource management (HRM) and strategic human resource management (SHRM). While some writers have associated HRM with the strategic aspects and concerns of 'best-fit',

34

Objectives provide an overview of the topics to be covered in each chapter, giving a clear indication of what you should expect to learn.

THE SYSTEMATIC APPROACH

Figure 2.2

Emergent strategy

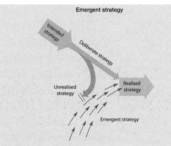

Source: Reprinted by permission of Harvard Business Review. From 'Crafting Strategy' by Mintzberg, H., July–August 1987. Copyright © 1987 by the Harvard Business School Publishing Corporation, all rights reserved.

is these pluralist tensions that are sometimes ignored in certain branches of the SHRM literature, most notably the 'best-practice' approach.

Stop & think

Can you think of reasons why an intended strategy might not be realised? Why do strategies sometimes emerge?

Illustrate your answers with examples from your own experience. If you do not have organisational examples, reflect upon your personal development so far.

What factors have influenced your choice of university? degree subject? career?, etc. Have you followed your original plans? What changes have you made? Have new strategies emerged? Using Mintzberg's model, you could plot your development so far on a time-line, identifying where and why planned strategies have failed to be realised while new ones have emerged.

The systemic approach

This leads us on to the final perspective identified by Whittington (1993, 2001), the systemic approach. The systemic approach suggests that strategy is shaped by the social system it operates within. Strategic choices, therefore, are shaped by the cultural and institutional interests of a broader society. So for example, state intervention in France and Germany has shaped HRM in a way which is different to the USA and the UK. A key theme of the systemic approach is that 'decision makers are not detached, calculating individuals interacting in purely economic transactions' (Whittington, 2001: 26) but are members of a community 'rooted in a densely interwoven social system'. Therefore in reality, organisations and their members' choices are embedded in a network of social relations (Whittington, 1993). Thus according to this approach, organisations differ according to the social and economic systems in which they are embedded.

41

Figures are used to illustrate key points, models, theories and processes.

Stop & think: readers are frequently invited to reflect critically, challenge their assumptions and relate to their own experience.

Activity

Try to answer these questions with regard to your organisation or one you are familiar with. Alternatively, you could use the case study 'Café Expresso' at the end of this chapter.

This approach has further implications for the role of human resource managers in a firm, as they need to understand the economic consequences of human resource practices and understand where they fit in the value chain. Barney and Wright (1998: 42) suggest that the human resources function needs to be able to explore the following questions:

- Who are your internal customers and how well do you know their part of the business?
- Are there organisational policies and practices that make it difficult for your internal clients to be successful?
- What services do you provide? What services should you provide? What services should you not provide?
- How do these services reduce internal customers' costs/increase their revenues?
- Can these services be provided more efficiently by outside vendors?
- Can you provide these services more efficiently?
- Do managers in the HR function understand the economic consequence of their jobs?

The value of an organisation's resources is not sufficient alone, however, for sustainable competitive advantage, because if other organisations possess the same value, then it will only provide *competitive parity*. Therefore an organisation needs to consider the next stage of the framework: rarity.

Rarity

The HR manager needs to consider how to develop and exploit rare characteristics of a firm's human resources to gain competitive advantage.

Nordstrom is an interesting case, because they operate in a highly competitive retail industry where you would usually expect a lower level of skill and subsequently high labour turnover. Nordstrom, however, focused on individual salespeople as a key source of its competitive advantage. It therefore invested in attracting and retaining young college-educated people who were looking for a career in retailing. To ensure horizontal integration, it also provided a highly incentive-based compensation system (up to twice the industry average)

Box 2.2

Please read the following extract:

Nordstrom exists in the highly competitive retailing industry. This industry is usually characterised as having relatively low skill requirements and high turnover for sales clerks. Nordstrom, however, has attempted to focus on individual salespersons as the key to its competitive advantage. It invests in attracting and retaining young, college-educated sales clerks who desire a career in retailing. It provides a highly incentive-based compensation system that allows Nordstrom's salespersons to make as much as twice the industry average in pay. The Nordstrom culture encourages sales clerks to make heroic efforts to attend to customers' needs, even to the point of changing a customer's tyre in the parking lot. The recruiting process, compensation practices, and culture at Nordstrom have helped the organisation to maintain the highest sales per square foot of any retailer in the nation.

Source: Barney J.B. and Wright P.M. On becoming a strategic partner: the role of human resources in gaining competitive advantage, *Human Resource Management*, Spring, 1998, vol. 37, no 1, 34.

Question

How did Nordstrom exploit the rare characteristics of their employees?

Activities appear throughout the text to reinforce learning with problems and practical exercises.

Boxes contain a variety of business examples to put theory into practice.

Summary

The chapter began by outlining seven key objectives and these are revisited here...

- Human resource planning can be interpreted in a number of different ways. For some it means the same as manpower planning, for others it is significantly different and has many similarities to HRM. The definition used in this chapter relates to HRP as a set of distinct activities that incorporates both the hard elements associated with manpower planning and some of the softer elements associated with HRM.
- The key stages in the traditional human resource planning process are investigation and analysis, forecasting demand and supply, developing action plans to address any imbalance, implementing the plans and evaluating their effectiveness.
- Methods of demand forecasting discussed are time series, ratio analysis, work study, managerial judgement, the Delphi technique and working back from budgets. Quantitative methods can be problematic as the extrapolation of past data might be inappropriate in a changing environment but they can provide a reasonable starting point for forecasts. Qualitative methods are more flexible but can be manipulated for political ends. Supply forecasting tends to focus mainly on various analyses of labour turnover and stability and movement through an organisation. Quantitative analysis can help to highlight problem areas but gives little indication about how problems might be addressed. Qualitative data can help to address this gap but can sometimes be difficult to obtain. Organisations can exacerbate problems if they are not seen to act on the information they receive.
- A more contemporary approach to HRP aims to enable the organisation to adapt to an uncertain and changing environment and emphasises the need to develop a well-trained and flexible workforce. Variants to HRP include micro-planning, contingency planning, succession planning, skills planning and soft human resource planning.
- The main advantages of HRP are that plans can help reduce uncertainty, can build flexibility and can contribute to vertical and horizontal integration. The key disadvantages relate to difficulties of predicting an uncertain future, the lack of necessary data to make accurate predictions and the absence of clear business plans.
- Evidence of HRP in practice is varied but the dominant approach seems to view HR as the 'dependent variable' and tends to be tentative and incremental rather than systematic.
- HRP's main role in SHRM is as a means to facilitate the integration of HR strategy with business strategy and to ensure that HR policies and practice are compatible with each other. In addition, some studies associate formal planning activity with improved organisational performance, particularly if planning is sustained over a number of years. The key emphasis, however, needs to be on building adaptability and managing change.

QUESTIONS

1 To what extent can forecasting activity influence the effectiveness of human resource plans?

2 Why should organisations be concerned with labour turnover and what steps can they take to address the issue?

3 Contemporary organisations increasingly operate in a dynamic and uncertain environment. Does this reduce or increase the need for human resource planning activity? Justify your answer.

The **Summary** allows you to recap and review your understanding of the main points of the chapter.

Questions can be used for self-testing, class exercises or debates.

CHAPTER 2 STRATEGIC HUMAN RESOURCE MANAGEMENT

CASE STUDY

Café Expresso

Café Expreso is one of the three main players in the 'coffee house' industry, which now has more than 6000 stores across the globe, 500 of which are in the UK and Ireland. They employ 7000 staff in the UK alone and serve 35 million customers in their stores across the globe each week.

The coffee industry is particularly robust, with coffee being the second most valuable commodity in the world after oil, with global retail sales estimated to be £39.2 billion. A total of 6.7 million tonnes of coffee were produced annually in 1998–2000, which is forecast to rise to 7 million tonnes by 2010.

The number of coffee bars in the high street has increased considerably in recent years, with the market being dominated by three main players. The 'coffee house' business therefore, is very competitive with coffee chains constantly looking for innovative ways of achieving sustainable competitive advantage, to remain ahead of their rivals.

Café Expresso had enjoyed first mover advantage in the marketplace and had rapidly grown to number one position, which they had retained for 15 years. In recent years, however, they have lost market share to rival competitors who have copied Café Expresso's business model and poached key staff to deliver it and subsequently customers had followed. This had resulted in Café Expresso slipping to the number three position. This loss of market share had forced them to rethink their strategy and a new charismatic chief executive, Ben Thomson, had been appointed in 2005 to turn the business around.

In reviewing Café Expresso's current strategy Ben Thomson embarked on an international fact finding tour of their coffee bars to meet staff and customers to get a feel for the nature of the business, together with rival coffee houses to gain an understanding of their source of competitive advantage. He wanted to return Café Expresso to the number one position in the marketplace. His review identified customers who were loyal to the brand of Café Expresso but had been enticed away by the experience, the variety of coffee and level of customer service offered by their competitors. His review of human resources found a high level of staff turnover, due to the minimum wage offered and the high percentage of international employees who tended to be employed on short-term contracts. The recent loss of market share and high employee turnover had led to low morale amongst remaining staff, as they felt Café Expresso's bars were

dated and the range of coffees limited. Ben Thomson's review of the competitors supported this, as he identified the significance of the 'coffee drinking experience' which was delivered through appropriate décor, ambience, variety in the range of products and most importantly of all, the *barista* or 'coffee seller'. He identified these as key sources of added value and competitive advantage.

Ben Thomson decided to relaunch Café Expresso's business strategy with a new vision: 'To be the number one coffee house of choice across the globe' and identified the following mission: Experience Café Expresso, we don't just sell coffee we provide customers with an unforgettable experience. This was encapsulated in his value statement: 'Nowhere else makes you feel this good.' which he believed should apply to staff as well as customers. He was convinced that the success of coffee bars lay not just in selling coffee as a product, but in selling the 'coffee house' experience. To achieve this he felt that Café Expresso's human resources would be crucial to the success of his strategy. He recognised that human resources would face a difficult task, as the coffee house industry is traditionally renowned for low pay (minimum wage being the norm) and high employee turnover (50–100 per cent being the norm), yet the baristas (coffee sellers) are crucial to the success of the business and the selling of the coffee house experience.

He identified the following priorities:

Business

- To be the number one coffee house across the globe.
- To attract new customers through reputation for providing the coffee house experience.
- To retain existing customers through loyalty service.

Customer service

- Commitment to excellence.
- Internal and external customers valued.
- Sell the barista experience.

People

- Diversity and individuality valued.
- Knowledge and talent encouraged and retained.
- Pride and enthusiasm valued.
- Reward to retain.

76

Case studies, at the end of each chapter and part, help consolidate your learning of major themes by applying them to real-life examples.

CHAPTER 2 STRATEGIC HUMAN RESOURCE MANAGEMENT

Useful websites

Confederation of British Industry	www.cbi.org.uk
Chartered Institute of Personnel and Development	www.cipd.co.uk
Department of Trade and Industry	www.dti.gov.uk
Detailed information about EVA	www.evanomics.com
Chartered Institute of Management	www.managers.org.uk
Personnel Today Journal	www.personneltoday.com
Strategic Management Society	www.csmintl.premierdomain.com/menu.htm

References and further reading

Those texts marked with an asterisk are recommended for further reading.

Abell, D.F. (1993) *Managing with Dual Strategies: Mastering the Present, Pre-empting the Future.* New York: Free Press.

Ahmad, S. and Schroeder, R.G. (2003) 'The impact of human resource management practices on operational performance: recognising country and industry differences', *Journal of Operations Management*, 21, 19–34.

Aktouf, O. (1996) *Traditional management and beyond: a matter of renewal.* Montreal: Gaetan Morin.

Alchian, A. and Demsetz, H. (1972) 'Production information costs and economic organisation', *American Economic Review*, 62, 777–795.

Amit, R. and Shoemaker, P. (1993) 'Strategic assets and organisational rent', *Strategic Management Journal*, 14, 33–46.

Ansoff, H.I., (1965) *Corporate Strategy.* Harmondsworth: Penguin.

Ansoff, H.I. and McDonnell, E. (1990) *Implanting Strategic Management* 2nd edn., Hemel Hempstead: Prentice Hall.

Applebaum, E., Bailey, T., Berg, P. and Kalleberg, A. (2000) *Manufacturing Competitive Advantage: Why high-performance systems pay off.* Ithaca, NY: ILR Press.

Applebaum, E. and Batt, R (1994) *The New American Workplace.* Ithaca, NY: ILR Press.

Armstrong, M. and Baron (2002) *Strategic Human Resource Management, A Guide to Action*, 2nd edn. London: CIPD.

Arthur, J. (1994) 'Effects of human resource systems on manufacturing performance and turnover', *Academy of Management Journal*, 37, 3: 670–687.

Atkinson, J. (1984) Manpower strategies for the flexible organisation', *Personnel Management*, August, 28–31.

Baden-Fuller, C. (1995) 'Strategic innovation, corporate entrepreneurship and matching outside-in to inside-out approaches to strategy research', *British Journal of Management*, 6 (special issue), 3–16.

Bae, J. and Lawler, J.J. (2000) 'Organisational and HRM strategies in Korea: impact on firm performance in an emerging economy', *Academy of Management Journal*, 43, 587–597.

Bahrami, H. (1992) 'The emerging flexible organisation: perspectives from Silicon Valley', *California Management Review*, 34, 4: 33–48.

Baird, L. and Meshoulam, I. (1988) 'Managing two fits of strategic human resource management', *Academy of Management Review*, 13 1: 116–28.

Bamberger, P. and Phillips, B. (1991) 'Organisational environment and business strategy: parallel versus conflicting influences on human resource strategy in the pharmaceutical industry', *Human Resource Management*, 30, 2: 153–82.

Barney, J.B. (1991) 'Firm resources and sustained competitive advantage', *Journal of Management*, 17, 1: 99–120.

Barney, J. (1995) 'Looking inside for competitive advantage', *Academy of Management Executive*, 9, 4: 49–61.

Barney, J.B. and Wright P.M. (1998) 'On becoming a strategic partner: the role of human resources in gaining competitive advantage', *Human Resource Management*, 37, 1.

Barr, P., Stimpert, J. and Huff, A. (1992) 'Cognitive change, strategic action, and organisational renewal', *Strategic Management Journal*, 13, 15–36.

Batt, R. (2002). 'Managing customer services: human resource practices, quit rates and sales growth' *Academy of Management Journal*, 45, 587–597.

Becker, B. and Gerhart, B. (1996) 'The impact of human resource management on organisational performance: progress and prospects', *Academy of Management Journal*, 39, 4: 779–801.

Becker, B.E., Huselid, M.A., Pickus, P.S. and Spratt, M.F. (1997) 'HR as a source of shareholder value: research and recommendations', *Human Resource Management*, 36, 1: spring, 39–47.

Beer, M., Spector, B., Lawrence, P.R., Quinn Mills, D. and Walton, R.E. (1984) *Managing Human Assets.* New York: Free Press.

Beer, M., Spector, B., Lawrence, P., Quinn Mills, D. and Walton, R., (1985) *Human Resource Management: A General Managers Perspective.* New York: Free Press.

Berg, P. (1999) 'The effects of high performance work practices on job satisfaction in the US steel industry', *Industrial Relations*, 54, 111–35.

Blyton, P. and Turnbull, P. (1992) (eds) *Reassessing HRM.* London: Sage.

Boxall, P. (1992) 'Strategic human resource management: beginnings of a new theoretical sophistication', *Human Resource Management Journal*, 2, 3: 60–79.

Boxall, P. (1996) 'The strategic HRM debate and the resource-based view of the firm', *Human Resource Management Journal*, 6, 3: 59–75.

*Boxall, P. and Purcell, J. (2003) *Strategy and Human Resource Management.* Houndmills: Palgrave Macmillan.

Boxall, P. and Steeneveld, M. (1999) 'Human resource strategy and competitive advantage: a longitudinal study of engineering consultancies', *Journal of Management Studies*, 36, 443–463.

78

References, **further reading** and **useful websites** support the chapter by giving printed and electronic sources for additional study.

Supporting resources

Visit **www.pearsoned.co.uk/beardwell** to find valuable online resources.

Companion Website for students

- Multiple choice questions for every chapter, with instant feedback
- Questions and exercises with suggested answers for self-directed study
- Links to useful websites to facilitate independent research
- Flashcards of key terms and definitions for reference and revision
- Online glossary

For instructors

- Lecturer's Guide with teaching notes and ideas
- PowerPoint slides, including figures and tables, for each chapter of the text

Also: The Companion Website provides the following features:

- Search tool to help locate specific items of content
- E-mail results and profile tools to send results of quizzes to instructors
- Online help and support to assist with website usage and troubleshooting

For more information please contact your local Pearson Education sales representative or visit **www.pearsoned.co.uk/beardwell**

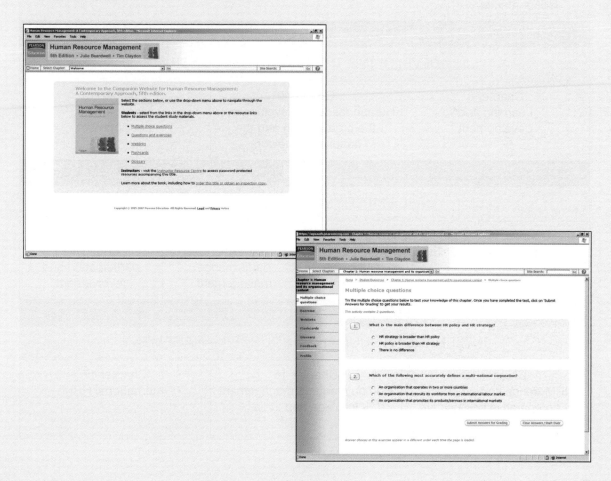

Plan of the book

Part 1		
HUMAN RESOURCE MANAGEMENT AND ITS ORGANISATIONAL CONTEXT		
Chapter 1 An introduction to human resource management	Chapter 2 Strategic human resource management	Chapter 3 Contextualising HRM: developing critical thinking

Part 2			
RESOURCING THE ORGANISATION			
Chapter 4 Human resource management and the labour market	Chapter 5 Human resource planning	Chapter 6 Recruitment and selection	Chapter 7 Managing equality and diversity

Part 3		
DEVELOPING THE HUMAN RESOURCE		
Chapter 8 Learning and development	Chapter 9 Human resource development: the organisation and the national framework	Chapter 10 Management development

Part 4			
THE EMPLOYMENT RELATIONSHIP			
Chapter 11 The employment relationship and employee rights at work	Chapter 12 Establishing the terms and conditions of employment	Chapter 13 Reward and performance management	Chapter 14 Employee participation and involvement

Part 5		
INTERNATIONAL HUMAN RESOURCE MANAGEMENT		
Chapter 15 HRM trends and prospects: a comparative perspective	Chapter 16 Human resource management in China and India	Chapter 17 International HRM

How to use this book

This text is designed to meet the needs of a range of students who are studying HRM either as a core or option subject on undergraduate degrees in Business and Social Science, MBAs, specialised Master's programmes, or for the CIPD's professional development scheme (PDS).

All the chapters are designed to take a critically evaluative approach to their subject material. This means that the book is not written in a prescriptive or descriptive style as are some other HRM textbooks, though there will be sections that must necessarily incorporate aspects of that approach. Some chapters will also be more easily absorbable by the novice student than others. For example. Chapters 1 (Introduction to HRM) and 2 (Strategic HRM) are good introductions to the subject, while Chapter 3 takes a more unusual perspective on contextualising HRM and developing critical thinking that will prove rewarding to the more able student. Likewise, Chapter 8 is a demanding and stimulating introduction to the processes of learning and development, whilst Chapter 9 contains more elements of what the student might expect in a chapter on HRD.

This edition features Activities and 'Stop and think' exercises throughout the text. These are to give readers pause for thought to help them absorb and understand the concepts and ideas in both a practical and theoretical context. As in earlier editions, there are case studies, exercises, activities and questions at the end of each part. These can be used by lecturers as course work exercises and the Lecturer's Guide that accompanies this edition gives detailed suggested answers. Additional material is also available on the companion website.

The outlines which follow are intended to indicate how the material in this book can be used to cover the requirements for a selection of post-graduate programmes. There is no corresponding outline for undergraduates because of the multiplicity of courses at this level which individual tutors will have devised. Nevertheless, it is hoped that these suggested 'routes' through the book will be helpful guidelines for tutors who have responsibility for some or all of these programmes.

MBA Route

Introduction: Chapters 1, 2, 3
Core: Chapters 4, 5, 6, 9, 11, 12, 13, 14, 15
Options: Chapters 7, 8, 10, 16, 17

MA/MSc Route

Introduction: Chapters 1, 2, 3, 4
Core: Chapters 5, 6, 9, 11, 12, 13, 14, 15
Options: Chapters 7, 8, 10, 16, 17

CIPD Professional Development Scheme

People Management and Development: Chapters 1, 2, 3, 4, 5, 6, 7, 9, 11, 12, 13
People Resourcing: Chapters 4, 5, 6, 7, 13
Learning and Development: Chapters 8, 9, 10
Employee Relations: Chapters 7, 11, 12, 14
Employee Reward: Chapter 13
Advanced Practitioner Standards: Chapters 1, 2, 15, 16, 17

CIPD specialist modules may be supported by the use of relevant chapters, for example:
Managing diversity and equality: Chapters 4, 7
Managing organisational learning and knowledge: Chapters 8, 9 and 10

Contributors

Phil Almond, BSc, MA, PhD, is Reader in International Human Resource Management at De Montfort University. His main research interests are international and comparative HRM and he also has an active research interest in industrial relations in France. He is a member of an international team of researchers investigating the HRM practices of American-owned multinational companies and has recently edited, *American Multinationals in Europe: Managing Employment Relations across National Borders*.

Julie Beardwell, BA, MA, CFCIPD is Associate Dean and Head of HRM/OB at Leeds Metropolitan University. She took up this post in 2006 after fifteen years in the HRM department at De Montfort University. She is joint series editor for the HR Series published by Elsevier and she is a member of the CIPD's standards moderating team. Her main research interests concern people management in small and medium-sized enterprises.

Peter Butler, BA, MA, PhD is Lecturer in Industrial Relations in the Department of Human Resource Management, De Montfort University. He teaches Industrial Relations at undergraduate and postgraduate level. Prior to his current appointment he was at the Centre for Labour Market Studies, University of Leicester, working on the ESRC funded project *Learning to Work*. He has written on non-union employee representation and the management of managerial careers in US-owned multinational companies.

Ian Clark, BA, MA, PGCE, PhD, is Reader in Industrial Relations and HRM at Birmingham University. Ian has written extensively on industrial relations and economic performance and the influence of the American business system on HRM and industrial relations in the UK. Recognised both nationally and internationally as an expert on Americanisation, in 2000 Ian published a well-received monograph on the international relations of industrial relations. Together with former colleagues at De Montfort, Ian recently completed a large ESRC and Anglo-German Foundation-funded

multi-country study which examined HRM and industrial relations in subsidiaries of US multinationals. An innovative aspect of this project was its corporate and subsidiary level empirical research. In addition to this, together with Trevor Colling, Ian developed the analysis of sector effects as a conceptual category that complements and further develops the analysis of country of origin and host country effects in international HRM. Ian is currently researching the impact of shareholder value approaches to corporate strategy on HRM and the role of private equity firms in the market for corporate control.

Tim Claydon, BSc, MSc (econ), PhD, is head of the Department of Human Resource Management at Leicester Business School, De Montfort University. He has written on trade union history, union derecognition, union–management partnership and ethical issues in HRM. His current interests include contemporary changes in work and employment and developments in trade unionism in the UK, Europe and the USA.

Audrey Collin, BA, DipAn, PhD, is Emeritus Professor of Career Studies, De Montfort University. Her early career was in personnel management, and she is now MCIPD. She was awarded a PhD for her study of mid-career change; she has researched and published on career and lifespan studies, mentoring, and the employment of older people. She has co-edited (with Richard A. Young) two books on career which reflect her questioning of traditional understandings of career and her commitment to interpretative research approaches. Now formally retired, she continues her writing on career for the international academic readership, while also addressing the relationship between theory and practice.

Trevor Colling, BA, MA, LLM is Senior Lecturer in Industrial Relations at the University of Warwick, having moved from De Montfort University in April 2005. He has written and published widely on public sector industrial relations, particularly the implications of privatisation and contracting out. More recently he has been researching and writing on employment practices of US multinationals and trade union roles in the enforcement of individual employment rights.

Mike Doyle, BA, MA, is Principal Lecturer in Human Resource Management, De Montfort University. He teaches on a range of postgraduate management programmes in the area of management development and organisational change. His current research interests include the exploration of major change initiatives in public and private sector organisations and the selection and development of middle managers as 'change agents'.

Linda Glover, BA, MBA, PhD, is Principal Lecturer in Human Resource Management, De Montfort University. She teaches on undergraduate and post-graduate programmes and is involved in a number of research projects. Linda has managed industry-funded research projects that have been investigating employee responses to quality management and HRM. She has also worked with Olga Tregaskis and Anthony Ferner on a CIPD-sponsored project examining the role of international HRM committees in transferring HR knowledge across borders within multinational companies. She has also collaborated with Noel Sui of Hong Kong Baptist University on a project examining the human resource issues associated with the management of quality in the People's Republic of China and she has written on the human resource problems associated with managing the subsidiaries of multinational companies.

Nicky Golding, BA, MSc, CIPD is a Senior Lecturer in Human Resource Management, De Montfort University. She lectures on a range of postgraduate and post experience courses in the area of Strategic Human Resource Management and Learning & Development. She has led and been involved in a range of consultancy projects in the public and private sector, advising senior management teams on SHRM and the management of change. Her current research interests are in exploring the relationship between SHRM and organisational performance.

Sue Marlow, BA, MA, PhD, is Professor of Small Business and Entrepreneurship at De Montfort University, Leicester. Sue has researched and published extensively in the area of small firms with a particular interest in women in self-employment, labour management, employment regulation, and training. She has recently co-edited a book for Routledge on employment relations in smaller firms and has been to the USA as a Visiting Professor to lecture on entrepreneurship and gender issues.

Mike Noon, BA, MSc, PhD, is Professor of Human Resource Management at Queen Mary, University of London. He has previously researched and taught at Imperial College, London; Cardiff Business School; Lancaster University; and De Montfort University. His research interests include: the effects of work transformation on employees and managers; equality and discrimination; and contemporary developments in HRM. He has published widely in academic journals, and his new books are: *The Realities of Work* (third edition, 2006, co-authored with Paul Blyton, published by Palgrave) and *A Dictionary of Human Resource Management* (second edition, 2007, co-authored with Ed Heery, published by Oxford University Press).

Julia Pointon, BA, MA, PGCE, CIPD, is Principal Lecturer in Organisational Behaviour and HRM in the Department of Human Resource Management at De Montfort University. She teaches on a range of undergraduate and postgraduate courses and is Course Director of the MA in International Business and HRM and the MA in Personnel and Development. She is a committee member of the CIPD National Upgrading Panel, serves on the CIPD membership and Education Committee and is Chair of the CIPD branch in Leicester.

Alan J. Ryan, BA, LLM, is a Senior Lecturer in the Department of HRM at De Montfort University. His teaching is focused on the implications of legal change for the management of people at work and the development of managerial responses to legislative activity. He teaches courses at undergraduate and postgraduate level as well as delivering courses and programmes to corporate clients. His research interest lies in the development of soft systems analysis as a way of understanding changes in managerial behaviour following the introduction of legislation. He has undertaken some consultancy work in both the private and the voluntary sector. He has written on reward management, participation regimes in SMEs and the legal implications of flexibility.

Amanda Thompson, BA, MA, CertEd, FCIPD, is Principal Lecturer in Human Resource Management at Leicester Business School, De Montfort University. She teaches gender studies at undergraduate level and leads modules in employee resourcing on both taught and distance learning postgraduate programmes. She is also Programme Leader of the Postgraduate Diploma in Personnel Management. Amanda is currently involved in a research project with Professor Susan Marlow to explore labour management processes in medium-sized enterprises.

Olga Tregaskis is a Senior Research Fellow in the Department of Human Resource Management at De Montfort University, having spent a number of years working at Cranfield School of Management where she also attained her PhD. She has published journal articles and book chapters on international and comparative HRM with a specific focus on organisational learning in multinational companies. Her research has attracted funding from international and national bodies including the European Union and Economic and Social Research Council (ESRC) and private companies including the Charter Institute of Personnel and Development.

Anita Trivedi, BA, MA, MSc, PhD, is a Lecturer in International Human Resource Management in the Department of Human Resource Management, De Montfort University. Her research interests include globalisation and its impact on economic development and social change; multinational corporations and international HRM; comparative industrial relations and social movements; spatial globalisation, urban processes and politics; and political economy of India. She has worked in industry for a few years and teaches on a range of undergraduate and postgraduate management programmes.

Mairi Watson, LLB, LLM, MBA, PGCE, MCIM is a Senior Lecturer in Organisational Behaviour and Human Resource Management at De Montfort University. Mairi brings her previous professional experience as a senior manager in the Prison Service and as director of a management and leadership development consultancy to her role. She teaches on a range of undergraduate, postgraduate and professional programmes. Mairi's research interests are managerial perceptions of the process of change, organisational experiences of learning and development and the pedagogic impact of online learning. Mairi received a Vice Chancellor's Distinguished Teaching Award in 2006 from De Montfort University.

Acknowledgements

Special thanks are due to the following reviewers, approached by the publishers, for their valued insightful and constructive comments that have helped shape the contents of this present edition:

Alhajie Saidy Khan, Keele University, UK
Andrew Charlwood, University of Leeds, UK
Chris Rowley, Cass Business School, City University, London
David Bright, University of Hull, UK
Denise Thursfield, University of Hull, UK
Geoff Tame, University of Northumbria, UK
James Richards, Herriot-Watt University, UK
John Geary, University College Dublin, Ireland
Marius Meyer, University of South Africa, SA
Mats Ehrnrooth, Swedish School of Economics and Business Administration, Finland
Mike Flynn, University of Wales Institute Cardiff, UK
Nigel Bassett-Jones, Oxford Brookes University, UK
Roger Brown, Coventry University, UK
Sheila McCallum, Thames Valley University, UK
Sue Hutchinson, Bath University, UK
Vaughan Ellis, Glasgow Caledonian University & Sterling University, UK

We are grateful to the following for permission to reproduce copyright material:
Figure 1.1 from *Strategic Human Resource Management*, John Wiley (Fornbrun, C.J. *et al.* 1984); Figure 1.2 from *Managing Human Assets*, Free Press (Beer, M. *et al.* 1984); Table 1.1 from *New Perspectives on Human Resource Management*, Thomson Learning (Storey, J. 1989); Figure 1.3 from *Strategy and Human Resource Management*, Palgrave Macmillan (Boxall, P. and Purcell, J. 2003); Table 1.4 from 'Role Call', in *People Management*, 16 June 2005, CIPD (Ulrich, D. and Brockbank, W. 2005) with permission from D. Ulrich and W. Brockbank; Figure 1.4 from 'Commonalities and contradictions in HRM and performance research', in *Human Resource Management Journal* Vol. 15 No. 3, Blackwell Publishing (Boselie, *et al.* 2005) adapted from Strategic human resource management and performance and introduction in *The International Journal of Human Resource Management*, Vol. 8 No. 3, http://www.tandf.co.uk/journals, Taylor & Francis Ltd (Paauwe, J. and Richardson, R. 1997); Figure 2.1 and Table 2.9 from *Contemporary Strategy Analysis: Concepts, Techniques, Applications*, 4/e, Blackwell Publishing (Grant, R.M. 2002); Figure 2.2 reprinted by permission of *Harvard Business Review*. From 'Crafting Strategy' by Mintzberg, H., July–August 1987. Copyright © 1987 by the Harvard

Business School Publishing Corporation, all rights reserved; Figure 2.3 and Table 2.1 from *What is Strategy and Does it Matter?*, Thomson Learning (Whittington, R. 2001), p. 3 and p. 39; Table 2.2 from ACADEMY OF MANAGEMENT EXECUTIVE by SCHULER, R. & JACKSON, S. Copyright 1987 by ACADEMY OF MANAGEMENT (NY). Reproduced with permission of ACADEMY OF MANAGEMENT (NY) in the format Textbook via Copyright Clearance Center; Table 2.3 from ACADEMY OF MANAGEMENT JOURNAL by DELERY J. & DOTY H. Copyright 1996 by ACADEMY OF MANAGEMENT (NY). Reproduced with permission of ACADEMY OF MANAGEMENT (NY) in the format Textbook via Copyright Clearance Center; Figure 2.4 from *Human Resource Management*, 4/e, Prentice Hall (Torrington, D. and Hall, L. 1998); Figure 2.5 ACADEMY OF MANAGEMENT REVIEW by WRIGHT, P.M. & SNELL, S.A. Copyright 1998 by ACADEMY OF MANAGEMENT (NY). Reproduced with permission of ACADEMY OF MANAGEMENT (NY) in the format Textbook via Copyright Clearance Center; Table 2.4 reprinted by permission of Harvard Business School Press. From *Competing for the future* by Hamel, G. and Prahalad, C. Boston, MA 1994, pp. 217–18. Copyright © 1994 by the Harvard Business School Publishing Corporation, all rights reserved; Table 2.5 reprinted by permission of Harvard Business School Press. From *The Human Equation: Building Profits by Putting People First* by Pfeffer, J., Boston, MA 1998. Copyright © 1998 by the Harvard Business School Publishing Corporation, all rights reserved; Table 2.7 reprinted by permission of Sage Publications Ltd from Wall, T.D. and Wood, S.J., 'The romance of human resource management and business performance, and the case for big science', in *Human Relations*, Vol. 58, No. 4. Copyright (© Sage Publications Ltd, 2005); Table 2.8 from *Strategic Human Resource Management: A Guide to Action*, 2/e, Kogan Page Becker & G (Armstrong, M. and Baron, A. 2002); Chaper 4, Activity, p. 126, table from *Census 2001*, ONS (ONS, 2001) reproduced under the terms of the Click Use Licence; Figure 4.1 from *UK Snapshot 2005*, www.statistics.gov.uk reproduced under the terms of the Click Use Licence; Figure 4.2 from *SCER Report 1 – Understanding the Labour Market*, Scottish Centre for Employment Research, University of Strathclyde (Scottish Centre for Employment Research 2001); Table 4.1 from *Labour Force Survey*, Spring 2004, ONS (ONS, 2004) reproduced under the terms of the Click Use Licence; Table 4.2 from *Sex and Power: Who Runs Britain?*, Equal Opportunities Commission, www.eoc.org.uk (Equal Opportunities Commission 2006); Table 4.3 from *Ethnic Penalties in the Labour Market: Employers and*

Discrimination, DWP Research Report No. 341, HMSO (Heath, A. and Cheung, S.Y. 2006) reproduced under the terms of the Click Use Licence; Table 4.4 and 4.5 from *Working Futures: New Projections of Occupational Attainment by Sector and Region 2002-2012*, Vol. 1: National Report, Institute for Employment Research, University of Warwick (Wilson, R., Homenikou, K. and Dickerson, A.2004); Figure 5.1 adapted from *Resourcing: HRM in Practice*, FT/Prentice Hall (Pilbeam, S. and Corbridge, M. 2002); Figure 5.5 adapted from 'Human resource planning' (Rothwell, S.) in *Human Resource Management: A Critical Text*, Routledge (Storey, J. (ed.) 1995); Figure 5.6 from *A Handbook of Human Resource Management Practice*, Kogan Page Becker & G (Armstrong, M. 2005); Table 6.1 from *Recruitment and Selection*, Advisory Booklet No. 6, Advisory, Conciliation and Arbitration Service (ACAS 1983); Figure 6.2 from *Successful Selection Interviewing*, Blackwell (Anderson, N. and Shackleton, V. 1993) with permission of Professor Neil Anderson; Figure 8.1 from 'Design for learning in management training and development: a view', in *Journal of European Industrial Training*, Vol. 4, No. 8, MCB University Press (Binsted, D.S. 1980); Table 9.1 from **www.bibb.de**; Table 13.1 adapted from *New Earnings Surveys*, HMSO (HMSO 1993-1997) reproduced under the terms of the Click Use Licence; Figure 13.2 from **http://ollie.dcccd.edu** reproduced with permission of Janet Caldwell-Cannedy, Director of Communications, Blue Rain Gallery; Figure 14.1 from *New Developments in Employee Involvement*, Department of Employment Research Series No. 2, HMSO (Marchington, M. *et al.* 1992) reproduced under the terms of the Click Use Licence; Table 14.1 reprinted by permission of Sage Publications Ltd from Hyman, J. and Mason, B., *Managing Employee Involvement and Participation*, Copyright (© Sage Publications Ltd, 1995); Table 14.4 and 14.5 adapted from *All Change at Work?: British Employment Relations 1980–1998, as portrayed by the Workplace Industrial Relations Survey series*, Routledge (Millward, N. *et al.* 2000); Table 14.6 from 'Bouquets, brickbats and blinkers: TQM and employee involvement in practice', *Organizational Studies*, Vol. 18 No. 5, Walter de Gruyter (Wilkinson, A. *et al.* 1997) with permission of G. Godfrey; Table 16.1 from 'Human resources in the People's Republic of China: the "three systems reforms"', in *Human Resource Management Journal*, Vol. 6, No. 3, Blackwell Publishing (Warner, M. 1996); Table 16.2 and 16.3 from 'Re-inventing China's industrial relations at enterprise level: an empirical field-study in four major cities', in *Industrial Relations Journal*, Vol. 30, No. 3, Blackwell Publishing (Ding. Z. and Warner, M. 1999); Figure 17.2 from Schuler, R., Dowling, P. and De Cieri, H., 'An integrative framework of strategic international human resource management', *Journal of Management* (Vol. 19, No. 2) pp. 419–459, copyright 1993 by Sage Publications, reprinted by permission of Sage Publications Inc.; Table 17.2 from 'Strategic human resource management: a global perspective' (Adler, N. and Ghadar, F.) in *Human Resource Management: An International Comparison*, Walter de Gruyter (Pieper, R. 1990).

John Wiley & Sons Inc., for extracts from 'On Becoming a Strategic Partner: The Role of Human Resources in gaining Competitive Advantage', by Barney J.B. and Wright P.M, published in *Human Resource Management*, Vol. 37, no. 1, 1998 and *Effective Mentoring and Teaching*, Jossey-Bass (Daloz, J.A. 1986). Reprinted with the permission of John Wiley & Sons, Inc.; DDB London for an extract from John Webster's 1985 advertisement for the *Guardian*; The Guardian for extracts from; 'Stuck on the "mummy track" – why having a baby means lower pay and prospects', by Patrick Barkham, published in the *Guardian*, 20 January 2006 Copyright Guardian Newspapers Limited 2006 and 'Chill enters cosy German Boardroom' by David Gow, published in the *Guardian*, 25 October 2004 Copyright Guardian Newspapers Limited 2004; *The Independent* for an extract from 'Systematic Racism At Car Plant Was Ignored By Ford', published in *The Independent*, 24 September 1999; The Employers Organisation for an extract from *Local government workforce profile and the top ten skills shortage areas – 2005: national recruitment and retention initiatives*, reproduced with kind permission from the IDeA (Improvement and Development Agency); The Chartered Institute of Personnel and Development for an extract from *The CIPD Learning and Development Generalist Standard: CIPD Practitioner-Level Professional Standards*, reproduced with the permission of the Chartered Institute of Personnel and Development, 151 The Broadway, London, SW19 1JQ; Investors in People UK for an extract about Wealden District Council, reprinted with the kind permission of Investors in People; The Institute of Administrative Management for an extract from Employee Engagement by Woodruffe, C., published in the *British Journal of Administrative Management* January 2006, 50, 28–29; Melcrum Publishing for an extract from 'Harley-Davidson', Scott *et al* published in the *Strategic HR Review*, Jan/Feb 2006, 5, 2, 28–31. **www.melcrum.com**; M@n@gement Journal and the authors; Cornelia Kothen, William McKinley and Professor Andreas Georg Scherer, for an extract from *Alternatives to organizational downsizing: a German case study*, published in *M@n@gement*, Vol. 2, No. 3 (special issue), reproduced with kind permission from *M@n@gement*, Professor Andreas Georg Scherer and William McKinley; The Economist for an extract from 'Mitsubishi company man' published in The Economist 9 December 1995 © The Economist Newspaper Limited; The Nikkei Weekly for their kind permission to reproduce an extract from *The Nikkei Weekly* special issue 6 March 2006.

We are grateful to the Financial Times Limited for permission to reprint the following material:

Box 2.5: 'Moving the goalposts', © *Financial Times*, 19 April 2006; and 'American to review bonus strategy', © *Financial Times*, 26 January 2006; Chapter 3 Case Study: 'Awkward squad promises a rough ride at Blackpool', © *Financial Times*, 9 September 2002; Part 1 Case Study: 'Human resources departments are unloved but not unnecessary', © *Financial*

Times, 18 April 2006; Chapter 8 Case Study (1): 'Growing pains let change blossom', © *Financial Times*, 25 March 2006; Chapter 8 Case Study (2): 'GE's corporate boot camp cum talent spotting venue', © *Financial Times*, 20 March 2006; Chapter 12 Case Study: 'Fears about job destruction proved to be unfounded', © *Financial Times*, 30 September 2005.

In some instances we have been unable to trace the owners of copyright material, and we would appreciate any information that would enable us to do so.

Part 1

HUMAN RESOURCE MANAGEMENT AND ITS ORGANISATIONAL CONTEXT

Introduction to Part 1

Human resource management has become a pervasive and influential approach to the management of employment in a wide range of market economies. The original US prescriptions of the early 1980s have become popularised and absorbed in a wide variety of economic settings: there are very few major economies where the nature of human resource management, to include its sources, operation and philosophy, is not actively discussed. As a result, the analysis and evaluation of HRM have become major themes in academic, policy and practitioner literatures.

These first three chapters are strongly related in that they consider the nature of HRM from a number of perspectives. The first chapter looks at the antecedents of HRM in the USA and its translation to other economies, with particular emphasis on Britain – where the HRM debate has been among the most active and has involved practitioner and academic alike. In tracing the key themes in this debate, the chapter considers the extent to which HRM differs from more traditional approaches to people management; the relationship between HRM and organisational performance; and the impact of HRM on the HR function.

The second chapter examines the strategic nature of HRM in more depth: how it is aligned to and configured with organisational strategy and how the debate has moved through a number of incarnations, from the 'best-fit approach' to the 'configurational approach' to the 'resource-based view' and 'best practice approach'. In considering claims for the importance of the strategic nature of HRM it raises questions as to its efficacy in helping meet organisational objectives, creating competitive advantage and 'adding value' through what has now become known as 'high-performance' or 'high-commitment work practices'. Whether or not the claims for these approaches are supportable, it is becoming clear that no one system or approach can be applied to all organisations owing to the increasing complexity of organisational forms and organisational contexts.

The third chapter continues this contextual theme and examines the context in which human resource management has emerged and in which it operates. This is important in understanding some of the assumptions and philosophical stances that lie behind it. The purpose of the discussion is to create a critical awareness of the broader context in which HRM operates, not simply as a set of operational matters that describe the functional role of personnel management, but as part of a complex and sophisticated process that helps us to understand the nature of organisational life.

The type of questions raised by HRM indicates the extent to which it has disturbed many formerly accepted concepts in the employment relationship. For some it has become a model for action and application; for others it is no more than a map that indicates how the management of employees might be worked out in more specific ways than HRM as a set of general principles can adequately deal with.

Chapter 1

An introduction to human resource management

Julie Beardwell and Ian Clark

Objectives

- To define Human Resource Management (HRM).
- To review and evaluate the main models of HRM.
- To explore the differences between HRM and more traditional approaches to people management.
- To explore the association between HRM and business performance.
- To consider HRM in multinational corporations.
- To review models of the HR function.

Introduction

When the first edition of this book was published in 1994 Human Resource Management (HRM) was described as a newly emerging phenomenon that added 'a powerful and influential perspective' to debates about the nature of the contemporary employment relationship (Beardwell and Holden, 1994: 5). A number of the substantial changes in the context of employment were also noted, including: a decline in trade union membership and collective bargaining; significant levels of organisational restructuring and the rise of atypical forms of employment, e.g. temporary work and contracted-out employment. The chapter suggested that:

> Any assessment of the emergence of Human Resource Management has, at least, to take account of this changing context of employment and provide some explanations as to the relationships that exist between the contribution HRM has made to some of these changes on the one hand and, on the other hand, the impact that such changes have had on the theory and practice of HRM itself.
> (Beardwell and Holden, 1994: 5)

HRM continues to both influence and be influenced by the changing context of employment but, whilst still relatively new, it is now a little long in the tooth to be described as an emerging phenomenon. Boxall and Purcell (2003) suggest that HRM has now become the most popular term in the English-speaking world to refer to the activities of management in the employment relationship. However, there is still little universal agreement of what HRM actually means and debates around the meaning of the term and the impact of the concept continue. When HRM first emerged in the UK a large part of the analysis and discussion that constitutes the HRM debate today had yet to reveal itself. Some initial studies of non-unionism were only just beginning to see the light of day (McLoughlin and Gourlay, 1994), while the role of HRM in transforming and adding value to organisational performance (Pfeffer, 1994, 1998), the relationship between HRM 'bundles'and business performance (McDuffie, 1995; Huselid, 1995), the role of the psychological contract in gaining employee assent (Guest and Conway, 1997) and wider changes in the infrastructure of the employment relationship (Cully *et al.*, 1999) would come later in the decade. In the early days, the key concerns were with the extent to which it represented something different from more established approaches to people management. As HRM has become more widely established the debate has moved more towards its impact, both for the employment relationship and for organisational performance. This chapter aims to explore the key themes within the debates surrounding HRM in order to show how our understanding has changed over time and to consider the impact this has had on the management of people. However, before we can do that it is important to clarify what we mean when we talk about HRM.

Definitions of HRM

Despite the popularity of the term HRM, there is still no universally agreed definition of its meaning. Watson (2002: 369) suggests that a 'rather messy situation currently exists whereby the term HRM is used in a confusing variety of ways'. In its broadest sense HRM can be used as a generic term to describe any approach to managing people; for example, Boxall and Purcell (2003: 1) use the term to refer to 'all those activities associated with the management of employment relationships in the firm'. In a similar vein, HRM can be used as a more contemporary phrase to describe the activities commonly associated with personnel management. For others, though, HRM encompasses a new approach to managing people that is significantly different to more traditional practices. Even in its specific sense there are a variety of perspectives on what makes HRM distinctive. One theme focuses on practices aimed at increasing employee commitment and capability to enhance business performance. For example, Storey (1995: 5) defines HRM as 'a distinctive approach to employment management which seeks to achieve competitive advantage through the strategic deployment of a highly committed and capable workforce, using an array of cultural, structural and personnel techniques'. Another theme emphasises the strategic nature of HRM; for example Buchanan and Huczynski (2004: 679) define HRM as 'a managerial perspective which argues the need to establish an integrated series of personnel policies to support organisational strategy'.

The ambiguity inherent in these different interpretations has led to the emergence of different terms as academics (and some practitioners) attempt to clarify the approach to managing people that is being described. The first attempts at clarification identified 'soft' and 'hard' variants of HRM (Guest, 1987; Storey, 1992) with 'soft HRM' used to describe approaches aimed at enhancing the commitment, quality and flexibility of employees whilst 'hard HRM' describes the emphasis on strategy where human resources are deployed to achieve business goals in the same way as any other resource. However, 'hard HRM' also has a harsher interpretation associated with strategies of cost minimisation (e.g. low wages, minimal training, close supervision) and lean production (downsizing, work intensification). These different interpretations can cause some confusion. For example, if hard HRM is used to describe a strategic approach to people management then soft and hard HRM are 'not necessarily incompatible' (Legge, 1995): hard variants can contain elements of soft practice, while soft variants can deliver hard outcomes in terms of tightness of fit with business strategy. However, if hard HRM is used to describe a cost minimisation approach then soft and hard HRM may be 'diametrically opposed' (Truss *et al.*, 1997: 54). What is probably more at issue than either of these two characterisations is the question of whether they are equally routes to work intensification and greater demands on the employment relationship by the organisation at the expense of the employee.

As the HRM debate has progressed further terms have also been introduced; for example 'high-commitment management (HCM)' instead of soft HRM and 'strategic HRM' instead of hard HRM. More recently the preoccupation in the relationship between HR practices and improved business performance has been reflected in the use of 'high-performance work practices (HPWP)' to describe 'a set of complementary work practices covering three broad categories: high employee involvement practices, human resource practices, and reward and commitment practices' (Sung and Ashton, 2005).

At least part of the explanation of the lack of a universally agreed definition of HRM lies in the absence of 'a coherent theoretical basis for classifying HRM policy and practice' (Guest, 1997: 266). Guest (1997) identifies three broad categories of general-level theory about HRM: strategic theories (e.g. Miles and Snow, 1984; Schuler and Jackson, 1987; Hendry and Pettigrew, 1990); descriptive theories (e.g. Beer *et al.*, 1984; Kochan *et al.*, 1986); and normative theories (e.g. Walton, 1985; Guest, 1987; Pfeffer, 1994). Each has its origin in a different theoretical base: contingency theory, systems theory and motivation theory respectively. However, what all these models have in common is an underlying assumption that the approach to people management being described or prescribed is distinctive in some way from earlier approaches to managing people

The origins of HRM

There is rather more consensus that the origins of HRM lie within employment practices associated with welfare capitalist employers in the United States during the 1930s. Both Jacoby (1997) and Foulkes (1980) argue that this type of employer exhibited an ideological opposition to unionisation and collective employment relations. As an alternative, welfare capitalists believed the organisation, rather than third-party institutions such as the state or trade unions, should provide for the security and welfare of workers. To deter any propensity to unionise, especially once President Roosevelt's New Deal programme commenced after 1933, welfare capitalists often paid efficiency wages, introduced health care coverage, pension plans and provided lay-off pay. Equally, they conducted regular surveys of employee opinion and sought to secure employee commitment via the promotion of strong centralised corporate cultures and long-term permanent employment. Welfare capitalists pioneered individual performance-related pay, profit-sharing schemes and what is now termed teamworking. This model of employment regulation had a pioneering role in the development in what is now termed HRM but rested on structural features such as stable product markets and the absence of marked business cycles. While the presence of HRM was well established in the American business system before the 1980s, it was only after that period that HRM gained external recognition by academics and practitioners.

There are a number of reasons for its emergence since then, among the most important of which are the major pressures experienced in product markets during the recession of 1980–82, combined with a growing recognition in the USA that trade union influence in collective employment was reaching fewer employees. By the 1980s the US economy was being challenged by overseas competitors, most particularly Japan. Discussion tended to focus on two issues: 'the productivity of the American worker', particularly compared with the Japanese worker, 'and the declining rate of innovation in American industries' (Devanna *et al.*, 1984: 33). From this sprang a desire to create a work situation free from conflict, in which both employers and employees worked in unity towards the same goal – the success of the organisation (Fombrun, 1984: 17). Beyond these prescriptive arguments and as a wideranging critique of institutional approaches to industrial relations analysis, Kaufman (1993) suggests that a preoccupation with pluralist industrial relations within and beyond the period of the New Deal excluded the non-union sector of the US economy for many years. In summary, welfare capitalist employers (soft HRM) and anti-union employers (hard HRM or no

HRM, are embedded features within the US business system, whereas the New Deal Model was a contingent response to economic crisis in the 1930s.

In the UK in the 1980s the business climate also became conducive to changes in the employment relationship. As in the USA, this was partly driven by economic pressure in the form of increased product market competition, the recession in the early part of the decade and the introduction of new technology. However, a very significant factor in the UK, generally absent from the USA, was the desire of the government to reform and reshape the conventional model of industrial relations, which provided a rationale for the development of more employer-oriented employment policies on the part of management (Beardwell, 1992, 1996). The restructuring of the economy saw a rapid decline in the old industries and a relative rise in the service sector and in new industries based on 'high-tech' products and services, many of which were comparatively free from the established patterns of what was sometimes termed the 'old' industrial relations. These changes were overseen by a muscular entrepreneurialism promoted by the Thatcher Conservative government in the form of privatisation and anti-union legislation 'which encouraged firms to introduce new labour practices and to re-order their collective bargaining arrangements' (Hendry and Pettigrew, 1990: 19).

The influence of the US 'excellence' literature (e.g. Peters and Waterman, 1982; Kanter, 1984) also associated the success of 'leading edge' companies with the motivation of employees by involved management styles that also responded to market changes. As a consequence, the concepts of employee commitment and 'empowerment' became another strand in the ongoing debate about management practice and HRM.

A review of these issues suggests that any discussion of HRM has to come to terms with at least three fundamental problems:

- that HRM is derived from a range of antecedents, the ultimate mix of which is wholly dependent upon the stance of the analyst, and which may be drawn from an eclectic range of sources;
- that HRM is itself a contributory factor in the analysis of the employment relationship, and sets part of the context in which that debate takes place;
- that it is difficult to distinguish where the significance of HRM lies – whether it is in its supposed transformation of styles of employee management in a specific sense, or whether in a broader sense it is in its capacity to sponsor a wholly redefined relationship between management and employees that overcomes the traditional issues of control and consent at work.

Models of HRM

This ambivalence over the definition, components and scope of HRM is apparent in the co-existence of a number of different models of HRM. Two models have been particularly influential in the interpretation of HRM. The 'Matching' model, developed by academics at the Michigan Business School, introduced the concept of strategic human resource management by which HRM policies are inextricably linked to the 'formulation and implementation of strategic corporate and/or business objectives' (Devanna *et al.*, 1984: 34). The model is illustrated in Figure 1.1.

The model emphasises the necessity of 'tight fit' between HR strategy and business strategy and the use of a set of HR policies and practices that are integrated with each other and with the goals of the organisation. Price (2004: 45–46) outlines the following key areas for the development of appropriate HR policies and systems:

- Selection of the most suitable people to meet business needs.
- Performance in the pursuit of business objectives.

Figure 1.1	The matching model of HRM

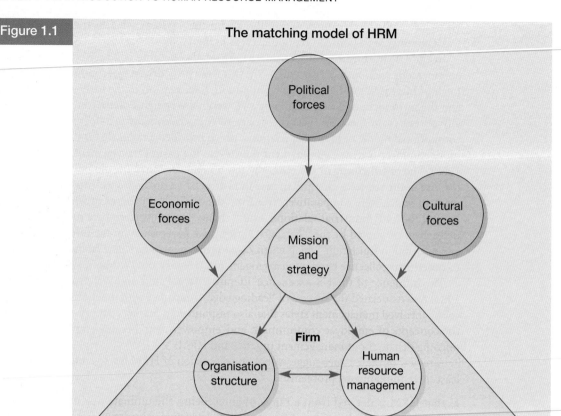

- Appraisal, monitoring performance and providing feedback to the organisation and its employees.
- Rewards for appropriate performance.
- Development of the skills and knowledge required to meet business objectives.

The matching model is closely allied with the 'hard' interpretation of HRM; that is, the deployment of human resources to meet business objectives. Two assumptions underpin this model: the first is that the most effective means of managing people will vary from organisation to organisation and is dependent on organisational context. The second assumption is that of unitarism, that is, the assumption that conflict or at least differing views cannot exist in the workplace because everyone (managers and employees) are working to achieve the same goal – the success of the organisation. This model has formed the basis of the 'best fit' school of HRM, discussed further in chapter 2.

A second influential model, illustrated in Figure 1.2, was developed by Beer *et al.* (1984) at Harvard University. 'The map of HRM territory', as the authors titled their model, recognises that there are a variety of 'stakeholders' in the corporation, which include shareholders, various groups of employees, the government and the community. The model recognises the legitimate interests of various groups, and assumes that the creation of HRM strategies will have to reflect these interests and fuse them as much as possible into the human resource strategy and ultimately the business strategy.

This recognition of stakeholders' interests raises a number of important questions for policy makers in the organisation:

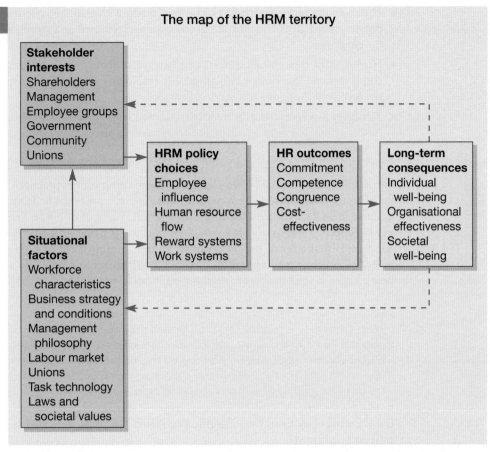

Source: Beer *et al.* (1984: 16). Reprinted with permission of The Free Press, a division of Simon & Schuster, from *Managing Human Assets* by Michael Beer, Bert Spector, Paul R. Lawrence, D. Quinn Mills and Richard E. Walton. Copyright © 1984 by The Free Press.

How much responsibility, authority and power should the organisation voluntarily delegate and to whom? If required by government legislation to bargain with the unions or consult with workers' councils, how should management enter into these institutional arrangements? Will they seek to minimize the power and influence of these legislated mechanisms? Or will they share influence and work to create greater congruence of interests between management and the employee groups represented through these mechanisms? (Beer *et al.*, 1984: 8)

The recognition that employees and their representatives are important stakeholders who at least need to be included in the equation initially led to greater acceptance of this model amongst academics and commentators in the UK although some academics still criticised it as being too unitarist (Hendry and Pettigrew, 1990). However, the main influence of this model has been less in considerations of stakeholder interests and situational factors and more in the prescriptive elements of the benefits to accrue from adopting a 'soft' approach to HRM, i.e. one that seeks to enhance the quality and commitment of the workforce. Building on this model Guest (1989: 42) developed a set of propositions that combine to create more effective organisations:

● *Strategic integration* is defined as 'the ability of organisations to integrate HRM issues into their strategic plans, to ensure that the various aspects of HRM cohere and for line managers to incorporate an HRM perspective into their decision making'.

9

- *High commitment* is defined as being 'concerned with both behavioural commitment to pursue agreed goals and attitudinal commitment reflected in a strong identification with the enterprise'.

- *High quality* 'refers to all aspects of managerial behaviour, including management of employees and investment in high-quality employees, which in turn will bear directly on the quality of the goods and services provided'.

- *Flexibility* is seen as being 'primarily concerned with what is sometimes called functional flexibility but also with an adaptable organisational structure with the capacity to manage innovation'.

This shows an assumption that it is possible to balance the strategic integration associated with 'hard' HRM with the 'softer' elements of high commitment practices. Guest also identifies a linkage between HRM aims, policies and outcomes as shown in Table 1.1.

These ideas have contributed to the 'best practice' school of HRM. Whereas the 'best fit' school adopts a *contingency* approach, 'best practice' is based on *universalism*. The assumption here is that a set of practices aimed at high commitment or high performance will benefit all organisations regardless of context. Which specific practices actually constitute 'best practice' is still open to debate although it can be noted that:

> There seems to be a growing consensus around the broad territory to be covered. There is a plausible list of practices that includes selection, training, communication, job design and reward systems. There are also practices on the margin such as family-friendly and equal opportunity practices as well as some that cannot apply across all sectors, such as profit-related pay and employee-share ownership schemes. (Guest, 2001: 1096)

The elements of best practices identified by Pfeffer (1998) are now widely recognised, if not universally accepted:

- Employment security.
- Sophisticated selection.
- Team-working and decentralisation.
- High wages linked to organisational performance.
- Extensive training.
- Narrow status differentials.
- Communication and involvement.

Best practice HRM is discussed more fully in Chapter 2 and will be revisited later in this chapter in relation to HRM and organisational performance. However, it is worth noting here that there are some challenges to the universal applicability of best practice HRM. For example, Marchington and Zagelmeyer (2005: 4) suggest that a high commitment approach to HRM is dependent on the ability of employers to take a long-term perspective and on the prospect of future market growth. They also suggest that it is easier to engage in high com-

Table 1.1 A human resource management framework

HRM aims	HRM policies	HRM outcomes
For example: • high commitment • quality	For example: • selection based on specific criteria using sophisticated tests	For example: • low labour turnover • allegiance to company • flexible working

Source: Storey (1989: 11)

mitment HRM when labour costs form a low proportion of total costs. Boxall and Purcell (2003) agree that any list of best practices is unlikely to have universal application because of the influence of organisational context but they also suggest that there are certain desirable principles which, if applied can bring about more effective people management, see Figure 1.3. They differentiate between the surface layer of policy and practice that is likely to be contingent on a range of internal and external factors and the underpinning layer that reflects 'certain *desirable* principles which, if applied, will bring about more effective management of people' (Boxall and Purcell, 2003: 69).

Figure 1.3	The 'best fit' versus 'best practice' debate: two levels of analysis

Surface layer: HR policies and practices – heavily influenced by context (societal, sectoral, organisational)

Underpinning player: generic HR processes and general principles of labour management

Source: Boxall and Purcell (2003: 69).

Phases in the HRM debate

In the twenty or so years since its emergence, HRM has continued to provoke interest and debate. It is possible to trace a number of key phases in the debate as each of these helps to clarify differing interpretations of HRM as well as identify the main preoccupations at the time. In the early days the main concerns were with the distinctiveness of HRM as a concept and the extent to which it represented a positive or negative phase in people management. In this respect, debate related to the difference between HRM and more traditional personnel management and concerns about whether the language associated with HRM was a true reflection of its intent.

HRM and personnel management

When HRM first emerged the debate largely focused on whether HRM represented a fundamental step-change in people management or was merely a phase in the historical development of personnel management. As an example of the step-change argument, Beer and Spector (1985: 231–232) stated that 'the transformation we are observing amounts to more than a subtle shift in the traditional practices of personnel or the substitution of new terms for unchanging practices. Instead, the transformation amounts to a new model regarding the management of human resources in organisations'. The opposing view was that HRM reflected a phase in the evolution of personnel management as affected by environmental and societal factors; for example, Gennard and Kelly (1997: 31) suggested that the delivery of the personnel function 'has always been flexible, adjusting historically and altering its dominant values . . . as macro circumstances change'. Bach and Sisson (2000: 14) argued that 'HRM emerged during a particular historical conjecture and its sentiments were the managerial version of Mrs Thatcher's dictum that "there is no such thing as society"'. In this respect, HRM can be seen to be as much a product of its time as the other historical phases of personnel management such as welfare, labour management or industrial relations.

11

Many of those who thought of HRM as something different also saw it as superior to personnel management. For example, the UK government suggested that personnel management was obsolete in the 1992 White Paper *People, Jobs and Opportunity*:

> Many employers are replacing *out-dated personnel practices* with new policies for *human resource management*, which put the emphasis on developing the talents and capabilities of each individual employee.   (Employment Department, 1992; emphasis added)

However, the limited examples of HRM in practice in the 1990s led to criticisms that the comparisons were unfair: comparing personnel management 'warts and all' with the more aspirational ideals of HRM. Legge (1995) therefore suggested that a more balanced approach might be to compare HRM with what personnel management aimed to be. Using this approach Legge (1995) identified a number of similarities between HRM and personnel management. Both models emphasised the importance of integration; both linked employee development with the achievement of organisational goals; both sought to ensure that the right people were in the right jobs. In addition, both gave people management to line managers; for example, the IPM (1963) definition stated that 'personnel management is the responsibility of all who manage people, as well as being a description of the work of those who are employed as specialists'.

Legge's (1995) analysis also identified three significant differences between personnel management and HRM. The first difference concerns the focus of activity as personnel management 'appears to be something performed on subordinates by managers rather than something that the latter experience themselves' (p. 74) whereas under HRM 'much greater attention is paid to the management of managers' (Storey, 2001: 7). This relates to the second difference which concerns the role of line managers; under personnel management their primary role is the implementation of personnel procedures whereas under HRM they are responsible for devising and driving a business-oriented HR strategy. The third difference, identified by Legge, relates to perceptions about organisational culture. The management of organisational culture is a central element of HRM models but not personnel management models, which often pre-date the interest in organisational culture. Legge (1995: 75) argues that 'these three differences in emphasis all point to HRM, in theory, being essentially a more central strategic management task than personnel management'.

Comparative models of personnel management and HRM

As part of this debate, several attempts were made to describe ways in which HRM differed from personnel management. Two comparative models from the UK were particularly influential in this respect: Guest's (1987) comparison between stereotypes of personnel management and human resource management; and Storey's (1992) '27 points of difference' (later modified to 25). In these, and in US comparative frameworks (e.g. Beer and Spector, 1985), it is possible to identify a number of common themes, as depicted in Table 1.2 and described more fully below.

Planning perspective

The advent of human resource management has brought forward the issue of the linkages between the employment relationship and wider organisational strategies and corporate policies. Historically, the management of industrial relations and personnel has been concerned either to cope with the 'downstream' consequences of earlier strategic decisions or to 'fire-fight' short-term problems that threaten the long-run success of a particular strategy. In these instances the role has been at best reactive and supportive to other managerial functions, at worst a hindrance until particular operational problems were overcome.

Human resource management lays claim to a fundamentally different relationship between the organisation's employment function and its strategic role. The assumption behind HRM is that it is essentially a strategically driven activity, which is not only a major contributor to that

Table 1.2 Stereotypes of personnel management and HRM

	Personnel management	HRM
Planning perspective		
Beer and Spector, 1985	Reactive Piecemeal interventions in response to specific problems	Proactive System-wide interventions with emphasis on fit
Guest, 1987	Short-term, reactive, ad hoc, marginal	Long-term, proactive, strategic, integrated
Storey, 1992	Piecemeal initiatives Marginal to corporate plan	Integrated initiatives Central to corporate plan
People management perspective		
Beer and Spector, 1985	People as variable cost	People are social capital capable of development
Guest, 1987	Cost-minimisation Compliance	Maximum utilisation (human asset accounting) Commitment
Storey, 1992	Monitoring Mutuality	Nurturing 'Can-do' outlook
Employment relations perspective		
Beer and Spector, 1985	Self-interest dominates; conflict of interest between stakeholders Seeks power advantages for bargaining and confrontation	Coincidence of interests between stakeholders can be developed Seeks power equalisation for trust and collaboration
Guest, 1987	Pluralist, collective, low trust	Unitarist, individual, high trust
Storey, 1992	Pluralist Institutionalised conflict Collective bargaining contracts	Unitarist Conflict de-emphasised Towards individual contracts
Structure/systems perspective		
Beer and Spector, 1985	Control from top Control of information flow to enhance efficiency, power	Participation and informed choice Open channels of communication to build trust and commitment
Guest, 1987	Bureaucratic/mechanistic Centralised, formal, defined roles External controls	Organic Devolved, flexible roles Self-control
Storey, 1992	Procedures High standardisation Restricted flow of communication	Business need Low standardisation Increased flow of communication
Role perspective		
Guest, 1987	Specialist/professional	Largely integrated into line management
Storey, 1992	Personnel/IR specialists	General/business/line managers

process but also a determining part of it. From this standpoint the contribution that the management of the employment relationship makes to the overall managerial process is as vital and formative as that of finance or marketing, for example. Indeed, the notion that HRM is central to such managerial decision-making indicates the extent to which its proponents feel that it has come out of the shadows to claim a rightful place alongside other core management roles. In this respect one of the traditional stances of the personnel practitioner – that of the 'liberal' conception of personnel management as standing between employer and employee, moderating and smoothing the interchange between them – is viewed as untenable: HRM is about shaping and delivering corporate strategies with commitment and results.

One of the key drivers that led to interest in HRM in the US was the challenge of increased overseas competition. Concern was expressed over the productivity of American workers (particularly in relation to Japanese workers) and 'the declining rate of innovation in American industries' (Devanna *et al.*, 1984: 33). In part, these failings were attributed to the failure of personnel management to promote the potential benefits of effective people management (e.g. Skinner, 1981). Traditional personnel management is seen as primarily concerned with enabling the organisation to maintain a steady supply of products or services free from any disruption whilst minimising labour costs (Thomason, 1998) so the prime focus is on reacting to specific problems as they arise. Legge (1978) describes this as the 'vicious circle in personnel management'. In this model the exclusion of the personnel department from organisational planning leads to human resource problems which the personnel department is expected to solve. However, time and work pressures result in crisis management which diminishes the credibility of the department resulting in its exclusion from organisational planning. In contrast, one of the key tenets of HRM is that human resources are a main source of competitive advantage and, as such, need to be managed in a way that is wholly consistent with the long-term goals of the organisation. This requires people management issues to be considered strategically.

As we have already seen, the 'matching model' (Devanna *et al.*, 1984) emphasises the importance of 'fit' between the organisational strategy, structure and HRM practices. The underpinning assumptions are that it is possible for an organisation to identify its key strategic focus and it is then possible to develop a matching set of human resource policies. Both assumptions have been criticised, e.g. Mintzberg (1994) on the nature and formulation of strategy and Sisson (1993) on management ability and willingness to embrace the paradigm shift from reactive to strategic management. Despite these criticisms, the contrast between reactive personnel management and strategic HRM continues to have currency.

A second emphasis within HRM is on internal fit, i.e. the integration of HR policies and practices with each other as well as with the business strategy. The nature of the fit can vary, for example Guest (1997: 271) differentiates between three types of internal fit: 'fit to an ideal set of practices', 'fit as gestalt' and 'fit as bundles'. The first type identifies a set of universally applicable 'best HRM practices' (e.g. Pfeffer, 1994) and the concern is with how close organisations get to this ideal list. 'Fit as gestalt' emphasises that finding an appropriate combination of practices is more important than the practices themselves. This concept of fit is seen as 'multiplicative'; if one key aspect is missing the fit is lost. 'Fit as bundles' also implies the existence of distinctive patterns or configurations of practices but in this case the results are additive. Generally speaking; the more HRM practices that are in place the better, provided some distinctive core exists (Marchington and Grugulis, 2000). Whatever approach is favoured, the integration of practices with each other and with business strategy is seen as being in direct contrast to the piecemeal and ad hoc nature of much traditional personnel management practice.

People management perspective

Comparative models suggest that there are fundamental differences in the assumptions underpinning the approach to the workforce in personnel management and HRM paradigms. Personnel management is based on the assumption that people are a variable cost and therefore the primary aim is to minimise this cost whilst maintaining or improving productivity and/or service levels. The cost minimisation model is associated with a belief in equitable selection and reward systems, efficient procedures for dismissal, discipline and redundancy, and clear and operable rules for administering large numbers of employees to avoid arbitrary judgements over individual cases. HRM, in contrast, assumes that people are a resource rather than a cost and practices are aimed at maximising employee commitment and/or improving the overall effectiveness of human resources. The specific practices used can vary depending on whether the dominant interpretation of HRM is soft or hard. Soft variants of HRM are likely to emphasise employee commitment through extensive employee development, internal labour markets and job security whereas hard variants are more likely to emphasise effective utilisation through flexibility, multi-skilling and performance-related pay.

A second key distinction relating to people management concerns the issue of organisational control. Differences between personnel management and HRM are often related to Walton's (1985) distinction between strategies of 'imposing control' and 'eliciting commitment'. The control model is based on Taylorist and Theory X (McGregor, 1960) assumptions about worker competence and motivation whereas the commitment model reflects Theory Y assumptions. Practices associated with the control model include fixed job definition, reliance on rules and procedures, differentiated status, equitable pay and restricted flow of information. In contrast, practices associated with the commitment model include flexible job design, emphasis on shared goals and values, minimum status differentials, performance-related pay and the encouragement of employee participation. Whilst Walton's model has been influential, the implication that seeking to maximise employee commitment is not a form of managerial control has been challenged. Guest (1991) acknowledges the differences between the two approaches but argues that both are forms of employee control. He therefore re-labels them as 'compliance' and 'commitment' and associates 'compliance' with personnel management and 'commitment' with HRM.

Employee relations perspective

Differences in the approach to the workforce adopted by HRM and personnel management are further reflected in the assumptions underpinning employee relations. The key distinction drawn is between unitarist and pluralist frames of reference with unitarism associated with HRM and pluralism with personnel management. When Fox (1966) coined the terms he perceived that pluralism reflected the true nature of organisations and dismissed unitarism as little more than wishful thinking which can 'distort reality and thereby prejudice solutions' (Fox, 1966: 2). In subsequent work, he suggests that pluralism is not only more realistic but also more effective: 'pluralism would certainly be defended by at least some of its exponents on the grounds that it is more likely than the unitary view to promote rational, efficient and effective management' (Fox, 1974: 280–281). However, by the 1980s the 'dominant orthodoxy' of the pluralist model was challenged by the emergence of HRM (Guest, 1991). Unitarist assumptions relating to HRM initially stemmed from the US where high commitment practices were identified primarily in large non-union companies (e.g. Foulkes, 1980). This does not necessarily preclude unions from HRM but does imply a shift in the union–management relationship from adversarial to cooperative. A related shift in thinking concerns the emphasis on extending management control over aspects of the collective relationship that were once customarily regarded as jointly agreed between employees (usually via their unions) and management. Treating employees as a primary responsibility of management, as opposed to the jointly negotiated responsibility of both unions and management, suggests an approach that is concerned to stress the primacy of the managerial agenda in the employment relationship, and marks a shift away from one of the fundamental assumptions of the approach (after the Second World War) to managing collective workforces. This shift was underlined in the 1993 employment legislation, which removed from the Advisory, Conciliation and Arbitration Service (ACAS) the duty, originally given to it on its inception in 1974, to promote collective bargaining. In reality, this duty was a reflection of a deeply rooted presumption stretching back throughout most of the twentieth century and, in the UK at least, largely shared by employers, unions and the state, that collective bargaining represented a 'politically' acceptable compromise between management and labour; for more discussion of this see Clark (2000).

The role of unions is further altered by the emphasis on individualism associated with HRM. This has coincided with a decline in trade union membership and a reduction in the coverage of collective bargaining, which historically, have together been regarded as the key means by which the independent employee voice was exercised. This individualism can manifest itself in a number of ways, including the use of individualised contracts and direct communication. Within the pluralist tradition communication is primarily filtered through union representatives on a 'need to know' basis. Under the auspices of HRM the emphasis is on both a wider dissemination of information directly to employees and the avoidance of any form of collective representation.

Structure/systems perspective

The conduct and systems of personnel management have the maintenance of organisational stability as one of their primary objectives (Hendry and Pettigrew, 1990). In this respect traditional personnel management is closely associated with bureaucratic, organisational structures. In contrast, HRM is seen as a response to the increased pace of change in the external context and the need for organisations to be flexible and adaptable. Delayering and devolved responsibility are frequently emphasised as one of the means by which this flexibility can be achieved as opposed to the hierarchical structures synonymous with traditional personnel management.

Role perspective

The final perspective apparent in comparative models concerns the management roles directly associated with different approaches to people management. Both Guest (1987) and Storey (1992) associate personnel management with a specialist function but place HRM firmly in the hands of line managers. The HRM model assumes that organisational culture lies in the hands of the CEO and line managers are involved as both deliverers and drivers of HR policy. This approach is consistent with the shift from bureaucratic, top-down organisations to more organic flatter structures but also represents a reaction to the poor credibility of specialists resulting from the 'vicious circle of personnel management' (Legge, 1978). The assumption underpinning HRM is that, as people are an organisation's main source of competitive advantage, the management of this resource is 'too important to be left to operational personnel specialists' (Storey, 2001: 7).

This comparison outlines a number of differences between HRM and traditional personnel management. For some commentators (e.g. Torrington and Hall, 1998: 17) this has been seen as a somewhat sterile argument 'of a strictly academic nature, similar to arguments about how many angels can dance on the head of a pin'. However, the distinction does appear to have a practical relevance. Hoque and Noon (2001) analysed data from the 1998 Workplace Employee Relations Survey (WERS 98) based on whether the specialist with senior responsibility for people management had 'human resource' or 'personnel' in their job title. The results showed that HRM practices such as psychometric tests, attitude surveys, off-the-job training and performance related pay were more likely to be found in workplaces that had an HR specialist rather than a personnel specialist.

The rhetoric of HRM

In many respects the use of rhetoric appears to be a defining feature of HRM. Legge (1995: xiv) argues that 'the importance of HRM, and its apparent overshadowing of personnel management, lies just as much (and possibly more so) in its function as a rhetoric about how employees should be managed to achieve competitive advantage than as a coherent new practice'. Similarly, Keenoy and Anthony (1992: 235) state that 'much of the real debate about HRM and the reconstruction of the employment relationship has been conducted through rhetoric and metaphor'. Within the comparative models the words used to describe HRM such as 'proactive', 'nurturing' and 'organic' instinctively seem more positive and attractive than the terms applied to personnel management, e.g. 'reactive', 'monitoring' and 'bureaucratic'. However, although much of the rhetoric of HRM is superficially seductive there is a strong body of literature that cautions against accepting it at face value. Legge (1995) suggests that rhetoric may be used to disguise actions that treat employees as a variable cost, rather than a resource, in the interests of business strategy. So, for example, if employees are transferred to other work in line with business requirements this can be portrayed in terms of employee development and enhanced opportunity. The rhetoric of soft HRM can be used to mask the negative elements of 'hard HRM' in order to manipulate and control the workforce (Bach and Sisson, 2000) or to disguise the introduction of practices that lead to a worsening of the terms and conditions for employees. Marchington and Grugulis (2000) suggest that some HRM practices, such as teamworking, may not offer universal benefits and empowerment but may actually lead to work intensification and more insidious forms of control.

Much of the criticism of HRM has also been conducted through metaphor with HRM variously described as 'old wine in new bottles', 'the emperor's new clothes' and a 'wolf in sheep's clothing' (Armstrong, 1987; Fowler, 1987; Legge, 1989; Keenoy, 1990a). Tom Keenoy is one of the most eloquent and persuasive of critics, and his examination of HRM has exposed many of the *a priori* assumptions and non-sequiturs that abound in the reasoning of its supporters. He claims that HRM is more rhetoric than reality and has been 'talked up' by its advocates. It has little support in terms of evidence, and has been a convenient dustbin of rationalisation to support ideological shifts in the employment relationship brought about by market pressures. It is also full of contradictions, not only in its meanings but also in its practice.

In examining the meanings of HRM Keenoy notes that a 'remarkable feature of the HRM phenomenon is the brilliant ambiguity of the term itself'. He later continues: 'On the "Alice principle" that a term means whatever one chooses it to mean, each of these interpretations may be valid but, in Britain, the absence of any intellectual touchstones has resulted in the term being subject to the process of almost continuous and contested conceptual elision' (Keenoy, 1990b: 363–384).

Stop & think

To what extent does the language used to describe HRM influence its meaning?

HRM and performance

Over the second half of the 1990s, a further turn in the HRM debate saw a move away from attempts to define what its 'input' characteristics might be in favour of examining what consequences flowed from applying HRM in fairly tightly defined circumstances. Whereas earlier analysis of HRM had been primarily concerned with its architecture, an 'output'-based model concerned itself with examining those organisations that not only constructed their HRM in particular configurations but also found that resultant outcomes could give them a competitive advantage. Analysing the links between best practice (or high commitment) HRM and organisational performance is now a major area of interest for research and policy (Marchington and Wilkinson, 2005). A recent overview of empirical work into the linkages between HRM and performance found 104 relevant articles published in 'pre-eminent, international refereed journals between 1994 and 2003' (Boselie *et al.*, 2005: 69).

The impetus for this approach was predominantly American, in particular the work of Arthur (1992, 1994), McDuffie (1995) and Huselid (1995). The unifying theme of these studies is that particular combinations of HRM practices, especially where they are refined and modified, can give quantifiable improvements in organisational performance. Arthur's work studied 54 mini-mills (new technology steel mills using smaller workforces and new working practices) and demonstrated that firms using a 'commitment' model of HRM saw higher productivity, lower labour turnover, and lower rates of rejected production. McDuffie's work examined 70 plants in the world car industry, and the use of HR techniques that were regarded as innovative. His analysis argued that it is when practices are used together, rather than simply in isolation or only for the specific effect of some more than others, that superior performance can be achieved. An important part of this analysis is the extent to which employees gave 'extra' in the form of discretionary effort that would otherwise have not been forthcoming without the effect of the chosen practices. Three factors were noted in particular: *buffers* (the extent to which plants adopted flexibility), *work system* (the work arrangements that complemented flexibility), and *HRM policies* (the HRM practices that complemented flexibility). The marked effect on performance was in the combined impact of all three factors working together.

Huselid's study examined the relationships between the HR system (the groups of practices rather than individual practices), outcome measures (such as financial performance as well as HR data on turnover and absence), and the fit between HR and competitive strategy in 986 US-owned firms employing more than 100 employees. Huselid's results indicated a lowering of labour turnover, higher sales performance, improved profitability and higher share valuations for those firms that performed well on his indices.

The benefits of adopting HRM are also evident in the study undertaken by Ichniowski *et al.* (1997). They identify four different types of HR system on the basis of innovative practices in relation to selection, reward, communication, work organisation, training and employment security. The HR systems are numbered from 1 to 4 with system 1 incorporating innovative practices in all areas and system 4, also labelled 'Traditional HRM', having no innovative practices. Systems 2 and 3 lie between the two extremes and have introduced innovative practices in some areas. The findings show a positive association between innovative HRM practices and both productivity and product quality. Furthermore, the authors claim that a move from system 4 to system 2, if maintained for ten years, would increase operating profits by over $10 million simply as a result of the HRM changes (Ichniowski *et al.*, 1997). A US study conducted by Chadwick and Cappelli (1998) identifies two approaches to managing people: an 'investment HR system' (including extensive training, employee involvement, teamworking) and a 'contractual HR system' (average pay, use of atypical workers, importance of industry credentials for selection). The findings suggest that not only are investment systems more likely to improve performance than contractual systems but also that contractual systems can have a detrimental effect on performance.

Similar findings have emerged from the UK. Thompson's (1998) study of the aerospace industry found that innovative HRM practices were positively associated with higher added value per employee. A longitudinal study of single-site, single-product manufacturing firms (Patterson *et al.*, 1997) concluded that HRM practices account for 19 per cent of variation in profitability and 18 per cent of variation in productivity. Positive results are not just limited to manufacturing. In 2002, a study of HR practices in NHS acute hospital trusts found that certain HR practices (the sophistication and extensiveness of appraisal and training for hospital employees and the percentage of staff working in teams) were significantly associated with measures of patient mortality (West *et al.*, 2002).

The results of these studies would seem to provide convincing evidence that HRM has a positive impact on organisational performance. However, a literature review of empirical studies that examine the link between HRM and performance (Hyde *et al.*, 2005) found little consistency in results. The elements of HRM most positively associated with performance were training, pay, employee involvement and 'bundles' of HR practices but these same elements also had the highest number of non-significant associations with performance. Pay and employee involvement also had the highest number of negative associations with performance. Table 1.3 provides an overview of the results.

Table 1.3 Numbers of empirical papers showing types of association between elements of HRM and performance

Element of HRM	Type of association			Main association between this element and performance	Total number of papers exploring this association
	Positive	Negative	Non-significant		
Training/development	24	1	19	Positive	44
Pay/incentives*	21	6	20	Positive	47
Involvement/voice**	16	5	17	Non-significant	38
Selection/recruitment	7	4	12	Non-significant	23
Teamworking	7	0	7	Positive or non-significant	14
Performance appraisal	6	0	12	Non-significant	18
HR index/bundle	37	3	20	Positive	60
Security	0	0	2	Non-significant	2
Job design (including work-life balance)	8	1	12	Non-significant	21
Equal opportunities	1	0	2	Non-significant	3
Career development (including mentoring)	2	0	6	Non-significant	8

*including 'pay for performance' **including 'information sharing/communication'

Source: Hyde *et al*. (2005) 'Improving Health through HRM', *Change Agenda*, CIPD.

Stop & think

What factors might account for the diversity of these results?

The extent to which it is possible to draw generalised conclusions from studies into the association between HRM and business performance is limited for a number of reasons. Firstly, there is a lack of consensus about which HR practices should be included. In their review of a range of studies into HRM and performance Marchington and Wilkinson (2005: 91) found that 'the number of HR practices in each of the lists varies substantially (from as few as six or seven to twenty or more) as does the inclusion or exclusion of specific techniques'. Secondly, there is considerable variety as to how these practices can be measured (Becker and Gerhart, 1996), (for a fuller discussion see Chapter 2) and little agreement about how organisational performance can be measured. The review of 97 academic papers undertaken by Hyde *et al.* (2005) found over 30 different performance measures used in the papers, with no single measure used in all the papers. There is also the danger that a concentration on the association between HRM and organisational performance can ignore other measures of managerial effectiveness and thus overstate the impact of HRM (Richardson and Thompson, 1999). A further concern relates to issues of causality: does the introduction of HRM practices lead to enhanced organisational performance or is it that better performing organisations can afford to invest in the more sophisticated practices associated with HRM. Figure 1.4 illustrates the association between HRM activities, HRM outcomes and business performance and 'indicates the possibility of two-way causation, i.e. that firm performance itself will give rise to a change (very often perceived as an improvement) in HRM practices' (Paauwe and Richardson, 1997).

| Figure 1.4 | HRM activities in relation to HRM outcomes and performance |

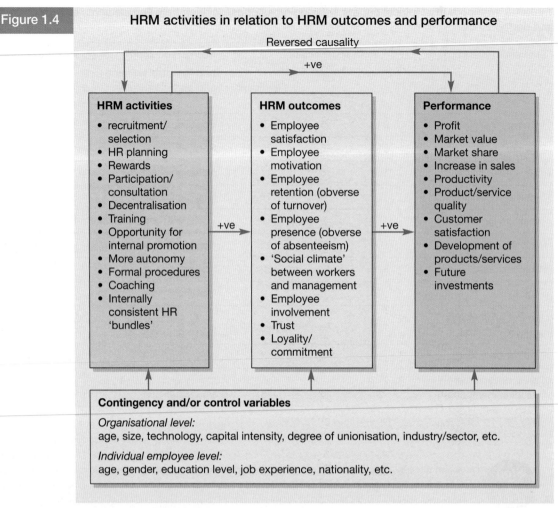

Source: Paauwe and Richardson (1997) cited in Boselie *et al.* (2005). http://www.tandf.co.uk/journals.

Issues about the direction of causation are revealed in a study exploring the relationship between HRM and performance in 366 UK companies in the manufacturing and service sectors (Guest *et al.*, 2003). The study covered nine main areas of HRM: recruitment and selection; training and development; appraisal; financial flexibility; job design; two-way communication; employment security and the internal labour market; single status and harmonisation; and quality. Measures of performance included employment relations items (e.g. labour turnover, absence and industrial conflict); labour productivity and financial performance compared to the average for the industry; and performance data such as value of sales and profit per employee. The findings show a positive association between HRM and profitability but appear to 'lend stronger support to the view that profitability creates scope for more HRM rather than vice versa' (p. 309). Overall, the results are described as 'very mixed and on balance predominantly negative':

> The tests of association show a positive relationship between the use of more HR practices and lower labour turnover and higher profitability, but show no association between HR and productivity. The test of whether the presence of more HR practices results in a change in performance shows no significant results.
>
> (Guest *et al.*, 2003: 307)

HRM, performance and the productivity gap

As Guest and his colleagues argue the focus of research on HRM and performance over the past decade has been slightly schizophrenic; it appeared on the one hand to establish that HRM has a positive effect on organisational performance but on the other hand as we establish in our summary of some of the recent research, such claims are premature. More critically, Wall and Wood (2005) demonstrate that the methodological limitations of most studies on HRM and performance undermine claims of any positive performance effect. In particular, Wall and Wood (2005: 450) claim that not all measures of improved performance, especially financial measures, are concurrent, that is they do not cover the same period of analysis. Thus, it is often the case that the data collected necessarily reflect prior performance and it follows from this that studies of HRM and performance may need to build a lag into their analysis. Alternatively, studies could be underestimating the strength of the relationship between HRM and performance because of inadequate measurement of HR practices.

The reason we make these points is because there are strong theoretical grounds for believing that the system deployment of HRM will not only improve employee involvement but enhance organisational performance and productivity. More significantly than this recent theoretical and empirical material on the UK productivity gap identifies the significance of people management. For example, one contemporary focus in the evaluation of the UK productivity gap centres on the evaluation of micro level productivity barriers/enhancers such as innovation, skill formation and management capability. In this respect the ESRC (2004) focuses not on the often quoted greater level of capital investment in American or German firms but the fact that 50 per cent of the UK/US productivity gap relates to management, ways of working and the application of technology. In addition to this the CIPD (2006) focuses on differences in productivity that relate to how available resources are used and managed, summarised as management capability.

The findings of the CIPD and the ESRC and other research such as the Conference Board (2005) make an important contribution to the wider debate about HRM and performance. First, the cited studies indicate that effective people management in conjunction with contemporary systems of work organisation can make a demonstrative difference to organisational performance and productivity. Second, and related, if, as the cited studies demonstrate, effective people management does make a difference in terms of performance and productivity a key question for both academics and practitioners is why so few firms deploy these practices? Third, both the UK and the USA are frequently cited as liberal market economies where short-termism and shareholder capitalism predominate over longer-term stakeholder approaches to management. The established research on HRM in the US does suggest that high performance, high commitment approaches to HRM do not have a widespread presence nonetheless their presence is greater than in the UK. So in conclusion whilst it is clear that HRM scholars and more mainstream economists demonstrate that HRM may have a positive effect on performance what is less clear is why the barriers to effective people management that relate to short-termism remain so embedded in the UK to limit the practice of HRM.

HRM in practice

What does seem clear from empirical studies into HRM and performance is that HRM is still only evident in a minority of organisations. The Sheffield study (Patterson *et al.*, 1997) concludes that the finding of a positive association between HRM and organisational performance is 'ironic, given that our research has also demonstrated that emphasis on HRM practices is one of the most neglected areas of managerial practice within organisations' (p. 21). A number of commentators (e.g. Storey, 1992; Guest, 1997; Gratton *et al.*, 1999) have noted that there appears to be fairly extensive use of individual HR practices in UK organisations. However, the extent to which these are linked together into a meaningful strategic whole is more contentious (Storey, 2001). The 1998 Workplace Employee Relations Survey (WERS98) (Cully *et al.*, 1999) investigated take-up of sixteen practices commonly associated with HRM, including team-working, employee involvement, guaranteed job security, etc. The survey found evidence of each of the sixteen practices identified by the survey, suggesting that 'there is evidence that a number of practices consistent with a human resource management approach are well entrenched in many British workplaces' (Cully *et al.*, 1999: 82). However, the practices appear to be adopted in a pragmatic and piecemeal way. Only three of the practices (formal disciplinary and grievance procedures, team briefing and performance appraisal) were evident in the majority of workplaces whilst practices rated as significant for a high commitment approach (e.g. job security, participation in problem-solving groups) were only evident in a small minority. Furthermore, only a fifth of workplaces had more than half of the sixteen practices in place. At the other extreme, only 2 per cent of workplaces reported having none of these practices in place. Findings from the Future of Work study (Guest *et al.*, 2000) reveal a generally low use of HRM practices:

> concentrating on a list of 18 typical practices, only 1 per cent of companies have more than three-quarters in place and applying to most workers, and only 26 per cent apply more than half of them. At the other extreme, 20 per cent of organisations make extensive use of less than a quarter of these practices.
>
> (Guest *et al.*, 2000: ix)

A more recent study (Sung and Ashton, 2005) investigated the adoption of thirty five 'high performance work practices'. The findings show that the more of these practices an organisation uses the more effective it is in delivering adequate training provision, motivating staff, managing change and providing career opportunities. However, the findings also show that about 60 per cent of the sample use less than 20 practices.

 Stop & think   *Why is the take-up of HRM practices generally low?*

Sisson (2001: 80–81) proposes two explanations for the limited adoption of an integrated set of HRM practices. The first is that the time resources and costs associated with change may tempt managers to adopt an incremental approach, that is 'try one or two elements and assess their impact before going further, even though this means forgoing the benefits of the integration associated with "bundles" of complementary practices'. The second, and in Sisson's words, 'less comfortable' explanation is that 'competitive success based on the quality and upskilling that HRM implies is only one of a number of strategies available to organisations' and other strategies such as cost-cutting, new forms of Taylorism, mergers and joint ventures may be applied instead. Legge (1989: 30) suggests the potential incompatibility between business strategies and best practice HRM: 'if the business strategy should dictate the choice of HRM policies, will some strategies dictate policies that . . . fail to emphasise commitment, flexibility and quality?'

The attractiveness of HRM to employers can depend on human resource requirements. Marchington and Wilkinson (2005: 97) suggest the rationale for adopting 'best practice' HRM is hard to sustain in workplaces where the time taken to train new staff is relatively short, work performance can be assessed simply and speedily and there is a supply of substitutable labour readily available. McDuffie (1995: 199) suggests three conditions that enable HRM to contribute to improved economic performance:

- When employees possess knowledge and skills that managers lack.
- When employees are motivated to apply this skill and knowledge through discretionary effort.
- When the organisation's business strategy can only be achieved when employees contribute such discretionary effort.

Cost considerations can also play a significant part. Godard (2004) suggests that many of the claims about the positive association between HRM and business performance underestimate the costs involved in adopting HRM practices. 'These costs can reflect higher wages, more training, possible inefficiencies arising from participatory decision-making processes and various resource requirements needed to maintain high involvement levels' (p. 367). As a result, Godard suggests that, for most employers, the use of an integrated set of HRM practices often has little or no overall advantage over traditional personnel practices with a few high performance practices grafted on and may even have negative effects for some employers. Thus, the 'pick and mix' approach to HRM practices (Storey, 1995), reflected in many UK organisations may make sound business sense.

An integrated set of practices may also be problematic for organisations operating across a range of countries or product markets. Legge (1989) poses the question: 'is it possible to have a corporation-wide mutually reinforcing set of HRM policies, if the organisation operates in highly diverse product markets, and, if not, does it matter, in terms of organisational effectiveness?' (p. 30). In addition, the belief that human resource management can transcend national cultures has attracted considerable critical comment (Pieper, 1990).

HRM in multinational corporations

The impact of increased globalisation of product and labour markets and the growth of multinational enterprises forms another theme in the HRM debate. The employment relationship is materially affected and defined by national and related institutional contexts and these variations in labour markets and national business systems give rise to a wide variety of employment policies and strategies for the management of labour within broadly defined capitalist economies. To the extent that an employer operates within the confines of a national business system, characteristics therein do not impinge upon neighbouring business systems. For example, the Americanness of US firms does not impinge on Canadian firms and their employment systems; similarly, the Britishness of UK firms does not impinge on the Irish business system. In contrast to this, in circumstances where employers operate across national borders, these different institutional characteristics may become factors that an employer wishes to change or override. Thus multinational corporations (MNCs) may seek to deploy centralised – more homogenous – employment strategies, regardless of the institutional character of national business systems where they locate subsidiary operations.

As global integration continues apace and more businesses from established and emerging industrial economies expand their operations across national borders issues around HRM in multinational firms have become critical to organisational sustainability and success. The key academic and practitioner issue that relates to HRM in multinationals is that the subject matter under evaluation does exist in a domestic context but has developed into an international focus from the operation of a firm in different cultural and national contexts. Initially focused on staffing decisions and the management of expatriates in particular, their development and remuneration international HRM holds the added complexity of diversity in national contexts and the inclusion of different national categories of worker. Since the early 1990s however, the focus of international HRM has moved beyond these issues towards the evaluation of more strategic issues in multinational firms in four areas. First, the analysis and deployment of international business strategies (Bartlett and Ghosal, 1989); Second, the transfer of management practices (see Hofstede, 1980, 1991); third, the evaluation of strategic issues relating to headquarters-subsidiary relations (Dowling and Welch, 2004). Fourth, and related to the previous category, the comparative analysis of country specific differences in (international) HRM in multinationals within institutional theory and national business systems (Whitley, 1992, 1999). Below these macro issues more micro empirical firm level issues in international HRM focus on the tensions between centralisation and global integration of business and HR strategies and the de-centralisation of these strategies to facilitate local responsiveness (see Ferner, *et al.*, 2004, Clark and Almond, 2004).

Multinational corporations are significant international actors in the world economy and play a key role in the trend towards 'globalisation', contributing to industrial development and restructuring within and across the borders of national business systems. But MNCs are not itinerant or transnational as is often suggested. Management style, strategies and policies are shaped by home business systems – the financial, institutional, legal and political frameworks in which they developed as domestic firms. Thus there is a persistent 'country of origin' effect in the behaviour of MNCs whereby the country from where an MNC originates exerts a distinctive effect on management style, particularly the management of human resources. Hirst and Thompson (1999: 84) demonstrate that the majority of MNCs are disproportionately concentrated in their country of origin, sell the majority of their goods and services there and hold the majority of their assets there. In addition to this home country or country of origin effect, government regulation in countries where subsidiary operations of MNCs are located may also have an effect on shaping company practices for the management of human resources. In some respects the impact of a 'host country' business system may constrain the preferred practices that reflect embedded patterns of regulation in an MNC's country of origin.

This interplay between home and host country influences raises important questions (for HR academics and practitioners employed in national and multinational firms) about the nature of international competitiveness and associated questions about how MNCs draw on and seek to diffuse competitive advantage from the business system in which they originate. International human resource management for global workforces is central to this question; policies to attract, retain, remunerate, develop and motivate staff are increasingly vital for the development of international competitive advantage. Thus the significance of these issues is not confined to theoretical debates on the nature and scope of globalisation; they are of considerable significance in respect of what becomes 'best practice' in and between different business systems. For example, in the UK, US MNCs are widely diffused and account for approximately 50 per cent of foreign direct investment (Ferner, 2003), and there is considerable evidence to suggest that subsidiaries of US MNCs diffuse international HRM, that is, within individual MNCs. But in addition to this there is evidence that US MNCs act as innovators in business systems where they operate. In the British context, productivity bargaining, performance-related pay, job evaluation, employee share option schemes, appraisal, single-status employment and direct employee involvement are now widely diffused in indigenous firms but were pioneered in subsidiaries of US MNCs; see Edwards and Ferner (2002) for a review of empirical material on US MNCs.

In summary, MNCs may seek to deploy centralised employment policies to subsidiary operations, a tendency that is more pronounced in US and Japanese subsidiaries but less so in the case of German MNCs. Some MNCs, notably US ones, have powerful corporate HR functions which 'roll out' programmatic approaches to HRM that monitor subsidiaries against an array of detailed performance targets. So within MNCs *international* HRM may create broad-based HR systems that minimise or override differences between national business systems and, by contrast, emphasise the importance of organisational cultures that are drawn from the strategic goals of the firm. Management style and practices for HRM in MNCs are shaped by the interplay between home and host country and, as Chapter 15 demonstrates, this interplay focuses ongoing debates about the institutional embeddedness of national business systems and the cultural impact of MNCs in overseas economies.

Evidence of the shifts in HRM that can occur when businesses come under pressure are apparent from examples such as BMW's handling of the Rover group sale and Barclays' branch closure programme. In BMW's case it sought to fuse a European style of communication and involvement with the Japanese style already existing within Rover as a result of the latter's Honda collaboration over the previous decade; in Barclays' case it saw the need to maintain its role as a 'big bank in a big world' by cutting 10 per cent of its branch network in one operation. Closures of plants owned by Corus, Ford and General Motors and relocation decisions made by the Prudential, British Telecom and Massey Ferguson demonstrate the

UK's exposure to MNCs. Here an emergent pattern of strategic decision-making, sometimes made on a pan-European basis, illustrates some embedded characteristics of the British business system, such as comparatively loose redundancy laws, to demonstrate that host country characteristics need not constrain MNCs (see Almond *et al.*, 2003). In each case the competitive pressures associated with the value of sterling, comparative labour costs, skill levels and unit labour costs, or delayed investment decisions overrode softer developmental aspects of HRM. This pattern illustrates how European consolidation in MNCs and the more general pursuit of 'shareholder value' further consolidate the cost-minimisation model of hard HRM.

The impact of HRM on the HR function

'There have been notable attempts to capture the changing nature of personnel roles in response to major transformations in the workplace and the associated rise of HRM' (Caldwell, 2003: 22). The personnel department has often been perceived as an administrative support function with a lowly status and a poor reputation, as depicted by Legge's (1978) 'vicious circle' discussed earlier in the chapter. The emergence of HRM and the emphasis on its contribution to the achievement of business goals has been perceived by many practitioners as an opportunity to 'raise the game'. In order to overcome the traditional marginality and poor reputation of the personnel function, Ulrich (1998) proposed that HR professionals should adopt four roles:

1 Business partner – working with senior and line managers in strategy execution. HR should identify the underlying model of the company's way of doing business, i.e. the organisational architecture, and undertake regular audits in order to identify aspects in need of change.

2 Administrative expert – improving administrative processes, often through the application of technology, in order to improve the efficiency of the HR function and the entire organisation.

3 Employee champion – ensuring that employees are 'engaged', i.e. feel committed to the organisation and contribute fully. This is achieved through acting as the voice for employees in management discussion as well as offering employees opportunities for personal and professional growth and providing the resources that help employees meet the demands put on them.

4 Change agent – building the organisation's capacity to embrace and capitalise on change by shaping processes by helping an organisation identify key success factors and assessing its strengths and weaknesses regarding each factor.

Ulrich (1998) suggests that the HR function needs to fulfil all four roles. Empirical evidence suggests that HR practitioners are more likely to aspire to the strategic roles of business partner and change agent rather than the more operationally-focused roles of administrative expert and employee champion. Survey findings in the UK (CIPD, 2003) show that a third of HR practitioners see their primary role as business partners and nearly three in five aspire to this role, whilst 28 per cent see themselves as change agents and a similar proportion (30 per cent) would like to play this role. In contrast a quarter of respondents see their primary role as administrative expert and only 4 per cent would like to play this role and 12 per cent see themselves as employee champions and only 6 per cent would wish to do so.

Stop & think *Why do you think so few HR professionals want to be employee champions?*

A recent variant of this model (Ulrich and Brockbank, 2005) redefines the employee champion and administrative expert roles, integrates the change agent role into the strategic

Table 1.4 Evolution of HR roles

Mid-1990s	Mid-2000s	Evolution of thinking
Employee champion	Employee advocate	Focuses on the needs of today's employee
	Human capital developer	Focuses on preparing employees to be successful in the future
Administrative expert	Functional expert	HR practices are central to HR value. Some HR practices are delivered though administrative efficiency and others through policies and interventions.
Change agent	Strategic partner	Being a strategic partner has multiple dimensions: business expert, change agent, strategic HR planner, knowledge manager and consultant
Strategic partner	Strategic partner	As above
	Leader	Being an HR leader requires functioning in each of these four roles. However, being an HR leader also has implications for leading the HR function, collaborating with other functions, setting and enhancing the standards for strategic thinking and ensuring corporate governance

Source: Ulrich, D. and Brockbank, W. (2005) 'Role call', *People Management*, 11,12: 24–28.

partner role and introduces the new role of HR leader, see Table 1.4. These 'subtle but important changes' are described as reflecting the 'changing roles we are observing in the leading organisations with which we work' (p. 24). So, employee champions are not only focused on the current needs of employees but also have to build the workforce of the future. Functional experts are not only concerned with administrative efficiency but also apply their expert knowledge to the design and implementation of HR practices that 'improve decisions and deliver results' (p. 26). Leaders are responsible for leading the HR function in order to enhance its credibility.

 Stop & think

To what extent do these new titles increase the attractiveness of operational HR roles?

Whilst many HR practitioners aspire to adopt a more strategic role survey data suggest that operational administrative work is still dominant. The CIPD survey (2003) into the roles and responsibilities of HR practitioners asked respondents to identify the three most time-consuming activities and the three most important activities in terms of their contribution to the organisation. The results are shown in Table 1.5.

These findings help to illustrate the ongoing tensions between competing role demands on the HR function and the difficulties in creating an entirely new role and agenda for the function that 'focuses it not on traditional HR activities such as staffing and compensation, but on outcomes' (Ulrich, 1998: 124). These problems are also reflected by the authors of the CIPD survey who comment that:

> It should perhaps be no surprise that, despite respondents' aspirations to be more strategic, they spend nearly three times as much time on administration as on business strategy, since 'urgent' matters notoriously drive out those that are only 'important'. (CIPD, 2003: 12)

Table 1.5 HR practitioners' perceptions of the most time-consuming and most important HR activities

HR activity	Most time-consuming (%)	Most important (%)
HR administration	46	4
Updating own HR knowledge	9	14
Providing support for line managers	70	44
Providing specialist HR input to wider business issues	47	60
Developing HR strategy and policy	45	71
Implementing HR policies	49	20
HR programme design	14	16
Business strategy	17	64

Source: CIPD (2003) 'HR Survey: where we are, where we're heading', p.12.

The findings may also reflect claims that although the role of the HR professional in contemporary organisations has become more multifaceted and complex, the negative counter-images of the past still remain (Caldwell, 2003: 22). Similar findings emerge from other studies. For example, Guest and King (2004) explore how far the advent of HRM offers a new basis for power and influence amongst HR professionals. From the findings they conclude that:

> While the rhetoric surrounding the importance of people management and people as key assets in the fight for competitive advantage has taken hold in industry, and while it is no longer quite right to claim that in the absence of a crisis HR is invariably a low priority for top management, neither it is a high priority. (Guest and King, 2004: 421)

Conclusion

HRM has now become the most popular term in the English-speaking world to refer to the activities of management in the employment relationship (Boxall and Purcell, 2003) but debates around the meaning of the term and the impact of the concept continue. This chapter has outlined the key themes in the HRM debate and has attempted to show how our understanding has changed over time and the impact this has had on the management of people. When HRM first emerged the main concerns appeared to be the distinctiveness of HRM and the extent to which it represented a positive or negative phase in people management. In this respect, the debate primarily related to the difference between HRM and more traditional personnel management and the extent to which the language associated with HRM was a true reflection of its intent. More recently, the HRM debate has been more concerned with outcomes, i.e. the consequences of applying HRM in specific circumstances and the extent to which HRM can provide competitive advantage. The results are somewhat ambiguous in that, whilst there appear to be associations between HRM and organisational performance, a question remains over which comes first: does HRM lead to better organisational performance or are better-performing organisations more able to invest in HRM practices? Either way it still seems that the majority of organisations have embraced HRM in a partial rather than a complete way. At the same time, it appears that the advent of HRM has had only partial impact on the role and status of the HR function and, whilst many HR practitioners aspire to more strategic roles the operational focus continues to be dominant.

Overall, it seems that HRM as a term is widely used but subject to so many different interpretations that 'it is easy to find slippage in its use' (Marchington and Wilkinson, 2005: 4). These different interpretations can be confusing but they are also part of the attraction of HRM for academics and practitioners and help ensure that 'the domain is still lively, vibrant and contested' (Storey, 2001: 16). Whatever the perspective taken, it seems that the advent of HRM has raised questions about the nature of people management that have stimulated one of the most intense and active debates to have occurred in the subject in the last 40 years and there is every likelihood that the debate will continue for some considerable time yet.

Summary

- There is no universally agreed definition of HRM and definitions can refer to people management activities in the broadest sense or in the specific meanings of high-commitment management or a strategic approach to people management.

- The origins of HRM may be traced back to the 1930s in the United States. By the early 1980s a number of US analysts were writing about HRM and devising models and explanations for its emergence. Among the most significant of these commentators are Devanna (the matching model), Beer (the Harvard model).

- Initially the debate about HRM was concerned with 'inputs', i.e. the extent to which the meaning and elements of HRM differed from more traditional models of personnel management and industrial relations.

- Much of the debate about HRM and the differences with more traditional approaches has been conducted through rhetoric and metaphor. However, although much of the rhetoric of HRM is superficially seductive there is a strong body of literature that cautions against accepting it at face value.

- Over recent years attention has shifted from inputs to outcomes, especially the impact of HRM on business performance. Results from empirical studies suggest that there is some association between HRM practice and business performance but the direction of causality is unclear as is the assumption that a set of practices can have universal applicability.

- HRM in multinational corporations is shaped by the interplay between home and host country. Within MNCs *international* HRM may create broad-based HR systems that minimise differences between national business systems and emphasise the importance of organisational cultures that are drawn from the strategic goals of the firm.

- The emergence of HRM and the emphasis on its contribution to the achievement of business goals has been perceived by many practitioners as an opportunity to improve the power and status of the HR function. One of the most influential models over years has been developed by Ulrich (1998). However, survey findings show that, whilst many practitioners aspire to adopt a more strategic role, the administrative role is still dominant.

CASE STUDY

Comparing different styles of people management

Organisation A

Bearing Co. was formed in 1990 from the merger of a British company and a Japanese company. The European HQ of the company is based in the UK and employs 470 people at a greenfield site in the East Midlands. The organisation as a whole employs approximately 20,000 people worldwide and produces a wide variety of bearings ranging from tiny

Case study continued

parts for computers to huge bearings used in construction. The market for bearings is not expanding so the only way to compete is by increasing market share. The company faces international competition, particularly from organisations in Sweden and Germany and seeks to compete with them on the basis of the volume and quality of production and the quality of service and technical support. Price is already at rock bottom so there is no further scope to compete on this basis.

People management matters are seen as high priority in the organisation and the HR director is a member of the board. The HR department policy is to integrate HR and business goals through 'best practice'. Over the last few years the role of HR has moved from being primarily a policing function, 'directly involved in managing other people's areas', to more of an advisory function providing support to line managers. The HR strategy, 'right people, right place, right time', is communicated through a series of management workshops and via a leaflet given to all employees that also lists the organisation's values of openness, trust, recognition, helping people develop, enthusiasm, teamwork, communication, fairness and courtesy.

The company adopts a relatively sophisticated approach to employee selection, using work-related exercises and psychometric tests when appropriate. For some roles, team members are included in the final interview panel. HR has an input into the selection process but the ultimate decision lies with line managers. Jobs are advertised internally and 30 per cent of the sales team were recruited from elsewhere in the organisation. This has caused some problems, especially if they have moved from engineering or technical posts that are harder to fill.

Pay is based on individual performance and line managers are given discretion to award within defined salary ranges. However, whilst performance should have the most impact, in practice most managers award similar rates to everyone and increases are usually very close to the cost of living.

The open-plan layout of HQ helps facilitate communication generally. Formal downward communication is mainly via department meetings/briefings although feedback suggests that the quality and quantity of information shared is variable. Upward communication channels include an attitude survey and an employee-produced newsletter. The attitude survey enables employees to influence management decision making; for example, working

teams have been set up to investigate particular areas of concern, including pay and communication.

Management are also currently considering a proposal for flexitime proposal that has come from a working group. The majority of employees work full-time and the organisation would like greater flexibility to break away from a 9–5 constraint which is inconvenient in a global business. The company may also consider more part-time working and job-share arrangements.

The training policy is geared towards continuous development. On average, employees have 5 days off-job training per year plus lots of on-job training and mentoring. Additional learning events are also identified during the annual performance development review (PDR). The PDR aims to raise awareness of the link between individual performance and business objectives. The system has proved popular with over 80 per cent completed on time.

The head office is non-union although trade unions are recognised in the manufacturing sites. Other forms of employee representation include various working teams and a health and safety committee. The company has sometimes found it difficult to whip up enthusiasm for working parties; 'it's usually the same people who want to be involved'. Overall, the relationship between management and the workforce is generally good.

Bearing Co. has recently become concerned that it has a huge amount of latent talent that is not fully utilised. Employees are not always very enthusiastic about company initiatives and need to be pushed to get more involved. People in the lower levels are perceived as not doing enough quality work and exit interviews suggest that people would like to be a bit more stretched. On the other hand, many managers are over-stretched; often this is because initiatives are driven from the top, managers need to report back and therefore end up doing a lot of monitoring.

Organisation B

PressCo is a family business that has been in existence for over 100 years. It manufactures rotary printing machines, mainly for export to the USA and Europe. Machines are built to order and each takes approximately 10 months to make. The main competitive advantage is the variety and quality of the product. Up until now this has proved to be successful and there has been a lot of repeat business. However, future orders are currently lower than expected.

The company employs approximately 220 people. Employees are apprentice-trained skilled manual work-

Case study continued

ers, designers, qualified engineers, administrative staff and managers. Shopfloor and support staff work the same hours but have different terms and conditions. Shopfloor workers are paid hourly and get overtime whilst technical and administrative staff are paid monthly and do not qualify for overtime payments.

The personnel and training manager is not a member of the board but reports directly to the managing director. The company philosophy is that employees are the key asset and the role of the personnel function is to maintain loyalty. The personnel strategy ethos is not written down but is 'to provide a cost effective and qualified workforce'. It manifests itself in personnel's role of recruiting people with the right qualifications and dealing with those not performing by 'making life uncomfortable for people who are not up to standard'.

Trade unions are recognised for shopfloor workers but not for administrative staff. The personnel manager describes the relationship between management and the workforce as very good and suggests this is because employees trust management and directors to look after their interests.

Over the last few years a supervisory layer has been removed from the organisational structure but this was achieved by natural wastage and re-organisation as redundancy is not a policy. The size of workforce is gradually decreasing as people leave; in an attempt to save costs the company encourages restructuring rather than replacement. However, labour turnover is low.

When vacancies are identified for shopfloor and technical staff, selection is primarily by interview plus a 'walkabout' to assess their attitudes to the working environment. The personnel manager is involved in all interviews. Administrative staff are initially sourced on a temporary basis from recruitment agencies and are offered a permanent post if their work is satisfactory.

Pay is reviewed annually and increases are based on cost of living. There is also an informal merit award for shopfloor workers. Collective bargaining determines the cost of living increase for shopfloor workers and the amount is usually close to the retail price index. Individual merit awards are determined by management but tend to be fairly modest. PressCo's main objective is to pay what the company can afford for the job being performed. It recognises it is not the top payer but rates tend to be average or above average. There is also a profit sharing arrangement based on percentage of gross sales.

Communication is mainly by the daily interface between management and workers. Details of new orders are put on noticeboards. The manufacturing director may give a specific brief if necessary but employees know it is something big if a briefing is called. If employees have any issues they are most likely to discuss this directly with their manager although they can ask to see the personnel manager or follow the grievance procedure. There are also regular meetings between union representatives and management.

The training and development policy has been written fairly recently and aims to provide training appropriate to company needs and individual development. It is communicated via management plus all employees know that the company will pay for work-related evening classes if requested. However, with the exception of apprentices it is difficult to quantify the time individuals spend on training. Performance appraisal has been introduced recently but only applies to managers.

Questions

1 What are the main similarities and differences between the approaches to people management adopted at organisations A and B?

2 What factors might account for these differences?

3 What is the likely impact of the chosen approach on business performance?

References and further reading

Those texts marked with an asterisk are recommended for further reading.

Almond, P., Edwards, T. and Clark, I. (2003) 'Multinationals and changing national business systems in Europe: towards the "shareholder value" model'? *Industrial Relations Journal*, 34, 5.

Armstrong, M. (1987) 'Human resource management: a case of the emperor's new clothes?', *Personnel Management*, 19, 8: 30–35.

Arthur, J.B. (1992) 'The link between business strategy and industrial relations systems in American steel mini-mills', *Industrial and Labour Relations Review*, 45, 3: 488–506.

Arthur, J.B. (1994) 'Effects of human resource systems on manufacturing performance and turnover', *Academy of Management Journal*, 37, 3: 670–687.

Bach, S. and Sisson, K. (eds) (2000) *Personnel Management*. Oxford: Blackwell.

Bartlett, C. and Ghosal, S. (1989) *Managing Across Borders*. Harvard, MA.: Transnational Solution.

Beardwell, I.J. (1992) 'The new industrial relations: a review of the debate', *Human Resource Management Journal*, 2, 2: 1–8.

Beardwell, I.J. (1996) 'How do we know how it really is?', in Beardwell, I.J. (ed.) *Contemporary Industrial Relations*. Oxford: Oxford University Press, pp. 1–10.

Beardwell, I. and Holden, L. (1994) *Human Resource Management: A Contemporary Perspective*. London: Pitman.

Becker, B. and Gerhart, B. (1996) 'The impact of human resource management on organizational performance: progress and prospects' *Academy of Management Journal*, 39, 4: 779–801.

Beer, M. and Spector, B. (1985) 'Corporate wide transformations in human resource management', in Walton, R.E. and Lawrence, E.R. (eds) *Human Resource Management Trends and Challenges*. Boston, MA: Harvard Business School Press.

*Beer, M., Spector, B., Lawrence P.R., Quinn Mills, D. and Walton, R.E. (1984) *Managing Human Assets*. New York: Free Press.

Boselie, P., Dietz, G. and Boon, C. (2005) 'Commonalities and contradictions in HRM and performance research', *Human Resource Management Journal*, 15, 3: 67–94.

Boxall, P. and Purcell, J. (2003) *Strategy and Human Resource Management*. Houndmills: Palgrave Macmillan.

Buchanan, D. and Huczynski, A. (2004) *Organizational Behaviour*, 5th edn. Harlow: FT/Prentice Hall.

Caldwell, R. (2003) 'The changing role of personnel managers: old ambiguities, new uncertainties', *Journal of Management Studies*, 40, 4: 983–1004.

Chadwick, C. and Cappelli, P (1998) 'Alternatives to generic strategy typologies in strategic human resource management' in P. Wright, L. Dyer, J. Boudreau and G. Milkovich (eds) *Research in Personnel and Human Resource Management*. Greenwich CT: JAI Press.

Clark, I. (2000) *Governance, The State, Regulation and Industrial Relations*. London: Routledge.

Clark, I., Colling, T., Almond, P., Gunnigle, P., Morley, M., Peters, R. and Portillo, M. (2002) 'Multinationals in Europe 2001–2002: home country, host country and sector effects in the context of crisis', *Industrial Relations Journal*, 33, 5: 446–464.

Clark, I. and Almond, P. (2004) 'Dynamism and embeddedness: towards a lower road? British Subsidiaries of American Multinationals, *Industrial Relations Journal*, 35, 6: 536–557.

CIPD (2003) 'Where are we: where are we heading?'. *HR Survey*, London: CIPD.

CIPD (2006) *People, Productivity and Performance – Work Smart*. London: CIPD.

Conference Board (2005) McGuckin, R. and van Ark, B. *Performance 2005: Productivity, Employment and Income in the World's Economies*. New York: Conference Board, August.

Cully, M., Woodland, S., O'Reilly, A. and Dix, G. (1999) *Britain at Work: As Depicted by the 1998 Workplace Employee Relations Survey*. London: Routledge.

*Devanna, M.A., Fombrun, C.J. and Tichy, N.M. (1984) 'A framework for strategic human resource management', in Fombrun, C.J., Tichy, M.M. and Devanna, M.A. (eds) *Strategic Human Resource Management*. New York: John Wiley.

Dowling, P. and Welch, D. (2004) *International Human Resource Management*, 4th edn. London: Thomson Learning.

Edwards, T. and Ferner, A. (2002) 'The renewed American challenge', *Industrial Relations Journal*, 33, 2: 94–111.

Employment Department (1992) 'People, Jobs and Opportunity', UK Government White Paper.

ESRC (2004) *The UK's Productivity Gap – what research tells us and what we need to know*. Swindon: ESRC.

Ferner, A. (2003) 'Foreign multinationals and industrial relations innovation in Britain', in Edwards, P. (ed.) *Industrial Relations in Britain*, 2nd edn. Oxford: Blackwell.

Ferner, A., Almond, P., Clark, I., Colling, T., Edwards, T., Holden, L. and Muller, M. (2004) 'The dynamics of central control and subsidiary autonomy in the management of human resources: case study evidence from US multinationals in the UK' *Organizational Studies*, 25, 3: 363–393.

Fombrun, C.J. (1984) 'The external context of human resource management', in Fombrun, C.J., Tichy, N.M. and Devanna, M.A. (eds) *Strategic Human Resource Management*. New York: John Wiley, p. 41.

Foulkes, F. (1980) *Personnel Policies in Large Non-Union Companies*. New Jersey: Prentice Hall.

Fowler, A. (1987) 'When chief executives discover HRM', *Personnel Management*, January: 3.

Fox, A. (1966) *Industrial Sociology and Industrial Relations*, Royal Commission on Trade Unions and Employers' Associations, Research Paper 3, London: HMSO.

Fox, A. (1974) *Beyond Contract: Work, Power and Trust Relations*. London: Faber.

Gennard, J. and Kelly, J. (1997) 'The unimportance of labels: the diffusion of the personnel/HRM function' *Industrial Relations Journal*, 28, 1: 27–42.

Godard, J. (2004) 'A critical assessment of the high-performance paradigm', *British Journal of Industrial Relations*, 42, 2: 349–378.

Gratton, L., Hope-Hailey, V., Stiles, P. and Truss, C. (1999) *Strategic Human Resource Management*. Oxford: OUP.

Guest, D. (1987) 'Human resource management and industrial relations', *Journal of Management Studies*, 24, 5: 503–521.

Guest, D. (1989) 'Human resource management: its implications for industrial relations and trade unions', in Storey, J. (ed.) *New Perspectives on Human Resource Management*. London: Routledge, pp. 41–55.

Guest, D. (1991) 'Personnel management: the end of orthodoxy?' *British Journal of Industrial Relations*, 29, 2: 149–175.

Guest, D. (1997) 'Human resource management and performance: a review and research agenda', *International Journal of Human Resource Management*, 8, 3: 263–276.

Guest, D. (2001) 'Industrial relations and human resource management' in J. Storey (ed.) *HRM: A Critical Text*. London: Thomson Learning.

Guest, D. and Conway, N. (1997) *Employee Motivation and the Psychological Contract, Issues in Personnel Management*, 21. London: IPD.

Guest, D., Michie, J., Sheehan, M., Conway, N. and Metochi, M. (2000) 'Effective people management: initial findings of the future of work study', *CIPD Research Report*. London: CIPD.

Guest, D., Michie, J., Conway, N. and Sheehan, M. (2003) 'Human resource management and corporate performance in the UK', *British Journal of Industrial Relations*, 41, 2: 291–314.

Guest, D. and King, Z. (2004) 'Power, innovation and problem solving: the personnel managers' three steps to heaven?' *Journal of Management Studies*, 41, 3: 401–423.

31

Hendry, C. and Pettigrew, A. (1990) 'Human resource management: an agenda for the 1990s', *International Journal of Human Resource Management*, 1, 1: 17–43.

Hirst, P. and Thompson, G. (1999) *Globalization in Question*, 2nd edn. London: Polity.

Hofstede, G. (1980) *Culture's Consequences: International Differences in Work Related Values*. London: Sage.

Hofstede, G. (1991) *Cultures and Organizations: Software of the Mind*. London: McGraw Hill.

Hoque, K. and Noon, M. (2001) 'Counting angels: a comparison of personnel and HR specialists', *Human Resource Management Journal*, 11, 3: 5–22.

*Huselid, M. (1995) 'The impact of HRM practices on turnover, productivity and corporate financial performance', *Academy of Management Journal*, 38, 3: 635–672.

Hyde, P., Boaden, R., Cortvriend, P., Harris, C., Marchington, M., Pass, S., Sparrow, P. and Sibbald, B. (2005) 'Improving health through human resource management: a starting point for change', *Change Agenda*. London: CIPD.

Ichniowski, C., Shaw, K. and Prennushi, G. (1997) 'The effects of human resource management practices on productivity: a study of steel finishing lines', *American Economic Review*, 87, 291–313.

IPM (1963) 'Statement on personnel management and personnel policies', *Personnel Management*, March, 11–15.

Jacoby, S. (1997) *Modern Manors: Welfare Capitalism Since the New Deal*. New Jersey: Princeton University Press.

Kanter, R. (1984) *The Change Masters*. London: Allen & Unwin.

Kaufman, B. (1993) *The Origins and Evolution of the Field of Industrial Relations*. New York: ILR Press.

Keenoy, T. (1990a) 'HRM: a case of the wolf in sheep's clothing?', *Personnel Review*, 19, 2: 3–9.

*Keenoy, T. (1990b) 'Human resource management: rhetoric, reality and contradiction', *International Journal of Human Resource Management*, 1, 3: 363–384.

Keenoy, T. and Anthony P. (1992) 'Human resource management: metaphor, meaning and morality', in Blyton, P. and Turnbull, P. (eds) *Reassessing Human Resource Management*. London: Sage, pp. 233–255.

Kochan, T., Katz, H. and McKersie, R. (1986) *The Transformation of American Industrial Relations*. New York: Basic Books.

Legge, K. (1978) *Power, Innovation and Problem Solving in Personnel Management*. London: McGraw-Hill.

*Legge, K. (1989) 'Human resource management: a critical analysis', in Storey, J. (ed.) *New Perspectives on Human Resource Management*. London: Routledge, pp. 19–40.

*Legge, K. (1995) *HRM: Rhetorics and Realities*. Basingstoke: Macmillan Business.

McDuffie, J.P. (1995) 'Human resource bundles and manufacturing performance', *Industrial and Labour Relations Review*, 48, 2: 197–221.

McGregor, D. (1960) *The Human Side of Enterprise*. New York: MacGraw Hill.

McLoughlin, I. and Gourlay, S. (1994) *Enterprise without Unions*. Buckingham: Open University Press.

Marchington, M. and Grugulis, I. (2000) 'Best practice human resource management: perfect opportunity or dangerous illusion?' *International Journal of Human Resource Management*, 11, 4: 905–925.

Marchington, M. and Wilkinson, A. (2005) *Human Resource Management at Work*, 3rd edn. London: CIPD.

Marchington, M. and Zagelmeyer, S. (2005) 'Foreword: linking HRM and performance – a never-ending search?' *Human Resource Management Journal*, 15, 4: 3–8.

Miles, R. and Snow, C. (1984) 'Designing strategic human resource systems', *Organisational Dynamics*, Summer: 36–52.

Mintzberg, H. (1994) *The Rise and Fall of Strategic Planning*. Hemel Hempstead: Prentice Hall.

Paauwe, J. and Richardson, R. (1997) 'Introduction' *International Journal of Human Resource Management*, 8, 3: 257–262.

Patterson, M., West, M., Lawthorm, R. and Nickell, S. (1997) *The Impact of People Management Practices on Business Performance, Issues in People Management*, 22. London: IPD.

Peters, T.J. and Waterman, R.H. (1982) *In Search of Excellence: Lessons from America's Best Run Companies*. New York: Harper & Row.

Pfeffer, J. (1994) *Competitive Advantage Through People*. Boston, MA: Harvard Business School Press.

Pfeffer, J. (1998) *The Human Equation*. Boston, MA: Harvard Business School Press.

Pieper, R. (ed.) (1990) *Human Resource Management: An International Comparison*. New York: Walter de Gruyter.

Price, A. (2004) *Human Resource Management in a Business Context*, 2nd edn. London: Thomson Learning.

Richardson, R. and Thompson, P. (1999) *The impact of people management practices on business performance: a literature review, Issues in People Management*. London: IPD.

Schuler, R. and Jackson, S. (1987) 'Linking competitive strategies with human resource management' *Academy of Management Executive*, 1, 3: 207–219.

Sisson, K. (1993) 'In search of HRM', *British Journal of Industrial Relations*, 31, 2: 201–210.

*Sisson, K. (2001) 'Human resource management and the personnel function: a case of partial impact?' in Storey, J. (ed.) *Human Resource Management: A Critical Text*, 2nd edn. London: Thomson Learning.

Skinner, W. (1981) 'Big hat, no cattle: managing human resources', *Harvard Business Review*, 59, 5: 106–114.

Storey, J. (1992) *Developments in the Management of Human Resources: An Analytical Review*. London: Blackwell.

Storey, J. (1995) *Human Resource Management: A Critical Text*. London: Routledge.

*Storey, J. (2001) 'Human resource management today: an assessment', in Storey, J. (ed.) *Human Resource Management: A Critical Text*, 2nd edn. London: Thomson Learning.

Storey, J. (ed.) (1989) *New Perspectives on Human Resource Management*. London: Routledge.

Sung, J. and Ashton, D. (2005) 'High Performance Work Practices: Linking Strategy, Skills and Performance Outcomes'. London: DTI/CIPD.

Thomason, G.F. (1998) 'Personnel Management' in Poole, M. and Warner, M. (eds) *The Handbook of Human Resource Management*. London: Thomson Business Press.

Thompson, M. (1998) 'Jet setters', *People Management*, 4, 8: 38–41.

Torrington, D. and Hall, L. (1998) *Human Resource Management*, 4th edn. Hemel Hempstead: Prentice Hall.

Truss, C., Gratton, L., Hope-Hailey, V., McGovern, P. and Stiles, P. (1997) 'Soft and hard models of human resource management: a reappraisal', *Journal of Management Studies*, 34, 1: 53–73.

Ulrich, D. (1998) *Human Resource Champions*. Boston: Harvard Business School Press.

Ulrich, D. and Brockbank, W. (2005) 'Role call', *People Management*, 11, 12: 24–28.

Wall, T. and Wood, S. (2005) 'The romance of human resource management and business performance and the case for big science', *Human Relations*, 58, 4: 429–462.

Walton, R.E. (1985) 'From control to commitment in the workplace', *Harvard Business Review*, 63, 2: March–April, 76–84.

Watson, T. (2002) *Organising and Managing Work*. Harlow: FT/Prentice Hall.

West, M. and Patterson, M. (1997) *The Impact of People Management Practices on Business Performance*, IPD Research paper 22. London: IPD.

West, M., Borrill, C., Dawson, J., Scully, J., Carter, M., Anelay, S., Patterson, M. and Waring, J. (2002) 'The link between the management of employees and patient mortality in acute hospitals', *International Journal of Human Resource Management*, 13, 8: 1299–1310.

Whitley, R. (1992) *Divergent Capitalisms: The Social Structuring and Change of Business Systems*. Oxford: Oxford University Press.

Whitley, R. (1999) *Divergent Capitalisms: The Social Structuring and Change of Business Systems*. Oxford: Oxford University Press.

For multiple-choice questions, exercises and annotated weblinks specific to the chapter visit the book's website at **www.pearsoned.co.uk/beardwell**

Chapter 2

Strategic human resource management

Nicky Golding

Objectives

- To indicate the significance of the business context in developing an understanding of the meaning and application of SHRM.
- To analyse the relationship between strategic management and SHRM.
- To examine the different approaches to SHRM including:
  - the best-fit approach to SHRM;
  - the configurational approach to SHRM;
  - the resource based view of SHRM
  - the best-practice approach to SHRM.
- To evaluate the relationship between SHRM and organisational performance.
- To present a number of activities and case studies that will facilitate the reader's understanding of the nature and complexity of the SHRM debate, and enable the reader to apply their knowledge and understanding.

Introduction to strategic human resource management

This chapter charts the development of strategic human resource management. It assumes a certain familiarity with the evolution of HRM, early HRM models and frameworks and their theoretical underpinning as discussed in other chapters and particularly Chapter 1. The aim of this chapter is to provide a challenging and critical analysis of the strategic human resource management literature, so that you will be able to understand the synthesis both within and between strategic human resource management and strategic management in its various forms.

Since the early 1980s when human resource management arrived on the managerial agenda, there has been considerable debate concerning its nature and its value to organisations. From the seminal works emerging from the Chicago school and the matching model of HRM (Fombrun, Tichy and Devanna, 1984) the emphasis has very much concerned its *strategic* role in the organisation. Indeed the now large literature rarely differentiates between human resource management (HRM) and strategic human resource management (SHRM). While some writers have associated HRM with the strategic aspects and concerns of 'best-fit', in vertically aligning an organisation's human resources to the needs of the organisation as expressed in the organisational strategy (Fombrun, *et al.* 1984) or by creating 'congruence' or 'horizontal alignment' between various managerial and HRM policies (Beer, *et al.*, 1984; Walton, 1985). Others have focused on HRM as a means of gaining commitment and linked this to outcomes of enhanced organisational performance and business effectiveness (Beer *et al.*, 1984; Guest, 1987; Guest *et al.*, 2000a; Wood and De Menezes, 1998); through best-practice models (Pfeffer, 1994; 1998; MacDuffie, 1995; Arthur, 1994) or high performance work practices (Huselid, 1995; Guest, 1987). Others have recognised the 'harder' nature of strategic HRM (Storey, 1992) emphasising its contribution to business efficiency. Interlaced with this debate has been the wider controversy concerning the nature of business strategy itself, from which strategic HRM takes its theoretical constructs.

Add to this, transformations in organisational forms, which have impacted simultaneously on both structures and relationships in organisations. Bahrami (1992) describes tensions in the US high technology sector that should be familiar to the UK audience. The need for increased flexibility (Atkinson, 1984), or 'agility' (Bahrami, 1992) in organisational structures and relationships, has led to 'delayering, team-based networks, alliances and partnerships and a new employer–employee covenant ' or psychological contract. These changes in organisational structuring and employer–employee relationships, have led to difficulties finding new organisational forms that both foster creativity but avoid chaos. Thus tensions can arise between 'innovation and maintaining focus, between rapid response and avoiding duplication, between a focus on future products and meeting time to market criteria, between long-term vision and ensuring performance today.' These tensions need to be considered within business and human resource strategies, as organisations grapple with remaining lean and focused, yet maintain a loose hands-off management style to encourage creativity and rapid response. These dilemmas are not new to the strategic HRM literature, Kanter in 1989 noted contradictions between remaining 'lean, mean and fit' on the one hand yet being seen as a great company to work for on the other.

Developments in SHRM thinking, explored in this chapter through the development of the best-fit approach, the configurational approach, the resource-based approach and the best- practice approach have a profound impact on our understanding of the contribution SHRM can make to organisational performance, through increased competitive advantage and added value. Indeed, it becomes clear that whether the focus of SHR practices is on alignment with the external context or on the internal context of the firm, the meaning of SHRM can only really be understood in the context of something else, namely organisational performance, whether that be in terms of economic value added and increased shareholder value; customer value added and increased market share or people added value through increased employee commitment and *reservoirs* of employee skills, knowledge and talent.

The debate therefore, becomes extremely complex in its ramification for analysing processes, evaluating performance and assessing outcomes. The observer therefore must come to the view, in the best postmodern tradition, that the profusion and confusion of policy makes straightforward analysis of SHRM in empirical and analytical terms extremely difficult and contingent on positional stances of the actors and observers involved in the research process. However, some kind of analytical context is useful in beginning our evaluations.

In order to understand the development of strategic human resource management, and recognise that SHRM is more than traditional human resource management 'tagged' with the word 'strategic', it is necessary to consider the nature of strategic management. This will provide an understanding of the 'strategic' context within which strategic human resource management has developed, and enable us to understand the increasingly complex relationship between strategic management and strategic human resource management.

Understanding the business context

The nature of business strategy

Boxall (1996) has commented that 'any credible attempt at model-building in strategic HRM involves taking a position on the difficult questions: what is strategy? (content) and how is strategy formed? (process)'. It is the intention of this section to explore these questions, and identify the difficulties and complexities involved in the 'strategy-making' process. This section provides an overview of some of the issues and debates, and sets the context for the SHRM debate discussed later in the chapter. It is not within the remit of this chapter, however, to provide a comprehensive review of strategic management theory. Readers are encouraged to seek further reading on strategic management, particularly if the material is completely new to you.

The roots of business strategy stretch far back into history (Alexander the Great 356–323 BC, Julius Caesar 100–44 BC), and early writers linked the term 'strategy' to the ancient Greek word 'strategos', which means 'general' and has connotations of 'to lead' and 'army'. Thus it is not surprising that many dictionary definitions convey a military perspective:

> Strategy. The art of war, especially the planning of movements of troops and ships etc. into favourable positions; plan of action or policy in business or politics etc.
>
> *Oxford Pocket Dictionary*

Early writings on business strategy adopted a military model combined with economics, particularly the notion of rational-economic man (Chandler, 1962; Sloan, 1963; Ansoff, 1965). This is known as the classical or rational-planning approach, and has influenced business thinking for many decades. The meaning of strategy has changed however, and become more complex over the last 20 years or so, as the literature has moved from emphasising a long-term planning perspective (Chandler, 1962) to a more organic evolutionary process occupying a shorter time frame. (Ansoff and McDonnell, 1990; Aktouf 1996). Thus strategic management in the late 1990s, early 2000s is seen to be as much about vision and direction as about planning, mechanisms and structure.

> Throughout the first half of our century and even into the early eighties, planning with its inevitable companion, strategy – has always been a key word, the core, the near ultimate weapon of 'good' and 'true' management. Yet many firms including Sony, Xerox, Texas Instruments ... have been remarkably successful ... with minimal official, rational and systematic planning. (Aktouf, 1996)

Activity

How would you define the word 'strategy'? Note down five words you associate with strategy.

Strategy is a difficult concept to define, sometimes it is easier to think in terms of metaphors. We have already been introduced to the military metaphor of 'strategy as the art of war'. What other metaphors might you use to define strategy?

What metaphor would best describe the 'strategy-making' process in your organisation? If you are unable to use your organisation, you can use the case study at the end of this chapter.

Approaches to the strategy-making process

This chapter uses the four distinctive approaches to strategy-making identified by Whittington (1993, 2001) as a model of analysis. These are the *classical* or *rational-planning approach*, the *evolutionary approach*, the *processual approach* and the *systemic approach*. As you will see, an organisation's approach to its 'strategy-making' process has implications for our understanding and application of strategic human resource management.

The classical or rational-planning approach

This view suggests strategy is formed through a formal and rational decision-making process. The key stages of the strategy-making process emphasise a comprehensive analysis of the external and internal environment that then enables an organisation to evaluate and choose from a range of strategic choices that in turn allows for plans to be made to implement the strategy. With this approach, profitability is assumed to be the only goal of business and the rational-planning approach the means to achieve it. Alfred Chandler (1962) a business historian, Igor Ansoff (1965) a theorist and Alfred Sloan (1963) President of General Motors identified these key characteristics of the classical approach in their work and writings. Chandler defined strategy as:

> the determination of the basic, long-term goals and objectives of an enterprise, and the adoption of courses of action and the allocation of resources necessary for those goals.

Grant (2002) highlighted the classical approach in his model of common elements in successful strategies (Figure 2.1): where clear goals, understanding the competitive environment, resource appraisal and effective implementation form the basis of his analysis.

Within the classical perspective, strategy can and often is viewed at three levels, firstly at the *corporate level*, which relates to the overall scope of the organisation, its structures, financing and distribution of key resources; secondly at a *business level* which relates to its competitive positioning in markets/products/services; thirdly at an *operational level* which relates to the methods used by the various functions: marketing, finance, production and, of

| Figure 2.1 | **Common elements in successful strategies** |

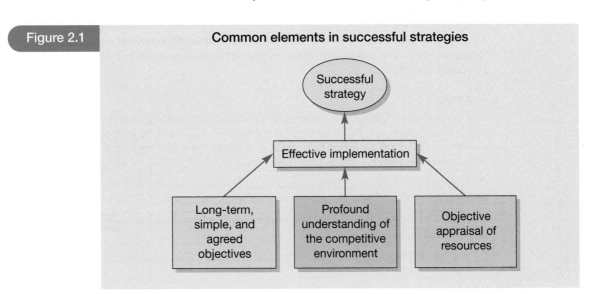

Source: Grant (2002: 11)

course, human resources to meet the objectives of the higher level strategies. This approach tends to separate out operational practices from higher level strategic planning. This is not always helpful in reality, as it is often operational practices and effective systems that are 'strategic' to success in organisations (Boxall and Purcell 2003), thus prompting Whittington (2001: 107) to comment that 'the rigid separation of strategy from operations is no longer valid in a knowledge-based age'. This is not to suggest that external analysis and planning should be ignored, but proposes a recognition that operational practices or 'tactical excellence' may provide sustainable competitive advantage by ensuring an organisation is adaptable and can flex with the environment. This becomes significant in contributing to our understanding of SHRM later in the chapter.

The classical approach, however, forms the basis of much of our early understanding of how organisations 'make strategy' and define competitive advantage. It is worth spending time on the activity below, which will enable you to understand and apply the strategic management process, from a classical rational-planning perspective. Drawing on Johnson and Scholes, (2002), it focuses on *strategic analysis*, which requires you to analyse the external and internal environment of an organisation and identify its key source of competitive advantage. This will then enable you to identify and evaluate the range of *strategic choices* open to the organisation. This in turn will enable you to consider the *implementation* stage of the strategy-making process in the organisation.

Activity — Analysing an organisation

Analyse the external environment

Analyse the external environment your business operates in. Consider the political, legal, technological, economic influences on your business. Now categorise these into opportunities and threats.

Analyse the internal environment

Now identify the internal strengths and weaknesses of the business. Consider the internal resources, structure, leadership, skills, knowledge, culture, etc.

Conduct a SWOT analysis

Put your analysis of the external and internal environment into a SWOT analysis. You might find it useful to prioritise the key strengths and weaknesses of the business, and the main threats and key opportunities available to the business. Remember it is important to be able to justify your decisions. You also need to be clear about differentiating between business and HR issues, although it is likely that certain HR strengths could be a core business competence/weakness.

Strategic choice

Now consider the organisation's strategy, review its vision statement, mission statement, corporate objectives and values. Does a comprehensive analysis of the external and internal environment of your organisation help you to understand the reasoning behind the organisation's strategy?

Can you identify the organisation's key sources of competitive advantage? Does this analysis help you to understand why the organisation has made certain strategic choices?

What other information do you think you would need to fully understand the strategy-making process in the organisation?

Do you think the organisation adopts a classical approach to 'strategy-making'?

Implementation

What changes has the organisation made in terms of culture, structures, leadership, functional strategies, specifically HR policies and practices to deliver their strategy. Have these changes been effective? Why? Why not?

You can either use the *case study* at the end of this chapter to complete this exercise, or you can use the organisation you work for or one you are familiar with and for which you have access to company information.

In the previous activity, you have probably raised more questions than answers, and you have probably identified some of the short-comings of the classical approach. Mintzberg (1990), clearly identified the 'basic premises' of the classical approach as being the disciplined 'readiness and capacity of managers to adopt profit-maximising strategies through rational long-term planning' Whittington (2001: 15). He questioned the feasibility of adopting this approach as either a model for prescription of best practice or as a model of analysis, as he considered it to be an inflexible and oversimplified view of the 'strategy-making' process, relying too heavily on military models and their assumed culture of discipline. Mintzberg (1987) argued that making strategy in practice tends to be complex and messy, and he preferred to think about strategy as 'crafting' rather than 'planning'.

The classical approach is, however, the basis for much strategy discussion and analysis, and, as we will see later, underpins much strategic HRM thinking, particularly the 'best-fit' school of thought and the notion of vertical integration. If, however, we accept that devising and implementing strategies in organisations is a complex and organic process, then it highlights the complexity of both defining and applying strategic human resource management.

The evolutionary approach

An alternative view of the strategy-making process is the evolutionary approach. This suggests that strategy is made through an informal evolutionary process in which managers rely less upon top managers to plan and act rationally and more upon the markets to secure profit maximisation. Whittington (2001) highlights the links between the evolutionary approach and the 'natural law of the jungle'. Henderson (1989: 143), argued that 'Darwin is probably a better guide to business competition than economists are' as he recognised that markets are rarely static and indeed likened competition to a process of natural selection, where only the fittest survive. Darwin noted that more individuals of each species are born than can survive, thus there is a frequently recurring struggle for existence. Evolutionists, therefore, argue that markets not managers, choose the prevailing strategies. Thus in this approach the rational-planning models that analyse the external and internal environment in order to select the most appropriate strategic choices and then to identify and plan structural, product and service changes to meet market need, become irrelevant. The evolutionary approach suggests markets are too competitive for 'expensive strategizing and too unpredictable to outguess' (Whittington, 2001: 19). From this perspective sophisticated strategies can only deliver a temporary advantage, and some suggest focusing instead on efficiency and managing the 'transaction costs'.

The processual approach

Quinn (1978) recognised that in practice strategy formation tends to be fragmented, evolutionary and largely intuitive. His 'logical incrementalist' view, therefore, while acknowledging the value of the rational–analytical approach, identified the need to take account of the psychological, political and behavioural relationships which influence and contribute to strategy. Quinn's view fits well within Whittington's processual approach which recognises 'organis-

Box 2.1 Playing the game of human capital hopscotch

Human capital is the 21st century equivalent of the 19th century dependence on natural resources. Modern wealth creation depends upon the development of people. You might think that this statement originated at the CIPD (Chartered Institute of Personnel and Development) or in a HRM textbook, but it came from the Prime Minister in 2005 and was supported by the introduction of Operating and Financial Reviews (OFRs) by the government in April, 2005. This required firms to report on their future strategy and prospects, including policies for managing their people, which was welcomed by the CIPD, and other professional bodies. Indeed voluntary OFRs had been recommended by the Institute of Chartered Accountants of England and Wales and the CIPD some years earlier, when they concluded 'organisations need to stop being shy about their human capital if they are to give a full view of their performance'.

By November, however, the Government had done a U-turn, with Gordon Brown announcing that he would be scrapping OFRs for all UK quoted companies. While some organisations welcomed this reduction in red tape, others lamented a missed opportunity in meeting the needs of investors and the business community. Friends of the Earth accused Chancellor Gordon Brown of 'short-term political expediency' and the Institute of Directors felt he 'demonstrated a cavalier and ill-thought-through approach to regulation'.

Source: Adapted from *Personnel Today*, January 2006.

Question

To what extent do you think the evolutionary approach to the strategic management process contributes to your understanding of Government strategy on Operating and Financial Reviews?

ations and markets' as 'sticky, messy phenomena, from which strategies emerge with much confusion and in small steps' (2001: 21).

The foundations of the processual school can be traced back to the work of the American Carnegie School according to Whittington (2001) and the work of Cyert and March (1956) and Simon (1947). They uncovered two key themes, firstly the cognitive limits of human action, and secondly that human beings are influenced by 'bounded rationality' (Simon, 1947). Thus no single human being, whether he be the chief executive or a production worker is likely to have all the answers to complex and difficult problems, and we all often have to act without knowing everything we would like to. Thus complexity, uncertainty and the need to take on board a range of interests become facts of life in strategic management and consequently in SHRM (Boxall and Purcell, 2003). It is important for organisations to recognise this to avoid falling into a fog of complacency or the 'success trap' (Barr, Stimpert and Huff, 1992), and it also highlights the limitations of some of the prescriptions for success advocated both in the strategic management and SHRM literature. In practice, an organisation's approach to SHRM has considerable influence here on the strategic management process, as to effectively manage the environment better than their competitors, some writers would suggest that the organisation needs to adopt a learning and open systems perspective. Mintzberg (1987) recognised this in his ideas on 'crafting strategy', and the fluid and organic nature of the strategy-making process. He compared the skills required of those involved in the process to those of a traditional craftsperson – traditional skill, dedication, perfection, mastery of detail, sense of involvement and intimacy through experience and commitment. Thus he recognised that planned strategies are not always realised strategies, and that strategies can often emerge and evolve (Figure 2.2). Thus the classic sequence of plan first, implementation second can become blurred, as 'strategy is discovered in action' (March 1976). Secondly, the processualists noted the significance of the micro-politics within organisations, a theme since developed by Pettigrew (1973, 1985) and Wilson (1992). This approach recognises the inherent rivalries and conflicting goals present within organisations and the impact this can have on strategy implementation. As we will see later in the chapter, it

Figure 2.2

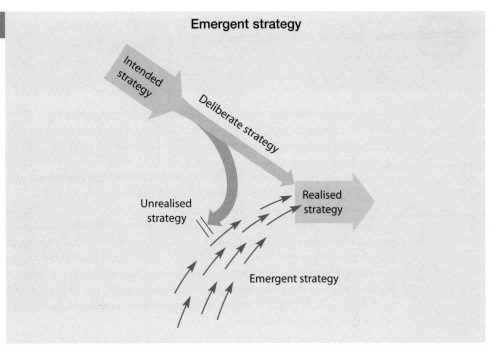

Emergent strategy

is these pluralist tensions that are sometimes ignored in certain branches of the SHRM literature, most notably the 'best-practice' approach.

 Stop & think

Can you think of reasons why an intended strategy might not be realised? Why do strategies sometimes emerge?

Illustrate your answers with examples from your own experience. If you do not have organisational examples, reflect upon your personal development so far.

What factors have influenced your choice of university? degree subject? career?, etc. Have you followed your original plans? What changes have you made? Have new strategies emerged? Using Mintzberg's model, you could plot your development so far on a time-line, identifying where and why planned strategies have failed to be realised while new ones have emerged.

The systemic approach

This leads us on to the final perspective identified by Whittington (1993, 2001), the systemic approach. The systemic approach suggests that strategy is shaped by the social system it operates within. Strategic choices, therefore, are shaped by the cultural and institutional interests of a broader society. So for example, state intervention in France and Germany has shaped HRM in a way which is different to the USA and the UK. A key theme of the systemic approach is that 'decision makers are not detached, calculating individuals interacting in purely economic transactions' (Whittington, 2001: 26) but are members of a community 'rooted in a densely interwoven social system'. Therefore in reality, organisations and their members' choices are embedded in a network of social relations (Whittington, 1993). Thus according to this approach, organisations differ according to the social and economic systems in which they are embedded.

Stop & think

What are the implications for multinational organisations if we assume a systemic view of strategy?

What are the implications for the HR professional involved in mergers and acquisitions?

The four approaches to strategy identified differ considerably in their implications for advice to management. Understanding that strategy formulation does not always occur in a rational, planned manner due to complexities in both the external and internal environment is significant for our understanding of strategic human resource management. Whittington (1993) summarised his four generic approaches of *classical, evolutionary, systemic* and *processual* approaches discussed above, in the model below (Figure 2.3).

By plotting his model on two continua of outcomes (profit maximisation – pluralistic) and processes (deliberate – emergent), Whittington (1993, 2001) recognises that the strategy process changes depending upon the context and outcomes. In terms of strategic human resource management, therefore, the term 'strategic' has broader and more complex connotations than those advocated in the prescriptive 'classical' strategy literature. As turbulence in the environment increases, organisations are recognising the importance of human resources to the competitive performance of the organisation, and therefore its role at a strategic level rather than an operational one.

Activity

Read the case study at the end of this chapter. Which of the approaches identified by Whittington (2001) best describes their approach to strategy formulation?

Why do you think it is important to consider the nature of strategy to aid our understanding of strategic human resource management?

By now you should be familiar with different approaches to understanding the nature of strategy and have gained an appreciation of the complexities involved in the strategic management process. You may have realised that our understanding and interpretation of SHRM

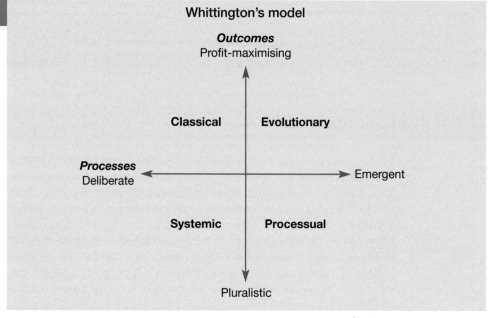

Figure 2.3

Whittington's model

Source: Whittington (2001: 3).

will, to a certain extent, be influenced by our interpretation of the context of strategic management. It is to the definition and the various interpretations of strategic human resource management that we turn next.

The rise of strategic human resource management

In the past 20 years or so, the management of people within organisations has moved from the sidelines to centre stage. The contribution that human resources may make to an organisation's performance and effectiveness has become the subject of much scrutiny. Much of this change has been linked to changes in the business environment, with the impact of globalisation leading to the need for increased competitiveness, flexibility, responsiveness, quality and the need for all functions of the business to demonstrate their contribution to the bottom line. As we have already recognised, it is against this backdrop that the traditional separation between strategy and operational activities, such as personnel and then HRM, has become blurred, particularly within a knowledge-based age.

There is confusion over the differentiation between human resource management and strategic human resource management. Part of the reason for this confusion will be familiar to you, as it arises from the varying stances of the literature, those of prescription, description or critical evaluation. Some writers see the two terms as synonymous (Mabey, Salaman and Storey, 1998), while others consider there are differences. A wealth of literature has appeared to prescribe, describe and critically evaluate the way organisations manage their human resources. It has evolved from being highly critical of the personnel function's contribution to the organisation, as being weak, non-strategic and lacking a theoretical base (Drucker, 1968; Watson, 1977; Legge, 1978; Purcell, 1985), through the development of human resource management models and frameworks (Beer *et al.* 1984; Fombrun *et al.* 1984; Schuler and Jackson, 1987; Guest, 1987), to critics of the HRM concept who question the empirical, ethical, theoretical and practical base of the subject (Legge, 1995; Keenoy, 1990; Blyton and Turnbull, 1992; Keenoy and Anthony, 1992; Clarke and Newman, 1997) to a wave of strategic human resource management literature focusing on the link or *vertical integration* between human resource practices and an organisation's business strategy, in order to enhance performance (Schuler and Jackson, 1987; Kochan and Barocci, 1985; Miles and Snow, 1984); and on the relationship between best practice or high commitment HR practices and organisational performance (Pfeffer, 1994, 1998; Huselid, 1995; MacDuffie, 1995; Guest 2001).

Confusion arises because embedded in much of the HRM literature is the notion of strategic integration (Guest, 1987; Beer *et al.*, 1984; Fombrun *et al.*, 1984) but critics have been quick to note the difference between the rhetoric of policy statements and the reality of action (Legge, 1995) and the somewhat piecemeal adoption of HRM practices (Storey, 1992, 1995) and the ingrained ambiguity of a number of these models (Keenoy, 1990; Blyton and Turnbull, 1992). Thus, while the early HRM literature appeared to emphasise a strategic theme, there was much critical evaluation that demonstrated its lack of strategic integration. Thus terms such as 'old wine in new bottles' became a familiar explanation for the development of personnel to HRM to SHRM.

Activity	Consider the reading you have done in Chapter 1 and draw your own model of HRM, demonstrating its theoretical and applied origins.

- In what ways do you believe strategic HRM to be different to your model of HRM?
- Would you make any alterations to your model to ensure its strategic nature?

Exploring the relationship between strategic management and SHRM: the best-fit school of SHRM

The best-fit (or contingency) school of SHRM explores the close link between strategic management and HRM by assessing the extent to which there is *vertical integration* between an organisation's business strategy and its HRM policies and practices. This is where an understanding of the strategic management process and context can enhance our understanding of the development of SHRM, both as an academic field of study and in its application in organisations.

The notion of a link between business strategy and the performance of every individual in the organisation is central to 'fit' or vertical integration. Vertical integration can be explicitly demonstrated through the linking of a business goal to individual objective setting, to the measurement and rewarding of attainment of that business goal. Vertical integration between business strategy or the objectives of the business and individual behaviour and ultimately individual, team and organisational performance is at the core of many models of SHRM. Inherent in most treatments of fit is the premise that organisations are more efficient and/or effective when they achieve fit relative to when a lack of fit exists (Wright and Snell, 1998: 757). This vertical integration or 'fit' where 'leverage' is gained through procedures, policies and processes is widely acknowledged to be a crucial part of any strategic approach to the management of people (Dyer, 1984; Mahoney and Deckop, 1986; Schuler and Jackson, 1987; Fombrun *et al.* 1984, Gratton, Hope-Hailey, Stiles and Truss 1999). Vertical integration therefore ensures an explicit link or relationship between internal people processes and policies and the external market or business strategy, and thereby ensures that competences are created which have a potential to be a key source of competitive advantage (Wright, McMahan and McWilliams, 1994).

Tyson (1997) identifies the move towards greater vertical integration (between human resource management and business strategy) and horizontal integration (between HR policies themselves and with line managers) as a sign of 'HRM's coming of age'. In recognising certain shifts in the HRM paradigm, Tyson identified 'vertical integration' as the essential ingredient that enables the HR paradigm to become strategic. This requires in practice, not only a statement of strategic intent, but planning to ensure an integrated HR system can support the policies and processes in line with the business strategy. It is worthwhile considering the earlier discussions on the nature of strategic management here, as a number of critics, notably Legge (1995) have questioned the applicability of the classical–rational models on the grounds that there is a dearth of empirical evidence to support their credibility. Legge (1995: 135) tends to prefer the processual framework (Whittington, 1993), which is grounded in empirical work and recognises that 'integrating HRM and business strategy is a highly complex and iterative process, much dependent on the interplay and resources of different stakeholders'.

In what way does Whittington's typology (1993, 2001) of strategy impact on your understanding of 'vertical integration'? You may find it useful to use Table 2.1 to guide your thinking.

There have been a number of SHRM models that have attempted to explore the link between business strategy and HR policies and practices, and develop categories of integration or 'fit'. These include the lifecycle models (Kochan and Barocci, 1985; Lengnick Hall and Lengnick Hall, 1988; Sisson and Storey, 2000) and the competitive advantage models of Miles and Snow (1978) and Schuler and Jackson, (1987) based on the influential work of Porter (1985).

Table 2.1

	Classic	Processual	Evolutionary	Systemic
Strategy	Formal and planned	Crafted and emergent	Efficient	Embedded
Rationale	Profit maximisation	Vague	Survival of the fittest	Local
Focus	Fitting internal plans to external contexts	Internal (politics)	External (markets)	External (societies)
Processes	Analytical	Bargaining/learning	Darwinian	Social/cultural
Key influences	Economics/military	Psychology	Economics/biology	Sociology
Emergence	1960's	1970's	1980's	1990's

Source: Adapted from Whittington (2001: 39).

Lifecycle models

A number of researchers have attempted to apply business and product lifecycle thinking or 'models' to the selection and management of appropriate HR policies and practices that fit the relevant stage of an organisation's development or lifecycle (Baird and Meshoulam, 1988; Kochan and Barocci, 1985). So, for example, according to this approach, during the start-up phase of the business there is an emphasis on 'flexibility' in HR to enable the business to grow and foster entrepreneurialism. Whereas in the growth stage, once a business grows beyond a certain size, the emphasis would move to the development of more formal HR policies and procedures. In the maturity stage, as markets mature and margins decrease, and the performance of certain products or the organisation plateaus, the focus of the HR strategy may move to cost control. Finally in the decline stage of a product or business, the emphasis shifts to rationalisation, with downsizing and redundancy implications for the HR function (Kochan and Barocci, 1985). The question for HR strategists here is firstly, how can HR strategy secure and retain the type of human resources that are necessary for the organisation's continued viability, as industries and sectors develop? Secondly, which HR policies and practices are more likely to contribute to sustainable competitive advantage as organisations go through their lifecycle (Boxall and Purcell, 2003)? Retaining viability and sustaining competitive advantage in the 'mature' stage of an organisation's development is at the heart of much SHRM literature. Baden-Fuller (1995) noted that there are two kinds of mature organisation that manage to survive industry development, 'one is the firm that succeeds in dominating the direction of industry change and the other is the firm that manages to adapt to the direction of change' (Boxall and Purcell, 2003: 198). Abell (1993), Boxall (1996) and Dyer and Shafer (1999) argue that the route to achieving human resource advantage as organisations develop and renew lies in the preparation for retaining viability and competitive advantage in the mature phase. The need for organisations to pursue 'dual' HR strategies, which enable them to master the present while preparing for and pre-empting the future, and avoiding becoming trapped in a single strategy is identified by Abell (1993), while Dyer and Shafer (1999) developed an approach that demonstrates how an organisation's HR strategy could contribute to what they termed 'organisational agility'. This implies an inbuilt capacity to flex and adapt to changes in the external context, which enables the business to change as a matter of course. Interestingly this work appears to draw on the resource-based view and best-practice view of SHRM discussed later in the chapter, as well as the best-fit approach, reflecting the difficulty of viewing the various approaches to SHRM as distinct entities.

How does the lifecycle approach contribute to your understanding of SHRM? How could Café Expresso (case study at the end of this chapter) have prepared better for organisational renewal and industry changes?

Competitive advantage models

Competitive advantage models tend to apply Porter's (1985) ideas on strategic choice. Porter identified three key bases of competitive advantage: cost leadership, differentiation through quality and service and focus on 'niche' markets. Schuler and Jackson (1987) used these as a basis for their model of strategic human resource management, where they defined the appropriate HR policies and practices to 'fit' the generic strategies of cost reduction, quality enhancement and innovation. They argued that business performance will improve when HR practices mutually reinforce the organisation's choice of competitive strategy. Thus in Schuler and Jackson's model (see Table 2.2) the organisation's mission and values are expressed through their desired competitive strategy. This in turn leads to a set of required employee behaviours, which would be reinforced by an appropriate set of HR practices. The outcome of this would be desired employee behaviours that are aligned with the corporate goals, thus demonstrating the achievement of vertical integration.

As you can see, the 'cost-reduction'-led HR strategy is likely to focus on the delivery of *efficiency* through mainly 'hard' HR techniques, whereas the 'quality-enhancement' and 'innovation' led HR strategies to focus on the delivery of *added value* through 'softer' HR techniques and policies. Thus all three of these strategies can be deemed 'strategic' in linking HR policies and practices to the goals of the business and the external context of the firm, and in therefore contributing in different ways to 'bottom-line' performance. Another commonly cited competitive advantage framework is that of Miles and Snow (1978), who defined generic types of business strategy as *defenders*, *prospectors* and *analysers* and matched the generic strategies to appropriate HR strategies, policies and practices. The rationale being that if appropriate alignment is achieved between the organisation's business strategy and its HR policies and practices, a higher level of organisational performance will result.

What are the advantages and disadvantages inherent in the competitive advantage models?

Can you see any difficulties in applying them to organisations?

Configurational models

One criticism often levelled at the contingency or best-fit school is that they tend to oversimplify organisational reality. In attempting to relate one dominant variable external to the organisation (for example, compete on innovation, quality or cost) to another internal variable (for example, human resource management), they tend to assume a linear, non-problematic relationship. It is unlikely, however, that an organisation is following one strategy alone, as organisations have to compete in an ever-changing external environment where new strategies are constantly evolving and emerging. How often in organisational change programmes have organisations issued new mission and value statements, proclaiming new organisational values of employee involvement, etc. on the one hand, with announcements of compulsory redundancies on the other? Thus cost-reduction reality and high-commitment rhetoric often go hand in hand, particularly in the short-termist UK economy. Delery and Doty (1996) noted the limitation of the contingency school, and proposed the notion of the configurational perspective. This approach focuses on how unique patterns

Table 2.2 Business strategies and associated HR policies

Strategy	Employee role behaviour	HRM policies
Innovation	A high degree of creative behaviour	Jobs that require close interaction and coordination among groups of individuals
	Longer-term focus	Performance appraisals that are more likely to reflect long-term and group based achievement
	A relatively high level of cooperative interdependent behaviour	Jobs that allow employees to develop skills that can be used in other positions in the firm
	A moderate degree of concern for quality	Pay rates that tends to be low, but allow employees to be stockholders and have more freedom to choose the mix of components that make up their pay package
	A moderate concern for quantity; an equal degree of concern for process and results	Broad career paths to reinforce the development of a broad range of skills
	A greater degree of risk-taking; a higher tolerance of ambiguity and unpredictability	
Quality enhancement	Relatively repetitive/predictable behaviours	Relatively fixed and explicit job descriptions
	A more long-term or immediate focus	High levels of employee participation in decisions Relevant to immediate work conditions and job itself
	A moderate amount of cooperative interdependent behaviour	A mix of individual and group criteria for performance appraisal that is mostly short-term and results orientated
	A high concern for quality	Relatively egalitarian treatment of employees and some guarantees of job security
	A modest concern for quantity of output	Extensive and continuous training and development of employees
	High concern for process; low risk-taking activity; commitment to the goals of the organisation	
Cost reduction	Relatively repetitive and predictable behaviour	Relatively fixed and explicit job descriptions that allow little room for ambiguity
	A rather short-term focus	Narrowly designed jobs and narrowly defined career paths that encourage specialisation expertise and efficiency
	Primarily autonomous or individual activity	Short-term results-orientated performance appraisals
	Moderate concern for quality	Close monitoring of market pay levels for use in making compensation decisions
	High concern for quantity of output	Minimal levels of employee training and development
	Primary concern for results; low risk-taking activity; relatively high degree of comfort with stability	

Source: ACADEMY OF MANAGEMENT EXECUTIVE by SCHULER, R. & JACKSON, S. Copyright 1987 by ACADEMY OF MANAGEMENT (NY). Reproduced with permission of ACADEMY OF MANAGEMENT (NY) in the format Textbook via Copyright Clearance Center.

or configurations of multiple independent variables are related to the dependent variable, by aiming to identify 'ideal type' categories of not only the organisation strategy but also the HR strategy. The significant difference here between the contingency approach and the configurational approach is that these configurations represent 'non-linear synergistic effects and higher-order interactions' that can result in maximum performance, Delery and Doty (1996: 808). As Marchington and Wilkinson (2002: 222) note, the key point about the configurational perspective is that it 'seeks to derive an internally consistent set of HR practices that maximise horizontal integration and then link these to alternative strategic configurations in order to maximise vertical integration'. Thus put simply, strategic human resource management according to configurational theorists, requires an organisation to develop a HR system that achieves both horizontal and vertical integration. Delery and Doty use Miles and Snow's (1978) categories of 'defender' and 'prospector' to theoretically derive 'internal systems' or configurations of HR practices that maximise horizontal fit, and then link these to strategic configurations of, for example, 'defender' or 'prospector' to maximise vertical fit (Table 2.3).

The configurational approach provides an interesting variation on the contingency approach, and contributes to the strategic human resource management debate in recognising the need for organisations to achieve both vertical and horizontal fit through their HR practices, so as to contribute to an organisation's competitive advantage and therefore be deemed strategic. While Table 2.3 below only provides for the two polar opposites of 'defender' and 'prospector' type strategies, the approach does allow for deviation from these ideal-type strategies and recognises the need for proportionate deviation from the ideal-type HR systems.

Activity

Chart the differences between the two theoretical perspectives identified in the discussion so far (contingency and configurational approaches). In what ways have these approaches contributed to your understanding of *strategic* HRM?

Table 2.3 Gaining maximum vertical and horizontal fit through strategic configurations

HR Practices	Internal career opportunities	Training and development	Performance management	Employment security	Participation	Role of HR
Defenders Low-risk strategies Secure markets Concentration on narrow segments Focus on efficiency of systems	Sophisticated recruitment and selection systems Build talent and skills Career development opportunities Retention of key skills valued	Focus longer-term development for the future and emphasis on learning	Appraisals development oriented Clear grading structure and transparency valued Employee share schemes	Job security highly valued	Employee voice valued, through established systems of employee involvement, grievance, trade unions where recognised Commitment to the organisation emphasised	Potential for strategic role Well established department, with established HR systems
Prospectors Innovative high-risk strategies Change and uncertainty Focus on entering new markets	Buy-in talent and skills Limited internal career paths	Focus short-term skill needs Onus on individual to take responsibility for personal learning and development	Appraisals results-oriented Reward short-term incentive based Performance related pay based on bottom-line measures	Employability valued	Participation and employee voice limited	Administrative role Support role

Source: Delery and Doty (1996: 802–835). ACADEMY OF MANAGEMENT JOURNAL by DELERY J. & DOTY H. Copyright 1996 by ACADEMY OF MANAGEMENT (NY). Reproduced with permission of ACADEMY OF MANAGEMENT (NY) in the format Textbook via Copyright Clearance Center.

In analysing the level of vertical integration evident in organisational practice, it soon becomes clear that organisations pursue and interpret vertical integration in different ways. Some organisations tend to adopt a top-down approach to HR 'strategy making', with senior management cascading defined strategic objectives to functional departments, who in turn cascade and roll out policies to employees, while other organisations recognise HRM as a business partner. Torrington and Hall (1998) have explored the varying interpretations of 'fit' or 'integration' by attempting to qualify the degree or levels of integration between an organisation's business strategy and its human resources strategy. They identified five different relationships or levels of 'vertical integration' (see Figure 2.4).

In the separation model, there is clearly no vertical integration or relationship between those responsible for business strategy and those responsible for HR, thus there is unlikely to be any formal responsibility for human resources in the organisation. The 'fit' model according to Torrington and Hall, recognises that employees are key to achieving the business strategy, therefore the human resources strategy is designed to fit the requirements of the organisation's business strategy. This 'top-down' version of 'fit' can be seen in the matching model (Fombrun *et al.* 1984) and in the best-fit models of Schuler and Jackson (1987) and Kochan and Barocci (1985). As you have probably already identified, these models assume a classical approach to strategy. Thus they assume that business objectives are cascaded down from senior management through departments to individuals.

The 'dialogue' model recognises the need for a two-way relationship between those responsible for making business strategy decisions and those responsible for making HR decisions. In reality, however, in this model the HR role may be limited to passing on essential information to the board to enable them to make strategic decisions. The 'holistic' model on the other hand recognises employees as a key source of competitive advantage rather than just a mechanism for implementing an organisation's strategy. Human resource

| Figure 2.4 | Torrington and Hall's five levels of 'vertical integration' |

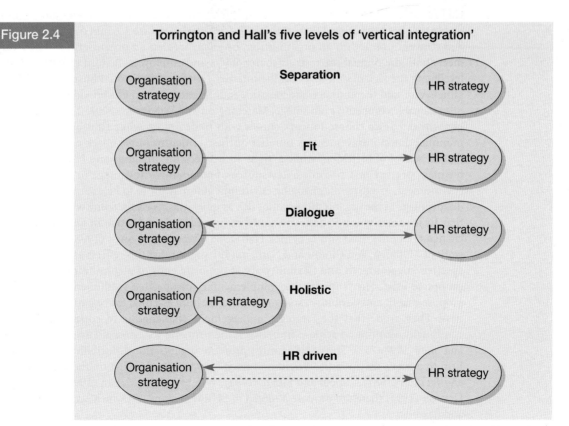

Source: Torrington and Hall (1998: 27).

strategy in this model becomes critical, as people competences become key business competences. This is the underpinning assumption behind the resource-based view of the firm (Barney, 1991; Barney and Wright, 1998), discussed later in this chapter. The final degree of integration identified by Torrington and Hall is the HR driven model, which places HR as a key strategic partner.

Having considered Torrington and Hall's (1998, 2005) levels of vertical integration, which of these approaches to HR strategy represents your organisation's approach to Human Resources? Alternatively, you can use the case study 'Café Expresso' at the end of this chapter.

Limitations of the best-fit models of SHRM

Criticisms of the best-fit approach have identified a number of problems, both in its underlying theoretical assumptions and its application to organisations. One of these key themes is the reliance on the classical rational-planning approach to strategy making, its reliance on determinism and the resulting lack of sophistication in its description of generic competitive strategies (Miller, 1992; Ritson, 1999; Boxall and Purcell, 2003), together with its rejection of societal and national cultural influences on HR strategy. As Boxall and Purcell (2003: 61) noted, the firm can never be the complete author of its own HRM. This criticism is partly answered by the configurational school, which recognises the prevalence of hybrid strategies and the need for HR to respond accordingly (Delery and Doty, 1996). A further criticism is that best-fit models tend to ignore employee interests in the pursuit of enhanced economic performance. Thus, in reality, alignment tends to focus on 'fit' as defined by Torrington and Hall (1998), and relies on assumptions of unitarism rather than the alignment of mutual interests. It has been argued that 'multiple fits' are needed to take account of pluralist interests and conventions within an organisation, by ensuring that an organisation's HR strategy meets both the mutual interests of shareholders and employees. A third criticism could be levelled at the lack of emphasis on the internal context of individual businesses within the same sector and the unique characteristics and practices that might provide its main source of sustainable competitive advantage. Marchington and Wilkinson (2002: 225) ask, for example, why did Tesco choose to work closely with trade unions while Sainsbury's preferred to minimise union involvement? A number of these criticisms imply a lack of flexibility in the best-fit school of SHRM as, while a 'tight' fit between an organisation's HR strategy and its business strategy may provide a key source of competitive advantage in a stable business environment, in a dynamic changing environment it may prove to be a source of competitive disadvantage as the organisation cannot flex as quickly as its rivals. Some writers have argued that fit is sometimes not desirable and can be counter productive in an environment of change (Lengnick Hall and Lengnick Hall, 1988). Wright and Snell (1998) drawing on the work of Milliman, Von Glinow and Nathan, 1991 suggest that this reflects an 'orthogonal perspective' suggesting fit and flexibility are at opposite ends of a continuum, and therefore cannot co-exist. They support the 'complementary perspective' (Milliman *et al.*, 1991) and propose that fit and flexibility can co-exist, and are both essential for organisational effectiveness. They argue that the strategic management challenge is to cope with change by continually adapting to achieve fit between the firm and its external environment (Wright and Snell, 1998: 757). Thus SHRM must promote organisational flexibility in order for the firm to achieve dynamic fit. Wright and Snell (1998: 759), drawing on the work of Schuler and Jackson (1987), Capelli and Singh (1992), Wright and McMahan (1992) and Truss and Gratton (1994) therefore propose a model of SHRM (Figure 2.5) which accounts for both fit and flexibility.

Figure 2.5

A fit/flexible model

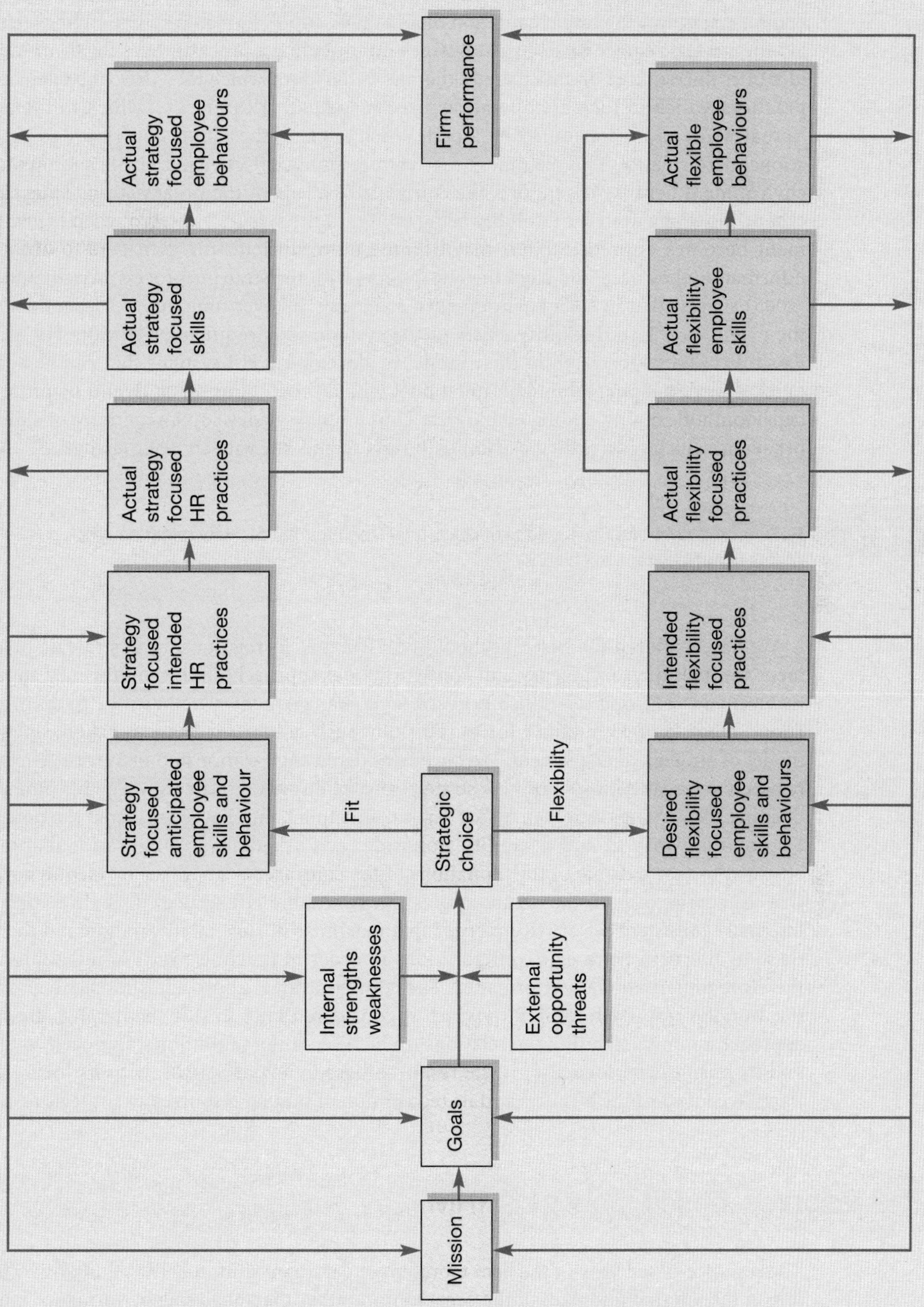

Source: Wright and Snell (1998: 758). ACADEMY OF MANAGEMENT REVIEW by WRIGHT, P.M. & SNELL, S.A. Copyright 1998 by ACADEMY OF MANAGEMENT (NY). Reproduced with permssion of ACADEMY OF MANAGEMENT (NY) in the format Textbook via Copyright Clearance Center.

The model assumes a classical stance towards the strategic management process, as it demonstrates how the implementation of an organisation's human resource strategy needs to 'fit' the strategic choice made by the business in providing a process where the firm's strategy identifies the required or anticipated skills and behaviours, which then drive the intended HR practices, which in turn are operationalised in 'actual' HR practices, which influence the 'actual' skills and behaviours developed. When aligned, these then contribute to organisational performance. This alignment may endure and be effective in a stable and predictable environment because it supports the competitive needs of the organisation. Thus fit may exist without any need for flexibility being built into the system. However, when the environment becomes unpredictable it may become more difficult for managers to obtain the information they need and align the HR systems with the strategic process. Wright and Snell (2005) suggest that in such environments, achieving 'fit' over time may be dependent upon the extent to which flexibility exists in the system, thus requiring a flexible HR system. Flexibility is demonstrated in their model by developing HR systems that can be adapted quickly, by developing a human capital pool with a broad range of skills and by promoting behavioural flexibility among employees. Thus employees develop a repertoire of skills and behaviour which reflects their capability to react to and flex with strategic changes.

Activity	Reflect on Wright and Snell's fit/flexibility model (see Figure 2.5). How might an HR professional facilitate flexibility?

We have explored the best-fit school of SHRM and its relationship to strategic management through the contingency and configurational approaches. The contingency approach recommends a strong relationship to strategic management, whether it be to an organisation's lifecycle or competitive forces. This obviously assumes a classical, rational-planning model of strategic management. We have considered this relationship or *vertical integration* between an organisation's business strategy and its human resource strategy in some detail, defining the varying degrees of 'fit' or vertical alignment, and have considered the possibility of providing both fit and flexibility alongside each other. The configurational approach attempts to answer some of the limitations of the contingency approach by identifying 'ideal type' categories of both the organisation strategy and the HR strategy. It 'seeks to derive an internally consistent set of HR practices that maximise horizontal integration and then link these to alternative strategic configurations in order to maximise vertical integration' and therefore organisational performance. The configurational approach is further explored in the 'bundles' approach to SHRM, which is considered later in this chapter. An alternative approach to understanding the relationship between an organisation's approach to SHRM and its business performance is the resource-based view of SHRM, with its focus on the internal context of the business and its recognition of human resources as 'strategic assets'.

The resource-based view of SHRM

The resource-based view of the firm represents a paradigm shift in SHRM thinking by focusing on the internal resources of the organisation rather than analysing performance in terms of the external context. It focuses on the relationship between a firm's internal resources, its profitability and the ability to stay competitive through its strategy formulation. (Delery, 1998; Ferris *et al.*, 1999). Advocates of the resource-based view on SHRM help us to understand the conditions under which human resources become a scarce, valuable, organisation-specific, difficult-to-imitate resource, in other words key 'strategic assets' (Barney and Wright, 1998; Mueller, 1998; Amit and Shoemaker, 1993; Winter, 1987).

Proponents of the resource-based view of the firm (Penrose, 1959; Wernerfelt, 1984; Amit and Shoemaker, 1993) argue that it is the range and manipulation of an organisation's resources, including human resources that give an organisation its 'uniqueness' and source of sustainable competitive advantage. Their work has resulted in an 'explosion of interest in the resource-based perspective' (Boxall and Purcell, 2003: 72), particularly in seeking ways to build and develop 'unique bundles' of human resources and technical resources that will lead to enhanced organisational performance and sustainable competitive advantage.

Barney (1991) and Barney and Wright (1998) contribute to the debate on strategic HRM in two important ways. Firstly, by adopting a resource-based view (Barney, 1991; Wernefelt, 1984), they provide an economic foundation for examining the role of human resource management in gaining sustainable competitive advantage. Secondly, in providing a tool of analysis in the VRIO framework (see next section), and by considering the implications for operationalising human resource strategy, they emphasise the role of the HR executive as a strategic partner in developing and sustaining an organisation's competitive advantage. The resource-based view therefore recognises the HR function (department) as a key 'strategic' player in developing sustainable competitive advantage and an organisation's human resources (employees) as key assets in developing and maintaining sustainable competitive advantage.

The VRIO framework

The resource-based view of SHRM explores the ways in which an organisation's human resources can provide sustainable competitive advantage. This is best explained by the VRIO framework:

- Value
- Rarity
- Inimitability
- Organisation

Value

Organisations need to consider how the human resources function can create value. It is quite common in organisations to reduce costs through HR such as the reduction in head-count and the introduction of flexible working practices etc., but it is also important to consider how they might increase revenue. Reicheld (1996) has identified human resources' contribution to the business as *efficiency*, but also as customer selection, customer retention and customer referral thus highlighting the impact of HR's contribution through enhanced customer service and *customer added value*. This view is reflected by Thompson (2001) in recognising the paradigm shift from traditional added value through economy and efficiency to ensuring the potential value of outputs is maximised by ensuring they fully meet the needs of the customers that the product or service is intended for. The suggestion of the resource-based view is that if the human resources function wishes to be a 'strategic partner', they need to know which human resources contribute the most to *sustainable competitive advantage* in the business, as some human resources may provide greater leverage for competitive advantage than others. Hamel and Prahalad (1993), therefore, identify that productivity and performance can be improved by gaining the same output from fewer resources (*rightsizing*) and by achieving more output from given resources (*leveraging*). In order to achieve this, the human resources function must ask themselves the following questions:

- On what basis is the firm seeking to distinguish itself from its competitors? Production efficiency? Innovation? Customer Service?
- Where in the value chain is the greatest leverage for achieving differentiation?
- Which employees provide the greatest potential to differentiate a firm from its competitors?

Activity Try to answer these questions with regard to your organisation or one you are familiar with. Alternatively, you could use the case study 'Café Expresso' at the end of this chapter.

This approach has further implications for the role of human resource managers in a firm, as they need to understand the economic consequences of human resource practices and understand where they fit in the value chain. Barney and Wright (1998: 42) suggest that the human resources function needs to be able to explore the following questions:

● Who are your internal customers and how well do you know their part of the business?
● Are there organisational policies and practices that make it difficult for your internal clients to be successful?
● What services do you provide? What services should you provide? What services should you not provide?
● How do these services reduce internal customers' costs/increase their revenues?
● Can these services be provided more efficiently by outside vendors?
● Can you provide these services more efficiently?
● Do managers in the HR function understand the economic consequence of their jobs?

The value of an organisation's resources is not sufficient alone, however, for sustainable competitive advantage, because if other organisations possess the same value, then it will only provide *competitive parity*. Therefore an organisation needs to consider the next stage of the framework: rarity.

Rarity

The HR manager needs to consider how to develop and exploit rare characteristics of a firm's human resources to gain competitive advantage.

Nordstrom is an interesting case, because they operate in a highly competitive retail industry where you would usually expect a lower level of skill and subsequently high labour turnover. Nordstrom, however, focused on individual salespeople as a key source of its competitive advantage. It therefore invested in attracting and retaining young college-educated people who were looking for a career in retailing. To ensure horizontal integration, it also provided a highly incentive-based compensation system (up to twice the industry average)

Box 2.2 Please read the following extract:

Nordstrom exists in the highly competitive retailing industry. This industry is usually characterised as having relatively low skill requirements and high turnover for sales clerks. Nordstrom, however, has attempted to focus on individual salespersons as the key to its competitive advantage. It invests in attracting and retaining young, college-educated sales clerks who desire a career in retailing. It provides a highly incentive-based compensation system that allows Nordstrom's salespersons to make as much as twice the industry average in pay. The Nordstrom culture encourages sales clerks to make heroic efforts to attend to customers' needs, even to the point of changing a customer's tyre in the parking lot. The recruiting process, compensation practices, and culture at Nordstrom have helped the organisation to maintain the highest sales per square foot of any retailer in the nation.

Source: Barney J.B. and Wright P.M. On becoming a strategic partner: the role of human resources in gaining competitive advantage, *Human Resource Management*, Spring, 1998, vol. 37, no 1, 34.

Question

How did Nordstrom exploit the rare characteristics of their employees?

and it encouraged employees to make a 'heroic effort' to attend customers' needs. Thus, by investing in its human resources and ensuring an integrated approach to development and reward, Nordstrom has taken a 'relatively homogeneous labour pool and exploited the rare characteristics to gain a competitive advantage' (Barney & Wright, 1998: 34).

Stop & think

Consider current advertising campaigns, either on television, radio or in the media. Can you identify any organisations that are attempting to exploit the rare characteristics of their employees, as a key source of their competitive advantage. Once you have identified an organisation, try to find more out about that organisation, their business strategy and their organisational performance in relation to their competitors.

Inimitability

If an organisation's human resources add value and are rare, they can provide competitive advantage in the short term, but if other firms can imitate these characteristics, then over time competitive advantage may be lost and replaced with *competitive parity*.

The third element of the VRIO framework requires the human resources function to develop and nurture characteristics that cannot be easily imitated by the organisation's competitors. Barney and Wright (1998) recognise the significance of 'socially complex phenomena' here, such as an organisation's unique history and culture, which can be used to identify unique practices and behaviours which enable organisations to 'leapfrog' their competitors. Alchian and Demsetz (1972) also identified the contribution of *social complexity* in providing competitive advantage in their work on the potential *synergy* that results from effective teamwork. They found that this ensured a rare and difficult-to-copy commodity for two reasons; firstly, it provided competitive advantage through its *causal ambiguity*, as the specific source of the competitive advantage was difficult to identify; secondly, a synergy resulted from its *social complexity* as team members were involved in socially complex relationships that are not transferable across organisations. So characteristics such as trust and good relationships become firm-specific assets that provide value, are rare and are difficult for competitors to copy.

Box 2.3

Please read the following extract:

Southwest Airlines exemplifies the role that socially complex phenomena such as culture play in competitive advantage. According to the company's top management, the firm's success can be attributed to the 'personality' of the company; a culture of fun and trust that provides employees with both the desire and the discretion to do whatever it takes to meet the customers' needs. The 'fun' airline uses an extensive selection process for hiring flight attendants who will project the fun image of the airline. Applicants must go through a casting call type exercise where they are interviewed by a panel that includes current flight attendants, managers and customers . . . Those who make it through the panel interview are then examined against a psychological profile that distinguished outstanding past flight attendants from those who were mediocre or worse.

In addition to the extensive selection process, employees are empowered to create an entertaining travelling environment by a strong organisational culture that values customer satisfaction. Herb Kelleher, CEO, says:

We tell our people that we value inconsistency. By that I mean that we're going to carry 20 million passengers this year and that I can't foresee all of the situations that will arise at the stations across our system. So what we tell our people is, 'Hey, we can't anticipate all of these things, you handle them the best way possible. You make a judgement and use your discretion; we trust you'll do the right thing. If we think you've done something erroneous, we'll let you know – without criticism, without backbiting.' (Quick, 1992.)

The extensive selection process and the strong organisational culture contribute to the differentiated service that has made Southwest Airlines the most financially successful airline over the past 20 years … with the fewest customer complaints.

Source: Barney J.B. and Wright P.M. On becoming a strategic partner: The role of human resources in gaining competitive advantage, *Human Resource Management*, Spring, 1998, vol. 37, no. 1, pp. 35.

Question

How did SW Airlines create a culture that was difficult to copy?

Box 2.3 demonstrates the strength of *Inimitability*: SW Airlines exemplify the role that socially complex phenomena such as culture can play in gaining competitive advantage. Top management attribute the company's success to its 'personality', a culture of 'fun' and 'trust', that empowers employees to do what it takes to meet the customers' needs. This is reinforced through an extensive selection process, and a culture of trust and empowerment reinforced by the CEO. SW Airlines attribute its strong financial success to its 'personality', which CEO Kelleher believes cannot be imitated by its competitors. So the human resources of SW Airlines serve as a source of sustained competitive advantage because they create value, are rare and are virtually impossible to imitate.

Organisation

Finally, to ensure that the HR function can provide *sustainable* competitive advantage, the VRIO framework suggests organisations need to ensure that they are *organised* so that they can capitalise on adding value, rarity and imitability. This implies a focus on horizontal integration, or *integrated, coherent systems of HR practices* rather than individual practices, that enable employees to reach their potential (Guest, 1987; Gratton *et al.*, 1999; Wright and Snell, 1991; Wright *et al.* 1996). This requires organisations to ensure that their policies and practices in the HR functional areas are coordinated and coherent, and not contradictory. Adopting such a macro view, however, is relatively new to the field of SHRM, as 'each of the various HRM functions have evolved in isolation, with little coordination across the disciplines (Wright and McMahan, 1992). Thus there is much best-practice literature focusing on the micro perspective, for example, on identifying appropriate training systems, or conducting performance appraisals, or designing selection systems. Although this literature has now evolved and recognised the 'strategic' nature of the functional areas, it has tended to focus on vertical integration at the expense of horizontal integration, thus there is still limited development in the interplay between employee resourcing, employee development, performance, reward and employee relations strategies. This discussion is explored in more detail in the section: Best-practice SHRM, page 59.

To conclude our remarks on the VRIO framework, if there are aspects of human resources that do not provide value they can only be a source of competitive disadvantage and should be discarded. Aspects of the organisation's human resources that provide value and are rare provide competitive parity only, aspects that provide value, are rare but are easily copied provide temporary competitive advantage, but in time are likely to be imitated and then only provide parity. So to achieve competitive advantage that is sustainable over time, the HR function needs to ensure the organisation's human resources provide value, are rare, are difficult to copy and that there are appropriate HR systems and practices in place to capitalise on this.

Stop & think

Which approach to strategic management identified by Whittington (1993) could be used to explain the resource-based view of SHRM?

How does the resource-based view contribute to your understanding of strategic HRM?

What implications does the resource-based view have for operationalising human resource strategy?

Mueller (1998) in advocating the resource-based view of SHRM argues that 'the existing theorising in strategic HRM needs to be complemented by an evolutionary perspective on the creation of human resource competencies'. He echoes Mintzberg's concerns (1987), that an overly rationalistic approach to strategy-making tends to focus too much attention on past successes and failures, when what is really needed is a level of strategic thinking that is radically different from the past. He identifies a lack of theoretical and empirical evidence to justify the emphasis on rational, codified policies of HRM, and reflects Bamberger and Phillips (1991) in describing human resource strategy as an 'emergent pattern in a stream of human-resource related decisions occurring over time'. Thus the strategic planning approach may be viewed by some as a 'metaphor employed by senior management to legitimise emergent decisions and actions' (Giojia and Chittipeddi, 1991). Unlike contingency and universalist theorists (Schuler and Jackson, 1987; Miles and Snow, 1978; Kochan and Barocci, 1985; Pfeffer, 1994, 1998; Huselid, 1995), Mueller (1998) is more wary of the claimed relationship between strategic HRM and the overall financial performance of an organisation. He recognises that enlightened best practice HR activities do not automatically translate into competitive superiority but rather require more complex and subtle conditions for human resources to become 'strategic assets'. He defines these as 'the social architecture' or 'social patterns' within an organisation which build up incrementally over time and are therefore difficult to copy. The focus on 'social architecture', rather than culture is deliberate as it provides an emphasis on developing and changing behaviours rather than values, which are notoriously difficult to change (Ogbonna, 1992). Mueller identifies an organisation's 'social architecture' as a key element in the resource-based view of SHRM. Together with an embedded 'persistent strategic intent' on the part of senior management and embedded learning in daily work routines, which enable the development of 'hidden reservoirs' of skills and knowledge, which in turn can be exploited by the organisation as 'strategic assets'. The role of human resources is then to channel these behaviours and skills so that the organisation can tap into these hidden reservoirs. This thinking is reflected in the work of Hamel and Prahalad (1993, 1994), discussed below.

Stop & think

How does Mueller's view on the rational-planning approach to strategic management aid your understanding of HR strategy in practise?

Compare Mueller's approach to Barney and Wright's VRIO framework.

Applying the resource based-view of SHRM

In adopting a focus on the internal context of the business, HR issues and practices are core to providing sustainable competitive advantage, as they focus on how organisations can define and build core competencies or capabilities which are superior to those of their competitors. One key framework here is the work of Hamel and Prahalad (1993, 1994) and their notion of 'core competencies' (Table 2.4) in their 'new strategy paradigm'. They argue that 'for most companies, the emphasis on competing in the present means that too much management energy is devoted to preserving the past and not enough to creating the future'. Thus it is organisations that focus on identifying and developing their core competencies that are more likely to be able to stay ahead of their competitors. The key point here is not to anticipate the future but create it, by not only focusing on organisational transformation and competing for market share, but also regenerating strategies and competing for opportunity share. Thus in creating the future, strategy is not only seen as learning, positioning and planning but also forgetting, foresight and strategic architecture, where strategy goes beyond achieving 'fit' and resource allocation to achieving 'stretch' and resource 'leverage'. The level of both tacit and explicit knowledge within the firm, coupled with the ability of employees to learn becomes crucial. Indeed, Boxall and Purcell (2003) argue that there is little point in

Table 2.4

Hamel and Prahalad's notion of 'core competency'
A core competency:
• is a bundle of skills and technologies that enable a company to provide particular benefits to customers
• is not product specific
• represents ... the sum of learning across individual skill sets and individual organisational units
• must be competitively unique
• is not an 'asset' in the accounting sense of the word
• represents a 'broad opportunity arena' or 'gateway' to the future

Source: Reprinted by permission of Harvard Business School Press. From *Competing for the future* by Hamel, G. and Prahalad, C., Boston, MA 1994, pp. 217–18. Copyright © 1994 by the Harvard Business School Publishing Corporation, all rights reserved.

making a distinction between the resource-based view and the knowledge-based view of the firm, as both approaches advocate that it is a firm's ability to learn faster than its competitors that leads to sustainable competitive advantage.

Alternatively, Boxall and Purcell present Leonard's (1998) similar analysis based on 'capabilities'. These are 'knowledge sets' consisting of four dimensions: employee skills and knowledge, technical systems, managerial systems and values and norms. In this model, employee development and incentive systems become a key driving force of achieving sustainable competitive advantage through core capability. Interestingly, Leonard emphasises the interlocking, systemic nature of these dimensions and warns organisations of the need to build in opportunities for renewal to avoid stagnation.

When organisations grow through mergers or acquisitions, as they appear to increasingly (Hubbard, 1999), it has been argued that the resource-based view takes on further significance. When mergers and acquisitions fail, it is often not at the planning stage but at the implementation stage (Hunt *et al.* 1987) and people and employee issues have been noted as the cause of one-third of such failures in one survey (Marks and Mirvis, 1982). Thus 'human factors' have been identified as crucial to successful mergers and acquisitions. The work of Hamel and Prahalad (1994) indicated that CEOs and directors of multi-divisional firms should be encouraged to identify clusters of 'know-how' in their organisations which 'transcend the artificial divisions of Strategic Business Units' or at least have the potential to do so. Thus the role of human resources shifts to a 'strategic' focus on 'managing capability' and 'know-how', and ensuring that organisations retain both tacit and explicit knowledge (Nonaka and Takeuchi, 1995) in order to become more innovative, as organisations move to knowledge-based strategies as opposed to product-based ones.

Stop & think

How does the work of Hamel and Prahalad (1993, 1994) contribute to the resource-based view debate?

Do you think the resource-based view model is appropriate for all organisational contexts?

The resource-based view of SHRM has recognised that both human capital and organisational processes can add value to an organisation, however they are likely to be more powerful when they mutually reinforce and support one another. The role of the human resources function in ensuring that exceptional value is achieved and in assisting organisations to build competitive advantage lies in their ability to implement an integrated and mutually reinforcing HR system that ensures that talent, once recruited, is developed, rewarded and managed in order to reach its full potential. This theme of *horizontal integra-*

tion or achieving congruence between HR policies and practices is developed further in the next section on the best-practice approach to SHRM.

Limitations of the resource-based view

The resource-based view is not without its critics however, particularly in relation to its strong focus on the internal context of the business. Some writers have suggested that the effectiveness of the resource-based view approach is inextricably linked to the external context of the firm (Miller and Shamsie, 1996; Porter, 1991). They have recognised that the resource-based view approach provides more added value when the external environment is less predictable. Other writers have noted the tendency for advocates of the resource-based view to focus on differences between firms in the same sector as sources of sustainable competitive advantage. This sometimes ignores the value and significance of common 'base-line' or 'table stake' (Hamel and Prahalad, 1994) characteristics across industries, which account for their legitimacy in that particular industry. Thus in the retail sector, there are strong similarities in how the industry employs a mix of core and peripheral labour, with the periphery tending to be made up of relatively low-skilled employees who traditionally demonstrate higher rates of employee turnover. Thus in reality, economic performance and efficiency tends to be delivered through rightsizing, by gaining the same output from fewer and cheaper resources, rather than through leverage by achieving more output from given resources. The example of B&Q in the UK, employing more mature people as both their core and particularly their peripheral workforce, is a good example of how an organisation can partially differentiate themselves from their competitors by focusing on adding value through the knowledge and skills of their human resources. Thus leverage is gained as the knowledge of B&Q's human resources add value to the level of customer service provided, which theoretically in turn will enhance customer retention and therefore shareholder value. An exploration of the empirical evidence to support this relationship between SHRM and organisational performance is discussed in more detail in the next section: the best-practice approach to strategic human resource management.

Best-practice SHRM: high commitment models

The notion of best practice or 'high commitment' HRM was identified initially in the early US models of HRM, many of which mooted the idea that the adoption of certain 'best' human resource practices would result in enhanced organisational performance, manifested in improved employee attitudes and behaviours, lower levels of absenteeism and turnover, higher levels of skills and therefore higher productivity, enhanced quality and efficiency. This can be identified as a key theme in the development of the SHRM debate, that of best-practice SHRM or universalism. Here, it is argued that all organisations will benefit and see improvements in organisational performance if they identify, gain commitment to and implement a set of best HRM practices. Since the early work of Beer *et al.* (1984) and Guest (1987), there has been much work done on defining sets of HR practices that enhance organisational performance. These models of best-practice can take many forms; while some have advocated a *universal* set of HR practices that would enhance the performance of all organisations they were applied to (Pfeffer, 1994,1998); others have focused on high-commitment models (Walton, 1985; Wood and de Menezes, 1998; Guest, 2001) or 'human capital-enhancing' practices (Youndt, *et al.* 1996) and high involvement practices (Wood, 1999; Guthrie 2001) which reflect an underlying assumption that a strong commitment to the organisational goals and values will provide competitive advantage. Others have focused on 'high-performance work systems/practices' (Berg,1999; Applebaum *et al.* 2000) This work has been accompanied by a growing body of research exploring the relationship between these 'sets of HR practices' and organisational performance (Pfeffer, 1994; Huselid, 1995; Huselid and Becker, 1996; Huselid, Jackson and Schuler, 1997; Patterson *et al.*, 1997; Guest, 2001; Guthrie, 2001; Batt, 2002; Guest *et al.*, 2003). Although there is a wealth of literature advocating the best-practice approach, with supporting empirical evidence, it is still difficult to reach generalised conclusions from these studies. This is mainly as a result of conflicting views about what constitutes an ideal set of HR best practices, whether they should be horizontally integrated into 'bundles' that fit the organisational context or not and the contribution these sets of HR practices can make to organisational performance.

Universalism and high commitment

One of the models most commonly cited is Pfeffer's (1994) 16 HR practices for 'competitive advantage through people' which he revised to seven practices for 'building profits by putting people first' in 1998. These have been adapted for the UK audience by Marchington and Wilkinson (2005), as shown in Table 2.5.

Pfeffer (1994) explains how changes in the external environment have reduced the impact of traditional sources of competitive advantage, and increased the significance of new sources of competitive advantage, namely human resources that enable an organisation to adapt and innovate. Pfeffer's relevance in a European context has been questioned due to his lack of commitment to independent worker representation and joint regulation (Boxall and Purcell, 2003), hence Marchington and Wilkinson's adaptation, highlighted in Table 2.6. With the universalist approach or 'ideal set of practices' (Guest, 1997), the concern is with how close organisations can get to the ideal set of practices, the hypothesis being that the closer an organisation gets, the better the organisation will perform in terms of higher productivity, service levels and profitability. The role of human resources therefore becomes one of identifying and gaining senior management commitment to a set of HR best practices and ensuring they are implemented and that reward is distributed accordingly.

The first difficulty with the best-practice approach, is the variation in what constitutes best practice. Agreement on the underlying principles of the best-practice approach is reflected in Youndt *et al.*'s (1996: 839) summary as follows:

> At the root, most (models) . . . focus on enhancing the skill base of employees through HR activities such as selective staffing, comprehensive training and broad developmental efforts like job rotation and cross-utilisation. Further (they) tend to promote empowerment, participative problem-solving and teamwork with job redesign, group based incentives and a transition from hourly to salaried compensation for production workers.

Lists of best practices, however, vary intensely in their constitution and in their relationship to organisational performance. A sample of these variations is provided in Table 2.6. This

Table 2.5

Building profits by putting people first	'High-commitment' HRM
Employment security	and internal labour markets
Selective hiring	and sophisticated selection
Extensive training	and learning and development
Sharing Information	Extensive involvement and voice
Self-managed teams/teamworking	Self-managed teams/teamworking and
Reduction of status differentials	harmonisation
High pay contingent on company	High compensation contingent on organisational
Performance	performance

Source: Reprinted by permission of Harvard Business School Press. From *The Human Equation: Building Profits by Putting People First*, by Pfeffer, J., Boston, MA 1998. Copyright © 1998 by the Harvard Business School Publishing Corporation, all rights reserved.

Table 2.6

Pfeffer (1998)	MacDuffie (1995)	Huselid (1995)	Arthur (1994)	Delery and Doty (1996)	Luthans and Sommer (2005)	Stavrou and Brewster (2005)
Employment security	Self-directed work teams	Contingent pay	Self-directed work teams	Internal career opportunities	Information-sharing	Training
Selective hiring	Job rotation	Hours per year training	Problem-solving groups	Training	Job design programmes	Share-options
Extensive training	Problem-solving groups	Information sharing	Contingent pay	Results-oriented appraisals	Job analysis methods	Evaluation of HR
Sharing information	TQM	Job analysis	Hours per year training	Profit-sharing	Participation programmes	Profit-sharing
Self-managed teams	Suggestions forum	Selective hiring	Conflict resolution	Employment security	Incentive-based compensation	Group bonus
High pay contingent on company performance	Hiring criteria, current job versus learning	Attitude surveys	Job design	Participation	Benefits	Merit pay
	Contingent pay	Grievance procedure	Percentage of skilled workers	Job descriptions	Training	Joint HR-management bundle
Reduction of status differentials	Induction and initial training provision	Employment tests	Supervisor span of control		Grievance	Communication on strategy
	Hours per year training	Formal performance appraisal	Social events		Selection and staffing	Communication on finance
		Promotion criteria	Average total labour costs		Performance appraisal	Communication on change
		Selection ratio	Benefits/total labour costs			Communication on organisation of work
						Career
						Wider-jobs
						Communication to management

Source: Adapted from Becker and Gerhart (1996: 785), *Academy of Management Journal*, vol. 39, no. 4, 779–801 and Stavrou, E.T. and Brewster, C. (2005) The Configurational Approach to Linking Startegic Human Resource Management Bundles with Business Performance: Myth or Reality? *Management Revue*, vol. 16, Iss. 2, 186–202.

results in confusion about which particular HR practices constitute high-commitment, and a lack of empirical evidence and 'theoretical rigour' (Guest, 1987: 267) to support their universal application. Capelli and Crocker-Hefter (1996: 7) note:

> We believe that a single set of 'best' practices may, indeed, be overstated . . . We argue that(it is) distinctive human resource practices that help to create unique competencies that differentiate products and, in turn drive competitiveness.

Integrated bundles of HRM: horizontal integration

A key theme that emerges in relation to best-practice HRM is that individual practices cannot be implemented effectively in isolation (Storey, 1992) but rather combining them into integrated and complementary bundles is crucial (MacDuffie, 1995). MacDuffie believes that a 'bundle' creates the multiple, reinforcing conditions that support employee motivation, given that employees have the necessary knowledge and skills to perform their jobs effectively (Stavrou and Brewster, 2005). Thus the notion of achieving horizontal integration within and between HR practices gains significance in the best-practice debate. Horizontal alignment with other functional areas has also been highlighted by some writers as a key element in enhancing the effectiveness of other organisational practices and therefore organisational performance. Lawler, Mohrman and Ledford (1995) identified the link between HRM and total quality management (TQM) and similarly MacDuffie (1995) identified human resource practices as integral to the effectiveness of lean production.

The need for *horizontal integration* in the application of SHRM principles is one element that is found in both the configurational school of thought, the resource-based view approach and in certain best-practice models. It emphasises the coordination and congruence between HR practices through 'a pattern of planned action' (Wright and McMahan, 1999). In the configurational school, cohesion is thought likely to create synergistic benefits, which in turn enable the organisation's strategic goals to be met. Roche (1999: 669) in his study on Irish organisations noted that 'organisations with a relatively high degree of integration of human resource strategy into business strategy are much more likely to adopt commitment-oriented bundles of HRM practices'. Where some of the best-practice models differ is in those that advocate the 'universal' application of SHRM, notably Pfeffer (1994, 1998). Pfeffer's argument is that best-practice may be used in any organisation, irrespective of product life cycle, market situation, workforce characteristics and improved performance will ensue. This approach ignores potentially significant differences between organisations, industries, sectors and countries however. The work of Delery and Doty (1996) has highlighted the complex relationship between the management of human resources and organisational performance, and their research supports the contingency approach (Schuler and Jackson, 1987) in indicating that there are some key HR practices, specifically internal career opportunities, results-oriented appraisals and participation/voice, that must be aligned with the business strategy or that, in other words, are context-specific. The 'bundles' approach, however, is additive, and accepts that as long as there is a core of integrated high commitment practices, other practices can be added or ignored, and still produce enhanced performance. Guest *et al.*'s analysis of the WERS data (2000a: 15), however, found that the 'only combination of practices that made any sense was a straightforward count of all the practices'. As with many high-commitment-based models, there is an underlying assumption of unitarism, which ignores the inherent pluralist values and tensions present in many organisations. Coupled with further criticisms of context avoidance and assumed rationality between implementation and performance, the best-practice advocates, particularly the universalists, are not without their critics.

Box 2.4 HR 'is still not strategic enough'

The annual Key Trends in Human Capital 2006 survey by Saratoga, the human capital metrics business of PricewaterhouseCoopers, found little evidence that the HR function was developing a higher level of strategic influence within the business.

The report stated: 'The centrality of human capital to organisational strategy would suggest that the HR function would move to a more influential position. There appears to be little evidence of this.'

In fact, although the number of HR professionals and managers has increased in Europe – from 62.1 per cent in 2003 to 64.5 per cent in 2004 – the findings do not suggest that their influence within the organisation has increased the same way.

The survey also found that the number of HR directors on the main boards of FTSE-100 companies had fallen to only six.

In the US, 63 per cent of HR directors report directly to the CEO, compared with 81% in 2003.

Richard Phelps, partner in HR Services at PwC, said one of the reasons behind the trend was the lack of skilled, strategically minded HR professionals. 'Moving to a shared services model and outsourcing administrative duties is supposed to free up HR and allow it to be more strategic in the business, but we are finding that organisations are experiencing skill gaps there' he said.

Source: People Management, March 2006: 13.

Ulrich (1998) and Ulrich and Brockbank (2005) identified the need for HR professionals to move away from traditional HR specialisms and create a range of new roles which focused on business outcomes and organisational performance. Specifically he identified the need for HR professionals to become 'business' or 'strategic' partners who were crucially involved with senior managers and line managers in strategy execution and value delivery, a further key role was identified as that of enabling and driving change, together with being an employee champion and administrative/functional expert. Ulrich's work struck a cord with the HR community in the UK and the CIPD's HR Survey 2003: where are we, where are we heading? indicated that HR professionals in the UK were aware of these roles as one in three senior HR practitioners saw their role predominantly as that of business partner, while 56 per cent indicated they aspired to become strategic partners and more than one in four saw themselves as change agents.

Source: CIPD report 2005.

Questions

1 Why do you think, therefore, there is still a skills gap in Senior HR professionals?

2 What do you think a 'strategically minded HR professional would look like?

3 How would you define the role and what key skills and knowledge would you identify?

HRM and performance

In recognising HRM systems as 'strategic assets' and in identifying the strategic value of a skilled, motivated and adaptable workforce, the relationship between strategic human resource management and organisational performance moves to centre stage. The traditional HR function when viewed as a cost centre, focuses on transactions, practices and compliance. When this is replaced by a strategic HRM system it is viewed as an investment and focuses on developing and maintaining a firm's strategic infrastructure (Becker *et al.* 1997). The strategic role of HRM then might be characterised as 'organisational systems designed to achieve *competitive advantage* through people' (Snell, Youndt and Wright, 1996: 62). In turn, competitive advantage may be defined as a set of capabilities or resources giving an organisation an advantage that leads to superior performance relative to that of its competitors (Wiggins and Ruefli, 2002: 84) thus the relationship between HRM and organisational performance becomes significant, both in terms of defining appropriate HR systems and in terms of identifying methods to evaluate and measure the contribution of HR systems.

It is not surprising, therefore that there is a growing body of work that focuses on the contribution of such HR systems to organisational performance (Stroh and Caligiuri, 1998; MacDuffie, 1995; Perry-Smith and Blum, 2000; Stavrou and Brewster, 2005). This systems approach and concentration on 'bundles' of integrated HR practices is at the centre of thinking on high performance work practices. The seminal work of Huselid (1995) and Huselid and Becker (1996) identified integrated systems of high performance work practices – those activities that improve employees' knowledge, skills and abilities and enhance employee motivation – as significant economic assets for organisations concluding that 'the magnitude of the return on investment in high performance work practices is substantial' (Huselid, 1995: 667) and that plausible changes in the quality of a firm's high performance work practices are associated with changes in market value of between $15,000 and $60,000 per employee. Zigarelli (1996; 63) identified that Huselid's study went beyond merely justifying the existence of the HR manager. In an increasingly competitive business environment where sources of competitive advantage are scarce, Huselid's work identified that strategic human resource management can provide such an edge, as a high quality, highly motivated workforce is a difficult advantage for competitors to replicate.

This differs from the universal approach, and is indicative of a configurational approach (Delery and Doty, 1996) in that high performance work practices are recognised as being highly idiosyncratic and in need of being tailored to meet an individual organisation's specific context in order to provide maximum performance. These high performance work practices will only have a strategic impact therefore, if they are aligned and integrated with each other and if the total HRM system supports key business priorities. Instead, therefore, of focusing on the effects of individual HR policies and practices on individual outcomes, it becomes necessary to explore the impact-specific configurations, or systems of HRM on organisational-level outcomes (Luthans and Sommer, 2005: 328). This requires a 'systems' thinking approach on the part of HR managers, which enables them to avoid 'deadly combinations' of HR practices which work against each other, for example, team-based culture and individual performance related pay, and seek out 'powerful connections' or synergies between practices, for example, building up new employees' expectations through sophisticated selection and meeting them through appropriate induction, personal development plans and reward strategies.

The impact of human resource management practices on organisational performance has been recognised as a key element of differentiation between HRM and strategic human resource management. Much research interest has been generated in exploring the influence of 'high performance work practices' on shareholder value (Huselid, 1995) and in human capital management (Ulrich, 1997; Ulrich *et al.* 1995). For example, Youndt *et al.*, (1996) demonstrated that productivity rates were higher in manufacturing plants where the HR strategy focused on enhancing human capital and Huselid, Jackson and Schuler (1997) found that increased HRM effectiveness corresponded to a 5.2 per cent estimated increase in sales per employee, 16.3 per cent increase in cash flow and an estimated 6 per cent in market value. Recent studies in the UK have demonstrated similar findings. A survey by Patterson *et al.*, (1997) published for the CIPD cited evidence for human resource management as a key contributor to improved performance. Patterson argued that 17 per cent of the variation in company profitability could be explained by HRM practices and job design, as opposed to just 8 per cent from research and development, 2 per cent from strategy and 1 per cent from both quality and technology. Other studies have reviewed the links between high commitment HRM and performance, and two recent studies by Guest *et al.* (2000a, 2000b) have argued the economic and business case for recognising people as a key source of competitive advantage in organisations and therefore a key contributor to enhanced organisational performance. Further, Gelade and Ivery (2003) noted significant correlations between work climate, human resource practices and business performance in the UK banking industry. Stavrou and Brewster (2005) however, have noted that while the connection between HRM and performance has been extensively researched in the US, there is a need for further studies to explore HRM approaches that are indigenous to the European Union.

In terms of HR managers, research has highlighted the need for the development of business-related capabilities, (an understanding of the business context and the implementation of competitive strategies) alongside professional HRM capabilities. Huselid, Jackson and

Schuler (1997) concluded that while professional HRM capabilities are necessary but not sufficient for better firm performance, business-related capabilities are not only underdeveloped within most firms, but they represent the area of greatest economic opportunity. The important message for HR managers is not only to understand and implement a systems perspective, but to understand how HR can add value to their particular business, so that they can become key 'strategic assets'.

Stop & think

How can HR demonstrate their business capability? What systems and measurement processes do they need to put in place, to demonstrate the contribution of HR practices to bottom-line performance?

SHRM and performance: the critique

While research studies devoted to demonstrating the link between SHRM and performance have increased (Wright and Haggerty, 2005), there is still much critique aimed at these studies. Criticisms aimed at advocates of the high commitment/performance link are mainly centred on the validity of the research methods employed (Wall and Wood, 2005); the lack of theoretical underpinning (Becker and Gerhart, 1996; Dyer and Reeves, 1995; Wright, Gardner and Moynihan, 2003); problems associated with inconsistencies in the best-practice models used (Becker and Gerhart, 1996; Marchington and Wilkinson, 2002; Wright and Gardner, 2003) and the lack of emphasis on the examination of the level of either vertical or horizontal alignment (Wall and Wood, 2005). This has led some researchers to be more circumspect in their analysis of the relationship between SHRM and performance (Marchington and Grugalis, 2000). In their 2003 study, Wright and Gardner suggest that HR practices are only 'weakly' related to firm performance (p. 312) and Godard (2004: 355) suggests that in liberal market economies the generalisability is likely to be low.

In terms of research methodology, Wall and Wood (2005), identified the least satisfactory survey method is to use single source respondents. In their review of 25 research studies, including many of the key studies on SHRM and performance, they identified that 21 of the studies had used single respondents as the sole source of data. A selection of the studies reviewed are included in Table 2.7. Wall and Wood (2005) therefore argue that future progress in justifying the relationship between SHRM and organisational performance depends on using large scale, long-term research or 'big science' in partnership between research, practitioner and government communities (Wall and Wood, 2005: 429).

In terms of evidence it is difficult to pinpoint whether it is the HR practices that in turn lead to enhanced organisational performance or whether financial success has enabled the implementation of appropriate HR practices. It is difficult to see how organisations operating in highly competitive markets, with tight financial control and margins would be able to invest in some of the HR practices advocated in the best-practice models. This is not to say that HR could not make a contribution in this type of business environment, but rather the contribution would not be that espoused by the best-practice models. Here, the enhanced performance could be delivered through the efficiency and tight cost control more associated with 'hard' HR practices (Storey, 1995) and the contingency school. A further difficulty is the underlying theme of 'unitarism' pervading many of the best-practice approaches. As Boxall and Purcell (2003) note, many advocates of best-practice, high commitment models, tend to 'fudge' the question of pluralist goals and interests. If the introduction of best-practice HR could meet the goals of all stakeholders within the business equally, the implementation of such practices would not be problematic. However, it is unlikely that this would be the case, particularly within a short-termist driven economy, where the majority of organisations are

Table 2.7 A review of research studies evaluating the SHRM/performance link

Research study and response rates	HRM dimensions	HRM measure and source	Dependent variable measures
Arthur (1994) 30 US mini steel mills: 56%	Control and commitment focus	Questionnaire: single source HR managers	Self report: scrap rates and productivity
Guest and Hoque (1994) 119 UK manufacturing sites mainly: 39%	Four *a priori* types 2 x 2: whether or not claim HRM strategy and use more or less than half of 22 HRM practices	Questionnaire: single source principal HR manager or line manager	Self-report: productivity and quality
Huselid (1995) 968 companies with 100+ staff: 28%	Two scales: skills and structures (communication, QWL, training, grievance procedures) and motivation (performance appraisals, promotion on merit)	Questionnaire: single source mailed to senior HRM professional	Objective: productivity, Tobin's Q and GRATE
MacDuffie (1995) 62 car assembly plants worldwide: 69%	Two scales: work systems (participation, teams, quality role) and HRM policies (selection, performance-related pay, training)	Questionnaire: a contact person, often the plant manager, sections completed by different people	Objective: productivity (labour hours per vehicle)
Delaney and Huselid (1996) 50 for-profit and non-profit US firms: 51%	Five scales: staffing, selectivity, training, incentive pay, decentralisation, internal promotion	Telephone survey: single source, multiple respondents in a few cases	Self-report, organisational and market performance
Delery and Doty (1996) 216 US banks, 101 in some analyses: 18%	Seven scales: internal promotion, training, appraisal, profit-sharing, security, participation, job specification and two strategy measures	Questionnaire: single source, senior HR manager (+ strategy from President)	Objective: return on assets (ROA), return on equity (ROE)
Youndt et al. (1996) 897 manufacturing plants in US: 19%	Two scales: administrative HR (appraisal, incentives) and human capital enhancing HR (selection and training for problem-solving, salaried pay)	Questionnaire: multiple source (at least two respondents per plant, mean score) general and functional managers	Self report: customer alignment (quality), productivity and machine efficiency
Huselid et al. (1997) 9293 US firms (manufacturing, finance, miscellaneous) response rate unclear	Two scales: strategic HRM (teamwork, empowerment) and technical HRM (recruitment, training). Ratings of perceived effectiveness	Questionnaire: single source, executives in HR (92%) and line (8%) positions (effectiveness of HR practices)	Objectivity: productivity, GRATE and Tobins Q
Wood and de Menezes (1998) Representative sample of 1693 UK workplaces	Four types of workplace, ranging from high to low high commitment management	Interviews: single source, HR manager or senior manager responsible for HR	Self report: productivity, productivity change over last 3 years and financial performance

Table 2.7 *Continued*

Research study and response rates	HRM dimensions	HRM measure and source	Dependent variable measures
Hoque (1999) 209 UK hotels: 35%	Overall HRM (21 practices used, including harmonisation, job design, training, merit pay)	Questionnaire: single source, respondents unclear	Self-report: productivity, service quality and financial performance
Capelli and Neumark (2001) 433–666 US manufacturing plants: response rates unclear	Extent of job rotation, self managed teams, teamwork training, cross-training pay for skill/ knowledge, profit/gain sharing, meetings and TQM	Telephone survey: single source: plant/site manager	Self-report: sales per employee, total labour cost per employee and sales/value/labour costs
Guthrie (2001) 164 New Zealand firms, heterogenous sample: 23%	Single high involvement work practices (HIWP) scale based on 12 practices (e.g. performance-based promotion, skill-based pay, training participation)	Questionnaire: single source, various staff from CEO to junior manager	Self-report: productivity (annual sales per employee)
Batt (2002) 260 call centres: 54%	Skill level (education and training); job design (discretion and teamwork); HR incentives (supportive HR-training, feedback, high pay, security)	Telephone survey: single source, general managers	Self-report: percent change in sales in prior 2-year period
Wright *et al.* (2003) 50 business units, US food service companies: response rate unclear	Single overall HR practices scale: nine items covering selection, pay for performance, training, participation	Employee attitude survey: multiple source: rank and file employees	Objective (from company records), productivity and profit-subsequent for period 3–9 months after measurement of HR practices

Source: Wall and Wood (2005: 429–463).

looking to primarily increase return on shareholder value. Thus if this return can best be met through cost reduction strategies or increasing leverage in a way that does not fit employees' goals or interests, how can these practices engender high-commitment and therefore be labelled 'best-practice'? It is not surprising, therefore, that ethical differences between the *rhetoric* of human resource best-practice and the *reality* of human resource real practices are highlighted (Legge, 1998). High-commitment models, therefore, which at first appear to satisfy ethical principles of deontology, in treating employees with respect and as ends in their own right, rather than as means to other ends (Legge, 1998), in reality can assume a utilitarian perspective, where it is deemed ethical to use employees as a means to an end, if it is for the greater good of the organisation. This might justify downsizing and rightsizing strategies, but it is difficult to see how this might justify recent tensions between shareholder interests and senior management goals. A common theme of the best-practice models is contingent pay, thus when an organisation is performing well, employees will be rewarded accordingly. There have been many recent cases, however, where senior managers of poorly performing organisations have been rewarded with large pay-offs.

Becker and Gerhart (1996) discuss and debate the impact of HRM on organisational performance further. They compare the views of those writers that advocate synergistic systems,

Box 2.5 Please read the following extracts:

Shareholders and employees fight back!

Vodafone's proposed executive bonus scheme includes a requirement for managers to reach certain levels of 'customer delight' before they go home with a smile on their own faces. It is a shame there is not a requirement for measuring investor delight.

The timing of this private consultation exercise with shareholders is awful. The last six months have not been pretty even by Vodafone standards, yet the board is asking to bring down the target range for earnings growth so managers can still get their share options. It may not like the answer.

Nevertheless, there is something to be said for more modest performance expectations. The company caused outrage in the past by rewarding expensive deal-making over returns on capital. It is the main reason, after all, that it now has to vet pay packages in advance with shareholders.

Source: Moving the Goalposts by Alison Smith, *Financial Times*, April, 2006.

American Airlines pledged to review its executive compensation strategy amid widespread employee discontent over plans that could see its top managers receive more than $70m in cash bonuses this year.

The loss-making carrier's largest unions this week filed a grievance claim over pay-outs due under a plan agreed by the airline's board in 2003 and tied to American's stock performance through to the end of last year.

While American's stock has soared over the past year and outperformed the sector, employee leaders feel the bonuses to be paid are inappropriate when the carrier remains in the red.

The concerns amongst American's employees mirror those of staff and creditors at United Airlines, who rallied against the compensation plan proposed for executives on its emergence from bankruptcy protection last week.

Source: Adapted from American Airlines to review bonus strategy, by Doug Cameron and Kevin Done, *Financial Times*, January 2006.

Time to thin down fat cat pay

Plato believed the income of the highest in society should never be more than five times that of the lowest. Ancient history, of course. In the past 10 years, median pay among FTSE 100 chief executives has grown by 92 per cent to £579,000, before bonuses and incentives, while male median pay sits at £21,000 having dribbled along with inflation.

According to pay consultants Hewitt, Bacon & Woodrow, in 84 per cent of European companies, decisions about executive pay are led by the remuneration committee, made up of non-executive directors. Yet in two or three meetings a year, these committees hardly have time to scratch the surface of what is a very complex subject, let alone go into the rival merits of an alphabet soup of performance indicators. In practice, they are heavily dependent on the advice they get. In 57 per cent of companies, that advice comes from the HR department. In 31% HR commissions assistance from external consultants, but in 41 per cent HR actually designs the package.

HR is therefore complicit in the great fat cat pay heist. It is time it gave some thought to improving the link between performance and reward.

Source: Article by Stephen Overell, *Personnel Today*, February 2004.

Question

How do you think this tension between shareholder interests, employee interests and senior management interests should be managed in determining executive reward strategies and what role should HR play in the process?

holistic approaches, internal–external fit, and contingency factors on the one hand (Amit and Shoemaker, 1993; Delery and Doty, 1996; Dyer and Reeves, 1995; Huselid, 1995; Milgrom and Roberts, 1995) with those that suggest there is an identifiable set of best practices for managing employees that have universal, additive, positive effects on organisation performance on the other hand (Applebaum and Batt, 1994; Kochan and Osterman, 1994; Pfeffer, 1994). They provide a useful critique of the best-practice school as they identify difficulties of generalisability in best-practice research and the inconsistencies in the best-practice models (Ferris *et al.*, 1999; Boxall and Steeneveld, 1999), such as Arthur's (1994) low emphasis on variable pay, whereas Huselid (1995) and MacDuffie (1995) have a high emphasis on variable pay.

Box 2.6 ## HR in practice – Rogas International

Rogas International (RI) owns a host of catalogue stores throughout Europe. They sell a broad range of goods from well-known electrical brands to children's toys to mobile phones at competitive prices. Rogas International operates stores in most medium-sized towns throughout the UK, as well as large stores in all major cities across Europe. Rogas has recently been taken over by a large multi-national retailer. The group trades in 1200 stores and online stores in 18 countries, and employs 30,000 people.

The challenge

As a result of the takeover, a two year change programme has been announced. This has restructuring implications and it is anticipated that staff headcount in the major distribution centres will be reduced by 25 per cent. Some sites will be closed down, with approximately a further 1000 job losses. It is anticipated that new centres will be also be required and this will involve redeployment and recruitment of new staff.

The Managing Director of RI is keen to maintain morale and performance during the change period. He recognises the need to involve all staff in the change programme and communicate Rogas' new business strategy and values transparently. He recognises that employees need to understand the reasons for change and the possible implications for their future job roles. As the planned change is over a two-year programme, he wants to avoid a mass exodus of staff in the early stages due to fears over job security.

Sally Smart, the HR Director, shared the Managing Director's concerns and wanted to avoid losing people in a way that Rogas couldn't control – if employees reacted badly to the news and simply walked out, many of the high street stores would come to a standstill. Rogas needed to maintain and enhance performance whilst restructuring, and they also needed to ensure that they retained key skills and knowledge, which could then be transferred to the new sites.

The solution

Rogas invited 70 of their top managers to a two-day communication event. Sally Smart commented 'We delivered the news about the intended changes in the first hour and spent the rest of the two days trying to understand what their concerns were and how we could deal with them'

To encourage buy-in to the new business strategy and the change programme, Rogas offered the managers a choice of personal and professional development courses so that if they did lose their job, they would feel better qualified to apply for another. For more junior staff, Rogas promised that if they could not find a role for them, they were entitled to £500 worth of training, their redundancy pay, a performance-related bonus and outplacement support.

'Most people don't like change, especially at work, the main reason they resist is because they feel they have no control. We wanted to make people feel more in control of their lives' added Sally Smart.

One of the ways RI did this was by inviting a training and development consultancy Gomad (Go Make a Difference) into its centres to run a series of workshops and personal development focusing on dealing with and surviving change, and challenging self development boundaries.

Many blue collar staff were cynical initially. Workshops were organised to coincide with the different shift patterns and were voluntary. The HR team worked in partnership with the trade union, and trade union stewards led by example and attended the workshops. Change champions were appointed who promoted the workshops, and posters designed in the initial workshops were used to encourage all employees to attend. The workshops were subsequently well-attended and productive feedback sessions were organised with the senior management team.

Cross-functional project teams were established to consider change solutions. They were empowered to deal with 'real' change problems as they arose and resourced to implement solutions. Their successes were publicised throughout the centres and solutions were rolled out throughout the group.

Line managers were encouraged to identify key potential in personal development planning sessions, and recommend individuals for succession. The Managing Director supported a talent management programme to support and retain key knowledge and potential.

The outcome

The year to May 2006 was successful in terms of the distribution team's performance in terms of delivery efficiency and reduced costs, with 70 per cent of staff on track to earn their performance bonus. Shop sales were buoyant, employee turnover and sickness rates had improved and morale appeared strong.

The Gomad programme and talent management programme in particular proved popular with employees. In feedback surveys, 90 per cent of the attendees said they would apply what they had learned, while all participants said they would recommend them to someone else.

Finally HR and the trade union had forged a constructive partnership, and the HR Director had demonstrated to the Board how HR can add value to the business.

Questions

1 Which approach to SHRM discussed in this chapter best explains Rogas International's approach to strategic human resource management and change?

2 How has Rogas International enhanced organisational performance through the implementation of human resource systems and practices?

3 What human resources advice would you give to Rogas International, to ensure that they can manage the consolidation stage of their strategy effectively? Which approach to SHRM has influenced your thinking and why?

Measuring the impact of SHRM on performance and the balanced scorecard

We have so far considered the complexity of the strategic human resource management debate and recognised that our understanding and application of strategic HRM principles is contingent upon the particular body of literature we cite our analysis in. What then are the implications for the HR practitioner, and particularly the HR strategist? We started to consider the role of the HR practitioner at the end of our consideration of the best-fit school. It is now appropriate to consider in more detail how strategic management processes in firms can be improved to deal more effectively with key HR issues and take advantage of HR opportunities. A study by Ernst & Young in 1997 cited in Armstrong and Baron (2002) found that more than a third of the data used to justify business analysts' decisions were non-financial, and that when non-financial factors, notably 'human resources', were taken into account better investment decisions were made. Their non-financial metrics most valued by investors are identified in Table 2.8 below.

This presents an opportunity for HR managers to develop business capability and demonstrate the contribution of SHRM to organisational performance. One method that is worthy of further consideration is the balanced score-card (Kaplan and Norton, 1996, 2001). This is also concerned with relating critical non-financial factors to financial outcomes by assisting firms to map the key cause–effect linkages in their desired strategies. Interestingly, Kaplan and Norton challenge the short-termism found in many Western traditional budgeting processes and as with the Ernst & Young study, they imply a central role for HRM in the

Table 2.8 Non-financial metrics most valued by investors

Metric	Question to which measurable answers are required
1 Strategy	How well does management leverage its skills and experience? Gain employee commitment? Stay aligned with shareholder interests?
2 Management credibility	What is management's behaviour? And forthrightness in dealing with issues?
3 Quality of strategy	Does management have a vision for the future? Can it make tough decisions and quickly seize opportunities? How well does it allocate resources?
4 Innovativeness	Is the company a trendsetter or a follower? What's in the R&D pipeline? How readily does the company adapt to changing technology and markets?
5 Ability to attract talented people?	Is the company able to hire and retain the very best people? Does it reward them? Is it training the talent it will need for tomorrow?
6 Management experience	What is the management's history and background? How well have they performed?
7 Quality of Executive Compensation	Is executive pay tied to strategic goals? How well is it linked to the creation of shareholder value?
8 Research Leadership	How well does management understand the link between creating knowledge and using it?

Source: Adapted by Armstrong and Baron (2002): Ernst & Young: *Measures that Matter*, 1997.

strategic management of the firm and importantly suggest practical ways for bringing it about (Boxall and Purcell, 2003).

Kaplan and Norton identify the significance of executed strategy and the implementation stage of the strategic management process as key drivers in enhancing organisational performance. They recognise, along with Mintzberg (1987), that 'business failure is seen to stem mostly from failing to implement and not from failing to have wonderful visions' (Kaplan and Norton, 2001: 1). Therefore, as with the resource-based view, implementation is identified as a key process which is often poorly executed.

Kaplan and Norton adopt a stakeholder perspective, based on the premise that for an organisation to be considered successful it must satisfy the requirements of key stakeholders, namely investors, customers and employees. They suggest identifying objectives, measures, targets and initiatives on four key perspectives of business performance. These are:

1 Financial: 'to succeed financially how should we appear to our shareholders'?
2 Customer: 'to achieve our vision how should we appear to our customers'?
3 Internal business processes: 'to satisfy our shareholders and customers what business processes must we excel at'?
4 Learning and growth: 'to achieve our vision, how will we sustain our ability to change and improve'?

They recognise that investors require financial performance, measured through profitability, market value and cash flow or EVA (economic value added). Customers require quality products and services, which can be measured by market share, customer service, customer retention and loyalty or CVA (customer value added). Employees require a healthy place to work, which recognises opportunities for personal development and growth. These can be measured by attitude surveys, skill audits, performance appraisal criteria, which recognise not only what they do, but what they know and how they feel or PVA (people value added). They can be delivered through appropriate and integrated systems, including HR systems. The balanced scorecard approach therefore provides an integrated framework for balancing shareholder and strategic goals, and extending those balanced performance measures down through the organisation, from corporate to divisional to functional departments and then on to individuals (Grant, 2002). By balancing a set of strategic and financial goals, the scorecard can be used to reward current practice and also offer incentives to invest in long-term effectiveness, by integrating financial measures of current performance with measures of 'future performance'. Thus it provides a template that can be adapted to provide the information that organisations require now and in the future for the creation of shareholder value. The balanced scorecard at Sears, for example (Yeung and Berman, 1997: 324; Rucci, Kirn and Quinn, 1998), focused on the creation of a vision that the company was 'a compelling place to invest,' 'a compelling place to shop', and 'a compelling place to work', whereas the balanced scorecard at Mobil North American Marketing and Refining (Kaplan and Norton, 2001) focused on cascading down financial performance goals into specific operating goals, through which performance-related pay bonuses were determined. An abridged version of this, including some of the strategic objectives and measures in Mobil's Balanced Scorecard, is included in Table 2.9.

Kaplan and Norton (2001) recognise the impact key human resource activities can have on business performance in the learning and growth element of the balanced scorecard. Employee skills, knowledge and satisfaction are identified as improving internal processes, and therefore contributing to customer added value and economic added value. Thus the scorecard provides a mechanism for integrating key HR performance drivers into the strategic management process. Boxall and Purcell (2003) highlight the similarities between Kaplan and Norton's (2001: 93) learning and growth categories of *strategic competencies*, skills and knowledge required by employees to support the strategy, *strategic technologies*, information support systems required to support the strategy and *climate for action*, the cultural shifts needed to motivate, empower and align the workforce behind the strategy; with the *AMO theory of performance*, where performance is seen as a function of employee *ability*, *motivation* and *opportunity*. Thus the balanced scorecard contributes to the development of SHRM, not only in establishing goals and measures to demonstrate cause–effect linkages, but also in encouraging a process that stimulates debate and shared understanding between the different areas of the business. However, the balanced scorecard approach does not escape criticism, particularly in relation to the measurement of some HR activities which are not directly linked to productivity, thus requiring an acknowledgement of the multidimensional nature of organisational performance and a recognition of multiple 'bottom-lines' in SHRM.

Table 2.9 Abridged balanced scorecard for Mobil North American Marketing and Refining

Values	Strategic objectives	Strategic measures
Finance *To be financially strong*	ROCE Cash flow Profitability Lowest cost Profitable growth	ROCE Cash flow Net margins Cost per gallon delivered to customer Comparative volume growth rate
Customer *To delight the customer*	Continually delight targeted customer	Market share Mystery shopper rating
Organisation *To be a competitive supplier*	Reduce delivered costs Inventory management	Delivered cost per gallon vs customer's inventory level
To be safe and reliable	Improve health and safety and environment	Number of incidents Days away from work
Learning and growth *To be motivated and prepared*	Organisation involvement Core competencies and skills Access to strategic information	Employee survey Strategic competitive availability Availability of strategic information

Source: Adapted from Grant, R.M. (2002: 58) based on Kaplan and Norton (2001).

Boxall and Purcell (2003) suggest the use of two others besides *labour productivity*, these being *organisational flexibility* and *social legitimacy*. So although the balanced scorecard has taken account of the impact and influence of an organisation's human resources in achieving competitive advantage, there is still room for the process to become more HR driven.

Activity

Either

Draw up a strategy map for your organisation or Café Expresso and identify appropriate balanced scorecard measures. Share your ideas with your colleagues and consider how you would audit HR.

Or

Evaluate your organisation's strategy map and balanced scorecard measures. How effective has this approach been in your organisation? Has it focused all stakeholders' attention on strategy implementation? Consult your colleagues, and prepare an audit of your HR provision.

Conclusion

Given the increasing profile of strategic human resource management in creating organisational competitive advantage and the subsequent complexity in interpreting and applying strategic human resource management principles, there appears to be agreement on the need for more theoretical development in the field, particularly on the relationship between strategic management and human resource management and the relationship between strategic human resource management and performance (Guest, 1997; Wright and McMahan, 1992; Wright and McMahan, 1999; Boxall and Purcell, 2003). This chapter has reviewed key developments and alternative frameworks in the field of strategic human resource management in an attempt to clarify its meaning so that the reader is able to make an informed judgement as to the meaning and intended outcomes of strategic human resource management. Thus strategic human resource management is differentiated from human resource management in a number of ways, particularly in its movement away from a micro-perspective on individual HR functional areas to the adoption of a macro-perspective (Butler, Ferris and Napier, 1991; Wright and McMahan, 1992), with its emphasis on vertical integration (Guest, 1989; Tyson, 1997; Schuler and Jackson, 1987) and horizontal integration (Baird and Meshoulam, 1988; MacDuffie, 1995). It therefore becomes apparent that the meaning of strategic human resource management tends to lie in the context of organisational performance, although organisational performance can be interpreted and measured in a variety of ways. These may range from delivering efficiency and flexibility through cost reduction driven strategies through the implementation of what may be termed 'hard HR techniques' (Schuler and Jackson, 1987), to delivering employee commitment to organisational goals through 'universal sets' of HR practices (Pfeffer, 1994, 1998) or 'bundles' of integrated HR practices (Huselid, 1995; Delery and Doty, 1996), to viewing human resources as a source of human capital and sustainable competitive advantage (Barney, 1991; Barney and Wright, 1998) and a core business competence and a key strategic asset (Hamel and Prahalad, 1993, 1994). There are therefore conflicting views as to the meaning of SHRM and the contribution strategic human resource management can make to an organisation. The implications of this are twofold: firstly for academics and researchers there is a need for further theory development to define the relationship between strategic management and strategic human resource management and to ensure more rigorous research methodology in evaluating the SHRM – organisational performance link (Wall and Wood, 2005) and secondly for HR professionals, there is a need to develop strategic knowledge and capabilities (Boxall and Purcell, 2003; Ulrich, 2005) so that they are credible strategic partners in the business.

Summary

- This chapter has charted the development of strategic human resource management, exploring the links between the strategic management literature and strategic human resource management. It has examined the different approaches to strategic human resource management identified in the literature, including the best-fit approach, the best-practice approach, the configurational approach and the resource-based view, in order to understand what makes human resource management strategic.

- A key claim of much strategic human resource management literature is a significant contribution to a firm's *competitive advantage*, whether it is through cost reduction methods or more often *added value* through best-practice HR policies and practices. An understanding of the business context and particularly of the 'strategy-making' process is therefore considered central to developing an understanding of strategic human resource management.

- Whittington's typology (1993, 2001) was used to analyse the different approaches to 'strategy-making' experienced by organisations and to consider the impact this would have on our understanding of the development of strategic human resource management. The influence of the classical, rational-planning approach on the strategic management literature and therefore strategic HRM literature was noted, with its inherent assumption that strategy-making was a rational, planned activity. This ignores some of the complexities and 'messiness' of the strategy-making process identified by Mintzberg and others. Other approaches that recognised the constituents of this 'messiness', namely the processual approach the evolutionary approach and the systemic approach, were identified. These took account of changes and competing interests both in the external and internal business environment. Significantly for human resource management, there is a recognition that it is not always appropriate to separate operational policies from higher-level strategic planning, as it is often operational policies and systems that may provide the source of 'tactical excellence', thus the traditional distinction between strategy and operations can become blurred.

- The best-fit approach to strategic HRM explored the close relationship between strategic management and human resource management by considering the influence and nature of vertical integration. Vertical integration, where leverage is gained through the close link of HR policies and practices to the business objectives and therefore the external context of the firm, is considered to be a key theme of *strategic* HRM. Best-fit was therefore explored in relation to life cycle models and competitive advantage models and the associated difficulties of matching generic business type strategies to generic human resource management strategies were considered, particularly in their inherent assumptions of a classical approach to the strategy-making process. The inflexibility of 'tight' fit models in a dynamic, changing environment was evaluated, and consideration was given to achieving both fit and flexibity through complementary SHR systems.

- The configurational approach identifies the value of having a set of HR practices that are both vertically integrated to the business strategy and horizontally integrated with each other, in order to gain maximum performance or synergistic benefits. This approach recognises the complexities of hybrid business strategies and the need for HRM to respond accordingly. In advocating unique patterns or configurations of multiple independent variables, they provide an answer to the linear, deterministic relationship advocated by the best-fit approach

- The resource-based view represents a paradigm shift in strategic HRM thinking by focusing on the internal resources of the firm as a key source of sustainable competitive advantage, rather than focusing on the relationship between the firm and the external business context. Human resources, as scarce, valuable, organisation-specific and difficult-to-imitate resources, therefore become key *strategic assets*. The work of Hamel and Prahalad (1994) and the development of core competencies is considered significant here.

- The best-practice approach highlights the relationship between 'sets' of good HR practices and organisational performance, mostly defined in terms of employee commitment and satisfaction. These sets of best practice can take many forms; some have advocated a universal set of practices that would enhance the performance of all organisations they were applied to (Pfeffer, 1994, 1998), others have focused on integrating the practices to the specific business context (high performance work practices). A key element of best-practice is horizontal integration and congruence between policies. Difficulties arise here, as best practice models vary significantly in their constitution and in their relationship to organisational performance, which makes generalisations from research and empirical data difficult.

- In endeavouring to gain an understanding of the meaning of strategic human resource management, it soon becomes apparent that a common theme of all approaches is enhanced organisational performance and viability, whether this be in a 'hard' sense, through cost reduction and efficiency driven practices or through high-commitment and involvement driven value-added. This relationship is considered significant to understanding the context and meaning of strategic human resource management. The need to conduct further empirical research, particularly in Europe, is identified (Stavrou and Brewster, 2005) and the lack of methodological rigour and the extensive use of single source respondents in current research studies evaluating the SHRM/performance link is noted (Wall and Wood, 2005).

- Finally the need for further theory development in the field of strategic human resource management was noted, and the need for human resource practitioners to develop strategic capability.

Activity

Defining the effective human resource professional

What does an effective HR professional look like? What skills, competencies and knowledge do they require to become a business partner? Try to collect information from a range of sources, for example: organisational websites, HR practitioner journals, (*Personnel Today*, *People Management*), other journals (*Human Resource Management Journal*, *Management Learning*); the CIPD website and HRM textbooks to develop a profile of an effective HR professional in the twenty-first century. Which skills, competencies and knowledge would you identify as *strategic* HR competencies?

QUESTIONS

1   In what way does an understanding of strategic management contribute to your understanding of strategic human resource management?

2   How would you differentiate human resource management from strategic human resource management?

3   Compare and contrast the best-fit and best-practice approach to strategic human resource management.

4   Evaluate the relationship between strategic human resource management and organisational performance.

5   Why do human resources practitioners need to develop strategic capabilities?

Café Expresso

Café Expresso is one of the three main players in the 'coffee house' industry, which now has more than 6000 stores across the globe, 500 of which are in the UK and Ireland. They employ 7000 staff in the UK alone and serve 35 million customers in their stores across the globe each week.

The coffee industry is particularly robust, with coffee being the second most valuable commodity in the world after oil, with global retail sales estimated to be £39.2 billion. A total of 6.7 million tonnes of coffee were produced annually in 1998–2000, which is forecast to rise to 7 million tonnes by 2010.

The number of coffee bars in the high street has increased considerably in recent years, with the market being dominated by three main players. The 'coffee house' business therefore, is very competitive with coffee chains constantly looking for innovative ways of achieving sustainable competitive advantage, to remain ahead of their rivals.

Café Expresso had enjoyed first mover advantage in the marketplace and had rapidly grown to number one position, which they had retained for 15 years. In recent years, however, they have lost market share to rival competitors who have copied Café Expresso's business model and poached key staff to deliver it and subsequently customers had followed. This had resulted in Café Expresso slipping to the number three position. This loss of market share had forced them to rethink their strategy and a new charismatic chief executive, Ben Thomson, had been appointed in 2005 to turn the business around.

In reviewing Café Expresso's current strategy Ben Thomson embarked on an international fact finding tour of their coffee bars to meet staff and customers to get a feel for the nature of the business, together with rival coffee houses to gain an understanding of their source of competitive advantage. He wanted to return Café Expresso to the number one position in the marketplace. His review identified customers who were loyal to the brand of Café Expresso but had been enticed away by the experience, the variety of coffee and level of customer service offered by their competitors. His review of human resources found a high level of staff turnover, due to the minimum wage offered and the high percentage of international employees who tended to be employed on short-term contracts. The recent loss of market share and high employee turnover had led to low morale amongst remaining staff, as they felt Café Expresso's bars were

dated and the range of coffees limited. Ben Thomson's review of the competitors supported this, as he identified the significance of the 'coffee drinking experience' which was delivered through appropriate décor, ambience, variety in the range of products and most importantly of all, the *barista* or 'coffee seller'. He identified these as key sources of added value and competitive advantage.

Ben Thomson decided to relaunch Café Expresso's business strategy with a new vision: 'To be the number one coffee house of choice across the globe' and identified the following mission: Experience Café Expresso, we don't just sell coffee we provide customers with an unforgettable experience. This was encapsulated in his value statement: 'Nowhere else makes you feel this good.' which he believed should apply to staff as well as customers. He was convinced that the success of coffee bars lay not just in selling coffee as a product, but in selling the 'coffee house' experience. To achieve this he felt that Café Expresso's human resources would be crucial to the success of his strategy. He recognised that human resources would face a difficult task, as the coffee house industry is traditionally renowned for low pay (minimum wage being the norm) and high employee turnover (50–100 per cent being the norm), yet the baristas (coffee sellers) are crucial to the success of the business and the selling of the coffee house experience.

He identified the following priorities:

Business

- To be the number one coffee house across the globe.
- To attract new customers through reputation for providing the coffee house experience.
- To retain existing customers through loyalty service.

Customer service

- Commitment to excellence.
- Internal and external customers valued.
- Sell the barista experience.

People

- Diversity and individuality valued.
- Knowledge and talent encouraged and retained.
- Pride and enthusiasm valued.
- Reward to retain.

Case study continued

Systems

- Customer feedback.
- Learning and development.
- Career and talent management.
- Performance management.
- Compensation and benefits.

Ben initiated a staged refurbishment programme starting with key stores and he appointed a new global HR director, Kam Patel, who came from a major airline, with a remit to introduce a new HR strategy to deliver Ben's vision of becoming the 'number one coffee house across the globe'. Kam Patel recognised the need to develop a human resource strategy which focused on the development and retention of key human resources, who could deliver the Café Expresso experience.

She reintroduced the HR strategy by relabelling the HR function as 'Partner Resources' and all staff became known as 'partners'. She decided to focus on key areas of human resources to deliver the business strategy, these were resourcing and retention, learning and development, talent management, employee involvement and communication and compensation and benefits, which she believed to be one of Partner Resources' most important roles in the company. Significantly, baristas were to be paid above minimum wage and store managers were offered a broad pay spectrum.

In terms of resourcing, Kam Patel focused on recruiting new 'partners' through window advertising and word of mouth. This was quite successful, and she acknowledged that a 'large number of their "partners" have grown to understand Café Expresso's market and approach through being a customer'. Store managers were responsible for interviewing and selection decisions and successful candidates were offered a half-day trial period.

The focus of the retention strategy is on the quality of compensation and range of benefits offered, particularly a share option scheme offered to all partners to encourage shared ownership in the business and reinforce the 'partner' ethos. A partner discount programme was also offered, which entitled staff to 30 per cent discount in stores.

All new recruits were encouraged to spend time 'on the floor' in the coffee bars, regardless of rank. They also spent a day at a central Café Expresso development centre learning about the company and the coffee industry. They also take part in the 'coffee master' programme, enabling them to become a Café Expresso ambassador. This development is then further supported through a mentor system where each new recruit, both baristas and managers are appointed a 'buddy', who will support them in their role and provide further advice.

A performance management system was introduced where all partners agreed objectives and development needs, both in terms of technical skills and knowledge and behavioural skills. Performance was to be reviewed on a six-monthly basis, and manager, peer and customer reviews were included in the process.

Team briefings were introduced where regular information on the performance of the business and each store was conveyed to all partners, and upward feedback and ideas were encouraged. A suggestion scheme was introduced where ideas subsequently implemented were rewarded and recognised in the company magazine, *Partner Voice*. Kam Patel also introduced an engagement survey annually, and the results and feedback were published and provided to all partners in the *Partner Voice*.

Gradually customer service feedback improved, and market share increased. Employee turnover reduced to 25 per cent, and Café Expresso moved to number two in the industry. Ben Thomson and Kam Patel had recognised that the HR strategic changes had supported this improved level of service and customer attraction/retention. They recognised, however, that it would not be long before their competitors copied their initiatives, particularly in terms of reward and benefits, so they were concerned about how they might maintain and develop the extent of their competitive advantage.

Activity

1 Reflecting on the approaches to strategic human resource management discussed in this chapter (the best-fit approach; the configurational approach; the resource-based view; the best-practice approach), analyse the approach to SHRM adopted by Ben Thomson and Kam Patel at Café Expresso

2 Drawing on your answer to question 1, and the concerns raised by Ben Thomson and Kam Patel in the final paragraph, how would you develop the HR strategy to ensure Café Expresso continues to attract and retain customers.

Useful websites

Confederation of British Industry	www.cbi.org.uk
Chartered Institute of Personnel and Development	www.cipd.co.uk
Department of Trade and Industry	www.dti.gov.uk
Detailed information about EVA	www.evanomics.com
Chartered Institute of Management	www.managers.org.uk
Personnel Today Journal	www.personneltoday.com
Strategic Management Society	www.csmintl.premierdomain.com/menu.htm

References and further reading

Those texts marked with an asterisk are recommended for further reading.

Abell, D.F. (1993) *Managing with Dual Strategies: Mastering the Present, Pre-empting the Future.* New York: Free Press.

Ahmad, S. and Schroeder, R.G. (2003) 'The impact of human resource management practices on operational performance: recognising country and industry differences', *Journal of Operations Management*, 21, 19–34

Aktouf, O. (1996) *Traditional management and beyond: a matter of renewal.* Montreal: Gaetan Morin.

Alchian, A. and Demsetz, H. (1972) 'Production information costs and economic organisation', *American Economic Review*, 62, 777–795.

Amit, R. and Shoemaker, P. (1993) 'Strategic assets and organisational rent', *Strategic Management Journal*, 14, 33–46.

Ansoff, H.I., (1965) *Corporate Strategy.* Harmondsworth: Penguin.

Ansoff, H.I. and McDonnell, E. (1990) *Implanting Strategic Management*, 2nd edn. Hemel Hempstead: Prentice Hall.

Applebaum, E., Bailey, T., Berg, P. and Kalleberg, A. (2000) *Manufacturing Competitive Advantage: Why high-performance systems pay off.* Ithaca, NY: ILR Press.

Applebaum, E. and Batt, R (1994) *The New American Workplace.* Ithaca, NY: ILR Press.

Armstrong, M. and Baron (2002) *Strategic Human Resource Management, A Guide to Action*, 2nd edn. London: CIPD.

Arthur, J. (1994) 'Effects of human resource systems on manufacturing performance and turnover', *Academy of Management Journal*, 37, 3: 670–687.

Atkinson, J. (1984) 'Manpower strategies for the flexible organisation', *Personnel Management*, August, 28–31.

Baden-Fuller, C. (1995) 'Strategic innovation, corporate entrepreneurship and matching outside-in to inside-out approaches to strategy research', *British Journal of Management*, 6 (special issue), 3–16.

Bae, J. and Lawler, J.J. (2000) 'Organisational and HRM strategies in Korea: impact on firm performance in an emerging economy', *Academy of Management Journal*, 43, 587–597.

Bahrami, H. (1992) 'The emerging flexible organisation: perspectives from Silicon Valley', *California Management Review*, 34, 4: 33–48.

Baird, L. and Meshoulam, I. (1988) 'Managing two fits of strategic human resource management', *Academy of Management Review*, 13, 1: 116–128.

Bamberger, P. and Phillips, B. (1991) 'Organisational environment and business strategy: parallel versus conflicting influences on human resource strategy in the pharmaceutical industry', *Human Resource Management*, 30, 2: 153–182.

Barney, J.B. (1991) 'Firm resources and sustained competitive advantage', *Journal of Management*, 17, 1: 99–120.

Barney, J. (1995) 'Looking inside for competitive advantage', *Academy of Management Executive*, 9, 4: 49–61.

Barney, J.B. and Wright P.M. (1998) 'On becoming a strategic partner: the role of human resources in gaining competitive advantage', *Human Resource Management*, 37, 1.

Barr, P., Stimpert, J. and Huff, A. (1992) 'Cognitive change, strategic action, and organisational renewal', *Strategic Management Journal*, 13, 15–36.

Batt, R. (2002). 'Managing customer services: human resource practices, quit rates and sales growth', *Academy of Management Journal*, 45, 587–597.

Becker, B. and Gerhart, B. (1996) 'The impact of human resource management on organisational performance: progress and prospects', *Academy of Management Journal*, 39, 4: 779–801.

Becker, B.E., Huselid, M.A., Pickus, P.S. and Spratt, M.F. (1997) 'HR as a source of shareholder value: research and recommendations', *Human Resource Management*, 36, 1: spring, 39–47.

Beer, M., Spector, B., Lawrence, P.R., Quinn Mills, D. and Walton, R.E. (1984) *Managing Human Assets.* New York: Free Press.

Beer, M., Spector, B., Lawrence, P., Quinn Mills, D. and Walton, R., (1985) *Human Resource Management: A General Managers Perspective.* New York: Free Press.

Berg, P. (1999) 'The effects of high performance work practices on job satisfaction in the US steel industry', *Industrial Relations*, 54, 111–135.

Blyton, P. and Turnbull, P. (1992) (eds) *Reassessing HRM.* London: Sage.

Boxall, P. (1992) 'Strategic human resource management: beginnings of a new theoretical sophistication', *Human Resource Management Journal*, 2, 3: 60–79.

Boxall, P. (1996) 'The strategic HRM debate and the resource-based view of the firm', *Human Resource Management Journal*, 6, 3: 59–75.

*Boxall, P. and Purcell, J. (2003) *Strategy and Human Resource Management.* Houndmills: Palgrave Macmillan.

Boxall, P. and Steeneveld, M. (1999) 'Human resource strategy and competitive advantage: a longitudinal study of engineering consultancies', *Journal of Management Studies*, 36, 443–463.

Butler, J.E., Ferris, G.R. and Napier, N.K. (1991) *Strategy and Human Resource Management*. Cincinnati, OH: Souhwestern Publishing Co.

Capelli, P. and Crocker-Hefter, A. (1996) 'Distinctive human resources are firms' core competencies', *Organisational Dynamics*, 24, 3: 7–22.

Capelli, P. and Neumark, D. (2001). 'Do "High performance work practices" improve establishment-level outcomes?' *Industrial and Labor Relations Review*, 54, 737–775.

Capelli, P. and Singh, H. (1992) 'Integrating strategic human resources and strategic management', in Lewin, D., Mitchell, O.S. and Sherer, P. (eds) *Research Frontiers in Industrial Relations and Human Resources*. Madison, WI: Madison Industrial Relations Research Association, 165–192.

Chandler, A.D., (1962) *Strategy and Structure: Chapters in the History of the American Industrial Enterprise*. Cambridge, MA: MIT Press

CIPD (2001) *Professional Standards for the Professional Development Scheme*, Chartered Institute of Personnel and Development. London: CIPD.

Clarke, J. and Newman, J. (1997) *The Managerial State*. London: Sage.

Cooper, C. (2000) 'In for the count', *People Management*, 28–34.

Cyert, R.M. and March, J.G. (1956) Organisational factors in the theory of monopoly, *Quarterly Journal of Economics*, 70, 1: 44–64.

Delaney, J.T. and Godard, J. (2001) 'An IR perspective on the high-performance paradigm', *Human Resource Management Review*, 40, 472–489.

Delaney, J.T. and Huselid, M.A. (1996) 'The impact of human resource management practices on perceptions of organisational performance', *Academy of Management Journal*, 39, 919–969.

Delery, J.E. (1998) 'Issues of fit in strategic human resource management: Implications of research', *HRM Review*, 8, 3: Autumn, 289–309.

Delery, J. and Doty, H. (1996) 'Modes of theorizing in strategic human resource management', *The Academy of Management Journal*, 39, 4: 802–835.

Drucker, P. (1968) *The Practice of Management*. London: Pan.

Dyer, L. (1984) 'Studying human resource strategy', *Industrial Relations*, 23, 2: 156–169.

Dyer, L. and Reeves, T. (1995) 'Human resource strategies and firm performance: what do we know and where do we need to go?' *The International Journal of HRM*, 6, 3: September, 656–670.

Dyer, L. and Shafer, R. (1999) 'Creating organisational agility: Implications for strategic human resource management', in Wright, P., Dyer, L., Boudreau, J. and Milkovich, G. (eds) *Research in Personnel and HRM*. Stamford, CT and London: JAI Press.

Ferris, G.R., Hochwater, W.A., Buckley, M.N., Harrell-Cook, G. and Frink, D. (1999) 'Human resource management, some new direction', *Journal of Management*, 25, 385–418.

Fombrun C., Tichy, N. and Devanna, M. (eds) (1984) *Strategic Human Resource Management*. New York: Wiley.

Gelade, G. and Ivery, M. (2003) 'The impact of human resource management and work climate on organisational performance', *Personnel Psychology*, 56, 383–401.

Giojia, D.A. and Chittipeddi, K. (1991) 'Sensemaking and sensegiving in strategic change initiation', *Strategic Management Journal*, 12, 6: 433–448.

Godard, J.A. (2004) 'A critical assessment of the high performance paradigm', *British Journal of Industrial Relations*, 42, 349–378.

*Grant, R.M. (2002) *Contemporary Strategy Analysis: Concepts, Techniques, Applications*, 4th edn. Oxford: Blackwell.

Gratton, L., Hope-Hailey, V., Stiles, P. and Truss, C. (1999) 'Linking individual performance to business strategy: The people process model', in Schuler, R.S. and Jackson S.E. (eds) *Strategic Human Resource Management*, 142–158.

Guest, D. (1987) 'Human resource management and industrial relations', *Journal of Management Studies*, 24, 5: 503–521.

Guest, D. (1989) 'Personnel and HRM: Can you tell the difference?' *Personnel Management*, 21, 48–51.

Guest, D. (1997) 'Human resource management and performance: A review and research agenda', *International Journal of Human Resource Management*, 8, 3: 263–276.

Guest, D. (2001) 'Human resource management: When research confronts theory', *International Journal of Human Resource Management*, 12, 7: 1092–1106.

Guest, D. and Hoque, K. (1994) 'The good, the bad and the ugly: Employee relations in new non-union workplaces', *Human Resource Management Journal*, 5, 1–14.

Guest, D.E., Michie, J. Conway, N. and Shehan, M. (2003) 'Human resource management and corporate performance in the UK', *British Journal of Industrial Relations*, 41, 291–314.

Guest, D., Michie, J., Sheehan, M. and Conway, N. (2000a) *Employment Relations, HRM and Business Performance: An Analysis of the 1998 workplace employee relations survey*. London: CIPD.

Guest, D., Michie, J., Sheehan, M., Conway, N. and Metochi, M. (2000b) *Effective People Management: Initial Findings of the future of Work Study*. London: CIPD.

Guthrie, J.P. (2001) 'High involvement work practices, turnover and productivity: Evidence from New Zealand', *Academy of Management Journal*, 44, 180–190.

Hamel, G. and Prahalad, C. (1993) 'Strategy as stretch and leverage', *Harvard Business Review*, 71, 2: 75–84.

Hamel, G. and Prahalad, C. (1994) *Competing for the Future*. Boston, MA: Harvard Business School Press.

Henderson, B.D. (1989) 'The origin of strategy', *Harvard Business Review*, November–December, 139–143.

Hoque, K. (1999). 'Human resource management and performance in the UK hotel industry', *British Journal of Industrial Relations*, 37, 419–443.

Hoque, K. (1999) 'HRM and performance in the UK hotel industry', *British Journal of Industrial Relations*, 37, September.

Hubbard, N. (1999) *Acquisition Strategy and Implementation*. Basingstoke: Macmillan.

Hunt, J., Lees, S., Grumber, J. and Vivian, P. (1987) *Acquisitions: The Human Factor*. London Business School and Egon Zehender International.

Huselid, M.A. (1995) 'The impact of human resource management on turnover, productivity, and corporate financial performance', *Academy of Management Journal*, 38, 635–672.

Huselid, M. and Becker, B. (1996) 'Methodological issues in cross-sectional and panel estimates of the HR-firm performance link', *Industrial Relations*, 35, 400–422.

Huselid, M.A., Jackson, S.E. and Schuler, R.S. (1997) 'Technical and strategic human resource management effectiveness as a determinant of firm performance', *Academy of Management Journal*, 40, 171–188.

Jackson, S.E. and Schuler R.S. (2000) *Managing Human Resources, A Partner Perspective*, 7th edn. Cincinatti: South Western Publishing.

Johnson G. and Scholes K. (2002) *Exploring Corporate Strategy*. London: Prentice-Hall.

Kamoche, K.N. (2001) *Understanding Human Resource Management*. Buckingham: Open University Press.

Kanter, R. (1989) 'The new managerial work', *Harvard Business Review,* Nov/Dec, 85–92.

Kaplan, R. and Norton, D. (1996) *The Balanced Scorecard: Translating Strategy into Action*. Boston, MA: Harvard Business School Press.

Kaplan, R. and Norton, D. (2001) *The Strategy-Focussed Organisation*. Boston, MA: Harvard Business School Press.

Keenoy, T. (1990) 'HRM: A case of the wolf in sheep's clothing', *Personnel Review*, 19, 2: 3–9.

Keenoy, T. and Anthony, P. (1992) 'HRM: Metaphor, meaning and morality', in Blyton, P. and Turnbull, P. (eds) *Reassessing Human Resource Management*. London: Sage.

Kochan T. and Barocci, T. (1985) *Human Resource Management and Industrial Relations*. Boston, MA: Little Brown.

Kochan, T.A. and Osterman, P. (1994) *The Mutual Gains Enterprise*. Boston, MA: Harvard Business School Press.

Lawler, E.E. Mohrman, S.A. and Ledford, G.E. (1995) *Creating High Performance Organisations*. San Francisco: Jossey-Bass.

Legge, K. (1978) *Power, Innovation and Problem-Solving in Personnel Management*. London: McGraw-Hill.

Legge, K. (1995) *Human Resource Management: Rhetoric and Realities*. London: Macmillan.

Legge, K. (1998) 'The morality of HRM', in Mabey C., Salaman, G. and Storey, J. (eds) *Strategic Human Resource Management, A Reader*. London: Open University/Sage, pp. 18–29.

Lengnick Hall, C.A. and Lengnick Hall, M.L. (1988) 'Strategic human resource management: A review of the literature and a proposed typology'. *Academy of Management Review*, 13, pp. 454–470.

Leonard, D. (1998) *Wellsprings of Knowledge: Building and sustaining the sources of innovation*, Boston, MA: Harvard Business School Press.

Luthans, K.W. and Sommer, S.M. (2005) 'The impact of high peformance work on industry-level outcomes', *Journal of Managerial Issues*, 17, 3: 327–346.

Mabey, C., Salaman, G. and Storey, J. (eds) (1998) *Strategic Human Resource Management, A Reader*, London: Open University/Sage.

MacDuffie, J.P. (1995) 'Human resource bundles and manufacturing performance', *Industrial Relations Review*, 48, 2: 199–221.

Mahoney, T. and Deckop, J. (1986) 'Evolution of concept and practice in personnel administration/human resource management', *Journal of Management*, 12, 223–241.

March, J.G. (1976) 'The technology of foolishness', in Marsh, J. and Olsen, J. (eds) *Ambiguity and Choice in Organisations* Bergen: Universitetsforlaget.

Marchington, M. and Grugalis, I. (2000) 'Best practice human resource management: Perfect opportunity or dangerous illusion?', *International Journal of Human Resource Management*, 11, 905–925.

Marchington, M. and Wilkinson, A. (2002) *People Management and Development*, 2nd edn. London: CIPD.

Marchington, M. and Wilkinson, A. (2005) *Human Resource Management at Work: People Management and Development*, 3rd edn. London: CIPD.

Marks, M. and Mirvis, P. (1982) 'Merging human resources: A review of current research', *Merger and Acquisitions*, 17, 2: 38–44.

Miles, R. and Snow, C. (1978) *Organisational Strategy, Structure and Process*. New York: McGraw Hill.

Miles, R.E and Snow, C.C. (1984) 'Designing strategic human resource systems', *Organisational Dynamics*, Summer, 36–52.

Milgrom, P. and Roberts, J. (1995) 'Complementarities and fit: Strategy, structure and organisational change in manufacturing', *Journal of Accounting and Economics*, 19 (2): 170–208.

Miller, D. (1992) 'Generic strategies; classification, combination and context', *Advances in Strategic Management*, 8, 391–408.

Miller, D. and Shamsie, J. (1996) 'The resource based view of the firm in two environments: The Hollywood Film Studios from 1936–1965', *Academy of Management Journal*, 39, 3: 519–543.

Miller, P. (1996) 'Strategy and the ethical management of human resources', *Human Resource Management Journal*, 6, 1: 5–18.

Milliman, J., Von Glinow, M.A. and Nathan, M. (1991) 'Organisational life cycles and international strategic human resource management in multinational companies: Implications for congruence theory', *Academy of Management Review*, 16, 318–339.

Millward, N., Bryson A. and Forth, J. (2000) *All Change at Work, British Employment Relations, 1980–1998, as portrayed by the Workplace Employment Relations Series*. London: Routledge.

Mintzberg, H. (1987) 'Crafting strategy', *Harvard Business Review*, July–August, 65–75.

Mintzberg, H. (1990) 'The design school: Reconsidering the basic premises of strategic management', *Strategic Management Journal*, 11, 171–195.

Mintzberg, H., Alhastrand, B. and Lampel, J. (1998) *Strategy Safari: a Guided Tour through the Wilds of Strategic Management*. London: Prentice-Hall.

Mueller, F. (1998) 'Human resources as strategic assets: An evolutionary resource-based theory', in Mabey, C., Salaman, G. and Storey, J. (eds) *Strategic Human Resource Management, A Reader*. London: Open University/Sage, pp. 152–169.

Nonaka, I. and Takeuchi, H. (1995) *The Knowledge-Creating Company*. New York: Oxford University Press.

Ogbonna, E. (1992) 'Organisational culture and human resource management, dilemmas and contradictions', in Blyton, P. and Turnbull, P. (eds) *Reassessing Human Resource Management*. London: Sage, pp. 74–96.

Patterson, M.G., West, M.A., Lawthom, R. and Nickell, S. (1997) *The Impact of People Management Practices on Business Performance*. London: IPD.

Penrose, E. (1959) *The Theory of the Growth of the Firm*. Oxford: Blackwell.

Perry-Smith, J. and Blum, T. (2000) 'Work-family human resource bundles and perceived organisational performance', *Academy of Management Journal*, 43, 1107–1117.

Pettigrew, A.M. (1973) *The Politics of Organisational Decision-Making*. London: Tavistock.

Pettigrew, A.M. (1985) *The Awakening Giant: Continuity & Change in ICI*. Oxford: Blackwell.

Pfeffer, J. (1994) *Competitive Advantage through People*. Boston: Harvard Business School Press

Pfeffer, J. (1998) *The Human Equation: Building Profits by putting People First*. Boston: Harvard Business School Press.

Porter, M. (1985) *Competitive Advantage: Creating and Sustaining Superior Performance*. New York: Free Press.

Porter, M. (1991) 'Towards a dynamic theory of strategy', *Strategic Management Journal*, 12 (Winter), 95–117.

Purcell, J. (1985) 'Is anybody listening to the corporate personnel department?' *Personnel Management*, September, 28–31.

Quick, J. (1992) 'Crafting an organizational culture: Herb's hand at Southwest', *Organizational Dynamics*, 21, 45–56.

Quinn J.B. (1978) 'Strategic change: Logical incrementalism', *Sloan Management Review*, 1, 20: 7–21.

Reicheld, F. (1996) *The Loyalty Effect: the hidden force behind growth, profits and lasting value*. Boston, MA: Harvard Business School Press.

Ritson, N. (1999) 'Corporate Strategy and the Role of HRM: critical cases in oil and chemicals', *Employee Relations*, 21, 2: 159–175.

Roche, W. (1999) 'In search of commitment-oriented HRM practices and the conditions that sustain them', *Journal of Management Studies*, 36, 5: 653–678.

Rucci, A. Kirn, S. and Quinn, R. (1998) 'The employee–customer–profit chain at Sears', *Harvard Business Review*, 76, 1: 82–97.

Schuler, R. and Jackson, S. (1987) 'Linking competitive strategies with human resource management', *Academy of Management Executive*, 1, 3: 207–219.

Schuler, R.S. and Jackson, S.E. (eds) (1999) *Strategic Human Resource Management*. Oxford: Blackwell Business.

Simon, H.A. (1947) *Administrative Behaviour*. New York: Free Press.

Sisson, K. and Storey, J. (2000) *The Realities of Human Resource Management*. Buckingham: Open University Press.

Sivasubramaniam, N. and Kroeck, K.G. (1995) 'The Concept of Fit in Strategic Human Resource Management', *Academy of Management Conference*, Vancouver.

Sloan, A.P. (1963) *My Years with General Motors*. London: Sidgwick & Jackson.

Snell, S.A., Youndt, M. and Wright, P.M. (1996) 'Establishing a framework for research in strategic human resource management: Merging resource theory and organisation learning', *Research in Personnel and Human Resources Management*, 14, 61–90.

Stavrou, E.T. and Brewster, C. (2005) 'The configurational approach to linking strategic human resource management bundles with business performance: Myth or reality?', *Management Revue*, 16, 2: 186–202.

Storey, J. (1992) *Developments in the Management of Human Resources*. Blackwell: Oxford.

Storey, J. (1995) *Human Resource Management, a Critical Text*. London: Routledge.

Storey, J. (ed.) (2001) *Human Resource Management, A Critical Text*. London: Thomson Learning.

Stroh, L. and Caligiuri, P.M. (1998) 'Strategic human resources: A new source for competitive advantage in the global arena', *International Journal of Human Resource Management*, 9, 1–17.

Thompson, J. (2001) *Understanding Corporate Strategy*. London: Thomson Learning.

Torrington, D. and Hall, L. (1998) *Human Resource Management*, 4th edn. Prentice-Hall, Europe.

Torrington, D. and Hall, L. (2005) *Human Resource Management*, 5th edn. Prentice-Hall, Europe.

Truss, C. and Gratton, L. (1994) 'Strategic human resource management: A conceptual approach', *International Journal of Human Resource Management*, 5, 663–686.

Tyson, S. (1997) 'Human resource strategy: A process for managing the contribution of HRM to organisational performance', *The International Journal of Human Resource Management*, 8, 3: 277–290.

Ulrich, D. (1997) 'Measuring human resources: An overview of practice and a prescription for results', *Human Resource Management*, 36, 3: (Fall), 303–320.

Ulrich, D. (1998) 'A new mandate for human resources', *Harvard Business Review*, January–February, 124–135.

Ulrich, D. and Brockbank, W. (2005) *The HR Value Proposition*. Boston: Harvard Business Review School Press.

Ulrich, D., Brockbank, W., Yeung, A. and Lake, D. (1995) 'Human resource competencies: An empirical assessment', *Human Resource Management*, 34, 473–495.

Vandenberg, R.J., Richardson, H.A. and Eastman, L.J. (1999) 'The Impact of high involvement work processes on organisational effectiveness', *Groups and Organisation Management*, 24, 300–399.

Ventrakaman, N. (1989) 'The concept of fit in strategy research: towards verbal and statistical correspondence', *Academy of Management Review*, 14, 423–444.

Wall, T.D. and Wood, S.J. (2005) 'The romance of human resource management and business performance, and the case for big science', *Human Relations*, 58, 4: April.

Walton, J. (1999) *Strategic Human Resource Development*. London: Prentice-Hall, Financial Times.

Walton R. (1985) 'From control to commitment in the workplace', *Harvard Business Review*, 63, March–April: 76–84.

Watson, J. (1977) *The Personnel Managers: A Study in the Sociology of Work and Employment*. London: Routledge & Kegan Paul.

Wernefelt, B. (1984) 'A resource based view of the firm', *Strategic Management Journal*, 5, 2: 171–180.

Whittington, R. (1992) 'Putting Giddens into action: Social systems and managerial agency', *Journal of Management Studies*, 29, 6: 693–712.

Whittington, R. (1993) *What is Strategy and Does it Matter?* 1st edn. London: Routledge.

*Whittington, R. (2001) *What is strategy and Does it Matter?* 2nd edn. London: Thomson Learning.

Wiggins, R.R. and Ruefli, T.W. (2002) 'Sustained competitive advantage: Temporal dynamics and the incidence and persistence of superior economic performance', *Organisation Science*, 13, 82–108.

Wilson, D. (1992) *A Strategy of Change*. London: Routledge.

Winter, S. (1987) 'Knowledge and competence as strategic assets', in Teece, D.J. (ed) *The Competitive Challenge: Strategies for Industrial Innovation and Renewal*. Cambridge, MA: Ballinger, pp. 159–184.

Wood, S. (1999) 'Human resource management and performance', *International Journal of Management Reviews*, 1, 4: 367–413.

Wood, S.J. and de Menezes, L. (1998) 'High commitment management in the UK: Evidence from the workplace industrial relations survey and employers' manpower and skills practices survey', *Human Relations*, 51, 485–515.

Wright, M.W. and Haggerty, J.J. (2005) 'Missing variables in theories of strategic human resource management: Time, cause and individuals', *Management Revue*, 16, 2: 164–174

Wright, P.M. and Gardner, T.M. (2003) 'The human resource-firm performance relationship: methodological and theoretical challenges', in Holman, D., Wall, T.D., Clegg, C.W., Sparrow, P. and Howard, A. (eds) *The New Workplace: a Guide to the Human Impact of Modern Working Practices*. Chichester: Wiley.

Wright, P.M., Gardner, T.M. and Moynihan, L.M. (2003) 'The impact of HR practices on the performance of business units', *Human Resource Management Journal*, 13, 21–36.

Wright, P., McCormick, B., Sherman, S. and McMahan, G. (1996) 'The role of human resource practices in petro-chemical refinery performance'. Paper presented at the *1996 Academy of Management*, Cincinnati.

Wright, P.M. and McMahan, G.C. (1992) 'Alternative theoretical perspectives for strategic human resource management', *Journal of Management*, 18, 295–320.

Wright, P.M. and McMahan, G.C. (1999) 'Theoretical perspectives for strategic human resource management', in Schuler, R.S. and Jackson, S.E (eds) *Strategic Human Resource Management*, pp. 49–72.

Wright, P. McMahan, G. and McWilliams, A. (1994) 'Human resources and sustained competitive advantage: A resource-based perspective', *International Journal of Human Resource Management*, 5, 2: 301–326.

Wright, P. and Snell, S. (1991) 'Towards an integrative view of strategic human resource management', *Human Resource Management Review*, 1, 203–225.

Wright, P.M. and Snell, S.A. (1998) 'Towards a unifying framework for exploring fit and flexibility in strategic human resource management', *Academy of Management Review*, 23, 4: 756–772.

Wright, P.M. and Snell, S.A. (2005) 'Creating value or living values: Challenges in balancing competing demands', *Human Resource Management Journal*, special issue.

Yeung, A. and Berman, B. (1997) 'Adding value through human resources: Reorienting human resource management to drive business performance', *Human Resource Management*, 36, 3: 321–335.

Youndt, M., Snell, S., Dean, J. and Lepak, D. (1996) 'Human resource management, manufacturing strategy and firm performance', *Academy of Management Journal*, 39, 836–866.

Zigarelli, M. (1996) 'Human resources and the bottom line', *Academy of Management Executive*, 10, 63–64.

For multiple-choice questions, exercises and annotated weblinks specific to the chapter visit the book's website at **www.pearsoned.co.uk/beardwell**

Chapter 3

Contextualising HRM: developing critical thinking

Audrey Collin

Objectives

- To indicate the significance of context for the understanding of HRM.

- To discuss ways of conceptualising and representing the nature of context generally and this context in particular.

- To look at the nature of the immediate context of HRM: the problematical nature of organisations and the need for management.

- To indicate the nature of the wider context of HRM and illustrate this through selected examples.

- To examine how our ways of interpreting and defining reality for ourselves and for others construct and influence the way we understand and practise HRM.

- To suggest the implications for the readers of this book.

- To present a number of activities and a case study that will facilitate readers' understanding of the context of HRM.

Introduction

The significance and nature of context

> An event seen from one point-of-view gives one impression. Seen from another point-of-view it gives quite a different impression. But it's only when you get the whole picture you fully understand what's going on.
>
> (Reproduced with kind permission of DDB London, in memory of John Webster (1934–2006))

The need to be aware of the context of human affairs was demonstrated dramatically in this prize-winning advertisement for the *Guardian* newspaper that is still remembered today. We can easily misinterpret facts, events and people when we examine them out of context, for it is their context that provides us with the clues necessary to enable us to understand them. Context locates them in space and time and gives them a past and a future, as well as the present that we see. It gives us the language to understand them, the codes to decode them, the keys to their meaning.

This chapter will carry forward your thinking about the issues raised in Chapter 1 by exploring the various strands within the context of HRM that are woven together to form the pattern of meanings that constitute it. As that chapter explained, and the rest of the book will amplify, HRM is far more than a portfolio of policies, practices, procedures and prescriptions concerned with the management of the employment relationship. It is this, but more. And because it is more, it is loosely defined and difficult to pin down precisely, a basket of multiple, overlapping and shifting meanings, which users of the term do not always specify. Its 'brilliant ambiguity' (Keenoy, 1990) derives from the context in which it is embedded, a context within which there are multiple and often competing perspectives upon the employment relationship, some ideological, others theoretical, some conceptual. HRM is inevitably a contested terrain, and the various definitions of it reflect this.

From the various models of HRM in Chapter 1, you will recognise that the context of HRM is a highly complex one, not just because of its increasing diversity and dynamism, but also because it is multi-layered. The organisation constitutes the immediate context of the employment relationship, and it is here that the debate over how that relationship should be managed begins. The nature of organisation and the tensions between the stakeholders in it give rise to issues that have to be addressed by managers: for example, choices about how to orchestrate the activities of organisational members and whose interests to serve.

Beyond the organisation itself lie the economic, social, political and cultural layers, and beyond them again the historical, national and global layers of context. Considerable change is taking place within those layers, making the whole field dynamic. It is not the purpose of this chapter to register these many changes; you will become aware of some of them as you read the remainder of this book. However, we need to note here that the events and changes in the wider context have repercussions for organisations, and present further issues to be managed and choices to be made. Indeed, Mayo and Nohria (2005) argue that successful managers have what they have coined 'contextual intelligence' that enables them to be deeply sensitive to their organisation's context.

The various layers of context and the elements within them, however, exist in more than one conceptual plane. One has a concrete nature, like a local pool of labour, and the other is abstract, like the values and stereotypes that influence an employer's views of a particular class of person in the labour market. The abstract world of ideas and values overlays the various layers of the context of HRM: the ways of organising society, of acquiring and using power, and of distributing resources; the ways of relating to, understanding and valuing human beings and their activities; the ways of studying and understanding reality and of acquiring knowledge; the stocks of accumulated knowledge in theories and concepts.

It is the argument of this chapter that to understand HRM we need to be aware not just of the multiple layers of its context – rather like the skins of an onion – but also of these conceptual planes and the way they intersect. Hence, 'context' is being used here to mean more than the surrounding circumstances that exert 'external influences' on a given topic: context gives them a third dimension. The chapter is arguing, further, that events and experiences, ideas and ideologies are not discrete and isolatable, but are interwoven and interconnected, and that HRM itself is embedded in that context: it is part of that web and cannot, therefore, be meaningfully examined separately from it. Context is highly significant yet, as we shall see, very difficult to study. Hence this chapter will present you with some challenging and abstract material that will encourage you to be a more analytical thinker. This is necessary not only for those studying HRM; today it is becoming essential for practitioners, too. It is predicted that HR will see a major transformation in the next few years, with its core becoming more analytical and critical (Czerny, 2005) and turned 'from a department and a transaction into a philosophy leading the organisation' (Pickard, 2005, p. 15). And from 2005 the concept of the 'thinking performer', 'who applies a critically thoughtful approach to their job' (Whittaker and Johns, 2004, p. 32), underpins the professional standards of the Chartered Institute of Personnel and Development.

Conceptualising and representing context

How can we begin to understand anything that is embedded in a complex context? We seem to have awareness at an intuitive level, perceiving and acting upon the clues that context gives to arrive at the 'tacit knowledge' discussed later in Chapter 8. However, context challenges our formal thinking. First, we cannot stand back to take in the complete picture, which has tradition-ally been one way to gain objective knowledge of a situation. Because we are ourselves part of our context, as defined in this chapter, it is not possible for us to obtain a detached perspective upon it. In that respect we are like the fish in water that 'can have no understanding of the concept of "wetness" since it has no idea of what it means to be dry' (Southgate and Randall, 1981: 54). However, humans are very different from the 'fish in water'. We can be *reflexive*, recognising what our perspective is and what its implications are; *open*, seeking out and recognising other people's perspectives; and *critical*, entering into a dialogue with others' views and interrogating our own in the light of others', and vice versa. The 'Stop and think' boxes, Activities and Exercises through-out the chapter are there to encourage you in this direction.

Second, we need the conceptual tools to grasp the wholeness (and dynamic nature) of the picture. To understand a social phenomenon such as HRM, we cannot just wrench it from its context and examine it microscopically in isolation. To do this is to be like the child who digs up the newly planted and now germinating seed to see 'whether it is growing'. In the same way, if we analyse context into its various elements and layers, then we are already distorting our understanding of it, because it is an indivisible whole. Rather, we have to find ways to examine HRM's interconnectedness and interdependence with other phenomena in its context.

The study of context, therefore, is no easy task, and poses a major challenge to our estab-lished formal, detached, and analytical ways of thinking. Nevertheless, as we shall discuss later in this chapter, there are ways forward that enable us to conceptualise the many loops and cir-cularities of these complex interrelationships in an often dynamic context.

Stop & think

Before you continue, spend a few minutes reflecting upon this way of understanding context. How different is it from the way in which you would have defined context? Does this have any implications for you as you read this chapter?

Meanwhile, we shall try to conceptualise context through metaphor: that is, envisage it in terms of something concrete that we already understand. We have already used the metaphor of the many-skinned onion to depict the multiple layers of context, but context is more com-plex than that and we need another metaphor to suggest its interconnectedness and texture. We could, therefore, think of it as a tapestry. This is a 'thick hand-woven textile fabric in which design is formed by weft stitches across parts of warp' (*Concise OED*, 1982). The warp threads run the length of the tapestry, the weft are the lateral threads that weave through the warp to give colour, pattern and texture. This metaphor helps us to visualise how interwoven and interrelated are the various elements of the context of HRM, both the concrete and the abstract; and how the pattern of HRM itself is woven into them. In terms of this metaphor, our ways of seeing and thinking about our world – the assumptions we make about our reality – could be said to be the warp, the threads which run the length of the tapestry contributing to its basic form and texture. Ideologies and the rhetoric through which they are expressed – ways of defining reality for other people – are the weft threads that weave through the warp threads, and give the tapestry pattern and texture. Events, people, ephemeral issues are the stitches that form the surface patterns and texture of HRM. We see this in Figure 3.1. In the case of the context of HRM, this tapestry is being woven continuously from threads of differ-ent colours and textures. At times one colour predominates, but then peters out. In parts of the tapestry patterns may be intentionally fashioned, while observers (such as the authors of this book) believe they can discern a recognisable pattern in other parts.

| Figure 3.1 | The metaphor of tapestry to convey HRM in context |

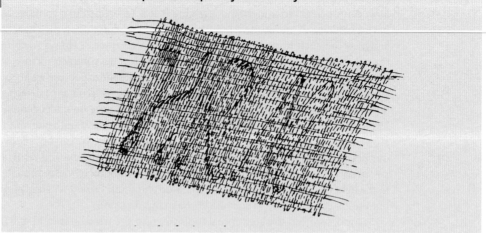

This metaphor again reminds us that an analytical approach to the study of context, which would take it apart to examine it closely, would be like taking a tapestry to bits: we would be left with threads. The tapestry itself inheres in the whole, not its parts. How, then, can the chapter begin to communicate the nature of this tapestry without destroying its very essence through analysis? The very representation of our thinking in written language is linear, and this undermines our ability to communicate a dynamic, interrelated complexity clearly and succinctly. We need to think in terms of 'rich pictures', 'mind-maps', or 'systems diagrams' (Checkland, 1981; Senge, 1990; Cameron, 1997).

It is not feasible here nor, indeed, necessary to attempt to portray the whole tapestry in detail; the chapter will focus instead upon a number of strands that run through it. You will be able to identify and follow them through the remainder of the book, and observe how their interweaving gives us changes in pattern and colour, some distinct, others subtle. Before beginning to read the exposition of the context of HRM, you will find it helpful to carry out the following activity.

| Activity | Look at the various models that were presented in Chapter 1 and identify some of the elements of context and the relationships between them that are explicit or implied there. This will help you develop your own view of the context of HRM before you read further, and give you some mental 'hooks' upon which to hang your new understanding. |

The concepts and language needed to understand context

To understand context, it has been suggested so far, we need to recognise its wholeness. We therefore need to incorporate both the concrete world and the world of abstract ideas. Although the appropriate language to enable us to do this may be largely unfamiliar to you, you will find that you already have considerable understanding of the concepts it expresses. Your own experience of thinking about and responding to one aspect of context – the natural, physical environment – will have given you the basic concepts that we are using and a useful set of 'hooks' upon which to hang the ideas that this chapter will introduce to you. It would be helpful to your understanding of this chapter, therefore, if you examined some of the 'hooks' you are already using, and perhaps clarify and refine them. (In this way, as Chapter 8 explains, the new material can now be more effectively transferred into, and later retrieved from, your long-term memory.)

Carry out the exercise at the end of the chapter. This will focus your thinking and enable you to recognise that you already have the 'hooks' you will need to classify the material of this chapter in a meaningful way. It will show you that, although you may not customarily use the terminology below, from your present knowledge of the environment you already recognise that:

- Context is *multi-layered, multidimensional, and interwoven*. In it, concrete events and abstract ideas intertwine to create issues; thinking, feeling, interpreting and behaving are all involved. It is like the tapestry described above.
- Our understanding depends upon our *perspective*.
- It also depends upon our *ideology*.
- Different groups in society have their own interpretations of events, stemming from their ideology. There are therefore *competing* or *contested interpretations* of events.
- These groups use *rhetoric* to express their own, and account for competing, interpretations, thus distorting, or even suppressing, the authentic expression of competing views.
- Powerful others often try to impose their interpretations of events, their version of reality, upon the less powerful majority: this is *hegemony*.

This subsection has perhaps given you a new language to describe what you already understand well. You will find some of these terms in the Glossary at the end of this book, and their definitions will be amplified in later sections of this chapter as it continues its exploration of the context of HRM.

The immediate context of HRM

Human resource management, however defined, concerns the management of the employment relationship: it is practised in organisations by managers. The nature of the organisation and the way it is managed therefore form the immediate context within which HRM is embedded, and generate the tensions that HRM policies and practices attempt to resolve.

The nature of organisations and the role of management

At its simplest, an organisation comes into existence when the efforts of two or more people are pooled to achieve an objective that one would be unable to complete alone. The achievement of this objective calls for the completion of a number of tasks. Depending upon their complexity, the availability of appropriate technology and the skills of the people involved, these tasks may be subdivided into a number of subtasks and more people employed to help carry them out. This division of labour constitutes the lateral dimension of the structure of the organisation. Its vertical dimension is constructed from the generally hierarchical relationships of power and authority between the owner or owners, the staff employed to complete these tasks, and the managers employed to coordinate and control the staff and their working activities. Working on behalf of the organisation's owners or shareholders and with the authority derived from them, managers draw upon a number of resources to enable them to complete their task: raw materials; finance; technology; appropriately skilled people; legitimacy, support and goodwill from the organisation's environment. They manage the organisation by ensuring that there are sufficient people with appropriate skills; that they work to the same ends and timetable; that they have the authority, information and other resources needed to complete their tasks; and that their tasks dovetail and are performed to an acceptable standard and at the required pace.

The very nature of organisation therefore generates a number of significant tensions: between people with different stakes in the organisation, and therefore different perspectives upon and interests in it; between what owners and other members of the organisation might desire and what they can feasibly achieve; between the needs, capabilities and potentials of organisational members and what the organisation demands of and permits them.

Management (see Watson, 2000) is the process that keeps the organisation from flying apart because of these tensions, that makes it work, secures its survival and, according to the type of organisation, its profitability or effectiveness. Inevitably, however, as Chapter 11 discusses, managerial control is a significant and often contentious issue.

The management of people and relationships is intrinsic to the managing of an organis-ation, but the very nature of people and the way they constitute an organisation make management complex. Although the organisation of tasks packages people into organisational roles, individuals are larger and more organic than those roles have traditionally tended to be. The organisation, writes Barnard (1938, in Schein, 1978: 17) 'pays people only for certain of their activities . . . but it is whole persons who come to work'. Unlike other resources, people interact with those who manage them and among themselves; they have needs for autonomy and agency; they think and are creative; they have feelings; they need consideration for their emotional and their physical needs, security and protection. The management of people is therefore not only a more diffuse and complex activity than the management of other resources, but also an essentially moral one (again, see Watson, 2000). This greatly complicates the tasks of managers, who can only work with and through people to ensure that the organ-isation survives and thrives in the face of increasing pressures from its environment.

Owners and managers are confronted with choices about how to manage people and resolve organisational tensions. The next subsection examines some of these choices and the strategies adopted to handle them. Before then, however, it must be noted that as organis-ations become larger and more complex, the division of managerial labour often leads to a specialist 'people' function to advise and support line managers in the complex and demand-ing tasks of managing their staff. This is now commonly called 'HRM', which has developed a professional and highly skilled expertise in certain aspects of managing people, such as selec-tion, training and industrial relations, which it offers in an advisory capacity to line managers, who nevertheless remain the prime managers of people. However, this division of managerial labour has fragmented the management of people: the development of human resource management beyond the traditional personnel approach can be seen as a strategy to reintegrate the management of people into the management of the organisation as a whole.

The approaches adopted by managers to resolve the tensions in organisations

The previous subsection suggested that there are inherent tensions in organisations. In brief, these are generated by:

- the existence of several stakeholders in the employment relationship;
- their differing perspectives upon events, experiences and relationships;
- their differing aims, interests and needs;
- the interplay between formal organisation and individual potential and needs.

In your own experience of being employed, however limited that might be so far, have you been aware of some of these tensions? What were their effects upon you and your colleagues at work? How did the management of the organisation appear to respond to these tensions? Has this coloured how you look at management and HRM?

Those tensions have to be resolved through the process of management or, rather, contin-uously resolved, for they are inherent in organisations. Thus Weick (1979: 44) writes that organising is a continuous process of meaning-making: 'organizations keep falling apart . . . require chronic rebuilding.' A continuing issue, therefore, is that of managerial control: how to orchestrate organisational activities in a way that meets the needs of the various stakeholders. The owners of organisations, or those who manage them on their behalf, have explored many ways to resolve these tensions: the emergence of HRM to develop alongside, subsume or replace personnel management is witness to this. The strategies they adopt are embodied in their employment policies and practices and the organisational systems they put in place (see also Chapter 11). They are also manifested in the psychological contract they have with their employees, the often unstated set of expectations between organisation and individual that embroiders the legal employment contract. (The notion of the psychological contract now in current use goes back to a much earlier literature – for example, Schein (1970) – and it is some of the earlier terminology that is used here.) This subsection will briefly outline some of the strategies that managers have adopted, while the next will discuss the interpretations by theorists and other commentators of those strategies. However, it must be kept in mind that managers are to some extent influenced by the concepts and language, if not the arguments, of these theorists.

In very crude terms, we can identify four strategies that managers have adopted to deal with these tensions. The first is represented by what is called scientific management, or the classical school of management theory. The second is the human relations approach, and the third is the human resource management approach. The fourth approach is perhaps more an ideal than a common reality. It must be emphasised that we cannot do justice here to the rich variety of approaches that can be found in organisations. You can elaborate upon the material here by reading about these differing views in an organisational behaviour textbook, such as Huczynski and Buchanan (2002) or Clark *et al.* (1994).

The first approach addressed the tensions in the organisation by striving to control people and keep down their costs: the *scientific management* approach. It emphasised the need for rationality, clear objectives, the managerial prerogative – the right of managers to manage – and adopted work study and similar methods. These led to the reduction of tasks to their basic elements and the grouping of similar elements together to produce low-skilled, low-paid jobs, epitomised by assembly-line working, with a large measure of interchangeability between workers. Workers tended to be treated relatively impersonally and collectively ('management and labour'), and the nature of the psychological contract with them was calculative (Schein, 1970), with a focus on extrinsic rewards and incentives. Such a strategy encouraged a collective response from workers, and hence the development of trade unions.

These views of management evolved in North America, and provided a firm foundation for modern bureaucracies (Clegg, 1990). In Britain they overlaid the norms of a complex, though changing, social class system that framed the relationships between managers and other employees (Child, 1969; Mant, 1979). This facilitated the acceptance of what Argyris (1960) saw were the negative outcomes of McGregor's (1960) X-theory of management which were hierarchy; paternalism; the attribution to workers of childlike qualities, laziness, limited aspirations and time horizons. While this strategy epitomised particularly the management approach of the first half of the twentieth century, it has left its legacy in many management practices, such as organisation and method study, job analysis and description, selection methods, an overriding concern for efficiency and the 'bottom line', appraisal and performance management. Moreover, it has not been completely abandoned (see Clegg, 1990; Ritzer, 1996 on 'McDonaldization'; and debates about employment in call centres, for example Callaghan and Thompson, 2002; Hatchett, 2000; Taylor *et al.*, 2002).

The *human relations* approach to the tensions in organisations emerged during the middle years of the twentieth century, and developed in parallel with an increasingly prosperous society in which there were strong trade unions and (later) a growing acceptance of the right of individuals to self-fulfilment. Child (1969) identifies its emergence in British management thinking as a response to growing labour tensions. It tempered scientific management by its recognition that people differed from other resources, that if they were treated as clock numbers rather than as human beings they would not be fully effective at work and could even fight back to the point of subverting management intentions. It also recognised the significance of social relationships at work – the informal organisation (Argyris, 1960). Managers therefore had to pay attention to the nature of supervision and the working of groups and teams, and to find ways of involving employees through job design (see Chapter 14), motivation, and a democratic, consultative or participative style of management. The nature of the psychological contract was cooperative (Schein, 1970).

The third and most recent major approach adopted by managers to address the tensions within the organisation has developed as major changes and threats have been experienced in the context of organisations (recession, international competition, and globalisation). It is a response to the need to achieve flexibility in the organisation and workforce (see Chapters 4 and 5) and improved performance through devolving decision-making and empowerment (see Chapter 14). As Chapter 8 notes, employees have had to become multi-skilled and to work across traditional boundaries. Unlike the other two strategies, the third approaches the organisation holistically and often with greater attention to its culture, leadership and 'vision', the 'soft' Ss of McKinsey's 'Seven S' framework (Pascale and Athos, 1982: 202–206). It attempts to integrate the needs of employees with those of the organisation in an explicit manner: the psychological contract embodies mutuality (Schein, 1970). It recognises that people should be invested in as assets so that they achieve their potential for the benefit of the organisation. It also pays greater attention to the individual rather than the collective, so that these notions of developing the individual's potential have been accompanied by individual contracts of employment (see Chapter 11), performance appraisal, and performance-related pay (see also Chapter 13).

The very title of *human resource management* suggests that this third approach to the management of organisational tensions is also an instrumental one. Although it differs greatly from the approaches that see labour as a 'cost', to be reduced or kept in check, it nevertheless construes the human being as a resource for the organisation to use. The fourth, idealistic, *humanistic* approach aims to construct the organisation as an appropriate environment for autonomous individuals to work together collaboratively for their common good. This is the approach of many cooperatives. It informed the early philosophy of organisation development (see Huse, 1980), although the practice of that is now largely instrumental. It also underpins the notion of the learning organisation (see Senge, 1990, and Chapters 7 and 8).

Although we have identified here four different strategies for managing the inherent tensions in organisations, they might be less easy to distinguish in practice. Some managers adopt a hybrid version more appropriate to their particular organisation. They will always be seeking new approaches to deal more effectively with those tensions, or to deal with variations in them as circumstances change (for example, with globalisation).

Activity   Comparing these managerial strategies

Many of you have worked in a call centre, or know someone who does. Working on your own or in a group, examine your experiences of working there. Could you identify one or more of these managerial strategies in your workplace? What might have been your experiences had the management adopted a different strategy?

When we look more deeply into these four managerial strategies, we can recognise that they implicate some much deeper questions. Underlying the management of people in organisations are some fundamental assumptions about the nature of people and reality itself, and hence about organising and managing. For example, managers make assumptions about the nature of the organisation, many interpreting it as having an objective reality that exists separately from themselves and other organisational members – they reify it (see Glossary). They make assumptions about the nature of their own and the organisation's goals, which many reify and interpret as rational and objective. They make assumptions about the appropriate distribution of limited power throughout the organisation, and how people in the organisation should be regarded and treated.

However, those assumptions are rarely made explicit, and are therefore rarely challenged. Moreover, many other members of the organisation appear to accept those premises on which they are managed, even though such assumptions might conflict with their own experiences, or virtually disempower or disenfranchise them. For example, many might assert the need for equal opportunities to jobs, training and promotion, but do not necessarily challenge the process of managing itself despite its often gender-blind nature (Hearn *et al.*, 1989; Hopfl and Hornby Atkinson, 2000). Nevertheless, those assumptions inform the practices and policies of management, and hence define the organisational and conceptual space that HRM fills, and generate the multiple meanings of which HRM is constructed. In terms of the metaphor used by this chapter, they constitute some of the warp and weft threads in the tapestry/context of HRM. They will be examined in greater detail in a later section.

Competing interpretations of organisations and management

When we turn from the concrete world of managing to the theories about organisations and management, we find that not only have very different interpretations been made over time, but that several strongly competing interpretations coexist. Again, this chapter can only skim over this material, but you can pursue the issues by reading, for example, Child (1969), who traces the development of management thought in Britain, or Morgan (1997), who sets out eight different metaphors for organisations through which he examines in a very accessible way the various ways in which theorists and others have construed organisations. Reed and Hughes (1992: 10–11) identify the changing focus of organisation theory over the past 30 or so years, from a concern with organisational stability, order and disorder, and then with organisational power and politics, to a concern with the construction of organisational reality.

The reification (see Glossary) of the organisation by managers and others, and the general acceptance of the need for it to have rational goals to drive it forward in an effective manner, have long been challenged. Simon (see Pugh *et al.*, 1983) recognised that rationality is 'bounded' – that managers make decisions on the basis of limited and imperfect knowledge. Cyert and March adopt a similar viewpoint: the many stakeholders in an organisation make it a 'shifting multigoal coalition' (see Pugh *et al.*, 1983: 108) that has to be managed in a pragmatic manner. Others (see Pfeffer, 1981; Morgan, 1997) recognise the essentially conflictual and political nature of organisations: goals, structures and processes are defined, manipulated and managed in the interests of those holding the power in the organisation. A range of different understandings of organisations has developed over time: the systems approach (Checkland, 1981), the learning organisation (Senge, 1990), transformational leadership and 'excellence' (Peters and Waterman, 1982; Kanter, 1983), knowledge management (see Chapter 7), the significance of rhetoric (see later, and Eccles and Nohria, 1992). This range is widening to include even more holistic approaches, with recent interest in the roles in the workplace of emotional intelligence (Cherniss and Goleman, 2001; Higgs and Dulewicz, 2002; Pickard, 1999), spirituality and love (Welch, 1998; Zohar and Marshall, 2001). The influence of many of these new ideas can be seen in the recently developed concern for work–life balance (for example, *People Management*, 2002).

The established views of managers are subject to further interpretations. Weick (1979) argues the need to focus upon the process of organising rather than its reified outcome, an organisation. As we noted earlier, he regards organising as a continuous process of meaning-making: '[p]rocesses continually need to be re-accomplished' (p. 44). Cooper and Fox (1990) and Hosking and Fineman (1990) adopt a similar interpretation in their discussion of the 'texture of organizing'.

Brunsson (1989) throws a different light on the nature and goals of organising, based on his research in Scandinavian municipal administrations. He suggests that the outputs of these kinds of organisations are 'talk, decisions and physical products'. He proposes two 'ideal types' of organisation: the *action* organisation, which depends on action for its legitimacy (and hence essential resources) in the eyes of its environment, and the *political* organisation, which depends on its reflection of environmental inconsistencies for its legitimacy. Talk and decisions in the action organisation (or an organisation in its action phase) lead to actions, whereas the outputs of the political organisation (or the organisation in its political phase) are talk and decisions that may or may not lead to action.

> . . . hypocrisy is a fundamental type of behaviour in the political organization: to talk in a way that satisfies one demand, to decide in a way that satisfies another, and to supply products in a way that satisfies a third.
>
> (p. 27)

There are similarly competing views upon organisational culture, as we see in Aldrich (1992) and Frost *et al.* (1991). The established view interprets it as a subsystem of the organisation that managers need to create and maintain through the promulgation and manipulation of values, norms, rites and symbols. The alternative view argues that culture is not something that an organisation has, but that it is.

Just as many managers leave their assumptions unaddressed and unstated, taken for granted, so that their actions appear to themselves and others based upon reason and organisational necessity, so also do many theorists. Many traditional theorists leave unstated that the organisations of which they write exist within a capitalist economic system and have to meet the needs of capital. They ignore the material and status needs of owners and managers, and their emotional (Fineman, 1993) and moral selves (Watson, 2000). Many also are gender-blind and take for granted a male world-view of organisations. These issues tend to be identified and discussed only by those writers who wish to persuade their readers to a different interpretation of organisations (for example, Braverman, 1974; Hearn *et al.*, 1989; Calas and Smircich, 1992).

Stop & think

At the close of the Introduction some of the concepts and terminology relevant to the understanding of context were noted. Have you been aware of any of these concepts in this discussion of the immediate context of HRM?

The wider context of HRM

Defining the wider context

The definition of the wider context of HRM could embrace innumerable topics (from, for example, demography to globalisation) and a long time perspective (from the organisation of labour in prehistory, as at Stonehenge, onwards). Such a vast range, however, could only be covered in a perfunctory manner here, which would render the exercise relatively valueless. It is more appropriate to give examples of some of the influential elements and how they affect HRM, and to encourage you to identify others for yourself. You can read about some of them in Chapters 4 and 7.

Activity

Go back to the models of HRM presented in Chapter 1 and, working either individually or in a group, start to elaborate upon the various contextual elements that they include. Look, for example, at the external forces of the 'matching model' illustrated in Chapter 1, Figure 1.1.

1 What in detail constituted the elements of the economic, political and cultural forces at the time Devanna *et al.* were writing? What would they be now?
2 What other elements would you add to those, both then and now?
3 What are the relationships between them, both then and now?
4 And what, in your view, has been their influence upon HRM, both then and now?

Echoes from the wider context

Here the focus will be on distant events from the socio-political sphere that have nevertheless influenced the management of the employment relationship and still do so indirectly. Although what follows is not a complete analysis of these influences, it illustrates how the field of HRM resonates with events and ideas from its wider context.

The First and Second World Wars

The two world wars, though distant in time and removed from the area of activity of HRM, have nevertheless influenced it in clearly identifiable and very important ways, some direct and some indirect. These effects can be classified in terms of changed attitudes of managers to labour, changed labour management practices, the development of personnel techniques, and the development of the personnel profession. We shall now examine these, and then note how some outcomes of the Second World War continue, indirectly, to influence HRM.

Changed attitudes of managers to labour

According to Child (1969: 44), the impact of the First World War upon industry hastened changes in attitudes to the control of the workplace that had begun before 1914. The development of the shop stewards' movement during the war increased demand for workers' control; there was growing 'censure of older and harsher methods of managing labour'. The recognition of the need for improved working conditions in munitions factories was continued in the postwar reconstruction debates: Child (1969: 49) quotes a Ministry of Reconstruction pamphlet that advised that 'the good employer profits by his "goodness"'. The outcome of these various changes was a greater democratisation of the workplace (seen, for example, in works councils) and, for 'a number of prominent employers', a willingness 'to renounce autocratic methods of managing employees' and 'to treat labour on the basis of human rather than commodity market criteria' (pp. 45–46). These new values became incorporated in what was emerging as a distinctive body of management thought, practice and ideology (see Glossary and later section on 'Ways of seeing and thinking'), upon which later theory and practice are founded.

Changed labour management practices

The need to employ and deploy labour effectively led to increased attention to working conditions and practices during both wars; the changes that were introduced then continued, and interacted with other social changes that ensued after the wars (Child, 1969). For example, the Health of Munitions Workers Committee, which encouraged the systematic study of human factors in stress and fatigue in the munitions factories during the First World War, was succeeded in 1918 by the Industrial Fatigue Research Board (DSIR, 1961; Child, 1969; Rose, 1978). During the postwar reconstruction period progressive employers advocated minimum wage levels, shorter working hours and improved security of tenure (Child, 1969).

'The proper use of manpower whether in mobilizing the nation or sustaining the war economy once reserves of strength were fully deployed' was national policy during the Second World War (Moxon, 1951). As examples of this policy, Moxon cites the part-time employment of married women, the growth of factory medical services, canteens, day nurseries and special leave of absence.

The development of personnel techniques

Both wars encouraged the application of psychological techniques to selection and training, and stimulated the development of new approaches. Rose (1978: 92) suggests that, in 1917, the American army tested two million men to identify 'subnormals and officer material'. Seymour (1959: 7–8) writes of the Second World War:

> the need to train millions of men and women for the fighting services led to a more detailed study of the skills required for handling modern weapons, and our understanding of human skill benefited greatly . . . Likewise, the shortage of labour in industry led . . . to experiments aimed at training munition workers to higher levels of output more quickly.

The wars further influenced the development of the ergonomic design of equipment, and encouraged the collaboration of engineers, psychologists and other social scientists (DSIR, 1961).

The exigencies of war ensured that attention and resources were focused upon activities that are of enormous significance to the field of employment, while the scale of operations guaranteed the availability for testing of numbers of candidates far in excess of those usually available to psychologists undertaking research.

The development of the personnel profession

Very significantly, the Second World War had a major influence on the development of the personnel profession. According to Moxon (1951: 7), the aims of national wartime policy were:

> (i) to see that the maximum use was made of each citizen, (ii) to see that working and living conditions were as satisfactory as possible, (iii) to see that individual rights were reasonably safeguarded and the democratic spirit preserved. The growth of personnel management was the direct result of the translation of this national policy by each industry and by each factory within an industry.

Child (1969: 11) reports how government concern in 1940 about appropriate working practices and conditions

> led to direct governmental action enforcing the appointment of personnel officers in all but small factories and the compulsory provision of minimum welfare amenities.

Moxon (1951) comments on the 'four-fold increase in the number of practising personnel managers' at this time (p. 7). Child (1969) records the membership of what was to become the Institute of Personnel Management as 760 in 1939, and 2993 in 1960 (p. 113). He also notes a similar increase in other management bodies. (The Institute has now become the Chartered Institute of Personnel and Development, with a membership of 124,000 in 2006.)

The postwar reconstruction of Japan

This subsection has so far noted some of the direct influences that the two world wars had upon the field of HRM. It now points to an indirect and still continuing influence. The foundation of the philosophy and practice of total quality management, which has been of considerable recent significance in HRM, was laid during the Second World War. Edward Deming and Joseph Juran were consultants to the US Defense Department and during the Second World War ran courses on their new approaches to quality control for firms supplying army ordnance (Pickard, 1992). Hodgson (1987: 40) reports that:

> Vast quantities of innovative and effective armaments were produced by a labour force starved of skill or manufacturing experience in the depression.

After the war, America 'could sell everything it could produce' and, because it was believed that 'improving quality adds to costs', the work of Deming and Juran was ignored in the West. However, Deming became an adviser to the Allied Powers Supreme Command and a member of the team advising the Japanese upon postwar reconstruction (Hodgson, 1987: 40–41). He told them that 'their war-ravaged country would become a major force in international trade' if they followed his approach to quality. They did.

Western organisations have since come to emulate the philosophy and practices of quality that proved so successful in Japan and that now feature among the preoccupations of human resource managers (see, for example, Chapter 14).

Stop & think

What other distant socio-political events have influenced HRM?

Contemporary influences on HRM

The two topics to be examined now also come from fields distant from that of HRM but nevertheless influence it. However, they differ from those examined above. First, they belong primarily to the world of ideas, rather than action. Secondly, whereas the influences discussed above contributed to the incremental development of HRM thinking and practice, those discussed below have the potential to unsettle and possibly disrupt established thinking, and hence practice. Thirdly, the two world wars are, for us, history: interpretations of them have by now become established and, to a large degree, generally accepted (though always open to question: see the later subsection 'Defining reality for others'). However, what are discussed below are ideas of our own time, not yet fully formed or understood. They both originated in fields outside social science, but have been introduced into it because of their potential significance for the understanding of social phenomena.

'Postmodernism'

It was in the fields of art and architecture, in which there had been early twentieth-century schools of thought and expression regarded as 'modernism', that certain new approaches came to be labelled 'postmodern'. In due course, the concepts of 'modernism' and 'postmodernism' spread throughout the fields of culture (Harvey, 1990) and the social sciences. However, 'postmodernism' is proving to be a challenging and unsettling concept for those socialised into what would now be called a 'modern' understanding of the world. One way to appreciate it is through the 2006 film *A Cock and Bull Story*, with Steve Coogan and Rob Brydon, which is about the famously idiosyncratic eighteenth century novel *Tristram Shandy* (Sterne, 1759–67). This stands out in the history of the novel for its reflexivity, the way the novelist shares with the reader his attempts to capture the wholeness of life in his pages. He wants to present his characters in context for, just as this chapter argues, without that understanding of them would be incomplete. So rather than following a traditional linear story-line, Sterne struggles to follow the interwoven threads of the tapestry of their life, causing him to digress and regress, and adopt unusual typography. Hence in the film Coogan, playing himself as an actor as well as two of the novel's characters, declares *Tristram Shandy* to be 'postmodern' before 'modernism' even existed. The film does not attempt a full adaptation of the novel, but captures its 'postmodern' spirit by using a reflexive, fractured and many-layered narrative.

'Modernism' and 'postmodernism' are now used to express a critical perspective in organisation studies (for example, Gergen, 1992; Hassard and Parker, 1993; Hatch, 1997; Morgan, 1997) and in the HRM field (Legge, 1995; Townley, 1993). Connock (1992) includes 'postmodern' thinking among the contemporary 'big ideas' of significance to human resource managers, while Fox (1990) interprets strategic HRM as a self-reflective cultural intervention responding to 'postmodern' conditions. Although questions about 'postmodernism' merge with others on post-industrialism, post-Fordism, and the present stage of capitalism (see Legge, 1995; Reed and Hughes, 1992), here we focus only on 'postmodernism'.

There is considerable debate about it. Does it refer to an epoch (Hassard, 1993), a period of historical time, namely the 'post-modern' present which has succeeded 'modern times'? If so, does it represent a continuation of or a disjunction with the past? Or does it refer to a particular, and critical, perspective, which Hassard (1993) calls an 'epistemological position' (see Glossary)? Many, such as Legge (1995), distinguish this from the epochal 'post-modern' by omitting the hyphen ('postmodern').

An example of the epochal interpretation is Clegg's (1990: 180–181) discussion of 'post-modern' organisations, the characteristics of which he identifies by contrasting them with 'modern' organisations. For example, he suggests that the latter (that is, the organisations that we had been familiar with until the last decade or so of the twentieth century) were rigid, addressed mass markets and were premised on technological determinism; their jobs were 'highly differentiated, demarcated and de-skilled'. 'Post-modern' organisations, however, are flexible, address niche markets, and are premised on technological choices; their jobs are 'highly de-differentiated, de-demarcated and multiskilled'. Since Clegg's analysis, the hierarchy of 'modern' organisations has often been contrasted with 'post-modern' networking.

It is less easy to pin down 'postmodernism' as an epistemological position but, in brief, it is somewhat like the little boy's response to the 'emperor's new clothes'. Whereas 'modernism' was based on the belief that there existed a universal objective truth which we could come to know by means of rational, scientific approaches (though often only with the help of experts), 'postmodernism' denies that. It assumes that truth is local and socially constructed (see Glossary and later section) from a particular perspective. It asks: 'What truth?', 'Whose truth?', 'Who says so?' Hence it challenges the authority of the established view, for example, of the 'meta-narratives' of 'progress', 'the value of science' or 'Marxism vs capitalism' which had become the accepted framework of twentieth-century understanding. Instead it recognises the claims of diverse and competing interpretations, and accepts that everything is open to question, that there are always alternative interpretations.

Hence 'postmodernism' has considerable significance for HRM. It recognises that multiple and competing views of organisations and HRM are legitimate; that the significance of theory lies not in its 'truth' but in its usefulness for practice. (This, perhaps, is a significant issue for the learning organisation, which is discussed in Chapter 7.) Moreover, it throws into question (Hassard and Parker, 1993; Kvale, 1992) the traditional (Western) understanding of the individual as a '"natural entity", independent of society, with "attributes" which can be studied empirically' (Collin, 1996: 9). That 'modern' interpretation has underpinned the understanding and practices of HRM, such as psychometric testing: the 'postmodern' view challenges the accepted way of dealing with, for example, competencies and assessment (Brittain and Ryder, 1999).

Moreover, 'postmodernism' recognises that, far from being objective and universal as 'modernism' assumed, knowledge is constructed through the interplay of power relationships and often the dominance of the most powerful. This makes a critical interpretation of established bodies of thought such as psychology (Kvale, 1992), which could be seen as a Western cultural product (Stead and Watson, 1999). Thus, whereas 'modernism' often ignored or, indeed, disguised ideologies (see Glossary and the section later on 'Ways of seeing and thinking'), 'postmodernism' seeks to uncover them. It also encourages self-reflexivity and, therefore, a critical suspicion towards one's own interpretations, and an ironic and playful treatment of one's subject.

Another important difference between 'modernism' and 'postmodernism' lies in the way they regard *language*. 'Modernism' assumes that language is neutral, 'the vehicle for communicating independent "facts"' (Legge, 1995: 306). The 'postmodern' argument, however, is that this is not the case (see Reed and Hughes, 1992; Hassard and Parker, 1993). Language 'itself constitutes or produces the "real"' (Legge, 1995: 306). Moreover, it is 'ideological' (Gowler and Legge, 1989: 438): both the means through which ideologies are expressed and the embodiment of ideology (see Glossary and later subsection). This can be seen in sexist and racist language, and in 'management-speak'.

'Postmodernism' highlights the significance of *discourse*. 'Why do we find it so congenial to speak of organizations as structures but not as clouds, systems but not songs, weak or strong but not tender or passionate?' (Gergen, 1992: 207). The reason, Gergen goes on to say, is that we achieve understanding within a 'discursive context', and the organisational context understands structure. A discourse is a 'set of meanings, metaphors, representations, images, stories, statements and so on that in some way together produce a particular version of events' (Burr, 1995: 48), a version belonging to a particular group of people. It provides the language and meanings whereby members of that group can interpret and construct reality, and gives them an identifiable position to adopt upon a given subject, thereby constituting their own identity, behaviour and reality (Gavey, 1989). By interpreting competing positions in its own terms, the group's discourse shuts down all other possible interpretations but its own.

For example, in order to engage in academic discourse, academics have to learn

> a vocabulary and a set of analytic procedures for 'seeing' what is going on . . . in the appropriate professional terms. For we must see only the partially ordered affairs of everyday life, which are open to many interpretations . . . as if they are events of a certain well-defined kind.
>
> (Parker and Shotter, 1990: 9)

Parker and Shotter (1990: 2–3), using the contrast between 'everyday talk' and academic writing, explain how academic text standardises its interpretations:

> The strange and special thing about an academic text . . . is that by the use of certain strategies and devices, as well as already predetermined meanings, one is able to construct a text which can be understood (by those who are a party to such 'moves') in a way divorced from any reference to any local or immediate contexts. Textual communication can be (relatively) decontextualised. Everyday talk, on the other hand, is marked by its vagueness and openness, by the fact that only those taking part in it can understand its drift; the meanings concerned are not wholly predetermined, they are negotiated by those involved, on the spot, in relation to the circumstances in which they are involved . . . Everyday talk is situated or contextualised, and relies upon its situation (its circumstances) for its sense.

There are many discourses identifiable in the field of organisation and management studies – managerial, humanist, critical, industrial relations – that offer their own explanations and rhetoric. You can explore them further in, for example, the chapters that follow, and Clark *et al.* (1994), but you should remain aware that academic discourse itself enables writers to exercise power over the production of knowledge and to influence their readers. Awareness of discourse is also important for the understanding of organisations:

> organisational life is made up of many 'discourses' – that is, flows of beliefs, experiences, meanings and actions. Each of these discourses shapes the behaviour of the organisation and of teams and individuals within it. These discourses are in turn created and reworked by individuals' actions and their expressed beliefs. This may not sound much, but it shifts the management of change, for example, from a simplistic view of changing culture, processes and structures to one of altering these aspects of organisational life by building on and reshaping the various discourses flowing around a company. (Baxter, 1999: 49)

The notion of discourse is relevant to our understanding of HRM. From today's vantage point we can now perhaps recognise that the way in which we once conceptualised and managed the employment relationship was influenced by 'modernism'. However, Legge (1995: 324–325) considers HRM to be both 'post-modern' and 'postmodern'. 'From a managerialist view' it is 'post-modern' in terms of epoch and its basic assumptions (p. 324), whereas 'from a critical perspective' it is a 'postmodernist discourse' (p. 312). HRM, with its ambiguous, or contested, nature, discussed in Chapter 1, emerged alongside the spread of 'post-modern' organisations and 'postmodern epistemology'. The recognition of multiple, coexisting yet competing realities and interpretations, the constant reinterpretation, the eclecticism, the concern for presentation and re-presentation – all of which you will recognise in this book – can be interpreted as a 'postmodern' rendering of the debate about the nature of the employment relationship. We must therefore expect that there will be even more, perhaps very different, interpretations of HRM to be made.

The way David Brent, in Ricky Gervais's The Office, *communicates with his staff is a caricature of managerial discourse. Can you identify from that what kind of managerial strategy (see earlier) he appears to have adopted?*

The 'new science'

We shall now turn briefly to another possible source of influence upon the HRM field. The so-called 'new science' derives from new developments in the natural sciences that challenge some of the key assumptions of Newton's mechanistic notion of the universe (see Wheatley, 1992, for a simplified explanation). Traditionally, science has been 'reductionist' in its analysis into parts and search for 'the basic building blocks of matter' (Wheatley, 1992: 32). It has assumed that 'certainty, linearity, and predictability' (Elliott and Kiel, 1997: 1) are essential elements of the universe. However, new discoveries have questioned those assumptions, generating the theories of complexity and chaos. Complexity refers to a system's 'interrelatedness and interdependence of components as well as their freedom to interact, align, and organize into related configurations' (Lee, 1997: 20). 'Because of this internal complexity, random disturbances can produce unpredictable events and relationships that reverberate throughout a system, creating novel patterns of change . . . however, . . . despite all the unpredictability, coherent order *always* [emphasis in original] emerges out of the randomness and surface chaos' (Morgan, 1997: 262). To understand complexity, new approaches that recognise the whole rather than just its parts – a holistic approach – and attention to relationships between the parts are needed, and these are being developed.

Although theories of complexity and chaos are sometimes referred to as a 'postmodern science', this is a 'common misconception', for 'while recognizing the need for a modification of the reductionist classical model of science, [these theories] remain grounded within the "scientific" tradition' (Price, 1997: 3). They are, nevertheless, recognised as relevant to the understanding of complex social systems. For example, 'chaos theory appears to provide a means for understanding and examining many of the uncertainties, nonlinearities, and unpredictable aspects of social systems behavior' (Elliott and Kiel, 1997: 1). The literature on the application of these theories to social phenomena tends to be very demanding (for example, Eve *et al.*, 1997; Kiel and Elliott, 1997). However, Morgan's (1997) and Wheatley's (1992) applications to organisations are more accessible. There has been some application in the HRM field. For example, Cooksey and Gates (1995) use non-linear dynamics and chaos theory as a way of conceptualising how common HRM practices translate into observable outcomes. Brittain and Ryder (1999: 51) draw on complexity theory in their attempt to improve the assessment of competencies, and conclude that 'HR professionals and psychologists need to challenge widely held beliefs about assessment processes, move away from simplistic assumptions about cause and effect and take a more complex view of the world'.

Ways of seeing and thinking

The chapter will now turn its attention to our ways of seeing and thinking about our world: ways that generate the language, the code, the keys we use in conceptualising and practising HRM. It is at this point that we become fully aware of the value of representing context as a tapestry rather than as a many-skinned onion, for we find here various strands of meaning that managers and academics are drawing upon to construct – that is, both to create and to make sense of – HRM. These ways of seeing are the warp, the threads running the length of the tapestry that give it its basic form and texture, but are generally not visible on its surface. They are more apparent, however, when we turn the tapestry over, as we shall do now, and examine how we perceive reality, make assumptions about it, and define it for ourselves. We shall then look at the weft threads of the tapestry as we examine how we define reality for others through ideology and rhetoric.

Perceiving reality

Perception

Human beings cannot approach reality directly, or in a completely detached and clinical manner. The barriers between ourselves and the world outside us operate at very basic levels:

> Despite the impression that we are in direct and immediate contact with the world, our perception is, in fact, separated from reality by a long chain of processing.
>
> (Medcof and Roth, 1979: 4)

Psychologists indicate that perception is a complex process involving the selection of stimuli to which to respond and the organisation and interpretation of them according to patterns we already recognise. (You can read more about this in Huczynski and Buchanan, 2002.) In other words, we develop a set of filters through which we make sense of our world. Kelly (1955) calls them our 'personal constructs', and they channel the ways we conceptualise and anticipate events (see Bannister and Fransella, 1971).

Defence mechanisms

Our approach to reality, however, is not just through cognitive processes. There is too much at stake for us, for our definition of reality has implications for our definitions of ourselves and for how we would wish others to see us. We therefore defend our sense of self – from what we interpret as threats from our environment or from our own inner urges – by means of what Freud called our 'ego defence mechanisms'. In his study of how such behaviour changes over time, Vaillant (1977: 7) wrote:

> Often such mechanisms are analogous to the means by which an oyster, confronted with a grain of sand, creates a pearl. Humans, too, when confronted with conflict, engage in unconscious but often creative behaviour.

Freudians and non-Freudians (see Peck and Whitlow, 1975: 39–40) have identified many forms of such unconscious adaptive behaviour, some regarded as healthy, others as unhealthy and distorting. We may not go to the lengths of the 'neurotic' defences which Vaillant (1977: 384–385) describes, but a very common approach to the threats of the complexity of intimacy or the responsibility for others is to separate our feelings from our thinking, to treat people and indeed parts of ourselves as objects rather than subjects. The scene is set for a detached, objective and scientific approach to reality in general, to organisations in particular, and to the possibility of treating human beings as 'resources' to be managed.

Making assumptions about reality

We noted earlier that the very term 'human resource management' confronts us with an assumption. This should cause us to recognise that the theory and practice of the employment relationship rest upon assumptions. The assumptions to be examined here are even more fundamental ones for they shape the very way we think. Some are so deeply engrained that they are difficult to identify and express, but they are nevertheless embodied in the way we approach life. They include the way we conceptualise, theorise about and manage the employment relationship, so our assumptions have important implications for our interpretation of HRM.

Writing about Kelly's (1955) personal construct theory, Bannister and Fransella (1971: 18) argue:

> we cannot contact an interpretation-free reality directly. We can only make assumptions about what reality is and then proceed to find out how useful or useless those assumptions are.

However, we have developed our assumptions from birth, and they have been refined and reinforced by socialisation and experience so that, generally, we are not even aware of them. We do not, therefore, generally concern ourselves with epistemology, the theory of knowledge, and we find the discussion of philosophical issues difficult to follow. Nevertheless, we are undoubtedly making significant assumptions about 'what it is possible to know, how may we be certain that we know something' (Heather, 1976: 12–13). These assumptions underpin thinking and contribute to the filters of perception: they therefore frame any understanding of the world, including the ways in which researchers, theorists and practitioners construe HRM. To understand something of HRM we need at least to recognise some of the implications of these epistemological and philosophical issues.

Pepper's (1942) 'world hypotheses' help us distinguish some fundamentally different assumptions that can be made about the world. He classifies them as two pairs of polarised assumptions. The first pair is about the universe. At one pole is the assumption that there is an ordered and systematic universe, 'where facts occur in a determinate order, and where, if enough were known, they could be predicted, or at least described' (Pepper, 1942: 143). At the other pole, the universe is understood as a 'flowing and unbroken wholeness' (Morgan, 1997: 251), with 'real indeterminateness in the world' (Harré, 1981: 3), in which there are 'multitudes of facts rather loosely scattered and not necessarily determining one another to any considerable degree' (Pepper, 1942: 142–143). Pepper's second polarity is about how we approach the universe: through analysis, fragmenting a whole into its parts in order to examine it more closely, or through synthesis, examining it as a whole within its context.

Western thinking stands at the first pole in both pairs of assumptions: it takes an analytical approach to what is assumed to be an ordered universe. Hence 'we are taught to break apart problems, to fragment the world' (Senge, 1990: 3); we examine the parts separately from their context and from one another, 'wrenching units of behaviour, action or experience from one another' (Parker, 1990: 100). These approaches, which underpin the positivism discussed in the next subsection, lead us in our research to examine a world that we interpret as

> abstract, fragmented, precategorized, standardized, divorced from personal and local contexts or relevance, and with its meanings defined and controlled by researchers.
>
> (Mishler, 1986: 120)

By contrast, and of particular relevance to this chapter, is 'contextualism', Pepper's world hypothesis that espouses the assumptions at the second pole of both pairs above. This regards events and actions as processes that are woven into their wider context, and so have to be understood in terms of the multiplicity of interconnections and interrelationships within that context. This is what our tapestry metaphor has attempted to convey. We can use further metaphors to glimpse just how different this view is from our orthodox understanding of the world: from the user's perspective, the latter is like using a library, while the former is more like using the internet (Collin, 1997). The information in a library is structured and classified by experts in a hierarchical system according to agreed conventions; users have to follow that system, translating their needs for information into a form recognised by that system. The Internet, however, is an open-ended network of providers of information, non-linear, constantly changing and expanding. It presents users with a multitude of potential connections to be followed at will and, moreover, the opportunity to participate through dialogue with existing websites or through establishing their own web page.

Differences as basic as those between Pepper's world hypotheses inevitably lead to very different ways of seeing and thinking about reality and, indeed, of understanding our own role in the universe. However, we are rarely aware of or have reason to question our deepest assumptions. Not only does our orthodox approach itself impede our recognition of these epistemological issues, but the processes of socialisation and education in any given society nudge its members in a particular direction (although some may wander off the highway into the byways or, like the author of *Zen and the Art of Motorcycle Maintenance* (Pirsig, 1976), into what are assumed to be badlands). It can be easier to discern these issues in the contrast offered by the epistemological positions adopted in other societies. We can, for example, recognise more of our own deeply embedded assumptions when we encounter a very different world view in an anthropologist's account (Castaneda, 1970) of his apprenticeship to a Yaqui sorceror. Of this, Goldschmidt (1970: 9–10) writes:

> Anthropology has taught us that the world is differently defined in different places. It is not only that people have different customs; it is not only that people believe in different gods and expect different post-mortem fates. It is, rather, that the worlds of different peoples have different shapes. The very metaphysical presuppositions differ: space does not conform to Euclidean geometry, time does not form a continuous unidirectional flow, causation does not conform to Aristotelian logic, man [sic] is not differentiated from non-man or life from death, as in our world . . . The central importance of entering worlds other than our own – and hence of anthropology itself – lies in the fact that the experience leads us to understand that our own world is also a cultural construct. By experiencing other worlds, then, we see our own for what it is . . .

Most of the epistemological threads in the tapestry examined in this chapter reflect Western orthodoxy. (Note how Western orthodoxy has exerted hegemony (see Glossary and below) over non-Western thinking (Stead and Watson, 1999).) And this orthodoxy itself might be gradually changing; some commentators have argued that it has reached a 'turning point' (Capra, 1983), that they can detect signs of a 'paradigm shift' (see Glossary). Indeed, over the last decade or so there have emerged new developments in the natural sciences (see the 'new science' above), and elsewhere (see feminist thinking: below) that challenge orthodoxy.

Stop & think

How could you use Pepper's ideas to explain the challenges of 'postmodernism' and the 'new science' to conventional thinking?

This chapter will now turn to a more accessible level of our thinking, easier to identify and understand, although again we do not customarily pay it much attention.

Defining reality for ourselves

The distinctions between the epistemological positions above and the philosophical stances examined here appear very blurred (Heather, 1976; Checkland, 1981). There is certainly considerable affinity between some of Pepper's (1942) 'world hypotheses' and the approaches noted below. The discussion here will be restricted to aspects of those approaches relevant to our understanding of concepts and practices like HRM.

Orthodox thinking

By orthodoxy we mean 'correct' or currently accepted opinions inculcated in the majority of members in any given society through the processes of socialisation and education and sustained through sanctions against deviation. In our society, for example, most people have traditionally trusted in rationality and 'orthodox medicine' and have had doubts about the paranormal and 'alternative medicine'. We do not generally question our orthodox beliefs: they 'stand to reason', they work, everyone else thinks in the same way. By definition, therefore, we do not pay much attention to them, nor consider how they frame the interpretations we make of our world, nor what other alternatives there could be. We shall therefore now first examine this orthodoxy and then some alternatives to it.

Activity   Either on your own or in a group, make a list of the characteristics of Western orthodoxy that have already been mentioned in this chapter.

The orthodox approach in Western thinking is based on positivism. Positivism forms the basis of scientific method, and applies the rational and ordered principles of the natural sciences to human affairs generally. It manifests itself (see Heather, 1976; Rose, 1978: 26) in a concern for objectivity, in the construction of testable hypotheses, in the collection of empirical data, in the search for causal relationships and in quantification. It is, therefore, uneasy with subjective experience, and attempts to maintain distance between the researcher and those studied (called 'subjects', though regarded more as objects). For example, the Western view is that the individual has (rather than is) a self, which is a natural object, bounded, reified, highly individualised, and autonomous (see Collin, 1996).

We can perceive the role of positivism in orthodoxy in the contrast Kelly draws between the assumptions underpinning his personal construct theory (see previous subsection) and those of orthodox science:

> A scientist . . . depends upon his [sic] facts to furnish the ultimate proof of his propositions . . . these shining nuggets of truth . . . To suggest [as Kelly does] . . . that further human reconstruction can completely alter the appearance of the precious fragments he has accumulated, as well as the direction of their arguments, is to threaten his scientific conclusions, his philosophical position, and even his moral security . . . our assumption that all facts are subject . . . to alternative constructions looms up as culpably subjective and dangerously subversive to the scientific establishment. (quoted in Bannister and Fransella, 1971: 17–18)

Positivism has informed most social science research, which in turn has reproduced, through the kind of new knowledge generated, Western orthodoxy. Hence, it 'reigns' in much HRM research (Legge, 1995: 308). It will be clear from the discussion of the immediate context of HRM that many managers and theorists of management espouse it. It underpins many organisational activities such as psychometric testing for selection and human resource planning models.

Challenging alternatives

There are several alternative ways of thinking that challenge orthodoxy, and you could read more about them in Denzin and Lincoln (1994). The approaches outlined here differ from one another, having different origins and, to some extent, values and constituencies, though they are largely similar in their express opposition to positivism. However, it is important to note that it is only the non-positivist forms of feminist and systems thinking that are covered here: in other words, there are also positivist versions.

Activity   Either on your own or in a group, make a list of the characteristics of alternatives to Western orthodoxy that have already been mentioned in this chapter.

Phenomenology, constructivism and social constructionism

These three approaches stand in marked contrast to positivism, being concerned not with objective reality, but with our lived, subjective, experience of it.

Phenomenology is concerned with understanding the individual's conscious experience. Rather than analysing this into fragments, it takes a holistic approach. It acknowledges the significance of subjectivity, which positivism subordinates to objectivity. Phenomenological researchers try to make explicit the conscious phenomena of experience of those they study, seeking access to them empathically, through shared meanings and inter-subjectivity. This is not a commonplace approach in the field of HRM and management (Sanders, 1982), although it is sometimes discussed in qualitative research studies.

Constructivism is also concerned with individual experience, but with emphasis upon the individual's cognitive processes: 'each individual mentally constructs the world of experience … the mind is not a mirror of the world as it is, but functions to create the world as we know it' (Gergen, 1999: 236). (Note that some constructivists appear to retain something of the positivist approach.)

Social constructionism holds that an objective reality is not directly knowable (and hence we cannot know whether it exists). The reality we do know is socially constructed: we construct it through language, discourse (see earlier), and social interaction.

> Human beings in the social process are constantly creating the social world in interaction with others. They are negotiating their interpretations of reality, those multiple interpretations at the same time constituting the reality itself.   (Checkland, 1981: 277)

To make sense of our experiences, we have to interpret and negotiate meaning with others. There can be no single objective meaning but, Hoffman (1990: 3) suggests,

> an evolving set of meanings that emerge unendingly from the interactions between people. These meanings are not skull-bound and may not exist inside what we think of as an individual 'mind'. They are part of a general flow of constantly changing narratives.

Knowledge is thus a social phenomenon (Hoffman, 1990), and language, rather than depicting objective reality, itself constructs meaning. Weick (1979: 1) quotes a baseball story that illustrates this nicely:

> Three umpires disagreed about the task of calling balls and strikes. The first one said, 'I calls them as they is.' The second one said, 'I calls them as I sees them.' The third and cleverest umpire said, 'They ain't nothin' till I calls them.'

As also suggested by Pepper's (1942) contextualism, discussed earlier, this view of the social construction of meaning implies that we cannot separate ourselves from our created reality: 'man [sic] is an animal suspended in webs of significance he himself has spun' (Geertz, 1973: 5). Again as with contextualism, this approach emphasises the significance of perspective, the position from which an interpretation is made (remember the *Guardian* advertisement at the start of this chapter?). Further, it also draws attention to the way in which some people contrive to impose their interpretations upon, and so define the reality of, others, with the result that less powerful people are disempowered, overlooked, remain silent, are left without a 'voice' (Mishler, 1986; Bhavnani, 1990). This is a point to which the chapter returns later.

While the social construction of meaning appears a very abstract notion, it is apparent in everyday life in the stories we tell: narrative is how we make meaning (Polkinghorne, 1988). 'We dream in narrative, daydream in narrative, remember, anticipate, hope, despair, believe, doubt, plan, revise, criticize, construct, gossip, learn, hate, and love by narrative' (Hardy, 1968: 5). Listening to narratives is an approach increasingly favoured by those trying to understand organisations (Gabriel, 2000).

Stop & think

Can you identify social constructionist perspectives among the competing interpretations of organisations and management discussed earlier in the chapter?

Feminist thinking

Feminist thinking, which recognises differences between the world-views of women and men, challenges what is increasingly regarded as the male world-view of the positivist approach (Gilligan, 1982; Spender, 1985). Gilligan's (1982) landmark study concluded that women value relationship and connection, whereas men value independence, autonomy and control. Bakan (1966) made a distinction between 'agency' and 'communion', associating the former with maleness and the latter with femaleness. Agency is 'an expression of independence through self-protection, self-assertion and control of the environment' (Marshall, 1989: 279), whereas the basis of communion is integration with others.

> The agentic strategy reduces tension by changing the world about it; communion seeks union and cooperation as its way of coming to terms with uncertainty. While agency manifests itself in focus, closedness and separation, communion is characterized by contact, openness and fusion.
>
> (Marshall, 1989: 289)

Therefore, Marshall (1989) argues, feminist thinking 'represents a fundamental critique of knowledge as it is traditionally constructed . . . largely . . . by and about men' and either ignores or devalues the experience of women:

> its preoccupation with seeking universal, immutable truth, failing to accept diversity and change; its categorization of the world into opposites, valuing one pole and devaluing the other; its claims of detachment and objectivity; and the predominance of linear cause-and-effect thinking. These forms reflect male, agentic experiences and strategies for coping with uncertainty. By shaping academic theorizing and research activities, they build male power and domination into the structures of knowledge . . .
>
> (p. 281)

Calas and Smircich (1992: 227) discuss how gender has been 'mis- or under-represented' in organisation theory, and explore the effects of rewriting it in. Those would include the correction or completion of the organisational record from which women have been absent or excluded, the assessment of gender bias in current knowledge, and the making of a new, more diverse organisation theory that covers topics of concern to women. Hearn *et al.* (1989) identify similar shortcomings in organisation theory in their discussion of the sexuality of organisations, while Hopfl and Hornby Atkinson (2000) point to the gendered assumptions made in organisations.

Systems and ecological thinking

Systems thinking offers particularly useful insights into the understanding of context. As with feminist thinking, there are both positivist and alternative views of systems, but here we are concerned with the latter. Checkland (1981), for example, employs systems not as 'descriptions of actual real-world activity' (p. 314) in his 'soft systems methodology', but as 'tools of an epistemological kind which can be used in a process of exploration within social reality' (p. 249). (Note that his later book – Checkland and Scholes, 1990 – updates the methodology but does not repeat the discussion of its philosophical underpinnings.) As with feminist thinking, systems thinking gives us a different perspective from that of orthodox thinking. It allows us to see the whole rather than just its parts and to recognise that we are a part of that whole. It registers patterns of change, relationships rather than just individual elements, a web of interrelationships and reciprocal flows of influence rather than linear chains of cause and effect.

The concept of system denotes a whole, complex and coherent entity, comprising a hierarchy of subsystems, where the whole is greater than the sum of its parts. Much of what has been written about systems draws upon General Systems Theory, a meta-theory that offered a way to conceptualise phenomena in any disciplinary area. Very importantly, the systems approach does not argue that social phenomena are systems, but rather that they can be modelled (conceptualised, thought about) as though they had systemic properties. The concept of system used in the social sciences is therefore a very abstract kind of metaphor. However, we can give only a brief outline of systems concepts here: you will find further detail in Checkland (1981), Checkland and Scholes (1990), Senge (1990) and Morgan (1997).

Systems may be 'open' (like biological or social systems) or 'closed' to their environment (like many physical and mechanical systems). As shown in Figure 3.2, the open system imports from, exchanges with, its environment what it needs to meet its goals and to survive. It converts or transforms these inputs into a form that sustains its existence and generates

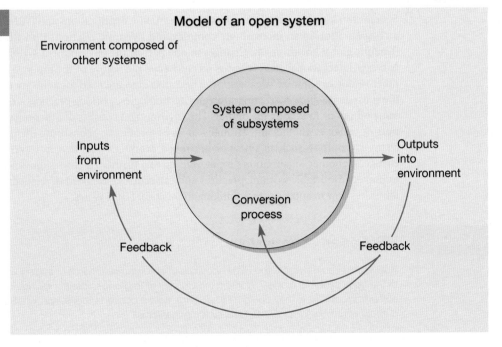

Figure 3.2   **Model of an open system**

Environment composed of other systems

System composed of subsystems

Inputs from environment

Outputs into environment

Conversion process

Feedback

Feedback

outputs that are returned to the environment either in exchange for further inputs or as waste products. The environment itself comprises other systems that are also drawing in inputs and discharging outputs. Changes in remote parts of any given system's environment can therefore ripple through that environment to affect it eventually. There are feedback loops that enable the system to make appropriate modifications to its subsystems in the light of the changing environment. Thus the system constantly adjusts to achieve equilibrium internally and with its environment.

Reflecting upon the management approaches identified earlier, we can now recognise that the scientific management, human relations and perhaps also the humanistic approaches treated the organisation as a closed system, whereas the human resource approach recognises it as open to its environment. Brunsson's (1989) identification of the 'action' and 'political' organisations could also be seen as an open system approach.

The significance of systems thinking, then, lies in its ability to conceptualise complex, dynamic realities – the system and its internal and external relationships – and model them in a simple, coherent way that is yet pregnant with meaning and capable of further elaboration when necessary. This means that we can use it to hold in our minds such complex ideas as those discussed in this book, without diminishing our awareness of their complexity and interrelationships.

According to Senge (1990: 12–13), systems thinking – his 'fifth discipline' – is essential for the development of the effective organisation – the learning organisation (Chapter 7):

> At the heart of a learning organization is a shift of mind – from seeing ourselves as separate from the world to connected to the world, from seeing problems as caused by someone or something 'out there' to seeing how our own actions create the problems we experience. A learning organization is a place where people are continually discovering how they create their reality. And how they can change it.

Stop & think

What similarities do you see between systems thinking and the 'new science'?

Systems thinking therefore enables us to contextualise organisations and HRM. It conceptualises an organisation in an increasingly complex and dynamic relationship with its complex and dynamic global environment. Changes in one part of the environment – global warming, poor harvests, international and civil wars – can change the nature of the inputs – raw materials and other resources – into an organisation. This can lead to the need for adjustments in and between the subsystems – new marketing strategies, technologies, working practices – either to ensure the same output or to modify the output. The environment consists of other organisations, the outputs of which – whether intentionally or as by-products – constitute the inputs of others. A change in output, such as a new or improved product or service, however, will constitute a change in another organisation's input, leading to a further ripple of adjustments. Consider, for example, how flexible working practices and call centres have been developed. Sherwood (2002) illustrates how to apply systems thinking to practical HRM issues.

Activity   HRM as an open system

How would you represent the HRM activities of an organisation in a changing world in terms of the open systems model? Working individually or in groups, identify its inputs (where they come from, and how they could be changing), how it converts these, and what its (changing?) outputs might be. What are its feedback mechanisms?

Defining reality for others

This chapter has defined the warp of the tapestry of context as our ways of seeing and thinking. It will now examine some of the weft threads – the ways in which others define our reality (or we define reality for others): ideology, hegemony, and rhetoric. These interweave through the warp to produce the basic pattern of the tapestry, but with differing colours and textures, and also differing lengths (durations), so that they do not necessarily appear throughout the tapestry. They constitute important contextual influences upon HRM, and in part account for the competing definitions of it.

Ideology

Gowler and Legge (1989) define ideology as 'sets of ideas involved in the framing of our experience, of making sense of the world, expressed through language' (p. 438). It has a narrower focus than the 'ways of thinking' we have been discussing above, and could be seen as a localised orthodoxy, a reasonably coherent set of ideas and beliefs that often goes unchallenged:

> Ideology operates as a reifying, congealing mechanism that imposes pseudoresolutions and compromises in the space where fluid, contradictory, and multivalent subjectivity could gain ground.
>
> (Sloan, 1992: 174)

Ideology purports to explain reality objectively, but within a pluralist society it actually represents and legitimates the interests of members of a subgroup. It is a 'subtle combination of facts and values' (Child, 1969: 224), and achieves its ends through language and rhetoric (see below). What we hear and what we read is conveying someone else's interpretations. The way those are expressed may obscure the ideology and vested interest in those interpretations. For example, in contrast to the orthodox view of culture, Jermier argues that culture is:

> the objectified product of the labor of human subjects . . . there is a profound forgetting of the fact that the world is socially constructed and can be remade . . . Exploitative practices are mystified and concealed.
>
> (Frost *et al.*, 1991: 231)

As you will recognise from earlier in the chapter, the organisation is an arena in which ideologies of many kinds are in contest: capitalism and Marxism, humanism and scientific approaches to the individual, feminism and a gender-biased view.

Child (1969) discusses the ideology embodied in the development of management thinking, identifying how the human relations approach chose to ignore the difference of interests between managers and employees and how this dismissal of potential conflict influenced theory and practice. Commentators such as Braverman (1974), Frost *et al.* (1991) and Rose (1978), and many of the readings in Clark *et al.* (1994), will help you to recognise some of the ideologies at work in this field.

Hegemony

Hegemony is the imposition of the reality favoured by a powerful subgroup in society upon less powerful others. Such a group exerts its authority over subordinate groups by imposing its definition of reality over other possible definitions. This does not have to be achieved through direct coercion, but by 'winning the consent of the dominated majority so that the power of the dominant classes appears both legitimate and natural'. In this way, subordinate groups are 'contained within an ideological space which does not seem at all "ideological": which appears instead to be permanent and "natural", to lie outside history, to be beyond particular interests' (Hebdige, 1979: 15–16).

It is argued that gender issues are generally completely submerged in organisations and theories of them (Hearn *et al.*, 1989; Calas and Smircich, 1992; Hopfl and Hornby Atkinson,

2000) so that male-defined realities of organisations appear natural, and feminist views unnatural and shrill. You could use the readings in Clark *et al.* (1994) to identify instances of hegemony and the outcomes of power relations, such as the 'management prerogative'; Watson (2000) throws light on the manager's experience of these.

Rhetoric

Rhetoric is 'the art of using language to persuade, influence or manipulate' (Gowler and Legge, 1989: 438). Its 'high symbolic content' '*allows it to reveal and conceal but above all develop and transform meaning*' (Gowler and Legge, 1989: 439, their italics). It '*heightens and transforms meaning by processes of association, involving both evocation and juxtaposition*'. In other words, its artfulness lies in playing with meanings, and can be used for various effects. It is something with which we are familiar, whether as political 'spin' or as the terminology used in effecting organisational change (Atkinson and Butcher, 1999). In the 'eco-climate' of an organisation, where meanings are shared and negotiated, power and knowledge relations are expressed rhetorically. For example, changes to structure and jobs might be described as 'flexibility' rather than as the casualisation of work (see, for example, Chapter 4), and increased pressures upon employees as 'empowerment' (see Chapter 14). Legge (1995) proposes that one way of interpreting HRM is to recognise it as 'a rhetoric about how employees should be managed to achieve competitive advantage' that both 'celebrates' the values of its stakeholders while 'at the same time mediating the contradictions of capitalism' (p. xiv). In other words, it allows those stakeholders to 'have their cake and eat it'. Nevertheless, Eccles and Nohria (1992: 10) regard rhetoric as

> something that can be used and abused, but it *cannot* be avoided [original italics]. Rather, it constantly serves to frame the way we see the world. In our view, rhetoric is used well when it mobilizes actions of people in a way that contributes both to the individuals as people and to the performance of organizations as a whole.

It is effective when it is flexible enough 'to incorporate the different meanings, emphases, and interpretations that different people will inevitably give it' (p. 35).

Conclusion . . . and a new beginning?

This chapter has examined something of the warp and weft that give the tapestry its basic form, pattern, colour and texture. To complete our understanding of the context of HRM we need to recognise that issues and people constitute the surface stitching that is drawn through the warp and weft to add further pattern and colour. You will be aware of examples from your own experience and the reading of this and other books, but we can instance the influences of recession, equal opportunities legislation, European directives, management gurus, Margaret Thatcher, 'New Labour', the euro debate, 11 September, that resonate with the warp and weft to produce the pattern that has come to be known as 'HRM'.

The tapestry of which HRM forms a part is continuously being woven, but we can now become aware of the sources of the differing approaches to organisation and management and of the contesting voices about the management of people. We can now recognise that their contest weaves multiple meanings into the organisational and conceptual pattern which is HRM. However, this awareness also allows us to recognise that yet other meanings, and hence potentials for the management of the employment relationship, remain to be constructed.

By pointing to the need to recognise the significance of the context of HRM, this chapter is also acknowledging that you will find therein more interpretations than this book of 'academic text' (Parker and Shotter, 1990: see 'Discourse' earlier), shaped by its writers' own agendas and values and the practicalities of commercial publication, can offer you. The process both of writing and of publication is that of decontextualisation, fragmentation, standardisation, and presentation of knowledge as 'entertaining education', in bite-sized chunks of knowledge or sound bites. But by urging you to become aware of the context of HRM, this chapter is at the same time inviting you to look beyond what this book has to say, to recognise the nature of its discourse or, rather, discourses, to challenge its assumptions (and, indeed, your own) and to use your own critical judgements informed by your wider reading and personal experience.

This, then, is why this book has begun its exploration of HRM by examining context. This chapter had a further aim (and this betrays this writer's 'agenda and values'). This is to orientate your thinking generally towards an awareness of context, to think contextually, for ultimately awareness of context is empowering. One of the outcomes could well be greater knowledge but less certainty, the recognition that there could be competing interpretations of the topic you are considering, that the several perspectives upon the area could all yield different conclusions. Attention to context, therefore, encourages us not to be taken in by our initial interpretations, nor to accept unquestioningly the definitions of reality that others would have us adopt (the 'hegemony' of the previous section). There are, however, no easy answers, and we have to make the choice between alternatives. Reality is much messier and more tentative than theory and, like 'everyday talk', it is 'marked by its vagueness and openness', its meaning open to interpretation through negotiation with others. The acceptance of this, however, as we shall later see in Chapter 7, is one of the marks of the mature learner: the ability to recognise alternative viewpoints but, nevertheless, to take responsibility for committing oneself to one of them.

By definition, one chapter cannot begin to portray the details of the context of HRM. Those, after all, are constantly changing with time. It will have achieved its purpose if it causes you to recognise the significance of context and the need to adopt ways of thinking that enable you to conceptualise it. It can point you in some directions, and you will find many others in the chapters that follow, but there are no logical starting points, because context is indivisible; and you will never reach the end of the story for, from the perspective of context, the story is never-ending.

Summary

- The chapter argues that the keys to the understanding of human affairs, such as HRM, lie within their context. Although context is difficult to conceptualise and represent, readers can draw on their existing understanding of environmental issues to help them comprehend it. Awareness and comprehension of context are ultimately empowering because they sharpen critical thinking by challenging our own and others' assumptions.

- Multiple interests, conflict, and stressful and moral issues are inherent in the immediate context of HRM, which comprises the organisation (the nature of which generates a number of lateral and vertical tensions) and management (defined as the continuous process of resolving those tensions). Over time, managers have adopted a range of approaches to their task, including scientific management; the human relations school; humanistic organisation development; and now HRM. To understand this layer of HRM's context calls for the recognition of the existence of some significant assumptions that inform managers' differing practices and the competing interpretations that theorists make of them.

- The wider social, economic, political and cultural context of HRM is diverse, complex and dynamic, but three very different and unconnected strands of it are pulled out for examination. The two world wars left legacies for the management of the employment relationship, while emerging 'postmodern' experiences and critiques and the 'new science' locate HRM within a contemporary framework of ideas that could eventually challenge some assumptions about the management of the employment relationship.

- The chapter, however, finds it insufficient to conceptualise context as layered, like an onion. Rather, HRM is embedded in its context. The metaphor of a tapestry is therefore used to express the way in which its meaning is constructed from the interweaving and mutual influences of the assumptions deriving from basic perceptual, epistemological, philosophical and ideological positions. The notions of 'warp' and 'weft' are used to discuss such key contextual elements as positivism, phenomenology, constructivism, social constructionism, feminist thinking, systems thinking, ideology, hegemony, and rhetoric. People, events and issues are the surface stitching.

- The nature of this tapestry, with its multiple and often competing perspectives, ensures that HRM, as a concept, theory and practice, is a contested terrain. However, the chapter leaves readers to identify the implications of this through their critical reading of the book.

<table><tr><td>Activity</td><td></td></tr></table>

Drawing on your understanding of the environment

The nature of our environment concerns us all. As 'environment' and 'green issues' have crossed the threshold of public awareness to become big business, we have become concerned about our natural environment as no previous generations have been. We are now aware of the increasing complexity in the web of human affairs. We recognise the interrelationships within our 'global village', between the world's 'rich' North and the 'poor' South, and between politics, economics and the environment, and at home between, for example, health, unemployment, deprivation and crime. Another feature of our environment that we cannot ignore is its increasingly dynamic nature. Our world is changing before our very eyes. Comparing it with the world we knew even ten years ago, and certainly with that known by our parents when they were the age we are now, it has changed dramatically and in ways that could never have been anticipated.

1 You will have considerable knowledge, and perhaps personal experience, of many environmental issues. These might be the problems of climate change, waste disposal and pollution, genetically modified food, the impact on the countryside of the construction of new roads, or the threats to the survival of many species of animals and plants.

　As a step towards helping you understand better the nature of context as defined in this chapter, and working individually or in groups, choose two or three such issues for discussion, and consider the following points.

(a) Identify those who are playing a part in them (the actors) and those who have an interest in them or are directly or indirectly affected by them (the stakeholders). How did the event or situation that has become an issue come about? Who started it? How do they explain it? Who benefits in this situation? How do they justify this? Who loses in it? What can they do about it? Why? Who is paying the cost? How and why?

(b) Look for concrete examples of the following statements.

　– 'We have an impact upon the environment and cause it to change, both positively and negatively.'

　– 'The environment and changes within it have an impact upon us and affect the quality of human life, both positively and negatively.'

　– 'The interrelationships between events and elements in the environment are so complex that they are often difficult to untangle.'

　– 'It may not be possible or even meaningful to identify the cause of events and their effects; the cause or causes may have to be inferred, the effects projected.'

　– 'Sometimes their effects are manifested far into the future, and so are not easily identifiable now, though they may affect future generations.'

　– 'Our relationship with our environment therefore has a moral dimension to it.'

- 'To deal with some of the negative causes may be gravely damaging to some other groups of people.'
- 'The understanding of these events will differ according to the particular perspective – whether of observer, actor, or stakeholder – and will arise from interpretation rather than ultimately verifiable "facts".'
- 'These issues often involve powerful power bases in society, each of which has its own interpretation of events, which it may wish others to accept.'
- 'The nature of our relationship with our environment challenges our traditional scientific ways of thinking, in which we value objectivity, analyse by breaking down a whole into its parts, and seek to identify cause and effect in a linear model.'
- 'It also therefore challenges our traditional methods of research and investigation, deduction and inference.'

2 The opening section of the chapter suggested that your examination of environmental issues would allow you to recognise that:

- Context is multilayered, multidimensional and interwoven, like a *tapestry*. Concrete events and abstract ideas intertwine to create issues, and thinking, feeling, interpreting and behaving are all involved.
- Our understanding of people and events depends upon our *perspective*.
- It also depends upon our *ideology*.
- There are therefore *competing or contested interpretations* of events.
- Different groups in society have their own interpretations of events, stemming from their *ideology*. Their *discourse* incorporates an explanation for competing interpretations. They use *rhetoric* to express their own interpretations and to explain those of other people, thus distorting, or even suppressing, the authentic expression of competing views.
- Powerful others often try to impose their interpretation of events, their version of reality, upon the less powerful majority: this is *hegemony*.

From your knowledge of the environmental issues you have just discussed, can you give concrete examples of these points?

QUESTIONS

1 In what ways does the conceptualisation of context adopted by this chapter differ from more commonly used approaches (for example, in the models of HRM in Chapter 1)? Does it add to the understanding they give of HRM and, if so, in what way?

2 What assumptions and 'world hypotheses' underpin those models, and what are the implications for your use of them?

3 What assumptions and 'world hypotheses' appear to underpin this chapter, and what are the implications for your use of the chapter?

4 Identify some recent events that are likely to play a significant part in the context of HRM.

5 This chapter has been written from a British perspective. If you were working from a different perspective – South African, perhaps, or Scandinavian – what elements of the context of HRM would you include?

6 The chapter has been written for students of HRM. Is it also relevant to practitioners of HRM and, if so, in what way?

EXERCISE

Having started to think in terms of context and to recognise the significance of our ways of thinking, you should be reading the rest of this book in this same critical manner. As you go through it, try to identify the following:

- the assumptions (at various levels) underlying the research and theory reported in the chapters that follow;

- the implications of these assumptions for the interpretations that the researchers and theorists are placing upon their material;

- the possibility of other interpretations deriving from other assumptions;

- the assumptions (at various levels) that the writers of the following chapters appear to hold;

- the implications of these assumptions for the interpretations that these writers are placing upon their material;

- the possibility of other interpretations deriving from other assumptions;

- the implications of the various alternatives for the practice of HRM.

CASE STUDY

FT

Awkward squad promises a rough ride at Blackpool

Blair faces bruising from less compliant union leaders, say David Turner and Christopher Adams

The awkward squad is up and running at this year's Trades Union Congress, and they have a ringleader with attitude and power promising a rough ride for Tony Blair. Yesterday, the eve of conference was the first big opportunity for this expanding group of left-wingers to grab attention – and they revelled in it.

None more so than Derek Simpson, who seized joint control of Britain's biggest private sector union two months ago and is now threatening a series of high-profile industrial disputes with a promise to tear up long-standing 'sweetheart' deals with employers. Many of the agreements bar strikes.

The left-winger and former communist, propelled to power at the Amicus union by grassroots discontent with the direction taken by Mr Blair's government, chose robust terms to signal that the days of compliant trade unionism were over.

Ramming home his campaign on workers' rights, Mr Simpson predicted the prime minister would leave Blackpool after his address to the TUC in Blackpool tomorrow with a 'fucking migraine'.

Bob Crow, leader of the RMT rail union, picked up the theme. Mr Blair, he quipped, would be need-ing Anadin to treat his headache and he would be happy to supply it.

Mr Blair's first address to the TUC for two years, having been called away from last year's conference by the September 11 attacks, is keenly awaited in Blackpool. Union leaders, moderate and militant, yesterday vented their dissatisfaction on a range of issues: Iraq, the demise of final salary pensions, privatisation of public services and the plight of manufacturing.

Discontent has boiled over in a series of hostile motions agreed for debate this week. The government is criticised for neglecting workers' rights and doing too little for public sector employees. Unions have united in support of the firefighters who, on Thursday, are expected to vote for strike action over a pay claim for the first time in 25 years.

But underlying all this venom directed at the government is a recognition by moderate union leaders that their members are being swayed by the arguments of the left and that they themselves need to toughen their rhetoric.

In truth, the TUC is more divided than at any time since Mr Blair became leader. Evidence of this is an

Case study continued

angry split on the euro, reflecting the 'anti' views of several new generation leaders. Bill Morris, TGWU leader and a close ally of chancellor Gordon Brown, is to defy a motion advocating euro membership.

The TUC line chiming with the government's 'in principle' policy on joining faces challenge at the hands of the anti-euro union leaders who include Dave Prentis of Unison, Mr Simpson and Mr Crow.

The split extends to Iraq, where union leaders have struggled for days to come up with a carefully constructed compromise opposing unilateral US action but leaving open the option of a military strike with United Nations support.

Already facing backbench unrest and public scepticism about the need for war against Iraq, the prime minister has the additional problem of a long battle over public sector reforms, peppered with disputes over pay.

Now Mr Simpson, who came from nowhere to unseat Sir Ken Jackson, is set on unpicking his Blairite predecessor's employer-friendly regime.

Amicus is to ask its million members whether they want to renegotiate agreements with employers that set out the terms for collective bargaining.

Mr Simpson said many deals negotiated in the 1980s and 1990s contained compulsory arbitration, no time off for union work and no right to negotiate pay and conditions.

The recognition process had become an unseemly 'beauty parade', he said. To secure sole recognition, unions were falling over themselves to offer favourable terms to employers rather than their members. 'We will tear up the form book on industrial relations and seek agreements that achieve real benefits for our members.'

The number of deals could run into several hundred, but union officials say they have already identified at least 30.

The move is a significant break with policy for a union that, under Sir Ken, pioneered the kind of 'partnership' agreements that have become commonplace through-out industry.

Mr Simpson said partnership had become a 'euphemism for exploitation'. Other unions like the sound of that – Ucatt, the construction workers' union, said it would 'bring to an end the practice of employers choosing a union for their workers'.

Mr Simpson, who has declined a meeting with the prime minister, personified the reception Mr Blair will face. There will be little escape from union leaders, awkward squad and moderates alike.

All this makes for a week of hard-talking and drawn-out debate that will define relations with the government up until the next election.

At the end of it, the unions may have found more common ground than they share now. On the other hand, and this is by far the more likely outcome, the true extent of the differences with the more vocal left will be clear. And the headache for Mr Blair is that the broad base of union support that underpinned him during his first term will be that little bit narrower.

Source: Turner, D. and Adams, C., *Financial Times*, 9 September 2002.

Questions

1 This article about the 2002 Trades Union Congress points to a number of elements within the context of HRM that threaten ultimately to affect HRM policies and practices within many organisations. Identify them, and develop a systems map to help you examine their likely influences upon the HRM of an organisation. (If you are working in a group, split in two, one half looking at this from the perspective of an HR director of a large private sector organisation, and the other from that of an HR director of a public sector organisation. Compare the two models. Are there differences between them? Why?)

2 What are the implications of changes in the wider context for the planning and development of an organisation's HRM policies and practices? What are the implications for HRM strategy?

3 How many different perspectives are evident in this article?

4 Identify the several instances of 'ideology', 'rhetoric', and 'discourse' recognisable in this article.

5 (You can carry out the following individually or in two groups.) First, as a member of Mr Blair's government, write a report on these TUC preoccupations for your colleagues. Next, as an HR director of a private sector organisation, write a report on them to your board. Now compare the two reports. How do they differ in rhetoric and discourse, and what do these differences suggest about their underlying ideology?

6 What are the implications of the significance of rhetoric and discourse for managing people in organisations?

References and further reading

Those texts marked with an asterisk are recommended for further reading.

Aldrich, H.E. (1992) 'Incommensurable paradigms? Vital signs from three perspectives', in Reed, M. and Hughes, M. (eds) *Rethinking Organization: New Directions in Organization Theory and Analysis*. London: Sage, pp. 17–45.

Argyris, C. (1960) *Understanding Organisational Behaviour*. London: Tavistock Dorsey.

Atkinson, S. and Butcher, D. (1999) 'The power of Babel: lingua franker', *People Management*, 5, 20, 14 October: 50–52.

Bakan, D. (1966) *The Duality of Human Existence*. Boston, MA.: Beacon.

Bannister, D. and Fransella, F. (1971) *Inquiring Man: The Theory of Personal Constructs*. Harmondsworth: Penguin.

Baxter, B. (1999) 'What do postmodernism and complexity science mean?', *People Management*, 5, 23, 25 November: 49.

Bhavnani, K.-K. (1990) 'What's power got to do with it? Empowerment and social research', in Parker, I. and Shotter, J. (eds) *Deconstructing Social Psychology*. London: Routledge, pp. 141–152.

Braverman, H. (1974) *Labor and Monopoly Capital: The Degradation of Work in the Twentieth Century*. New York: Monthly Review Press.

Brittain, S. and Ryder, P. (1999) 'Get complex', *People Management*, 5, 23, 25 November: 48–51.

Brunsson, N. (1989) *The Organization of Hypocrisy: Talk, Decisions and Actions in Organizations*. Chichester: Wiley.

Burr, V. (1995) *An Introduction to Social Constructionism*. London: Routledge.

Calas, M.B. and Smircich, L. (1992) 'Re-writing gender into organizational theorizing: directions from feminist perspectives', in Reed, M. and Hughes, M. (eds) *Rethinking Organization: New Directions in Organization Theory and Analysis*. London: Sage, pp. 227–253.

Callaghan, G. and Thompson, P. (2002) 'We recruit attitude: the selection and shaping of routine call centre labour', *Journal of Management Studies*, 39, 2: 233–254.

Cameron, S. (1997) *The MBA Handbook: Study Skills for Managers*, 3rd edn. London: Pitman.

Capra, F. (1983) *The Turning Point: Science, Society and the Rising Cultures*. London: Fontana.

Castaneda, C. (1970) *The Teachings of Don Juan: A Yaqui Way of Knowledge*. Harmondsworth: Penguin.

Checkland, P. (1981) *Systems Thinking, Systems Practice*. Chichester: Wiley.

Checkland, P. and Scholes, J. (1990) *Soft Systems Methodology in Action*. Chichester: Wiley.

Cherniss, C. and Goleman, D. (eds) (2001) *The Emotionally Intelligent Workplace: How to Select for, Measure, and Improve Emotional Intelligence in Individuals, Groups, and Organizations*. San Francisco, CA: Jossey-Bass.

Child, J. (1969) *British Management Thought: A Critical Analysis*. London: George Allen & Unwin.

*Clark, H., Chandler, J. and Barry, J. (1994) *Organisation and Identities: Text and Readings in Organisational Behaviour*. London: Chapman & Hall.

Clegg, S.R. (1990) *Modern Organizations: Organization Studies in the Postmodern World*. London: Sage.

Collin, A. (1996) 'Organizations and the end of the individual?', *Journal of Managerial Psychology*, 11, 7: 9–17.

Collin, A. (1997) 'Career in context', *British Journal of Guidance and Counselling*, 25, 4: 435–446.

Concise Oxford English Dictionary (1982) 7th edn. Oxford: Clarendon Press.

Connock, S. (1992) 'The importance of "big ideas" to HR managers', *Personnel Management*, June, pp. 24–27.

Cooksey, R.W. and Gates, G.R. (1995) 'HRM: A management science in need of discipline', *Asia Pacific Journal of Human Resources*, 33, 3: 15–38.

Cooper, R. and Fox, S. (1990) 'The "texture" of organizing', *Journal of Management Studies*, 27, 6: 575–582.

Czerny, A. (2005) 'Lean future looms for HR functions', *People Management*, 11, 11, 2 June: 9.

Denzin, N.K. and Lincoln, Y.S. (eds) (1994) *Handbook of Qualitative Research*. Thousand Oaks, CA: Sage.

Department of Scientific and Industrial Research (1961) *Human Sciences: Aid to Industry*. London: HMSO.

*Eccles, R.G. and Nohria, N. (1992) *Beyond the Hype: Rediscovering the Essence of Management*. Boston, MA: Harvard Business School Press.

Elliott, E. and Kiel, L.D. (1997) 'Introduction', in Kiel, L.D. and Elliott, E. (eds) *Chaos Theory in the Social Sciences: Foundations and Applications*. Ann Arbor, MI: The University of Michigan Press, pp. 1–15.

Eve, R.A., Horsfall, S. and Lee, M.E. (eds) (1997) *Chaos, Complexity, and Sociology: Myths, Models, and Theories*. Thousand Oaks, CA: Sage.

Fineman, S. (ed.) (1993) *Emotion in Organizations*. London: Sage.

Fox, S. (1990) 'Strategic HRM: postmodern conditioning for the corporate culture', in Fox, S. and Moult, G. (eds) *Postmodern Culture and Management Development*, Special Edition: Management Education and Development, 21, 3: 192–206.

*Frost, P.J., Moore, L.F., Louis, M.R., Lundberg, C.C. and Martin, J. (1991) *Reframing Organizational Culture*. Newbury Park, CA: Sage.

Gabriel, Y. (2000) *Storytelling in Organizations: Facts, Fictions, and Fantasies*. Oxford: Oxford University Press.

Gavey, N. (1989) 'Feminist poststructuralism and discourse analysis: contributions to feminist psychology', *Psychology of Women Quarterly*, 13, 459–475.

Geertz, C. (1973) *The Interpretation of Cultures*. New York: Basic Books.

Gergen, K.J. (1992) 'Organization theory in the postmodern era', in Reed, M. and Hughes, M. (eds) *Rethinking Organization: New Directions in Organization Theory and Analysis*. London: Sage, pp. 207–226.

Gergen, K.J. (1999) *An Invitation to Social Construction*. London: Sage.

Gilligan, C. (1982) *In a Different Voice: Psychological Theory and Women's Development*. Cambridge, MA: Harvard University Press.

Goldschmidt, W. (1970) 'Foreword', in Castaneda, C., *The Teachings of Don Juan: A Yaqui Way of Knowledge*. Harmondsworth: Penguin, pp. 9–10.

Gowler, D. and Legge, K. (1989) 'Rhetoric in bureaucratic careers: managing the meaning of management success', in Arthur, M.B., Hall, D.T. and Lawrence, B.S. (eds) *Handbook of Career Theory*. Cambridge: Cambridge University Press, pp. 437–453.

Hardy, B. (1968) 'Towards a poetics of fiction: An approach through narrative'. *Novel*, 2, 5–14.

Harré, R. (1981) 'The positivist-empiricist approach and its alternative', in Reason, P. and Rowan, J. (eds) *Human Inquiry: A Sourcebook of New Paradigm Research*. Chichester: Wiley, pp. 3–17.

Harvey, D. (1990) *The Condition of Postmodernity*. Oxford: Blackwell.

Hassard, J. (1993) 'Postmodernism and organizational analysis: An overview', in Hassard, J. and Parker, M. (eds) (1993) *Postmodernism and Organizations*. London: Sage, pp. 1–23.

Hassard, J. and Parker, M. (eds) (1993) *Postmodernism and Organizations*. London: Sage.

Hatch, M.J. (1997) *Organization Theory: Modern, Symbolic and Postmodern Perspectives*. Oxford: Oxford University Press.

Hatchett, A. (2000) 'Call collective: ringing true', *People Management*, 6, 2, January: 40–42.

*Hearn, J., Sheppard, D.L., Tancred-Sheriff, P. and Burrell, G. (1989) *The Sexuality of Organization*. London: Sage.

Heather, N. (1976) *Radical Perspectives in Psychology*. London: Methuen.

Hebdige, D. (1979) *Subculture: The Meaning of Style*. London: Methuen.

Hendry, C. and Pettigrew, A. (1990) 'Human resource management: an agenda for the 1990s', *International Journal of Human Resource Management*, 1, 1: 17–43.

Higgs, M. and Dulewicz, V. (2002) *Making Sense of Emotional Intelligence*, 2nd edn. London: nferNelson.

Hodgson, A. (1987) 'Deming's never-ending road to quality', *Personnel Management*, July, pp. 40–44.

Hoffman, L. (1990) 'Constructing realities: an art of lenses', *Family Process*, 29, 1: 1–12.

Hopfl, H. and Hornby Atkinson, P. (2000) 'The future of women's career', in Collin, A. and Young, R.A. (eds) *The Future of Career*, Cambridge: Cambridge University Press, pp. 130–143.

Hosking, D. and Fineman, S. (1990) 'Organizing processes', *Journal of Management Studies*, 27, 6: 583–604.

Huczynski, A. and Buchanan, D. (2002) *Organizational Behaviour: An Introductory Text*, 4th edn. Harlow: FT/Prentice Hall.

Huse, E.F. (1980) *Organization Development and Change*, 2nd edn. St Paul, MN: West Publishing.

Kanter, R.M. (1983) *The Change Masters*. New York: Simon & Schuster.

Keenoy, T. (1990) 'Human resource management: rhetoric, reality and contradiction', *International Journal of Human Resource Management*, 1, 3: 363–384.

Kelly, G.A. (1955) *The Psychology of Personal Constructs*, Vols 1 and 2. New York: W.W. Norton.

Kiel, L.D. and Elliott, E. (eds) (1997) *Chaos Theory in the Social Sciences: Foundations and Applications*. Ann Arbor, MI: The University of Michigan Press.

Kvale, S. (ed.) (1992) *Psychology and Postmodernism*. London: Sage.

Lee, M.E. (1997) 'From enlightenment to chaos: toward non-modern social theory', in Eve, R.A., Horsfall, S. and Lee, M.E. (eds) *Chaos, Complexity, and Sociology: Myths, Models, and Theories*. Thousand Oaks, CA: Sage, pp. 15–29.

Legge, K. (1995) *Human Resource Management: Rhetorics and Realities*. Basingstoke: Macmillan Business.

Mant, A. (1979) *The Rise and Fall of the British Manager*. London: Pan.

Marshall, J. (1989) 'Re-visioning career concepts: a feminist invitation', in Arthur, M.B., Hall, D.T. and Lawrence, B.S. (eds) *Handbook of Career Theory*. Cambridge: Cambridge University Press, pp. 275–291.

Mayo, A.J. and Nohria, N. (2005) *In Their Time: The Greatest Business Leaders of the 20th Century*. Boston, MA: Harvard Business School Press.

McGregor, D. (1960) *The Human Side of Enterprise*. New York: McGraw-Hill.

Medcof, J. and Roth, J. (eds) (1979) *Approaches to Psychology*. Milton Keynes: Open University Press.

Mishler, E.G. (1986) *Research Interviewing: Context and Narrative*. Cambridge, MA: Harvard University Press.

*Morgan, G. (1997) *Images of Organization*. Thousand Oaks, CA: Sage.

Moxon, G.R. (1951) *Functions of a Personnel Department*. London: Institute of Personnel Management.

Parker, I. (1990) 'The abstraction and representation of social psychology', in Parker, I. and Shotter, J. (eds) *Deconstructing Social Psychology*. London: Routledge, pp. 91–102.

Parker, I. and Shotter, J. (eds) (1990) 'Introduction', in *Deconstructing Social Psychology*. London: Routledge, pp. 1–14.

*Pascale, R.T. and Athos, A.G. (1982) *The Art of Japanese Management*. Harmondsworth: Penguin.

Peck, D. and Whitlow, D. (1975) *Approaches to Personality Theory*. London: Methuen.

People Management (2002) *The Guide to Work–Life Balance*. London: *People Management* (www.peoplemanagement.co.uk/work-life).

Pepper, S.C. (1942) *World Hypotheses*. Berkeley, CA: University of California Press.

Peters, T.J. and Waterman, R.H. Jr (1982) *In Search of Excellence: Lessons from America's Best Run Companies*. New York: Harper & Row.

Pfeffer, J. (1981) *Power in Organizations*. London: Pitman.

Pickard, J. (1992) 'Profile: W. Edward Deming', *Personnel Management*, June, p. 23.

Pickard, J. (1999) 'Emote possibilities: sense and sensitivity', *People Management*, 5, 21, 28 October: 48–56.

Pickard, J. (2005) '"HR will be a philosophy rather than a department"', *People Management*, 11, 22, 10 November: 15.

Pirsig, R.M. (1976) *Zen and the Art of Motorcycle Maintenance*. London: Corgi.

Polkinghorne, D.E. (1988) *Narrative Knowing and the Human Sciences*. Albany, NY: State University of New York Press.

Price, B. (1997) 'The myth of postmodern science', in Eve, R.A., Horsfall, S. and Lee, M.E. (eds) *Chaos, Complexity, and Sociology: Myths, Models, and Theories*. Thousand Oaks, CA: Sage, pp. 3–14.

Pugh, D.S., Hickson, D.J. and Hinings, C.R. (1983) *Writers on Organizations*, 3rd edn. Harmondsworth: Penguin.

*Reed, M. and Hughes, M. (eds) (1992) *Rethinking Organization: New Directions in Organization Theory and Analysis*. London: Sage.

Ritzer, G. (1996) *The McDonaldization of Society: An Investigation into the Changing Character of Contemporary Social Life*. Thousand Oaks, CA: Pine Forge Press.

Rose, M. (1978) *Industrial Behaviour: Theoretical Development since Taylor*. Harmondsworth: Penguin.

115

Sanders, P. (1982) 'Phenomenology: a new way of viewing organizational research', *Academy of Management Review*, 7, 3: 353–360.

Schein, E.H. (1970) *Organizational Psychology*, 2nd edn. Englewood Cliffs, NJ: Prentice Hall.

Schein, E.H. (1978) *Career Dynamics: Matching Individual and Organizational Needs*. Reading, MA: Addison-Wesley.

*Senge, P. (1990) *The Fifth Discipline: The Art and Practice of the Learning Organization*. London: Century.

Seymour, W.D. (1959) *Operator Training in Industry*. London: Institute of Personnel Management.

Sherwood, D. (2002) *Seeing the Forest for the Trees: A Manager's Guide to Applying Systems Thinking*. London: Nicholas Brealey.

Sloan, T. (1992) 'Career decisions: a critical psychology', in Young, R.A. and Collin, A. (eds) *Interpreting Career: Hermeneutical Studies of Lives in Context*. Westport, Conn.: Praeger, pp. 168–176.

Southgate, J. and Randall, R. (1981) 'The troubled fish: barriers to dialogue', in Reason, P. and Rowan, J. (eds) *Human Inquiry: A Sourcebook of New Paradigm Research*. Chichester: Wiley, pp. 53–61.

Spender, D. (1985) *For the Record: The Making and Meaning of Feminist Knowledge*. London: Women's Press.

Stead, G.B., and Watson, M.B. (1999) 'Indigenisation of psychology in South Africa', in Stead, G.B. and Watson, M.B. (eds) *Career Psychology in the South African Context*. Pretoria, South Africa: Van Schaik, pp. 214–225.

Sterne, L. (1759–67) *The Life and Opinions of Tristram Shandy, Gentleman*. Published by Penguin Classics, 1997, edited by M. New and J. New. Harmondsworth: Penguin.

Taylor, P., Mulvey, G., Hyman, J. and Bain, P. (2002) 'Work organisation, control and the experience of work in call centres', *Work, Employment and Society*, 16, 1: 133–150.

Townley, B. (1993) 'Foucault power/knowledge, and its relevance for human resource management', *Academy of Management Review*, 18, 3: 518–545.

Vaillant, G.E. (1977) *Adaptation to Life: How the Brightest and Best Came of Age*. Boston, MA: Little, Brown.

*Watson, T.J. (2000) *In Search of Management: Culture, Chaos and Control in Managerial Work*. London: Thomson Learning.

*Weick, K.E. (1979) *The Social Psychology of Organizing*. New York: Random House.

Welch, J. (1998) 'The new seekers: creed is good', *People Management*, 4, 25, 24 December: 28–33.

Wheatley, M.J. (1992) *Leadership and the New Science: Learning about Organization from an Orderly Universe*. San Francisco, CA: Berrett-Koehler.

Whittaker, J. and Johns, T. (2004) 'Standards deliver', *People Management*, 10, 13, 30 June: 32–34.

Zohar, D. and Marshall, I. (2001) *Spiritual Intelligence: The Ultimate Intelligence*. London: Bloomsbury.

For multiple-choice questions, exercises and annotated weblinks specific to this chapter visit the book's website at **www.pearsoned.co.uk/beardwell**

How well are we doing at work?

FT

Some of the world's cleverest people have struggled to develop ways of measuring how well we are doing at work. You can choose from grand-sounding methodologies such as Economic Value Added or the Balanced Scorecard, among many others. But I always think the George Bailey test is pretty revealing.

Younger readers may need reminding that George Bailey is the hero of Frank Capra's classic 1946 film *It's A Wonderful Life*. In the film Bailey, played by James Stewart, is in despair on Christmas Eve and on the point of suicide when a guardian angel descends and takes him on a magical trip, showing him how dreadful life would have been in his home town had he not lived. Bailey is forced to reconsider his suicide plans and . . . well, it will be on again at Christmas, so why not watch it then?

In business, several disciplines pass the George Bailey test with ease. Without finance there are no accounts to file and no commercial record of performance. Without sales there is no business at all. But take away the human resources department and . . . what? Recruitment might seize up a bit. People will still get paid, presuming you have automated or outsourced these things. The employment lawyers will be busy clearing up some of the mess caused by untutored line managers. But how much would your company actually suffer? And would managers feel exposed or liberated by the sudden absence of their HR colleagues?

This is not going to be another of those 'Isn't HR rubbish?' articles. I raise these questions more in sorrow than in anger. The tragedy of HR is that it is, potentially, the most significant and rewarding work any manager could want to get involved in. Helping people to build a career and find work more fulfilling is a serious and worthwhile task. But HR is rarely discussed in these terms. Instead, people refer dismissively to the 'human remains' department. Less than 10 per cent of FTSE100 companies have a HR director on the board. The truth is the profession is at a crisis point, with its credibility – and future – at stake.

Yet HR's plight is not inevitable. A pathway to salvation has been plotted by Dave Ulrich, professor of business administration at the University of Michigan and HR's leading guru. In his 1997 book *Human Resources Champions*, he offers an ambitious four-pillared approach to the task.

HR professionals, he says, need to be 'administrative experts', that is, make sure that the 'pay and rations' element of HR (what we used to call personnel) is in immaculate order. Second, HR needs to be a 'strategic partner': it must understand the commercial realities of the business and work with managers to help them execute the company's strategy.

Third, HR needs to be a 'change agent', helping the organisation understand the need for change and cope with it. And finally, HR should be the 'employee champion', listening and responding to employees, and making sure their voices are heard at the top table.

A fine model, we can all agree. But now look at the reality. Business leaders are simply not persuaded that most HR professionals have a serious contribution to make to the commercial success of their organisation. According to a recent UK survey carried out by PwC, while 73 per cent of HR directors say they see their role as strategic, 51 per cent of CEOs look on HR primarily as 'an administrative centre'.

Another survey, conducted by the Hay Group in the US last year, found that only about 50 per cent of workers below manager level believed their companies took a genuine interest in their well-being. Clearly, HR's performance is in doubt.

Why have HR managers failed to rise to the Ulrich challenge? Lack of nerve (and ability) maybe, but perhaps the hostility of some corporate environments has made it difficult for them to speak up. Clearly, if CEOs and finance chiefs do not really believe the phrases they sign off on the annual report – 'our people are our biggest asset', 'we are a people business' – then HR staff face a fairly hopeless task.

The difficulty of their position, in the UK at least, is symbolised by the unhappy fate of the operating and financial review (OFR), which was to come into force this year but has now been watered down.

Among other things, the OFR was an attempt to find better ways to account for the people side of business. HR professionals saw in it an opportunity finally to exert some influence at a strategic level. But

➤

like a hapless HR manager being excluded from a crucial meeting, OFRs were suddenly swept aside by government after a moment's reflection.

Nor does the fashionable debate over 'human capital management' seem to offer HR much encouragement. According to a recent report by Saratoga, the human capital consultancy that is now part of PwC: 'The strategic importance of human capital may mean that CEOs and other senior executives are taking more personal responsibility and control over human capital issues.'

When line managers are competent it is hard to see what HR can add. But that is why we need HR. There is always management mess to clear up and hand-

holding to be done. Sadly, this condemns HR to its traditional 'tea and sympathy' role.

As core administrative tasks are outsourced, and headcount in HR departments falls, those who remain will have to stand and deliver – preferably something that is valuable to the business.

But even if HR can, like George Bailey, pull itself back from the brink, there will always be that other unnerving question to answer – the one posed by the child who pointed at Lord Randolph Churchill when he was out campaigning, and said: 'Dearest Mama, pray tell me what is that man for?'

Source: Stern, S (2006) 'Human resources departments are unloved but not unnecessary', *Financial Times*, 18 April.

Questions

1 Why do you think that the HR function failed to rise to the 'Ulrich challenge'?

2 Why does the HR function struggle to justify its contribution when finance and marketing functions do not?

3 Do contextual factors increase or decrease the need for a specialist HR function?

4 What effect are the different models of HRM discussed in this part of the book likely to have on the HR delivery?

Part 2

RESOURCING THE ORGANISATION

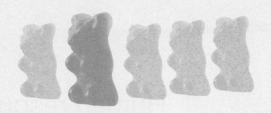

Introduction to Part 2

This part deals with how organisations define and meet their needs for labour and how they are influenced by factors internal and external to the organisation.

For students and practitioners of management the main theme of the past decade has been change, uncertainty and risk. Technological change has transformed the nature of products and production systems, services and their delivery. Markets have become more unpredictable and competition more intense. The response has been to reduce the size of workforces and look for ways to achieve greater labour flexibility. These changes have called established approaches to human resource planning and the management of labour into question. At the same time, a tightening labour market and growing competition for skilled workers has increased the importance attached to effective recruitment and selection.

Chapter 4 explains the labour market context within which employee resourcing decisions are taken. It starts by explaining the concept of the labour market and why different organisations adopt different approaches to recruitment, retention and reward. Next it examines the nature of labour supply and demand in the UK, looking at the determinants of labour supply and how the demand for labour is structured and how it has changed over the last two decades. Finally it goes on to examine how changes in labour demand have affected the quality of employment opportunities available to different labour market groups. It concludes with a brief discussion of some of the practical and theoretical implications of these developments.

Chapter 5 looks at the role of human resource planning in helping to integrate human resource strategy with business strategy. It discusses how approaches to human resource planning have changed as the organisational context has become more fluid and how the right approach to human resource planning can reduce uncertainty and develop organisational flexibility.

Chapter 6 explains how contemporary developments are increasing the potential importance of having effective methods of recruitment and selection. These developments include the growing need to ensure that diverse groups are treated fairly in terms of employment opportunity and the growing emphasis on the need for flexible, adaptable and cooperative workers. It goes on to explore the principles of employee recruitment and selection and recent developments in this area of HRM.

Chapter 7 takes up the theme of advantage and more specifically, disadvantage in employment in depth by examining the nature and effects of unfair discrimination in employment, why managers should act to promote fairness at work and the different, sometime conflicting ideas about how they should do so. It highlights the complex nature of the issues raised by attempts to tackle disadvantage due to unfair discrimination. For example, should managers treat all employees the same regardless of ethnicity or gender, or should they take these differences into account when framing their employment policies? Should policies for combating disadvantage aim at equality of opportunity or equality of outcome? It also discusses the significance of the recent tendency to shift the focus of discussion away from the traditional idea of 'equal opportunities' to the concept of 'managing diversity'.

Chapter 4

Human resource management and the labour market

Tim Claydon and Amanda Thompson

Objectives

- To explain the nature and composition of the UK labour market.

- To identify the major social forces responsible for shaping the nature and extent of people's engagement with paid employment.

- To highlight developments in the nature of work and employment in the late twentieth and early twenty first century and to show how these trends have influenced organisational requirements for labour.

- To present a critical assessment of workers' experiences of employment in contemporary Britain.

Introduction

This chapter is concerned principally with the size, composition and condition of the UK labour market and more specifically with how the labour market shapes employers' choices concerning people management and utilisation. An appreciation of labour markets and how they operate is especially relevant for students of HRM, particularly as HRM claims to offer a strategic approach to managing people. A strategic stance is attractive because it offers organisations the latitude to select an appropriate employment system and a set of complementary HR practices to 'fit' the external operating environment, thus placing the firm in a better position to exploit competitive advantage. From a practical perspective therefore, knowing and understanding labour market issues is likely to be of prime value to the organisation in its bid to formulate a strategic approach to HRM, through which superior business outcomes can, with fortune, be realised.

We divide the chapter into four main sections to draw upon a range of contemporary labour market issues and to consider the significance of each for the practice of HRM. In the first we briefly consider the nature of labour markets and discuss the considerations that influence the employment strategies of firms. In the second we explore recent political and social developments and the implications of these for the supply of labour. The third section explores the changing nature of work and employment and is designed to focus on emergent themes in employers' demand for labour. The final section of the chapter considers key dimensions of job quality and discusses these in relation to workers' experiences of employment in contemporary Britain.

The nature of labour markets

The most general definition of the labour market is that it consists of workers who are looking for paid employment and employers who are seeking to fill vacancies. The amount of labour that is available to firms – *labour supply* – is determined by the number of people of working age who are in employment or seeking employment and the number of hours that they are willing to work. This number will be determined by the size and age structure of the population and by the decisions made by individuals and households about the relative costs and benefits of taking paid employment. These decisions are influenced by various factors, one of which is the level of wages on offer. Generally speaking a higher wage will attract more people into the labour market while a lower wage will attract fewer, as long as other factors, such as the level of welfare benefits and people's attitudes towards work, remain constant.

The number of jobs on offer to workers – *labour demand* – is the sum of people in employment plus the number of vacancies waiting to be filled. The demand for labour is determined by the level of demand for the goods and services produced by firms in the market. When sales and production are rising, firms' demand for labour rises. When sales fall and production is cut back, firms' demand for labour falls.

The simplest view of the labour market is that it is an arena of competition. Workers enter the arena in search of jobs and employers enter it in search of workers. Competition between employers for workers and between workers for jobs results in a 'market wage' that adjusts to relative changes in labour demand and supply. Thus, when labour demand rises relative to labour supply, the market wage rises as firms try to outbid each other for scarce labour. When labour demand falls relative to labour supply, the market wage falls as workers compete with each other for the smaller number of available jobs.

Competition means that no individual firm can set a wage that is out of line with the competitive market wage. Neither can workers demand such a wage. Should a firm try to offer a wage that is below the market rate, it will be unable to hire workers. Should a firm set a wage above the market rate, it will go out of business because its costs of production will be above those of its competitors. For the same reason, workers who demand a wage higher than the market rate will price themselves out of jobs. No firm will hire them because to do so would increase their costs of production relative to those of their competitors.

While it is undeniable that competitive forces operate in the labour market to a degree, few would seriously pretend that this is a wholly accurate description of the real world. There are limits to competition between firms and among workers. Wages do not respond instantly to changes in labour demand. Nor is there a uniform wage in the labour market. Empirical research has shown that rates of pay vary between firms, even in the same industry and operating in the same local labour market (Nolan and Brown, 1983). Other employment policies also vary among firms. For example, some firms employ labour on a hire and fire basis and make heavy use of casualised forms of employment such as temporary work while others offer long-term employment security and career development. The policies that employers adopt are influenced to a great extent by the characteristics they seek in their workforce:

● **The need for a stable workforce.** A stable workforce is advantageous to employers because it reduces the costs of labour turnover, i.e. disruption of production due to the unplanned reductions in the workforce that result from workers leaving, costs of recruitment and selection, such as the financial costs of advertising for recruits and the cost in terms of management time spent in recruiting and selecting replacements, and the cost of training new recruits. These costs may be particularly high where skilled labour is scarce and replacements hard to find, or where employers have invested considerable amounts in training workers. In these situations employers have a strong interest in limiting the extent of labour turnover.

What types of workforce will have low turnover costs and why? What types of workforce will have high turnover costs?

● **The need for worker cooperation in production.** A central issue in managing people at work is how to manage their performance. One way of trying to ensure that workers supply the required level of effort is by subjecting them to direct controls (Friedman, 1977). Traditionally this took the form of direct personal supervision by a superior and externally imposed discipline. Today direct supervision is supplemented with electronic surveillance, 'mystery customers' and customer questionnaire surveys in a managerial effort to make workers' effort levels increasingly visible. However, there are limits to the extent that employers can rely on direct controls. To a great extent employers rely on sufficiently motivated workers using their initiative to ensure efficiency and quality in the production of goods and the delivery of services. The nature of the product or the production process often makes it difficult to define what the appropriate effort levels are for each worker and to measure how hard they are actually working. This makes it difficult for managers to impose effort levels without the workers' agreement. Heavy reliance on supervision and surveillance may also be counterproductive because of the resistance that it can generate among workers. The alternative is to encourage workers to exercise *responsible autonomy* at work (Friedman, 1977). In other words it may be more cost-effective for managers to offer positive incentives to ensure that workers cooperate voluntarily with management and use their job knowledge and their initiative to maintain and improve efficiency and quality.

The greater are employers' needs for a stable, highly cooperative workforce, the more likely they are to introduce policies to retain workers and create a basis for mutual trust and cooperation while also raising the cost to the employee of losing their job should they fall short of the standards demanded by management. These policies, which are associated with the 'best practice HRM' principle of treating employees as valued assets rather than disposable commodities (see Chapter 1), *internalise* employment by fostering long-term employment relationships and giving workers a degree of protection from external labour market pressures. They include guarantees of long-term employment security, opportunities for training and internal promotion, fringe benefits and pay that is higher than the market rate. However these policies are themselves costly. Therefore the extent to which employers seek to internalise employment depends on the cost of labour turnover and the limits to direct control. Where these are low, employers are more likely to treat labour as a disposable commodity, in other words *externalising* the employment relationship.

Activity

During 1998 two leading supermarket chains converted two-thirds of their temporary staff onto permanent contracts. Temporary workers had been hired to cope with seasonal peaks in demand or to enable stores to adjust more easily under uncertain trading conditions. However, workers who remained on temporary contracts for too long lost motivation and this had a damaging effect on the quality of customer service. Other problems that managers associated with employing workers on temporary and zero hours contracts were lack of training and difficulty of communication.

Source: People Management, June 1998.

Question

What is it about the nature of customer service work that leads employers to require voluntary cooperation from workers? Why does this set limits to the extent to which management can externalise the employment relationship?

From this we can see that employers make strategic choices concerning the extent to which they internalise or externalise employment. However, these choices are influenced by the specific labour market contexts in which they operate. As we shall see later in this chapter, the overall state of the labour market is one important influence, while another is the way in which the labour market is segmented, giving rise to advantaged and disadvantaged labour market groups. To be able to understand how these influences operate, we first need to examine the two key dimensions of the labour market, labour supply and demand.

The supply of labour

'In being bought and sold in the labour market, labour becomes a commodity' (SCER, 2001: 5). It follows that firms in competition with one another for labour will be interested in the current and future availability of this commodity. Conventionally the process of human resource planning involves forecasting the supply and demand for labour so that suitable plans can be put in place to address situations of labour shortage or surplus (see Chapter 5). Despite the apparent logic of this approach Taylor (2005) suggests there is some evidence of firms rejecting systematic human resource planning as they find it impossible to predict labour supply and demand with any degree of accuracy in a climate of uncertainty. Even so, some understanding of where the future supply of labour can be sourced from and how plentiful that source is expected to be is important in informing employers' actions in the labour market.

The number of people seeking work in the labour market is influenced by factors relating to the size and composition of the population. Within this section of the chapter we consider the main demographic factors affecting total labour supply, namely population and population change, the age structure of the population, gender and ethnicity.

Population

The supply side of the labour market derives from the country's population, specifically men aged between 16 and 65 years and women between the ages of 16 and 60 (working age). Information on the total size of the current population and predictions of future patterns of population growth and decline are thus important in estimating the current and future supply of labour.

Population is affected by birth and death rates. When live births exceed the number of deaths a net natural population increase arises and when mortality rates exceed birth rates a net natural decline in population occurs. Population change is also influenced by net migration; that is the effect caused by people moving into and out of the country. In the 1950s and 1960s population growth was largely attributable to net natural change. Within this period a relatively stable death rate coupled with the baby boom that followed the Second World War triggered net natural growth. Since 1983 net migration has played an increased part in the expansion of the population as the number of people migrating into the United Kingdom continues to surpass the number leaving. In 2004 nearly 222,600 more people migrated to the United Kingdom than left it. This net inflow represents the highest since the present methods of estimation began in 1991. The net effects of migration are forecast to continue to play a major role in population growth alongside net natural change (ONS, 2006a). For illustrative purposes Home Office statistics (ONS, 2006a) show that between 1991 and 2004 the total number of people accepted for permanent settlement in the United Kingdom more than doubled. The biggest increase in acceptances was for people from Europe (excluding EEA nationals) followed by those from Africa.

Latest data from the ONS (2006a) shows that the population of the United Kingdom has been climbing steadily since 1971 and had reached 59.8 million people by 2004. Predictions of population from the 2004 base estimate that by 2011 the population will be 61.9 million, rising to 64.7 million in 2021 and extending still further to 67 million by 2031. Growth is projected to occur most rapidly and over a sustained period in England compared with the rest of the United Kingdom. In line with trends emerging in the 1980s more of the anticipated expansion in the population of the United Kingdom in the period 2004 to 2031 is expected to result from net migration (57 per cent) than from natural increase (43 per cent).

The way in which the country's population expands affects the gender composition, age profile and ethnic diversity of the labour market. Changes to the composition of labour supply arising from fluctuations in birth and death rates and shifting patterns of migration may call into question the appropriateness of established human resource management practices aimed at attracting and retaining suitable labour. Similarly, at a localised level, patterns of regional population density resulting from a combination of natural causes, international migration *and* internal migration (the movement of people between regions within the United Kingdom) lead to variations in the amount and type of labour available in different parts of the country. While labour tends to move to parts of the country where work is more plentiful (ONS, 2001) those organisations reliant on local labour in areas of the country with low population density and/or net population loss are confronted with a different set of labour market circumstances from those operating in areas of higher population density.

Age structure of the population

The age structure of the population is a key determinant of labour supply as firms draw labour from the portion of the total population that is of working age. The age structure is closely associated with past trends in migration; such trends can also be used to explain regional differences in the population's age profile as migrants establish communities in certain areas of the country. ONS (2006a) shows that white ethnic groups, particularly the white Irish population, have an older age structure than other ethnic groups as a consequence of past fertility and immigration patterns. Among non-white ethnic groups younger age profiles are exhibited within groups migrating to the United Kingdom relatively recently whilst, as might be expected, those groups with an earlier history of large-scale migration to the United Kingdom have now begun to display larger proportions of people within older age brackets. For example ONS data (2006a) shows that just 2 per cent of the country's Black African population are aged 65 and over compared with 11 per cent of Black Caribbeans, large-scale migration from countries such as Jamaica and Trinidad having taken place several decades prior to the large-scale arrival of migrants from Nigeria, Ghana and other African countries which began in earnest in the 1980s.

Activity

Examine the information provided in the table below summarising the age structure of the populations of Eastbourne and Leicester at the time of the last census in April 2001.

Age structure of the population	Eastbourne	Leicester
% of the resident population aged 0–4	5.31	6.83
% of the resident population aged 5–15	12.69	15.46
% of the resident population aged 16–19	4.32	5.92
% of the resident population aged 20–44	30.49	38.75
% of the resident population aged 45–64	22.47	19.52
% of the resident population aged 65 or over	24.72	13.52
Average age of the population (years)	43.2	35.5

Source: Census 2001 (ONS, 2001).

Questions

1 Suggest why the proportion of residents over the age of retirement in Eastbourne is almost double the proportion of those aged 65 and over in Leicester.

2 Explain why Leicester has a greater proportion of residents in all age brackets below 65.

3 Consider the possible implications of the above data for the current and future supply of labour in Leicester and Eastbourne.

As well as past trends in migration, the age structure of the total population and of regional populations is affected by births and deaths and past trends in these key indices. Records depict a fairly erratic pattern in the number of live births occurring in the United Kingdom at different phases throughout the twentieth century (ONS, 2006a). Notable decreases in the number of births occurred during the two world wars (1914–1918 and 1939–1945), and apart from a sharp increase in the number of births in the immediate aftermath of the First World War, births fell again and remained relatively subdued for most of the inter-war period. A further baby boom occurred after the Second World War causing another, but this time more modest, increase in the late 1980s and early 1990s as the baby boomer generation produced children of their own. Since this time the number of live births per year has fallen as women average fewer children and delay the age at which they give birth to their first child (ONS, 2005b).

Together with birth rates, the age structure of the population is influenced by the death rate. The ONS (2006a) charts a decline in death rates as the population has grown in size. In the 33-year period between 1971 and 2004 the ONS cites a 9 per cent decline in the death rate for all females and a 21 per cent fall in the death rates for all males (ONS, 2006a). General improvements in living standards and advancements in health and medicine have contributed to an increased life expectancy for both men and women, although women continue to outlive men. Whilst women born in the United Kingdom in 2004 could expect to live to the age of 81, men could expect to live to 77; this contrasts sharply with the life expectancy of men and women born at the start of the last century, a time when boys could expect to live to just 45, and girls to 49 (www.statistics.gov.uk). Projections of life expectancy based on 2004 data (Figure 4.1) foretell an extrapolation of past trends, adding some substance to the claim 'by this time tomorrow you can expect to live for five hours longer!' (Jah, 2006: 6)

Figure 4.1

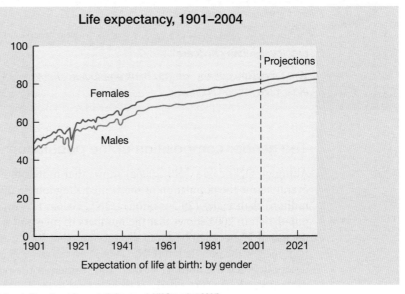

Life expectancy, 1901–2004

Expectation of life at birth: by gender

Source: Government Actuary's Department (www.statistics.gov.uk *UK Snapshot 2005*).

We have seen in this section that the age structure of the population is affected by migration, births and deaths. While some non-white ethnic groups display relatively young age profiles, the overall picture is of an ageing population. In short 'there are increasing numbers of people aged 65 and over and decreasing numbers of children under 16' (ONS, 2006a: 11). In recent decades these trends in the age structure of the population can be attributed to lower fertility rates combined with declining mortality rates amongst the elderly. Such trends show little sign of abating; on the contrary it is projected that 'by 2014 the number of people over the age of 65 will *exceed* those under the age of 16 for the first time and the gap will widen' (ONS, 2006a: 12).

In terms of human resource management the implications of changes in the age structure of the population are numerous. The following points indicate some of the challenges presented by an ageing population:

- The prospect of a shrinking pool of people of working age as the 'baby boomers' born in the 1950s and 1960s move into retirement.
- Intensified competition for school leavers/young workers.
- Identifying employment strategies which succeed in attracting and retaining older workers.
- Meeting the needs and aspirations of older workers in work.
- Career management and development.
- Managing sickness absence.
- Growing elder care responsibilities for those in employment.
- Concerns over the adequacy of pension arrangements and the viability of retaining the current State retirement ages. The second report of Lord Turner's Pensions Commission published in November 2005 includes a proposal to increase the state pension age. The Commission also recommends the default retirement age of 65 written into the Age Discrimination Regulations, due to be implemented on 1 October 2006 is removed so that older people can remain in employment beyond 65 if they so choose (CIPD, 2006).
- The need to scrutinise policies and practice to ensure equal opportunities are afforded to workers of all ages to comply with the Employment Equality (Age) Regulations 2006, due to be implemented on 1 October 2006.

Stop & think

How might employees' care responsibilities for elderly relations impact upon their presence and attention to paid work?

Do you think elder care will soon begin to pose a greater challenge to employers and employees than childcare? Why?

What measures, if any, do you think employers should introduce to assist employees with elder care responsibilities?

The gender composition of the population

Although ONS data (ONS, 2006a) shows that more boys are born each year than girls, in overall terms the population of the United Kingdom in 2004 contained more females (30.6 million) than males (29.3 million) (ONS, 2006a: 11). Analysis by gender of the country's population in 2004 shows that the numbers of men and women were broadly in step up to the age of 22 but then began to diverge such that by the age of 30 there were more women than men in the population (ONS, 2006a). In the older age groups (post retirement age) the fissure between the number of men and women in the population broadens, and 'is most pronounced in the very elderly, as women tend to live longer than men' (ONS, 2006a: 11).

As 'the inflow of females has always been higher than the outflow' (ONS, 2006a: 17) net in-migration is one of the key ways in which the female population of the country has expanded. In every year since 1994 the outflow of males *and* females from the United Kingdom has been lower than the inflow of both sexes into the country causing a net in-migration effect to both the male and female population; the more pronounced population gains falling to the female population. In 2003 for example, the net gain for the United Kingdom's female population was more than 15,000 higher than the net gain to the male population (ONS, 2006a: 17). It is highly probable that, at least in numerical terms, the labour market will benefit from net in-migration as migrants (both in and out) are least likely to be over the age of retirement, or children under the age of 15 (ONS, 2006a: 18).

Later in the chapter we consider the ways in which gender shapes people's experiences of work. In particular we explore the interplay of gender and age and look at gendered roles within the family to understand differences in the patterns of male and female participation in the labour market.

Ethnicity and the population

In previous sections we have referred to migration and demonstrated that in the post-war period the United Kingdom has granted residency to people from a variety of different countries including Pakistan, India, Bangladesh, China, parts of Africa and the Caribbean and more recently from countries within Eastern Europe. As a consequence a number of distinct minority ethnic groups have joined the nation's historically white British heritage to form a more multicultural, ethnically and religiously diverse Britain. The census collects ethnicity data by asking people which group they see themselves belonging to. When the census was last conducted in April 2001 it showed England's population to be 87 per cent white British, 3.9 per cent white other, 1.3 per cent mixed, 4.6 per cent Asian, 2.3 per cent Black and 0.9 per cent Chinese and other (ONS, 2001). In terms of religious denomination almost 70 per cent of respondents considered themselves to be of Christian religion and white British ethnicity, other main faiths include Pakistani Muslims, Indian Hindus, black Caribbean Christians, Indian Sikhs and black African Christians.

Whilst in general terms the total population is becoming more ethnically diverse, certain local authority districts contain high concentrations of (non-white) ethnic minority groups, in excess of the national average of 9 per cent non-white (ONS, 2001). The census conducted in 2001 shows that sixteen of the twenty authorities with the highest concentrations of non-white ethnic minority groups are London boroughs (ONS, 2001); of these Newham and Brent both have a majority non-white population (61 per cent and 55 per cent respectively). Outside of London, Leicester, Slough, Birmingham and Luton record the highest concentrations of non-white ethnic minority groups. In some other regions of the country (for example, the south-west and the north-east), non-white ethnic minority groups form a very small percentage of the population, significantly below the national average.

The limited geographic dispersal of non-white ethnic minority groups means that some local labour markets remain practically monocultural whilst others are considerably diverse. As we shall see, men and women from non-white ethnic minority groups tend to experience greater disadvantage in the labour market; they are less likely to be active in the labour market than their white counterparts, more likely to suffer high levels of unemployment and when they are in work, people from ethnic minority groups as a whole have lower levels of occupational attainment and progression than white people (Strategy Unit, 2003). The Strategy Unit report for the Cabinet Office on the position of ethnic minorities in the labour market (2003) suggests that men and women from ethnic minority groups still fare less well in the labour market than their white contemporaries even when factors such as age, gender and qualifications are controlled for and the report concludes that this can partially be explained by the existence of racism and discrimination in the labour market. The role of HRM in combating discrimination at work and embracing diversity is the subject of debate and discussion in Chapter 7.

The workforce

The workforce is conventionally drawn from the segment of the population between the ages of 16 and state retirement age, although some men and women will continue to work beyond the state pension age. Of those aged 16 or older, not everyone will be in employment at any one time. Figure 4.2 is a useful framework within which to define and discuss the activities of people of working age.

A proportion of those over the age of 16 will not be in work or seeking work; this portion of the workforce is classified as *economically inactive*. There are a number of reasons why people might be economically inactive. This group typically includes those with caring responsibilities for children or other dependents, those who have retired from work, students, people who are incapacitated through ill health or disability and those choosing not to work or seek work. People within this group may voluntarily decide to enter (or re-enter) the labour market once their circumstances alter. Others may need to be enticed back to work through incentives and/or government-orchestrated benefit reforms directed at this purpose. For example, the Department for Work and Pensions recently announced plans to radically reform the current system of incapacity benefit in an effort to reduce benefit dependency and get some of the long-term sick back into work (DWP, 2005).

In real terms the amount of labour available to firms at any one time will be influenced by the number of people of working age who are in employment or are seeking employment, in other words those classified as *economically active*. A number of factors affect individuals' propensity to furnish their labour, including the availability and proximity of employment opportunities to meet their personal needs and aspirations, travel links, the levels of pay and benefits offered by organisations, the type of contract offered and so forth. These factors also influence people's decisions to move between jobs within the labour market. The employed segment of the workforce contains those in paid work; this incorporates those working full time or part time, temporarily or permanently as employees (under a contract *of service*), workers (under a contract *for services*) or on a self-employed basis.

Those seeking work are typically registered as unemployed but could also be those who have recently left work but are not eligible to claim unemployment benefit, for example, those who have been made redundant. Job seekers might also include recent school leavers and those completing programmes of study in further and higher education. The term *unemployed* is used to describe those people who are currently not in work but would like to be. To

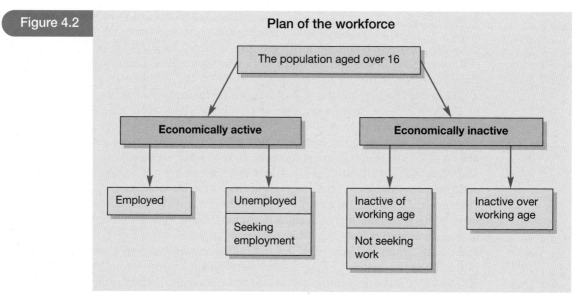

| Figure 4.2 | **Plan of the workforce** |

Source: Adapted from *SCER Report 1 – Understanding the Labour Market*, 2001.

remain in receipt of unemployment benefit unemployed workers must be able to show that they are actively seeking work. The unemployed group comprises people affected by different types of unemployment:

- *Long-term unemployment or structural unemployment* – those unemployed as a result of the demise of whole industries or distinct occupations, for example mineworkers, ship-builders, textile workers.
- *Frictional unemployment* – those temporarily out of work because they are between jobs.
- *Seasonal unemployment* – those made jobless as a result of seasonal fluctuations in the availability of work. Seasonal unemployment is typically experienced by land workers and those whose work is connected with holiday seasons.

In addition it is also likely that some of those registered unemployed will never work again as they lack the skills and competencies sought by employers. This group of unemployed workers is sometimes referred to as the *residual* unemployed.

The latest ONS data, drawn from the Labour Force Survey (ONS 2006a) shows that over the period 1971 to 2005 the number of both economically active and economically inactive people has increased. The ONS (2006a: 50) attributes much of the climb in the number of those in work or actively seeking work to the increased participation of women in the workforce. By spring 2005 over 30 million people in the United Kingdom were economically active and some 17.6 million economically inactive (if those over the state pension age are included). The employment rate (the proportion of the working age population of the United Kingdom in employment) stood at 75 per cent in the spring of 2005 (ONS, 2006a: 52) although differences in rates exist both within and between different regions of the country.

Unemployment rates also vary across regions of the United Kingdom. In spring 2005 (ONS, 2006a: 60) the lowest rate was recorded in the south-west region (3.4 per cent) and the highest rate in London (7.2 per cent). Nationally the unemployment rate in the United Kingdom stood at 4.7 per cent in spring 2005 (1.4 million people), this compares very favourably with 1984 when unemployment peaked at 3.3 million and more recently 1993 when the number of people out of work again approached the 3 million mark.

Patterns of labour market participation

This subsection of the chapter explores patterns of participation in paid employment by gender, parental/family status, age, and ethnicity.

The operation of the labour market is shaped and constrained by broader societal developments and the behaviour and attitudes of government, employees and employers. In social terms, attitudes to marriage and partnership and men and women's respective responsibilities for childcare and domestic duties shape the labour market decisions made by individuals, couples and families. In so far as government behaviours and attitudes are concerned, the policy direction of government, for example over such issues as the school curriculum and funding for post-compulsory education, affects the skills set and level of educational attainment with which young people join the labour market and influences the age at which young people enter employment. As we saw earlier, the government also acts to stimulate labour supply by implementing policies designed to get the unemployed into work and schemes to encourage the economically inactive to enter into employment.

Further potential constraints on people's participation in employment stem from their inability to understand the labour market and acquire and exploit 'social capital' (SCER, 2001: 17). In other words some people will lack the necessary information and contacts to search for and take advantage of employment opportunities and so tend to be less successful within the labour market. The SCER notes that this is particularly likely to be the case for the unemployed and for new entrants to the labour market. In addition the SCER suggests that 'even with the right information, skills and qualifications, there still exist barriers to full or appropriate labour market participation for some people . . . one such barrier is discrimination, typically race and sex discrimination' (2001: 18). Whilst anti-discrimination legislation exists to help eradicate unfair discrimination in employment, employers' policies and practices may still harbour prejudice and unfairness resulting in patterns of disadvantage in the labour market for certain groups and individuals.

Patterns of male and female participation in employment

Over the last 30 years or so the employment rates of men and women have converged considerably. The period 1971 to spring 2005 saw the employment rate for men fall from 92 per cent to 79 per cent and the employment rate for women rise 14 percentage points from 56 per cent to 70 per cent (ONS, 2006a). A major doorway to the world of work has clearly opened up for women but as we shall see, the career paths and fortunes of men and women in the labour market are often distinctly gendered.

One of the deeper influences attributable to gender that serves to structure women's participation in paid employment is domestic work. Women continue to perform the bulk of housework and to shoulder the primary responsibility for childcare in the majority of households and this shapes the amount of paid work they do. A glimmer of change is offered by Hardill *et al.* (1997) who present evidence of a small move towards more egalitarian relationships in professional/managerial, dual-career households but this is dashed by Laurie and Gurshuny (2000) who find that women continue to do more than 60 per cent of the domestic work even in couples where both partners work full time.

A major element of domestic work is childcare. Table 4.1 below clearly shows the differences in employment rates between those people of working age with and without responsibilities for the care of dependent children. The data illustrates that parenthood affects the employment rates of mothers and fathers in patently different ways; while mothers of working age were *less* likely to be in employment than working age women without any dependent children, fathers were *more* likely to be in employment than men of working age without dependent children. It is noteworthy that mothers of working age in the two elder age brackets had considerably higher employment rates than younger women with dependent children. Within the elder age brackets the employment rates of working age mothers were not remarkably different to the employment rates of women of the same ages without dependent children.

Table 4.1 Employment rates of people[1] with and without dependent children:[2] by age and sex, 2004[3] (percentages)

	16–24	25–34	35–49	50–59/64	All
Mothers with dependent children	35	59	73	68	67
Married/cohabiting mothers	45	63	76	72	71
Lone mothers	25	46	62	55	53
Women without dependent children	62	90	81	68	73
Fathers with dependent children	81	89	92	84	90
Married/cohabiting fathers	82	89	93	85	91
Lone fathers	26	55	72	61	67
Men without dependent children	61	87	85	69	74
All parents with dependent children	45	70	82	78	77
Married/cohabiting parents	57	75	84	80	81
Lone parents	25	47	64	56	54
All people without dependent children	61	88	83	69	74

[1] Men aged 16–64 and women aged 16–59. Excludes people with unknown employment status
[2] Children under 16 and those 16–18 who are never-married and in full-time education
[3] At spring. Data are not seasonally adjusted and have been adjusted in line with population estimates published in spring 2003.

Source: Labour Force Survey, Spring 2004 (ONS)

Stop & think *Why might older mothers of dependent children display higher employment rates than younger women with children?*

While parenthood continues to affect women's employment rates disproportionately to men's, the proportion of working age mothers with dependent children who are in employment has risen from 47 per cent in 1973 to 67 per cent in 2004 (EOC, 2006). In 2004 in all but the youngest age category (mothers aged 16–24 with dependent children) the majority of married *and* lone mothers of working age were engaged in paid employment. The speed with which women return to work following maternity leave has also hastened significantly in the period since 1979; according to EOC figures (2006) 70 per cent of mothers are back at work eight months after giving birth, compared with just 15 per cent in 1979. The average amount of time women spend away from waged work for general family care is falling rapidly too (Bradley, 1999).

Further key points to emerge from the data in Table 4.1 are:

- Mothers of dependent children are less likely to work than fathers of dependent children.
- Lone fathers are more likely to be in employment than lone mothers.
- Married and cohabiting parents have higher employment rates than lone parents.

Ethnicity and patterns of labour market participation

Employment participation rates for ethnic minorities are significantly lower than those for the population as a whole. In autumn, 2005 66.2 per cent of ethnic minority people of working age were either in work or seeking work compared with 78.8 per cent among the population as a whole. The employment rate among ethnic minorities was 59.1 per cent as against 74.9 per cent for the population as a whole, while unemployment was higher among ethnic minorities at 10.7 per cent compared with 4.9 per cent of the entire workforce (LFS, 2006). It has been argued that low participation rates among ethnic minorities are related to low levels of educational attainment and low skills, aspects of family structure, poor access to childcare, poor housing and a lack of public transport facilities (Strategy Unit, 2003). However, research by Wadsworth (2003) found that age, region and educational attainment explained hardly any of the difference in employment rates as between ethnic minorities and British-born whites.

There are noticeable variations in activity and employment rates as between different ethnic minority groups. For example, the employment rate among people of Indian origin is 69.8 per cent compared with just 38.5 per cent among Bangladeshis (LFS, 2006). Activity and employment rates also vary within each ethnic group, generally being higher among British-born members of ethnic minorities than among immigrants (Wadsworth 2003). Also, ethnic minority women are less likely to participate in employment than men, with the differential tending to be greater among immigrants rather than British-born ethnic minorities. Nonetheless, British-born Indian women had the same employment rate – 73 per cent – as British born white women in 2002 (Wadsworth, 2003).

Labour demand

Aggregate demand for labour

The aggregate demand for labour consists of total employment plus unfilled vacancies. As the demand for labour is derived from the demand for goods and services it follows the economic cycle, rising in upswings and falling in recessions. Changes in labour demand are reflected in changes in the unemployment rate.

Low levels of unemployment are usually taken as a sign that the economy is growing and is in good shape. For employers however, the combination of record employment, low unemployment and high numbers of economically inactive people exacerbates labour market pressures contributing to what is referred to as a 'tight labour market'. In tight labour markets employers are likely to experience recruitment difficulties and skill shortages (CIPD, 2005). *The CIPD Barometer of HR Tends and Prospects* (2005) suggested further tightening of the labour market had occurred for these reasons during 2004 but problems had partially been off set by firms employing immigrant workers, including those from countries such as Latvia, Poland and Slovenia, which joined the EU on 1 May 2004 (CIPD, 2005).

Tight labour markets mean that employers have to compete more actively for workers and workers have a wider choice of employment opportunities. This will lead to higher rates of labour turnover as workers leave organisations for better jobs elsewhere. In response, firms may be forced to increase pay. They may also adopt other policies aimed at retaining employees, since vacancies arising from labour turnover will be hard to fill. Therefore there will be more internal promotion and redeployment and this may necessitate increased investment in training. While these responses might be seen as moves towards internalising employment they are not driven by the technical and skill requirements of production or a long-term employment strategy but by immediate pressures from the labour market. These pressures may be reinforced by stronger trade union bargaining power as a result of low unemployment and unfilled vacancies. Once established, these employment practices may become embedded, although employers may seek to reverse them should labour demand slacken and unemployment rise.

In addition to changes in aggregate demand for labour, we need to look at how demand conditions for different labour market groups vary as the result of structured patterns of inequality of employment opportunity. We also need to examine the changing pattern of demand for labour and how it affects different labour market groups.

Labour market inequality

The quality of jobs on offer in the labour market varies. Some workers are in 'good jobs' with high earnings, good working conditions, employment security and opportunities for training and career development. Others are in 'bad jobs' with low status and pay, poor working conditions, little access to training and few if any opportunities for promotion. How good and bad jobs get created has been a matter of ongoing debate surrounding the theory of labour market segmentation. One line of explanation, advanced by two economists, Doeringer and Piore (1971), is based on the analysis of employers' labour requirements outlined above. Some firms face strong pressures to internalise the employment relationship in order to train, develop and retain suitably skilled workers and gain their voluntary cooperation in production. Others do not and are able to meet their labour requirements by following the commodity labour approach and externalising the employment relationship.

Another explanation (Gordon, Edwards and Reich, 1982) is that some firms enjoy monopoly power in their product markets and are able to use this power to increase the selling price of the product, thereby increasing profits. Some of these companies are faced by workers who have developed strong trade unions that can use their bargaining power to gain a share of these profits in the form of high wages and other benefits, including job security provisions. At the same time, management seeks to limit union solidarity and bargaining power by dividing the workforce into horizontal segments and offering the prospect of promotion to those who are cooperative and trustworthy. Firms that are unable to use monopoly power to raise their prices do not have surplus profits to share with trade unions, so terms and conditions of employment are less favourable. Since it is more likely that large, rather than small firms are able to exercise monopoly power, primary sector employment is concentrated in large, rather than small firms.

One of the central predictions of the labour segmentation thesis is that there will be little movement of workers between the primary and secondary sectors of the labour market. Workers in the primary sector are unwilling to move to the secondary sector and the high level of employment security that they enjoy means that they are unlikely to be forced to through job loss. Workers who make up the disadvantaged segments of the labour market are unable to move up into the primary sector because employers see them as undesirable candidates for jobs. Primary sector employers want disciplined, cooperative workers with good work habits, so when selecting from among applicants for jobs, primary sector employers will tend to reject those with unstable employment histories that involve frequent unemployment and job changes because they will assume that this indicates a poor quality worker. This will automatically rule out secondary sector workers, regardless of their personal qualities, since by definition secondary workers are in unstable, insecure jobs. It is also the case however, that because of their experience of poor work, some secondary sector workers will tend to develop negative attitudes and poor patterns of work behaviour that reinforce employers' prejudices against secondary sector workers as a whole.

These explanations for labour market segmentation emphasise the way in which firms' employment decisions influence the wider labour market by dividing it into advantaged and disadvantaged groups. However, the question of whether the labour market *is* divided into primary and secondary sectors as a result of employers' labour policies has generated considerable debate. Numerous empirical studies to test the theory have been carried out in Britain and the United States, with mixed results (see Joll, McKenna, McNab and Shorey, 1983; King, 1990 for a discussion of these).

What is not in doubt is that the quality of the jobs that people do is not determined simply by their abilities, educational attainment and skills acquired through training. The chances of someone being in a good or a bad job are also influenced by their membership of particular socio-economic groups. There is clear evidence that the labour market is segmented along lines that reflect 'broader social forces leading to discrimination within the labour market' (Rubery, 1994: 53).

Discrimination in the labour market means that workers' chances of gaining access to 'good' or 'bad' jobs are unfairly influenced by non-work characteristics such as gender, race, class, work-unrelated disability and age. Thus two equally skilled workers will find themselves in different sectors of the labour market because one is a white male from a middle-class social background and the other is a working-class black woman. This reflects deep-seated patterns of discrimination within society in general as well as in the labour market. Here we focus on how gender and ethnicity influence people's experiences in the labour market.

Women and ethnic minority groups occupy a disadvantaged place in the labour market. Women's employment disadvantage reflects deep-seated societal norms concerning the family and the respective roles of women and men in domestic roles and paid work. The domestic roles played by many women mean that their employment opportunities are restricted geographically and contractually. This is particularly true of women with children. In the absence of highly developed systems of state support for childcare, childcare responsibilities mean that many women cannot travel long distances to work and also that they cannot work 'standard' hours. Therefore they are restricted to part-time work in the immediate locality. This means that they have limited choice of employment and therefore little bargaining power and may have to accept secondary sector terms and conditions of employment. Ethnic minority workers, as well as facing racial prejudice and discrimination, may be faced with additional limits to their choice of employment because they live in areas where business activity is low and public transport facilities are poor (Strategy Unit, 2003).

Gender-based inequalities in employment opportunity

The social forces identified above mean there are major differences in the types of work that men and women tend to do and the way in which male and female employment is segregated by time. Patterns of occupational segregation are strongly in evidence in the labour market, creating a division between male and female work. Bradley (1999) suggests that 66 per cent of men and 54 per cent of women work only or mainly with their own sex, with women typically crowded into administrative and secretarial work, catering, cleaning and caring occupations and men in skilled trades, construction and information technology (EOC, 2005). As shown in Table 4.2, patterns of vertical segregation also loom large with men continuing to dominate highly rewarded, senior roles in politics, business, media and culture and the public and voluntary sectors (EOC, 2006).

The work that men and women do in the labour market is also segregated by hours of work. Women are disproportionately represented in part-time work; women hold over 90 per cent of part-time jobs and nearly half of all female employees (44 per cent) work part time compared with just 8 per cent of men (ONS, 2004). Part-time working is most closely associated with women who have dependent children, although students and semi-retired older people are also attracted to working in this way (Hakim, 1998). Part-time working is invariably low-paid and this is reflected in the stubbornly persistent gender pay gap that exists between women working part time and men working full time (EOC, 2005).

Female heterogeneity

The population, and hence the labour market, comprises different sorts of women, fractured by age, class, ethnicity, qualification level, background and experience. So, whilst generalisations about the relative positions of men and women in employment serve some purpose, an understanding of the different experiences of different sorts of people in the labour market is more useful.

While we have seen that women are typically casualties of segregation in employment, some women will be in a more advantageous labour market position than other women (and some men). For example, the spring 2004 Labour Force Study (ONS, 2006a) shows us that a far greater proportion of women with a degree or equivalent qualification were in employment than women without. Some women are making significant strides in training and occupations traditionally dominated by men, for example, women now comprise the majority of medical students, there was also a 24 per cent rise in the number of female law students in the period 1971 to 1990 and a 61 per cent rise in women entering managerial work (Crompton, 1997).

Management is one of the areas in which women have made the most progress. In 2004, 33 per cent of all managers and senior officials were women (ONS, 2004). However, a closer look at the gender composition at different levels of management and at management in different sectors reveals gendered patterns of horizontal and vertical segregation *within* management careers. The dominance of men in the most senior management positions is aptly illustrated by the following findings from the Cranfield Female FTSE Index 2005:

Table 4.2 Women's share of a selection of senior ranked roles in the three consecutive years 2003–2005.

	2003 % women	2004 % women	2005 % women
Members of Parliament	18.1	18.1	19.7
Local Authority Council Leaders	n/a	16.6	16.2
Directors in FTSE 100 companies (executive and non-executive directors)	8.6	9.7	10.5
Small businesses with women the majority of directors	12.3	14.4	n/a
Editors of national newspapers	9.1	9.1	13.0
Directors of major museums and art galleries	21.1	21.1	21.7
Chief executives of national sports bodies	14.3	6.3	6.7
Local authority chief executives	13.1	12.4	17.5
Senior ranks in the armed forces	0.6	0.8	0.8
Senior police officers	7.6	8.3	10.2
University vice chancellors	12.4	15.0	11.1
Health service chief executives	28.6	27.7	28.1

Source: EOC (2006).

- 22 of the FTSE100 companies have all-male boards.

- 6 of the FTSE 100 companies appointed female directors for the first time in 2005.

- Only 11 companies have female executive directors, representing just 3.4 per cent of all executive directorship positions.

- Only one company (Pearson) has a female chief executive.

A similar picture emerges in the professions. Women make up some 40 per cent of those working in the autonomous liberal (traditional) professions, for example law, medicine, veterinary science, accountancy and teaching (EOC, 2001) but there are still some very entrenched areas such as engineering and sciences that are heavily male dominated. Again, even where women formed a sizeable proportion of the profession as a whole, their share of higher-level jobs is low and they tend to be channelled into different branches of the profession to men as the following example illustrates:

- Women made up 34 per cent of hospital medical staff in 1999 (compared with 26 per cent in 1989).

- The number of female general practitioners increased by a similar amount in the same period.

But . . .

- Men made up 79 per cent of consultants (the highest grade) and 95 per cent of consultant surgeons

- Women made up 38 per cent of paediatric consultants, 32 per cent of the psychiatry group and over 20 per cent of gynaecologists.

Source: EOC (2001)

It is evident that higher-level qualifications afford women greater opportunities within the labour market but such credentials do not entirely safeguard against disadvantage. Becoming a member of an esteemed profession is an added advantage to women in the labour market but underpinning their experiences are deeper influences attributable to gender. 'Women can stretch the ties that bind but cannot sever them' (Marlow and Carter, 2004: 16). Moreover, if highly educated women remain at a disadvantage in employment terms, this is even truer of lesser educated women from lower income and lower social class backgrounds (Taylor, 2002b).

Ethnically based labour market inequality

People from ethnic minorities experience disadvantage compared to whites in terms of their access to employment, their level of occupational attainment, and pay. Average unemployment among ethnic minority workers in autumn 2005 was 10.7 per cent compared with 4.9 per cent across the workforce as a whole (LFS, 2006). Ethnic minority men are paid less than white men. Ethnic minority women earn as much or more than white women but this is mainly because they are more likely than white women to take full-time jobs, which are better paid than part-time jobs. Ethnic minorities in general are less likely than whites to be employed in professional and managerial occupations and more likely to be in semi-routine and routine occupations (Heath and Cheung, 2006).

These disadvantages could theoretically reflect differences in education and skills. We know that unemployment is higher and wages are lower among lower educated, unskilled workers. However, these disadvantages remain even when educational qualifications are taken into account. Most ethnic minority workers are paid less than white workers having the same educational qualifications. This means that the return to investments in education, that is the amount that each extra year of education beyond minimum school leaving age adds to lifetime earnings, is lower for most ethnic minority groups than for comparable white workers. While this does not prove conclusively that people from ethnic minorities are being discriminated against unfairly it does make it a distinct possibility.

Stop & think

What are the costs to employers of discriminating against ethnic minority groups? In view of these costs why might employers still engage in unfair discrimination?

Ethnic heterogeneity

Although people from ethnic minorities as a whole are disadvantaged in the labour market, there is noticeable variation in the experience of different ethnic groups and between men and women within ethnic groups. Differences have also been found between members of ethnic minorities born in Britain and more recent immigrants (Wadsworth, 2003).

Unemployment varies considerably between groups; for example in autumn 2005 the unemployment rate among Pakistanis at 14 per cent was twice as high as that for Indians (LFS, 2006). Levels of occupational attainment also vary between different ethnic minority groups, as shown in Table 4.3. Chinese and Indians of both sexes are more likely to be in professional and managerial occupations than whites, as are black African and black Caribbean women. With the exception of Indians and Chinese, ethnic minority workers are more likely to be in semi-routine or routine occupations than whites.

There are also variations in average earnings across ethnic minorities. Thus Indian and Chinese men's average hourly earnings in the period 2001–2004 were 5 per cent higher and 11 per cent higher respectively than British and other white men's earnings. All other ethnic minority men earned less than British and other whites. Black Caribbean workers' average hourly earnings were 90 per cent of whites'; Pakistanis' earnings were 80 per cent and Bangladeshis received just 59 per cent. Ethnic minority women's earnings were as high or higher than those of British and other white women. Chinese earned 16 per cent more than whites while the lowest paid, the black Africans, earned 98 per cent (Heath and Cheung, 2006). At first glance this is surprising but it is explained by the fact that ethnic minority women are less likely to take part-time jobs than white women. Full-time jobs are noticeably better paid than part-time jobs, and it is this that accounts largely for the apparent lack of pay disadvantage among ethnic minority women.

Stop & think

How might you explain the differences in the labour market experiences of ethnic minority groups in the UK?

Table 4.3 Occupational attainment among ethnic groups in the UK 2001–2004

| | Proportion (per cent) of ethnic group in | | | |
| | High and low professional and managerial occupations | | Semi-routine and routine occupations | |
	Men	Women	Men	Women
British/other white	41.8	37	24.5	31.1
Black African	38.8	43	35.6	33.2
Black Caribbean	30.8	39.4	36.5	31.9
Indian	45.3	37	23.7	31.2
Pakistani	27.9	30	29.7	39
Bangladeshi	17.8	20.7	50.2	52.9
Chinese	46	41.6	18.2	26.7

Source: Heath and Cheung (2006: 15) .

Heath and Cheung (2006) have found that men and women in most ethnic minority groups face what they call 'ethnic penalties' in the labour market, i.e. disadvantages that cannot be explained by factors such as educational achievement and appear to be related to ethnicity alone. These penalties relate to access to employment, occupational attainment, and pay. All ethnic minorities apart from the Chinese experience ethnic penalties relating to access to employment. Once in employment, most groups – apart from Indians and Chinese – face ethnic penalties in terms of access to professional and managerial jobs and in terms of pay. The highest penalty in this respect is paid by black Africans. From Table 4.3 this group appears quite successful, particularly women, who are more likely to be in professional and managerial roles than whites. However, they remain significantly under-represented when qualifications are taken into account. Black Africans are more highly qualified than whites in the UK. Some 27 per cent have degrees compared with 18 per cent of whites and only 11 per cent have low or no qualifications compared with 13 per cent of whites. On the basis of their qualifications a higher proportion of black Africans should be in professional and managerial occupations and black Africans should also have higher average earnings than whites, rather than lower.

The presence of disadvantaged groups in the labour market increases the range of options open to some employers by allowing them to fulfil their requirements for a stable, cooperative workforce without having to offer the positive incentives associated with internalised employment relationships (Rubery, 1994). This is because, as indicated above, disadvantaged groups have few employment alternatives so they have to take what they can get. The absence of better alternatives makes these jobs more attractive than they would otherwise be and therefore more highly valued by workers. This is reflected in the willingness of many disadvantaged workers to remain with their employer and cooperate with management in order to keep their jobs. This is illustrated in Box 4.1.

Stop & think

Is it rational for an employer to refuse to hire workers on the basis of their ethnicity or nationality? Do employers who hire ethnic minority workers nevertheless benefit from the presence of racism in society as a whole?

Changing patterns of demand

The period since the 1980s has seen significant changes in the pattern of demand for labour and therefore in the types of jobs available to workers. These shifts reflect inter-linked changes in the structure of the economy, government policy for the labour market, and employers' labour requirements.

Box 4.1 ## Advantages to employers of using immigrant labour from Eastern Europe

Recent research carried out for the Joseph Rowntree Foundation into the position of Central and Eastern European immigrant workers in the UK found that immigrant workers from Central and Eastern Europe often had skills and qualifications that were significantly higher than those needed in their jobs. Many of these workers were willing to take low-paid work in the UK because there were even fewer employment opportunities in their home countries. The research also found that employers regarded them as 'high quality workers for low-skilled work' and that employers 'were often trying to balance the requirement for workers who were easy to hire and fire on the one hand but were also reliable and easy to retain'.

Source: Anderson, B., Ruhs, M., Royally, B. and Spencer, C. (2006).

A shift of employment from manufacturing to services

The proportion of workers employed in manufacturing has declined in the UK, USA and all the major European Union economies since the 1960s. This reflects the effects of economic growth and rising incomes on people's consumption patterns. As people get richer, the proportion of their income that they spend on manufactured goods declines (although people may still spend more money on them in absolute terms) and the proportion spent on services increases. This means that output and hence employment grow faster in the service sector than the manufacturing sector. This trend is reinforced by the fact that the long-run rate of growth of labour productivity is higher in manufacturing than in services. Higher productivity growth plus slower growing demand mean slower growth or even decline of employment in manufacturing.

The decline of manufacturing has been particularly rapid in the UK since 1980. This has reflected additional forces such as the effects of government monetary and exchange rate policy during the 1980s which raised the price of British exports in foreign markets and cheapened foreign imports; the long-term inability of UK manufacturing to respond adequately to foreign competition; and organisational restructuring whereby manufacturing firms have tried to cut costs by hiving off certain 'non-core' and specialist activities, such as security, cleaning and catering to outside suppliers of these services. This has meant that the workers who used to deliver these services are now counted as being in the service sector rather than manufacturing. The trend of employment away from manufacturing towards services is predicted to continue, as shown in Table 4.4.

The growth of service sector employment has been a major factor in the increase in part-time employment in the UK and has therefore expanded employment opportunities for women with dependent children and also, more recently, young people in full-time education.

Stop & think

How specifically has the growth of the service sector boosted part-time and female employment?

Changes in the occupational structure of employment

The occupational structure refers to how employment is apportioned among different jobs in the economy. Changes in the occupational structure of employment reflect changes in the types of skill demanded by employers. The declining relative importance of manufacturing means that, over time, the share of occupations associated with manufacturing has also declined while the share of occupations associated with the delivery of business services, retail services, etc. has increased. Changes in the occupational structure also reflect changes in the demand for skills *within* industries. These changes are generated by new technologies and by organisational changes that alter the way in which goods are produced and services deliv-

Table 4.4 Changes in the distribution of employment by broad sector 1982–2012 (percentage share of total employment)

	1982	1992	2002	2007*	2012*
Primary goods and utilities	5.2	3.5	2.2	2.0	1.8
Manufacturing	22.7	16.6	13.2	11.7	10.5
Construction	6.7	7.0	6.3	6.1	5.9
Distribution, transport, etc.	28.3	29.5.	29.6	29.5	29.6
Business and other services	16.5	21.1	25.6	26.9	28.6
Non-marketed services	20.6	22.7	23.1	23.8	23.6

*Projected figures

Source: Wilson, R., Homenikou, K. and Dickerson, A. (2006: 26).

ered; for example, the introduction of new robotic equipment has reduced the requirement for semi-skilled workers in vehicle manufacture. Over the last twenty-five years the effect of technical change has been to increase demand for skilled workers relative to unskilled workers. A national survey of skills trends for the period 1986–2001 found evidence of an overall increase in the skill requirements of jobs, with the proportion of jobs requiring degree qualifications increasing from 9.7 per cent to 17.3 per cent over the period and the proportion requiring no qualifications falling from 38.4 per cent to 26.5 per cent. (Felstead, Gallie and Green, 2002).

We can see further evidence of this in the way in which the occupational structure has changed since the early 1980s. From Table 4.5 we can see that the most highly skilled groups – managers and senior officials, professionals, and associate professional and technical occupations – increased their overall share of employment from 28.3 per cent in 1982 to 40.2 per cent in 2002. Meanwhile the share accounted for by the remaining categories fell from 71.8 per cent to 59.8 per cent. The projections suggest that by 2012 the three most highly skilled categories will have increased their share to 45.1 per cent while that of the rest will fall to 55 per cent.

We need to be careful in interpreting what these trends mean for actual employment opportunities. They do not mean that there will be no employment opportunities in declining occupations. The figures in Table 4.5 refer to the total number of jobs in each occupation that results from its net expansion or decline – the 'expansion demand' (Wilson *et al.*, 2006). However, we also need to take account of the fact that in addition to net growth or decline, there will be a demand for workers to replace those leaving occupations, mainly for reasons of retirement. Replacement demand means that, although total employment in an occupation may be declining, there will still be a large number of jobs on offer within it at any one time. For example, employment in elementary clerical and service occupations (e.g filing clerks, check-out operators) is predicted to fall by 408,000 over the period 2002–2012 but replacement demand is estimated at 1,108,000. This means that there will be a net labour requirement of an extra 647,000 workers over that period, higher than for most of the professional and associated professional groups, which are predicted to grow (Wilson *et al.*, 2006: 73). It may be for this reason that employers report skill shortages in skilled trades and personal services. These reported shortages do not relate to a dearth of applicants to vacancies

Table 4.5 Changes in the occupational structure (percentage share of total employment)

	1982	1992	2002	2007*	2012*
Managers and senior officials	10.7	12.6	14.9	15.4	16.2
Professional occupations	8.0	9.4	11.3	12.2	12.9
Associate professional and technical occupations	9.6	11.3	14.0	15.1	16.0
Administrative, clerical and secretarial occupations	15.5	15.8	13.2	12.2	11.4
Skilled trades	17.0	14.6	11.4	10.2	9.1
Personal service	3.7	4.9	7.3	8.2	9.4
Sales and customer service	6.1	6.7	7.9	8.5	9.0
Transport and machine operatives	11.8	9.7	8.4	7.7	7.2
Elementary occupations	17.7	15.0	11.6	10.4	8.9

*Projected figures

Source: Wilson, R., Homenikou, K. and Dickerson, A. (2006: 58) .

but to what employers see as a lack of necessary skills among applicants. For example, the 2004 National Employers' Skills Survey reported that 50 per cent of applicants to skill short-age vacancies in skilled trades lacked technical and practical skills (Learning and Skills Council, 2005: 9).

Higgs (2004) observes that in response to a shortage of skills in certain areas, some employers have elected to focus on potential ability rather than current ability when hiring staff, this approach, he suggests 'opens up a larger talent pool and at the same time offers potential employees skill development as part of the 'deal' to attract and retain them' (Higgs, 2004: 20). However, in the light of the evidence of continuing discrimination against women and ethnic minorities in the labour market employers could also put more effort into making fuller use of the skills and abilities of workers from disadvantaged labour market groups.

While employers claim to experience skill shortages in specific areas, there is evidence of a growing mismatch between the qualifications held by workers and those required in their jobs. The supply of workers with intermediate qualifications, i.e. Levels 2 and 3, is outstrip-ping the demand for them and a growing proportion of workers as a whole are in jobs where they are over-qualified. This proportion increased from 30.6 per cent in 1986 to 37 per cent in 2001 (Felstead, Gallie and Green, 2002). This suggests that, in general, the demand for skilled labour has not kept pace with the increased supply of qualified workers, so that more people are experiencing job dissatisfaction as a result of the mismatch between their qualifi-cations and the demands of their jobs.

This growing mismatch may be in part a reflection of a growing polarisation of employ-ment in the UK. While there has been an overall shift in favour of more highly skilled jobs, some of the most rapid growth has been in low skilled jobs such as sales assistants and check-out operators, telephone sales workers and security guards. A recent study found that employment growth was concentrated among the best paying and the worst paying jobs. Those in the top 20 per cent of the pay distribution and those in the bottom 10 per cent increased their share of total employment while the share of the rest declined (Goos and Manning, 2003). This suggests that the labour market is polarising into good jobs and bad jobs as intermediate jobs decline.

Activity Review the sections of this chapter that discuss differences in employment opportunity between socio-economic groups and then consider the likely consequences of polarisation of employment for these different groups.

Changing forms of employment

During the 1980s and 1990s, senior managers initiated programmes of organisational change aimed at reducing costs and increasing the speed with which their organisations could respond to changes in market conditions. A central feature of organisational change pro-grammes was workforce 'restructuring' that involved large-scale reductions in headcount, achieved partly through redundancies, early retirement and non-replacement of departing workers and partly by contracting out non-core and specialist services. This was accompa-nied by the reorganisation of work and in many cases, wider use of part-time, fixed-term contract and temporary labour and in a minority of cases, highly casualised forms of employment such as zero hours contracts (Cully, Woodland, O'Reilly and Dix, 1999; Millward, Bryson and Forth, 2000). These changes were aimed at increasing managers' ability to achieve greater *numerical labour flexibility*, in other words to be able to adjust the size of the workforce more easily in response to changes in demand.

The result was that, although the total number of jobs grew, there was a net reduction in the number of *full-time* jobs in Britain during the 1990s. All of the growth in employment was accounted for by a growth of part-time jobs, which increased from 22.9 per cent of total employment in 1992 to 24.6 per cent in 1999. The early and mid-1990s also saw an increase in the share of fixed-term and temporary employment from 5.9 per cent in 1992 to 7.6 per cent in 1997. These developments led some to argue that the full-time, permanent job was likely to become the exception rather than the rule (Bayliss, 1998). However, while part-time employment has continued to increase its share of total employment since 1997, reaching 25.8 per cent in 2004, the trend of temporary and fixed-term employment has been downward, with the share falling to 5.9 per cent in 2005 (ONS 2003, 2005).

Stop & think

What factors might explain why the share of employment accounted for by temporary and fixed-term jobs has fallen back in recent years while that of part-time jobs has continued to rise?

Labour market outcomes: the quality of employment

In this section of the chapter we examine how changes in the labour market have affected the quality of employment experience. How should we assess the quality of jobs? What indices should we use? Traditionally economists have used pay as the measure of job quality. Other social scientists have stressed the level of skill as a key measure on the grounds that skilled work not only provides workers with better pay but also more variety, personal autonomy and involvement and ultimately more control over their effort. We have seen that there has been an overall trend towards increased skill requirements in jobs so on the face of things at least it seems plausible that the quality of jobs available in the labour market has, on balance, improved. However, recent research has uncovered unexpected disjunctures between skill and other measures of job quality such as employment security, the ability to control one's level of effort and exercise control over how the job is done. In this section we review evidence relating to these dimensions of job quality to assess whether recent changes in the demand for labour have improved the quality of employment experience in the UK.

Job security

Job security is generally regarded as an important factor determining job quality. Employment security has also been linked positively to skill level, with skilled workers enjoying greater job security than unskilled workers. However, management-led organisational change during the 1980s and 1990s was seen by some to be undermining job security with disproportionately large effects on skilled workers such as managers and professionals.

The erosion of internalised employment systems

As we have seen, in recent years more organisations have restructured their workforces. They have reduced headcount, contracted out non-core and specialist jobs and increased their use of part-time, temporary and fixed-term contracts of employment and self-employed 'freelance' workers. Employers have also reduced their commitment to providing long-term employment security for 'permanent' employees. They have done this in order to achieve greater numerical flexibility of labour and reduce labour costs. However, they have sought to justify it in moral terms by arguing that workers should rely less on employers to provide long-term employment security and planned career paths and take greater responsibility for their own careers and 'employability'.

During the 1990s growing awareness of these changes led to concern at what appeared to be an increase in employment insecurity. It was argued widely in the press and by some academics that changing patterns of labour demand were creating a new era of insecurity for workers and the disappearance of 'jobs for life' (see Heery and Salmon (2000) for a review of these arguments). So have changes in the labour market made jobs more insecure? Before attempting to answer this question we need to define what we mean by employment insecurity. The most commonly used indicators of employment insecurity are the risk of involuntary job loss the costs of job loss, and the subjective feelings of workers.

The risk of job loss

The risk of job loss is affected by movements in the labour market, particularly changes in the rate of unemployment. The risk of job loss is greater when unemployment is rising than when it is constant or falling. However, during the 1990s some observers argued that the risk of job loss was increasing independently of the level of unemployment; in other words for any given level of unemployment the risk of job loss was higher than it used to be. Proponents of this argument pointed to redundancy dismissals and the replacement of permanent, full-time jobs with part-time and temporary jobs among previously secure groups such as managerial and professional workers and public sector workers. These developments were seen by some as marking the end of internalised employment relationships that offered 'jobs for life' and clear career paths linked to length of service.

The costs of job loss

The costs of job loss consist of three main elements. First is the immediate loss of income caused by having to live on social security benefits until a replacement job is found. Second is the likelihood of not being able to find a replacement job as good as the one that was lost. Third, long periods of unemployment lead to psychological and physical deterioration that reduces the chances of re-employment. Supporters of the insecurity thesis argued that the costs of job loss had risen because the level of social security payments had fallen relative to average wages and workers who had lost permanent full-time jobs were less able than previously to find equivalent replacements because of the trend away from full-time, permanent jobs to part-time and temporary jobs.

Subjective feelings of insecurity

These developments were seen as generating heightened feelings of insecurity among workers. However, the argument that workers were entering a new age of employment insecurity was challenged by other observers, who argued that it was largely a media creation that had been fuelled some well-publicised but unrepresentative instances where permanent, full-time employees had been replaced by freelance workers on fixed-term contracts, mostly in the media themselves (Doogan, 2001).

So has job insecurity increased? The evidence is that there has not been a significant increase in employment insecurity in general. While there was a slight increase in the proportion of workers in jobs lasting less than one year, from 18.6 per cent to 19.9 per cent during 1991–1998, there was also an increase in the proportion of people employed in long-term jobs, i.e. those lasting ten years or more, from 29 per cent to just over 32 per cent (Sparrow and Cooper, 2003: 77). Neither, as Table 4.6 shows, was there a long-term increase in people's feelings of employment insecurity.

Table 4.6 shows that workers' perceptions of the risk of job loss moved in line with unemployment, showing a tendency to increase in the early and mid-1990s and decline thereafter. However, the proportion of workers who felt that there was an even chance or greater of losing their jobs rose very little between 1986 and 1997, the period when employment insecurity was supposed to be increasing. Table 4.6 also shows that over the period 1986–2001 workers became more confident of being able to find an equivalent replacement job should they lose their current one. In particular the proportion of male and female workers who thought it would be very difficult to do so halved over the period. Therefore there is no strong evidence that a long-term increase in employment insecurity has led to a decline in the quality of people's employment experience. Significantly too, over the past five years employment insecurity has figured less and less in public discussion.

Although restructuring may not have increased the risks of job loss significantly, it may have contributed to a loss of valued features of jobs, which has led workers to feel less secure

Table 4.6 Workers' perceptions of employment insecurity in the UK 1991–2001

Perceived likelihood of job loss (%)	All employed workers		
	1986	1997	2001
No chance	80.0	77.1	83.4
Very unlikely	1.3	1.3	1.0
Quite unlikely	3.5	5.2	3.7
Evens	6.6	9.2	5.9
Quite unlikely	4.0	3.5	3.1
Very likely	4.6	3.6	2.9

Perceived difficulty of re-employment
How easy do you think it would be to get another job as good as your current one?

	Men			Women		
	1986	1997	2001	1986	1997	2001
% replying:						
Very easy	4.9	5.5	9.9	4.5	8.5	10.8
Quite easy	14.9	21.8	28.5	18.4	27.2	29.8
Quite difficult	37.2	39.7	39.5	41.8	41.8	42.1
Very difficult	43.0	33.0	22.2	35.3	22.6	17.3

Source: Green, F. (2004) p. 26.

about their long-term futures. One example of this is how organisational restructuring has eroded internal promotion ladders. 'Downsizing' has been accompanied by 'delayering'. Not only have jobs been cut; the number of job levels has also been reduced. The result is that workers have fewer opportunities to gain access to internal promotion ladders. This has been particularly noticeable in the banking and finance sector and in supermarkets, where jobs that used to provide stepping stones from junior to more senior grades have largely been eliminated (Grimshaw, Ward, Rubery and Beynon, 2001; Hudson 2002). This may also be contributing to the polarisation of employment opportunities that has been noted above.

> **Activity**
>
> Discuss with fellow students your perceptions of your own job security or insecurity. What factors influence your assessment?

Effort and work pressure

Feelings of insecurity at work may also result from being under pressure at work and more particularly being unable to control the pressure of work. Since the 1980s many have argued that work pressure has been increasing on two fronts in the UK. First, managers have been putting workers (and each other) under increasing pressure to work long hours. The prevalence of the 'long hours culture' in the UK is indicated by the fact that average working hours are higher than elsewhere in the European Union (EU). The British government has been accused of supporting a long hours culture by seeking to limit the effect of the EU Working Hours Directive in the UK. Second, since the mid-1980s analysts have argued that work is being intensified; in other words, workers are being made to work harder during their working hours.

Green (2006) notes that there is a widespread perception that work is encroaching on other aspects of life, restricting the time available for non-work activities and subjecting people to increased time pressures. This has fuelled recent discussion of 'work–life balance' (see below, p. 148). Statistical evidence, however, shows that there has not been a long-term increase in average hours worked in the UK. Average hours worked per employed person fell from the 1950s to the 1980s. The decline was halted during the 1980s but has resumed since. In 2003 average annual hours worked per employed person were 1673 compared with 1767 in 1990, 1713 in 1983 and 1833 in 1979 (Green, 2006: 46). What have increased are working hours per household as the proportion of households where all the adults are working has grown. The growing proportion of women with dependent children who are in work has been a major influence here. According to Green it is the increase in the total hours worked per household rather than an increase in hours worked per worker that has made it more difficult to balance between work and non-work activities and put people under pressure of time. Even so, there is widespread dissatisfaction over working hours among the UK workforce as a whole. Boheim and Taylor (2004) found that over 40 per cent of male and female full-time workers were dissatisfied with their hours of work, with the majority wanting to work fewer hours.

If the average amount of time that workers spend in work has not increased since the 1980s, people are nevertheless working harder during working time. Workers' self-reports show that the amount of effort required of them has increased, that they have had to work faster to cope with their workload and that they have increasingly been working under a great deal of tension. Thus the proportion of workers reporting that they worked at very high speed all the time or almost all the time rose from 17.3 per cent in 1992 to 25.6 per cent in 2001 and the proportion agreeing or strongly agreeing that they worked under a great deal of tension rose from 48.4 per cent to 58.4 per cent over the same period (Green, 2006: 54). A growing proportion of workers also reported that they found it difficult to unwind after work, that they kept worrying about work problems after work and that they felt 'used up at the end of a workday' (Green 2006: 156).

Work intensification has been driven mainly by the 'effort-biased' nature of technical change (Green, 2006), which enables management to exercise closer control over workers' effort. A clear example of this is the automated call distribution technology that is used in call centres. This ensures that call centre operators receive a continuous stream of incoming and outgoing calls, setting the pace of work in a similar way to the assembly line of an automated manufacturing plant. Another factor contributing to work intensification may be change in the labour market environment, particularly the decline of collective bargaining. This has given employers greater freedom to introduce new pay systems that are designed to extract higher effort from workers (Green, 2006).

Stop & think

Think about your own workplace. What systems and technologies are in place to regulate your effort? Have you noticed an increase or decrease in the intensity of your work over time?

Worker discretion and autonomy

Worker discretion and autonomy are usually associated with skill. In fact the skill content of a job is partly defined in terms of the extent to which workers are required to exercise their own judgement in deciding how the job should be done, the other elements being task complexity and variety. The fewer the prescribed instructions to workers and the greater the number of decisions that workers have to make in the course of the job, the more skilled it is (Noon and Blyton, 1997). We have already seen that changes in the demand for labour have led to an increase in the average skill requirements of jobs. But does this mean that workers are enjoying increasing influence and control over how they work? The trend towards work intensification noted above suggests that workers have been losing control over effort levels and the pace of work. What has happened to their ability to influence other aspects of their work?

Various studies have cast doubt on how far recent upskilling of jobs has been accompanied by increased discretion and control for workers. Ramsay, Baldry, Connolly and Lockyer

(1991) found that white-collar workers in local government reported increased supervision following the introduction of information technology. Dent (1991) found that doctors and academics were being subject to increased bureaucratic control and a large survey carried out by Gallie *et al.*, (1998) found that skilled workers were subject to increased supervision, particularly when they worked with new technology.

National survey data also shows that the overall increase in skill levels has not been accompanied by increased worker discretion; if anything the reverse has occurred. The proportion of all workers reporting that they had a great deal of choice over the way they did their job fell from 51.8 per cent in 1986 to 38.6 per cent in 2001, a decline of 13.2 percentage points. While all broad occupational categories reported a decline in discretion, it was most marked among professional workers, where the proportion reporting that they had a lot of choice over how they did their work fell from 71.5 per cent to 38.3 per cent, a drop of 33.4 percentage points (Green, 2006: 105).

Rather than the shift in favour of more skilled jobs providing workers with greater control over their work, there has been a marked overall decline in discretion, particularly among professionals, who are among the most highly skilled workers. The reasons for this probably include the effects of new technology, financial pressures in the public sector, the spread of subcontracting and the increased public accountability to which professions have been subjected in the interests of improving public services such as health and education. New technologies allow the implementation of routine processes and the closer monitoring of individual workers. Professional workers are also concentrated in the public sector, where government-imposed financial constraints have encouraged closer managerial control of professional workers. At the same time, political pressure to reform and improve public services has involved criticisms of established standards and practices among professional groups that have led to managerial interventions to limit professional autonomy.

Stop & think

Identify as many examples as you can of politically inspired managerial interventions that have affected public service sector professional workers. Here is one to start you off – the National Curriculum in schools.

Job quality – an assessment

The evidence that we have reviewed in this section suggests that in important respects workers' experience of employment has deteriorated since the 1980s. While there has not been a general, long-term increase in job insecurity, work has become more intense and pressured and workers have less control over how they do their jobs. At the same time, the increase in the number of households where all adults are working has led to difficulties of balancing work and non-work areas of life. These changes have led to a significant decline in job satisfaction among British workers with just over 40 per cent of workers reporting high levels of job satisfaction in 2001 compared with just over 50 per cent in 1992 (Green, 2006: 154).

Dissatisfaction appears to be particularly strong among older workers and women. A comparison of the 1992 and 2000 Employment in Britain surveys by Taylor (2002b) showed that among workers aged 50 and over the proportion who were completely or very satisfied with pay fell from 37 per cent in 1992 to just 12 per cent in 2000 while the proportion expressing satisfaction with hours of work halved from 53 per cent to 25 per cent. Dissatisfaction with work intensification was revealed in drop in the proportion who were satisfied with the amount of work they had to do from 51 per cent to 26 per cent (p. 12).

Among women there was a decline in job satisfaction at all occupational levels. However, the decline was greatest among women in intermediate and routine occupations. While the proportion of women in higher level professional and managerial posts expressing satisfaction with their jobs fell from 38 per cent to 26 per cent between 1992 and 2000, the proportion of lower administrative, clerical and sales workers who did so fell from 61 per cent to 35 per cent and that of skilled manual workers from 44 per cent to 17 per cent (Taylor, 2002b: p. 14)

Responses to work pressure – the quest for 'work–life balance'

One important response to the growing sense of work pressure being experienced by people has been the emergence of demands for an improved balance between work and non–work aspects of life. Taylor (2002a) argues that work–life balance is about how to deal with the conflicting demands of corporate profitability on the one hand and the concerns of workers who are under work pressure and strain on the other. In this sense it is an expression of declining job satisfaction over hours and workload. While the increased employment partici-pation of women with dependent children and an ageing population have raised issues of how to combine work with the care of relatives, dissatisfaction with workload and hours is not directly linked to having caring responsibilities. Therefore we need to take a wider view of work–life balance and not just see it in terms of the 'family friendly' agenda (Taylor 2002a).

What do we mean by work–life balance?

Work–life balance is not an easily defined term. The word 'balance' suggests the search for equi-librium between work and life; a settled point perhaps at which work and the rest of life's activities can comfortably reside side by side. Part of the problem associated with the notion of striking a balance or equilibrium is that work and non-work aspects of life are often entwined rather than entirely separate, compartmentalised spheres. For example, we might read a report for work on the train on the way home, we may look up the cinema show times on the web at work or chat to colleagues about non-work related issues during working hours; in essence what we are doing is seeking to find ways to *integrate* work and other aspects of our lives in ways that are workable and beneficial. Sparrow and Cooper (2003: 219) suggest therefore that 'work–life balance concerns those practices that enhance the flexibility and autonomy of the employee in this process of integration and in the negotiation over the attention and presence required'. They suggest that autonomy can either be guided by the provision of specific organ-isational arrangements to enable employees to split work and non-work aspects of their lives, for example, options to work part time or full time, to work in school term time only or to job share, or it can be achieved by the organisation making available practices which allow individ-uals to draw their own lines between and around work and non-work, for example, unpaid leave, career breaks, parental leave, sabbaticals, paid holidays. Work–life balance strategies are thus often associated with the provision of greater flexibility in terms of working arrangements.

Work–life balance and government policy

Legal imperatives for employers to address issues of work–life balance began to emerge at the end of the 1990s. In 1998 we saw the introduction of the Working Time Regulations, aimed at curtailing the working week to a maximum of 48 hours and requiring employers to formally secure an 'opt-out' agreement with those employees willing to contract in excess of the 48-hour cap. On the heels of the Working Time Directive, the Employment Rights Act 1999 contained provisions to bolster the position of working parents and carers within the work-place whilst the Employment Act 2002 propelled the legislative agenda underpinning work–life balance provisions yet further (see Chapter 11 for further details of the legislation). At the time of writing it is anticipated that the government will extend the right to request flexible working to carers of adults with effect from April 2007.

The Government's concern for work–life balance was formally highlighted in Spring 2000 at the launch of the Work–Life Balance Campaign (Hogarth *et al.*, 2000). The objective of the campaign was to alert employers to the business case in favour of introducing practices to help employees strike a better balance between work and other non-work areas of their lives. Importantly the campaign sought to promote the merits of work–life balance *for all* rather than identifying those with caring responsibilities as key beneficiaries of support.

The pattern of employer responses to work–life balance issues

There are potentially strong business reasons why employers should offer arrangements to employees to help achieve a better integration of work and non-work aspects of their lives. Specifically they may aid recruitment and retention at a time when organisations are competing for highly qualified, talented workers. Edwards and Wajcman (2005) refer to international survey evidence that shows that graduates give a higher priority to work–life balance than to pay. Clutterbuck (2004) suggests that creating an enabling culture in which employees can amend and re-apportion the time and attention they pay to work to meet their particular needs and circumstances can be a source of sustainable competitive advantage (Clutterbuck, 2004).

Employers' responses to the work–life balance issue have, however, been mixed. Some appear to welcome and encourage work–life balance initiatives while others are more reticent. Work undertaken by Wood (1999) for the National Centre for Economic Research suggests that employers' motives for introducing work–life balance initiatives can be summarised within a four-fold theoretical classification;

- institutional theory;
- organisational-adaption theory;
- high-commitment theory;
- practical response theory.

Wood explains that whilst some firms will apparently willingly and proactively adopt work–life balance initiatives, others will only do so to respond to pressing and immediate circumstances.

In adopting the classification Wood argues that those organisations whose behaviour shows them to be eager to reflect broader societal values in their practices conform to *Institutional theory*. Typically these firms operate in the public sector and need to be seen to be proactive, or they are large private sector firms in the public gaze for whom there is visible kudos to be earned from setting the lead in developing and implementing work–life balance solutions. Additionally firms with trade union presence are more likely to conform.

Organisational adaption theory relates to those organisations in which societal norms are interpreted in ways that are seen to be consistent with the views and interests of senior management, so alongside the pre-mentioned conditions favourable for the adoption of work–life balance initiatives, firms conforming to organisational adaption theory are likely to be drawn towards work-life balance initiatives because of specific organisational circumstances. Such firms may be especially reliant on a predominantly female workforce or require skill sets that are difficult to secure and retain and employee retention issues therefore critical. Organisational adaption theory also captures the propensity for firms to implement work–life balance initiatives when existing working patterns and systems are conducive to or compatible with them.

Within Wood's framework *high-commitment theory* is used to explain the uptake of work–life balance initiatives among those organisations with developed HRM systems and practices, where it is understood that mechanisms to help employees achieve a better work–life balance may in turn engender greater levels of employee commitment.

Finally, *practical response theory* applies to organisations who display a rather more *ad hoc* approach to the development and introduction of work–life balance initiatives; resorting to implementing work–life balance practices if they are perceived to be beneficial in helping to address particular organisational difficulties.

The following organisations all have in place work–life balance practices:

(a) *British Telecom*

(b) *Asda*

(c) *Lloyds TSB Plc*

(d) *The University of Leicester Hospitals Trust*

In each case, which of Wood's theories do you think most closely relates to the organisation's particular motives for embracing work–life balance practices?

In commenting on Wood's analysis Clutterbuck (2004) suggests that the primary drivers for work–life balance in the EU differ from those typically forwarded by US organisations. In the US he recognises a model firmly centred upon work–life balance as a source of competitive advantage whilst in the EU motives typically push social responsibility to the fore.

Stop & think

Think of an organisation you have worked for where some work–life balance practices were available. Why do you think this organisation elected to develop and introduce WLB initiatives?

The take-up of work–life balance initiatives by employers

The first findings of the 2004 WERS survey (Kersley *et al.* 2005) reported an increase in the proportion of employers who believe that employees' work–life balance is their responsibility. Latest findings from WERS 2004 (Kersley *et al.*, 2005: 31) show an increase in the availability of parental leave, paid paternity/discretionary leave for fathers and special paid leave in emergencies for at least some non-managerial employees in the period 1998 to 2004. WERS data continues, however, to reflect a chequered picture in terms of employees' access to a range of work–life balance provisions, suggesting that not all employers feel pressured to prioritise provision for work–life balance. The WERS panel survey showed the proportion of workplaces providing access to zero hours contracts, annualised hours, job sharing, home working, term-time only contracts, flexi-time and the facility to switch from full-time to part-time employment to at least some of their non-managerial employees increased during the period 1998 to 2004. However, Kersley *et al.* admit that 'generally these practices were more common in larger workplaces, the public sector and where unions were recognised' (2005: 28). This pattern is illustrative of the sway of institutional theory. In a pattern resonant with organisational adaption theory, Kersley *et al.* (2005) have found that workplaces in which female employees outnumber male employees are more disposed to permit some employees to use all of the practices listed in Table 4.7 apart from homeworking and flexi-time (2005: 28).

In light of this, the trend to smaller workplaces combined with sparse trade union presence suggests that progress in addressing work–life balance issues will continue to be uneven. Moreover, even in those organisations where opportunities for flexible working are offered barriers to their take-up by employees remain. These include the irreducible nature of work tasks in many cases, possible damage to career prospects resulting from taking flexible work options and for low earners, loss of earnings resulting from some options. Workers may also be unwilling to take advantage of work–life balance initiatives because they are worried that it will generate hostile responses from colleagues who are unable or do not wish to do so

Figure 4.7 Availability of flexible working arrangements

Flexible working arrangements	Per cent of workplaces offering the arrangement to some employees
Reduced hours	70
Increased hours	57
Change working pattern	45
Flexi-time	35
Job sharing	31
Homeworking	26
Term-time only	20
Compressed hours	16
Annualised hours	6
Zero-hours contracts	5

Source: Kersley *et al.* (2005: 29), Inside the workplace: first findings from the 2004 Workplace Employment Relations Survey.

(Sparrow and Cooper, 2003). More optimistically, there is evidence that the incidence of long hours working and work intensification is declining. The proportion of workers working long hours peaked at 36 per cent in 1995 and fell to 30 per cent by the end of 2002 (Green, 2003: 140). Also, while work was more intense in 2001 than in 1992, the process of intensification halted in 1997, since when there has been little change (Green, 2003: 144).

Conclusion: labour market developments, job quality and the implications for the employment relationship

The evidence discussed in this chapter suggests that, despite the widespread rhetoric of high commitment and high involvement and the tendency among advocates and practitioners of HRM to present the employment relationship in terms of mutual consent, it continues to be characterised by conflicts of interest. Currently these centre on hours of work, work intensity, lack of discretion and control over how work is performed, and structured inequalities in the labour market.

The main labour market development over the last ten years has been a sustained growth of employment accompanied by increasing inequality in the distribution of pay as a result of the polarised nature of employment growth. While employment and pay have risen for all groups of workers since 1993, the *relative* position of less-skilled workers in terms of unemployment, access to jobs, and pay is worse than it was at the start of the 1980s. This is despite recent government interventions such as the national minimum wage and measures aimed at improving the employability of young school leavers (Goos and Manning, 2003)

In addition, long-standing patterns of inequality and disadvantage remain. The difference in employment rates between women and men has not really changed over the last ten years, the employment rate among women remaining 11 percentage points below that of men. Neither has there been much change in the quality of jobs occupied by women. They are still concentrated in occupations and industries where rates of pay are low and working conditions are poor. While the overall pay gap between women and men has narrowed, it is the minority of women who are working full time in higher-paid occupations who have benefited. This group have also benefited from statutory maternity leave provisions, which have given them the right to return to their jobs after childbirth. The pay gap for the majority of working women, who are in part-time jobs, has not narrowed and may even have increased slightly (Robinson, 2003). Moreover the position of these women, employed mainly in low skill occupations, has deteriorated to an even greater extent than that of low skilled men in relation to unemployment, access to employment, and pay (Gregg and Wadsworth, 2003).

Established patterns of labour market inequality between ethnic minorities and whites have also persisted. There has been an increase in the employment rate and a consequent reduction in the employment gap relative to whites among some, but not all British born ethnic minority groups and a slight reduction in the degree of occupational segregation. However there is less evidence for a reduction in the pay gap. The position of ethnic minority immigrants has shown no sign of improving relative to whites (Wadsworth, 2003).

These features of the contemporary labour market suggest that employers have a number of serious issues to face. First, it is clear that there is a growing mismatch between the way managers are organising work and designing jobs on the one hand and how workers' job aspirations are developing on the other. Widespread job dissatisfaction is weakening employees' commitment to their employers and eroding the goodwill that is necessary for cooperative behaviour in the workplace. Given the particularly steep decline in job satisfaction among the over-50s and women, employers need to take action to address these workers' grievances.

Second, if, as is widely predicted, the ageing of the population means that the future supply of skilled labour is likely to become increasingly tight, government and employers will need to develop and utilise more effectively under-employed skills in the ethnic minority population, among women and older workers as well as making greater use of migrant workers from the expanded EU. This implies a stronger commitment to valuing diversity in the workforce and managing it effectively.

However, employers individually may benefit from the presence of disadvantaged groups who can be exploited because they lack alternative job opportunities. Therefore there is a case for stronger state intervention to combat unfair discrimination in the labour market. There is also a case for strengthening workers' rights to trade union membership and representation.

Finally, the evidence reviewed in this chapter should lead you to think about the nature of HRM and the extent of its adoption in the UK. What do we consider to be HRM? Is it a set of practices aimed at generating high levels of employee commitment or high performance through employee involvement? If so, there would appear to be little evidence that it has spread widely in the UK since the 1980s.

Summary

- Labour markets are often seen as arenas of competition in which forces of supply and demand determine wage and employment levels. In reality however, there are limits to competition in labour markets.

- Employers have some freedom to make a strategic choice between internalising or externalising the employment relationship. Their choices are influenced although not completely determined by the nature of their labour requirements and by features of the labour market context in which they operate.

- The aggregate supply of labour – the size of the workforce – is determined by demographic factors such as the size and age structure of the population and by social and political factors that influence the participation rate of different socio-economic groups within the population. In the UK differential participation rates can be observed between men and women of different age groups and different ethnic groups.

- Aggregate labour demand consists of total employment plus unfilled vacancies. The demand for labour is derived from the demand for goods and services. In conditions of low unemployment – tight labour markets – employers have to compete more actively to attract and retain workers.

- The demand for labour is segmented into jobs offers of varying quality. Unfair discrimination along lines of gender and ethnicity mean that women and ethnic minorities are disadvantaged in terms of access to good jobs.

- There has been a long-term change in labour demand away from manufacturing to services. This has been an important force driving the long-term growth of part-time employment and women's employment.

- Since the 1980s there has been a shift in the occupational structure of labour demand mainly towards highly skilled occupations but also leading to the growth of some low-skilled occupations. There has been a relative decline in intermediate occupations.

- Since the 1980s managers have restructured their organisations and their workforces. This has involved a retreat from internalised employment relationships.

- Contrary to what might have been predicted from the overall trend towards more highly skilled work, the quality of jobs has deteriorated in terms of work pressure and worker autonomy, although not in terms of job stability leading to falling levels of job satisfaction compared with the early 1990s. The demand for better work–life balance is a recent response to growing work pressure.

- Declining job satisfaction and the presence of disadvantaged groups in the labour market indicate the continued presence of conflict in the employment relationship.

1 Explain the factors that influence the differential labour market participation rates of women and men and ethnic minorities and whites.

2 How has the structure of demand for labour changed since the 1980s?

3 Why have levels of job satisfaction declined since the early 1990s?

4 Who have been the man beneficiaries of changes in the labour market since the 1980s and who have been the main losers?

CASE STUDY

Stuck on the 'mummy track' – why having a baby means lower pay and prospects

From the moment they give birth, women get stuck on a 'mummy track' of low pay and low prospects as their wages fall and never fully recover – even when their children have left home, a new study has found.

Far from being a liberating release, the point when their children start school marks another sudden slump in the average growth of women's pay compared with male wages, according to the report by the Institute for Fiscal Studies.

Before they have children, the average hourly wage for female workers is 91 per cent of the male average but declines to 67 per cent for working mothers juggling jobs and childcare.

Their wages relative to men then stagnate for 10 years before showing a modest recovery, reports the study, Newborns and New Schools. But even when children have left home, the average hourly wage for their mothers remained at 72 per cent of the male average.

Rather than facilitate a large-scale return to the workforce for women, the moment their children enter full-time school accelerates relative wage decline. The average wage growth over two years for women before having children was 11 per cent, but fell to 8 per cent for women with newborn children. While it recovered to 9 per cent for those with pre-school children, it fell again to less than 5 per cent when their children entered school. The aggregate proportion of mothers in work before their children began school compared with afterwards only rose slightly from 53 per cent in June to 57 per cent when term began in September.

'There is a huge assumption that suddenly because the child is at school the mother can return to work,' said Gillian Paull, a co-author of the study for the Department for Work and Pensions. 'But school hours are far too short to cover most jobs and school brings with it a new set of responsibilities in terms of children needing input from parents and parents being involved in school life. Finding childcare that fits around school hours and the holidays is difficult unless you pay for expensive full-time care.'

Only a small part of this gender wage gap is because mothers choose to work part time. For full-time workers, the gender wage ratio suffered a similar slump between childless women and working mothers, with a decline from women commanding 94 per cent of male wages before children to just 74 per cent for those with children and 79 per cent for the group after children.

When researchers took account of other factors which might determine the gender wage gap such as gender differences in demographic background, educational attainment and work characteristics and conditions they still found 'a substantial "unexplained" gender wage gap' of 11 per cent for those before children, 30 per cent for those living with children and 23 per cent for those whose children have grown up or left home.

'The million-dollar question is: "Are the wage levels different because working mothers are treated differently or is it that they choose a different way to behave in the labour market?"' Dr Paull said.

Working mothers could be suffering a wide pay gap because of pure discrimination. Or, controversially, some employers claim they do not pay as much because working mothers are not as productive as men. Thirdly, Dr Paull said, it could be that women were choosing jobs that fit in with the demands of motherhood, finding work that was less physically demanding, for instance, so they could devote more energy to their families.

Case study continued

'Too many women get stuck on a "mummy track" of low pay and low prospects. The pay gap for women working part-time, at nearly 40 per cent, has barely improved since the Sex Discrimination Act was introduced 30 years ago,' said Caroline Slocock, the chief executive of the Equal Opportunities Commission.

'Many women choose to work part-time, but they don't choose low pay. Four in five part-time workers – 5.6 million people, most of whom are women – are working in jobs which do not use their potential, because flexible and part-time work is too often low-status and underpaid. This is a colossal waste of talent for employers and the economy as well as individuals.'

The IFS study is published days before the Women and Work Commission reports to Tony Blair after spending 18 months looking at the problem of the gender pay gap. The prime minister is expected to help launch the report next month, which is expected to outline radical proposals to help women return to well-paid work.

Children represent a 'major part' of the gender pay gap, according to Margaret Prosser, who chairs the Women and Work Commission. 'Once women have children, their job choices are hugely constrained, either because they have to choose local work which provides fewer options or choose part-time employment, where there are few jobs at a professional or senior level.'

Lady Prosser said she was not surprised that figures showed women's pay stagnating even years after they have raised young children.

'The majority of women who have children want to spend some time with those children. What they would like is work that is sufficiently flexible but what they do not want is work that is always at the bottom of the ladder.

'There is no silver bullet answer to this. There has to be a whole range of policy proposals around edu-cational choices, encouragement for girls and more widely available childcare facilities.'

Source: Patrick Barkham, 20 January 2006, *The Guardian*

Questions

1 To what extent do you believe that women get stuck on the 'mummy track' because they *choose* to prioritise responsibilities to their children over and above paid work?

2 Are New Labour's promises to improve access to affordable childcare and plans to introduce school 'wrap around time' (the provision of breakfast clubs and after school activities to extend the school day) the 'green light' needed for working mothers to be able to compete on equal terms with men in the workplace?

3 Whilst organisations might not deliberately set out to discriminate against working mothers, consider ways in which norms and expectations in the contemporary workplace may make it difficult for working mothers to gain promotion and hence access to better paid positions. What steps could organisations take to help more women off the 'mummy track'?

Activity

You have been invited to a campus debate to discuss the proposition outlined below:

> Given employers' demand for low skill workers to fill low-paid jobs in the service sector, the existence of receptive pockets of labour (for example, working mothers, students, migrant workers) prepared to accept these jobs is beneficial for organisations and the economy at large.

Using the article 'Stuck on the Mummy track' as a starting point, consider positions both *in support of and against* the above statement. You should be able to draw upon several segments of this chapter to inform your arguments.

References and further reading

Adkins, L. (1995) *Gendered Work, Sexuality, Family and the Labour Market*. Buckingham: OUP.

Anderson, B., Ruhs, M., Rogaly, B. and Spencer, C. (2006) *Fair Enough? Central and Eastern European Migrants in Low-Wage Employment*. York: Joseph Rowntree Foundation.

Bayliss, V. (1998) *Redefining Work: An RSA Initiative*. London: Royal Society for the Encouragement of Arts, Manufactures and Commerce.

Boheim, R. and Taylor, M.P. (2004) 'Actual and preferred working hours', *British Journal of Industrial Relations*, 42, 1: 149–166.

Bradley (1999), *Gender and Power in the Workplace: Analysing the Impact of Economic Change*. Basingstoke: Macmillan Press Ltd.

Browning, G. (2005) 'The Search for Meaning', *People Management*, 11, 25: December.

CIPD (2005) *A Barometer of HR Trends and Prospects, Overview of CIPD Surveys*. London: CIPD.

CIPD (2006) 'Jobs blow to women as economic slowdown hits consumer services', Press Release, London, CIPD, 15 March.

CIPD and KPMG (2006) Labour Market Outlook, *Quarterly Survey Report*, London, CIPD Spring.

Clutterbuck, D. (2004) *Managing Work–Life Balance in the 21st Century*. London: CIPD

Connor, H., Tyers, C., Davis, S. and Tackey, N. (2003) *Minority Ethnic Students in Higher Education*. London: DFES

Cooper, C. (2005) 'Another Year Down?' *People Management*, 11, 25: December.

Crompton, R. (1997) *Women and Work in Modern Britain*, Oxford: Oxford University Press Ltd.

Cully, M., Woodland, S., O'Reilly, A. and Dix, G. (1999) *Britain at Work. As depicted by the 1998 Workplace Employee Relations Survey*. London: Routledge.

Dent, M. (1991) 'Autonomy and the medical profession: medical audit and management control', in Smith, C., Knights, D. and Willmott, H. (eds) *White-Collar Work: The Non-Manual Labour Process*. Basingstoke: Macmillan, pp. 65–88.

Doeringer, P.B. and Piore, M.J. (1971) *Internal Labor Markets and Manpower Analysis*. Lexington, Mass.: Heath.

Doogan, K. (2001) 'Insecurity and long term employment', *Work, Employment and Society*, 15, 3: 419–441.

Drucker, P. (2001) 'Beyond the Information Revolution' in Giddens, A. (ed.) *Sociology: Introductory Readings*. Cambridge: Polity Press.

DWP (2005) Speech given by the Rt Hon Alan Johnson MP, Secretary of State for Work and Pensions, 7 February, www.dwp.gov.uk.

Edwards, P. and Wajcman, J. (2005) *The Politics of Working Life*. Oxford: Oxford University Press.

EOC (2001) *Women and Men in Britain: Professional Occupations*.

EOC (2005) Facts about Men and Women in Britain 2005, an EOC Fact Sheet

EOC (2006) Then and Now; 30 years of the Sex Discrimination Act, an EOC Fact Sheet.

Felstead, A., Gallie, D. and Green, F. (2002) *Work Skills in Britain 1986–2001*. Nottingham: DfES publications.

Friedman, A. (1977) *Industry and Labour*. London: Macmillan.

Gallie, D., White, M. and Cheng, Y. (1998) *Restructuring the Employment Relationship*. Oxford: Clarendon Press.

Goos, M. and Manning, A. (2003) 'McJobs and MacJobs: The growing polarisation of jobs in the UK', in Dickens, R., Gregg, P. and Wadsworth, J. (eds) *The Labour Market under New Labour: The State of Working Britain*. Basingstoke: Palgrave, pp. 70–85.

Gordon, D.M., Edwards, R. and Reich, M. (1982) *Segmented Work, Divided Workers: The Historical Transformation of Labor in the United States*. Cambridge: Cambridge University Press.

Green, F. (2003) 'The demands of work', in Dickens, R., Gregg, P. and Wadsworth, J. (eds) *The Labour Market under New Labour: The State of Working Britain*. Basingstoke: Palgrave, pp. 137–149.

Green, F. (2004) 'The rise and decline of job insecurity', Department of Economics Discussion Paper, Kent University.

Green, F. (2006) *Demanding Work: The Paradox of Job Quality in the Affluent Economy*. Oxford: Princeton University Press.

Gregg, P. and Wadsworth, J. (2003) 'Labour market prospects of less skilled workers over the recovery', in Dickens, R., Gregg, P. and Wadsworth, J. (eds) *The Labour Market Under New Labour: The State of Working Britain*. Basingstoke: Palgrave, pp. 87–97.

Grimshaw, D., Ward, K.G., Rubery, J. and Beynon, H. (2001) 'Organisations and the transformation of the internal labour market', *Work, Employment and Society*, 15, 1: 25–54.

Hakim, C. (1998) *Social Change and Innovation in the Labour Market*. Oxford: OUP.

Hardill, I., Duddlestone, A. and Owen, D.W. (1997) 'Who decides what? Decision making in dual career households', *Work, Employment & Society*, 11, 2: 313–326.

Heath, A. and Cheung, S.Y. (2006) *Ethnic Penalties in the Labour Market: Employers and Discrimination*. DWP Research Report 341.

Heery, E. and Salmon, J. (2000) 'The insecurity thesis', in Heery, E. and Salmon, J. (eds) *The Insecure Workforce*. London: Routledge, pp. 1–24.

Higgs, M. (2004) 'Future Trends in HR', in Rees, D. and McBain, R. (eds) *People Management Challenges and Opportunities*. Basingstoke: Palgrave.

Hogarth, T., Hasluck, C., Pierre, G., Winterbotham, M. and Vivian, D. (2000) *Work-life Balance, 2000: Baseline Study of Work-Life Balance Practices in Great Britain*. Warwick: Institute for Employment Research: Warwick University.

Hudson, M. (1999) 'Disappearing pathways and the struggle for a fair day's pay', in Burchell, B., Day, D., Hudson, M., Ladipo, D., Mankelow, R., Nolan, J., Reed, H., Wichert, I. and Wilkinson, F. *Job Insecurity and Work Intensification: Flexibility and the Changing Boundaries of Work*. York: Joseph Rowntree Foundation, pp. 77–93.

Hudson, M. (2002) 'Disappearing pathways and the struggle for a fair day's pay', in Burchell, B., Day, D., Hudson, M., Ladipo, D., Mankelow, R., Nolan, J., Reed, H., Wichert, I. and Wilkinson, F. *Job Insecurity and Work Intensification: Flexibility and the Changing Boundaries of Work*. York: Joseph Rowntree Foundation, pp. 77–93.

Jah, A. (2006) 'The future of old age', *The Guardian*, 8 March 2006, p. 6.

Joll, C., Mckenna, C., McNab, R. and Shorey, J. (1983) *Developments in Labour Market Analysis*. London: George Allen & Unwin.

Kersley, B., Alpin, C., Forth, J., Bryson, A., Bewley, H., Dix, G. and Oxenbridge, S. (2005) *Inside the Workplace: First Findings from the 2004 Workplace Employment Relations Survey*. London: DTi.

King, J.E. (1990) *Labour Economics*, 2nd edition. London: Macmillan.

Laurie, H. and Gershuny, J. (2000) 'Couples, Work and Money' in Berthoud, R. and Gershuny, J. (eds) *Seven Years in the Lives of British Families*. Bristol: Polity Press.

Learning and Skills Council (2005) *National Employer Skills Survey: Key Findings*. Coventry: Learning and Skills Council.

Leonard, D. and Speakman, M.A. (1986) 'Women in the family: companions or caretaker?', in Beechey, V. and Whitelegg, E. (eds) *Women in Britain Today*. Milton Keynes: Open University Press.

LFS (2006) 'Ethnic minorities in the labour market: Autumn 2005', *LFS Update*, www.emetaskforce.gov.uk.

Marlow, S. and Carter, S. (2004) 'Accounting for change: professional status, gender disadvantage and self-employment', *Women in Management Review*, 19, 1: 5–17.

Miller, H. (1991) 'Academics and the labour process', in Smith, C., Knights, D. and Willmott, H. (eds) *White-Collar Work: The Non-Manual Labour Process*. Basingstoke: Macmillan, pp. 109–138.

Millward, N., Bryson, A. and Forth, J. (2000) *All Change at Work? British Employment Relations as Portrayed by the Workplace Industrial Relations Survey Series*. London: Routledge.

Nolan, P. and Brown, W. (1983) 'Competition and workplace wage determination', *Oxford Bulletin of Economics and Statistics*, 45, 269–287.

Noon, M. and Blyton, P. (1997) *The Realities of Work*. Basingstoke: Macmillan.

ONS (2001), Census 2001.

ONS (2003) *Labour Market Trends*, 111, 12.

ONS (2004) *Labour Force Survey*, Spring 2004 dataset.

ONS (2005a) *Labour Market Trends*, 113, 12.

ONS (2005b) *Population Trends*, 121, Autumn 2005.

ONS (2005c) *Annual Earnings Survey*, Office for National Statistics.

ONS (2006a) *Social Trends*, 36th edn, Office for National Statistics.

ONS (2006b) 'Diversity within and between ethnic groups', *Social Trends*, 36th edn, News Release, 21 February.

Ramsay, H., Baldry, C., Connolly, A. and Lockyer, C. (1991) 'Multiple microchips: the computerised labour process in the public service sector', in Smith, C., Knights, D. and Willmott, H. (eds) *White-Collar Work: The Non-Manual Labour Process*. Basingstoke: Macmillan, pp. 35–64.

Robinson, H. (2003) 'Gender and labour market performance in the recovery', in Dickens, R., Gregg, P. and Wadsworth, J. (eds) *The Labour Market Under New Labour*. Basingstoke: Palgrave, pp. 232–247.

Rubery, J. (1994) 'Internal and external labour markets: towards an integrated analysis', in Rubery, J. and Wilkinson, F. (eds) *Employer Strategy and the Labour Market*. Oxford: Oxford University Press, pp. 37–68.

Scottish Centre for Employment Research (2001) *SCER Report 1 – Understanding the Labour Market*, Department of Human Resource Management, University of Strathclyde.

Sparrow, P.R. and Cooper, C.L. (2003) *The Employment Relationship: Key Challenges for HR*. London: Butterworth Heinemann.

Stanworth, C. (2000) 'Flexible working patterns', in Winstanley, D. and Woodall, J. (eds) *Ethical Issues in Contemporary Human Resource Management*. Basingstoke: Palgrave.

Strategy Unit (2003) *Ethnic Minorities and the Labour Market: Final Report*. London: Cabinet Office.

Taylor, R. (2002a) *The Future of Work–Life Balance*. Swindon: Economic and Social Research Council.

Taylor, R. (2002b) *Britain's Diverse Labour Market*. Swindon: Economic and Social Research Council.

Taylor, S. (2005), *People Resourcing*, 3rd edn. London: CIPD.

TUC (2005) 'Challenging Times'. London: TUC

Wadsworth, J. (2003) 'The labour market performance of ethnic minorities in the recovery', in Dickens, R., Gregg, P. and Wadsworth, J. *The Labour Market under New Labour: The State of Working Britain*. Basingstoke: Palgrave, pp. 116–133.

Wilson, R., Homenikou, K. and Dickerson, A. (2006) *Working Futures: New Projections of Occupational Attainment by Sector and Region 2002–2012. Volume 1: National Report*. Coventry: Institute for Employment Research, University of Warwick.

Wood, S. (1999) Family-friendly management; testing the various perspectives, *National Institute for Economic Research*, 168, April 2/99: 99–116.

For multiple-choice questions, exercises and annotated weblinks specific to this chapter visit the book's website at **www.pearsoned.co.uk/beardwell**

Chapter 5

Human resource planning

Julie Beardwell

Objectives

- To identify multiple interpretations of human resource planning and define the concept.
- To discuss key stages in the traditional human resource planning process.
- To analyse and evaluate quantitative and qualitative methods of demand and supply forecasting.
- To identify and discuss contemporary approaches to human resource planning.
- To discuss the advantages and disadvantages of human resource planning.
- To investigate the application of human resource planning in practice.
- To explore the link between human resource planning and strategic HRM.

Introduction

Planning for human resources has had a fairly chequered history (Torrington *et al.*, 2002). The subject, initially termed 'manpower planning', first rose to prominence in the 1960s when the emphasis was on the means of achieving growth in production against a backdrop of skills shortages and relatively stable, predictable world markets. At this time, much of the emphasis was on the application of statistical and mathematical techniques (see, for example, Bartholemew, 1976). However, by the early 1980s manpower planning was seen by many as largely irrelevant as it had become associated with growth, five-year plans and bureaucracy at a time when many organisations were preoccupied with having to contract and become more flexible (Cowling and Walters, 1990: 3). Since then, human resource planning has often been denigrated, with the result that it has received relatively little attention in the literature and has become less widely used in organisations (Taylor, 2005). The demise of HRP can seem rather ironic as it appears to have occurred at the same time as there have been increasing calls for people management to become a more strategic activity. After defining the terminology, the chapter outlines the traditional approach to HRP; it then considers more contemporary variants; explores the application of HRP in practice; and finally explores the link between HRP and strategic HRM.

Defining human resource planning

In *Through the Looking Glass* Humpty Dumpty tells Alice, 'When I use a word it means exactly what I choose it to mean, neither more nor less.' The same might be said of 'human resource planning' (HRP) as the phrase can be used in a number of different ways. The main distinction is between those who view the term as synonymous with 'manpower planning' and those who believe that 'human resource planning' represents something rather different (Taylor, 2005).

Manpower planning has been defined as 'a strategy for the acquisition, utilisation, improvement and retention of an enterprise's human resources' (Department of Employment, 1974). The prime concern is generally with enabling organisations to maintain the status quo; 'the purpose of manpower planning is to provide continuity of efficient manning for the total business and optimum use of manpower resources' (McBeath, 1992: 26), usually via the application of statistical techniques. The term 'human resource planning' emerged at about the same time as 'human resource management' started to replace 'personnel management', and for some (e.g. McBeath, 1992; Thomason, 1988) the terminology is just a more up-to-date, gender-neutral way of describing the techniques associated with manpower planning.

For others, human resource planning represents something different but the extent of this difference can vary. In some instances, human resource planning is seen as a variant of manpower planning more concerned with qualitative issues and cultural change, than with hierarchical structures, succession plans and mathematical modelling (e.g. Cowling and Walters, 1990). In other instances, the term can be used to signal a significant difference in both thinking and practice (Liff, 2000). For example, Bramham (1989) argues that there are fundamental differences between the two approaches:

> There are particularly important differences in terms of process and purpose. In human resource planning the manager is concerned with motivating people – a process in which costs, numbers, control and systems interact to play a part. In manpower planning the manager is concerned with the numerical elements of forecasting, supply-demand matching and control, in which people are a part. There are therefore important areas of overlap and interconnection but there is a fundamental difference in underlying approach.
>
> (Bramham, 1989: 147)

This broad interpretation of HRP can be seen as rather vague and lacking explicit practical application or specification. For example, Marchington and Wilkinson (1996) argue that Bramham's conception of HRP is synonymous with HRM in its entirety and, as such, loses any distinctive sense. Indeed, in his book *Human Resource Planning*, Bramham (1989) discusses a very wide range of people management issues, including employee development, reward management and employee relations, and only focuses on specific planning issues in one chapter.

A third approach is to define HRP as a distinct process aimed at predicting an organisation's future requirements for human resources that incorporates both the qualitative elements of human resource planning and the quantitative elements of manpower planning. These two elements are often labelled as 'soft' and 'hard' human resource planning respectively. Tansley (1999: 41) summarises the general conceptions of 'hard' HRP in the literature as follows:

● emphasis on 'direct' control of employees – employees are viewed like any other resource with the need for efficient and tight management;

● akin to the notion of manpower planning – with emphasis on demand–supply matching;

● undertaken by HR specialists;

● related HR strategies are concerned with improving the utilisation of human resources.

In contrast, she summarises the general characteristics of 'soft' HRP as:

- emphasis on 'indirect control of employees – with increasing emphasis on employee involvement and teamwork;
- a wider focus to include an emphasis on organisational culture and the clearer integration between corporate goals and employee values and behaviour;
- involves HR specialists, line managers and possibly other employees;
- greater emphasis on strategies and plans for gaining employee commitment.

Like the broader interpretations of HRP, definitions of 'soft' HRP tend to assume a 'best practice', high-commitment approach to people management. Although there is emphasis on the need to integrate human resource planning activity with corporate goals, the implicit assumption is that this will be achieved via the design and application of plans aimed at developing employee skills and securing their commitment to organisational goals. However, as we shall discuss later in the chapter, there may be some business strategies, e.g. cost minimisation, that require different approaches to people management.

Stop & think

Which definition of human resource planning do you prefer and why?

In order to convey the meaning of HRP as a set of activities that represent a key element of HRM but are distinct from it, and to include both the soft and hard aspects of the planning process, the definition used in this chapter is as follows:

> HRP is the process for identifying an organisation's current and future human resource requirements, developing and implementing plans to meet these requirements and monitoring their overall effectiveness.

There are a number of ways in which this process can be undertaken. The chapter begins with an exploration of the key stages in the traditional approach to HRP (incorporating many of the 'hard' elements) and then considers more contemporary variants.

The traditional approach to HRP

The prime concern within traditional or 'hard' HRP relates to balancing the demand for and the supply of human resources. Demand reflects an organisation's requirements for human resources while supply refers to the availability of these resources, both within the organisation and externally. Key stages within the traditional HRP process are largely derived from the techniques associated with manpower planning. The approach can be depicted in a number of different ways (see, for example, Armstrong, 2005; Bramham, 1988; Torrington *et al.*, 2002) but the models have a number of key features in common. All are essentially concerned with forecasting demand and supply and developing plans to meet any identified imbalance resulting from the forecasts.

The Bramham model has proved to be one of the most influential. It was initially devised in 1975 and the basic structure is still relevant, albeit with minor modifications, for example by Pilbeam and Corbridge (2002). This is the model used in this chapter as a framework for the key stages of traditional HRP; see Figure 5.1.

| Figure 5.1 | The process of human resource planning |

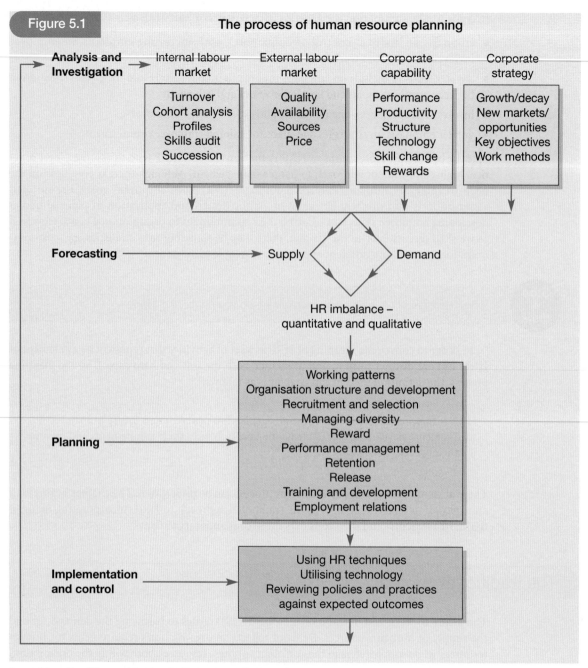

Source: Adapted from Pilbeam and Corbridge (2002), adapted from Bramham (1994).

Investigation and analysis

This stage is not explicit in all models but, arguably, those responsible for human resource planning need to know something about the current situation in order to assess the extent to which it is likely to alter or be affected by future developments.

Internal labour market

A combination of quantitative and qualitative data can provide a 'snapshot' of the existing workforce. This can include analysis of the workforce on a variety of levels such as skills, qualifications, length of experience and job type as well as on factors relating to equal opportunities, i.e. gender, ethnic origin, disability and age. This can help to ensure that the organisation is making most effective use of existing resources and can identify any potential problem areas; for example, if the composition of the workforce does not reflect the local community or if the organisation is not fully utilising the skills it has available. Movement through the organisation can also be investigated by tracking promotions, transfers and the paths of those in more senior positions.

External labour market

Investigation and analysis are primarily concerned with the availability of the type of labour the organisation requires at the price it can afford. It is likely that those responsible for human resource planning will need to collect data from local, national and international labour markets depending on the nature of jobs and the skills required. Data can be collected by formal and informal means, including local and national surveys, benchmarking and information provided by applicants on application forms and CVs. Analysis and investigation can potentially cover a broad range of issues as the external supply of labour can be affected by a number of factors.

Stop & think

What factors are likely to affect the external supply of human resources?

A number of factors can influence the availability of people and skills at both local and national level, for example:

- *competitor behaviour* – the activity of other firms operating in the same labour markets, i.e. expansion or contraction; whether organisations secure the necessary skills through training or poaching from other firms; comparative pay and conditions;
- *location* – whether or not the organisation is based in a location that is attractive and affordable for potential recruits; factors to be considered here might include the availability and cost of housing and the reputation of local schools;
- *transport links* – the availability and cost of public transport and accessibility of the organisation;
- *economic cycle* – can affect people's willingness to move jobs, e.g. people may be more concerned with job security in times of high unemployment;
- *unemployment levels* – nationally and regionally;
- *education output* – numbers and qualifications of school and college leavers, numbers going on to higher education;
- *legislation* – e.g. working hours, minimum wage, employment protection, flexible working.

Corporate capability

Data can be gathered to provide a snapshot of the current situation within the organisation in order to identify current strengths and weaknesses. Information on organisational performance can include productivity and service levels, turnover and profitability and these may be measured at organisational, unit or department level. Analysis may also relate to ways in which human resources are currently managed, e.g. the extent to which the current workforce structure, job design and reward systems enhance or restrict productivity and performance levels.

Corporate strategy

Whereas corporate capability is primarily concerned with the current situation in the organisation, corporate strategy focuses on future direction. Factors to be considered here might include the organisation's stage in its life cycle (see, for example, Kochan and Barocci, 1985); plans for consolidation or diversification; mergers, acquisitions and key organisational objectives. Each of these factors is likely to have some impact on the numbers and types of human resources required in the future. For example, a common consequence of mergers is for the rationalisation of merged activities to lead to a significant number of redundancies (CIPD, 2000).

Forecasting

The next stage in the process involves predicting how the need for and availability of human resources is likely to change in the future. Demand and supply forecasting can involve quantitative and qualitative techniques and the most popular approaches are outlined below.

Activity

This is an example of demand forecasting in a tyre and exhaust centre using the work study method. The main tasks have been classified as follows:

Key tasks	Hours per task
Exhausts	0.6
Tyres	0.3
Brakes	1.1

Forecasts jobs in 000s

	Year 1	Year 2	Year 3
Exhausts	30	31	32
Tyres	100	115	130
Brakes	25	29	34

Convert into total work hours (000s)

	Year 1	Year 2	Year 3
Exhausts	18	18.6	19.2
Tyres	30	34.5	39
Brakes	27.5	31.9	37.4
TOTAL	75.5	85	95.6

Convert into employees required (assuming 1800 hours/employee)

	Year 1	Year 2	Year 3
Employees (full-time equivalents)	41.9	47.2	53.1

What key external and internal factors are likely to affect the accuracy of these forecasts?

Forecasting the demand for human resources

Demand forecasting is concerned with estimating the numbers of people and the types of skills the organisation will need in the future. There are three main approaches to demand forecasting: objective methods, subjective methods and budgets.

Objective methods

Objective methods identify past trends, using statistical and mathematical techniques, and project these into the future to determine requirements. Three methods frequently referred to in the literature are time trends, ratio analysis and work study. Time trends consider patterns of employment levels over the past few years in order to predict the numbers required in the future. This can be undertaken either for the organisation as a whole or for sub-groups of employees. It can also be used to identify cyclical or seasonal variations in staffing levels. Ratio analysis bases forecasts on the ratio between some causal factor, e.g. sales volume, and the number of employees required, e.g. sales people (Dessler, 2003). Work study methods break jobs down into discrete tasks, measure the time taken to complete each component and then calculate the number of people-hours required. The effectiveness of this approach is largely determined by the ease with which the individual components of jobs can be measured. For many jobs, e.g. knowledge workers, this is extremely difficult and therefore work study will only be appropriate in certain circumstances. Even when it is appropriate, care has to be taken to avoid manipulation of timings by either employee or employer.

One of the major criticisms levelled at objective methods is that they are based on assumptions of continuity between past, present and future and are therefore only appropriate if the environment is relatively stable and productivity remains the same. In less stable environments, supplementary data on the causes of particular trends are necessary to distinguish between changes that are likely to recur and those that are not. Alternatively, past data can be used as a starting point and then amended to reflect potential or real productivity improvements.

Activity

Return to the forecasting exercise in the tyre and exhaust centre. This time management estimate that productivity improvements can be made each year as follows:

| | Time per job: | | |
	Year 1	Year 2	Year 3
Exhausts	0.6	0.55	0.5
Tyres	0.3	0.25	0.2
Brakes	1.1	1.05	1.0

Calculate the full-time equivalent employees required for each year, incorporating these improvements.

How does this affect employee demand?

Subjective methods

The most common approach used in demand forecasting is managerial judgement, i.e. managers estimate the human resources necessary for the achievement of corporate goals. Estimates are likely to be based on a combination of past experience, knowledge of changing circumstances and gut instinct. The approach is more flexible and adaptable than objective methods but is inevitably less precise. There is also a danger that forecasts will be manipulated due to organisational politics and 'empire building'. For example, managers may inflate estimates of future requirements because they want to increase the size of their department (and thus possibly protect or improve their own position) or because they expect that estimates will be cut and want to secure at least some improvements in staffing levels.

A more systematic use of the subjective approach is via the Delphi technique. A group of managers make independent forecasts of future requirements. The forecasts are then amalgamated, recirculated and managers then modify their estimates until some sort of consensus is reached. The process can help to minimise problems of manipulation in forecasts produced on an individual basis but, although the literature frequently refers to the technique as a common approach, empirical data suggest that it is rarely used in practice (Torrington et al., 2002).

Budgets

In this method the starting point is not past data but future budgets, i.e. what the organisation can spend if profit and market targets are met. According to Bramham (1988: 59), this is an extremely attractive approach: 'it has the supreme advantage that, in working from the future to the present, the manager is not necessarily constrained by past practices'. However, future budgets are likely to be determined, at least in part, by assumptions about changes to past and current performance and are still reliant on the accuracy of predictions.

These different approaches to demand forecasting can be combined to provide more comprehensive forecasts. So, for example, objective methods may be used to give an indication of future requirements but projections can then be modified by managerial judgement or to take account of budgetary constraints. Similarly, estimates based on ratio data may be adjusted to take account of productivity improvements resulting from new working methods or the introduction of new technology.

Forecasting the supply of human resources

Forecasts of internal supply are based primarily on labour turnover and the movement of people within the organisation. As with demand, the process for forecasting supply uses a combination of quantitative and qualitative techniques.

Measuring labour turnover – quantitative methods

The most common method of measuring labour turnover is to express leavers as a percentage of the average number of employees. The labour turnover index is usually calculated using the following formula:

$$\frac{\text{Number of leavers in a specified period}}{\text{Average number employed in the same period}} \times 100\%$$

This measure is used most effectively on a comparative basis and frequently provides the basis for external and internal benchmarking. Labour turnover can vary significantly between different sectors and industries; for example, a recent survey into labour turnover (CIPD, 2005) reports that the average labour turnover rate in the UK is 15.7 per cent but this varies between different industries and sectors. For example, 65 per cent in hotels, catering and leisure, 36 per cent in call centres and 12 per cent in the public sector. There is no single best level of labour turnover but external comparisons can be useful to benchmark labour turnover against other organisations in the same industry, sector or location. However, even organisations with lower than average turnover rates can experience problems if people have left from critical jobs or from posts that are difficult to fill. Conversely, high turnover is not necessarily problematic and might even prove useful if an organisation is seeking to reduce costs or reduce the numbers employed (Sadhev *et al.*, 1999). The main limitation of the labour turnover index is that it is a relatively crude measure that provides no data on the characteristics of leavers, their reasons for leaving, their length of service or the jobs they have left. So, while it may indicate that an organisation has a problem, it gives no indication about what the specific problem might be, nor what might be done to address it.

> *Example*
> Company A has 200 employees. During the year 40 employees have left from different jobs and been replaced. The turnover rate is 20 per cent.
>
> Company B also has an average of 200 employees. Over the year 40 people have left the same 20 jobs (i.e. each has been replaced twice). The turnover rate is also 20 per cent.

Limitations about the location of leavers within an organisation can be addressed to some extent by analysing labour turnover at department or business unit level or by job category. For example, managers generally have lower levels of resignation than other groups of employees (CIPD, 2005). Any areas with turnover levels significantly above or below organisational or job category averages can then be subject to further investigation. Most attention is levelled at the cost and potential disruption associated with high labour turnover. CIPD survey data (2005) estimates the average cost per leaver to be £4625. However, low levels of labour turnover should not be ignored as they may be equally problematic.

What are the key problems associated with low labour turnover?

Low labour turnover can cause difficulties as a lack of people with new ideas, fresh ways of looking at things and different skills and experiences can cause organisations to become stale and rather complacent. It can also be difficult to create promotion and development opportunities for existing employees.

Nevertheless, many organisations are keen for some levels of stability. While the labour turnover index focuses on leavers, the stability index focuses on the percentage of employees who have stayed throughout a particular period, often one year. This therefore allows organisations to assess the extent to which they are able to retain workers. The formula used to calculate stability is:

$$\frac{\text{Number of employees with 1 year's service at a given date}}{\text{Number employed 1 year ago}} \times 100\%$$

This can be a useful indicator of organisational stability but does require a pre-set decision about a relevant period for which it is important to retain staff. To return to our earlier example:

Company A has 160 employees with more than one year's service and has a stability rate of 80%.

Company B has 180 employees with more than one year's service and has a stability rate of 90%.

As with demand forecasting, labour turnover and stability indices are frequently used to project historical data into the future. So, for example, if an organisation identifies an annual turnover rate of 8 per cent it may build this into future projections of available supply. Alternatively, managerial judgement may predict a reduction or an increase in turnover rates in the light of current circumstances and forecasts can be adjusted accordingly.

More data on the length of service of leavers can be provided through the census method. This is essentially a 'snapshot' of leavers by length of service over a set period, often one year. Length of service has long been recognised as an influential factor in labour turnover. Hill and Trist (1955) identified three phases in labour turnover, the 'induction crisis', 'differential transit' and 'settled connection'. People are more likely to leave during the first few months, as the relationship between the individual and the organisation is unsettled and insecure, and less likely to leave the longer they are in the organisation. The census method can help to identify patterns of leavers and any key risk periods.

Another way of investigating the relationship between labour turnover and length of service is to consider the survival rate, i.e. the proportion of employees recruited in a specific year who are still with the organisation at a certain later date. So, for example, plotting the survival rate of a cohort of 30 graduate trainees might show that 12 remain with the organisation after five years, giving a survival rate of 40 per cent. It is also common to measure the half-life of a cohort, i.e. the time taken for the cohort to reduce to half its original size. Both survival rates and half-life measures can be useful for identifying problem periods and for succession planning purposes.

The major drawback with all quantitative methods of turnover analysis is that they provide no information on the reasons why people are leaving. So, for example, the census method may show that the highest proportion of people leave in the first six months but the information on its own does not show whether this is due to poor recruitment or induction practices, the nature of the job, management style or other factors. Thus, quantitative analyses can help to highlight problems but they give those responsible for planning no indication about how these problems might be addressed.

Measuring labour turnover – qualitative methods

Investigations into reasons for turnover are usually undertaken via qualitative means. A variety of approaches are used in UK organisations. The CIPD undertakes an annual survey of recruitment, retention and labour turnover and the most recent report (CIPD, 2005) shows the popularity of different methods (see Figure 5.2).

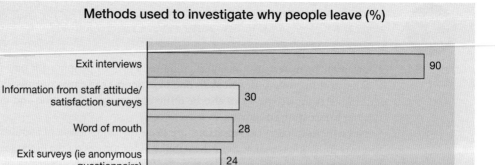

Figure 5.2 — Methods used to investigate why people leave (%)

Source: CIPD (2005: 29).

Exit interviews are by far the most commonly used methods of finding out why people leave. The benefits of exit interviews are that they are flexible enough to investigate reasons for leaving, identify factors that could improve the situation in the future and gather information on the terms and conditions offered by other organisations. Generally, exit interviews collect information on the following (IRS, 2001a):

- reasons for leaving;
- conditions under which the exiting employee would have stayed;
- improvements the organisation can make for the future;
- the pay and benefits package in the new organisation.

There can also be a number of problems. The interview may not discover the real reason for leaving, either because the interviewer fails to ask the right questions or probe sufficiently or because some employees may be reluctant to state the real reason in case this affects any future references or causes problems for colleagues who remain with the organisation, for example in instances of bullying or harassment. Conversely, some employees may choose this meeting to air any general grievances and exaggerate their complaints. Some organisations collect exit information via questionnaires. These can be completed during the exit interview or sent to people once they have left the organisation. They are often a series of tick boxes with some room for qualitative answers. The questionnaire format has the advantage of gathering data in a more systematic way which can make subsequent analysis easier. However, the standardisation of questions may reduce the amount of probing and self-completed questionnaires can suffer from a low response rate.

Reasons for leaving can be divided into four main categories:

- voluntary, controllable – people leaving the organisation due to factors within the organisation's control, e.g. dissatisfaction with pay, prospects, colleagues;
- voluntary, uncontrollable – people leaving the organisation due to factors beyond the organisation's control, e.g. relocation, ill-health;
- involuntary – determined by the organisation, e.g. dismissal, redundancy, retirement;
- other/unknown.

Attention is usually concentrated on leavers in the voluntary, controllable category as organisations can potentially take action to address the factors causing concern. However, distinctions between controllable and uncontrollable factors can become blurred. For example, in some instances, advances in technology and greater flexibility can facilitate the adoption of working methods and patterns to accommodate employees' domestic circumstances, while the 'reasonable adjustments' required under the Disability Discrimination Act can reduce the numbers of people forced to leave work on health grounds. The involuntary category is also worthy of attention as high numbers of controlled leavers can be indicative of organisational problems, e.g. a high dismissal rate might be due to poor recruitment or lack of effective performance management, while a high redundancy rate might reflect inadequate planning in the past.

The CIPD survey (CIPD, 2005) asked organisations to identify the main reasons for employee turnover and the most commonly cited reasons were as follows:

- Promotion outside the organisation (53%).
- Lack of development or career opportunities (42%).
- Change of career (41%).
- Level of pay (37%).

However, whilst exit interviews or exit surveys can provide some information about why people are leaving, they do not necessarily identify the triggers that made someone decide to leave. For example, someone might say that they are leaving to go to a job with better pay but this does not show what led the person to start looking for another job in the first place. In order to produce human resource plans that address labour turnover problems, organisations need to differentiate between 'push' and 'pull' factors. The former relate to factors within the organisation (e.g. poor line management, inadequate career opportunities, job insecurity, dissatisfaction with pay or hours of work) that weaken the psychological link between an individual and their employer (IRS, 2001a). Once an individual has decided to look for another job they are likely to base their decision on 'pull' factors, i.e. the attractions of the new job or organisation in relation to their existing circumstances. A report from the HR benchmark group (cited in IRS, 2002) listed the top five factors affecting an employee's decision to stay or leave an organisation as:

- the quality of the relationship with their supervisor or manager;
- an ability to balance work and home life;
- the amount of meaningful work and the feeling of making a difference;
- the level of cooperation with co-workers;
- the level of trust in the workplace.

One way to identify potential 'push' factors is to conduct attitude surveys within the organisation. Attitude surveys have an advantage over exit interviews and leaver questionnaires in that they can identify potential problems experienced by existing employees rather than those that have already decided to leave. This means that any response can be proactive rather than reactive. However, it also means that organisations can make problems worse if they do not act on the findings. 'Telling employees that an organisation cares enough to get their opinion and then doing nothing can exacerbate the negative feelings that already existed, or generate feelings that were not present beforehand' (IRS, 2002a: 40).

The final method to investigate labour turnover to be discussed here is risk analysis. This involves identifying two factors: the likelihood that an individual will leave and the consequences of the resignation (Bevan et al., 1997). Statistically, people who are younger, better qualified and who have shorter service, few domestic responsibilities, marketable skills and relatively low morale are most likely to leave (IRS, 2001b). The consequences of any resignations are likely to be determined by their position in the organisation, performance levels and the ease with which they can be replaced. The risk analysis grid (Bevan, 1997) shows how the two factors can be combined (Figure 5.3). This then enables the organisation to target resources or action at the people it would be most costly to lose.

Within human resource planning literature most attention is concentrated on forecasts of people joining and leaving the organisation but internal movement is also a key factor in

Figure 5.3	Risk analysis grid

Risk analysis grid

		Likelihood of leaving	
		High	*Low*
Impact on organisation	*High*	Danger zone	Watching brief
	Low	'Thanks for all you've done'	No immediate danger

Source: Bevan (1997: 34).

internal supply. Techniques to analyse movement of employees within an organisation are potentially more sophisticated than the techniques for analysing wastage rates but the most sophisticated tools, e.g. Markov chains and renewal models, are rarely used (Torrington et al, 2002). A simpler approach is to track employee movement to identify patterns of promotion and/or lateral mobility between positions as well as movement in and out of the organisation or function, see Figure 5.4.

In many respects forecasting is *the* key stage of traditional human resource planning. A combination of quantitative and qualitative methods can be used to determine the organisation's future requirements and the availability of human resources. Therefore much hinges on the accuracy of forecasting but there are a number of potential problems that can affect the reliability of any predictions. The first issue here is the difficulty of relying on past data to cope with a volatile and uncertain environment. Other problems can include the lack of reliable data, the manipulation of data for political ends and the low priority given to forecasting in many organisations.

Human resource plans

The likely results of forecasting activity are the identification of a potential mismatch between future demand and supply. If future demand is likely to exceed supply, then plans need to be developed to match the shortfall but if future supply is likely to exceed demand, then plans need to be developed to reduce the surplus. A number of options are illustrated in Figure 5.5.

While the detailed content of action plans will be determined by the nature of the imbalance between demand and supply and HR and corporate objectives, they are likely to cover at least some of the following areas:

- *working patterns* – e.g. balance of full-time and part-time workers, overtime, short-term contracts, annualised hours, job sharing, remote working;
- *organisation structure and development* – e.g. workforce size and structure, degree of centralisation, use of subcontracting;
- *recruitment and selection* – e.g. skills and experience required, main sources of applicants, methods to attract suitable candidates, recruitment freezes;

Figure 5.4 | Employee 'movements' in an organisation

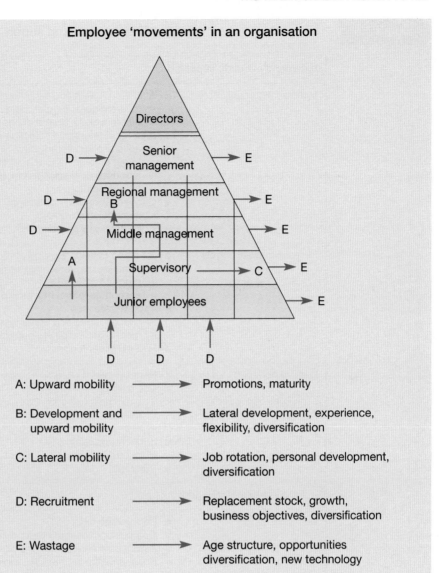

- *workforce diversity* – e.g. monitoring of current and prospective employees, equal opportunities/diversity policies, awareness training;
- *pay and reward* – e.g. mix of financial and non-financial rewards, use of contingent pay, market position;
- *performance management* – e.g. type of performance appraisal, links to reward, attendance management;
- *retention* – e.g. family friendly policies, terms and conditions, employee development;
- *training and development* – induction, training programmes, development reviews, education;
- *employment relations* – e.g. union recognition, communication, grievance and disciplinary policies;
- *release* – e.g. natural wastage, redundancy programmes, outplacement support.

Figure 5.5	Reconciling demand and supply

If demand exceeds supply:

Increase external supply	• Alter recruitment and selection criteria
	  – different ages, gender, ethnic origin
	  – different skills, qualifications and experience
	• Alter recruitment and selection practices
	  – advertise in different ways
	  – target different labour markets
	  – introduce new selection techniques
	  – offer relocation
	• Change terms and conditions
	  – more flexible working
	  – improve pay and benefits

Increase internal supply	• Train and develop existing staff
	• Alter internal movement patterns
	  – promote differently
	  – encourage lateral movement
	• Improve retention
	  – change terms and conditions
	  – more flexible working patterns
	• Reduce absenteeism

Reduce demand	• Redesign work
	• Use existing staff differently
	  – overtime
	  – multi-skilling
	  – high performance work teams
	• Subcontract work
	• Relocate work
	• Automate

If supply exceeds demand:

Decrease supply	• Early retirement • Compulsory/voluntary redundancy • Assisted career change and alternative employment • Secondments, sabbaticals, career breaks
Discourage retention	• Short-term contracts • Part-time contracts
Increase demand	• Increase markets for products and services • Diversification

Source: Adapted from Rothwell (1995).

The scope and content of plans are also influenced by the time-scales involved. Schuler (1998) suggests that the main phases of HRP should be undertaken for three different time horizons – short term (1 year), medium term (2–3 years) and long term (3 years+).

Advocates of human resource planning argue that the process helps to ensure vertical and horizontal integration, i.e. the alignment of human resource policies and practices with corporate goals and with each other. So, for example, plans to address supply shortages by altering selection criteria can influence the type of training required, the level of pay and reward offered to existing and prospective employees and the way the employment relationship is managed. However, in practice the situation is likely to be complicated by the fact that

Box 5.1 | Tackling skills shortages with overseas recruitment

In 2004, First's UK Bus Division was facing significant challenges in recruiting bus drivers and skilled engineers. These shortages were not unique to First, but a problem for the entire UK bus industry. Various recruitment drives within the UK had failed to fill the gaps and so First turned to Eastern Europe.

The initial pilot for overseas recruitment involved recruiting Polish bus drivers to First's biggest areas of driver shortage, its Bath depot. Poland was chosen for the pilot recruitment drive because the combination of high unemployment, low wages and a high proportion of graduates made the labour force an attractive proposition. First worked with EURES (the European Employment Services network) – the overseas wing of Jobcentre Plus and their corresponding agencies across Europe. This helped to establish strong European contacts and ensured that First was seen as a credible employer.

First looks for experienced people who also have basic grasp of the English language. Drivers must also pass the UK bus driver competency test covering the Highway Code, numeracy, safety and customer care. Once they have passed this assessment, the overseas recruits are offered a contract of employment on identical terms to any UK recruit. First further supports overseas recruits by arranging transport to the UK and finding suitable, high-quality rented accommodation, as well as providing help with opening bank accounts and applying for UK driving licences.

As a result of the initial recruitment programme, 36 Polish drivers and engineers arrived at Bath bus depot in May 2004 to start a four-week orientation and induction programme. By the following year more than 250 skilled drivers and engineers have been recruited to First's operating companies throughout the UK and the company is now working on recruiting 100 overseas workers every month. So far, the company has managed to retain all its overseas workers. First has now expanded its overseas recruitment activity to include Slovakia, Slovenia, Hungary, the Czech Republic and Portugal as well as Poland.

Source: based on IRS (2005)

Questions

1 What are the main short- and long-term implications of addressing UK skills shortages by recruiting from overseas?

2 What other options could be considered to address skills shortages?

the balance between demand and supply may vary in different parts of the organisation; for example, supply shortages may be identified in some areas while surpluses are predicted in others. The development of action plans can potentially help to ensure that managers are aware of significant inconsistencies. The adoption of a more holistic approach can therefore reduce some of the problems associated with these complexities; for example, an organisation may need to recruit some staff at the same time as it is making others redundant but knowledge of this can help to ensure that both activities are handled sensitively.

Implementation and control

The final stage of the traditional HRP process is concerned with implementation of HR plans and evaluation of their overall effectiveness. This stage of the model tends to be rather neglected in the literature but there is little point in developing comprehensive plans if they are not put into practice. Implementation of plans is likely to involve a number of different players, including line managers, employee representatives and employees, but the extent of involvement can vary considerably. The shift towards 'softer', more qualitative aspects of human resource planning places far more emphasis on the need to involve employees throughout the process (e.g. through the use of enhanced communication and tools such as attitude surveys) than is apparent in a 'harder' focus on headcount. Control relates to the extent to which the planning process has contributed to the effective and efficient utilisation of human resources and ultimately to the achievement of corporate objectives. The IPM (now CIPD) suggests three criteria for evaluating the effectiveness of the HRP process (IPM, 1992):

- the extent to which the outputs of HR planning programmes continue to meet changing circumstances;
- the extent to which HRP programmes achieve their cost and productivity objectives;
- the extent to which strategies and programmes are replanned to meet changing circumstances.

This latter point emphasises the need for the constant review and modification of human resource plans in the light of changing circumstances. One of the main criticisms levelled at traditional approaches to HRP has been the inflexibility of plans resulting from the extrapolation of past data and assumptions about the future. The emphasis on flexibility is much more explicit in later models of HRP as the purpose of HRP has become less concerned with ensuring continuity and more on enabling organisations to adapt within unpredictable environments.

Human resource planning – a contemporary approach

Armstrong (2005) has modified the phases of traditional human resource planning to reflect aims more appropriate for contemporary circumstances. He outlines these aims as:

- to attract and retain the number of people required with the appropriate skills, expertise and competences;
- to anticipate problems of potential surpluses or deficits of people;
- to develop a well-trained and flexible workforce, thus contributing to the organisation's ability to adapt to an uncertain and changing environment;
- to reduce dependence on external recruitment when key skills are in short supply by formulating retention and development strategies;
- to improve the utilisation of people by introducing more flexible systems of work.

This approach differs from traditional HRP in that it puts greater emphasis on the 'soft' side of HRP but there are still elements of the 'hard' approach, e.g. in the balance between demand and supply forecasting. It also differs from the traditional approach in its emphasis on the internal labour supply. The key stages of the model are shown in Figure 5.6.

A fundamental difference between this model and the traditional HRP model is the underlying assumption that much of the process might be rather vague:

> It cannot be assumed that there will be a well-articulated business plan as a basis for the HR plans. The business strategy may be evolutionary rather than deliberate; it may be fragmented, intuitive and incremental. Resourcing decisions may be based on scenarios that are riddled with assumptions that may or may not be correct and cannot be tested. Resourcing strategy may be equally vague or based on unproven beliefs about the future. It may contain statements, about for example building the skills base, that are little more than rhetoric.
>
> (Armstrong, 2005: 369)

Such statements could lead one to question whether there is any point to the process at all! Armstrong (2005) goes on to argue that even if all that is achieved is a broad statement of intent, 'this could be sufficient to guide resourcing practice generally and would be better

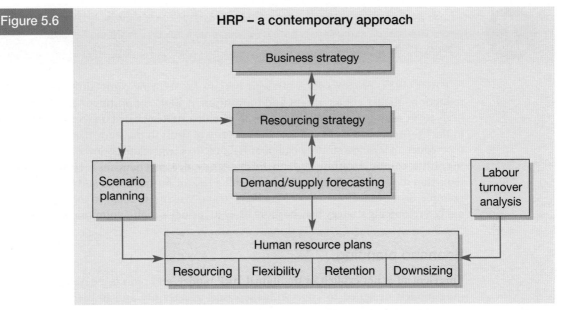

Source: Adapted from Armstrong (2005) *A Handbook Resource Management Practice*, p. 370. Reprinted with permission of Kogan Page.

than nothing at all'. However, this does suggest that any plans inevitably have to be tentative, flexible and reviewed and modified on a regular basis.

Business strategy

The first key element of this model is business strategy. Strategy has been defined as:

> the direction and scope of an organisation over the long-term, which achieves competitive advantage for the organisation through its configuration of resources within a changing environment and to fulfil stakeholder expectations.
> (Johnson and Scholes, 2002: 10)

Business strategy can be either deliberate or emergent (Whittington, 1993). Deliberate strategies assume a rational evaluation of external and internal circumstances and an identification of the best way to ensure competitive advantage. Emergent strategies, on the other hand, are the product of market forces: 'the most appropriate strategies . . . emerge as competitive processes that allow the relatively better performers to survive while the weaker performers are squeezed out' (Legge, 1995: 99).

Resourcing strategy

In this model the resourcing strategy derives from the business strategy and also feeds into it. For example, the identification of particular strengths and capabilities might lead to new business goals, especially if strategy formation is emergent rather than deliberate. The rationale underpinning Armstrong's perception of this strategy is related to the resource-based view of the firm (see Chapter 2): 'the aim of this strategy is therefore to ensure that a firm achieves competitive advantage by employing more capable people than its rivals' (Armstrong, 2005: 371). Thus, the implicit assumption is that the vertical integration between business strategy and resourcing strategy will include practices designed to attract and retain a high-quality workforce, such as offering rewards and opportunities that are better than competitors and seeking to maximise commitment and trust.

Stop & think

Under what circumstances might a high-commitment resourcing strategy not be appropriate for an organisation?

Porter (1985) proposes three strategic options for securing competitive advantage: cost reduction, quality enhancement and innovation. A high-commitment approach is more likely to 'fit' with the latter two strategies than with a strategy based on cost reduction. Work in the US (Arthur, 1992) found that the majority of firms in the study that were following a cost reduction business strategy had poor HR practices (e.g. relatively low pay, minimal training, little communication and no formal grievance mechanisms). However, the cost reduction model is frequently associated with a lack of formalisation and planning (see, for example, Sisson and Storey, 2000; Marchington and Wilkinson, 2005) so the process of developing a resourcing strategy may be more likely to include a high-commitment approach.

Scenario planning

This element is not explicit in traditional HRP models and reflects a development in planning models designed to cope with increased uncertainty and unpredictability in the environment. Scenario planning can be used to supplement or replace more traditional demand and supply forecasting. This approach is 'predicated on the assumption that if you cannot predict *the* future, then by speculating on a variety of them, you might just hit upon the right one' (Mintzberg, 1994: 248). Mintzberg (1994) argues that it is difficult to determine the required number of scenarios, i.e. enough to have a good chance of getting it right but not so many as to be unmanageable. The ease with which scenario planning can be undertaken has been greatly improved by the use of computer modelling, in which figures and formulae can be altered to calculate the implications of different predictions. However, this can in itself lead to problems of information overload and difficulties in how to respond to the results. Porter (1985) suggests five key options:

- Bet on the most probable one.
- Bet on the best one for the organisation.
- Hedge bets so as to get satisfactory results no matter which one results.
- Preserve flexibility.
- Exert influence to make the most desirable scenario a reality.

This approach can help to broaden perspectives and consider a number of future options but each decision has its own costs and these also need to be considered. For example, opting to preserve flexibility might be at the expense of following a clear-cut business strategy to secure competitive advantage. Similarly, devoting resources to the best scenario for the organisation might be little more than wishful thinking.

Scenario planning has been described here as a fairly formal process but it can also be regarded as an informal approach to thinking about the future in broad terms, based upon an analysis of likely changes in the internal and external environment (Armstrong, 2005).

Forecasting and labour turnover

Demand and supply forecasting in the model includes all the objective and subjective techniques described in the traditional model. The key difference lies in the emphasis given to labour turnover analysis; in the traditional model this is seen as an element of supply forecasting but here it is deemed worthy of its own category. Nevertheless, the techniques used to measure it are the same as discussed earlier in the chapter.

Human resource plans

Human resource plans are derived from the resourcing strategy and take into account data from a combination of scenario planning, demand and supply forecasting and labour turnover analysis. The model again reflects the lack of certainty and predictability: 'the plans often have to be short term and flexible because of the difficulty of making firm predictions about human resource requirements in times of rapid change' (Armstrong, 2005: 382). The plans can be divided into four broad areas: resourcing, flexibility, retention and downsizing.

Resourcing plan

This is primarily concerned with effective use of the internal labour market as well as attracting high-quality external applicants. Armstrong (2005) identifies three main components to the resourcing plan: internal resourcing, i.e. the availability of suitable people from within the organisation and plans to make better use of existing employees; the recruitment plan (e.g. numbers and types of people required, sources of candidates, recruitment techniques, etc.) and the 'employer of choice' plan. Steps that organisations have taken to find additional sources of applicants to address skills shortages and improve the diversity of the workforce are discussed in Chapter 6, so here we highlight some of the initiatives used to make employers more attractive to high-quality applicants. The CIPD Recruitment, Retention and Labour Turnover Survey (2005) found that over a third of employers have increased starting salaries or benefits for recruits and a quarter have offered flexible working hours. Some organisations also offer 'golden hellos' (financial inducements to new recruits), particularly to graduates. The CIPD survey (2005) found that only 4 per cent of respondents offered 'golden hellos' but this may be because the practice is mainly restricted to larger organisations. This practice originated in the private sector but over recent years has been used to address skills shortages in the public sector, e.g. teaching and some areas of local government. The main reasons for introducing a golden hello (IRS, 2001c) are:

- to ease recruitment difficulties;
- as a response to competition;
- to help graduates settle in a new job;
- to help retain staff.

 Stop & think

To what extent would you be more attracted to an employer that offered a 'golden hello' than one that did not? What other factors would you take into account?

In addition to being able to attract high-quality applicants, organisations also have to be able to keep them. Other initiatives to become an 'employer of choice' might include providing opportunities for development and career progression and addressing work–life balance issues. Williams (2000) takes this a step further by arguing that organisations need to create the right environment in order to win 'the war for talent':

> In essence, creating a winning environment consists of developing a high-achieving company with values and brand images of which employees can be proud. At the same time, their jobs should permit a high degree of freedom, give them a chance to leave a personal mark and inject a constant flow of adrenalin. Leadership, of course, should be used to enhance, enable and empower, rather than to inhibit, constrain or diminish. (Williams, 2000: 31)

Flexibility plan

The flexibility plan is likely to involve the use of functional and numerical flexibility (discussed more fully in Chapter 4). Armstrong (2005: 384) suggests that the aim of the flexibility plan should be to:

- provide for greater operational flexibility;
- improve the utilisation of employees' skills and capabilities;
- reduce employment costs;
- help to achieve downsizing smoothly and avoid the need for compulsory redundancies;
- increase productivity.

From this perspective, flexibility appears to be mainly employer-driven rather than a means to help employees achieve work–life balance and therefore there may be some potential contradictions between this and the 'employer of choice' plan described above. Alternatively, it may be that different plans can be applied to different sections of the workforce. Purcell (1999) suggests that distinctions are growing in the treatment of core workers, who may be nurtured owing to their contribution to competitive advantage, and non-core peripheral or subcontracted workers.

The retention plan

Manfred Kets de Vries (cited in Williams, 2000: 28) stated that 'today's high performers are like frogs in a wheelbarrow: they can jump out at any time'. It seems that increasing numbers of organisations recognise this and are turning their attention to the retention of key staff. The exact components of the retention plan will be largely determined by the outcomes of labour turnover analysis and risk analysis and initiatives are likely to focus on 'pull' factors. Findings from the CIPD recruitment, retention and turnover survey (CIPD, 2005) show the most common steps taken by organisations to improve retention:

- Improved employee communication/involvement.
- Increased learning and development opportunities.
- Improved induction process.
- Increased pay.
- Improved selection techniques.
- Changes to improve work–life balance.
- Improved line management HR skills.
- Revised the way staff are rewarded so their efforts are better recognised.
- Offered coaching/mentoring/buddy systems.

Stop & think

How might these different practices improve retention? Which might be most effective for the retention of graduates?

Attention to the skills and abilities of managers is perceived by some as a key element of retention: 'put simply, employees leave managers not companies' (Buckingham, 2000: 45). Buckingham (2000) argues that employees are more likely to remain with an organisation if they believe that their manager shows interest and concern for them; if they know what is expected of them; if they are given a role that fits their capabilities; and if they receive regular positive feedback and recognition. However, he also suggests that 'most organisations currently devote far fewer resources to this level of management than they do to high-fliers' (p. 46).

Box 5.2 | **Improving retention at the Student Loans Company**

The Student Loans Company employs approximately 600 staff at its call centre in Glasgow. The city is home to a large proportion of the UK's call centre operations and so the organisation faces stiff competition for staff and the risk of losing them to other companies is always present. As a non-departmental government body, the organisation is constrained in how it can compete with other companies, some of whom may be able to offer higher salaries and perks.

Staff retention is particularly important for the Student Loans Company because operator roles are complex and require in-depth knowledge. There is also a long training period and the annual cycle of student loans means that it takes a year for a new employee to experience the different demands and issues associated with the job. As a result of the lengthy training and the time it takes for employees to be fully productive, the organisation estimates the cost of labour turnover as almost £5000 per person.

The Student Loans Company has introduced a competency-based approach to recruitment and selection, which enables the organisation to assess whether or not applicants can demonstrate competency in the necessary core qualities and thus helps to recruit the right people for the job. The complexity and knowledge requirements of the role mean that call centre operators enjoy more variation than in many call centres. However, the front-line nature of the work requires a certain amount of resilience.

The organisation is very supportive of new starters: induction begins with a formal two-week classroom-based programme before new employees join their teams in the call centre. This is followed by feedback meetings at the end of the first and second months of employment and a formal review at the end of the three-month probationary period. In addition, ongoing on-the-job training is provided by coaches and team leaders.

These improvements in recruitment and training have helped to reduce staff turnover from 40% to 20%.

Source: based on IRS (2006).

Questions

1 What steps would you recommend to improve retention even further?

2 How might your recommendations be best implemented?

3 How would you monitor the effectiveness of action taken?

Downsizing plan

The fourth element of the human resource plan is the downsizing plan. This is concerned with the numbers to be 'downsized', the timing of any reductions and the process itself. Methods of reducing the size of the workforce include natural wastage, redeployment, early retirement, voluntary and compulsory redundancy. Armstrong (2005: 387) implies that this plan is implemented as a last resort: 'if all else fails, it may be necessary to deal with unacceptable employment costs or surplus numbers of employees by what has euphemistically come to be known as downsizing'. However, other commentators suggest that downsizing is fairly endemic in the UK:

> The lack of labour market protection, the weakness of unions and the intense pressure on private and public sector companies alike to improve their profitability and efficiency have meant that the fashionable doctrine of downsizing has spread like contagion.
>
> (Hutton, 1997: 40)

Hutton was writing in the late 1990s but it is still relatively easy to find examples of organisations radically reducing the size of the workforce. For example, Shell plans to lay off 4000 staff (Griffiths, 2003) and Corus plans to lose a further 3000 (Harrison, 2003). Several studies (e.g. Bennet, 1991; Cascio, 1993) suggest that downsizing frequently fails to bring the anticipated cost savings for organisations, leading Redman and Wilkinson (2001: 319) to state that 'despite the real sufferings of many workers in an era of redundancy there have been few long-term benefits to justify its level of severity, nor an overwhelming economic justification for its continuing blanket use'.

'It's human resource planning, Jim, but not as we know it'

Changes in organisational structures and the uncertainty of the environment have led to the development of more flexible and focused approaches to planning. Taylor (2005) suggests a number of variants on the traditional planning process that may be more appropriate to organisations with unpredictable markets and structures.

Micro-planning uses similar techniques to more traditional HRP but concentrates on key problem areas rather than the organisation as a whole. The more limited scope, both in terms of coverage and time, makes the process more manageable and the results more immediately visible. Micro-planning is likely to be a one-off activity rather than an ongoing process. It can be used to address a variety of issues such as skills shortages, new legislation, competitor activity or a new business opportunity.

Contingency planning is based on scenario planning and enables organisations to draw up a number of different plans to deal with different scenarios. This can enable HRP to switch from being a reactive process undertaken in order to assist the organisation achieve its aims, to become a proactive process undertaken prior to the formulation of wider organisational objectives and strategies (Taylor, 2005: 107). On the other hand, Mintzberg (1994: 252) argues that, in practice, contingency planning presents several problems. Firstly, the contingency that does occur may not be one that was thought of; and secondly, the presentation of a number of different options may lead to no action at all – 'paralysis by analysis'.

In succession planning the focus is primarily on recruitment and retention and the ability of the organisation to fill key posts. It is likely that this will relate to a relatively narrow group of people. There is nothing new about organisations identifying and grooming people to fill key posts; in fact, succession planning has always been an element of traditional HRP. The traditional approach relied on identifying a few key individuals who would be ready to take on senior roles at certain points in time. However, to be effective, this requires a stable environment and long-term career plans. In response to a rapidly changing environment where the future is uncertain, the focus has moved away from identifying an individual to fill a specific job towards developing talent for groups of jobs and planning for jobs that do not yet exist. In addition, the emphasis is on balancing the needs of the organisation with the aspirations of employees and on increasing the diversity of the senior management group in terms of competencies and qualities (IRS, 2002).

Succession planning is often linked to competency frameworks and the key challenge is to identify the competencies that will contribute to future organisational performance rather than those that have been valued in the past. Astra Zeneca identifies seven leadership competencies: provides clarity about strategic direction, builds relationships, ensures commitment, develops people, focuses on delivery, builds self-awareness and demonstrates personal conviction (IRS, 2002: 42). Holbeche (2000) cites the five key types of skills, knowledge and aptitude critical to future success identified by Brent Allred et al.:

- *technical specialisms, including computer literacy* – the ability to make practical use of information is more likely to lead to career advancement than the management of people;
- *cross-functional and international experience* – the ability to create and manage multidisciplinary teams and projects;
- *collaborative leadership* – the ability to integrate quickly into new or existing teams;

Box 5.3 Succession planning at Britvic Soft Drinks

Britvic employs more than 3000 people across 20 different UK sites. The company has taken a formal approach to career development and succession planning for several years and has developed a Senior Management Development Programme (SMDP) to help identify, develop and retain a succession pool of senior talent.

Line managers are closely involved in assessing people's potential through the performance management system and can nominate people who they believe are suitable. Twice a year the company holds an assessment event to identify potential for the SMDP. The event includes a business simulation, two personality questionnaires, competency-based interviews and role-plays.

The programme comprises a range of leading-edge learning opportunities. Britvic collaborates with specialised management and leadership schools, including Cranfield and Henley, in order to design executive-level development programmes. The learning programme is tailored to an individual's specific learning needs and activities include internal job moves with a big emphasis on cross-functional work experience. There is an online learning facility and all participants have a mentor. At least half of the people currently on the programme are also involved in a large-scale strategic project in addition to their main role.

Source: based on IRS (2005).

Questions

1 What are the main benefits of this type of succession planning for the organisation and individuals?

2 What potential drawbacks also need to be considered?

- *self-managing skills* – with an emphasis on continuous development and the ability to manage work–life balance;
- *flexibility* – including the ability to take the lead on one project and be a team-member on another.

Another key issue in contemporary succession planning concerns the balance between internal and external labour markets. Succession planning can be used as a means to retain and motivate key members of the existing workforce but there is a danger that the organisation can become stale in the absence of 'new blood'. Some senior external appointments are therefore necessary to improve diversity and to bring on board people with different skills and experience but too many can result in frustration and the loss of some key talent.

Skills planning, an adaptation of traditional HRP, moves away from a focus on planning for people to one that looks primarily at the skills required (Taylor, 2005). Forecasting concentrates on the identification of competencies necessary for future organisational performance rather than on the numbers and types of people required. Skills planning builds on the ideas inherent in Armstrong's (2005) flexibility plan in its assumption that the required skills might be secured by a variety of means, including short-term contracts, agency workers, subcontracting, outsourcing, etc.

Various meanings of soft human resource planning were discussed earlier in the chapter. Taylor (2005: 111) interprets this in its relatively narrow sense, i.e. as a distinct range of activities focusing on forecasting the supply and demand for particular attitudes and behaviours rather than attitudes and skills. Part of this process involves gathering data on employee attitudes in a number of areas, e.g. motivation, job satisfaction, management effectiveness and commitment to the organisation. This can be done in a variety of ways, such as employee interviews, attitude surveys and focus groups. Attitude surveys continue to grow in popularity: survey data (IRS, 2001d) found that 66 per cent of respondents are currently using them and a further 21 per cent are either planning to use them in the next year or are seriously considering their use in the future. The same study (IRS, 2001d: 8) found the main topics covered in attitude surveys to be:

- management style and performance;
- internal communication;
- personal morale;
- job satisfaction;
- organisation's values;
- career development opportunities;
- personal motivation;
- working environment;
- working conditions;
- teamwork;
- training opportunities;
- assessment of senior management;
- training needs;
- relations with immediate colleagues;
- pay and benefits.

As in traditional HRP, forecasting is also concerned with external supply issues. The main difference is that soft HRP is less concerned with the availability of people and skills than with the attitudes and expectations of potential employees. Schuler (1998: 79) highlights the different expectations and values of three distinct age groups in today's workforce:

- *Traditionalists* (born between 1925 and 1945) value job security, employment security and income security.
- *Baby Boomers* (born between 1946 and 1964) tend to value trust and authority; see work as a duty and a means to financial wealth; and expect that performance will be rewarded more than years of experience.
- *Generation X* (born between 1965 and 1985) value recognition and praise; time with their managers; opportunities to learn new things; fun at work; unstructured, flexible time; and small, unexpected rewards for jobs well done.

 Stop & think *What are the main implications of these different expectations and values for effective people management?*

Acting on the results of attitude surveys and assessments of broader societal expectations can help organisations attract and retain the attitudes believed necessary for future success. Retention can be viewed as one of the key aims of soft HRP, but again the concern is less with keeping specific people and more to do with securing commitment and loyalty to the organisation. One way to achieve this is through career management, i.e. processes to encourage the progression of individuals in line with personal preferences and capabilities and organisational requirements. Like succession planning, this can provide a potential win–win situation in that employees gain opportunities for development and feel valued while the organisation is able to fill posts internally. However, it can be difficult to sustain in times of uncertainty when job security is threatened.

The advantages and disadvantages of human resource planning

HRP, in both its traditional and more contemporary forms, can be perceived to have a number of distinct advantages. Firstly, it is argued that planning can help to reduce uncertainty as long as plans are adaptable. Although unpredictable events do occur, the majority of organisational change does not happen overnight so the planning process can provide an element of control, even if it is relatively short term. Taylor (2005: 102) suggests that in the HR field there is potentially more scope for change and adaptation in six months than there is in relation to capital investment in new plant and machinery. Thus he argues that many of the assumptions about the difficulties of planning generally are less relevant to HR.

Other advantages relate to the contribution of planning to organisational performance. For example, the planning process can make a significant contribution to the integration of HR policies and practices with each other and with the business strategy, i.e. horizontal and vertical integration. Marchington and Wilkinson (2005: 159) suggest that HR plans can be developed to 'fit' with strategic goals or they can contribute to the development of the business strategy, but conclude that 'either way, HRP is perceived as a major facilitator of competitive advantage'. Another way that HRP can contribute is by helping to build flexibility into the organisation, either through the use of more flexible forms of work or through identification of the skills and qualities required in employees.

One of the key problems with planning relates to the difficulties of developing accurate forecasts in a turbulent environment but this does not reduce the need for it. Rothwell (1995: 178) suggests that 'the need for planning may be in inverse proportion to its feasibility', while Liff (2000: 96) argues that 'the more rapidly changing environment . . . makes the planning process more complex and less certain, but does not make it less important or significant'. Bramham (1988, 1989) states that the process is more important in a complex environment and uses a navigation metaphor to emphasise the point:

> The good navigator uses scientific methods in applying his [sic] knowledge and skills, within the limits of the equipment available, in order to establish first his position and then his best possible course and speed, with a view to arriving at the chosen destination by the most suitable route. From time to time during the voyage he will take fresh readings; calculate what action is necessary to compensate for hitherto unforeseen changes in wind, current and weather; and adjust his course accordingly. If the wind changes dramatically the navigator is not likely to abandon compass and sextant, go below and pray to God to get him to port. He is more likely to apply his knowledge and skills to a reassessment of his position and course as soon as it is practicable.
>
> (Smith, 1976, cited in Bramham, 1988: 6)

This metaphor suggests that HRP can make a significant contribution to the achievement of strategic goals but does imply that the destination remains constant even if other factors change. It also suggests that the person responsible for planning has sufficient information on which to make accurate judgements. Sisson and Storey (2000) argue that the planning process is based on two, highly questionable assumptions: firstly, that the organisation has the necessary personnel information to engage in meaningful HR and succession planning; and secondly, that there are clear operational plans flowing from the business strategy. Furthermore, they suggest that business planning is incremental rather than linear and therefore 'the implication is that the would-be planner will never have the neat and tidy business plan that much of the prescriptive literature takes for granted' (p. 55).

Other key criticisms of the process relate particularly to the difficulties of forecasting accurately. Mintzberg (1994) highlights problems in predicting not only the changes to come but also the type of changes, i.e. whether they are likely to be repeated or are a one-off event. Incorrect forecasts can be expensive but accurate forecasts might provide only limited competitive advantage if other organisations also adopt them:

> The ability to forecast accurately is central to effective planning strategies. If the forecasts turn out to be wrong, the real costs and opportunity costs . . . can be considerable. On the other hand, if they are correct they can provide a great deal of benefit – if the competitors have not followed similar planning strategies.
>
> (Makridakis, 1990, cited in Mintzberg, 1994: 229)

Furthermore, Mintzberg (1994) argues that the reliability of forecasts diminishes as the time-scale of projections increases: two or three months may be 'reasonable' but three or four years is 'hazardous'. This is because predictions are frequently based on extrapolations from the past, adjusted by assumptions about the future so there is considerable room for error in both.

The relevance of HRP to contemporary organisations can also be questioned. Taylor (2005) argues that the traditional systematic approach is still appropriate for large organisations operating in relatively stable product and labour markets but other conditions might be less compatible. For example, moves towards decentralisation and the devolution of HR matters to managers at business unit level can make detailed planning impractical. At the same time, the increased fluidity in some organisational structures (e.g. the emphasis on flatter structures, the absence of clearly delineated jobs and the variety of contractual arrangements) can be incompatible with some objective methods of forecasting. Finally, the short-term focus evident in many UK organisations means that long-term planning is just not given high priority.

Human resource planning in practice

While much is written about HRP in theory, evidence about its application in practice is harder to obtain. The 1998 Workplace Employee Relations Survey (Cully *et al.*, 1999) reports that 91 per cent of managers with senior responsibility for employment relations include 'staffing or manpower planning' in their list of tasks. Analysis of data from this and the two previous workplace surveys (Millward *et al.*, 2000) shows a shift in responsibility for HRP. The proportion of HR specialists with responsibility for HRP declined from 87 per cent in 1984 to 80 per cent in 1990 and remained stable at 80 per cent in 1998, while the proportion of non-specialists with responsibility for HRP has increased from 85 per cent in 1984 to 90 per cent in 1998. This could be seen as indicative of a general trend in the devolution of people management matters to line and general managers. However, HRP seems to be a unique case as, of the six HR functions covered in the surveys, reduced responsibility for HRP is 'the only enduring change' (Millward *et al.*, 2000: 62). There are significant sectoral variations in this shift: the proportion of HR specialists with responsibility for 'staffing or manpower planning' declined in the private sector but increased substantially in the public sector. However, the scope for different interpretations inherent in the term 'staffing or manpower planning' means that we know little about the type of HRP activity actually carried out and so are unable to draw firm conclusions about the reasons for shifts in responsibility.

There is also the potential danger that the high proportion of respondents reporting HRP activity could be indicative of intent rather than actual practice. A number of authors (see, for example, Liff, 2000; Rothwell, 1995) have noted the gap between widespread claims and relatively limited activity. Storey (1992) observed that the majority of companies in his sample would have 'ticked' survey questions about HRP, but a substantial number were not doing it. In the past, studies investigating HRP in practice (e.g. Mackay and Torrington, 1986; Cowling and Walters, 1990) have tended to find evidence of only partial activity and limited implementation of any plans. Rothwell (1995: 178–179) suggests four principal reasons for the lack of empirical proof of HRP activity:

- The extent of change impacting on organisations makes planning too problematic, even though there is a growing need for it. This might also explain why plans, even if developed, are rarely implemented.

- The need to account for the 'shifting kaleidoscope of policy priorities' (p. 178) and the relatively weak power-base of the HR function meaning that either inadequate resources are devoted to planning activities or there is a lack of ability to ensure implementation of plans.

- The preference for pragmatism and the distrust of theory and planning prevalent amongst UK management and the potential inconsistencies in organisational goals, e.g. need for consistency and flexibility, for prediction and planning and speed of response, etc.

- Research into HRP is often over-theoretical and fails to take sufficient account of organisational reality. A lot of HRP activity is undertaken but because it is on an ad hoc rather than a systematic basis it is frequently discounted by researchers.

This last reason could help to account for the potential discrepancy between the proportion of managers reporting involvement in 'staffing or manpower planning' in WERS and the limited evidence of systematic planning activity in more detailed studies. In his study into people management practices in SMEs, Hendry (1995) found some evidence of HRP-related activities (e.g. managers considered recruitment and selection, training and pay in relation to issues identified in labour and product markets) but approaches tended to be tentative and incremental rather than classical and rational.

The need for human resource planning activity has been identified in some areas of the public sector, particularly in response to specific skills shortages. The Local Government Pay and Workforce Strategy (2005: 6) identifies the 'top ten' public sector skills shortages as social workers, occupational therapists, environmental health officers, trading standards officers, residential social workers, planning officers, building control officers, educational psychologists, teachers and librarians. In order to address this issue the report advocates 'an appropriate system of workforce planning that:

- Projects workforce trends for individual authorities and identifies future staff numbers and skills needed

- Includes gender, race and disability data

- Analyses future changes such as use of technology in service improvement and reduction in needs for services' (www.lg-employers.gov.uk)

This suggests that human resource planning activity still has contemporary relevance, at least in intent if not in practice

HRP and strategic HRM

The concept of strategic human resource management (SHRM) has many different interpretations (as discussed in Chapter 2) and 'different definitions carry different assumptions, assert different causal relationships, even seek different goals' (Mabey *et al.*, 1998: 58). Nevertheless, there are two key assumptions that are particularly relevant to the role of HRP: firstly, human resources are the key source of competitive advantage; and secondly, the importance of vertical and horizontal integration. The need for planning is therefore a key component of SHRM in that it can help organisations determine the best use of human resources to meet organisational goals and can facilitate the integration of HR policies and practices with each other and with the business strategy.

Planning is such a key component of SHRM that the terms planning and strategy are sometimes used interchangeably, for example: 'the key message of the HRM literature is the need to establish a close, two-way relationship between business strategy or planning and strategic HRM strategy or planning' (Beaumont, 1992: 40). However, it is useful to differentiate between the HRP process and the long-term HR strategy of the organisation. Brews and Hunt (1999) highlight the difference between ends and means; ends relate to what an organisation desires to achieve while means relate to how it intends to achieve them. Thus, the HRP process produces action plans (means) to help the organisation achieve its key objectives or strategy (ends).

Many of the SHRM models are particularly concerned with the notion of 'fit', i.e. the matching of HR policies and practices with the business or product strategy (see, for example, Kochan and Barrocci, 1985: Fombrun *et al.*, 1984; Schuler and Jackson, 1987). The models have been subject to criticism on a number of grounds (see Chapter 2 for a more detailed discussion of the key criticisms). Criticisms relate principally to the over-simplification of the concepts of strategy and 'fit'; for example, 'both these elements are much more complex and uncertain in reality than they are in many SHRM models' (Mabey *et al.*, 1998: 81). This complexity and ambiguity challenges a number of assumptions underpinning SHRM models, for example: the assumption that a preferred business strategy can be identified; that consistency in HR practices can be achieved; and that these practices can be implemented with no resistance from the human resources involved. While these logistical problems are recognised, the process of HRP can help to identify the preferred approach (or approaches, if scenario planning is used) and attempt to predict any potential barriers to implementation.

At the very least, HRP allows managers to consider a range of solutions rather than feeling pressurised into adopting a knee-jerk reaction to avoid a crisis. Lam and Schaubroeck (1998: 5) go further and argue that:

> Planning is critical to strategy because it identifies gaps in capabilities which would prevent successful implementation; surpluses in capabilities that suggest opportunities for enhancing efficiencies and responsiveness; and poor utilisation of highly valued organisational resources because of inappropriate HR practices.

This emphasises the need for a two-way relationship between business strategy and HR strategy. However, in the UK it appears that 'the dominant model of the link between business plans and HR plans sees HR as the 'dependent variable' – fleshing out the personnel implications of pre-determined business plans, implementing appropriate policies to fulfil the requirements identified' (Liff, 2000: 98). Lam and Schaubroeck (1998) found that, in the majority of organisations in their study, the approach to planning was operational rather than strategic. This reflects findings from another study into HRP in large UK organisations (Hercus, 1992) which noted that the priority given to HRP was largely determined by a mismatch between demand and supply. Four of the eight firms had made significant staff reductions in response to difficult economic conditions and 'as they emerged from this period, HR planning has been given priority ... because of the shortages of professionals and skilled employees, and corporate goals emphasising productivity improvement and quality' (Hercus, 1992: 422). Thus, even if HR is the 'dependent variable', HRP can contribute to the achievement of organisational goals.

HRP has a role to play even in the absence of a clear-cut strategy. Sisson and Storey (2000) suggest that:

> The would-be HR planner will never have the neat and tidy business plans that so much of the prescriptive literature takes for granted. Even so, pressure has to be applied to secure operational plans, however rudimentary, if there is to be any sensible attempt to forecast the number of employees and their skills.
> (Sisson and Storey, 2000: 59)

However, Boxall and Purcell (2003: 235) argue that 'it is not a question of choosing between short-term or long-run planning systems. Both forms of planning are important and HR planning needs to play an appropriate role in both.' They also cite research (Koch and McGrath, 1996) that shows that labour productivity is better in organisations that formally

plan for their future human resource needs. The study by Brews and Hunt (1999) also identifies a link between improvements in organisational performance and the HRP process but
the findings indicate that this only becomes apparent after at least four years of formal planning. Thus, organisations who prioritise HRP only on a 'needs-must' basis may miss out on
the potential advantages.

Hercus (1992: 425) found that 'the role of senior management and the board, and that of
the HR director, appears to be particularly important to the success of the HR planning
process'. Findings from the Workplace Industrial Relations Survey series show an overall
decline in HR representation at board level, thus suggesting that HR issues are not given priority by senior management in many UK workplaces, particularly smaller, non-union
workplaces (Millward *et al.*, 2000). The 1998 survey (Cully *et al.*, 1999) found that over two-
thirds (68 per cent) of workplaces had a strategic plan which included employee development
issues and in more than half of workplaces (57 per cent) the strategic plan was drawn up with
some input from the person with responsibility for employment relations. This strategic
approach was most likely to be found in larger workplaces and in the public sector.

Stop & think

*What factors might account for the discrepancy between the proportion of workplaces with
strategic plans that include employee development issues and the proportion of
workplaces that involve HR in the development of these plans?*

Future directions

Much of the criticism levelled at traditional HRP concerned its inflexibility and inability to
cope with changing circumstances. Many of the more contemporary variants attempt to
address these problems in some way. For example, contingency planning provides greater
flexibility by considering the implications of a number of different scenarios while other
approaches (e.g. succession planning) focus on specific issues rather than attempting to
tackle everything at once. It seems likely that this drive for greater flexibility will continue and
HRP will become increasingly dynamic. Boxall and Purcell (2003) argue that 'it is vital to
accept that change is inevitable and that some preparation for the future is therefore crucial'
(p. 232). They further suggest that short-term planning is necessary for survival but long-
term planning is a good thing providing it does not make the organisation inflexible. Schuler
(1998: 176) makes a similar point, suggesting that planning will become more tentative and
short-term to deal with the rapidly changing environment but long-term needs are still
important because some changes take time. These arguments can be seen to underpin the
need for both traditional HRP techniques for short-term forecasting and for more contemporary variants such as scenario planning for longer-term plans.

HRP appears to have moved a long way from the mechanistic approach associated with
traditional manpower planning. Contemporary approaches are less concerned with maintaining stability and more with shaping and managing change. Brews and Hunt (1999) argue
that unstable environments make HRP more, rather than less, necessary but the key focus
needs to be on adapting to change:

> When the going gets tough, the tough go planning: formally, specifically, yet with flexibility
> and with persistence. And once they have learned to plan, they plan to learn.
>
> (Brews and Hunt, 1999: 906)

Summary

The chapter began by outlining seven key objectives and these are revisited here.

- Human resource planning can be interpreted in a number of different ways. For some it means the same as manpower planning, for others it is significantly different and has many similarities to HRM. The definition used in this chapter relates to HRP as a set of distinct activities that incorporates both the hard elements associated with manpower planning and some of the softer elements associated with HRM.

- The key stages in the traditional human resource planning process are investigation and analysis, forecasting demand and supply, developing action plans to address any imbalance, implementing the plans and evaluating their effectiveness.

- Methods of demand forecasting discussed are time series, ratio analysis, work study, managerial judgement, the Delphi technique and working back from budgets. Quantitative methods can be problematic as the extrapolation of past data might be inappropriate in a changing environment but they can provide a reasonable starting point for forecasts. Qualitative methods are more flexible but can be manipulated for political ends. Supply forecasting tends to focus mainly on various analyses of labour turnover and stability and movement through an organisation. Quantitative analysis can help to highlight problem areas but gives little indication about how problems might be addressed. Qualitative data can help to address this gap but can sometimes be difficult to obtain. Organisations can exacerbate problems if they are not seen to act on the information they receive.

- A more contemporary approach to HRP aims to enable the organisation to adapt to an uncertain and changing environment and emphasises the need to develop a well-trained and flexible workforce. Variants to HRP include micro-planning, contingency planning, succession planning, skills planning and soft human resource planning.

- The main advantages of HRP are that plans can help reduce uncertainty, can build flexibility and can contribute to vertical and horizontal integration. The key disadvantages relate to difficulties of predicting an uncertain future, the lack of necessary data to make accurate predictions and the absence of clear business plans.

- Evidence of HRP in practice is varied but the dominant approach seems to view HR as the 'dependent variable' and tends to be tentative and incremental rather than systematic.

- HRP's main role in SHRM is as a means to facilitate the integration of HR strategy with business strategy and to ensure that HR policies and practice are compatible with each other. In addition, some studies associate formal planning activity with improved organisational performance, particularly if planning is sustained over a number of years. The key emphasis, however, needs to be on building adaptability and managing change.

QUESTIONS

1 To what extent can forecasting activity influence the effectiveness of human resource plans?

2 Why should organisations be concerned with labour turnover and what steps can they take to address the issue?

3 Contemporary organisations increasingly operate in a dynamic and uncertain environment. Does this reduce or increase the need for human resource planning activity? Justify your answer.

London Olympics 2012

A briefing document produced by the People 1st Research Team (2005) draws on a range of public research to outline the major issues resulting from London hosting the Olympic Games in 2012.

It is estimated that 12,000 new jobs will be created as a result of the development of the Olympic Park area. The biggest economy legacy from the games will be the creation of the employment opportunities and improvements in education, skills and knowledge of the local labour force in an area of high unemployment.

In addition, there will be 7000 full-time equivalent construction workers required to develop the infrastructure for the games.

London 2012 estimates that up to 70,000 volunteers will be required to help run the Olympic and Paralympic Games in 2012. This will require the biggest volunteer recruitment drive in UK peacetime, providing a unique boost both to sport-specific and general volunteering in the UK.

The opportunities presented to local communities by the Olympics are immense in terms of tackling unemployment, lack of basic skills and poor health Hackney Borough Council suggests that the games offer a unique chance for Hackney people to access new employment opportunities in East London and in the wider economy. Training and employment opportunities for Hackney's residents stem from the potential development of the food and catering services industry. The Olympics will also provide a fantastic opportunity to equip local people with vital new skills, in areas like construction, IT and hospitality.

Key lessons that arose for the people involved with the Manchester Commonwealth games were:

- Significant changes in the scale and complexity of the event resulted in a corresponding change in the number and types of roles needed.
- As staffing gaps became obvious the timescales were tight, and so experienced staff were recruited rather than multi-tasking existing staff.
- Staff were generally hired on the basis of existing expertise, all staff were given training in areas such as First Aid and Health and Safety.

Source: People 1st (2005).

Questions

1 Identify key priority areas to ensure optimum levels of staff and volunteers for the games in 2012.

2 Identify the key stakeholders likely to be involved in the process.

3 Outline the main contribution that human resource planning can make to the successful staffing of the games.

References and further reading

Armstrong, M. (2005) *A Handbook of Human Resource Management Practice*, 10th edn. London: Kogan Page.

Arthur, J. (1992) 'The link between business strategy and industrial relations systems in American steel mini-mills', *Industrial and Labor Relations Review*, 45, 3: 488–506.

Bartholemew, D. (ed.) (1976) *Manpower Planning*. Harmondsworth: Penguin.

Beaumont, P. (1992) 'The US human resource management literature', in Salaman, G. *et al.* (eds) *Human Resource Strategies*. London: Sage.

Bennet, A. (1991) 'Downsizing doesn't necessarily bring an upswing in corporate profitability', *The Wall Street Journal*, 6 June, p. 1.

Bevan, S. (1997) 'Quit stalling', *People Management*, 20 November.

Bevan, S., Barber, L. and Robinson, D. (1997) *Keeping the Best: A Practical Guide to Retaining Key Employees*. London: Institute for Employment Studies.

Boxall, P. and Purcell, J. (2003) *Strategy and Human Resource Management*. London: Palgrave.

Bramham, J. (1988) *Practical Manpower Planning*, 4th edn. London: IPM.

Bramham, J. (1989) *Human Resource Planning*. London: IPM.

Bramham, J. (1994) *Human Resource Planning*. London: IPD.

Brews, P. and Hunt, M. (1999) 'Learning to plan and planning to learn: resolving the planning school/learning school debate', *Strategic Management Journal*, 20, 889–913.

Buckingham, G. (2000) 'Same indifference', *People Management*, 17 February: 44–46.

Cascio, W. (1993) 'Downsizing: what do we know, what have we learned?', *Academy of Management Executive*, 7, 1: 95–104.

Chartered Institute of Personnel and Development (2000) *The People Management Implications of Mergers and Acquisitions, Joint Ventures and Divestments*. CIPD Research Report, September.

Chartered Institute of Personnel and Development (2005) *Recruitment, Retention and Labour Turnover*. CIPD Survey Report.

Cowling, A. and Walters, M. (1990) 'Manpower planning – where are we today?', *Personnel Review*, 19, 3: 3–8.

Cully, M., Woodland, S., O'Reilly, A. and Dix, G. (1999) *Britain at Work*. London: Routledge.

Department of Employment (1974) *Company Manpower Planning*. London: HMSO.

Dessler, G. (2003) *Human Resource Management*, 9th edn. Englewood Cliffs, New Jersey: Prentice Hall.

Fombrun, C., Tichy, N. and Devanna, M. (1984) *Strategic Human Resource Management*. New York: John Wiley.

Griffiths, K. (2003) 'The face of corporate Britain', *The Independent*, 24 April: 1.

Harrison, M. (2003) 'Sir Brian Moffat forced out at Corus', *The Independent*, 24 April: 21.

Hendry, C. (1995) *Human Resource Management: A Strategic Approach to Employment*. Oxford: Butterworth-Heinemann.

Hercus, T. (1992) 'Human resource planning in eight British organisations: a Canadian perspective' in Towers, B. (ed.) *The Handbook of Human Resource Management*. Oxford: Blackwell.

Hill, J. and Trist, E. (1955) 'Changes in accidents and other absences with length of service', *Human Relations*, 8, May.

Holbeche, L. (2000) 'Work in progression', *People Management*, 8 June.

Hutton, W. (1997) *The State to Come*. London: Vintage.

IPM (1992) *Statement on Human Resource Planning*. London: IPD.

IRS (2001a) 'Benchmarking labour turnover 2001/02, part 1', *IRS Employment Review 741*, 3 December.

IRS (2001b) 'Risk analysis and job retention', *IRS Employee Development Bulletin 141*, September.

IRS (2001c) 'Hanging up the welcome sign', *IRS Employee Development Bulletin 135*, March.

IRS (2001d) 'Reality check: using attitude surveys to manage retention', *IRS Employee Development Bulletin 137*, May.

IRS (2002) 'The changing face of succession planning', *IRS Employment Review 756*, 22 July: 37–42.

IRS (2005) 'In quick succession', *IRS Employment Review 833*, 14 October.

IRS (2006) 'Recruitment and retention', *IRS Employment Review 839*, 20 January.

Johnson, G. and Scholes, K. (2002) *Exploring Corporate Strategy*. Harlow: Prentice Hall.

Koch, M. and McGrath, R. (1996) 'Improving labor productivity: human resource management policies do matter', *Strategic Management Journal*, 17: 335–354.

Kochan, T.A. and Barocci, T. (1985) *Human Resource Management Industrial Relations: Text, Readings and Cases*. Boston, Mass.: Little, Brown.

Lam, S. and Schaubroeck, J. (1998) 'Integrating HR planning and organisational strategy', *Human Resource Journal*, 8, 3: 5–19.

Legge, K. (1995) *Human Resource Management: Rhetorics and Realities*. Basingstoke: Macmillan.

Liff, S. (2000) 'Manpower or human resource planning – what's in a name?', in Bach, S. and Sisson, K. (eds) *Personnel Management: A Comprehensive Guide to Theory and Practice*, 3rd edn. Oxford: Blackwell.

Local Government (2005) *Local Government Pay and Workforce Strategy* (www.lg-employers.gov.uk).

Mabey, C., Salaman, G. and Storey, J. (1998) *Human Resource Management: A Strategic Introduction*, 2nd edn. Oxford: Blackwell.

Mackay, L. and Torrington, D. (1986) *The Changing Nature of Personnel Management*. London: IPM.

Marchington, M. and Wilkinson, A. (1996) *Core Personnel and Development*. London: IPD.

Marchington, M. and Wilkinson, A. (2005) *Human Resource Management at Work*, 3rd edn. London: CIPD.

McBeath, G. (1992) *The Handbook of Human Resource Planning*. Oxford: Blackwell.

Millward, N., Bryson, A. and Forth, J. (2000) *All Change at Work?* London: Routledge.

Mintzberg, H. (1994) *The Rise and Fall of Strategic Planning*. Hemel Hempstead: Prentice Hall.

People 1st (2005) *London Olympics 2012*, briefing document, February. Accessed via the Internet at www.people1st.co.uk.

Pilbeam, S. and Corbridge, M. (2002) *People Resourcing: HRM in Practice*. Harlow: FT/Prentice Hall.

Porter, M. (1985) *Competitive Advantage: Creating and Sustaining Superior Performance*. New York: Free Press.

Purcell, J. (1999) 'The search for best practice and best fit in human resource management: chimera or cul-de-sac?', *Human Resource Management Journal*, 9, 3: 26–41.

Redman, T. and Wilkinson, A. (2001) *Contemporary HRM*. Harlow: FT/Prentice Hall.

Rothwell, S. (1995) 'Human resource planning', in Storey, J. (ed.) *Human Resource Management: A Critical Text*. London: Routledge.

Sadhev, K., Vinnicombe, S. and Tyson, S. (1999) 'Downsizing and the changing role of HR', *International Journal of HRM*, 10, 5: 906–923.

Schuler, R.S. (1998) *Managing Human Resources*, 6th edn. Cincinnati, Ohio: South-Western College Publishing.

Schuler, R. and Jackson, S. (1987) 'Linking competitive strategies with human resource management', *Academy of Management Executive*, 1, 3: 207–219.

Sisson, K. and Storey, J. (2000) *The Realities of Human Resource Management*. Buckingham: Open University Press.

Storey, J. (1992) *Developments in the Management of Human Resources*. Oxford: Blackwell.

Tansley, C. (1999) 'Human resource planning: Strategies, systems and processes', in Leopold, J., Harris, L. and Watson, T. (eds) *Strategic Human Resourcing: Principle, Perspectives and Practice*. Harlow: FT/Pitman.

Taylor, S. (2005) *People Resourcing*, 3rd edn. London: CIPD.

Thomason, G. (1988) *A Textbook of Human Resource Management*. London: IPM.

Torrington, D., Hall, L. and Taylor, S. (2002) *Human Resource Management*. Harlow: FT/Prentice Hall.

Whittington, R. (1993) *What is Strategy and Does It Matter?*, London: Routledge.

Williams, M. (2000) 'Transfixed assets', *People Management*, 3 August: 28–33.

For multiple-choice questions, exercises and annotated weblinks specific to this chapter visit the book's website at **www.pearsoned.co.uk/beardwell**

Chapter 6

Recruitment and selection

Julie Beardwell

Objectives

- To define recruitment and selection.
- To examine the external and internal contextual factors that can influence recruitment and selection practices.
- To identify key stages in the systematic approach to recruitment and selection.
- To explore trends in the use of recruitment and selection methods.
- To evaluate the effectiveness of different recruitment and selection practices.

Introduction

The importance of ensuring the selection of the right people to join the workforce has become increasingly apparent as the emphasis on people as the prime source of competitive advantage has grown. Beaumont (1993) identifies three key issues that have increased the potential importance of the selection decision to organisations. First, demographic trends and changes in the labour market have led to a more diverse workforce, which has placed increasing pressure on the notion of fairness in selection. Second, the desire for a multi-skilled, flexible workforce and an increased emphasis on teamworking has meant that selection decisions are concerned more with behaviour and attitudes than with matching individuals to immediate job requirements. And third, the emphasis between corporate strategy and people management has led to the notion of strategic selection: that is, a system that links selection processes and outcomes to organisational goals and aims to match the flow of people to emerging business strategies.

Selective hiring (i.e. the use of sophisticated techniques to ensure selection of the 'right' people) is frequently included in the 'bundles' of best HR practice (see, for example, Pfeffer, 1998). The contribution of effective recruitment and selection to enhanced business performance is also illustrated by the findings of empirical studies. For example, a study into small and medium-sized manufacturing establishments (Patterson *et al.*, 1997) found the acquisition and development of employee skills through the use of sophisticated selection, induction, training and appraisals to have a positive impact on company productivity and profitability. Thus the practice of recruitment and selection is increasingly important from an HRM perspective.

At the same time, however, many of the traditional methods of recruitment and selection are being challenged by the need for organisations to address the increased complexity, greater ambiguity and rapid pace of change in the contemporary environment. This chapter, therefore, discusses key contemporary approaches to recruitment and selection, and examines the influence of external and internal factors on the process. After clarifying what is meant by recruitment and selection, the chapter begins by exploring the key elements of a systematic approach and discusses recent developments at each stage of the process. It then explores external and internal factors that might account for variations in recruitment and selection practice. In the final section the chapter emphasises the two-way nature of recruitment and selection, and considers ethical issues in the treatment of individuals. The chapter concludes with a summary and a number of self-test exercises.

Definitions

Stop & think

What do you see as the key differences between recruitment and selection?

The recruitment and selection process is concerned with identifying, attracting and choosing suitable people to meet an organisation's human resource requirements. They are integrated activities, and 'where recruitment stops and selection begins is a moot point' (Anderson, 1994). Nevertheless, it is useful to try to differentiate between the two areas: Whitehill (1991) describes the recruitment process as a positive one, 'building a roster of potentially qualified applicants', as opposed to the 'negative' process of selection. So a useful definition of recruitment is 'searching for and obtaining potential job candidates in sufficient numbers and quality so that the organisation can select the most appropriate people to fill its job needs' (Dowling and Schuler, 1990); whereas selection is concerned more with 'predicting which candidates will make the most appropriate contribution to the organisation – now and in the future' (Hackett, 1991).

The external context

The processes of recruitment and selection take place within a framework of external and internal influences. External direction, through legislation and published codes of practice, suggests that approaches will be standardised, in the UK at least. However, other factors in both external and internal contexts result in variations in both philosophy and practice.

External labour market factors

When organisations choose to recruit externally rather than internally, the search takes place in local, regional, national and/or international labour markets, depending on numbers, skills, competences and experiences required, the potential financial costs involved and the perceived benefits involved to the organisation concerned. External recruitment often poses problems for organisations: 85 per cent of respondents to the CIPD Recruitment, Retention and Turnover Survey (CIPD, 2005a) report recruitment difficulties. The main causes cited are:

- a lack of the specialist skills required;
- a lack of experience required;
- applicants want more pay than can be offered;
- no applicants.

Recruitment difficulties are most frequently reported in the voluntary, community and not-for-profit sector and by larger organisations. Initiatives aimed at addressing these difficulties include:

- appointing people who have potential to grow but do not currently have all that is required;
- increasing starting salaries or the benefits package;
- taking account of a broader range of qualities, such as personal skills instead of qualifications;
- redefining the job;
- appointing people who do not exactly match what the job requires.

In addition, around one in five organisations have opted for overseas recruitment to ease skills shortages (CIPD, 2005a). This approach is most likely to be used by public sector employers. EU accession countries, such as Poland, are currently the most popular source of migrant labour (CIPD, 2005b).The appetite among Polish workers to relocate to the UK has been widely documented and is attributed to the high unemployment rate in Poland and the comparatively high wages on offer in the UK (IDS, 2005).

Technological developments

Technological developments can influence recruitment and selection in a number of ways. First, technological advancements such as the automation of production processes can influence the types of knowledge and skills required by organisations. Second, developments in information and communication technology have affected the labour markets for some types of jobs. A growing number of UK organisations have moved their contact centre operations overseas, especially to the Indian sub-continent, to take advantage of the 'huge, well-educated, English speaking labour force' and significantly lower wage rates (Crabb, 2003: 30). Third, the growth of the internet has influenced the means by which organisations attract and select candidates. Many UK organisations have experimented with online recruitment and further growth is likely, aided by public and private investment in the internet, including broadband access and the continual development of corporate websites (IRS, 2005a).

Government policy and legislation

While organisations have considerable freedom of choice in the type of people they want to recruit, legislation plays a significant role in the recruitment and selection process, particularly in attempts to prevent discrimination on the grounds of sex, race, disability and age (see also Chapter 7).

Sex and race discrimination

Two Acts are specifically designed to prevent discrimination in employment on the basis of sex or race. The Sex Discrimination Act 1975 makes it unlawful to discriminate against a person directly or indirectly in the field of employment on the grounds of their sex or marital status. The Race Relations Act 1976 makes it unlawful to discriminate against a person in the field of employment on the grounds of their race, colour and nationality, including ethnic or national origin.

Both Acts prohibit direct and indirect discrimination. Direct discrimination occurs when an individual is treated less favourably than another because of their sex, marital status or race. Indirect discrimination occurs when requirements are imposed that are not necessary for the job, and that may disadvantage a significantly larger proportion of one sex or racial group than another. Thus, organisations have to ensure that selection criteria are job relevant and applicable to all.

Both Acts make it lawful for employers to take positive action to encourage applications from members of one sex or of racial groups who have been under-represented in particular work over the previous 12 months. However, positive discrimination is unlawful, which means that, although advertisements can explicitly encourage applications from one sex or particular racial group, no applicant can be denied information or be discriminated against in selection because they do not fit the 'preferred' category. Sex or race discrimination is permitted only where sex or race is a defined 'genuine occupational qualification' (GOQ). Examples of GOQs include those for models, actors and some personal welfare counsellors.

These Acts have had some success in achieving sexual and racial equality and there has undoubtedly been a significant reduction in overt discrimination, particularly in recruitment advertising. However, there is less evidence of equality in employment practices generally. Women are still more likely to be in lower paid work including catering, clerical, care working, cleaners and customer service whilst men are more likely to be in managerial, skilled trade or machine operative positions (see Chapter 4 for more detail). At the same time, a higher proportion of black and ethnic minority groups are likely to be unemployed. A study for the TUC found that the unemployment rate for black women was almost twice that for white women and black and Asian women also had to settle more often for work which they were over-qualified to do (TUC, 2006).

Indications of continued inequalities in the labour market may be partly due to the fact that, until relatively recently, legislation was aimed at ending discrimination rather than requiring organisations to promote equality. The situation has now changed, at least in the public sector. In 2001 the Race Relations (Amendment) Act imposed a positive duty on public authorities to promote racial equality. In relation to recruitment and selection this specifically requires public sector organisations to:

- ensure that employment practices attract good candidates from all ethnic groups;
- set targets and take action to encourage applicants from ethnic groups currently under-represented in particular areas of work;
- monitor employees and applicants for employment, training and promotion by ethnic group.

From April 2007 public authorities will have to adopt a similar approach in relation to gender equality. The Gender Equality Duty requires public authorities to pay due regard to promoting gender equality and eliminating sex discrimination. This involves looking at employment practices, e.g. recruitment and selection, development and pay, and considering the needs of all staff, including those that identify themselves as transgender or transsexual.

Findings of the fourth Workplace Employee Relations Survey, WERS 4 (Cully *et al.*, 1999), suggest that monitoring does not occur as much as one might expect. Fewer than half of organisations with a formal equal opportunity policy collect statistics on posts held by men and women, or keep employee records with ethnic origin attached, and only a third review selection procedures to identify indirect discrimination. As yet, there is little indication that private sector workplaces are mirroring the practices required in the public sector.

Some organisations appear to have adopted a more flexible approach to recruitment and selection in order to increase the diversity of the workforce. The CIPD Recruitment, Retention and Turnover Survey (CIPD, 2005a) highlights a number of measures aimed at improving the diversity of the workforce, including:

- Training interviewers in equal opportunities/diversity issues.
- Operating policies that go beyond basic legislative requirements.
- Checking that any tests used are culture-free and tested on diverse norm groups.
- Ensuring the recruitment team reflects diversity criteria.
- Advertise vacancies beyond traditional media to target under-represented groups.
- Using specific images or words in advertisements to target under-represented groups.

Other initiatives to increase the diversity of the workforce include building up relationships with community groups. Pre-employment training can also help to increase the number of employees from previously under-represented groups, but is used by only a small number of organisations (Dickens, 2000). These forms of positive action may be aimed at improving opportunities for previously disadvantaged groups by creating a 'level playing field'. However, these types of initiatives can be seen as counter-productive because people who are perceived to have gained advantage through positive action may be viewed negatively by others. In addition, offering extra training and help to under-represented groups implies 'that they are deficient in some way and that consequently they are the problem . . . [when] invariably the problem lies not with the targeted group itself but elsewhere in an organisation's own processes or culture' (Kandola, 1995: 20).

Disability discrimination

The Disability Discrimination Act (1995) came into force at the end of 1996. The Act defines disability as a physical or mental impairment that has a substantial and long-term adverse effect on a person's ability to carry out normal day-to-day duties, and includes progressive conditions such as cancer and multiple sclerosis. The legislation makes it unlawful for companies to treat people with disabilities less favourably than they do others unless they can justify their actions. In addition, employers are required to make 'reasonable adjustment' to the workplace or to working arrangements where this would help to overcome the practical effects of a disability. The requirement for reasonable adjustment includes modifying the recruitment and selection procedure if required: for example, providing application forms in large print or accepting applications by audio tape. The use of testing during the selection process may present a potential problem for people with disabilities, and reasonable adjustments might include modifying test materials, allowing a disabled candidate assistance during a test, or flexibility in the scoring and interpretation of test results (IRS, 1999a).

Discrimination against disabled people has been unlawful only since 1996. Before then, legislation relating to the treatment of disabled people at work was primarily to 'secure for the disabled their full share, within their capacity, of such employment as is ordinarily available' rather than preventing discrimination. It is therefore not surprising that disabled people still appear to be disadvantaged in the labour market. *Labour Force Survey* (ONS, 2002) statistics show that:

● 1 in 5 people of working age in the UK has a long-term disability.

● 52 per cent of disabled people are economically active compared with 79 per cent for the whole working age population.

● Disabled people are more likely than non-disabled people to be unemployed (9 per cent and 5 per cent respectively) and are also more likely to have been unemployed for at least a year.

From December 2006 public sector organisations are required to comply with the Disability Equality Duty. This is similar to the duty imposed in relation to gender and race equality and, in part, requires organisations to outline arrangements for gathering information in relation to the recruitment, development and retention of disabled people; put these arrangements into practice; and make use of the information collected.

Age discrimination

From October 2006 age discrimination in recruitment, promotion and training is unlawful in the UK. In terms of recruitment and selection this means that employers should not use age, age-related criteria and age ranges in adverts other than to encourage applications from age groups who would not normally apply. Where this is the case it should be clearly stated (CIPD, 2006a). The legislation is likely to lead to a broadening out of recruitment campaigns; for example, employers will need to ensure that graduate recruitment schemes do not indirectly discriminate against older workers.

Stop & think

What impact might this legislation have on recruitment and selection practice?

In terms of recruitment and selection, the major requirements of legislation relating to gender, race, disability and age are that employers should focus on the basis of skills and abilities necessary to do the job rather than imposing discriminatory selection criteria or making stereotypical judgements based on personal characteristics. Employers also need to ensure that the recruitment media used to advertise vacancies are widely accessible; there is some concern that online recruitment may pose difficulties for people with certain disabilities (IRS, 2005a). Finally, employers need to ensure that their selection methods, including interviews and tests, do not unfairly disadvantage any group.

Employment of people with criminal records

There are 7.3 million people in England and Wales on the Home Office Offenders Index, the official register of all those with criminal convictions and these people are likely to be disadvantaged in the workplace. Evidence shows that of all things to put an employer off, a criminal record is the worst; estimates suggest that it is at least eight times harder for someone with a criminal record to obtain employment (CIPD, 2006b). The Rehabilitation of Offenders Act (ROA) 1974 provides some protection for certain categories of ex-offenders, as it enables offenders who have received sentences of 30 months or less to have their convictions 'spent'. This means that, after a specified period, they can reply 'no' when asked if they have a criminal record. Although it is unlawful for an employer to discriminate on the grounds of a 'spent' conviction, the candidate who is discriminated against has no individual remedy (IDS, 1992). In addition, a wide range of jobs and professions are exempt from the provisions of this Act, including teachers, social workers, doctors, lawyers and accountants.

Recruiters' ability to undertake pre-employment screening increased with the launch of the Criminal Records Bureau in 2002 (IRS, 2005b). Part V of the Police Act, 1997 makes provision for three different levels of criminal record checks:

- *Basic disclosure*: shows current, unspent convictions. This type of disclosure has not yet been introduced in England and Wales.

- *Standard disclosure*: contains details of spent and unspent convictions and is available for posts exempt from the ROA, e.g. those involved with children or vulnerable adults and for certain professions such as law and accountancy.

- *Enhanced disclosure*: standard disclosure plus relevant, non-conviction information held on police records. This level of disclosure is only for posts involving regular care for, training, supervising or being in sole charge of children or vulnerable adults.

Government research (cited in IRS, 2002b) concludes that the availability of these checks will make it more difficult for people with criminal records to get a job, or may increase their chances of dismissal through the discovery of previously undisclosed convictions. However, whilst employers need to maintain a duty of care towards employees and customers, there are strong social and business arguments to support the employment of ex-offenders. The social argument is that employment is the single most important factor in reducing re-offending (CIPD, 2006b). The business argument is that, in the light of recruitment difficulties, employers cannot afford to exclude such a large group of people.

The internal context

The discussions above relate to external factors influencing recruitment and selection activities and go some way to explaining why we see both similarities and differences in recruitment activity. While legislation and codes of conduct would suggest a certain approach in the UK, differences in job/occupation being recruited, labour markets and skills availability might cause this approach to be modified. However, factors within organisations also affect the way recruitment and selection is handled. In this section we explore the extent to which recruitment and selection activities are aligned with overall business strategy; the impact of an organisation's approach to HRM, its financial position, the size of the organisation, its industrial sector, and its culture. This section also considers the approaches adopted by multinational corporations.

Business strategy

The advantages to adopting an integrated and complementary 'bundle' of HR practices have already been outlined in Chapter 1. Different models of HRM propose that HR practices, including recruitment and selection, should be both vertically integrated with the organisation's position or preferred business strategy and horizontally integrated with each other. Parallel strategies in recruitment, selection, development and reward, in particular, are suggested. For example, the Kochan and Barocci model, outlined in Figure 6.1, argues that organisations have lifecycles, and that recruitment, selection and staffing policies vary according to an organisation's perceived stage in the cycle. Other models attempt to link recruitment and selection to product strategies (e.g. Fombrun *et al.*, 1984) or overall business strategy (e.g. Miles and Snow, 1984).

Schuler and Jackson (1996) argue that HR practices are associated with an organisation's competitive strategy, e.g. cost reduction, quality improvement or innovation (see also Chapter 2):

> These different ways of competing are significant for managing human resources because they help determine needed employee behaviors. That is, for competitive strategies to be successfully implemented, employees have to behave in certain ways. And for employees to behave in certain ways, human resource practices need to be put in place that help ensure that those behaviors are explained, are possible, and are rewarded.

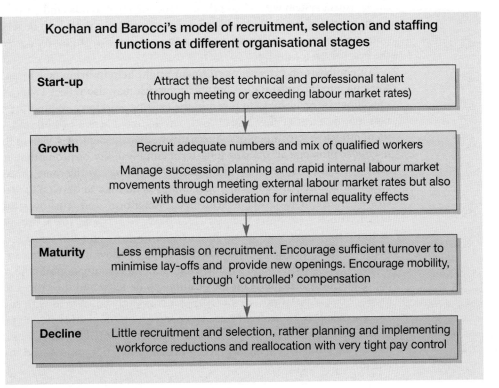

Figure 6.1   **Kochan and Barocci's model of recruitment, selection and staffing functions at different organisational stages**

Start-up   Attract the best technical and professional talent (through meeting or exceeding labour market rates)

Growth   Recruit adequate numbers and mix of qualified workers

Manage succession planning and rapid internal labour market movements through meeting external labour market rates but also with due consideration for internal equality effects

Maturity   Less emphasis on recruitment. Encourage sufficient turnover to minimise lay-offs and provide new openings. Encourage mobility, through 'controlled' compensation

Decline   Little recruitment and selection, rather planning and implementing workforce reductions and reallocation with very tight pay control

Source: Adapted from Storey and Sisson (1993).

Organisations following a cost reduction strategy are likely to use ad hoc methods of recruitment and selection and rely on agencies and subcontractors. Organisations following a quality enhancement strategy are likely to adopt sophisticated methods to recruit and select employees and organisations following an innovation strategy are likely to focus on core competencies and transferable skills (Sisson and Storey, 2000).

The models serve to highlight possible reasons for variations in approach to recruitment and selection. However, there is considerable debate about the extent to which a classical and rational approach to decision-making in organisations is either sensible or even exists. The problems include:

- the difficulties in agreeing what corporate strategy is, and the extent to which it is perceived as planned rather than emergent;
- a perception of critical time lag between 'strategic decision-making' and implementation of the policies deemed necessary to achieve corporate objectives;
- pressures to recruit and select in the short term via the external labour market to meet urgent needs, which may conflict with the chosen longer-term strategy of internal labour market development.

A further explanation of different approaches to recruitment and selection might therefore be the lack of a strategic approach to HRM within organisations.

The balance between external and internal recruitment

Whether or not an organisation is pursuing a strategic approach to the management of people, there still needs to be a choice about the balance between internal or external recruitment. Some organisations prefer to fill as many vacancies as possible with existing employees in order to motivate and develop people and retain critical skills. This approach requires considerable investment in training and development and the support of a performance management system with an emphasis on identifying potential and on securing commitment from employees. However, the internal recruitment pool is likely to be relatively small so the potential downside of internal recruitment is that the organisation does not necessarily get the best person for the job.

An emphasis on external recruitment might help to bring new ideas and new styles of working into the organisation but this approach may also reflect a short-term focus and an unwillingness or inability to invest in the existing workforce. Within the UK the unwillingness may be a fear of engaging in costly development activities with staff, which could make them attractive to competitors. Alternatively, management may believe that future changes may pose problems in offering long-term employability or promotion and do not wish to raise unrealistic expectations amongst the workforce. At the same time, rapidly changing organisational requirements may mean there is no time to develop the required competencies in-house. The CIPD Recruitment, Retention and Turnover Survey found that organisations were more than twice as likely to respond to recruitment difficulties by 'appointing people who have the potential to grow but don't currently have all that is required' than to 'provide additional training to allow internal staff to fill posts' (CIPD, 2005a: 6). In practice, many organisations adopt a combination of both external and internal recruitment depending on the positions to be filled and the skills available in-house. A number of organisations are becoming increasingly concerned with succession planning (see also Chapter 5), i.e. having enough people with the right skills and leadership potential to step into business-critical positions at the right time (IRS, 2005c). This is likely to involve identifying potential during the recruitment and selection process and then developing and retaining this 'talent'.

Financial position of the organisation

The financial position of an organisation can impact significantly on recruitment and selection practices. 'Cash rich' organisations may find it easy to find agreement for the budgets required for an investment in sophisticated selection processes and an emphasis on employee development. Financial constraints can forestall the investment in training and development necessary to tap the potential of the internal labour market, with decision makers seeing training budgets as costly 'extras'. Financial constraints can push an organisation towards an external focus on recruitment but, at the same time, might limit the number and quality of recruitment and selection methods available for use. Assessment centres may be deemed appropriate in terms of their purpose and suitability, but remain unused because cheaper selection tools exist. In addition, tight budgets may limit the amount of cash available to fund higher reward packages expected by the best applicants.

Size of the organisation

While large organisations with over 500 employees comprise only 3 per cent of total workplaces, they account for nearly a third of all employees in the UK (Cully *et al.*, 1999) and 'size matters, all other things being equal, because larger units increase the complexity of the management task . . . and the greater the need for rules and procedures to achieve consistency of behaviour on the part of individual managers' (Sisson and Marginson, 1995).

Within the largest organisations HR policy may be decided by a powerful central function, developed over time, with individual business or service units expected to maintain strict adherence to written policy and procedure. Small organisations (25–49 employees), on the other hand, account for over half of UK workplaces. Within them, well-developed personnel functions or recruitment and selection systems may not exist. Recruitment may be irregular, with a heavy reliance on informal methods of recruitment, especially if these have worked well previously. Responsibility for the recruitment activity, in particular, may be passed to enthusiastic 'amateurs' within the organisation, or outsourced to a third party. Overall, smaller workplaces are more likely to rely on more traditional methods of recruitment and selection, namely CVs and interviews whilst some of the more sophisticated methods, such as assessment centres, are most likely to be found in larger organisations.

Industrial sector

'The output of a workplace, and the type of environment in which it operates, are likely to be significant determinants of how work is organised' (Cully *et al.*, 1999) and marked differences between public and private sector recruitment and selection practice are reported (CIPD, 2005a). WERS 4 data suggest that 72 per cent of all workplaces in the UK are in the private sector, with financial services, manufacturing, wholesale/retail, hotels and restaurants almost totally within private ownership (Cully *et al.*, 1999). The probable usage of third parties in recruitment appears high within this group, and the financial services and manufacturing industries are key users of executive search and selection. Financial services, information technology, customer care, engineering and design organisations are also predicted to grow the extent to which they outsource their processes, including HR, in the next five years (Crabb, 2003).

Conversely, public administration and education are firmly located in the public sector, where third-party recruitment has traditionally been very limited, with both recruitment and selection being maintained in-house by teams of professionals and specialists. The use of application forms and structured panel interviews are more prevalent, as is requesting references before the interview. At the same time, employee referrals and telephone interviews are much less likely in the public sector (CIPD, 2005a). In addition, public sector organisations tend to have policies which require all posts to be advertised externally (as well as internally) in the pursuit of equal opportunities.

Cultural differences between organisations

Differences exist even within similar industries, sectors and sized organisations. Several factors need to be considered: perhaps those who hold power in organisations have a strong preference for one particular recruitment method or have a dislike of any selection method except one-to-one interviewing. Perhaps expectations of the processes are based on custom and practice built over many years, which may or may not include a well-established routine, backed by written policies, procedures and monitoring systems, and an insistence on formal training for individuals in recruitment and selection. Perhaps recruitment is seen as a marginal activity, undertaken as required in an ad hoc manner by some delegated employee or outsourced to a third party as and when need arises. The roles and ability of those engaged in recruitment and selection may vary from one business unit to another, as may the extent to which divergence from organisational policy is permitted (Cully *et al.*, 1999).

Regional differences may also influence methods used. Head offices tend to be in London and the south-east, and here the use of headhunters is far greater (with more than 50 per cent using them), the use of Job Centres is lower, as is the use of local press in advertising. In Northern Ireland strong anti-discrimination legislation leads to less use of informal recruitment methods or headhunters.

Recruitment and selection in multinational organisations

Four distinct approaches have been identified for recruitment in multinational companies. They imply different patterns of control over the overseas' activities, and can have varying impacts on career development for the employees concerned:

- *Ethnocentric*, where the majority of key positions are filled by nationals of the parent company. This is a typical strategy employed in the early days of the new subsidiary, and suggests that power, decision-making and control are maintained at parent headquarters.

- *Polycentric*, where host country nationals fill the majority of key positions in the subsidiary. Each subsidiary is treated as a distinct national entity, although key financial targets and investment decisions are controlled by parent headquarters, where key positions remain with parent country nationals.

- *Regiocentric*, where decisions will be made on a regional basis (the new subsidiary will be based in one country of the region), with due regard to the key factor for success of the product or service. For example, if local knowledge is paramount, host country nationals will be recruited; if knowledge of established product is the key factor, parent country nationals are likely to be targets, though anyone from the geographical region would be considered.

- *Geocentric*, where the 'best people' are recruited regardless of nationality for all parent and subsidiary positions: for example, a national of a country in which neither the parent nor subsidiary is based could be considered. This results in a thoroughly international board and senior management, and is still relatively uncommon.

Increased globalisation of business generates other issues of relevance when considering recruitment and selection. Hendry (1995) identifies an increasing number of managers and professionals affected by international assignments, leading to increased importance of managing international careers. Selection criteria for managers operating internationally include (CIPD, 2006c):

- Technical and managerial ability.

- Stress tolerance and resilience (e.g. dealing successfully with cultural adaptation and individual anxieties relating to this).

- Emotional maturity (ability to cope with and manage complexity and diversity).

- Flexibility (ability to adapt to role changes and possible conflict).
- Communication (listening and articulating skills in order to build social and business relations).
- Cultural empathy (having an understanding of and an ability to work within the local culture).

Stop & think

What might be the most effective ways of identifying these skills and abilities?

Sparrow (1999: 40) concludes that there are 'no simple recipes that can be followed when selecting for international assignments. Rather there are choices to be made and opportunities to be pursued'. He identifies three main resourcing philosophies. The first is a traditional, predictive approach, using psychometrics and competence frameworks to assess a person's suitability; the second is a risk assessment approach, which concentrates on cultural adaptability. His third philosophy involves reversing the process, and designing the assignment to match the skills of the manager. Specific training and preparation become vitally important to ensure that such relocation is effective, and that high levels of expatriate failure are avoided. Likely interventions include pre-move visits to the proposed host country (often with family members), language and cross-cultural training for managers and families, and briefing by both host country and in-house representatives.

Key stages in the recruitment and selection process

The key stages of a systematic approach can be summarised as: defining the vacancy, attracting applicants, assessing candidates, and making the final decision. Another way of expressing this is as a series of questions:

- Who do we want?
- How can we attract them?
- How can we identify them?
- How do we know we have got it right?

In addition, a supplementary question that is increasingly asked is:

- Who should be involved in the process?

Here we describe the main components of each stage, and indicate ways in which recruitment and selection activities are changing to meet current and future demands.

Who do we want?

Authorisation

When someone leaves a job they are not automatically replaced. Securing authorisation ensures that the need to start the recruitment process is agreed by management as being compatible with the organisational/departmental objectives: that is, necessary, timely and cost-effective. At the same time, it provides an opportunity to consider options other than recruitment and selection, for example:

- restructure workloads/departments and redeploy existing staff;
- delay recruitment to save costs;
- cover vacancy with temporary workers or overtime.

None of these opportunities are risk-free: redeployment of existing staff may mean that the incoming jobholder is not necessarily the 'best person for the job' and result in management resentment against the system; inadequately thought-through restructuring or short-term cost-saving measures may damage the department and organisation in the long term, as opportunities fail to be exploited for lack of suitable human resources.

These decisions may be made on an operational or strategic basis. The latter emphasises the contribution of effective staffing levels to the achievement of organisational goals and may include long-term human resource development (HRD) objectives and succession planning alongside the immediate requirement to fill a post.

Defining the job and the person

The traditional approach involves writing a comprehensive job description of the job to be filled. This enables the recruiter to know exactly what the purpose, duties and responsibilities of the vacant position will be and its location within the organisation structure. The next step involves drawing up a person specification that is based on the job description, and which identifies the personal characteristics required to perform the job adequately. Characteristics are usually described within a framework consisting of a number of broad headings. Two frequently cited frameworks are the seven-point plan (Rodger, 1952) and the five-fold grading system (Munro Fraser, 1954), illustrated in Table 6.1. Both frameworks are somewhat dated now, and some headings can appear to be potentially discriminatory (e.g. physical make-up and circumstances), but nevertheless they continue to form the basis of many person specifications in current use. It is common to differentiate between requirements that are essential to the job and those that are merely desirable.

The person specification is a vital part of the recruitment and selection process as it can form the basis of the recruitment advertisement, it can help determine the most effective selection methods and, if applied correctly, can ensure that selection decisions are based on sound, justifiable criteria. However, the compilation of a person specification needs to be handled with care. Predetermined criteria can contribute to effective recruitment and selection only if full consideration has been given to the necessity and fairness of all the requirements. Preconceived or entrenched attitudes, prejudices and assumptions can lead,

Table 6.1 Person specification frameworks

Rodger (1952)	Munro Fraser (1954)
Physical make-up: health, appearance, bearing and speech	*Impact on others*: physical make-up, appearance, speech and manner
Attainments: education, qualifications, experience	*Acquired qualifications*: education, vocational training, work experience
General intelligence: intellectual capacity	
Special aptitudes: mechanical, manual dexterity, facility in use of words and figures	*Innate abilities*: quickness of comprehension and aptitude for learning
Interests: intellectual, practical, constructional, physically active, social, artistic	*Motivation*: individual goals, consistency and determination in following them up, success rate
Disposition: acceptability, influence over others, steadiness, dependability, self-reliance	*Adjustment*: emotional stability, ability to stand up to stress and ability to get on with people
Circumstances: any special demands of the job, such as ability to work unsocial hours, travel abroad	

Source: ACAS (1983).

consciously or unconsciously, to requirements that are less job-related than aimed at meeting the assumed needs of customers, colleagues or the established culture of the organisation. Examples of this might include insistence on a British education, unnecessary age restrictions, or sex role stereotyping.

The job-based approach to recruitment and selection can be inflexible in a number of ways. For example, the job description may fail to reflect potential changes in the key tasks or the list of duties and responsibilities may be too constraining, especially where teamworking is introduced. This concentration on a specific job and its place in a bureaucratic structure may be detrimental to the development of the skills and aptitudes needed for the long-term benefit of the organisation. In order to accommodate the need for greater flexibility and the desire to encourage working 'beyond contract', some organisations have replaced traditional job descriptions with more generic and concise job profiles, consisting of a list of 'bullet points' or accountability statements.

The recognition that jobs can be subject to frequent change can also reduce the importance of the job description and increase the relative importance of getting the 'right' person. This approach has the potential for greater flexibility as it enables organisations to focus 'more on the qualities of the jobholder and the person's potential suitability for other duties as jobs change' than on the job itself (IRS, 1999b). For example, research into call centre recruitment and selection found that a positive attitude was more important in candidates than their ability to use a keyboard (Callaghan and Thompson, 2002).

In many instances, a combination of the job-oriented and person-oriented approaches may be adopted, in order to recruit people who can not only do the job but also contribute to the wider business goals of the organisation. One way to achieve this is via the use of competencies. The term has many definitions but most refer to 'the work-related personal attributes, knowledge, experience, skills and values that a person draws on to perform their work well' (Roberts, 1997: 6). Competency-based recruitment and selection involves the identification of a set of competencies that are seen as important across the organisation, such as planning and organising, managing relationships, gathering and analysing information, and decision-making. Each competency can then be divided into a number of different levels, and these can be matched to the requirements of a particular job.

Feltham (in Boam and Sparrow, 1992) argues that a competency-based approach can contribute to the effectiveness of recruitment and selection in three main ways:

- the process of competency analysis helps an organisation to identify what it needs from its human resources and to specify the part that selection and recruitment can play;

- the implementation of competency-based recruitment and selection systems results in a number of direct practical benefits; and

- where systems are linked to competencies, aspects of fairness, effectiveness and validity become amenable to evaluation. These competence frameworks can be used for more than just recruitment and selection.

The application of the same competency framework to all areas of HRM can ensure consistency and aid vertical and horizontal integration. Occasionally competencies can be identified at national levels. For example, in answer to calls for increased effectiveness of non-executive directors in the wake of corporate scandals in the USA and UK, Derek Higgs, appointed to lead an independent review of the role and effectiveness of non-executive directors in the UK, identified a set of competencies to be assessed via assessment centres, psychological testing and competency-based interviews, to ensure that appropriate non-executive directors make up at least half of organisations' boards (Dulewicz, 2003).

What a competency-based approach may discover is that recruitment is not always the answer. There is usually a variety of strategies for achieving a particular competency mix and no 'right' solutions. For example, if specialist skills are scarce, an organisation may choose to replace the skills with new technology, train existing staff, or hire specialist consultants when needed in preference to employment of permanent staff (Feltham, 1992). Where recruitment and selection is deemed appropriate, a competency-based approach achieves a visible set of agreed standards which can form the basis of systematic, fair and consistent decision-making.

Agree terms and conditions

Decisions on terms and conditions are made at various points in the process. Some of these are often not negotiated (e.g. hours, reward) until the final selection stages. There is a case for deciding the salary band (if not the specific amount) and other elements of the reward package before attracting candidates. This can take time (for example, if the position has to be processed through a job evaluation exercise), but potential candidates may fail to apply without some indication of the reward offered, as this often gives an indication of the level and status of the position.

The alternative is to wait and see who applies and then negotiate terms and conditions with the favoured candidate. This is a less restrictive approach, and may provide a better chance of employing high-calibre people who match the long-term aims of the organisation. However, it can be problematic on a number of grounds: the organisation may project a poor image if it appears to be unsure of what is on offer or may damage its reputation by being perceived to pay only what it can get away with. Furthermore, this reactive approach could lead to breaches of equal pay legislation. In practice, the approach adopted is likely to be determined by the organisation's reward strategy, including the relative importance of internal pay equity and external competitiveness and the emphasis on individual and collective pay-setting.

Stop & think

What key skills, qualities and experience do you possess? How might you determine their worth in relation to the type of job you want to do? What other factors do you need to take into account?

How do we attract them?

> ... the actual channels or vehicles used to attract candidates ... seem to influence whether the right kinds of applicants are encouraged to apply, and to persist in their application.
>
> (Iles and Salaman, 1995: 211)

Recruitment methods

Organisations can choose from a wide variety of methods, including the use of:

- informal personal contacts, such as word of mouth and speculative applications;
- formal personal contacts, such as employee referral schemes, careers fairs and open days;
- notice boards, accessible by current staff and/or the general public;
- advertising, including local and national press, specialist publications, radio and TV
- the internet;
- external assistance, including job centres, careers service, employment agencies and 'headhunters'.

The relative popularity of these different methods are shown in Table 6.2.

Decisions about the most appropriate method (or methods, as many organisations will use more than one) are likely to be influenced by the level of the vacancy and its importance within the organisation. The CIPD survey (2005a) found that recruitment agencies were rated as most effective for senior management and director level posts, whereas the local press was more likely to be rated effective for administrative and manual vacancies. Other factors to be taken into account when choosing the most appropriate method include the

Table 6.2 Percentage of organisations using particular recruitment methods

Local newspaper advertisements	85	Employee referral scheme	38
Recruitment agencies/search	80	Links with schools/colleges/universities	35
Own website	67	Apprentices/work placements/secondments	32
Specialist journals/trade press	59	Commercial website	30
National newspaper advertisements	55	Physical posters/billboards/vehicles	14
Jobcentre Plus	54	Radio or TV advertisements	9
Speculative application/word of mouth	52	Other	7

Number of employers in survey = 713

Source: CIPD (2005a: 10)

resources available within the organisation (in terms of personnel and finance), the perceived target groups, and the organisation's stance on internal versus external recruitment. Human resource management literature emphasises the need to have well-developed internal labour market arrangements for promotion, training and career development, which would suggest that many openings can and should be filled internally (Beaumont, 1993). However, a number of organisations, particularly those in the public sector, have policies that require the majority of posts to be advertised externally. Findings from the 2004 Workplace Employment Relations Survey (WERS, 2004) (Kersley *et al.*, 2005) show that, although the majority of workplaces treat external and internal applicants equally, one-fifth give preference to internal candidates and one in ten prefer to recruit externally.

Design of advertisements

The most popular formal recruitment method continues to be press advertising. Good communication from the employer to potential applicants requires thought and skill, and many organisations use the services of a recruitment agency for the design of the advertisement and advice on the most effective media. The aim of the advertisement is to attract only suitable applicants, and therefore it should discourage those who do not possess the necessary attributes while, at the same time, retaining and encouraging the interest of those with potential to be suitable. Taylor (2005) suggests a number of key decisions faced by recruiters in the style and wording of advertisements:

- Wide trawls or wide nets – i.e., whether the advert aims to attract a wide range of candidates or only those with very specific qualities. For example, an advertisement for the Royal Marines claims that 99 per cent of candidates won't make it.

- Realistic or positive – in terms of the language used and information provided on the job and the organisation.

- Corporate image or specific job – the emphasis most likely to appeal to the target audience can depend on a number of factors, e.g. whether the organisation is a household name or has a good reputation in the area, or whether the type of job is well known or highly sought-after.

- Precise vs vague information – variations are especially apparent in relation to salary information: some organisations (particularly in the public sector) provide very precise information, e.g. 'salary up to £23 889 dependent on qualifications and experience (pay award pending)', whereas others include little more than 'competitive salary'.

Online recruitment

Over recent years there has been a growth in the use of online methods of recruitment. Over two-thirds of organisations advertise vacancies on their own website, 72 per cent accept emailed CVs and just under half accept application forms by email (CIPD, 2005a). The impact of this on the recruitment and selection process is variable and depends on whether

203

ional versus Internet-based recruitment

ditional	Internet
A job vacancy is advertised in the press	A job vacancy is advertised on the Internet
A job seeker writes or telephones for more details and/or an application form	All the company and job details are on the website together with an online application form
3 A job seeker returns the application form and/or CV by post	A job seeker returns the completed application form electronically
4 Personnel review the written application forms or CVs	Specialised computer software reviews the application forms for an initial match with the organisation's requirements

Source: CIPD (2002)

online methods are used to supplement or replace more traditional approaches. Corporate and external websites can be used to advertise vacancies in addition to press adverts, while the handling of enquiries and applications via e-mail can lead to a duplication of activity (electronic as well as paper-based systems) rather than a replacement of one system with another. Alternatively, the impact may be more substantial and can alter the process up to and including the selection stage, as illustrated in Table 6.3

These two approaches are not necessarily exclusive and activities can be combined at almost any stage. For example, a press advertisement may direct readers to a website providing further information or a corporate website may require applicants to request an application form via e-mail or telephone that will then be processed manually (CIPD, 2002).

Stop & think

What are the key advantages and disadvantages of using the internet for recruitment?

The key advantages of online recruitment (CIPD, 2005c) are that it can:

- provide a shorter recruitment cycle and streamlined administration;
- reduce recruitment costs if used instead of rather than as well as other methods;
- reach a wide pool of applicants;
- provide the image of an up-to-date organisation;
- provide global coverage 24/7;
- be a cost-effective way to build a talent bank for future vacancies;
- help handle high volume job applications in a consistent way;
- make internal vacancies known across multiple sites and separate divisions.

The key disadvantages (CIPD, 2005) are that online recruitment can:

- limit the applicant audience as the internet is not the first choice for all job seekers;
- cause applications overload or inappropriate applications;
- exclude those who cannot or do not want to search for a new job online;
- give rise to allegations of discrimination, particularly in the use of limited key words to screen CVs;
- make the process impersonal which may be off-putting for some candidates;
- turn off candidates if the website is badly designed;
- lose out on candidates particularly if the organisation's website is below the search engine ranking of competitors.

An IRS survey (IRS, 2005a: 48) compared online recruitment with more traditional methods and found that online recruitment was just as able to produce the most suitable candidate, even though a larger number of applicants sometimes required recruiters to 'search for a needle in a haystack'. Many respondents also found it easier to administer than traditional recruitment and the majority reported that total costs were lower. The use of online recruitment is likely to continue to grow as the take up of broadband increases.

Recruitment documentation

The response to applicants should indicate the overall image that the organisation wishes to project. Some organisations prepare a package of documents, which may include the job description, the person specification, information about the organisation, the equal opportunities policy, the rewards package available, and possible future prospects. Some give candidates the opportunity to discuss the position with an organisational representative on an informal basis. This allows the candidate to withdraw from the process with the minimum activity and cost to the organisation. Much relevant information can now be supplied via the Internet: for example, BT uses a question and answer approach to supply information on a wide range of issues, including salary and benefits, development opportunities and career prospects (IRS, 2002c).

The design of application forms can vary considerably, but the traditional approach tends to concentrate on finding out about qualifications and work history, and usually includes a section in which candidates are encouraged to 'sell' their potential contribution to the organisation. A more recent development is the adoption of a competency-based focus, requiring candidates to answer a series of questions in which they describe how they have dealt with specific incidents such as solving a difficult problem, or demonstrating leadership skills. Some organisations, particularly in the retail sector, include a short questionnaire in which applicants are asked to indicate their preferred way of working.

A variant on the traditional application form, 'biodata' (short for biographical data), may also be used. Forms usually consist of a series of multiple-choice questions that are partly factual (e.g. number of brothers and sisters, position in the family) and partly about attitudes, values and preferences (Sadler and Milmer, 1993). The results are then compared against an 'ideal' profile, which has been compiled by identifying the competencies that differentiate between effective and non-effective job performance in existing employees. Biodata questionnaires are costly to develop and need to be designed separately for each job (Taylor, 2005). There are also problems with potential discrimination and intrusion into privacy, depending on the information that is sought. For these reasons, biodata is used by only a small number of employers.

Stop & think

How much time and effort does it take an individual to obtain details about a post and complete an application form that attempts to show how their skills and experiences match the requirements of the job?

Why is it important for an organisation to be aware of the answers to the above question?

How do we identify them?

The stages described above constitute recruitment, and are primarily concerned with generating a sufficient pool of applicants. The focus now shifts to selection and the next stages concentrate on assessing the suitability of candidates.

Shortlisting

It is extremely unlikely that all job applicants will meet the necessary criteria, and so the initial step in selection is categorising candidates as probable, possible or unsuitable. This should be done by comparing the information provided on the application form or CV with the predetermined selection criteria. The criteria may either be explicit (detailed on the person specification) or implicit (only in the mind of the person doing the shortlisting). However, this latter approach is potentially discriminatory, and would provide no defence if an organisation was challenged on the grounds of unlawful discrimination (see discussion on legislative requirements earlier in this chapter). Potentially suitable candidates will continue to the next stage of the selection process. CIPD guidelines state that unsuccessful candidates should be informed as soon as possible. In practice, written notification of rejection is increasingly less common, and many application forms warn candidates that if they have not had a response by a set date they can assume they have been unsuccessful.

The increased emphasis on personal characteristics rather than job demands may result in some changes to the way shortlisting is undertaken. For example, the use of biodata can provide a clearer focus than more traditional methods, as 'selectors can concentrate solely on those areas of the form found in the biodata validation exercise to be particularly relevant to the prediction of effective performance in the job concerned' (IRS, 1994). Other developments chiefly reflect a desire to reduce the time and effort involved in shortlisting from large numbers of applicants. One option is to encourage unsuitable candidates to self-select themselves out of the process. Advances in technology allow for the provision of self-selection questionnaires and feedback on the answers on corporate websites. A variant on this is to use 'killer' questions; these are asked at certain stages of an online application process and the wrong answer will terminate the application at that point (IRS, 2003). Another option is to use a software package that compares CVs with the selection criteria and separates the applications that

Box 6.1   Online screening at Woolworths

Woolworths was one of the first large retailers to develop a web-based recruitment strategy. The organisation employs over 28,000 staff across 800 stores and head office and has had to develop a resourcing strategy that is able to cope with high volume recruitment. Its online recruitment focuses on store and assistant manager vacancies and the organisation receives up to 5000 applicants a year for these posts.

There are three stages to the online screening process. The first stage is 'biographical', in that applicants answer a series of questions designed to screen them against the essential criteria for the role. These include areas such as specific work experience, education, the right to work in the UK and unspent criminal convictions. Some 'killer' questions are also included. If an unacceptable response is received, the applicant is informed at the end of this section that their application is unlikely to be successful but they are still welcome to complete the selection process.

In the second stage of the screening process applicants are matched against the competency-based criteria for the role. The questions are based on asking applicants about their actual past experience and typically start with 'In the past, I have….' Each statement is accompanied by a series of tick boxes that allows the individual to indicate their level of experience associated with each competency.

The third stage gives applicants the opportunity to inform the organisation about their career expectations. This provides the organisation with a further screening process but also enables individuals to screen themselves out if they have unrealistic expectations about the job. Any potential mismatches can be followed up in the telephone interview that forms the next stage in the process.

Feedback is provided after each stage. On completion of the application and screening process, applicants receive an automated response thanking them for their application and advising them that the company will be in touch. The online screening process rates candidates from 'A' (great candidate) to 'C' (not suitable). Promising applications are followed up with a telephone interview but the approach taken will differ depending on the ranking: an interview with a 'straight A' candidate aims to hook the person and invite them to the final selection event – an assessment centre – whereas an interview with a 'B' candidate is likely to be more exploratory.

Source: based on IRS (2005d: 46).

match the criteria from those that do not. This has the advantage of removing some of the subjectivity inherent in human shortlisting, but does rely on the selection criteria being correctly identified in the first instance. It can also reject good candidates who have not used the right keywords so needs to be handled with caution. A third option is to reduce large numbers of applicants via random selection. Although there is concern that this may operate against equal opportunities, it is also claimed that 'randomised selection may produce a better shortlist than one based on human intervention where the wrong selection criteria are used consistently or where the correct selection criteria are applied inconsistently' (IRS, 1994: 6).

Selection techniques

Various selection techniques are available, and a selection procedure will frequently involve the use of more than one. The most popular techniques are outlined here, and their validity and effectiveness are discussed later in the chapter.

Interviews

Interviewing is universally popular as a selection tool. Torrington *et al.* (2002: 242) describe an interview as 'a controlled conversation with a purpose', but this broad definition encompasses a wide diversity of practice. Differences can include both the number of interviewers and the number of interview stages. The format can be biographical, i.e. following the contents of the application form or it can be based on the key competencies required for the job. Over the years interviews have received a relatively bad press as being overly subjective, prone to interviewer bias, and therefore unreliable predictors of future performance. Such criticisms are levelled particularly at unstructured interviews, and in response to this, developments have focused on more formally structuring the interview or supplementing the interview with less subjective selection tools such as psychometric tests and work sampling.

There are different types of structured interview, but they have a number of common features (Anderson and Shackleton, 1993: 72):

- The interaction is standardised as much as possible.
- All candidates are asked the same series of questions.
- Replies are rated by the interviewer on preformatted rating scales.
- Dimensions for rating are derived from critical aspects of on-the-job behaviour.

The two most popular structured interview techniques are behavioural and situational interviews. Both use critical incident job analysis to determine aspects of job behaviour that distinguish between effective and ineffective performance (Anderson and Shackleton, 1993). The difference between them is that in behavioural interviews the questions focus on past behaviour (for example, 'Can you give an example of when you have had to deal with a difficult person? What did you do?'), whereas situational interviews use hypothetical questions ('What would you do if you had to deal with a team member who was uncooperative?'). Table 6.4 shows the popularity of different types of interview by industrial sector.

Decisions about the number of interviewers, the type of interview and the number of interview stages are likely to take account of the seniority and nature of the post and the organisation's attitude towards equal opportunities.

Activity

Imagine you are responsible for selecting operators to work in a call centre. Prepare a set of behavioural questions suitable for the interview. You are looking for evidence of strong social skills, e.g. good verbal communication, positive attitude, good sense of humour, energy and enthusiasm; and good technical skills, e.g. numeracy and keyboard skills.

Test out these questions on friends and colleagues to assess their effectiveness. What do you see as the key strengths and weaknesses of this approach?

Table 6.4 Interview types by sector (%)

	All	Manufacturing and production	Voluntary, community and not-for-profit	Private sector services	Public services
Interviews following contents of CV/application form (i.e. biographical)	68	80	56	73	38
Competency-based interviews	58	56	40	61	59
Structured interview (panel)	56	45	84	45	61
Structured interviews (one-to-one and critical incident/behavioural)	41	40	31	50	25

Source: CIPD (2005a: 12).

Telephone interviewing

The use of telephone interviewing is increasing. The CIPD recruitment survey (CIPD, 2005a) found that 30 per cent of all organisations and 45 per cent of organisations in private sector services use telephone interviews as part of the selection process. Telephone interviews can be used to screen out unsuitable applicants or as an integral part of the selection process (IRS, 2005e: 43):

Screening

- Short, rigidly structured interviews based on essential criteria.
- A competency-based, screening interview, where candidates are asked a number of multiple-choice questions to gauge suitability for the job role.

Selection

- A structured telephone role play when roles require advanced telephone communication skills.
- A sales telephone interview where a candidate is asked to sell something to the interviewer over the phone.
- An in-depth, semi-structured interview for senior or managerial positions. Where it is more difficult to capture experience and skills on paper an initial telephone interview can help both parties assess suitability for the next stage of the process.
- An alternative to face-to-face interviews for people who are based overseas or unavailable for long periods of time.

Advances in technology continue to facilitate other forms of 'remote' interviewing, for example by video link or via the internet, but take-up is still relatively low.

What are the main benefits and drawbacks of telephone interviews?

Telephone interviews have a a number of benefits, including (CIPD, 2001a; IRS, 2002d):

- They can be quicker to arrange and conduct than more conventional methods.
- They can be cost-effective as an initial screen.
- They can maintain a degree of confidentiality about the post as these details will only be provided once initial screening is complete (particularly useful for senior posts).

- They provide an ideal way to assess a candidate's telephone manner.
- There are fewer interpersonal distractions.
- They provide less opportunity to discriminate on grounds of race, disability, age or other non-job-related factors.

One of the major drawbacks cited in the same reports is that telephone interviews cannot take account of non-verbal communication, e.g. facial expressions, gestures and body language, which accounts for 60 per cent of total interpersonal communication. However, research into telephone and face-to-face interviewing suggests that what is said and how it is said is more influential in selection decisions than non-verbal clues: 'while 60 per cent of communication may be non-verbal, it would appear that the remaining 40 per cent that involves verbal communication is key to selection' (IRS, 2005e: 43).

Tests

'Testing is essentially an attempt to achieve objectivity, or, to put it more accurately, to reduce subjectivity in selection decision-making' (Lewis, 1985: 157). The types of test used for selection are ability and aptitude tests, intelligence tests and personality questionnaires. Ability tests (such as typing tests) are concerned with skills and abilities already acquired by an individual, whereas aptitude tests (such as verbal reasoning tests or numerical aptitude) focus on an individual's potential to undertake specific tasks. Intelligence tests can give an indication of overall mental capacity, and have been used for selection purposes for some considerable time. Personality questionnaires allow quantification of characteristics that are important to job performance and difficult to measure by other methods (Lewis, 1985). The debate about the value of personality tests is ongoing, and centres around lack of agreement on four key issues (Taylor, 2005):

- the extent to which personality is measurable;
- the extent to which personality remains stable over time and across different situations;
- the extent to which certain personality characteristics can be identified as being necessary or desirable for a particular job;
- the extent to which completion of a questionnaire can provide sufficient information about an individual's personality to make meaningful inferences about their suitability for a job.

Table 6.5 shows the use of psychometric testing across a range of organisations.

Tests have the benefit of providing objective measurement of individual characteristics, but they must be chosen with care. Armstrong (2006: 462) lists four characteristics of a good test:

Table 6.5 The use of psychometric testing by sector (%)

	All	Manufacturing and production	Voluntary, community and not-for-profit	Private sector services	Public services
Tests for specific skills	50	39	65	49	61
General ability tests	40	41	51	33	48
Literacy and/or numeracy tests	39	40	49	35	42
Personality questionnaires	36	37	35	38	31
Online tests (selection/ self-selection)	5	5	4	7	2

Source: CIPD (2005a: 12).

- It is a *sensitive* measuring instrument which discriminates well between subjects.

- It has been *standardised* on a representative and sizeable sample of the population for which it is intended so that any individual's score can be interpreted in relation to others.

- It is *reliable* in the sense that it always measures the same thing. A test aimed at measuring a particular characteristic should measure the same characteristic when applied to different people at the same time, or to the same person at different times.

- It is *valid* in the sense that it measures the characteristic which the test is intended to measure. Thus, an intelligence test should measure intelligence and not simply verbal facility.

One relatively recent development has been the growth of interest in online testing. Online testing has the potential to reduce delivery costs, thus making testing more affordable for lower-paid jobs. However, there are also some potential disadvantages, including lack of control of the environment in which the test takes place, problems verifying candidates' identity and the need for candidates (under data protection legislation) to have access to any personal information stored about them (IRS, 2002e).

Assessment centres

An assessment centre is not a place but rather a process that 'consists of a small group of participants who undertake a series of tests and exercises under observation, with a view to the assessment of their skills and competencies, their suitability for particular roles and their potential for development' (Fowler, 1992). There are a number of defining characteristics of an assessment centre:

- A variety of individual and group assessment techniques are used, at least one of which is a work simulation.

- Multiple assessors are used (frequently the ratio is one assessor per two candidates). These assessors should have received training prior to participating in the centre.

- Selection decisions are based on pooled information from assessors and techniques.

- Job analysis is used to identify the behaviours and characteristics to be measured by the assessment centre.

Assessment centres are used by just over a third of organisations (CIPD, 2005a). The assessment centre process allows organisations to observe candidate behaviour in a work-related setting; and the combination of techniques used helps to improve the consistency and objectivity of the selection process. The use of such a sophisticated technique, if handled well, can also help the organisation to display a positive image to potential candidates. The drawbacks primarily relate

---

Box 6.2 | **Online testing at Cadbury Schweppes**

Cadbury Schweppes receives around 4000 applications each year for just 20 places on its graduate programme. Four years ago, the company moved its recruitment process online and has now gone even further and introduced online verbal and numerical reasoning tests in place of paper-based versions.

The company has always used psychometric assessment as part of its selection process. However, it was taking candidates in the region of 90 minutes to complete the paper-based tests during assessment centres. The company trialled an online test from assessment specialist PSL last year and has now cut this down to a 45-minute test that is conducted prior to the interview stage.

Source: based on IRS (2005f: 44)

Question

What are the advantages and disadvantages of this approach for the organisation and individual applicants?

to the costs and resources required. For this reason, assessment centres are most likely to be used in public sector organisations and by larger private sector employers. A number of trends has been identified in the design and delivery of assessment centres (IRS, 2002f), including:

- More emphasis on the integration of exercises (i.e. using the same business context and same characters in different exercises).
- A clearer link between exercises and work content.
- More candidate friendly (i.e. better briefing on how people will be assessed, more comprehensive feedback).
- A focus on core values to identify candidates who will contribute most in rapidly changing circumstances.

Job simulation/work sampling

A key component of an assessment centre is the job simulation exercise, which is designed to be an accurate representation of performance in the job itself. Candidates are placed in situations that they are likely to face if selected: examples include in-tray exercises and role-play interviews.

An extension of job simulation is work sampling: that is, giving the candidate the opportunity to perform in the role for a specified length of time. An example of this is given in the Pret A Manger case on page 216.

References

These are used to obtain additional information about candidates from third parties such as previous employers, academic tutors, colleagues or acquaintances. The accuracy of the information is variable; Armstrong (2006) suggests that factual information (e.g. nature of previous job, time in employment, reason for leaving, salary, academic achievement) is essential, but opinions about character and suitability are less reliable. He goes on to say that 'personal referees are, of course, entirely useless. All they prove is that the applicant has at least one or two friends' (p. 435).

References can be used at different stages in the selection process: some organisations use them only to confirm details of the chosen candidate after the position has been offered, whereas others will request references for all shortlisted candidates prior to interview. The format may also vary, with some organisations requesting verbal references by telephone and others requiring written references. In either case, organisations may require referees to answer specific structured questions or provide some general comments on the candidate's performance and suitability. The most popular types of information requested by employers include absence record, opinion of candidate's personality and suitability for the vacancy, work history, punctuality and disciplinary record (IRS, 2002a: 752). Many employers consider references to be 'only marginally effective' (Industrial Society, 1994), yet there is little doubt that they remain a popular component of the selection process, particularly in the public sector.

Other methods

One of the more unconventional and controversial selection tools is graphology, based on the idea that handwriting analysis can reveal personal traits and characteristics. Although it is not widely used in the UK, its effectiveness as a selection tool has been the subject of considerable debate. Having reviewed the available data on graphology, the CIPD concludes that 'the evidence in favour is inconclusive, anecdotal and therefore prone to bias and misinterpretation' (CIPD, 2001b).

Factors influencing choice of selection techniques

What determines the choice of different techniques? One could reasonably assume that a key factor in determining the type of method would be its ability to predict who is suitable and unsuitable for the position. In other words, whatever technique is used, people who do well should be capable of doing the job and people who do badly should not.

Accuracy

'No single technique, regardless of how well it is designed and administered, is capable of producing perfect selection decisions that predict with certainty which individuals will perform well in a particular role' (Marchington and Wilkinson, 2005: 175). Figure 6.2 shows the accuracy of selection methods measured on the correlation coefficient between predicted and actual job performance, with zero for chance prediction and 1.0 for perfect prediction.

The increased use of more accurate methods such as assessment centres and selection testing can help to improve the effectiveness of the selection process. However, findings from the CIPD survey (2005a) show that interviews are rated as the most effective selection method for all occupational groups. Nevertheless, doubts about accuracy appear to have encouraged employers to adopt more structured interview formats or supplement the interview with other selection methods such as tests or work simulation.

Statistics on the accuracy of different types of selection techniques mask wide variations within each technique. Two key criteria to be considered are reliability and validity. Reliability generally relates to the ability of a selection technique to produce consistent results over time or among different people, whereas validity relates to the extent to which the technique is able to measure what it is intended to measure. These have already been discussed in relation to selection testing, but can be applied to other techniques too. For example, the reliability of interviews can vary if interviewers have differing levels of interviewing skills or different perceptions of the selection criteria. Reliability can also vary when just one person is involved in interviewing, as the conduct of the interview can be affected by the timing of the interview and by how many interviews have been conducted already.

Figure 6.2	The predictive accuracy of selection methods

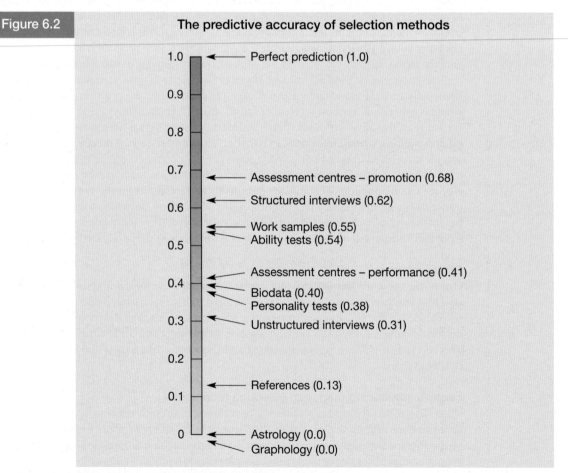

Source: Adapted from Anderson and Shackleton (1993).

In assessment centres, the effectiveness of the exercises in predicting job performance is dependent on the extent to which they represent the performance content and competency requirements of the job they are designed to sample. In practice, the standard of assessment centres can vary from organisation to organisation:

> Because properly designed and applied ACs work well, it does not mean that anything set up and run with the same name is equally good. A lot of so-called ACs in the UK use badly thought-out exercises and inadequately trained assessors; they probably achieve little other than to alienate candidates, who are usually quick to spot their shortcomings.
>
> (Fletcher, 1993: 46)

The same can be said of tests that are relevant only if the behaviours and attitudes they measure are those necessary for effective job performance. Additional problems are also associated with the use of tests. Both the British Psychological Society (BPS) and the CIPD have issued codes of practice on the use of tests, which stress that everyone responsible for the application of tests, which includes evaluation, interpretation and feedback, should be trained to at least the level of competence recommended by the BPS (CIPD, 2001c). The guidelines also make it clear that 'the results of a single test should not be used as the sole basis for decision-making' (IPD, 1997). However, a survey conducted by Newell and Shackleton (1993) found that, although companies used trained personnel to administer tests, the majority did not always give feedback of results to candidates, and some were using the tests to make definitive judgements about people.

Level of vacancy

IRS (1997: 16) argues that the type of job is 'the most significant influence on the choice of selection methods for any one vacancy'. Assessment centres, in particular, are more likely to be used for managerial and graduate posts. This may indicate an organisation's willingness to invest more heavily in future managers than in other parts of the workforce, but may also be due to candidate expectations and the organisation's need to attract the highest-quality applicants. A growing number of organisations have started to use assessment centre techniques for non-managerial appointments but the process tends to be shorter and therefore cheaper. For example, easyJet holds half-day assessment centres for cabin crew (IDS, 2002).

Cost of selection techniques

There is no doubt that recruitment and selection can be costly activities, and the costs incurred by some selection techniques can make them prohibitive for all but a few 'key' vacancies in an organisation. For example, assessment centres require considerable investment of resources and are particularly demanding in terms of the time commitment required from assessors (IDS, 2002). However, in deciding on the most cost-effective methods, the 'up-front' costs need to be balanced against the costs of wrong decisions, which may include costs associated with labour turnover owing to lack of ability. Jaffee and Cohen (cited in Appelbaum *et al.*, 1989: 60) suggest that consideration should include some or all of the following:

- the start-up time required by a replacement for the jobholder;
- the downtime associated with the jobholder changing jobs internally or externally;
- training and/or retraining for the replacement and the jobholder;
- relocation expenses;
- the shortfall in productivity between an effective and ineffective jobholder;
- the psychological impact on the 'failed' jobholder and the morale of others in the department.

The CIPD recruitment survey (CIPD, 2005a) found that, although half the respondents reported that they calculate the cost of recruitment, only a small proportion were able to supply figures.

Custom and practice

A possible explanation for the continued use of interviews is the simple fact that people are familiar with them. Although, at an academic level, the general consensus is that interviews are unreliable, invalid and provide ample opportunity for personal prejudice (Herriot, 1989), at a practical level many interviewers feel that they are good judges of people and can make effective selection decisions, and most of us would probably feel unhappy in starting a job without undergoing some form of face-to-face meeting with our prospective employer.

Making the decision

The aim of the overall recruitment and selection process is to provide enough information to enable recruiters to differentiate between those who can do the job and those who cannot. The prescriptive approach stresses that the final decision should involve measuring each candidate against the selection criteria defined in the person specification and not against each other (Torrington *et al.*, 2002). Searle (2003: 114–116) suggests a number of sources of error and bias in interviewers' decision-making process, including:

- 'similar to me effect', where interviewers enhance the ratings of those who look like themselves, respond in a similar way, or appear to have equivalent experiences;
- 'halo effect', where one aspect of the candidate's qualities (most commonly physical attractiveness) influences all other aspects and so boosts their overall rating;
- 'horns effect', where over-attention to some negative aspect reduces a candidate's overall rating.

The combination of a number of different selection methods and the increased use of more objective methods can enhance the quantity and quality of information about each candidate, although Anderson and Shackleton (1993) warn of the dangers of information overload in selection. Armstrong (2006: 459) points out that the ultimate decision may be judgemental:

> There may be one outstanding candidate, but quite often there are two or three. In these circumstances you have to come to a balanced view of which one is more likely to fit the job and the organisation and have potential for a long-term career, if this is possible.

How do we know if we've got it right?

The final stage of the recruitment and selection process concerns measurement of its success, both qualitatively and quantitatively. ACAS guidelines suggest that any recruitment and selection system should be based on three fundamental principles: effectiveness, efficiency and fairness (ACAS, 1983). Effectiveness is concerned with distinguishing accurately between suitable and unsuitable candidates: Mayo (1995) suggests a number of ways in which this can be measured for recruits, including retention rates, promotion rates, and percentage of recruits perceived as having high potential after three to five years. However, these factors can also be influenced by working conditions and the emphasis on employee development within the organisation. Efficiency is concerned more with the costs of the exercise, and measures here may include average cost per recruit, average time lapsed between various stages, percentage of offers made, and offer-acceptance rate (Mayo, 1995). The CIPD recruitment survey (CIPD, 2005a) found that the average time taken to fill a vacancy varied between seventeen-and-a-half weeks for senior management to five-and-a-half weeks for manual workers. However, as this period was measured from the decision that there was a vacancy to the new employee's actual start date, different notice periods also have to be considered. Fairness is concerned with dealing with all applicants fairly and honestly, but has often been taken to refer to equal opportunity monitoring, and has been limited to record keeping on the gender, ethnic origin and disability of successful and unsuccessful candidates.

Who is involved in the process?

Recruitment and selection have long been seen as two of the key activities of the HR function. However, increasingly organisations are choosing to involve other parties such as line managers or specialist agencies, or to outsource the activity altogether.

Line managers

A key feature of HRM is the extent to which activities once seen as the remit of HR specialists are devolved to others, particularly line managers and supervisors. Findings from WERS 98 (Cully *et al.*, 1999) showed that around 80 per cent of managers considered they had responsibility for employment relations matters, with 94 per cent of these including 'recruitment and selection of employees'. In workplaces (with supervisors and over 25 employees), 30 per cent of private sector and 17 per cent of public sector supervisors had the final say in decisions about taking on the people who worked for them, though relevant training was not given in the majority of cases. However, it appears that line managers are likely to be involved in selection rather than recruitment activity. First-line management respondents to a survey (IRS, 2004) reported that recruitment was one of the HR practices for which they had little responsibility (along with performance pay, promotions and welfare). In contrast, (Lupton, 2000) found that hospital consultants made decisions about the selection of doctors, with HR input limited to administrative support.

Box 6.3 **Monitoring the effectiveness of recruitment**

Between 2000 and 2002 the Government spent £50 million on recruitment advertising for essential services such as the police, the NHS and teachers.

The police recruitment campaign, which featured celebrities such as Lennox Lewis, Bob Geldorf and Patsy Palmer saying that they could not cope with everyday situations faced by the police, cost £12 million.

A BBC survey found that only 13 forces could verify the number of officers attracted by the campaign – a paltry 120. Extrapolating this figure across all of the UK's 43 regional forces would mean that the campaign led to the recruitment of only 400 officers, i.e. £30,000 per recruit.

The advertising agency, M&C Saatchi, argued against these findings, stating that the number of recruits between September 2000 and 2001 was 70 per cent up on the previous year, thus making it one of the most successful police recruitment campaigns ever. However, the Home Office admits that it is unable to find out whether or not recruits were inspired by the adverts or were joining for other reasons. Recruitment is conducted regionally and it is up to regional forces to check why recruits have joined. There are some suggestions that regional forces are reluctant to acknowledge the success of the campaign, since this would detract from their role in recruitment and could jeopardise the jobs of local recruitment officers

Source: Benady (2002: 24–27).

Questions

1 What methods could have been used to monitor the effectiveness of the recruitment campaign?

2 What could be done to integrate national and regional recruitment?

Peers

Employees can be involved at various stages in the recruitment and selection process. The most popular level of involvement is to encourage existing employees to introduce candidates to the organisation. Over a third (38 per cent) of respondents to the CIPD recruitment survey (2005a) operate employee referral schemes. Companies using this approach include Alliance and Leicester, Asda, Amazon, BUPA, first direct, Nationwide, Sainsbury's and Vodafone with payments for successful appointments ranging from £200 to £2500 (IDS, 2004). A less common approach is to involve peers or team members in the selection of candidates, as illustrated in the example below.

Recruitment agencies

More than eight in ten organisations used recruitment agencies in 2004 (CIPD, 2005a). The same survey also identifies the main reasons for using agencies to fill vacancies as:

- Speed (63 per cent).
- Challenge of recruiting scarce skills (57 per cent).
- Direct advertising did not work (38 per cent).
- Specialist expertise (30 per cent).

Recruitment agencies can be used to fill temporary and permanent positions. Their involvement in the recruitment and selection process can vary from supplying 'temps' to address short-term needs, to undertaking recruitment administration and initial stages of selection, i.e. short-listing. The CIPD (2005a) survey differentiates between different types of recruitment agency:

- *Contingency* – i.e. ad hoc recruitment using agency database of candidates.
- *Advertised selection* – agency runs online/press campaign on organisation's behalf.
- *Search* – 'head-hunting'.

Box 6.4 | ## Selection at Pret A Manger

Pret A Manger, the sandwich chain, employs 2400 staff in its 118 shops. In 2001 the company received 55,000 applications for fewer than 1500 vacancies. The first stage of selection consists of a competency-based interview. To be successful at this stage candidates have to demonstrate an outgoing personality, a positive attitude to life, some knowledge of the company and enthusiasm to work there. Those who successfully complete this interview are then invited to undertake a day's on-the-job experience at the shop with the vacancy. Candidates are required to start at 6.30 a.m., the same time as their future colleagues. An existing team member will be assigned to act as a guide and mentor for the day but candidates will work with as many other team members and do as many different jobs as possible. Team members will assess each candidate on a number of competencies, including enthusiasm and ability to follow instructions, and then vote on whether or not they want to offer them a job. Candidates will also be interviewed by the shop manager who does not get a vote but can lobby for or against someone. Towards the end of the day, the manager gathers team members' votes and lets the candidate know the outcome. Feedback is provided for both successful and unsuccessful candidates.

Source: Carrington (2002).

Questions

1 What are the benefits and drawbacks of including peer assessment as part of the selection process?

2 What factors need to be considered before introducing peer assessment?

'Executive search and selection' tends to be used mainly for senior level appointments. Search (or head-hunting) refers to the recruitment of executives through direct or personal contact by a specialist consultancy acting as an intermediary between the employer and prospective candidate(s). Selection concerns the identification of potential candidates and preliminary screening to produce a viable short-list of suitably qualified individuals. The individuals targeted by executive search consultants generally work at senior levels, and may have responsibility at regional, national or international level. Key reasons for using executive search and selection consultants include the need for confidentiality, a lack of in-house recruitment knowledge and skills at this level, and simply a lack of senior management time to devote to the activity. The main advantage of using specialist consultants is 'the opportunity they give to open up confidential channels of communication with high-flying employees working for competitor organisations . . . [allowing] recruitment managers to tap into a reservoir of interesting potential applicants who are not actively seeking new jobs' (Taylor, 2005:188). However, there can be considerable variations in the quality of service provided and a number of large corporations are employing their own researchers rather than using head-hunters (Hirschkorn, 2004).

Outsourcing

'Outsourcing' is the term used to describe the transfer of a distinct business function from inside the business to an external third party. Outsourcing of parts of the HR function has become more common. Lonsdale and Cox (1998) argue that outsourcing decisions can be classified under the following three headings:

● Outsourcing for short-term cost and headcount reductions.

● Core-competence-based outsourcing, where peripheral activities are passed to third parties and core activities are retained in-house.

● Iterative and entrepreneurial outsourcing, where periodic reviews of critical market activities are undertaken, with subsequent decisions to retain or outsource.

Outsourcing certain HR activities, such as payroll administration, is nothing new but only a minority of organisations appear to have outsourced recruitment activity according to an IRS survey (IRS, 2005h). The survey findings show that the activities likely to be outsourced are at the early stages of the process, i.e. advertising, managing responses from applicants and undertaking an initial sift of applications. Only 2 per cent of respondents have given a third party responsibility for making final selection decisions.

Stop & think

What are the advantages and disadvantages of outsourcing recruitment activity to a third party?

The same survey found that the main reasons why employers had decided to outsource recruitment activities were to speed up recruitment; gain access to greater expertise; help make HR more strategic; make recruitment more flexible and responsive; and achieve cost savings. At the same time, the reasons why other employers had decided not to outsource recruitment activity was that recruitment was seen as too important to outsource; it would not be cost effective to do so; the issues had not been raised; and it would not add value (IRS, 2005h).

Ethical issues in recruitment and selection

Up to now we have focused on recruitment and selection from an organisational perspective. We should not forget that recruitment and selection is a two-way process, and so our final topic for discussion concerns the extent to which any approach respects the rights of individuals participating in the process. Ethical issues arise concerning the treatment of people during recruitment and selection. To a large extent, whether certain activities are perceived as ethical or unethical reflects the prevailing attitudes within the society or societies in which an organisation operates. However, differences in attitudes also reflect the judgement and positioning chosen by major stakeholders, and can be determined by traditional values inherent within the organisation itself.

Recruitment

Providing equality of opportunity for a diverse number of groups is considered important by certain organisations. However, opportunity to apply for positions can be restricted through the (sometimes unnecessary) insistence on previous experience, or prior development of skills and competences. 'Glass ceilings' can exist in internal labour markets for women and minority groups. In the case of third-party recruitment, particularly executive search, opportunities to widen the net can be forestalled, with organisations frequently relying on the knowledge and networking of one consultant to deliver the chosen recruit, often to a specification that ensures that the status quo is maintained. The continued existence of such practices suggests a society in which those in power tolerate them as rational and sound, and where there is insufficient groundswell of opinion from society at large to insist on change. As Goss (1994: 173) remarks:

> If HRM is to be serious in its commitment to the development of all human resources, it may need to face the challenge of wider patterns of social inequality. This means looking not only at disadvantage, but also addressing the issue of who benefits from the status quo.

In a similar vein, multinational and other organisations that have overseas supplier links have to consider their ethical position in relation to both employment conditions and more particularly targeted recruits. To some extent a similar discussion can be held concerning UK organisations where work is subcontracted to UK agencies and suppliers, on relatively poor conditions of employment, or where schoolchildren (already 'fully employed') are recruited in lieu of those already available in the external labour market.

The business decision may be difficult and involve weighing up important economic, financial, marketing and public relations considerations. While component costs may fall dramatically through the use of overseas subsidiaries and suppliers, bad publicity and loss of sales can ensue through dealing with an organisation where, for example, child labour is found to be extensively used, employment conditions are unsafe, or recruits are paid less than a living wage. Model codes of practice have been drawn up, but for many organisations the ethical issues in 'make or buy' decisions will continue to be debated.

Selection

Issues in selection revolve around areas of individual rights, the potential for abuse of power, issues of control and social engineering, use of certain assessment techniques, and the issues of equality of opportunity implied in the above.

The ownership of information about an individual passes in the recruitment and selection process from the individual to the organisation. While some protection is afforded by data protection legislation, the organisation is perceived to increase its power over the individual by holding such information and by accumulating more through the use of various selection techniques, the findings of which are not always made known to the candidate.

An individual's right to privacy is further challenged by the impact of scientific developments assisting the prediction of future employment scenarios. For example, tests now exist to enable organisations to conduct pre-employment medicals that predict the future health of candidates. As genetic tests become increasingly available, will employers use them to screen out anyone whom they see as potentially expensive to employ? As certain genes occur more frequently in particular ethnic groups, the issues become even more complex.

Apart from questions about the technical effectiveness of various selection techniques, ethical questions remain about their use at all:

> There are questions of a more ethical nature surrounding personality tests. It has been suggested that organisations have no right to seek to control access to jobs on the grounds of individual personality.
>
> (Goss, 1994: 47)

Professional guidance in the area of occupation testing exists, both in specific codes of practice (CIPD and BPS) and as part of ethical codes of practice within large organisations in particular. However, research has shown that, while selectors claim to recognise the rights of those being tested (for example, to be fairly treated, to expect counselling where needed, to confidentiality of data, to know the tests used are valid), these rights are not always upheld in practice (Baker and Cooper, 2002). In addition, questions remain to be asked as to whether:

- the selection of one personality type leads to a weakened 'inbred' profile of employees in organisations, incapable of thinking or acting in original ways when the situation demands;
- an organisation has the right to enforce a unitarist perspective on employees – some selection tests, for example, are designed to filter out those who are 'prone to unionise' (Flood *et al.*, 1996), others to ensure that potential employees' values are in line with the organisation's thinking:

> At the heart of these concerns seems to be a fear about the totalitarian possibilities of work organisations and the role of personality profiling as a form of 'social engineering' for corporate conformity.
>
> (Goss, 1994: 47)

The use of interviews as a selection method has long been open to criticism on the grounds of subjectivity and stereotyping. Using biodata as a basis of selection has potential for misuse, discriminating against individuals and groups on factors that are beyond their control (education, social class and gender, for example). Graphology attracts criticism for similar reasons of social stereotyping and superficial judgements.

In conclusion, the use of both external and internal labour markets and associated selection techniques can raise ethical issues. Poaching experienced people from the external labour market implies an approach that only 'takes' from society, in terms of the costs of education and previous training and development, and the higher wages needed to attract applicants can be perceived as inflationary. Alternatively, one can view the use of the internal labour market through in-house development around organisation-based objectives as somewhat menacing, tying the individual closely to the organisation from which escape is perceived as increasingly difficult and from which the measurement of individual freedom, and the quality of the conditions of employment enjoyed, become more difficult to judge.

Conclusion

The focus of this chapter has been to outline contemporary approaches to recruitment and selection, and to consider the influence of external and internal factors on the process. We conclude that the systematic approach to recruitment and selection still provides a useful framework for analysing activity. The key stages – defining the vacancy, attracting applicants, assessing candidates, and making the final decision – are applicable most of the time, but the way in which each stage is tackled can vary considerably. Key developments within the process itself include the increased use of technology. The internet has emerged as a new recruitment medium, and its use is likely to continue to grow. At the same time, the availability of software to aid the selection process is increasing. Developments in selection techniques appear to reflect growing awareness of the limitations of interviews, and so there is evidence of a growth in the use of more structured formats as well as greater use of supplementary tools such as tests and job simulations. For some organisations, however, it is business as usual and little has changed.

The current state of recruitment and selection is complex because a variety of internal and external factors continue to influence the process. The underlying philosophy regarding the management of human resources and the degree of adoption of technological advances affects the way work is organised and the resultant skills needed by employees. Externally, labour market conditions, legislation and government policy in training and education dictate who is available to fill contemporary jobs. Further complexity is added by the growth of multinational enterprises. These factors are constantly changing, and the environment in which the recruitment and selection process operates is dynamic and increasingly ambiguous. What is certain, however, is that there is no universal solution to this complexity – no 'one size that fits all' – and this is how one can account for the coexistence of both new and traditional approaches to the recruitment and selection of employees. Organisations tend to adopt a pragmatic approach to the attraction and selection of employees based on their assessment of current and future conditions and their response to the critical questions outlined in this chapter. Thus, one will find differences in approaches not only between organisations but also within organisations, depending on the level of vacancies and organisational requirements.

Although this chapter has concentrated on recruitment and selection from an organisational perspective, readers should not forget that recruitment and selection is a two-way process. Not all the developments can be endorsed wholeheartedly. On the positive side, the use of more sophisticated techniques can be seen as an attempt to improve the quality of the selection decision, through increasing objectivity and reducing the scope for bias and prejudice. On the negative side, the emphasis on personality and behavioural characteristics can be used to create and manipulate a workforce that is more amenable to management initiatives. Ethical considerations continue to be important, and care must be taken in the use of these techniques, particularly in handling the increasingly large amount of information that can be gained about prospective workers.

The most appropriate recruitment and selection techniques will continue to be those that balance the requirements of organisations with those of current and prospective employees, and the approach adopted is likely to be determined, at least in part, by external circumstances. If predictions about the demise of 'jobs for life' and the growth of 'portfolio careers' are true, then the experience of recruitment and selection may become an increasing feature in all our lives, regardless of the techniques involved.

Summary

The chapter began with five key objectives. Here we revisit those objectives and outline our key responses:

- Recruitment and selection are integrated activities. Recruitment is primarily concerned with generating a pool of suitable candidates whereas selection is concerned with identifying those that meet the organisation's requirements.

- The external factors most likely to affect recruitment and selection practices are conditions in external labour markets, technological developments, and legislation. The combination of these factors can be contradictory: on the one hand, legislative requirements can suggest a common 'best' practice, whereas on the other hand variations in labour supply and market conditions can indicate the need for a more diverse, pragmatic approach.

- A range of internal organisational factors can influence approaches to recruitment and selection, including the organisation's business strategy and the preferred balance between external and internal recruitment . Additional factors include industrial, sectoral and size variation and the growth in multinational enterprises. The combination of organisational diversity and pressures from the external environment can account for variations in recruitment and selection practice.

- The key stages of a systematic approach to recruitment and selection can be summarised as defining the vacancy, attracting applicants, assessing candidates, making appropriate decisions, and evaluating the effectiveness of the process. Recent developments within this framework include greater use of the Internet for recruitment, greater emphasis on competencies and the increased use of more sophisticated selection techniques such as psychometric tests and assessment centres. At the same time, more traditional methods such as press advertising, interviews and references continue to be very popular. In addition, recruitment and selection activities are increasingly devolved to other parties both inside and outside the organisation.

- There is considerable variation in the effectiveness of recruitment and selection techniques. Although the use of selection methods with higher predictive validity is increasing, the most widely used methods are not necessarily the most accurate at differentiating between people who can and cannot do the job. Effectiveness can also be considered in relation to equal opportunity and ethical issues, such as the extent to which employment of people from previously under-represented groups is encouraged, and the existence of checks that selection methods are 'fair' – that is, discriminate only on job ability. In measuring effectiveness, organisations need to balance the costs involved in the actual process against the costs of selecting the wrong person.

QUESTIONS

1 What factors should be taken into account to determine the most appropriate recruitment methods and how can effectiveness be measured?

2 What can an organisation do to minimise potential indirect discrimination during the recruitment and selection process?

3 To what extent can improving the structure of interviews increase their validity and reliability as a selection tool?

CASE STUDY

International graduate recruitment at GKN

GKN is a global manufacturing and technological company. It recruits 20 engineering graduates each year to its 'International leadership development programme' (ILDP) and receives more than 1000 applications for places on the programme. GKN recruits graduates from the UK, US, Germany, Italy, France and Spain. Assessment centres form a very important part of the selection process. Candidates invited to take part will already have successfully completed an initial interview with a member of the ILDP team and the results will have been considered by a pre-assessment centre board. Assessment centres are held over one-and-a-half days and could take place at one of GKN's corporate sites or at a hotel or conference centre, depending on location. Typically, around 12 candidates attend each assessment centre.

Case study continued

The centre starts in the afternoon of the first day with a presentation about the GKN group and the ILDP programme. This is followed by a written in-tray exercise that lasts for 90 minutes and is based on similar tasks and scenarios to those the candidate would be likely to encounter in the role. The evening provides an opportunity for candidates to interact socially and they are often joined by current GKN employees who themselves joined the company through the ILDP route. The second day consists of two group exercises and a technical interview.

Internal staff act as assessors and observers at the centres and are typically quite senior people drawn from a range of business areas. Many have worked around the world and so are aware of cultural differences and may speak several languages. This can contribute to the fairness and the diversity of a process involving candidates from more than one country.

A competency-based approach is used to assess candidates. Candidates are rated against a competency framework that includes technical, personal and managerial competencies. A matrix profile is produced for each candidate to give the assessment team an overall picture of each individual's performance across all exercises. Feedback is given to both successful and unsuccessful candidates.

Source: based on IRS (2005g) 'Centres of attention', p. 47.

Questions

1 What further action might GKN take to ensure that the selection process fully reflects the global nature of the business?

2 What criteria should GKN use to measure the effectiveness of the assessment centres?

References and further reading

Those texts marked with an asterisk are recommended for further reading.

ACAS (1983) *Recruitment and Selection*, Advisory Booklet No. 6. London: Advisory, Conciliation & Arbitration Service.

Anderson, A.H. (1994) *Effective Personnel Management: A Skills and Activity-Based Approach*. Oxford: Blackwell Business.

*Anderson, N. and Shackleton, V. (1993) *Successful Selection Interviewing*. Oxford: Blackwell.

Appelbaum, S., Kay, F. and Shapiro, B. (1989) 'The assessment centre is not dead! How to keep it alive and well', *Journal of Management Development*, 8, 5: 51–65.

Armstrong, M. (2006) *A Handbook of Human Resource Management Practice*, 10th edn. London: Kogan Page.

Baker, B. and Cooper, J.N. (2002) 'Occupational testing and psychometric instruments: an ethical perspective', in Winstanley, D. and Woodall, J. (eds) *Ethical Issues in Contemporary Human Resource Management*. Houndmills: Palgrave.

Beaumont, P. (1993) *Human Resource Management: Key Concepts and Skills*. London: Sage.

Benady, D. (2002) 'Money for nothing?', *Marketing Week*, 22 August: 24–27.

Boam, R. and Sparrow, P. (eds) (1992) *Designing and Achieving Competency: A Competency-based Approach to Developing People and Organisations*. Maidenhead: McGraw-Hill.

Callaghan, G. and Thompson, P. (2002) 'We recruit attitude: the selection and shaping of routine call centre labour', *Journal of Management Studies*, 39, 2: 233–254.

Carrington, L. (2002) 'At the cutting edge', *People Management*, 8, 10: 30–31.

CIPD (2001a) Telephone interviewing, *Quick Facts*. London: CIPD.

CIPD (2001b) Graphology, *Quick Facts*. London: CIPD.

CIPD (2001c) Psychological testing, *Quick Facts*. London: CIPD.

CIPD (2002) Recruitment on the Internet, *Quick Facts*. London: CIPD.

CIPD (2005a) *Recruitment, Retention and Labour Turnover Survey*. London: CIPD.

CIPD (2005b) *Labour Market Outlook*. London: CIPD.

CIPD (2005c) Online recruitment, *Factsheet*. London: CIPD

CIPD (2006a) Age and employment, *Factsheet*. London: CIPD.

CIPD (2006b) Employment of people with criminal records, *Factsheet*. London: CIPD.

CIPD (2006c) International management and development: an overview, *Factsheet*. London: CIPD.

Crabb, S. (2003) 'East India companies', *People Management*, 8, 4: 28–32.

Cully, M., Woodland, S., O'Reilly, A. and Dix, G. (1999) *Britain at Work: As Depicted by the 1998 Workplace Employee Relations Survey*. London: Routledge.

Dickens, L. (2000) 'Still wasting resources? Equality in employment', in Bach, S. and Sisson, K. (eds) *Personnel Management: A Comprehensive Guide to Theory and Practice*, 3rd edn. Oxford: Blackwell, pp. 137–169.

Dowling, P.J. and Schuler, R.S. (1990) *International Dimensions of HRM*. Boston, Mass: PWS-Kent.

Dulewicz, V. (2003) 'How to prepare for the board', *People Management*, 6 March: 54.

Feltham, R. (1992) 'Using competencies in selection and recruitment', in Boam, R. and Sparrow, P. (eds) *Designing and Achieving Competency: a Competency-based Approach to Developing People and Organisations*. Maidenhead: McGraw-Hill.

Fletcher, C. (1993) 'Testing times for the world of psychometrics', *People Management*, December: 46–50.

Flood, P.C., Gannon, M.J. and Paauwe, J. (1996) *Managing Without Traditional Methods: International Innovations in Human Resource Management*. Wokingham: Addison-Wesley.

Fombrun, C., Tichy, N. and Devanna, M. (1984) *Strategic Human Resource Management*. New York: Wiley.

Fowler, A. (1992) 'How to plan an assessment centre', *PM Plus*, December: 21–23.

Goss, D. (1994) *Principles of Human Resource Management*. London: Routledge.

Hackett, P. (1991) *Personnel: The Department at Work*. London: IPM.

Hendry, C. (1995) *Human Resource Management: A Strategic Approach to Employment*. Oxford: Butterworth-Heinemann.

Herriot, P. (1989) *Recruitment in the 1990s*. London: IPM.

Hirschkorn, J. (2004) 'Research and employ', *People Management*, 15 January: 33–35.

IDS (1992) Employment Law Supplement: Recruitment, *IDS Brief 64*, April.

IDS (2002) Assessment Centres, *Study* 569, January.

IDS (2004) HR Studies Update, September.

IDS (2005) HR Studies Update 795, April.

Iles, P. and Salaman, G. (1995) 'Recruitment, selection and assessment', in Storey, J. (ed.) *Human Resource Management: A Critical Text*. London: Routledge, pp. 203–233.

Industrial Society (1994) *Recruitment and Selection*, Managing Best Practice 4. London: The Industrial Society.

IPD (1997) *Psychological Testing*, key facts. London: IPD, August.

IRS (1994) 'Ensuring effective recruitment' and 'Random selection', *Employee Development Bulletin 51*, March: 2–8.

IRS (1997) 'The state of selection: an IRS survey', *Employee Development Bulletin 85*, January: 8–18.

IRS (1999a) 'Testing time for people with disabilities', *Employee Development Bulletin 113*, May: 5–9.

IRS (1999b) 'The business of selection: an IRS survey', *Employee Development Bulletin 117*, September: 5–16.

IRS (2002a) 'Going beyond the DDA', *IRS Employment Review 758*, 19 August.

IRS (2002b) 'The uses and abuses of the new Criminal Records Bureau', *IRS Employment Review 753*, 10 June: 37–40.

IRS (2002c) 'Internet recruiting the FTSE-100 way', *IRS Employment Review 746*, 25 February: 35–40.

IRS (2002d) 'I've got your number: telephone interviewing', *IRS Employment Review 756*, 22 July: 34–36.

IRS (2002e) 'Psychometrics: the next generation', *IRS Employment Review 744*, 28 January: 36–40.

IRS (2002f) 'Focus of attention', *IRS Employment Review 749*, 15 April: 36–42.

IRS (2003) 'Spinning the recruitment web', *IRS Employment Review 767*, 10 January: 34–40.

IRS (2004) 'Welcome the new multitasking all-purpose management expert', *IRS Employment Review 793*, 6 February: 8–13.

IRS (2005a) 'E-recruitment', *IRS Employment Review 822*, 29 April.

IRS (2005b) 'Checking out the activities of the Criminal Records Bureau', *IRS Employment Review 828*, 29 July: 42–48.

IRS (2005c) 'In quick succession', *IRS Employment Review 833*, 14 October: 46–48.

IRS (2005d) 'First line filter: screening candidates for selection', *IRS Employment Review 837*, 16 December: 44–48.

IRS (2005e) 'Got your number: using telephone interviewing', *IRS Employment Review 832*, 30 September: 43–45.

IRS (2005f) 'Selecting graduates: doing it online, on time', *IRS Employment Review 836*, 2 December: 42–45.

IRS (2005g) 'Centres of attention', *IRS Employment Review 816*, 28 January: 43–47.

IRS (2005h) 'Outsourcing recruitment: a minority pursuit?', *IRS Employment Review 830*, 26 August: 42–48.

Kandola, B. (1995) 'Firms must rework race bias policies', *Personnel Today*, 25 October: 20.

Kersley, B., Alpin, C., Forth, J., Bryson, A., Bewley, H., Dix, G. and Oxenbridge, S (2005) Inside the Workplace: first findings from the 2004 Workplace Employment Relations Survey.

Lewis, C. (1985) *Employee Selection*. London: Hutchinson.

Lonsdale, C. and Cox, A. (1998) 'Falling in with the out crowd', *People Management*, 15 October: 52–55.

Lupton, B. (2000) 'Pouring coffee at the interview? Personnel's role in the selection of doctors', *Personnel Review*, 29, 1: 48–68.

McLuhan, R. (2000) 'Change management', *Personnel Today* 18 April: 25–26.

Manocha, R (2002) 'Unlocking potential', *People Management*, 8, 19: 28–34.

Marchington, M. and Wilkinson, A. (2005) *Human Resource Management at Work*. London: CIPD.

Mayo, A. (1995) 'Economic indicators of HRM', in Tyson, S. (ed.) *Strategic Prospects for HRM*. London: IPD, p. 34.

Miles, R.E and Snow, C.C. (1984) 'Designing strategic human resource systems', *Organisational Dynamics*, Summer: 36–52.

Munro Fraser, J. (1954) *A Handbook of Employment Interviewing*. London: Macdonald & Evans.

Newell, S. and Shackleton, V. (1993) 'The use and abuse of psychometric tests in British industry and commerce', *Human Resource Management Journal*, 4, 1: 14–23.

Office for National Statistics (2002) *Labour Force Survey*, London.

Patterson, M., West, M., Lawthorn, R. and Nickell, S. (1997) *Impact of People Management Practices on Business Performance*, Issues in People Management 22. London: IPD.

Pfeffer, J. (1998) *The Human Equation: Building Profits by Putting People First*. Boston, Mass: Harvard Business School Press.

*Roberts, G. (1997) *Recruitment and Selection: A Competency Approach*. London: IPD.

Rodger, A. (1952) *The Seven Point Plan*. London: National Institute of Industrial Psychology.

Sadler, P. and Milmer, K. (1993) *The Talent-Intensive Organisation: Optimising your Company's Human Resource Strategies*, Special Report P659. London: The Economist Intelligence Unit.

Schuler, R.S. and Jackson, S.E. (1996) *Human Resource Management: Positioning for the 21st Century*, 6th edn. St Paul, Minn.: West Publishing Company.

Searle, R. (2003) *Selection and Recruitment: A Critical Text*. Milton Keynes: The Open University.

Sisson, K. and Marginson, P. (1995) 'Management: systems, structures and strategy' in Edwards, P. (ed) *Industrial Relations: Theory and Practice in Britain*. Oxford: Blackwell.

Sisson, K. and Storey, J. (2000) *The Realities of HRM*. Buckingham: Open University Press.

Sparrow, P. (1999) 'Abroad minded', *People Management*, 20 May: 40–44.

Storey, J. and Sisson, K. (1993) *Managing Human Resources and Industrial Relations*. Buckingham: Open University Press.

*Taylor, S. (2005) *People Resourcing*, 3rd edn. London: CIPD.

Torrington, D., Hall, L. and Taylor, S. (2002) *Human Resource Management*, 5th edn. Harlow: Prentice Hall.

TUC (2006) *Black Women and Employment*, TUC Report, April.

Whitehill, A.M. (1991) *Japanese Management: Tradition and Transition*. London: Routledge.

For multiple-choice questions, exercises and annotated weblinks specific to this chapter visit the book's website at **www.pearsoned.co.uk/beardwell**

Chapter 7

Managing equality and diversity

Mike Noon

Objectives

- Define discrimination and describe its potential impact on different groups.
- Describe and compare the social justice and business case arguments for pursuing policies of equality and diversity.
- Explain the purpose of equality and diversity policies and assess their limitations.
- Explain the concepts of 'sameness' and 'difference', and evaluate their importance in guiding policy within organisations.
- Describe and critically evaluate the concept of institutional discrimination.
- Assess the process of discrimination in an organisation and outline its possible consequences.

Introduction

There is a short story by H.G. Wells called *The Country of the Blind* in which a mountaineer falls into a hidden valley in South America where all the inhabitants have been blind for fifteen generations. His initial reaction is that among such a disadvantaged group of people he can easily establish himself as superior because of his sight; indeed, as the saying expresses it, 'in the country of the blind the one-eyed man is king'. However, he soon learns that the whole of this society is constructed around the norm of blindness, so his sightedness provides no advantages and in many ways disadvantages him from becoming integrated and accepted into the community. For instance, all work is undertaken in the dark at night (when it is cool); there are no lights and the buildings have no windows; his descriptions and explanations based on sight, colour and so forth have no meaning to the inhabitants; and his under-developed alternative senses mean he cannot participate fully in the culture of the community. In the end, in order to fit in, he has to choose either to conform to the dominate norms and have his eyes removed or else leave the community.

The relevance of this story is that it illustrates how being different to the dominant social group can produce disadvantages for an individual irrespective of his or her qualities and abilities. In this example the disadvantage suffered by the main character is due to his sight in a society in which sight is undervalued. In the real world, of course, key characteristics such as gender, race/ethnicity, disability, age, religion, and sexuality are typically the bases for disadvantage. People can suffer rejection, non-acceptance and unfair treatment within a particular setting (especially the workplace) because they differ from the dominant social group across one of more of these characteristics. They can feel excluded and marginalised, or in extreme cases become the victims of abuse and harassment. This disadvantage can manifest itself in many of the key processes within organisations that are explained in other chapters: recruitment and selection, training and development; appraisals; promotion; career development; remuneration; and work organisation.

The purpose of this chapter is to explore how managers can take action to minimise the disadvantages and provide a working environment that supports equality and diversity. To investigate these issues the chapter is divided into six main sections. First, there is an examination of the meaning of discrimination; the second section addresses the question of why managers should be concerned about equality and diversity; the third section explains the role of equality and diversity policies; the fourth section analyses the different approaches to devising such policies; the fifth section evaluates the concept of institutional discrimination and the sixth section explains the process of discrimination within organisations.

The nature of discrimination

One of the assumptions sometimes made is that discrimination is experienced in the same way by different groups of people. In other words, discrimination based on sex, race/ethnicity, disability and age is often assumed to be the same. While it is certainly the case that the effects of discrimination (the disadvantage suffered) are the same or very similar for the victims, the nature of the discrimination often differs and the response and attitudes of the social groups can also differ. It is important to elaborate these statements to show how there might be differences between social groups and within social groups.

One starting point for this is to consider the characteristics that identify a person as different: sex, age, ethnicity, etc. In particular, these characteristics differ in terms of whether they can be considered *stable* and *visible*.

- *Stable* characteristics are features such as race and sex – with the exception of the tiny minority of people that undergo gender reassignment. In contrast a person's age differs throughout their life, thus everyone is susceptible to being a victim of ageism, and the type of ageism will change at different life stages.

- *Visible* characteristics are features that a person cannot hide – such as sex, race/ethnicity and some forms of disability. Others, such as sexual orientation, can be hidden and so although discrimination occurs, some potential victims can dodge it through behaviour that disguises their true identities.

A further consideration concerns the differences between the perpetrators and the victims. Whereas discrimination is perpetrated typically by one group against a different group (men over women, able-bodied over less able, ethnic majority over minority) this is not true of age discrimination. For instance, research by Oswick and Rosenthal (2001) reveals that older workers are frequently discriminated against by managers of similar ages; it is not simply the case that the 'old' are discriminated against by the 'young' (or vice-versa). As the authors vividly express it, 'the purveyors of ageism are also in other circumstances its recipients'. Thus there is 'same-group' discrimination, rather than 'different-group' discrimination.

Turning to the victims of discrimination it is important to recognise differences within social groups, rather than consider each group to be homogeneous. For instance, Reynolds *et al.* (2001) point out how disability can be a diverse and wide-ranging categorisation. People may move into a state of disability from ill-health, work accidents or ageing, and so while some people are 'born disabled', there is an increasing proportion of employees who 'become disabled'. Moreover, the needs of those with different 'disabilities' are so wide-ranging that it might be suggested there is very little meaning in such a broad category as 'disability'. The same conclusion might be reached for race/ethnicity. Increasingly commentators (for example, Modood *et al.*, 1997; Pilkington, 2001) are arguing that research evidence suggests there is so much ethnic diversity that to describe discrimination as being the same across different ethnic groups fails to take into account its differential impact. This means it is essential to recognise the differences between ethnic groups not only in terms of their experiences of discrimination, but also in their varied requirements for redressing the discrimination. Furthermore, it is possible to challenge the assumptions that a person's ethnic group can be clearly defined and remains stable (note the discussion above). First, there are increasingly people with multiple cultural identities who simply do not 'fit' the ethnic categories, and second, exposure to varied cultural influences means that ethnic identity is likely to change across one's lifetime.

It is important to acknowledge differences between social groups. Indeed, if people within the same social group experience discrimination in different ways and in different circumstances, there is little reason to suppose that people from different social groups will have similar experiences. They may be victims of discrimination but there is little reason to suppose that the experience of being discriminated against because you are a woman is the same as that of being discriminated against on the grounds of sexual orientation; or that the discrimination experienced by disabled employees is the same as that endured by ethnic minority employees. Box 7.1, The Royal Mail, illustrates these sometimes competing interests (see also Liff, 2003).

A final issue that further underlines the diversity of the nature of discrimination is that some people experience multi-discrimination. For example, an employee may be discriminated against because she is both a women and Asian, and might therefore not identify with or share the same concerns as her white women colleagues or black male colleagues. Similarly consider the following comment:

> I'm a 54 year-old fitter who has been made redundant, and I've been trying for months to get back into work. I've even done all these special courses at the Job Centre to make myself more employable and to practice interviews and things. The problem is that when an employer sees 54 on the application form the majority of them don't want to know – but of course I can't prove that. Then, after weeks of trying I got an interview, and I was really excited because it was a chance to get back to doing something useful and earning again. I can remember I was full of enthusiasm and hope when I walked into the interview room, but then I saw the look on the faces of the panel as I walked through the door and they realised I'm black.

Box 7.1   The Royal Mail

The UK's postal service, the Royal Mail, has traditionally operated a system of seniority for employees who sort and deliver the mail. This means that the greater the length of service the postal workers have behind them, then the more privileges they get. In particular, this means that they get first choice of holidays, overtime and shifts. The system was designed to reward loyalty and experience, but with the introduction of new technology and different forms of working, the managers required far greater flexibility from employees and so they proposed changes to working practices that would lead to the abolition of the seniority system. Interestingly, this led both sides (the trade unions and the management) to claim they were working in the interest of equal opportunities.

The trade unions argued that seniority protected equal opportunities because it produced a rational, transparent and equitable means of allocating duties. In particular they said that it protected employees against favouritism and prejudice by managers in the allocation of duties – an issue of importance to ethnic minority members of the trade unions.

The management argued that it was not fair on part-time employees who were at the back of the queue because their length of service was less yet they nevertheless made an important contribution to the business. In particular, they suggested that it had a discriminatory effect on women because the majority of part-timers were women.

These two viewpoints illustrate how both parties were able to make a claim that their position was in defence of equal opportunities. Indeed, the logic of both cases can be seen. It provides a vivid illustration of how different groups might require different (and, in this case, competing) policies and action in order to ensure fairness. Part-time employees, particularly those who were women, might have felt betrayed by the trade unions. Similarly ethnic minority employees might have felt that management were attempting to remove a system that had protected them against discrimination.

The picture is of diversity in the nature of discrimination and difference in the needs of the various groups and individuals that experience discrimination. These are important issues because it means:

- Managers should not assume that discrimination means the same thing irrespective of group concerned.

- Managers should not assume that a policy solution for one social group (for example, women) will be appropriate or welcomed by a different social group (for example, disabled people).

- Managers should expect that attitudes will differ within social groups (for example, Asian employees and black employees).

The recognition of this diversity has led some commentators to argue that rather than defining people by their similarities to others, managers should see all employees as individuals with unique skills and needs. This is an issue that will be returned to later in the chapter.

Stop & think

On the basis of the preceding discussion reflect on your own experiences of disadvantage by identifying the ways you might have been disadvantaged personally in your past or current employment (or in any other aspect of your life). You do not necessarily need to restrict the criteria to the categories noted above: there might be other features which you feel have resulted in negative treatment or disadvantage – for example, your accent, physical appearance (size, height, haircut, piercings, tattoos), class or social background, schooling and lack of belonging to the right social network.

Why be concerned with equality and diversity?

A key question that needs to be addressed is why managers should care whether some people are disadvantaged and suffer unfair treatment. In answering this question, it is useful to distinguish between two different sets of arguments, which can be labeled 'the social justice case' and 'the business case'.

The social justice case

The social justice case is that managers have a moral obligation to treat employees with fairness and dignity. Part of this involves ensuring that decisions are made without resorting to prejudice and stereotypes. You may already be familiar with these concepts, but in case not, they can be defined as follows:

Prejudice. In the context of discrimination at work, prejudice means holding negative attitudes towards a particular group, and viewing all members of that group in a negative light, irrespective of their individual qualities and attributes. Typically we think of prejudice as being against a particular group based on gender, race/ethnicity, religion, disability, age and sexual orientation. However, prejudice extends much further and is frequently directed at other groups based on features such as accent, height, weight, hair colour, beards, body piercings, tattoos and clothes. It is extremely rare to find a person who is not prejudiced against any group – although most of us are reluctant to admit to our prejudices.

(Heery and Noon 2001: 279)

Stereotyping. Stereotyping is the act of judging people according to our assumptions about the group to which they belong. It is based on the belief that people from a specific group share similar traits and behave in a similar manner. Rather than looking at a person's individual qualities, stereotyping leads us to jump to conclusions about what someone is like. This might act against the person concerned (negative stereotype) or in their favour (positive stereotype). For example, the negative stereotype of an accountant is someone who is dull, uninteresting and shy – which, of course, is a slur on all the exciting, adventurous accountants in the world. A positive stereotype is that accountants are intelligent, conscientious and trustworthy – which is an equally inaccurate description of some of the accountants you are likely to encounter. The problem with stereotypes is that they are generalisations (so there are always exceptions) and can be based on ignorance and prejudice (so are often inaccurate). It is vital for managers to resist resorting to stereotyping when managing people, otherwise they run the risk of treating employees unfairly and making poor-quality decisions that are detrimental to the organisation.

(Heery and Noon, 2001: 347)

If decisions are made free from prejudice and stereotyping then there is a lower risk of any particular group being disadvantaged and therefore less chance of an individual feeling that he or she has been discriminated against.

Discrimination is very much a core concept for the social justice case so its meaning needs to be considered. 'Discrimination' is the process of judging people according to particular criteria. For example, in the selection process for a teaching post, the appointment panel might discriminate in favour of a candidate who answers their questions clearly and concisely, and discriminate against a candidate who mutters and digresses from the point. However, when most people use the term 'discrimination' they tend to mean *unfair* discrimination. The word is mainly used to denote that the criteria on which the discrimination has occurred are unjust. It is likely that most people would not describe the example above as 'discrimination' because they would not consider the criteria the panel used (clarity, conciseness) as unfair. However, if the criterion the appointment panel used to choose between candidates was gender or race, then most people would recognise it as discrimination. Essentially it is the problem of deciding upon the 'fairness' of the process which makes it a concern for social justice.

There is a further complication to the social justice case. This concerns the question of whether the focus should be on justice in terms of procedures ('a level playing field') or outcomes ('a fair share of the cake'). For example, in a recruitment process, this would mean either a person is selected according to merit (procedural justice) or he/she is selected in order to fill a quota (to ensure representativeness of different social groups). Selection on merit alone will not produce representativeness unless such merit is evenly distributed throughout all groups. Of course, such even distribution is highly unlikely due to structural disadvantages and inequalities (schooling, economics support, connections, social stereotypes, and so forth) which limit a person's potential to acquire meritorious characteristics (Noon and Ogbonna, 2001:4).

As shall be seen later in the chapter, this dilemma leads to different policy suggestions as to how organisations should address the problem of ensuring fairness. Those who favour procedural intervention tend to advocate a 'light touch' in terms of legal regulation and best practice guidelines, while those who focus on outcomes advocate stronger legislation and/or more radical changes to organisational processes and practices.

Limitations of the social justice argument

Critics of the social justice case tend to argue that while the pursuit of fairness is laudable, it is not the prime concern of organisations. The goals of managers in organisations are profit and efficiency, rather than morality. If social justice were to guide their decision making it might have a detrimental effect on the operation of the business and ultimately the bottom line. This line of argument has led to an additional rationale for equality and diversity: the business case.

The business case

The second set of arguments that can be used to justify why managers should be concerned with eliminating disadvantage is based on making a business case. The point is that, aside from any concerns with social justice, fair treatment simply makes good business sense for four main reasons.

1 *It is a better use of human resources.* By discriminating on the basis of sex, race/ethnicity, disability, and so on, managers run the risk of neglecting or overlooking talented employees. The consequence is that the organisation fails to maximise its full human resource potential and valuable resources are wasted through under-utilising the competences of existing employees or losing disgruntled, talented staff to other organisations.

2 *It leads to a wider customer base.* By broadening the diversity of the workforce, managers might help the organisation to appeal to a greater range of customers. This might be particularly important where face-to-face service delivery is a central part of the business and requires an understanding of the diverse needs of customers.

3 *It creates a wider pool of labour for recruitment.* By being more open-minded about the people they could employ for various jobs, managers will have a wider pool of talent from which to recruit. This is particularly important when an organisation is attempting to secure scarce resources, such as employees with specific skills or experience.

4 *It leads to a positive company image.* By having a clear statement of the organisation's commitment to fair treatment, backed by meaningful practices that result in a diverse workforce, managers will be able to project a positive image of the organisation to customers, suppliers and potential employees. In terms of employees, the organisation will be perceived as good to work for because it values ability and talent, and so is more likely to attract and retain high-calibre people.

Limitations of the business case arguments

Although these arguments are quite persuasive, there might be some circumstances when 'good business sense' provides the justification for not acting in the interest of particular groups. For example, Cunningham and James (2001) find that line managers often justify the decision not to employ disabled people on the grounds that the necessary workplace adjustments would eat into their operating budgets. Indeed, equality and diversity initiatives often have a cost associated with them, the recovery of which cannot always be easily measured and might only be realised in the long term. The danger (highlighted by commentators such as Dickens, 1994, 2000 and Webb, 1997) is that such initiatives can only be justified as long as they contribute to profit. For example, in Webb's (1997) case study of an international computing systems manufacturer, the corporate philosophy was to encourage employee diversity to bring in new ideas, meet customer needs and achieve success in the global market place.

However, at divisional level in the UK, the requests from women for childcare provision and flexible hours were rejected on the basis that these would adversely affect profitability. Furthermore, although managerial opportunities were open to women this was clearly on men's terms, as Webb (1997: 165) explains:

> Women graduate engineers are aware that they have to fit in as 'one of the boys' and however supportive the line manager, these are all men: 'I think the difficulty is still being able to sit down, map out your career and possibly say that at a certain time you many well wish to have a family . . . (graduate sales rep.). . . . Even for those willing to adopt male work norms, the corporate orientation to innovation and change mean that the uncertainties experienced by managers are likely to result in the continuing exclusion of women, who continue to be regarded as a riskier bet than men.

This type of problem is common and is expressed vividly by Liff and Wajcman (1996: 89) in the following quote:

> Managers' perceptions of job requirements and procedures for assessing merit have been shown to be saturated with gendered assumptions . . . Feminists can argue (as they have for years) that not all women get pregnant, but it seems unlikely that this will stop managers thinking 'yes, but no men will'.

For an alternative example of how the business case argument can work against a particular group of employees, attempt the following activity.

Activity

The department store

The following quote is from a research interview with a personnel manager of a large departmental store in a city in the UK. She had been asked why there were no ethnic minority employees on the sales floor, even though the city had an ethnic minority population of over 5 per cent.

> Our customers are mainly white, middle-class women. They would be uncomfortable being served by ethnic minorities and they would probably shop elsewhere. That is why we don't have black sales assistants and only have men in certain areas such as the electrical department. We have some Asian employees in the stockroom and doing other vital jobs behind the scenes.

Question

What are the potential problems for the organisation in taking this approach?

A further problem is the issue of measuring the effects of extending opportunities. The underlying assumption is that any initiatives will have a positive effect on business (hence they make good business sense). But this logic requires that they are subsequently measured and evaluated to assess their effects. This poses two difficulties:

1 *Finding a meaningful measure.* In some instances this is feasible. For example, it would be possible to recruit more Asian salespeople in order to increase sales to Asian customers, and in this case appropriate measures would be the number and value of sales and the number of Asian customers (identified by their family name). However, in other instances measurement is very difficult. For example, how would you measure the impact of ethnic-awareness training? Or the effects of flexible working arrangements? In both these cases it might be possible to measure the effects in terms of attitudes or changes in performance, but it would be more difficult to attribute these solely to the specific initiatives.

2 *Measuring in the short term.* In many instances the full effects of an equality or diversity initiative would only be realised in the long term. For many managers within organisations this would be a disincentive to invest in such initiatives, particularly if the performance of their department was measured in the short term. Moreover, it would be an even greater disincentive to invest if the manager's salary or bonus was affected by the short-term performance of their department.

Overall, the business case argument can make an impact – for example, in circumstances of skills shortages, needs for particular types of employees, or local labour market conditions – but this is likely to be variable and patchy. As Dickens (1999: 10) states:

> The contingent and variable nature of the business case can be seen in the fact that business case arguments have greater salience for some organisations than others. . . . The appeal of a particular business case argument can also vary over time as labour or product markets change, giving rise to 'fair weather' equality action.

Stop & think

Should the absence or weakness of a 'business case' for eliminating unfair discrimination and disadvantage absolve managers from trying to do so?

Justice and business sense

As you might have noticed, the two sets of arguments are not necessarily mutually exclusive. Indeed, it is feasible and practical for managers to use both sets to justify equality or diversity initiatives in their organisations. It reflects a pragmatic realisation that by stressing both arguments there is more chance of gaining commitment to equality and diversity from a wider group of people. Whether a manager is committed to equality because of justice or business sense reasons does not really matter – it is the fact he or she is committed that counts. Of course, this is not quite as simple in practice because once commitment has been gained, there is then the question of what policies to put in place.

Before proceeding with a discussion of policy choices, there is an important point to note that underpins much of the following discussion. Efforts to tackle unfair discrimination have not been able to develop through a simple reliance on voluntary commitment to social justice by managers or their rational acceptance of the business case. In most countries legislation has been introduced which sets limits to lawful managerial action and places obligations on managers to act in accordance with principles of fairness. In other words, some equality and diversity practices are the result of a legal obligation, rather than management choice. Bearing this general point in mind, you should also note the following:

- The type and extent of this legislation varies from country to country, so it is important to read about the specific legislation in your own national context.

- Opinion varies as to whether state regulation is necessary or the extent to which it is legitimate or practical to legislate to prevent discrimination and promote equality of opportunity.

- Even when legislation is in place there is no guarantee that this ensures equality of opportunity. This might be because the legislation is flaunted (unlawfully) or because it is ineffective (too weak, too many loopholes, easily ignored, difficult to enforce, and so on).

In Europe there has been a move towards a common platform of human rights in relation to equality and fairness. One of the key developments has been the attempt to harmonise the protection against discrimination at work. Within each country there have been changes in national legislation – either amendments to existing laws or the introduction of new laws – in compliance with European Union directives. The basic principle behind the directives is a right to equal treatment irrespective of racial or ethnic origin, religion or belief, disability, age or sexual orientation. This principle is breached by direct and indirect discrimination, harassment or an instruction to discriminate. As well as providing a shared platform of protection, the directives have established common legal definitions of these four terms, such that they now have the same meaning in the different countries (although of course interpretation of the meaning might still vary in different judicial contexts).

1 *Direct discrimination* is where a person is treated less favourably than another is, has been or would be treated in a comparable situation on one of the grounds of racial or ethnic origin, religion or belief, disability, age, or sexual orientation.
2 *Indirect discrimination* is where a provision, criterion or practice that appears to be neutral and non-discriminatory would in fact disadvantage someone of a particular racial or ethnic origin, religion or belief, disability, age or sexual orientation, compared to others, unless it is objectively justified by a legitimate aim and it is an appropriate and necessary means of achieving that aim.
3 *Harassment* is where unwanted conduct related to any of the listed grounds of discrimination takes place with the *purpose or effect* of violating someone's dignity and of creating an intimidating, hostile, degrading, humiliating or offensive environment.
4 *An instruction to discriminate* is where one person obliges another to act in a discriminatory manner against a third party on the grounds noted above.

Equality and diversity policies

If the issue of disadvantage is to be addressed in a systemic and consistent way within an organisation, then it is advantageous to have an overall policy that guides decision making and action. Increasingly such policies are being created, although the terminology differs from organisation to organisation: some call them equal opportunity policies, others diversity policies and still others use both terms. The rationale for such policies can be based on a mix of justice and business sense arguments, as was noted above. The form of these policies varies between organisations and the next section will explain why this is the case. Before this, it is necessary to make some general points about the purpose and forms of equal and diversity policies and to note some of the criticisms made of them.

The ten points that follow are from the website of the UK's Commission for Racial Equality (www.cre.gov.uk) and are typical of the recommended good practice that employers are encouraged to adopt. The initiatives from 3 to 10 are often described as 'positive action' (or 'affirmative action') and organisations are encouraged to adopt some, if not all, of these.

1 Develop an equal opportunities policy, covering recruitment, promotion and training.
2 Set an action plan, with targets, so that you and your staff have a clear idea of what can be achieved and by when.
3 Provide training for all people, including managers, throughout your organisation, to ensure they understand the importance of equal opportunities. Provide additional training for staff who recruit, select and train your employees.
4 Assess the present position to establish your starting point, and monitor progress in achieving your objectives.
5 Review recruitment, selection, promotion and training procedures regularly, to ensure that you are delivering on your policy.
6 Draw up clear and justifiable job criteria, which are demonstrably objective and job-related.
7 Offer pre-employment training, where appropriate, to prepare potential job applicants for selection tests and interviews; consider positive action training to help ethnic minority employees to apply for jobs in areas where they are under-represented.

8 Consider your organisation's image: do you encourage applications from under-represented groups and feature women, ethnic minority staff and people with disabilities in recruitment literature, or could you be seen as an employer who is indifferent to these groups?

9 Consider flexible working, career breaks, providing childcare facilities, and so on, to help women in particular meet domestic responsibilities and pursue their occupations; and consider providing special equipment and assistance to help people with disabilities.

10 Develop links with local community groups, organisations and schools, in order to reach a wider pool of potential applicants.

The willingness of organisations to adopt such guidelines varies considerably. Moreover, there is also considerable variation in the extent to which all the points are adopted. This can be thought of as a sliding scale: at one extreme are those organisations that adopt a policy that meets very few of the points, and at the other extreme those organisations that have addressed all 10 points. Another way of looking at this is to think of different categories into which an organisation might be placed according to its approach to equality and diversity. Table 7.1 is an example of this type of categorisation.

One particular technique recommended by advocates of equality and diversity is 'discrimination proofing' the organisation. This entails auditing the processes to assess the potential areas where unfair practice might occur. This might be through an absence of clear policy or procedures, or from managerial lack of knowledge or training. The purpose of such an exercise is to identify the areas of vulnerability and to take action to make improvements where they carry an unacceptable level of risk.

In which category in Table 7.1 would you place your own organisation (or an organisation you are familiar with)?

Even where organisations have equality and diversity policies in place, it does not necessarily mean that these lead to organisational practices that ensure fair treatment within the workplace. This point can be illustrated by looking at the findings from an analysis of data from a nationally representative sample of British workplaces with 10 or more employees (Hoque and Noon, 2004). The study assessed the frequency of equality policies and whether such policies have any substance to them (meaning that they are backed up by practices that result in fair treatment) or whether they are simply 'empty shells', with few or no practices to ensure their

Table 7.1 Types of equal opportunity organisation

The *negative* organisation	Has no equal opportunity policy
	Makes no claims of being an equal opportunity employer
	Might not be complying with the law
The *minimalist* organisation	Claims to be an equal opportunity employer
	Has no written equal opportunity policy
	Has no procedure or initiatives, but will react to claims of discrimination as they arise
The *compliant* organisation	Has a written equal opportunity policy
	Has procedures and initiatives in place to comply with some aspects of good practice recommendations
The *proactive* organisation	Has a written policy backed up with procedures and initiatives
	Monitors the outcomes of initiatives to assess their impact
	Promotes equality using full set of good practice guidelines, and might even go beyond these

Source: Based on Healy (1993) and Kirton and Greene (2005)

effectiveness. The analysis, drawing on the Workplace Employee Relations survey data from managers in over 2000 workplaces and over 28,000 employees, led to the following conclusions.

- Equal opportunity (EO) policies are more likely to be adopted in:
  - large organisations;
  - organisations with a human resource or personnel specialist;
  - organisations with trade union representation.

- Almost 60 per cent of workplaces have an EO policy that covers gender, race/ethnicity and disability, and 40 per cent covering age.

- But, less than half the workplaces with an EO policy had introduced equal opportunity practices to back the policy up. In other words, such policies are often 'empty shells'.

- EO policies are more likely to be empty shells in:
  - small organisations;
  - private sector organisations;
  - organisations with no HR specialist.

- Unionised workplaces are more likely to have formal EO policies, but those policies are no less likely to constitute empty shells.

- Even where organisations have practices in place to back up their EO policies, not all employees have access to those practices – in other words, for such employees, they are no better than empty shells.

Two key components: positive action and monitoring

To ensure the effectiveness of equal and diversity policies, the organisation needs to adopt positive action initiatives and ensure monitoring takes place. These two components are a feature of those organisations categorised as 'proactive', so they need some elaboration.

Positive action

Positive action (sometimes called affirmative action) means one or more specific initiatives designed to encourage under-represented groups to apply for jobs or promotion within the organisation. Positive action might also be concerned with making changes to working arrangements to encourage the retention of employees by making the environment more suited to the needs they have that differ from the majority of employees. It is important not to confuse the term 'positive action' with 'positive discrimination'. The latter means the preferential treatment of a person because of their sex, ethnicity, age and so forth, and this is unlawful under most discrimination law within Europe. Elsewhere – most notably in parts of the United States – positive discrimination is sometimes used as part of a programme of initiatives designed to redress existing imbalances in the composition of the workforce for particular organisations (usually public sector).

There are examples of positive action initiatives throughout this chapter, but to illustrate the variety of forms that might occur within a single organisation, consider the UK police force. In 1999 there was a government report on the police force, branding it as racist and criticising it for failing to have enough ethnic minority police officers. In 2003 there was a BBC undercover investigation that revealed blatant racism among recruits and in 2004 a further government report condemning the lack of diversity in the force. A range of initiatives was launched in various police forces throughout the UK, which included the following specific actions designed to improve the recruitment and retention of ethnic minorities.

- Running pre-joining courses for ethnic minority groups, giving prospective candidates a chance to experience the reality of life in the force, and dispelling any myths.

- Introducing a national recruitment campaign featuring black role models.

- Placing advertisements in Bollywood cinemas, ethnic minority press and radio stations that carried the message, 'It's not where you're from, it's where we're going'.
- Creating Positive Action Teams to run roadshows.
- Setting up recruitment stalls at high-profile minority events and in locations where there is a large ethnic minority population.
- Encouraging senior officers to visit religious venues.
- Allowing Muslim female officers to wear the hijab (a scarf that covers the head and shoulders worn by some Muslim women) on duty.
- Allowing officers wishing to observe Ramadan (when it is forbidden to drink or consume food from sunrise to dusk) to take later breaks rather than the set ones.
- Introducing prayer rooms to allow Muslim officers to pray during working hours.
- Providing halal food in staff canteens.
- Introducing mentors to provide career guidance.
- Introducing a High Potential Development Scheme (HPDS) to seek out those with the potential to be future leaders.

Initiatives such as these are considered a central component in encouraging a more diverse workforce. However, it is not sufficient simply to put such actions into place, they have to be regularly audited to ensure they are working. For example, in the case of the police, there has been an increase in ethnic minority recruits, but the rate of resignation or dismissal within 12 months of joining is twice as high as white recruits. This 'revolving door syndrome' (where recruitment is counterbalanced by exit) suggests that the initiatives might be working to attract ethnic minorities, but there are problems of retention and progression. However, such an assessment is only possible if data are collected prior to the introduction of a particular initiative in order to be able to establish a benchmark and then assess the effect it is having. This is why monitoring is the second key component.

Stop & think

In Norway it is a legal requirement for large private companies to have at least 40 per cent of the board made up of women members. The penalty for non-compliance is the disbandment of the organisation. The Norwegian government argued that voluntary measures had failed, so legislation was necessary.

What is your view about this approach?

Monitoring

One of the key ways of helping to ensure the effectiveness of policies is through the use of equality monitoring. This is a process of systematically collecting and analysing data on the composition of the workforce, particularly with regard to recruitment and promotion. The rationale behind monitoring is that it is impossible for managers to make an assessment of what action to take (if any) unless they are aware of the current situation. Of course, the supposition behind this is that managers might want to take action – but if this is not the case then logically managers might not see the value in collecting the data in the first place. Therefore, equality monitoring has both advocates and detractors who will marshall different arguments to justify their position. These are summarised in Table 7.2. Once again there is also variation in practice depending on the national context. For example, in France it is unlawful for data to be collected on the ethnic composition of the workforce because this contravenes French policy on ethnic integration. In contrast, in the UK, public authorities now have a legal requirement to collect ethnic monitoring data on staff in post, applications for employment, promotion and training, and then to analyse this data and act upon any evidence of unfairness or disadvantage.

Table 7.2 The arguments for and against monitoring

The case in favour of equal opportunities monitoring	The case against equal opportunities monitoring
It allows an organisation to demonstrate what they are doing and identify particular problem areas so that they can take action	It stirs up trouble and discontent, and can create problems that would otherwise not arise
It encourages managers to think creatively about positive action initiatives	It puts undue pressure on managers, and might encourage them to lower standards or appoint for the wrong reasons
It removes the need for stronger legislation such as quotas (positive discrimination)	It is positive discrimination by the back door
The data can be kept confidential, just like any other information	It is an invasion of privacy and open to abuse
It provides useful information to help management decision making	It creates the requirement to collect information that is unnecessary
Organisations conducting their activities in line with the legal requirements have nothing to fear	Organisations with no problems regarding equal opportunities do not need this burdensome bureaucratic mechanism
The costs are modest	It is an unnecessary expenditure
It is good business practice	The business needs to focus on its commercial activities

Activity

Equality initiatives

Read these four examples of equality initiatives.

1 The big four accountancy firms – KPMG, Deloitte, Ernst & Young and PricewaterhouseCoopers – are actively seeking to recruit women and ethnic minorities because they are under-represented in the organisations, especially at senior levels. Their tactics have been to hold career events specifically targeted at female and ethnic minority undergraduates.

2 The UK Environment Agency has set regional targets for recruiting ethnic minority employees and linked these to the bonuses of all executive managers. Within 18 months the percentage of black and ethnic minority applicants for advertised vacancies had doubled (from 3 to 7 per cent) and the number of ethnic minority candidates offered jobs increased from 2 to 5 per cent.

3 The disability charity Scope introduced a reserved-post policy which means that a certain percentage of jobs are to be filled by people who are registered disabled. The charity have set a target of 20 per cent of posts to be reserved for disabled employees.

4 Time Warner Books recognised how white-dominated their organisation was (along with most other book publishers) and decided to offer a paid internship to someone from an ethnic minority. The plan involved recruiting the person by word-of-mouth rather than formal advertising.

Questions

1 Assess the pros and cons of each approach.
2 Which of the initiatives can be described as positive action and which are forms of positive discrimination?

Criticism of equal and diversity policies

Naturally, there are some criticisms of equal and diversity policies. The first of these is that they are sometimes not worth the paper they are written on. Just because an organisation has a policy, it does not mean that the policy is effective. An example of this point of view was noted above in relation to the equality policies of organisations in Britain (Hoque and Noon, 2004). Indeed, it might be argued that in some organisations managers want to present the positive image of being aware of equality concerns, but do not wish to introduce procedures or initiatives that might (in their opinion) constrain or limit their decisions about who to appoint, train, promote and so on.

A second criticism is that formal policies do not prevent managers from finding ways of evading or distorting the procedures. For example, in their case study of a local government authority in the UK, Liff and Dale (1994) interviewed a black woman on a clerical grade who had been told that she needed to get a professional qualification if she wanted promotion. 'After obtaining the qualification she was turned down again, this time in favour of a white woman without qualification: a decision justified [by the managers] on the grounds of "positive action"' (Liff and Dale, 1994: 87). In another study (Collinson *et al.*, 1990) even the personnel/HR managers, who are supposedly the guardians and promoters of good practice, were colluding with line managers to avoid equal opportunity guidelines.

A third criticism is that even where managers are working within the procedures, there is a huge amount of informal practice and discretion that means unfair treatment can persist. In the quote below, Liff (2003: 434) gives examples from two studies that show how this might occur during selection interviewing.

> Collinson *et al.* (1990) during detailed observation of interviews, found that managers used different (gender-based) criteria to assess whether applicants were able to meet the job requirements. For example, a form of behaviour described as 'showing initiative' and assessed as desirable when demonstrated by a male applicant, in a woman applicant was seen as 'pushy' and undesirable. Similarly Curran (1988: 344) showed that managers often found it hard to separate the assessment of a characteristic such as leadership from the concept of masculinity, or a 'requirement for a pleasant personality and one for a pretty girl with a smile'. What is important about these findings is that they show that for some managers at least gender becomes part of their assessment of suitability criteria . . . Such findings also reduce the force of the prescriptive advice to excluded groups that they can succeed simply by gaining the necessary skills and demonstrating their ability at job-related tasks.

It will be noted that these three types of criticism are concerned with the ineffectiveness of equality and diversity policies, however, there are other critics who simply reject the whole idea of the needs for such policies. They tend to suggest that policies and positive action initiatives are providing special privileges for particular groups. It is a viewpoint that is common among those of an extreme right-wing political persuasion and sometimes stems from a belief in the inferiority of some groups over others. Within organisations it can manifest itself in the form of verbal abuse and harassment – in these extreme circumstances the issue is not simply an organisational concern, but might also be a criminal matter. A dramatic example of the way that such extreme views can cause misery for employees is the case of a Ford UK employee.

> Mr Parma suffered years of routine abuse by his foreman and his team leader. Once, he opened his sealed pay packet to find the word 'Paki' scrawled inside. In another incident, he saw graffiti threatening to throw him to his death.[. . .]
>
> On one occasion he was ordered into the 'punishment cell', a small booth in which oil is sprayed over engines, but he was not allowed to wear protective clothing. He became ill and needed medical attention.

On another occasion Mr Parma had his lunch kicked out of his hands and was told: 'We're not having any of that Indian shit in here.' He was also warned that he would have his legs broken if he ever named any of his tormentors. The police were called in at one stage, but the Crown Prosecution Service decided to drop charges. (*The Independent*, 24 September 1999).

Incidents such as this may be extreme but their existence makes the case for all organisations both to have an equality/diversity policy and to ensure that it is enforced through positive action initiatives and audited through monitoring procedures.

Devising equality and diversity policies

It has been noted above that equality and diversity policies are seen as desirable and that recommendations are often made to organisations about how to frame such policies. Ultimately, however, it is up to the decision makers within organisations to choose the form and content of their policies – although there might be certain legal requirements within which they are expected to operate.

When formulating policy, managers are faced with addressing the key question of how to treat people at work in order to ensure fairness. Or, to express this more specifically: to ensure fairness, should managers ignore the differences between people and treat them the same, or should managers acknowledge differences and treat people differently?

In many respects this is a key question that lies at the heart of any discussion about equality and diversity. The reason why people often vehemently disagree about equality initiatives is because they are approaching the issue from very different perspectives. In other words, if you believe that for example, men and women, or different ethnic groups are fundamentally (as human beings) the same, then you are approaching the issues from an alternative perspective to someone who sees people as fundamentally different.

These contrasting perspectives also lead to different ways of dealing with the issues of ensuring fairness at work. It is therefore important to understand the two perspectives and look at the organisational initiatives that each might lead towards. To help explain this, Figure 7.1 puts the perspectives in diagrammatic form and the following sections analyse each one in detail.

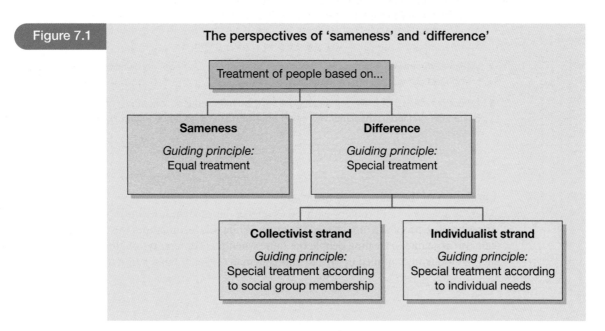

Figure 7.1   **The perspectives of 'sameness' and 'difference'**

The sameness perspective

A word of warning is needed here. This concept of 'sameness' acknowledges genuine differences between people, but means that the variations of attributes such as intelligence, potential to develop skills, values, emotions, and so forth are distributed across different social groups. Consequently, it is argued that any differences between people on these attributes are not determined by their gender, ethnicity, age, sexual orientation and so forth, but arise from their upbringing, experiences, socialisation and other contextual factors. Therefore, the important guiding principle for managers is that people should be treated equally regardless of their sex, ethnic group, age and so forth.

Below are a few examples of the kinds of practices that this perspective might lead organisations to adopt.

- Ensure that age is not used as a criterion to decide whether an employee is suitable for retraining.
- Ensure the same questions are asked of men and women during selection interviews.
- ensure that gender specific language does not appear in job adverts, job descriptions and other organisation documents.
- Ensure part-time working opportunities are available to men and women.
- Ensure any company benefits (for example, pensions, insurance rights, health scheme subsidies) are available to partners of non-married couples and same-sex partners.
- Ensure the same pay for the same job.

The guiding policy behind these types of initiative is *equal treatment*. Obviously any such organisational initiatives are influenced by the legal context in which the organisation is based. There is likely to be legislation that requires organisations to undertake some actions. For instance in the UK the legislation sets some of the parameters in the recruitment process (see Chapter 6) in terms and conditions of employment (Chapter 12) and in reward systems (Chapter 13).

Activity | **Equality and diversity initiatives**

1 Draw up a list of the initiatives designed to address equality and diversity in your organisation (if you work full time or part time) or an organisation with which you are familiar (if you are a full-time student). Your list does not need to be exhaustive, but try to include initiatives additional to the examples already given.

2 Which of the initiatives have arisen because of legal requirements and which have been introduced out of choice (i.e. voluntarily)?

3 Select one or two of those initiatives that have been introduced voluntarily and assess the influences that led to the initiatives being adopted. These could be internal or external pressures.

Limitation of the sameness approach

There is a substantial problem with this sameness approach. It assumes that disadvantage arises because people are not treated the same. While this is sometimes the case, disadvantage can also arise due to treating people the same when their differences ought to be considered. This is eloquently summed up by Liff and Wajcman (1996: 81) in relation to gender:

All policies based on same/equal treatment require women to deny, or attempt to minimize, differences between themselves and men as the price of equality. This, it is suggested, is neither feasible nor desirable. Such an approach can never adequately take account of problems arising from, say, women's domestic responsibilities or their educational disadvantage. Nor does it take account of those who want to spend time with their children without this costing them advancement at work. Sameness is being judged against a norm of male characteristics and behaviour. . . . [The sameness approach to equal opportunities takes] an over-simplistic view both of the problem of inequality (seeing it as a managerial failure to treat like as like) and its solution ('equality' can be achieved by treating women the same as men).

The difference perspective

The 'difference' perspective assumes that key differences exist between people and that these should be taken into account when managers are making decisions. In other words, it can be argued that ignoring differences can lead to disadvantage.

Again there is a word of warning. There tends to be two strands to this perspective and this must be taken into account: (1) the collectivist strand; (2) the individualist strand.

1 The collectivist strand

This approach argues that the differences are associated with the social groups to which a person belongs. For example, as the quote above from Liff and Wajcman (1996) underlines, women's domestic responsibilities are different in general from those of men – most notably in the time spent on childcare – so, to ignore this difference will disadvantage women. In practical terms, it means that when faced with job or promotion candidates of similar ages and both with families, the female candidate is more likely to have less direct experience because she has had to take time out to have children and might have chosen to take extended maternity leave. By ignoring the differences, the woman may appear a weaker candidate; by recognising them, the woman's achievements during her more recent periods of employment can be assessed.

The collectivist strand therefore argues that differences between social groups exist and should be considered in relation to ensuring fairness at work. This means that it might be relevant to introduce practices that are based on recognising differences between social groups, rather than ignoring differences. Below are some examples of the types of initiatives that might arise from taking this collectivist difference perspective.

- Single-sex training schemes (developing skills to allow access to a wide range of jobs).
- Payment for jobs based on principles of equal value (see also Chapter 13).
- Job advertisements aimed at encouraging applications from under-represented groups.
- Reassessment of job requirements to open opportunities up to wider range of people.
- Choice of food in the workplace cafeteria that reflects different cultural needs.

The guiding policy behind these types of positive action initiative is *special treatment according to social group membership*. There is a wide range of such initiatives, the most extreme sort being quotas that set a requirement for organisations to recruit and promote a specific percentage of people from disadvantaged groups. Setting quotas in this way is a type of positive discrimination – unlawful in most European countries – although setting targets is allowed and normally encouraged under discrimination law provisions. Again the legal context is important because some principles, such as equal value, might be a legal requirement for all organisations, while others are left entirely to the discretion of managers within organisations.

One of the notable problems with this perspective is that it leads some people to argue that special treatment constitutes an unfair advantage. There is a tendency among critics to emphasise the extreme examples, and there has been considerable backlash to some affirmative action programmes in the United States where quotas are used. Some of this criticism is politically driven, but it also comes from some of the supposed benefactors of positive discrimination, particular ethnic minorities. These critics argue that it demeans their achievements because it leads others to suspect that they only got the job or promotion to meet the required 'quota', rather than because they were the best candidate. Furthermore, some commentators argue that it is simply wrong in principle to redress the disadvantage suffered by one group of people because of favouritism and privilege with measures that are specifically designed to favour and privilege an alternative group of people. Indeed, this is the perspective of the UK's Chartered Institute of Personnel and Development who use the term 'reverse discrimination' to describe extreme measures such as quota systems.

Although the policy of special treatment presents some problems, it also offers a persuasive approach for some people because it recognises that disadvantage is often an intrinsic part of existing organisational structures, practices and culture. Simply adopting a policy of equal treatment would not remove this existing disadvantage, instead something more radical has to be done to get to the root of the problem and redress the existing imbalance. One of the best expressions of this comes from former US President Lyndon Johnson at the time of the introduction of race legislation in 1965.

> Imagine a hundred yard dash in which one of the two runners has his legs shackled together. He has progressed 10 yards, while the unshackled runner has gone 50 yards. At that point the judges decide that the race is unfair. How do they rectify the situation? Do they merely remove the shackles and allow the race to proceed? Then they could say that 'equal opportunity' now prevailed. But one of the runners would still be forty yards ahead of the other. Would it not be the better part of justice to allow the previously shackled runner to make up the forty yard gap; or to start the race all over again?   (Quoted in Noon and Blyton, 2002: 278)

 Stop & think

Look again at the questions raised in President Johnson's analogy. What would you do and how would you justify it?

2 The individualist strand

The second way of looking from a difference perspective can be called the individualist strand because the main focus is the individual rather than the social group. This approach emphasises the individuality of all employees. People have unique strengths and weaknesses, abilities and needs. Therefore it is not important to focus on characteristics that associate people with a particular group – for instance their sex or whether they have a disability – rather it is their individuality that becomes the pertinent issue.

A label that is often associated with this approach is 'managing diversity'. It is increasingly being used by organisations as a term to describe their approach to ensure fairness and opportunities for all. However, a particular problem is that the term 'managing diversity' can have various meanings. It has become one of those widely used management phrases, so can mean different things in different organisations. At one extreme it is simply a synonym for 'equal opportunities' – used because the latter is seen as old-fashioned or backward looking – and therefore has no distinct or special meaning of its own. At the other extreme managing diversity represents a new approach to dealing with disadvantage at work.

A notable example of the new approach based on recognising individual differences is Kandola and Fullerton (1994). They argue that managing diversity is superior to previous approaches to equality at work for five reasons.

1 It ensures all employees maximise their potential and their contribution to the organisation.
2 It covers a broad range of people – no one is excluded.
3 It focuses on issues of movement within an organisation, the culture of the organisation, and the meeting of business objectives.
4 It becomes the concern of all employees and especially all managers.
5 It does not rely on positive action/affirmative action.

Below are some examples of the types of initiatives that might arise from taking this individualist difference perspective.

- Offer employees a choice of benefits from a 'menu' so they can tailor a package to suit their individual needs.
- Devise training and development plans for each employee.
- Provide training to ensure managers are aware of and can combat their prejudices based on stereotypes.
- Explore and publicise ways that diversity within the organisation improves the organisation – for example, public perceptions, sensitivity to customer needs, wider range of views and ideas.
- Re-evaluate the criteria for promotion and development and widen them by recognising a greater range of competences, experiences and career paths.

The guiding policy behind these types of initiative is *special treatment according to individual needs*. Of course, this approach has its critics, and in particular three objections can by raised.

1 The approach tends to understate the extent to which people share common experiences. It has a tendency to reject the idea of social groups which is somewhat counter to people's everyday experiences. For example, while several disabled people might differ considerably across a whole range of attributes and attitudes, their common experience of disability (even different forms of disability) might be sufficient to create a feeling of cohesion and solidarity. In particular some people might actively look for social group identity if they feel isolated or vulnerable.
2 The approach ignores material similarities between social groups. For example, Kirton and Greene (2005) note that 'women of all ethnic groups typically take on the responsibility for children and are less able to compete for jobs with men, not withstanding qualitative ethnic differences in how women may "juggle" their multiple roles.'
3 The approach has a tendency to emphasise the value of diversity in terms of the business sense arguments outlined earlier in the chapter. As was noted such arguments have their limitations because they focus only on those initiatives that can be shown to contribute to the profitability or other performance indicators of the organisation. In practice this extends opportunities only to a selective number of individuals whose competencies are in short supply or have been identified as being of particular value.

Sameness and difference

As has been shown in the discussion above, disadvantage can arise by treating people the same or by treating people differently, so any policy that emphasises one perspective more than the other runs the risk of leaving some disadvantages unchecked. What is called for is a mixed policy that recognises that to eliminate disadvantage it is necessary in some circumstances to treat people the same, and in other circumstances to treat people differently. Of course, this is a challenge in itself because in what circumstances do you apply one criterion and not the other? For example, imagine the following situation.

A woman applies for a job as an adviser selling financial products in a company that is dominated by men.

Scenario 1: she has the same qualifications and experience as male applicants, but the all-male selection panel might reject her because they consider that she would not 'fit in' with the competitive, aggressive culture of the organisation.

Scenario 2: she has the same qualifications as male applicants but has taken a career break for childcare purposes. The selection panel reject her because compared with men of the same age she has less work experience.

In the first scenario the panel are rejecting her by using the criterion of difference (recognising gender); in the second by using the criterion of sameness (ignoring gender). But if the panel were to reverse their logic of difference and sameness, it might lead them to different conclusions. In the first scenario, if the panel ignored gender, they would arrive at the conclusion that she was appointable. In the second scenario, if they recognised that, because of her gender, she has had extra domestic commitments so cannot be compared with men of the same age then again they might conclude she is appointable.

This illustrates that managers have a key role in dealing with disadvantage because they determine the criteria and define the circumstances in which sameness and difference are either recognised or ignored.

Institutional discrimination

One of key issues that managers must face is whether their organisation operates in ways that are fundamentally discriminatory. This is sometimes referred to as institutional racism, institutional sexism, institutional homophobia, and so on. The term means that rather than discrimination being seen simply as the actions of individuals, it is deep-rooted in the processes and culture of the organisation.

Examples of processes that are sometimes described as evidence of institutional discrimination are:

- Word-of-mouth methods for recruitment.
- Dress codes that prevent people practising their religious beliefs.
- Promotions based on informal recommendations, rather than open competition.
- Informal assessments rather than formal appraisals.
- Assumptions about training capabilities.
- Assumptions about language difficulties and attitudes.

Often these types of processes are not recognised as being discriminatory and have been in operation for many years. It is only when a company is faced with a legal challenge that such practices are seen to be having a discriminatory impact. Managers should regularly scrutinise organisational procedures, and the use of data collected through equality monitoring can be particularly effective in highlighting areas whether the processes might be disadvantaging particular groups.

Activity

Recruitment at SewCo

Consider the following case.

SewCo is a family-run business that makes garments. Most of its employees are sewing machine operators (all women) who assemble the garments. It has a stable core workforce, but there is fluctuation in demand for its products, so extra employees are brought in when the order books are full and 'let go' at slack periods. When managers need to recruit extra employees, or when they need to replace someone, they rely on word-of-mouth methods. This means that the women on the shopfloor ask around their friends and family. When likely candidates are identified their names are given to the factory manager. He calls them in for a chat and assesses their suitability. If he approves them he asks the supervisor to check if the candidate has the required sewing skills.

Questions

1 Identify the problems with this approach to recruitment process in terms of equality and diversity.

2 Suggest an alternative approach that might address the problems you have identified.

Just as pernicious are workplace cultures that have the effect of excluding people from particular social groups by making them feel unwelcome or uncomfortable. This is key issue for managers because organisations might have cultures that are long established and deeply embedded. An interesting review of the way organisational cultures can marginalise social groups is provided by Kirton and Greene (2005). Most notable among their conclusions are the following points:

- Organisational cultures are infused with gendered meanings, which are often unarticulated and thus rendered invisible. The gendered hierarchy is an example, as are various unwritten codes, rules, customs and habits which guide gendered behaviour and underpin expectations of organisational members.

- Sexual harassment and the use of sexual humour are pervasive and the outcome of workplace gendered social relations, which are powerful mechanisms for the control and subordination of women.

- Stereotypes (based on gender, race, disability, sexual orientation and age) are reinforced through jokes and humour, leading to negative organisational experiences for some people.

- Non-disabled people's lack of contact with disability reinforces their fear and ignorance surrounding the issue.

Stop & think

Consider whether your own employing organisation, university or college operates practices that might support institutionalised discrimination.

Problems with institutional discrimination

The first problem is inertia. Even when institutional discrimination has been identified there is no incentive to make changes because those people in positions of influence have benefited (and continue to benefit) from the system. Furthermore, those people most likely to change policies within the organisation (the 'victims' of discrimination) are denied access to decision-making processes.

The second problem is with the concept of institutional discrimination itself. Some critics argue that it can lead to a tendency to blame 'the system', rather than focusing on the people who shape and sustain the system. In some circumstances this can be helpful because by removing blame from individuals it might be easier to encourage action to address the problem. In other circumstances it can result in nothing being done because no one is deemed responsible or held accountable.

In defence of the concept of institutional discrimination, it can be argued that it alerts people to the way that the fundamental structures and processes can be detrimental to equality and diversity, and that unless action is taken to address these fundamentals, nothing will improve. This is an important point because it suggests that in many instances the drive to equality and diversity requires some radical changes, rather than just equality/diversity statements and positive action initiatives.

The need for radical changes: the long agenda

The existence of institutional discrimination leads some commentators to argue that fundamental change is needed if the elimination of disadvantage is to be achieved. Foremost among these commentators is Cockburn (1989, 1991) who has pointed out that many of the positive action initiatives adopted by managers in organisations are concerned only with the short term. Typically these initiatives are fixing current problems, responding to outside pressures, or perhaps seeking to make a pre-emptive move to impress customers and clients. This ignores the possibilities of more radical, long-term initiatives that might fundamentally change the structures and processes that produce disadvantage.

The proposition forwarded by Cockburn is that as well as this short agenda (with its laudable aim of eliminating bias) there is the need to consider the long agenda. This would be a challenging project of organisational transformation, requiring fundamental changes to the processes, roles, norms, attitudes and relationships within organisations. Cockburn (1989: 218) explains:

> As such it brings into view the nature and purpose of institutions and the processes by which the power of some groups over others in institutions is built and renewed. It acknowledges the needs of disadvantaged groups for access to power. [. . .] But it also looks for change in the nature of power, in the control ordinary people of diverse kinds have over institutions, a melting away of the white male monoculture.

The obvious problem for enacting the long agenda is that those in positions of influence within organisations have little incentive to make changes that might challenge their own power and dominance. The long agenda therefore has to be led by activists and advocates. This might be through committed individuals within organisations, but it would also require collective voice and action. It might also require a political context that encourages a more active approach by organisations to ensuring equality of opportunity – through, for example, compulsory monitoring or employment quotas for disadvantaged groups.

The process of discrimination in an organisation

The discussion so far has explored many of the complex and sometimes contradictory issues surrounding equality and diversity. It makes sense to bring this together by considering the range of pressures and influences that are brought to bear when managing equality and diversity. Figure 7.2 is a flowchart that maps the relationship between the key components and thereby show how the process of discrimination occurs in organisations (Noon and Blyton, 2002). Each of the components of this flowchart is discussed in this section, and is linked with many of the issues raised in the earlier part of the chapter.

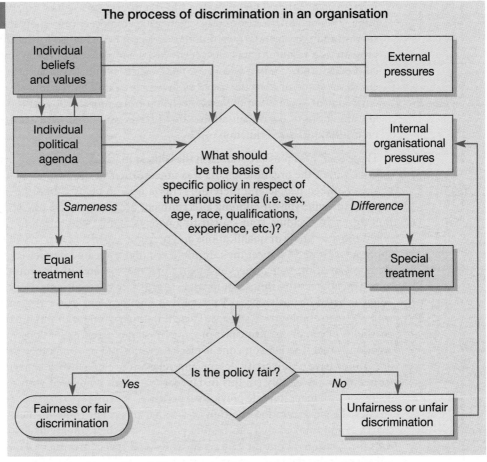

Figure 7.2 — **The process of discrimination in an organisation**

Source: Adapted from Noon and Blyton (2002).

At the centre of the process lie two vital questions: 'what should be the basis of any specific policy?' and 'is the policy fair?'. Try to envisage this in terms of specific policies, such as promotion, awarding of merit pay, entitlement to career development opportunities, and so on. The first question is of vital concern to managers since their decisions are going to shape a particular policy. However, as the diagram shows, such decisions are not made in isolation but are subject to a range of influences: personal influences (belief, values and political agenda), external pressures and organisational pressures.

1 *Personal influences.* A manager will have his or her individual beliefs and values that fundamentally guide behaviour and influence decisions. So, for instance, a strong belief in social justice is going to affect the choices that a manager makes, as is a particular prejudice or stereotype about a social group. Combined with this is the individual political agenda of the manager, which might moderate the values and beliefs in some way. For example, a male manager might believe that women do not make good leaders but knows that in order to get promotion he must suppress this view in order not to alienate his boss – who is a woman. This, of course, is the *realpolitik* of normal organisational life and will operate at all levels. This intermixing of beliefs, values and political manoeuvring is going to have an influence on the manager's decisions.

2 *External pressures.* In addition to these personal pressures, the manager is faced with external pressure. This could be legislation requiring (or prohibiting) certain action, public opinion, customer or client pressure, supplier influence, labour supply issues, and so forth. For instance, it was noted in the discussion about the business case how managers might adopt equal and diversity initiatives in order to improve the public image of their organisations, or access a wider customer base.

247

3 *Internal organisational pressures.* The final set of pressures comes from within the organisation. They might arise from other managers, employees (especially through satisfaction surveys and grievances), trade unions, works councils, and so forth. There might also be pressure as a result of data collected within the organisation. For example, high levels of employee turnover might encourage positive action initiatives that help to retain employees, develop and make better use of skills, and provide a more supportive and encouraging environment. In addition there are likely to be pressures because of the workplace culture and traditions of the organisation – the sorts of issues that were discussed in the section on institutional discrimination.

These combined pressures establish the context in which decisions are made about specific policies within the organisation. As was noted earlier in the chapter, managers must make choices between people and therefore criteria have to be used to differentiate people. For example, imagine you are running a recruitment process and have received a pile of application forms. In deciding your shortlisting policy (that is, who to call for an interview) you might use the criteria of qualifications and previous experience as a way of choosing between applicants. Those who meet the minimum requirements are interviewed, those who do not are rejected. At the same time, you might think that age and ethnic group are irrelevant and so you do not take this into account when shortlisting the applicants. Hence your shortlisting policy is based on 'difference' with regard to qualifications and experience, and 'sameness' with regard to ethnic group and age. There is nothing wrong with this mixture – it reflects the possibility of combining principles of sameness and difference. The consequence of this combination is that whether someone is black or white, old or young they get equal treatment, but if they have a university degree and relevant previous work experience they will get treated more favourably (in this instance, shortlisted) compared with someone without a degree or with inappropriate previous experience.

Logically, this raises the question of whether this is fair (note the next stage in the flowchart). If you think such a shortlisting policy is fair then you are likely to be in agreement with the decisions about the criteria for equal and special treatment. However, if you think this is unfair this might be because you feel:

- equal treatment was applied inappropriately (for example, age should have been taken into account), and/or
- special treatment was given inappropriately (for example, previous experience should not have been taken into account).

If you were an employee in the organisation then this feeling of unfairness might simply produce a feeling of discontent. On the other hand it might drive you to take action such as voicing your opinion to managers, going to the trade union, discussing the issue with other employees or leaving. This in turn might produce internal organisational pressures on future decisions (shown by the feedback loop in Figure 7.2).

Mapping out the process in this way reveals that every managerial decision over appointments, promotions, allocation of work, merit pay, training opportunities and so forth, is likely to be met with a variety of responses: some individuals and groups will interpret the decision as fair and others as unfair, depending on whether they consider the equal or special treatment to be justifiable. The extent to which employees concern themselves with issues of fairness will vary according to the circumstances and is likely to reflect whether they are directly involved with, or affected by, the outcome.

Have you directly experienced treatment you considered unfair? If so, what did you do about it? What other options did you have?

Concluding comment

It can be seen from the preceding sections that managing equality and diversity is about making choices between various courses of action. It was also shown that there are competing viewpoints as to why particular approaches should be taken. In many instances there is no clear-cut right or wrong method – rather it is a matter of judgement and conscience. What is important, however, is that any action or policy is backed up by a clear rationale.

Obviously, this chapter cannot conclude by recommending a particular approach because it depends on whether you are persuaded by the rationale behind that approach. The chapter's purpose has been to show you the approaches and provide you with an understanding of the key concepts and dilemmas. These should allow you to make your own choices and equip you to predict and challenge opposing viewpoints. The summary provides you with a review of the key points to reflect upon in forming your opinions.

Summary

- The differences that define disadvantaged groups are far more imprecise than might at first appear. It is important to recognise the diversity between social groups and within the same social group. Such diversity means policies need to be sensitive to different experiences of discrimination and different needs of disadvantaged groups and individuals.

- The reason for managers to intervene in order to prevent discrimination can be based on arguments of social justice or business needs – or both. The social justice case stresses the moral case for fairness, but critics argue that managers should be concerned with profit and efficiency, not morality. The business case stresses ways that equality and diversity are good for business, but critics point to instances where it can make good business sense *not* to act in the interests of equality and diversity.

- Equality and diversity policies vary between organisations; they range from those that are simply empty statements to others which are backed up by effective action programmes. For policies to be effective they need to have positive action initiatives to ensure policy is implemented, and monitoring to assess the effectiveness of the initiatives over time.

- When devising policies to ensure fairness managers can base them on assumptions of sameness or assumptions of difference. These two perspectives help to explain why there is often a lack of agreement about how to ensure fairness. The sameness perspective emphasises similarities between people and advocates equal treatment. The difference perspective emphasises diversity either between social groups or between individuals. These two variations of the difference perspective are similar in that they both advocate special treatment that takes the differences between people into account, but they differ in their suggestions about the types of initiatives that organisations should adopt.

- The term managing diversity is often used to describe the approach to fairness that emphasises the individual differences between people. In some instances it is an alternative approach advocated by commentators who think traditional equal opportunities policies have failed and are fundamentally flawed.

- It is important for managers to recognise that unfair treatment sometimes results from treating people differently when they ought to be treated the same, and sometimes from treating people the same when key differences ought to be recognised. Policies, procedures and attitudes within an organisation should therefore be based on recognising both the similarities and differences between people.

- Institutional discrimination is a term used to describe organisations that have processes and practices that are fundamentally discriminatory – sometimes without managers realising – and are reinforced through existing organisational structures and workplace cultures. Tackling such fundamental problems might require a more radical agenda than that being proposed by many advocates of equality and diversity.

- The process of discrimination can be seen as the combination of personal, external and internal pressures on managers to make choices in their decisions about appointments, promotions, allocation of work, training opportunities, and so forth, according to principles of sameness or difference. Perceptions of unfairness are the result of a mismatch between the expectations of employees and the manager's decisions. Viewed in this way, all decisions are susceptible to claims of unfairness, depending on the perspective of the individuals concerned, the perceived appropriateness of the criterion for the decision and the individual and social acceptability of the type of treatment (special or equal).

QUESTIONS

1 'We don't employ people over 50 years old because they find it difficult to learn new skills.' This statement was made by a training manager in a call centre.

   Comment on the statement using the concepts of stereotyping, prejudice, social justice and the business case.

2 What is the purpose of equality and diversity policies? Why do they sometimes fail to live up to expectations?

3 Without looking back through the chapter, give at least one example of a workplace initiative from each of the following approaches:

   a) The sameness perspective.
   b) The collectivist strand of the difference perspective.
   c) The individualist strand of the difference perspective.

4 'I treat everyone the same – so that's how I ensure fairness.' This quote is from a section manager in a supermarket. Explain why such an approach can sometimes lead to unfairness.

5 'Everyone is unique. Everyone is an individual. As a manager you should treat them as such.' If you were being critical of this opinion, what points would you make?

6 The Fire Service in the UK has been described as institutionally racist, sexist and homophobic. What does this mean? How would you evaluate whether such a description was legitimate?

CASE STUDY 1

A short case scenario

Branch X of a large bank is disproportionately white and the manager decides to employ more people from ethnic minorities, in line with the organisation's corporate equality and diversity statement of being, 'A bank that considers opportunity based on merit and respect for differences to be the principles that ensure fairness guides all action and decision making.' A Muslim woman is recruited and she asks if she can wear the hijab; the manager agrees to this. After a few weeks, some of her work colleagues have begun to refer to her as 'the suicide bomber' (behind her back) and she does not socialise with any of the

Case study continued

other employees at lunchtime or during other breaks. Overall, the manager is pleased about the quality of work of the new employee, but is concerned that she is not fitting in. In addition, one of the regular customers to the bank (an influential local businessman) has refused to be served by the new employee – threatening to take his account elsewhere.

The new employee is on a probationary period which is due for review. The manager is seriously considering 'letting her go'.

Questions

1 Using your knowledge of concepts explored in this chapter, identify the key issues that this scenario raises?

2 What should the manager do?

Safe future finance

The following is a true story, although for legal reasons names have been changed.

Gordon Burrows graduated from university last year with a business degree, took some time out to go travelling around the world and then returned back to his University town. He was unsure about his career but he saw an advert pinned to the notice board in the University careers office that read as follows.

> Are you qualified to degree level, highly self-motivated, diligent and keen to make a fortune?
> Then you could be the person for us!
> We are looking for confident, young graduates to join our financial advisory team. Excellent prospects and high earning potentials. Call us to find out more.

With nothing to lose, Gordon made the phone call and within the week found himself outside the offices of Safe Future Finance, about to go for an interview with Mr Fletcher. The woman at reception escorted Gordon into a large open plan office, full of desks occupied by men in dark suits and brightly coloured ties. Mr Fletcher was among them and, it turned out, was not much older than Gordon.

'I have your interviewee, Mr Fletcher.'

'Thanks Brenda. Could you fetch us a couple of coffees? Is coffee okay for you Gordon? Sorry I can't offer you anything stronger! Call me Dave, by the way.'

Gordon soon learned that the job involved being part of Dave's team selling financial products – particularly investment plans with life cover. There was no fixed salary but he would be paid on a commission-only basis and would have 'self-employed' status.

However, the bonuses were good; potentially they were very high if he reached Dave's level who, as a team leader, also received a percentage cut of all his sales team.

During the next half-an-hour Dave read through Gordon's application form and asked a series of questions. He enquired about Gordon's background and seemed particularly interested that Gordon had been to a private school. He also noted that Gordon was a keen golfer. The interview was not as Gordon had expected – it was more like a chat than the formal process he had learned about at business school.

'Right' said Dave, 'Let's give you a tour of the office then we'll finish this off in the bar across the road. That's where I can find out if you're the right man for the job – you know, find out if we'd be able to work together.'

As they wandered around the large air-conditioned office, Dave explained that the teams were in competition with each other so a good team spirit with everyone 'singing from the same hymn sheet' was essential. He added, 'There's no room for mavericks in my team. We work together and we play together – it's all part of building up good team spirit and getting sales. There's a lot of banter – you know nicknames, piss-taking, that sort of thing – but it's all part of the culture of the place. They must have taught you all about organisational culture at business school.'

Gordon nodded although this was not quite what he remembered about organisational culture.

As they walked between the desks Dave exchanged a few pleasantries and a few light-hearted insults with

Case study continued

the various sales advisors. He explained to Gordon, 'One of the most important things you need to know about this place is that you are very much seen as an individual. Okay, you'd be part of my team but you work on your own and you sink or swim according to your own abilities. You could come to me for advice but I'd be expecting you to work your balls off. I've got no room for passengers on my team.'

Gordon was unsure whether to respond but commented. 'I work well on my own and I'm not scared of hard work.'

Dave nodded approvingly. 'Good. This is a tough job. It is all about closing a deal. I can teach you the basics but the drive comes from within. Sometimes you've got to be ruthless for the sake of your own bonus and the team. You see the chart on the wall over there? You see the long line?'

Gordon stared at a multicoloured chart that had everyone's name listed down the side and a performance line alongside. One of the lines stretched noticeably further than the rest.

'The longest line is me', said Dave loud enough for the men at the nearby desks to hear. 'I clean up on the amount of business I sign up. None of these tossers can get anywhere near me!' There were a few smirks and some obscene gestures before Dave said in a mocking tone, 'Come on, let's leave these ladies to it.'

'Funny you should say that', ventured Gordon. 'Aren't there any women working here?'

'Sure' said Dave, 'All the girls are on the next floor. They handle the paperwork.'

'So don't they apply for sales advisor jobs?' asked Gordon.

'Yes, they apply, but they don't get them because they tend not to have the drive and hard-nosed atti-

tude to sales. But we're not prejudiced here, it's just that skills are used where they are best suited. For instance, you'll see we've got some Asians in the office. They've got excellent contacts, particularly among their families, who have money and are willing to invest it in the financial products we sell. On the other hand, you won't see any black faces because they have a different attitude to investments and they aren't well-connected. Being well-connected to people with money to invest is one of the key factors for success in this job. In fact we've just recruited a couple of shirt-lifters because the company is hoping they'll bring in "pink cash" from their community.'

Dave checked his watch, and announced that it was time for them to finish off the interview in the bar across the road. He added, 'Besides, I'm desperate for a cigarette. That's one of the downsides of working here – it's a no-smoking office. Bloody discrimination if you ask me.'

Questions

1 Evaluate Dave's attitude using your knowledge of the social justice and business case arguments.

2 Evaluate the recruitment procedure used in this instance drawing upon your knowledge of Equal Opportunity best-practice guidelines.

3 Does Dave treat people according to principles of sameness or difference?

4 Assess whether or not there is evidence of institutional discrimination at Safe Future Finance.

5 Using Figure 7.2 as a process map, identify the critical junctures where problems have or could occur and where change interventions could/should be made.

References and further reading

Cockburn, C. (1989) 'Equal opportunities: the short and long agenda', *Industrial Relations Journal*, 20, 3: 213–225.

Cockburn, C. (1991) *In the Way of Women*. Basingstoke: Macmillan.

Collinson, D.L., Knights, D. and Collinson, M. (1990) *Managing to Discriminate*. London: Routledge.

Cunningham, I. and James, P. (2001) 'Managing diversity and disability legislation', in Noon, M. and Ogbonna, E. (eds) *Equality, Diversity and Disadvantage in Employment*. Basingstoke: Palgrave, pp. 103–117.

Curran, M. (1988) 'Gender and recruitment: people and places in the labour market', *Work, Employment and Society*, 2, 3: 335–351.

Dickens, L. (1994) 'The business case for women's equality', *Employee Relations*, 16, 8: 5–18.

Dickens, L. (1999) 'Beyond the business case: a three-pronged approach to equality action', *Human Resource Management Journal*, 9, 1: 9–19.

Dickens, L. (2000) 'Still wasting resources? Equality in employment', in Bach, S. and Sisson, K. (eds) *Personnel Management*, 3rd edn. Oxford: Blackwell, pp. 137–169.

Healy, G. (1993) 'Business and discrimination' in Stacey, R. (ed.) *Strategic Thinking and the Management of Change*. London: Kogan Page.

Heery, E. and Noon, M. (2001) *A Dictionary of Human Resource Management*. Oxford: Oxford University Press.

Hoque, K. and Noon, M. (2004) 'Equal Opportunities Policy and Practice in Britain: Evaluating the "Empty Shell" Hypothesis', *Work, Employment and Society* 18, 3: 481–506.

Kandola, R. and Fullerton, J. (1994) *Managing the Mosaic*. London: IPD.

Kandola, R., Fullerton, J. and Ahmed, Y. (1995) 'Managing diversity: Succeeding where equal opportunities has failed', *Equal Opportunities Review*, 59: 31–36.

Kirton, G. and Greene, A-M. (2005) *The Dynamics of Managing Diversity*, 2nd edn. Oxford: Butterworth-Heinemann.

Liff, S. (2003) 'The industrial relations of a diverse workforce', in Edwards, P. (ed.) *Industrial Relations*, 2nd edn. Oxford: Blackwell, pp. 420–446.

Liff, S. and Dale, K. (1994) 'Formal opportunity, informal barriers: Black women managers within a local authority', *Work, Employment and Society*, 8, 2: 177–198.

Liff, S. and Wajcman, J. (1996) '"Sameness" and "difference" revisited: Which way forward for equal opportunity initiatives?', *Journal of Management Studies*, 33, 1: 79–94.

Modood, T., Berthoud, R., Lakey, J., Nazroo, J., Smith, P., Virdee, S. and Beishon, S. (1997) *Ethnic Minorities in Britain: Diversity and Disadvantage*. London: Policy Studies Institute.

Noon, M. and Blyton, P. (2002) *The Realities of Work*, 2nd edn. Basingstoke: Palgrave.

Noon, M. and Ogbonna, E. (2001) 'Introduction: The key analytical themes', in Noon, M. and Ogbonna, E. (eds) *Equality, Diversity and Disadvantage in Employment*. Basingstoke: Palgrave, pp. 1–14.

Oswick, C. and Rosenthal, P. (2001) 'Towards a relevant theory of age discrimination in employment', in Noon, M. and Ogbonna, E. (eds) *Equality, Diversity and Disadvantage in Employment*. Basingstoke: Palgrave, pp. 156–171.

Pilkington, A. (2001) 'Beyond racial dualism: Racial disadvantage and ethnic diversity in the labour market', in Noon, M. and Ogbonna, E. (eds) *Equality, Diversity and Disadvantage in Employment*. Basingstoke: Palgrave, pp. 171–189.

Reynolds, G., Nicholls, P. and Alferoff, C. (2001) 'Disabled people, (re)training and employment: A qualitative exploration of exclusion', in Noon, M. and Ogbonna, E. (eds) *Equality, Diversity and Disadvantage in Employment*. Basingstoke: Palgrave, pp. 172–189.

Webb, J. (1997) 'The politics of equal opportunity', *Gender, Work and Organisation*, 4, 3: 159–169.

For multiple-choice questions, exercises and annotated weblinks specific to this chapter visit the book's website at www.pearsoned.co.uk/beardwell

Teacher shortages

Over the past 50 years, the UK has lurched from one crisis to another in the recruitment and retention of teachers, particularly for secondary schools. Now the shortage of teachers looks set to become even more of a problem as large numbers of people currently in the profession near retirement. Shortages are especially acute in subjects like maths, science and modern languages and in specific geographical areas like inner London, where there are many alternative careers. A growing body of economic research on the labour market for teachers is seeking to understand these shortages and provide insights into potential policy measures.

To some extent, the labour market for teachers functions like any other labour market, with schools acting as employers. But there are two notable characteristics shared with some other public service occupations like healthcare professionals. These are that the state has both monopoly power in the provision of credentials – the state determines who is qualified to teach – and near 'monopsony' (monopoly buyer) power in the recruitment of teachers – since most teachers are employed in state schools. What's more, teaching is highly unionised and the government generally determines pay.

England has an ageing teaching profession, especially in primary schools. 40 per cent of all teachers are aged 45–55, and those aged over 55 account for another 6 per cent of the workforce. Within the next ten years, nearly 50 per cent of the current workforce is likely to have retired. Currently, the official retirement age is 65 but teachers can retire as early as 55 and many do so. Since the number of pupils is not forecast to decrease significantly, at the current level of recruitment, there is likely to be a large shortage of teachers.

There has been an excess demand for teachers almost continuously throughout the post-war period. The main problem has been a shortage of secondary teachers, although the difference in excess demand between primary and secondary teachers disappeared towards the end of the 1990s.

Since 1992 teachers' pay has fallen by 6 per cent relative to average non-manual earnings (although the decline 'bottomed out' in the late 1990s. Over the longer run, teachers' pay follows a repetitive cyclical pattern; a period of sustained decline followed by a dramatic increase, usually as a result of a major government report on the crisis in teacher supply.

A key aspect of teacher supply is the relative popularity of the profession with women graduates. Feminisation of the teaching profession adds some difficulties to planning teacher supply as many women will at some point interrupt their career for family reasons. Women are also more likely to leave teaching than men so policies to facilitate work and child-rearing, such as subsidised childcare or reduced workload, may increase teacher supply.

As with other public sector service professions, there have also been shortages of teachers in certain areas of the country, most markedly in inner London and the South East. Official vacancy rates are two to three times higher than the national average in London despite it being the area that relies most on temporarily filled positions. Recruiting difficulties in London are thought to stem from the better alternative careers for potential teachers and the upward pressure on living costs associated with a more competitive labour market. But it is possible that recruiting difficulties in London have more to do with job conditions in inner city schools than outside job opportunities and living costs.

Most government policies to retain teachers concentrate on financial incentives but surveys of teachers reveal that pay is not the only determinant of their dissatisfaction. Compared with other graduates, teachers are more likely to claim to be dissatisfied with their hours of work. Compared with other employees, teachers' hours are concentrated during term time with an average working week of 52 hours.

It has long been asserted that many people become teachers because of the non-pecuniary benefits, such as long holidays. However, the national curriculum and rigours of the inspection procedure may have given teachers an excessive administrative burden. Interviews with teachers leaving the profession confirm that heavy workloads and other characteristics of schools rank higher than pay as a reason for quitting.

National recruitment and retention initiatives

Training bursaries

Training bursaries from the Teacher Development Agency (TDA) encourage recruitment into Initial Teacher Training (ITT) courses via postgraduate routes. It is not a loan and is tax-free for full-time postgraduate students. Bursaries from September 2006 are £9000 for maths, science and other secondary shortage subjects and £6000 for secondary non-shortage subjects and primary.

Golden hellos

This initiative was introduced to increase the number of trainees achieving Qualified Teacher Status (QTS) and finding employment in shortage subjects. Payment is made through salaries after a successful induction period – normally a year – and is taxable. From September 2006 'golden hello' payments are £5000 for maths and science and £2500 for secondary shortage subjects.

Payment of fees

From 2006–7 all trainees on postgraduate certificate in education (PGCE) courses will be required to pay variable fees. However, all PGCE students will be eligible for a £1200 grant from DfES to help pay for fees.

Graduate Teacher Programme (GTP)

The GTP is a one-year programme offering graduates the opportunity to train as a teacher and gain QTS while employed in a school. The school pays a salary at the rate for an unqualified teacher but receives a grant towards employment costs and training costs.

Registered Teacher Programme (RTP)

The RTP is normally a two-year programme, offering candidates who have completed two years of higher education (or equivalent) to train as a teacher and gain QTS while employed in a school. The school pays a salary at a rate for either a qualified or unqualified teacher and receives a grant to cover training costs.

Fast track teaching

The Fast Track Teacher programme is a leadership development programme providing professional development opportunities and coaching to help teachers reach leadership positions more quickly.

Overseas Trained Teachers Programme (OTTP)

The OTTP runs for a maximum of a year and offers teachers trained overseas the opportunity to gain QTS while working as a teacher. The school pays the salary at a rate for either a qualified or unqualified teacher.

Source: Employers Organisation (2005) Local government workforce profile and the top ten skills shortage areas – 2005: national recruitment and retention initiatives.

Questions

1 To what extent are these national initiatives likely to ease the shortages identified in the extract above?

2 What other options might be considered to improve recruitment and retention of teachers?

3 What are the cost implications of your recommendations?

DEVELOPING THE HUMAN RESOURCE

Introduction to Part 3

Human resource development (HRD), like HRM, is a term that is often used loosely, and indeed poses problems of definition. Stewart and McGoldrick (1996: 1), who write authoritatively in the HRD area, suggest that the question of what it is 'is not yet amenable to a definitive answer', but offer the following 'tentative' definition:

> Human resource development encompasses activities and processes which are intended to have impact on organisational and individual learning. The term assumes that organisations can be constructively conceived of as learning entities, and that the learning processes of both organisations and individuals are capable of influence and direction through deliberate and planned interventions. Thus, HRD is constituted by planned interventions in organisational and individual processes.

This definition emphasises HRD of the individual and her or his relation to the organisation. It can, however, be viewed much more broadly than this. In Asian and African countries, for example, HRD encompasses government initiatives and policies to improve knowledge and skills to enhance economic growth. As Rao (1995: 15) states:

> at the national level HRD aims at ensuring that people in the country live longer; live happily; free of disease and hunger; have sufficient skill base to earn their livelihood and well being; have a sense of belongingness and pride through participation in determining their own destinies. The promotion of the well-being of individuals, families and societies provides a human resource agenda for all countries the world over.

And, indeed, over the last decade it has become recognised that the HRD that takes place in organisations can play an important role in the overall economy and hence in the well-being of society. This concept is represented by the three concentric circles in Figure P3.1. The more overlap (the shaded area) there is between these three elements, the more likely HRD is to be mutually beneficial for the individual, the organisation and the economy as a whole. It is therefore not surprising that training and development are important issues, to which governments give careful consideration. For example, support from government initiatives, such as legislation on vocational training, enhances the skills and knowledge of those seeking work in the labour market, which enhances the efficiency of organisations, which in turn enhances the growth and development of the economy. For these reasons Part 3 looks beyond and beneath organisational HRD and examines both its national context and the basic processes that constitute it; where appropriate, it invites readers to reflect on their own individual learning and development.

Although Stewart and Harris (2003: 58) encountered an 'uneasy' relationship between HRM and HRD, with training 'the Cinderella of the HR function', HRD is now increasingly being recognised as having a significant part to play in achieving and maintaining the survival and success of an organisation. Managers have not only to acquire appropriate people to resource it, as discussed in Part 2, they also need to train and develop them, for the following reasons:

Figure P3.1   HRD: the individual, the organisation and the economy

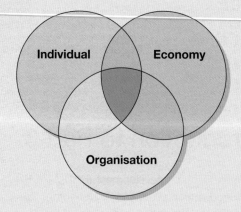

- New employees are, in some respects, like the organisation's raw materials. They have to be 'processed' to enable them to perform the tasks of their job adequately, to fit into their workgroup and into the organisation as a whole, but in a manner that respects their human qualities.
- Jobs and tasks may change over time, both quantitatively and qualitatively, and employees have to be updated to maintain adequate performance.
- New jobs and tasks may be introduced into the organisation, and be filled by existing employees, who need redirection.
- People need training to perform better in their existing jobs.
- People themselves change their interests, their skills, their confidence and aspirations, their circumstances.
- Some employees may move jobs within the organisation, on promotion or to widen their experience, and so need further training.
- The organisation itself, or its context, may change or be changed over time, so that employees have to be updated in their ways of working together.
- The organisation may wish to be ready for some future change, and require (some) employees to develop transferable skills.
- The organisation may wish to respond flexibly to its environment and so require (some) employees to develop flexibility and transferable skills.
- Management requires training and development. This will involve training for new managers, further development and training for managers, management succession, and the development of potential managers.

However, as the chapters that follow show, changes in the context of the organisation increase the need to train and develop its members to ensure effectiveness, quality and responsiveness. Because these changes are not being made once and for all, employees are having to adjust to continuous change, and their managers to pay greater attention to HRD than ever before. Nevertheless, HRD does not take place in an organisational vacuum. To be effective, it presupposes effective selection, effective supervision and an appropriate management style, the opportunity to transfer learning to the workplace, career paths and promotion possibilities, appropriate incentives and rewards. It also presupposes some degree of planning and linkage to the strategy of the organisation, and is therefore implicit within organisation development. Indeed, for the organisation that espouses 'human resource management' and addresses the human resource implications of its strategic positioning, training and development become investment decisions and operations that are as important as investments in new technology, relocation or entry into new markets.

Part 3 examines the several forms that HRD takes: the development of the employee both as an individual and as an employee; development of the employee by the employer or by self; training; education; career development; group development; staff development; professional development, management development and, even more widely, organisation development. These differ not only in terms of the hierarchical levels of the organisation but also in purpose and form. While recognising these different kinds of training and development in organisations, we have to understand that they are not necessarily easily distinguishable in practice, and that some activities contribute to more than one form of development.

Chapter 8 identifies the need for HRD in the organisation, and considers the basic processes of learning and development involved and the ways in which they can be facilitated in the organisation. This chapter underpins the subsequent chapters of Part 3 and introduces some of the concepts they use. Chapter 9 examines the processes and activities intentionally undertaken within organisations to enable employees to acquire, improve or update their skills, and then explores the national framework for vocational education and training, with some international comparisons, which is the context within which organisational HRD operates. Chapter 10 examines the development of managers, noting both their formal and informal modes of development, and relates management to organisation development. There is necessarily some overlap between the chapters of Part 3. Thus specific training to enable an employee to perform more effectively can now also contribute to that person's overall career development. What is intended as instrumental by the employer may be construed as empowering by the individual. This raises the question about who owns the individual's development, one of the controversial issues addressed in Chapter 8.

References and further reading

Rao, T.V. (1995) *Human Resource Development.* New Delhi: Sage.

Stewart, J. and Harris, L. (2003) 'HRD and HRM: an uneasy relationship', *People Management,* 9, 19, September: 58.

Stewart, J. and McGoldrick, J. (eds) (1996) *Human Resource Development: Perspectives, Strategies and Practice.* London: Pitman.

Chapter 8

Learning and development

Audrey Collin

Objectives

- To highlight the learning and development demanded by the significant changes taking place in organisations.
- To note the characteristics of different types of learners.
- To indicate the outcomes of learning.
- To outline the process of learning.
- To discuss the concept of development.
- To note various kinds of development.
- To discuss the implications of learning and development for human resource managers.
- To consider the context of learning and development within and beyond the organisation.
- To examine how learning and development can be facilitated and designed within organisations.
- To pose some controversial issues for reflection and discussion.
- To offer some activities that encourage readers to review their own learning and development.

Introduction

Learning is 'the central issue for the twenty-first century', asserts Honey (1998: 28–29):

> Changes are bigger and are happening faster, and learning is the way to keep ahead . . . to maintain employability in an era when jobs for life have gone. It enables organisations to sustain their edge as global competition increases. Learning to learn . . . [is] the ultimate life skill.

This makes human resource development a key activity in today's organisations, and lifelong learning crucial for individuals.

The purpose of this chapter, which forms a foundation for Chapters 9 and 10, is to explain what learning and development are. It starts by identifying some of the ways in which work and organisations are changing, and why those changes demand continuous learning in individuals and organisations. It then explains what learning and development are, identifies how their context influences them, and examines how they can be facilitated in work organisations.

The changing world of work and organisations

By the end of the twentieth century, the firmly established nature of work and organisations was changing so dramatically that some observers had foreseen the 'end of work' (Rifkin, 1995) and workplaces without jobs (Bridges, 1995). Changes were being brought about through the new information and communications technologies, and through the way in which organisations were responding to the need to achieve and maintain their competitive edge in increasingly global markets. Globalisation affects employment, too: it is predicted that by 2030 50 per cent of the global workforce will be located in China and India (Smethurst, 2005a). Castells (1996) argued that a new 'network society' was emerging. The new technologies have made economies interdependent, organised around global networks of capital, management and information, and thereby are profoundly transforming capital and labour. While capital and information flow around the globe, unconfined in space and time, labour is local: individuals live and work in time and place. 'Labor is disaggregated in its performance, fragmented in its organization, diversified in its existence, divided in its collective action' (Castells, 1996: 475).

Although great effort is made to understand what changes may take place (for example, the ESRC Future of Work Programme), predictions about the future are difficult to make. Bayliss (1998) suggests that many of the traditional boundaries and distinctions – between organisations, between jobs, between employment and self-employment – will shift or become eroded. The relationship that individuals will have with employing organisations will change: individuals will move more frequently, have projects rather than long-term jobs, work in different locations and at different times, make their own work, no longer have fixed working lives. Many careers will be 'boundaryless', transcending traditional boundaries between organisations (Arthur and Rousseau, 1996). To express those changes in metaphors: whereas during much of the twentieth century jobs were like pigeon-holes, or boxes piled up to form organisations, at the start of the twenty-first century organisations are more like nets and networks.

In this changing context, organisations have had to become more flexible, innovative, quality-conscious, customer-oriented, constantly improving their performance to remain competitive. During the past 25 years or so they have undertaken what amount to massive experiments with ways of achieving those ends. During the 1980s the imperatives were excellence, world-class and 'lean' manufacturing (a collection of techniques contributing significantly to organisational performance), total quality management (TQM), downsizing, delayering, and the breaking of bureaucracies down into business units. During the early 1990s the new soft approaches were multi-skilling and the learning organisation, while the hard approach was business process re-engineering (BPR). In the later 1990s, attention turned to knowledge management and innovation, with a further emphasis on teamworking. As the twenty-first century opened, the key issues have become the management and measurement of human capital, 'the contribution of human skills and knowledge to the production of goods and services' (Scarborough, 2003: 32) and, more recently, the re-configuration of the HR function (Ulrich and Brockbank, 2005) and outsourcing (Pickard, 2006). Thus wave after wave of new approaches have brought about new tasks, new ways of working, new roles, relationships and skills, so that lifelong learning and human resource development are now central to the effectiveness of organisations.

For example, TQM (see also Chapter 14) holds that quality is achieved through continuous improvement in the processes, products and services of the organisation: Deming's 'journey of never-ending improvement' (Hodgson, 1987: 41). It requires new relationships between organisations and their suppliers and customers and the transformation of the management of people 'so that employees become involved in quality as the central part of their job' (Sheard, 1992: 33). BPR, which radically restructured bureaucratic organisations by focusing on their lateral processes rather than their vertical functions, not only 'downsized' organisations, but also redesigned the nature of jobs within them:

> For multi-dimensional and changing jobs, companies don't need people to fill a slot, because the slot will be only roughly defined. Companies need people who can figure out what the job takes and people to do it, people who can create the slot that fits them. Moreover, the slot will keep changing.
>
> (Hammer and Champy, 1994: 72)

Whereas work had previously been packaged into jobs, Martin (1995: 20) argues, it is now being reconstructed into the competences needed to achieve customer satisfaction. 'The future will see a world based more on skills than on organisations' (Tyson and Fell, 1995: 45).

If TQM and BPR can be seen as natural heirs – in spirit if not in practice – of scientific management and Taylorism (see Chapters 3 and 11), then knowledge management (Nonaka, 1991) could be recognised as an echo of Trist and the Tavistock school (Pugh *et al.*, 1983). They saw the working group as a socio-technical system: to be effective, the introduction of new technology had to take that into account. Fifty years later, it is once more being recognised (Malhotra, 1998) that it is people who make the difference. The wealth of information generated by information technology becomes meaningful and of competitive advantage to the organisation only when people share, interpret and elaborate it. This enables them to anticipate challenges to the organisation's goals and practices, and thus to adapt the organisation in appropriate and timely fashion.

> Creating, disseminating and embodying knowledge – tacit and explicit – becomes a key strategic resource to be leveraged. It holds the key to unlocking the organisation's ability to learn faster than its environment is changing. In summary, learning and development lie at the heart of innovation in organisations.
>
> (Guest *et al.*, 1997: 3)

Knowledge management embraces knowledge creation, validation, presentation, distribution, and application. In the first generation of knowledge management, its focus was on the role of information technology. The second generation recognised that different kinds of knowledge had to be managed in different ways. Some knowledge was explicit, and could easily be documented, whereas other knowledge was tacit. 'The knowledge needed to develop a new product is largely in people's heads . . . [it] cannot be written down, because an individual may not even know it is there until the situation demands a creative response' (Dixon, 2000: 37). The third generation (Snowden, 2002) is even more challenging to scientific management orthodoxy. Knowledge is now no longer regarded as 'abstract, objective' truth but a cultural construction within 'communities of practice', and hence 'essentially pragmatic, partial, tentative and always open to revision' (Blackler, 2000: 61). It highlights the significance of organisational culture, meaning-making, narrative, context, and systems thinking (see Chapter 3). The challenge to HRD is to promote the kind of learning that, through critical thinking and reflection, can recognise, appraise, transmit, and apply contextually-embedded meanings (Hwang, 2003). That calls for understanding of the process of learning, development of higher-order thinking skills and of the learning organisation.

Research suggests that financial results account for only 50 to 70 per cent of a firm's market value, the remainder being attributed to 'intangibles' (Ulrich and Smallwood, 2002), such as intellectual property and human capital. Scarborough (2003: 32–34) suggests that the human capital approach is 'more than a recycling of clichés about the importance of our employees. It also reflects a shift in thinking about ways to make the best use of the whole range of abilities that people bring to the workplace.' He cites the television programme *Jamie's Kitchen*, in which cook Jamie Oliver turned a team of inexperienced and unemployed young people into top-class chefs. 'This blending of new skills and attitudes into high-level performance sums up exactly what human capital can be and why it is so important to business' (Scarborough, 2003: 32).

Ulrich and Smallwood (2002: 43) include learning or knowledge management among the seven 'critical organisation capabilities that [create] intangible shareholder value': 'Learning capacity is an intangible value when organisations have the ability to move ideas across vertical, horizontal, external and global boundaries.' However, accountants have traditionally not found satisfactory ways of measuring human capital, and so have treated employees as costs to an organisation rather than assets. Considerable effort is being made to change that as the significance for competitiveness of investment in human capital is increasingly recognised (Manocha, 2005). Once again, this highlights the significance of HRD and the understanding and promotion of learning in organisations. It is also becoming clear that employees are beginning to recognise the need to invest in their own learning and development – their human capital – and so employers have to take steps to retain talent, nurture it, and manage it effectively, which in turn calls for effective means of measuring human capital (Mayo, 2002).

Activity — Identifying contextual changes leading to HRD

Before proceeding further, on your own or in a small group identify some of the changes taking place in organisations you know in response to changes in their context. What are the implications for human resource development and for the learning and development of individuals?

The strategic importance of learning and development

'Change matters more than ever before', said the president of the Chartered Institute of Personnel and Development (CIPD, formerly IPD) in his message in the Annual Report for 2000 (Beattie, 2002: 2–3). 'People are our only source of differentiation and sustainable competitive advantage. Essential to that is learning.' Hence the director general of the IPD claimed that 'staff management and development will become the primary weapon available to managers to generate success' (Rana, 2000). The continuous learning and development of individuals are, therefore, of crucial and strategic importance to organisations, and thereby also to the overall economy.

The new ways of working are demanding not just extensive training in new task skills, but completely new ways of thinking about work, doing work, and relating with one another. Individuals at all levels need to be able to challenge traditional ways of thinking and working; think and work 'outside the box' of traditional job descriptions; and work without prior experience, clear guidelines or close supervision; be flexible, prepared to change, undertake new tasks or move to a different organisation. In the struggle to 'think global and act local', organisations need people who have 'a "matrix of the mind"'; sharing learning and creating new knowledge are among the key capabilities that organisations must have (Ulrich and Stewart Black, 1999). Overall, this amounts to the need for using high levels of cognitive skills.

Human resource developers and trainers now have to address the new responsibilities of their increasingly strategic role (Chartered Institute of Personnel and Development, 2002a). That calls for more than training new employees: organisations have to invest in their human capital. It means that they have to train and develop their existing workforce, facilitate their learning within a learning culture, with appropriate resources, and develop a learning organisation (see Chapters 9 and 10). Hence human resource managers need to understand the processes and nature of the learning of the higher-order and other task skills in order to be able to facilitate that learning and development. It is the purpose of this chapter to explain these.

Importantly, organisations have to invest not just in their knowledge workers but in their lower-skilled employees as well (Chartered Institute of Personnel and Development, 2002a). For much of the industrial age, higher-order abilities were expected mainly in the upper echelons of organisations. However, in the twenty-first century, competitive organisations need to find those abilities much more widely in their workforce, in what Castells (1998: 341) calls the 'self-programmable' labour in the global economy. This has 'the capability constantly to redefine the necessary skills for a given task, and to access the sources for learning these skills'.

Nevertheless, there will still be work that does not require those particular abilities – for example, serving in fast food outlets – jobs that will be undertaken by what Castells (1998: 341) calls 'generic' labour, which, lacking self-programmable skills, would be:

> 'human terminals' [which could] be replaced by machines, or by any other body around the city, the country, or the world, depending on business decisions. While they are collectively indispensable to the production process, they are individually expendable . . .

(It should not be assumed, however, that all jobs giving personal service demand low-level skills: they may require high levels of social, emotional and other non-cognitive intelligences (Gardner, 1985, 1999; Pickard, 1999b).)

Although many employers are now recognising the need to invest in their employees' learning, it is held that individuals must also take some responsibility for it; that they must invest in their own learning and development to ensure their own employability (Arnold, 1997). This personal investment changes the balance of the 'psychological contract' (see Chapters 3 and 13), and raises the question of who owns the individual's learning (see Controversial issues on page 295 at the end of this chapter).

The need for higher order skills

According to Wisher (1994: 37), among the 'competencies that occur frequently in the most successful clusters of different organisations' are conceptual, 'helicopter' and analytical thinking. The Chartered Institute of Personnel and Development, for example, now underpins its professional standards with the concept of the 'thinking performer', 'who applies a critically thoughtful approach to their job' (Whittaker and Johns, 2004: 32). Organisations are thus now requiring higher-order thinking skills, and not just from their managers.

However, there is a long way to go for many organisations. According to Myers and Davids (1992: 47):

> workers are a resource which has not been well understood by management in the past. Blue-collar workers in particular have been regarded as a static commodity incapable of innovation and self-development. Consequently reservoirs of skill and ability remain untapped.

Cooley (1987) reports how the Lucas Aerospace Shop Stewards' Combine Committee, as long ago as 1975, recognised the value of human capital. It challenged the organisation not to lay off its highly skilled workforce when its market was failing, but to retain it by moving into new markets for 'socially useful' products:

> What the Lucas workers did was to embark on an exemplary project which would inflame the imagination of others. To do so, they realised that it was necessary to demonstrate in a very practical and direct way the creative power of 'ordinary people'. Further, their manner of doing it had to confirm for 'ordinary people' that they too had the capacity to change their situation, that they are not the objects of history but rather the subjects, capable of building their own futures.
> (Cooley, 1987: 139)

As this chapter will show, 'ordinary people' have the capacity to learn and develop.

The need for a learning society

The need for learning and development is not just an issue for individuals and their employers. It is now widely recognised that we need to become a learning society, in which there is a culture of, and opportunities for, lifelong learning in order to provide the skills required for competitiveness in a global economy. This national significance is now fully recognised by the government which, for example, passed the Learning and Skills Act (2000), launched learndirect (1998) to deliver workforce development and lifelong learning, set up the Learning and Skills Council (2001), developed a Skills Strategy (2003) which led to support of the employer-led, independent Sector Skills Councils (see Smethurst, 2005b), and published the Skills White Paper: Getting on in Business, Getting on at Work (2005) (see Chapter 9).

Stop & think

What are the implications of the issues raised so far in this chapter for your own learning and development needs? How would you attempt to meet these needs? In the light of this, what would you seek from any prospective employer?

Learning and development

> Deep down, we are all learners. No one has to teach an infant to learn. In fact, no one has to teach infants anything. They are intrinsically inquisitive, masterful learners who learn to walk, speak . . . Learning organizations are possible because not only is it our nature to learn but we love to learn.
>
> (Senge, 1990: 4)

From birth, humans, like all animals, learn and develop: learning is a natural process in which we all engage. It is not just a cognitive activity, and it affects the person as a whole. Learning and development lead to skilful and effective adaptation to and manipulation of the environment, which is one element in a much-quoted definition of intelligence (Wechsler, 1958, in Ribeaux and Poppleton, 1978: 189). People continue learning throughout life, whether encouraged or not, whether formally taught or not, whether the outcomes are valued or not. Moreover, the process of their learning knows no boundaries: learning in one domain, such as employment, hobbies or maintenance of home and car, cross-fertilises that in another and thereby achieves a wider understanding and more finely honed skills.

> Most of us have learned a good deal more out of school than in it. We have learned from our families, our work, our friends. We have learned from problems resolved and tasks achieved but also from mistakes confronted and illusions unmasked. Intentionally or not, we have learned from the dilemmas our lives hand us daily.
>
> (Daloz, 1986: 1)

Society fosters and facilitates these activities of its members, but also channels and controls them through socialisation and education so that they yield outcomes that contribute to and are acceptable to it. However, although individuals have a lifetime's experience of being learners, some of their experiences (especially those in formal educational settings) might not have been happy ones (Honey, 1999). They might be experienced learners, but not necessarily competent or confident learners.

Defining learning and development

To understand the processes of learning and development and use this understanding to good effect in developing people and their organisations, you have to be able to think clearly about the concepts you are using. The concepts 'learning' and 'development' are frequently used loosely and even interchangeably, so it is important to define how they are being used here. The following definitions will enable you to distinguish them and understand the relationship between them.

Learning is

> a process within the organism which results in the capacity for changed performance which can be related to experience rather than maturation.   (Ribeaux and Poppleton, 1978: 38)

It is now widely recognised that intelligence is not just a unitary concept (see Gardner (1985, 1999) on multiple intelligences; Mayo and Nohria (2005) on 'contextual intelligence') nor just a cognitive capacity (see Pickard (1999b) on emotional intelligence). Hence learning is not just a cognitive process that involves the assimilation of information in symbolic form (as in book learning), but also an affective and physical process (Binsted, 1980). Our emotions, nerves and muscles are involved in the process, too. Learning leads to change, whether positive or negative for the learner. It is an experience after which an individual 'qualitatively [changes] the way he or she conceived something' (Burgoyne and Hodgson, 1983: 393) or experiences 'personal transformation' (Mezirow, 1977). Learning can be more or less effectively undertaken, and it could be more effective when it is paid conscious attention.

Development, however, is the process of becoming increasingly complex, more elaborate and differentiated, by virtue of learning and maturation. (As will be noted later, it is sometimes assumed that development connotes progression and advancement.) In an organism, greater complexity, and differentiation among its parts, leads to changes in the structure of the whole and to the way in which the whole functions (Reese and Overton, 1970: 126). In the individual, this greater complexity opens up the potential for new ways of acting and responding to the environment. This leads to the need and opportunity for even further learning, and so on.

Development, whether of an organism, individual or organisation, is a process of both continuity and discontinuity. Quantitative changes lead to qualitative changes or transformations; development is irreversible, although regression to earlier phases can occur.

> The disintegration of the old phase of functioning . . . creates the conditions for the discontinuous 'step-jump' to a new phase. This succeeding phase incorporates yet transforms the repertoire of principles, values, etc., of earlier phases and adds to them. The new phase is therefore not entirely new – it is a transformation. Each succeeding phase is more complex, integrating what has gone before.   (Pedler, 1988: 7–8)

Overall, then, learning contributes to development. It is not synonymous with it, but development cannot take place without learning of some kind. Lifelong learning means continuous adaptation. Increased knowledge and improved skills enlarge the individual's capacities to adapt to the environment and to change that environment. As the systems model in Chapter 3 implies, such external changes will lead on to further internal changes, allowing new possibilities for the individual to emerge. Moreover, these changes feed the individual's self-esteem and confidence, and enhance social status. Hence learning generates potentially far-reaching changes in the individual: learning promotes development. In his very warm-hearted and insightful book on 'the transformational power of adult learning experiences', Daloz (1986: 24–26) draws on mythology to convey the nature of this development:

> The journey tale begins with an old world, generally simple and uncomplicated, more often than not, home . . . The middle portion, beginning with departure from home, is characterized by confusion, adventure, great highs and lows, struggle, uncertainty. The ways of the old world no longer hold, and the hero's task is to find a way through this strange middle land, generally in search of something lying at its heart. At the deepest point, the nadir of the

descent, a transformation occurs, and the traveler moves out of the darkness toward a new world that often bears an ironic resemblance to the old.

Nothing is different, yet all is transformed. It is seen differently . . . Our old life is still there, but its meaning has profoundly changed because we have left home, seen it from afar, and been transformed by that vision. You can't go home again.

(Daloz, 1986: 24–26. Reprinted with permission of John Wiley & Sons, Inc.)

Stop & think

Has your learning caused you to develop? What has the experience of that been for you?

The outcomes of a person's learning and development are the way they think, feel and interpret their world (their cognition, affect, attitudes, overall philosophy of life); the way they see themselves, their self-concept and self-esteem; and their ability to respond to and make their way in their particular environment (their perceptual-motor, intellectual, social, and interpersonal skills). Some of the transformational impact of learning can be seen in Daloz's description above of the journey of development. Learning and development are therefore significant experiences for individuals and hence for organisations. Following from this, it should also be noted, the facilitation of another's learning is a moral project: it has the potential to promote changes that may have a profound effect in the other's life. This, too, has implications for the debate about the ownership of learning, one of the controversial issues at the end of the chapter.

Learning and development are processes that we all experience, active processes in which we all engage: we do not have learning and development done to us. However, we rarely pay conscious attention to them and so might not fully understand them. This chapter therefore addresses you, the reader, directly, and here and throughout this chapter invites you to draw upon your own experience in order to understand and make use of the issues that are discussed.

Your very reading of this book might itself entail some of these issues. Before proceeding further, therefore, it makes sense to identify and reflect on them so that you will then have ready in your mind the 'hooks' on to which to hang the information this chapter will give you. In the language of a learning theory to be noted later, you will be ready to 'decode' these new 'signals'.

Activity | **Your aims and motivation for learning**

List your reasons for reading this book, noting:

- both short-term and long-term aims;
- those aims that are ends in themselves and those that are means to an end;
- the most important and the least important;
- the aims that you can achieve by yourself;
- those that require others to facilitate them;
- what else you need to achieve these aims;
- what initiated your pursuit of these aims;
- who or what has influenced you during this pursuit.

This chapter will examine how people learn, and what helps or hinders them. By paying attention now to how you are reading this book, you can begin to understand your own processes of learning and development. Later you will have the opportunity to identify those who benefit from and pay for your learning. This will help you to understand something of the problematical issues inherent in employee development.

Many types of learner

Much of what we know about learning and teaching derives from the study of children and young people (pedagogy). However, learners in organisations are not children, and have different needs and experiences.

From your own experience and observing others' behaviour, how do adult learners differ from young learners? What are likely to be the implications for human resource developers?

Adult learners

Instead of a pedagogical model of learning, an androgogical model is needed to understand adult learning. According to Knowles and Associates (1984), this needs to take into account that adult learners are self-directing, and motivated by their need to be recognised, to prove something to themselves and others, to better themselves, and achieve their potential. Their learning does not take place in a vacuum. Not only are they ready to learn when they recognise their need to know or do something, but they have experience on which to draw and to hang their new learning, and to assess its utility. Earlier (especially formal) learning experiences might have been far from effective or comfortable, so that many adults have developed poor learning habits or become apprehensive about further learning.

Human resource development has to address these various needs appropriately, as will be suggested in the later section on the organisation as a context for learning.

Learners in the organisation
Older workers

Traditionally, older people have been widely discriminated against when seeking employment and when employed (Naylor, 1987; Dennis, 1988; Laslett, 1989; Waskel, 1991). They have been commonly stereotyped as having failing cognitive and physical abilities, as being inflexible, unwilling and unable to learn new ways. However, the Carnegie Inquiry into the Third Age (Trinder *et al.*, 1992: 20) reports:

> There does seem to be a decline in performance with age . . . but such deterioration as there is, is less than the popular stereotype . . . Except where such abilities as muscular strength are of predominant importance, age is not a good discriminator of ability to work; nor of the ability to learn.

Trinder *et al.* (1992) also note that performance is influenced as much by experience and skill as by age: skill development in earlier years will encourage adaptability in later life.

Although older people are 'at a disadvantage with speedy and novel (unexpected) forms of presentation', Coleman (1990: 70–71) reports little or no decline with age in memory and learning, particularly 'if the material is fully learned initially'. (The role of rehearsal and revision in memory will be examined later in this chapter.) Pickard (1999a: 30), discussing changing attitudes to the employment of older people, and the possibility of retirement age rising to the upper 70s, quotes a 72-year-old Nobel prize-winning scientist as saying: 'You may forget where you were last week, but not the things that matter.' Coleman (1990) goes on to cite a study in which the majority of the 80 volunteers aged 63 to 91 years learned German from scratch, and in six months reached the level of skill in reading German normally achieved by schoolchildren in five years.

Until recently, there were few examples to cite of organisations that employed older people. The do-it-yourself retail chain B&Q was a notable exception, staffing one store solely by people over the age of 50. It was 'an overwhelming success . . . In commercial terms the store has surpassed its trading targets' (Hogarth and Barth, 1991: 15). In this trial these older workers were found to be willing to train, although initially reluctant to use new technology, and did not require longer or different training from other workers. Since then, as Pickard (1999a) reports, B&Q has been joined by other employers in giving employment opportunities to older people. For example, BMW has an apprenticeship programme for older workers which is completed in 60 per cent of the time taken by the youth apprenticeship scheme; 'They already had life skills and were used to factory work, making it easier to acquire new skills. But they were also motivated and knew what they wanted to do' (*People Management*, 2005a: 17). These older workers demonstrate the ability to continue to learn through life. Their learning will be facilitated if employers adopt appropriate approaches, which will be examined in the section on the organisation as a context for learning.

However, traditional attitudes towards older workers are starting to change because of today's concern for knowledge management and investment in human capital (*People Management*, 2005b) and demographic changes. By 2020 young people are expected to comprise 11 per cent of the workforce compared with 16 per cent in 2005 (Griffiths, 2005a). At the same time, the proportion of older people in the population is growing, putting considerable pressure on pensions provision, and causing the government to raise the compulsory retirement age. Moreover, its legislation to deal with age discrimination will enable more older people to continue in employment. These changes have implications for HR managers, who have to consider introducing part-time working for older people, gradual retirement arrangements, the provision of career planning, continuing training opportunities (which have hitherto been scarce), and lifelong learning (Hope, 2005; Reday-Mulvey, 2005). Such ideas, and new appraisals of older workers, can be found in Smethurst (2006), and via the Centre for Research into the Older Workforce at Surrey University.

Other classes of employees

Three classes of people – disabled people, women, and individuals from cultural and ethnic minorities – are often socialised and educated in ways that do not advantage them in labour markets or organisations; they may develop correspondingly low expectations and aspirations. Negative stereotyping of them in employment is frequently discussed (Gallos, 1989; Thomas and Alderfer, 1989). This section will briefly note some aspects of their experience that will influence them as learners in the organisation: these need to be viewed in terms of the barriers to learning referred to later.

Until recently, little seems to have been written about the training of disabled people in organisations. Moreton (1992) identified the role of the Training and Enterprise Councils in providing training programmes for them, and Arkin (1995) summarised the implications for employers of the 1995 Disability Discrimination Act (DDA). The 2003 Amendment to the DDA is now raising further challenges to employers to treat disabled people as individuals, which would embrace training and career development (Edwards, 2004; Griffiths, 2005b). A continuing impediment to providing opportunities for them is the attitudes of colleagues and customers, so organisations are providing for them awareness training on the difficulties faced by those with disabilities (Edwards, 2004). Nevertheless, e-learning (discussed later; see also Chapter 9) has the potential to enable those with disabilities to learn and update skills, though appropriate accessibility is not always available (Jarvis and Hooley, 2004).

There is now a considerable body of theory, including feminist critiques, that addresses the nature of women and their experiences in their own right, rather than as a subset of a supposed 'universal' (but often Eurocentric, middle-class male) nature. For example, as was noted in Chapter 3, Marshall (1989) states that knowledge is traditionally constructed from a male perspective, and Gilligan (1977: see Daloz, 1986: 134–135) argues that unlike men, who see their world as 'a hierarchy of power', women see theirs as 'a web of relationships'. The connected self interprets the environment differently, and so responds to it differently, from the separate self. These and other ways in which women may differ from men (Bartol, 1978) will influence their approach to, experience of, and outcomes from, learning; they may, indeed, give advantage in the development of some of the higher-order skills needed in organisations. However, it has also been suggested (Griffiths, 2005c) that competency frameworks may be biased against women.

Different cultures imbue their members with different basic assumptions about the nature of reality and the values and the roles in social life. Cultural experiences differ, and hence the accumulated experience of the members will also differ. The concept of intelligence is not culture-free. Gardner (1985), who expounds a theory of multiple intelligences that include interpersonal and intrapersonal intelligence, recognises that

> because each culture has its own symbol systems, its own means for interpreting experiences, the 'raw materials' of the personal intelligences quickly get marshaled by systems of meaning that may be quite distinct from one another . . . the varieties of personal intelligence prove much more distinctive, less comparable, perhaps even unknowable to someone from an alien society.
> (p. 240)

Hence some members of cultural and ethnic minorities may have ways of learning that are dissimilar to those of the dominant culture, and also different outcomes from their learning. It is therefore important to assess such constructs as intelligence in as culture-fair a manner as possible (Sternberg, 1985: 77, 309), and to seek appropriate means to facilitate learning of the skills required in organisations. Clements and Jones (2002) point to the importance of self-learning when addressing diversity. Learning through action might also be particularly appropriate.

Understanding of and fluency with English are not the only language issues in organisations. As discussed in Chapter 3, language is ideological and can embody racism and sexism. Similarly, the construction of knowledge is a social and ideological process. Through the very nature of language and knowledge, these learners may be internalising constructions of themselves that ultimately undermine their self-esteem, alienate them from self-fulfilment, and erect barriers to their effective learning. Mentoring to support such learners could be particularly valuable.

The outcomes and process of learning

Managers responsible for human resource development need to understand the nature of learning and development. This section will, therefore, first examine the outcomes of learning, such as skill, competence and tacit knowledge, and employability, an indirect outcome. It will then look at the process of learning, the various levels of cognitive and other skills, at models of learning, and finally at barriers to learning.

The outcomes of learning

Skill

> . . . the performance of any task which, for its successful and rapid completion, requires an improved organisation of responses making use of only those aspects of the stimulus which are essential to satisfactory performance.
> (Ribeaux and Poppleton, 1978: 53–54)

> . . . an appearance of ease, of smoothness of movement, of confidence and the comparative absence of hesitation; it frequently gives the impression of being unhurried, while the actual pace of activity may of course be quite high . . . increasing skill involves a widening of the range of possible disturbances that can be coped with without disrupting the performance.
>
> (Borger and Seaborne, 1966: 128–129)

These definitions are particularly appropriate to perceptual-motor skills, which involve physical, motor responses to perceived stimuli in the external world. Such skills are needed at every level of an organisation, from the senior manager's ability to operate a desktop computer to the cleaner's operation of a floor-scrubbing machine. High levels of such skills are particularly needed to operate complex and expensive technology. There are many other kinds of skills needed in organisations, such as cognitive, linguistic, social and interpersonal skills, that could also be defined in these terms. However, their complexity suggests that various levels of skill have to be recognised, which is what a later subsection will do in presenting some hierarchies of skills.

Competence

Competence – also referred to as competency in the literature – has been defined as:

> an underlying characteristic of a person which results in effective and/or superior performance in a job.
>
> (Boyatzis, 1982)

> the ability to perform the activities within an occupational area to the levels of performance expected in employment.
>
> (Training Commission, 1988)

The core of the definition is an ability to apply knowledge and skills with understanding to a work activity.

Competences are now a major element in the design of training and development in Britain (Cannell *et al.*, 1999), and seem to fit well with what is happening in organisations. Martin (1995: 20) proposes that they are a means of 'aligning what people can offer – their competencies – against the demands of customers rather than against the ill-fitting and ill-designed demands of jobs'. Nevertheless, the notions of competence and competency are still matters of debate: from the confusion suggested by differences between the definitions above (Woodruffe, 1991) to, arguably, some inherent weaknesses (see Ford, 2002), and the challenge of 'postmodern' (see Chapter 3) thinking (Brittain and Ryder, 1999). Despite considerable variation in the number of competences being used in competence frameworks (one study suggested between 21 and 30 and 300–400), and often a lack of validation of such frameworks, there is claimed to be a 'dramatic increase' in the number of companies using them. 'Personnel professionals must stop dismissing competencies as fads' (Walsh, 1998: 15).

What needs to be noted at this point is that the concept of competence integrates knowledge and skill that are assessed via performance. This leads on to the distinction between formal knowledge and 'know-how', in which tacit knowledge has a significant part to play.

'Know-how' and tacit knowledge

'Knowing how to do something' is a very different matter from knowing about 'knowing how to do something'. This truism is captured in the everyday suspicion and disparagement of 'the ivory tower': 'those who can, do; those who can't, teach'.

Gardner (1985) makes the distinction between 'know-how' and 'know-that'. For him, 'know-how' is the tacit knowledge of how to execute something, whereas 'know-that' is the statement of formal thinking (propositional knowledge) about the actual set of procedures involved in the execution:

> Thus, many of us know how to ride a bicycle but lack the propositional knowledge of how that behaviour is carried out. In contrast, many of us have propositional knowledge about how to make a soufflé without knowing how to carry this task through to successful completion.
>
> (p. 68)

This distinction highlights the significance for learning of action. Book ('propositional') knowledge is not enough.

Tacit knowledge is an essential ingredient of 'know-how' and action. Sternberg (1985: 169) recognises this in his definition of practical intelligence:

> Underlying successful performance in many real-world tasks is tacit knowledge of a kind that is never explicitly taught and in many instances never even verbalized.

The example that he gives is of the tacit knowledge relevant to the management of one's career. The individual also draws upon tacit knowledge in the fluent performance of perceptual-motor skills, as seen in the definition of skill above; indeed, Myers and Davids (1992) write of 'tacit skills'. It would appear to be acquired through experience rather than through instruction, and is embedded in the context in which this experience is taking place. This can be seen in Stage 2 of the model of Dreyfus *et al.* (see below), in which the learner becomes independent of instruction through the recognition of the contextual elements of the task, and thereafter develops the ability to register and 'read' contextual cues. However, unlike the formal knowledge that it accompanies, this tacit knowledge never becomes explicit, although it remains very significant. It has to be apprehended in context, and one way of doing this is to pay attention to the stories that are told in organisations (for example, Gabriel, 2000). Myers and Davids (1992: 47) question whether 'tacit skills' can be taught, and identify that they are often transmitted in 'an environment of intensive practical experience' and in task performance: 'We may yet be able to learn much from "sitting next to Nellie"!' They also note the need to take account of both formal and tacit knowledge in selection.

Traditionally, practical knowledge tends to feature at a lower level in any representation of the social hierarchy of skills, and is thereby institutionalised in lower-level occupations. In discussing the public's understanding of science, Collins (1993: 17) writes about:

> the all too invisible laboratory technician . . . Look into a laboratory and you will see it filled with fallible machines and the manifest recalcitrance of nature . . . Technicians make things work in the face of this . . . Notoriously, techniques that can be made to work by one technician in one place will not work elsewhere. The technician has a practical understanding of aspects of the craft of science beyond that of many scientists. But does the technician 'understand science'?

Cooley (1987: 10–13) draws attention to the way in which practical knowledge, craft skill, is devalued in the face of technological progress. This is the starting point for his reflections upon the way 'ordinary people' could achieve something extraordinary. He believes that technological systems

> tend to absorb the knowledge from ['ordinary people'], deny them the right to use their skill and judgement, and render them abject appendages to the machines and systems being developed.

Myers and Davids (1992: 47) come to a similar conclusion after their discussion of the significance of 'tacit skills'.

It is clear that organisations need both 'know-how' and 'know-that'. Hence the concept of competences, as defined above, is important, although it can be argued that the institutionalised, transorganisational process of identifying and defining them has wrenched them from their context and hence from the tacit knowledge that contributes so significantly to them. However, knowledge management, action learning, and mentoring all explicitly contextualise knowledge and learning and hence draw out tacit knowledge.

Employability

An indirect outcome of learning and development is employability, a notion that became current because of the proliferation of flexible contracts of employment and insecurity in employment during the 1990s. According to Kanter (1989a), employability was the 'new security': if individuals have acquired and maintained their employability then, should their job come to an end, they would be able to find employment elsewhere.

Employability results from investment in the human capital of skills and reputation. This means that individuals must engage in continuous learning and development, update their skills and acquire others that might be needed in the future by their current or future employer (Fonda and Guile, 1999). It is also argued that, as part of the 'new deal' in employment, good employers will ensure that their employees remain employable (Herriot and Pemberton, 1995) by keeping them up to date through training and development.

The process of learning

The chapter will now first consider theories of the process of learning and of elements within it, and then examine that process in terms of various levels, stages, and cyclical models of learning. This is a very rich and complex field, to which justice cannot be done here, and you are recommended to read a text such as Atkinson *et al.* (1999) or Ribeaux and Poppleton (1978).

Theories of the process of learning

Behaviourist approach to learning

The behaviourist approach has been one of the most influential in the field of psychology. It proposes that learning is the process by which a particular stimulus (S), repeatedly associated with, or conditioned by, desirable or undesirable experiences, comes to evoke a particular response (R). This conditioning can be of two kinds. Classical conditioning occurs when a stimulus leads automatically to a response. Dogs, for example, salivate at the presentation of food; Pavlov demonstrated that they could also be conditioned to salivate at the sound of a bell rung before food is presented. Operant conditioning (Skinner) takes place after a desired response, which is then reinforced, or rewarded, to increase the probability of the repetition of the same response when the stimulus recurs.

There has been much experimental research (including many animal studies) into such issues as the nature of the reinforcement (negative reinforcement, or punishment, is not as effective for learning as positive reward); the schedule of reinforcement (whether at fixed or variable intervals: intermittent reinforcement is more effective than continuous reinforcement). This form of conditioning is also used to shape behaviour: that is, to continue to reinforce responses that approximate to the desired behaviour until that behaviour is finally achieved. We are familiar with this kind of approach to the encouragement of simple behaviours: we use it with small children, with animals, and in basic forms of training.

Cognitive learning theory

The S–R approach pays no attention to the cognitive processes whereby the stimulus comes to be associated with a particular response: it does not investigate what is in the 'black box'. Cognitive learning theory, however, offers a more complex understanding of learning, proposing, again originally on the basis of animal studies, that what is learned is not an association of stimulus with response (S–R), but of stimulus with stimulus (S–S). The learner develops expectations that stimuli are linked; the result is a cognitive 'map' or latent learning. Hence insightful behaviour appropriate to a situation takes place without the strengthening association of S–R bonds. Social learning theory also addresses what is in the 'black box'. It recognises the role in learning of the observation and imitation of the behaviour of others, but as seen in, say, the debates over the influence of the media upon young people's behaviour, there are clearly many moderating variables.

Information-processing approach to learning

This approach regards learning as an information processing system in which a signal, containing information, is transmitted along a communication channel of limited capacity and subject to interference and 'noise' (Stammers and Patrick, 1975). The signal has to be decoded before it can be received, and then encoded to pass it on. In learning, data received through the senses are filtered, recognised and decoded through the interpretative process of perception; this information is then translated into action through the selection of appropriate responses. The effectiveness of learning depends on attention being paid only to the relevant parts of the stimuli, the rapid selection of appropriate responses, the efficient performance of them, and the feeding back of information about their effects into the system. Overload or breakdown of the system can occur at any of these stages.

Gagné (1974, in Fontana, 1981: 73) expresses this as a chain of events, some internal and others external to the learner. It begins with the learner's readiness to receive information (motivation or expectancy), and continues as the learner perceives it, distinguishes it from other stimuli, makes sense of it and relates it to what is already known. The information is then stored in short- or long-term memory. Thereafter it can be retrieved from memory, generalised to, and put into practice in, new situations. Its final phase is feedback from knowledge of the results obtained from this practice. Those concerned to facilitate learning in others can use their understanding of this chain to prevent failure to learn, which can take place at any one of these levels.

Elements in the process of learning

This subsection will deal briefly with other important elements in the process of learning that need to be taken into account when designing or facilitating learning.

Feedback (or knowledge of results)

The feedback to learners of the results of their performance is recognised as essential to their effective learning. This is discussed in Ribeaux and Poppleton (1978) and Stammers and Patrick (1975). Feedback will be either intrinsic or extrinsic (or augmented). Learners receive visual or kinaesthetic feedback (intrinsic) from their responses to stimuli in the learning situation; they need to be encouraged to 'listen' to such bodily cues in order to improve performance. They may also receive feedback (extrinsic, augmented) from an external source while they are performing (concurrent feedback) or after it (terminal). Learners may also benefit from guidance given before their performance about what to look out for during it. The sources cited above set out the characteristics, advantages and disadvantages of these different kinds of feedback.

The notion of feedback is frequently discussed in terms of learning perceptual-motor or similar skills. It is also of considerable importance in the learning of the higher-order skills discussed in this chapter, but here it is very complex in nature, and difficult for the learner to be aware and make sense of it. However, by reflecting and engaging in the whole-loop learning, the learner will have opportunity to pay attention to both intrinsic and extrinsic feedback.

The choice of whole or part learning

Psychologists continue to debate the appropriateness of whole or part learning in learning to perform various tasks: that is, whether the task is learned as a whole, or in parts. Ribeaux and Poppleton (1978: 61) report on one approach that classifies tasks according to their 'complexity' (the difficulty of the component subtasks) and 'organisation' (the degree to which they are interrelated). Where complexity and organisation are both high, whole methods appear superior; where either is low, part methods are superior in most cases; when both are low, part and whole methods are equally successful. Stammers and Patrick (1975: 85–88), however, report on research that appears to draw opposite conclusions: where the elements of a task are highly independent the task is best learned as a whole, but where they are interdependent, they should be learned in parts.

It tends to be the whole method in operation when learning takes place during the performance of a job, through action learning, or through observing others.

The role of memory in learning

Memory plays a significant role in learning, and some understanding of it can therefore be used to make learning more effective. Once again, it is not possible to do more than present an outline here, but texts such as Stammers and Patrick (1975), Ribeaux and Poppleton (1978), Fontana (1981) and Atkinson *et al.* (1999) give further information.

Memory involves three kinds of information storage: the storage of sensory memories, short-term or primary memory, and long-term or secondary memory. Unless transferred to short-term memory, the sensory memory retains sense data for probably less than two seconds. Unless incoming information is paid particular attention or rehearsed, short-term memory holds it for up to 30 seconds and appears to have limited capacity, whereas long-term memory appears to have unlimited capacity and to hold information for years. What is therefore of concern for effective learning is the ability to transfer information to the long-term memory. There are two aspects to such transfer. The first is 'rehearsal' – that is, paying attention to and repeating the information until it is coded and enters the long-term store; it is otherwise displaced by new incoming information. The second aspect of the transfer of information to long-term memory is coding: the translation of information into the codes that enable it to be 'filed' into the memory's 'filing system'. Information is largely coded according to meaning (a semantic code) or through visual images, but sometimes (where the meaning itself is unclear) according to sound.

The ability to retrieve information from long-term memory depends in part upon how effectively it has been organised ('filed') in storage (for example, words may be stored according to sound and meaning), but also upon having the most appropriate retrieval cue. We experience this when we are searching for something that we have lost: we think systematically through what we were doing when we believe we last used the lost object. Recognition is easier than recall from memory because it follows the presentation of clear retrieval cues.

Difficulty in retrieving information, or forgetting, occurs for several reasons apart from those concerning the degree of organisation in storage. Interference from other information can disrupt long-term as well as short-term memory (where new items displace existing items in the limited capacity). Interference may be retroactive, when new information interferes with the recall of older material, or proactive, when earlier learning seems to inhibit the recall of later information. Forgetting also takes place through anxiety or unhappy associations with the material to be learned, which might become repressed. Unhappy childhood experiences, for example, might be repressed for many years.

Finally, memory does not just operate as a camera recording what is experienced: it is an active and a constructive process. This is particularly so when learning the kind of complex material that constitutes the world of organisations and human resource management. As well as recording its data inputs, the process of memory draws inferences from the data and so elaborates upon them, filtering them through the individual's stereotypes, mindset and world-view. What is then stored is this enhanced and repackaged material.

An understanding of the nature of memory suggests various ways in which it might be improved to make learning more effective. The transfer of new information to long-term memory is clearly crucial: attention, recitation, repetition and constant revision (known as *overlearning*) are needed. The coding and organisation of material to be stored are also important: this is helped by associating the new information with what is already familiar, especially using visual imagery, by attending to the context giving rise to the information to be learned, and by making the effort to understand the information so that it can be stored in the appropriate 'files'. Importantly, facilitators of learning need to ensure that the learning context or event does not provoke anxiety.

Levels of learning

This chapter has highlighted the need for organisational members to practise higher-order thinking skills. This implies that there are several types and levels of skill. This subsection presents several classifications, some of different types of skill, others of different levels or stages. Some are couched in terms of stages rather than levels: the individual can progress from the lower to the higher stages, but does not necessarily do so. The lower levels are pre-requisites for, and subsumed by, the higher. (See The process of development on page 280 for a discussion of the concept of stages.)

Organisations require several types and levels of skills, not only the higher-level thinking skills. The human resource manager can therefore use these classifications, first to identify the prior learning needed before skills of various levels can be attained, and then to plan ways of facilitating their learning.

Fitts's stages of skills acquisition

Fitts (1962, in Stammers and Patrick, 1975) distinguished three stages of learning, in particular of perceptual-motor skills acquisition. It is recognised that they may overlap.

- *Cognitive stage.* The learner has to understand what is required, its rules and concepts, and how to achieve it.

- *Associative stage.* The learner has to establish through practice the stimulus–response links, the correct patterns of behaviour, gradually eliminating errors.

- *Autonomous stage.* The learner refines the motor patterns of behaviour until external sources of information become redundant and the capacity simultaneously to perform secondary tasks increases.

Dreyfus et al.'s stage model of skills acquisition

Dreyfus *et al.* (1986, in Cooley, 1987: 13–15 and Quinn *et al.*, 1990: 314–315) set out a more elaborate model of the acquisition of skills that is relevant to understanding the development of cognitive skills. Their five-stage model moves from the effective performance of lower- to higher-order skills.

- *Stage 1: the novice.* Novices follow context-free rules, with relevant components of the situation defined for them: hence they lack any coherent sense of the overall task.

- *Stage 2: the advanced beginner.* Through their practical experience in concrete situations learners begin to recognise the contextual elements of their task. They begin to perceive similarities between new and previous experiences.

- *Stage 3: competent.* They begin to recognise a wider range of cues, and become able to select and focus upon the most important of them. Their reliance upon rules lessens; they experiment and go beyond the rules, using trial and error.

- *Stage 4: proficient.* Those who arrive at this stage achieve the unconscious, fluid, effortless performance referred to in the definitions of skill given earlier. They still think analytically, but can now 'read' the evolving situation, picking up new cues and becoming aware of emerging patterns; they have an involved, intuitive and holistic grasp of the situation.

- *Stage 5: expert.* At this stage, according to Cooley (1987: 15), 'Highly experienced people seem to be able to recognise whole scenarios without decomposing them into elements or separate features'. They have 'multidimensional maps of the territory'; they 'frame and reframe strategies as they read changing cues' (Quinn *et al.*, 1990: 315). With this intuitive understanding of the implications of a situation, they can cope with uncertainty and unforeseen situations.

Managers' levels of learning (Burgoyne and Hodgson)

A similar hierarchy has been proposed specifically for the learning of managers. Burgoyne and Hodgson (1983) suggest that managers have a gradual build-up of experience created out of specific learning incidents, internalise this experience, and use it, both consciously and unconsciously, to guide their future action and decision-making. They identify three levels of this learning process:

- *Level 1 learning*, which occurs when managers simply take in some factual information or data that is immediately relevant but does not change their views of the world.

- *Level 2 learning*, which occurs at an unconscious or tacit level. Managers gradually build up a body of personal 'case law' that enables them to deal with future events.

- *Level 3 learning*, when managers consciously reflect on their conception of the world, how it is formed, and how they might change it.

Perry's continuum of intellectual and ethical development

Perry's (1968) schema (see Daloz, 1986) emerged from his research into his students' experiences. He interpreted their intellectual and ethical development as a continuum, and mapped out the way in which individuals develop multiple perspectives while at the same time becoming able to commit themselves to their own personal interpretation. At one extreme is basic dualism, where everything is seen as good or bad. This moves through the perception of the diversity of opinion; of extensive legitimate uncertainty; through perception that all knowledge and values are contextual and relativistic; to the recognition of the need to make a commitment to a viewpoint; the making of that commitment; experiencing its implications; and, finally, to the affirmation of identity as this commitment is expressed through lifestyle.

Bloom et al.'s taxonomy of cognitive skills

Bloom *et al.* (1956) offer a classification of skills in which a hierarchy is implied:

- knowledge (simple knowledge of facts, of terms, of theories etc.);
- comprehension (an understanding of the meaning of this knowledge);
- application (the ability to apply this knowledge and comprehension in new concrete situations);
- analysis (the ability to break the material down into its constituent parts and to see the relationship between them);
- synthesis (the ability to reassemble these parts into a new and meaningful relationship, thus forming a new whole);
- evaluation (the ability to judge the value of material using explicit and coherent criteria, either of one's own devising or derived from the work of others) (Fontana, 1981: 71).

Single- and double-loop learning

Another useful classification of learning is found in the concept of two different types of learning: single- and double-loop learning. Individuals do not necessarily progress from single- to double-loop learning, nor is the former an essential prerequisite for the latter.

Single-loop learning refers to the detection and correction of deviances in performance from established (organisational or other) norms, whereas double-loop learning (Argyris and Schön, 1978) refers to the questioning of those very norms that define effective performance. Learning how to learn calls for double-loop learning.

Gagné's classification of learning

Gagné (1970, in Stammers and Patrick, 1975) studied both the process of learning and the most effective modes of instruction, and has made several classifications of types of learning, again implying a hierarchy. For example, he identified the ability to make a general response to a signal; to develop a chain of two or more stimulus–response links, including verbal chains and associations; to make different responses to similar though different stimuli; to achieve concept learning and identify a class of objects or events; to learn rules through the acquisition of a chain of two or more concepts; and, finally, to combine rules and so achieve problem-solving.

Gagné's classification allows us to identify the processes whereby skills of all levels are acquired, and hence suggests how to facilitate learning and prevent failure to learn at the various levels.

Activity

Higher-order thinking skills

On your own or in a small group, return to the section 'The changing world of work and organisations' and identify the higher-order thinking skills it suggests are now needed in organisations. Where would they be classified in the various classifications above? What does this tell you about those skills and how they could be developed?

Cyclical models of learning and learning styles

Another, and more dynamic, way of conceptualising the learning process is to see it as cyclical. The process has different identifiable phases, and individual learners have preferred learning styles. If methods appropriate to the various phases and individual styles are used, more effective learning will result. (The assumptions about phases echo those underlying the concept of development, which is to be discussed in the next section.) The various models below offer a number of important insights to the human resource manager concerned to facilitate higher-order skills in the organisation. They draw attention to the significance of learning through action and reflection, as well as through the traditional channels of teaching/learning. They recognise that individuals might prefer different phases of the cycle and have different styles: they offer means to identify those preferences; to engage in dialogue with individuals about their preferences; and to identify means of helping individuals to complete the whole cycle.

Kolb's learning cycle

The best-known learning cycle in the field in which we are interested is that of Kolb. There are two dimensions to learning (Kolb *et al.*, 1984): concrete/abstract (involvement/detachment) and active/reflective (actor/observer). Learning is an integrated cognitive and affective process moving in a cyclical manner from concrete experience (CE) through reflective observation (RO) and abstract conceptualisation (AC) to active experimentation (AE) and so on (Kolb, 1983).

Effective learning calls for learners:

- to become fully involved in concrete, new experiences (CE);
- to observe and reflect on these experiences from many perspectives (RO);
- to use concepts and theories to integrate their observations (AC);
- to use those theories for decision-making and problem-solving (AE).

However, many people have a preference for a particular phase and so do not complete the cycle: thus they do not learn as effectively or as comprehensively as they could. Kolb's

Learning Styles Inventory identifies these preferences (Mumford, 1988: 27). The 'converger' (AC and AE) prefers the practical and specific; the 'diverger' (CE and RO) looks from different points of view and observes rather than acts; the 'assimilator' (AC and RO) is comfortable with concepts and abstract ideas; and the 'accommodator' (CE and AE) prefers to learn primarily from doing.

Honey and Mumford's learning styles

Honey and Mumford (1992) also identify four learning styles, based on the individual's preference for one element in the learning cycle, and have developed norms based on the results of those who have completed their Learning Styles Questionnaire. Their activists learn best when they are actively involved in concrete tasks; reflectors learn best through reviewing and reflecting upon what has happened and what they have done; theorists learn best when they can relate new information to concepts or theory; pragmatists learn best when they see relevance between new information and real-life issues or problems (Mumford, 1988: 28). This information can be used to design effective learning events, including, Mumford (2002) reminds us, e-learning. Individuals, too, can use it to build on their strengths and reduce their weaknesses in learning.

The Lancaster cycle of learning

A cyclical model said to represent 'all forms of learning including cognitive, skill development and affective, by any process' (Binsted, 1980: 22) is the Lancaster model based on managers' learning. This identifies three different forms of learning: receipt of input/generation of output, discovery and reflection. As Figure 8.1 shows, they take place in both the inner and outer world of the individual. The receipt of input results from being taught or told information, or reading it in books. Learners follow the discovery loop (action and feedback) through action and experimentation, opening themselves to the new experiences generated, and becoming aware of the consequences of their actions. They follow the reflection loop (conceptualising and hypothesising) when making sense of the information they receive and the actions they undertake, and when, on the basis of this, theorising about past or future situations.

Each form of learning is cyclical, and the cycles can be linked in various ways (for example, learning in formal classroom settings links the receipt of input with reflection), but in effective learning the learner will complete the overall cycle.

The learning curve

Though not a cyclical model, the learning curve is included here for convenience.

The notion of a curve is based on the recognition that there is a relationship between the rate of learning and the passage of time. Managers working on the introduction of a new system, for example, might say 'we are on a learning curve'. This curve is often represented as being S-shaped, that is, proficiency in a new skill begins slowly at first, increases steadily over time, and then remains on a plateau. However, since the shape of the curve must clearly depend on the nature and circumstances of the learning, this notion of a learning curve perhaps adds little of value to the understanding of learning.

Activity **Achieving effective learning**

Reflect on your own learning about HRM. Identify where you are in terms of the classifications and cycles above. What do you have to do to make your learning more effective? Note this in your learning diary, and discuss with your mentor (see Exercises on page 299 at the end of this chapter).

Figure 8.1	The Lancaster model of the learning cycle

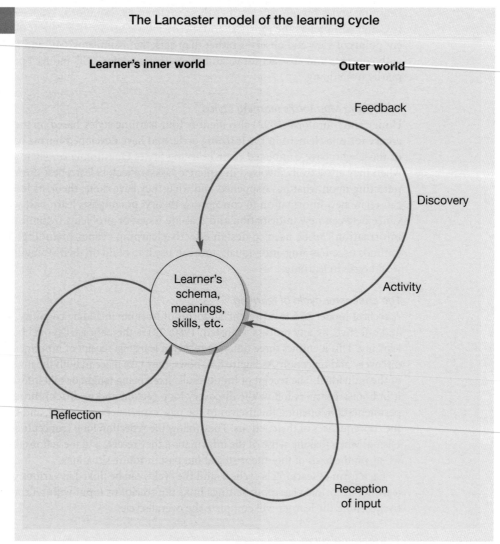

Source: Binsted (1980). Reproduced with permission of Emerald Group Publishing Limited.

Barriers to learning

Although learning is a natural process, people can experience significant barriers, particularly to their learning in formal settings such as school and work. Some of these barriers can be internal: the learner might have poor learning skills or habitual learning styles that constrain them; poor communications skills; unwillingness to take risks; fear or insecurity. Anxiety and lack of confidence are frequently emphasised as significant impediments to learning. Other barriers can be thrown up by the situation: lack of learning opportunities or of support, inappropriate time or place (see Mumford, 1988). This emphasises the need for HR managers to understand the nature and process of learning, and to design learning experiences and events accordingly.

The process of development

The word 'development' is often used quite loosely, but here we use it to mean the process whereby, over time, the individual becomes more complex and differentiated through the interaction of internal and external factors. Learning plays a part in development. For example, the individual's innate tendencies towards growth and maturation are facilitated or constrained – shaped – by the influences in the individual's specific context, and by how the individual responds to them. Development is difficult to conceptualise, though the systems thinking discussed in Chapter 3 is helpful. It is also difficult to study, embracing as it does both the individual's (or organisation's) inner life and the changing nature of a complex world, often with the lifespan as the time dimension. Researchers and theorists may therefore have focused upon segments of the lifespan and drawn implications for the remainder, or upon aspects, rather than the whole range, of development.

Some developmental theorists have devised models to represent universal, normative patterns of experience – making the assumption that all individuals follow similar patterns of experience – and those models suggest that some degree of prediction could be made about the basic outline of individual lives (for example, Levinson *et al.*, 1978). Further, as has already been noted, development – as in 'career development' – is sometimes used to connote progression or advancement. In other words, it is being assumed that there are accepted norms against which an individual's development can be calibrated, and that those norms and the individuals' experiences can be clearly identified. If you recall the nature of various assumptions about social and personal reality discussed in Chapter 3, you will recognise that these are positivist assumptions. Positivist assumptions about individuals and the social and economic environment within which their lives are led (construed as an objective, orderly, stable framework) give rise to the definition of development in terms of sequential phases or stages, often with their own developmental tasks. However, those models frequently interpret the experiences of women and black people in terms of those of white males. Those working with such assumptions might also recognise that individuals have subjective experiences that cannot be studied in this scientific manner. They might therefore disregard them, although individuals base decisions about their life on their subjective experiences.

However, as Chapter 3 outlined, there are alternative approaches. The phenomenological approach acknowledges the significance of a person's subjective experiences, and the social constructionist approach recognises that, because individual experiences are socially constructed, the context of the individual has to be taken into account. Such alternative assumptions lead to a focus upon individual cases and the search for insights rather than generalisable conclusions. They also emphasise the significance of context, and the dynamic, intersubjective processes through which individuals interpret and make decisions about their lives and careers.

When trying to understand development, then, it is important to be aware of the kind of assumptions that are being made about it.

Lifespan development

Lifespan development embraces the total development of the individual over time, and results from the interweaving of the biological, social, economic and psychological strands of the individual's life. People develop through their lifespan, achieving greater degrees of complexity, even transformation. They are therefore continuously engaging in learning processes as they seek balance between changing self and changing environment. The theories and models of lifespan development have several implications for human resource development, for the organisation is one of the major arenas in which adult development takes place.

The influence of the socio-cultural context

One perspective upon the influence of the socio-cultural context on the individual's lifespan experiences interprets that there are tendencies towards common patterns in individual experiences resulting from socialisation. In any given social setting, whether culture, class or organisation, the members of a social group experience pressures to conform to certain patterns of behaviour or norms. Sometimes these pressures are expressed as legal constraints: the age of consent, marriage, attaining one's majority (becoming an adult); or as quasi-legal constraints such as the age at which the state pension is paid and hence at which most people retire from the labour force; or as social and peer group expectations. For example, Neugarten (1968) recognises how family, work and social statuses provide the 'major punctuation marks in the adult life', and the

> way of structuring the passage of time in the life span of the individual, providing a time clock that can be superimposed over the biological clock . . . (p. 146)

Stable organisations in the past also had their own 'clocks'. Sofer (1970) writes of his respondents' 'sensitive awareness' of the relation between age and organisational grade, for they were:

> constantly mulling over this and asking themselves whether they were on schedule, in front of schedule or behind schedule, showing quite clearly that they had a set of norms in mind as to where one should be by a given age. (p. 239)

There is another perspective, however, that emphasises that the environment offers different opportunities and threats for individual lives. The process of development or elaboration takes place as the individual's innate capacity to grow and mature unfolds within a particular context, which in turn facilitates or stunts growth, or prompts variations upon it. For example, it is argued that there are significant differences in physical, intellectual and socio-economic attainments between children from different social classes (Keil, 1981). The interaction and accommodation between individuals and their environment therefore cannot be meaningfully expressed in a model that is cross-cultural or universal. Hence Gallos (1989) questions the relevance of many of the accepted views of development to women's lives and careers, while Thomas and Alderfer (1989) note that 'the influence of race on the developmental process' is commonly ignored in the literature.

Models of lifespan development

There are many different models of the lifespan: here you can see two that have been influential in lifespan psychology. It is important to be aware of the assumptions underlying those models, as discussed above. Their implications for human resource development will be noted below.

Erikson's psychosocial model

Erikson (1950) conceives of development in terms of stages of ego development and the effects of maturation, experience and socialisation (see Levinson *et al.*, 1978; Wrightsman, 1988). Each stage builds on the ones before, and presents the expanding ego with a choice or 'crisis'. The successful resolution of that 'crisis' achieves a higher level of elaboration in individuality and adaptation to the demands of both inner and outer world, and hence the capacity to deal with the next stage. An unsuccessful or inadequate resolution hinders or distorts this process of effective adaptation in the subsequent stages.

For example, the adolescent strives for a coherent sense of self, or identity, perhaps experimenting with several different identities and as yet uncommitted to one; entry to work and choice of work role play a part here. A choice, however, has to be made and responsibility assumed for its consequences: unless this occurs, there is identity confusion. Young adults have to resolve another choice. This is between achieving closeness and intimate relationships *or* being ready to isolate themselves from others.

Erikson paid less attention to the remainder of the lifespan, but indicated that the choice for those aged 25 to 65 is between the stagnation that would result from concern only for self, indulging themselves as though they were 'their own only child' (Wrightsman, 1988: 66), *or* 'generativity'. This is the reaching out beyond the need to satisfy self in order to take responsibility in the adult world, and show care for others, the next generation, or the planet itself. The choice of the final stage is between construing life as having been well *or* ill spent.

The model of Levinson et al.

Levinson *et al.* (1978) studied the experiences of men in mid-life, and from those constructed a model of the male lifespan in terms of alternating, age-related, periods of stability and instability. In the stable period, lasting six to eight years, a man builds and enriches the structure of his life: work, personal relationships and community involvement. That structure, however, cannot last, and so there follows a transitional period, of four to five years, when the individual reappraises that structure and explores new possibilities. Those can be uncomfortable or painful experiences, but they are the essential prelude to adapting or changing the life structure, and so achieving a further stable period.

You can read more about this model in Daloz (1986) and Wrightsman (1988), but should be aware of the assumptions underpinning it. Its definition of the periods within the lifespan in terms of chronological age – for example, between ages 22 and 28 a man embarks on a stable period and entry into the adult world, and between ages 33 and 40 enters another stable period in which he settles down – reflects its assumption about the universal, normative patterning of experiences.

What are the implications of your personal development so far for your effectiveness, or potential effectiveness, as an employee?

Career development

Individual development interacts with the organisation and its development through the individual's career. Career development therefore is of significance for both individual and organisation, and hence for human resource development.

Defining career

Although the term 'career' is well understood in everyday language, the concept is a complex one with several levels of meaning, making it open to several definitions (see Glossary, p. 669; Collin and Young, 2000). The core of the concept suggests the experience of continuity and coherence while the individual moves through time and social space. As with development generally, an individual's career results from the interaction of internal and external factors. As individuals become more skilled and flexible through learning and development, they gain more opportunities for intra- or inter-organisational moves, including promotion. Their learning and development also influence the rewards they gain from their work, their relationship with their employer, the role of work in their lives, and the way they view themselves and are viewed by others. However, 'career' refers not only to their observable movement through and experiences in organisations and the social structure generally. That is their objective career, while the personal interpretation they make of those experiences, the private meaning and significance it has for them, is their subjective career.

Because career is such a broad, often ambiguous, yet widely used concept, there are many perspectives that can be taken upon it, as can be seen in Greenhaus and Callanan (2006). For example, it can be considered as a concept in both social science and everyday speech. Collin and Young (2000) point out that there are various stakeholders in it, including the individual, the employer, the career counsellor, the government, and society itself, and draw attention to how power relationships are glossed over by its rhetorical use. (For a discussion of rhetoric see Chapter 3.) They also suggest that career may be changing from being a linear, future-oriented trajectory to becoming more of a collage of experiences. Another viewpoint upon career, found within vocational psychology, and underpinning career guidance theories and practice, focuses upon career choice and the most effective ways of matching people to jobs (for example, Holland, 1997). Or the concern may be with career development through life (for example, Cytrynbaum and Crites, 1989; Dalton, 1989). A further perspective looks at the nature and management of careers in organisations (for example, Arnold, 1997; Arthur *et al.*, 1989; Arthur and Rousseau, 1996; Chartered Institute of Personnel and Develoment, 2003; Hall and Associates, 1996; Herriot, 1992; Jackson, 1999), while yet another adopts a self-help approach to careers (for example, Bolles, 1988).

Traditional theories of career development

There are many theories that have attempted to explain career. Although it is not possible to examine all these theories here (for further details see Arthur *et al.*, 1989; Greenhaus and Callanan, 2006; Watts *et al.*, 1996), by classifying them into families we can see something of their range and major concerns:

- Theories concerned with external influences upon the individual's career:
  - the economic system and labour markets;
  - social class, social structure and social mobility;
  - organisational and occupational structure and mobility.
- Theories concerned with factors internal to the individual:
  - factors such as age, gender;
  - psychoanalytical explanations;
  - personality traits;
  - lifespan development;
  - implementation of self-concept.
- Theories concerned with the interaction of internal and external factors:
  - decision making;
  - social learning.
- Theories concerned with the interpretation of the individual's subjective experiences:
  - narrative approaches;
  - social constructionist approaches (see Chapter 3).

The theories of career development have similar characteristics to those of lifespan development. Because of the assumptions commonly made about objectivity and subjectivity (see Chapter 3, and the discussion about the concept of development above), frequently they:

- are formulated from a positivist rather than from a phenomenological or constructionist stance (see Chapter 3);
- focus upon objective rather than subjective experience;
- emphasise intra-individual rather than contextual factors;
- make assumptions about the universality of career, disregarding the significance of diversity: gender, race and social class (see Hopfl and Hornby Atkinson, 2000; Leong and Hartung, 2000; Marshall, 1989; Thomas, 1989).

When reading about career (for example, Greenhaus and Callanan, 2006), then, one must be aware of their underlying assumptions.

Careers in the twenty-first century

The theories above reflect our traditional understandings of career. However, the flatter and more flexible forms of today's organisations, and the changing relationship between employees and employers ('the new deal', according to Herriot and Pemberton (1995)) could well change the nature of career dramatically. There are also some slow, deep-seated changes taking place in the context of career. Demographic changes and shifts in public and private values, for example, may over time have significant impacts upon individuals' opportunities, attitudes and aspirations. It is for this reason that questions are being asked not only about future careers (Chartered Institute of Personnel and Development, 2002b), but also about the future of the concept of career itself (Collin and Young, 2000).

The potentials and implications of some of these changes – for individuals, employers, educationalists, careers guidance practitioners and policy makers of various kinds – are being discussed widely (see Jackson *et al.*, 1996). It has been suggested that it is the traditional 'onward and upward' form of career that is under threat. However, Guest and McKenzie Davey (1996: 22), who have found little evidence of major organisational transformations in their own research, caution 'don't write off the traditional career'. Moreover, Moynagh and Worsley (2005), drawing on the ESRC's Future of Work research programme, also consider that long-term jobs and careers will continue to be found.

Theorists are attempting to understand what career is likely to become in the twenty-first century: three examples of their views are given here.

Bureaucratic, professional and entrepreneurial forms of career

Kanter (1989b: 508) draws our attention to the way in which, although only one of three forms of career, the 'bureaucratic' form, defined by a 'logic of advancement', has come to dominate our view of organisational careers generally. The 'professional' form of career (Kanter, 1989b: 516) is wider than that pursued by members of professional bodies. It is defined by craft or skill; occupational status is achieved through the 'monopolization of socially valued knowledge' and 'reputation' is a key resource for the individual. Career opportunities are not dependent in the same way as in the 'bureaucratic' career upon the development of the organisation, nor is satisfaction as dependent upon the availability of extrinsic rewards. Some professional careers may be only weakly connected to employing organisations. The 'entrepreneurial' career develops 'through the creation of new value or new organisational capacity' (Kanter, 1989b: 516). Its key resource is the capacity to create valued outputs, and it offers freedom, independence and control over tasks and surroundings. However, while those with a 'bureaucratic' career have (relative) security, and 'professionals' can command a price in the marketplace, 'entrepreneurs' 'have only what they grow'.

It is the 'bureaucratic' form of career that is now under threat, but attributes of the 'professional' and 'entrepreneurial' forms are likely to be found far more extensively in the twenty-first century (Collin and Watts, 1996; Chartered Institute of Personnel and Development, 2002b).

The subjective career

Weick and Berlinger (1989) argue that in 'self-designing organizations' (the learning organisation of a later section), the focus will be on the subjective career. In the absence of the typical attributes of career such as advancement and stable pathways, 'the objective career dissolves' and the subjective career 'becomes externalized and treated as a framework for career growth' (Weick and Berlinger, 1989: 321), and a resource for the further organisational self-design. They liken career development in such organisations to what Hall (1976) describes as the 'Protean career', in which people engage in 'interminable series of experiments and explorations'. Such a career calls for frequent substantial career moves in order to incorporate a changing, complex and multi-layered sense of self; the 'decoupling' of identity from jobs; the preservation of the ability to make choices within the organisation; the identification of distinctive competence; and the synthesis of complex information (Weick and Berlinger, 1989: 323–326).

The boundaryless career

Arthur and Rousseau (1996: 3) indicate that whereas careers traditionally took place 'through orderly employment arrangements' within organisations, many are now 'boundaryless', crossing traditional boundaries – between organisations, and home and work.

How do you envisage your future career? How will it be likely to differ from the career of your parents' and grandparents' generations?

What are the implications for your learning and development needs?

Implications of the changing nature of career

Many have regarded the traditional career as elitist, available to only a few from a relatively privileged social background and education. The future career may also be elitist, available to a few, but perhaps a different few. At this point it is possible to identify some of the winners and losers from the changes that are taking place. So far the losers have included workers in manufacturing, unskilled workers of many kinds, clerical workers of many kinds, middle managers of many kinds, and full-time workers of many kinds; many of those have been men. The winners have been the knowledge workers, those with the skills required by the new technologies, those with the attitudes and skills needed in service jobs, those who are able (or want) to work only part time. Women may be benefiting from some of the changes. To be employed and to have a career in the future – to be self-programmable (Castells, 1998, see earlier) – individuals will have to remain employable, as this chapter has reiterated, with the ability to learn new knowledge and skills, and above all to learn how to learn.

The changing nature of career is of considerable significance for society as a whole, as well as for individuals and for the economy. For example, the future orientation that a career gives an individual is essential when making decisions about such key issues as starting a family, taking out a mortgage, changing one's occupation, re-entering education, or retiring from employment. Uncertainty about career could therefore over time affect the structure of the population or the housing market, while the effects of unemployment could damage the social fabric severely.

Activity | Implications for human resource development

On your own or in a small group, identify and discuss the implications of an individual's

- lifespan development,
- career development

for the ways in which an organisation sets out to develop its employees

Development of the individual within organisations

We shall now note some ways in which individuals develop within organisations – or are developed by their organisations.

Employee development

One definition of employee development is:

> . . . the skilful provision and organization of learning experiences in the workplace . . . [so that] performance can be improved . . . work goals can be achieved and that, through enhancing the skills, knowledge, learning ability and enthusiasm at every level, there can be continuous organizational as well as individual growth. Employee development must, therefore, be part of a wider strategy for the business, aligned with the organization's corporate mission and goals.
> (Harrison, 1992: 4; see also Harrison, 2002)

Although, as the chapter has already argued, it is important for the organisation to develop its employees generally, many British employers have traditionally neglected employee development. This is reflected in the quotations from Cooley (1987) used in this chapter. However, recent interest in knowledge management, human capital and the learning organisation, and the establishment of the Investors in People award (see Chapter 9), are witness to employers' awareness of the need for employee development and the benefits that flow from it. Furthermore, those employers who have already recognised their own self-interest in their employees' continuous learning and employability often encourage their employees to engage in learning activities for self-development. Many organisations have now established learning centres that often support opportunities for learning beyond what those organisations specifically need. Others have set up corporate universities, such as Motorola and Unipart (Miller and Stewart, 1999; see also Coulson-Thomas, 2000). (See also the subsection on e-learning.) Nevertheless, even though their employers may not formally 'develop' them or encourage them to develop themselves, people still continue to learn, as we shall note later in the chapter.

Staff development

This is similar to employee and professional development, but generally refers to the development of administrative, technical and professional staff in organisations, such as local authorities, in which such staff form a large proportion of those employed. Its aim is to enable such employees to perform their current and future roles effectively, but does not generally include their systematic development as managers.

Self-development

It is now becoming widely recognised that, with the increasing flexibility of organisations and their contracts of employment, individuals need to engage in lifelong learning. However, many (including managers) do not receive from their employers the training and continuous development they need, so their need for self-development, associated with their need for employability, is likely in the future to be greater than ever.

'Self-development' is used to denote both 'of self' and 'by self' types of learning (Pedler, 1988). People developing themselves take responsibility for their own learning, identify their own learning needs and how to meet them, often through the performance of everyday work, monitor their own progress, assess the outcomes, and reassess their goals. The role of others in self-development is not to teach or to train, but perhaps to mentor, counsel or act as a resource.

Although self-development is regarded positively as proactive and entrepreneurial, it can be difficult for the individual to provide evidence of it without some form of accreditation. Once the study programmes available were largely dictated by the traditions and values of the educational providers, but now the Credit Accumulation and Transfer Scheme, and the Accreditation of Prior Learning and of Experiential Learning allow individuals to claim accreditation for a range of learning experiences, while S/NVQs (see Chapter 9) allow them to gain recognition for aspects of their work performance. Employee development schemes should also help individuals in their self-development, whether systematic or sporadic.

Management and organisation development

It should be noted that organisations, like people, need to develop to become more flexible, differentiated and adaptable to their environment. Indeed, the very development of organisational members will contribute to the development of the organisation itself, and the developing organisation can stimulate and foster individual learning. For example, as Chapter 10 recognises, management development is both needed by the developing organisation and sets in train further organisation development. However, it is not within the remit of this chapter to examine management development – this forms the subject of Chapter 10 – or organisation development, but they are included here for completeness.

Continuing professional development

Many professional institutions (see Arkin, 1992) require their members to engage in continuing professional development (CPD) because the changing environment is rendering obsolete some of their original professional skills and knowledge, and demanding the development of others. However, CPD is more than updating: it calls for a continuous process of learning and of learning-to-learn, and so is likely to have considerable benefits for organisations employing professionals, especially when part of the overall corporate strategy (Young, 1996).

Likely to be of particular relevance to readers of this book is the requirement for CPD that the Chartered Institute of Personnel and Development (CIPD) places on its members. For the Institute, Whittaker (1992) states that CPD is needed to ensure that members remain up to date in a changing world and that the reputation of the profession is enhanced; and to encourage members to aspire to improved performance and become committed to learning as an integral part of their work. She identifies the following principles underlying CPD:

- Development should always be continuous, the professional always actively seeking improved performance.
- Development should be owned and managed by the learner.
- Development should begin from the learner's current learning state – learning needs are individual.
- Learning objectives should be clear, and where possible serve organisational as well as individual goals.
- Investment in the time required for CPD should be regarded as being as important as investment in other activities.

CIPD members ensure their continuing development by engaging in professional activities, formal learning, and self-directed and informal learning (Megginson and Whitaker, 2003; see also Haistead, 1995). However, recent research (Rothwell and Arnold, 2005) indicated that, in practice, the high value that members attached to CPD has not translated into active engagement in it.

The subsection on career development referred briefly to the 'professional' form of career, and suggested that it might be more widely adopted in future. Continuing development, even where not required or monitored by a professional body, would be an important element of that.

The organisation as context for learning and development

This chapter has already noted how the process of learning knows no boundaries. People bring the fruits of this naturally occurring and continuous process into their place of work and so, as Cooley (1987: 169) shows, 'ordinary people' have the potential to contribute the knowledge, skills, attitudes and creative thinking that organisations need for survival, flexibility and development. Moreover, individuals' learning and development continue within the organisation, so here we shall examine how human resource managers can provide an environment in which the capacity to learn and adapt can be harnessed to benefit the organisation.

Employers benefit from – indeed, depend on – their employees' naturally occurring learning. Some recognise this and encourage, facilitate and extend those aspects of their employees' learning that are essential for the organisation, and support them informally or undertake formal employee development activities. However, organisations themselves can sometimes make inhospitable environments for the learning and development individuals bring to them (e.g. Honey, 2002). The section on learning and development noted that learning involves the whole person, but organisations are systems of roles (see Chapter 3), and those roles can distort or straitjacket individuals, as Argyris (1960) and McGregor (1960) argue. Moreover, some employers ignore the significance for the organisation of their employees' learning, and do little either to overcome the way in which the organisation may thwart the development of their employees, or to foster that learning and development. In those cases, employee development is not a planned or systematic process. It takes place nevertheless: employees learn for themselves how to carry out their jobs, or improve their performance; how to make job changes or achieve promotions; how to become managers and develop others. It must therefore be recognised that much employee learning might not be intended, planned or systematic. Nevertheless, individuals may:

- learn how to carry out their initial and subsequent jobs through doing and observing, through trial and error, through the influence of and feedback from their peers and supervisors, through modelling themselves on others, and through informal mentors;

- develop themselves through their own more or less systematic analysis of their learning needs;

- take the initiative to acquire additional knowledge or understanding by attending educational and other courses, *via*, for example, learndirect (see Chapter 9).

Because of this, employee learning is problematical. Employers may receive many of its benefits without effort on their part, while at the same time, unlike recruitment and selection, they cannot fully control or contain it. Some employers might feel threatened by the potential of their employees' learning and development, seeing it as 'potentially subversive' (Garratt, in Pickard, 2005: 16), and not welcome significant changes in the people they had been at pains to select as employees. Through their work, employees might acquire knowledge and skills that make them marketable to other employers, and perhaps less than fully committed to their present employer. Equally, not exposed to best practice, they might learn poor lessons; they might also learn ineffectively and in an unnecessarily uncomfortable, effortful or wasteful manner. Thus they might not necessarily benefit from the learning and development they contribute to their organisation, although they would not be able to withhold some of its benefits from their employers.

To manage people effectively and fairly, and in a way that benefits the organisation, therefore, it is important to be aware of these thorny and, at times, moral issues. (You will have the opportunity to consider them in greater depth in the section on controversial issues.)

At the end of the twentieth century learning was advocated with missionary zeal, as is apparent in the words of Honey (1998: 28–29), quoted in the Introduction to this chapter, when setting out the Declaration of Learning drawn up by some of the 'leading thinkers on learning in organisations'. Many organisations heeded that message and, as many reports in *People Management* testify, are now committed to HRD. (See also CIPD's annual learning and development survey.) However, within a few years that Declaration had 'sunk without trace' (Pickard, 2005: 16). In a recent post-mortem, those same 'leading thinkers' discussed whether its demise might be due to HRD's tendency to control individuals through, for example, competency frameworks, rather than to develop them by developing the organisation. It was also suggested that, with the overall economy changing, HR was 'trying to make the industrial model work in the knowledge management world' (Burgoyne, in Pickard, 2005: 17). Nevertheless, the need for learning and development remains, and the organisation remains a significant context for it. It is, therefore, necessary to understand how the processes of learning and development can be facilitated in the organisation and, indeed, how the organisation itself can learn.

Influences upon learning and development from outside the organisation

Many significant influences upon learning and development emanate from outside the organisation. Government-driven education and training initiatives and changes, stemming from increasing concern over the country's need for learning and skills development, have contributed to the institutionalisation of competence-based education and training. The history, purpose and nature of these developments are discussed by Harrison (1992: 17–77; see also Harrison, 2002). Within a comprehensive and continually updating national framework agreed across all sectors and occupations (see Chapter 9), elements in an individual's learning and development, whether achieved through formal education, training or experiential learning across the lifespan, are identified and assessed against nationally agreed standards. The language, philosophy and procedures of this framework are likely to shape individuals' perceptions of their learning and learning needs, and to influence how employers articulate the learning needs of their employees. Moreover, the Investors in People initiative (see Chapter 9 and Arkin, 1999) also both prompts, shapes and supports human resource development practices.

Facilitating learning and development within the organisation

Employees learn and develop through carrying out their jobs: this chapter has already noted the significance of action for learning. For example, the design of those jobs and the organisation structure, the degree to which it is centralised and bureaucratised, all influence employees' learning opportunities. People need to be able to grow in their jobs, and might outgrow their jobs as they learn, or to move into new jobs that would allow them to continue the process of their development. An organisation that is growing or changing is more likely to offer those opportunities than one that is static or declining.

Here, then, are some of the features of organisation and management that would facilitate learning and development within organisations.

The style of management

Reporting on the results of research by the New Learning for New Work Consortium, Fonda and Guile (1999) set out the guiding principles for managing 'capable' organisations that seek to develop the learning of their employees. These are 'respect for the views of the workforce and clarity about the capabilities that the whole workforce will need; the creation of both challenge and support for developing and sustaining these capabilities; and an individualised approach to potential' (p. 41).Thus, as well as specific training, individuals need feedback on their performance, encouragement, support, and resources to give them self-confidence, to stimulate and sustain their learning and development. To develop the higher-order skills needed in organisations, employees need the opportunity to take risks and hence to make mistakes. This presupposes not only a risk-taking and confident approach on the part of employees, but also a risk-taking and supportive management. Effective learning and development in the organisation therefore call for a managerial style that is compatible with this need. The existence and nature of an appraisal scheme (see Chapter 13) could have positive or negative effects upon employees' learning (Thatcher, 1996). Essentially, organisations that want to develop those characteristics need also themselves to learn to learn, to become learning organisations, to have a learning culture and a learning centre (Coulson-Thomas, 2000).

The learning organisation

The structure and operation of an organisation can influence the process of learning within it. It is evident that the human resource development argued for throughout this chapter would be achieved in a learning organisation. (See also Chapter 9.)

The concept of the learning organisation is open to criticism, not least because it is often expressed in theoretical terms. This is recognised by Senge (Pickard, 2000: 39), one of its early and influential proponents (Senge, 1990), who has elaborated his thinking in more concrete terms (Senge *et al.*, 1998). Nevertheless, the learning organisation continues to be 'an aspirational concept' (Burgoyne, 1995: 24), a 'transitional myth' that makes sense both in the world that is passing and in the one that replaces it. Hence it enables people to bridge the gap – in this case as 'more emotionally involving, inclusive forms of organisation' emerge from the information-based organisation. However, Burgoyne (1999: 44), another early and key proponent, acknowledges that it has not 'delivered its full potential or lived up to all our expectations', and sets out what the characteristics of the second generation will have to be.

Today's interest in knowledge management gives new relevance to Morgan's (1997) 'holographic organisation'. Using the metaphor of the organisation as a brain, he offers a new way of appreciating how the organisation itself can facilitate, constrain or repress the learning of its members. Both brain and organisation can be understood as holograms, 'where qualities of the whole are enfolded in all the parts so that the system has an ability to self-organize and regenerate itself on a continuous basis' (p. 100). The holographic nature of the learning organisation provides the stimulus, prompts and cues for individuals to learn and develop the higher-order skills they need to sustain and develop the organisation in a changing world, and 'to develop a discursive, networking culture in which everyone constantly questioned their own assumptions' (Pickard, 2000: 39).

Reminding us that the brains of employees and the brain-like capacities of computers and the internet already have holographic features, Morgan considers how to design those features into organisations as well. He identifies five principles: the 'whole' built into the 'parts', redundant functions, requisite variety, minimum critical specification, and learning to learn.

Building the 'whole' into the 'parts'

One way of building the 'whole' into the parts of the organisation is through its culture. When that embodies the organisation's 'vision, values, and sense of purpose', then it will act like a 'corporate "DNA"' (Morgan, 1997: 102), which carries the holographic code of the human body in each of its parts. Another way is to network information throughout the organisation, so that it can be widely accessed, enabling organisational members 'to become full participants in an evolving system of organizational memory and intelligence' (Morgan, 1997: 104). Further ways are to have the kind of structure that allows the organisation to 'grow large while remaining small' (Morgan, 1997: 104), and to organise work tasks not into specialised jobs but into holistic teams of individuals having multiple skills.

Redundancy

In the traditional mechanistic design of organisations, each part has a specific function, with additional parts for backup or replacement. This allows a degree of passivity and neglect in the system ('"that's not my responsibility"', (Morgan, 1997: 111)). With the capacity for redesigning the system delegated to specialised parts, the capacity to self-organise is not generalised throughout the system. Instead, Morgan suggests that the organisation needs an 'excess capacity that can create room for innovation and development to occur' (1997: 108–110). It needs redundancy of functions rather than redundancy of parts (1997: 111–112). Where each part has additional functions currently redundant but potentially available – through multi-skilling and teamworking, for example – the capacities for the functioning of the whole are built into the parts. Thus the system as a whole has flexibility, with the capacity to reflect on and question how it is operating and to change its mode of operating.

Requisite variety

The internal diversity of a self-regulating system must match the variety and complexity of its environment in order to deal with the challenges from that environment. All elements of the organisation should therefore 'embody critical dimensions' of the environment with which they have to deal; this variety can be achieved, where appropriate, through 'multifunctioned teams' (Morgan, 1997: 112).

Minimum critical specification

Overdefinition and control, as in a bureaucracy, erode flexibility and stifle innovation. Hence the manager should define no more than is essential, but should instead focus on 'facilitation, orchestration and boundary management, creating "enabling conditions" that allow a system to find its own form' (Morgan, 1997: 114). The challenge is to avoid the extremes of anarchy and overcentralisation.

Learning to learn

Finally, the organisation needs to engage in double-loop learning (see earlier), allowing its operating norms and rules to change as the wider environment changes.

Morgan concludes by noting that these five interconnected principles should not be regarded as 'a blueprint or recipe' (Morgan, 1997: 115), but as a way of looking at how organisations could ensure that they remain adaptive.

Mentoring

Mentor was the friend to whom Ulysses entrusted the care of his young son before embarking on his epic voyages. Although the notion of mentoring is, therefore, a very old one, its value in organisations started to be recognised 25 or so years ago, and knowledge management now gives it particular relevance. You can read about mentoring in Kram (1985), Collin (1988), Fowler (1998), Clutterbuck (2004), Whittaker and Cartwright (1999), and Klasen and Clutterbuck (2001).

The nature and purpose of mentoring

In organisations, mentors are more experienced employees (and often managers) who guide, encourage and support younger or less experienced employees, or 'protégés'. Their relationship is a developmental one that serves career-enhancing and psychosocial functions for the protégé while also benefiting the mentor. Overall, the mentor stimulates, encourages, guides, supports and cautions, acts as a role model, nurtures learning through action, learning-to-learn, and the adoption of a future orientation. While meeting the developmental needs of employees, mentoring is also contributing to the process of meaning-making in the organisation (see Chapter 3) and hence to its responsiveness to its environment. (Note that coaching, which is now gaining in popularity (Clutterbuck and Megginson, 2005; Jarvis *et al.*, 2005), has traditionally differed from mentoring in its focus on role or task needs rather than the developmental needs of the protégé.)

Although being or having a mentor can occur naturally both outside and within organisations, this does not necessarily occur universally or systematically. To reap the benefits of mentoring, organisations set up formal programmes. Their purpose might be to support a graduate intake or other trainees and develop 'high fliers' or senior managers; encourage career advancement of women or those from minority groups (see Crofts, 1995); nurture employees with skills in short supply; stimulate and foster innovation in the organisation; and support managers in training, or other learners in the organisation. Examples are to be found in a wide range of private and public sector organisations in Britain, Europe and North America.

Protégés are not the only beneficiaries of mentoring: mentors also gain greatly from being challenged to understand their own jobs and the organisation, and to find ways of helping their protégés share this understanding and work effectively. Mentors might also find that they, too, need mentoring.

Have you had, or been, a mentor? What does your experience suggest would be the benefits of a mentoring programme in an organisation? How could it be made to work effectively?

The requirements for effective mentoring

This literature generally agrees on the following requirements for effective mentoring.

● *The status and characteristics of the mentor.* Mentors will generally be senior to protégés in status, experience and probably age; it is highly desirable that senior managers act as mentors, and that top management be involved with the programme. Mentors should have the skills and qualities that protégés respect, good empathic and people-developing skills, good organisational knowledge and personal networks, and patience and humility to be able to learn from the protégé. Not all managers, therefore, would make appropriate mentors. Mentors should not have a line relationship with their protégé because the element of control inherent in that would conflict with the developmental nature of the mentoring relationship.

- *The protégé.* Protégés should have potential, and be hungry to learn and develop in order to realise it. There will be many more potential protégés in the organisation than can be effectively mentored; it is therefore commonly noted that mentoring is elitist.

- *The relationship.* The relationship should be one of mutual trust, and will develop over time. Unless limits are set by a mentoring programme, it might continue until the protégé no longer needs its support. Sometimes it develops into a full friendship.

- *The activities.* Mentors encourage their protégés to analyse their task performance and to identify weaknesses and strengths. They give feedback and guidance on how weaknesses can be eliminated or neutralised. They help them recognise the tacit dimensions of the task skills, an important element in the development of competence and 'know-how'. Mentors act as a sounding board for their protégés' ideas, and support them as they try out new behaviours and take risks. They give honest, realistic but supportive feedback, an important element in learning generally and learning-to-learn in particular. They encourage their protégés to observe and analyse the organisation at work through their own and others' actions. Through this process the protégé begins to identify and then practise tacit knowledge and political skills. Mentors help protégés to identify and develop potentials, question and reflect on experiences and prospects within the organisation, apply formal learning to practice, and learn more widely about the organisation. Mentors draw upon their own networks to give experience and support to their protégés, and encourage them to develop networks of their own. In this way, the practice and benefits cascade through the organisation.

Activity | **Developing higher-order skills through mentoring**

On your own or in a small group, identify the higher-order skills that mentoring could develop, and discuss how it might do so.

Designing learning in the organisation

Formal programmes

The messages about how to design effective learning are very consistent. For example, the advice that Sternberg (1985: 338–341), a theorist of intelligence, gives on how intelligent performance can be trained includes the following: make links with 'real-world' behaviour; deal explicitly with strategies and tactics for coping with novel tasks and situations; be sensitive to individual differences, and help individuals capitalise on their strengths and compensate for their weaknesses; be concerned with motivation. The implications of the androgogical model of learning introduced in an earlier section (Knowles and Associates, 1984: 14–18) are that the facilitator of adult learning needs to:

- set a climate conducive to learning, both physical and psychological (one of mutual respect, collaborativeness, mutual trust, supportiveness, openness and authenticity, pleasure, 'humanness');
- involve learners in mutual planning of their learning;
- involve them in diagnosing their own learning needs;
- involve them in formulating their learning objectives;
- involve them in designing learning plans;
- help them carry out their learning plans – use learning contracts;
- involve them in evaluating their learning.

Belbin and Belbin (1972) draw upon their experience of studying training in industry for this advice on training 40- to 55-year-old adults:

1 Reduce anxiety and tension in the adult learner:
   – provide social support and allow social groups to form;
   – use acceptable instructors;
   – offer a secure future.
2 Create an adult atmosphere.
3 Arrange the schedule:
   – use sessions of appropriate length;
   – give preference to whole rather than part method;
   – start slowly.
4 Correct errors:
   – at the appropriate time.
5 Address individual differences:
   – different instructional approaches;
   – effects of previous education and work;
   – spare-time interests.
6 Follow up after training.

The value of these approaches is illustrated in the lessons drawn from the adoption in Britain of the Deming-inspired quality and continuous improvement programmes (Hodgson, 1987: 43):

> Train with extreme sensitivity – pick trainers who have operators' confidence, are alert to remedial training needs and people's fears about going back to class; minimise the gap between awareness, training and use; gear course contents to people's learning needs – don't impose blanket programmes.

However, if those principles of design are ignored, barriers to effective learning, such as anxiety and lack of confidence, would be set up (see earlier). Barry (1988: 47), for example, notes that the considerable apprehension felt by the fitters and electricians who were returning to college after 20 years was an obstacle in the introduction of a multi-skilling programme. Their anxieties were dissipated once they learned that some of the tutors belonged to the same union and had the same craft background as themselves.

e-learning

Information technology has provided the opportunity for e-learning, through which learning can be customised, and individuals can learn at their desks, rather than taking time out to study in a classroom (Sloman, 2001). For e-learning to be effective, it is not only the technology that has to be considered. The purpose of this form of learning has to be clear: it is more appropriate where knowledge is to be acquired than where interpersonal interactions are required.

Despite initial apparent enthusiasm for it, e-learning has not taken off as had been expected (Sloman, 2002). However, major lessons have been learned. An overall systematic approach, that includes e-learning, classroom and on-the-job learning, has to be developed, and it has to be recognised that e-learning is learner-centred, requiring new relationships between learners, trainers and line managers. Very importantly, it demands that effective support be provided for the learner (Sloman, 2002).

Informal and tacit learning

Other people are major actors in the context of the individual's learning, and significant for an individual's learning and development, providing instruction and feedback (see earlier), support and encouragement, confidence-building, perhaps even inspiration. They might be, perhaps unknown to themselves, mentors, models or points of comparison for learners who learn not just from their formal instructors or supervisors, but also from peers and subordinates. This informal method of learning, including 'sitting next to Nellie', might have its weaknesses, but it also has strengths. It can offer whole rather than part learning, and the opportunity to apprehend tacit knowledge (see earlier).

Some organisations attempt to capture and use formally some of these otherwise informal ways of learning through people. Knowledge management and mentoring are examples of this. Shadowing is a method that gives the opportunity for a learner to observe the actions of a senior manager systematically and over a period of time. From this observation the learner can infer certain general principles, grounded in everyday organisational realities. However, as the novel *Nice Work* (Lodge, 1988) suggests, without feedback from the manager, the 'shadow' can misinterpret some of the situations witnessed.

Action learning

> There can be no action without learning, and no learning without action.　(Revans, 1983: 16)

Revans was the 'father of action learning' and 'one of the great unsung heroes of modern management' (Pedler, Brook and Burgoyne, 2003). His original concept (Pedler, 1983) has been adapted somewhat to changing circumstances, but as now applied is 'a method for individual and organisational development. Working in small groups [or 'learning sets'], people tackle important organisational issues or problems and learn from their attempts to change things' (Pedler *et al.*, 2003: 41).

Action learning (see also Chapter 10) embodies key aspects of learning that have been noted earlier. Whereas traditional instruction presents the kind of programmed knowledge needed to deal with puzzles that can be solved, action learning addresses problems for which there is no right answer, and which call for critical reflection and questioning insight (Pedler and Wilde, 2003). It stimulates learning through action, engages in double-loop learning as its participants start to examine their underlying assumptions, demands reflection, and draws on tacit knowledge. It offers human resource managers a way of developing the higher-order skills needed in an organisation.

Reflective practice

Reflection, as well as action, we have already noted, plays a key part in learning. Schön (1983) suggested that effective professionals engage in reflective practice: they build reflection into their actions. When faced with a unique and uncertain situation, they enter into a 'reflective conversation' with it, hypothesise on the basis of their existing knowledge and theories about how it could be changed, reframe it, experiment to identify the consequences and implications of this frame, listen to the situation's 'talk back' and, if necessary, 'reframe' again.

Other kinds of employee could also be encouraged to engage in Schön's (1983) reflective practice, thereby strengthening their learning to learn. See also Brockbank *et al.* (2002).

Controversial issues

Although the argument for the need for learning and development within organisations is incontrovertible, it nevertheless raises some controversial issues, which you should consider. For example,

- Who owns the employee's learning and development?
- As generally presented, the value and purpose of human resource development is not questioned. Are there other ways of interpreting it?

295

> **Activity** **Who owns the employee's learning and development?**
>
> Reflect on your own experience. Then, on your own or in a small group, identify the stakeholders in the individual's learning and development.
>
> *Reflect on your own experience*
>
> - What is it costing you to learn? For example, take your reading of this book: what does this cost you?
> - How do you benefit from your learning and development?
>
> *Who are the stakeholders in the individual's learning and development?*
>
> - What other costs are incurred in your learning and development? Who pays them?
> - Who else benefits from your learning and development?
> - What benefits do they receive?
> - Who could impede your learning and development?

> **Activity** **As generally presented, the value and purpose of human resource development is not questioned. Are there other ways of interpreting it?**
>
> The philosophy underpinning this chapter's presentation of its material is humanistic – learning and development have largely been interpreted as empowering of the individual. The chapter has not questioned whether the harnessing of individual learning and development by the organisation could be interpreted differently.
>
> - Should the question that Legge (1995) asked of human resource management also be asked of human resource development – rhetoric or reality?
>
> The awareness that the ownership of individual learning is a matter of debate, however, presents the opportunity to look for other interpretations. Consider this on your own or in a small group.
>
> - What interpretations might the other chapters of this book make of human resource development?
> - How idealistic or cynical are calls for activities such as mentoring and the learning organisation in today's flexible organisations?
> - Is mentoring elitist or empowering?
> - Is the learning organisation rhetoric or reality?
> - Are there other possible interpretations?
>
> (You may find it helpful to return to the section on ideology and rhetoric in Chapter 3.)

Conclusions

This chapter has identified the significance of learning and development for individuals and organisations. Many organisations have recognised this, and have invested in their human resource development, as *People Management* reports in its regular company profiles and annual features on the National Training Awards. These reports suggest that both organisations and their employees have benefited.

However, by reflecting upon your own motivation and experiences, you will already have an insight into some of the thorny issues inherent in human resource development (others are discussed by Rainbird and Maguire, 1993). These issues can be summarised as follows:

- Learning and development take place throughout life, and in every aspect of life, as well as through performance of the job.

- Employer-initiated and sponsored and delivered learning can constitute only a small part of an individual's total learning.

- Some of such activities are undertaken as part of planned development; some are random or opportunistic.

- The employer cannot ring-fence such employer-provided learning.

- Employer-provided learning will be infiltrated by learning from other arenas – from home or social life, but also from undertaking the daily job, or observing boss or colleagues. Such learning may influence, strengthen, challenge or undermine employer-provided learning.

- The processes of learning and development might work counter to the processes of matching and control in which some employers invest heavily through the selection process.

- Learning and development are difficult to evaluate, because they often need an interval of time for their outcomes to be manifested.

- It is not easy to apportion their benefits to either employer or employee.

- It is not easy to calculate their costs, nor apportion them between employer and employee.

- Some of the costs are not borne by either of these; partners, families and the state through the educational and vocational training systems also pay some of the price of employee development.

- Individuals expect reward for their training or development – when they have put effort in, and become more skilled, they expect greater reward. This reward might be either extrinsic (promotion, increase in pay) or intrinsic (greater fulfilment through a more demanding or higher-status job).

- As employees learn and develop, they might become less compliant to their employer and more demanding of changes at work and further development.

- This might result in the employee's dissatisfaction with his or her present job or employer.

- Because of all the above, some employers might be reluctant to pay to develop their employees.

- Some of the processes, activities and benefits depend upon the individual's context (including the presence of significant others), age and stage of development in life.

- It is difficult formally to ensure effective learning – it often seems false in comparison with the ongoing spontaneous learning from life in general, and there are often difficulties in transferring from formal learning situations to everyday work.

The issue of the ownership of the learning and development of individuals, as employees, reminds us that managing people has a moral dimension – human resource management juggles with empowering and controlling. This is the unanswered (and unanswerable?) question at the heart of human resource development, and poses dilemmas to both employer and employee.

Summary

- This chapter addressed the issue of why individuals generally and human resource managers in particular need to understand learning and development.

- It began with a series of definitions of learning that rested on the view that the acquisition of knowledge and understanding facilitates change in perceptions and practice. Such acquisition is increasingly essential in today's world of work, in which employees are expected to cope with change and new technology, take more responsibility, become more skilled and knowledgeable, and develop the ability for problem solving and creative thinking.

- The attributes that today's organisations need for their survival were examined – in particular, the need for quality and continuous improvement, flexibility, adaptability, and the exploitation of knowledge. Individual employees therefore must engage in a continuous process of learning how to learn, and managers must learn how to facilitate this.

- The nature of the learner was examined; but it was also emphasised that learning is a lifelong process that means making continuous adaptations. In many senses it is a journey. In the process of learning, many barriers are thrown up, including anxiety and lack of confidence on behalf of the learner. Discrimination also exists and often creates barriers for certain groups such as older workers, women, disabled people and cultural and ethnic minorities. This might impair their ability to learn by undermining their confidence and/or preventing them from taking courses and training programmes that will lead to greater opportunities. Many in those groups belong to the most disadvantaged in our society.

- The outcomes of learning – the acquisition of new skills, competence, 'know-how', tacit knowledge and employability – were highlighted. It is equally important for managers to have an awareness of the hierarchies of learning, the various levels of learning through which learners proceed. Each level adds a further layer of sophistication to that process, from the simple acquisition of knowledge of facts through to the ability to understand complicated analyses involving complex abstract processes. Such understanding will take the learner through the various stages of learning: novice, advanced beginner, competent, proficient and, finally, expert. Various theories and models of learning and learning styles were also examined.

- The concept of development was explored. It is a process in which the learner 'becomes increasingly complex, more elaborate and differentiated, and thereby able to adapt to the changing environment'. A number of theories and models of lifespan, career and other forms of development were then examined and their implications for human resource development noted.

- Much learning and development takes place within the organisational context, itself influenced from outside by national training initiatives. Although learning knows no frontiers, organisations can often make inhospitable environments for the learning and development of individuals, and with this in mind it must be recognised that learning has to be supported by managers, mentors, and the overall learning climate of a learning organisation.

- The final part of the chapter examined two controversies for the reader to reflect on. These questioned who owned the individual's learning and development, and whether human resource development should be accepted at face value. Rather than giving answers the author posed a number of probing questions for the reader to reflect upon – a form of self-development in itself.

QUESTIONS

1 What do human resource managers need to know about learning and development and how they take place? Draw up a list of questions that they could ask a learning specialist.

2 How can practical knowledge be developed in an organisation?

3 How might learning transform an individual? What are the implications of such transformation for an organisation?

4 What are the implications for an individual's career of new flexible forms of organisation?

5 The chapter has highlighted two controversial issues for discussion. What other thorny issues do learning and development in organisations raise?

EXERCISES

1 Keep a learning diary

Reflection is essential for effective learning. Systematically reflect upon what and how you learn by keeping a learning diary. It will also help you remember issues to discuss with your tutor (and, if you have one, mentor), and might also contribute to your continuing professional development portfolio. Spend half an hour every week recording the following:

- the most meaningful or stressful events of the week;
- how they came about and who was involved;
- your interpretation of them;
- the emotions evoked by them;
- how you dealt with them;
- the outcomes of your actions;
- your evaluation of your actions;
- what you would do or avoid doing in future;
- what further skills, knowledge and understanding you need to perform more effectively;
- how you could acquire these;
- your action plan.

2 Find yourself a mentor

If you are not fortunate enough to have a mentor already, then find yourself one. Phillips-Jones (1982) suggests the following steps:

- Identify what (not who) you need.
- Evaluate yourself as a prospective protégé.
- Identify some mentor candidates.
- Prepare for the obstacles that they might raise.
- Approach your possible mentors.

3 How can you make and keep yourself employable?

- Assess your present employability.
- What do you need to do to achieve, maintain or improve this?
- What would be the implications for the nature and quality of your life overall if your career proved to be flexible and/or fragmented?

4 Review and make plans for your career development

To make effective plans for your future development, you need to be aware of how you have arrived at where you are and become who you are.

- Write a brief story of your life and career to date. Why and how have you become who you are today? What are your strengths and weaknesses?
- Now write your story again through the eyes of people who know you well: your parents or partner; your best friend or boss. Would they have a different interpretation of your life and career from you? Does that tell you anything about yourself that you might not have noticed before?
- Are you content with yourself and your present life? What would you like to be different? Why? What are the opportunities and threats to your life and career? What would you have to do (and forgo) to bring that change about? Would it be worth it? And what would the effect(s) be?
- Who else would such changes affect? Who could help or hinder you in those changes? What resources would you need to effect them? In what sequence would those changes have to come about, and how do they fit into the other timetables of your life?
- Now draw up an action plan, identifying the actions you will have to carry out over the short, medium and long term.
- Take the first step in implementing it today. Commit yourself to it by telling someone else about it and enlist their support to keep you motivated.
- At the end of the first month and every three months thereafter, review the progress of your plan and make any necessary adjustments.

There now follow two cases that you need to compare.

CASE STUDY 1

Growing pains let change blossom

Jonathan Moules

Published: 24 March 2006, 16:50; last updated: 24 March, 2006, 16:50

The heavenly choir would probably argue that when it comes to all things bright and beautiful, the Lord God ultimately makes them all. But here on earth, Hillier Nurseries does a large amount of the work.

Hillier, a 142-year-old family-owned business, whose customers include the Royal Family, is one of the UK's largest independent plant growers and as such sees itself as one of the last big manufacturing operations in the UK.

Although the Hampshire-based company has expanded into operating garden centres in recent years, growing shrubs and flowers is still its core business.

Its wholesale nursery division produces about two million container-grown plants a year for garden centres nationwide.

Hillier even reinvests the margins it receives from its retail outlets to support the growing operations.

Like many manufacturers, Hillier also feels under threat from cheaper foreign imports.

At one point it produced 5000 varieties of flowers and shrubs, but this has shrunk to 1500 varieties.

Robert Hillier, managing director and the fourth generation of the family at the helm, says: 'Nurseries in this country were the largest plant growers in Europe at one stage.'

'We have lost that position but I can help us hang on in there by taking costs out.'

The main way Hillier has achieved this is by adopting the lean manufacturing techniques of industrialists, reasoning that the process of improving productivity is fundamentally the same whether you make potted plants or washing machines.

For instance, the company has been able to save £80,000 a year from its transport costs by reorganising the weekly schedules for its delivery trucks.

This was a complicated exercise, involving customers and Hillier's sales staff as well as the drivers. But by agreeing to deliver plants to customers on specific days of the week, Hillier has minimised the periods where vehicles travel around empty.

It also saved £46,000 on the annual cost of its potted plant production line by retraining the six operators to be more rigorous on aligning the pots with the machinery filling them with soil and discarding substandard plants before potting.

The efficiency savings have even been found in the production of the colour picture labels attached to plants. The annual bill for these items was £120,000, but Hillier trimmed this by halving the label size.

John Woodhead, the board director responsible for nurseries, says such efficiency improvements have been particularly important in recent years when colder than average temperatures have hit sales in the horticultural industry.

'The last couple of years have been pretty damn tough. We have had to become as efficient as we possibly can to reduce crop losses.'

He believes that part of the reason why such an old company is able to continue to change the way it operates is because the family owners delegate so much responsibility to non-family members such as himself.

The director of each of Hillier's three operating divisions is responsible for the cash flow and resources of their operations, making the role more fulfilling and encouraging improvement, Mr Woodhead says.

'It is as near as you can possibly get to it being my own business without my owning it,' he adds.

The company tries to encourage as many of its 500 staff as possible, not just the board directors, to take the initiative in their day-to-day work, according to Mr Hillier.

Hillier was the first business in Hampshire to use the Investors in People training programme in 1992 and Mr Hillier actively encourages staff to sort out problems as they find them.

Within each of the business divisions, work is divided into smaller units with section leaders responsible for their individual team's operations.

'Our processes are largely driven by the people who have to follow them,' Mr Hillier says.

Although the company has been run by a member of the family since it was founded in 1864, Mr Hillier stresses that it is more important for his relatives to own the equity of the business than it is to maintain operational control.

'The style of management has changed dramatically since my father's day when an autocratic style still worked,' he says.

'I have raised the importance of training and developing people. For the future success of the business we have got to get the right people running it.'

Several years ago Mr Hillier and his brother John moved the family's entire equity holding into a family trust to secure the Hilliers' long-term ownership of the business.

Case study continued

'We don't have the pressure of outside shareholders, which is perhaps why it has been possible for us to create these autonomous teams within the business,' he says.

At 63 years old, Mr Hillier is considering the future management of the business and he is certain the next managing director will be the first person outside the family to run Hillier. He believes that the key benefit of family ownership is the ability to plan for the long term and not the need to pass the business to his son.

'We have a great way of life which is unusual for a medium-sized business. We don't have the pressure of outside shareholders, so perhaps it has been easier to create a greater sense of teamwork and not put people under the cosh.

'As the family has grown up we have accepted that we cannot achieve success on our own. It has got to depend on the other people.'

Source: Financial Times, 24 March 2006.

Questions

Working on your own or a small group, answer the following questions:

1 What are the contextual changes impacting on Hillier Nurseries?

2 What responses is the company making?

3 What new demands are those responses placing on the owners, managers, and staff of the company ?

4 What are the learning and development needs in the company now?

5 How could those needs be met?

6 How would you see your future if you were a young person who had recently joined the company? What would you do to ensure that it was bright?

7 How would you see your future if you were a middle-aged, established member of the staff of Hillier Nurseries? What would you do to ensure that it was bright?

CASE STUDY 2

GE's corporate boot camp cum talent spotting venue

Rebecca Knight

Published: 20 March 2006, 10:54; last updated: 20 March 2006, 10:54

Every year hundreds of GE employees are sent to the John F Welch Leadership Center in Crotonville, NY, a bucolic town nestled in the Hudson River Valley, to take part in what you might call business school boot camp.

The participants read case studies, take classes and pull all-nighters working on real-life business problems and putting together recommendations for senior management.

'There's lot of reading and a lot of homework,' explains one recent Crotonville graduate. 'It's like graduate school on steroids.'

The Leadership Center, which opened in 1956 as part of a GE campaign to train its managers better, offers various courses ranging in duration from one day to three weeks.

Throughout the curriculum, there are general units on professional skills development including classes on hiring the right people, delegation skills and time management.

There are also specialised courses on risk analysis, loan structuring and capital markets securitisation.

The bulk of the courses, however, are designed to tackle the specific, nitty-gritty issues that GE faces in one of its many businesses – how to improve a supply chain in its jet engine division, how to market a particular product in its plastics unit, or how to improve margins in its financial services group.

Rob Phillips, vice-president of training at GE Capital Solutions, views the Leadership Center as the company's way of 'getting employees to the next level'.

He says: 'GE realises it can run the company better if Bill Smith is smarter, so it sends him to Crotonville.'

Mr Phillips started at the company 24 years ago on an assembly line in Binghamton, New York and has since obtained his bachelor's and master's degrees in engineering.

He comments: 'Whether you need to learn to make presentations better or underwrite deals better, this place accelerates your learning curve.'

The Center's in-house staff teach most of the classes, but there are often guest lecturers from professors at Harvard Business School and Wharton.

There are also visits from top company management.

Jeff Immelt, GE's chief executive officer, for instance, drops in on the Center about three times a month, both to lecture and mingle with employees.

Case study continued

'They're looking for talent, trying to see if someone has a brilliant idea we should be using,' says Mr Phillips.

Anne Alzapiedi, a human relations specialist at GE Capital Solutions, has taken six classes at the Leadership Center during her eight-year career at the company.

She says that the courses help her 'feel connected to the company'. 'When I come here, it's a big deal because I feel like the company is investing in me,' she says.

'I get to meet people from all over the world and I get exposure to business leaders I wouldn't ordinarily get to see.'

Participants are selected to attend a course at Crotonville based on merit. GE managers evaluate their workforce and each year nominate those employees who have achieved a certain career milestone or have displayed a great deal of potential.

'It's all part of managers reviewing the talent and determine how we're going to grow them,' according to Ms Alzapiedi.

'I see Crotonville as a place to drive the culture at GE,' she says.

Sven Jurgal, who works for the equipment-financing department at GE Capital Solutions in London, recently undertook an 18-day management course at Crotonville with 69 other managers.

'It's a recognition of contribution and potential,' he says of being selected to attend. 'What I am taking away is a great network of people and the moulding from the senior people in the company.'

Despite the gruelling schedule, there is some built-in fun at Crotonville. There are regular movie nights as well as shopping and theatre trips to New York City, which is about 35 miles due south of the Center.

In addition, the 53-acre campus features state-of-the-art fitness and recreation facilities as well as a softball field, volleyball court and jogging paths.

The campus also features a 140-year-old farmhouse that has been converted into a multi-purpose recreation centre, complete with billiards, darts and table tennis.

Participants often meet there to unwind after rigorous all-day sessions. 'No matter how tired I am, I always stop by,' says Ms Alzapiedi of GE Capital Solutions.

The GE Leadership Center also offers tailored courses for its customers, free of charge. Typically, a company's senior management team arrives at Crotonville with a particular project or issue they'd like to focus on.

Through discussions, workshops and other exercises, Crotonville instructors help the team work their way through the problem. Last year, about 200 customers participated in classes.

'Customers are like sponges, they just soak this stuff up,' says Mr Phillips. 'It doesn't matter if you're making money or making widgets, companies across the board all have the same problems. Our job is to come up with solutions. There are basic processes that seem to work.'

Then again, he says, GE also learns from its customers. 'We don't have the answers for everything. There are many instances where we're scribbling madly as customers are talking,' says Mr Phillips.

Source: Financial Times, 20 March 2006.

Questions

Working on your own or in a small group, answer the following questions:

1 Although GE is a very different kind of company from Hillier Nurseries (because of the industry, size, country etc.), what are the similarities between them in terms of their need for learning and development?

2 What could Hillier Nurseries learn, and adapt, from GE?

Useful websites

Career management surveys:	www.cipd.co.uk/surveys
Future of work and skills required:	www.cipd.co.uk
	www.dfes.gov.uk
	www.leeds.ac.uk/futureofwork
	www.toscagroup.com
	www.TUC.org.uk
	www.workforce-dev.com
Learning theories:	www.emtech.net/learning_theories.htm
Older workers:	www.agepositive.gov.uk
	www.surrey.ac.uk/crow/
	www.pjb.co.uk/npl/bp21.htm
Reflective practice:	www.nursesnetwork.co.uk/ nurses%20office/02_06_29reflpract.shtml

References and further reading

Those texts marked with an asterisk are recommended for further reading.

Argyris, C. (1960) *Understanding Organizational Behaviour.* London: Tavistock Dorsey.

Argyris, C. and Schön, D.A. (1978) *Organisational Learning: A Theory of Action Perspective.* Reading, Mass.: Addison-Wesley.

Arkin, A. (1992) 'What other institutes are doing', *Personnel Management*, March: 29.

Arkin, A. (1995) 'How the act will affect you', *People Management*, 16 November: 20, 23.

Arkin, A. (1999) 'Investors in future: above and beyond', *People Management*, 5, 3: 40–41.

Arnold, J. (1997) *Managing Careers into the 21st Century.* London: Paul Chapman.

Arthur, M.B., Hall, D.T. and Lawrence, B.S. (eds) (1989) *Handbook of Career Theory.* Cambridge: Cambridge University Press.

Arthur, M.B. and Rousseau, D.M. (1996) (eds) *The Boundaryless Career: A New Employment Principle for a New Organizational Era.* Oxford: Oxford University Press.

*Atkinson, R.L., Atkinson, R.C., Smith, E.E., Bem, D.J. and Nolen-Hoeksema, S. (1999) *Hilgard's Introduction to Psychology*, 13th edn. New York: Harcourt Brace College Publishing.

Barry, A. (1988) 'Twilight study sheds new light on craft development', *Personnel Management*, November: 46–49.

Bartol, K.N. (1978) 'The sex structuring of organizations: a search for possible causes', *Academy of Management Review*, October: 805–815.

Bayliss, V. (1998) Redefining Work: An RSA Initiative. London: The Royal Society for the Encouragement of the Arts, Manufactures and Commerce.

Beattie, D. (2002) President's Message, Annual Report 2002, London: Chartered Institute of Personnel and Development.

Belbin, E. and Belbin, R.M. (1972) *Problems in Adult Retraining.* London: Heinemann.

Binsted, D.S. (1980) 'Design for learning in management training and development: a view', *Journal of European Industrial Training*, 4, 8: whole issue.

Blackler, F. (2000) 'Collective wisdom', *People Management*, 22 June: 61.

Bloom, B.S. *et al.* (1956) *Taxonomy of Educational Objectives,* Handbook 1: The Cognitive Domain. London: Longmans Green.

Bolles, R.N. (1988) *What Color is Your Parachute?* Berkeley, Calif.: Ten Speed.

Borger, R. and Seaborne, A.E.M. (1966) *The Psychology of Learning.* Harmondsworth: Penguin.

Boyatzis, R.E. (1982) *The Competent Manager: A Model for Effective Performance.* New York: Wiley.

Bridges, W. (1995) *Job Shift: How to Prosper in a Workplace Without Jobs.* London: Nicholas Brealey.

Brittain, S. and Ryder, P. (1999) 'A certain *je ne sais quoi*: get complex', *People Management*, 25 November: 48–51.

Brockbank, A., McGill, I. and Beech, N. (2002) (eds) *Reflective Learning in Practice.* Aldershot: Gower.

Burgoyne, J. (1995) 'Feeding minds to grow the business', *People Management*, 21 September: 22–25.

Burgoyne, J. (1999) 'Better by design: design of the times', *People Management*, 3 June: 39–44.

Burgoyne, J.G. and Hodgson, V.E. (1983) 'Natural learning and managerial action: a phenomenological study in the field setting', *Journal of Management Studies*, 20, 3: 387–399.

Cannell, M., Ashton, D., Powell, M. and Sung, J. (1999) 'Training: auditory perceptions: ahead of the field', *People Management*, 22 April: 48–49.

Castells, M. (1996) *The Information Age: Economy, Society and Culture. I: The Rise of the Network Society.* Oxford: Blackwell.

Castells, M. (1998) *The Information Age: Economy, Society and Culture. III: End of Millennium.* Oxford: Blackwell.

Chartered Institute of Personnel and Development (2002a) *Training in the Knowledge Economy.* London: Chartered Institute of Personnel and Development.

*Chartered Institute of Personnel and Development (2002b) *The Future of Careers.* London: Chartered Institute of Personnel and Development.

Chartered Institute of Personnel and Development (2003) *Reflections: Trends and Issues in Career Management.* London: Chartered Institute of Personnel and Development.

Clements, P. and Jones, J.J. (2002) *Diversity Training: A Practical Guide to Understanding and Changing Attitudes.* London: Kogan Page.

Clutterbuck, D. (2004) *Everyone Needs a Mentor*, 4th edn., London: Chartered Institute of Personnel and Development.

Clutterbuck, D. and Megginson, D. (2005) *Making Coaching Work.* London: Chartered Institute of Personnel and Development.

Coleman, P. (1990) 'Psychological ageing', in Bond, J. and Coleman, P. (eds) *Ageing and Society: An Introduction to Social Gerontology.* London: Sage, pp. 62–88.

Collin, A. (1988) 'Mentoring', *Industrial and Commercial Training*, 20, 2: 23–27.

Collin, A. and Watts, A.G. (1996) 'The death and transfiguration of career – and of career guidance?', *British Journal of Guidance and Counselling*, 24, 3: 385–398.

Collin, A. and Young, R.A. (eds) (2000) *The Future of Career.* Cambridge: Cambridge University Press.

Collins, H. (1993) 'Untidy minds in action', *The Times Higher Education Supplement*, 1066, 9 April: 15, 17.

*Cooley, M. (1987) *Architect or Bee? The Human Price of Technology.* London: Hogarth Press.

Corney, M. (1995) 'Employee development schemes', *Employment Gazette*, 103, 10: 385–390.

Coulson-Thomas, C. (2000) 'Carry on campus', *People Management*, 17 February: 33.

Crofts, P. (1995) 'A helping hand up the career ladder', *People Management*, 7 September: 38–40.

Cytrynbaum, S. and Crites, J.O. (1989) 'The utility of adult development theory in understanding career adjustment process', in Arthur, M.B., Hall, D.T. and Lawrence, B.S. (eds) *Handbook of Career Theory.* Cambridge: Cambridge University Press, pp. 66–88.

*Daloz, L. A. (1986) *Effective Mentoring and Teaching.* San Francisco, Calif.: Jossey-Bass.

Dalton, G.W. (1989) 'Developmental views of careers in organizations', in Arthur, M.B., Hall, D.T. and Lawrence, B.S. (eds) *Handbook of Career Theory.* Cambridge: Cambridge University Press, pp. 89–109.

Dennis, H. (1988) *Fourteen Steps in Managing an Aging Work Force*. Lexington, Mass.: D.C. Heath.

Dixon, N. (2000) 'Common knowledge: the insight track', *People Management*, 17 February: 34–39.

Dreyfus, H.L., Dreyfus, S.E. and Athanasion, T. (1986) *Mind Over Machine: The Power of Human Intuition and Expertise in the Era of the Computer*. New York: Free Press.

Edwards, C. (2004) 'Assister act', *People Management*, 10, 17, 2 September: 26–30.

Erikson, E. (1950) *Childhood and Society*. New York: W.W. Norton.

Fitts, P.M. (1962) 'Factors in complex skills training', in Glaser, R. (ed.) *Training Research and Education*. New York: Wiley.

Fonda, N. and Guile, D. (1999) 'A real step change: joint learning adventures', *People Management*, 25 March: 38–44.

Ford, J. (2002) 'The use of competency models is widespread, but new research highlights their shortcomings', *People Management*, 10 October: 56.

Fontana, D. (1981) 'Learning and teaching', in Cooper, C.L. (ed.) *Psychology for Managers: A Text for Managers and Trade Unionists*. London: The British Psychological Society and Macmillan, pp. 64–78.

Fowler, A. (1998) 'How to run a mentoring scheme: guide lines', *People Management*, 15 October: 48–50.

Gabriel, Y. (2000) *Storytelling in Organizations: Facts, Fictions, and Fantasies*, Oxford: Oxford University Press.

Gagné, R.M. (1970) *The Conditions of Learning*, 2nd edn. New York: Holt, Rinehart & Winston.

Gagné, R.M. (1974) *Essentials of Learning for Instruction*. Hinsdale, Ill.: Dryden Press.

Gallos, J.V. (1989) 'Exploring women's development: implications for career theory, practice, and research', in Arthur, M.B., Hall, D.T. and Lawrence, B.S. (eds) *Handbook of Career Theory*. Cambridge: Cambridge University Press, pp. 110–132.

Gardner, H. (1985) *Frames of Mind: The Theory of Multiple Intelligences*. London: Paladin.

Gardner, H. (1999) *Intelligence Reframed: Multiple Intelligences for the 21st Century*. New York: Basic Books.

Gilligan, C. (1977) 'In a different voice: women's conception of the self and of morality', *Harvard Educational Review*, 47: 481–517.

Greenhaus, J.H. and Callanan, G.A. (2006) (eds) *Encyclopedia of Career Development*. Thousand Oaks, CA: Sage.

Griffiths, J. (2005a) 'Firms must plan for dearth of young', *People Management*, 2 June: 10.

Griffiths, J. (2005b) 'Open and shut case', *People Management*, 1 September: 20–21.

Griffiths, J. (2005c) 'Masculine wiles', *People Management*, 27 October: 20–21.

Guest, D. and McKenzie Davey, K.M. (1996) 'Don't write off the traditional career', *People Management*, 22 February: 22–25.

Guest, D., Storey, Y. and Tate, W. (1997) *Opportunity Through People*. IPD Consultative Document, June. London: IPD.

Haistead, N. (1995) 'A flexible route to life-long learning', *People Management*, 21 September: 40.

Hall, D.T. (1976) *Careers in Organizations*. Pacific Palisades, CA: Goodyear.

Hall, D.T. and Associates (1996) *The Career is Dead – Long Live Career: A Relational Approach to Careers*, San Francisco, CA: Jossey-Bass.

Hammer, M. and Champy, J. (1994) *Reengineering the Corporation: A Manifesto for Business Revolution*. New York: Harper Business.

Harrison, R. (1992) *Employee Development*. London: Institute of Personnel Management.

Harrison, R. (2002) *Learning and Development*. London: Chartered Institute of Personnel and Development.

Herriot, P. (1992) *The Career Management Challenge*. London: Sage.

Herriot, P. and Pemberton, C. (1995) *New Deals: The Revolution in Managerial Careers*. Chichester: John Wiley.

Hodgson, A. (1987) 'Deming's never-ending road to quality', *Personnel Management*, July: 40–44.

Hogarth, T. and Barth, M.C. (1991) 'Costs and benefits of hiring older workers: a case study of B&Q', *International Journal of Manpower*, 12, 8: 5–17.

Holland, J.L. (1997) *Making Vocational Choices: A Theory of Vocational Personalities and Work Environments*, 3rd edn. Odessa, Fl.: Psychological Assessment Resources.

Honey, P. (1998) 'The debate starts here', *People Management*, 1 October: 28–29.

Honey, P. (1999) 'Not for the faint-hearted', *People Management*, 28 October: 39.

Honey, P. (2002) 'Tough love on learning', *People Management*, 2 May: 42.

Honey, P. and Mumford, A. (1992) *Manual of Learning Styles*, 3rd edn. London: Peter Honey.

Hope, K. (2005) 'New for old', *People Management*, 28 July: 14–15.

Hopfl, H. and Hornby Atkinson, P. (2000) 'The future of women's career', in Collin, A. and Young, R.A. (eds.) *The Future of Career*, Cambridge: Cambridge University Press, pp. 130–143.

Hwang, A.-S. (2003) 'Training strategies in the management of knowledge', *Journal of Knowledge Management*, 7, 3, July: 92–104.

Jackson, C., Arnold, J., Nicholson, N. and Watts, A.G. (1996) *Managing Careers in 2000 and Beyond*. Brighton: Institute for Employment Studies.

Jackson, T. (1999) *Career Development*. London: IPD.

Jarvis, J. and Hooley, A. (2004) 'Access all areas', *People Management*, 9 December: 40–42.

Jarvis, J., Lane, D. and Fillery-Travis, A. (2005) *The Case for Coaching*. London: Chartered Institute of Personnel and Development.

Kanter, R.M. (1989a) *When Giants Learn to Dance*. New York: Simon & Schuster.

Kanter, R.M. (1989b) 'Careers and the wealth of nations: a macro-perspective on the structure and implications of career forms', in Arthur, M.B., Hall, D.T. and Lawrence, B.S. (eds) *Handbook of Career Theory*. Cambridge: Cambridge University Press, pp. 506–521.

Keil, T. (1981) 'Social structure and status in career development', in Watts, A.G., Super, D.E. and Kidd, J. M. (eds) *Career Development in Britain: Some Contributions to Theory and Practice*. Cambridge: CRAC, Hobson's Press, pp. 155–192.

Klasen, N. and Clutterbuck, D. (2001) *Implementing Mentoring Schemes: A Practical Guide to Successful Programs*. London: Butterworth-Heinemann.

Knowles, M.S. and Associates (1984) *Androgogy in Action*. San Francisco, CA: Jossey-Bass.

Kolb, D.A. (1983) *Experiential Learning*. New York: Prentice Hall.

Kolb, D.A., Rubin, I.M. and MacIntyre, J.M. (1984) *Organizational Psychology: An Experiential Approach*, 4th edn. New York: Prentice Hall.

Kram, K.E. (1985) *Mentoring At Work: Developmental Relationships in Organizational Life*. Glenview, Ill.: Scott, Foresman.

Laslett, P. (1989) *A Fresh Map of Life: The Emergence of the Third Age*. London: Weidenfeld & Nicolson.

Legge, K. (1995) *Human Resource Management: Rhetorics and Realities*. Basingstoke: Macmillan.

Leong, F.T.L. and Hartung, P.J. (2000) 'Adapting to the changing multicultural context of career', in Collin, A. and Young, R.A. (eds) *The Future of Career*, Cambridge: Cambridge University Press, pp. 212–227.

Levinson, D.J., Darrow, C.M., Klein, E.B., Levinson, M.H. and McKee, B. (1978) *The Seasons of a Man's Life*. New York: Alfred A. Knopf.

Lodge, D. (1988) *Nice Work: A Novel*. London: Secker & Warburg.

Malhotra, Y. (1998) *Knowledge Management for the New World of Business*, WWW Virtual Library on Knowledge Management, http://www.brint.com/km/.

Manocha, R. (2005) 'Grand totals', *People Management*, 7 April: 26–31.

Marshall, J. (1989) 'Re-visioning career concepts: a feminist invitation', in Arthur, M.B., Hall, D.T. and Lawrence, B.S. (eds) *Handbook of Career Theory*. Cambridge: Cambridge University Press, pp. 275–291.

Martin, S. (1995) 'A futures market for competencies', *People Management*, 23 March: 20–24.

Mayo, A. (2002) 'A thorough evaluation', *People Management*, 4 April: 36–39.

Mayo, A.J. and Nohria, N. (2005) *In Their Time: The Greatest Business Leaders of the 20th Century*. Boston, Mass.: Harvard Business School Press.

McGregor, D. (1960) *The Human Side of Enterprise*. New York: McGraw-Hill.

Megginson, D. and Whitaker, V. (2003) *Continuing Professional Development*. Maidenhead: CIPD.

Mezirow, J. (1977) 'Personal transformation', *Studies in Adult Education* (Leicester: National Institute of Adult Education), 9, 2: 153–164.

Miller, R. and Stewart, J. (1999) 'U and improved: opened university', *People Management*, 5, 12, 17 June: 42–46.

Moreton, T. (ed.) (1992) 'The education, training and employment of disabled people', *Personnel Review*, 21, 6: 2–87.

*Morgan, G. (1997) *Images of Organization*, 2nd edn. Thousand Oaks, CA: Sage.

Moynagh, M. and Worsley, R. (2005) *Working in the Twenty-First Century*, Leeds/Norfolk: ESRC/The Tomorrow Project.

Mumford, A. (1988) 'Learning to learn and management self-development', in Pedler, M., Burgoyne, J. and Boydell, T. (eds) *Applying Self-Development in Organizations*. New York: Prentice Hall, pp. 22–27.

Mumford, A. (2002) 'Horses for courses', *People Management*, 27 June: 51.

Myers, C. and Davids, K. (1992) 'Knowing and doing: tacit skills at work', *Personnel Management*, February: 45–47.

Naylor, P. (1987) 'In praise of older workers', *Personnel Management*, November: 44–48.

Neugarten, B.L. (1968) 'Adult personality: toward a psychology of the life cycle', in Neugarten, B.L. (ed.) *Middle Age and Aging: A Reader in Social Psychology*. Chicago, Ill.: University of Chicago Press, pp. 137–147.

Nonaka, I. (1991) 'The knowledge creating company', in *Harvard Business Review on Knowledge Management*. Cambridge, Mass.: Harvard Business School Press, pp. 21–45.

Pedler, M. (1988) 'Self-development and work organizations', in Pedler, M., Burgoyne, J. and Boydell, T. (eds) *Applying Self-Development in Organizations*. New York: Prentice Hall, pp. 1–19.

Pedler, M. (ed.) (1983) *Action Learning in Practice*. Aldershot: Gower.

Pedler, M., Brook, C. and Burgoyne, J. (2003) 'Motion pictures', *People Management*, 17 April: 40–44.

Pedler, M., Burgoyne, J. and Boydell, T. (eds) (1988) *Applying Self-Development in Organizations*. New York: Prentice Hall.

Pedler, M. and Wilde, A. (2003) *Action Learning Toolkit*, Ely, Cambs.: Fenman.

People Management (2005a) 'Older staff train faster at BMW', 27 October: 17.

People Management (2005b) 'Troubleshooter', 27 October: 64–65.

Perry, W.G. (1968) *Forms of Intellectual and Ethical Development in the College Years: A Scheme*. New York: Holt, Rinehart & Winston.

Phillips-Jones, L. (1982) *Mentors and Protégés: How to Establish, Strengthen and Get the Most from a Mentor/Protégé Relationship*. New York: Arbor House.

Pickard, J. (1999a) 'Lifelong earning: grey areas', *People Management*, 29 July: 30–37.

Pickard, J. (1999b) 'Emote possibilities: sense and sensitivity', *People Management*, 28 October: 48–56.

Pickard, J. (2000) 'Profile: high-mileage meditations', *People Management*, 6, 7: 38–43.

Pickard, J. (2005) 'Out of control', *People Management*, 24 November: 16–17.

Pickard, J. (2006) 'Multiple choice', in *The Guide to HR Outsourcing, People Management*, London: Chartered Institute of Personnel and Development, pp. 7–11.

Pugh, D.S., Hickson, D.J. and Hinings, C.R. (eds) (1983) *Writers on Organizations*. Harmondsworth: Penguin.

Quinn, R.E., Faerman, S.R., Thompson, M.P. and McGrath, M.R. (1990) *Becoming a Master Manager*. New York: Wiley.

Rainbird, H. and Maguire, M. (1993) 'When corporate need supersedes employee development', *Personnel Management*, February, pp. 34–37.

Rana, E. (2000) '2000 predictions: Enter the people dimension', *People Management*, 6 January: 16–17.

Reday-Mulvey, G. (2005) 'The tide turns', *People Management*, 30 June: 36–38.

Reese, H.W. and Overton, W.F. (1970) 'Models of development and theories of development', in Goulet, L.R. and Baltes, P.B. (eds) *Life-Span Developmental Psychology: Theory and Research*. New York: Academic Press, pp. 115–145.

*Revans, R. (1983) *ABC of Action Learning*. Bromley: Chartwell-Bratt (Publishing and Training).

Ribeaux, P. and Poppleton, S.E. (1978) *Psychology and Work: An Introduction*. London: Macmillan.

Rifkin, J. (1995) *The End of Work: The Decline of the Global Labor Force and the Dawn of the Post-Market Era*. New York: Putnam.

Rothwell, A. and Arnold, J (2005) 'How professionals rate "continuing professional development"', *Human Resource Management Journal*, 15, 3: 18–32.

Scarborough, H. (2003) 'Recipe for success', *People Management*, 23 January: 32–35.

Schön, D.A. (1983) *The Reflective Practitioner: How Professionals Think in Action.* New York: Basic Books.

*Senge, P. (1990) *The Fifth Discipline: The Art and Practice of the Learning Organization.* London: Century.

Senge, P., Kleiner, A., Roberts, C., Ross, R., Roth, G. and Smith, B. (1998) *The Dance of Change.* London: Nicholas Brealey.

Sheard, M. (1992) 'Two routes to quality: why Dow went for BS 5750', *Personnel Management*, November, pp. 33–34.

Sloman, M. (2001) *The E-Learning Revolution.* London: Chartered Institute of Personnel and Development.

Sloman, M. (2002) 'Don't believe the hype', *People Management*, 21 March: 40–42.

Smethurst, S. (2005a) 'The great beyond', *People Management*, 27 January: 28–31.

Smethurst, S. (2005b) 'And … action!', *People Management*, 24 March: 12–13.

Smethurst, S. (2006) 'State of mind', *People Management*, 12 January: 24–29.

Snowden, D. (2002) 'Complex acts of knowing: paradox and descriptive self-awareness', *Journal of Knowledge Management*, 6, 2, May: 100–111.

Sofer, C. (1970) *Men in Mid-Career.* Cambridge: Cambridge University Press.

Stammers, R. and Patrick, J. (1975) *The Psychology of Training.* London: Methuen.

Sternberg, R.J. (1985) *Beyond IQ: A Triarchic Theory of Human Intelligence.* Cambridge: Cambridge University Press.

Thatcher, M. (1996) 'Allowing everyone to have their say', *People Management*, 21 March: 28–30.

Thomas, D.A. and Alderfer, C.P. (1989) 'The influence of race on career dynamics: theory and research on minority career experiences', in Arthur, M.B., Hall, D.T. and Lawrence, B.S. (eds) *Handbook of Career Theory.* Cambridge: Cambridge University Press, pp. 133–158.

Thomas, R.J. (1989) 'Blue-collar careers: meaning and choice in a world of constraints', in Arthur, M.B., Hall, D.T. and Lawrence, B.S. (eds) *Handbook of Career Theory.* Cambridge: Cambridge University Press, pp. 354–379.

Training Commission (1988) *Classifying the Components of Management Competences.* Sheffield: Training Commission.

Trinder, C., Hulme, G. and McCarthy, U. (1992) *Employment: the Role of Work in the Third Age*, The Carnegie Inquiry into the Third Age, Research Paper Number 1. Dunfermline: The Carnegie United Kingdom Trust.

Tyson, S. and Fell, A. (1995) 'A focus on skills, not organisations', *People Management*, 19 October: 42–45.

Ulrich, D. and Brockbank, W. (2005) 'Role call', *People Management*, 16 June: 22–28.

Ulrich, D. and Smallwood, N. (2002) 'Seven up', *People Management*, 16 May: 42–44.

Ulrich, D. and Stewart Black, J. (1999) 'All around the world: worldly wise', *People Management*, 25 October: 42–46.

Walsh, J. (1998) 'Competency frameworks give companies the edge', *People Management*, 17 September: 15.

Waskel, S. A. (1991) *Mid-Life Issues and the Workplace of the 90s: A Guide for Human Resource Specialists.* New York: Quorum.

Watts, A.G., Law, B., Killeen, J., Kidd, J. M. and Hawthorn, R. (1996) *Rethinking Careers Education and Guidance: Theory, Policy and Practice.* London: Routledge.

Wechsler, D. (1958) *The Measurement and Appraisal of Adult Intelligence*, 4th edn. London: Baillière, Tindall & Cox.

Weick, K.E. and Berlinger, L.R. (1989) 'Career improvisation in self-designing organizations', in Arthur, M.B., Hall, D.T. and Lawrence, B.S. (eds) *Handbook of Career Theory.* Cambridge: Cambridge University Press, pp. 313–328.

Whittaker, J. (1992) 'Making a policy of keeping up to date', *Personnel Management*, March, pp. 28–31.

Whittaker, J. and Johns, T. (2004) 'Standards deliver', *People Management*, 30 June: 32–34.

Whittaker, M. and Cartwright, A. (1999) *The Mentoring Manual.* London: Gower.

Wisher, V. (1994) 'Competencies: the precious seeds of growth', *Personnel Management*, July: 36–39.

Woodruffe, C. (1991) 'Competent by any other name', *Personnel Management*, September: 30–33.

Wrightsman, L.S. (1988) *Personality Development in Adulthood.* Newbury Park, CA: Sage.

Young, C. (1996) 'How CPD can further organisational aims', *People Management*, 30 May: 67.

For multiple-choice questions, exercises and annotated weblinks specific to this chapter visit the book's website at **www.pearsoned.co.uk/beardwell**

Chapter 9

Human resource development: the organisational and national framework

Mairi Watson

Objectives

- To examine the strategic nature of HRD and its relationship to the organisational and UK national context.
- To outline and explain the development of HRD plans and the link to the organisational and national context.
- To examine the national framework for workforce development in the UK.
- To examine systems of national vocational education in Europe.
- To examine the implications of these European comparisons for the UK.
- To identify future issues for HRD.

Introduction

The world in which organisations, managers and human resource management (HRM) professionals operate today would be unrecognisable to their peers 35 years ago. The pace of innovation, the development of technology, the turbulence of economic conditions and the professionalisation of management and human resource management are just some areas where the 'escalating and seemingly impossible demands' (Kanter, 1989) that face organisations have had an enduring impact on the context in which they function today.

As a consequence, the ways in which organisations develop their people have altered. Three decades ago in the UK, the Employment and Training Act (1973) set the foundations for the transformation of the national and organisational learning and development landscape. Since then an 'evolution' has occurred as organisations have changed in size, purpose, structure, philosophy, work methods, technology and relationships (Garavan *et al.*, 1995). Approaches to learning have shifted as the practice and purpose of training and developing people have grown in importance, broadened in scope and become more sophisticated in method (Reid, Barrington and Brown, 2004: 9). The change in strategic pressures for organisations have led to developments in training and learning technology, the role of external consultants, new perspectives on learning and knowledge and the increased emphasis on individual responsibility for learning.

While the environmental changes have had a significant impact on organisations at a general level, for human resource development (HRD) there appear to be two fundamental shifts in the way that the learning and development of people is managed and delivered:

- **From training to learning:** Training is defined as a set of activities which react to present needs and is focused on the instructor and contrasts with learning as a process that focuses on developing individual and organisational potential and building capabilities for the future (Reynolds, 2004: 1; Sloman, 2005: 2).

- **From human resource development to strategic human resource development:** This emphasises the link between how people in the organisation are developed and the achievement of organisational goals, and that competitive advantage comes from the strategic development of people.

The underlying issues and broader implications of these two shifts are developed in this chapter. While the previous chapter considered the meanings, outcomes and processes of learning in the context of the organisation, this chapter explores this contemporary context at the organisational, strategic, national and international levels and considers the link between the development of people and organisations' business performance and competitiveness.

Training, learning, HRD and HRM

Training and learning

> The slide of the formal training course from its once pre-eminent role in workplace learning continues. 56% of learning and development professionals now tell us that on-the-job training is the most effective way for people to learn in their organisation. Only 17% say that formal training course takes this accolade in their organisation.
>
> (CIPD, 2006)

The role of formal training in organisations today appears to have declined significantly. Firstly, the speed with which skills requirements change in some sectors means that formal, time-consuming, classroom based learning fails to deliver efficiently as required. Secondly, the growing recognition of HRD as a tool to achieve competitive advantage has raised awareness of the need to embrace learning as a central strategic concern and to be part of the culture of the organisation (Senge, 1990, Pedlar, Burgoyne and Boydell, 1997) of which formal training is just one, often small, component. Thirdly, a government-policy-driven emphasis on individual responsibility for life-long learning means that individuals are encouraged to take more responsibility for their own learning with spin-off benefits for the organisation, which reduces the relevance of off-the-shelf, one-size-fits-all group learning. On the other side of this coin is the need to provide employees with workplace-specific skills to reduce the 'poaching' of skilled employees which reduces the value of traditional training methods.

Finally, the availability of more efficient and more effective alternatives (e.g. e-learning, distance learning, individualised learning, coaching and workplace learning) means that in achieving competitive advantage organisations can calculate a greater return on their investment with alternative methods of delivery and application. The extract in Box 9.1 emphasises that training as a standalone strategy for learning is likely to be worthless.

One allied issue which underpins the shift from training to learning is the growing and developing role of stakeholders in the process (Garavan *et al.*, 1998). These stakeholders have varying degrees of power and influence, hold varying roles, have different values, use different tactics to achieve their aims, engage in different learning experiences, have different aims, objectives and structure, in different contexts and cultures, with different expectations. Employees, employers, managers, leaders, government, European and international bodies, customers, HRD specialists, consultants and trade unions all have a stake in developing the area to their advantage. Furthermore, investors value highly an organisation's ability to attract and retain the very best of people, and their investment in training them for the future (Ernst and Young, 1997; CIPD, 2006).

Box 9.1 The death of training?

The instructional side of training needs to be left behind, the director of learning and strategy evangelism at Microsoft has said. Bob Mosher told delegates that just as Microsoft's own learners had grown out of the classroom model, the same would happen in every organisation.

Quoting research from KPMG Consulting, which found that up to 80 per cent of learning occurred informally, Mosher questioned how many firms were actually supporting such learning. 'A lot should be, but most don't', he said.

And while Mosher admitted that there was still a place for instructor-led training at the beginning of someone's career, he argued that from then on, formal training failed to meet the needs of the learner.

He cited e-communities, peer support, internet references and electronic performance systems as tools to aid informal learning. These should also be used alongside formal training where it does occur, because employees need to be supported between courses.

'The average person gets 26 hours of instruction a year – but what are you doing to support them in between?' he asked.

Mosher also stressed the need to monitor informal learning. 'You can then help employees to choose learning that is appropriate for them,' he argued.

Source: 'An informal approach gets better results' *People Management*, 30 June 2005, Vol. 11, No. 13, 14.

Questions

1 Given the emphasis on informal learning, what are the difficulties that organisations face in monitoring and controlling it?

2 As this chapter considers HRD to be a strategic resource, how can informal learning be linked to the strategy of the organisation?

One set of influential stakeholders are the professional organisations, and their influence is pervasive in this area. The Chartered Institute of Personnel Development's (CIPD) professional standards for 'Learning and Development' (2001a) established this phrase as one which intends to capture the breadth and depth of the role of learning and development in organisations. They have underpinning them the explicit assumption that if organisations make the shift from training to learning, and to the strategic development of learning, then they will achieve competitive advantage (Sloman, 2005: 1).

The performance indicators (shown below) allied to the CIPD's professional standards help to illustrate just how far the understanding of workplace training and learning has moved in the last three decades.

1 Integrating learning and development activity and organisational needs.
2 Providing a value-adding learning and development function.
3 Contributing to the recruitment and performance management processes.
4 Contributing to the retention of employees.
5 Contributing to building organisational capacity and facilitating change.
6 Stimulating strategic awareness and the development of knowledge.
7 Designing and delivering learning processes and activity.
8 Evaluating and assessing learning and development outcomes and investment.
9 Achieving ethical practice.
10 Ensuring continual professional self-development.

(CIPD, 2001a)

These indicate that 'learning and development' as a phenomenon exists, and exists on several levels:

- At the practical level of delivering or facilitating training, learning and development interventions, e.g. training, on-the job learning, e-learning, coaching, mentoring, secondments, etc.

- At a professional level in hosting a set of plans, policies and strategies to achieve a predetermined set of strategic goals, to coordinate the production of information and evaluation, providing expertise and advice on learning and development as experts in the practice of ethical learning and development, who understand the nature of effective design and delivery.

- At a partnership level in building relationships intra-organisationally between HRD and HRM, HRD and the wider organisation.

- At a strategic level in ensuring that learning and development activity contributes to plugging performance gaps identified in strategic planning.

- At a cultural level in developing a culture that values learning and principles associated with it.

- At an extra-organisational level in building strategically beneficial relationships outside the organisation to ensure that learning and development in the organisation are up-to-date, relevant and appropriately develop the organisation's skills base.

This is some way from the definition of and emphasis on training in the Employment and Training Act (1973) and demonstrates the growing importance of training and development for human resource management in companies (Saggers, 1994; Brewster and Hegewisch, 1993; Sloman, 2002) and the increasing financial investment in the area (Learning and Skills Council (LSC), 2004; CIPD, 2006).

The CIPD's 2005 document, *Reflections on the 2005 Training and Development Survey*, noted that 79 per cent of respondents identified that the skills of the people in the organisation needed to develop in order to meet the requirements of the organisation's strategy, indicating that people within organisations appreciate that if the organisation wants to get to where it wants to go, HRD has a strategic role to play. Two-thirds of respondents in the 2006 Training and Development survey believe that learning and training is now taken more seriously by senior and line managers (63 per cent and 68 per cent), and 58 per cent believed the department has far more credibility than before (CIPD, 2006).

Until 2006, the CIPD annually produced a 'Training and Development' Survey. During 2006 (and for the first time), the CIPD named the survey 'Learning and Development', perhaps representing the final nail in the coffin of an enduring emphasis on training as the primary mode of learning in the workplace.

HRD and HRM

With the shift from training to learning comes the need to understand where HRD 'fits' in the organisation. The growing understanding of the contribution that HRD can make to organisational performance has much to do with the growth in interest in HRM and in the contribution that people can make to a business. Most of the models of HRM considered in Chapters 1 and 2 have as part of their aims, policies or outcomes that are directly related to HRD (Beer *et al.*, 1984; Storey, 1989; Storey, 1992). Some commentators argue that it is self-evident that HRD is not a subset of HRM, but that each has its own separate, equally important (and problematic) space (Stewart and McGoldrick, 1996: 9; Hall, 1984; Nadler, 1984). They view HRM and HRD as separate but complementary processes in the analysis of contemporary organisations. However, it is more common to consider HRD as a section or part of an organisation's approach to HRM, one of the many tools at its disposal, and the existence of human resource management policies, generally, as being the distinguishing factor in successful organisations (Sloman, 2002).

Organisational approaches vary greatly, but organisations that demonstrate a high commitment to HRM policies include as part of this commitment extensive training learning and development (Sung and Ashton, 2004; Purcell, 2003; Pfeffer, 1998) enabling them to achieve superior performance through their people. In some organisations this is no small undertaking, and they have created their own 'Universities', for example UnipartU (www.unipart.co.uk) where training and learning, and ultimately, being a learning organisation are considered part of the company's competitive strategy. However, this level of expenditure is reserved for the very large organisation.

While the links to HRM are clear, this does not mean that training and learning are solely the responsibility of HR managers or departments. The commitment and involvement of line managers, as well as top management support are evident in companies that have a strong learning culture and a strategic approach to learning and development (McCracken and Wallace, 2000).

The reality of the relationship between a business's strategy and HRD is somewhat at odds with the aspirations: the CIPD's 2006 Learning and Development Survey reveals that 45 per cent of reorganisations only involve learning and development professionals after all the major decisions have been made or at the final stages of the project. A further 9 per cent do not involve learning and development professionals at all. On the plus side, 27 per cent of organisations involve learning and development professionals from the initial planning stages, and in a further 19 per cent of organisations they are brought in at the initial implementation stage (CIPD, 2006).

Furthermore, while many organisations have a staff development budget, this is not uniform across sector or organisation size: while private sector organisations are least likely to have a specific budget for development, they have the highest average spend (CIPD, 2006); the larger the organisation, the smaller the budget per employee, with employers with fewer than 100 employees spending £898 per employee, compared with organisations with 500 or more spending just £344 (CIPD, 2006); and in organisations with fewer than 5 employees, only 49 per cent arranged any training at all (LSC, 2004).

HRD: The organisational context

Planning human resource development

Planning businesses are more likely to be training businesses.   (LSC, 2005: 52)

Popular practitioner textbooks on HRD and learning and development (Harrison, 2005; Reid, Barrington and Brown, 2004; Marchington and Wilkinson, 2005; Walton, 1999) recommend that in order to design, implement and evaluate effective learning events or HRD interventions (including training, but sometimes covering learning and development more broadly), a cyclical process or system of formal planning ought to be followed. Its origins can be traced to the work of the Industrial Training Boards set up in 1964 and developed by Tom Boydell in 1971 (Harrison, 2005: 13).

However, its popularity is more evident in the rhetoric of the literature than in organisational reality with only 44 per cent of employers having a training plan specifying in advance the level and types of training employees will need in the coming year and only 34 per cent with a budget for training expenditure. Organisations with more than 25 people were much more likely to see these activities as 'standard' and to have them in place. Where businesses had a formal plan of business objectives, they were more likely to have a training plan, and where there was a training plan, it was more likely that there would be a training budget (LSC, 2005: 77).

Typically the learning cycle (see Figure 9.1) comprises a number of logical stages in a step-by-step process to: ensure the consideration of the needs of the individual and the organisation at the early stages; establish appropriate aims and objectives; ensure optimum methods of design and delivery; and carry out effective evaluation of the learning intervention.

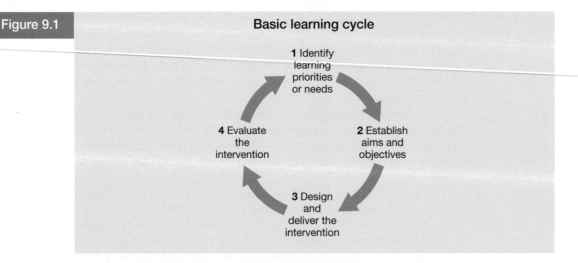

Figure 9.1   Basic learning cycle

This approach stems from strategic planning approaches and has been popular for several decades (Rothwell and Kanazas, 1989, Walton, 1999). It matches most organisations' tendency to treat strategic issues formally, using written documents with aims, objectives, targets, priorities and performance indicators. It relies heavily on analysis, planning and foresight, logical thinking and clarity of organisational objectives. As such the approach pays scant attention to the likelihood of iterations of or interruptions in or to the process, changes in aspects material to the process, and influences internal and external to the process. It does not take account of the need for evaluation to happen at all stages of the process, or the way that needs change and develop as the process moves on. It matches well the classical or rational planning approach to strategy which suggests that organisational strategy is formed through a formal, rational decision making process (see Chapter 2 on SHRM), but not with alternative approaches (e.g. evolutionary, processual or systemic (Whittington, 1993, outlined in Chapter 2) which conceptualise strategy as something more informal, fragmented and embedded in the social systems (cultural and institutional aspects) of the business.

Most commentators are not blind to the need to link the learning or training cycle to the strategic processes of the organisation. This consideration usually appears in the first stage of analysis of learning needs in the form of an organisational or strategic review, but it fails to appreciate the role of strategic considerations throughout the whole process, and doesn't account for other internal or external contextual issues such as power and politics, stakeholders, values, structure, culture, management perspectives and much, much more.

While the basic model is useful in order to structure consideration of the key aspects of planning HRD in organisations, the sequential presentation of the issues does not imply their sequential occurrence in practice. In particular, there is a need at all stages of the process to consider how the strategic intentions of the whole business are being served, and how this contribution will be measured. The adapted cycle shown in Figure 9.2 captures the overlapping and interactive nature of the development of HRD at a strategic level, and the concomitant consideration of needs. It underlines that this occurs in the internal and external context of the organisation. It goes on to emphasise the ongoing nature of evaluation, explored more fully below.

Stop & think

Which aspects of the cycle, or which interactions in the cycle, are likely to be neglected and why?

One of the areas that receives the least attention is closing the loop between evaluation and strategy. We explore this in detail below. Why do you think this area is paid so little attention?

Figure 9.2

The HRD/learning and development process, developed

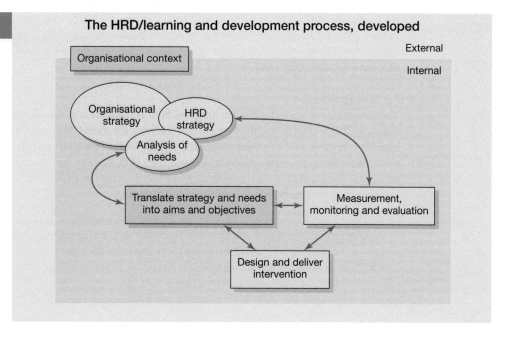

Stages in the process

The next sections cover in sequence:

- Analysing learning needs.
- Design and delivery of learning.
- Evaluation.

Analysing learning needs

The purpose of analysing learning needs is to establish how learning and development strategies, policies, practices and activities can bridge the gap between where the organisation is now and where it needs to be in order to achieve its strategic objectives.

Given the multi-level nature of the learning and development process, one would expect multi-level analysis of learning and development needs. So, while this section considers the analysis of learning needs at just three levels: organisational, job and individual, others consider more. McGoldrick, Stewart and Watson (2002), for example, offer a comprehensive structure which suggests seven levels of analysis:

- *Extra-organisational*: beyond organisational boundaries, attempting to understand, anticipate and create change in the environment and translate it into the advantage of the organisation. This involves practical and analytical research and learning and changing in response to this.
- *Inter-organisational*: between organisations, transferring learning and information, sharing best practices through collaboration and exchange.
- *Intra-organisational*: between departments, cross-fertilisation of ideas, encouraging diversity.
- *Organisational*: recognising the uniqueness of the organisation and responding to its needs for learning and change.
- *Departmental*: encouraging self-development and creativity through learning by experimentation.
- *Group*: through good communication identifying and solving problems to lead to learning and improvement.
- *Individual*: personal responsibility for identifying learning and improvement needs in knowledge, skills, aptitude and performance.

However, despite the aspirations of authors, articles and textbooks, only half of employers (52 per cent) formally assess the extent to which employees currently have gaps in their skills against formal written job descriptions, and 30 per cent do not have formal written job descriptions (LSC, 2005: 84).

For the organisation

The first stage of analysing the learning needs of the business is 'the identification of needed skills and active management of employees learning for their long-range future in relation to explicit corporate and business strategies' (Hall, 1984). This step provides the link between the broader strategy of the organisation and the HRD strategy and ensures that the learning processes, systems and interventions support the direction in which the business is heading. However it is not one that has always received attention:

> Many organisations invest considerable resources in training and development but never really examine how training and development can most effectively promote organisational objectives, or how developmental activities should be altered in the light of business plans.
>
> (Hall, 1984)

If learning and development are to be effective, then it is necessary to identify not only the needs of the individual and the job, but how these fit the overall organisational strategy and objectives. Therefore, this level of review has as its aim the identification of the learning needs of the whole organisation as evidenced in its strategy. However costly or complex, organisations have no alternative but to embrace this as an essential first step. This is also central to the 'Investors In People Standard' (considered below).

Considering what has been said here about the need to understand the broader context of the organisation, it is important that in the analysis of learning needs considers the 'fit' with the values and priorities of the organisation and considers the feedback provided by evaluation of previous learning and development interventions. Hirsh and Reilly (1998: 40) warn that 'organisational structures and employee attitudes have an impact. Simply having appropriate skilled individuals does not automatically yield high performance'.

In practice, this level of analysis can consist of (Reid, Barrington and Brown, 2004: 243):

- A global review: where the organisation examines its short- and longer-term objectives and the skills and knowledge required to meet them. This takes the form of a detailed whole-organisation job analysis.

- Competence based global review: where competence and performance management approaches are used to align training and development to organisational objectives. It is attractive because it is firmly related to the organisation's objectives and can be the basis of performance related pay.

- Critical incident analysis: this is a positive, key event focused strategy which considers the main processes in the organisation and considers the learning needs associated with them.

- Priority problem analysis: where the aim is not to consider comprehensively learning needs, but to identify and prioritise the main problems of the organisation and respond using HRD interventions.

For the job

Job level analysis has as its purpose the identification of the skills knowledge and attributes of the job. The outcomes of this level of analysis are usually a job description, job specification and job training specification. Job level analysis can be categorised on three levels (Stewart, 1999; Harrison, 2005):

Box 9.2   **Practice in focus: how do we take a business goal and convert it to learning goals?**

Andrew Mayo takes a refreshingly clear view of the link between organisational goals and learning goals. He suggests that managers easily fall into the trap of jumping to tried and trusted solutions, especially to training courses. He argues that we need to be very sure whether it is a learning solution that is needed or whether there is change required in resources or systems instead, or as well as. Only then, should managers proceed to set clear learning objectives and choose the most effective learning solution.

The eight steps shown in Figure 9.3 represent a methodology for doing this systematically:

Figure 9.3   **From business goals to learning goals in eight steps**

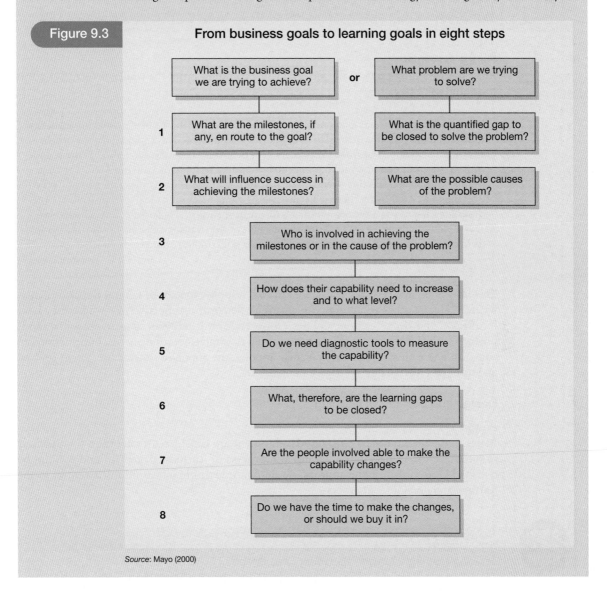

Source: Mayo (2000)

● Comprehensive analysis: which consists of a full and exhaustive analysis of the job, producing a detailed job specification of all the tasks, roles and performance levels associated with the job and the level of knowledge, skills and attitudes required to perform the job effectively.

- Key task analysis: this consists of an analysis of the tasks central to effective performance of the job.

These first two levels have as their outcome a job training specification which forms the basis of planning for HRD interventions for each post-holder. The third level is:

- Problem-centred analysis: this focuses on problems or performance deficiencies and seeks to identify HRD solutions.

How can you gather information to inform job analysis?

The most commonly used approaches include interviews with job holders, managers and supervisors, job logs, questionnaires and group discussions. What else can you think of?

For the individual

Analysis of training needs at the job level while common is not the whole picture, and nor is it without its critics:

> It is tempting to address training needs at [job] level: deciding the training needed for particular roles then rolling out this training to all employees with that job. This approach has the benefit of ensuring all employees have the skills to perform their role effectively. Yet it also has drawbacks, with its 'sheep dip' tactics resulting in people attending training they do not need. The consequences are wasted training spend, poor perception of the training department and wasted working time. Addressing training needs analysis at the most individual level possible is time-consuming and can be more costly. But it yields greater benefits . . . financially . . . organisationally . . . . and individually. What can make us more a part of the strategic direction of the organisation than delivering the employee resource with the exact skills profile required to realise it?
>
> (Ashworth, 2006)

This level of analysis is often considered to be a response to gaps or failures in performance, where there are areas where individuals aren't performing effectively or where they have insufficient knowledge, skills or abilities. However, Ashworth (2006), above, argues that this is potentially the best way for organisations to address strategic learning needs. Information can come from person specifications, personal profiles, the appraisal system, assessment centres, and through individual or managerial initiative.

Design and delivery of learning

Design

Issues in the design of learning and development are considered in depth in the previous chapter (see the section on Outcomes and process of learning, page 270) and will not be revisited here. However, the appropriate design of learning interventions is central to the learning and development process.

What impact can the learning theories discussed in the previous chapter have on the design of learning interventions in your organisation?

Delivery

The distinction between design on the one hand, and delivery on the other is not always an easy one to make. The overlapping and intertwined nature of the relationship makes it difficult to identify where design stops and delivery begins. However, there are some issues not covered in the previous chapter related to design and delivery which are worthy of mention here.

What do organisations do?

The average spend on learning, training and development per employee in 2005 was £469 employee (CIPD, 2006) and collectively, employers funded or arranged the equivalent of 5.9 days of training for every worker in the country, representing a training spend of £4.4 billion per annum, which does not include the cost of staff time, only the direct costs of providing the training (LSC, 2004).

Over the last few years, employers have made greater use of external training providers, including external consultants and training courses (CIPD, 2006) and of further and higher education colleges (LSC, 2004; CIPD, 2006). In most organisations, decisions about the learning and development needs of the organisation are made by learning and development specialists or the HR department. Senior managers also have a significant part in determining the level of investment (CIPD, 2006).

Given the size of expenditure on training activity in organisations, the cost effective use of training methods ought to be an investment which companies and organisations consider carefully. However, many commentators report that organisations choose inappropriate methods which are costly, time consuming, have a deleterious affect on employees' perceptions of the value of training and development and ultimately do little to increase skills levels in organisations (LSC, 2004).

Stop & think

The CIPD and the Learning Skills Council produce annual reports which include information on training and development activity in organisations.

These are available online:

- *National Employers Skills Survey 2004 (published July 2005) www.lsc.gov.uk.*

- *Annual Survey Report 2006: Learning and Development (published 4 April 2006) www.cipd.co.uk.*

Compare and contrast the findings in each of the most recent surveys. Notice the different perspectives from which they are written and the different information presented.

Questions

1 *How can you account for the differences in findings?*

2 *How closely does your organisation match with organisations mentioned in the reports?*

3 *What can you learn from reading through the reports about the way your organisation needs to develop its people?*

The National Employer Skills Survey notes the division of training into (LSC, 2004):

- *Off-the-job training:* which takes place away from the individual's immediate work position.

- *On-the-job training:* defined as activities that would be recognised as training by staff, **but not** the sort of learning by experience which takes place on an ongoing basis.

The type of provision of training by employer varies, with 17 per cent providing on the job training only, 13 per cent providing off the job training only and 33 per cent providing both. Some 36 per cent of employers reported that they did not train at all (LSC, 2004). By size, larger companies (25+) are more likely to provide training, although almost all provide at least some training, with managers being the most trained occupational groups. (LSC, 2004). Most employers that train arrange and fund a number of types of training and development interventions, with the most common being 'job specific' training (81 per cent of employers that train) which by its nature varies from occupation to occupation. 80 per cent have arranged health and safety training, 66 per cent induction training, 59 per cent training in new technology, 42 per cent supervisory training and 41 per cent management training (LSC, 2004).

The **CIPD** (2005d) reports that by far the most popular method of training is on-the-job training, with 99 per cent of employers using this group of methods as a way of developing their staff. (See Figure 9.4.)

A summary of some of the main methods of learning is given below. In order to broaden the definitions and provide recognition of the many ways that staff are developed, here the reference is to on- and off-the-job *learning* rather than *training*

On-the-job learning

By far the most popular way of training and learning at work, on-the-job learning, includes staff meetings, discussion, reflection, observation, teamworking, undertaking a project, assignment or consultancy, taking on a new area of responsibility, changing work practices or systems and much more. It is popular because it is job-specific and relevant, immediate and flexible. In 2006, the CIPD survey identified that it was also the most *effective* method of training. However, both positive and negative behaviours and skills can be passed on, underlining the need for suitable role models and opportunities to be identified and developed as part of the organisation's HRD strategy. On-the-job training ought not to be haphazard and accidental. The most commonly used planned methods are discussed under the following five headings.

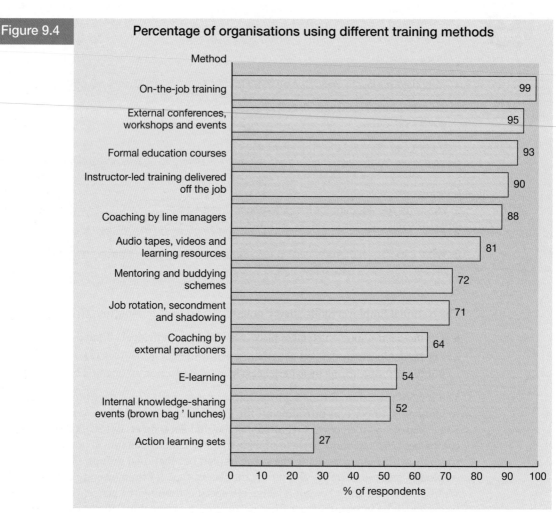

Figure 9.4 **Percentage of organisations using different training methods**

Source: CIPD (2005f).

Sitting by Nellie

Both the strengths and the limitations of this approach are based on its central premise – that people learn well by watching others. It is a truism that most employees gain most of their job knowledge from colleagues and not from books or courses. It is popular because it is immediate and accessible to most employees. While much of this type of learning happens in an ad hoc, unplanned way, it can be a valid, planned way of transferring learning and knowledge in the workplace. In order to be effective, it relies on good structuring, planning and monitoring.

However, the limitations of this approach are well documented. The underlying assumption is that the role model is an experienced, well practiced and skilled performer who has a good understanding of what needs to be passed on. However, they may not be good at their job, may exhibit inefficient job practices or inappropriate behaviour. There might be someone else who is better, or the role model may not have been trained in the practices they are modelling. Often this is a result of poor structure, design and planning but it can result in the passing on of bad or even dangerous working practices (Cannell, 1997).

This approach has been superseded in rhetoric at least, by mentoring and coaching (covered below and in the previous chapter) both of which aim to develop on-the-job, continuous learning.

Mentoring

The terms mentoring and coaching are sometimes used interchangeably, but it is broadly understood that there is a difference in the relationship between the participants in the process. The previous chapter gives a detailed consideration of mentoring, but a short summary is given here.

> The mentoring relationship is most often oriented towards an 'exchange of wisdom, support, learning or guidance for the purpose of . . . career growth; sometimes [it is] used to achieve strategic business goals . . . content can be wide ranging'.
> (Parsloe and Wray, 2000)

Thus, mentoring usually takes the form of a senior or experienced employee taking a supporting role in the development of a new or younger employee. It can be formal or informal and relies on the development of a positive advisory relationship. As such it includes the skills of coaching, facilitating, counselling and networking. Mentoring is part of a range of 'talent management' activities which organisations engage in to identify, develop, engage, retain and deploy the most talented individuals (Warren, 2006; CIPD, 2005d). Mentoring and buddying schemes are used by 32 per cent of employees with this purpose (CIPD, 2005d).

Coaching

> The coach does not need to impart knowledge, advice or even wisdom. What he or she must do is speak, and act, in such a way that others learn and perform at their best.
> (Downey, 2003)
>
> Coaching . . . requires people to see things from others' perspectives, suspend their judgment and listen at a higher level.
> (Hall, 2005)

The coaching market has grown exponentially in the last decade. Coaching, along with e-learning, represents the largest growth area identified by the CIPD's Training and Development 2005 survey. Coaching is delivered either by in-house staff (90 per cent of employers) or external practitioners (64 per cent of employers) (CIPD, 2005d) and often forms part of managers' job descriptions.

At the centre of coaching are models of *structure* and *skills*. The **structure** of coaching, or the coaching process is firmly focused on the outcome or longer-term objective that the participants want to achieve. The most popular model is the 'GROW' model (Gallwey, 1986;

Whitmore, 2002; Downey, 2003). The model takes the participants through four overlapping stages in an iterative process of interaction between the coach and the coachee. Usually this takes the form of the coach asking questions in order to raise the awareness and responsibility of the coachee, and allows them to develop practicable solutions or actions in order to achieve the goal. It enables the coach to structure the conversation and deliver a result which emphasises the accountability and responsibility of the coachee and the will to achieve the outcome.

Box 9.3 **Typical GROW model**

Goal: What is the longer term objective? What is the objective for *this* discussion?

Reality: What is the situation now? Who is involved? What is it costing? What is happening?

Options: What are the possible (not necessarily practicable) solutions? What *could* be done?

Will: What will be done? When? With whose support?

Within this conversational process the coach is using a range of **skills**: Downey (2003) suggests that the coach can use all of the skills on the spectrum shown in Figure 9.5. He indicates that the most effective skills of the coach lie at the non-directive end of the spectrum. For Downey, the skills of the coach are more valuable than his experience of the problem the coachee is attempting to resolve. He indicates that while there will be times when the coachee is stuck and the coach knows the solution, there are limitations to the directive approach – namely, the coach has to know the answer already or be able to work it out, the answer is unlikely to be the one that fits the problem best, and the experience of the coachee is excluded.

Coaching is beset by a number of debates, not least the one which concerns the appropriate way to regulate the profession and develop the skills of those who practice it (Hall, 2005). Many universities and professional bodies have introduced development programmes for would-be coaches, and most organisations have a system to measure the abilities or performance of the coaches they use.

Figure 9.5

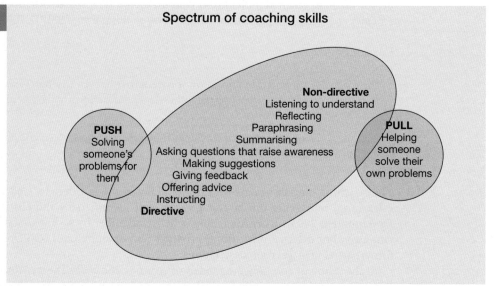

Spectrum of coaching skills

Source: Downey (2003).

The emphasis has shifted in the last few years from developing effective coaches and processes to developing a coaching culture (CIPD, 2006; Clutterbuck and Megginson, 2005) with the aim of improving individual and organisational performance.

Job rotation, secondment and shadowing

Job rotation aims to reduce boredom, vary activities, and develop or increase skill levels by encouraging employees to change jobs periodically. Its popularity was established in the 1970s, and if properly structured can be a positive learning experience for employees and have spin-off benefits for business performance. It is usually part of a larger agenda of *job enrichment* which aims to motivate staff and increase productivity. However, it has been criticised for being insufficiently planned and structured, with less focus on employee development and more on achieving organisational outcomes of flexibility and efficiency.

Secondment encourages the cross-fertilisation of ideas, and usually involves an employee leaving, temporarily, their workplace to work for another organisation. Usually it will be a similar job in a different sector, or a similar area of work with a different focus, e.g. practical vs theoretical. It is usually for a fixed period of time with a structured procedure for feedback and learning.

Shadowing is another popular technique where employees gain an understanding of a job or role in a different department. Usually, the participant is not expected to carry out the job role they are shadowing, but learn about a job by walking through the work day as a shadow to a competent worker. Normally it is temporary, and allows the participant to view at first hand the work environment and skills in practice, with the intention of gaining skills and experience in that area in order to inform job choices, or to develop cross-departmental understanding.

E-learning

There is little doubt that e-learning is big business in the UK. e-learning is, at its simplest, learning that uses information and communication technologies.

In that sense, it refers to computer-based learning which encourages the learner to interact with the technology to achieve specified learning objectives. It can use the whole range of electronic resources, e.g. e-mail, intranet, internet, software packages, PDAs, CDs/DVDs and beyond as technologies develop and advance. It requires the learner to take a high level of responsibility for their own learning and motivation to learn.

At its best, it provides learning which is more accessible, more flexible and adaptable to individual circumstances, provides a broader range of alternatives and is cheaper than alternatives. Its greatest potential lies in how it links learners together and learners to resources through online learning platforms. Its limitations lie in its use simply as a high-tech alternative to textbook learning – only a quarter of respondents to the CIPD 2006 Learning and Development Survey believe that e-learning has significantly altered learning and training offerings. For organisations it is attractive because of its flexibility and accessibility whereby learning is available when learners are available to learn. It allows for learning to be completed in 'granules' in the workplace during working hours, rather than through the traditional training course.

According to a CIPD e-learning survey (2004a) most organisations still rely on CD-Roms (73 per cent), with around half relying on generic or specific modules. Reynolds *et al.* (2002) distinguish three types of e-learning: web-based learning, supported online learning, and informal e-learning. *Web-based learning* is content-focused and relies on minimal interaction between the learner and the tutor and no collaboration with other learners. *Supported online learning* has its focus as the learner, and involves significant interaction with the tutor and other learners. Finally, *informal e-learning*, usually through e-mail and discussion boards, is focused on group interaction, with the participants acting as learners and tutors, interacting with each other in order to achieve organisational learning and the building of the organisation's knowledge base.

Stop & think

Can you find examples in your workplace or on the web of each of Reynolds et al's three types of e-learning?

1 Web-based learning.

2 Supported online learning.

3 Informal e-learning.

www.learndirect.co.uk has hundreds of e-learning courses available on their website. You can find many examples of web-based learning and supported online learning there.

The most successful and effective reports of e-learning come from businesses which use a 'blended learning' approach (CIPD, 2004a) – e-learning combined with multiple additional routes that support and facilitate learning (Sloman and Rolph, 2003). This can be through e-learning supported by periodic face-to-face learning, or with the knowledge component delivered through e-learning and skills component delivered face-to-face, perhaps supported by online discussions and resource links. The possibilities and combinations are endless and changing.

Off-the-job learning

Off-the-job learning is simply learning which takes place away from the place of work of the employee. However, it is frequently pigeon-holed as the 'old' way of doing things – and typified as teacher-centred, classroom-based, process-focused and providing learning that is difficult to transfer to the workplace. It is often criticised as wasteful of time and money, taking the employee away from the practical context in which he or she will have to apply the theoretical knowledge. That said, learning which takes place away from the place of work gives the employee time and space to consider the new learning, and if the event includes learners from other departments, workplaces or sectors, allows the cross-fertilisation of ideas and innovations, the chance to consider notions free from distractions, and the opportunity to network with likeminded individuals.

In order to make off-the-job learning credible and valuable, it has to be, like other learning interventions, identified as organisationally useful at the analysis stage of the process; providing training or learning opportunities which make little or no contribution to the business seriously affects the credibility of those in the organisation responsible for learning and development.

Box 9.4 **e-learning – some secrets of success?**

The Priory Group have taken their e-learning one step further than most. Their Foundations for Growth programme is a 'blended learning system' which delivers all online learning materials and acts as a signpost to other training opportunities, venues and dates. All employees have individual programmes created for them and are allocated whatever modules their line managers request for them, plus certain ones that everyone takes. At the end of each module is an evaluation form. Face-to-face courses, normally lasting a half or full day, have become on average 30–40 minute modules. No-one has asked for extra time to complete this learning – it makes the most of 'downtime' in jobs where people have 20 minutes to sit at a computer and, if disturbed, can return to where they left off easily and without disruption. Learning administrators support the process by providing a point of contact at each of the Group's sites. Although it's early days, the Group expects that there will be significant return on their investment. 'Training costs were huge in the past and are expected to fall…we're not just seeing time savings. If you take a nurse off a ward, you have to replace her. Now they can usually fit training into the working day.'

Source: Smethurst, S. (2006) 'Course of Treatment' *People Management*, 9 March 2006.

Consider an off-the-job learning experience you have had recently. Did you enjoy it? Did you learn something that you were able to apply to your job on return to the workplace? If it was successful, what contributed to this? If it was unsuccessful, why do you think this was the case?

Reading the previous chapter, you will see that the selection of training and learning methods is a complex business, and in order for learning to be effective, there has to be a match between the purpose of the event, your learning preferences and the learning methods employed.

Off-the-job learning is epitomised by formal education courses or instructor-led training delivered off the job. The CIPD learning and development survey (2006) identifies these as being used by 95 per cent and 93 per cent of organisations respectively. Formal education courses normally take place in further or higher education colleges or universities. Instructor-led training is usually delivered by training professionals either directly employed by the organisations or contracted to deliver the event as a training consultant.

What would be the advantages and disadvantages of each method of training delivery for the people in your organisation?

Which methods would be best for which skills?

Evaluating HRD – an integrated approach

> On the one hand, CEOs understand the essential strategic value of a skilled, motivated and flexible labour force. On the other hand, the traditional HRM function has not typically been thought of as a strategic asset, and consequently is under pressure to reduce expenses and demonstrate efficiency in the delivery of it services. (Becker and Huselid, 1998)

> Organisations seriously committed to achieving competitive advantage through their people make measurement of their efforts a critical component of the overall process.
>
> (Pfeffer, 1994)

The assumption that HRD can add something to 'the bottom line' of a business and that it can be measured springs from the literature on high performance work practices and the best-practice literature (see Chapter 2 on SHRM). The best-practice work (e.g. Beer *et al.* (1984), Guest (1987)) highlights the link between sets of good HR practices and organisational performance (e.g. productivity and quality) and argues these are applicable across all organisations. High performance work practices, typified by the work of Huselid (1995) sees integrated sets of HR practices as *economic* assets which are context specific, with a high potential magnitude of return on investment.

However, despite the strategic importance of HRD, the evaluation of it is rarely carried out in any organisationally useful way. Six out of ten HR and financial directors have little or no idea what return they get on their company's investment in training and many in the HRD profession do not have a predisposition toward measurement and evaluation (Swanson, 2001). Furthermore, this goes beyond the reach of the responsibilities of HR managers, as only 23 per cent of workplaces with more than 25 employees have HR specialists (Millward *et al.*, 2000). Evaluation is therefore important to all managers, and where the contribution of HRD cannot be, or is not, demonstrated it is likely to be an easy target for cost reductions and efficiencies.

Usually, evaluation is focused on *training* events, and on participants' *immediate reactions* to the event. This can take place during or after the event and may include:

- Questionnaires or 'happy sheets' to measure participants immediate responses to training or learning events.

- Interviews or questionnaires at a later stage after the event to measure the application of learning in the workplace.

- Tests or examinations: which are common on formal or skills courses in order to measure the progress of trainees.

- Case studies which provide participants with the opportunity to apply their newly applied knowledge, and tutors to observe the ability of the trainees in applying this knowledge.

- Discussion which, as above, allows the opportunity to consider openly the application of new skills or knowledge.

Often these approaches are combined to achieve a fuller picture of the learning of the participants and the extent to which they have applied their learning in the workplace. While this information is useful, it is such a small part of the picture that it can only be incomplete. In this chapter we have considered the strategic importance of HRD in making a contribution to business performance. We have treated it seriously as a business resource. Thus, evaluating the impact of HRD strategy and interventions ought to be treated equally seriously in order to close the loop and ensure that there is learning for the organisation from the learning of the individuals within it and to consider how aspects of the HRD have contributed to the organisation's achievement of its strategy.

This goes beyond considering the outcome of training courses and the transfer of learning to the workplace to considering how HRD can add value to the organisation. HRD can add value to an organisation by improving its position as an employer of choice, through a positive effect on motivation and morale, enhancing employee contribution, supporting the delivery of company objectives by developing the skills in line with organisational needs. It is a key part of the psychological contract in organisations and potentially skills the workforce to be better than the competition. At the very least, HRD sometimes means a business can operate within legal requirements. Measurements go beyond post-course evaluation to measuring wastage, error rates, cost benefit, customer satisfaction, staff opinions and motivation, and can attempt to link specific outcomes to the training delivered, analyse cost effectiveness, demonstrate contribution to strategic objectives, and linking HRD to performance via performance management system.

That said, evaluation is less of a calculation than it is a *judgement* (Kearns, 2005). A rigorous scientific approach to evaluation, although in theory desirable, is not practicable (Kenney *et al.*, 1979). Therefore, it involves a number of subjective considerations – the measurement itself is subjective, the interpretation of the results is subjective, and the values and goals of the stakeholders in the process are different and potentially conflicting. Attaching a financial value to HRD, which means estimating the financial impact of employee behaviour, is at least challenging. However, one might argue, no less challenging than assessing the impact on the organisation or marketing efforts such as advertising or networking. Isolating the impact of HRD is therefore not insurmountable: for example, alongside the many tools suggested in this section, one might establish a control group, consider the impact of other influences (e.g. market or financial changes in the environment) or use professional judgement.

One remaining conundrum is that which concerns what evaluation purports to measure: most models we consider here are concerned with *intermediate* outcomes which may or may not lead to business success e.g. cost of training, reduction of turnover or absence, improved morale or motivation, all of which it is hoped will have some broader business impact. These *performance* indicators may not give the best information as they measure only the specific outcome they purport to measure and nothing more. Writers still struggle to elevate the measures associated with HRD to a higher, strategic level.

However, there are a number of reasons why organisations fail to carry out evaluation even at the simpler, and strategic, levels. Often it is simply because they are not sure how to do it, beyond tried and tested approaches and techniques. Or, if sure how to do it, not sure what to do with the results. There is also a fear that it will be expensive and time-consuming, and offer little in the way of results. Finally, because evaluation is often tagged on at the end of training, learning or development, the event or intervention will not have been designed with the end (evaluation and feedback into the next intervention) in mind.

Green (1999) argues that businesses rarely give sufficient emphasis to researching the impact that specific interventions or tools can make to improved performance. He says that business success will be achieved by asking challenging questions such as: why is the organisation doing this activity? What difference does it make? Does the difference (return) justify the investment? Could we get the same results in a more cost-effective way? Does the difference anticipated align with our business strategy and objectives? These can be simplified to: why should we do this? What difference do we want? How are we going to measure it? Is it cost-effective?

Such questions are at the heart of evaluation, and this section outlines some of the key models and approaches to judging the contribution HRD behaviour can make to organisational performance. Evaluation at its best flows throughout learning in the organisational context, and happens as events unfold using multiple methods of feedback and communication, rather than on a piece of paper at the end of a training course.

Stop & think

- *What are the benefits of investing in measuring the impact of training and learning on organisational outcomes?*

- *Why are most organisations reluctant to carry out any meaningful analysis?*

- *What evaluation techniques have you used or been subject to?*

Categorising evaluation

Three themes are apparent in the development of measurement and evaluation in HRD (Wang and Spitzer, 2005):

- *Practice-oriented stage*: typified by the seminal work of Kirkpatrick (1960) (see below) and considering the impact of (usually) training interventions.

- *Process-driven stage*: typified by the return on investment (ROI) work seeking to justify training and HRD expenditure based on the measurements of benefits vs costs of training.

- *Research-oriented, practice-driven stage*: based on an awareness of business reality and by extension, of the strategic contribution that HRD can make, which is still an emerging field of analysis.

Practice-oriented stage

Kirkpatrick's (1960) enduring work, while much criticised, has had enviable staying power in the world of learning evaluation. Kirkpatrick proposed four levels of evaluation of learning and training, and while much criticised, a close examination reveals that Kirkpatrick was more concerned with the transfer of learning to the workplace and organisational results than is often represented:

1 *Reactions* for Kirkpatrick are defined as 'how well the trainees liked a particular training program'. Reactions are typically measured formally, and immediately, at the end of training, but can be measured informally by the trainer/facilitator during the event.

   Measures include: reaction questionnaires, observation of reactions, relationships, body language, participant interactions, questioning by trainer and questions asked by participants.

2 *Learning* is defined by Kirkpatrick as the 'principles, facts, and techniques [that] were understood and absorbed by the conferees'. This has the purpose of measuring the change in the knowledge of the learner post-event, compared to the knowledge pre-event.

Measures include: written, verbal and practical tests, interviews with participants and managers at pre-determined times after the event, self-assessment, performance review procedures, questionnaires, interviews, peer group discussion.

3 *Behaviour* is about changes in on-the-job behaviour, which must be evaluated in the workplace itself.

Measures include: self, peer and manager appraisals, observation, measurement of outputs/results, interviews, product/service sampling.

4 *Results*. Kirkpatrick relied on a range of examples to make clear his meaning here: 'Reduction of costs; reduction of turnover and absenteeism; reduction of grievances; increase in quality and quantity or production; or improved morale which, it is hoped, will lead to some of the previously stated results.'

Measures include: measurement of performance indicators, e.g. absenteeism, grievances, production, customer satisfaction, turnover, targets, stakeholder feedback, return on investment measures (see below).

It is difficult to over-estimate the popularity of Kirkpatrick's model. Some 91 per cent of those surveyed in the CIPD's Learning and Development Survey 2006 evaluated training, learning and development activities and 98 per cent of those used exercises to measure Kirkpatrick's level 1 outcomes. Some 75 per cent used level 2 evaluation exercises, 62 per cent level 3 and 36 per cent go as far as level 4.

Missing from Kirkpatrick's model is any consideration of the pre-event state of affairs or an assessment of how level four results affect the business. Hamblin (1974) added this 'ultimate level' to consider the extent to which the event has affected the ultimate profitability and survival of the organisation.

Another popular model is from Warr *et al.*'s work in 1970. They suggested a similar four level model, considering:

- *Context*: conditions in the operational context, e.g. the aims and objectives, problems to be overcome, strengths and weaknesses of the approach chosen. This allows the evaluator to consider how the preparation underpinning the training did or did not support the achievement of the objectives of the event.

- *Input*: the processes and resources involved in the event itself, how these were chosen and deployed.

- *Reactions*: the reaction of the learners during and after the event, measuring what the participants feel, rather than what they have learned.

- *Outcome*: what happened as a result of the event, the learning and changes which can be related to the training. This comprises four stages – definition of training objectives, building evaluation tools, using them and reviewing the results.

These models have operational and practitioner appeal, and have a role in demonstrating the value that learning and development activities can add to organisations. Even at this level, organisations identify that their efforts to measure the impact of learning and development activities do not go far enough, and while there is an increasing emphasis on evaluation, cost, time, lack of effective measures, organisational priorities and lack of knowledge and understanding act against the best attempts of those who seek to establish the contribution that learning and development makes to business performance (CIPD, 2006).

Process-driven stage
This second level of evaluation is driven by an increasing awareness of the business reality of increasing global competition, increasing pressure from adverse economic conditions and increased demands for managerial accountability (Wang and Spitzer, 2005).

Return on investment (ROI) measures represent the main theme of the work in this area, and these measures have stimulated much critical debate in the world of HRD (Phillips, 2005).

At its simplest, ROI calculates of the costs and benefits of training events, and it is usually represented as an (apparently) straightforward formula:

$$\frac{\text{Benefits from training} - \text{Costs of training}}{\text{Costs of training} \times 100\%} = \%\ \text{ROI}$$

There the simplicity ends, as measuring the costs and benefits of the training is often far from straightforward. Thompson (2005) argues that to measure ROI effectively, training has to be divided into two categories: knowledge and technical skills (content or 'hard' training), and attitude and interpersonal skills (process or 'soft' training). The former is fairly easy to assess for ROI purposes, but the latter (often the larger proportion of companies' training effort in terms of time, money or profile) is a 'problem area of evaluation'. Its complexity may be the cause of the limited use of ROI measures in practice; less than a fifth of those surveyed in the CIPD's Learning and Development survey (2006) used ROI as a measure of learning, training and development activities in their organisation.

The usefulness or otherwise of the measure is dependent on the quality of the information which feeds it. Sophisticated models (Phillips, 2002; Swanson, 2001; Kearns, 2005) emphasise the importance of:

- the collection of information post-event or programme, including evaluation instruments which are purposeful, timely, and multilevel;
- isolating the effects of the training or programme;
- converting the data to monetary value;
- calculating ROI;
- identifying other, intangible benefits.

Potentially, the sophisticated emphasis on financial and strategic measurement of outputs is at odds with the values-based practice of training and development and Dee and Hatton, 2006 argue for an incremental approach. 'Learning and Development should demonstrate a business benefit, but it is often impossible to go from training straight to ROI. A possible alternative is a staged process which focuses on improving the quality of programmes, increasing the transfer of learning to the workplace and measuring against specific metrics established from the outset' (Dee and Hatton, 2006).

Ford (1993) suggested measures (or metrics) covering three broad areas which he argues that most HRD practitioners find essential within the ROI calculation:

- *Measures of training activity*: how much training and development occurs? Percentage of payroll, training amount spent per employee per annum, average number of training days per employee/manager per annum, HRD staff per 100 employees.
- *Measures of training results*:
  - at reaction level: average percentage of positive course ratings;
  - at learning level: average percentage gain in learning per-course based on difference between pre- and post-course results;
  - at behaviour level: average percentage of improvement in on-the-job performance after training;
  - bottom line: profits per employee per year;
  - cost savings as a ratio of training expenses.
- *Measures of training efficiency*: training cost per delegate hour.

Despite the limitations, discussion of ROI has increased the awareness among HRD practitioners that in order to justify the existence of HRD interventions, there has to be some attempt to measure the financial contribution it makes to the organisations, however challenging this is in practice (Thompson; 2005, Phillips, 2005).

Practically speaking, how would you gather the information required to inform an ROI judgement?

Thompson (2005) suggests a few methods of gathering information to inform an ROI judgement:

- Refining end-of-course 'happy sheets' to ask 'What will you do/do differently as a result of this training?' and 'How exactly will each element of this course help you to do a better job?'

- Following up with line managers and participants at a later date asking for feedback on the things they have used from the training.

- E-mailing a sample of people, asking them about past 'critical incidents' (for example, in management of communication), what skills they used to deal with them, and where they acquired those skills without hinting that training could be the primary source.

- Interviewing participants, their managers and other significant stakeholders before and after training.

- Asking participants to complete pre- and post-event evaluations.

Benchmarking can also provide information on the evaluation of process in HRD. See Box 9.5. Benchmarking is a set of related activities which support and enhance strategies of imitation or collaboration leading to a competitive advantage (Ellis and Williams, 1995). Walton (1999: 303) notes that 'some organisations have relied excessively on comparative performance data as a key plank in their competitive strategy . . . this may help a company meet competitors' performance, but it is unlikely to reveal practices to beat them'. Harrison (2005: 250) also argues that benchmarking measures best-value or best-practice and not the value added to the organisation by the training or learning intervention. To measure added value, Harrison argues, means asking and answering a different question: 'what critical difference has the service made to the organisation's capability to differentiate itself from other similar organisations, thereby giving it a leading edge?'

There are three types of benchmarking: competitive benchmarking which assesses key parts of the organisation's processes, systems and procedures with those of chosen competitors in the field; best-practice/functional benchmarking which compares particular aspects of an organisation's product or service against organisations considered to be 'the best' in this area, and may involve collaboration; and internal benchmarking which considers and compares similar processes within an organisation to achieve internal best-practice, e.g. induction, appraisal.

Green (1999) is not a supporter of an approach which values 'best-practice' (above) as a guide for HR behaviour: 'The response that is often given by HR professionals when challenged on their activities is to refer to them as best practice, as if this in itself is enough to justify the often substantial investment. If probed further, it often turns out to mean "everybody else is doing something on this, so we'd better too" . . . the eventual result of the best-practice syndrome is a cynical and negative view of the HR function as the purveyor of fads and gimmicks. But the best-practice approach also creates a defensive way of looking at HR needs and constrains the innovation and creativity that is needed now, more than ever, to make full use of people as the value drivers in organisations'.

Research-oriented, practice-driven stage

As a categorisation for evaluation of learning and development, this group is not closed, settled or firmly established (Wang and Spitzer, 2005). It has arisen as a result of the awareness of a need to demonstrate overall contribution to business performance in a way that goes beyond the previous section. Therefore, this section contains a number of approaches or ideas which attempt to go beyond measures of process and of intermediate outcomes, to measures of strategic contribution, added value, or ultimate business performance outcomes.

Box 9.5 For HRD, Walton (1999: 313) suggests three levels at which benchmarking can operate:

1 The level of organisational learning:
   ● How have other organisations generated a learning climate?

2 The level of organisation-wide HRD processes
   ● How have other organisations identified and developed competences for staff?
   ● How have other organisations balanced on and off the job learning?

3 The level of training and development activity and resource allocation:
   ● What percentage of payroll is devoted to training and development in other organisations?

Questions

1 How can you use this model of benchmarking in your organisation to assess the effectiveness of HRD activity?

2 Where can you find the information you need to answer the questions successfully?

Stop & think

In Chapter 2, you were introduced to the idea that the principal purpose of measuring HR performance is to drive performance improvement (Yeung and Berman, 1997) and to establish performance improvements from HR evaluation, organisations need to establish the timely and ongoing collection of data, analyse this data, and have managers accountable for those measures.

Question

*How could the **balanced scorecard** approaches which are raised in this context be applied to HRD?*

This *added value* literature is often considered to be synonymous with the ROI literature, however, that is not the case. Commentators on added value focus on more than just financial metrics such as ROI, and usually go beyond to consider broader aspects of pre- and post-intervention measurement, with ROI as, if desired, a part of the broader measurement portfolio.

Green (1999) challenges the limited view that comes with approaches like those in the previous section and instead, he suggests that organisations ought to focus on taking a more 'offensive approach' to HR, and by extension to HRD. For him, measurement is a vital part of the picture but more is required. He argues that to establish added value, organisations must achieve:

● *alignment*, which means pointing people in the right direction;

● *engagement*, which means developing belief and a commitment to the organisation's purpose and direction; and

● *measurement*, which means providing data that demonstrates the improved results of this new approach.

Holton (1996) raises similar issues in his critique of Kirkpatrick's model and refers to three primary learning outcome measures: learning: achievement of the learning outcomes desired in the intervention; individual performance: change in individual performance as a result of the learning being applied on the job; and organisational results: consequences of the change in individual performance. Holton, like many other writers in this area use outcome based models as the basis of their analysis.

Brinkerhoff (2005) supports this view that traditional evaluation models and methods do little to improve organisational performance. His 'success case method' argues that 'the main challenge for organisations is how to leverage learning – consistently, quickly, and effectively – into improved performance'. Responsibility for this does not lie solely with HRD professionals, and while the diffusion of responsibility poses challenges, especially for evaluation, it opens the way for a consideration of a 'whole organisation approach' to evaluation, which will ultimately be more effective in turning learning into organisational advantage. He uses the metaphor of marriage to explain that most evaluation considers the wedding (the training) whereas what we really need to know about is the whole marriage (the training, plus what comes afterwards), the entire training to organisational performance process.

The learning organisation

The notion of the learning organisation is all about creating organisational results from individual learning.

(Senge, 1990)

The notion of the learning organisation has been, and continues to be an influential one. While its roots can be traced in literature on organisational excellence (Peters and Waterman, 1982), total quality management (Deming, 1986), action learning (Revans, 1982, 1983), and organisational learning (Argyris, 1992; Argyris and Schon, 1878), Peter Senge (1990) is usually credited with bringing the concept to organisational life in the early 1990s in the US, and the work of Pedlar, Burgoyne and Boydell (1991) on 'The Learning Company Project' in the late 1980s and early 1990s in the UK provided organisationally useful tools for establishing a *learning climate*.

It has at its heart a 'whole company' perspective (not just an HR one) on learning and development. It links the development of the potential of *everyone* (not just managers, or 'talent' in the business) to the development of the company as a whole. It emphasises the importance of organisational flexibility, responsiveness, adaptability and conscious approach to change (Senge, 1990) and underlines the importance of breaking down outmoded ideas, attitudes and practices before building new skills, structures and values (Pettigrew and Whipp, 1991). It is a 'systemic' rather than 'systematic' approach seeing everything as interconnected, rather than simple cause and effect, and because of this complexity, is probably much less commonly adopted than the rhetoric would suggest (Gibb and Megginson, 2002: 153).

Pedlar, Burgoyne and Boydell (1991, 1997) explained that at its heart, the learning *company* was about releasing the 'massive underdeveloped potential in our organisations' (1997: 3) and seek to differentiate the type of learning as one that happens 'at the whole organisation level' (1997: 3). For them, it is about being 'an organisation that facilitates the learning of all its members and consciously transforms itself and its context' (1997: 3) and is about 'understanding and mastering the art of corporate learning . . . as learning is the key to survival and development for the companies of today' (1997: 6).

Diagnostic tools are popular in the literature of the learning organisation. Pedlar, Burgoyne and Boydell (1991, 1997) developed an 11-point diagnostic jigsaw (Figure 9.6). Honey and Mumford (1989) generate an 11-point checklist and Bartram *et al.* (1993) a 70-item questionnaire centred around seven broad categories (supportive management style, time pressures, degree of autonomy, encouraging team style, opportunities to develop, availability of written guidelines, atmosphere of satisfaction). These tools are intended as a structure for a gap analysis to establish the journey the business must make between where it is now and where it wants to be.

Figure 9.6a   **The learning company profile**

Company regularly takes stock and modifies direction and strategy as appropriate.

Policy and strategy formation structured as learning processes.

All members of the company take part in policy and strategy formation.

Policies are significantly influenced by the views of stakeholders.

1. The learning approach to strategy

2. Participative policy making

Managerial acts seen as conscious experiments.

Business plans are evolved and modified as we go along.

Commitment to airing differences and working through conflicts.

Company policies reflect the values of all members, not just those of top management.

1.

Deliberate small scale experiments and feedback loops are built into the planning process to enable continuous improvement.

Appraisal and career planning discussions often generate visions that contribute to strategy and policy.

2.

Information is used for understanding, not for reward or punishment.

Information technology is used to create databases and communication systems that help everyone understand what is going on.

Systems of accounting, budgeting and reporting are structured to assist learning.

Everyone feels part of a department or unit responsible for its own resources.

3. Informating

4. Formative accounting and control

You can get feedback on how your section or department is doing at any time by pressing a button.

We really understand the nature and significance of variation in a system, and interpret data accordingly.

Accountants and finance people act as consultants and advisers *as well as* score keepers and bean counters

Control systems are designed and run to delight their customers.

3.

Information technology is used to create databases, information and communication systems that help everyone to understand what is going on and to make sound decisions.

The financial system encourages departments and individuals to take risks with venture capital.

4.

Departments see each other as customers and suppliers, discuss and come to agreements on quality, cost, delivery.

Each department strives to delight its internal customers *and* remains aware of the needs of the company as a whole.

The basic assumptions and values underpinning reward systems are explored and shared.

The nature of 'reward' is examined in depth.

5. Internal exchange

6. Reward flexibility

Departments speak freely and candidly with each other, both to challenge and to give help.

Managers facilitate communication, negotiation and contracting, rather than exerting top-down control.

Alternative reward systems are examined, discussed, tried out.

We are all involved in determining the nature and share of reward systems.

5.

Departments, sections and units are able to act on their own initiatives.

Flexible working patterns allow people to make different contributions and draw different rewards.

6.

Source: Pedlar, Burgoyne and Boydell (1991: 26–27).

Figure 9.6b — The learning company profile

Roles and careers are flexibly structured to allow for experimentation, growth and adaptation.

Appraisals are geared more to learning and development than to reward and punishment.

It is part of the work of all staff to collect, bring back, and report information about what's going on outside the company.

All meetings in the company regularly include a review of what's going on in our business environment.

7. Enabling structures

8. Boundary workers as environmental scanners

We have rules and procedures but they are frequently changed after review and discussion.

Departmental and other boundaries are seen as temporary structures that can flex in response to changes.

We meet regularly with representative groups of customers, suppliers, community members and so on to find out what's important to them.

We receive regular intelligence reports on the economy, markets, technological developments, socio-political events and world trends and examine how these may affect our business.

7.

We experiment with new forms of structures.

There are systems and procedures for receiving, collating and sharing information from outside the company.

8.

People from the company go on attachments to our business partners, including suppliers, customers and competitors.

If something goes wrong around here you can expect help, support, and interest in learning lessons from it.

People make time to question their own practice, to analyse, discuss and learn from what happens.

We regularly meet with our competitors to share ideas and information.

9. Inter-company learning

10. Learning climate

We engage in joint ventures with our suppliers, customers and competitors, to develop new products and markets.

We participate in joint learning events with our suppliers, customers and other stakeholders.

There is a general attitude of continuous improvement – always trying to learn and do better.

When you don't know something, it's normal to ask around until you get the required help or information.

3.

We use benchmarking in order to learn from the best practice in other industries.

Differences of all sorts, between young and old, women and men, black and white, etc. are recognized and positively valued as essential to learning and creativity.

10.

People here have their own self-development budgets – they decide what training and development they want, and what to pay for it.

There are lots of opportunities, materials and resources available for learning on an 'open access' basis around the company.

11. Self-development opportunities for all

With appropriate guidance people are encouraged to take responsibility.

11.

Self-development resources are available to external stakeholders.

The exploration of an individual's learning needs is the central focus of appraisal and career planning.

Source: Pedlar, Burgoyne and Boydell (1991: 26–27).

Stop & think

Pedlar, Burgoyne and Boydell (1991, 1997) explain that the diagnostic jigsaw ought to be used by organisations to test how they measure up against the concept of the learning organisation. Apply the jigsaw to your organisation.

Questions

1 *To what extent is my company like this?*

2 *If this is how my company is at the moment, how would I like it to be in the future?*

There are, however, criticisms of the concept. Its popularity peaked in the early 1990s, and since 2002 there has been considerably less discussion of the impact of the idea than in previous years. Even strong supporters point to the fact that it has not lived up to 'all our aspirations . . . or delivered its full potential' (Burgoyne, 1999). Garvin (1993) identifies that important writers' work, Senge and Nonaka particularly is 'utopian . . . filled with near mystical terminology'.

Garvin (1993) also highlights the aspirational nature of the ideas:

. . . idyllic? Absolutely. Desirable? Without question. But does it provide a framework for action? Hardly. These recommendations are far too abstract, too many questions remain unanswered. How, for example, will managers know when their companies have become learning organisations? What concrete changes in behaviour are required? What policies and programmes must be in place? How do you get from here to there?

Sloman (1999: 3) agrees – 'the concept of the learning organisation should be redefined or declared redundant'. In its current manifestations, 'The idea of learning organisations cannot be said to be capable of operationalisation in any meaningful sense' (Stewart and Sambrook, 2002: 183).

Overall, the models lack a convincing link between theory and practice (Lahteenmaki *et al.*, 1999), practice and outcomes. However, it must be noted that the original authors did not promise the learning organisation as a quick fix or simple solution (Pedlar, Burgoyne and Boydell, 1991) and that organisations face challenges of culture, time, ownership and commitment (Chase, 1997) is hardly surprising given the nature and size of the task.

However, the debate is still live on how to promote individual learning for organisational advantage. Organisations still place 'enormous importance' on the creation of cultures that support learning and development for individuals, and for business benefit (CIPD, 2004c: 14), but the discussion has moved on, in part at least to the development of a coaching culture.

Making evaluation work: closing the loop

The initial diagrams for HRD strategy planning represented the process as a loop, where evaluation ultimately fed into the development of future plans.

Easterby-Smith and Mackness (1992) state that 'Training evaluation is commonly seen as a feedback loop, starting with course objectives and ending by collecting end-of-course reactions which are then generally filed away and not acted on' and the same likely applies to other learning and human resource development activities.

Closing the loop gives purpose to the evaluation activities, and without that there is little point in engaging in what is potentially difficult, complex and judgemental.

Stop & think

How can HRD evaluation make a contribution to the development of future plans and approaches?

HRD and national frameworks for vocational education and training

Introduction

This section presents a European perspective on National Vocational Education and Training (NVET or VET). Considering the broader national and international context of skills development has clear relevance for organisational HRD strategies often, the approaches spoken about here are how new recruits have acquired and continue to acquire knowledge and skills relevant to work. At this level it gives a practical understanding to how individuals and ultimately organisations learn. Furthermore, it allows consideration of how weaknesses in the national approach to skills development translate into skills deficiencies and shortages in organisations and correspondingly how strengths translate into innovation and organisational strength. Finally, it helps to underline the increasing importance of workplace learning as a source of competitiveness and supports similar arguments in previous sections.

There is a large body of evidence that suggests that organisational differences in human resource (HR) practices, including training and development, are related to variations in national legislation and cultural frameworks of a country and the national context is a primary factor which must not be ignored in the examination of determinants of training and development activity (Tregaskis and Dany, 1996). Learning and development are not solely the concern of individuals and their employers, but to ensure that a country achieves the level of skills it needs to compete internationally, they are also the concern of governments and European bodies. Trends in technology, the decline in the need for traditional skills, the aging of the population and changes in career and life spans are international issues and comparison works to aid comprehension of the issues and the position of vocational education in the UK as it appears to its competitors.

Since 1996, the UK government has published National Employers Skill Surveys which identify, among other things, the skills gaps and shortages experienced by the UK and academics have for many years drawn attention to the link between skills development and national productivity. Most attention has been focused on discovering the elements of education and training that can create successful companies, which then contribute to the economic strength of the nation. Wilson and Briscoe (2004) attribute a 1–3 per cent increase in GDP per capita growth to a 1 per cent increase in school enrolment rates. There is the assumption that since 'some education makes some of us rich, more would make more of us richer' (Wolf, 2002: 28). However, the relationship is not uncomplicated or uncontroversial. The national characteristics impact on the manner in which business systems, such as education and training, operate.

Finegold and Soskice (1988) discussed the two-way relationship between education and training and international competitiveness. They characterised Britain as trapped in a low skills equilibrium, which means 'a self-reinforcing network of societal and state institutions which interact to stifle the demand for improvements in skill levels' (1988: 22). The notion of and trend in developing a low-skills equilibrium meant that many UK organisations persisted in producing low added-value products and services that demanded low skills, so that UK employers had little incentive to invest in skills development (Hendry, 1994: 102).

Hall and Soskice (2001) provide another international perspective and a different dimension by placing the UK in a broader economic landscape. They examine critically the link between national level institutional structures and organisation level skills strategies. Using international data and drawing international comparisons, they identify two types of economy, namely *coordinated* market economies, and *liberal* market economies. The strength of the relationship between the national structures and organisational strategies determines the skills levels of the employees, and thus the competitiveness of the national economy.

Coordinated market economies, typified by Scandinavian countries such as Denmark, Sweden and the Netherlands, as well as Germany, are underpinned by strong inter-organisational relationships between investors and organisations, product differentiation strategies and cooperative networks between organisations. They rely on the development of high-value skills and task or sector specific skills development.

Liberal market economies (e.g. the UK, Australia, and the US) by contrast have less well-structured relationships between national structures and organisational strategies, employment security and protection is weaker, and as such economies rely on the development of portable and generic skills, fundamental shifts in products and services are more likely to be supported. (For a more detailed discussion of cross-national variety in employment policy and practice, see the section in Chapter 15 entitled 'National employment systems' (page 566).)

However, researching the link between education and training and economic growth is limited by the poor quality of data, particularly in inter-country comparisons, and by the fact that human capital is mostly measured by *formal* education, training and qualifications (Descy and Tessaring, 2005: 16).

Furthermore, the research underemphasises macro-social outcomes (crime, social cohesion, citizenship, civic and political participation) and individual benefits of education and training beyond the impact on company performance (Green *et al.*, 2005). Drawing conclusions about the link between education and macro-social outcomes is difficult as these 'effects are mostly indirect and conditional on other – often more powerful – contextual determinants' (Descy and Tessaring, 2005: 37). Furthermore, for the individual, there are likely to be substantial personal benefits – including better health, parenting, crime reduction and social inclusion (Descy and Tessaring, 2005: 39).

> Education and training are complex systems that do not exist in isolation but have social and economic roles. Reforming them is a process that requires debate and compromise on what is to be changed and for what reasons, not only between those in the systems but also other stakeholders, especially social partners. It is essential to envisage and to evaluate the internal consistency of a new policy with other elements of the system . . . but reforms also have to take into account the needs – and be coherent with the modes of functioning – of the productions system and of society more generally (external consistency). Traditional evaluations of policies or programmes focus strictly on policy as a separate entity, treating it as if it were self-contained and independent from the historical, structural and institutional context. This reinforces the tendency to design policies that are limited in scope and do not take into account the existing institutions and interventions as well as the modes of functioning of economic and social systems.
>
> (CEDEFOP/Descy and Tessaring, 2005: 21)

At the level of the business, there is strong evidence that investment in training and development generate substantial gains for firms (Descy and Tessaring, 2005: 38; Ballot, 2003; CIPD, 2005d). However, most investors do not appreciate the link, leading to under investment in profitable training programmes (DfES, 2005a: 38; Bassi *et al.*, 2001).

The consideration of national vocational education and training (NVET) systems is therefore complex and context bound, however, it is essential to ensure an understanding of national competitiveness.

The European dimension – VET in Europe

National vocational education and training systems (NVETs), providing training beyond compulsory school age exist internationally, but with differences in key features, aims and objectives and underlying principles. Particularly within Europe, the difficulty with this area is not that there is a dearth of information available, but that there is so much, in so many places. The European Commission (EC), the Organization for Economic Co-operation and Development (OECD), the European Centre for the Development of Vocational Training (CEDEFOP) and the Chartered Institute of Personnel and Development (CIPD) all provide information across a range of national systems of vocational education and training. However, despite the ease with which information can be found, realistic comparison is *not* easy given different political, social, economic, technological and legal development paths as well as different styles of management and cultural understanding.

This section of the chapter will consider comparative aspects of national systems of VET across Europe. There are a number of uniting themes in this context which allow side-by-side consideration of national VET systems, policies and procedures, not least because the European context is one which faces particular labour market challenges and changes (Descy and Tessaring, 2005: 21):

- Higher skills levels are needed, especially in modern, knowledge intensive, global economies.
- At the same time labour markets are becoming more polarised, with more precarious and repetitive jobs for the less educated.
- The population of the EU is aging, and this trend will be accelerated by the accession of new countries.
- The initial education level of the EU population is improving, but a substantial proportion is still typified by a low level of formal education.
- Unemployment is a concern, particularly after enlargement.
- Skill renewal through lifelong learning is becoming increasingly desirable in EU countries.

Furthermore, Europe is united by common goals in this area. The Lisbon European Council in 2001 set a strategic goal to make the EU, by 2010 'the most competitive and dynamic knowledge-based economy in the world, capable of sustainable economic growth with more and better jobs and greater social cohesion'. Subsequently, the Barcelona European Council in 2002 set the goal of making 'Europe's education and training systems a world quality reference by 2010'. These goals are to be achieved through comprehensive systems of lifelong learning, from nursery school to retirement.

Common objectives for education and training have been established to measure five reference levels of European average performance in education and training. These educational benchmarks (the 'Lisbon Goals') are intended to provide all citizens with the basic education they need in a knowledge-based society (EC, 2002):

By 2010:

- at least 85 per cent of 22-year olds should have completed upper secondary education;
- no more than 10 per cent of those aged 18–24 should have left school before completing upper secondary education or vocational or other training;
- the total number of graduates in mathematics, science and technology should have increased by 15 per cent while the gender imbalance should decrease;
- the percentage of 15-year olds with low achievement in reading literacy should have decreased by at least 20 per cent compared to 2000 levels;
- the average level of participation in lifelong learning of those aged 25 to 64 should be at least 12.5 per cent.

This has opened the door for a greater level of Europe-wide comparison and provided common targets for the EU.

Within this context then, this section attempts to outline the main components of Germany and France, to allow comparison with the UK approach to NVET considered later in this section.

The German system of VET

Germany's 'dual system' has remained one of the most frequently copied training systems in the world (Deissinger, 2000: 605) and is frequently given as an example of best practice. Germany's vocational education system relies on a dualism of learning venues, funding and legal responsibilities, placing responsibility for the funding and development of the programmes on a number of stakeholders. Training is workplace led and practical and skill requirements are defined around the workplace. Over the two to three years of the process, participants spend 30 per cent of their time in a vocational school, and 70 per cent in the workplace. The cost of the system is split between the employers and the state, in fact, employers have a legal responsibility to provide funding and resources for training. This 'dual system' is determined by the involvement of the federal and state administration, as well as employers' associations and trade unions, making occupational standards and conditions of apprenticeship legally enforceable.

Germany, like France, takes a process-oriented approach to education; that is, education paths are largely anchored in institutional (vocational or academic) communities. This contrasts with the fundamentally outcomes-oriented approach taken by English-speaking countries that is an essential element of vocational education and training (Deissinger, 2000).

Some 51 per cent of school leavers take part in one of the 370 training vocations across 23.3 per cent of all companies who provide training (www.bibb.de, March, 2006). For the employers, the cost of recruitment is low and businesses have an influence on the content and organisational of training. The trainees have the opportunity to earn while they are learning and acquire labour market relevant training. The on- and off-the-job instruction is carefully coordinated, producing a vocational course that provides development of three areas of skills: occupational competence (of systems and equipment), methodological competence (in reasoning and problem solving) and personal and social competence (team working and creativity) (Dybowski, 2005: 16).

Underpinning this is a strong sense of cooperation between the state and private organisations which is envied by the UK. The LSC's second (2005) Statement of Priorities (LSC, November 2005: 01) argues

> . . . we have to take a more collaborative, less transactional approach if we are to get the provision of learning right. That means building meaningful relationships with colleges, schools, providers and employers. Increasingly, our business will feature strategic discussions with local partners that recognise the need to channel resources to our priority areas for funding.

Activity ▶ **On the web 2**

The German Federal Institute of Vocational Education and Training has a multi-language website which provides a substantial amount of information and context on the German system of VET (www.bibb.de).

Explore this website for current issues and debates in the German system.

While much envied and mimicked, the German system is not immune to the challenges being faced across Europe. By early 2006, the number of in-company training places on offer had decreased noticeably since German reunification in 1999, largely as a result of a significant decline in the level of employment across Germany (Table 9.1). In the absence of a sufficiently large number of in-company training places, school leavers are opting for full-time courses of training (at an all-day vocational school). The Vocational Training Act has allowed the review of school-based training to place it on par with in-company 'dual' vocational training (Section 43 of the Act to Reform Vocational Education and Training). The predicted downward trend in the number of young people in Germany means that this problem is not easily resolvable. This trend is all the more problematic because the number of young people is predicted to decrease dramatically, leading to a substantial shortage of skilled workers in the future. Furthermore, the number of newly concluded training contracts in 2005 (550, 180) was at its lowest since 1999. This overall drop in participation has arguably provided the impetus for reform of the Vocational Training Act 1969 in the form of the Vocational Training Reform Act 2005. The first significant changes to the system in 35 years provide greater flexibility in the provision of training and a reduction of bureaucracy.

Table 9.1 Changes in newly concluded training contracts in 2005 compared to 2004 by fields of training

	2004	2005	Changes from previous year Absolute	In %
Industry/commerce*	322.759	316.165	−6.594	−2.0
Trades	168.290	157.025	−11.265	−6.7
Public service	15.130	14.171	−959	−6.3
Liberal professions	46.538	43.617	−2.921	−6.3
Home economics	4.876	4.119	−757	−15.5
Ocean shipping	196	298	102	52
Total	572.980	550.180	−22.800	−4.0

*Newly concluded training contracts per area of responsibility.
Periods of coverage: 1 October to 30 September.

Source: Results of BIBB survey for 30 September 2005: as of 13 December 2005, www.bibb.de, 19 January 2006.

&
think

Deissinger (2000: 605) argues that Germany's 'dual system' continues to exist because of a 'deeply rooted disinclination to reform' and because 'it has remained one of the most frequently copied training systems in the world'.

Question

What are the disadvantages of the German system?

The French system of VET

The French system of vocational training is a complex and comprehensive one, with a long period of historical development (CEDEFOP, 2000: 32). In short, the French Government's commitment to VET and lifelong learning (la formation professionnelle permanente) is embodied in three levels of provision:

1 The secondary education system:
    ● Baccalauréat Professionelle: a four-year course which confers a qualification in a given occupation;
    ● the Baccalauréat Technologique: which confers a qualification in a given *technology.*
2 Higher education: which offers job-related courses.
3 Formation Professionnelle Continué (CVT): continuing education post school.

There is a growing emphasis in France on *alternance* training or apprenticeship which involves the employer in the provision of training, gives the participant the status of employee rather than student, and has the aim of bringing training closer to practice and ease the transition to working life (CEDEFOP, 2000).

The French system relies on the training tax or levy introduced in 1971 and the need for the provision of training to be measurable and accountable has resulted in an emphasis on the use of formal courses at the expense of informal on-the-job learning (CIPD, 2001c). Each company and the self-employed, pay a percentage of their wage bill to fund employee training and leave, initial vocational training, and encourage the development of training plans. The levy represents 1.5 per cent of the wage bill of companies with over 10 employees. The funds are used to address both the training needs of particular industries and to develop generic skills across the industries. The French system offers compulsory paid training leave with up to 95 per cent of wages paid during the leave. However, as companies must provide training, or pay the levy, it is seen by many as a penalty, and companies unwilling or unable to train staff opt to pay the levy (CIPD, 2001c; Finegold and Levine, 1997).

The French system is, like others, under some considerable pressure. Rising, and dramatic, youth unemployment, with 20 per cent of 18- to 25-year-olds unemployed (more than twice the national average) is being tackled under the 'Battle for Jobs' (www.premier-ministre.gouv.fr, 16 March 2006). However, the French Prime Minister was forced to abandon a new first-job contract or CPE (contrat première embauche) on 10 April 2006, after prolonged and extensive public demonstrations and unrest.

&
think

Greinert (2002) presents three paradigms which lend shape and form to the institutions in the countries they relate to. How far can you see Greinert's paradigms reflected in the NVET systems in France, Germany and the UK?

● *In Britain the production relationship is regarded as no more than a market process in which the market participants are members of society. The image of law is correspondingly negative.*
● *In France, the production relationship is seen as a political entity. Central control of working life is given to the state.*
● *In Germany the production relationship is regarded as a kind of community which has a tradition of reciprocal responsibility and consideration of the whole. It is based on active social partnership.*

Implications of European comparisons for the UK

We can see from this section's introduction that the performance of the economy in the UK is dependent on the development of the skills required in the labour market. The internationalisation of markets means that this is done on a globally competitive stage, and the comparative state of the UK is one which sees a narrowing productivity gap between the UK and other nations, and lower unemployment, but still a lower output per hour than France, Germany and the USA (LSC, 2004).

Each country we have considered has a number of routes through education and training. While the sequential nature of the French system contrasts with the dual system of the German system, we will see from the next section that the UK's approach is the most diffuse, complex and lacking in clarity. Keep and Mayhew (2001) describe the UK approach as a 'blizzard of initiatives' with a system of qualifications that is a 'sprawling, complex mess, incomprehensible to employers and trainees alike' which involves 'near-ceaseless organisational change' that does not produce results, and fails to deliver lasting and significant change on a number of fronts.

The link between learning and work is less well cemented in the UK than in the other countries we have considered. Thanks to the German Dual System, young people there spend a longer period of time in education, with signification participation in work during study, than in the UK (OECD, 2005).

While the proportion of educational attainment has grown in France and the UK, Germany's rate is the highest, and is similar among the 25–34 and 40–54 age groups. In 17 out of 20 OECD countries, upper secondary graduation rates exceed 70 per cent. The UK sits right on this boundary for 25–34 year-olds, and below it for 45–54 year olds. France and Germany both exceed 80 per cent for 25–34 year-olds. As people grow older, they participate less in education (OECD, 2005; LSC, 2004).

Westwood (2001) identifies that access to workforce development in the UK is unequal, with management and professionals or those with a degree up to five times more likely to receive work-based training than people with no qualification and/or in an unskilled job (Westwood, 2001: 19). Green *et al.* (2002) report that 71 per cent of unskilled workers in their study were excluded from training in the preceding five years.

These issues raise questions about the role of skills development in the UK and the following consideration of the UK's approach attempts to answer some of these.

VET in the UK

Introduction

> We seek a fair society which ensures that every individual irrespective of background, ethnicity, gender, faith, disability or postcode, is helped to realise their own capability for learning, and raise their quality of life. We also seek a dynamic economy where our national and regional productivity is enhanced through high-skilled, well-rewarded employees working in companies committed to long-term investment and leading the world in their business sectors.
>
> (DfES, 2005b)

> Unless Britain has the requisite stock of skills, including entrepreneurship, innovation and technical capability, then the goal of achieving a high-value added, high-productivity economy [will] remain elusive.
>
> (LSC, 2004: iii)

The history of workforce development is well documented elsewhere (Cannell, 2004, Harrison, 2005), and this section focuses on more contemporary aspects of government approaches and initiatives to developing an economically productive workforce. This brief summary will help to outline the background to skills development, and the nature of the changes in the last 35 years.

1973–1997: national survival

Until 1979 there was no clear vision for national education and training policy. Attempts to raise the national profile of the issues in 1973 were embodied in the Employment and Training Act which had introduced the Manpower Services Commission (MSC) and a national Training Services Agency (TSA). This underlined the growing role of training in national competitiveness and indicated a stronger role for the government in regulating training. A major outcome of the MSC was the Youth Opportunities Programme (YOP) offering work experience and work preparation courses. This was a major part of the government's attempts to reduce unemployment as it grew dramatically in the late 1970s.

In 1979, the new Conservative government, led by Margaret Thatcher, heralded a less interventionist and market-led approach which continued the voluntaristic view of individual and employer responsibility for workplace training and development. However, the level of intervention grew as academic criticism of the UK's approach to training and skills development gathered pace. The 'cradle-to-grave' approach to skills development included the introduction of National Vocational Qualifications (NVQs) in 1986 and the Education Reform Act in 1988 which changed the system of GCSEs with the aim of enhancing educational standards and vocational choice and providing greater parity between vocational and academic qualifications. The notion of competence was central to these approaches and has remained at the heart of the UK's NVET since then.

Training Enterprise Councils (1989, replaced in 2001 by Learning Skills Councils) completed this tranche of changes and had as their aim to make training policy sensitive and responsive to local business needs, and to accelerate business growth.

The 1991 White Paper *Education and Training for the 21st Century*, although focused still on individual and employer responsibility, set out seven aims for national vocational education and training. Investors in People was launched in 1991 and provided national accreditation for workplaces who met a set of standards which valued learning and development. A piecemeal approach continued during the boom and bust entrepreneurial age of the late 1990s until the change of government in 1997.

1997–2006: national competitiveness and upskilling

The new Labour government in 1997 recognised that the approach taken by the previous government had had limited impact on the competitiveness of the nation, as, despite having the fourth largest economy in the world, the UK's productivity lagged, and lags, behind the most advanced countries. While the UK's productivity has improved significantly over the last 10 years compared with that in other countries, the level of productivity in the UK remains below that in other developed countries and on a Gross Domestic Product (GDP) per worker basis, is lower than that of France and the USA, similar to that of Germany, and above that of Japan (ONS, 2004, 2006). Economic growth rates in the UK are no higher now than at the end of the Second World War (Elliot, 2004). Combined with increased competition from the Far East and challenging demographic trends as the population ages, the UK faces new challenges in developing skills to match the global competitive environment (LSC, 2005: 6). That said, the UK labour market has been, since 1997, characterised by reducing unemployment, increased educational attainment and the increased participation of women in employment and in 2003/4, investment in education and training as a proportion of GDP rose from 4.7 per cent in 1996/7 to 5.3 per cent (Cuddy and Lenny, 2005).

One of the first tasks of the Labour government which came to power in 1997 was to establish the National Skills Task Force (NSTF) which embraced the case, made for many years by academics and researchers, that developing the skills of the workforce was a way of improving the UK's productivity and competitiveness in the global marketplace. The problem has been a lasting one, as recent government documents highlight the issues still persists. *The National Employers Skills Survey* (LSC, 2004) reiterates the findings of previous years (LSC, 2001; LSC, 2003); one in five employers reported skills gaps in their workforce (representing 7 per cent of the total workforce in England), and, specifically, employers identify shortages among applicants for vacant posts in technical and practical skills, communication skills, customer handling, team-working and problem-solving skills. While overall, there has been little change in the proportions of vacancies attributed to shortages in these main skill areas, there has been 'a relatively large increase in the incidence of literacy and numeracy skill shortages being reported (LSC, 2004: 8).

In order to combat the limitations of previous approaches, the focus in the last decade in the UK has been one of up-skilling the workforce and developing a focus on lifelong learning through a variety of initiatives which have had a major effect on HRD in the UK (Lee, 2004: 334). Some 94 per cent of employers agree that up-skilling their workforce is important to achieving their business strategy (CIPD, 2005), so at both an organisational and national level, the development of workforce skills is vitally important. *Learning to Succeed 1999*, the government's White Paper on lifelong learning specifies local authorities, employers, the voluntary sector and trade unions as vital partners in up-skilling the workforce in the context of lifelong learning.

Since 1997, the Labour government has taken a proactive approach to developing the skills base of the UK's workforce. The new millennium has seen a proliferation of initiatives in order to raise the bar on workforce development. The Learning and Skills Act 2000, the February 2005 White Paper, *14–19 Education and Skills*, the *Skills Strategy White Papers* in 2003 and 2005, which followed the launch of *Skills for Life* in 2001, and the Strategy Units comprehensive action plan for skills development to 2010 (Strategy Unit, 2001, 2002) set out the government's agenda for the demand-led development of workforce skills at a national, organisational and individual level. The *Skills Strategy* is at the heart of the Government's attempts to improve skills in the UK and runs alongside specific reforms aimed at 14-19 year-olds. It aims to 'ensure that employers have the right skills to support the success of their businesses and individuals have the skills they need to be both employable and personally fulfilled (Strategy Unit, 2003: 11).

The strategy, which is essentially demand- and market-led, and is still voluntary for the most part, is underpinned by a number of government initiatives and bodies which are outlined below. There is very little substantive legal regulation in this area and almost without exception the government's role is one of providing a policy context rather than a legal one. However, there is clear evidence of increasing involvement by the state (Cuddy and Lenny, 2005).

Finally, the Government commissioned the Leitch Review of Skills 'to identify the UK's optimal skills mix in 2020 to maximise economic growth, productivity and social justice, and to consider the policy implications of achieving the level of change required' (www.hm-treasury.gov.uk, 5 April 2006). It published its interim report 'Skills in the UK: The long-term challenge' on 5 December 2005, and was due to report to the Government during 2006 on the gap between the likely skills profile in 2020 and the skills profile that ought to be aimed for, and the consequences of this.

However, despite this activity to raise levels of qualification in the population, to increase employability and improve competitiveness and productivity in the UK, major decisions about workplace training and HRD are still in the hands of employers and the VET system is still a voluntaristic one (Lenny *et al.*, 2004).

Government initiatives in the UK: vocational education and training

The UK has one of the highest levels of participation in continuing vocational training courses in the EU (beaten only by the Netherlands, Sweden and Germany) (Cuddy and Lenny, 2005: 22) with 87 per cent of all employees. In the UK, schooling to the standards of the national curriculum is compulsory from 5–16 years. At 16 most pupils take public examinations – GCSEs – in a range of single subjects and thereafter choose to continue at school, attend a sixth form college, undertake an apprenticeship, or leave and enter employment. Those remaining at school choose between academic and vocational subjects and from 16–19 can undertake GCEs (A-levels). Since September 2004, there has been a statutory requirement for schools to provide all students with work-related learning opportunities (Cuddy and Lenny, 2005).

While there is no required distinction between academic and vocational qualifications in the UK, there is a clear inequality between them, and within the systems as vocational qualifications are viewed as second-class to the academic and disadvantaged groups are badly served, with staying-on rates poor, and drop-out rates high among low-income learners (DfES, 2005b: 21). This separation between vocational and academic learning is criticised as being counter to the reality of people's lives where 'individual, societal and industrial challenges are interwoven' (Stevenson, 2003).

Vocational qualifications

In the UK, vocational education and training includes a wide range of qualifications, structures and awarding bodies. Broadly speaking, vocational qualifications offer an introduction to a career or industry sector, are practically focused and result in a recognisable qualification or award. The awards are based on the achievement of competencies.

> At the core of the term skill is the idea of competence or proficiency . . . skill is the ability to perform a task to a pre-defined standard of competence . . . but also connotes a dimension of increasing ability . . . skills therefore go hand in hand with knowledge.　　(NSTF, 2000)

This competency-based approach is at the heart of vocational qualifications in the UK and across the world. While this approach is sometimes criticised (Armstrong, 1996; Kandola, 1996) there is no sign of it disappearing.

Vocational qualifications include:

- Vocational subjects at GCSE level.

- A Vocational Certificates of Education (VCE) which are groups of A-levels in a range of work-related subjects.

- National Vocational Qualifications (GNVQs and NVQs) which demonstrate the skills and knowledge required for particular occupations, covering the main aspects of an occupation, including current best practice, the ability to adapt to future requirements and the knowledge and understanding to enable an employee to perform well. At the heart of NVQs are National Occupational Standards which describe the work competencies required of an individual in a range of occupations.

- Higher National Certificates and Diplomas (HNCs and HNDs) which are vocational higher education qualifications. They are an alternative route for students who want to get a higher education without studying for a degree and normally last two years, as opposed to the three years normally required of an academic higher education qualification.

- Vocational qualifications (VQs) offered by a number of other awarding bodies with the National Qualifications Framework (NQF) ensuring the consistency and reliability of all the qualifications. There are vocational qualifications covering almost every industry sector, and every level of the NQF (www.directgov.co.uk).

All qualifications are classified in the 'National Qualifications Framework' introduced in 2000 and updated in 2006 to classify all qualifications from entry level to level 8. Entry level qualifications recognise basic knowledge and skills and the ability to apply learning in everyday situations under direct guidance or supervision. Learning at this level involves building basic knowledge and skills and is not geared towards specific occupations. Level 8 qualifications by contrast recognise leading experts or practitioners in a particular field. Learning at this level involves the development of new and creative approaches that extend or redefine existing knowledge or professional practice. This scale makes the qualifications transparent for users, learners and potential employers so that the former know what they have to learn and the latter know what they can expect.

Apprenticeships as part of the VET framework provide work-based training in a range of sectors and combine working with gaining recognised qualifications. They consist of three elements – an NVQ (an occupationally specific qualification assessed and delivered in the workplace), Key Skills at an appropriate level (including communication, ICT, application of number) and a technical certificate (underpinning knowledge of the technical or business terms, delivered in an FE college). They are not age limited. Funded and managed by the LSCs, they had as a central aim the reduction of the 'skills gap' in the UK and a target of getting 28 per cent of 16–21 year-olds entering apprenticeships by 2005 (http://www.apprenticeships.org.uk). There are over 60 apprenticeships and advanced apprenticeships available in over 80 different industries (Cuddy and Lenny, 2005).

Academic qualifications

The government's growing reliance and emphasis on the importance of tertiary (university/higher) education in the UK is not without consequence. Keep and Mayhew (2004: 298) argue that underpinning the government's policy of expanding higher education are the beliefs that it is necessary to transform economic performance and that it can aid social justice by opening up higher-earning jobs to those from lower socio-economic backgrounds.

However, they go on to argue that the evidence for a positive economic impact is at best ambiguous (Keep and Mayhew, 1996b; Keep *et al.* 2002), and the rest of the vocational and educational system is likely to suffer as a result. This ambiguity is evidenced in the fact that 'There will remain a substantial number of jobs with vocational requirements below degree level, not least in craft and technical operations. It is doubtful whether graduate courses (honours or foundation) are an effective or efficient means of meeting such demand' (Keep and Mayhew, 2004: 299; Mayhew, *et al.*, 2004).

Additionally, the emphasis on academic participation has not resulted in sound economic growth. 'The explosion in graduate output over the last 15 years has not been accompanied by any concomitant uplift in productivity growth (Keep and Mayhew, 2004: 299).

Foundation degrees, introduced in 2001, are an attempt at bridging the gap between the skills required by employers and the skills acquired during academic qualifications. They are degree-level qualifications designed in partnership with employers to create the knowledge and skills to improve business performance and profitability (www.foundationdegree.org.uk). They offer work placement opportunities within them, and are assessed on a blend of academic and vocational ability, through part-time distance learning, e-learning, workplace learning, modular provision and where students do need to attend college or university, local provision. There is some resemblance between these and the German 'dual system' considered earlier in the chapter.

Lifelong learning

In the UK, the decision on access to further education beyond statutory school age is left to the individual except in cases where a job requires certain entry qualifications (an individualistic approach). Although government places increasing importance on upskilling the workforce, training policies are left to employers (a voluntaristic approach). The UK performs comparatively well on short, workplace training courses, but overall levels of qualification compare unfavourably with several other EU countries.

(Cuddy and Lenny, 2005: 36)

The notion of lifelong learning embodies the greater attention paid to vocational education by policy makers in the UK. In the most recent government White Paper on this area *Skills: Getting on in business, Getting on at work* (March 2005) the government outlines its plans to increase skills levels through lifelong learning initiatives. Lifelong learning is understood to mean 'the provision of an interconnected, universal system of education and training that permits high quality learning from early years to retirement. It allows learners to earn recognised and clearly understood qualifications, and to build on them over their lives' (DfES, 2005b).

The UK has a comparatively high level of participation in adult learning, with the largest percentage in the OECD of workers aged 30–39 who report having been enrolled in full- or part-time training (OECD, 2004).

Box 9.6 **Too much apple pie?**

Thompson (2001) argued that 'Lifelong learning is something of an "apple pie" concept. Hardly anyone is actively against the encouragement of perpetual access to education and training, but, beyond the warm rhetoric, lifelong learning proves to be a tricky term, full of tensions, contradictions and questions about what sort of learning is valued, who it's for and who ought to be funding it . . . Equally depressing is the suspicion, voiced recently by John Field, professor of lifelong learning at the University of Warwick, that the share of all learning taken by people aged over 25 may have fallen dramatically over the past five years, while the share among the 16–24 age group has risen. Indeed, government policies may be making little, if any, difference to opportunities for learning later in life . . . It is not unreasonable for a business to focus training and development on areas of immediate benefit and to concentrate learning opportunities among those who might be expected to deliver the greatest short-term returns on its investment. The problem is that, overall, this results in a volume and pattern of opportunity distribution that everyone agrees is insufficient, wasteful of human potential and not conducive to an inclusive business culture.'

Learning and Skills Council

The Learning and Skills Act (2000) overhauled the funding and planning of post-compulsory education and training in the UK by establishing the Learning and Skills Council (LSC). The LSC is responsible for planning and funding all post-16 education (but not university education) and training in England. In the financial year 2006–2007, the LSC received £10.4 billion to invest in learning and skills (LSC, 2005). This expenditure covers (LSC, 2005):

- School sixth forms.
- 16–19 further education.
- Work-based learning.
- 19+ further education.
- National Employer Training Programmes (NETP).
- Personal and Community Development Learning.
- Learners with learning disabilities and/or difficulties.
- Learner Support Funds.
- University for Industry/learndirect.
- 14–19 years skills and quality reform.

A network of local LSCs serve counties across England and the priorities are delivered through an array of local and national bodies, both government and private bodies (LSC, 2005).

Trade union learning representatives

Trade unions play a growing role in the government's learning and skills agenda. They have representatives on Regional Development Agencies (and devolved equivalents in Scotland, Wales and Northern Ireland), at the Sector Skills Councils boards and on LSCs. Additionally, Union learning representatives were established by legislation in 2002 to provide advice and guidance to union members on their training, educational and development needs. Particularly, their role is to encourage members to think about the benefits of training and learning, understand the options available to them, encourage the low skilled into education and training, and to support those with higher level skills to engage in continuing professional development (Cuddy and Lenny, 2005).

Sector Skills Councils

The Sector Skills Development Agency (SSDA), launched in September 2002, is a UK-wide non-departmental body network of 25 (and increasing) employer-led sector skills councils covering 85 per cent of the UK's workforce.

The aims of the agency are to reduce skills gaps and shortages; improve productivity, business and public service performance; increase opportunities to boost the skills and productivity of everyone in the sector's workforce and improve learning supply including apprenticeships, higher education and National Occupational Standards (NOS). SSC provide a forum for discussion and network building to ensure that skills and productivity needs of employers and employees are met by course providers.

Investors in People

The Investors in People (IiP) Standard was developed in 1990 and revised in 2004 (placing emphasis on employee involvement and on maximising their potential) and is a national quality standard setting a level of good practice for improving an organisation's performance and competitiveness through a planned approach to setting and communicating business objectives and developing people to meet these objectives.

The IiP Standard is based on three principles:

- *Strategy*: developing strategies to improve the performance of the organisation.
- *Action*: taking action to improve the performance of the organisation.
- *Evaluation*: evaluating the impact on the performance of the organisation.

There are ten indicators grouped under these key principles which form the basis of measurement against the standard. Organisations are assessed against the standard on the basis of evidence and self-assessment. Once the organisation has achieved the standard, and been recognised as such, this can be maintained through reassessment at no more than three-yearly intervals. The achievement of the standard requires investment and effort on the part of the business, but the processes followed to achieve this and the outcomes are likely to have considerable organisational benefits (Taylor and Thackwray, 1995).

LSCs and Business Links provide guidance and advice on the IiP Standard and assessment and recognition are considered by a network of nine Regional Quality Centres across England, and four others to cover Scotland, Wales and Northern Ireland. In practice LSCs provide advice to organisations with over 250 employees, and Business Links to smaller organisations. Organisations' first point of contact in order to start the assessment process would be one of these organisations.

Despite the popularity of the Standard, particularly among larger employers, in 2001, IiP had reached only 1.5 per cent of all employers 11 years after its creation (CIPD, 2001c: 56). However, Spellman (2001) estimates that this represents a third of the working population, as most organisations that have achieved recognition are larger, prominent, high-profile businesses with high numbers of employees.

Professional organisations

Professional organisations, particularly those with 'Chartered Status' (see Box 9.7) have a clear role in developing the skills of those in the professions they represent. Some have formal links with the Sector Skills Development Agency (SSDA) and make a contribution to the development of the National Occupational Standard in their area of work.

The scope of each individual organisation is different, but all require a level of assessed membership based on experience, competence or qualifications. Many offer different levels of membership reflecting different levels within each profession, some with designatory letters. Three organisations which may be of particular interest to readers of this text are shown in Table 9.2. A full list of all Chartered bodies is available at the Privy Council's website, www.privy-council.org.uk.

Scotland, Wales and Northern Ireland

Throughout this section, the predominant view has been that of the UK, but in many sections this applies only to England as the devolution of governance in the UK means that the govern-

Table 9.2

Chartered body, date charter granted and professional grades of membership	Website	Aims, objectives and central functions
Chartered Management Institute (2002) ACMI (Associate) MCMI (Member) FCMI (Fellow) CCMI (Companion)	www.managers.org.uk	The mission of the Institute is to promote the art and science of management by encouraging and supporting the lifelong development of managers, by raising the level of management, by initiating, developing, evaluating and disseminating management thinking, tools, techniques and practices, by influencing employers, policy makers and opinion formers on management, by ensuring all Institute members all work to a code of professional management practice that sets high standards of conduct, competence, judgement and integrity for practising managers. The Institute is home to the Management Standards Centre which is the nationally recognised standard setting body for management which continues the work carried out by the 'Management Charter Initiative' (MCI). The Centre is an independent unit within the Institute under contract to the Sector Skills Development Agency (SSDA).
Chartered Institute of Personnel Development (2000) MCIPD (Member) FCIPD (Fellow) CCIPD (Companion)	www.cipd.co.uk	The Chartered Institute of Personnel and Development (CIPD) is the professional body for those involved in the management and development of people. It aims to lead in the development and promotion of good practice in the field of the management and development of people, for application both by professional members and by their organisational colleagues, to serve the professional interests of members and to uphold the highest ideals in the management and development of people.
Chartered Institute of Management Accountants (CIMA) (1919) ACIMA (Associate) FCIMA (Fellow)	www.cimaglobal.com	To promote and develop the science of Management Accountancy. To research the best means and methods of developing and applying the science, and promoting knowledge, education and training, and the exchange of ideas and information in the field.

Box 9.7	**What is chartered status?**

Royal Charters are normally reserved for bodies that work in the public interest (such as professional institutions, charities and companies of which there are around 400 in the UK) that can 'demonstrate pre-eminence, stability and permanence in their particular field' (www.privy-council.org.uk). Many older universities in England, Wales and Northern Ireland are also chartered bodies.

A Royal Charter is granted by the Privy Council. The Privy Council is the part of the Government of the UK which advises on the exercise of prerogative powers and certain functions assigned to The Queen and the Council by Act of Parliament. Members of the Privy Council, who are primarily former and current members of both Houses of Parliament, including all Cabinet ministers, are appointed for life, but only ministers of the Government of the day have a role to play in its policy work. Chartered bodies that are incorporated by Royal Charter, and their affairs are a large part of the day to day work of the Privy Council (www.privy-council.org.uk).

ment and institutional frameworks differ between England, Wales, Northern Ireland and Scotland. (For a fuller description of the divisions of responsibility see Cuddy and Lenny, 2005.) For example,

- While overall policy responsibility for vocational education and skills lies with the Department for Education and Skills in England, in Wales this is the Welsh Assembly Government Department for Training and Education, in Northern Ireland it is the Department for Employment and Learning Northern Ireland (DELNI), and in Scotland it is the Scottish Executive Enterprise, Transport and Lifelong Learning Department.

- Funding of Providers in the learning and skills sector (colleges of further education, adult learning and work-based providers is the responsibility of National Learning and Skills Councils (LSC) in England, but in Wales it is the Welsh Assembly Government Department for Training and Education and in Scotland it falls to Scottish Enterprise (SEn) and Highlands and Islands Enterprise (HIE) working with local enterprise companies (LECs).

Areas where there are no differences include:

- Department of Trade and Industry (DTI):
- Improvements in productivity and skills
- Sector Skills Development Agency (SSDA):
- Overall responsibility for developing occupational standards and the licensing of sector skills bodies.
- Development of occupational standards for specific economic sectors, together with work to identify and reduce sectoral skills gaps and increase opportunities for workforce.

Conclusions

It is easy to find criticisms of the UK's 'myriad of national, regional and local agencies' (Unwin, 2004) which make up its approach to vocational education and training. Critics reflect on (Unwin, 2004):

- employer inertia;
- lack of investment and interest in training;
- policy makers' short-sightedness and ultimate failure;

- low quality training provision;
- lack of information for employees;
- the dual standards between academic and vocational learning and training.

However, the UK government is investing heavily in developing its skills strategy, the LSC and SSDA, all of which represent unifying initiatives in the previously disparate system. Yet, the proliferation of initiatives underneath these bodies mean that employers are often confused by what is available, or reluctant to invest where the outcomes are not clear. The continuity of the systems in France and German are examples of where consistency has meant strength and clarity.

What ought to be done to improve the UKs system of VET? What practical recommendations would you make to policy makers to clarify the system and the responsibilities of the key players within it?

What are the challenges ahead?

The UK now has the emergent institutional infrastructures to move from a low-skills/low-tech equilibrium to a high-skills/high-tech economy. Given the rapidity and strength of the competitive challenges globalisation is bringing, the case for this is unanswerable. However, much political and institutional will is required to ensure that the UK, along with the rest of the European Union, becomes a dynamic knowledge economy in the future . . . Despite the widespread perception that the UK's training system is largely dysfunctional, the cumulative impact of reforms undertaken since 1997 is beginning to be significant – if so far largely unremarked on. Action is being taken . . . and the UK can close our 'human capital gap'.

(Hutton, W. and The Work Foundation, 2005)

Whether the UK can or cannot close the 'human capital gap' remains a pressing issue. The following issues are proposed as the main themes for debate on the future of HRD:

- *Skills and knowledge.* Britain can (probably) never compete with the 'large armies of inexpensive offshore workers' (Gentleman, 2005) offered by countries in the Far East and Africa and so it must find other ways of differentiating itself in the global market place to be competitive and successful as a nation. For some time now, the role of knowledge as a strategic resource has been recognised:

Knowledge and information are becoming the strategic resource and transforming agent of the post-industrial society . . . just as the combination of energy, resources and machine technology were the transformational agencies of industrial societies.

(Bell, 1980: 531)

The productivity of knowledge and knowledge workers will not be the only competitive factor in the world economy. It is however, likely to become the decisive factor, at least for most industries in the developed countries.

(Druker, 1998: 17)

Knowledge-based industries (e.g. financial services, information technologies etc.) . . . operate by . . . selectively appropriating information as a key resource to be exploited . . . [with] highly specialised knowledge as a key resource from which . . . significant returns on investments can be earned.

(Cooke, 2002: 71)

Many writers argue that there has been a profound change in the nature of work so that there is a reliance on 'creativity . . . and intellective skills' (Frenkel *et al.*, 1995: 780). If this is the case then, the future of UK skill development is likely to be twofold: developing the 'intellective' skills of the workforce, and in capturing the knowledge on which they rely.

The rise in interest in 'knowledge management' over the years is evidence of the growing importance of this area. (Issues relating to this are covered in the previous chapter.)

- *The link between workplace training and competitiveness.* This section identifies that the problematic relationship between workplace training and development and national competitiveness remains.

  Firstly, Crouch and Sako (2001) argue that improved skills levels do not necessarily solve unemployment, and improved levels of education and training may simply produce overqualified workers. Furthermore, if employers, as they do in the UK, provide skills training independent of government initiatives, then the government is left to sweep up the 'bottom third, the less able' (Unwin, 2004) who have been excluded from the investment of their employers in the past and may be unemployed in the present. The contribution that this level of development makes to national competitiveness is unclear. We have seen from the French VET system that high unemployment, especially among young people has proved problematic and can note the challenges that now face the German system as unemployment rises. Thirdly, while most recognise the value and worth of training and development, few claim to be able to isolate the effects of it on economic growth. Attempts have been made with varied results.

It remains to be seen then, whether the continuing voluntarist approach of the Labour government can carry the country forward in a competitive global market.

Summary

- This chapter has considered the shifts in the HRD landscape, especially the change in rhetoric and reality from training to learning, and the contribution that learning can make to business performance.

- The discussion of practical issues of HRD in an organisational context provided a clear structure for the strategic assessment of the contribution of HRD to organisational performance: from establishing needs, through designing and delivering learning and training, to closing the loop through evaluating the value added by the interventions. There was also an outline of the central methods for the delivery of training and their relative effectiveness.

- Of particular contemporary interest were the issues which surround coaching and e-learning, and the enduring interest in 'learning organisations'.

- Then, the chapter set the scene for the discussion of NVET by considering the link between education and economic growth and then discussed the European context of vocational education and training (VET) and provided a comparative analysis of the approaches in Germany, France and the UK, drawing critical conclusions in assessing the value and effectiveness of the individual national approaches as they strive to achieve the Lisbon Goals.

- Finally, the chapter concluded with identifying the key challenges ahead if the UK is to be competitive in a global marketplace.

1 The learning cycle is aspirational and textbook and does not bear comparison with messy organisational reality. How far would you agree with this statement?

2 Human Capital Reporting is now required by law in Operating and Financial Reviews for Companies. To what extent is the evaluation of HRD interventions truly possible? How can businesses demonstrate the contribution to the 'bottom line'?

3 To what extent is there a business benefit in developing a coaching culture? Is it just the latest management fad or are there demonstrable benefits for businesses?

4 What impact do government initiatives really have on business performance?

EXERCISES

1 The notion of the learning organisation – is it alive or dead? Is it something that is worth working towards? Working in two groups, prepare your case for each side of the argument and present it to the whole group.

2 What steps would you take if you were tasked with achieving Investors In People status for your organisation? What would be the benefits of achieving it? What would be the spin-off benefits of simply going through the process?

3 Compare the UK, French and German systems of VET. Read further in the CEDEFOP, CIPD and other information. What can the UK learn from the approaches of other nations? What does the UK do well, or less well than other countries?

CASE STUDY 1

Wealden District Council

The organisation

Wealden District Council was established as a local authority in 1974. Embracing 320 miles of East Sussex, it stretches from the Kent borders to the sea, and is the largest district council in the South East. Its 135 000 population is scattered among rural villages and four substantial market towns.

It provides a range of services, including planning and development, refuse collection, environmental health, housing and leisure services. A staff of 560 is divided between two offices, four leisure centres, two depots and 19 sheltered dwellings. The Council, with no overall control, has 58 elected councillors, serving on ten committees and subcommittees.

The challenge

The Council aims to offer the highest possible standard of service within the constraints of its budget, customer care being of paramount importance.

Particular challenges have continued to include:

- the introduction of compulsory competitive tendering, with the cost of services being tested in the open market against commercial operators;
- new legislation affecting large areas of the Council's work;
- the consolidation of Audit Commission performance indicators against which service performance is stringently measured;
- the requirement to work to constrained budgets, while delivering consistently high levels of service;
- introducing and developing new indicators for the benefit of the customer.

The objective continues to be to deliver a consistently high standard of service across an organisation widespread in location and function, with all the elements working harmoniously together, against a background of change.

Source: Printed with the kind permission of Investors in People.

Question

What strategy would you recommend Wealden District Council to follow in order to achieve its aims?

Smart cookies

This case study is concerned with a training programme instituted in Fox's Biscuits that won a training award from the CIPD.

The Fox's Biscuits factory near Kirkham, near Preston, was the poorest performing site within Northern Foods five years ago. Today it is viewed as the jewel in the group's crown.

The plant, which produces 12 000 biscuits every minute for the likes of Marks and Spencer, Asda and Sainsbury's, has an impressive list of achievements since 1995. Of the 345 employees in manufacturing, 181 have achieved NVQ level 1 in food and drink, 128 have completed level 2 and 25 are about to finish level 3. Absence rates have decreased significantly, while staff turnover has dropped from 11 per cent to 9 per cent.

According to its managers, it is also now the most cost-effective biscuit manufacturer in the industry. It has even opened its doors to share best practice with household names such as Guinness, Eden Vale and Ross Young.

'We have used training to revolutionise both the manufacturing process and the company's culture,' says Charlotte Greenwood, senior personnel and training officer.

What's more, it has achieved all this without external help. 'It's unusual not to use consultants for this type of project,' says Linda Atkins, personnel manager. 'But we felt that we had enough skills and expertise on site and the right people to carry it through.'

Before 1995, millions of pounds had been invested in new technology for the site, but little had been spent on giving employees the skills to operate it. Several other key people management problems also needed tackling, so the senior management team had to act.

'We have a long-serving workforce with a low skills base and, in some cases, poor literacy. There were also communication problems,' Atkins says. 'Because of the way in which the work teams were structured, there was little accountability or ownership. We had a traditional, autocratic culture and there was a lack of trust in managers. There were also too many layers of management – about seven or eight – and a very complex shift system that created huge problems.'

The first stage of the turnaround saw the reorganisation and delayering of the management team. Areas of responsibility were defined more clearly and appraisals were introduced to identify skills gaps among managers.

The restructuring also applied to the factory floor. Previously, separate teams of mixers, bakers and packers had worked across all six production lines. The employees now work in multidisciplinary teams, which are responsible for all processes from mixing ingredients to packing the finished products on each line. 'Under the old system, the process could – and did – fall down quickly,' says Ian Jackson, factory manager. 'There were grey areas surrounding who was responsible for what stage of the process. Each of the teams operated as its own little unit. They didn't talk to each other. In fact there was very little communication along the manufacturing process.'

While members of each team are now able to do each other's work, the company has introduced the concept of 'principal job' to allow people to specialise. It has also established standard working practices for each job type and rationalised the shift system.

The company then turned its attention to developing the skills of the operating teams. Senior managers and factory staff worked with advisers from Blackpool and Fylde College to tailor an NVQ course in food and drink that would meet their specific requirements. The training was delivered through the time-honoured system of 'sitting by Nellie'.

'People have different speeds of learning, so we wanted to help them to get the most out of the training without feeling pressured to keep up – as they might have been on a structured programme,' Atkins says.

While the NVQ was developed, charge hands and managers on the production line received accreditation as internal D32 assessors. The college acted as an internal verifier. With all the employees working towards the same study goals, they were able to help each other improve – in effect becoming trainers themselves.

'It helps to know that there is someone you can go to if there are things you don't know,' says Trish Butcher, a hygiene operator with 18 years' experience. 'It also means that you're not afraid to admit that you don't know something. Before now we would have been too scared to show a lack of knowledge.'

The confidence that learning has given many employees has inspired a high proportion of them to carry on studying. They include Sean Mangan, who has been with the company 15 years. A charge hand and D32 assessor, he is working towards an NVQ level 3.

'When I started here, there was nothing in the way of training,' he says. 'You were shadowed for six weeks on the job and then simply told to get on with it.

Case study continued

Training has come on in leaps and bounds. Having an NVQ qualification shows people that you know your job and it sets a good example to new starters. It's also a qualification that you have under your belt if you go anywhere else.'

The pride that many employees now take in their work is evident in the five core action teams (Cats) that have been established. Ideas for improvement are invited from all parts of the workforce and every week a Cat member logs all of these ideas and posts them on notice boards around the site. Voluntary action teams then get together and develop these ideas. Their proposals are submitted to Cats for scrutiny. Approved ideas are then developed further and, every five weeks, each Cat updates the senior management team on the progress it has made. It's at this point that the senior managers approve any expenditure required or ask for more work to be carried out on a proposal.

In the past year alone, ideas from employees have saved the site more than £350 000. One person submitted 40 ideas, most of which were implemented.

'We put about half the ideas into action, and there's more than 60 per cent participation in these projects, which is a tremendous figure,' Atkins says. 'There's a culture here now of everyone wanting to be involved and wanting to work towards improving the quality of everything we do.'

The company's £300 000 investment in its employees over the past five years has obviously paid off. As Dave Smith, the general manager, puts it: 'Improving capability through developing and involving our people has been the catalyst for our success.'

Source: Celia Poole, *People Management*, 25 January 2002: 46, 47.

Questions

1 How do you think this training programme contributed to improving employee attitudes towards the company?

2 What aspects of a 'blended learning' approach can you identify at Fox's Biscuits?

3 In what ways has the HRD strategy of Fox's Biscuits paid off for all its stakeholders?

4 Could Fox's Biscuits be called a learning organisation?

(*A full answer to this question is given in the Lecturer's Guide that accompanies this texbook.*)

Useful websites

Organisation	URL	Summary of contents
Chartered Institute of Personnel and Development (CIPD)	www.cipd.co.uk	Professional organisation for HR professionals
Chartered Management Institute	www.managers.org.uk	Professional organisation for managers
Investors in People	www.iipuk.co.uk	Validating body for the IIP standard
Qualifications and Curriculum Authority	www.qca.org.uk	Maintains and develops school curricula and associated assessments, as well as accrediting and monitoring qualifications in schools, colleges, and at work
Sector Skills Councils	www.ssda.org.uk	The Skills for Business network is made up of 25 Sector Skills Councils (SSCs). Each SSC is an employer-led, independent organisation that covers a specific sector across the UK
University for Industry/Learn Direct	www.learndirect.co.uk	Government driven, hundreds of online courses, 1350 learndirect centres to help deliver learning to excluded sections of the population

Organisation	URL	Summary of contents
Department for Education and Skills	www.dfes.gov.uk	Government Department with responsibility for learning and skills in the UK
National Qualifications Framework	www.qca.org.uk/nq/framework	Explains how the National Qualifications Framework (NQF) works
The European Centre for the Development of Vocational Training	http://www.cedefop.eu.int	Established in 1975, is a European agency that helps the European Union (EU). It is the EU's reference centre for vocational education and training
Training Village	www.trainingvillage.gr	Sponsored by CEDEFOP
Organisation for Economic Co-operation and Development (OECD)	www.oecd.org	An international organisation helping governments tackle the economic, social and governance challenges of a globalised economy

References and further reading

Alberga, T. (1997) 'Investors in People: Time for a check up', *People Management*, 30–32.

Argyris, C. (1992) *On Organizational Learning*. Oxford: Blackwell Business.

Argyris, C. and Schon, D.A. (1978) *Organizational Learning: A Theory in Action Perspective.* Needham Heights, MA: Allyn & Bacon.

Armstrong, G. (1996) 'A qualifications cuckoo in the competency nest?', *People Management*, 23.

Ashworth, L. (2006) 'Training Needs Analysis is better carried out at an individual level than as a "sheep-dip", *People Management*, 12, 6: 1.

Ballot, G. (2003) Firms investment in human capital: sponsoring and effect on performance. *European Conference on The Future of Work: Challenges for the European Employment Strategy*. Athens.

Barnes, M. and Asogbon, G. (2004) *International Comparisons of Productivity: Better Data Improve UK Productivity Position: Detailed results for the February 2004 release of International Comparisons of Productivity covering 1990 to 2002.* London: Office for National Statistics.

Barrington, H. and Reid, M.A. (1999) *Training Interventions: Promoting Learning Opportunities.* London: IPD.

Bartram, D., Foster, J., Lindley, P.A., Brown, A.J. and Nixon, S. (1993) *The Learning Climate Questionnaire.* Employment Service and Newland Park Associates Ltd.

Bassi, L.J. *et al.* (2001) *Human Capital Investments and Firm Performance.* Washington: Human Capital Dynamics.

Becker, B.E. and Huselid, M.A. (1998) 'High Performance Work Systems and Firm Performance: a synthesis of research and managerial implications', in G.R. Ferris (ed.) *Personnel and Human Resource Management*. Greenwich, CT: JAI Press. 16: 53–101.

Beer, M., Spector, B., Lawrence, P.R., Quinn Mills, D. and Walton, R.E. (1984) *Managing Human Assets.* New York: Free Press.

Bell, D. (1980) 'The social framework of the information society' in *The Microelectronics Revolution*, T. Forester. Oxford: Blackwell.

Blake, R.R. (1995) 'Memories of HRD', *Training and Development*, 49, 3: 7.

Blyth, A. (2003) 'A worthwhile investment?', *Personnel Today*, 21–22.

Brewster, C. and Hegewisch, A. (1993) 'A continent of diversity', *Personnel Management*, January: 36–40.

Brinkerhoff, R.O. (2005) 'The Success Case Method: A Strategic Evaluation Approach to Increasing the Value and Effect of Training', *Advances in Developing Human Resources*, 7, 1: 86–102.

Burgoyne, J. (1999) 'Design of the Times', *People Management*, 3 June.

Cannell, M. (1997) 'Practice Makes Perfect', *People Management*, 26–33.

Cannell, M. (2004) *Training – A Short History*. London: CIPD.

CEDEFOP (2000) *Vocational Education and Training in France.* CEDEFOP.

CEDEFOP (2002) *Towards a History of Vocational Education and Training in Europe in a Comparative Perspective: Proceedings of the First International Conference: Vols 1 and 2.* Florence Luxembourg: Office for Official Publications of the European Communities, 2004.

Chase, R. (1997) 'The knowledge based organisation: an international study', *Journal of Knowledge Management*, 1, 1: 38–49.

CIPD (2001a) *The Learning and Development Generalist Standard: CIPD Practitioner-Level Professional Standards.* London: CIPD.

CIPD (2001b) *The future of Learning for Work: Executive Briefing.* London: CIPD.

CIPD (2001c) *Workplace Learning in Europe.* London: CIPD.

CIPD (2002) *Who Learns At Work? Survey Report.* February. London: CIPD.

CIPD (2004a) *E-learning Survey Results Report.* London: CIPD.

CIPD (2004b) *Quarterly Trends and Indicators: Survey Report Autumn 2004.* London: CIPD.

CIPD (2004c) *Reflections: New Trends in Training and Development: Experts' Views on the 2004 Training and Development Survey Findings.* London: CIPD.

CIPD (2004d) *Trade Union Learning Representatives: the Change Agenda*. London: CIPD.

CIPD (2004e) *Why Accessible e-learning Makes Business Sense: Inclusive Learning for All*. London: CIPD.

CIPD (2005a) *A Barometer of HR Trends and Prospects 2005: Overview of CIPD Surveys*. London: CIPD.

CIPD (2005b) *Basic Skills in the Workplace: Opening Doors to Learning*. London: CIPD.

CIPD (2005c) 'An informal approach gets better results', *People Management*, 11, 13: 14.

CIPD (2005d) *Latest Trends in Learning, Training and Development: Reflections on the 2005 Training and Development Survey*. London: CIPD.

CIPD (2005e) *Quarterly HR Trends and Indicators: Survey Report 2004/5*. London: CIPD.

CIPD (2005f) *Training and Development: Annual Survey Report 2005*. London: CIPD.

CIPD (2006) *Learning and Development: Annual Survey Report 2006*. London: CIPD.

Clutterbuck, D. and Megginson M.D. (2005) *Making Coaching Work: Developing a Coaching Culture*. London: CIPD.

Cooke, P. (2002) *Knowledge Economies*. London: Routledge.

Crouch, C.F.D. and Sako, M. (2001) *Are Skills the Answer? The Political Economy of Skill Creation in Advanced Industrial Nations*. Oxford: Oxford University Press.

Cuddy, N. and Lenny, T. (2005) *Vocational Education and training in the United Kingdom*. CEDEFOP.

Dee, K. and Hatton, A. (2006) 'How to face training evaluation head-on', *People Management*, 12, 6: 40–41.

Deissinger, T. (2000) 'The German "Philosophy" of linking academic and work-based learning in Higher Education: the case of vocational academies', *Journal of Vocational Education and Training*, 52, 4: 605–626.

Deming, W.E. (1986) *Out of Crisis*. Cambridge: Cambridge University Press.

Department for Education and Skills (2002) *Delivering Skills for Business*. Department for Education and Skills, Skills Sector Development Agency: 8.

Department for Education and Skills (2004) *The Story So Far*. Sector Skills Development Agency.

Department for Education and Skills (2005a) *Skills Sector Agreements*. Skills Sector Development Agency.

Department for Education and Skills (2005b) *White Paper – Skills: Getting On in Business, Getting On at Work*. Department for Education and Skills.

Department for Education and Skills (2005c) *Department for Education and Skills: Departmental Report 2005*. London: DfES.

Descy, P. and Tessaring, M. (2005) *The Value of Learning: Evaluation and Impact of Education and Training. Third Report on Vocational Training Research in Europe*. CEDEFOP.

Downey, M. (2003) *Effective Coaching*. New York: Thompson Texere.

Druker, P. (1998) 'The future has already happened.' *The Futurist*, 32, 8: 16–18.

Dybowski, D.G. (2005) *The Dual Vocational Education and Training System in Germany*. Keynote speech on Dual Vocational Training International Conference, Taiwan.

Easterby-Smith, M. and Mackness, J. (1992) 'Completing the Cycle of Evaluation', *Personnel Management*, June: 50–55.

E-Learning Strategy Unit (8 July 2003) *Towards a Unified e-learning Strategy*. London: Department for Education and Skills.

Elliot, L. (2004) 'Why we shouldn't just be topping up the number of graduates', *Guardian*, 12 January.

Ellis, J. and Williams, D. (1995) *International Business Strategy*. London: Pitman.

Ernst and Young (1997) *Measures that Matter*. London: Ernst and Young.

European Commission (2002) *Communication from the Commission – European Benchmarks in Education and Training: Follow-up to the Lisbon European Council*. Luxembourg: EUR–OP.

Finegold, D. and Levine, D.I. (1997) 'Institutional incentives for employer training', *Journal of Education and Work*, 10, 2: 109–127.

Finegold, D. and Soskice, D. (1988) 'The failure of training in Britain: analysis and prescription', *Oxford Review of Economic Policy*, 4, 3: 21.

Finegold, D. and Soskice, D. (1999) 'Creating self-sustaining high-skill ecosystems', *Oxford Review of Economic Policy*, 15, 1: 60–79.

Ford, D. J. (1993) *Benchmarking HRD*. London: ASTO.

Frenkel, S., Korczynski, M., Donoghue, L. and Shire, K. (1995) 'Re-constituting work: trends towards knowledge work and info–normative control', *Work, Employment and Society*, 9, 4: 773–796.

Gallwey, T. (1986) *The Inner Game of Golf*. London: Pan.

Garavan, T.N. (1991) 'Strategic Human Resource Development', *Journal of European Industrial Training*, 15, 1: 17–30.

Garavan, T.N., Costine, P. and Heraty, N. (1995) 'The emergence of strategic human resource development', *Journal of European Industrial Training*, 19, 10: 4–10.

Garavan, T.N., Heraty, N. and Morley, M. (1998) 'Actors in the HRD process', *International Studies of Management and Organization*, 28, 1: 114–135.

Garvin, D. (1993) *Building a Learning Organisation*. Harvard Business Review on Knowledge Management. Cambridge, MA: Harvard Business School Press.

Gentleman, A. (2005) 'Painful truth of the call centre cyber coolies', *The Observer*, 30 October.

Gibb, S. and Megginson, D. (2001) 'Employee Development' in, T. Redman and A. Wilkinson (eds) *Contemporary Human Resource Management*. London: FT Prentice Hall.

Gilley, J.W. and Eggland, S.A. (1989) *Principles of Human Resource Development*. Wokingham: Addison-Wesley Publishing.

Green, A., Preston, J. and Malmberg, L.-E (2005) 'Non-material benefits of education, training and skills at the macro level', in P. Descy and M. Tessaring (eds) *The Value of Learning: Evaluation and Impact of Education and Training. Third Report on Vocational Training Research in Europe*. CEDEFOP.

Green, F., Felstead A. and Gallie, D. (2002) *Works Skills in Britain 1986–2001*. Nottingham: DfES Publications.

Green, K. (1999) 'Offensive Thinking', *People Management*, 5, 8: 27.

Greinert, W.-D. (2002) 'European vocational training systems: the theoretical context of historical development', in CEDEFOP, *Towards a History of Vocational Education and Training in Europe in a Comparative Perspective: Proceedings of the First International Conference Volume 1*.

Grieves, J. (2003) *Strategic Human Resource Development*. London: Sage.

Guest, D. (1987) 'Human Resource Management and Industrial Relations', *Journal of Management Studies*, 24, 5: 503–521.

Hall, D. T. (1984) 'Human resource development and organisational effectiveness', in C. Forbum, N. Tichny and M. Devanna (eds) *Strategic Human Resource Management*. New York: John Wiley.

Hall, L. (2005) 'Coach Class', *People Management*, 1 September.

Hall, P.A. and Soskice, D. (2001) *Varieties of Capitalism: The Institutional Foundations of Comparative Advantage*. Oxford: Oxford University Press.

Hamblin, A.C. (1974) *Evaluation and Control of Training*. Maidenhead: McGraw-Hill.

Harrison, R. (2005) *Learning and Development*. London: CIPD.

Harrison, R. and Kessells, J. (2004) *Human Resource Development in a Knowledge Economy: An Organisational View*. Basingstoke: Palgrave Macmillan.

Hendry, C. (1994) 'The Single European Market and The HRM Response', in P.A. Kirkbride (ed.) *Human Resource Management in Europe: Perspectives for the 1990s*. London: Routledge, pp. 93–113.

Hirsch, W. and Reilly, P. (1998) 'Cycling proficiency: how do large organisations identify their future skill needs among their thousands of employees?', *People Management*, 9 July: 36–41.

Holden, L. and Liviad, Y. (1993) 'Does Strategic training policy exist? Evidence from ten European Countries', in A. Hegewisch and C. Brewester *European Development in HRM: The Cranfield Management Research Series*. Aldershot: Kogan Page.

Holton, E. R., III. (1996) 'The flawed four-level evaluation model', *Human Resource Development Quarterly*, 7: 5–21.

Honey, P. (1999) 'A declaration on learning', *Human Resource Development International*, 2, 1: 9–17.

Honey, P. and Mumford, A. (1989) *Manual of Learning Opportunities*. Maidenhead: Peter Honey.

Huselid, M.A. (1995) 'The impact of human resource management on turnover, productivity and corporate financial performance', *Academy of Management Journal*, 38: 635–672.

Hutton, W. and The Work Foundation (2005) *Where are the Gaps? An analysis of UK Skills and Education Strategy in the Light of the Kok Group and European Commission Midterm Review of the Lisbon Goals*. Department for Education and Skills.

IDS (2004) 'TNT UK recognised as an IiP champion', *IDS HR Studies Update*, 782: 19–23.

Investors in People, UK (2001) *A Decade of Success: 10 Years of Making a Difference to Working Life in the UK*. London: IIP UK.

Kandola, B. (1996) 'Are competences too much of a good thing?', *People Management*, 2 May.

Kanter, R.M. (1989) *When Giants Learn to Dance*. New York: Simon and Schuster.

Kearns, P. (2005) 'From Return on Investment to Added Value Evaluation: The Foundation for Organizational Learning', *Advances in Developing Human Resources*, 7, 1: 135–146.

Keep, E., Mayhew, K. and Corney, M. (2002) *Review of the Evidence on the Rate of Return to Employers of Investment in Training and Employer Training Measures*. SKOPE Research Paper. Coventry: University of Warwick.

Keep, E. and Mayhew, K. (1996a) 'Economic Demand for Higher Education – A Sound Foundation for Further Expansion?', *Higher Education Quarterly*, 50, 2: 89–190.

Keep, E. and Mayhew, K. (1996b) 'Evaluating assumptions that underlie training policy', in A. Booth and D.J. Snower *Acquiring Skills*. Cambridge: Cambridge University Press, pp. 305–334.

Keep, E. and Mayhew, K. (2001) *The Skills System in 2015. The future of learning for work*. Executive Briefing. London: CIPD.

Keep, E. and Mayhew, K. (2004) 'Expansion Questioned', *Times Higher Education Supplement*, 30 July.

Kenney, J. et al. (1979) *Manpower Training and Development*. London: Institute of Personnel Management.

Kessels, J. and Harrison, R. (1998) 'External consistency: the key to management development', *Management Learning*, 29, 1: 39–68.

Kirkpatrick, J. (1960) 'Techniques for evaluating training programmes', *Journal of American Society for Training and Development*, 14, 13–18: 25–32.

Lahteenmaki, S., Holden, L. and Roberts, I. (eds) (1999) *HRM and the Learning Organisation*. Turku, Finland: Turku School of Economics and Business Administration.

Learning and Skills Council (2001) *National Employers Skills Survey: Key Findings*. Department for Education and Skills.

Learning and Skills Council (2003) *National Employers Skills Survey: Key Findings*. Department for Education and Skills.

Learning and Skills Council (2004) *National Employers Skills Survey: Key Findings*. Department for Education and Skills.

Learning and Skills Council (2005) *Transforming Learning and Skills: Our Annual Statement of Priorities*. Department for Education and Skills.

Lee, M. (2004) 'National Human Resource Development in the United Kingdom', *Advances in Developing Human Resources*, 6, 3: 334–345.

Leitch, S. (2005) *Skills in the UK: The Long-Term Challenge*. London: H.M. Treasury.

Lenny, T. et al. (2004) *Thematic Overview of VET in England and the Devolved Administrations of the UK*. CEDEFOP.

Marchington, M. and Wilkinson, A. (2005) *Human Resource Management at Work*. London: CIPD.

Matthews, J.-J., Megginson, D. and Surtees, M. (2004) *Human Resource Development*. London: Kogan Page.

Mayhew, K., Deer, C. and Dua, M. (2004) 'The move to mass higher education in the UK: many questions and some answers', *Oxford Review of Education*, 30, 1: 65–82.

Mayo, A. (2000) *Building a Training and Development Strategy*. www.cipd.co.uk/subjects/training/trnstrgy/buildtdstr.htm

McCracken, M. and Wallace, M. (2000) 'Towards a redefinition of Strategic HRD', *Journal of European Industrial Training*, 24, 5.

McGoldrick, J., Stewart, J. and Watson, S. (2002) *Understanding Human Resource Development: A Research Based Approach*. London: Routledge.

Miller, R. and Stewart, J. (1999) 'Opened University', *People Management*, 17 June.

Millward, N., Bryson, A. and Forth, J. (2000) *All Change at Work: British Employee Relations 1980–1998*. London: Routledge.

Nadler, L. (1984) *The Handbook of Human Resource Development*. New York: John Wiley.

NAO (2005) *Employer Perspectives on Improving Skills for Employment*. London: National Audit Office.

National Skills Task Force (2000) *Skills for All: Proposals for a National Skills Agenda*. London: Department for Education and Employment.

Noon, M. and Blyton, P. (2002) *The Realities of Work*. Basingstoke: Palgrave.

OECD (2004) *Education at a Glance*. Paris: OECD.

OECD (2005) *The Role of Qualifications Systems in Promoting Life-long Learning*. Paris: OECD.

Office for National Statistics (2004) *Economic Trends*, December 2004, available from www.statistics.gov.uk.

Office for National Statistics (2006) *Economic Trends*, March 2006, available from www.statistics.gov.uk.

Overton, L. (2004) 'Fighting Fit', *E-Learning Age*. December 2003–January 2004.

Parsloe, E. and Wray, M. (2000) *Coaching and Mentoring: Practical Methods to Improve Learning*. London: Kogan Page.

Payne, J. (2003) *Vocational Pathways at Age 16–19*. DfES Research Report. Nottingham: DfES.

Pearn, M., Roderick, C. and Mulrooney, C. (1995) *Learning Organisations in Practice*. Maidenhead: McGraw Hill.

Pedlar, M., Burgoyne, J. and Boydell, T. (1991) *The Learning Company*. Maidenhead: McGraw-Hill.

Pedlar, M., Burgoyne, J. and Boydell, T. (1997) *The Learning Company*. Maidenhead: McGraw-Hill.

Peters, T.J. and Waterman, R.H. (1982) *In Search of Excellence: Lessons from America's Best Run Companies*. New York: Harper and Row.

Pettigrew, A. and Whipp, R. (1991) *Managing Change for Competitive Success (ESRC Competitiveness Surveys)*. Oxford: Blackwell.

Pfeffer, J. (1994) *Competitive Advantage Through People: Understanding the Power of the Workforce*. Boston, MA: Houghton Mifflin.

Pfeffer, J. (1998) *The Human Equation: Building Profits by Putting People First*. Cambridge, MA: Harvard Business School Press.

Pfeffer, J. (2003) *Understanding the People and Performance Link: Unlocking the Black Box*. London: CIPD.

Phillips, J. (2002) *How to Measure Training Success: A Practical Guide to Evaluating Training*. New York: McGraw Hill.

Phillips, J. (2005) 'Measuring Up', *People Management*, 7 April.

Pullinger, D. (2004) 'Capture learning to capitalise value', *People Management* (Study notes, 27 October).

Purcell, J. (2003) *Understanding the People and Performance Link: Unlocking the Black box*. London: CIPD.

Rae, L. (2002) *Assessing the Value of Your Training: The Evaluation Process from Training Needs to the Report to the Board*. London: Gower.

Reid, M.A., Barrington, H. and Brown, M. (2004) *Human Resource Development: Beyond Training Interventions*. London: CIPD.

Revans, R. (1982) *The Enterprise as a Learning System. Action Learning in Practice*. Aldershot: Gower.

Revans, R. (1983) *The ABC of Action Learning*. Bromley: Chartwell Bratt.

Reynolds, J., Caley, L. and Mason. R. (2002) *How do People Learn?* London: CIPD.

Reynolds, J. (2004) *Helping People Learn: Strategies for Moving from Training to Learning. Research Report*. London: CIPD.

Rothwell, W.J. and Kanazas, H.C. (1989) *Strategic Human Resource Development*. Englewood Cliffs, N.J.: Prentice Hall.

Saggers, R. (1994) 'Training Climbs the Corporate Agenda', *People Management*, July: 55–57.

Senge, P. (1990) *The Fifth Discipline*. London: Random House Business Books.

Sloman, M. (1999) 'Learning Centre: Seize the Day', *People Management*, 20 May: 31.

Sloman, M. (2002) 'Don't believe the hype', *People Management*, 21 March: 41.

Sloman, M. (2005) *Change Agenda: Training to Learning. Research Report*. London: CIPD.

Sloman, M. and Rolph, J. (2003) *E-learning: The Learning Curve*. Change Agendas, CIPD.

Smethurst, S. (2006) 'Course of Treatment', *People Management*, 12, 5: 34–36.

Soskice, D.W. (1993) 'Social Skills from Mass Higher Education: Rethinking the Company Based Initial Training Paradigm', *Oxford Review of Economic Policy*, 9, 3: 101–113.

Spellman, R. (2001) 'Training for success: the case for IiP.' *Training Journal*, 14–16.

Stevenson, J. (2003) *Developing Vocational Expertise*. London: Crows Nest, Allen and Unwin.

Stewart, J. (1999) *Employee Development Practice*. London: FT Pitman Publishing.

Stewart, J. and McGoldrick, J. (1996) *Human Resource Development: Perspectives, Strategies and Practice*. London: Pitman.

Stewart, J. and Sambrook, S. (2002) 'Reflections and discussion', in J. Stewart, S. Tjepkema, S. Sambrook, M. Mulder, H. Horst and J. Schreerens (eds) *HRD and Learning Organisations in Europe*. London: Routledge.

Storey, J. (ed.) (1989) *New Perspectives on Human Resource Management*. London: Routledge.

Storey, J. (1992) *Developments in the Management of Human Resources: an Analytical Review*. Oxford: Blackwell.

Storey, J. (1995) *Human Resource Management: A Critical Text*. London: Routledge.

Strategy Unit (2001) *In Demand: Adult Skills in the 21st Century*. London: Strategy Unit.

Strategy Unit (2002) *In Demand: Adult Skills in the 21st Century – Part 2*. London: Strategy Unit.

Strategy Unit (2003) *Skills Strategy White Paper*. London: Department for Education and Skills.

Sung, J. and Ashton, D. (2004) *Achieving Best Practice in Your Business: High Performance Work Practices: Linking Strategy and Skills to Performance Outcomes*. London: DTI.

Swanson, R.A. (2001) *Assessing the Financial Benefits of Human Resource Development*. Cambridge, MA: Perseus.

Symon, G. (2002) 'The "Reality" of Rhetoric and the Learning organization in the UK', *Human Resource Development International*, 5, 2: 155–174.

Taylor, P. and Thackwray, B. (1995) *Investors in People Explained*. London: Kogan Page.

Thompson, A. (2001) 'Too Much Apple Pie?', *People Management*, 3 May.

Thompson, I. (2005) *Training Evaluation: Making it Happen*. http://www.cipd.co.uk/subjects/training/trneval/treva.htm.

Tracey, W.R. (1968) *Evaluating Training and Development Systems*. American Management Association.

Tregaskis, O. and Dany, F. (1996) 'A comparison of HRD in France and the UK', *Journal of European Industrial Training*, 20, 1: 20–30.

Ulrich, J.G., Flemming, S., Granath, R-O, and Krekel, E.M. (2006) 'Number of newly concluded training contracts drops to lowest level since German reunification', www.bibb.de, 16 March.

Unwin, L. (2004) 'Growing Beans with Thoreau: rescuing skills and vocational education from the UK's deficit approach', *Oxford Review of Education*, 30, 1: 147–160.

Walton, J. (1999) *Strategic Human Resource Development*. Harlow: Pearson Education Limited.

Wang, G.G. and Spitzer, D.R. (2005) 'Human Resource Development Measurement and Evaluation: Looking Back and Moving Forward', *Advances in Developing Human Resources*, 7, 1: 5–16.

Warr, P., Bird, M.W. and Rackham, N. (1970) *Evaluation of Management Training*. Aldershot: Gower.

Warren, C. (2006) 'Curtain Call', *People Management*, 23 March.

Westwood, A. (2001) 'Drawing a line – who is going to train our workforce?', in D. Wilson, E. Lank, A. Westwood, E. Keep, C. Leadbetter and M. Sloman (eds) *The Future of Learning for Work: Executive Briefing.* London: CIPD, pp. 17–22.

Whitmore, J. (2002) *Coaching for Performance.* London: Nicholas Brearley Publishing Ltd

Whittington, R. (1993) *What is Strategy and Why Does it Matter?* London: Routledge.

Wilson, J. (ed.) (1999) *Human Resource Development.* London: Kogan Page.

Wilson, R.A. and Briscoe, G. (2004) 'The impact of human capital on economic growth: a review', in *Impact of Education and Training: Third Report of Vocational Training Research in Europe: Background Report.* Luxembourg.

Wolf, A. (2002) *Does Education Matter: Myths About Education and Economic Growth.* London: Penguin.

Wolf, A. (2004) 'Education and economic performance: simplistic theories and their policy consequences', *Oxford Review of Economic Policy*, 20, 2: 315.

Woodall, J. *et al.* (eds) (2004) 'New frontiers in HRD', *Routledge Studies in Human Resource Development*, 8.

Yeung, A. and Berman, B. (1997) 'Adding value through human resources: reorienting human resource management to drive through business performance', *Human Resource Management*, 36, 3: 321–335.

Young, M.F.D. (2003) 'National Qualifications Frameworks as a Global Phenomenon: a comparative perspective', *Journal of Education and Work*, 16, 3: 223–237.

For multiple-choice questions, exercises and annotated weblinks specific to this chapter visit the book's website at **www.pearsoned.co.uk/beardwell**

Chapter 10

Management development

Mike Doyle

Objectives

- To explain the meaning and nature of management development in organisations.
- To acknowledge the significance of management development to organisational success.
- To contrast 'piecemeal' and open system approaches to management development.
- To examine the methods, techniques and processes used to develop managers.
- To draw attention to the way management development can be varied to meet special needs and different contexts.
- To speculate about the future direction of management development in the UK and beyond.

Introduction

The main aim of this chapter is to assist you in exploring contemporary management development from within increasingly complex and diverse organisational contexts. Our exploration begins with a discussion of management development: how it is defined, and how it might be differentiated from management training and education. Consideration is then given to the role and objectives of management development and its contribution to organisational strategies.

We then move to examine the more functional aspects of organising, implementing and evaluating management development programmes. Here, the analysis begins with an examination of those who have responsibility for development and how that responsibility is shared. We reaffirm the need for management development to be supported by a robust HR infrastructure. We then explore the range of formal and less formal methods and techniques employed in the development of managers – making the argument that the choice and implementation of methods must be contingent to meet diverse organisational or individual situations.

Picking up this theme of contingency and diversity, the chapter then explores how management development meets special needs in different contexts. Areas that are examined include management development in the public sector and small firms and the special needs of professionals, international and women managers.

Management development, like management itself, is now in a state of considerable flux. As you would expect, this is giving rise to considerable controversy and tension, and against that backdrop, the final section of the chapter examines some of the issues that face management development in the future.

The chapter concludes with questions, exercises and a case study. These will help you to review and consolidate what you have learned. There is also a list of recommended and further reading included for guidance and reference purposes.

Defining management development

What is management?

The nature of management and the work that managers do was explored in detail in Chapter 3. In that chapter, an argument was made that managers have to deal with the ambiguities and complexities that arise from tensions in the employment relationship, the different aims and interests that reside in organisations and the varying interpretations of managerial roles and what they represent. It would appear reasonable to contend, therefore, that management development approaches should seek to accommodate the functional complexities of the managerial role and the diverse needs of those individuals who occupy those roles. For instance, different people, at different times, have different conceptions of what 'management' is about. This will shape individual views about the development of managers and this, in turn, may give rise to a number of tensions and contradictions which themselves have to be managed (Watson, 1994, 2002). Logically, if development activity is to be effective, it has to be pragmatic in its approach and implemented within what managers consider is *their* unique organisational context. It has to help them adapt and cope with the diversity and complexity that resides therein and meet their specific needs (Hales, 1993). In other words, any investment in development has to be congruent with the 'reality' of what managers do, and not (however well intentioned) be rooted in abstract or increasingly redundant models of what others might think they should do or used to do (Salaman, 1995).

It therefore follows that during an era of rapid and far-reaching change, the use of rigid and inflexible approaches to management development can no longer be tolerated if they create frustration and disillusionment among managers. Such approaches will inevitably lead to lower levels of morale and motivation amongst managers and ultimately waste resources and threaten future organisational success (Doyle, 1995, 2000a; Currie, 1999).

As you study the rest of this chapter you will become aware that there are in existence different interpretations of what we mean by the terms 'management', 'managing' and 'the manager'. You should also note that these differences will influence the way organisations, professional bodies, government agencies and academic institutions view and approach management development. This gives rise to a number of issues and debates and these will be identified and critically explored throughout the chapter.

What is management development?

There are many definitions of management development to select from, but most contemporary definitions share the characteristics contained in the view of development suggested by Thomson *et al.* (2001).

We have used the term in a comprehensive sense to encompass the different ways in which managers improve their capabilities. It includes management education, which is often taken to refer to formal, structured learning in an institutional context, and management training which is often used to mean acquiring knowledge and skills related to work requirements, also by formal means. But our use of the term 'development' goes beyond the sum of these to mean a wider process than the formal learning of knowledge and skills, which includes informal and experiential modes of human capital formation. Management development is thus a multi-faceted process in which some aspects are easier to identify and measure than others.

(Thomson *et al.*, 2001: 10)

A key point to note from Thomson *et al.*'s definition is the distinction they make between what constitutes management education, training and development. Unfortunately, these terms are often used in overlapping and interchangeable ways within organisations and as such they can generate confusion, leading to ineffective development. For example, management development is often seen as synonymous with 'sending people on training or education courses' – even when such courses may be the least appropriate way to develop individuals or groups of managers and may even generate resistance and frustration (Roberts and McDonald, 1995; Mole, 1996, 2000; Currie, 1999).

Management development as a strategic imperative

Major environmental shifts are now demanding a more strategic perspective from those who manage and lead in organisations. Many organisations are now 'globalising' in their quest for markets that will bring them new opportunities for growth and prosperity (Anderson *et al.*, 1998). Advances in technology, especially in the field of information technology and telecommunications, are leading to greater efficiencies, reduced costs and opportunities to launch new products and services. The nature of organisational life itself is changing.

Organisations are becoming more complex and diverse. Change and its impact is now the dominant feature of organisational life. Employee adaptability and flexibility are the essential characteristics for organisational survival and success. As a consequence, organisations are now espousing values that regard people not as costs to be minimised but as assets to be maintained and developed.

Such changes are setting new challenges for managers and employees alike. Managers are being challenged to respond as strategic leaders and perform in the role of change agent (Salaman, 1995; Rosenfeld and Wilson, 1999; Doyle, 2002). Their task is to establish a clear mission, linked to a set of strategic business objectives that enable organisations to acquire, control and allocate resources to maximise the opportunities available and to minimise any threats to their survival and success. But managers need the knowledge and skills to do this and in this sense, management development has now become a *strategic imperative* within many organisations (Woodall and Winstanley, 1998; Thomson *et al.*, 2001).

An illustration of how management development is being integrated with and used to support business strategy can be found in the major international company Unilever (see Box 10.1).

Devising a management development policy

> Management development will fail if there is no clear policy. (Margerison, 1991)

Policy statements are useful because they express an organisation's commitment to development, and set out clearly a framework within which it can take place. It makes it explicit who is responsible for development, the support that is available, methods used etc. Research has also suggested that those organisations having a formal policy for developing their managers 'undertook significantly more management training than did companies without such a policy' (Thomson *et al.*, 2001).

However, what is sometimes less clear is the extent to which organisations are committed to and prepared to implement their policies. Policies may be viewed with some scepticism – especially during times of radical downsizing involving the loss of managerial jobs (Thomson *et al.*, 2001). There are also difficulties evaluating the effectiveness of policies in achieving desired outcomes. The difficulties associated with evaluating management development outcomes will be explored later in the chapter.

Box 10.1 A management development strategy for Unilever

Unilever is a huge international organisation with 1000 brands, employing some 255,000 people in 300 operating units across 88 countries. In recent years the business strategy has been refocused to achieve significant economies of scale, reduce the number of products offered and increase penetration in successful product markets.

This refocusing has had a major impact on HR strategies and policies. One area that the company has identified as a priority has been the development of its managers as 'global players' with the ability to implement the new business plan.

Success in developing managers is based on the following principles:

- Management development is a business responsibility.
- Responsibility for development is shared between Unilever and the manager.
- Individuals drive their own learning and development.
- Explicit responsibilities are placed on line and senior managers for developing their managers.

Unilever aims to create a 'seamless' system of management development – delivered in one language worldwide in a way that facilitates the transfer of people across different operating units. A framework of worldwide competences and skills is available on the Internet for managers to plan their personal development. An emphasis is placed on managers developing both professional and generalist skills that are transferable to different global contexts. Development activity is closely linked to performance management and measurable outcomes. Managers are required to produce an improvement development plan and advancement is tightly linked to meeting performance targets.

Source: Adapted from Reitsma, 2001.

Extracts from a management development policy

- We accept that it is the Group's responsibility to provide every manager with the opportunity to develop his/her ability and potential so that he/she does their existing job effectively.

- We believe that people derive more satisfaction from working when they themselves have helped to establish and are committed to the objective of their job.

- The policy requires that through the Divisions we create an environment in which all managers contribute to the objectives of the business to their maximum ability.

- We have undertaken to support this policy by providing an organisational structure within which the responsibilities of each manager are clearly defined.

- We expect that increasing the influence and scope for initiative and self-motivation of managers and their subordinates will lead to increasing job satisfaction and to direct improvement in the Group's commercial performance.

Source: Mumford, 1997: 11. This extract is taken from *Management Development* (1997) by Alan Mumford.

Does your organisation have a management development policy? If it does, how far does it reflect the aims listed in the extract above?

If it doesn't have a policy, what has been the impact on management development outcomes?

Having determined its policy guidelines, the next step for the organisation is to consider how it should *approach* the development of its managers.

Organisational approaches to management development

Why develop this manager?

Having devised a clear and communicated policy for management development, those responsible for implementing development need to think through and be able to justify why they are developing an individual manager (or a group of managers). The reasons for developing managers are varied. For example:

- to introduce new attitudes and behaviours to promote culture change;
- to encourage more empowerment and innovation;
- to develop the knowledge and the skills to seek new market opportunities;
- to develop the knowledge to maximise the use of new technology;
- to facilitate the introduction of new systems, processes and working practices.

You will have noted that in addition to developing new knowledge and skills, management development is a way of shaping individual and collective attitudes and behaviours – an important consideration when implementing organisational change.

As well as organisations ensuring that development is linked to the philosophies and strategic objectives of the organisation, they must also take account of individual needs, expectations and aspirations. This can often be a difficult balance to achieve, and frequently becomes a source of tension (Hopfl and Dawes, 1995; Currie, 1999).

For instance, senior managers who are seeking a quick-fix solution to a deep-rooted managerial or organisational problem will often consult with development 'experts', who are only too pleased to solve the problem by introducing them to the latest development fad. When the 'quick-fix' solution fails to produce the anticipated results or (worse) exacerbates an existing problem, management development is at risk of being undermined and discredited (Roberts and McDonald, 1995; Currie, 1999). It is therefore vital that organisations view management development as a long-term investment and select an approach that is suited to their specific needs and requirements.

Selecting the right approach

Management development can be approached in a number of different ways. Mumford (1997) describes three different types of approach that are broadly representative of current UK management development (see Box 10.2).

Burgoyne (1988) argues that management development may be considered as progressing through different levels of maturity (see Table 10.1). At Level 1 there is no systematic approach to management development, and at Level 6 management development not only shapes and informs corporate strategy, it actually enhances the process of strategy formation. In practice, management development approaches for most organisations rarely extend beyond Levels 1 and 2. Those who reach Levels 5 and 6 find it is 'often precariously achieved and lost' (p. 44). Burgoyne argues that to progress through the levels of maturity to the point where management development is making the fullest contribution to organisation development demands a much more holistic approach to development. In this approach, both 'hard' (roles, duties, technical competence, etc.) and 'soft' (career, quality of life, ethos, values, etc.) managerial issues are considered when framing approaches to development.

Activity | Study Mumford and Burgoyne's models. Identify where you believe your organisation is positioned in relation to the different 'types' and 'levels of maturity'.

| Box 10.2 | **Type 1: 'Informal managerial' – accidental processes** |

Characteristics:

- occurs within manager's activities
- explicit intention is task performance
- no clear development objectives
- unstructured in development terms
- not planned in advance
- owned by managers.

Development consequences:

- learning real, direct, unconscious, insufficient.

Type 2: 'Integrated managerial' – opportunistic processes

Characteristics:

- occurs within managerial activities
- explicit intention is both task performance and development
- clear development objectives
- structured for development by boss and subordinate
- planned beforehand and/or reviewed subsequently as learning experiences
- owned by managers.

Development consequences:

- learning is real, direct, conscious, more substantial.

Type 3: 'Formalised development' – planned processes

Characteristics:

- often away from normal managerial activities
- explicit intention is development
- clear development objectives
- structured for development by developers
- planned beforehand or reviewed subsequently as learning experiences
- owned more by developers than managers.

Development consequences:

- learning may be real (through a job) or detached (through a course)
- is more likely to be conscious, relatively infrequent.

Source: The material above first appeared in *Management Education and Development*, Vol. 18, Part 3 (1987).

A 'piecemeal' approach

Many approaches to development have characteristics similar to Mumford's Type 1 and Type 3 development and Burgoyne's Levels 1 and 2 and accordingly may be labelled as *piecemeal*. Implementing piecemeal approaches will almost certainly lead to inefficient and ineffective development.

Piecemeal approaches to development are characterised by the following:

- There is no management development infrastructure. Development is not linked to business strategy. Activities are unrelated, and lack overall direction or philosophy. They fail to reinforce each other, and reduce the potential for organisational effectiveness.

- Development often focuses on the needs of the organisation, and fails to meet the learning needs and aspirations of individuals and groups.

- Development is largely defined in terms of a range of universal, off-the-shelf internal or external courses.

Table 10.1 Levels of maturity or organisational management development

1 No systematic management development	2 Isolated tactical management development	3 Integrated and coordinated structural and development tactics	4 A management development strategy to implement corporate policy	5 Management development strategy input to corporate policy formation	6 Strategic development of the management of corporate policy
No systematic or deliberate management development in a structural or developmental sense; total reliance on *laissez-faire*, uncontrived processes of management development	There are isolated and ad hoc tactical management development activities, of either structural or developmental kinds, or both, in response to local problems, crises, or sporadically identified general problems	The specific management development tactics that impinge directly on the individual manager, of career structure management, and of assisting learning, are integrated and coordinated	A management development strategy plays its part in implementing corporate policies through managerial human resource planning, and providing a strategic framework and direction for the tactics of career structure management and of learning, education and training	Management development processes feed information into corporate policy decision-making processes on the organisation's managerial assets, strengths, weaknesses and potential, and contribute to the forecasting and analysis of the manageability of proposed projects, ventures, changes	Management development processes enhance the nature and quality of corporate policy-forming processes, which they also inform and help implement

Source: Burgoyne (1988).

- There is tacit support for management education and training because it is seen as a 'good thing to be doing' irrespective of organisational needs.

- There is a lack of common vision among those responsible for management development. For instance, some managers see development as a central part of their job, others see it as peripheral and a nuisance.

- Management development effort can be wasted because it is used as a solution to the wrong problem. Rather than developing managers, the correct solution may be to change aspects of organisation structure or systems.

- It is difficult to evaluate the effectiveness of a piecemeal approach that lacks clear direction and established objectives.

Sadly, piecemeal and fragmented approaches to management development are all too commonplace (Roberts and McDonald, 1995; Mole, 2000). Such approaches are a significant contributor to the failure of management development to fulfil personal and organisational expectations (Temporal, 1990; Mumford, 1997; Mole, 2000). Not only do they waste investment, time and effort, there is also a risk of damage to existing levels of morale and commitment among managers as efforts to develop them founder on organisational barriers to change (Doyle, 1995, 2000a). As Molander and Winterton (1994: 89) contend:

> Where such conditions exist, what is required is an organisation-wide assessment of the elements in the culture which require changing, followed by an effective change programme. Focusing attention on individual managers . . . will not bring about required change. In this case the organisation itself should be the focus of change.

An open systems view of management development

In Chapter 3, the *open systems model* was introduced as a way of conceptualising and making sense of the complexity of organisational life (Kast and Rosenweig, 1985; Morgan, 1997). In this section, it will be argued that if organisations can be persuaded to adopt an open systems perspective in relation to management development, then they are likely to overcome many of the problems created by a piecemeal approach to development. Instead of looking at management development in isolation (as a closed system) it is now being considered as an integral part of a wider organisational system, and, more importantly, is linked to the context and 'reality' of managerial work (see, for example, Mumford's Type 2 development).

Viewing management development from an open systems perspective recognises and focuses attention on the following factors:

● Management development is viewed as both a *system* and a *process* (see Figure 10.1). It is composed of identifiable parts or components that act together in an organised way. Inputs to the process of development are transformed into a range of outputs that affect both the individual and the organisation in some way.

Figure 10.1	**Management development as an open system**

- Figure 10.1 also demonstrates that in an open system the management development process *interacts with* and is *influenced by* variables from other environmental and organisational subsystems (structural, social, technological and cultural). For example, prevailing ideologies, values and beliefs within the organisation represent a *cultural subsystem*. Management development can be used as a way of reinforcing this cultural subsystem by shaping and moulding managers' attitudes and values and exerting pressure upon them to conform and display 'acceptable' behaviour patterns – an important consideration during times of radical change.

- Management development becomes *integrated* with, and *mutually dependent* upon, other organisational subsystems, activities and processes. For example, as we saw earlier in this chapter, the system for strategic planning and the setting of organisational goals must interact with a management development system that seeks to develop the managerial skills and knowledge to organise and implement the business strategy (Ready *et al.*, 1994; Thomson *et al.*, 2001).

- Such an interaction means that *if you develop the manager, you develop the organisation*, and vice versa (see Figure 10.2). As the organisation changes and develops, so positive influencing 'loops' are created that lead to the further development of managers (Morgan, 1997). Similarly, as managers are developed, positive influencing 'loops' lead to changes in the organisation which produce greater effectiveness. It can, of course, work the other way. Poor or ineffective development can create negative influencing 'loops' that undermine organisational or managerial effectiveness. The need therefore is to focus on *managing* management development as well as *doing* management development.

- Viewing management development in open systems terms reveals the full extent of its influence on the organisation, and is likely to lead to more detailed and objective assessment of the performance and overall effectiveness of managers who are developed.

In the subsequent sections of this chapter, an open systems perspective of management development will become the basis for both theoretical and practical analysis and discussion.

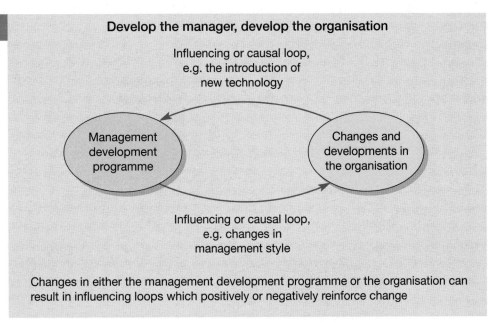

Figure 10.2 **Develop the manager, develop the organisation**

Influencing or causal loop, e.g. the introduction of new technology

Management development programme

Changes and developments in the organisation

Influencing or causal loop, e.g. changes in management style

Changes in either the management development programme or the organisation can result in influencing loops which positively or negatively reinforce change

Organising management development programmes

Working from open system principles, if management development is to succeed it requires the support of a robust HR infrastructure that addresses issues such as:

- who is responsible for development;
- how managers are selected for development;
- performance management;
- career progression.

Determining who is responsible for management development

If a development programme is to be successfully planned and implemented, there has to be clear and unambiguous allocation of responsibility and a willingness to accept that responsibility by the parties involved.

Traditionally, responsibility for development has rested with the HR function, with some input from the manager's boss. The individual manager was often passive in the process: they were only required to 'turn up and be developed'.

To be effective, development demands the involvement of a range of stakeholders, or 'helpers', each of whom will have an impact on the development process and its outcomes (Mabey and Salaman, 1995; Mumford, 1997). Figure 10.3 identifies a number of key stakeholders who each share a measure of responsibility. At the core of the process, the main responsibilities are shared between the personnel specialist, the boss and the individual (Davis, 1990).

An active process of discussion and negotiation should ensure that they each accept and own a share of the responsibility for setting development objectives, planning and imple-

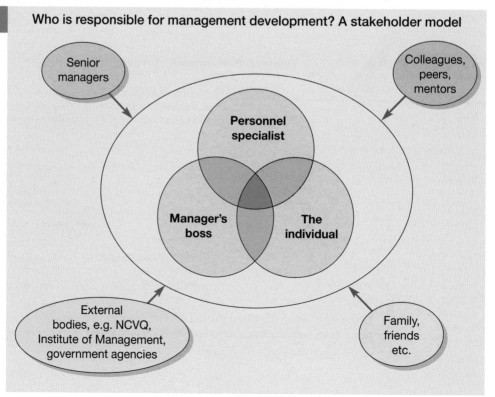

Figure 10.3   **Who is responsible for management development? A stakeholder model**

menting the process. However, although these three parties are central to the development process, other stakeholders will have an input (Mabey and Salaman, 1995; Mumford, 1997). For example, the role of senior management is vital in terms of resourcing, commitment and establishing a supportive culture. Colleagues and mentors will advise and assist in overcoming particular problems and issues (Mumford, 1997).

Activity Prepare a list of those who are responsible for your development. How effective is the support you receive? Does it need to be improved in any way?

National bodies such as the Chartered Management Institute, NVQ lead bodies and Learning and Enterprise Councils are influential in shaping management development policies and direction through mechanisms such as funding, reports, lobbying, and contact with industry representatives. Similarly, academic and vocational institutions are able to influence development methods and agendas through their research, teaching, awards and other activities (see Chapter 9). And finally it must be remembered that the individual's friends and family have a crucial role to play in providing support and encouragement (Mumford, 1997). As Mabey and Salaman (1995: 176) point out, the linkages between each stakeholder are complex and each will 'help shape the ethos and practice of training and development within organisations'.

Ensuring the availability of suitable managers

To achieve their strategic objectives, organisations must ensure that they have the right number of managers, with the right skills and available at the right time. A core element of human resource planning (explored in more detail in Chapter 5) is the assessment of existing managerial stock and, where necessary, the replenishment of that stock through the recruitment of new managers. A *managerial audit* is normally carried out, utilising information from sources such as assessment centres, performance appraisals, personnel files and discussions with bosses, to reveal the skills available to meet forecast demand. These skills are then compared with the organisation's HRM plan, and development objectives are established (Vineall, 1994; Woodall and Winstanley, 1998; Prokopenko, 1998).

In certain cases, it may not be feasible or appropriate to develop the existing stock of managers, and organisations may choose or be forced to enter the marketplace to 'buy-in' the required skills, e.g. in the case of small businesses (Woodall and Winstanley, 1998).

Performance management

Growing attention is now being paid to performance management systems that both motivate and reward those managers who contribute to strategic goals and objectives and, by implication, to exert sanctions on or to 'punish' those who fail to deliver anticipated performance levels.

Performance management can be conceptualised in the form of a cycle consisting of five elements (Mabey and Salaman, 1995):

- setting performance objectives;
- measuring outcomes;
- feedback of results;
- rewards linked to outcomes;
- amendments to objectives and activities.

Within the performance management cycle, performance-related pay (PRP) and performance appraisal are key components: the former to produce the extrinsic financial rewards in the form

369

of shares, income differentials, profit-sharing schemes and bonuses, and the latter to provide the essential mechanism for setting objectives and feeding back performance criteria (Hendry, 1995).

In terms of management development, there is a close interaction with performance management systems. First and foremost, performance management systems must be seen to reward personal development and achievement. This is leading a number of organisations to link their systems of reward more closely to the attainment of higher levels of competence, which is one way of overcoming 'the subjectivity and arbitrariness of assessment' (Hendry, 1995: 309). The achievement of objectives is also closely linked to management training and education, which act to provide the skills and knowledge required to meet objectives. Performance appraisal provides the forum for identifying development needs. It also serves as the mechanism for feeding back information to the manager about current levels of performance, enabling them to identify and negotiate adjustments or further development needs.

Although the focus of performance management is on extrinsic rewards, intrinsic rewards through praise, encouragement and reassurance are vital components in management development, particularly in the area of coaching and mentoring. For example, for younger managers who may be on fast-track graduate programmes (see section on graduate development later in this chapter), continuous positive feedback during the early stages of the programme is vital to sustain motivation and commitment. Older, more experienced managers also need regular praise, encouragement and, above all, reassurance that their skills and experience are still valued and appreciated, and that any investment in personal development is seen as being positive from the organisation's viewpoint (Mumford, 1997).

Career development

Management development can only be effective if careful consideration is given to career paths and opportunities for promotion and progression (Mumford, 1997; Margerison, 1994a). This requires a well-prepared human resource plan that is future oriented. In the past, career development very much reflected more traditional organisational structures and cultures. Hierarchical progression was seen to be upwards through clearly defined junior, middle and senior management roles based on tenure and the possession of specialist skills and the display of patterns of expected behaviours. However, in the face of radical organisational change such pathways are now giving way to a more uncertain and less clearly defined progression where 'automatic' promotion is no longer available to many. Citing research by Benbow, Thomson *et al.*, (2001: 181) capture the mood amongst UK and US managers about their future career development:

> A high proportion of respondents do not feel in control of their future career development. The pace of change over the last decade has shattered career and financial expectations, generating a need for individuals to re-examine many of the inherited wisdoms of the past. The demise of the job for life and the trend towards a wholly flexible employment market are clear examples of the extent to which new agendas are being set.

Such concerns reflect in part the emphasis now being placed on managers to ensure their employability and marketability. This in turn reflects a redefining of the psychological contract that exists between managers and their employing organisation (Herriot and Pemberton, 1995). In terms of career progression, the emphasis is shifting towards individuals who display greater flexibility, adaptability and personal characteristics such as emotional resilience (Watson, 2002). Some will find themselves facing a 'boundaryless' career in which there will be less job security and career progression opportunities will be limited. Instead, career progression is likely to involve a greater emphasis on horizontal or diagonal rather than vertical movement, e.g. projects, overseas secondments and postings, departmental and job shifts, internal consultancy roles, acting as mentors and coaches etc. (Arnold, 1997; Thomson *et al.*, 2001).

In terms of management development strategies, some significant rethinking of HR policies and approaches will be required at both an individual and an organisational level if they are to fit and support these significant shifts in management career prospects. Organisational policies in terms of career planning workshops, mentoring arrangements, performance management systems and processes etc. will all require reviewing. The new imperative for organisations will be to ensure that their managers are made fully aware of the realities of the changing nature of their careers, with concomitant efforts being made to reward, retain and motivate those who find themselves moving sideways, not upwards. The risk of not attending to these issues is that the relationship between managers and their employing organisation becomes one that is short termist and calculative, stifling innovation, creativity and a developmental outlook (Watson and Harris, 1999). Unfortunately, there is evidence to suggest that some organisations appear to be unaware or unwilling to communicate the harsh reality of the changing nature of managerial careers to their managers.

> The picture emerging then is one of traditional career management structures and approaches struggling to balance and reconcile organisational and individual goals which themselves are changing in response to an increasingly self-centred, instrumental climate.
>
> (Doyle, 2000b: 231)

In respect of management development approaches therefore, it is important that these reflect shifts in philosophy about managerial careers and that they encourage managers first and foremost to take a greater responsibility for their own development. In addition, managers will require the knowledge and skills to progress horizontally and diagonally, e.g. how to work in and lead a project team or how to make a success of an overseas posting. In this sense, management development approaches will have to reflect the required self-reliant, adaptive and intellectual capacities that such career moves suggest.

Implementing and evaluating management development programmes

Earlier in this chapter the question was posed: 'Why are we developing this manager?' In this section attention will turn to the techniques and choices available to organisations when they seek to implement their development programmes. Again, in keeping with our open systems principles and ideas, it is important that any implementation plan acknowledges the diversity of management roles and responsibilities and the contexts in which they operate.

Acknowledging the diversity of management

We saw earlier that development has to be linked to the reality of managerial work. When organising development programmes, it is important to cater for the diversity of management skills, attitudes and experience that reside within the organisation. One useful example is given by Odiorne (1984), who advocates a *portfolio* approach to development to improve the overall efficiency of the process and ensure the optimal allocation of resources (see Box 10.3). This requires organisations to make a range of decisions and develop a 'mix' of contingent objectives and techniques arranged to match the profile of the management team in the organisation.

Shaping development activity in this way to accommodate the diverse needs of the managers and their employing organisations requires certain questions to be considered before development commences:

'*Stars*': high-performing, high-potential managers

Aim:

- create challenge
- provide incentives and reward
- allocate adequate resources and effort.

'*Workhorses*': high-performing, limited-potential managers

Aim:

- emphasise value and worth of experience
- motivate and reassure
- utilise experience on assignments, projects, coaching.

'*Problem employees*': high-potential, underperforming managers

Aim:

- identify weaknesses
- channel resources to address weaknesses
- regular performance monitoring and feedback.

'*Deadwood*': low-performing, low-potential managers

Aim:

- identify weaknesses, resolvable?
- if not, consider release, early retirement, demotion.

(*Source*: adapted from Odiorne, 1984)

- *Who is being developed?*
    - Is it older managers seeking new challenges or younger 'high fliers' on a fast-track development programme?
    - Is it senior managers seeking to enhance their strategic skills, middle managers seeking to update and broaden existing skills, or junior-level managers looking to acquire additional managerial skills?
    - Is it technical specialists or professionals seeking to expand their cross-functional capabilities, or supervisors receiving training for the first time?
- *What is being developed?*
    - Does the programme seek to develop new attitudes and values, as in the case of a recently privatised public utility or a private sector company that has just undergone a takeover?
    - Does the programme aim to develop technical, financial, business or interpersonal skills? What are the priorities?
    - Does the programme seek to change existing managerial behaviours and styles to reflect an internal organisational restructuring, such as the introduction of new technology?
- *Where will the development take place?*
    - Should development be on-the-job in the office, factory or sales territory, or off-the-job in a residential hall, academic institution or individual's home, or a combination of all of these?
- *What are the most appropriate techniques to achieve the best fit between individual and organisational requirements?*
    - What are the most cost-effective/appropriate techniques available?
    - How much scope is there to accommodate individual learning needs and preferences?
    - How much choice is delegated to the individual over the choice of development techniques?
    - How is conflict resolved between individual and organisational needs?

(You should note that some of these questions are explored later in the chapter in the section that deals with special needs in different contexts.)

It is only when these questions have been considered that the organisation is in a position to construct a framework of development that best fits its needs and the needs of its managers. In practice, however, this can prove problematical. Organisations may be unclear about the aims and objectives of their development activities and how they meet their needs, e.g. longer-term supply of future managers or short-term expediency to meet sudden strategic changes in structure? There may be confusion about different learning methods and what they mean in different contexts, e.g. are special projects the same as in-company job rotation? There may be a failure to fully assess the implications of different methods when they are used in these different contexts, e.g. managers may prefer on-the-job, work-based development (Woodall, 2000). But without effective support from motivated and competent line managers and HRD professionals, such approaches may become piecemeal and ineffective or even lead to resentment and frustration (Doyle, 1995; Currie, 1999).

Development needs analysis

If managers are to be developed effectively, their individual development needs must be assessed in a careful and systematic fashion. There are several ways to do this. Traditionally, the diagnosis of development needs for managers has often relied upon an ad hoc and piecemeal process of selective observation in the role joined with the 'constructive' but often subjective input from others in the organisation (usually senior managers or HR professionals).

To counter this, organisations are turning to performance appraisal as a structured way of identifying the skills and behaviours that are required to meet business objectives (Mumford, 1997; Woodall and Winstanley, 1998). During the appraisal process, both the individual and their boss review performance against departmental/organisational objectives and other performance criteria to determine development needs. Once analysed, the development needs form the basis of a negotiated and agreed *personal development plan*, which is regularly reviewed and modified in the light of changing organisational and individual circumstances. However, as Thomson *et al.*, (2001) point out, issues such as a lack of line manager support and weaknesses in the appraisal process mean that 'individuals rarely walk away from such discussions with clear plans for personal development' (p. 126).

Activity | Have you got a personal development plan? If you haven't, make a mental note to discuss this with your boss at your next appraisal interview. If you have got a plan, when was it last reviewed? Is it still valid and up to date?

In addition to performance appraisal, more and more organisations are turning to the use of assessment/development 'centres' to analyse development needs. These 'centres' are 'workshops which measure the abilities of participants against the agreed success criteria for a job or role' (Lee and Beard, 1994). It should also be borne in mind that the term 'development centre' relates to the process of identifying needs, not to a specific place (Munchus and McArthur, 1991).

The main aim of a development centre is to 'obtain the best possible indication of people's actual or potential competence to perform at the target job or job level' (Woodruffe, 1993: 2). Most development centres operate in the following way:

- There is careful selection of job-related criteria. These may be in the form of competences, dimensions, attributes, critical success factors, etc.

- A group of managers is identified and brought together in the form of a workshop normally lasting one or two days. In the workshops a series of diagnostic instruments and/or multiple assessment techniques are administered that aim to measure an individual's ability to perform against the job-related criteria. These can take the form of psychometric tests, planning exercises, in-tray exercises, interviews, games, or simulations.

- A team of trained assessors observe and measure performance, evaluate and provide structured feedback and guidance to individuals.
- After the workshop, line managers and/or trainers utilise the feedback to help the individual construct a personal development plan.

Although the use of development centres is growing, there have been a number of criticisms, which tend to revolve around: assessment techniques that do not relate to the task or job, poor organisation, poorly trained assessors, ineffective feedback and the lack of follow-up action (Dulewicz, 1991; Whiddett and Branch, 1993).

Whichever method or combination of methods is selected, it is vital that each manager's needs are carefully assessed before implementing a development programme, and that an effective system of providing feedback is established.

Formalised methods for developing managers

A great deal of management development is formalised, planned and structured. It can take place 'on-the-job' – within the workplace environment, for instance a training centre. Or it can take place 'off-the-job' – away from the workplace in a college, university or conference/seminar (Mumford, 1997; Prokopenko, 1998; Woodall and Winstanley, 1998; Woodall, 2000).

Research by Burgoyne and Stuart (1991) reveals that the following methods are likely to be used in more formalised and structured approaches (in order of predominance of use):

- lectures;
- games and simulations;
- projects;
- case studies;
- experiential (analysis of experience);
- guided reading;
- role playing;
- seminars;
- programmed instruction (computerised/packaged).

Although these methods are widely used in education and training, they can often appear to be abstract, detached and somewhat artificial in nature (Burgoyne and Stuart, 1991). Criticisms have been levelled at the relevance of much of the taught material and the problems of transferring knowledge and skills into the reality of the workplace (Roberts and McDonald, 1995; Mumford, 1997).

Competency-based development programmes

Competency-based development is a good example of a formalised and structured method for developing managers. This approach to development was introduced with the aim of improving the overall effectiveness of UK managers following severe criticism of their performance and its impact on the national economy in the late 1980s.

National standards for management competency (competency here is defined as an ability to apply knowledge and skills to a required standard of performance) were originally devised in the early 1990s by the then lead body for management standards – the Management Charter Initiative (MCI). The aim was to integrate the standards into the UK system of National Vocational Qualifications (see Chapters 8 and 9). Responsibility for design administration and promotion of the standards has now shifted to the Management Standards Centre (MSC) which has close affiliations to the Chartered Management Institute (www.management-standards.org.uk).

The original standards consisted of a complex framework of Units of Competence which 'defined' the manager's role. Managerial competency in each unit was assessed using exacting performance criteria. Assessment was carried out by trained assessors. The standards were revised in 1997 to take account of concerns and reservations expressed about the design, administration and implementation of the original standards. The aim was to produce a more flexible framework of mandatory and optional units from which managers could select the pathway of competence that best suited their circumstances and the qualification they wished to pursue.

In 2003–4, the 1997 suite of standards was again modified to reduce the number of units from 77 to 47 'to reflect the fact that many managers felt that the 1997 suite was too unwieldy to make large use of and contained large areas of duplication' (www.management-standards.org.uk). The latest standards now consist of the following areas of competence:

A Managing self and personal skills
B Providing direction
C Facilitating change
D Working with people
E Using resources
F Achieving results

The Management Standards Centre points out that a greater emphasis has now been given to softer skills and that 'it is intended that this suite will be subject to incremental change using feedback collected from new and existing users of the standards'.

Since their inception, competence-based development programmes on national standards of competence have attracted considerable criticism, in both philosophical and practical terms. Philosophically, there has been a long-standing, fundamental disagreement about the whole basis on which competences were conceived and the way in which they were being enacted. For instance, attention has been drawn to the behaviourist orthodoxy that underpins competence-based training and development, which, ideologically, grew from the 'social efficiency' movement in the USA, and which, some argue, represents a form of 'social engineering' in which habitual behaviour is a key principle (Hyland, 1994).

Others have challenged the functional, reductionist, mechanistic approach and the extent to which it leads to an 'abstraction of reality'. They have questioned how far competences can be generalised from a particular managerial context (Antonacopoulou and Fitzgerald, 1996; Loan-Clarke, 1996). As Kilcourse (1994: 14) remarks: 'competencies thought to have general application will fit where they touch when it comes to specific organisations'. In other words, managers who may be viewed as competent in one contextual setting may be deemed 'incompetent' when faced with new challenges in another context.

Some have argued that there has been too much emphasis on assessment and not enough on learning (Loan-Clarke, 1996). This might be interpreted as a way of saying that the focus on practical, workplace outcomes is subordinating learning and understanding to the extent that the competence approach might be seen as almost anti-theory/anti-academic. There may therefore be a case for reasserting the role of established methodologies within the existing and expanding educational and vocational framework (Stewart and Hamlin, 1992a and 1992b). However, many managers might argue (and regularly do) that the gulf between learning and knowledge and its application in the workplace still remains. Theory, it would seem, does not travel easily into the workplace, and competence-based management development is presented as one attempt to overcome this problem.

At an operational, practical level, there are major concerns about the way competence-based approaches are seen to operate (cost, time, bureaucracy, inflexibility etc.), and many of these concerns carry over into the way management development strategies and approaches are being implemented to generate frustration and resentment in some contexts when this approach is seen not to be appropriate or relevant to the needs of managers (Stewart and Hamlin, 1992a; Currie and Darby, 1995; Antonacopoulou and Fitzgerald, 1996; Loan-Clarke, 1996).

What can we conclude in respect of competency-based approaches? Despite the criticisms, it would appear that the notion of competence-based development has now been established within the framework of UK management development (Thomson et al., 2001).

More recent evidence suggests that there are moves away from the generic model originally developed by MCI to a more flexible and contextually based approach such as that defined in the latest standards. However, it would still seem that many organisations prefer to 'do their own thing'. Rather than engage with a somewhat costly, bureaucratic, prescriptive and rigid framework of national standards, organisations are now developing competence frameworks for managers that are more fragmented and differentiated as they seek to adapt to changing circumstances, for example, shortened organisational lifecycles (Sparrow and Bognanno, 1994; Roberts, 1995).

This adjustment may be seen as an inevitable consequence of what some would judge to be inherent flaws in a nationally driven, generic framework – now on its third set of standards. But although this more pragmatic, flexible response by organisations is likely to be welcomed by many in the field of management development, it does raise a number of issues, not least how to maintain and guarantee a system of assessment and national accreditation for management qualifications with any measure of confidence. Finally, it is important to remember that 'competence-based development is not seen to be a panacea for all management development ills but is one approach which may be taken with others' (Currie and Darby, 1995: 17).

Activity

● List what you see as the pros and cons of Competency Based Development (CBD).

● To what extent would CBD make a difference to the way managers in your organisation are currently being developed?

● If your organisation already operates CBD, how effective has it been?

Less formal methods for developing managers

There is a growing interest in less formalised methods for developing managers and such methods are proving increasingly effective (Thomson *et al.*, 2001). As we saw earlier, this may in part reflect a general dissatisfaction with generic, formal off-the-shelf courses or education programmes that do not meet unique organisational or individual needs (Roberts and McDonald, 1995; Mole, 2000; Thomson *et al.*, 2001). It may also reflect the desire by individuals and organisations to take advantage of more flexible and cost-effective methods that fit with changing lifestyles and rapidly changing organisational situations.

Action learning

In Chapter 8, the significance of experiential learning processes to the development of managers was identified. Much of the theory relating to experiential learning is drawn from the theoretical work of Kolb (1984) and Honey and Mumford (1986), who introduced the concept of a learning cycle in which managers learn through a process of:

● implementation;

● reflection;

● making changes;

● initiating further action.

Burgoyne and Stuart (1991) point out that a greater focus on experiential learning in the workplace, coupled to a reaction against the 'remoteness', complication and institutionalisation of management development, has encouraged organisations to adopt new methods of learning. Many of these new approaches are built around the principles of action learning pioneered by writers such as Reg Revans.

Revans' key principles of action learning

1. Management development must be based on real work projects.
2. Those projects must be owned and defined by senior managers as having a significant impact on the future success of the enterprise.
3. Managers must aim to make a real return on the cost of the investment.
4. Managers must work together and learn from each other.
5. Managers must achieve real action and change.
6. Managers must study the content and process of change.
7. Managers must publicly commit themselves to action.   (Margerison, 1991: 38)

Revans saw learning (L) as a combination of what he terms 'programmed knowledge' (P) and 'questioning insight' (Q): thus $L = P + Q$. When facing unprecedented changes, managers cannot know what programmed knowledge they will need. Instead, they need to 'understand the subjective aspects of searching the unfamiliar, or learning to pose useful and discriminating questions'. Therefore action learning becomes a 'simple device of setting them to tackle real problems that have so far defied solution' (Revans, 1983: 11).

Revans argues that managerial learning has to embrace both 'know-how' and 'know-that', and be rooted in real problem-solving, where 'lasting behavioural change is more likely to follow the reinterpretation of past experiences than the acquisition of fresh knowledge' (p. 14). Managers will be more able to make their interpretations, which are 'necessarily subjective, complex and ill-structured' (p. 14), and reorder their perceptions by working with colleagues who are engaged in the same process, rather than with non-managers such as management teachers who are 'not exposed to real risk in responsible action'. In other words, managers form 'learning sets' (groups of four to six people) who, with the aid of a facilitator, work together and learn to give and accept criticism, advice and support. Margerison (1994b), citing Revans, likens this approach to 'comrades in adversity'. Managers will only 'learn effectively when they are confronted with difficulties and have the opportunity to share constructively their concerns and experiences with others' (p. 109).

Margerison (1991), drawing on case studies and personal experience of supervising action learning programmes, points out that managers learn a considerable amount:

- about themselves,
- about their job,
- about team members, and most of all
- about how to improve things and make changes.

However, there are some doubts about the efficacy of action learning. For example, will managers truly engage in action learning if this challenges current management cultures and political structures with concomitant risks for the individual (Pedler, 1997)?

Coaching and mentoring

Coaching

To many managers, coaching and mentoring represent the most tangible, practical and, if carried out effectively, possibly most useful forms of relatively informal on-the-job development.

Coaching is defined by Torrington *et al.* (1994: 432) as 'improving the performance of somebody who is already competent rather than establishing competence in the first place'. It is analogous to the sports coach who is seeking to improve performance by continually analysing and offering constructive criticism and guidance to an athlete or player. The coach (boss) must be willing to share tasks and assignments with the individual. Each task must have scope, responsibility and authority to challenge and test the individual. Coaching usually begins with a period of instruction and 'shadowing' to grasp the essential aspects of the task. There is then a transfer of responsibility for the task to the individual. Throughout the process there is a dialogue, with regular feedback on performance in the form of constructive criticism and comments. The effectiveness of this feedback is dependent upon a sound working relationship.

In most organisations, coaching is done on an informal basis and is dependent on the boss having the inclination, time and motivation to do it, as well as possessing the necessary expertise and personal qualities for it to succeed.

Activity

Have you recently experienced coaching – either being coached or coaching one of your own staff? List the benefits you or your staff felt they gained from the experience.

Mentoring

Mentoring was described more fully in Chapter 8. It differs from coaching in two ways:

- The relationship is not usually between the individual and his or her immediate boss. An older, more experienced manager unconnected with the individual's immediate workplace is normally selected or agrees to act as mentor.
- Mentoring is about developing and sharing relationships rather than engaging in specific activities.

Mentoring represents a powerful form of management development for both the parties involved. For the individual, it allows them to discuss confusing, perplexing or ambiguous situations, and their innermost feelings and emotions, with somebody they can trust and respect. They gain the benefit of accumulated wisdom and experience from somebody who is knowledgeable and 'street-wise' in the ways of the organisation, especially its political workings. For older managers looking for new challenges and stimulation in their managerial role, mentoring represents an ideal development opportunity. It gives them an opportunity to achieve satisfaction and personal reward by sharing in the growth and maturity of another individual.

Stop & think

If you haven't already done so, think seriously about finding yourself a mentor to provide you with support and guidance in your managerial role.

Projects and secondments

Project management is increasing in prominence as the role and function of a manager changes within an increasingly turbulent, uncertain and often ambiguous world (Watson and Harris, 1999). Managers are developing new skills and having to take on board new values (Rosenfeld and Wilson, 1999). Buchanan and Boddy (1992) highlight the need to develop the notion of the 'flexible manager' who has the ability to:

- understand and relate to the wider environment;
- manage in that environment;
- manage complex, changing structures;
- innovate and initiate change;
- manage and utilise sophisticated information systems;
- manage people with different values and expectations.

One way to develop these attitudes and competences is to delegate responsibility for managing a cross-functional team of people, tasked with achieving a specific organisational goal within a fixed time-scale and to a set budget. This cross-functional project management role not only improves core management skills such as communication and motivation but is also effective at developing 'higher order' diagnostic, judgemental, evaluative and political skills (Buchanan and Boddy, 1992).

Secondments are also increasingly being used for manager development. Multinational companies have highly sophisticated management exchange programmes that are used not only to develop important language and cultural skills in managers, but also to reinforce the organisation's central belief and value systems (see the example of Unilever earlier in this chapter and the later section that explores international management development).

Exchange programmes also exist between public and private sector organisations to transfer knowledge and broaden understanding. Some larger organisations are seconding their managers to various initiatives designed to assist small business ventures and community programmes.

Activity Projects and secondments offer many developmental benefits. Identify a possible project or secondment opportunity that you could take advantage of in your organisation.

Outdoor management development

During the 1980s and 1990s increasing attention was focused on the benefits of outdoor management development (OMD) as a development tool. OMD has its roots in the Outward Bound movement founded by Kurt Hahn (Burnett and James, 1994). The aim is to provide opportunities for personal growth and for managers to realise the potential of their 'inner resources' (Irvine and Wilson, 1994). In OMD, managers are exposed to emotional, physical and mental risks and challenges in which skills such as leadership and teamwork become *real* to the individuals and groups concerned (Burnett and James, 1994) and where 'the penalties for wrong decisions are painful; the consequence of bad judgements can be as real as being lost in a cold rainstorm at the edge of a dark forest' (Banks, 1994: 11). Others have likened OMD to 'outdoor action learning' in which 'the physical tasks at the core of outdoor development courses, whether they be abseiling down a cliff, climbing a mountain peak or navigating rapids in canoes are real tasks which present real problems to real people in real time with real constraints' (Banks, 1994: 9).

However, following a 1993 TV documentary from the Channel 4 *Cutting Edge* series, which featured a group of managers being 'damaged in body and mind' while on such a course (Banks, 1994), some began to questions the benefits of OMD as a form of management development. Some were critical of the degree of risk and adventure that managers *actually* experience, and argue that many of the claimed 'benefits' of OMD can be attained within existing development frameworks (Irvine and Wilson, 1994). Jones and Oswick (1993) identify a plethora of claimed benefits for OMD, many of which they say are anecdotal and unsubstantiated. Tarrant (2005) relating OMD to management team development, captures this shift when she states 'Depending on your bent or glee at seeing a difficult colleague disappear down a river without a paddle, the experience [of OMD] invariably delivered "war stories" of hilarity and terror with widely questioned benefits to the team at the real coalface back at the office' (p. 25).

Whilst physical challenges are still popular, there has been a noticeable shift to more sophisticated forms of OMD that focuses on problem solving, innovation and changing behaviour in the classroom and beyond. For example, Arkin (2003) describes how Sony (Europe) took its senior managers on a 'leadership journey' across Europe linked to team and individual exercises designed for them to experience the anxiety and uncertainty their employees felt during radical change. Allen (2003) describes how managers are engaging with community-based projects linked to corporate social responsibility. As Allen (2003: 36) argues, OMD is moving towards 'experiences that are carefully designed to provide a true metaphor for the workplace'.

Self-development

Organisations that invest in effective management development programmes are encouraging their managers to take more responsibility and control of their own development. As Boydell and Pedler (1981: 3) remark:

> Any effective system for management development must increase the manager's capacity and willingness to take control over and responsibility for events, and participating for themselves in their own learning.

If managers take responsibility for their own development they are likely to:

- improve career prospects;
- improve performance;
- develop certain skills;
- achieve full potential/self-actualisation.

What arrangements have you made for your self-development?

A range of techniques exist for managers to undertake self-development. Some involve managers helping each other by sharing experiences in self-managed learning groups (see the previous section on action learning). Other approaches are more personally focused, using techniques such as distance learning materials, computer-based training and interactive videos. (For a fuller discussion of the methods used for self-development, see Pedler *et al.*, 1990.)

In summary, this section has outlined some of the formal and informal methods that are currently being used to develop managers. However, it must be borne in mind that a great deal of development takes place in ways that are not only less formal, they are incidental and opportunistic (Mumford, 1997). There may be times when the individual manager is unaware that development has even taken place, e.g. trial and error, learning from mistakes, playing political games etc. This suggests that development may have as much to do with the provision of organisational support and facilitation for the creation of a learning culture (Woodall, 2000) and managing the influence of organisational context (social, political, cultural) in which managers operate (Doyle, 2000a) as it does with the selection and implementation of specific development methods.

Evaluating management development

If management development is to be effective in meeting individual needs and delivering organisation goals, the whole process must be effectively evaluated to make judgements about its cost-effectiveness and aid ongoing organisational learning and improvement (Easterby-Smith, 1994). Traditionally, the literature on evaluation has focused heavily on the training and education 'components' of development (Warr *et al.*, 1970; Rae, 1986). Evaluation is concerned with the immediate training or educational 'event': measuring the inputs to the event, the process itself and immediate outcomes (see Figure 10.4). Measurement is against identified development needs and training objectives within the framework of a systematic training cycle (Harrison, 1997). There is often less concern with the longer-term impact and effects of the event or activity (Rae, 1986).

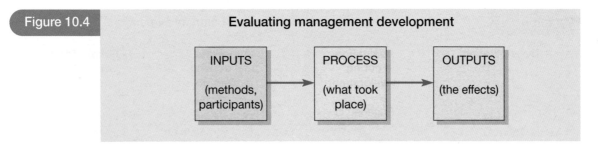

Figure 10.4   Evaluating management development

INPUTS (methods, participants) → PROCESS (what took place) → OUTPUTS (the effects)

Approaching evaluation

There are different approaches to evaluation. Some are regarded as being objective, rigorous and scientific, while others are much more pragmatic, subjective and interpretative in orientation (Easterby-Smith, 1994). In collecting data, it is normal to employ a range of quantitative and qualitative methods (Smith and Porter, 1990).

Methods will include:

- in-course and post-course questionnaires;
- attitude surveys and psychological tests before and after the event;
- appraisal systems;
- observations by trainers and others;
- self-reports and critical incident analysis.

Thomson *et al.* (2001) reported a similar range of methods in their survey. Formal methods included: appraisals, surveys, training needs audits, comparison with strategic plans. Informal methods included: consultations with line managers, mentors, training managers and consultants.

Some issues in evaluation

In attempting to evaluate management development, a number of issues emerge. Most evaluation is short-termist in outlook – captured in the ubiquitous 'happy sheet' questionnaire where questions focus on the immediacy of development activity rather than its longer-term outcomes. But to be effective, development must permit managers (a) the opportunity to transfer and apply new knowledge and skills and (b) a period of learning and adjustment in respect of newly acquired attitudes and behaviours. This implies that any evaluation of development outcomes has to have a longer-term orientation.

Figure 10.5 presents a more developed view of the evaluation process. It incorporates pre- and post-development evaluation but critically, it suggests that attention must be given to evaluating post development activity after a period of time has elapsed – ideally somewhere between 6 and 12 months. This permits those responsible for development to make informed judgements about knowledge and skills transfer to the management role and attitudinal and behavioural change.

In addition to assessing changes in the performance and behaviour of individual managers, evaluation must include some assessment of the impact of the organisational context in which managers are seeking to apply their new knowledge, e.g. the cultural and political environment that may promote or inhibit development. As Smith (1993: 23) observes, 'management development programmes are not context free but dependent on the cultural baggage of the participants and the organisation'. Therefore any judgement about the outcomes of management development programmes must be viewed within the context in which they are embedded. This raises further issues about the way management development outcomes themselves are interpreted and justified. For example, any claims about the efficacy of management development investment may fall prey to political games. As Fox (1989: 192) explains, 'because a pseudo-scientific approach [to evaluation] does not deal with human issues and

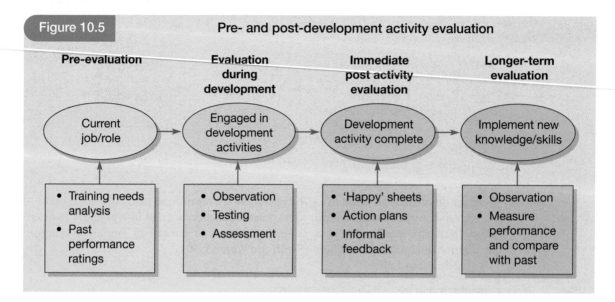

Figure 10.5   Pre- and post-development activity evaluation

value judgements, it is not surprising that they fall into disuse or are simply done by token [then] politics takes over'. Both Fox (1989) and Currie (1994), who have examined the evaluation of management development programmes in the National Health Service, conclude that political and cultural factors were heavily influential in shaping the evaluation process.

Another issue relates to the way development outcomes are measured. It is common to encounter evaluation methodologies that are left striving to display some form of pseudo-scientific objectivity to win or protect investment in development activity. For example, those responsible for development might be tempted to make unsubstantiated causal links between an investment in development and some aspect of organisational performance, e.g. annual sales. Another problem is that the environment in which evaluation is taking place is often highly complex and subjective and evaluation methodologies may be judged simplistic and inadequate (Smith, 1993; Mole, 1996, Mole, 2000). For example, some of the criticisms levelled at competency-based development discussed earlier revolve around the doubts and reservations over supposedly objective and structured internal and external verification procedures as a means of determining the level of an individual's competency (Loan-Clarke, 1996). In other words, 'the complexity of management training and development demonstrates the point that measuring its effectiveness cannot be adequately accomplished by using a single, generic formula' (Endres and Kleiner, 1990).

Concerns surround the need to ensure that emotional, attitudinal and behavioural outcomes are measured and have an equal validity alongside harder aspects such as financial performance and technical competence. This necessitates the use of carefully constructed and focused methodologies incorporating ethnographic, interpretative techniques (Fox, 1989; Currie, 1994). But this presupposes that those tasked with evaluation have the time, commitment and skills to conduct research in these areas.

Looking at all these issues, it seems inevitable that the evaluation of management development will always be a somewhat difficult, complex and at times contentious process where it involves the measurement of changes in some aspect of human behaviour. One way to improve evaluation is for organisations to adopt a more systemic, holistic perspective of evaluation. This can be done by:

● Examining the extent to which development activity fits with individual needs and organisational context.

● Assessing how far new behaviours can be transferred and applied in the workplace, whether or not new behaviour corresponds with espoused organisational culture and values.

● Adopting methodologies that can measure both hard and soft aspects of performance (Easterby-Smith, 1994; Mole, 1996).

● From a more practical perspective, rather than focus on the benefits of development, consider the ramifications of not doing development.

● Rather than looking forward to eventual outcomes, it might be more prudent to look back at, for example, past mistakes, which can often be quantified. Improvements can be measured from that point, i.e. how mistakes and associated cost have been eliminated through development activity.

But are we asking too much? Is evaluation a chimera? As Easterby-Smith (1994: 143) states:

> Thus attempts to evaluate development methods may fail to satisfy the purist, and much of this stems from the diffuseness of the target that is being examined and the difficulty of isolating procedures from the real constraints and politics of the organisations in which they are taking place.

Management development for different contexts and special needs

Up until now we have stressed an open systems perspective in which the need for management development to acknowledge contextual diversity and complexity is a significant consideration. This section will explore a variety of different contexts in which development takes place and looks at the needs of different managers.

Senior manager development

Many of those involved in planning, organising and facilitating management development in organisations encounter a paradox when they seek to address senior management development. On the one hand, senior managers are viewed as a valuable and critical resource to the survival and success of the organisation (Woodall and Winstanley, 1998; Syrett and Lammiman, 1999). Logic therefore dictates that during periods of radical change their knowledge and skills must be maintained at levels consistent with meeting the challenges of change. And yet on the other hand, their development often appears to be inadequate or neglected. For instance, a survey of 295 HR specialists in the 1990s revealed that 50 per cent of organisations surveyed did not have a strategy for developing their senior managers (Industrial Society, 1997).

Barriers to senior manager development?

What might explain this apparent neglect of senior manager development activity? Explanations range from the pressure of work and a lack of time that prevent them from engaging in their personal development – individually and collectively – to deeper emotional and political attitudes about their perceived need for development. As Syrett and Lammiman (1999: 148) identify:

> the distressing thing about boardroom education at the end of the 20th century is not the availability of suitable courses, which has improved immensely in the last decade, but the lack of take-up at a time when the need for properly educated directors has never been clearer

Reflecting on the earlier sections of this chapter, can you spot an important issue arising from this statement by Syrett and Lammiman?

In identifying the problem, Syrett and Lammiman may also have uncovered a contributory factor when they appear to suggest that development should revolve around the availability of *suitable courses*. However, as we have already seen in the preceding sections, management development should be viewed as being far broader than merely sending people on management training courses – important as they are.

But there may be a deeper reason inhibiting some senior managers from participating in development activity. Simply put, they do not believe they need it! Logically in their mind, the very fact they have attained senior level shows that they possess the skills and capabilities to perform at that level. There may also be political and credibility considerations which prevent them participating. Admitting you may need developing could offer your opponents a political advantage or undermine your credibility with senior management colleagues.

How should senior managers be developed?

Individually, the role of a senior manager demands a considerable emphasis on strategic leadership coupled to legal and regulatory duties that are not found in other management roles. Collectively, senior managers have to be developed to work as an effective team while at the same time maintaining a required independence of thought and behaviour (Mumford, 1988).

Woodall and Winstanley (1998) identify four stages in the process of developing senior managers:

- *Grooming* – managers are prepared for the transition to the boardroom by giving them wider responsibilities and exposure to a range of managerial experiences.

- *Induction* – having entered the boardroom, senior managers are familarised with the cultures, processes and practices that prevail there – both formal and informal.

- *Competencies within the role* – an assessment of the individual's current level of skills and ability benchmarked against what is required to develop senior manager competence. Individual development plans are prepared through joint discussion and negotiation.

- *Team effectiveness* – the collective development needs of the senior manager team are assessed in areas such as group interaction, team roles etc. and a development plan for the top team is implemented.

Research suggests that senior managers prefer to learn through informal learning processes. They are 'less comfortable with formal settings where the agenda is written by someone else and they do not have control over whom they exchange views with' (Syrett and Lammiman,

Box 10.2

The author was engaged by a company to act as a development mentor and adviser to a newly appointed operations director. The hidden agenda communicated to the author by the CEO was to 'persuade' him that he lacked the necessary skills to perform his increasingly strategic role and if he did not develop those skills, his position was under threat. Despite a number of meetings with the operations director in which issues such as career planning, development needs, etc. were discussed, it was clear that he was not prepared to admit he needed development and always found an excuse not to participate in framing a development plan. The author concluded from his observations that the operations director felt that any admission that he needed development would weaken his power and credibility in the boardroom. His lack of strategic skills was a major reason for him being asked to leave the company 18 months later.

1999). In many ways, development for senior managers mirrors the approaches that are used at lower levels. They will incorporate a blend of formal and informal methods, e.g. job rotation, secondments, mentoring, role shadowing, project working, special assignments, action learning combined with management education, conferences, seminars, forums etc. (Mumford, 1988, 1997; Industrial Society, 1997; Syrett and Lammiman, 1999). However, it is important to note that the content and emphasis given to aspects such as political, leadership and change skills are likely to differ markedly to reflect strategic, legal, regulatory and fiduciary roles as well as the added emotional and psychological burden that is inherent in such roles.

Developing professionals as managers

The development of professionals (scientists, doctors, engineers, accountants etc.) as managers presents those responsible for management development with a number of interesting challenges.

Activity

Think about the way that professionals are being developed in your organisation (this may include you). List what you see as the challenges facing developers in your organisation.

The special characteristics of professionals

Woodall and Winstanley (1998) identify professionals as having the following characteristics:

- expertise based on a distinct body of knowledge;
- altruistic service orientation to work;
- autonomy and independence;
- restrictive entry;
- collective peer group collegiate relations;
- code of professional ethics;
- power through expertise;
- professional goals above the organisation.

Bittel (1998) argues that the main challenge for developers stems from the highly individualistic approach that professionals have towards their work. They view professional work as rewarding and intellectually challenging. They are generally loyal to their profession and the values it espouses. But when faced with the challenge of moving into management, they may display a number of what Bittel deems are 'counterproductive characteristics'. They:

- over-apply their analytical skills and can become paralysed by analysis;
- are insensitive to others and feel they are above organisational politics;
- expect their technical expertise to solve organisational problems;
- respect logic and intuition over emotion;
- lack feeling and empathy;
- lack awareness of common-sense solutions to problems.

There is, of course, a danger of generalising too far here and becoming a prey to stereotyping. Undoubtedly, some professionals make very good managers and are particularly good with people (Woodall and Winstanley, 1998). But others face conflict between their role as professional and their role as manager. For example, research in secondary education amongst heads of department and deputy heads highlights the clash between the professional role as teacher and the role of middle manager (Adey, 2000). In the NHS, similar clashes were identified. Some doctors who found themselves moving into management by default became more concerned with protecting their corner and loyalty to their professional colleagues. However, other doctors welcomed their move into management, were loyal and committed to the organisation and viewed themselves as a member of the management team (Woodall and Winstanley, 1998).

How to approach the management development of professionals?

As we have seen, one area that demands close attention is the conflict between professional and managerial value systems. Clearly, approaches to development that challenge these values are likely to be resented and resisted. For example, in the NHS, competence-based approaches that were seen to be generic, highly prescriptive and structured did not go down well with professional groups (Currie and Darby, 1995). As Currie (1999: 58) remarks:

> Whilst recognising that every organisation is unique, the history and professional elaboration of groups in the public sector make a hospital particularly unique. The weakness of the competence approach and insensitivity of delivery to context reinforce the ideological gap between managerial and professional values.

Other research highlights the potential dangers of using what are perceived to be generic, simplistic, off-the-shelf training courses for developing professionals as managers. For example, in education, the government has made the management development of head teachers a key priority. But amongst some head teachers management theory is seen as 'applied social science' offering simplistic recipes to complex problems. Research suggests that overall, professionals in education may prefer a more contingent, personalised approach to their development and the issues it raises (Bolam, 1997).

The spirit of this personalised approach is captured in the notion of continuous professional development (CPD).

> The essential principles of CPD are that development should be continuous; it should be owned and managed by the learner; learning objectives should be clear and wherever possible, serve both organisational needs as well as individual goals. And regular investment of an individual's time in learning should be seen as an essential part of professional life.
>
> (Little, 1997: 28)

Stop & think

What arrangement have you made/are you making for your professional development to include management knowledge and skills?

As most professions now incorporate elements of management and being a manager into their requirement for CPD, the issue then becomes one of identifying what is the best approach for professionals to adopt and what, from the requisite professional body viewpoint, constitutes 'good' management development.

In summary, it would seem that in terms of developing professionals as managers, the issue is not so much one of access and the availability of management development but recognising that professionals have special needs and prefer to plan and organise their own management development to meet those needs in a contingent manner. For developers the message is clear: resist the temptation to direct professionals into structured, mechanistic and simplistic approaches. Instead, offer advice and support within the framework and spirit of CPD where reflective and experiential on-the-job approaches such as multidiscipline projects and individual assignments linked to coaching and mentoring seem to work best in developing their managerial skills.

Graduate management development

Research has revealed that 68 per cent of organisations surveyed viewed graduate recruitment and development as a key feature of their business strategy (The Industrial Society, 1998). Graduates are recruited – usually directly from university or shortly after they graduate – for broadly two purposes. Firstly, they provide essential specialist knowledge and skills, e.g. scientific, engineering, computing etc. Secondly, they 'create a pool of intelligent people with high potential as a means of providing for management of the future' (Mumford, 1997: 222).

Developing graduates as managers

Following a rigorous selection process – usually involving an assessment centre – successful graduates will work with their organisation to prepare a personal development plan. The plan will normally focus on the development of both hard and soft managerial skills – building on the information obtained at the assessment centre and other identified needs.

In respect of the way in which graduates are developed as managers, Mumford (1997: 223) argues:

> There is no mystery about what to do with graduates. There needs to be a formal development programme for them which will include appropriate courses; they need to have assignments in particular units or departments long enough to establish that they have done a definable piece of work.

In most cases, management development will last between one and two years and involve joint and independent project working across a number of functional areas. Increasingly, there is the probability of being seconded to other divisions and undertaking overseas assignments (see the section on international management development later in this chapter). Development at all stages should be supported by a comprehensive system of mentoring and performance appraisal to provide essential feedback at critical stages in the development plan. Upon successful completion of the development plan, graduates will normally assume a junior management position and progress in their chosen career.

Management development in the small firm

The economic role of small firms (defined generically as less than 50 people) in creating wealth and employment is widely acknowledged in the UK and beyond. For example, small firms account for 90 per cent of employing companies in the EU and employ some 30 million people (Kerr and McDougall, 1999). In the UK, 75 per cent of employers are classified as small firms. However, while small firms employ the bulk of the workforce, they also display a high failure rate. In Australia, for example, an estimated 30,000 small firms fail each year, 50 per cent fail in the first two years and only 20 per cent survive beyond ten years (Saee and Mouzytchenko, 1999). In the UK 65–75 per cent collapse or are sold during first-generation ownership tenure (Syert and Lammiman, 1999).

Management development as a strategic issue for the small firm

While there are many factors that may be cited as contributing to this high rate of failure, the lack of management knowledge and expertise is viewed as a major factor (Saee and Mouzytchenko, 1999). Certainly, there appears to be sound evidence to suggest that few managers in small firms receive formal management training. For instance, research indicates that one in four managers receives no training and only 15 per cent of managers had received a maximum of two weeks' training over two years – comparable to larger firms (IRS Employment review, 1997). A similar picture is revealed by Thomson *et al.* (2001), who found that while there had been improvements in the development of managers in small firms in recent years, one in five managers received no training at all.

Stop & think

To what extent are the problems facing the development of managers in small firms similar or different to those in larger firms?

Why the apparent lack of management development in the small firm?

The quoted statistics above may be a cause for some pessimism but you should note that, in the main, they relate to formal modes of development such as training and management education rather than less formal, on-the-job development. Nevertheless, research suggests that the reasons why small firms appear to ignore or avoid investing in management development are fairly clear and consistent. The following reasons are identified as the main barriers to development (Saee and Mouzytchenko, 1999; Kerr and McDougall, 1999; Thomson *et al.*, 2001):

- lack of time;
- lack of resources to fund formal training;
- lack of previous formal education;
- concerns about realising returns on investment in management training;
- not knowing where or how to get advice and assistance;
- complicated procedures and bureaucracy when applying for assistance.

Another significant barrier arises from the peculiarities, idiosyncrasies and diversity of the small firm sector. This often makes the transfer and take-up of mainstream, large-organisation-focused methods problematical (Tolentino, 1998). Problems also emerge when management development is reduced to the provision of 'enterprise training' encompassing basic skills in operations, HRM marketing, finance etc.

> This view however, springs from an economic model of small businesses as large firms scaled down, a model which many consider to be deeply flawed. . . . Management development is seen as a subordinate priority to the need to improve the institutional and structural framework within which small firms operate.
>
> (Thomson *et al.*, 2001: 205)

Other barriers may arise from the attitudes and values that are to be found in small firms. Kerr and McDougall (1999), researching 130 small firms in Scotland, found that a short-term outlook, pragmatism, a desire for informality and the need to survive were considerations that often took precedence over training or business planning. In another study of small firms in the hotel and leisure industry, Beaver and Lashley (1998: 234) found that 'managers running small firms have a wider variety of roles and different priorities than those running larger enterprises'; for instance, the assumption that all owner/managers are motivated solely by commercial objectives 'is naïve'. Many in fact attach more significance to personal lifestyle considerations. In the same vein, Tolentino (1998) makes the point that small firm managers have a different outlook to managers in larger firms in areas such as entrepreneurship, risk-taking, personal achievement and control. They have a much closer identification with the business and the family/community in which it is located.

Promoting management development in the small firm

Considerations for a strategy for developing managers in the small firm would include the following:

- identifying the knowledge and skills required by small firm owner/managers;
- delivering development in a way that acknowledges the sector's diversity and uniqueness;
- finding ways to overcome the bureaucracy and provide accessible and affordable approaches to development.

Managerial knowledge and skills for the small firm

In terms of the knowledge and skills required, these are seemingly well understood and documented. Thomson *et al.* (2001) cite Bolton's list of skills as typical of those that are felt to be required:

- raising and using finance;
- costing and control information;
- organising and delegating;
- marketing;
- using information;
- personnel management;
- dealing with technological change;
- production scheduling and purchase control.

Other studies have shown that while these areas were important, many small firm managers were lacking the required level of knowledge and skills in these key areas. For example, one survey found that small firm managers were particularly lacking in areas such as: the ability to appraise performance; strategic planning; teamworking and communication (IRS Employment Review, 1997).

So what might constitute a suitable framework of delivery methods and approaches? Tolentino (1998) suggests that the following points should constitute a framework for good management development practice:

- Identify training needs in conjunction with managers.
- Adopt a demand-led approach to learning.
- Ensure that training is close to the workplace and at suitable times.
- Provide support with costs but ensure that the firm makes some contribution.
- Use of consultancy-led approach.
- Work with managers from other small firms for advice and benchmarking.

In terms of support to facilitate development of managers, the role of the CEO/owner is seen as a crucial factor, as is the support given by experienced external consultants/advisers (Wong *et al.*, 1997; Kerr and McDougall, 1999). Other studies highlight the role of various government agencies, tax incentives and loans, and the impact of the Investors in People initiative in promoting and supporting management development in small firms (Beaver and Lashley, 1998).

In summary, it is clear that the needs of the small firm manager have similarities to those of managers in larger organisations but they also differ sharply in a number of important respects. Success in developing these managers has to begin with a careful and considered examination of the context in which they are managing, allied to an understanding of their individual and collective motives and needs; and ensuring that whatever methods or approaches that are adopted are relevant and affordable.

Management development in the public sector

Management in the UK public sector has often been the butt of criticism from politicians, journalists and other commentators about its seemingly bureaucratic, inefficient and unfocused approach to organisation and management. Cooper (2002) captures the mood in a recent newspaper article:

> many senior public sector managers thought that 'management' was about changing organisational systems, committee structures, and hierarchy charts rather than developing and investing in their vision/long-term objectives and the people who achieve them. For them management meant bureaucratic action, fiddling with committees, setting up control systems and dealing with detail.

While some of this criticism may be justified, other criticisms of public sector management often come from those who are ill-informed about the many conflicting and competing pressures that face many public sector managers. According to Bicker and Cameron (1997), managers in public sector organisations face a number of conflicting demands stemming from:

- resource constraints;
- a hostile owner;
- pressure to emulate private sector practices;
- the need to maintain the public sector ethic;
- union pressures and demands.

It is not difficult to see how these demands may conflict when, for example, pressures to emulate profit-driven commercial organisations have to be reconciled with attitudes and behaviours that give primacy to values such as public service and patient care. Similarly, public sector managers increasingly have to motivate employees to attain higher standards of national or local government-imposed performance standards in situations where working conditions are often inferior to those in the private sector and where incentive opportunities are severely curtailed by public sector spending constraints.

With these pressures in mind, the choice of management development methods is important. The focus for management development in the public sector should, according to Bicker and Cameron, be on 'key enablers':

- *roles and responsibilities* – providing clarity and accountability;
- *leadership skills* – including influencing, decision-making and communication skills;
- *attitudes* – including risk-taking and openness.

For many public sector organisations, expensive management training courses are not an option – given the resource restrictions they face. As a recent study of a management training initiative in the NHS revealed, there may be resistance to externally driven courses that are premised on values that run counter to or deviate from those that predominate in the public sector (Currie, 1999).

Given these resource or value-driven constraints, managers in the public sector are more likely to be predisposed towards less formal, on-the-job methods that are rooted in their organisational context and meet the challenges they face (Currie, 1999). Methods such as project working, coaching, mentoring, action learning and, where appropriate, professional partnerships with colleges and universities are likely to receive greater support (Mavin and Bryans, 2000).

International management development

For multinational organisations such as Unilever, development is focused on the creation of elite cadres of international managers tasked with building efficient networks of organisations operating across national boundaries (Anderson *et al.*, 1998). We saw earlier in this chapter that Unilever's aim is to develop a common philosophy and system of management development that is 'seamless' and permits managers to move easily between different countries (Reitsma, 2001).

However, while organisations such as Unilever may adopt a strategic, integrated approach to development, others are adopting an approach to international management development that – like UK management development – is best described as 'piecemeal' in orientation (Woodall and Winstanley, 1998). In addition to piecemeal approaches, those who develop international managers are faced with the perception that many managers in the USA and UK are 'simply not global animals' (Ferner, 1994: 91). The problem is rooted in what might be termed a 'cultural blindness' which seemingly limits the ability of many Western managers to work in multicultural environments (Miroshnik, 2002). It is axiomatic therefore that an inability to address cultural diversity has the potential to undermine management development strategies in an international context (Liu and Vince, 1999). The primary focus for international management development therefore becomes the need to ensure that 'working effectively in multiple cross-cultural contexts is . . . a vital competence' (Harris and Kumra, 2000).

It is crucial that managers who are going to undertake an international assignment are properly prepared for the experience of expatriation. Preparation may include company briefings, short visits to host countries, cultural awareness and a language skills course. If families are accompanying the manager, an increasing number of organisations will involve spouses and partners in such preparation activities to include relocation, housing and education considerations (Woodall and Winstanley, 1998). Alongside this, the development of social, cultural, communication and empathetic knowledge and skills will be a priority. As Miroshnik (2002: 524) points out, 'Different cultural environments require different managerial behaviours . . . managing relations between multicultural organisations and cultural environments is thus a matter of accurate perception, diagnosis and appropriate adaptation'. It is clear that to be effective, this process of cultural awareness must begin well before the manager arrives at his or her international destination (Harris and Kumra, 2000).

As well as effective pre-preparation, successful development of the international manager must also be predicated on the establishment of clear international management development policies supported by and integrated with an appropriate international manager selection, recruitment, appraisal, career and reward infrastructure (Harzing and Van Ruysseveldt, 1995). For instance, Unilever's strategic approach ensures that managers are fully supported to work overseas through the implementation of detailed HR policies aimed at a global alignment of management development. Policies must also support the reintegration of the managers following their overseas assignment where there are issues such as status, ongoing career development, and adapting to a different lifestyle to consider.

Who are these international managers?

Before we discuss the methods used to develop managers for international assignments, it is useful to reflect on what we mean by the term 'international manager'. Unpacking the concept, we find that there are different types of international manager:

- local nationals employed by multinational to manage locally (host);
- managers who live abroad and run overseas divisions or companies (expatriates);
- managers on short missions or projects (sales teams, plant installation);
- managers who work across national boundaries (Euro-manager, Middle East).

In the past, the emphasis has been on expatriate managers whose primary role was to protect the interests of the multinational organisation (Rosenfeld and Wilson, 1999). They were generally male, married and working overseas was a permanent career for them. However, this type of international manager is giving way to a more 'flexible' type of international manager – one who may undertake 'one or two assignments in the course of their careers in order to gain international experience' (Harris and Kumra, 2000: 603). In addition, a small but growing number of these managers are women. But as we shall see shortly, this raises a further set of issues for developers to consider.

The knowledge and skills required for effective international management?

Phillips (1992) summarises the views of most commentators and practitioners in the following list:

- *technical skills and experience* often beyond those normally required at home, for example the engineer who needs sound financial management skills;
- *people skills* – cultural empathy, team-building and interpersonal skills;
- *intellectual skills* – seeing the big picture, and thinking in a macro not micro way;

- *emotional maturity* – being adaptable, independent, sensitive, self-aware;
- *motivation* – drive, enthusiasm, stamina, resilience and persistence.

But despite the recognition of the importance of softer skills, there is a risk that technical expertise may come to dominate and dictate the development agenda at the expense of softer skills development. Other risks include:

- the reliance on selection processes that rest heavily on personal recommendations;
- a successful track record in a national rather than an international context;
- selection criteria based on Western competences and personality traits which may have to be for an overseas appointment.

If such risks are not addressed, organisations may be in danger of setting their international managers up to fail, with serious consequences for the organisation and the individual.

Methods to develop international skills are eclectic and will vary according to the organisation, the type of international assignment that is planned, the nature of the host country etc. They will include formal programmes of management education to develop language skills and cultural awareness. They will also include on-the-job activities such as international exchanges, projects and action learning programmes to develop technical expertise, communication and interpersonal skills.

Developing women as international managers

A KPMG survey of 164 Western companies found that 94 per cent said it was important to send people on international assignments; however, they also pointed out that finding the right people for international assignments was a major HR concern (Caligiuri and Cascio, 1998). This is leading some Western organisations to break with tradition and consider women managers as candidates for international assignments. In addition to women managers meeting a growing demand for international assignments, organisations are recognising that women managers may have personality and communication skills that are better suited to international assignments (Caligiuri and Cascio, 1998). Their non-aggressive and more subtle, process-oriented approach to business, it is argued, has a better fit with many non-Western cultures (Wah, 1998).

But a paradox emerges. If women managers possess the qualities that make them suited for international assignments, why is it that only 3 per cent of expatriate managers are women (Linehan and Walsh, 2000)? There are a number of possible reasons. The first possibility stems from a lack of organisational support and the continuing stereotyping and prejudice women may face from within their own organisation about their suitability for overseas responsibilities (Varma *et al.*, 2001). In addition, while organisations may be good at providing training in areas such as cultural sensitivity, they rarely address gender specific issues facing potential women expatriate managers (Wah, 1998).

The second possibility revolves around the threat of hostility from host country male managers. The role of women in the host society may be viewed differently to that of the home country, e.g. women do not have a role to play in business (Linehan and Walsh, 2000; Owen and Scherer, 2002).

> In Brazil, male managers will automatically address their male counterparts assuming that any woman manager in the team is a subordinate. In the Middle East, male managers will only address women managers if they do not shake their hands or look into their face.
>
> (Wah, 1998)

The third possible reason relates to the practical and emotional issues that seemingly face women expatriate managers, such as the 'trailing male spouse' who may have difficulty in adjusting to life overseas in his new role. In addition, there is the challenge of caring for and educating children in unfamiliar surroundings (Woodall and Winstanley, 1998). The final possible reason relates to the single woman manager. Here, the threat is of sexual harassment and possible exclusion from decision making when business is done in male-dominated bars and clubs (Wah, 1998).

So what can be done to assist women managers faced with international assignments? In terms of development needs, the focus needs to be on helping women to cope with the cultural clashes and hostilities outlined above. Measures would include: the use of mentors, short visits to host countries to learn about attitudes to women managers and how to deal with them, preparing host countries to accept women managers (Caligiuri and Cascio, 1998; Wah, 1998).

International management development: embarking on a 'world tour'

In this section we will embark on a 'world tour' to explore the way managers are being developed in different countries. You will recall the point made earlier, that it is difficult to separate development approaches from the cultural, social and economic context in which they are located. This raises a number of issues, not least the problems associated with transferring Western models to other countries. This will become even clearer as the 'tour' progresses.

United States/United Kingdom

In respect of management development, both the USA and the UK are very similar in their approach. Management development is often viewed as a separate, discrete and heavily individualised activity, aimed at correcting identified 'weaknesses' in skills and knowledge or 'deviances' in individual attitudes and behaviour (Mumford, 1997). In essence, development approaches are dominated by a powerful rational-functional philosophy, which views the main justification for any development programme as being its direct contribution to business strategy and organisational performance. In other words, the view is that management development must add value to the business and maintain competitiveness in the face of environmental threats (Woodall and Winstanley, 1998; Thomson *et al.*, 2001).

Increasingly, the aim is to develop generalist managerial rather than narrow specialist skills to improve mobility and the ability to take on new assignments and challenges – especially in a global environment (Heisler and Benham, 1992). Development has often been synonymous with management education and/or short, intensive training courses. For example, both countries now focus attention on competence-based approaches. In the UK such approaches are institutionalised and championed through competency based development (see the earlier discussion on competency-based development, found on page 271). However, as we have seen in this chapter, there is now a growing emphasis on more holistic, contextual, work-based forms of development that are experientially based, e.g. action learning projects, coaching and mentoring (Vicere, 1998).

Europe

In contrast to the Anglo-Saxon model described above, many continental European approaches have in the past been less concerned with management development as a discrete activity. In France, for example, the development of managers is linked more closely to its social and historical context. Rather than management being something that can be explicitly developed in individuals, it is perceived as 'more a state of being' (Lawrence, 1992). Those who become managers form part of a social elite (*cadre*), and much of their development begins within the higher education institutions (*grandes écoles*), where the study of natural sciences and mathematics predominates. However, concerns are now being expressed about the ethnocentrism and insularity that is permeating French business schools (*grandes écoles de commerce*), creating structural and cultural barriers to a wider system of management education that is adapted to global market situations (Kumar and Usunier, 2001).

In Germany, the approach to development is much more functional, with specialist expertise, especially in engineering and science, being closely linked to the vocational system of education built around the concept of 'Technik' and the production of 'Technikers' – technical experts who dominate in management (Randlesome, 2000). As in France, the concept of management is not considered as something to be seen as separate, but more as part of the overall functional system within the organisation. Managers have less mobility than in the USA/UK, tending to stay in their functional role much longer.

In terms of the content of management development activity, there is less perceived need for generalist skills development and generalist business education such as that represented by the MBA, which in the past has been 'regarded with great suspicion' (Randlesome, 2000). Discrete management development activity is seen as less salient, and does not flourish to the same extent (Lawrence, 1992). Where management development is carried out it is mainly in-house (Thomson *et al.*, 2001). For instance, German managers tend to favour 'structured learning situations with precise objectives, detailed assignments and strict timetables' (Hill, 1994).

Despite their relatively weak tradition and the problem of 'cultural insularity' in terms of management development, France, Germany and other European countries are beginning to establish institutions specifically aimed at developing managers. For example, despite past reservations, there has been a growth of MBA activity in both Germany and France (Easterby-Smith, 1992; Randlesome, 2000). In major German companies such as Siemens and BMW there is a greater awareness of the importance of managerial competencies (Randlesome, 2000) and in France there is a belated emergence of US-style business schools (Hill, 1994; Kumar and Usunier, 2001).

Another important influence on management development is the increasing monetary, economic and social convergence and cooperation across the European Union. This has focused attention on the 'Europeanisation' of management and, more recently, on how to develop what might be termed the *Euro-manager*. This is seen by some as an essential requirement if Europe is to be properly equipped to fend off the competitive challenges posed by global markets (Tijmstra and Casler, 1992). However, some take a more cautious view. Hilb (1992) argues that there are major disparities in selection, appraisal and reward systems across Europe, and that management development is neither strategically oriented nor properly evaluated. Additionally, HRD practices in general are too heavily influenced by variations in national labour markets, cultures and legislative frameworks. Kakabadse and Myers (1995), studying 959 chief executives in Europe, found wide variations in terms of management orientation across a number of criteria that are predicted to have implications for management development. For Thornhill (1993), any move towards Europeanisation raises significant issues for management trainers, who have to contend with variations over job content, context, expectations, experiences and work-related values.

Thurley and Wirdenhuis (1991) also point to these cultural and other national variations, arguing that the concept of the Euro-manager will be relevant only in certain industrial contexts. Storey (1992) identifies managerial parochialism and the lack of a European 'mindset' as a barrier, concluding that:

> The notion of the Euro-manager may not quite be a myth but the extent to which there is a clear conceptual and practical difference between this species and the international manager is open to question.
>
> (p. 2)

Far East

In the past, considerable attention was focused on the prowess of Japanese (and more recently, Korean and Taiwanese) management practices in attaining organisational success in a global marketplace. This success may have as much to do with social and cultural factors as the ways in which Japanese managers are developed, since the two are inextricably linked. For Japanese managers, the experience of development is much more likely to be a long-term affair rather than the short-term, 'sink-or-swim' approach that characterises development in Western, Anglo-Saxon countries. In Japan there is a strong foundation of individual loyalty to the organisation, and an emphasis on providing job security for employees. The approach to development is likely to be much more systematic, structured and carefully planned (Neelankavil, 1992). Whereas Anglo-Saxon models stress individualism and development through short, intensive bursts of training to prepare managers for assignments characterised by challenge and risk, Japanese development programmes are longer and more culturally reflective in focusing on collectivism and group/team effort. The influence of role models is also strong. Unlike the USA/UK, where management development is in the hands of specialists, the Japanese view the relationship between the individual and the boss as a significant factor in developing the manager. The aim is to nurture growth, loyalty, commitment and retention (Storey *et al.*, 1991).

In China there is a massive shortage of managers with global management skills. Management training has therefore become a national imperative as the country opens itself up to global markets and Western capitalism: 'There is a pressing need for a class of professional managers in China capable of facing the challenges of a market economy' (Chak-Ming Wo and Pounder, 2000). However, as with other countries, China has experienced the problems of discrepancies between the models of Western management development and Chinese culture and society. For example, many imported Western models of management development are based on techniques such as group discussion and classroom participation, with an emphasis on reflection and abstract reasoning and a free and open critique and challenging of ideas and assumptions. Such techniques are often in conflict with Chinese culture where there is a strong emphasis on collective ideals, conformity, social status, the need to preserve 'face' and self-esteem, an unchallenged acceptance of the 'expert' and associative rather than abstract reasoning. All of these cultural factors, it is argued, tend to militate against the adoption of Western models (Bu and Mitchell, 1992; Cumber *et al.*, 1994). In the past, this has led to a preference for more didactic development methods such as formal management courses. In the past experiential methods were almost unheard of (Kirkbride and Tang, 1992). But more recently there are signs that Chinese managers are becoming more receptive to Western approaches as their own approaches to management education prove too basic and focused on technical skills rather than the softer skills required to manage in complex global enterprises (Chak-Ming Wo and Pounder, 2000).

In Hong Kong, Western management education and know-how have been much in demand as managers in Hong Kong seek the adaptive, flexible skills and knowledge required to handle the challenges of the Confucian, bureaucratic, centralising society of the PRC (Chong *et al.*, 1993). More recently, the economy of Hong Kong has had to cope with an unprecedented economic downturn in the Far East in recent years that has forced them to shed labour and rationalise their organisational structures. This has posed a further challenge for management development, especially in how to develop managers to deal with the human resource issues raised by such events. (See Chapter 17 for more information on HRM in Asia, including China, Japan, Hong Kong, South Korea and Singapore.)

Central and Eastern Europe

The main force driving the development of managers in countries such as Russia, Poland, Hungary, Bulgaria and Romania is the rapid transition from a centrally planned to a market-based economy and more recently to some of them attaining membership of the EU. However, as Vecsenyi (1992) observes in relation to development in these countries, there are no 'road maps' in respect of management development, and it is often carried out in an atmosphere of crisis. The strategy in the past has been to import ready-made Western models to provide know-how and practical skills. In Russia, for example, management education is booming, and demand massively outstrips supply as the country struggles to adapt to major economic, social and political upheavals. However, in a number of cases Western models have been found wanting as they have failed to adapt to local economic, political and social conditions (Kwiatkowski and Kozminski, 1992). For instance, when faced with the problems of backward technology and hyperinflation, Bulgarian managers said that what they wanted was emergency solutions to pressing problems, not grandiose views about longer-term strategy (Hollingshead and Michailova, 2001).

Western 'recipes for success' may therefore be accused of failing because they do not take into account the context confronting them, they lack strategic credibility, and they have not responded to the variations in learning styles of Eastern European managers (Lee, 1995; Redman *et al.*, 1995a; Hollingshead and Michailova, 2001). Taking a pessimistic outlook, therefore, Western-oriented business schools may be accused of contributing to rampant capitalism and engendering resentment. But if they can adapt they may contribute positively to a more sophisticated economic infrastructure, changing social attitudes, and new forms of political decision-making (Puffer, 1993). This is confirmed by recent research which suggests that Western approaches are more effective if they can be customised to meet local needs. For example, in a recent study of management training in Central and Eastern Europe, Gobell *et al.* (1998) found that when Western trainers took the time to understand their needs, Central and Eastern European managers were as receptive as their US counterparts to open discussion and debate. This was viewed as a welcome change from the 'brute force lectures' they had previously endured as students!

Africa

Over the whole of Africa, there are considerable variations in approaches to management development and these reflect the different stages of economic, social, cultural and political development across different regions.

South Africa, for example, has undergone massive social and political upheaval in recent years. However, the key issue now currently confronting the country is how to use management development as a tool to overcome major societal gulfs in respect of the disadvantaged black majority and the well-educated white minority (Templer *et al.*, 1992). Recent research indicates that fewer than 5 per cent of blacks occupy managerial posts (McFarlin *et al.*, 1999).

The argument therefore is for the need to 'South Africanise' development through a more holistic, integrative approach that unifies the country by providing and sharing opportunities. Some progress has been made; for instance, the introduction of a strategy of educating black managers, coaching them and then allowing them to practise their management skills in the workplace. But problems can emerge when existing organisational structures and cultures are denying black managers access to the practical opportunities to apply those newly acquired skills. This has led to powerful arguments for a policy of 'aggressive affirmative' action in which the percentage of black managers more closely reflects the population mix (McFarlin *et al.*, 1999).

But is aggressive affirmative action enough? McFarlin *et al.* argue for the need to develop new management styles that are embedded in an African cultural context. They point to the concept of *Ubuntu* as the basis for development. *Ubuntu* is a metaphor for life that stresses support, sharing, community and solidarity that in the past has been essential to survive the harshness of African life. Within this philosophy, management development is premised on the introduction of collective, participative approaches; teaching managers how to build trust, bonding and solidarity with employees and each other while at the same time seeking to mesh with the imperatives of Western materialism. Such approaches have worked well in organisations such as South African Airways where policies towards customer care are meshed with the notion of managers and employees seeing themselves as part of an extended African family. These arguments made by McFarlin *et al.* and others reinforce the point made earlier in this chapter about the need to manage development as well as doing it – in other words, focusing on those social, structural and cultural barriers that 'interfere with development' (Doyle, 1995, 2000a).

By way of contrast to South Africa, in less developed regions such as Eastern Africa (Ethiopia, Kenya, Uganda, Tanzania) there is a different set of challenges facing management development. Here, the problem is centred on the economic underdevelopment of the region creating a huge disparity between 'the African reality and the application of imported theories' (Mitiku and Wallace, 1999). Management development approaches are largely geared towards the imperatives of trying to govern or manage donor-aid from institutions such as the World Bank. But this focus, however well intentioned, may be robbing the region of essential wealth-creating skills required to lift the area out of poverty. The need therefore according to Mitiku and Wallace is to refocus management development at a more local level – building on successful examples of enterprise while lowering the costs of training to local entrepreneurs.

To conclude this review of international management development, you have seen that there is a considerable and growing interest in developing the skills and mindsets of the 'global' or 'international' manager. There is also a desire by many countries across the world to import Western (mainly Anglo-Saxon) conceptions and models of management development and to utilise them as powerful tools in their quest for social and economic transformation and renewal. However, you will also have noted that, although Western models are considered by many to be dominant across the world, efforts to import them by different countries have not been entirely successful. This reinforces a point made earlier, that there is growing evidence to suggest that management development cannot easily be removed or separated from the wider cultural, social, political and economic context in which it is embedded (Hansen and Brooks, 1994). It therefore becomes clear that just as in the UK national context, any international development policy, activity or programme is likely to be more effective if it is made *contingent* upon the unique set of circumstances that confront it and proactive efforts are made to manage that context. However, such a perspective of development sets new challenges for those professionals involved in developing international managers.

The progression and development of women managers

There is now overwhelming evidence to suggest that women are generally under-represented in UK management, but measuring the extent of this under-representation has not been easy. The problem rests mainly with comparisons between different interpretations of the term 'manager' – defined in terms of work content and scope of responsibility (Davidson and Burke, 1994). In 1989 it was estimated that 44 per cent of the UK labour force were women (this proportion was forecast to rise to some 50 per cent by the year 2000 and has now gone slightly above 50 per cent), and yet only 11 per cent of UK general management were women (Davidson, 1991). At chief executive level the picture was even bleaker, with only 1 per cent of senior management positions occupied by women (Davidson and Cooper, 1992).

More recent evidence seems to suggest an improving picture, with the proportion of women 'managers' now approaching some 26 per cent of the managerial workforce (Vinnicombe and Colwill, 1995). However, this figure appears to include all levels of management. Closer examination reveals a less rosy picture. Estimates vary, but it would seem that for middle managers the proportion is still around 8–10 per cent of the managerial workforce (Woodall and Winstanley, 1998). And in respect of senior management positions, the situation has hardly improved at all since the 1980s. For example, a 1995 survey of some 300 enterprises in the UK revealed that only 3 per cent of board directors were women, and in another cited study of 100 major companies it was estimated that only 4 per cent of directors were women (International Labour Organization, 1997). It would seem that the so-called 'glass ceiling' is proving to be stubbornly unbreakable at the higher levels of UK management.

There are a number of explanations cited for the increasing, albeit slowly, proportion of women managers in Western organisations. These include: better educational attainment; better access to training opportunities; and the removal of the more overt forms of gender discrimination in the workplace that have deterred or prevented women from entering management in the past (Larwood and Wood, 1995; Lewis and Fagenson, 1995). But there is less cause for celebration when we examine more closely the type of work that women managers are doing. Traditionally, women have suffered a degree of ghettoising in terms of their managerial roles. For example, women managers are concentrated mainly in the banking, retail and catering industries, at the lower managerial levels, and in the 'softer' areas such as personnel and customer service. It would appear that progress out of the ghetto into more front-line, business-focused roles is a slow process (Ohlott *et al.*, 1994).

Research also suggests a risk that women managers may find themselves caught in a vicious circle. Their very success in these softer roles may serve to stereotype them and encourage organisations to retain them in these roles. Where efforts are made to move them into front-line positions without adequate development there is a risk of creating a self-fulfilling prophecy. For example,

> putting a woman in a highly visible job she is unprepared for could result in visible confirmation of prejudice. The glass ceiling becomes real because in an effort to protect women, hiring managers do not give them the same challenges as men. (Ohlott *et al.*, 1994: 62)

What are the factors inhibiting the development of women managers?

Woodall and Winstanley (1998) argue that forging a successful career in management is more difficult for women because it involves them having to jump through a series of 'hoops'. They have to:

- enter management at an early age;
- already have appropriate management qualifications;
- have experience or rapidly gain experience in functions that are seen to be core to the organisation;
- be continuously employed;
- work long hours and conform to the organisation's age-related concept of career;
- be geographically mobile (see the preceding discussion regarding the development of women as international managers);
- conform to promotion criteria (which will invariably be determined in a male-oriented way).

As Woodall and Winstanley remark, 'Thus it should not be surprising that women find career progress more difficult than most of their male counterparts' (p. 224).

Not only do women have to jump through hoops to conform to certain organisational expectations, they have to overcome a number of barriers that inhibit their managerial career progression. Woodall and Winstanley identify three barriers:

- the attitude and behaviour of women managers, e.g. their lack of confidence and perceived low career orientation and lack of competition;
- structural factors such as HR policies and practices which discriminate against women managers, e.g. appraisal and selection criteria that foreclose consideration for certain positions;
- organisational cultural factors such as the attitudes of male managers and informal clubs and networks which serve to exclude women and reinforce gender stereotypes.

Stop & think

Do you detect any barriers to women's development in your organisation?

Any subsequent strategy for developing women managers therefore has to be aware of and prepared to address these barriers if it is to be successful.

What can be done to remove these barriers?

Davidson (1991) makes the telling point that those organisations that fail to utilise the potential of their women managers will be committing 'economic suicide'. Earlier in the chapter it was pointed out that in the case of international management, the availability of a pool of women with the right qualities for overseas assignments gave organisations a 'tactical advantage'.

The barriers are twofold – barriers to entry and barriers to progression. Hammond (1998) stresses the need for the organisation to conduct a thorough review and diagnosis of the structural and cultural factors that may be acting as barriers at both levels. For example, Hammond advocates a 'Women's experience profile' in which organisations are asked questions such as:

- Are women currently employed as managers?
- What is the proportion at different levels and what jobs do they do?
- Do women apply for managerial jobs in sufficient numbers?
- How do the careers of men and women compare?
- What is the ratio of success in selection between men and women?

In a similar manner, Woodall and Winstanley (1998) suggest that as an *aide-mémoire* to those responsible for promoting women's development the following questions should be investigated:

- What is the pattern of representation in management positions?
- What is the business case?
- Which women want or need development?
- What are the structural or cultural constraints?
- How can politics be used to overcome any barriers?

At a more novel and practical level, Mattis (2001) argues that male middle and senior managers should ask themselves: 'What can one manager do to . . .

- actively intervene in meetings where the behaviour of others stifles women's contributions;
- assign a proportional representation of women on task forces/projects/committees;
- organise two social events per year in which women can participate comfortably;
- join a committee where he is in the minority;
- have a zero tolerance for overt discrimination, inappropriate behaviour or inappropriate entertainment venues;
- become a diversity thought leader and raise diversity and gender issues for discussion;
- provide feedback, coaching and evaluating the work of their women direct reports?'

Other writers argue that women's development is helped when male and female managers learn to value each other's differences and aim to cooperate in their personal development to increase organisational effectiveness (Fischer and Gleijm, 1992; Whitaker and Megginson, 1992).

So what practical measures can be taken to develop women managers?

Much of the literature dealing with the development of women managers makes the point that the tasks facing men and women managers are similar but that women managers do face special difficulties. So what practical help/advice can be given? The literature contains many ideas and suggestions. The following list is by no means exhaustive:

- integrating women's development into mainstream HRD;
- mentoring/providing role models;
- reviewing childcare provisions;
- reviewing equal opportunities policies;

- auditing attitudes towards women;
- providing women-only training;
- encouraging women into management education;
- putting equality on the organisational agenda;
- reviewing selection/promotion/appraisal processes;
- promoting the networking of women;
- assertiveness training;
- moving women out of the 'ghetto' into front-line positions;
- career planning strategies for women;
- training before promotion.

Activity

Looking at this list, identify the initiatives that your organisation is doing to facilitate the entry and progression of women managers. How does it compare with the list above?

It is clear from this extensive list that the progression and development of women managers is complex, and will require a more strategic approach than has hitherto been the case. However, Woodall and Winstanley (1998) sound a cautionary note. They make the point that while these factors are indeed relevant and that a lack of attention to them may help to explain the underachievement of women in management, 'they are by no means universal'. Each factor may apply to different women in different organisational contexts at different times. It is therefore important that organisations carry out a 'prior analysis' before selecting any intervention to improve entry and progression in management. And again echoing a core theme in this chapter, it is also important to ensure that any strategic approach to women's management development takes account of and deals with the wider structural and cultural impediments that continue to give rise to a more covert and often unconscious prejudice.

However, these impediments are deeply ingrained and give grounds for some pessimism. For instance, Veale and Gold (1998), in a study of a UK local authority, conclude that the main cause of the so-called glass ceiling still remains an 'anti-women ethos' permeating the organisation and reflects widely held attitudes that still persist in British society.

Many commentators have in the past advocated special forms of treatment such as positive discrimination and quotas for women or gender-exclusive development programmes. But paradoxically, and somewhat controversially, some commentators are arguing that viewing women managers as requiring 'special' treatment may be exacerbating many of the problems they are experiencing. While organisations should acknowledge the problems to which women managers are exposed, this should be done in a less gender-focused way. Instead, development should seek to integrate women managers both socially and professionally with men in work-related activities (Snyder, 1993; Larwood and Wood, 1995). For Snyder, this means 'systematically and systemically attacking potential sources of segregation' (Snyder, 1993: 104). This suggests less concern with 'special' development arrangements such as women-only training courses – although these remain important. Instead, the focus should be on locating men and women as part of the organisation 'system' and analysing their strengths and weaknesses as individuals in the situational context in which they find themselves, irrespective of their gender, and developing them accordingly (Davidson and Burke, 1994).

In summary, the issue of women's development and career progression remains an area of controversy and debate – not least because of the seeming slow progress that women managers have made in the workplace over the past 15–20 years when compared with the rapid growth in the overall proportion of women in the workforce. Although there are structural issues to address, the root cause of the problem would appear to lie in the attitudes of wider society being carried into and enacted both individually and collectively within work organisations by male managers.

One might draw a rather pessimistic inference from this and argue that the development and progression of women managers will hardly improve (especially at senior level) until work organisations rid themselves of the current generation of male senior and middle managers. The argument is that it these managers who have the power to determine the future of women in management and real progress will only be made when they are replaced by a new generation of men and women in senior positions who do not have the social 'hang-ups' of their predecessors. (See also Chapter 7 for further issues relating to women and women managers.)

The future for management development: the need for new thinking and new practices?

Activity

- Before you read this section of the chapter, list what you believe to be the way in which management development might evolve over the next 10–15 years. Add a short sentence against each point to explain your reasoning.

- If time and/or circumstances permit, discuss your ideas with a colleague(s). How do your ideas compare with theirs?

In concluding this chapter, we might speculate on the future direction of management development. Perhaps the first thing to note is that the development of managers – like so many aspects of organisational life – is in a state of considerable flux and transformation. This is giving rise to a number of issues and tensions that are continuing to influence the way management development is interpreted, planned, organised and implemented across a wide range of contexts, and these have been touched on in this chapter, e.g. competency-based development. To close the chapter it is useful to pause and, building on the preceding discussion, to speculate about the future shape and direction of management development.

Is management development fulfilling its strategic role?

It has been argued throughout this chapter that an open systems perspective offers a valid and useful perspective within which to view management development. In practical terms, management development has to be integrated with organisational development and change in a way that recognises their mutuality and interdependence. As we have seen, for many organisations, management development has now become a strategic imperative for organisational success. But if we are to achieve and maintain the required level of strategic fit, management development has to be managed in a way that accepts and accommodates contextual diversity and organisational complexities. 'Managing' development therefore has to be seen as being just as important as 'doing' development.

So to what extent is management development fulfilling its strategic role in this contextual and contingent manner? The answer has to be a qualified one. There is evidence of success – cited mainly in organisational case studies and wider surveys (Prokopenko, 1998; Syrett and Lammiman, 1999, Thomson *et al.* 2001). But there is also evidence that in some situations management development might be considered to be 'failing' in the sense that it is not fully delivering anticipated organisational and individual outcomes (Meldrum and Atkinson, 1998; Currie, 1999; Doyle, 1995, 2000a).

Stop & think

To what extent do you feel that management development is 'failing' to deliver anticipated outcomes in your organisation?

The notion that management development is somehow 'failing' is not a new one. A number of highly critical reports published in the late 1980s (Handy, 1987, Constable and McCormick, 1987) identified managerial 'underdevelopment' in the UK as undermining UK competitiveness.

Since those critical reports, research has shown that organisations have increased their commitment and investment in management development (Storey *et al.*, 1997; Thomson *et al.*, 2001). But while investment and commitment may have increased, there are still reservations and doubts about the overall *efficacy* of management development and its ability to deliver increased performance and organisational success during times of radical and far-reaching change (Doyle, 1995, 2000a). With a sense of *déjà vu* perhaps, and on a somewhat depressing note, we see that managers are once again being singled out by the government and others as being a key factor in the poor performance of UK companies:

> Recent reports from the consulting firm McKinsey & Company and Proudfoot Consulting identified weak management skills as key in the disappointing performance of UK-owned companies. And last month, the DTI appointed Professor Michael Porter of Harvard University to examine the link between poor management and low UK productivity.
>
> (Dearlove, 2002)

Of course, it is legitimate to point out that management development is only one of a myriad of influencing factors determining UK performance and evaluating the relationship between managerial and organisational performance. Cynics might argue that UK managers are once again a convenient political scapegoat for government ministers to blame.

But there are grounds for critically evaluating the contribution that management development is making. As we have already noted in this chapter, just increasing commitment and investment in management training by itself may not be enough to deliver managerial effectiveness. In complex, diverse and radically changing organisational contexts there may be internal and external factors preventing management development delivering what stakeholders expect and need it to deliver. There may be structural, political, social and cultural barriers that may be 'interfering' with measures to develop managers and contribute to improvements in organisational performance (Hopfl and Dawes, 1995; Currie, 1999). Another possibility lies in a fundamental lack of awareness amongst key stakeholders as to what constitutes management development, e.g. the dominance of formalised models and practices at the expense of more contextual, work-oriented models (Simpson and Lyddon, 1995).

The future challenge, therefore, for those with responsibilities for developing managers may be to shift from merely 'doing' development (designing and delivering training courses) to managing development in ways that address the wider contextual barriers that inhibit or block effectiveness (Doyle, 2000a; Mole, 2000). But as we have seen throughout this chapter, any shift towards a more systemic perspective to manage development may require a significant reorientation in thinking and practice amongst the professionals involved. For instance, one such reorientation emphasises the greater use of work-based approaches to development (Woodall, 2000).

The need to increase the emphasis on work-based development?

One way to address the issue of contextual diversity and complexity is to place a growing emphasis on developing *managers within the context in which they manage* rather than just in the classroom, the training suite or the hotel conference room.

Of course, work-based development has always occurred in less formalised ways through activities such as coaching and mentoring. However, with cost considerations, time pressures, desire for flexibility and relevance in development activity, the need is for organisations to turn towards the greater use of 'reality-based' tasks, projects and assignments (Vicere, 1998; Paauwe and Williams, 2001). Premised upon an experiential, action learning philosophy, such approaches offer the possibility of overcoming some of the simplistic, generic and contextual problems that have bedevilled management development for so long. However, as Paauwe and Williams note, work-based development does have some disadvantages in terms of the level of cost, commitment and support required. Woodall (2000) cautions that the whole issue of work-based development is not well understood – even amongst those HR professionals who purport to organise and manage development in the workplace (see above).

The evolution of the corporate university

A significant development in recent years has been the growth of corporate universities. In the USA, corporate universities grew from 400 in the late 1980s to some 1000 in the late 1990s (Greco, 1997). A similar pattern is emerging in the UK where there are now an estimated 200 organisations professing to have established a corporate university. Organisations include: Anglian Water, Unipart, Lloyds TSB and British Aerospace. What has led to this expansion? There are a number of factors:

- Dissatisfaction with the generic nature of academic programmes which do not always address localised and unique management problems and issues (see above).
- Technological development facilitating new approaches to learning and networking that can be delivered with ease and cost-effectively.
- As organisations grow increasingly more complex and ambiguous, the establishment of a corporate university becomes an important symbol and mechanism for knowledge management.
- It raises the status and prestige of the HRD department.
- It delivers HR benefits, e.g. access to a high standard of development facilities, aiding recruitment by demonstrating commitment to develop.

We can thus see that corporate universities represent a coherent attempt by organisations to plan and organise the whole panoply of training and management development in such a way that it meets the needs of the organisation and the individuals within their workplace reality. In other words, it becomes a way of directly addressing the issue of strategic fit and overcoming the problem of how to meet the needs of contextual diversity and complexity by customising and shaping HRD to suit contingent circumstances. Their aim is 'to align training and development with business strategy while also sending out a clear message to employees that the organisation is prepared to invest in them' (Arkin, 2000: 42).

However, there are a number of issues to address. First, there is a risk that some so-called corporate universities may be nothing more than re-badged training departments where the motive is more political or PR than learning or development (Prince and Beaver (2001). Secondly, at forecasted rates of growth, there is a fear that corporate universities will overtake and become a challenge to traditional universities (Vine, 1999). However, organisations refute this. Rather, what they say they are seeking is a collaboration with Higher Education institutions, e.g. to validate their degree offerings. But there are fears that the values that underpin university education (independence of thought and critical analysis and debate) may not be welcome in certain types of organisational culture. Thirdly, there are practical concerns too. What happens if students are part-way through their studies and the company decides to close its corporate university as a cost-cutting exercise? Universities too may be chary of linking themselves too closely to a single partner when there is a risk of commercial failure (Arkin, 2000). It remains to be seen how far this ideal will evolve in the years to come.

Filling the gaps and meeting the challenges?

A final item for our futuristic 'agenda' is the extent to which the whole notion of management development is seen to fit with the everyday experience and reality of the changing nature of the managerial role. Recent evidence points to some fairly significant shifts in the context and nature of managerial roles, e.g. a greater emphasis on intellectual and influencing capacities (Chapman, 2001). There is also evidence of a growing awareness of how management development should respond – in both theoretical and practical terms (Vicere, 1998; Thomson *et al.*, 2001).

If we look more critically at the current frameworks, approaches and methods still employed in designing and implementing management development, it is not too difficult to identify the gaps, the incompleteness and the sometimes oversimplification that exists when compared with the challenges facing most managers. For example, the development of political skills is often cited as a crucial competence for managerial effectiveness (especially during times of radical change), so why does it not appear in the mainstream course syllabus or competency blueprints and frameworks discussed earlier? Why is there so little apparent attention paid to developing political skills (Baddeley and James, 1990; Buchanan and Badham, 1999)?

The development of change management knowledge and skills is another area that, superficially, receives attention but on closer examination, it becomes clear that the provision for developing change expertise and capability is inadequate (Buchanan *et al.*, 1999; Doyle *et al.*, 2000; Doyle, 2002).

Finally, while the acquisition of functional knowledge and skills dominates individual and organisational development activity, has the time arrived for managers to acknowledge and accept that they are not 'Masters of the Universe' – that they cannot control everything and everyone through the application of rational models of managing? Should development now focus on turning the heads of managers away from generic theories and models of managing that may now have little to offer and instead develop within them the intellectual and personal capacities required to accept, live and cope with diversity and complexity in its myriad forms? The indicators suggest that the answer to both questions is 'yes'.

Summary

- The terms 'management' and 'manager' have different meanings within different contexts. The role and 'reality' of managing in organisations is often more complex, confusing and chaotic than many management texts would suggest.

- Management development is more than just management education and training. It involves the holistic development of the manager, taking account of such factors as: the needs, goals and expectations of both the organisation and the individual; the political, cultural and economic context; structures, and systems for selection, reward and monitoring performance.

- As part of an overall human resource strategy, management development is now identified by many organisations as a source of competitive advantage and one of the key ingredients for success. However, if management development is to be effective it must link to, and support, the organisation's business strategy. This enables those responsible for development to respond to the question, 'Why are you developing this manager?'

- Development programmes cannot be isolated from other organisational systems and processes in a series of 'piecemeal' approaches. An open systems perspective takes account of the interactions and dependences that exist between the organisation's context and management development programmes. An open systems approach offers a way of constructing a unified, integrated framework within which the organisation can organise and implement development programmes.

- Development is more effective when a stakeholder partnership exists between the individual, their boss and others in the organisation. A wide range of development techniques exist. The selection of the most appropriate techniques will depend upon the learning preferences and needs of managers. To be effective, development must reflect organisational context and the 'reality' of managerial work. An increasing reliance is being placed on the use of experiential techniques.

- A greater emphasis is now required on management development attending to contextual complexity and diversity and meeting the needs of diverse groups of individuals, e.g. public sector and international managers and the specific needs of women and professionals.

- Like many aspects of organisational life, management development cannot be isolated from controversy and debate. Areas of future challenge, conflict, tension and ambiguity remain to be resolved.

QUESTIONS

1 What do you understand by the term 'management development'? Distinguish between management development, management education and management training.

2 To what extent does management development influence the human resource strategy in an organisation?

3 Who is responsible for management development? What are their roles and responsibilities?

4 What management skills and knowledge do international managers require? In what way do they differ from those required by UK managers?

5 'To develop managerial effectiveness in today's complex organisations means that the development of social political and emotional skills is just as important as developing functional capabilities'. Discuss.

EXERCISES

1 List the different methods and techniques used to develop managers. How would you judge and evaluate their effectiveness?

2 Organisations are increasingly turning to self-development as a management technique. Imagine you are the manager responsible for a group of young graduates about to embark upon your organisation's graduate development programme. Working in groups, develop an action plan for achieving a self-learning culture.

CASE STUDY

Management development in Mid-County NHS Trust

Introduction

In recent years, Mid-County NHS Trust has undergone radical and far-reaching change. The aim has been to improve the overall standard of patient care while at the same time increasing efficiency and reducing costs. To this end, the Trust set out to re-engineer its key structures, systems and processes. It employed a firm of external change consultants who are acknowledged experts in the field of business process re-engineering (BPR). The firm's BPR methodology was employed to act as a framework for change. It involved the systematic analysis, mapping and reconfiguration of key structures and processes to deliver cost and efficiency benefits.

To assist the consultants, the Trust identified staff from a range of professions across the organisation. These individuals were then seconded to work with the consultants on a full-time basis – acting in the role of internal change agents – and at any one time there were some 30 individuals in the re-engineering

➤

Case study continued

team. The team were coached and received extensive training in BPR from the consultants.

The implementation of redesigned processes and structures had a profound impact on the Trust. On a positive front, there were major improvements in the level of service and quality of patient care. But there were negative effects too. For a few individuals, change meant a loss of job. Others found their jobs radically redesigned, involving significant retraining – often for roles far removed from their existing jobs. Some individuals were demoted from their present roles.

Process management

One outcome of BPR was a radical reappraisal of the way the various Directorates were managed. To improve efficiency, the Trust created a new position of Process Manager. Process managers, as their name suggests, were responsible for the patient care process from start to finish. Working alongside their clinical colleagues, their role was primarily to manage the operational and business elements of the process. Many of the newly promoted managers were ex-nursing staff or staff from occupational and support professions. Most had been involved as internal change agents in the BPR change process since its inception.

Shortly after occupying their new positions, it was clear that a sizeable minority of staff found coming to terms and dealing with managerial issues difficult. While most were competent in their profession, few had any prior managerial training. Areas such as strategic planning, budgets and finance, dealing with organisational politics and handling conflict were a burden and a strain. Some were also uncomfortable with the philosophy of their new role. They felt it took them away from their previously held 'caring' role.

Their views were communicated to the Trust's senior management who promised to initiate steps to improve the level of managerial capability among this key group.

Management development for process managers

The Trust found the resources and embarked on an urgent management development programme designed to develop the managerial skills required to operate in a more flexible and business-focused cul-

ture. It organised a series of in-house management training courses in core subjects delivered by a range of internal and external tutors. Details were circulated to the process managers and they were invited to put their names forward. The number of nominations received was lower than expected given the perceived scale of the 'problem'. When the courses were run, attendance was poor. When individuals were asked why they were not attending, most replied that they did not have the time. However, informally, a number questioned whether – given the changes they and the Trust had gone through – this was the right way to approach their management development. Few changes were made to the programme and eventually it was decided to terminate the programme and channel scarce resources into other training areas.

Recently, a firm of independent management consultants visited the Trust to review and evaluate the organisational change outcomes. They were highly critical of the management capabilities of some process managers. They felt that this lack of skills was severely hampering the anticipated benefits of the overall BPR change programme. They also commented unfavourably on the 'attitudes' of some managers whose view of their new role did not conform to the 'expected professional management behaviours'. They cited a lack of overall organisation and leadership, for example too much time spent concerned with non-managerial problems in a hands-on capacity.

Note: This case study is based on real events. Names have been altered to preserve confidentiality.

Questions

You are a member of the Trust's senior management team and have been asked by the Chief Executive to investigate this problem and design an overall strategy for improving the development of process managers.

1 Adopting a systemic view of the management development 'problem', what do you see as the main issues to be explored in relation to the development of process managers?

2 How should the Trust address them?

Present your findings in the form of a short report/oral presentation to your senior management colleagues.

References and further reading

Those texts marked with an asterisk are recommended for further reading.

Adey, K. (2000) 'Professional development priorities: the views of middle managers in secondary schools', *Educational Management and Administration*, 28, 4: 419–431.

Allen, A. (2003) 'Out of the Ordinary', *People Management*, 9, 24: 36–38.

Anderson, V., Graham, S. and Lawrence, P. (1998) 'Learning to internationalise', *Journal of Management Development*, 17, 7: 492–502.

Antonacopoulou, E. and Fitzgerald, L. (1996) 'Reframing competency in management development', *Human Resource Management Journal*, 6, 1: 27–48.

Arkin, A. (2000) 'Combined honours', *People Management*, October, 6, 20: 42–46.

Arkin, A. (2003) 'Shaken and stirred', *People Management*, 9, 24: 32–34.

Arnold, J. (1997) *Managing Careers into the 21st Century*. London: Paul Chapman Publishing Ltd.

Baddeley, S. and James, K. (1990) 'Political management: developing the management portfolio', *Journal of Management Development*, 9, 3: 42–59.

Banks, J. (1994) *Outdoor Development for Managers*, 2nd edn. Aldershot: Gower.

Beaver, G. and Lashley, C. (1998) 'Barriers to development in small hospitality firms', *Strategic Change*, June, 7, 4: 223–235.

Bicker, L. and Cameron, A. (1997) 'From manager to leader: facing up to the challenge of change', *EFMD Forum*, 1: 30–32.

Bittel, L. (1998) 'Management development for scientific and engineering personnel', in Prokopenko, J. (ed.) *Management Development: A Guide for the Profession*. Geneva: International Labour Office, pp. 426–445.

Bolam, R. (1997) 'Management development for head teachers: retrospect and prospect', *Educational Management and Administration*, 25, 3: 265–283.

Boydell, T. and Pedler, M. (1981) *Management Self-Development*. Westmead: Gower.

Bu, N. and Mitchell, V. (1992) 'Developing the PRC's managers: how can Western Europe become more helpful?', *Journal of Management Development*, 11, 2: 42–53.

*Buchanan, D. and Badham, R. (1999) *Power Politics and Organisational Change: Winning the Turf Game*. London: Sage.

*Buchanan, D. and Boddy, D. (1992) *The Expertise of the Change Agent*. Hemel Hempstead: Prentice Hall.

Buchanan, D., Claydon, T. and Doyle, M. (1999) 'Organisation development and change: the legacy of the nineties', *Human Resource Management Journal*, 9, 2: 20–37.

Burgoyne, J. (1988) 'Management development for the individual and the organisation', *Personnel Management*, June: 40–44.

Burgoyne, J. and Stuart, R. (1991) 'Teaching and learning methods in management development', *Personnel Review*, 20, 3: 27–33.

Burnett, D. and James, K. (1994) 'Using the outdoors to facilitate personal change in managers', *Journal of Management Development*, 13, 9: 14–24.

Caligiuri, P. and Cascio, W. (1998) 'Can we send her there: maximising the success of Western women on global assignments', *Journal of World Business*, Winter, 33, 4: 394–416.

Chak-Ming Wo and Pounder, J. (2000) 'Post-experience management education and training in China', *Journal of General Management*, 26, 2: 52–70.

Chapman, J.A. (2001) 'The work of managers in new organisational contexts', *Journal of Management Development*, 20, 1: 55–68.

Chong, J., Kassener, M.W. and Ta-Lang Shih (1993) 'Management development of Hong Kong managers for 1997', *Journal of Management Development*, 12, 8: 18–26.

Constable, J. and McCormick, R. (1987) *The Making of British Managers*. London: BIM/CBI.

Cooper, C. (2002) 'Wanted: leaders to transform public services', *Sunday Times*, 13 January, p. 17.

Cumber, M., Donohoe, P. and Ho Sai Pak (1994) *Making Asian Managers*. Hong Kong: The Management Development Centre of Hong Kong.

Currie, G. (1994) 'Evaluation of management development: a case study', *Journal of Management Development*, 13, 3: 22–26.

*Currie, G. (1999) 'Resistance around a management development programme: negotiated order in an NHS Trust', *Management Learning*, 30, 1: 43–61.

Currie, G. and Darby, R. (1995) 'Competence-based management development: rhetoric and reality', *Journal of European Industrial Training*, 19, 5: 11–18.

Davidson, M. (1991) 'Women managers in Britain: issues for the 1990s', *Women in Management Review*, 6, 1: 5–10.

Davidson, M. and Burke, R. (eds) (1994) *Women in Management: Current Research Issues*. London: Paul Chapman Publishing.

Davidson, M. and Cooper, C. (1992) *Shattering the Glass Ceiling: The Woman Manager*. London: Paul Chapman Publishing.

Davis, T. (1990) 'Whose job is management development: comparing the choices', *Journal of Management Development*, 9, 1: 58–70.

Dearlove, D. (2002) 'Why workers distrust bosses', *The Times*, 31 October, p. 11.

Doyle, M. (1995) 'Organisational transformation and renewal: a case for reframing management development?', *Personnel Review*, 24, 6: 6–18.

*Doyle, M. (2000a) 'Management development in an era of radical change: evolving a relational perspective', *Journal of Management Development*, 19, 7: 579–601.

Doyle, M. (2000b) 'Managing careers in organisations', in Collin, A. and Young, R. (eds) *The Future of Career*. Cambridge: Cambridge University Press, pp. 228–242.

Doyle, M. (2002) 'From change novice to change expert', *Personnel Review*, 31, 2: 465–481.

Doyle, M., Claydon, T. and Buchanan, D. (2000) 'Mixed results, lousy process: contrasts and contradictions in the management experience of change', *British Journal of Management*, 11, Special Issue: 59–80.

Dulewicz, V. (1991) 'Improving assessment centres', *Personnel Management*, June: 50–55.

Easterby-Smith, M. (1992) 'European management education: the prospects for unification', *Human Resource Management Journal*, 3, 1: 23–36.

*Easterby-Smith, M. (1994) *Evaluation of Management Education, Training and Development*. Aldershot: Gower.

Endres, G. and Kleiner, B. (1990) 'How to measure management training and effectiveness', *Journal of European Industrial Training*, 14, 9: 3–7.

Ferner, A. (1994) 'Multi-national comparisons and HRM: an overview of research issues', *Human Resource Management Journal*, 4, 3: 79–102.

Fischer, M. and Gleijm, H. (1992) 'The gender gap in management', *Industrial and Commercial Training*, 24, 4: 5–11.

Fox, S. (1989) 'The politics of evaluating management development', *Management Education and Development*, 20, Pt 3: 191–207.

Gobell, D., Przybylowski, K. and Rudlelius, W. (1998) 'Customising management training in Central and Eastern Europe', *Business Horizons*, May/June, 41, 3: 61–72.

Greco, J. (1997) 'Corporate home schooling', *Journal of Business Strategy*, May/June, 18, 3: 48–52.

Hales, C. (1993) *Managing Through Organisation*. London: Routledge.

Hammond, V. (1998) 'Training and developing women for managerial jobs' in Prokopenko, J. (ed.) *Management Development: A Guide for the Profession*. Geneva: International Labour Office, pp. 446–462.

Handy, C. (1987) *The Making of Managers*. London: MSC/NEDO/BIM.

Hansen, C.D. and Brooks, A.K. (1994) 'A review of cross-cultural research on human resource development', *Human Resource Development Quarterly*, 5, 1: 55–74.

Harris, H. and Kumra, S. (2000) 'International manager development: cross-cultural training in highly diverse environments', *Journal of Management Development*, 19, 7: 602–614.

Harrison, R. (1997) *Employee Development*, 2nd edn. London: IPM.

*Harzing, A.-M. and Van Ruysseveldt, J. (1995) *International Human Resource Management*. London: Sage.

Heisler, W.J. and Benham, P. (1992) 'The challenge of management development in North America in the 1990s', *Journal of Management Development*, 11, 2: 16–31.

Hendry, C. (1995) *Human Resource Management: A Strategic Approach to Employment*. Oxford: Butterworth-Heinemann.

Herriot, P. and Pemberton, C. (1995) *New Deals: The Revolution in Managerial Careers*. Chichester: John Wiley.

Hilb, P. (1992) 'The challenge of management development in Western Europe in the 1990s', *International Journal of Human Resource Management*, 3, 3: 575–584.

Hill, R. (1994) *Euro-Managers and Martians*. Brussels: Euro Publications.

Hollingshead, G. and Michailova, S. (2001) 'Blockbusters or bridge builders? The role of Western trainers in developing new entrepreneurialism in Eastern Europe', *Management Learning*, 32, 4: 419–436.

Honey, P. and Mumford, A. (1986) *Manual of Learning Styles*, 2nd edn. Maidenhead: Peter Honey.

Hopfl, H. and Dawes, F. (1995) 'A whole can of worms! The contested frontiers of management development and learning', *Personnel Review*, 24, 6: 19–28.

Hyland, T. (1994) *Competences, Education and NVQs: Dissenting Perspectives*. London: Cassell Education.

Industrial Society (1997) 'Senior management development', *Managing Best Practice*, 80, London.

Industrial Society (1998) 'Graduate recruitment and development', *Managing Best Practice*, 53, London.

International Labour Organization (1997) *Breaking Through the Glass Ceiling: Women in Management*. Geneva: ILO Publications.

IRS Employment Review (1997) 'Developing Managers in Small Firms', April, 630: 15–16.

Irvine, D. and Wilson, J.P. (1994) 'Outdoor management development: reality or illusion?', *Journal of Management Development*, 13, 5: 25–37.

Jones, P. and Oswick, C. (1993) 'Outcomes of outdoor management development: articles of faith?', *Journal of European Industrial Training*, 17, 3: 10–18.

Kakabadse, A. and Myers, A. (1995) 'Qualities of top management: comparisons of European manufacturers', *Journal of Management Development*, 14, 1: 5–15.

Kast, F.S. and Rosenweig, J.E. (1985) *Organisation and Management: A Systems Approach*, 4th edn. New York: McGraw-Hill.

Kerr, A. and McDougall, M. (1999) 'The small business of developing people', *International Small Business Journal*, Jan/March, 17, 66: 65–74.

Kilcourse, T. (1994) 'Developing competent managers', *Journal of European Industrial Training*, 18, 2: 12–16.

Kirkbride, P. and Tang, S. (1992) 'Management development in the Nanyang Chinese societies of S.E. Asia', *Journal of Management Development*, 11, 2: 54–66.

Kolb, D. (1984) *Experiential Learning*. New York: Prentice Hall.

Kumar, R. and Usunier, J.C. (2001) 'Management education in a globalising world', *Management Learning*, 32, 3: 363–391.

Kwiatkowski, S. and Kozminski, A. (1992) 'Paradoxical country: management education in Poland', *Journal of Management Development*, 11, 5: 28–33.

Larwood, L. and Wood, M. (1995) 'Training women for changing priorities', *Journal of Management Development*, 14, 2: 54–64.

Lawrence, P. (1992) 'Management development in Europe: a study in cultural contrast', *Human Resource Management Journal*, 3, 1: 11–23.

Lee, G. and Beard, D. (1994) *Development Centres: Realising the Potential of Your Employees through Assessment and Development*. Maidenhead: McGraw-Hill.

Lee, M. (1995) 'Working with choice in Central Europe', *Management Learning*, 26, 2: 215–230.

Lewis, A. and Fagenson, E. (1995) 'Strategies for developing women managers: how well do they fulfil their objectives?', *Journal of Management Development*, 14, 2: 39–53.

Linehan, M. and Walsh, J. (2000) 'Work–family conflict and the senior female international managers', *British Journal of Management*, 11, special issue: S49–58.

Little, B. (1997) 'I have a plan', *Management Skills and Development*, September: 26–30.

Liu, S. and Vince, R. (1999) 'The cultural context of learning in international joint ventures', *Journal of Management Development*, 18, 8: 666–675.

*Loan-Clarke, J. (1996) 'The Management Charter Initiative: critique of management standards/NVQs', *Journal of Management Development*, 15, 6: 4–17.

Mabey, C. and Salaman, G. (1995) *Strategic Human Resource Management*. Oxford: Blackwell.

Margerison, C. (1991) *Making Management Development Work*. Maidenhead: McGraw-Hill.

Margerison, C. (1994a) 'Managing career choices', in Mumford, A. (ed.) *Gower Handbook of Management Development*. Aldershot: Gower.

Margerison, C. (1994b) 'Action learning and excellence in management development', in Mabey, C. and Iles, P. (eds) *Managing Learning*. London: Routledge.

Mattis, M. (2001) 'Advancing women in business organisations: key leadership roles and behaviours of senior leaders and middle managers' *Journal of Management Development*, 20, 4: 371–388.

Mavin, S. and Bryans, P. (2000) 'Management development in the public sector: what role can universities play?', *International Journal of Public Sector Management*, 13, 2: 142–152.

McFarlin, D., Coster, E. and Mogale, P. (1999) 'South African management development in the twenty-first century: moving towards a more Africanised model', *Journal of Management Development*, 18, 1: 63–78.

*Meldrum, M. and Atkinson, S. (1998) 'Is management development fulfilling its organisational role?', *Management Decision*, 36, 8: 528–532.

Miroshnik, V. (2002) 'Culture and international management: a review', *Journal of Management Development*, 21, 7: 521–544.

Mitiku, A. and Wallace, J. (1999) 'Preparing East African managers for the twenty-first century', *Journal of Management Development*, 18, 1: 46–62.

Molander, C. and Winterton, J. (1994) *Managing Human Resources*. London: Routledge.

Mole, G. (1996) 'The management training industry in the UK: an HRD director's critique', *Human Resource Management Journal*, 6, 1: 19–26.

*Mole, G. (2000) *Managing Management Development*. Buckingham: Open University Press.

*Morgan, G. (1997) *Images of Organisation*, 2nd edn. Beverley Hills, Calif.: Sage.

Mumford, A. (1988) *Developing Top Managers*. Aldershot: Gower.

*Mumford, A. (1997) *Management Development: Strategies for Action*, 3rd edn. London: IPD.

Munchus, G. and McArthur, B. (1991) 'Revisiting the historical use of assessment centres in management selection and development', *Journal of Management Development*, 10, 1: 5–13.

Neelankavil, J. (1992) 'Management development and training programmes in Japanese firms', *Journal of Management Development*, 11, 3: 12–17.

Odiorne, G.S. (1984) *Strategic Management of Human Resources: A Portfolio Approach*. San Francisco, Calif: Jossey-Bass.

Ohlott, P., Ruderman, M. and McCauley, C. (1994) 'Gender differences in managers' developmental job experiences', *Academy of Management Journal*, 37, 1: 46–67.

Owen, C. and Scherer, R. (2002) 'Doing business in Latin America: managing cultural differences in perceptions of female expatriates', *SAM Advanced Management Journal*, Spring, 67, 2: 37–41, 47.

Paauwe, J. and Williams, R. (2001) 'Seven key issues for management development', *Journal of Management Development*, 20, 2: 90–105.

Pedler, M. (1997) 'Interpreting action learning', in Burgoyne, J. and Reynolds, M. (eds) *Management Learning: Integrating Perspectives in Theory and Practice*. London: Sage, pp. 248–264.

Pedler, M., Burgoyne, J., Boydell, T. and Welshman, G. (1990) *Self-Development in Organisations*. Maidenhead: McGraw-Hill.

Phillips, N. (1992) *Managing International Teams*. London: Pitman.

Prince, C. and Beaver, G. (2001) 'Facilitating organisational change: the role of the corporate university', *Strategic Change*, June/July, 10, 4: 189–199.

*Prokopenko, J. (1998) *Management Development: A Guide for the Profession*. Geneva: International Labour Office.

Puffer, S. (1993) 'The booming business of management education in Russia', *Journal of Management Development*, 12, 5: 46–59.

Rae, L. (1986) *How to Measure Training Effectiveness*. Aldershot: Gower.

Randlesome, C. (2000) 'Changes in management culture and competences: the German experience', *Journal of Management Development*, 19, 7: 629–642.

*Ready, D., Vicere, A. and White, A. (1994) 'Towards a systems approach to executive development', *Journal of Management Development*, 13, 5: 3–11.

Redman, T., Keithley, D. and Szalkowski, A. (1995a) 'Management development under adversity: case studies from Poland', *Journal of Management Development*, 14, 10: 4–13.

Reitsma, S.G. (2001) 'Management development in Unilever', *Journal of Management Development*, 20, 2: 131–144.

*Revans, R. (1983) *ABC of Action Learning*. Bromley: Chartwell-Bratt.

*Roberts, C. and McDonald, G. (1995) 'Training to fail', *Journal of Management Development*, 14, 4: 1–16.

Roberts, G. (1995) 'Competency management systems: the need for a practical framework', *Competency*, 3, 2: 27–30.

Rosenfeld, R. and Wilson, D. (1999) *Managing Organisations: Texts, Readings and Cases*, 2nd edn. London: McGraw-Hill.

Saee, J. and Mouzytchenko, O. (1999) 'The role of multinational entrepreneurs within the Australian economy: strategic entrepreneurs management training and institutional responses and solutions', *Journal of European Business Education*, December, 9, 1: 62–79.

*Salaman, G. (1995) *Managing*. Buckingham: Open University Press.

Simpson, P. and Lyddon, T. (1995) 'Different roles, different views: exploring the range of stakeholder perceptions on an in-company management development programme', *Industrial and Commercial Training*, 27, 4: 26–32.

Smith, A. (1993) 'Management development evaluation and effectiveness', *Journal of Management Development*, 12, 1: 20–32.

Smith, A. and Porter, J. (1990) 'The tailor-made training maze: a practitioner's guide to evaluation', *Journal of European Industrial Training*, 14, 8: complete issue.

*Snyder, R. (1993) 'The glass ceiling for women: things that don't cause it and things that won't break it', *Human Resource Development Quarterly*, 4, 1: 97–106.

Sparrow, P. and Bognanno, M. (1994) 'Competency forecasting: issues for international selection and assessment', in Mabey, C. and Iles, P. (eds) *Managing Learning*. London: Routledge.

*Stewart, J. and Hamlin, B. (1992a) 'Competence-based qualifications: the case against change', *Journal of European Industrial Training*, 16, 7: 21–32.

*Stewart, J. and Hamlin, B. (1992b) 'Competence-based qualifications: a case for established methodologies', *Journal of European Industrial Training*, 16, 10: 9–16.

Storey, J. (1992) 'Making European managers: an overview', *Human Resource Management Journal*, 3, 1: 1–10.

*Storey, J., Mabey, C. and Thomson, A. (1997) 'What a difference a decade makes', *People Management*, June: 28–30.

Storey, J., Okazaki-Ward, L., Gow, I., Edwards, P.K. and Sisson, K. (1991) 'Managerial careers and management development: a comparative analysis of Britain and Japan', *Human Resource Management Journal*, 1, 3, Spring: 33–57.

Syrett, M. and Lammiman, J. (1999) *Management Development: Making the Investment Count*. London: Profile Books.

Tarrant, D. (2005) 'Building a better team', *Management Today Australia*, May 14: 25–27.

Templer, A., Beatty, D. and Hofmeyer, K. (1992) 'The challenge of management development in South Africa: so little time, so much to do', *Journal of Management Development*, 11, 2: 32–41.

Temporal, P. (1990) 'Linking management development to the corporate future: the role of the professional', *Journal of Management Development*, 9, 5: 7–15.

*Thomson, A., Mabey, C., Storey, J., Gray, C. and Iles, P. (2001) *Changing Patterns of Management Development*. Oxford: Blackwell Business.

Thornhill, A. (1993) 'Management training across cultures: the challenge for trainers', *Journal of European Industrial Training*, 17, 10: 43–51.

Thurley, K. and Wirdenhuis, H. (1991) 'Will management become European? Strategic choice for organisations', *European Management Journal*, 9, 2: 127–135.

Tijmstra, S. and Casler, K. (1992) 'Management learning for Europe', *European Management Journal*, 10, 1: 30–38.

Tolentino, A. (1998) 'Training and development of entrepreneur-managers of small enterprises', in Prokopenko, J. (ed.) *Management Development: A Guide for the Profession*, Geneva: International Labour Office, pp. 471–492.

Torrington, D., Weightman, J. and Johns, K. (1994) *Effective Management: People and Organisations*, 2nd edn. Hemel Hempstead: Prentice Hall.

Varma, A., Stroh, L. and Schmitt, L. (2001) 'Women and international assignments: the impact of supervisor–subordinate relationships', *Journal of World Business*, 36, 4: 380–388.

Veale, C. and Gold, J. (1998) 'Smashing into the glass ceiling for women managers', *Journal of Management Development*, 17, 1: 17–26.

Vecsenyi, J. (1992) 'Management education for the Hungarian transition', *Journal of Management Development*, 11, 3: 39–47.

Vicere, A. (1998) 'Changes in practice, changes in perspectives: the 1997 international study of executive development trends', *Journal of Management Development*, 17, 7: 526–543.

Vine, P. (1999) 'Back to school', *British Journal of Administrative Management*, March/April: 18–21.

Vineall, T. (1994) 'Planning management development', in Mumford, A. (ed.) *Gower Handbook of Management Development*, 4th edn. Aldershot: Gower.

Vinnicombe, S. and Colwill, N. (1995) *The Essence of Women in Management*. Hemel Hempstead: Prentice Hall.

Wah, L. (1998) 'Surfing the rough seas', *American Management Association*, September: 25–29.

Warr, P., Bird, M. and Rackham, N. (1970) *Evaluation of Management Training*. London: Gower.

*Watson, T. (1994) *In Search of Management*. London: Routledge.

*Watson, T. (2002) *Organising and Managing Work*. Harlow: Financial Times/Prentice Hall.

*Watson, T. and Harris, P. (1999) *The Emergent Manager*. London: Sage.

Whiddett, S. and Branch, J. (1993) 'Development centres in Volvo', *Training and Development UK*, 11, 11: 16–18.

Whitaker, V. and Megginson, D. (1992) 'Women and men working together effectively', *Industrial and Commercial Training*, 24, 4: 16–19.

Wong, C., Marshall, N., Alderman, N. and Thwaites, A. (1997) 'Management training in small and medium-sized enterprises: methodological and conceptual issues', *The International Journal of Human Resource Management*, 8, 1: 44–65.

Woodall, J. (2000) 'Corporate support for work-based management development', *Human Resource Management Journal*, 10, 1: 18–32.

*Woodall, J. and Winstanley, D. (1998) *Management Development: Strategy and Practice*. Oxford: Blackwell.

Woodruffe, C. (1993) *Assessment Centres: Identifying and Developing Competence*. London: IPM.

For multiple-choice questions, exercises and annotated weblinks specific to this chapter visit the book's website at **www.pearsoned.co.uk/beardwell**

Transforming Anglian Water

The history

Anglian Water is geographically the largest of the ten regional water companies in the UK, delivering clean drinking water and removing sewage and waste-water from the homes and premises of some 5 million customers. Throughout the 1980s there were growing concerns over the standards and level of service delivery afforded by public sector organisations, and in line with the then government ideology and policy Anglian Water was privatised in 1989. Following privatisation, the company introduced a major reorganisation of its business, involving a rationalisation of existing structures and a diversification into new markets – many of them overseas operations. Between 1993 and 1995 the company reduced management layers from eleven to five, and 33 per cent of white-collar jobs were eliminated, bringing a saving of £40 million. However, senior management were conscious that if the organisation was to transform itself into a successful, high-performing international company, a fundamental realignment of its existing culture was required.

Prior to privatisation, the company's culture could be described as 'militaristic' – and with some justification. The risks were high. Any mistake in delivering water to customers could prove disastrous, and the company abided by the principle that 'contaminated water cannot be recalled'. The management solution was to introduce strict rules and procedures that were to be followed to the letter and obeyed without question. Any diversion from routine procedures was alien to an organisation where small risks or mistakes could rapidly and seriously jeopardise health and safety. The result was a culture in which playing by the rules, obeying orders, the acceptance and non-questioning of procedures was (and in the eyes of many had to be) the norm.

Forging a learning organisation

Senior management were under no illusions: the company's future success and survival in an increasingly competitive and aggressive marketplace depended on replacing the company's command-and-control culture with a more outward-looking, entrepreneurial, customer-focused, innovative approach to doing business. But how could this be achieved?

Philosophically, the company's approach was rooted in the need to reorient and prepare its employees for continuing and radical change, and to do this meant creating a more flexible, empowering, learning culture. The need to move in this direction was highlighted by a series of employee attitude surveys carried out after the restructuring of the early 1990s. Among other things, the surveys highlighted a discontent with the existing management style and communication policies. This led the senior management of Anglian Water into a considered debate about the future cultural direction of the business and the decision to create what they termed a *learning organisation*.

As a learning organisation the company would move away from the old public sector, keep your head down, jobs for life, follow the procedure mentality towards an environment in which employee creativity, innovation and challenge would be encouraged and valued. Employees would be empowered to take the lead in change. Individually and in cross-functional teams they would involve themselves in continuous improvement, not only in the area of technological development but – more significantly for a highly rational, technical organisation – in the area of customer service to meet changing needs and demands.

Steps along the way

There were two central, interlocking components designed to transform Anglian Water into a learning organisation. The first was the *Transformation Journey*. The concept of the Journey evolved from a development programme for attitudinal and behavioural change among senior managers. Following its success, a decision was taken to roll it out to all employees. The Journey was not a training programme. Instead it was a holistic strategy designed to prepare and equip employees for the technical and emotional challenges of operating in a turbulent and uncertain environment. The Journey was aimed at changing mindsets and creating self-awareness. It sought to promote teamworking and cooperation, and ultimately to have a direct bearing on operational effectiveness and business performance.

Any employee could 'sign up' for the Journey, and participation was entirely voluntary. However, clear signals were sent to the workforce that individuals were expected to participate, and enrolment on the Journey was regarded as an indication of their commitment to the company and its future.

Employees formed themselves into teams. Sometimes these were work related, but on other occasions individuals from disparate backgrounds came together. The only proviso was that any activity they engaged in was to benefit themselves, their group, and Anglian Water. There were four guiding principles for 'Travellers':

- a willingness to get to know myself;
- a desire to develop myself;
- a desire to realise my full potential with and through others;
- an ability to link my personal development to the development of Anglian Water.

A typical Journey lasted two years and was an essentially self-managed exercise. Each group was expected to acquire its own funding and sponsorship and to arrange its own support and skills development. Regular reviews along the way ensured that there was a basis for learning and reflection.

Journeys included groups who went outside Anglian Water, for example to build a toilet block on top of England's highest mountain, to refurbish a children's hospice, or to dig a well in Africa. Other groups focused on internal projects to improve overall business functioning and 'make things happen'. They involved themselves in more cross-functional teamworking, sought to improve their business knowledge and commercial awareness, became more creative and lateral in their thinking, conducted detailed research into business problems, and explored different options for change.

Between 1995 and 1997, 3000 employees had enrolled on the Journey, with some 300 groups being formed. In a 1996 survey, 88 per cent of respondents felt the Journey had benefited Anglian Water, and 99 per cent said that participation in a Journey had been a 'good learning experience'. Coincident with this survey, it was reported that customer satisfaction ratings had risen from 70 per cent in March 1995 to 90 per cent in March 1996.

The second component in Anglian's strategy to transform itself into a learning organisation was the establishment of the *University of Water* (colloquially known as Aqua Universitas). Knowledge creation and sharing were seen as vital in promoting best-practice networks and better customer service, and in enhancing commercial success. The University was aimed at acknowledging, integrating, supporting and accrediting all forms of learning taking place in the company. Its role was to define and develop the skills and competences – especially management skills – that were required to move Anglian into the twenty-first century and ensure its future as a global player. To this end, considerable resources were made available – for example, a dedicated 'campus' on the shores of Rutland Water and the installation of an intranet to promote information exchange and communication.

Around these two central components throughout the 1990s the company introduced a raft of supporting initiatives, including total quality management, leadership coaching, mass communication strategy development, change agent networks, new HR performance management policies, and vision and values statements designed to inculcate new attitudes and behaviours.

So have efforts to transform Anglian Water into a learning organisation culture been a success? Certainly there are considerable references to the 'old Anglian Water' and the 'new Anglian Water', reflecting a perception of behaviour and attitudinal change. And according to Clive Morton, ex-HR Director of Anglian, there is no doubt that a change in culture has occurred:

> The combination of the Journey and the University of Water with its universal access has created the conditions for a learning business, helping to assure the future for Anglian Water and its stakeholders.
>
> (Morton, 1998: 98)

The future

In 1998 Ofwat (the government's regulatory body for the water industry) recommended a price reduction of at least 17.5 per cent (about £45 on the average bill) in 2000. This one-off cut in charges represented about £130 million loss of revenue, and compares with 1998 profits of £268 million on turnover of £850 million. 'Costs must come down', the company warned. During 1999 the company initiated a major cost-reduction strategy, and this has translated into 400 job losses (10 per cent of the workforce).

References

Morton, C. (1998) *Beyond World Class*. Basingstoke: Macmillan Business Press.

Source: Extracts from *Anglian Water News*

Questions

You are an external consultant(s) advising a company facing similar challenges to those experienced by Anglian Water. It has read an account similar to the one described above, and is interested in exploring the whole concept of the learning organisation as a way of helping it to transform and succeed in the face of radical change. However, the board is cautious, and slightly sceptical of the cultural transformation process that Anglian has undergone. It has asked you to make an assessment. Specifically, they want you to report:

1 on the extent to which Anglian Water's claim to be a learning organisation can be justified. On what grounds should any claims or justifications be made?

2 against the backdrop of recent major job losses, whether or not Anglian can/should sustain the ideals and practices of a learning organisation. Are there any factors that might eventually undermine the concept and call into question the massive investment Anglian has made?

You are to prepare a report for the board of between 1000 and 1500 words, and follow this up with a short presentation (ten minutes).

Part 4

THE EMPLOYMENT RELATIONSHIP

Introduction to Part 4

The employment relationship is a key feature in the nature of managing employment. It brings together the sources of power and legitimacy, rights and obligations, that management and employees seek for themselves and apply to others. This part of the book is concerned with explaining this relationship and examining how it works out through a variety of applications such as the law, collective bargaining, performance and reward, and employee involvement.

Chapter 11 deals with the role and influence of the law in determining the nature of contract. The contract of employment is not simply a document that is presented to employees on appointment, but is a complex set of formal and informal rules which govern the whole basis of the employment relationship. Thus, the way employees and managers conform with, or break, those rules determines how that relationship works out in practice. Moreover, the nature of contract can have an important bearing on whether such newer concepts as human resource management can fundamentally change a relationship that is so dependent upon the interaction of formal and informal legal regulation.

Chapter 12 introduces the concept and practice of collective bargaining. In recent years the collective determination of pay has reduced in coverage and scope in many market economies, but it still remains the most important single method of arriving at broad pay settlement for many employees, and its impact and effect is often felt throughout economies. For these reasons its nature, structure and outcomes form the basis of analysis.

Chapter 13 discusses the processes that go towards settling pay for individuals when criteria which test their own performance are introduced. In recent years there has been an increasing use made of individualised pay, performance-related pay and performance management. This chapter examines some of the problems and issues in operating and evaluating such processes.

Chapter 14 is concerned with the development of employee involvement. This is a topic that has seen great interest recently, but there are contradictory elements within it which this chapter explores, among them whether involvement can genuinely bring employee and managerial interests together and whether involvement is a vehicle for 'empowerment' or simply a further way in which the managerial prerogative is asserted in the employment relationship.

Chapter 11

The employment relationship and employee rights at work

Ian Clark

Objectives

- To introduce readers from a variety of backgrounds to the central significance of contract in the employment relationship.
- To examine employment contracts and the legal regulation of employee activity within them.
- To provide the personnel practitioner or other interested reader with the necessary basic information to enable them to make fair and reasonable decisions within the employment relationship.
- To examine the contractual and statutory regulation of employment contracts in a manner that is reader friendly, non-technical but taking as its central focus the manner in which employment rights need to be regulated and proceduralised in the workplace.
- To add critical observations on the limitations of employee rights in the UK.

Introduction

This chapter examines the employment relationship and its contractual regulation. In particular, it outlines the central significance of contractual regulation in the employment relationship, and how this legitimises the managerial prerogative. The employment relationship is visualised as a process of socio-economic exchange. That is, unlike other contractual relationships, for example, something as mundane as the purchase of a railway ticket, the employment relationship is an open-ended contractual relationship. By this we mean that both parties intend the contract to continue until either party indicates a desire to terminate the relationship. Thus an employment contract is not an immediately closed relationship of exchange. The employment relationship contains an economic component – the exchange of work for payment – but also includes a sociological dimension centred on power and authority. The economic and sociological components of the employment relationship are structured by the contract of employment. In addition to this, the employment relationship is subject to a range of other processes, for example management competence and efficiency, work group control, management and worker motivation and the potential for workplace conflict and disagreement. These factors make the apparently rational process of economic exchange much more complicated and to some extent indeterminate – that is, a relationship in which the specific details are subject to ongoing negotiation and change.

All employees are protected by a series of basic contractual and statutory employment rights which the employment practices of an employer must abide by. In order to provide readers with the necessary basic information on these matters the chapter is divided into seven sections:

- Distinguishing contractual and statutory employment rights
- The contract of employment
- Discrimination in employment
- The regulation of working time
- Termination of the employment contract
- Enforcement of contractual and statutory employment rights
- New rights at work?

Throughout the chapter there is a series of Activity boxes and Stop and think boxes that aim to assist the reader apply and digest particular points. Readers should work through these individually or in discussion with their teachers. The material in each part of the chapter, although necessarily legal in nature, is explained as far as possible in terms that are general and straightforward, that is, in a manner that will assist the reader in their application. Some points are repeated as they impact on areas of employment regulation detailed in successive parts of the chapter. Because the aim is to present the material in a 'reader friendly' manner there are few direct references to legal texts or statutes; however, at the end of the chapter a list of law texts is provided for further reading. The reader should view this chapter as a general introduction to the contract of employment and its regulation and readers should be aware that more specialist information may be required in applying the general principles to specific situations.

Distinguishing contractual and statutory employment rights

In a chapter such as this, it is impossible to provide a complete and comprehensive analysis of the employment relationship and its legal regulation – employment contracts and employment statutes are subject to change as practices that were previously 'outwith the law' become subject to legal regulation, for example the recent emergence of paid paternity leave for fathers and more recently still protection against discrimination in employment due to sexual orientation, hence the law may be further updated after this edition is published. Equally, many areas of contractual and statutory regulation are extremely complicated and disputes between an employer and an employee may require specialist analysis by employment lawyers. Examples of these areas include discrimination claims with respect to pension rights for part-time women employees, disability discrimination claims that relate to the status of an employee as HIV positive and the interpretation of working time regulations for a particular group of employees. Thus, bearing in mind that contractual and statutory regulation of the employment relationship is a 'moving target', our examination of regulation within the employment relationship divides between a discussion of contractual and statutory employment rights.

Contractual rights

All employees have a contract of employment that governs the relationship between the employer and an individual employee. As we discuss below, an employment contract has three types of terms and conditions within it – express terms that are usually written down and which govern the specific details of the employee's contract of employment, implied terms that are unlikely to be written down but which nevertheless are considered to be part of an employee's contract of employment. For example, an employer is under a legally enforceable duty to provide a healthy and safe workplace. Equally, employees are likely to find themselves subject to various duties that are derived from custom and practice arrangements in the workplace even though many of them may be unwritten. The third type of term and condition within a contract of employment relates to statutory protection against unfair or unreasonable treatment by an employer and these statutory terms and conditions are incorporated into individual employment contracts. In summary, contractual rights flow from the express, implied and statutory incorporated terms and conditions that create an individual contract of employment. It is important to point out that while employees receive protection via elements of these terms and conditions they are also subject to regulation by them; hence the contract of employment is made up of a balance of rights and obligations between the employer and the employee.

Statutory rights

Statutory employment rights provide a basic floor of rights for all workers. Statutory employment rights are created by legislation in the form of Acts of Parliament and, increasingly, European Union directives that must be incorporated into UK law. A recent example of the latter is the emergence in the UK of the statutory regulation of working time and the introduction, from April 2003, of paid paternity leave for fathers.

In the drafting process, government and European Union civil servants seek to ensure that the legislation covers most eventualities. However, because legislation is necessarily general in its coverage of a particular issue an employer, trade unions and the judiciary must interpret legislation. Interpretation of legislation is a complicated and controversial matter and often turns on the issue of what is 'reasonable'. For an employer's interpretation of a statute to be reasonable the employer must be able to demonstrate to an employee, trade union or, in a matter of dispute, an employment tribunal that another employer faced with the same or a similar situation would have acted in the same way. In a matter of dispute an employee or a trade union must be able to demonstrate that another employer would not have acted in a particular manner. For example, until recently it was common practice for many employers to exclude their part-time workforce from occupational pension schemes on the basis that the salary or wage level of part-timers was too low to generate a sufficient pension fund, particularly as this would reduce the take-home pay of such workers because of the necessary deduction of an employee's contribution to the pension scheme. After a long legal campaign several trade unions, supported by the Equal Opportunities Commission, have established that this practice is unreasonable because many part-time workers are women and their exclusion from company pension schemes amounts to indirect sex discrimination. This is the case because, although the exclusion of part-time workers from pension schemes appears to be sex neutral in its effects, such exclusion has a disproportionate effect on women, so the practice is discriminatory. Common law precedent, that is, judicial decisions of interpretation, guide decisions in disputes where there is no relevant Act of Parliament and thus has the status of an Act of Parliament.

Summary

A central principle of the English legal system operative in contract law, the common law and statute law is that of *reasonableness*. In employment contracts, the common law terms and conditions and statutory interventions both have to be reasonable in their effects on the employer and employee. Thus in many cases judgments in disputes between employer and employee often turn on the question of reasonableness. The notions of reasonable and unreasonable behaviour or instructions are questions of interpretation in the circumstances of particular cases. As explained above, an express, implied or incorporated term in a contract of employment is reasonable if, in a matter of dispute, it is held that a similar employer would have done the same thing, for example, discipline or dismiss an employee, in similar circumstances. The discussion of this point is important for the following reasons. As statutory rights are subject to interpretation, challenge and eventual updating either in the form of statutory amendment or a binding precedent created by a court or employment tribunal, personnel practitioners must keep abreast of developments in employment law to ensure that the procedures set in place by their employer reflect the spirit and the letter of the law.

Stop & think

Try to think of five contractual rights and five statutory rights that you have or that your parents or partner have in employment.

The contract of employment

This part of the chapter divides into six subsections. The first distinguishes employment contracts from commercial contracts; this is followed by a brief discussion of contract theory. The third subsection examines the effects of the common law on employment contracts; this is followed by a discussion of different types of employment contracts. The fifth subsection discusses terms and conditions of employment contracts, and finally statutory rights that relate to employment contracts are examined in some detail.

Distinguishing commercial contracts and employment contracts

In order to explain the concept of contract, it is useful to distinguish between commercial contracts and employment contracts, the area of our particular focus. Commercial contracts, for example something as simple as buying a bus ticket or something as complex as a house purchase, contain four elements:

- offer;
- acceptance;
- consideration;
- the intention to create legal relations.

To illustrate these four elements we can draw on the example of a house purchase. An individual may visit a particular house and decide they would like to buy it. As a result of this they decide to make an offer. The current property owner may decide to accept this offer – subject to contract. 'Subject to contract' will necessarily involve the person who wishes to buy the house – the offeror – receiving a satisfactory structural survey and acquiring the necessary purchase price either in cash or (more likely) through a mortgage. If these requirements are satisfactorily fulfilled, a contract can be drawn up. In consideration for the agreed purchase price, the existing property owner – the offeree – agrees to give up their property rights in the house and exchange them through contract to the offeror. Thus consideration is the mechanism that validates the contract: that is, each party gives something to the contract, in this case a house for money by the offeror and money for a house by the offeree. If a contract contains offer, acceptance and consideration, the presence of these factors indicates that the parties to the contract wish to create a legally binding relationship.

A legally binding contract must also satisfy the following factors. First, the contents of the contract, to which the parties have agreed, must be reasonable. Second, the contract in itself must be legal, in terms of the prevailing law. For example, a contract to assassinate a person may contain offer, acceptance and consideration and an intention to create a legally binding relationship between the parties. However, conspiracy to murder is a criminal offence, thus any contractual relationship is void – the legal term for invalid. Third, there must be genuine consent between the parties, and the parties themselves must have the capacity to consent to the agreement. For example, minors and bankrupts have only limited capacities in contract. From this brief introduction we can now proceed to look at employment contracts, which are a very specialised form of contract.

A contract of employment is a *contract of service*, where an employee – the subject of the contract – is in the personal service of their employer. It is necessary to distinguish an employment contract of personal service from a commercial *contract for services*. As Wedderburn (1986: 106) makes clear, the law marks off the employee under a contract of service from independent contractors – self-employed workers – who may provide services to an organisation under a commercial contract. For example, a commercial contract whereby catering or cleaning services are provided to one firm by a second firm is a contract for services, not an employment contract, even though the work is performed by labour. Catering staff may be employees in the offeror firm, but the offeree firm has bought their services under a commercial contract for catering services.

A contract of employment differs from a commercial contract for services in the sense that an employment contract of personal service to an employer is intended to be an open-ended relationship. It is a relationship that continues until either party decides to end it through due notice, whereas a commercial contract is more likely to be a precise exchange of services over a clearly defined period of time. Some employment contracts today are of a temporary or fixed-term nature, but nonetheless an employment relationship is created, whereas in commercial contracts of a long-term duration, for example computer or photocopier servicing, an employment relationship is not created. Equally, such commercial contracts are likely to contain clear and precise contractual duties for each party. Thus commercial contracts are a purely contractual relationship and, unlike employment contracts, are not subject to the *common law duties* of an employer and employee which operate as implied terms and conditions within the contract of employment. The common law refers to areas of law that are not covered by parliamentary or European Union legislation. The common law has been developed by the judiciary: that is, the common law is *judge-made law*. Now that we have defined contract and distinguished between commercial and employment contracts, it is possible to proceed with a discussion of the underlying assumptions behind contract theory.

> **Activity**
>
> List the differences between commercial and employment contracts. Explain how commercial contracts might create employment. Compare and contrast your views with those of a colleague or the teacher.

Equality and freedom of entry: market individualism

The philosophical basis of contract is derived from the principle of market individualism. Market individualism suggests that the individual is the best judge of his or her own interests. From this suggestion the notion of *freedom of contract* is introduced, which assumes that individuals are self-determining agents, who are primarily self-interested. Thus individuals are able to fulfil their own self-interest most effectively if they are free to enter into contracts between themselves within the market mechanism.

Freedom of contract suggests that individuals act as free agents when they enter into contracts as both parties to a contract have equal status before the law and they jointly determine the terms and conditions of the contract. It follows from this assumption that the component elements of a contract – offer, acceptance and the consideration between the parties – are arrived at through a process of negotiation and then agreement to create legal relations. This may be the situation in the case of a house purchase, but in relation to employment the situation is somewhat different. As Fox (1985: 6) points out, contract theory alone, with all that it entails in terms of equality and references to adjudication by an outside body, cannot be an effective mode of regulation in the case of employment if the parties to the contract are in dispute. In the UK this is the case because the employment relationship remains one of *status*. The notion of status derives from paternalism in the master and servant relationship inherent in 'employment' prior to the rise of industrial economies. Examples of paternal employment include domestic service and tied cottages for estate farmers and general agricultural labourers. In the nineteenth century, domestic servants and agricultural labourers were not employees in the modern sense of the word; rather they were subject to a crude form of commercial contract whereby they provided their labour services to a master in return for board and lodgings. However, once employment became contractually determined in a formal legal sense it did not constitute a clean break with the past. By this we mean that the contractual process incorporates characteristics from pre-industrial 'paternal' employment: for example, the status bias of the master and servant relationship.

Fox (1985: 3–5) identifies paternalism as the basis of status within employment. Paternalism refers to a situation of subordination to legitimate authority. Prior to the contractual determination of employment the process of subordination to legitimate authority was entirely within the master–servant relationship. Within contractually determined employment, the employee subordinates him or herself to the greater legal authority of the employer, the superiority of which is derived from the status-based relationship of master and servant.

So, although employment contracts provide employees with a degree of independence from their employer – for example, employees can terminate their employment through due notice – employees remain subordinate parties to the employment contract. They are subject to the reasonable and legitimate authority of their employer, to whom they provide personal service.

From the above discussion it is clear that equality before the law in employment contracts is a fiction because employer authority is derived from their paternal status which underpins the employment relationship. This is often referred to as the *managerial prerogative*. In most contracts the agreeing parties are assumed to be the best judges of their own interests. However, in employment the status bias of the employer gives them the privilege of determining their self-interest and a partial say in the determination of employee interests. This privilege derives from the concept of *subordination*, which implies that the junior partner to the employment contract cannot perceive all their real interests. Kahn-Freund (1984) described the individually based contract of employment as an act of submission on the part of the employee:

> In its operation it is a condition of subordination, however much the submission and the subordination may be concealed by that indispensable figment of the legal mind known as the contract of employment.

An employer may determine the organisation of work, levels of payment and duration of working time. The employee is bound by such impositions if they are reasonable. Thus the notion of free employment contracts bears little resemblance to the real world (Hyman, 1975: 23). Relatedly, although all employees have an individual contract of employment, the terms and conditions of an individual's contract of employment are likely to be determined and regulated by means of a collective agreement, the details of which are normally incorporated in an individual's contract of employment. These agreements are often negotiated by a trade union through the process of collective bargaining. In the absence of a trade union and collective bargaining 'collective agreements' are unilaterally determined by management on behalf of the employer; they are not the subject of negotiation. This point again illustrates that the notions of individual negotiation and freedom of contract exist at only a superficial level of relations between employer and employee.

Activity Summarise what you understand by the terms 'managerial prerogative' and 'subordination' in the employment relationship. Provide two examples of the managerial prerogative and subordination in your employment. Lastly, explain how the notion of 'equality before the law' is not necessarily the same as equality in law within the employment relationship.

Common law regulation of employment contracts

There are two features of the English legal system that highlight the contexts within which all aspects of the law operate. First, the English legal system, unlike most other legal systems (for example, those of other European Union states), does not operate in conjunction with a written constitution or a Bill of Rights. In the specific area of employment the absence of a written constitution or a Bill of Rights means that British subjects do not possess any specific inalienable rights as employees: for example, the right to strike. Second, and relatedly, the system is very conservative – some would say obsessed with the past. This conservatism explains why 'precedent' has so prominent a role in the common law. Precedent operates on the basis of decisions previously arrived at in a higher court. It is judge-made law that creates a rule for lower courts and subsequent future cases of a similar nature. Thus a precedent creates an example for subsequent cases or acts as a justification for subsequent decisions.

Advocates of Britain's unwritten constitution argue that its major benefit is adaptability over time, which contrasts with the rigid mechanism of a written constitution around which new developments have to be moulded. In matters of employment many of the rights held by British subjects result from case law and precedent and from trade union activity in collective bargaining. Equally, trade unions have a consultative role in the formulation of statutory protections and provisions such as the national minimum wage or the statutory procedure for trade union recognition under the Employment Relations Act 1999.

Common law duties of employer and employee

Earlier in this part of the chapter, the concept of 'freedom of contract' was introduced. This concept assumes that individuals are self-determining agents who are primarily self-interested. It follows from this that individuals both freely enter into contractual arrangements and jointly determine the terms and conditions of an employment contract. In the case of employment, the notion of freedom of contract operates in conjunction with the common law duties of employer and employee. That is, although contracts of employment may be entered into freely, the contract of employment itself incorporates the common law duties of employee and employer.

Common law duties of the employer
These are to:

- Provide a reasonable opportunity for the employee to work and pay the agreed wages as consideration for work performed. It is a matter of some debate as to whether the employer has a common law duty to actually provide work; the issue appears to turn on the notion of reasonableness, which will depend on the details of any particular case.

- Take reasonable care to ensure that all employees are safe at the workplace, and indemnify any employee for injury sustained during employment. Employers have a vicarious common law duty to provide a safe working environment for their employees. Vicarious means that a legal duty is delegated to an employer to provide a safe working environment for employees, that is, it is a duty imposed on employers. Aspects of this liability are codified in statute under the Health and Safety at Work Act 1974.

- Treat all employees in a courteous and polite manner. That is, employers should not 'bully' or abuse their employees, or subject them to racist or sexist remarks. Aspects of this liability are codified in the Sex Discrimination Act 1975 (as amended) and the Race Relations Act 1976 (as amended). The common law duties of the employer contrast with those of an employee.

Common law duties of the employee

These are to:

- be ready and willing to work for their employer;
- offer personal service to the employer: that is, not hold a second job without agreement;
- take reasonable care in the conduct of their personal service;
- work in the employer's time, obey reasonable orders during that time, and undertake not to disrupt the employer's business on purpose;
- not disclose any trade secret to their employer's competitors.

The common law duties of the employee and employer are not always detailed in the written particulars of a contract of employment, and may be implied terms in the contract derived from custom and practice or statutes.

In market economies the contract of employment is freely entered into; however, the terms and conditions, whether they are express or implied, are not jointly determined, and in terms of employee and employer obligations they are not equal in terms of their scope and coverage. In most cases the employer is in the dominant bargaining position because they are offering employment. Hence the employer is able unilaterally to determine how the common law duties of the employee are to be fulfilled. The common law duties of the employee, as listed above, are clear and precise but open to considerable interpretation. In contrast to this, the common law obligations of the employer are imbued with the tenet of limited reasonableness: that is, the obligations imposed on the employer should not be unreasonable. Thus the general concept of reasonableness can only be tested in individual cases. As Hyman (1975: 24) argues, the symmetrical equality within the concept of self-determining individuals freely entering into contracts of employment is really asymmetrical because of the form that the notion of equality (before the law) and freedom of entry actually take. Clearly, equality before the law belies the market power held by an employer. Individual equality before the law places firms that have access to necessarily expensive legal advice on the formulation of employment contracts and individuals bereft of such a capability on the same plane. As we pointed out earlier, within the contract of employment freedom and equality are fused with the traditional status bias of employment, and it is this that appears to reduce the equality of the employee and raise the equality of the employer. This dealignment of equality creates the asymmetrical situation described by Hyman.

Types of employment contract

Every employee has a contract of employment. However, not all workers have a contract of employment. Where an employer provides regular work, defines working hours, the place of work and deducts income tax and National Insurance through the PAYE system, an employment relationship is created and anyone engaged on these terms is likely to be an employee. In contrast to this situation, a worker who is not an employee will pay their own income tax and National Insurance contributions, decide when, where and how they work and make their own holiday and sick pay arrangements. Hence many workers work under a contract for services as described above. However, in addition to self-employed contractors and freelance IT specialists, journalists, consultants etc., some agency workers, casual workers and 'home workers' may be classified as having worker status rather than employee status. A contract of employment is not always written down in one document, and sometimes the contract may not be written down at all.

There are several types of employment contract, as detailed below.

Permanent, ongoing or open-ended contracts

This type of employment contract is assumed to continue until either side gives notice of an intention to terminate the contract.

Temporary contract

This type of contract has a specified duration, but does not contain any restrictive fixed terms or waivers, for example, the requirement that the employee waive their right to statutory protection against a claim for unfair dismissal or redundancy. A temporary contract may be made permanent, and in this case the clause that relates to the specified duration will be removed, and the time served under the temporary contract will constitute continuity of service. Hence in the case of employment rights that are based on an employee's length of service – for example, unfair dismissal, which is currently set at one year's length of service – it is unnecessary for the employee to serve another full year to acquire this protection. However, although the general principle is clear, it is a complex area of law subject to the particular circumstances of individual cases.

Fixed-term contract

This type of contract has a specified duration: that is, a clear start date and a clear and unequivocal termination date. Examples of this might include situations where employment is subject to 'funding arrangements' that are not renewable, a specific one-off project or matters such as maternity and paternity leave. Both parties to a fixed-term contract should be aware that the contract is not renewable. More significant than this, many employees who are subject to fixed-term contracts are required to waive their statutory protections against unfair dismissal and redundancy. The Employment Relations Act 1999 prohibits employers from using waiver clauses against unfair dismissal; however, redundancy waivers continue. Since November 2001, employees under fixed-term contracts have equal rights to those of permanent employees in terms of pay rates and pension provision.

'Casual', 'spot' or zero hours contracts

Under this type of contract the employee must be available for work, but the employer does not have to guarantee work: for example, a retired teacher may be on call to cover for sick colleagues. Equally, banks use call staff to cover busy periods such as lunchtime, whereas the Post Office employs many casual workers at Christmas. In most situations this type of contract is mutually beneficial and not open to abuse; however, if a worker is required to be at work but clock off during slack periods – a practice once common in many fast-food outlets – zero hours contracts are open to abuse. For example, such a worker could remain at the workplace for long periods yet have a very low rate of hourly pay owing to continual clocking off. In an effort to overcome some of the abuses of zero hours contracts a person employed on such a contract is now entitled to the national minimum wage, whereas the Working Time Directive entitles the person to a paid holiday provided they worked during the preceding 13 weeks. The vast majority of individuals who are engaged under a zero hours contract will be classified as an employee; however, some employers have attempted to argue that engagement under a zero hours contract is compatible with worker status. The basis of this argument centres on the 'mutuality of obligation' between the employer and the worker or employee. If someone engaged under a zero hours contract does not have regular hours of work and is able to decline offers of work and/or work elsewhere, there is unlikely to be a mutuality of obligation between the two parties. It is the presence of mutual obligation that creates the employment relationship establishing the employer and employee. This is a controversial area and the distinction between worker status and employee status is persistently criticised by the TUC and other employee groups. Up to nine million workers in the UK may have worker status, many of whom are arguably *de facto* employees, for example, long-term agency workers or temps engaged in one organisation. The TUC is campaigning for all workers to have the status of an employee and therefore receive the basic contractual and statutory protections outlined earlier in the chapter. On the specific issue of agency and temporary workers, the UK's forthcoming adoption of European Union directives may provide the basis of some improvement in employment protection.

We have established that in the vast majority of cases the employer is the dominant party in the employment relationship. This dominance enables the employer to determine many terms and conditions contained within the employment contract.

What types of employment might be offered on the basis of a casual, spot or zero hours contract of employment? What reasons might an employer have to engage an employee on a fixed-term contract of employment?

Terms and conditions within employment contracts

There are three types of terms and conditions within a contract of employment.

Express terms and conditions

These form an explicit part of an individual contract of employment. They are often referred to as the *written* terms and conditions of the contract that are included in the written *statement of the contract*. Any employee, irrespective of the number of hours they work, must be given a statement of the written terms and conditions of their contract within two months – eight weeks – of starting work. The statement must include the following items:

- Name and address of employer.
- Date employment began.
- Place or places of work.
- Rate of pay or salary point; for lower-paid employees the rate must adhere to the statutory national minimum wage, from 1 October 2005, £5.05 per hour for workers aged 22 or over, £4.25 per hour for those aged 18–21 and £3.00 for 16 and 17 year-olds. From October 2006 the full adult rate will rise to £5.35 per hour and to £4.45 for those aged 18–21 and to £3.30 for those aged 16–17 years. For more details see www.dti.gov.uk/er/nmw.
- Hours of work; as a result of the Human Rights Act, 1998 it may be necessary for employers to specify the reasons for, frequency of and need to telephone employees at home. This legislation establishes that an employer does not have an automatic right to demand an employee's home phone number unless the express terms of an employment contract state that an employee has a duty to be available outside normal working hours.
- Holiday entitlements; as a result of the working time regulations (see the section 'The regulation of working time' on page 435) all employees are now entitled to four weeks' paid holiday, part-time workers on a pro-rata basis. The situation with respect to temporary or agency workers is more complicated. All employees are entitled to a minimum of four weeks' paid holiday but to qualify for this an employee must work for an employer for 13 weeks. Temps employed by an agency are entitled to paid holidays if they work for 13 weeks. This is the case even if they move between different workplaces as long as the employment is continuous. In March 2006 the European Court of Justice threw the commonplace practice of 'rolled up holiday pay' into potential disarray after an application by a group of shift and contract workers. This practice describes the situation where employees are paid for their holiday entitlement instead of being given leave, the European Court described the practice as unlawful, however, at the time of writing the full judgment is not available and it is likely that the decision will be appealed. On the one hand the decision, if upheld, would prevent rogue bosses and poor practice employment agencies from denying employees their full workplace rights, yet on the other hand if upheld the decision would make personnel practice in respect of remuneration and leave much more complicated and potentially over-regulated.
- Sick pay arrangements.
- Notice entitlements.
- Pension rights.
- For firms employing more than 20 employees, details of the grievance procedure.
- For firms employing more than 20 employees, details of the discipline procedure.

- Job title.
- Period of employment if job not permanent.
- Name of employee.

Implied terms and conditions

These are terms and conditions that are not explicitly stated in an individual contract of employment but which are assumed to be included in the contract: for example, workplace custom and practice arrangements and the common law duties of the employer and employee.

Incorporated terms and conditions of employment

These are terms and conditions that are incorporated into individual contracts of employment as either express or implied terms. Incorporated terms and conditions of employment include the provisions of collective agreements negotiated between an employer and a recognised trade union and statutory protections passed by Parliament or the European Union. In English law, collective agreements negotiated between employers and trade unions through the process of collective bargaining are not legally binding. However, elements within collective agreements are legally binding if they are incorporated into individual contracts of employment: for example, working hours and pay rates.

Changing terms and conditions of employment

Employers are able to change terms and conditions of employment; however, employees have some rights if an employer seeks to change terms and conditions without consultation and agreement. A unilateral change in pay rates represents a serious breach of contract, as does the unilateral removal of a company car, reductions in holiday entitlements and suspension of an employer's pension contribution. Employees can accept unilateral changes and work normally under protest – object to the changes and seek to minimise the effects of the unilateral change and seek representation through a trade union – or leave and claim 'constructive dismissal'.

Stop & think

Ensure that you are clear on the differences between express, implied and statutory incorporated terms and conditions of employment. Check your understanding with a class colleague and the teacher.

Activity

Examine the points above on express, implied and statutory incorporated terms and conditions of employment against your own job and see if you can state what your express terms are or where details of them can be found.

Statutory rights relating to employment contracts

All employees have a contract of employment; equally, all employees receive some level of statutory protection against arbitrary and unreasonable treatment by an employer. Statutory protection can be framed in individual terms, for example protection against sexual and racial discrimination in the workplace; alternatively, rights may be collective, for example the statutory procedure for trade union recognition introduced by the Employment Relations Act 1999.

Since 1995 all workers, either full-time or part-time, have been subject to the same *day one statutory rights* irrespective of how many hours they work. Statutory day one rights provide a minimum level of protection to all workers. Some workers may have additional contractual rights negotiated by their employer and a recognised trade union. In addition to day one rights, other rights depend on an employee's length of service.

Day one employment rights

Equal pay/equal value

The Equal Pay Act 1970 (EPA) as amended inserts an *equality clause* into contracts of employment that can be enforced by an employment tribunal. Under the EPA clauses within a contract of employment must be equal between the sexes. The equality clause enforces equal terms and conditions in the contracts of men and women employed in the same organisation. The clause covers pay and all other contractual terms of employment. The EPA is applicable in three situations:

- *Like work.* Where men and women are employed to perform like work, that is, the same work or work that is broadly similar, men and women must receive the same rate of pay or be paid on the same salary scale. This is the case even if part-time men and women work fewer hours than full-time men and women, that is, a part-time worker may compare themselves to a full-time employee.

- *Work rated as equivalent under an analytical job evaluation scheme.* Job evaluation describes a set of methods that compare jobs with the view to assessing their relative and comparative worth. The process of job evaluation ranks jobs based on rational and objective assessment of key factors – such as skill, effort and decision-making – from a representative sample of jobs in a particular organisation. The purpose of job evaluation is to produce a reasonable and defensible ranking of jobs. By formalising and making explicit the basis of payment systems and associated differences in pay levels, employers can expose discriminatory practices and remove them; for more detail on job evaluation see Armstrong and Baron (1995) and Chapter 6.

- Where work is of *equal value*, even though it is not like work or work covered by a non-discriminatory job evaluation scheme in the same employment. Equal value is measured in terms of the demands upon the worker in terms of skill levels, effort and decision-making. If different work is held to be of equal value under these criteria then the two groups of workers must have the same pay levels. Pay is constituted in its widest sense and includes salary scales or pay rates, access to occupational pension schemes, redundancy protection, sick pay, travel concessions and other perks. In the 1980s, USDAW (the shop workers' trade union) and the Equal Opportunities Commission successfully fought equal value cases on behalf of supermarket checkout workers, who are predominantly women, against delivery dock and warehouse workers who were predominantly men. An employer may defend an equal value case on the grounds that differences in pay between men and women are justified on the grounds of a genuine material factor that is both relevant and significant in the particular case. The fact that a particular group of workers who are predominantly women includes a male worker does not constitute a genuine material factor: that is, men who receive lower pay than other men employed in the same organisation are able to claim that their work is of equal value. For example, the presence of a 'token' male checkout worker or school lunch assistant appears insufficient to defeat a claim for equal value. In summary, a claim to equal pay for work of equal value normally involves women in comparison to men; however, the presence of lower-paid men cannot undermine a claim because men are also protected in respect of equal pay for work of equal value.

Sex discrimination/harassment

It is unlawful to discriminate against an employee, that is offer them them less favourable treatment on grounds of their sex, sexual orientation or marital status, or because of maternity or pregnancy. Employment protection legislation covers discrimination in respect of pay, whereas the Sex Discrimination Act 1975 as amended (SDA) covers discrimination in respect of selection, training, promotion, termination (e.g. selection for redundancy) or any other detriment in employment (e.g. sexual harassment). The SDA applies equally to men and women except with respect to pregnancy provisions, and defines discrimination in three ways:

- *Direct discrimination.* For example, denying a woman a job or promotion on the grounds that she is a woman, a married woman, a single woman, is pregnant and/or has children.

- *Indirect discrimination.* This category refers to apparently sex-neutral job requirements that have a disproportional effect on men or women, for example height requirements, dress codes or age and length of service requirements for promotion that may preclude married women with children from having sufficient length of service to apply by an upper age limit. Some cases of indirect discrimination appear to be intentional, whereas other cases result from a failure to update personnel procedures in accordance with the law: for example, dress codes that prevent women from wearing trousers. An employer may choose to defend a charge of indirect discrimination on the grounds that the apparently discriminatory provision is a necessary requirement of the job. For example, in selection exercises for the fire service candidates must be able to expand their lung capacity by a certain measurement. Many women applicants are unable to meet this requirement: hence it appears to have a disproportionate effect on women. However, many men are unable to meet the requirement. Lung expansion is a requirement of a firefighter's job because it plays a part in assessing whether or not a candidate would be able to escape from a variety of smoke-filled situations. Claims of direct and indirect sex discrimination are in the majority of cases launched by women; however, the law is equally applicable to men and women, an equality that was recently demonstrated in the decision of an employment tribunal. In this case a male worker in a Stockport job centre won a claim for sexual discrimination because he refused to wear a tie at work. The basis of this claim was that he was told what to wear whereas female colleagues were not and that female colleagues were allowed to wear tee shirts as opposed to more formal blouses. The Department of Work and Pensions appealed this decision and as a result the case was withdrawn and settled on a voluntary basis that involved re-working dress codes for both male and female employees.

- *Victimisation.* This category covers verbal abuse or suggestive behaviour or harassment. It may also result from an employee's enforcing a statutory right. Harassment and bullying occur when a person engages in unwanted conduct which has the purpose or effect of violating another's dignity. Alternatively bully and harassment may create an intimidating, hostile degrading humiliating or offensive environment for another person. Certain types of employment are exempt from the provisions of the SDA: for example, employment that is mainly or wholly outside the UK, photographic modelling, and some areas of social work such as child protection from abuse and rape counselling.

Racial discrimination and harassment

The Race Relations Act 1976 (as amended) (RRA) follows the model set by the SDA and defines racial discrimination as direct, indirect and victimisation. Cases of direct racial discrimination in employment on the grounds that a person is black, Asian, or Afro-Caribbean are less in evidence than during the 1960s. However, examples of indirect racial discrimination in employment turn on the relevance of apparently race-neutral job requirements that have a disproportionate effect on ethnic minorities: for example, requirements that preclude candidates on the basis that their grandparents were not British, or English language requirements. If these requirements are unrelated to the job they may well be indirectly discriminatory. Racial victimisation in employment covers matters such as racial abuse, suggestive behaviour or harassment as a result of an employee attempting to enforce a statutory right. Certain types of employment are exempt from the provisions of the RRA: for example, staff in specialised restaurants and community social workers who are required to speak particular ethnic languages.

Activity Think of two examples of employer or organisational behaviour that might constitute direct discrimination, indirect discrimination and victimisation in employment in terms of racial and sexual discrimination. Compare your list with one of your class colleagues.

Maternity rights

The rules and regulations in respect of maternity rights are very complicated. It is important that both the employer and the employee follow them carefully. Some employees have better maternity arrangements than the statutory arrangements; this is usually the result of collective bargaining arrangements in the workplace.

All women are entitled to maternity leave, which under the provisions of the ERA was set at 26 weeks and was further extended by the maternity and paternity leave regulations to 52 weeks of which up to 26 weeks are paid maternity leave. In April 2007 paid maternity leave will be extended to nine months and the government has made a further commitment to increase paid leave to one year by the end of this Parliament (at the latest 2010). In addition to this the government is also examining a new right for mothers to transfer up to three months of their paid maternity leave entitlement to fathers. The entitlement to paid maternity leave is unrelated to the number of hours worked or length of service. A pregnant employee must conform to the following requirements:

- provide written notice of pregnancy and due date;
- provide a medical certificate if requested;
- indicate the date the employee intends to begin leave – this cannot be before the 11th week;
- return to work within 26 weeks for paid maternity leave or 52 weeks if the employee is taking a futher 26 weeks unpaid maternity leave.

Maternity leave may be extended if the employee is sick or has an illness related to confinement. The day one employment rights listed above and below establish that employees who are either pregnant or on maternity leave cannot be dismissed or made redundant because of pregnancy or a pregnancy-related illness contracted or diagnosed as commencing before or after the birth of the child.

An employee who fulfils the following criteria is entitled to *statutory maternity pay* when:

- their earnings are equal to £106 per week – the lower earnings limit;
- the employee provides the employer with a maternity certificate giving the due date;
- they were employed up to and including the 15th week before the baby was due;
- they have stopped working;
- they have given the employer 21 days' notice of their intention to stop working;
- at the end of the 15th week of confinement before the baby was due, the employee had worked for this employer for 26 weeks.

Statutory maternity pay is calculated on the basis of 6 weeks at 90 per cent of average earnings plus 20 weeks at the basic rate of statutory sick pay, currently £106 per week. Employees who do not qualify for maternity pay may receive maternity allowance from the Department of Social Security. Awards for maternity allowance depend on an employee's National Insurance contribution. Finally, an employer can compel a new mother to take maternity leave. There is a two-week period of compulsory maternity leave (four weeks for employees who work in a factory) following the birth of a child. It is unlawful for an employer to allow or compel a new mother to work during this period. After a period of maternity leave an employee is entitled to return to the same job they held before going on leave. In the case of extended maternity leave for employees working in a firm employing fewer than five workers an employer may be able to demonstrate that keeping a job open is unreasonable and offer the returning employee a similar job.

Disability discrimination

There are approximately seven million disabled working age people in the UK but only half that figure are actually in employment and many more would like to work but are unemployed or in receipt of incapacity benefit. The Disability Discrimination Act 1995 (DDA) makes it unlawful for an employer to discriminate against applicants for employment and employees who have a disability in relation to job applications, promotion, training and contractual terms and benefits. The provisions of the statute cover all employees from permanent to casual. In addition, subcontract workers are also covered. The DDA is now universal in application, since October 2004 employers with fewer than 15 workers are now covered by its provisions. The 2005 Disability Discrimination Act further extends the coverage of disability in the workplace, for example, the framework of protection now covers employees with 'asymptomatic' conditions such as MS, HIV, ADDHS and some forms of cancer from the time they are diagnosed by a doctor. This provision detailed in the 2005 legislation is intended to cover so-called 'hidden disabilities'.

The DDA defines *disability* as mental or physical impairment that has a long-term and substantial adverse effect on the ability of an individual to perform normal daily activities. The legislation goes on to amplify this definition under several headings. First, the nature of impairment is broadly interpreted in terms of its daily impact on an employee rather than being confined to those that are recognised medical conditions, for example, HIV-positive status, schizophrenia, ADDHS and other forms of mental illness. Second, the requirement for a substantial effect rules out minor complaints such as hay fever or colour-blindness. Third, and related, a condition of impairment must last at least a year or the rest of a person's life to qualify as a long-term effect. This requirement rules out impairments such as whiplash resulting from minor motor accidents and other temporary debilitating illnesses. Last, the ability to undertake normal daily activity covers issues such as the ability to hear and learn, comprehend the perception and risk of physical danger, continence, eyesight, hearing, manual dexterity, memory, speech and physical coordination.

The DDA outlines three tests for disability discrimination:

- *Less favourable treatment.* This situation arises when a disabled employee is able to demonstrate less favourable treatment – in comparison with an able-bodied person – that is related to their disability that cannot be justified by the employer. An employer can defend a claim for disability discrimination on the grounds of less favourable treatment if they can demonstrate a relevant or substantial reason for the treatment.

- *A duty to make reasonable adjustments.* A failure to make reasonable adjustments in the workplace may result in disability discrimination. It is likely to be unlawful and unreasonable where a disabled employee is substantially disadvantaged by work arrangements or the layout of the workplace when compared with an able-bodied employee. In this situation the employer is under a legal duty to make reasonable adjustments: for example, the installation of wheelchair ramps and the provision of ground floor office space for wheelchair users. An employer can justify the discrimination on the grounds that they were unaware that a job applicant or employee was disabled, however employers must demonstrate that they did not unlawfully, that is the burden of proof lies with the employer. In addition to this, an employer can no longer justify disability discrimination with a substantial reason. Lastly, from December 2006 public sector employers will be charged with a duty to promote disability equality as best practice.

- *Victimisation.* It is unlawful under the DDA to bully, harass or victimise a person who alleges disability discrimination, enforces statutory rights under the DDA or gives evidence in a disability case.

Miscellaneous

In addition to the above day one rights, all employees have the following day one rights where relevant:

- time off for trade union duties;
- protection against victimisation due to involvement in trade union duties – for example, unfair selection for redundancy;
- protection against victimisation due to involvement in health and safety activity;
- the right to itemised payslips;
- protection against unlawful deductions from wages and or claims that relate to entitlements under the provision of the national minimum wage or the provisions of the working time directive, for example, entitlements to paid holidays.
- written reasons for dismissal during pregnancy or maternity leave;
- time off for antenatal visits;
- basic maternity leave of 26 weeks (rising to nine months from April 2007);
- Sunday working rights, where relevant;
- protection against victimisation for enforcing a day one or length of service statutory right;
- disclosure of wrong-doing under the provisions of the Public Interest Disclosure Act, 1998, that is 'whistleblowing'.

Rights that depend on length of service

Access to the following statutory rights is dependent upon an employee's length of service, but is unrelated to how many hours they work.

- *Written statement of main terms and conditions of employment*: 2 months.
- *Extended maternity leave*: 1 year. Employees who have at least one year's employment service at the beginning of the 11th week before the baby is due are entitled to a longer period of maternity leave, termed extended maternity leave. This leave may extend up to 40 weeks, starting 11 weeks before the birth and lasting up to 29 weeks after birth. As with basic maternity leave, it does not matter how many hours the employee works. An employee who claims extended maternity leave has to follow several procedural rules:
  - work up to the 11th week before the baby is due;
  - give the employer at least 21 days' notice before the start of leave;
  - provide the employer with a statement that she is going on maternity leave and will return afterwards, and state the date the baby is due;
  - provide a certificate of due date signed by a GP or midwife if requested;
  - provide the employer with 21 days' written notice of the date she intends to return to work;
  - return to work within 29 weeks of the start of the week in which the baby is born.
- *Written reasons for dismissal*: 1 year.
- *Protection against unfair dismissal*: 1 year.
- *Protection against unfair dismissal due to 'whistle blowing', i.e. public interest disclosure*: 1 year. Such cases can be expensive for an employer because the public interest disclosure legislation does not impose a cap on tribunal awards. Connex, the train operating company, was ordered to pay £55,000 to a train driver who successfully demonstrated his victimisation after he published concerns over safety risks. £18,000 of the award was for aggravated damages and injury to feelings. Connex declined to appeal the tribunal decision.
- *Dismissal due to job redundancy*: 2 years.
- *Guaranteed lay-off pay*: 1 month.
- *Medical suspension pay*: Absence or suspension from work on medical grounds – 1 month.

- *Paid parental leave for fathers*: 1 year, 2 weeks' paid paternity leave at the same rate as statutory maternity pay. This supplements the government decision to introduce the EU minimum 13 weeks' unpaid leave provision.
- *Paid adoption leave*: 1 year, in order to allow one adoptive parent 2 weeks' paid leave at the same rate as statutory maternity pay.

Employers are required to provide employees with the periods of paid notice listed in Table 11.1. Employers must give employees full pay for the notice period even if the worker is off sick or on maternity leave.

Table 11.1 Minimum notice periods

Length of service	Notice	Length of service	Notice
4 weeks–2 years	1 week	7–8 years	7 weeks
2–3 years	2 weeks	8–9 years	8 weeks
3–4 years	3 weeks	9–10 years	9 weeks
4–5 years	4 weeks	10–11 years	10 weeks
5–6 years	5 weeks	11–12 years	11 weeks
6–7 years	6 weeks	Over 12 years	12 weeks

Activity

On the basis of the material on day one and length of service rights, discuss any situation in your employment where such rights may have been infringed. The discussion should test your argument against the law. In areas of disagreement between you and your class colleagues, confer with the teacher.

Discrimination in employment

As the second part of this chapter establishes, employees have statutory protection against discrimination on grounds of sex, race, disability and unequal treatment in terms of pay. However, the presence of discrimination in employment is still evident (see Dickens, 2005 for general discussion of the problem); for example, the Equal Opportunities Commission (2001) reported that women in full-time employment earn 82 per cent of male full-time hourly earnings, a figure that stood at 69 per cent in 1971. Equally, part-time women employees receive only 61 per cent of male full-time hourly earnings against a European Union average of 73 per cent. Further, in some female-dominated occupations, for example nursing, women earn 6 per cent less than average male hourly earnings and survey material continues to demonstrate that female employees argue that pay discrimination remains a persistent problem. For example, a survey of 1500 women managers found that a third of the sample claimed that pay discrimination persists in their organisation (Public Affairs, 2001). More dramatically than this, a recent report by the National Association of Citizens Advice Bureau found that many women are still sacked or threatened with the sack when they become pregnant.

In 2002, in its submission to the Hicks review of non-executive directors, the Equal Opportunities Commission provided evidence that of over 600 senior executive positions of the top 100 firms in the FTSE only 10, or 2 per cent, are filled by women, a proportion that has remained unchanged for the past ten years (EOC, 2002). Only one FTSE 100 company has a woman chief executive – Marjorie Scardino – chief executive of the Pearson Group. Women now account for 30 per cent of managers but earn 24 per cent less than male managers.

The categories of sex and race discrimination – direct discrimination, indirect discrimination and victimisation – are relatively easy to define, and many organisations have taken procedural steps in terms of pay audits, greater transparency over pay, analytical job evaluation schemes and equal opportunities policies to combat such discrimination, yet discriminatory practices remain in evidence. There are four reasons that help to explain the continued presence of discrimination in employment.

Firstly, much discrimination goes unreported and is tolerated by employees, who feel that they have no voice mechanism to complain about such treatment; this is particularly the case in small firms and some non-union employers. That is, some employers know they are breaking the law but hope to get away with ignoring it. However, it is necessary to point out that within workplaces that have collective bargaining and otherwise well-ordered personnel policies, discrimination may occur; for example, recently there was a well-publicised case of racial discrimination at the Ford Dagenham plant. This case was settled by an employment tribunal in 2002 when two former employees were awarded a total of £500,000 in damages for racial discrimination and medical disability. The Ford motor company accepted the decision of the tribunal but added that a policy of zero tolerance of racial abuse had been introduced at the Dagenham plant and further noted that the complaints of both employees had been thoroughly investigated.

A second explanation for the continued presence of discrimination relates to the rather limited nature of employment protection legislation during the 1980s. For much of its period of office the last Conservative government operated differential employment protection legislation for full-time and part-time workers. The results of much of this legislation, for example the lawful exclusion of part-time workers from occupational pension schemes, are now unlawful. However, many claims against this type of discrimination, unequal pay and indirect sex discrimination, lodged on the basis that more part-time workers were women than men, remain in the process of redress and resolution.

In an effort to reduce discrimination between full-time and part-time employees the Part-time Workers' Regulations came into force in July 2000. These regulations state that part-time workers should receive the same pay rates as full-time colleagues and receive the same hourly overtime rate once they exceed normal working hours. In addition to these equal rights, part-time workers must receive the same holiday, maternity and paternity leave entitlements as full-time colleagues on a pro-rata basis. Finally, part-time workers must be included in the provision of workplace training, that is, there must be a single framework for training in the workplace and not separate sets of arrangements for full-time and part-time workers.

The part-time regulations cover seven million workers working fewer than 30 hours per week, including home workers and those employed on temporary, casual or short-term contracts or by an employment agency. The regulations, although a marked improvement on the previous situation – which forced female part-timers who alleged discrimination to seek redress through the indirect route of the Sex Discrimination Act – are limited. For example, while the regulations call for comparability of pay between full-time and part-time workers, they contain no mechanism to measure or quantify such comparison. Currently a 'comparable worker' – a comparator that a part-time employee uses for comparison – is defined as 'a full-time worker with the same type of employment contract doing the same or similar work'.

A third explanation of the emergence of newly defined forms of discrimination in employment is the UK's further integration within the EU and the adoption by the incoming Labour government of the EU's Social Charter of employment and social rights in 1997. This accession further exposed the limited protection provided for many British employees; for example, prior to November 2001 individuals employed on fixed-term contracts did not have the same rights as full- and part-time employees in terms of pay, pension entitlement and paid holidays. Further, at the time of writing, agency workers or 'temps' employed directly by employment agencies can be lawfully discriminated against in terms of pay, holiday pay and dismissal. A recently announced EU directive – once approved at EU level – may eventually remedy this source of currently lawful discrimination in the workplace (see the section 'New rights at work' on page 442).

Lastly, in the UK some areas of discriminatory practice, for example, discrimination on the grounds of age, sexual and racial harassment, remained 'lawful' if omitted from specific mention in relevant statutes – racial and sexual harassment are not categorised by Race Relations legislation or Sex Discrimination legislation. Until October 2006 age discrimination was regulated by a voluntary code of practice but is now regulated due to the implementation of the EU directive on age discrimination. The age discrimination regulations contain the following provisions. They make it unlawful for employers to specify age when recruiting staff, promoting staff or training staff. Similarly terms such as 'youngish', 'recently qualified' 'under forty' become unlawful unless an employer is able to provide a clear business-related reason for the specification of the requirement. In addition to these provisions the regulations suggest that advertisements which seek 'experienced' workers will require careful wording and person specifications to ensure that it is clear that recruitment decisions are not made on the basis of age and experience. Furthermore, the regulations ban compulsory retirement on age grounds for employees below 65 years and place a duty on employers to consider requests made by an employee to work beyond 65 years. On a related matter, employees beyond the statutory retirement age have traditionally found themselves beyond employment protection but the regulations remove the upper age limits for protection against unfair dismissal and redundancy.

The emergent issue of workplace bullying further demonstrates the limited nature of the UK's discrimination and employment protection laws. In 2002 a survey of 3500 employees found that 20 per cent of the sample had experienced workplace bullying in the past year, with 8 per cent of the sample claiming to have experienced bullying on a regular basis. Bullying is not confined to employees further down the organisational hierarchy; 24 per cent of middle managers and 17 per cent of senior managers reported that they had been bullied at least once over the past year (Mercer Human Resource Consulting, 2002). Currently, workplace bullying is not specifically categorised in employment legislation, and while the practice may constitute victimisation, disability discrimination or indirect racial or sexual discrimination, in other cases employees may have to resign and claim constructive dismissal, see the section 'Termination of the employment contract' on page 437.

It is important for the personnel practitioner to note that an employer is liable to defend an allegation of discrimination in the workplace and act upon it even if the employer is not directly responsible for it; that is, where another employee is responsible for the discriminatory behaviour. As some recent cases in City of London financial institutions demonstrate, it is not sufficient for an employer to argue that racist and sexist behaviour constitutes workplace 'banter' or that they were unaware that such behaviour occurred or that such behaviour is not discriminatory because all employees are subject to it. Further, other recent cases in financial institutions demonstrate the continued presence of indirect sex discrimination due to unequal pay, such as in the calculation of bonus payments. For example, a female analyst employed by Schroder Securities recently won £1.4 million damages in a sex discrimination case where the applicant to the employment tribunal successfully argued that her results were similar to those of male colleagues but that her bonus payments (£25,000) were significantly lower than those of her colleagues who received 'six-figure' bonuses. The employer, while denying the claim, accepted the tribunal decision and withdrew its application to the Employment Appeal Tribunal. Since April 2003 employees have had the right to require employers to complete equal pay questionnaires on co-workers. The evidence suggests that employers who conduct regular pay reviews and those who are committed to pay transparency are far less likely to have pay systems that discriminate against women workers.

The main themes that emerge from this part of the chapter centre around three issues, each of which is pertinent to the personnel practitioner. First, statutory protection is updated at Parliamentary or EU level and it is essential for personnel practitioners to audit and monitor workplace practices and procedures that are likely to be affected by new legislation. Second, workplaces that have proceduralised systems for personnel management must be vigilant and act quickly to prevent apparently one-off incidents developing into persistent behaviour consistent with emergent bullying or victimisation. Last, much remains to be done in order to remove discriminatory practices in the workplace and it is clear that the discrimination agenda gets not only longer but wider as new areas of activity are drawn into the scope of existing measures; for example, the extension of equal pay legislation to cover pension entitlements and before that, in the 1980s, the introduction of the equal value amendments for different work of equal value to an employer in terms of skill, effort and decision making.

Stop & think

At the end of the third point on continued sources of discrimination in the workplace the text refers to 'this source of currently lawful discrimination in the workplace'. Is it fair and reasonable to argue that lawful discrimination actually exists?

The regulation of working time

As Chapter 12 demonstrates, historically the UK's industrial relations system exhibits only a few areas of specific regulation. The voluntary nature of the British system witnessed a reliance on the negotiation of voluntary agreements over pay and conditions of employment and working time arrangements in particular (see Clark, 2000 and Edwards, 2003 for a general discussion of voluntarism). The 1999 Working Time Regulations provide one of the first serious attempts to provide for the regulation of hours at work. However, the voluntary and unregulated nature of the British industrial relations system remains significant. Currently, the UK's application of the EU working time directive illustrates the pervasive nature of voluntarism via the inclusion of opt-outs that allow employers – sometimes unilaterally, sometimes in negotiation with trade unions – to regulate working hours as they see fit.

The UK's working time regulations provide the following working time rights for all employees:

- A maximum of 48 hours on the average working week over a 17-week period. 'Working time' includes overtime, workplace training provided by the employer, work time travelling to meet clients or business partners when this is a regular part of a job and hospitality arrangements such as attendance at receptions and working lunches. Working time excludes travelling time to and from work, training at educational institutions, work time breaks and periods 'on call' but not working.

One aim of the working time regulations that remains unfulfilled is a reduction in the effects on employees, of all grades, of the burden of the UK's previously unregulated work culture. In 2002 The Department of Trade and Industry reported that 16 per cent of workers work 60 hours a week in comparison to 12 per cent in 2000 (see *Financial Times*, 30 August 2002) with 4.5 million workers working more than 48 hours per week. Comparatively, British working hours are the longest in Europe and remain so even in face of the provisions contained in the Working Time Directive (see European Commission, 2003). The long-hours work culture prevalent in the UK has resulted in the emergence of workplace stress as a major issue for British employers, with work overload often cited as the main cause of stress. The magnitude of the long-hours culture and workplace stress was demonstrated by a survey of 5000 employers which found that while 80 per cent of the sample felt vulnerable to possible legal action over workplace stress, 66 per cent of the sample had no stress policies in place. In 2001, over 6000 firms paid an average of £51,000 in damages for workplace stress; this figure represents a twelve-fold increase on the number of employees who successfully sued their employer for stress compared to 2000 (Work Stress Management, 2002). Whilst the length of the average full-time working week fell to 37.4 hours in 2005 overall the long hours work culture remains in evidence. Just under a quarter of the employed population (6.3 million people) worked more than 45 hours per week in 2005 with British workers on average also having fewer paid holidays than employees in other EU states, 20 compared to 25–30 in most EU nations, see (CIPD, 2006a, b).

The limit of opt-out arrangements

An employer cannot require employees to opt-out of the provisions listed below:

- four weeks' paid holiday;
- a work time break where the working day exceeds 6 hours;
- an 11-hour rest period every working day;
- a 24-hour rest period once every 7 days;
- a maximum of an average of 8 hours' night work in every 24 hours and free health assessments for night workers.

Unlike other EU nations, the British government provides employers with a series of exemptions and also allows employers to seek voluntary opt-outs from the 48-hour working time rule, although not the other provisions within the working time directive. The effect of opt-out provision is that many employers 'ask' their employees to waive this protection against what has become known as 'the long-hours culture'. The opt-out provision allows employers to exclude workers provided for by the regulations, whereas the exemptions negotiated by the British government exclude workers in several sectors of employment and in several job types from the regulations completely. Specific categories of worker exempted from the regulations include:

- train drivers;
- domestic employees who work in private households, e.g. cleaners, domestic staff and servants;
- members of the police and the armed forces;
- junior doctors;
- employees who have 'unmeasured or undetermined' working time.

The last category represents a catch-all mechanism that covers many white-collar workers who have some measure of autonomy over how and when they perform their work. Junior doctors have voiced strong opposition to their exclusion from the regulations and the British Medical Association has negotiated reductions in the length of their working week. Equally, school teachers in England and Wales are currently campaigning for a 35-hour working week to bring them into line with their colleagues in Scotland.

The EU Commission reviewed the UK's opt-out provisions in 2003 and it is likely to be made unlawful. If this is the case, it will remain possible to work beyond the 48-hour rule as long as the 17-week average is not greater than 48 hours. In 2002, after a submission by the Amicus trade union, the EU Commission began legal proceedings against the UK in respect of the failure by the British government to implement the Working Time Directive correctly. The Amicus trade union cited several areas of complaint in their submission to the EU Commission; these included the exclusion of night-time overtime from the calculation of normal working time, failure by employers to measure and record overtime work beyond normal working hours and the failure of some employers to enforce worker entitlement to breaks and holidays (see *Financial Times*, 29 April 2002). At the time of writing the situation regarding the UK's opt-out from the 48-hour rule is unresolved and, in effect, continues to operate. However, in May 2005 the European Parliament voted to outlaw national provisions that permit working time opt-outs by 2010. This decision builds on the earlier decision of the EU Commission that as a precursor to the complete removal of the opt-out provision individual employees are to be prevented from agreeing to an opt-out when they sign a contract of employment. Instead of this, individuals will be allowed to opt-out from the working hours provision but agreement must be in writing and valid for a maximum of one year at a time subject to annual renewal. In addition to these provisions no employee will be allowed to work more than 65 hours.

The regulation of working time in the UK demonstrates the partial nature of an apparently inalienable right – the provision of opt-outs creates voluntary exclusion and illustrates the persistence of aspects of Britain's voluntary industrial relations system. In contrast to this, the exclusion via exemptions of many groups of autonomous workers renders working time unregulated in several sectors of employment. Further, low-paid workers who earn only the basic national minimum wage per hour are in effect forced to sign opt-outs to earn a living wage. Lastly, young workers over 16 but younger than 18 are beyond the regulations and covered by the Young Workers' Working Time Directive, which is similar to the regulations for older workers but provides for better rest breaks during working time.

Activity

In what ways is the exclusion and opt-out provision from the working time regulations fair and reasonable? Is your job included, excluded or opted-out?

If your job is exempt or subject to an opt-out clause in your contract of employment, consider the implications for your employer if, in the future, your job were to be included in the regulations on the 48-hour working week.

Termination of the employment contract

Employment contracts can terminate in a variety of ways, for example job redundancy, voluntary resignation, death in service, non-renewal of a fixed-term contract and summary termination due to conduct – 'the sack'. This part of the chapter examines the issue of termination due to dismissal under the headings of fair dismissal, unfair dismissal, wrongful dismissal and constructive dismissal.

Fair dismissal

To be fair a dismissal must be contractually lawful, that is not in breach of any contractual provision and in addition a dismissal must be lawful according to statute. In the majority of situations when an employee is dismissed from employment, the reasons for the dismissal are likely to be fair. An employer can fairly dismiss an employee on several grounds; dismissal is likely to be fair if it relates to the following categories:

- Employee conduct – theft or fraud in the workplace, gross insubordination, fighting etc.
- Job redundancy – where a job is no longer needed and the employee is dismissed due to job redundancy through no fault of their own and has been correctly consulted about the situation and fairly selected for redundancy via an agreed process of selection. If an employee has two years of continuous service with the employer, they must be compensated for the redundancy.
- Capability, competence and qualifications. An employer can fairly dismiss an employee on these grounds but must demonstrate that dismissal relates to job capability, not the employee. For example, to obtain dismissal due to capability on the grounds of illness or disability an employer must demonstrate that they have already made changes to the work situation of an employee and cannot make further changes. Without this evidence the employee may have a claim under the Disability Discrimination Act. If an employee has falsified their qualifications or if they lose a practitioner qualification, for example, by being struck off the medical register if they are a doctor, dismissal is likely to be fair. If an employee is deemed to be incompetent it will be necessary to demonstrate this, for example, that they have been through an internal disciplinary procedure and been given a reasonable opportunity to improve their performance but failed to do so.
- Statutory bar or other legal requirement that prevents the continuation of employment. For example, if an employee is a driver or needs to be able to drive to perform their job, the loss of a driving licence is likely to be a fair reason for dismissal. Similarly, if there is

another legal requirement that the employee can no longer meet, dismissal is likely to be fair; for example, for deep sea divers there are strict age and hours limits due to health and safety considerations. Equally, lorry drivers may have to pass eyesight checks and pilots meet strict health requirements. While dismissals may be fair in some situations, an employer may offer the employee another job. This is more likely if the firm has a collective bargaining agreement with a trade union.

● Some other substantial reason. Here an employer must demonstrate, in a case where a dismissal is disputed, that the dismissal, while it does not relate to the categories listed above, is nonetheless substantive, fair and reasonable.

Unfair dismissal

A dismissal is fair if an employer can demonstrate that the reason for the dismissal fits into one of the five categories listed above. However, as pointed out earlier in the chapter, many aspects of employment law turn on questions of interpretation and the reasonableness of a particular interpretation. So while an employer may deem a dismissal fair, an employee may disagree. For example, they may claim that they were unfairly selected for redundancy, or that they have been victimised for whistle-blowing or that their dismissal on any of the grounds listed above was motivated by discrimination such as disability, race, sex, marital status, pregnancy etc.

In situations where the fairness of a dismissal is disputed and proceeds to an employment tribunal, there are several tests that the tribunal will apply to rule on a dismissal. Dismissals due to conduct, redundancy, statutory bar, competence and qualification and some other substantive reason are termed *potentially fair* reasons for dismissal. A tribunal will examine the dismissal against the facts of a particular case to test whether the dismissal was *fair in the particular circumstances of the case*. If the details of a particular case do not meet the criteria for a potentially fair dismissal then the dismissal is unfair. In some circumstances a reason for dismissal may be fair yet the dismissal may have been conducted in an unfair manner, that is, a dismissal may be *procedurally unfair*. Hence, if there are internal procedures that should be followed that relate to grievance and discipline in the workplace it is vital that an employer follows these procedures and is further able to demonstrate to the employee, their representatives and a tribunal that they have done so.

As the section 'The contract of employment' on page 419 states, employees need one year of continuous employment service to qualify for protection against unfair dismissal. This extends to unfair dismissals that relate to job redundancy, that is, unfair selection for redundancy, whereas dismissal due to job redundancy requires two years' employment service before an employee qualifies for compensation. Unfair dismissals that relate to race or sex discrimination, including those for unequal pay and those that relate to pregnancy, are automatically unfair and are available to employees as day one rights. For example, a group of part-time women workers employed on a particular pay grade made redundant after six months' service may be able to demonstrate unfair selection for redundancy if no male employees were made redundant and they can establish that they were made redundant because they were the cheapest employees to terminate.

Other situations where no length of service is necessary to claim unfair dismissal include those that relate to trade union membership, participation in lawful industrial action that lasted less than eight weeks, participation as an employee representative for purposes of consultation (where there is no trade union presence), refusal to work on grounds of health and safety or where an employee seeks to assert a statutory right.

Wrongful dismissal

A wrongful dismissal is a dismissal that is in breach of contract, for example dismissal without notice or a failure to pay all due wages and remuneration during the notice period. Many wrongful dismissal cases relate to highly paid business executives who are dismissed but denied some aspect of their remuneration package. Other cases may relate to employees in government service who are dismissed by ministers. In the early 1990s, Michael Howard, the Conservative government Home Secretary, dismissed Derek Lewis, head of the prison service, without notice in a dispute about who held overall operational responsibility for prisons. Mr Lewis sued for wrongful dismissal and the Home Office later met his claim.

Constructive dismissal

Constructive dismissal refers to a situation where an employee alleges that an employer has acted so contrary to the operation of their contract of employment that the contract is deemed to be unlawful and immediately terminated. Events that may trigger constructive dismissal include financial loss due to unilateral changes in pay and remuneration, racial or sexual harassment, unilateral relocations to undesirable areas, being unilaterally stripped of authority or persistent victimisation.

Claims for constructive dismissal are risky because an employee has to satisfy a tribunal that they had no alternative but to leave and in the majority of cases it is unlikely that the employee will get their job back. Normally employees who are constructively dismissed pursue a claim for breach of contract where employment tribunals can make an award of up to £25,000. In addition to this, the employee can pursue a statutory award for unfair dismissal.

Redundancy rights

Under current legislation – the Employment Protection Acts and the Employment Rights Act 1996 – employees require two years of continuous service in a particular employment from the age of 18 to qualify for a lump sum compensation award. Further, the employee must have a contract of employment and for each complete year of service between the ages of 18 and 21 they will receive half a week's pay. This increases to one week's pay for employees between the ages of 22 and 40 and rises to one and a half week's pay between the ages of 41 and 65. Redundancy payments and unfair dismissal compensation are unaffected by the number of hours an employee works but the statutory limit for one week's pay is £290 and redundancy payments up to the value of £30,000 are tax free. An employer must make the payment as soon as the employee is dismissed.

Employers are required to consult the workforce about redundancy and, where collective bargaining is present, a trade union must be consulted. In non-union workplaces employers must establish a representative body of the workforce to consult over redundancy, for example multinational corporations may use an already established European Works Council for this purpose. The employer must notify the consultative body or the trade union of the reasons for redundancy, the numbers involved and the grades of job affected, the method of determining which jobs are redundant and how any payments that supplement the statutory requirements are to be worked out. If an employer has collective bargaining it is likely that there will be an established redundancy procedure negotiated with the trade union.

There is a statutory period for consultation that relates to the number of jobs being made redundant. If over 100 jobs are made redundant the employer must consult over a 90-day period, but only 30 days of consultation are necessary where the number of job redundancies is fewer than 100. Throughout the consultation period an employer must seek alternatives to job redundancy and act in good faith. Both these issues are controversial. Many trade unions argue that it is easier to dismiss British employees than employees in other EU nations because consultation occurs once the decision to make jobs redundant is taken, rather than before the decision is made as is required by law in most other EU nations. In extreme cases some employees, for example, those employed at Vauxhall's Luton plant, have first heard of their impending redundancy through the local and national media. The enforcement of a European Union directive on employee consultation may improve this situation, see section 'New rights at work?' on page 442.

The section 'The contract of employment' on page 419 detailed the contractual and statutory rights of employees; the section 'Discrimination in employment' on page 432 examined the continued presence of discrimination and the section 'The regulation of working time' on page 435 demonstrated the difficulty of establishing employee rights that relate to working time. This part of the chapter illustrated how employers can fairly dismiss employees and how employees can claim unfair, wrongful or constructive dismissal. The next section of the chapter examines the issues that relate to the enforcement of employee rights in the employment relationship.

Activity

Provide two potential examples of unfair, wrongful and constructive dismissal. In each case suggest how an employer might avoid the situation.

Enforcement of contractual and statutory employment rights

For the vast majority of employees, enforcement of employment rights is not an issue. Good employers, large and small, ensure that employment contracts reflect existing and new employment rights. Moreover, large employers are likely to have a dedicated personnel function to do this. Furthermore, larger firms are likely to recognise trade unions for the purposes of individual and collective representation and this presence is likely to ensure that terms and conditions of employment and internal procedures reflect employee rights, be they contractual or statutory. In summary, it is not in the interests of employers to 'short change' their employees, particularly in a period of full employment when staff recruitment and retention are recognised personnel problems. Equally, if, as many employers claim, employees are the most valued assets within a firm, demonstrating this through good employment practice and not merely in management rhetoric is one measure of being a good employer. However, some employers do seek to short-change employees by withholding certain rights, such as the minimum wage, or subjecting employees to arbitrary and unreasonable treatment.

If employees feel that a contractual or statutory employment right is either absent or incorrectly proceduralised or not enforced, there are several routes that they can take. Discussion of the situation with a supervisor, line manager or the personnel function may result in corrective action. Alternatively, an employee might raise their grievance with a trade union representative or other employee representative. Lastly, and more often in cases of alleged unfair dismissal, an employee can instigate proceedings against their employer or former employer by making an application to an employment tribunal. In many cases such an application may be sufficient to persuade the employer that they need to take corrective action. However, some cases will go to tribunal either because the dispute cannot be settled in any other way due to employer intransigence or because an employer feels the case must be defended because of its future implications for themselves and other similar employers.

Employment tribunals are now long established and operate as specialist employment 'courts'. Tribunals have a legally qualified chair and two lay members acting as employee and employer nominees. Tribunals are less formal than other courts but over the years they have become more legalistic than was originally intended and more time consuming, particularly in situations where a test case is being heard. Virtually all claims in relation to the employment relationship are heard in tribunals; however some, notably claims for constructive and unfair dismissals that involve a breach of contract, are heard in civil courts.

To begin an application to a tribunal an employee or former employee must complete an application form ET1 within three months of the incident or event they intend to complain about. The ET1 will contain details of the employee's claim and the remedy they are seeking – reinstatement, re-engagement or compensation. The tribunal service will send the ET1 and an ET2 to the employer or former employer; the ET2 summonses the employer to appear before the tribunal. The employer must also complete an ET3, which details their defence.

In 1999 there was a 32 per cent increase in applications to the tribunal service – 164,000, up from 124,000 in 1998; 2000 witnessed a further increase to 167,000, whereas in the year to March 2001 there were 130,408 applications to the tribunal service. However, ACAS reported only 94,000 applications to the tribunal service in 2002 (*Financial Times*, 9 September 2003) and 100,000 applications for 2003, (ACAS, 2004), the latest full-year figures for 2004 show a 25 per cent reduction in applications on the previous year (TUC, 2005). Employer bodies such as the Engineering Employers Federation argue that on an annual basis only 6 per cent of claims against their members are upheld, with 70 per cent settled or withdrawn. In contrast, the TUC argues that 95 per cent of cases it backs are won. Moreover, employer bodies argue that there are too many applications to tribunals that employers have to defend unnecessarily as many applications are frivolous or vexatious. Even so, the introduction of a fine of up to £10,000 in such cases in July 2001 has only recently begun to stem the large number of applications most of which relate to claims of unfair dismissal.

The statutory award for unfair dismissal is made up of two components. First, the basic award of up £290 for each year of completed employment and second the compensatory award of up to a maximum of £58,400. However, in cases that relate to discrimination because of disability, race or gender there is no upper limit on tribunal awards. For example, a City drinks sector analyst employed by Schroder Securities won £1.4 million in a sex discrimination case after successfully claiming that male colleagues were given six-figure bonus payments while she received only £25,000 while delivering similar results in the workplace. While denying the allegation, the employer withdrew an appeal against the decision of an employment tribunal. For details of the case see the *Financial Times*, 11 January 2002 and 20 June 2002.

While these compensation awards seem large, the average award is much lower in the majority of cases. Equally, in most cases former employees do not get their job back; for example, in 1999 in only 3 per cent of unfair dismissal cases was the applicant re-employed. Compensation, as opposed to re-employment or re-engagement, is the preferred remedy of most tribunals.

There is, in addition to this argument, evidence that employers, and small employers in particular, lack confidence on the issue of employee rights. The DTI found that only 20 per cent of small employers have confidence in their knowledge of employment legislation, with only 50 per cent aware of the employee right to paid paternity leave (see *Financial Times*, 13 August 2002). The government has recently taken some steps to allow employees to exercise their rights more effectively by compelling employees to follow internal grievance procedures before taking a case to tribunal. This measure, while sensible and reasonable, rests on the premise that all employers have these procedures in place.

The evidence suggests that employer claims of 'excessive red tape' and the burden of defending unnecessary tribunal applications are not proven. Many employees are denied the opportunity to go through internal grievance procedures. Equally, the growth in employment rights caught some employers – good and bad – off guard, particularly in the area of unfair dismissal. Employer claims of red tape and the cost of defending at a tribunal must be measured against better regulation of the employment relationship and the need for improved best practice. While the majority of applications to tribunals to enforce employee rights are settled on a voluntary basis and withdrawn, the growth in the number of applications demonstrates the absence of best practice in many areas of employment. Lastly, claims that a 'compensation culture' is emerging which is likely to damage the competitiveness of British industry is a very doubtful argument, because if employees win a case at tribunal it demonstrates that their rights were in some way infringed. Alternatively, if an employer settles a claim or takes corrective action in the workplace, this demonstrates that some aspect of employment practice was poorly proceduralised. High-profile compensation awards involving large sums, such as those associated with the 'sexism in the City' cases, are rare if of great interest to the media, but more significantly demonstrate that poor employment practice occurs in all types of employment and that enforcement can be expensive for employers. Furthermore, the actions of some employers in recent cases undermine claims of bureaucracy and red tape and time wasting in the defence of applications to employment tribunals. Applications to tribunals that are withdrawn or settled voluntarily may be settled 'out of court' by employers. For example, Nomura International reached an out of court settlement with an employee made redundant while on maternity leave, who prior to that had been asked to wear short skirts at work and give a male colleague a massage. The former employee dropped her discrimination claim but reached a £70,000 out-of-court settlement with Nomura, which maintained that the claim was unfounded. In a similar City case, Cru Publishing settled a case of constructive dismissal out of court even though an employment tribunal found that the employee was 75 per cent to blame for her dismissal.

While the growth of out-of-court settlements does undermine employers' claims of red tape and excessive costs in employment regulation, there are three specific problems with them in respect to the enforcement of employment rights. First, out-of-court settlements often prevent full disclosure of the facts and while a former employee may be generously compensated, the provisions of a settlement usually remain confidential. Second, withdrawing a claim and settling out of court often enables employers to deny the charges made against them and, more importantly, prevents the creation of what might be a reference point – a precedent for future cases. Third, an employer that settles a case out of court but denies the basis of the claim may fail to improve personnel procedures – a measure often enforced by tribunals, the Equal Opportunities Commission and the Commission for Racial Equality.

In summary, a well-resourced personnel function staffed by CIPD-qualified practitioners is one route to employer best practice in the area of employment rights; trade union recognition is another, and the latter is likely to lead to negotiation and partnership in the management of employee rights. Both routes are likely to become more fruitful for employers, bearing in mind the likelihood of further growth in employee rights and the medium- to longer-term impact of the 1999 Employment Relations Act.

New rights at work?

This final part of the chapter examines the emergence of new rights at work codified within the 1999 Employment Relations Act and subsequent legislation, several of which are currently at the consultation stage.

The Employment Relations Act 1999 (ERA)

The ERA established many new rights, both collective and individual, that represent a significant improvement in workplace rights, bringing many into line with those found in other European Union states. The ERA complements other measures that aim to improve fairness at work, such as the Working Time Directive and the national minimum wage. The legislation aims to achieve decent minimum standards at work that will underpin a flexible labour market and facilitate good industrial relations in the workplace, via trade unions and collective bargaining where desired by employees.

The provisions of the ERA divide into four categories: new and improved individual rights for all employees, new collective rights for all employees, maternity and paternity rights, and rights to representation in the workplace. These areas are briefly reviewed below and where necessary are already incorporated into relevant parts of this chapter, in particular the sections 'The contract of employment' (page 419) and 'The regulation of working time' (page 435).

New rights for all workers

Improved protection against unfair dismissal

This protection is now available after one year's service rather than two years. Estimates suggest that up to 270,000 workers with between one and two years' employment service are dismissed each year. Some of these employees are 'fairly' unfairly dismissed, hence many will directly benefit from this new right. Moreover, the ERA increased top-level payments in cases of unfair dismissal from £12,000 to £50,000, a figure that has recently been increased further to £53,000. In addition to these improvements, the ERA makes it automatically unfair to dismiss an employee taking part in lawfully organised industrial action for eight weeks. After two months, dismissal will be fair only if the employer can establish that they have taken all reasonable procedural steps to try to resolve the dispute.

Blacklisting

Blacklisting of individual employees for trade union membership or activity is prohibited. This provision relates to blacklists compiled by an employer or by any organisation such as the Economic League or the Freedom Association.

Unpaid parental leave

The ERA established the right of employees with one year's employment service to parental leave (if named as a parent on a birth certificate) for any child born after December 1999 up to the age of 5 years or an adopted child below 18 born after the same date. A parent is entitled to 13 weeks for each eligible child, and this extends to multiple births. The employee remains 'employed' during the leave and on return the employee is entitled to their old job or – if this is unreasonable or impossible – a better job or one of the same standard in terms and conditions. Some employees had paid or unpaid parental leave clauses in their contracts of employment before the provisions of the ERA became effective. These arrangements, many of them arrived at through the process of collective bargaining, remain operative. On return from leave an employee must not have any seniority or pension rights denied as a result of taking leave. If a job is made redundant while an employee is on leave, they must be treated as if they are working normally. In January 2000 the TUC, after taking legal advice, declared an intention to undertake a legal challenge to the December 1999 cut-off date. The TUC was advised that the directive should be retrospective in covering all children under the age of 5 at the date of its implementation, and after the threat and instigation of legal action the government amended the UK's regulations and subsequently introduced paid paternity leave for fathers the details are outlined in the section 'The contract of employment' on page 419). The 2004 Workplace Employment Relations Survey found that 92 per cent of employees eligible for paid parental leave exercised this employment right, (Kersley *et al.*, 2004).

Personal contracts

The ERA makes it unlawful for an employer to dismiss, omit or otherwise act detrimentally towards an employee who refuses to sign a personal contract that excludes the employee from collectively negotiated terms and conditions of employment. This right was recently further strengthened by a ruling in the European court that established that such measures breached the human rights of individual employees. This case concerned a *Daily Mail* journalist and dates from 1989. The journalist was denied a pay increase after he refused to give up the right to have terms and conditions of employment determined through the process of collective bargaining. The Court of Appeal found in favour of the journalist but his employer appealed to Law Lords who held that collective bargaining over terms and conditions of employment fails to represent a defining characteristic of trade union membership. Thus, in this case the use of financial incentives to end collective bargaining and personal contracts that may result in less or more favourable treatment for individual employees does not represent a breach of human rights. However, the European Court of Human Rights held that a state is responsible for ensuring that union members are not restrained from using a union to represent them. As a result of this decision it is now clear that individuals and trade unions can enforce the right to collective representation. Equally, laws that permit British employers to discriminate against, i.e. treat less favourably, workers who seek to retain collective bargaining and collective representation is a breach of human rights.

Prohibition of waiver clauses for unfair dismissal rights in fixed-term contracts

Under the provisions of the ERA it is no longer possible for employers to ask or compel employees on fixed-term contracts to waive the right to complain of unfair dismissal if the contract is not renewed. Waiver clauses in operation before the provisions of the ERA became effective can continue. Equally, the provisions within the ERA make no mention of redundancy rights waivers in fixed-term contracts: hence these waivers remain lawful.

Family emergencies

The ERA provides the right for employees to have reasonable time off work to deal with family emergencies such as accidents or illness to family members, bereavements and severe damage to property. These new rights aim to provide workers with a more effective voice mechanism in the workplace where it was previously restricted or where they had none. Where employers are obstructive over access to new or extended individual employment rights the law will work in favour of employees in imposing trade union recognition where employees desire this.

Maternity and parental leave

The material in the section 'The contract of employment' on page 419 on day one rights and length of service rights established that all employees are entitled to basic maternity leave, whereas those with at least one year's length of service are entitled to extended maternity leave. The ERA increased the period of paid basic maternity leave from 14 to 18 weeks subsequently increased further to 26 weeks and reduced the qualification period for extended maternity leave from two years to one year. The ERA also introduced the provision for parental leave that is discussed above under new individual employment rights. The present government has stated its commitment to increase statutory maternity leave to nine months by the end of the current Parliament.

The right to representation

The ERA establishes that whether a trade union is recognised or not, individual union members and non-union members alike have the right to be accompanied by a trade union official in disciplinary and grievance hearings. If the employer obstructs or denies this, there is a compensatory penalty of up to two weeks' pay.

A lasting effect of the ERA centres on the enforcement of employee rights in the workplace. Trade union recognition and the emergence of collective bargaining in the workplace is one mechanism to monitor the introduction of new employment rights. By negotiating with an employer and seeking partnership in the implementation of new rights, trade unions can ensure that an employer meets their legal obligations. In addition, collective representation may create a workplace 'voice mechanism' that can prevent the emergence of issues that might otherwise lead to conflict, dispute and eventually application to an employment tribunal.

In addition to the contractual and statutory rights examined in the section 'The contract of employment' (page 419) and the collective and individual employment rights associated with the ERA, the following measures either offer new employment rights or will establish them in the near future.

Collective employment rights: trade union recognition

ERA establishes that a claim for trade union recognition can be made with 10 per cent membership and majority support. To demonstrate support for trade union recognition a union can call upon the findings of a survey or petition. Where a trade union already has over 50 per cent membership within the proposed bargaining group, recognition will be automatic except on two grounds: first, where an employer appeals to the central arbitration committee for a secret ballot on the grounds that a ballot will be good for workplace industrial relations; second, where despite a high level of union membership a significant number of employees express a desire not be union members or to be represented by the union in collective bargaining, or where the central arbitration committee concludes either situation to be the case. The evidence concerning the impact of the legislation leads to two conclusions. First, where there is a majority of union members in a non-unionised workplace employers are likely to offer guarded support for a recognition claim. Second, before the ERA became effective some employers anticipated its provisions and negotiated voluntary recognition before the legislation became operative. Further, where a majority of union members is very high the evidence suggests that employers wish to avoid negative media coverage and so negotiate voluntary recognition agreements. For example, erstwhile anti-union employers such as Dixon's Electrical Stores and Noon's Foods, both of which have very high union membership, negotiated voluntary recognition deals with the AEEU and GMB unions respectively. Survey evidence for 1999 found 74 recognition agreements covering 21,000 workers. Of more significance, almost 50 per cent of the trade unions in the survey said that recognition deals resulted from an employer approach (TUC, 2000). Equally, in the year to March 2001 trade union membership rose by 46,000 to 7.9 million, the second annual rise in succession after a sustained fall in union membership since the early 1980s (Labour Market Trends, 2001). The data in this report indicate that the period of large-scale decline in union membership has ended and that membership has begun to stabilise since 1997. This suggests that employers are likely to view the issue of trade union recognition more favourably than they did during the 1980s and 1990s when more assertive programmes of trade union de-recognition in the workplace were supported by government policy (see Clark, 1996 and Claydon, 1996). For example, HSBC, formerly Midland Bank, has recently restored union representation for 12,500 junior and middle managers four years after withdrawing recognition for this group of workers.

In 2002, a TUC report, *Focus on Recognition*, found that there were 300 recognition deals in the year up to October 2002, the vast majority of which were concluded on a voluntary basis covering firms such as American Airlines, Boots, Meridian TV, the Church of Scotland, Kwik-Fit, Green Peace and Air New Zealand (TUC, 2002). The overwhelming majority of agreements covered pay, hours and holidays and 91 per cent covered representation at grievance and discipline hearings, 62 per cent covered training, over 50 per cent covered equal rights and information and consultation in the workplace. Lastly, 36 per cent covered pension arrangements. Many of the recognition deals reviewed in the report were concluded in smaller employers, the average size being 260 employees; notwithstanding this, a recent review of the Employment Relations Act excludes any alteration to the rules and procedures on recognition, in particular the exclusion of workplaces employing fewer than 20 workers from the provision of the Act. The latest workplace employment relations survey found that 30 per cent of workplaces have recognised trade unions and that 39 per cent of workplaces employing 25 or more workers recognised trade unions whereas only 18 per cent of workplaces employing between 10–24 employees recognise trade unions, (Kersley *et al.*, 2004: 12–16).

In situations where workplace ballots are necessary, a trade union is able to address the workforce directly as well as mail information to employees. When recognition is won, the trade union acquires a legal right to negotiate terms and conditions to include hours, pay, and work allocation and discipline. Equally significant to these collective rights, recognition imposes a duty on the employer to inform and consult about training. In cases where an employer proves to be obstructive in establishing a bargaining procedure, the ERA allows for one to be imposed upon them. In cases where a trade union is unable to prove 50 per cent membership, the statutory procedure for a recognition award will be triggered where there is majority support in a ballot with at least 40 per cent of those eligible to vote taking part. Tthe Central Arbitration Committee has enforced recognition after successful ballots, for example

Saudi Arabian Airways at Heathrow airport was compelled to introduce collective bargaining after the employer ignored a successful ballot in favour of recognition. Staff employed by the airline voted nine to one in favour of recognition by the MSF technicians' union. Similarly, the Central Arbitration Committee intervened in a dispute between Honda and the AEEU after the firm refused to hold a recognition ballot. As a result of the subsequent ballot the AEEU won recognition for full collective bargaining at Honda's Swindon plant where 1600 of the 4000 workforce were already union members.

EU Information and Consultation Directive

Regulations relating to the EU's Information and Consultation Directive came into force in the UK in April 2005. These regulations require employers to establish a democratic and collective mechanism in order to consult with a workforce on substantial changes to the terms and conditions of employment such as changes in work organisation, redundancy and the sale of subsidiaries. Employers must set up a consultation mechanism if 10 per cent of the workforce supports the initiative. The regulations cover workplaces with more than 150 employees and will be extended to workplaces with 100 or more workers in April 2007 and those with 50 or more in 2008.

Employer groups have voiced concern about the effects of this requirement on the competitiveness of British firms, suggesting that the mechanism will add further 'red tape' but no positive business outcomes. However, this is a familiar argument that was voiced previously against the provisions of the national minimum wage, the Working Time Directive and the ERA. None of the projected claims such as growth in unemployment and reduced competitiveness occurred and are unlikely to occur in this case. The persistence of employer opposition to new employment legislation illustrates that a deeply embedded preference for voluntary and unregulated employer 'best practice' remains in the UK. Equally though, the partial failure of voluntary best practice is amply illustrated by the partial enforcement of employment rights and the persistence of discrimination in employment highlighted in earlier parts of this chapter. The information and consultation directive may go some way to improve employee consultation over *proposed* (as opposed to the current situation of *actual*) redundancies, which is a major concern of British trade unions. In January 2003, Alan Johnson, the then employment relations minister, argued that information and consultation committees, when introduced in British firms, would not constitute co-determination or joint decision making on the continental model and emphasised the consultative nature of the committees (*Financial Times*, 17 January 2003).

European Union Agency Workers Directive

The Agency Workers Directive is more controversial and seeks to establish equality between employment rights for workers employed directly by an employment agency as 'temps' and those directly employed in the workplace to which they are assigned by the agency. The directive is likely to have a dramatic impact because the majority of temps employed across the EU work in the UK – over one million workers. The areas of comparability between agency workers and employees in a particular organisation covered by the directive include pay, pensions, holiday entitlement and other benefits such as protection against unfair dismissal. The government estimates that the provisions contained within the directive will lead to a rise of approximately £1000 a year in pay levels for temps. The British government, after lobbying by employer groups, is seeking a six-week exemption to the equal pay rule, provided that an employer demonstrates that 'an adequate level of pay is provided from day one'. In September 2002 the draft directive was complete and ready to be considered by the EU social affairs committee (see *Financial Times*, 3 September 2002). The Agency Workers Directive is likely to come into force in the UK in 2006

'Two-tier working' in the provision of public services

'Two-tier' working refers to the situation where a local government service or aspects of health care previously provided by a local authority or the National Health Service is fully or partially contracted out to a private sector provider. The term describes the situation where public sector workers or those transferred to the private sector have terms and conditions of employment that are different from – better than – those of new employees engaged by the private sector provider but working in the provision of the service.

Trade unions such as UNISON and the GMB argue that all workers should have the same terms and conditions of employment guaranteed by statutory guidance written into contracts between local authorities and private sector contractors. In July 2002 the government promised legislation to provide for comparability of terms and conditions of employment. However, in January 2003 the row over the two-tier workforce was reignited because of disagreement over the proposed wording of the government code of practice, which cites a form of wording preferred by the CBI that calls for the terms and conditions of new recruits to be 'broadly comparable' to those of existing employees. A specific area of disagreement relates to the proposed exclusion of pensions from the broadly comparable formula. Some trade unions have expressed guarded support for this, yet experience with previous measures such as paternity leave, the Working Time Directive and the Equal Pay Act suggest that such terms may be broadly reasonable in application and coverage but subject to different interpretation by employers and employees. Differences of interpretation on this issue may result in future legal challenges in particular situations. The situation is Scotland is somewhat different. The Scottish Finance Minister signed a protocol agreement with trade unions that represent workers in the public sector. The framework contract guarantees that all workers recruited by private sector contractors under public/private partnership deals will receive fair pay, pension, holiday and sick pay entitlements commensurate with those of existing pubic sector workers. The difference between broadly comparable and commensurate could create problems for contractors who operate in both England and Scotland in respect of the EU Equal Treatment Directive. Further, a key difficulty for trade unions who support the formula and those that do not and the government is that the term 'broadly comparable' in its present constitution appears to allow for the presence of a two-tier workforce and not its elimination as pledged by the Prime Minister in July 2002. The government recognised this as problematic and, following a meeting with prominent trade unions in February 2002, announced that the government will insist that private sector firms taking public services contracts must provide employment contracts that are 'no less favourable' for future employees than contracts enjoyed by public sector workers. This commitment was given an unexpected fillip when the Cleaning and Support Services Association announced its support for the provision, arguing that it would prevent 'cowboy' operators cutting their members out of the market by reducing costs irresponsibly (*Financial Times*, 17 March 2003).

Flexible employment for parents

The Employment Act 2002 has provided a legal framework for aspects of flexible working and since April 2003 all parents of children under six, with six months continuous employment service, have been entitled to ask their employer to 'seriously consider' requests for flexible work arrangements. Up to four million parents are eligible to submit such requests and first findings from the latest workplace employment relations study found that 28 per cent of employees work only during term time compared to 14 per cent in 1998 (the date of the previous survey) and that 26 per cent of workers work on a flexi-time basis compared to 19 per cent in 1998. The growth of term-time and flexi-time working suggests that some employers are treating requests for flexible working more sympathetically than before the introduction of the 2002 legislation, (Kersley *et al.*, 2004: 28–32). Parents must make written requests and meet with the relevant manager within four weeks to discuss the request and a decision must be made in a further two weeks. Employers are expected to meet the majority of requests and ministers have included in the guidance an 82 per cent success rate target. If an employer denies a request they must provide the employee with a written explanation of the business reasons for the decision and set out proposals for an internal appeal procedure. In situations where a case remains unresolved, binding mediation and arbitration will be made available. It is important to make clear that the right to flexible working is limited to serious consideration of the request and that this is not the same as a right to flexible working arrangements. The seriousness of this limitation is brought into sharp focus by the results of a survey conducted by the employment law firm Peninsula. Seventy per cent of small firms in the survey asserted that claims for flexible working hours will damage their competitiveness and more than 80 per cent of the companies surveyed said they would attempt to dodge the rules (Peninsula, 2003). Applications for flexible working arrangements can be refused on eight specific grounds these are currently:

1 The burden of additional costs.
2 A detrimental effect on the ability to meet customer demand.
3 An inability to reorganise work among existing staff.
4 An inability to recruit additional staff.
5 A detrimental impact on quality.
6 A detrimental impact on performance.
7 Insufficient work during the period(s) the employee proposes to work.
8 Planned structural changes.

The Human Rights Act, 1998

The Human Rights Act, while wide-ranging in its provisions, fails to create any specific employment rights. To enforce their human rights employees must cite an existing employment right, the infringement of which impacts on their human rights, for example until 2004 unfair dismissal due to sexual orientation was not necessarily unlawful and was not covered specifically by the UK's sex discrimination legislation; but at this time a dismissal on these grounds may have been unfair if it infringed rights to privacy that are protected by the Human Rights legislation.

However, the basis of the human rights legislation is a balancing of (employer and employee) interests and, where those of an employer and employer conflict, an employment tribunal will have to make a judgment on the balance of these interests.

The emergence of new employment rights such as protection against dismissal due to sexual orientation and age discrimination reinforces the need for good employer practice to be both operational and strategic. The evidence suggests that in relation to the national minimum wage, the ERA and the Working Time Directive, many employers – large and small – were 'off the pace'. Employers with a personnel function staffed by CIPD-qualified practitioners are more likely to be on the pace, as are those who have a trade union presence that works in partnership or structured negotiation with an employer.

Conclusion

While the employment relationship and within that the employment contract is viewed by many as a private exchange between an employer and an employee, the employment relationship is subject to significant contractual and statutory regulation.

All employees have a contract of employment and some measure of statutory protection against unfair and unreasonable treatment by an employer. However, in the contemporary period since 1997 the contractual and statutory regulation of the employment relationship has tightened. As a result of this, employees have greater protection in the employment relationship than previously; this greater protection creates the need for improved vigilance by employers and reinforces the need in all areas of employment for an effective personnel function. In large and small employers, a personnel function staffed by CIPD-qualified professionals is likely to increase employer confidence in the regulation of employment and may help avoid the infringement of employee rights. Equally, trade unions through the process of collective bargaining – partnership or structured negotiation – have a role to play in the enforcement of employee rights at work. This is the case because although there has been a significant growth in statutory protection for individual employees since 1997, a question remains about its effectiveness. The growth in the number of applications to employment tribunals illustrates that the application of best practice principles in the regulation of the employment relationship is far from universal. Similarly, the continued search for labour market flexibility, as demonstrated by the UK's idiosyncratic application of the working time directive and the weakness in the framework for applications for flexible working, may infringe the employment rights of some workers but go unnoticed. Thus, individual employment rights must be enforced, yet the search for labour market flexibility and the relative weakness of trade unions across the employed labour force (only 29 per cent of the labour force is represented by trade unions) suggests that measures to improve collective representation are more likely to improve the enforcement of individual employment rights than individuals acting alone. This argument is borne out by some of the recent recognition cases where employees in banking, motor manufacturing and civil aviation cited enforcement of employment rights and protection against future consolidation or downsizing in their organisations as two reasons for seeking union recognition. This feature in the trend towards union recognition extends within traditional non-union firms such as Virgin Atlantic and those cited earlier in this chapter. Virgin Atlantic signed a recognition agreement with the AEEU for its 2800 cabin crew after previously signing an agreement with BALPA for pilots and flight engineers. Virgin signed these agreements on a voluntary basis after consultation with its employees.

The emergence of employer and employee interest in trade union recognition for purposes of collective bargaining and collective enforcement of individual employment rights flies in the face of arguments put forward by Alan Johnson, the then employment relations minister. In an interview with the *Financial Times* (17 September 2002) the minister argued that the expansion of individual employment rights under the current government empowers individual employees and demonstrates that the government is well ahead of trade unions which emphasise rights through union membership rather than individual rights. However, the minister made no points on the issue of enforcement. For a more critical examination of the provisions contained in the Employment Relations Act see Glyn and Wood (2001: 61–63).

If, as many employers assert, employees are the most valued assets within an organisation, fair and reasonable treatment consistent with contractual and statutory rights regulated on an individual or collective basis is one measure of good employment practice. Moreover, the voluntary enforcement of employee rights by employers demonstrates the 'good employer' ethos – best practice in the regulation of the employment relationship. Employees who receive fair and reasonable treatment in the employment relationship are more likely to be retained by an employer, better motivated, more committed and deliver higher productivity than those employees who are not. As this chapter demonstrates, employee rights are extensive but not prohibitive in terms of coverage or the 'red tape' they create. Reasonable treatment requires regulation and enforcement. The evidence suggests that what some employers term 'red tape' is created when unreasonable treatment occurs, that is, when employers deviate from the good employer ethos and fail to follow best-practice procedures.

Summary

This chapter examined the employment relationship and its regulation through the contract of employment under six different headings.

Distinguishing contractual and statutory employment rights

- All employees have a contract of employment.
- All employees are protected by some statutory rights – day one rights; other rights require some length of service.

The contract of employment

- Employment contracts are contracts of personal service between an employer and an employee.
- Employment contracts are based on the theory of market individualism, where individuals are seen as rational and self-interested.
- Employment contracts are subject to the common law.
- There are different types of employment contract.
- Employment contracts contain express, implied and statutory incorporated terms and conditions.

Discrimination in employment

- Discrimination remains a persistent feature of the employment relationship.
- Some types of 'discrimination' remain lawful.

The regulation of working time

- Traditionally, working time has been unregulated in the UK.
- The Working Time Directive regulates hours of work but contains many exceptions and allows employees to opt out from the provision.
- The Working Time Directive has failed to counter the UK's 'long-hours' culture.
- The UK's application of the directive may soon be challenged.

Termination of the employment contract

- Employees can be fairly, unfairly, wrongfully or constructively dismissed.
- Dismissals may be fair and potentially fair, otherwise they are unfair.

Enforcement of contractual and statutory employment rights

- Most employees are treated fairly.
- If employees are treated unreasonably or unfairly they can complain to an employment tribunal.
- Tribunals, personnel departments, the Equal Opportunities Commission, the Commission for Racial Equality and trade unions play a role in enforcing employment rights.

New rights at work?

- The Employment Relations Act consolidated some employment rights and introduced other individual and collective rights.
- Further employment rights are in the process of introduction or are at the consultation stage and will be introduced in the near future.

1 How is a contract formed in the following situations?

(a) Buying a magazine in a newsagent's.
(b) An offer of full-time permanent employment.
(c) The hiring of a subcontractor to perform maintenance work on a firm's computers.

2 How does employment protection legislation actually protect full-time and part-time employees?

3 Do you think that the employment protection legislation provides for effective and reasonable protection of employees?

CASE STUDY

The pitfalls that follow a failure of best-practice

In June 1996 Jane Smith was engaged by the department of media studies at Cromwell University as a part-time administrative assistant. For non-academic staff and casual employees decisions over recruitment, selection, remuneration and terms and conditions of employment are decentralised to departmental managers who should follow procedures laid down in best-practice manuals supplied by the personnel function. At the time, Jane was given a 'casual contract' that excluded her from the terms and conditions of employment applied to permanent staff and academic staff employed by the university. Jane was not given a copy of the contract even though she regularly asked for a copy. Two years later, Jane was given a copy of the casual contract. On examining the contract Jane noticed that, although the contract specified that a termination date must be included, no termination date was included. In addition to this omission, Jane's hours of work were not specified. Jane queried both these omissions but was told by her line manager, Professor Clarke, not to worry about them. On average Jane worked 15 hours per week and was paid at an hourly rate of £10. By June 1999 the hourly rate had risen to £11. In order to receive her pay Jane merely had to include a code on her wage claims and get the signature of Professor Clarke. The code related to funds held and controlled by the department of media studies and as long as this was included on wages claims the wages and salaries section would not query any claims.

In June 1999 Jane became pregnant, and she informed her line manager Professor Clarke, indicating that she would soon seek maternity leave, and asked him what procedures she needed to follow in order to do this. Professor Clarke replied that he didn't know but would find out for her. Since her engagement Jane had worked continuously at the university and had been allowed to take holidays by arrangement with her line manager even though at the time of her engagement this was clearly prohibited within the terms of her casual contract.

Eventually, Jane approached the wages and salaries section of the personnel function to inquire about maternity leave and maternity pay. She was told that as a casual employee she was not entitled to these benefits because she was engaged by the university on a term-by-term basis. Jane countered this argument by stating that she had worked at the university for the past three years, had a staff pigeon-hole and an entry in the university telephone directory. The staff in the wages and salary section, although nominally part of the personnel function, are actually controlled by the university treasury function and are not qualified personnel practitioners. They refused to process her inquiry because as she had no employee reference number she must be an hourly paid casual worker. An argument ensued and Jane was told to stop wasting their time and go away.

Jane went directly to see the head of personnel but found that he was away on holiday; perplexed, Jane sought legal and trade union assistance. Her representatives contacted the pro vice chancellor responsible for staff relations and demanded a meeting. At the meeting, all the above information was presented to the pro vice chancellor, who was unable to deal with it effectively because the head of personnel was on holiday. However, he promised to get this matter sorted out by the middle of the following week and arranged a meeting for the Wednesday.

Case study continued

Activity

Assume you are the personnel manager and a summary of the above lands on your desk when you return from holiday on the Monday morning together with a note from the pro vice chancellor asking you to sort all this out by Wednesday. How would you sort the situation out? And how would you diagnose the situation? The following pointers may help guide you in this task:

- Does the university have to provide Jane with maternity leave and maternity pay? If so, why?

- Is Jane an employee? Does it matter that she is a casual employee?

- Does Jane have continuous service with the university?

- Does Jane's situation suggest that there might be a wider problem in the university? For example, would the apparently less than satisfactory situation concerning Jane's employment go unnoticed if she had not become pregnant or if Jane was a male employee?

- How will you rectify Jane's situation?

Useful websites

Confederation of British Industry	www.cbi.org.uk
Commission for Racial Equality	www.cre.gov.uk
Department of Trade and Industry	www.dti.gov.uk
Equal Opportunities Commission	www.eoc.org.uk
Chartered Institute of Personnel and Development	www.cipd.org.uk
Disability Rights Commission	www.disability.gov.uk
Trade Union Congress	tuc.org.uk
Workplace Bullying: The Andrea Adams Trust	www.andreaadamstrust.org
UK national workplace bullying advice line	www.bullyonline.org

References and further reading

Those texts marked with an asterisk are recommended for further reading.

ACAS (2004) *Employment Relations Matters*. Issue 1, page 6. London: ACAS.

*Allen, R. and Crasnow, R. (2002) *Employment Law and Human Rights*. Oxford: Oxford University Press.

*Anderman, S. (2000) *Labour Law, Management Decisions and Worker Rights*. London: Butterworths.

Armstrong, P. and Baron, A. (1995) *The Job Evaluation Handbook*. London: CIPD.

Bach, S. (ed.) (2005) *The Management of Human Resources – Personnel Management in Transition*. Oxford: Blackwell

*Barnet, D. and Scrope, H. (2002) *European Employment Law*. London: Butterworths.

CIPD (2006a) 'Working Hours in the UK', www.cipd.co.uk.

CIPD (2006b) 'Work–Life Balance', www.cipd.co.uk.

Clark, I. (1996) 'The state and new industrial relations', in Beardwell, I. (ed.) *Contemporary Industrial Relations: A Critical Analysis*. Oxford: Oxford University Press.

Clark, I. (2000) *The State, Regulation and Industrial Relations*. London: Routledge.

Claydon, T. (1996) 'Union derecognition: a re-examination', in Beardwell, I. (ed.) *Contemporary Industrial Relations: A Critical Analysis*. Oxford: Oxford University Press.

*Deakin, S. and Morris, G. (2001) *Labour Law*, 3rd edn. Oxford: Hart Publishing.

Dickens, L. (2005) 'Walking the Talk? Equality and Diversity in Employment' in Bach, S. (ed.) *The Management of Human Resources: Personnel Management in Britain*. Oxford: Blackwell.

Edwards, P. (ed.) (2003) *Industrial Relations: Theory and Practice*. Oxford: Blackwell.

Equal Opportunities Commission (2001) Annual Report: Manchester: EOC.

Equal Opportunities Commission (2002) – evidence submitted to the Hicks' Inquiry into Non-Executive Directors' Pay. Manchester: EOC.

European Commission (2003) *Employment in Europe 2003. Recent Trends and Prospects*. Luxembourg: Office for Official Publications of the European Communities.

Financial Times, 11 January 2002, 'Analyst gets £1.4 million payout for "insulting bonus"'.

Financial Times, 29 April 2002, 'Brussels starts legal action over working hours'.

Financial Times, 20 June 2002, 'Sex discrimination appeal dropped'.

Financial Times, 13 August 2002, 'Employers lack confidence on rights of workers'.

Financial Times, 30 August 2002, 'More women work even longer hours'.

Financial Times, 3 September 2002, 'Anger at EU Directive on temporary workers'.

Financial Times, 17 September 2002, 'Minister blows his own trumpet at the unions'.

Financial Times, 17 January 2003, 'Managers still rule, unions told'.

Financial Times, 17 March 2003, 'Support for union demand on equal treatment'.

Financial Times, 9 September 2003, 'Call for more radical workers' rights'.

Fox, A. (1985) *History and Heritage*. London: Allen & Unwin.

Gall, G. and McKay, S. (1999) 'Developments in union recognition and derecognition in Britain 1994–1998', *British Journal of Industrial Relations*, 37, 4: 601–614.

Glyn, A. and Wood, S. (2001) 'Economic policy under New Labour: how social democratic is the Blair Government?' *Political Quarterly*, 72, 1: 50–66.

*Grant, B. (2002) *Employment Law: A Guide for Human Resource Managers*. London: Thomson Learning.

Health and Safety Commission (2002) Annual Report. London: HSC.

Hyman, R. (1975) *Industrial Relations: A Marxist Introduction*. London: Macmillan.

Kahn-Freund, O. (1984) *Labour and the Law*, 2nd edn. London: Stevens.

Kersley, B., Carmen, A., Forth, J., Bryson, A., Bewley, H., Dix, S. and Oxenbridge, S. (2004) *Inside the Workplace – First Findings from the 2004 Workplace Employment Relations Survey*. London: DTI, ESRC, ACAS, PSI and Routledge.

Labour Market Trends (2001) London: Office for National Statistics

Mercer Human Resource Consulting (2002) *The Prevalence of Bullying in the Workplace*. London: MHRC. Mercer.Pressoffice@ mercer.com.

National Association of Citizens Advice Bureau (2002) *Report on equal opportunities OECD Economic Outlook*. Paris: OECD.

*Novitz, T. and Skidmore, P. (2001) *Fairness at Work: A Critical Analysis of the Employment Relations Act, 1999 and its Treatment of Collective Rights*. Oxford: Hart Publishing.

Peninsula (2003) *Survey on Flexible Hours*. London: Peninsula.

Public Affairs (2001) *A Women's Place*. public.affairs@imgt.org.uk.

TUC (2000) *Trade Union Recognition*. London: TUC.

TUC (2002) *Focus on Recognition*. London: TUC.

TUC (2005) '*Government Should Investigate Cause of Tribunals Drop*', press release, 12 July.

Wedderburn, W. (1986) *The Worker and the Law*. London: Penguin.

*Willey, B. (2000) *Employment Law in Context*. Harlow: Prentice Hall.

Work Stress Management (2002) *Survey on Workplace Stress*. www.workstressmanagement.com.

 For multiple-choice questions, exercises and annotated weblinks specific to this chapter visit the book's website at **www.pearsoned.co.uk/beardwell**

Chapter 12

Establishing the terms and conditions of employment

Sue Marlow and Trevor Colling

Objectives

- To describe and evaluate the efficacy of the collective bargaining process in establishing and amending the terms and conditions of employment.
- To discuss the manner in which terms and conditions of employment are decided and amended within the public sector.
- To outline and discuss how terms and conditions are decided and amended within organisations which do not recognise trade unions or union bargained agreements.
- To outline and discuss how terms and conditions are decided and amended within small firms.
- To consider the influence of contemporary government regulation upon the terms and conditions of employment.

Introduction

Critical to the structure of capitalist economies in the modern era has been the manner in which labour is rewarded for the effort made to produce goods and services – the 'effort – wage bargain' (Behrend, 1957). As capitalism developed and began to mature at the beginning of the nineteenth century, the foundations of a wage economy were formalised, this led to contention regarding how work should be measured and valued. In response to the exploitative nature of early capitalism, trade unions developed as collective organisations to protect the employment conditions of skilled labour; by the early part of the twentieth century, unions had expanded their influence to semi- and un-skilled workers (Hyman, 2003). The state, after some resistance, made union representation legal and laid basic protective rights for employees on statute. Employers, albeit reluctantly, accepted these constraints upon their prerogative, and so the concept of negotiating the terms and conditions of employment emerged into modern society (Coates and Topham, 1986). Regarding the establishment, protection and improvement of the terms and conditions of employment, it was accepted that the most efficient and equitable manner for the effort – wage bargain to be negotiated was through free collective bargaining (Webb and Webb, 1902; Brown, 1993). Collective bargaining is a process of negotiation undertaken between employers' federations or representatives and trade unionists to agree the terms and conditions under which employees should work. During the latter part of the nineteenth century, and for most of the twentieth century, collective bargaining came to be accepted as a legitimate process by which the terms and conditions of employment were established and to this end has, to differing degrees, been accepted by the state and employers (Brown, 1993).

However, with the election of a Conservative administration in 1979, the political and economic environment changed. With a clear affiliation to a free market philosophy, successive Conservative governments (1979–1997) introduced legislation, policies and practices to ensure a decline in trade union influence and power in the UK (Hutton, 1997). Along with the constraint and control of trade union power, came a concomitant decline in the coverage of collective bargaining. This decline has been recorded by successive workplace surveys undertaken during this period such that in 1984, it was found that over 70 per cent of employees were covered by collectively bargained agreements but this figure had dropped to approximately 48 per cent by 2004 (Kersley *et al.*, 2005: 13), although the decline would appear to have stabilised.

So, until recently, in any debate upon how the terms and conditions of employment are agreed, the critical focus would have been upon the collective bargaining process. However, within the contemporary UK economy, whilst a substantial minority of employees still benefit from collective bargaining coverage, the majority do not (Kersley *et al.*, 2005). Bacon and Storey (1996: 43) refer to the 'fracturing of collectivism' by the structural changes in the labour market and the pursuit of individualism by management. This is evident in the increasing number of firms who do not recognise unions as either employee representatives or bargaining agents and some contraction of bargaining in traditional bastions of strength such as the public sector (Bach and Winchester, 2003). So, it is recognised that overall, collective negotiation of the terms and conditions of employment no longer dominates in the UK. Yet, there is little evidence for a credible alternative model of employment relations emerging to replace the collective bargaining approach, leaving what Beaumont (1995) describes as an institutional vacuum. Towers (1997: 64) meanwhile, suggests that a growing representation gap has emerged in the UK, where no formal methods for the articulation for employee voice has emerged with any coherence to effectively replace collective representation. It is noted that the latest information emerging from WERS 2004 (Kersley *et al.*, 2005: 18) finds that over 90 per cent of organisations engage with some type of direct communication and some information sharing but this is varied in type and degree, offering limited opportunity for dialogue and negotiation. This may be partially addressed by the European directive upon information and consultation which has been transposed into UK legislation as the Information and Consultation of Employees Act (2005) (ICE). Given its relatively recent enactment, it remains to be seen how effective ICE might be. However, firms with fewer than 50 employees are exempted, plus, as the provisions of the act have to be 'triggered' by employee request, it has been argued that the impact is likely to be limited in sectors where voice is currently constrained (Marlow and Gray, 2005).

Consequently, given the contraction of union representation and the growth of less effective communication and consultation channels, there would appear to be some foundation for concerns regarding employee voice. It should be noted that there are considerable differences between the process of negotiation and that of consultation and communication. Within the former, each party involved has a degree of power underpinned by the use of sanctions to influence the outcome of the negotiation whereas in the latter, information might be shared and responses noted but not necessarily acted upon. As Dundon and Rollason (2004: 156) commented when considering voice mechanisms in non-union firms, 'management assumed that because they circulated information, employees had received and understood the message . . . management relied on a series of top-down communications and took these to mean that they consulted and informed employees which was not the case in practice'.

Stop & think

What do you understand by the term 'the representation gap'?

The extent of collective bargaining coverage in the UK has experienced some change since the election of successive Labour governments in 1997 and the introduction of a statutory recognition procedure within the Employment Relations Act for firms with more than 20 employees (1999). Gall and McKay (1999) drew attention to union recognition campaigns aimed at over 300 companies with over 235,000 employees in total where the indications were that many firms planned to accept such agreements in advance of statutory obligations. Reviewing the latest data from WERS (Kersley *et al.*, 2005: 13), it emerges that whilst only 27 per cent of workplaces recognise unions for bargaining purposes, coverage extends to 48 per cent of all employees. This particular survey also recognises that coverage of bargained agreements may extend beyond workplaces where unions are actively recognised (where employers recognise industry-wide agreements). On this basis, coverage extends to 30 and 50 per cent accordingly. It should also be noted that this WERS was the first to include findings from small firms with between 10 and 24 employees, this has an adverse effect upon the calculation of union recognition given the very low rates amongst this sector. Consequently, Kersley *et al.*, (2005: 13) comment that, 'Among workplaces with 25 or more employees, the incidence of recognition remained stable at around two-fifths (39 per cent in 2004, compared with 41 per cent in 1998). The continual decline in the rate of recognition seen among this group over the 1980s and 1990s therefore, appears to have been arrested'.

The public sector however, retains a strong union presence being recognised in 90 per cent of workplaces (Kersley *et al.*, 2005). So, public sector unions have maintained a presence in the workplace, but even here there can be little doubt that they have lost influence regarding the determination of the terms of employment. As in the private sector, there has been some contraction of bargaining agendas and shifts in bargaining level. During the 1980s, for example, successive Conservative governments made greater use of pay review bodies, which, although consulting with unions, effectively by-passed the collective bargaining process (Bach, 2002). In the contemporary economy there has been some decline in the use of such bodies particularly for the NHS as the Agenda for Change takes effect.

The debate surrounding the contraction and expansion of bargaining coverage in both the private and public sector is set to continue but it is clear that a majority of employees within the contemporary economy now work in firms which do not recognise trade unions for bargaining purposes (Kersley *et al.*, 2005). Within the non-union sector, a range of approaches – from individual negotiation to unilateral management determination – have been identified and these differing approaches will be explored to illuminate this debate further with a particular focus upon smaller firms. So, in recognition of the growing diversity in establishing terms and conditions of employment, this chapter will:

- offer a comprehensive overview of the collective bargaining process in both the private and public sector;

- discuss recent modernising initiatives and agendas which might impact upon this process

- consider the manner in which terms and conditions are established in firms which do not recognise trade unions for bargaining purposes.

Collective bargaining – a short overview

As has been noted above, the extent to which collectively bargained agreements establish the terms and conditions of employment has declined quite markedly since the 1980s (Edwards, 2003). However, it is important to recognise that collective bargaining has been of critical importance within the study of industrial relations in the UK, as Rose (2004: 305) notes, 'collective bargaining . . . is the very essence of industrial relations and an important institution in all democratic societies where freedom of association is common'. Collective bargaining is deemed to be of such importance as it underpins the notion of *voluntarism* or *collective laissez faire* which defined the British approach to the employment relationship until the growing regulatory approach, emerging at the end of the 1970s and gathering pace since (Dickens *et al.*, 2005). As such, voluntarism arises from the practice of establishing the terms and conditions of employment through freely negotiated, collectively bargained, voluntary agreements between trade unions and employers federations or management representatives. Such agreements are not legally binding although it is noted that some legislative actions were necessary to establish the conditions to enable unions to apply sanctions within the bargaining process. Collective bargaining is so important because the process focuses upon voluntary negotiation, where each party has a degree of power and can apply sanctions so it enables employees, through trade unions, to have some input into shaping their own employment conditions. This should be contrasted with consultation and communication processes which share information and enable feedback but do not offer employees substantive collective power to challenge managerial decisions. Consequently, even though collective bargaining coverage has declined – markedly so in the private sector – it still shapes the terms and conditions of a substantial minority of the labour force whilst its importance and influence in the recent past should not be underestimated.

The term 'collective bargaining' was first utilised by Sidney and Beatrice Webb (Webb and Webb, 1902) who believed that this activity was the collective equivalent to individual bargaining, where the prime aim was to achieve economic advantage. So, bargaining had an *economic* function and was undertaken between trade unions and employers or employers' organisations. This classical definition of collective bargaining has been subject to a number of critical analyses. In the late 1960s, Flanders (1968) argued that this view was erroneous; rather, collective bargaining should be understood as a *rule-making process* which established the rules under which the economic purchase of labour could initially take place. Flanders also argued that collective bargaining entails a power relationship; the imbalance of economic power, status and security between the single employee and that of the management can, to some degree, be addressed by collective pressure such that agreements are compromise settlements of power conflicts. Fox (1975) disputes Flanders' argument that an individual bargain is an economic exchange which always concludes with an agreement, whereas collective bargaining is essentially a process to establish rules for exchange. In fact, Fox argues that there is no assurance that either process will achieve agreement on terms acceptable to the parties involved in negotiation. Moreover, he believes that the economic function of collective bargaining has not been afforded sufficient attention by Flanders. Drawing from these arguments, it is useful to recognise that Flanders moves the discussion forward with the emphasis on regulation but the contrast between collective regulation and individual bargaining is debateable as Fox notes.

Rather than isolating one major function of collective bargaining, Chamberlain and Kuhn (1965) offer an analysis which outlines three distinct activities which interact to form the bargaining process:

- *Market or economic function.* This determines the price of labour to the employer, thus the collective agreement forms the 'contract' for the terms under which employees will work for the employer, i.e. the *substantive terms* (see below) of employment.

- *Decision-making function.* In this role, collective bargaining offers employees the opportunity, if they wish, to 'participate in the determination of the policies which guide and rule their working lives' (Chamberlain and Kuhn, 1965: 130).

- *Governmental function.* Collective bargaining establishes rules by which the employment relationship is governed. Thus, bargaining is a political process as it establishes a 'constitution' (Salamon, 1992).

From the above points it is clear that collective bargaining is concerned with the establishment of:

- *Substantive rules.* These regulate all aspects of pay agreements and hours of work.

- *Procedural rules.* These establish the rules under which negotiation over the terms and conditions of employment can take place and establish grievance and dispute procedures.

Bargaining principles

The aim of collective bargaining is to reach negotiated agreements upon a range of issues pertaining to the employment relationship. From this range of issues, some will hold the potential for a conflict situation where the distribution and division of scarce resources are under negotiation (for example, division of profit as dividends or wage increase). Others, however, will have mutual benefit for employees and management with the major debate focusing upon the most beneficial manner in which to implement change (for example, introduction of health and safety procedures). These differences were noted by Walton and McKersie (1965) who outlined two approaches to collective bargaining:

- *Distributive bargaining.* One party will seek to achieve gains at the expense of the other; the aim is the division of a limited resource between groups both of whom wish to maximise their share. Pay bargaining is distributive bargaining as one party's gain is the others loss.

- *Integrative bargaining.* This approach seeks mutual gains in areas of common interest with a problem-solving approach from the parties involved. Successful integrative bargaining depends upon a relatively high level of trust between parties and a willingness to share information.

Discuss the differences between negotiation, consultation and communication in workplace.

Summary

Collective bargaining remains an important part of the contemporary employment relationship, although since the early 1980s, it has been subject to contraction and decline. Recently, however, due to limited political support and new statutory rights, this decline in influence would appear to have halted (Kersley *et al.*, 2005). There has been considerable debate regarding the fundamental nature and purpose of the bargaining process, but any definition of collective bargaining must take account of historical and contemporary influences which impinge upon those involved in bargaining practices.

The collective agreement

At the end of the negotiating and bargaining process, collective agreements are reached. Traditionally, British collective bargaining has been notable for the informality with which agreements are reached but from the early 1970s there has been a growing trend to establish formal written contracts to avoid any potential problems given the possibility of differing interpretations of negotiation outcomes. Written agreements also contributes to a rationalisation and codification of employment relations procedures but the existence of such agreements will not prevent informal bargaining at local level. Indeed, there are a number of levels, outlined below, at which collective agreements can be reached.

Multi-employer agreements

Such agreements cover specific groups of employees (described within the contract) from a particular industry and are negotiated by employers' associations or federations and full-time national trade union officials. Multi-employer agreements also form guidelines for employers who are not members of the industry association, and for firms who do not recognise unions.

Single-employer bargaining (organisational bargaining)

Organisational bargaining may occur at a number of levels for example:

- *Corporate* – all those employed by the organisation are covered by agreements bargained by the company and relevant trade union officials.

- *Plant* – the collective agreement is negotiated for a specific site or plant within the corporate structure affecting only the employees of that location. These agreements may be totally independent of national terms or constructed upon an industry agreement.

Determinants of bargaining level within organisations

It is indicated that company-level bargaining is associated with large organisations and the presence of professional HR specialists in corporate level management (CBI, 1988). Site bargaining is associated with firms where labour costs are a high percentage of total costs and there are substantial numbers of workers on each site. At present, the choice of bargaining level falls within managerial prerogative influenced by a number of variables; for example, corporate-level bargaining may be favoured as one channel to neutralise potentially powerful plant-based union pressure and avoid inter-plant comparisons (Rose, 2004).

A brief historical analysis of collective bargaining in Britain 1945–1980

During the immediate post-war period, the influence of corporatism, where joint negotiations between employers and trade unions are encouraged by the state, ensured that industry-level collective bargaining became firmly established. The nationalisation programme and the advent of the welfare system ensured that the state became a major employer and, indeed, the post-war Labour government enacted legislation which obliged management in the newly nationalised industries to establish negotiating procedures for all employees. It is incorrect, however, to presume that local or domestic bargaining ceased to be of relevance because of the formal establishment of national bargaining machinery for the majority of British labour by the early 1950s. In fact, by the 1960s, the conditions of full employment, coupled with high demand for goods, offered considerable leverage for local bargaining by shop stewards in the less bureaucratic, private manufacturing sector. The toleration of local bargaining eventually led to 'wages drift' which occurred when national agreements were utilised as a bargaining floor upon top of which local agreements were added, leading to inflationary pressures. This latter point generated concern from a then Labour government, given the problems of introducing and operating incomes policies in the face of informal, unregulated local bargaining and growing inflation. The growth and economic effect of domestic bargaining was deemed an 'industrial relations problem'.

Given, however, that domestic bargaining was a problem for employers who faced increasing international competition and found wage costs difficult to control and was also a potential threat to government economic policy, a Royal Commission was established to examine industrial relations practices and procedures in both the public and private sector. The Donovan Commission reported in 1968, arguing that Britain had two systems of industrial relations, the formal and informal (Donovan Commission, 1968: 12). In private-sector manufacturing, the formal system was based upon national bargaining between employers' organisations and full-time trade union officials. The informal system was based upon local bargaining between management and shop stewards under the influence of full employment and buoyant demand for goods. Overall, the Donovan Commission argued that workplace bargaining had become of greater importance than national bargaining in the private manufacturing sector. This local-level of bargaining, it was suggested, was 'largely informal, largely fragmented, and largely autonomous' (Flanders, 1970: 169) as it was based upon verbal agreements backed by custom and practice. Fragmented bargaining was undertaken by individual or small groups of stewards negotiating with individual or small groups of managers who did not consult with employers' organisations or full-time trade union officials, and did not respect national agreements.

The Commission argued that multi-employer bargaining on a national industry level could no longer effectively accommodate differentiated working practices throughout the private sector. The responsibility for introducing reform lay with management but local informal agreements were not dismissed, but it was insisted that local agreements should achieve a level of formality such that they did not totally ignore and undermine national agreements. Moreover, the system of local informal bargaining hampered the development of effective and orderly workplace bargaining: '. . . the objection to the state of plant bargaining at that time therefore, was its doubtful legitimacy and furtive character' (Clegg, 1979: 237). What was required was a rationalisation of the existing system which would effectively combine the two systems of industrial relations into one coherent, ordered process which did not then undermine the formal rules in multi-employer agreements.

The reform of local-level bargaining

In consequence, most organisations, encouraged by the Conservative government (1970–74) and the Labour government (1974–79) undertook voluntary reform of collective bargaining procedures. As such, management facilitated the formalisation of domestic bargaining by recognising shop stewards, supporting union organisation through closed shop agreements and check-off procedures (whereby union subscriptions are deducted by the company from wages and then paid to the trade union account). The reform of collective bargaining during the 1970s offered clear benefits to trade unions with increased formal recognition and better facilities (for a critique of the incorporation of shop stewards into formal management/trade union bargaining hierarchy – 'the bureaucratisation thesis' – see Hyman, 1977). It became apparent however, that rapidly rising inflation, growing international competition and greater foreign ownership combined with state intervention in industrial relations issues, created a climate favourable for management to press for further reforms. So, for example, there emerged a trend towards decentralisation of bargaining and a growth in formal recognition of domestic bargainers, but there remained considerable variation in collective bargaining processes within British industry during the 1970s.

When the Donovan Committee (1968) reported that the UK had two approaches to bargaining, informal and formal, what do you think this meant?

Summary

In the post-war period there was a rapid expansion in domestic bargaining at local level in private sector manufacturing industry despite the existence of national agreements negotiated by multi-employer organisations and full-time trade union officials. The Labour government of 1964–70 was concerned that local bargaining was compromising its incomes policy programme, adding to inflationary pressure and adversely affecting Britain's competitive performance. The Donovan Commission was charged with investigating contemporary industrial relations and concluded that Britain had two systems of industrial relations, informal and formal. The solution was to incorporate the two, establishing formal bargaining processes and procedures at the domestic level with an emphasis upon productivity bargaining. Governments throughout the 1960s and 1970s continued to support collective bargaining as the most appropriate and equitable manner in which to establish the terms and conditions of employment.

Changes in collective bargaining since the 1980s

From the late 1970s to the mid-1990s the British economy suffered cyclical economic recession, and volatile levels of unemployment (Rose, 2004). Such structural changes, combined with the election of successive Conservative governments from 1979 to 1997, hostile to the ethos of collective representation by trade unions, have prompted substantial change in the nature of collective bargaining in both the public and private sector. It is important to note that such changes arose from joint pressures from industry, successive Conservative governments plus a failure by unions to develop a strategy to protect their presence in the workplace. It was a combination of such factors which prompted substantial changes within the scope and influence of the collective bargaining process (Edwards, 2003). Contemporary workplace studies (Gall and McKay, 1999; Kersley *et al.*, 2005) have found that, while the nature, scope and processes of collective bargaining have changed, it remains an important vehicle for fixing pay and conditions in the public sector, and for a substantial minority of employees elsewhere.

Decentralisation of bargaining

There has been a growing trend towards the decentralisation of collective bargaining away from multi-employer/industry level, to organisation or plant level. This trend has continued during the 1980s and 1990s with encouragement from successive Conservative governments during this period who attempted to promote the practice in the public sector. Indeed, the 1990 White Paper, *Employment for the 1990s*, stated that plant- or company-level negotiations result in more realistic pay settlements and thus, avoided wage inflation. From the corporate stance, decentralised bargaining offers the opportunity to link pay and productivity together at local level where regional variations and conditions can be accounted for accurately by local management and trade union officials. The weakened state of contemporary trade unions ensure they are less able to resist managerial strategy to utilise local bargaining to review labour costs and reform working practices, for example, the introduction of new technology, flexible working practices, etc. (Rose, 2004).

There is a need for a note of caution regarding whether decentralised bargaining is a useful strategy for all corporate structures and also regarding the true extent of the 'decentralisation' process. Considering the issue of decentralisation in more detail, Kinnie (1990) found a false image of local autonomy in bargaining, suggesting that local management are subject to head office directive even when there is an appearance of local autonomy. This is supported in more recent work with Cully *et al.* (1999: 106) commenting that 'the pay setting process is often handled beyond the workplace and may be opaque to managers at a local level').

Activity

A corporate enterprise has always undertaken centralised bargaining, with a specialised team of negotiators bargaining annually with full-time trade union officials. However, the corporation is considering a complete restructuring whereby local 'profit centres' would be developed as single business units. As part of this restructuring it has been suggested that collective bargaining should be devolved to local level, with outline directives issued from head office regarding acceptable bargaining agendas and final settlements.

As HRM consultants, outline the presentation you would make to the board to include the following issues:

(a) the origins and extent of local bargaining;
(b) the advantages and potential problems of local bargaining to both management and trade unions;
(c) possible solutions to such problems;
(d) recommendations concerning the move to local bargaining.

Flexibility issues

The introduction of flexible working has been made possible by the de-regulation of the labour market, the weakness of trade unions to resist such change, the growth of managerial prerogative and market pressure to cut costs (see Chapter 4 for further discussion). Where changes aimed at promoting flexibility within the labour process have been introduced, the following points have emerged:

- If a company introduces flexible working, not subject to statutory regulation, such changes usually form an overlapping agreement to become part of a complete package which constitutes a flexibility agreement. The terms and conditions of contemporary flexibility agreements evident will depend on such factors as the state of union–management relations, the bargaining environment and the nature of technology employed.

The implications for collective bargaining of flexibility agreements are as follows:

- Trade unions are no longer bargaining terms and conditions for a specific craft or activity. Flexibility between tasks blurs lines of demarcation such that the possession of a specific skill or talent is no longer exclusive as tasks are spread throughout the workforce. Thus, bargaining leverage is reduced.

- As employees undertake a wider range of tasks throughout the labour process, fewer 'core' workers are required with an increasing dependence upon numerically flexible labour, thus leading to redundancies and a consequent fall in trade union membership and growth in unemployment.

- Growth in atypical labour (employees not working under a standard employment contract) has implications for union membership given the difficulties of attracting and retaining such employees as union members.

- The growing links between flexibility bargaining and pay increases means that there is a growing trend to bargain around issues of exchange, for example, for wage increases in exchange for changes in work organisation, manning levels and redundancies.

This latter point is of some importance. This notion of exchange between improved pay and acceptance of changes in working methods is reminiscent of productivity bargaining during the 1960s. In return for accepting flexibility agreements, employees have been offered a range of benefits including pay increases, enhanced status and greater job security. Trade unions have been forced to bargain for better conditions on the basis of making concessions allowing significant changes in the labour process (Rose, 2004). Indeed, a reflection of this stance can clearly be seen in the Labour government's attitude toward the 2002–3 fire fighters' dispute where agreement to changed working practices was demanded in order for meaningful negotiations to ensue.

As with many other issues discussed, there is a robust critique of the ideas surrounding the flexible workforce idea. In a succinct, critical review of the flexibility debate, Pollert (1988) and Legge (1995) argue that this is not a new strategic attempt by employers to establish a labour force suitable to meet the needs of changing markets. Rather, employers have always made *ad hoc* attempts to make labour more flexible, but have been hampered by state and union regulation of terms and conditions of employment. Recently, employers have been able to take advantage of a weakened labour movement to introduce greater flexibility encouraged by governments sympathetic to such changes. Moreover, Legge (1995) argues that flexible working arrangements have largely been introduced in an opportunistic fashion with the emphasis upon short term cost savings rather than as any constituent of a longer term strategic change to working practices.

So, while there is some evidence concerning the development of flexible working and the inclusion of flexibility agreements in the bargaining forum, there is only a limited indication of a link between improved productivity and flexibility initiatives (Nolan and O'Donnell, 2003). This, together with the critique of flexibility, suggests that, while flexibility issues are undoubtedly an important HRM initiative to effect change in the labour process, with implications for collective bargaining, caution is required in interpreting the extent of such change. This is particularly pertinent in respect to what degree the utilisation of flexibility represents a strategic or coherent approach to fragmenting the labour force, or to undermining collective coverage.

Successive Labour administrations from 1997 have offered continued support for flexible working, but have recognised the need to ameliorate the worst effects of such initiatives (Dickens, 2004). It was intended that the statutory protection offered in the Minimum Wage Act (1998), the Employment Relations Act (1999), the Employment Act (2002) and the recognition and adoption of EU Directives would go some way towards offering vulnerable labour greater protection. Moreover, there has been a clear focus upon the development of family friendly policies which aim to allow parents to accommodate both work and family commitments. It is recognised that statutory provision for individual employment rights might challenge the need for collective bargaining (if not for collective representation to ensure rights are observed: see below). This stance is indicative that contemporary Labour governments have focused mainly upon regulation and individualisation with considerable sensitivity towards business needs rather than supporting free collective bargaining and any ensuing collaboration with trade unions (Dickens *et al.*, 2005). However, such agreements may be used as a floor of rights in some organisations whilst scope exists for unions to police the provisions and ensure they are properly represented within the collective bargaining agenda or act to support individual employees should they decide to pursue their new rights.

Contemporary bargaining initiatives

Since the reform of collective bargaining in the 1980s, a number of discrete initiatives have emerged which have, on the whole, enabled management to reform the bargaining process quite considerably. A number of these are briefly considered.

- Single union deals are largely associated with Japanese management strategies given their initiation within Japanese subsidiaries locating on greenfield sites in the UK (Salamon, 1992). The single union agreement occurs where management grants recognition to only one trade union to represent employees in the bargaining process. The major objection to single union deals is the promotion of what Salamon describes as a 'beauty contest approach' between trade unions. Management outline the envisaged approach to industrial relations and a personnel strategy, inviting trade unions to state how they might measure up to the managerial view of employment relations – with the reward being a new pool of members during a time when trade unions were experiencing decline. However, it could be argued that, given the labour process of organisations who adopted single union deals (single status working, flexibility, fewer separate job titles), the scope for a differentiated approach to bargaining is significantly narrowed. A further constraint upon the bargaining process in single union firms is the association between single union deals, no-strike deals and pendulum arbitration (Rose, 2004).

- A no-strike clause, once accepted by a trade union on behalf of the membership, effectively deprives union negotiators of the threat of strike action should bargaining break down and, moreover, denies employees the option of withdrawing their labour unilaterally.

- No-strike clauses are usually (but not always) accompanied by pendulum arbitration facilities where a third party will arbitrate on behalf of the two principals should they fail to reach agreement. Where both sides are aware that an arbitrator will adopt one side or the other's position and this will represent a cost to the other party, they are more likely to bargain in good faith, making every effort to settle (Singh, 1986; Milner, 1993). The limited use of this practice in Britain makes it difficult to assess the impact upon the bargaining process.

- Single table bargaining offers employers similar benefits to single union deals whilst maintaining a multi-union site. Bargaining takes place between unions to establish a negotiation proposal, which is then articulated by one bargaining unit which negotiates on behalf of all employees (Rose, 2004).

Stop & think

List the major reforms to collective bargaining levels and processes in the 1980s.

HRM and collective bargaining

The early conceptual notion of HRM being focused upon, and only possible in, the unitary firm has not emerged in the modern British economy. In contemporary usage, HRM is employed as a set of strategic initiatives focused upon the employee with the aim of improving competitiveness, where any firm, depending on product and market demands, may utilise any number from a range of initiatives included under the HRM umbrella (see Chapter 2 for further discussion). Yet, introducing and managing HRM practices in a collective bargaining environment does raise a number of contentious issues, primarily whether a series of initiatives aimed at the individual employee can be compatible within the collective approach.

Overall, there is little evidence for the emergence of a strategic approach to managing labour in the UK economy (Mabey and Salamon, 1995) but it appears that HRM initiatives are more evident in unionised firms. This can be taken as evidence that the two practices, HRM and collective bargaining, are not mutually exclusive (Mishel and Voos, 1992). Guest (1989) argues that the values underpinning HRM – strategic integration and the pursuit of quality – are not incompatible with collective representation where bargaining channels can be effectively utilised to introduce change. Evidence from the 1998 Employment Relations Survey found 'high commitment management practices going hand in hand with a union presence' and also found this to be the case for high productivity firms (Cully *et al.*, 1999: 294). Storey (1995) argues that the two systems can coexist in harmony where HRM initiatives are focused upon areas which do not pose a threat to the scope of collective bargaining, or where they do not attempt to by-pass established bargaining channels. Consequently, it is not axiomatic that if HRM initiatives are to be utilised, collective bargaining must be removed from the agenda; the critical issue here is the motivation for the introduction of HRM. If individualised HRM practices are aimed at undermining union effectiveness, there is a real threat to existing procedures. However, if change is deployed after discussion and/or negotiation with existing unions, there is an opportunity for joint regulation of new working practices. This is not to argue that collective bargaining will be unaffected by the adoption of HRM. Storey (1995), found that whilst collective bargaining had become less of a management priority, new HRM practices and collective bargaining tended to exist as parallel arrangements.

Considering the issue of HRM and collective bargaining processes specifically, it appears that the former can coexist with the latter and indeed, HRM initiatives may be introduced through bargaining channels. In established plants, while HRM initiatives are evident, they have not seriously challenged the main focus of collective bargaining upon pay issues, but the scope of bargaining has been narrowed, with consultation being employed as a preferred channel of communication.

Summary

A number of bargaining initiatives have emerged during the 1980s which have changed the level and structure of the collective bargaining process. These initiatives have facilitated the exercise of managerial prerogative in the bargaining relationship and further narrowed the scope of bargaining channels. Overall, where it persists, the collective bargaining function has remained intact but has been constrained in scope.

'New Labour' and the contemporary employment relationship

With the election of 'New Labour' in 1997 there has emerged a rather contradictory programme of change and continuity in employment relations. A modernising agenda has been actioned which moves away from the philosophy of state sponsored wealth redistribution through social ownership to the support of private capital, private enterprise, individualism and a continuation of Conservative expenditure limits (Edwards, 2003). The new administration made it quite clear that the vast majority of the initiatives undertaken by the previous Conservative administration to reform the employment relationship would remain in place. Hence, the anti-union legislation enacted in the last 20 years remains largely untouched such that Britain still has the most restrictive regime of any Western developed nation towards collective representation at work (Howell, 2004). There has been no noticeable resurgence of the special relationship between Labour and unions evident in previous administrations whilst the Labour government has retained an enthusiasm for a de-regulated labour market with flexibility as a key factor (Rose, 2004). Whilst retaining some of the frameworks which shaped employment relations over the last 20 years, successive Labour governments have introduced policies which necessitate the state to develop a model of 'good' employment relations. The key focal points of the administration to date have been the notions of social partnership, fairness at work for the individual and the constrained recognition of European employment regulation (Howell, 2004).

In his commentary, McIlroy (1998) emphasises the difficult choices facing the trade union movement in reaching a compromise with the new Labour administration, who were not prepared to abandon the Thatcherite foundation of the contemporary employment relationship. There is some speculation regarding the future of the party-union link – whether it goes further down the path McIlroy (1998) describes as 'arms-length organisational relationships'. Given the current tension between public sector unions and the government where Bach (2002: 320) notes, 'public sector trade unions leaders were disappointed by the lack of progress in improving their members' pay and working conditions' plus, the bitter Fire Service dispute and the election of more left-leaning trade union officials recently, a distanced toleration would seem, at best, most likely.

However, the notion of social partnerships is one issue where moderate unions have indicated a willingness to comply with political will but as McIlroy argues, these partnerships do not reflect the robust Rhineland model where consultation, communication and representation are strongly regulated. Hence, suspicion and doubt remains regarding their real utility to employees as the weak UK version clearly underpins the desire to retain flexibility, de-regulation and competitiveness (Martinez-Lucio and Stuart, 2005). In consequence, the current government refers to the mutual responsibilities between employers and employees and is equally encouraging to both unions and management to engage in dialogue to introduce change, improve productivity and resolve disputes.

From trade unions, there has been some support for the social partnership concept (Monks, 1996) although this has been with an element of pragmatism, recognising that the 'New Unionism' agenda must be seen to be moderate and conciliatory to maintain support from employers and the state (McIlroy, 1998). Support for partnerships from unions is, of course, not entirely based on pragmatism. In a number of polls commissioned by the GMB in the late 1980s and early 1990s, it became apparent that employees had concerns relating to issues which were beyond the traditional remit of collective bargaining. These included job fulfilment, worthwhile work, and job security, all of which were ranked above pay in importance. John Edmonds (1997), the GMB General Secretary argued that the former are most effectively addressed through partnership discussion rather than collective negotiation. This union stance towards social partnerships has fuelled the contemporary debate surrounding the most appropriate strategies for unions to adopt in the workplace to ensure their continued relevance as both employee representatives and bargainers. More recently, there is some indication that the union movement is growing disillusioned with the notion of partnership, particularly as practised by the Labour government. Based on their disappointment with the nature of proposed changes in the public sector, in July 2001 the TUC openly expressed doubts about the government's ability to generate meaningful partnerships. If the union movement feels those who are supposed to be most supportive of the notion of partnerships are not committed to them, this must surely raise questions regarding the whole ethos. Union disillusionment with this process has been further emphasised with Serwotka, the General Secretary of the Public and Commercial Services Union (PCS) openly declaring a clear break with the partnership agenda in his determination to return outsourced employment to the public sector and to use strike action if necessary to achieve this goal (Turner, 2003a).

The radical critique of the concept of social partnerships, however, questions the whole feasibility of such relationships in the first instance. Kelly (1996) argues that it is difficult to form meaningful relationships with a party who wishes you did not exist. Equally, Kelly argues that in an inequitable power arrangement, as exists between capital and labour, the likelihood of meaningful partnerships being established is impossible unless far reaching coercive measures can be applied. Briefly, Kelly believes that given the current state of management strength and the ambivalence towards unions from the current government, that there is little rationale for employers to enter into true partnerships with unions when they can achieve their goals through flexing their prerogative. Critically, Kelly also believes that a partnership stance will undermine the role of collective bargaining and narrow current agendas further. Bacon and Storey (1996: 43) however, describe the 'fracturing of collectivism' and instead argue that unions must find new ways of representing the individual in the workplace and engage with partnership channels. At the same time they recognise that partnership initiatives have been frustrated in a number of firms, owing to the lack of management commitment to the process leading to nothing more than a rhetoric of partnership. Indeed, Martinez-Lucio and Stuart (2005), draw attention to these risks for those entering into such partnerships suggesting that they are, in fact, inherently unstable.

While it is not yet evident how collective bargaining will be affected by the notion of partnership, a number of suppositions are possible. The enactment of the Employment Relations Act (1999) has signalled the current government's intention to tacitly support union recognition, if rather cautiously. In his comment upon the impact of employment regulation upon union influence, Howell (2004: 10), argues that, 'These collective rights at work are, again, fairly limited, particularly in the context of 18 years of legislation restricting collective representation, collective bargaining and collective action at work'. There has also been some indication of an emergence of new consultation and partnership agendas (Roche and Geary, 2002). This may be unpalatable to unions but, if they are to be seen to support partnerships, they may have to accept a continued restriction of negotiation, and expansion of consultation. However, management will still have to enter into debate around key issues, and demonstrate progress if partnerships are to be maintained. What is not in doubt is that partnerships are contentious and their success will depend upon employer and employee representatives being able to demonstrate that they are reaching consensus through cooperation without one set of interests being consistently subordinated. From limited evidence based upon partnerships in the water industry in the UK and vehicle manufacturing in the USA, Towers (1997: 226) comments that there is 'an essential need for equal partnership reinforced by collective bargaining which accepts the legitimacy of conflict or interests as well as encouraging and institutionalising co-operation'. Further evidence will be required to assess the impact and success of social partnerships. However, recent empirical examinations of partnership in practice found that, whilst there are mutual gains for both employees and management, the advantage is skewed in the favour of management, who set the partnership agenda and appear to protect their own prerogative (Guest and Peccei, 2001; Roche and Geary, 2002).

Stop & think

Briefly outline the major reforms introduced by the Labour government since 1997 which have affected the manner in which the terms and conditions of employment are agreed.

Whilst the changes to national policy regarding the management of employment relations might be viewed as cautious at best and highly conservative at worst, New Labour have actively engaged with recognition of European regulation which is a notable change from their Conservative predecessors. Whereas the Conservatives had rejected the social aspect of European Union membership, preferring to maintain their autonomy to foster free market individualism, the Blair administrations have recognised this dimension. However, it should be noted that Labour still favours minimal compliance and in some cases, has not recognised measures in full or met agreed deadlines. So, for example, the Working Time Directive can be applied in such a way that the impact on the working week is minimal. Equally the initial attempt to use 'employees' rather than 'workers' in the Part Time Workers Directive would have effectively excluded most of those who might benefit from the regulation.

Summary

When the Labour government was elected to power in 1997, it was anticipated that there would be some revival of trade union influence over policy and economic development. However, successive Labour administrations have not demonstrated any enthusiasm to develop a close relationship with the trade union movement. Rather, they have enacted legislation which has strengthened union rights but the overall focus has been upon the individual at work and incorporating weak versions of European regulation rather than supporting collective labour rights. The outcome of this distancing stance has been a growing disillusionment by the union movement with successive Labour governments. This has been articulated by the election of 'left wing' activists to positions of prominence, and protracted disputes in the public sector such as that in the Fire Service with the government threatening the union with legal action which would enable them to impose a settlement. There can be little doubt that the ERA (1999) did strengthen unions' ability to influence terms and conditions of employment. However, this fell short of what the trade union movement expected of the Labour government and it appears unlikely that any further government support will be forthcoming. Another outcome of the focus upon individuality has been a notable expansion in cases brought to the Employment Tribunal as traditional collective solutions to disputes have declined, 'the collapse in union membership and collective bargaining coverage of the past two decades have forced the tribunal system to undertake work previously handled by voluntary collective procedures' (Howell, 2004: 11). It should be noted that the Employment Act (2002) was enacted as a response to the increase in tribunal cases, aiming to compel greater formality around grievance and discipline issues whilst encouraging other routes to avoid tribunals.

Establishing the terms and conditions of employment in the public sector

For much of the period following the Second World War, public sector employment relationships were distinctive, and designedly so. Managers were held accountable through political and administrative mechanisms, rather than through the market, and links between management practice and public policy were viewed as obvious and entirely legitimate. Public organisations were required to exemplify 'model employer' practice. Employment procedures were prescribed explicitly, sometimes by statute, and were subject to informal ministerial influence. Collective bargaining and consultation with trade unions were well established where national bargaining forums sat atop complex local and regional structures setting uniform national pay rates and conditions of service.

Since 1979, there has been some considerable reform of this process with successive Conservative governments intent on privatisation, cost cutting and the introduction of market forces into service provision. Contemporary Labour governments have broadly supported many of the Conservative ideas and reforms but within a new framework of a modernising agenda which recognises the need for increasing investment if service provision is to be improved and recruitment and retention problems addressed. Whilst demonstrating more sympathy towards the notion of public sector provision, the current government is determined to continue to foster increasing co-operation with the private sector through the private finance initiative (PFI) and public private partnerships (PPP) (Bach, 2002). To explore these issues in more detail, this section will outline the 'golden era' of public sector development, consider how this has changed in recent years and discuss current government initiatives regarding pay and conditions for public sector employees.

The 'golden era': Morrisonian organisations and model employment

That which until recently was recognised as the public sector developed in the immediate post-war period (Winchester, 1983). Between 1945 and 1950, the Labour government took into public ownership a number of basic industries including coal, steel and the railways. Together these accounted for approximately 10 per cent of the country's total productive capacity (Dearlove and Saunders, 1984: 268). Services that were to constitute the welfare state, including health and social security, were established under public administration and expanded rapidly. By 1959, almost a quarter (23.9 per cent) of the labour force worked in the public sector (Fairbrother, 1982: 3). Over the next 30 years this diverse range of enterprises, utility industries and services was gradually restructured more or less according to the principles of public corporations established by the Labour politician, Herbert Morrison. During this 'golden era', there was little doubt that employment practice in the public sector was different from that prevailing elsewhere in the economy (Winchester, 1983).

Morrisonian principles were informed by two policy objectives: first, to ensure that the priorities pursued by key industries and services were consistent with macroeconomic, industrial and social policy; and second, to provide within this framework some autonomy for professional managers. These large, integrated organisations were managed therefore, through independent industry boards that had responsibility for day-to-day operational matters. But these boards were accountable directly to the relevant ministers, who were also empowered to give 'general direction' (Pendleton and Winterton, 1993). In the interests of equality of treatment, uniform standards of product or service were a priority, and departments would be deployed to ensure consistency across the organisation. Guaranteeing probity in the public interest required complex internal control systems and hierarchies of management and committee structures (Pratchett and Wingfield, 1995).

The public sector as a whole was also assigned a particular industrial relations mission: to be a 'model employer' and implement 'a range of practices which today constitute good management' (Priestly Commission, 1955, cited in Farnham and Horton, 1995: 8). The state sector's role in macroeconomic policy was important in this regard. Though the depth of the post-war consensus can be exaggerated, commitments to full employment and the welfare state structured the programmes of both of the key political parties for as long as they could be combined with economic growth (Hills, 1990). The public sector was assigned a key role in job creation, 'mopping up' under-employment created by restructuring in the broader economy. Expanding public sector employment enabled managers to offer meaningful job security.

'Model employer' practices also implied a range of procedures intended to set an example to organisations across the economy which included promoting collective employment relations. Union growth was consequently stimulated directly (through the promotion of trade union membership) and indirectly (through the involvement of unions with collective bargaining). This growth continued in the 1970s as union membership expanded alongside the growth in public sector employment. Given the strategic importance of public industries in particular, great emphasis was also attached to the collective involvement of employees as a means of identifying and resolving grievances, and thereby avoiding potentially costly disruption. The requirement on public enterprises 'to consult with organisations which appear to them to be representative' was legally specified in their respective nationalisation acts (Pendleton and Winterton, 1993: 3). Elaborate, formal and bureaucratic systems for negotiation and consultation, often referred to as Whitleyism, also developed across the public services. Created with the brief to establish viable industrial relations systems following the end of the First World War, the Whitley Committee advocated centralised bargaining through joint industrial councils with a view to securing 'cooperation in the centre between national organisations' (Clegg, 1979: 31).

Consequently, industrial relations were marked by a significant degree of centralisation but there were important variations in this general picture (Fogarty and Brooks, 1986). For example, traditions of local bargaining in some of the nationalised industries (such as coal, docks and steel) remained entrenched long into the golden era, and local government employers came to full national bargaining relatively late in the day (Kessler, 1991: 7). Such centralisation was also evident in influencing the determination and negotiation of terms and conditions and cost constraints, and their ramifications for the management of the public sector, were more prominent features of the 'golden era' than is often acknowledged. Ministerial responsibilities for containing public expenditure generated a compelling interest in the outcome of collective bargaining. As early as the 1950s, government departments intervened to veto agreements in health and public transport that set precedents potentially which were deemed undesirable (Crouch, 1979; Thornley, 1994).

So, 'model employer' principles developed during this period resulted in relatively coherent frameworks for bargaining and consultation and a prominent role for trade unions in the management of change. It is important to maintain an appropriately nuanced perspective however, and exhortations to 'good management' were laced intermittently with cost pressures backed by ministerial pressure. Whilst public employment was secure, low pay and discriminatory employment procedures remained characteristic of large parts of the public sector (Thornley, 1994).

Summary

The scope and depth of public sector activity grew dramatically during the 'golden era' from the 1940s to the late 1970s. Principles established by Herbert Morrison underpinned management structures and behaviour. A key feature was the need to ensure some degree of congruence between the goals of particular public organisations and espoused public policy. Organisations were highly integrated, characterised by bureaucratic procedures, and managed by professional specialists subject to general direction by the relevant government ministers with a clear emphasis on centralised bargaining and collective industrial relations.

The Conservative era and market reform

From 1979 to 1997 the focus shifted to market-based approaches with expansion halted by public expenditure constraints and then reversed, as 'rolling back the frontiers of the state' became a priority (Hutton, 1996). Public enterprises were transferred to the private sector, and market mechanisms and competitive pressures were introduced into the remaining public services. Organisations were fragmented as distinct roles were created for service purchasers and providers (Bach and Winchester, 2003). Conservative ministers from 1979, and the New Right thinkers who influenced them, were inclined to view trade unions as an impediment to the effective operation of markets (Rose, 2004). At a more pragmatic level, they also recognised that public sector unions had become a potent source of opposition to government policy, and had contributed in no small measure to the downfall of the 1974–79 Labour government therefore, promoting national collective bargaining and trade union organisation became less of a priority. More important perhaps, the very notion of a single set of employment principles was not attractive to policy makers, who regarded the ability to tailor terms and conditions of employment to specific trading contexts as the hallmark of effective management. During the period of market-based reform, the emphasis shifted from promoting 'model employment' to providing the space in which managers could assume the *right* to manage (Bach and Winchester, 2003).

The extent to which this philosophy was reflected in changed management practice is a different matter. As Colling (1997) argues, government's interest in employment levels and pay remained undiminished and constrained the extent to which decision making could be left entirely to local actors. Paradoxically, promoting market pressures in these and other areas often required government to intervene more determinedly rather than stand back. Alongside measures promising greater discretion therefore, initiatives were developed to test performance and to set targets for change and improvement.

Reform of the centralised bargaining and consultation structures, characteristic of the Morrison era, has been one of the most tangible indicators of changing employment practice. After 1979, market orientations fostered an approach to pay determination founded on aligning pay with local labour markets and affordability considerations at the level of service providers. Decentralisation was thus, the primary motif of Conservative governments throughout the 1980s and 1990s. It was pursued pragmatically (rather than strategically), however, and was held in tension by a contending desire to maintain central control of the overall pay bill (Bach and Winchester, 2003).

The growth of indexation and independent pay review mechanisms played a significant role in reducing the scope of collective bargaining (Bach, 2002). Where they have been introduced, pay issues are decided through either predetermined formulae, in the case of indexation, or the deliberations of a panel following the submission of evidence from managers, unions and government. While some argue that the latter amounts to 'quasi-bargaining forums' (Winchester, 1996: 10), the removal of formal collective bargaining, and notionally thereby, the threat of strike action, was a common element. Although it was reserved initially for judges, doctors and the armed forces, other significant occupational groupings were incorporated gradually. The fire and police services were surprisingly late additions at the end of the 1970s, and schoolteachers, nurses and midwives were added subsequently. One-third of public sector employees were no longer affected by collective pay bargaining by the end of the period of market-based reform (Bailey, 1996: 136).

Throughout the 1980s, centralised bargaining structures came under informal pressure through changes to public sector financial procedures. The switch to cash rather than volume planning required employers to balance increases in pay against levels of service. From the late 1980s, managers in the NHS used the discretion available to them to vary starting salaries and job descriptions for ancillary and administrative staff (Grimshaw, 1999). The creation of market relationships, such as those stemming from competitive tendering, provided additional impetus. Decisions about the allocations of service contracts were based primarily on price, of which labour costs are usually a substantial element. Quests for savings prompted service managers locally to redesign work organisation and terms and conditions of employment (Colling, 1993). Ad hoc adjustments to employment packages became common, irrespective of whether or not the work was retained by public sector employers. In local government, for example, reform of bonus payments and working hours disorientated pay and grading structures, increasing pay inequalities, particularly between women and men (Escott and Whitfield, 1995).

From the early 1990s attempts were made to extend decentralised bargaining across and up grading structures to include professional and technical staff whose pay and conditions remained subject usually to national negotiations. This required a more direct approach to reform. The 1992 White Paper *People, Jobs and Opportunity* promised to:

> encourage employers to move away from traditional, centralised collective bargaining towards methods of pay determination which reward individual skills and performance; respond to the wish of individual employees to negotiate their own terms and conditions, and take full account of business circumstances.
>
> (Cited in White, 1994: 7)

The government's determination to decentralise is further illustrated by the escalation of pressure on NHS trust managers. Local managers, aware of the considerable opposition of the unions and professional associations, sought initially to innovate through job redesign and to maximise the grading flexibility offered by existing national agreements rather than negotiate locally for professional groups (Bach and Winchester, 1994). Following the 1992 election, however, burgeoning entrepreneurial spirit was galvanised by increasingly explicit exhortations from ministers and the NHS Executive and, after a protracted stand-off with the unions, the 1995 pay settlement eventually permitted some element of local bargaining for health service staff with the exception of doctors (Grimshaw, 1999).

Activity	Make a note of the key elements which differentiate the 'golden era' of public sector development from the market reform era of successive Conservative Governments 1979–1997.

Decentralisation and market-based reform contributed significantly to changing expectations surrounding public sector pay. Comparability gave way to affordability, and earnings growth considerably fell behind that of the private sector (Elliot and Duffus, 1996; Winchester, 1996). They also generated difficulties of their own, confusion within pay structures, and the inequalities that emerged subsequently (Escott and Whitfield, 1995) arguably did little for morale and provided the basis for substantial legal challenges. The Acquired Rights Directive and its UK variant, the Transfer of Undertakings (Protection of Employment) Directive (TUPE), provide rights to consultation and prohibit changes to pay and conditions when staff are transferred from one employer to another (e.g. from the public sector to a private contractor). Equal pay legislation makes it illegal to pay different rates to women and men when they carry out similar work, work rated as equivalent by a job evaluation scheme, or work that is of equal value in terms of effort or skill (see Chapter 7). Though the extent and security of such protections have been far from total (Napier, 1993; Dickens, 2000), unions became adept at selecting test cases to inhibit or reverse market-driven reform of pay systems, and won some notable victories in both domestic and European courts (Colling, 2000). The threat of further proceedings underpinned subsequent bargaining strategies, particularly in health and local government, where potential equal value cases became intertwined with union demands for coordinated reviews of pay and grading.

Summary

The election of successive Conservative governments during the 1980s and 1990s saw the introduction of far reaching reform into the public sector. There was a marked shift from the centralised, 'model employer' policy to that which focused upon market forces and cost constraints. This stance, combined with the government's evident hostility toward organised labour, substantially reduced the influence of trade unions upon employment issues. The uneven implementation of Conservative policies, however, led to a degree of confusion and problems in achieving desired outcomes regarding cost savings, productivity and performance.

'New Labour' and the modernising agenda

A modernisation agenda, developed and pursued by successive Labour governments since 1997, reveals a 'third way' approach to managing the public sector based on a combination of planning and market-driven strategies (Howell, 2004). The denigration of public services has ceased, and their contribution to national economic and social priorities is acknowledged to a greater degree. Some market-driven pressures have been removed, including the internal market in health and CCT in local government, and organisations have been re-integrated. Explicit target-setting has reintroduced elements of planning by ensuring compliance with national policy priorities within and across public services. Although important aspects of policy towards the public sector have changed, current emphases on employment flexibility and performance targets can be clearly identified as key aspects of previous Conservative government policy. So, the 'model employer' model has shifted somewhat from its dominant market focus, the critical notion underpinning current reforms is now that of 'performativity' (Bach, 2002).

This modernisation agenda of the Labour Government articulates a desire to reintroduce coordination into public service employment. Fundamental reviews of pay, grading and bargaining arrangements are in progress for many parts of the sector (Cabinet Office, 1999). For example, in health, comprehensive local reviews have aimed to extend functional flexibility further within and across a broader range of occupational groupings (NHS Executive, 1999) whilst the 'Agenda for Change' programme has established a simplified pay structure for the NHS with the intention of enabling greater flexibility and addressing persistent equal pay discrepancies. Regarding the Civil Service, existing performance-related pay (PRP) schemes have been reviewed and reformed and the Makinson Report (2000) has recommended a shift to team bonuses which will also be linked into target attainment. In education, headteachers were assimilated on to new scales incorporating performance elements in 1999 and pay review body recommendations that classroom teachers should be included in this scheme from 2000 have been acted upon. The majority of teachers applying to this scheme (93 per cent) were successful in achieving awards, which, in essence, were pay awards linked to performance and attainment. So, continuities from the previous period of market-based reform are notable with commitments to link pay with performance sustained and indeed, intensified (Cabinet Office, 1999).

As the first Comprehensive Spending Review progressed through 1999, the Chancellor announced higher than expected general settlements for health and for education, but pressure on pay was sustained. New money was tied explicitly to funding capital projects, such as improved information technology, and meeting previously established service targets, such as hospital waiting lists. Interventions by the Prime Minister made it clear that government did not expect to see pay levels increasing at the same rate as general expenditure unless they were 'linked to results' (Peston and Timmins, 1999).

After re-election in 2001, the second public spending review (2001–2004) committed the government to growth in expenditure of almost 4 per cent per year with a considerable proportion of this still focused upon health and education. The government's intent is to demonstrate clear improvements in the level of service and also to address recruitment and retention issues through selective improvements in pay and conditions. However, accompanying increasing expenditure was increased pressure from the Treasury to meet set targets regarding service provisions and performance standards, a task which will present considerable challenges to public sector employers, managers and employees. An apposite example of such pressures was the Fire Service dispute which rumbled on from 2002 until the summer of 2003. The Fire Brigades Union (FBU) made an original pay claim of 40 per cent, eventually settling for a 16 per cent deal phased in over two years and subject to modernisation of terms and conditions. The government were determined that public sector pay rises were to reflect their modernising agenda, in this case to include the recommendations of the Bain Report (2002) which linked pay issues to the reform of working practices and so, vetoed an early settlement between the local employers and the FBU. Discontent with the final settlement emerged again in 2004 when the employers were reluctant to award a tranche of the pay increase claiming the union were not fully committed to the modernisation agenda (www.news.bbc.co.uk/firefightersdispute2002), hence, ill feeling and distrust have prevailed.

In terms of other areas of public sector pay, Bach (2002: 331) notes 'For the third year in succession, from 1 April (2002), the government implemented in full recommendations of the pay review bodies for more than one million public-sector workers . . . Headline pay increases clustered around 3.7 per cent'. By agreeing to pay review recommendations, public sector pay is now making some gains in regard to the private sector as the government accepts that if critical recruitment and retention issues (for examples, in teaching, health and police services) are to be addressed, comparative pay issues must be addressed. A difficult area here for the current government is that of pay equality in the public sector. In 2005, after years of campaigning and negotiation, a Unison full-time organiser representing 1600 women health workers in Cumbria won a £300 million equal pay deal; the impact of this settlement has been somewhat muted as the government does not want to encourage such claims (despite a rhetoric of fairness at work). Even Unison have not taken this as a template for other test cases recognising that if this settlement were to be reflected throughout the public sector the financial and political implications would be considerable (Campbell, 2006).

Successive Labour governments, whilst investing substantially in the public sector, have certainly not abandoned their support for private sector involvement in public services (Howell, 2004). The PFI was first introduced by the Conservative Government in 1992 with the aim of securing private sector funding for public sector provision of new hospitals, prisons, schools. Essentially, private contractors construct the buildings or provide the service which the government then leases back over an agreed term (Bach and Winchester, 2003).

Stop & think

What do you understand by the term 'public private partnership' in respect of public sector provision?

Some concessions have been offered by the government to reassure public sector unions regarding private sector involvement, for example, since April 1998, NHS unions have had the right to interview prospective bidders for PFI projects on their employment practices, equal opportunities and health and safety records. Similar rights were extended to Civil Service unions in October of the same year (Unison, 1998: para. 6.3). Best-value guidelines emphasise repeatedly the need to involve staff in reviews of service provision. This falls short of explicit reference to union representation, but unions have indicated their readiness to use TUPE legislation to secure rights similar to those available in PFI contexts (Unison, 1999: para. 17).

In February 2003, however, in what the *Financial Times* described as a 'U turn', the government has made substantial concessions to the unions regarding terms and conditions of employment for private sector workers employed on local government contracts. These concessions require 'all new contractors providing services for local authorities to offer new workers such as cleaners and care workers terms and conditions "no less favourable" than those already enjoyed by colleagues transferred from the local authority to the new contractor' (Turner, 2003a). This agreement has come as a shock to the CBI who expected a rather more 'business-friendly' agreement with a voluntary code of enforcement whereas new agreements will now have to be written into forthcoming contracts. They believe this policy will make competitiveness within public private partnerships more challenging and so impede what they describe as 'public sector reform' (Turner, 2003b). However, it should be noted that in supporting this reform the government is merely undertaking a commitment which it made in 2001 to address the two-tier workforce (Labour Party, 2001). Whilst the union movement perceives this to be a very positive event, it should be noted that this agreement only applies to Local Government contracts at the moment. However, unions have already expressed the wish to see this agreement extended to cover all public private partnerships both in the future and those already in existence. This may, however, be an optimistic hope; when the equal pay claim pursued by health workers in Cumbria (see above) was settled, one of the hospitals involved, the Cumberland Infirmary was to be rebuilt through the PFI. Equal pay would certainly be unwelcome and indeed, the union organiser involved was keen to lodge a claim for it before the contract was signed aiming to thwart private involvement. However, it emerged that the government had indemnified the private investors for 15 years so the deal was able to continue (Campbell, 2006).

On a final note regarding the PFI schemes which are now well established in the prison service and to a lesser extent in health and education, recent assessments of their efficiency would suggest that the evidence regarding their value for money is by no means certain. Reports from the Institute of Public Policy Research (IPPR, 2001) and the Audit Commission (2003) raised questions about the efficacy of public private partnerships particularly regarding the provision of value for money. Whilst the IPPR were able to point to success in the Prison Service, the Audit Commission found that in schools, construction projects, 'traditional funding delivered, on average, better school buildings' (2003: 1). Although both the IPPR and the Audit Commission are supportive of PFI, they drew attention to weaknesses in provision and the need for further monitoring and reform.

Summary

Public sector workforces remain predominantly collectivised despite these substantial challenges, and continued rapid decline in other sectors of the economy means that public sector unions still constitute the core of the labour movement. Data from Kersley *et al.* (2005) indicates that there is a recognised union in almost all public sector workplaces (95 per cent), but in only a quarter (25 per cent) of private sector ones (Cully *et al.*, 1999: 92). There is some variation in union density – that is, in the proportion of the workforce in union membership. Overall density though remains markedly higher, at 61 per cent, than elsewhere in the economy. However, there is still considerable frustration with the government's determination to keep an 'arms length' attitude towards the union movement. As noted, the TUC has expressed criticism and doubt regarding the government's commitment to partnership working and the PCS has overtly expressed its intent to move away from this agenda with the intention of lobbying for the abandonment of the current outsourcing policy and a declared intention to use industrial action, if necessary, to achieve this (Turner, 2003a). Regarding the PFI, this is regarded with suspicion by trade unions in that it is perceived as quasi-privatisation. Unions are intent upon protecting terms and conditions for their members and extending protection to new employees in PFI ventures. The government appears to be supportive of this stance but will also ensure that sufficient employer freedom and flexibility persists to encourage further private sector investment.

So far, this chapter has explored the establishment of the terms and conditions of employment largely in organisations where trade unions still bargain or where they in a context still have considerable influence, such as within the public sector. However, it has been established that in the contemporary economy, most employees are no longer covered by collectively bargained agreements (Milward *et al.*, 1992; Cully *et al.*, 1999; Kersley *et al.*, 2005) The reasons underpinning this decline can be summarised thus:

- Constraint and control of the power and influence of trade unions by successive Conservative governments since 1979 hostile to the notion of collective labour organisation.

- Active derecognition strategies and support for such from Conservative administrations.

- The enactment of employment legislation to constrain and control the power of trade unions.

- The encouragement and facilitation of the exercise of management prerogative.

- Mass unemployment in the manufacturing sector, an area of traditional strength for trade unions and an expansion in the service sector, an area of traditional weakness.

- The growth of new managerial strategies such as human resource management which focused upon the individual at work and managerial prerogative.

- A move away from collective bargaining in the public sector through a shift in 'model employer' policies based on union recognition to a focus on market values and the introduction of competitive tendering whereby private sector firms took over public sector tasks and employment.

- Encouragement of self-employment and the growth of new small firms, a sector where union presence is negligible.

- The failure of trade unions to develop effective strategies to expand existing membership and to enter growth areas of the economy such as smaller firms and the private sector service.

- A focus by successive Labour governments upon creating fairness at work by creating new individual employment rights whilst remaining reluctant to expand collective union power.

This list is by no means exhaustive and greater consideration can be found in texts such as Noon and Blyton (2002), Edwards (2003) and Rose (2004). Clearly then, many contemporary employees work in organisations which do not recognise trade unions or bargained agreements so it is important to consider how the terms and conditions of employment are decided in such firms.

Establishing terms and conditions of employment in non-union organisations

The combination of the changes listed above and wider market shifts have encouraged and facilitated the growth of the non-union sector. Yet it is important to remember that even when collective bargaining coverage was at its peak in the 1970s, at least a third of the labour force were excluded from such agreements. In reality, the figure was probably greater given the tendency to ignore the small firm sector and exclude it from employment surveys prior to the late 1990s. However, it is evident that the non-union sector has grown over the last 25 years but, whilst such organisations may share their representation status, they differ in the manner this is articulated given the influence of managerial style, size, sector, markets, location etc. However, to facilitate an overview of the non-union sector, the useful distinction based upon the notion of substitutionists and suppressionists, outlined by Flood and Toner (1997), will be used as a descriptive tool whilst the particular characteristics of smaller firms will be considered separately. It is acknowledged that a crude categorisation of firms will be a blunt tool at best; as Dundon and Rollason (2004: 152) argue this leads to a tendency to 'obscure the dynamic processed within these relationships'. As such, these categories are better seen as forming ends of a continuum with differing degrees of coercion and consent evident throughout.

So, *substitutionist* strategies involve developing sophisticated policy and practice to ensure that employees will not experience either the motivation or desire to seek union recognition as a collectively bargained agreement are unlikely to improve terms and conditions. Such an approach must ensure, that for the majority of employees, terms and conditions are at the least as good as, if not better than, those in comparative firms who recognise trade unions for bargaining purposes (McLoughlin and Gourley, 1994). Clearly, the aim is to ensure that employees would not find a union presence or collective bargaining beneficial. Such firms might be described as having a 'soft' HRM style with a focus upon employee involvement, consultation and participation to ensure high performance and individual commitment to the firm. To maintain this situation, the organisation must be able to provide what are perceived as a floor of excellent terms and conditions of employment but also promote an environment which rewards individuality whilst offering effective channels for employee involvement (Dundon and Rollason, 2004).

This stance has been described as a somewhat 'pyrrhic' victory by Flood and Toner (1997) who argue that if one of the aims of non-unionism is cost containment through the avoidance of collective bargaining and collective leverage, this is unlikely to be achieved through such costly substitution policies. Given the investment required in terms of finance and management time for high reward, consultation, communication etc., the rewards do seem uncertain. However, the key strategic focus must, of course, be upon the retention of prerogative over decision making, change management, flexibility and the avoidance of disruptive collective resistance. Moreover, in the absence of unions there is a blurring of the divisions between management and employees promoting the unitarist ethos of shared focus and ambition. It might be expected that if there has been an expansion in non-union firms developing this type of substitutionist strategies to avoid recognition that there should be some evidence for an expansion in 'soft' HRM practices and policies in the UK. However, drawing on the latest WERS data, not yet available in detail, indicates that the presence of high commitment practices largely reflects that reported in the previous survey such that they are relatively rare and indeed, most frequently found in unionised firms (Cully *et al.*, 1999). Thus, it would appear that this type of 'soft' HRM, non-union organisation remains limited in the UK which suggests that most non-union firms are not pursuing these strategies.

Some non-union firms have, in the past, recognised trade unions, so rather than having a dedicated substitutionist philosophy as described above, they have achieved non-union status by other means such as overt union derecognition. Claydon (1997) notes that this process can occur incidentally, when membership density and employee support for the recognised union is low and falling to the extent that management is able to by-pass the bargaining agenda over time until it withers altogether with little union or employee resistance. Alternatively, management develop specific strategies, such as consultation and communication forums, to gradually eliminate union presence over a relatively lengthy period of time with the clear intent of by-passing and undermining the union presence. Overall, derecognition has not been extensively pursued in the UK despite the political hostility towards collective organisation and legislation enacted to facilitate the process (Rose, 2004). This is largely because as unions became weaker in the 1980s and 1990s, management have been able to narrow the bargaining agenda substantially whilst using union channels to introduce change secure in the knowledge that collective resistance would be unlikely. Hence, there have been relatively few aggressive derecognition campaigns and those which have occurred have, in fact, encouraged renewed union affiliation whilst generating poorer employment relations at a time when union influence was minimal.

Firms which have neither derecognised unions nor employed substitutionist strategies are most likely to be found in sectors where unions have been traditionally weak, such as private services or in firms which have grown during the 1980s and 1990s. Such firms are either unlikely to have considered union recognition, avoid employing or intimidate those who might pursue recognition or have been able to ignore any approaches from a relatively weak union movement. As such, these firms *suppress* moves to achieve union recognition. Within such organisations, managerial prerogative, with limited avenues for consultation and commitment are likely to dominate when imposing terms and conditions (Dundon and Rollinson, 2004) although, the recently enacted ICE legislation may curtail such prerogative to some degree.

Hence, within the non-union sector the determination of terms and conditions of employment would appear to be contingent upon a number of issues. These include the organisation's preferred management style regarding the employment relationship and the manner in which management prerogative is exercised; issues which themselves are contingent upon the firm's market position, sector, product and the perceived value of their employees. However, even where relatively extensive routes are in existence to provide employees with input to decisions over their terms of employment, as Dundon and Rollinson comment, 'these schemes were all designed and controlled by management and where employees could contribute, it is important to recognise that these contributions were on matters deemed appropriate by management' (2004: 157). In other words, management set the agenda and the boundaries for the employee voice.

It is important to note however, that in recent years, management prerogative has been somewhat constrained by employment regulation introduced by successive Labour governments and also, recognition and implementation of European regulation by such administrations. So, for example, the Employment Relations Act (1999) legislated for statutory recognition of trade unions where the necessary degree of support could be demonstrated, the Works Council Directive requires representation and consultation in multinational enterprises. Of particular relevance for this discussion will be the impact of the Information and Consultation with Employees Directive (ICE). This was transposed into legislation in April 2005 for undertakings with at least 150 people covering all undertakings with more than 50 employees by 2008 with employment calculated upon an annual average. The aim of the European Directive (2002/14/EC) is to 'establish a general framework for informing and consulting employees' and to strengthen opportunities for dialogue between management and employees. Storey (2005: 7) summarises these aspects into three categories:

1 Information on the recent and probable development of the undertakings . . . activities and economic situation.
2 Information and consultation on the situation and probable development of employment – in particular, if there is a threat to employment.
3 Information and consultation on decisions likely to lead to substantial changes in work organisation or in contractual relations.

In terms of the relevance of ICE for the non-union organisation, it should be noted that unless at least 10 per cent of employees (or a minimum of 15 and maximum of 2500) request an agreement – described as 'pulling the trigger', employers are not obliged to introduce new arrangements or amend those in existence. Consequently, for many organisations, particularly smaller firms where employees work in proximity to employers, little is likely to change. Where pre-existing agreement exists, a ballot is required to endorse that agreement which has to be a formal, written agreement extending to all employees. If a new agreement is concluded, it must meet the minimum standards laid down in ICE in order to comply with the legislation which again requires a written agreement covering all employees. It must also provide for the election or appointment of employee representatives or establish how direct information and consultation is to be provided (ACAS, 2004). Whilst ICE does offer employees the right to be informed and consulted regarding their employment conditions and indeed, makes provision for the election of employee representatives as Storey (2005: 11) argues there is, 'considerable scope for interpretation of the meaning and implications of much of this new legislation. These spaces for ambiguity are likely to be exploited'. There is, of course, the 'trigger' issue in that unless employees request a change to existing provision, no actions will be taken. Moreover, as Dundon and Rollison (2004) have noted, it is management who still set the agenda regarding how information will be disseminated; there is reference to 'a duty of cooperation' within the regulation but how the spirit of that is to be interpreted remains vague. In suppressionist organisations described above, it is difficult to envisage a full and open spirit of cooperation with elected representatives consulting freely with management. Finally, the use of the notion 'undertaking' – a public or private venture undertaking an economic activity – leaves some uncertainty regarding the level at which engagement will take place given the complexity of the contemporary organisation. Consequently, it would appear that whilst ICE will have some impact upon the opportunities for employee voice as Storey suggests, the 'outcome in the medium term . . . is that organisations will introduce a series of adjustments to current arrangements, but these will in all probability be of a "bolt-on" nature' (2005: 5).

To summarise this section, generalising cautiously, it would appear that the non-union firm sector has grown for a number of reasons. Since the 1980s, the political environment in the UK has supported a non union stance whilst market and sector shifts have made this approach increasingly likely. The manner in which non-unionism has emerged in larger enterprises has taken a number of forms; for some firms, there has been the adoption of clear substitution policies to avoid union recognition in the first instance. Given the level of political encouragement and union weakness, a relatively small number have pursued (either strategically or in an ad hoc fashion) derecognition policies with only limited resistance from unions and their members. Those firms falling outside of these categories are those which have grown in sectors where unions have not traditionally had a strong presence and they have not been able to generate an organising agenda to successfully generate a demand for recognition. For employees the consequences differ; for those working in 'high performance' firms, employment conditions will be favourable but on the basis of fulfilling high expectations in terms of productivity, loyalty and commitment. For others, their terms and conditions will depend upon the manner in which management prerogative is exercised within the constraints of the firms market and sector. However, as is noted above, the unrestrained exercise of managerial prerogative in such firms will be subject to the constraints of both national and European employment regulation which has been growing since 1997. However, the manner in which much of this regulation has been transposed into legislation in the UK will enable the employer to retain considerable control over the level and degree of impact. Having offered a brief commentary on the manner in which large non-union firms manage their employees, this is now compared and contrasted to the situation within smaller firms.

> **Activity**
>
> Make a list of advantages and disadvantages of working in a non-union firm from the perspective of the HR manager and from that of a production worker.

Establishing terms of employment in small non-union firms

There are a number of differing definitions of a 'small' firm. In 1971, the Bolton committee report referred to criteria of independence and a small market share, the Companies Act of 1985 combined turnover and employment criteria, with the EU having the most comprehensive criteria of turnover, employees and independence. In the UK, governments rely on the somewhat simplistic measure of the number of employees within the enterprise such that:

- small firm = 0–49 employees
- medium firm = 50–249 employees
- large firm = over 250 employees   (DTI, 2004)

Given the heterogeneity of the small and medium-sized firms (SME) sector, it is difficult to find a definition which adequately encompasses all relevant firms. Regardless of how the sector is defined, it is appropriate to consider small firms as a separate entity within the economy. For some time, they have been recognised as being essentially different in their approach to management, markets and business outlook from their larger counterparts; it is no longer presumed that such firms are enterprises which have merely failed to grow to corporate dimensions (Storey, 1994). As Cully *et al.* (1999: 251) remark, 'small businesses occupy a distinct part of the lexicon in academic and policy debates', they have their own associations and government representative at ministerial level. This is not to suggest that small firms can be easily studied as a single entity. A significant challenge in analysing small firm behaviour is identifying common themes and trends in a sector noted for its heterogeneity. So, any conclusions drawn and observations made must always be qualified with the same caution applied to large firms, that there will always be a substantial number of enterprises which refute established trends.

The number of small businesses in the UK economy has grown somewhat since the early 1980s, levelling out in the early 1990s (Stanworth and Purdy, 2003). As the DTI (2004) note, SMEs account for 99.8 per cent of all private sector businesses, 58 per cent of employment and 52 per cent of turnover although it should be noted that the majority of these are sole traders. It is apparent that small firms are important employers in the modern economy and so insight into how labour is managed in such firms is critical. However, until quite recently the study of employment relations in small firms had been much neglected (Marlow *et al.*, 2004). The earliest evidence pertaining to the management of people of small firms initially indicated an environment where the close proximity of owner and worker could overcome the traditional tensions between labour and capital (Goss, 1991). In the late 1960s, a number of studies portrayed employment conditions in small firms as a relative haven of peace and harmony. It was recognised that financial rewards were lower in the sector but this was more than compensated for by low levels of industrial unrest, team working with colleagues and low labour turnover (Ingham, 1970; Bolton Report, 1971). This image has since been dispelled by a number of empirical studies undertaken in the 1980s. These studies found that most small firm employees would prefer to work in larger firms, that there were higher levels of job insecurity and labour turnover and owner/manager strategies for labour control were largely authoritarian or based on benevolent autocracy (Rainnie, 1989; Goss, 1991).

More recent work which has advanced the analysis of the employment relationship in small firms recognises the complex interplay between the position of the organisation in the wider economy and the components which make up the 'black box' of the firm itself (Ram, 1994; Holliday, 1995; Moule, 1998). This case study material, gathered in the 1990s, proved to be both sensitive to market constraints whilst acknowledging how the internal dynamics within the firm led to heterogeneity within the sector. This work illustrated how owners actually managed their employees *in situ* and also, how employees experienced their work in small firms and were, in fact, able, to differing degrees, to manipulate their own labour process. Reminiscent of the classic case studies of large firms in the 1970s and 1980s (Beynon, 1979; Cockburn, 1983) studies of labour management in smaller firms echoed this approach with their intimate portrayals of how the employment relationship was constructed, changed and challenged in such firms. This work, as part of the wider evidence to analyse the complexity of employment relations in small firms which emerged in the 1990s (see also Ram, 1999; Matlay, 1999) advanced the debate by demonstrating the manner in which firm size facilitates social negotiation between employees and employers around the labour process.

These case studies have been particularly helpful in revealing the interaction between markets, firms, owners, managers and employees which then in turn, shapes the manner in which labour is managed. The findings support the notion that it is somewhat simplistic to argue that the employment relationship in small firms is determined solely by the market and so, from necessity autocracy, not harmony, dominates. It would appear that market influence is critical but equally, the particularistic social relations of production generated within a context of smallness and proximity, facilitate differentiated degrees of negotiation between employers and employees regarding the terms and conditions of employment. As such, the form and content of the employment relationship in small firms arises from the interplay of these factors rather than either one alone. A critical outcome of this more complex analysis focused around the importance of informal management approaches in small firms. In this context, informality and formality are presented as opposing constructs where the former is perceived to encompass an approach where labour management is largely emergent, flexible and loosely structured. As such, in the small firm this would appear to be an outcome from a number of factors. Of importance amongst these is the preference of owners to maintain their prerogative by managing labour personally and a reluctance to recognise trade unions. Consequently, in the absence of unions and informed professional HR management, contemporary and appropriate HR policies and practices are unlikely to be in place, and management by the uninformed facilitates and encourages the intrusion of personal idiosyncrasies and priorities (Wynarczyk, *et al.*, 1993; Marlow, 2002). In contrast, formality might usefully be described as:

> where terms and conditions of employment are formally contracted so both labour and management have recourse to a set of rules, should they feel it appropriate to use them. Moreover . . . the presence of HR professionals who can be called upon to formulate policy and apply rules and regulations facilitates a more 'arms length' or anonymous application of formality which emphasises bureaucratic rationality.
>
> (Marlow, 2002: 4)

This notion of informality in small firms is a useful construct as a general indicator of difference between the employment relationship in small and large enterprises with empirical evidence, drawn from both fine grained research (Marlow and Patton, 2002) and large surveys (Matlay, 2002) supporting this notion, whilst, of course, exception is recognised. So, for example, Cully *et al.* (1999) in the WER Survey did find that smaller firms were likely to have some formal policies in place – particularly regarding discipline issues. It is interesting to note that Marlow (2002), in a qualitative study of labour management in manufacturing firms, also found some degree of co-existence between formality and informality but upon closer analysis, found that whilst policy was in place, owners were reluctant to use it. This occurred as the close proximity between employer and employee generated a social relationship into which formality would not readily intrude. This social relationship emerged in a number of ways, some of which were highly exploitative but whether harsh or based around friendships and team working, the resort to formality was unlikely as this, in fact, professionalised the employment relationship where previously, there had been no precedent for this.

However, it is recognised that it is overly simplistic to subscribe to a dichotomy of formality and informality without recognising the dynamic nature of such constructs as noted by Ram *et al.* (2001: 846), who argued that 'informality . . . is therefore, a matter of degree and not kind' when arguing that the manner in which informality is articulated changes over time and is sensitive to context. Drawing upon a study of the impact of regulatory shock, specifically the introduction of the National Minimum Wage (NMW), Ram *et al.* argued that informality was not solely an outcome of owner prerogative but is also a necessary response to accommodating fluctuating product and labour market demands. In essence firms were combining flexibility and informality to remain viable.

So, it would appear that within all firms there is a differentiated degree of co-existence between informal and formal labour management approaches which suggests that it is too simplistic to develop an uncritical correlation between firm size and these concepts. Whilst recognising this, Marlow (2002) draws attention to the fact that within larger firms, the dynamic of control and consent is bounded by formality in that if, and when, line managers have to overtly assert authority, they have the channels by which to do so or indeed, where necessary or preferred, they can even delegate this task to the professional HR function. Equally, the recourse to formal policy and practice is available to employees or their trade union representatives should they wish to individually, or collectively, assert their rights within the employment relationship.

Empirical evidence relating to the manner in which regulatory compliance is managed by smaller firms is a good illustration of the impact of external change upon the articulation and accommodation of informality. Overall, the introduction of an increasing tranche of employment regulation has been seen to be particularly problematic for smaller firms. If, as the evidence would indicate, many such firms rely on differing degrees of informal, flexible, even idiosyncratic labour management, adopting a regulatory approach will be challenging as it is axiomatic that compliance is demonstrated by inclusion within existing, established policy. There has been considerable resistance to the regulation agenda by pressure groups representing small businesses in particular (FSB, 2000) with dire predictions made regarding the impact of increasing regulation upon the performance of the small firm sector *per se* (Oldfield, 1999). However, the empirical evidence which has emerged regarding this issue suggests that the impact of compliance has been considerably less disastrous than predicted with negative perceptions outweighing experiential effects (Blackburn and Hart, 2001: 764).

This brief overview of some of the critical developments in the literature pertaining to employment relations in small firms serves to demonstrate the growing sophistication of this analysis. Contrary to the belief of Barrett and Rainnie (2002), the literature has moved forward from the generalised dichotomy focused upon notions of 'small is beautiful' or 'bleak house scenarios'. Rather, as evidence has accumulated around analyses which delve into the nature of employment relations in small firms, knowledge has become more detailed and far more sensitive to issues of heterogeneity within the sector as well as the dynamic between these enterprises and their larger counterparts. What has emerged is an argument which suggests that the effort wage bargain is an outcome of the interaction between the external market positioning of the firm and the internal dynamics of the enterprise. Gilman *et al.* (2002: 54) usefully summarise this commenting that 'the balance between some form of negotiation and direct employer autocracy and the whip of the market is likely to be determined by employee skill, scarcity value, and the extent to which there are fraternal or familial relationships'.

Stop & think

How does a firm's size impact upon its propensity to recognise a trade union for bargaining purposes.

To summarise, although there will always be exceptions, it is apparent that establishing terms and conditions of employment in small firms is more likely to be conducted on an informal basis, focused on the individual in a framework unilaterally devised by the firm owner. For some employees, there will still be room to construct their own social relations of production and engage in mutual adjustment strategies but, for many there will be little opportunity to exercise any discretion over the manner in which they work and are rewarded. To some extent, increasing employment regulation should address these issues but this does depend upon employer awareness and observation of the legislation. As Earnshaw *et al.* (1998) found, increasing regulation and legislation is not a problem for many small owners because they simply do not know about it. In terms of the new ICE regulation which will eventually apply to firms with more than 50 employees, as noted above, the necessity of the 'trigger' mechanism is likely to prove an impediment to adoption in firms where the proximity between employers and employees dominates the social relations of production. Given the number of employees within the small firm sector, there is some cause for concern regarding the level of informality and ignorance that persists surrounding the management of labour. However, this overview must again be qualified with the recognition of heterogeneity amongst small firms such that exceptions to these generalisations will be evident throughout the sector.

Summary

- Collective bargaining has customarily been defined in Britain as the process of joint regulation of job control, undertaken by management and trade unions who negotiate to establish the terms and conditions which govern the employment relationship. Human resource management might be viewed as posing a threat to this joint process by its emphasis on the managerial dominance of the relationship which requires that employees accept a managerially derived employment agenda.

- Contemporary developments in collective bargaining in the private sector have seen a narrowing of its coverage as a result of the decline in unionisation and managerial pressure to limit its scope amongst employees. In the public sector, there have been considerable changes regarding the 'model employer' perception during the post war period. The 'golden era' associated with centralisation, trade union influence and collectivity was replaced in the 1980s with a market approach which focused far more on cost constraints in a context of privatisation and decentralisation. Since 1997, a modernising agenda has been developed to bring greater coherence between cost issues, performance elements and service provision with implications for pay-setting where emphasis is upon 'performativity' with some evident resistance from public sector employees. Whilst public private partnerships and PFI remain a feature of public sector provision, a recent change in contract conditions to challenge the 'two tier' workforce in local authorities has signalled more sympathy with the union perception of this issue and a greater focus upon quality rather than cost.

- The current Labour government promoted 'social partnerships' based on fairness, equity, information sharing, employee representation and consultation and a consensual approach to problem solving. Most trade unions and many employers have embraced the ethos of partnership but recently, the failure of these to deliver in regard to improved conditions of employment and clear avenues of information sharing has led to some discontent and indeed, disaffection from the notion by the trade union movement. In becoming a full signatory to the Maastricht agreement, the Labour government has committed the UK to the implementation of European Directives on employment but as McKay (2001) and Howell (2004) have observed, a rather dilute, weakened form of adoption would seem to be preferred by the present government adding to union cynicism regarding the desire to establish a new, strong framework of employee rights.

● There has been a significant increase in the number of organisations in the UK which have no form of union representation for employees and it would appear that there is a range of policies and practices employed to establish the terms and conditions of employment for labour in such organisations. Broadly, however, it is possible to examine this sector on the basis of firm size where larger firms would appear to adopt union substitution/suppressionist approaches, have de-recognised unions for bargaining purposes or to have grown in sectors where unions have little presence so have not engaged with recognition. Larger non-union firms have however, had their degree of prerogative bounded by employment regulation in recent years. This would not appear to be the case in small firms. Until relatively recently, there was a presumption that small businesses enjoyed harmonious industrial relations, this was based on the absence of overt conflict and a perception of greater team working due to the owner and managers close working proximity with labour. Recently, this image has been questioned with evidence suggesting that employees in many small firms have lower rewards, limited benefits and fewer prospects than that of most larger firms. It has also been revealed that agreeing terms and conditions of employment is likely to be undertaken unilaterally by owners or management upon an informal, ad hoc basis and, through a combination of ignorance and resistance, has only been marginally affected by new employment regulation.

QUESTIONS

1 What have been the major developments in British collective bargaining since 1979?

2 'Collective bargaining processes contradict the basic assumptions of the HRM approach'. Discuss.

3 Discuss the manner in which the Employment Relations Act (1999) impacted upon collective bargaining in the workplace.

4 Critically evaluate the extent to which the partnership approach would appear to be under some stress within the public sector.

5 State and comment upon the underlying reasons for the shifts in the manner in which the terms and conditions of employment have been agreed in the public sector since 1980.

6 Compare and contrast the manner in which the terms and conditions of employment are determined in small and large non-union enterprises.

EXERCISES

1 Debate the proposition that 'collective bargaining is the most appropriate channel to redress the power imbalance within the employment relationship'.

2 You are the HR director of a private firm wishing to bid for a public sector project as part of the private finance initiative. If the bid were successful, what new challenges would arise in the management of the employment relationship under such circumstances?

3 What are the major challenges facing small firm employees in achieving fair and equitable conditions of employment which observe current regulations?

4 Prepare a workshop presentation which outlines the differing types of non-union firms in the contemporary economy and the labour management strategies employed by such firms.

CASE STUDY

Fears about job destruction proved to be unfounded

Scheherazade Daneshkhu

In the run-up to the National Minimum Wage in April, 1999, there were claims that it could destroy up to 2 m jobs and lead to higher inflation and interest rates because better paid workers were likely to demand similar pay increases to their lower paid colleagues. None of these fears materialised. In a recent study of the impact of the national minimum wage, the Centre for Economic Performance at the London School of Economics concluded that 'there is no evidence of significant job losses for the workers most affected by the minimum wage and there have been no obvious knock-on effects on the wages of better-paid workers'.

The main reason why jobs were not lost, according to Alan Manning, professor of economics at the LSE, was because 'it was set at such a modest level [£3.60 an hour] that its impact has been much less than originally estimated'. He estimated that it had raised the pay of 5 to 6 per cent of workers by about 15 per cent on average. That was important for the 1.2 m to 1.3 m workers affected but was not significant for the economy as a whole.

However, since its introduction, it has increased in excess of retail price inflation each year and is set to rise to £5.35 in October 2006. This represents a 49 per cent increase in nominal terms and a rise of 14 per cent in real terms 'stripping out the effective of inflation' since 1999. The Institute for Fiscal Studies, the think-tank, says that the value of the minimum wage relative to the average hourly rate has been increasing. In 1999 the rate was equivalent to 37 per cent of the average wage in that year but by 2004 it had increased to 40 per cent of the respective average wage.

These above-inflation increases have alarmed businesses. This week, Kevin Hawkins, director-general of the British Retail Consortium, said 'ahead of tomorrow's rise in the minimum wage to £5.05' that retailers were finding it increasingly difficult to afford the minimum wage. The consortium has estimated that the rise to the current £4.85 cost retailers £1.7 bn. 'Above-inflation increases to the minimum wage are proving very difficult for both larger and smaller retailers to absorb, especially in today's tough trading conditions,' he said. The consortium wants next year's recommended level of £5.35, pledged by the Labour party, to be reviewed next autumn. Mike Brewer of the Institute for Fiscal Studies believes even though there is no clear evidence that the minimum wage has led to job losses, that could change.

'While it is possible that the proposed further increases in the minimum wage may have little effect on employment, there is the possibility of a negative effect, especially if the growth in the minimum wage continues to outpace growth in average earnings,' he wrote in a recent study. And Martin Weale, director of the National Institute of Economic and Social Research, has warned that it would be a mistake to think that just because unemployment has not risen the minimum wage has had no effect. The institute's research into Labour's New Deal to raise employment for young people suggests the programme has promoted employment but the minimum wage has reduced it. In other words, employment rates might have been higher had the minimum wage not been introduced. But Professor Manning thinks there is no question about the social benefits of the minimum wage. 'There is some pretty bad exploitation at the bottom of the labour market and the minimum wage has done something to prevent that.'

Source: Financial Times, 30 September 2005.

References and further reading

Those texts marked with an asterisk are particularly recommended for further reading.

ACAS (2004) 'Information and Consultation', www.acas.org/infoconsut/consultation.html.

Audit Commission (2003) 'Early PFI Schools Not Significantly Better, Says Audit Commission', www.audit-commission.gov.uk/reports, 30 January 2003.

*Bach, S. (2002) 'Public Sector Employment Relations Reforms under Labour: Muddling through on Modernization?', *British Journal of Industrial Relations*, 40, 2: 319–341.

Bach, S. and Winchester, D. (1994) 'Opting out of pay devolution? Prospects for local pay bargaining in the UK public services', *British Journal of Industrial Relations*, 32, 2: 82–96.

*Bach, S. and Winchester, D. (2003) 'Industrial Relations in the Public Sector' in Edwards, P. (ed.) *Industrial Relations: Theory and Practice*. Oxford: Blackwell.

Bacon, N. and Storey, J. (1996) *Individualism and Collectivism* in Ackers, P., Smith, C. and Smith, P. (1997) *The New Workplace and Trade Unionism*. London: Routledge.

Bailey, R. (1996) 'Public sector industrial relations', in Beardwell, I.J. (ed.) *Contemporary Industrial Relations: A Critical Analysis.* Oxford: Oxford University Press, pp. 121–151.

Bain Report (2002) 'The Future of the Fire Service: reducing risk, saving lives', 16 December. London: HMSO.

Barrett, R. and Rainnie, A. (2002) 'What's so special about small firms? Developing an integrated approach to analysing small firm industrial relations', *Work, Employment and Society*, 16, 3: 415–433.

Bates Report (1997) 'Review of the Private Finance Initiative', 30 October. London: HMSO.

Beaumont, P.B. (1995) *The Future of Employment Relations.* London: Sage.

Behrend, H. (1957) 'The Effort Bargain', *Industrial and Labor Relations Review*, 10, 4: 503–15.

Beynon, H. (1979) *Working for Ford.* Harmondsworth, Penguin.

Blackburn, R. and Hart, M. (2001)'Ignorance is bliss, knowledge is blight? Employment rights and small firms', Paper to the 24th ISBA National Small Firms Conference, Leicester, November.

Bolton, J.E. (1971) *Report of the Command of Inquiry on Small Firms*, Cmnd. 0811. London: HMSO.

Brown, W. (1993) 'The Contraction of Collective Bargaining in Britain', *British Journal of Industrial Relations*, 31, 2.

Cabinet Office (1999) *Modernising Government*, Cmnd. 4310. London: The Stationery Office.

Campbell, B. (2006) 'Embarrassment of Riches', *The Guardian Weekend*, 18 February, 28–31.

Chamberlain, N.W. and Kuhn, J.W. (1965) *Collective Bargaining.* New York: McGraw-Hill.

*Claydon, T. (1997) 'Union de-recognition: A Re-examination', in Beardwell, I. (ed), *Contemporary Industrial Relations: A Critical Analysis.* Oxford: Oxford University Press.

Clegg, H. (1979) *The Changing Systems of Industrial Relations in Great Britain.* Oxford: Blackwell.

Coates, K. and Topham, T. (1986) *Trade Unions and Politics.* Blackwell: Oxford.

Cockburn, C. (1983) *Brothers, Male Dominance and Technological Change.* London: Pluto.

Colling, T. (1993) 'Contracting public services: the management of CCT in two county councils', *Human Resource Management Journal*, 3, 4: 1–15.

Colling, T. (1997) 'Managing human resources in the public sector', in Beardwell, I. and Holden, L. (eds) *Human Resource Management: A Contemporary Perspective.* London: Pitman, pp. 654–679.

Colling, T. (2000) 'Personnel Management in the extended organisation', in Bach, S. and Sisson, K. (eds) *Personnel Management: A Comprehensive Guide to Theory and Practice.* Oxford: Blackwell, pp. 70–91.

Confederation of British Industry (1988) *The Structure and Processes of Pay Determination in the Private Sector: 1979–1986.* London: CBI.

Crouch, C. (1979) *The Politics of Industrial Relations.* London: Fontana.

*Cully, M., Woodland, S., O'Reilly, A. and Dix, G. (1999) *Britain at Work: As Depicted by the 1998 Workplace Employee Relations Survey.* London: Routledge.

Dearlove, J. and Saunders, P. (1984) *Introduction to British Politics.* Cambridge: Polity Press.

Department of Trade and Industry (2004) *Small and Medium Enterprise, SME – Definitions*, September. London: The Stationery Office.

Dickens, L. (2000) 'Still Wasting Resources. Equality in Employment', in Bach, S. and Sisson, K. (eds) *Personnel Management: A Comprehensive Guide to Theory and Practice.* Oxford: Blackwell, pp. 137–171.

*Dickens, L., Hall, M. and Wood, S. (2005) 'The Impact of employment legislation: reviewing the research', DTI Employment Relations Series, 45, URN 05/1257, London.

*Dickens, L. (2004) 'Problems of Fit: Changing Employment and Labour Regulation', *British Journal of Industrial Relations*, 42, 4: 595–616.

Donovan Commission (1968) *Report of the Royal Commission on Trade Unions and Employers' Associations, 1965–68*, Cmnd. 3623. London: HMSO.

Department of Trade and Industry, Small Business Service (2004) SME Statistics for the UK, 2003, www.sbs.gov.uk/content/statistics/stats2001.xls.

*Dundon, T. and Rollason, D. (2004) *Employment Relations in non-union firms.* London: Routledge.

Earnshaw, J., Goodman, J., Harrison, R. and Marchington, M. (1998) 'Industrial tribunals, workplace disciplinary procedures and employment practice', *Employment Relations Research Series 2.* London: DTI.

Edmonds, J. (1997) 'Unions and Employers, How Can Partnership Work?', in *Creating Social Partnerships.* London: Unions21.

*Edwards, P. (2003) *Industrial Relations Theory and Practice in Britain.* Oxford: Blackwell.

Elliott, R. and Duffus, K. (1996) 'What has been happening to pay in the public services sector of the economy? Developments over the period 1970–1992'. *British Journal of Industrial Relations*. 34, 1: 51–85.

Escott, K. and Whitfield, D. (1995) *The Gender Impact of Compulsory Competitive Tendering in Local Government.* Manchester: Equal Opportunities Commission.

Fairbrother, P. (1982) *Working for the State*, Studies for Trade Unionists, 8.29. London: Workers Educational Association.

Farnham, D. and Horton, S. (1995) 'The New People Management in the UK's public services: a silent revolution?', paper presented to the International Colloquium on Contemporary Development in HRM, École Supérieure de Commerce, Montpellier, France, October.

Federation of Small Business (2000) 'FSB Delivers damning "Red Tape" dossier to government', 23 May, www.fsb.org.

Flanders, A. (1968) 'Collective bargaining: a theoretical analysis', *British Journal of Industrial Relations*, 6, 1: 1–26.

Flanders, A. (1970) 'Collective bargaining: prescription for change', *Management and Unions: The Theory and Reform of Industrial Relations.* London: Faber.

*Flood, P. and Toner, B. (1997) 'Large Non-Union Companies: How Do They Avoid a Catch 22', *British Journal of Industrial Relations*, 35, 3: 257–277.

Fogarty, M. and Brooks, D. (1986) *Trade Unions and British Industrial Development.* London: Policy Studies Institute.

Fox, A. (1975) 'Collective bargaining, Flanders and the Webbs', *British Journal of Industrial Relations*, 13, 2: 151–174.

Gall and McKay, S. (1999) 'Developments in Union Recognition and Derecognition in Britain, 1994–1998', *British Journal of Industrial Relations*, 37, 4: 601–614.

Gilman, M. Edwards, P., Ram, M. and Arrowsmith, J. (2002), 'Pay Determination in small firms in the UK: the case of the response to the National Minimum Wage', *Industrial Relations Journal*, 33, 1: 52–68.

Goss, D. (1991) *Small Business and Society*. London: Routledge.

Grimshaw, D. (1999) 'Changes in skills-mix and pay determination among the nursing workforce in the UK', *Work, Employment and Society*, 13, 2: 295–328.

Guest, D. (1989) 'Personnel and HRM: can you tell the difference?', *Personnel Management*, January.

Guest, D. and Peccei, R. (1998) *The Partnership Company*. London: Involvement and Participation Association.

Hills, J. (1990) *The State of Welfare: The Welfare State in Britain since 1974*. Oxford: Clarendon Press.

Holliday, R. (1995) *Investigating Small Firms, Nice Work?* London: Routledge.

Howell, C. (2004) 'Is there a third way for Industrial Relations?', *British Journal of Industrial Relations*, 42, 1: 1–22.

Hutton, W. (1996) *The State We're in*. London: Vintage.

Hutton, W. (1997) *The State to Come*. London: Vintage.

Hyman, R. (1977) *A Marxist Introduction to Industrial Relations*. London: Macmillan.

Hyman, R. (2003) 'The Historical Evolution of British Industrial Relations', in Edwards, P. (ed.) *Industrial Relations; Theory and Practice*. Oxford: Blackwell.

Ingham, G.K. (1970) *The Size of Industrial Organisation and Worker Behaviour*. London: CUP.

Institute for Public Policy Research (IPPR) (2001) *Building Better Partnerships*. London: IPPR.

Kelly, J. (1996) 'Union Militancy and Social Partnership', in Kelly, J. (1998) *Rethinking Industrial Relations*. London: Routledge.

*Kersley, B., Alpin, C., Forth, J., Bryson, A., Bailey, H., Dix, G. and Oxenbridge, S. (2005) 'Inside the Workplace; First findings from the 2004 Workplace Employment Relations Survey'. DTI; URN 05/1057. London: Institute of Public Policy Research.

Kessler, I. (1991) 'Workplace industrial relations in local government', *Employee Relations*, special issue, 13, 2: complete issue.

Kinnie, N. (1990) 'The decentralisation of industrial relations? Recent research considered', *Personnel Review*, 19, 3.

Labour Party (2001) *Ambitions for Britain: Labour's Manifesto 2001*. London: The Labour Party.

*Legge, K. (1995) *HRM: Rhetoric and Realities*. London: Routledge.

Mabey, C. and Salamon, G. (1995) *Strategic Human Resource Management*. Oxford: Blackwell.

Makinson, J. (2000) *Incentives for Change: Rewarding performance in National Government Networks*. London: The Stationery Office.

Marlow, S. (2000) 'People in the small firm' in *Enterprise and Small Business: Principles, Policy and Practice*. London: Addison Wesley.

*Marlow, S. (2002) 'Managing Labour in Smaller Firms', *Human Resource Management Journal*, 12, 2: 26–47.

Marlow, S. and Gray, C. (2005) 'Information and Consultation in small and medium sized enterprises', in Storey, J. (2005), *Adding value through information and consultation*. London: Palgrave.

Marlow, S. and Patton, D. (2002) 'Minding the Gap: managing the employment relationship in smaller firms'. *Employee Relations*, 24, 5.

*Marlow, S., Patton, D. and Ram, M. (2004) (eds) *Managing Labour in Small Firms*. London: Routledge.

Martinez-Lucio, M. and Stuart, M. (2005) 'Partnership and new industrial relations in a risk society', *Work, Employment and Society*, 19, 4: 797–817.

Matlay, H. (1999) 'Employee Relations in small firms: A micro-business perspective', *Employee Relations*, 21, 3: 285–295.

Matlay, H. (2002) 'Industrial Relations in the SME sector of the British economy: An empirical perspective', *Journal of Small Business and Enterprise Development*, 9, 3: 307–319.

*McIlroy, J. (1998) 'The Enduring Alliance: Trade Unions and the Making of New Labour, 1994–1997', *British Journal of Industrial Relations*, 36, 4: 537–564.

*McKay, S. (2001) 'Between flexibility and regulation: rights, protection and equality at work', *British Journal of Industrial Relations*, 39, 3: 285–303.

McLoughlin, I. and Gourlay, S. (1994) *Enterprise Without Unions: Industrial Relations in the Non-Union Firm*. Buckingham: Open University Press.

Milner, S. (1993) 'Dispute deterrence: Evidence on final offer arbitration', in Metcalf, D. and Milner, S. (1993) *New Perspectives on Industrial Disputes*. London: Routledge.

Millward, N., Steven, M., Smart, D. and Hawes, W.R. (1992) *Workplace Industrial Relations in Transition*. Aldershot: Dartmouth.

Mishel, L. and Voos, P.B. (eds) (1992) *Unions and Economic Competitiveness*. New York: Sharpe.

Monks, J. (1996) 'Interview: John Monks', *New Statesman*, 6 September.

Moule, M. (1998) 'Regulation of Work in Small Firms: A View from the Inside', *Work, Employment and Society*, 12, 4: 635–653.

Napier, B. (1993) *CCT, Market Testing and Employment Rights: The Effects of TUPE and the Acquired Rights Directive*. London: Institute of Employment Rights.

NHS Executive (1999) *Agenda for Change: Modernising the NHS Pay System. Joint Framework of Principles and Agreed Statement on the Way Forward*. Health Service Circular 1999/227.

Nichols, T. and Beynon, H. (1977) *Living with Capitalism: Class Relations and the Modern Factory*. London: Routledge and Kegan Paul.

Nolan, P. and O'Donnell, K. (2003) 'Industrial Relations and Productivity', in Edwards, P. (ed.) *Industrial Relations Theory and Practice in Britain*. Oxford: Blackwell.

Noon, M. and Blyton, P. (2002) *The Realities of Work*. London: Palgrave.

Oldfield, C. (1999) 'Red Tape is Strangling Enterprise', *Sunday Times*, 31 October, p. 7.

Pendleton, A. and Winterton, J. (1993) 'Public enterprise industrial relations in context', in Pendleton, A. and Winterton, J. (eds) *Public Enterprise in Transition*. London: Routledge.

Peston, R. and Timmins, N. (1999) 'Brown to boost NHS and schools', *Financial Times*, 13 July, p. 1.

Pollert, A. (1988) 'Dismantling flexibility', *Capital and Class*, 34, Spring: 42–75.

Pratchett, L. and Wingfield, M. (1995) *Reforming the Public Service Ethos in Local Government: A New Institutional Perspective*, Leicester Business School Occasional Paper 27. Leicester: De Montfort University.

Rainnie, A. (1989) *Industrial Relations in Small Firms*. London: Routledge.

Ram, M. (1994) *Managing to Survive*. London: Routledge.

Ram, M. (1999) 'Managing Autonomy: Employment Relations in Small Professional Service Firms', *International Small Business Journal*, 17, 2.

*Ram, M., Edwards, P. Gilman, M. and Arrowsmith, J. (2001) 'The dynamics of informality: employment relations in small firms and the effects of regulatory change', *Work, Employment and Society*, 15, 4: 845–861.

Ram, M. and Edwards, P. (2003) 'Praising Caesar not burying him: What we know about employment relations in small firms', *Work, Employment and Society*, 17, 4: 719–730.

Roche, W. and Geary, J. (2002) 'Advocates, Critics and Union involvement in Workplace Partnerships: Irish Airports', *British Journal of Industrial Relations*. 40, 4: 659–689.

*Rose, E. (2004) *Employment Relations*. London: Prentice Hall.

Salamon, M. (1992) *Industrial Relations, Theory and Practice*. Englewood Cliffs, NJ: Prentice Hall.

Singh, R. (1986) 'Final offer: arbitration in theory and practice', *Industrial Relations Journal*, Winter: 329–330.

Sisson, K. (1987) *The Management of Collective Bargaining, An International Comparison*. Oxford: Blackwell.

Sisson, K. (1993) 'In search of HRM', *British Journal of Industrial Relations*, 31, 2.

Stanworth, J. and Purdy, D. (2003) *SME Facts and Figures*, Report to the All-Party Parliamentary Small Business Group, Westminster.

Storey, D.J. (1994) *Understanding the small business sector*. London: Routledge.

Storey, J. (1992) *Developments in the Management of Human Resources*. Oxford: Blackwell.

Storey, J. (1995) (ed.) *HRM A Critical Text*. London: Routledge.

Storey, J. (2005) (ed.) *Adding value through information and consultation*. London: Palgrave.

Thornley, C. (1994) 'Nursing pay policy: chaos in context', paper presented to Employment Research Unit Annual Conference, Cardiff Business School, September.

Timmins, N. (2000) 'PRP: Team bonuses for civil servants'. *Financial Times*, 12 February, p. 11.

Towers, B. (1997) *The Representation Gap: Change and Reform in the British and American Workplace*. Oxford: Oxford University Press.

Turner, D. (2003a) 'CBI attacks misguided employment proposals', *Financial Times*, 28 January.

Turner, D. (2003b) 'Union chief to campaign on privatised services', *Financial Times*, 29 January.

Unison (1998) *A Step by Step Guide to the PFI Process*. London: Unison.

Unison (1999) *Unison's Response to Implementing Best Value: A Consultation Paper on Draft Guidance*. London: Unison.

Walton, R.E. and McKersie, R.B. (1965) *A Behavioural Theory of Labor Negotiations*. New York: McGraw-Hill.

Webb, S. and Webb, B. (1902) *Industrial Democracy*. London: Longman.

White, G. (1994) 'Public sector pay: decentralisation versus control', paper to Employment Research Unit Annual Conference, The Contract State: The Future of Public Management, September.

Winchester, D. (1983) 'The public sector', in Bain, G.S. (ed.) *Industrial Relations in Britain*. Oxford: Blackwell, pp. 155–179.

Winchester, D. (1996) 'The regulation of public services pay in the united Kingdom', paper to the Industrial Relations in the European Community (IREC) Network Annual Conference, Industrial Relations in Europe: Convergence or Diversification? University of Copenhagen: FAOS.

Wynarczyk, P., Storey, D., Shot, H. and Keasey, K. (1993) *The Managerial Labour Markets in Small Firms*. London: Routledge.

For multiple-choice questions, exercises and annotated weblinks specific to this chapter visit the book's website at **www.pearsoned.co.uk/beardwell**

Chapter 13

Reward and performance management

Alan J. Ryan and Julia Pointon

Objectives

- To present the historical and theoretical foundations of reward and performance management strategies.
- To consider and evaluate the issues concerned in designing performance management and reward systems.
- To critically assess the objectives of various reward systems.
- To analyse theories of motivation in the context of performance management.
- To consider the psychological contract in the context of the employment relationship.
- To discuss the interactive links between current trends in human resource management and performance management.

Introduction

This chapter demonstrates the level to which human resource management has developed existing theoretical and practical issues surrounding the management of labour performance within modern organisations. A central element of these debates is the management of reward structures, strategies and systems. In this chapter we introduce the concept of reward(s) as a core function in the development of a strategic role for HR functionaries and offer some explanation of the objectives of current links to performance management.

The often heard comment across many organisations runs along the lines of 'There's only one reason we come here – the money'. Unsurprisingly, these comments reflect the nature of the employment relationship as a reward/effort bargain (Chapters 11 and 12). Whether openly, covertly, personally or collectively, we all become involved in the resolution of this bargain at some time during our working life. This chapter discusses how management have attempted to resolve their problem of converting the labour potential, obtained by their transactions in the labour market, into the labour performance they desire; i.e., securing the required effort levels without rewarding at levels detrimental to the generation of sufficient profit. In this sense we view reward as a core function for HR managers and rewards as composed of more than the mere 'notes' in the pay packet.

The development of reward systems

As a separate management concern the issue of reward systems is fairly recent, indeed reward management has often been viewed as the 'poor relation' of HRM concerned with 'systems, figures and procedures'. During the development of a 'factory'-based economy, owners found that they were unable to control the 'effort' side of the bargain effectively. Workers, who were previously self-controlled and motivated in many respects by subsistence, worked in small 'cottage' industries within which the product of their labour was owned by the producers (workers themselves; notably in regard to the skilled artisans) and they worked as hard as necessary in order to meet their subsistence needs. As Anthony suggests, 'A great deal of the ideology of work is directed at getting men [sic] to take work seriously when they know that it is a joke' (1977: 5). Owners found that getting workers to keep regular hours and to commit the effort owners considered to constitute 'a fair day's work' was problematic. In response to this dilemma they employed the 'butty' system of reward management. Under this system owners committed a specific level of investment to a selected group of workers (normally skilled artisans) who then hired labour on 'spot contracts' by the day. The major problem for the owners with this system was that these 'subcontractors' had control over the effort/reward bargain and were able to enrich themselves at the expense of the owners. The owners enjoyed little or no control over the process of production so the system was economically inefficient and failed to deliver the returns (rents/profits) required or more importantly that were possible from the process of industrialisation.

From this group of 'favoured' workers, along with the introduction of some university graduates there grew a new management cadre. This was a slow process, as Gospel notes that generally, in UK industry, this group (management, technical and clerical) amounted to only 8.6 per cent of the workforce in most manufacturing organisations (1992: 17), within which development was uneven and patchy. These changes did little to address the problems associated with the effort/reward bargain, meaning productivity was below optimum levels. In part the problem was generated by the fact that 'the managers' brain was still under the workers' cap', more precisely that these managers rarely possessed the skills or knowledge of the production process held by the workers. This led to lower than optimum levels of production and reduced profits, a system F.W. Taylor described as 'Systematic Soldiering'. This activity was engaged in by workers, according to Taylor, 'with the deliberate object of keeping their employers ignorant of how fast work can be done' (Taylor, 1964). From his observations Taylor took the view that workers acting in this manner were merely behaving as 'economically rational actors' desiring their own best interests. It was clear therefore that management needed to take the reins of the production process and assert their right to determine the outcome of the wage/effort bargain. Taylor, as the so-called 'father of Scientific Management', developed a system of measuring work which assisted the process of reclaiming managerial rights. Jobs were broken down into specific elements which could then be timed and rated, whilst in the process, returning the determination of the speed of work to management and allowing for the development of pay systems which reflected, however crudely, performance. This scientific system devised by Taylor became the basis of countless pay systems operating effectively alongside the routinisation and deskilling of work which is often associated with Scientific Management within the literature (see, for example, Braverman, 1974; Burawoy, 1985; Hill, 1981; Littler, 1982, 1985; Thompson, 1983; and Wood, 1982). Whilst this allowed management to reassert their control over the level of outputs, to relocate the managers' brain under their own hats and hence the determination of the wage/effort bargain, it did generate problems in relation to managerial attempts to convince workers to take work seriously. In straightforward terms we can suggest that the 'Measured-Work' techniques advocated by adherents of Taylorism further separated conception from execution and led to feelings of alienation. Alienation can be defined as 'various social or psychological evils which are characterised by a harmful separation, disruption or fragmentation which sunders things that properly belong together' (Wood, 2000); in our terms that means the separation of workers from that which they produce. Blauner (1964) argued that such an objective state is created as an offshoot of the subjective feelings of separation which workers experience under modern production systems. These feelings and their outcomes can be briefly outlined in the following manner:

- Powerlessness – the inability to exert control over work processes.

- Meaninglessness – the lack of a sense of purpose as employees only concentrated on a narrowly defined and repetitive task and therefore could not relate their role to the overall production process and end product.

- 'Self-estrangement' – the failure to become involved in work as a mode of self-expression.

- Isolation – the lack of sense of belonging.   *Source*: Adapted from Blauner (1964)

Although Scientific Management originated at the beginning of the twentieth century, its legacy has lived on in many areas. Similar experiences have been reported in the design of work in service industries and call centres (Ritzer, 1997, 2000; Taylor and Bain, 1999; Taylor and Bain, 1999; Callaghan and Thompson, 2001). The solution to this problem has been sought, following Taylor's notion of man as an economic actor (see below), by the introduction of various performance and reward systems and mechanisms, the core objectives of which were originally to operationalise effective control over the wage/effort bargain and later with current systems to alleviate the feelings of alienation and generate commitment to organisational goals.

Design and debates

Whilst this section discusses reward systems in a manner which appears to offer a chronological explanation, we should note that the development of 'new' systems does not indicate the total removal of other mechanisms; indeed in many organisations we find that both 'old' and 'new' pay systems operate in tandem, delivering control on different levels for various groups of workers.

In terms of the types of reward mechanism applied we can note the application of a number of different mechanisms based on 'time worked'. Time rates are mechanisms whereby reward is related to the number of hours worked and are often applied to manual workers in the form of hourly rates and non-manual workers by the application of monthly or annual salaries. A criticism of these mechanisms is that they are often related to historic rather than current value, and can result in discrimination, demarcation disputes and a sense of injustice.

Time-related mechanisms are often based on the notion of a pay spine in which groups of skills are banded. Although widely applied in their heyday, basic versions of these instruments are poor in terms of relating wage to current effort; often rewarding effort which has been applied externally (gaining a recognised skill) and are inappropriate to current tasks. The advantages of these systems are that management can control wage costs by limiting the access to various grades on the spine, can limit the range of the grade (say, 4 per cent top to bottom) and can demonstrate they are fair in relation to agreed procedures. The problems created are not necessarily with the pay spine system *per se* but with the manner in which skills relating to specific grades are defined; solutions must then address the structure, strategy and rationale of the reward system rather than the application of such mechanisms.

Conboy (1976) noted that the key advantage of these instruments is that both parties have a clear idea of the 'wage' element of the bargain. For management the problem is that these mechanisms do not give any clear indication of the 'effort' element of the bargain. This led to time rate instruments being complicated by the addition of 'performance' elements, often in the

| Figure 13.1 | The traditional form of time rate instruments |

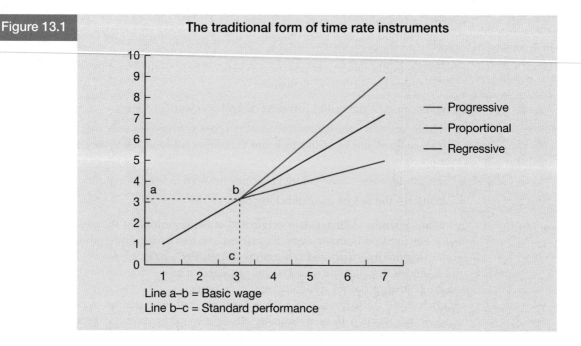

Line a–b = Basic wage
Line b–c = Standard performance

form of 'piece-rates' or other complex 'bonus' calculations in an attempt to determine acceptable effort levels (e.g. Predetermined Motion Time Systems and Measured-Day-Work). The traditional form of such schemes can be demonstrated using the diagram shown in Figure 13.1.

Many schemes give guaranteed basic earnings which are then supplemented in ways which we can class as proportional (wages increase in direct relationship to output), progressive (wages increase more than output) or regressive (wages increase at a slower rate than output).

An important element in this discussion regards the manner in which the 'base' element is decided. We have become familiar with the notion of a National Minimum Wage, which sets the minimum rate for specified groups; outwith this scheme, organisations need some mechanisms by which to assign values to various roles within the organisation. Traditional mechanisms (and in a slightly modified manner 'new pay' systems) have related to job evaluation schemes. A job evaluation scheme operates by allocating values to each of a series of elements (e.g. skill or responsibility) and then measuring each 'job' in order to arrive at an agreed 'score'. The scores are then placed on the pay spine in relation to accepted criteria. These criteria will be formed by the interaction of two sets of relativities. Scores will need to reflect 'external relativities', by which we mean the situation that appears to hold in relation to external markets and environmental conditions, and 'internal relativities', meaning an appearance of fairness in relation to other jobs/roles within the organisation. In the basic form these schemes introduce us to the notion of reward packages under which different elements can be rewarded in various ways. However, these schemes fell out of favour in some respects because they are seen to 'pay-the-job' rather than 'pay-the-worker', and as such were difficult to relate to individual performance.

This is clearly the simplest form of wage payment system, easily understood by both parties; it allows the development of 'overtime' payments for work completed in addition to the contracted hours in any given period and formed the basis of the creation of systems classed as payment by results (PBR).

We can conclude then that such payment by results systems, whilst originally crude, developed alongside the more extensive division of labour achieved by the increasing use and application of technology, ergonomics (pseudo-scientific work measurement) and mechanical production methods. These early techniques can be easily applied to such divided work because of four basic characteristics of such work (adapted from Conboy, 1976):

- short job cycles;
- high manual content (which, using sophisticated ergonomic processes, can be measured);
- batch production (with repeated orders/processes);
- no marked fluctuations in required outputs.

The simplistic assumptions underlying these and other PBR systems are twofold. Firstly, workers are motivated to increase performance (work harder) by money, and secondly, any increases in output will result in equivalent increases in wages. The schemes are intended to be self-financing and designed to reduce 'wasteful activity' in that they can be used to redesign the labour process. Whilst such schemes now enjoy less popularity than they have in previous decades, there is still evidence that they are used in relation to specific groups of workers.

Stop & think

To what extent do you think such wage systems reflect management's inability to clearly determine the 'effort' of the bargain?

Table 13.1 shows that while there has been an overall decline in the application of PBR techniques, the decline is not as marked as some proponents of 'new pay' (see below) would argue. The heart of this debate suggests that such schemes can be seen as various techniques designed to act upon worker motivation and as such provide incentives for an individual to reassess the wage/effort bargain.

Table 13.1 Percentage of employees receiving PBR

Class of worker	1993	1995	1997
Manual	29.6	28	24
Non-manual	13.9	14.5	12
All	19.4	19.3	16.1

Source: New Earnings Surveys (1993–1997).

In order to assess the effectiveness, validity and reliability of such arguments we need to consider the underlying assumptions in a little more detail.

Motivation as a mechanism

Early in the new millennium, Miner (2003: 29) concluded that motivation continues to hold a significant position in the eyes of scholars. 'If one wishes to create a highly valid theory, which is also constructed with the purpose of enhanced usefulness in practice in mind, it would be best to look to motivation theories . . . for an appropriate model.'

But, what is 'motivation' and how do we understand it in the context of work? At a very basic level it is characterised by a certain level of willingness on the part of the employee to increase their effort, to the extent that this exertion also satisfies a predefined need or desire they hold. It is therefore all about individual behaviours directed towards realising a goal, it is about 'motives' and 'needs'. In slightly more detail, work motivation is often considered as a set of energetic forces that originate both within as well as beyond an individual's being, to initiate work-related behaviour and to determine its form, direction, intensity, and duration (Pinder, 1998: 11). Thus, motivation can be understood as a psychological process resulting from the interaction between the individual and the environment. Understanding work motivation in this way draws attention to the fact that it will probably vary from individual to individual and over time. In addition, because it is based on needs and motives that alter over time, and on an interaction with the environment, which will also change, the dynamic process is subject to constant reconfiguration.

To summarise, motivation can be regarded as:

- an individual phenomenon – people are unique, and this means that motivation theories usually allow for uniqueness to be reflected in individual behaviour;
- intentional and results in behaviours that are the result of conscious choices;
- a multifaceted concept, which involves (a) factors that arouse people to action (b) choice of behaviour and (c) choices abut the persistency and intensity of behaviour;
- valid as a theory because it helps predict behaviour by explaining what prompts the behaviour of people, which means that it has very little concern with simply describing or categorising behaviour.

Since the level of employee motivation influences productivity, organisations generally and managers and line managers in particular need to understand what motivates employees to reach peak performance. It is not an easy task to increase employee motivation because employees respond in different ways to their jobs and their organisation's practices. Factors that affect work motivation include individual differences, job characteristics and organisational practices. Individual differences are the personal needs, values, attitudes, interests and abilities that people bring to their jobs. Job characteristics are the aspects of the position that determine its limitations and challenges. Organisational practices are the rules, human resources policies, managerial practices, and rewards systems of an organisation. An understanding of work motivation is important in the context of performance management and the development of reward strategies for a number of reasons:

First, it enables organisations to 'humanise' work for employees so that work is inherently more satisfying, the assumption being that organisations have a responsibility to try to provide work that is meaningful, satisfying and as enjoyable as possible.

Second, an appropriate understanding of work motivation allows organisations to make the jobs more satisfying for employees within the company. The underlying assumption is clearly that if employees are happier at work then they will be more productive.

Third, such an understanding enables management to control the behaviour of subordinates more effectively and therefore enables management to 'pull the right strings' in order to achieve organisational goals.

Stop & think

To what extent and why do you agree with the suggestion that organisations have a responsibility to try to provide work that is meaningful, satisfying and as enjoyable as possible?

The theory of motivation has a long history and continues to evolve as we understand more about employees and work. Essentially, there are two main approaches to motivation theory: content and process theories.

Content theory of motivation

Content (or need) theories of motivation focus on factors internal to the individual that energise and direct behaviour. In general, such theories regard motivation as the product of internal drives that compel an individual to act or move (hence, 'motivate') toward the satisfaction of individual needs. Major content theories of motivation are Maslow's hierarchy of needs, Alderfer's ERG theory, Herzberg's motivator-hygiene theory, and McClelland's learned needs or three-needs theory.

Key features from each of the main theories will be considered in the next part of this chapter.

Maslow's hierarchy of needs

This is probably one of the best known. He first presented the five-tier hierarchy in 1942 to a psychoanalytic society and published it in 1954 in *Motivation and Personality* (New York: Harper and Row). His theory identifies five levels of needs (see Figure 13.2), which are best seen as a hierarchy with the most basic need emerging first and the most sophisticated need last. People move up the hierarchy one level at a time. Gratified needs lose their strength and the next level of needs is activated. As basic or lower-level needs are satisfied, higher-level needs become operative. A satisfied need is not a motivator. The most powerful employee need is the one that has not been satisfied.

- *Level I* – Physiological needs are the most basic human needs. They include food, water, and comfort. The organisation helps to satisfy employees' physiological needs by providing a financial reward – pay!

- *Level II* – Safety needs are the desires for security and stability, to feel safe from harm. The organisation helps to satisfy employees' safety needs by benefits.

- *Level III* – Social needs are the desires for affiliation. They include friendship and belonging. The organisation helps to satisfy employees' social needs through sports teams, parties and celebrations. The supervisor can help fulfil social needs by showing direct care and concern for employees.

- *Level IV* – Esteem needs are the desires for self-respect and respect or recognition from others. The organisation helps to satisfy employees' esteem needs by matching the skills and abilities of the employee to the job. The supervisor can help fulfil esteem needs by showing workers that their work is appreciated.

- *Level V* – Self-actualisation needs are the desires for self-fulfilment and the realisation of the individual's full potential. The supervisor can help fulfil self-actualisation needs by assigning tasks that challenge employees' minds while drawing on their aptitude and training.

The theory, especially in relation to reward and performance management, has an uncomplicated appeal because its message is clear – find out what motivates your employees at each of the levels and, more importantly still, at which level each employee is operating, and develop a reward strategy accordingly. However, evaluations have revealed a number of significant flaws that suggest that 'needs' do not always group together in the ways predicted. From this follows the proposition that the theories are unable to predict when a particular need will be manifest because there is no clear relationship between needs and behaviour, so that, for example, the

Figure 13.2

Maslow's hierarchy of needs

Self-actualisation needs

Social needs

Esteem needs

Safety needs

Physiological needs

Source: http://ollie.dcccd.edu.

same behaviour could reflect different needs, and different needs the same behaviour. This criticism is further developed as we note that 'needs' are generally imprecisely defined in part due to the notion of need as a biological phenomenon being problematic. Applications of the hierarchy of needs to management and the workplace are obvious. According to the implications of the hierarchy, individuals must have their lower level needs met by, for example, safe working conditions, adequate pay to take care of one's self and one's family, and job security before they will be motivated by increased job responsibilities, status, and challenging work assignments. Despite the ease of application of this theory to a work setting, it has received little research support and therefore is not very useful in practice.

Despite these limitations, Maslow's thinking remains influential and continues to influence management deliberations in respect of job design, pay and reward structures. Huczynski and Buchanan (2001: 242) highlight this stating: 'Many subsequent management fashions, such as job enrichment, total quality management, business process re-engineering, self-managing teams, the "new leadership" and employee empowerment incorporated his ideas in the search for practical motivational methods'.

Stop & think

To what extent do you consider the achievement of self-actualisation to be a realistic possibility?

Alderfer's ERG theory

The ERG theory is an extension of Maslow's hierarchy of needs. Alderfer suggested that needs could be classified into three categories, rather than five. These three types of needs are Existence, Relatedness, and Growth. Existence needs are similar to Maslow's physiological and safety needs categories. Relatedness needs involve interpersonal relationships and are comparable to aspects of Maslow's belongingness and esteem needs. Growth needs are those related to the attainment of one's potential and are associated with Maslow's esteem and self-actualisation needs.

The ERG theory differs from the hierarchy of needs in that it does not suggest that lower-level needs must be completely satisfied before upper-level needs become motivational. ERG theory also suggests that if an individual is continually unable to meet upper-level needs that the person will regress and lower-level needs become the major determinants of their motivation. The ERG theory's implications for managers are similar to those for the needs hierarchy: managers should focus on meeting employees' existence, relatedness, and growth needs, though without necessarily applying the proviso that, say, job-safety concerns necessarily take precedence over challenging and fulfilling job requirements.

Herzberg's motivator–hygiene theory

Frederick Herzberg developed the motivator–hygiene theory. This theory is closely related to Maslow's hierarchy of needs but relates more specifically to how individuals are motivated in the workplace. Based on his research, Herzberg identified two factors central to our understanding of motivation:

1 *Motivators*. These were such things as 'a sense of achievement', 'an opportunity for personal growth', 'the sense of having done a job well', 'having responsibility', and 'achieving recognition for your work'.
2 *Hygiene* factors. These included such things as money, working conditions, job security, company policies, the quality of supervision and interpersonal relationships at work.

Herzberg argued that meeting the lower-level needs (hygiene factors) of individuals would not motivate them to exert effort, but would only prevent them from being dissatisfied. Only if higher-level needs (motivators) were met would individuals be motivated. For Herzberg therefore, the opposite of satisfaction is not dissatisfaction, it is merely no satisfaction and equally, the opposite of dissatisfaction is not necessarily satisfaction, simply no dissatisfaction. The implication for managers of the motivator–hygiene theory is that meeting employees lower-level needs by improving pay, benefits, safety, and other job-contextual factors will prevent employees from becoming actively dissatisfied but will probably not motivate them to exert additional effort toward achieving peak performance. To motivate workers, managers must focus on changing the intrinsic nature and content of jobs themselves by 'enriching' them to increase employees' autonomy and their opportunities to take on additional responsibility, gain recognition, and develop their skills and careers.

Bassett Jones and Lloyd (2004) undertook research to determine if Herzberg's two factor theory of motivation was still relevant. The results, derived from a survey of over 3200 responses, indicated that money and recognition do not appear to be primary sources of motivation. In line with Herzberg's predictions, factors associated with intrinsic satisfaction play a more important part. They concluded that, despite the criticism, Herzberg's two-factor theory still has utility nearly 50 years after it was first developed.

McClelland's learned needs theory

McClelland's theory suggests that individuals learn needs from their culture. The three primary needs are first, the need for affiliation (n Aff), characterised as a desire to establish social relationships with others. Second, the need for power (n Pow) reflects a desire to control one's environment and influence others. Finally the need for achievement (n Ach) is associated with a desire to take responsibility, set challenging goals, and obtain performance feedback. The main point of the learned needs theory is that when one of these needs is strong in a person, it has the potential to motivate behaviour that leads to its satisfaction. The implication for managers is they should develop an understanding of whether and to what degree their employees have one or more of these needs, and the extent to which their jobs can be structured to satisfy them.

Criticisms of content theories

There are two observations of content or needs theories that are worth highlighting.

First, at the heart of these theories lies the suggestion that there is a single factor – money, social needs or psychological growth that motivates behavior. The implication is that if managers can identify the key motivational factor and reinforce it, then an employee will 'naturally' be motivated. The reality is that for most employees motivation will be a messy and complicated relationship between a number of factors that are difficult to separate out or identify individually.

Second, content theories also assume that the task of any reward and performance management system is to identify standard motivational strategies that can be applied in any context (e.g. all jobs can be rationalised, redesigned or enriched). But as it is difficult to predict when certain needs become important, we can argue that the application of 'standardised' solutions is neither possible or desirable. It is clear that as the different needs are very difficult to isolate, define or describe and further, that any suggestion that needs have a biological origin is problematic, performance management involves issues to which there is no 'off the shelf' one-size-fits-all response.

Process theories of motivation

Process (or cognitive) theories of motivation focus on conscious human decision making as a process which helps explain motivation. The process theories are concerned with determining how individual behaviour is energised, directed, and maintained. Process theories of motivation are based on early cognitive theories, which hold that behaviour is the result of conscious decision-making processes. The major process theories of motivation are expectancy theory, equity theory, goal-setting theory and reinforcement theory.

Vroom's expectancy theory

In the early 1960s, Victor Vroom applied concepts of behavioural research conducted in the 1930s by Kurt Lewin and Edward Tolman directly to work motivation. Vroom suggested that individuals choose work behaviours they believe will result in the achievement of specific outcomes they value. In deciding how much effort to put into work behaviour, individuals are likely to consider:

- Valence, which is the extent to which the expected outcome is attractive or unattractive.
- Instrumentality, or the degree to which they believe that a given level of performance will result in the certain achievement of the outcome or desired rewards.
- Expectancy, meaning the degree to which the employee believes that putting in effort will lead to a given level of performance – Is the type of effort appropriate to achieving the goal?

All three of these factors, often referred to as 'VIE', are considered to influence motivation in a combined manner. Thus, for an individual to be highly motivated, all three of the components of the expectancy model must be present. If even one of these is zero (e.g., instrumentality and valence are high, but expectancy is completely absent), the employee will not be motivated. Managers therefore need to attempt to ensure that their employees believe that increased effort will improve performance and that performance will lead to valued rewards.

In the late 1960s, Porter and Lawler published an extension of the Vroom expectancy model, which is known as the Porter–Lawler expectancy model or simply the Porter–Lawler model. Although the basic premise of the Porter–Lawler model is the same as for Vroom's model, the Porter–Lawler model is more complex in a number of ways. It suggests that increased effort does not automatically lead to improved performance because individuals may not possess the necessary abilities needed to achieve high levels of performance, or because they may have an inadequate or vague perception of how to perform necessary tasks. Without an understanding of how to direct effort effectively, individuals may exert considerable effort without a corresponding increase in performance.

There are criticisms of expectancy theory that argue that the theory attempts to predict a choice of effort. However, because no clear specification of the meaning of effort exists, the variables cannot be measured adequately. As a process theory, it does not specify the outcomes relevant to a particular individual situation and therefore offers little guidance to the human resource manager seeking to design a performance management and reward system as there is an implicit assumption that all motivation is conscious. The employee is assumed to consciously calculate the pleasure or pain that he/she expects to attain or avoid and then a choice is made.

Equity theory

The equity theory of motivation is based on the principle that since there are no absolute criteria for fairness, employees generally assess fairness by making comparisons with others in similar situations. Therefore, motivation to put effort into a task will be influenced by perception of whether the rewards are fair in comparison to those received by others. To assess fairness an employee is likely to make a comparison between the level of inputs and outputs they are making compared to the level of input and output they consider the comparator to be making. Inputs are often multiple and consist of things an employee may bring to the task – education, previous experience, effort. Outputs are the rewards for the inputs – salary, performance related pay, praise. Inputs are essentially costs while the outputs are the benefits. If, following the subjective comparison, a feeling of inequity prevails, it can give rise to tensions and feelings of psychological discomfort. This may result in a desire to 'do something about it' and take action designed to lessen the tension being experienced. Adams (1965) suggests that there are six basic options available to an employee (adapted from Rollinson, 2002: 235):

- Modify inputs.
- Seek to modify outputs.
- Modify perception of self.

- Modify perception of comparator.
- Change comparator.
- Leave the situation.

Adams (1963) suggests that adopting one or a combination of the options may result in a feeling of restored balance or equity resulting in the employee accepting the situation.

This theory is straightforward and easy to understand, however, it can not cover every contingency. For example, some employees are far more sensitive to perceptions of inequity than others. There is some evidence to suggest that even where inequity is perceived to exist, employees have some tolerance providing the reasons for the inequity are explained and justified.

This has two major implications for managers when designing performance management and reward schemes.

First, it is important to be aware that employees will make comparisons; further, because comparisons are subjective, care must be taken to relate similar jobs in terms of the wage/effort bargain; and if managers wish to avoid inaccurate conclusions about equity it is necessary to be open concerning the basis on which the rewards are made. Generally speaking, it is important for managers to be aware of what employees perceive to be fair and equitable and to recognise that this will vary from group to group. By taking adequate consideration of the employee's perceptions, by providing an adequate explanation of any changes in work process or design and by ensuring policies etc. are applied consistently and in an unbiased manner, employees are more likely to believe the organisation is trying to reduce any perceived inequality and that they are being treated fairly in comparison with the treatment received by others. For the human resource manager equity theory illustrates how important it is to provide a performance management and reward system in which the outcomes are perceived by individuals to be relevant and acknowledge the truth that different employees value different things.

Second, it is clear that human resource managers need to (re)design current compensations systems in order to avoid the performance destroying effects of perceived inequities which result from employee perceptions that the wage/effort bargain provides insufficient rewards and that these redesigned systems need to avoid over-rewarding performance as this does not necessarily result in higher productivity or improved performance.

Goal setting theory

This approach to motivation by Locke and Latham (1984) is based on a simple premise: performance is caused by an employee's intention to perform. What follows is clear: an employee with higher goals will do better than an employee with lower goals. If an employee knows precisely what they want to do, or are expected to do, that employee will perform better than someone whose goals or intentions are vague. In other words there is a positive relationship between goal precision, difficulty and performance. This, however, does not hold for extremely difficult goals which are beyond an employee's ability. Using this prism we can argue that specific goals lead to higher performance than general or vague 'do your best' goals. Specific goals seem to create a precise intention, which in turn aids individual employees in shaping their behaviour with the same precision. Further, the theory proposes that knowledge of results (feedback) is essential if the full performance benefits of setting more difficult goals are to be achieved. Hence feedback offered in an appropriate manner can have a motivating effect on the employee. It is suggested that the beneficial effects of goal setting depend in part on the employee's goal commitment, that is their determination to succeed and unwillingness to abandon or reduce it.

These four principles establish the core of goal setting theory and make it one of the more consistently supported theories of motivation. Locke *et al.* (1981) suggests that financial incentives can enhance performance by raising the level of the goal or by increasing an employee's commitment to a goal which can be achieved where the employee is involved in establishing the required performance. We can therefore argue that, in the workplace, the value of goal setting is enhanced by the provision of adequate, timely feedback.

Goal-based theories of motivation emphasise the importance of feedback in order to:

- increase the employee's feeling of achievement;
- increase the sense of personal responsibility for the work;
- reduce uncertainty;
- refine performance.

However, many systems do not systematically provide for line managers to communicate feedback on performance to those employees for which they have responsibility. This may be for many reasons such as leadership style, protection of power bases or the information system not providing data for management functions. Often employees are provided with feedback 'by exception', typically when performance has fallen below a certain acceptable level and managers are themselves under pressure to improve performance. However, managers have to maintain a careful balance in providing feedback – too little, too late can be demotivating but too much and too frequently can be 'stifling' and perceived as indicative of a lack of trust or respect.

Reinforcement theory

This theory can be traced to the work of the pioneering behaviourist B.F. Skinner. It is considered a motivation theory as well as a learning theory. Reinforcement theory posits that motivated behaviour occurs as a result of 'reinforcers', which are outcomes resulting from the behaviour that makes it more likely the behaviour will occur again. Behaviour that is reinforced in a positive manner is likely to continue, but behaviour that is not rewarded or behaviour that is punished is not likely to be repeated. Reinforcement theory suggests to managers that they can improve employees' performance by a process of behaviour modification in which they reinforce desired behaviours and punish undesired behaviours.

Criticisms of process theories

A key criticism of process theories is that they tend to assume an overly rational view of human decision making. For example, decision making is often habitual or unconscious rather than conscious and rational. Furthermore, when making choices people do not have complete knowledge of the possible results of their behavioural options, and are not normally aware of the full range of options available to them. Another weak assumption of process theories is that individuals have a comprehensive and consistent scale of values with which they might evaluate the value of the various outcomes they are able to identify. Ultimately process theories do not consider why an individual values or does not value particular outcomes, only how the motivation develops.

New motivational techniques

During the last two decades, there has been a shift in organisations towards more team- and group-based work and towards an increased use of mentoring and coaching as strategies designed to enhance levels of employee motivation and performance. This section considers research studies into the design of work for autonomous work teams, the effects of group goal setting which is an extension of individual goal setting research, the role of mentoring and the use of non-financial rewards.

Two studies in particular have examined the effect of job characteristics or work design on the affective and behavioural responses of autonomous work teams. Cordery, Mueller and Smith (1991) conducted a study comparing semi-autonomous work teams and traditionally organised work groups. They found that semi-autonomous teams reported higher levels of freedom in their work, a characteristic associated with intrinsic job satisfaction as well as experiencing extrinsic satisfaction and organisational commitment. Cordery *et al.* (1991) concluded that employees in autonomous work groups report more favourable work attitudes and levels of motivation.

In 1993, Jin examined the effect of work group formation in China, that is how the members of the work groups were selected. Jin found that work groups which had formed voluntarily reported higher levels of work motivation, higher cooperative intentions, better interpersonal relations, greater work satisfaction, had fewer disciplinary problems and produced higher quantity and quality output.

The increased use of teams has resulted in an increase in the need to establish team-based goals – or group goals. A study conducted by Crown and Rosse (1995) found that when group members received individual goals, the group performed less well and were less motivated than when employees received group goals. Group-oriented goals were associated with more cooperative strategies better performance and better reported level of motivation. Individual goals were associated with more competitive strategies that interfered with the group's ability to perform and reduced levels of motivation.

Both studies concluded the use of autonomous work teams and work groups had a positive impact on both levels of employee motivation and performance. One interesting point is that although Cordery et al. (1991) also found work groups report more favourable work attitudes their research also revealed higher levels of turnover and absenteeism for semi-autonomous teams. So, while they concluded that employees in autonomous groups were more motivated, they also cautioned that the turnover and absence data may have illustrated some of the pressures associated with autonomous work groups, and which may ultimately become de-motivating.

The current work on mentoring is equally positive. Research results from a study conducted by Orpen in 1997 indicated the better the relationship between mentors and mentees in the mentoring programme, the more mentees were motivated to work hard and felt committed to their organisation. More specifically, it found that mentees who were in a close working relationship with their mentors, were more motivated and committed than those who were physically distant from their mentors. In addition, mentees were more motivated and committed when their mentors on the programme liked and respected them, and enjoyed interacting with them. The study found that when mentees performed poorly or were unmotivated it was frequently due to situational factors beyond the control of either party. Among the more pervasive negative factors that fell into this category were breakdowns in machinery, lack of consumer demand, non-cooperation from colleagues, weak marketing, outdated equipment, inappropriate organisational structure, and lack of training.

What such factors serve to demonstrate yet again is the multifaceted nature of motivation. They illustrate how interaction with the environment and associated difficulties make it sometimes impossible for employees to perform really well, even when they are strongly motivated as individuals and are committed to the organisation.

Non-financial rewards

The extent to which money is a motivator to improved performance remains a bit of an unresolved debate. It has traditionally been held that employees are likely to 'over-report' the importance of pay in any employee survey. However, recent research (Rynes et al., 2004) suggested the opposite was actually true. They reviewed evidence showing the discrepancies between what people say and do with respect to pay and concluded that although pay is not equally important in all situations or to all individuals it is such an important general motivator that many managers underestimate its importance. Although now a little dated, previous research also demonstrates how non-financial motivators have always been identified as significant, see Table 13.2.

Non-financial motivations

According to research by Woodruffe (2006: 29) non-financial factors, such as those he identified in the following list, remain the most important motivators of employee performance.

- *Advancement* – People value the extent to which they perceive that their job is giving them the opportunity for career advancement.

Table 13.2

Year	Most important motivational factor
1946	Appreciation
1980	Interesting work
1986	Interesting work
1992	Good wages
1997	Good wages, full appreciation of work done

Source: Kovach, K.A. (1987) 'What motivates employees? Workers and supervisors give different answers', *Business Horizons*, Sept–Oct, 58–65; Wiley, C. (1997) 'What motivates employees according to over 40 years of motivation surveys', *International Journal of Manpower*, 18, 3: 263–280.

- *Autonomy* – Most people like to be able to get 'on a roll' as far as work is concerned and a degree of real autonomy, where someone can really get 'into' their job, is likely to be welcome.

- *Civilised treatment* – Too many organisations treat people in a brusque, even uncivilised, way. The problem often arises because a line manager responsible for the people in question is working under great stress and, in effect, 'kicks downwards'. This can easily wipe out a great deal of effort by a human resources department in recruiting and motivating the right person.

- *Employer commitment* – People like to feel that their employers are genuinely committed to them and to their careers.

- *Environment* – A pleasant working environment is always essential: stress can be caused by an unpleasant environment.

- *Exposure to senior people* – Most employees like to feel that they are being noticed by an organisation's senior people and that they could approach these people if necessary for advice and guidance.

- *Praise is awarded when praise is due* – One of the classic signs of poor management occurs when staff are given *negative* feedback for what is perceived as poor performance, but never given *positive* feedback. The emotional benefits of praise can be enormous.

- *Support is available* – Employees like to feel that there is someone available to whom they can turn for advice if they need it.

- *Challenge* – Employees like to feel challenged, given that they believe they have the tools and skills to respond to the challenge successfully. Sometimes employees can respond with surprising resilience, energy and commitment to even a really demanding challenge.

- *Trust* – As social animals, humans will habitually, and often for very good reasons, withhold trust until they believe that extending this is justified. Employees know this, so the bestowal of trust is quite rightly regarded as extremely important. Employees, who feel trusted, are more likely to feel a useful and important part of an organisation and therefore are more likely to be loyal.

- *Reliable organisation* – People want to be proud of their jobs and of the organisations for which they work.

- *Assignments* – Every employee, no matter which rung they occupy in the corporate hierarchy, wants to feel important and valued, and there is no better way of helping an employee feel this than by giving him or her some genuinely significant assignments on which to work. The work–life balance is respected – employees know they are going to have to work hard, but an employer who shows sensitivity to work–life balance issues is very likely to outsource one who doesn't.

Box 13.1   Sara Lee Corporation

Chicago-based Sara Lee Corporation is a global manufacturer of brand-name products for consumers throughout the world. Sara Lee has operations in 58 countries, market-branded products in nearly 200 nations and 137,000 employees worldwide.

The Sara Lee Corporation needed to improve levels of employee motivation fast! Managers focused on 'recognition' as the key to raising employee motivation and developed an employee nomination scheme.

Using an online 'Nomination Wizard', every employee could nominate anyone they considered worthy of recognition. The online system asks a series of questions in order to determine the appropriate level of recognition and after approval from the appropriate people the awards, which can be given daily, are presented. Successful employees receive a certificate with an online code that allows them to browse and select a gift from their eligible level of achievement.

For Sara Lee Foods' managers and employees the question was not whether or not to recognise, but when and how. 'You have to find time to recognise', commented a leading manager. 'People certainly appreciate their salaries, but I see people stay and thrive as a group when they understand the vision and the challenges, and when they're appreciated. Appreciation is a critical part of the work experience.

In the experience of a 'recognised' employee 'To be recognised formally gave me extra motivation and made me wonder what I could do to keep the momentum going'.

Source: Case Studies, Melcrum Publishing Ltd (2006).

Box 13.2   Harley-Davidson

Harley-Davidson has been producing motorbikes, parts and accessories, MotorClothes and other merchandise since 1903. There are now 1300 Harley-Davidson dealerships in 60 countries worldwide and its corporate headquarters are based in Wisconsin, USA. The company employs 9000 people across the globe.

Over the past four years Harley-Davidson have witnessed unprecedented growth. Because the attention to growth had effectively forced the HR function to focus almost solely on recruiting, other critical HR practices were not prioritised.

This, in turn, was creating a potentially difficult situation and the HR function recognised that it had to more effectively manage the motivation and performance of its employees.

An emerging tool, called the 'Accenture Human Capital Development Framework', provided critical guidance in this effort. The Framework is a diagnostic approach to assessing human capital capabilities and the processes that motivate them, and then linking human capital assets and approaches to business performance outcomes.

It helps organisations do more than look at levels of spending to get a sense of their human capital development strengths; it also highlights how complete the underlying practices are, how effectively they support employees, and how aligned they are with the organisation's competitive strategy and mission. The framework demonstrates the link between different elements at four distinct levels, or tiers and so recognises the inherent complexity of employee motivation and performance.

- *Tier 1*: Business results – the financial measures of organisational success, such as capital efficiency, revenue growth, return on invested capital and total return to shareholders.
- *Tier 2*: Key performance drivers – the intermediate organisational outcomes, such as customer satisfaction and innovation, that are typically captured on a balanced scorecard.
- *Tier 3*: Human capital capabilities – or the most immediate and visible people-related qualities that human capital processes produce, such as workforce performance, employee engagement and workforce adaptability.

● *Tier 4*: Human capital processes – the specific practices and activities such as performance appraisal, workforce planning and learning management that organisations undertake to develop their human capital capabilities.

Harley-Davidson's 10-week implementation of the Framework began in January 2004. Factual, financial and HR data were collected through interviews with nine business and HR executives (including the CEO and vice president of HR) and a representative sample of five HR executives and 69 employees.

Compelling findings

The results of the Framework confirmed that the organisation was performing above the average in seven of the 13 human capital processes, but executives weren't surprised to learn that there was room for improvement in the remaining six processes:

1 career development;
2 workforce planning;
3 rewards and recognition;
4 employee relations;
5 human capital strategy; and
6 human capital infrastructure.

Subsequent attention to these areas helped the organisation improve employee motivation and performance levels and supported its ongoing success.

Source: Scott, H., Cheese, P. and Cantrell, S. (2006) 'Harley-Davidson'. *Strategic HR Review*, Jan/Feb 2006, 5, 2: 28–31.

New day, new way, new pay?

This discussion indicates that early PBR mechanisms, discussed above, were in some respects aiming at the wrong target. By concentrating simplistically on the cash nexus they avoided more complex motivators which determine the effort side of the bargain. The realisation amongst managers and academics that the application of greater levels of effort could be achieved more effectively by the application of methods other than money led to the development of a wider discussion.

By the 1980s it had become clear that the traditional (old pay) systems were not effectively delivering in terms of key organisational goals. The developing HRM rhetoric and the more apparent interest in business performance led HR managers to reassess the role of reward management in the delivery of organisational efficiency. As White and Drucker (2000) note, these developments have been accompanied by broader economic and social changes which challenged the belief in traditional personnel practices. Within this process of change, reward management underwent a metamorphosis of major proportions in that it was no longer simply about rewarding people for previous attainment but became linked to future performance. According to Armstrong (2002), reward is now 'about how people are rewarded in accordance with their value to the organisation' (2002: 3) and as such can no longer be seen as the mere administration of set procedures and policies. From this perspective the development of HRM has led to an evaluation of reward systems in an attempt to link them more effectively to organisational strategies (fitting in with notions of strategic HRM). Reward strategies then, are viewed as a key organisational contribution and a central element in the work of HR functionaries.

As we can note from the models and maps of HRM (see Chapter 1), reward systems are seen as one of the four key policy choices (Beer *et al.*, 1984) out of which organisations can aim to develop commitment, competence, congruence and cost-effectiveness, while Storey

(1992) indicates reward management as one of the points of difference between personnel and HRM. The older mechanisms, including graded spines based on job evaluation, are in part considered inappropriate in modern business. Rewards, or more precisely reward strategies, are seen as techniques which organisations can apply in order to secure various behaviours and values. Millward *et al.* (2000) note that in 1990 the major influence which determined pay settlements in organisations where collective bargaining was not dominant was individual employee performance (2000: 207); by 1998 the focus had shifted, with the main influence in this group of respondents being economic factors and more recognition of limits set by higher authority (2000: 211). These changes have not resulted in reward systems which are any easier for workers to understand or are less complex than their predecessors. That reward management developed in a manner which encouraged this occupation of a position of central importance has various causes. As we noted above, control of costs is at the heart of managerial responsibilities and, within that, control of labour costs is fundamental to organisational performance. Further, we have suggested that reward systems form part of the employees' notion of organisational justice and as such underlie a sense of loyalty. This simple statement needs unpacking in terms of the manner in which policy and practice have developed as a result of these changes.

In the 1990s, US writers (Lawler, 1990; Schuster and Zingheim, 1992) offered concepts they labelled 'new pay' as a prism through which we can view these changes. The central idea is intended to signify the realisation that reward strategies have to relate to organisational culture, values, aims and strategies, which in turn must take into account the challenges of a modern economy. As Schuster and Zingheim (1992) note, the rudimentary elements of 'new pay' include an acknowledgement that employees form a core ingredient in the recipe for organisational success. They suggest that the change cannot be one of rhetoric (from reward to compensation) alone but must also be demonstrated in the design of 'total compensation' packages which consistently reward required actions and attitudes. They indicate that a key element in such a total compensation package is variable pay, suggesting that pay remains a crucial mechanism for sending messages to employees in regard to the managerially desired effort levels. In this light, reward strategy needs to be integrated with wider organisational and managerial processes rather than being viewed as a 'bolt-on' optional extra. This whole package approach means that all elements (base, variable and indirect rewards) need to support each rather than compete for supremacy. Base pay remains the foundation of the policy and should be set in line with organisational and societal norms in order to ensure 'felt justice' across the organisation. Alongside this element however, the organisation may develop variable elements which do not become permanent, remaining subject to criteria related to either individual or organisational performance. These variable elements can therefore go down as well as up, addressing the issue of wage rigidity which adds damaging costs in periods of downturn. There are a number of means by which this variable element can be determined but they are often grouped under the generic term performance-related pay (PRP), indicating that the measurement of such performance may be based on the individual, the team or the organisation.

In this section we begin with consideration of the organisational element commonly called performance management and link this to a discussion of modern job evaluation schemes, profit-related pay and modern managerial practice. The underlying idea in the introduction of variable/contingent elements was that employees would identify more readily with organisational goals where part of their compensation package was linked to performance/profit. In simple terms, when the organisation did well they would share in the gain and therefore would also share the suffering in bad times. This may work where employees can be encouraged to swap a percentage of their base pay for this variable element but many organisations introduced these schemes as additional to existing compensation levels (see Kellaway, 1993). Current research (Freeman, 2001) looking at these schemes indicates two main findings:

- They have some positive impact on performance.
- Employees can view the rewards as unrelated to individual performance.

The second point is reason enough to move towards systems which apparently reward individual performance more directly. This has been achieved by the introduction of schemes that are based on modern job evaluation, and grading schemes within which the compensation increases the variable/contingent element rather than the base as in the past. Such contingency pay can be based upon:

- competence;
- skills;
- length of service;
- contribution and/or
- performance.

Each of these elements can be included in the development of job evaluation schemes, which are designed to influence employees' perceptions of distributive justice.

Modern job evaluation schemes

Modern organisations base such grading schemes on notions of competencies. Competency can be defined as:

> an underlying characteristic of an individual which is causally related to effective or superior performance in a job. (Mitrani *et al.*, 1993: 5)
>
> The characteristic set of knowledge, skills, abilities, motivations and procedures that individuals working in specific jobs should possess to allow them to perform their work to minimum standards. (Cornelius, 2001: 366)

From these comments, we can suggest a list of competencies adapted from Gooch and Cornelius (2001) which includes:

- leadership;
- communication skills;
- presentation skills;
- interpersonal skills;
- workflow management;
- adaptability;
- customer service.

Competence-based payment (CBP) schemes have grown alongside the interest in variable compensation and are often part of modern job evaluations schemes. HR functionaries have expended significant time and energy in the development of 'competence frameworks' which link pay to the achievement of specific behaviours, attitudes and the attainment of required competencies. These schemes are popular with both parties, in part due to the fact that it is clear what is valued by the organisation and hence what will receive increased reward. This differs from traditional 'pay-by-skill' in that it is applied across the organisation to all workers (rather than just the traditional skills) and the required 'competencies' are somewhat broader than the definition of 'skill(s)'. This breadth of definition allows the application and adaptation of traditional job evaluation schemes by taking into account current changes in the organisation of work and the utilisation of new technology. Thus job evaluation techniques were rescued from decline by becoming more flexible, broader in coverage and applicable to modern multi-skilled workers (Pritchard and Murlis, 1992).

Hastings and Dixon (1995) suggest that CBP systems can take three major forms in which the attainment of indicated competencies is:

- the basis for progression within scales;
- the basis upon which the scales are founded;
- the basis both for progression and for the scale.

A second system, which is adopted within modern organisations, is based on employee input and relates to the acquisition of new skills. Within a modern job evaluation scheme development of firm-related skills can be used as a mechanism which allows individuals to move beyond 'bars within grades'. Therefore a grade may contain five or six spine points with a bar after three which limits progression and can only be passed following the acquisition of clearly identified skills.

A length of service approach relates the contingent element to time served. As Daniels (2006: 236) notes it is 'still very popular in the voluntary and public sector'. The basis upon which such an element is included into calculations within job evaluation schemes relates to the idea that longer service equals more experience. Such experience may be seen to allow the individual the possession of more organisational knowledge and hence value to the organisation. However, following recent age discrimination legislation, this has to be objectively justified.

Contribution, as a contingent element of a reward package, is designed to evaluate employee competencies and performance in a more holistic manner. It attempts to measure, albeit subjectively, the overall value of the employee in the pursuit of organisational objectives. In this manner it can be linked to the authentication of a cohesive in-house culture and hence support programmes of cultural change.

Many modern job evaluation schemes continue to use pseudo-scientific mechanisms to measure and reward performance. Such measurement is normally made with reference to defined organisational objectives. Objectives are agreed between the parties and often form part of the appraisal scheme (see below).

Whichever system is applied, a main advantage lies in the ability of organisations to set their own 'characteristic set of knowledge, skills, abilities and motivations'. From such a development, they can develop job families, which allow equality issues to be addressed across various functions. The use of job families, based on broad role profiles, allows a series of job descriptions to be aligned within a single framework, hence financial rewards can be linked to individual performance against a set of organisationally specific competencies.

In recent debates much attention has turned to discussion of a contract which is unwritten and yet seen as being as important as any written terms and conditions. The psychological contract is seen to underpin all reward and performance management systems in that it conceptualises the wage/effort bargain for a new generation of workers and owners. In the following section we consider the formation of the contract and identify the 'agreed' terms (if such they can be called) forming the basis from which human resource managers seek to develop performance norms, organisational values and note the psychological contract as a mechanism in the continuing strategy to encourage 'men [sic] to take work seriously when they know that it is a joke' (Anthony, 1977: 5).

The psychological contract

Defining the psychological contract

As with many aspects of human resource management – such as motivation and performance – the psychological contract is somewhat elusive and challenging to define (for a discussion of this, see Guest, 1998a). However, it is generally accepted that it is concerned with an individual's subjective beliefs, shaped by the organisation, regarding the terms of an exchange relationship between the individual employee and the organisation (Rousseau, 1995). As it is subjective, unwritten and often not discussed or negotiated, it goes beyond any formal contract of employment. The psychological contract is promise based, and over time assumes the form of a mental schema or model, which like most schema is relatively stable and durable. (For a more detailed analysis on how the psychological contract is formed see Rousseau, 2001.) A major feature of psychological contracts is the concept of mutuality – that there is a common and agreed understanding of promises and obligations the respective parties have made to each other about work, pay, loyalty, commitment, flexibility, security and career advancement.

Research undertaken by Herriot *et al.*, (1997) sought to explore the content of the psychological contract in the UK. They researched the perceived obligations of two parties to the psychological contract by identifying the critical incidents of 184 employees and 184 managers representing the organisation. From the results they inferred seven categories of employee obligation and twelve categories of organisation obligation.

In relation to employee obligations, they make reference to both concrete and abstract inputs the organisation hopes/expects the employee will bring to the organisation. At the first level these involve an expectation that the employee will work the hours contracted and consistently do a good job in terms of quality and quantity. The organisation will desire that their employees deal honestly with clients and with the organisation and remain loyal by staying with the organisation, guarding its reputation and putting its interests first, including treating the property which belongs to the organisation in a careful way. Employees will be expected to dress and behave correctly with customers and colleagues and show commitment to the organisation by being willing to go beyond their own job description, especially in emergency. It is possible to suggest that many of these expectations reflect the common law terms implied in the contract of employment and as such it is the 'manifestation' of the required behaviours more than the existence of a psychological contract which is used to manage 'norms' within the organisation.

On the other side of the contract we can note the obligations placed on the organisation in terms of the expectations each employee has of the deal. Most employees would want the organisation to provide adequate induction and training and then ensure fairness of selection, appraisal, promotion and redundancy procedures. While recent legislation has centred on the notion of work–life balance, it is argued that an element of this agreement is an employee expectation that the organisation will allow time off to meet personal and family needs irrespective of legal requirements. It has long been held that workers ought to have the right to participate in the making of the decisions which affect their working lives (see Adams, 1986; Bean, 1994; Freeman and Rogers, 1999); the debate relating to the psychological contract suggests that employees further expect organisations to consult and communicate on the matters which affect them. With the increasingly high levels of 'knowledge' workers it is accepted that organisations ought to engage in a policy of minimum interference with employees in terms of how they do their job and to recognise or reward for special contribution or long service. Organisations are generally depended upon to act in a personally and socially responsible and supportive way towards employees, which includes the provision of a safe and congenial work environment. We have already noted that in relation to reward and performance management systems there is a need to act with fairness and consistency; the expectation goes further in that the application of rules and disciplinary procedures must be seen to be equitable. This perceived justice should extend to market values and be consistently awarded across the organisation, indicating the link therefore to a consistency in the administration of the benefit systems. The final element that many workers expect their employer to provide is security in terms of the organisation trying hard to provide what job security is feasible within the current economic climate.

1   Write down your expectations of your employer and what you consider to be their expectations of you.

2   Reflect on which aspects can be described as formal and which could be considered as unwritten.

3   Consider how you reached this 'psychological contract' – did you, for example, negotiate and agree it or have you assumed aspects?

4   To what extent are both parties, i.e. you and your employer, aware of the existence and the content of the contract; to what extent do you share the same expectations?

5   What might be the issues for you and for the employer if there is a mismatch of expectations?

6   Finally, consider with whom you have the contract – a named individual within the organisation or do you have multiple contracts with different agents within the organisation?

Previous decades have seen many organisations forced, by increased competition and the globalisation of business, to seek to remain competitive by cutting costs and increasing efficiency. This has, in part, given rise to the restructuring endemic in UK and US organisations under the various guises of business process re-engineering, downsizing and rightsizing, all of which apply performance-related pay systems aimed at increasing productivity. The restructuring has also given rise to redundancies, had the significant impact of reducing job security of those who remained, removed many of the middle-level management grades and consequently reduced possible promotion opportunities for junior employees.

While long-term job security, promotion and career progression were perceived by many employees, whose psychological contract was possibly formed many years earlier, to be the 'key' obligations which were owed by the organisation in return for their loyalty and commitment, modern organisations (and in some respects the 'modern' employee) are learning to live without such elements in the psychological contract. The consequences have been predictable; employees feel angry at the apparent unilateral breaking of the psychological contract and at the same time insecure, having lost trust in the organisation. Commitment is reduced, with motivation, morale and performance being adversely affected. This is potentially dangerous for the organisation, as lean organisations need effort and commitment in order to get work done and at the same time a willingness to take risks in the pursuit of innovation. It is suggested (Rousseau, 2001; Guest and Conway, 2002) that negative change in the employment relationship may adversely affect the state of the psychological contract.

Sparrow (1996) claims that the psychological contract underpins the work relationship and provides a basis for capturing complex organisational phenomena by acting in a similar manner to that of Herzberg's hygiene factors. Good psychological contracts may not always result in superior performance, or indeed in satisfied employees; but poor psychological contracts tend to act as demotivators, which can be reflected in lower levels of employee commitment, higher levels of absenteeism and turnover, and reduced performance. Herriott and Pemberton (1995: 58) suggest that the captains of industry have set in motion a revolution in the nature of the employment relationship, the like of which they never imagined. For they have shattered the old psychological contract and failed to negotiate a new one.

It has long been accepted that two forms of psychological contract, termed relational and transactional, operate in the employment relationship (Table 13.3). The former refers to 'a long-term relationship based on trust and mutual respect. The employee offers loyalty, conformity to requirements, commitment to their employer's goals and trust in their employer not to abuse their goodwill' (Arnold et al., 1998: 388). In return, the organisation supposedly offered security of employment, promotion prospects, training and development and some flexibility about the demands made on the employees if they were in difficulty.

Table 13.3 Relational and transactional contracts

	Transactional	Relational
Primary focus	Concerned about economic factors	Concerned about people
Time frame	Closed ended and short term	Open ended and indefinite
Stability of the relationship	Static, rarely changing	Dynamic and frequently changing
Scope of relationship	Narrow	Broad and pervasive
Tangibility of terms	Well defined	Highly subjective

However, as a result of the changes outlined above it is suggested that some employers have had difficulty in maintaining their side of the bargain. As a result, the old relational contracts have been violated and have been replaced by new, more transactional contracts, which are imposed rather than negotiated and based on a short-term economic exchange. As Arnold *et al.* (1998: 388) suggest, 'the employee offers longer hours, broader skills, tolerance of change and ambiguity . . . In return the employer offers (to some) high pay, rewards for high performance and simply a job'.

If the psychological contract is changing as current research appears to suggest, what are the organisational implications for managing the psychological contract in the future? The psychological contract needs careful management; although it is unwritten it remains a highly influential aspect of the employment relationship. In flatter, delayered organisations with limited opportunities for career progression and the absence of any guarantee of a job for life, attaining and maintaining employee commitment becomes increasingly more challenging for management. To manage the psychological contract in the future, organisations need to offer 'realistic job previews' to new entrants, recognise the impact of change on those remaining and 'invest in the survivors'. Further, there is a need to change the management style and to push towards cross-functional teamwork, design tasks and structures to allow employees to feel a sense of accomplishment and develop their skills to increase their own 'employability security'. Such activities are intended to create a new kind of commitment through the creation of meaning and values between employees, not just from a top-down mission statement, to be attentive to the need to balance work and other aspects of life and to be continuous in communication with employees. (For further reading, see the work of Jean Hiltrop.)

Guzzo and Noonan (1994) take the perspective that psychological contracts can have both transactional and relational elements. Employers may have to demonstrate to employees that they can keep to a sound and fair transactional deal before attempting to develop a relational contract based on trust and commitment. Furthermore, as Herriot *et al.* (1997: 161) suggest: 'Organisations may be in danger of underestimating the fundamentally transactional nature of the employment relationship for many of their employees'. The essential point is to recognise that all psychological contracts are different. It is important for the organisation to appreciate the complexities of transactional and relational contracts and to recognise that psychological contracts will have elements of all dimensions and that contracts are individual, subjective and dynamic. The significance of the psychological contract in relation to performance management is that it highlights how easy it is for organisations to assume that employees seek primarily monetary rewards; this is not necessarily the case. The evidence suggests that effective performance management and reward structures in organisations must attend to the quality of the relationships employees experience while at work which are an integral aspect of the psychological contract. The message appears simple: improved performance is affected by more than money.

HRM and performance management

We can see that the key issue related to the determination of the wage/effort bargain is not simply a matter of setting a wage relative to the level of effort and letting things 'tick along'. From the dawn of the industrial era, managers have sought to control the effort side of the agreement by utilising their power to determine the wage. Performance management (or more accurately forms of performance-related pay) has formed a key activity for managers and management in the quest to increase the benefits gained by the application of labour power. There have been various mechanisms applied in order to secure this advantage which were based on the 'current fad' or understanding of the labour process (for a discussion of the influence of the emergence of SHRM, see Schuler and Jackson, 1999). The choice of which management system to adopt has been driven by the answer proposed to the basic question 'what motivates workers to perform at higher levels?' and more often than not can be located within the various schools of thought outlined above. We can see the development of reward management along the lines suggested by Etzioni (1975) in terms of coercive (work harder or lose your job), remunerative (work harder and receive more money) and normative (work harder to achieve agreed organisational goals). Current trends in the management of worker performance fail to be considered in the area of normative managerial practices, but are fraught with difficulty in an era where emotional labour and the knowledge worker hold such a central place in organisational success. These developments need to be considered alongside the evolution of an ambiguous employment relationship (the breakdown of the psychological contract) and the rise of insecurity of modern organisations (reflected in the growth of 'butterfly workers'). As Fisher notes, 'Insecurity is a common phenomenon in organisations' (1999: 167), be it the feelings of insecurity within line managers who have not previously been responsible for the range of issues they now enjoy or that of the HR manager attempting to demonstrate they have put in place all the necessary procedures required to measure performance and show their organisational worth in a modern competitive environment. HR managers, lost in a landscape where memory no longer serves the function of creating security (Schama, 1995), argue that they can apply the techniques presented within expectancy and/or goal-setting theory to the development of procedures which will secure competitive advantage for the organisation. Such procedures are borne within the all-encompassing 'HRM mantra' which declares, for self-assurance as much as public consumption, that the HR function is a strategic player in the organisation network, bringing new understanding to the application of personnel practices and organisational changes.

We can suggest from Figure 13.3 that the HRM mantra, which can be considered as the 'self-reassuring' chant of HR managers, indicates the importance of HR procedures in the success of the organisation and note how a number of these link into our discussion of reward systems and performance management. The notions of 'productivity through our people', customer focus, strong(er) leadership, flatter structures and cohesive cultures all suggest a management framework which seeks to improve individual and organisational performance in ways that can be measured, a concentration on competence (inputs) alongside attention to attainment (outcomes).

These elements turn attention to the fact that in modern organisations it is the quality and behaviours of the employees that generate, as much as other inputs, competitive advantage. While much of the business strategy literature since the 1980s has concentrated on the 'setting and achievement' of organisational goals, what has often been lost is the role of human resources in the attainment of competitive advantage (a trend addressed by the application of the ideas associated with the resource-based view of the firm in recent years; see Chapter 2 on strategic HRM in this edition). However, a set of key questions still remain: 'what motivates workers to perform at higher levels?', 'how do we manage this motivation to the best effect?' and 'how do we measure resulting performance levels?'

Some attempt has been made to answer the first of these questions in the preceding sections using the theoretical constructs offered by Maslow, Herzberg, Taylor, Vroom and Locke.

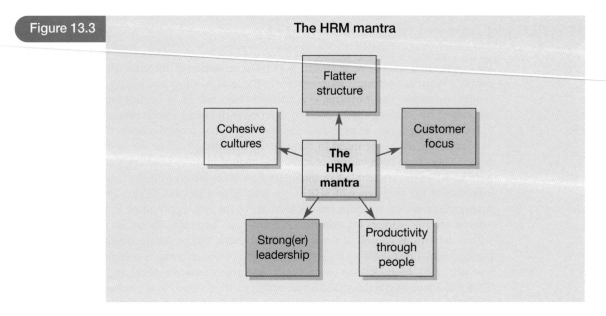

Figure 13.3   The HRM mantra

These, as our discussion of the psychological contract suggested, leave us with some confusion and inconsistencies which present management with as many questions as answers. The recent developments in this area, as suggested above, involve two themes:

- the performance management process, and
- contingent pay.

As Lowry (2002) argues, the management of employee performance is usually seen as a necessary function of the managerial cadre. Centrally, it links a number of themes, including the extent to which the organisation has identified strategic goals reflecting the needs of the business and the degree to which these are communicated to and shared by each employee. We can further note that general definitions suggest that performance management involves a formal and systematic review of the progress towards achieving these goals. In response to the problems this creates, theorists have developed the idea of a performance management cycle within which the elements of the process can be identified, investigated and implemented by HR managers in the attempt to create organisational advantage. The cycle consists of five elements which provide a framework within which we can audit the delivery of strategic objectives with a view to developing continuous improvement. These elements are presented as a common link between organisational and individual performance, which underlies the development of a committed, motivated, loyal workforce. In simple terms, it is suggested that the cycle indicates a system within which performance objectives are set, outcomes are then measured, results are fed back, rewards are linked to outcomes and changes are made before new objectives are set for which the outcomes can be measured. We now consider each of these elements individually.

Setting objectives

There is any amount of prescriptive advice which indicates that the objectives need to be achievable and linked to organisational objectives. Where the purpose of setting such objectives is to direct, monitor, motivate and audit individual performance they must fulfil both of these criteria, otherwise the process will result in the opposite effects being secured. The application of expectancy and goal-setting theories implies that this is best achieved where the individual has an important role in the determination of the objectives for the period concerned. As suggested in the discussion above, this will encourage the selection of appropriate goals which are specific, attainable and owned by the individual. The process, as a management tool, is established on the basis that organisational objectives can be broken down and translated into individual goals, the attainment of which can then be effectively measured.

In recent debates we find that organisations are said to make frequent use of the acronym SMART to assist in establishing effective objectives:

S – Specific or Stretching
M – Measurable
A – Agreed or Achievable
R – Realistic
T – Time bound

There are, however, difficulties in setting objectives for some jobs, e.g. doctors, lecturers and lower levels in the organisation hierarchy, as they may not have the opportunity to improve their performance or demonstrate merit, and may be unable to identify or relate to organisational goals.

Measuring the outcomes

Where the objectives relate to numbers, increased sales or an increased production of widgets, for example, the measurement appears unproblematic. However, not all of us are sales representatives or widget-makers; indeed, in the current economic climate such crude measures may be inappropriate and in some respects a return to 'old pay' notions of piecework. The growth of 'knowledge' workers has been accompanied by a change to competence-based approaches to measurement which centre on the three stages of competence development (know-what, know-why and know-how; see Raub, 2001). Therefore the outcomes can be measured in relation to the individual's success in deploying, integrating and improving their competence in the identified field of activity. This allows the organisation to refocus on the development of competitive advantage through the application of 'core knowledge', including tangible and intangible assets. It allows the application of 'just enough discipline' to establish a relevant 'core knowledge' base which is defined by strategic business drivers and monitored to maintain balance (see Klien, 1998).

The outcomes are often measured by the application of appraisal schemes. The purpose of performance planning, review and appraisal needs to be made clear if employees at all levels in the organisation are to play an active part in the process. It is possible that some employees and line managers may meet performance appraisal schemes with distrust, suspicion and fear, but an integrated and effective process can lead to increased organisational performance and employee motivation. It is important for employees to be genuinely involved in the design of an appraisal scheme, the evaluation of performance, and the objective-setting process. An appraisal scheme should be set up in an atmosphere of openness, with agreement between management, employees and employee representatives on the design of the scheme (Grayson, 1984: 177). Employees need to have a clear understanding of the purpose of the process (evaluative or developmental).

From this we can suggest that the key principles in the design of a performance appraisal scheme are that it should be congruent with the organisation's competitive strategy. It needs to provide direction for continuous improvement activities and identify both tendencies and progress in performance. Manifestly, it needs to facilitate the understanding of cause and effect relationships regarding performance while remaining intelligible to those employees to which it applies. It ought to be dynamic, covering all of the company's business processes, and provide real-time information about all aspects of performance. A scheme that does not include employees' attitudes is unlikely to allow performance to be compared against benchmarks because it will not be composed of effective performance measures. Finally, we can note that a performance appraisal system should provide a perspective of past, present and future performance which is visible to both employees and management.

On the basis of seven case studies, IDS produced the following list of factors which were typically appraised (IDS, 1992):

- job knowledge and abilities (ability to perform all aspects of the job);
- adaptability/flexibility (ability to cope with change; multi-skilling for craft workers);
- productivity (individual work output);
- quality of work (attention to detail; consistent quality);
- attitude to work (commitment; motivation; enthusiasm);
- interaction with others (communication skills; teamworking ability);
- originality of thought/initiative (problem-solving);
- perception (ability to correctly interpret job requirements);
- judgement, use of resources (setting priorities; ability to plan and organise work);
- attendance and time keeping (number of and reasons for absence; punctuality);
- safety awareness (awareness of health and safety standards);
- need for supervision (leadership; ability to develop others);
- performance against targets (extent to which previously set targets have been achieved).

From this we can suggest that assessment of these factors is achieved by a mixture of 'subjective' and 'objective' measures, almost always carried out by the employee's immediate superior. The most commonly used measures will therefore relate to the individual's attitude to work as well as the quality of their work and their attendance and time keeping. These will be assessed alongside their knowledge of the job and productivity, while more subjective measures involving a judgement of their ability to interact with others will be included in a good scheme in order to develop an insight into the effectiveness of recruitment procedures. In terms of 'rating' or 'scoring' individual employees, a number of 'target areas' can be identified for assessment.

Accountabilities

Accountabilities define the responsibilities of a certain job and the results that jobholders are expected to achieve. The employee's actual output in terms of measurable productivity, timeliness and quality may be directly assessed as part of the appraisal scheme. This presupposes the employee's job role is open to such quantitative assessment.

Skills acquisition

Employees may be assessed on their acquisition of new skills required to further improve their performance in the job or the continued development of essential skills. Jones the Bootmaker, a footwear company in the Midlands, have recently developed a new performance appraisal scheme in which they specifically appraise managers on the job they are currently required to do rather than place undue emphasis on developing skills and competences for future positions. Andrew White, company representative, stated 'We found that the previous scheme was appraising managers on competences beyond their current job role, which in some cases led to demotivation' (White, November 2002).

Self-assessment

This approach is mainly concerned with the identification of self-development needs by the actual employee. Margerison (1976) has suggested that self-assessment is the only way to give a complete picture of the performance of the employee and to avoid a 'criticise–defend' scenario. It does, however, require the employee to have a detailed and informed understanding of both the current and future needs of the job role and the organisational needs against which they can accurately assess their current performance and so their future development needs.

Paired comparisons

This is a comparative method of performance assessment in which a superior assesses the performance of pairs of individuals, until each employee has been judged relative to each other employee, or until every possible combination of employees has been considered. A rating scale is then devised to show the number of times an individual employee was judged as 'better' (Roberts, 2001: 542).

Ranking

This is another comparative measure of assessment in which employees are assessed against pre-set and documented measures of effectiveness and placed in a hierarchy from best to worst. At Cummins Engines the appraisal system is based on a 10:80:10 ranking scheme. Those employees ranked in the top 10 per cent are identified for promotion and special development. Those identified within the next 80 per cent are maintained within the organisation and the remaining 10 per cent are effectively 'managed out' of the organisation. In Cummins the appraisal scheme is very open and there are no secrets over how it operates in practice!

Rating scale

This is considered to be an 'absolute' method of performance assessment. The method, according to Roberts (2001: 542), lists a number of factors such as job-related qualities or behaviours or can include certain personality traits. Individual employees are then rated on the extent to which they possess these factors. The rating scale can be numerically, alphabetically or graphically represented on a continuum, i.e. from 'very high' to 'very low'. However, when scoring is involved it can get ugly. The attraction of rating systems – the school-report model that ranks you as a team player from one to five, or rates your customer focus from A to E – is that the feedback is easy to gather and produces lots of data that can be aggregated and turned into bar charts. In this respect the HR department is happy because they have made a 'fuzzy' process look scientific, and someone from client services is proud because they got a 4 on knowledge leadership and their colleague only got a 3. But a number may not offer much insight on how to improve. For that you need thoughtful, qualitative comments – harder to gather, but much more helpful.

Behaviourally anchored rating scale (BARS)

This is an attempt to assess actual performance and behaviour, so, for example, it is concerned not with whether an employee has 'initiative', but with specifically identifying what he or she actually does that demonstrates initiative – or the lack of it!

The development of a BARS approach typically involves the following stages:

- Meetings are held with superiors and/or outside consultants to identify several key aspects or categories of performance in particular jobs.
- The same or other sources of information are used to provide examples of good, average and poor performance for each category of performance in an individual's job.
- A number of such categories or anchors are generated (frequently 6–9 per job) and each is ascribed a value, for instance 1–7, or 'average', 'above average', etc. Essentially these define the 'most efficient' through to the 'least efficient' behaviour and performance for the job.
- Appraisers use this format to evaluate the expected behaviour of individual employees holding the jobs concerned.

The underlying job analysis is critical to the success of this approach and many proponents argue that the employee and their superiors should be actively involved in the process to ensure it is relatively realistic.

Development plan approach

In some organisations the link between personal development and the business strategy is weak but is crucial to effective performance management. Effective development plans consider the future skills, knowledge and experiences that will be required by the employee to enable them to do their current job effectively. The identification of needs should also be linked to what the employee may require in the future – needs identification must therefore be closely linked to organisational succession and business plans. The plan may be in the style of an essay or a controlled report which asks for responses to certain headings or sections.

360-degree appraisals

This approach to performance management has grown in popularity and when undertaken correctly is effective, reasonably inexpensive, widely applicable and clearly focused on individual performance.

The idea behind 360-degree feedback is that employees benefit from feedback gathered from a wide range of sources. Characteristically this includes peers, superiors, subordinates and customers; essentially it is designed to obtain comments from 'all directions', above, below and to the side of the employee concerned. It is intended to give a more complete and comprehensive picture of the individual's performance and contribution.

The process typically follows a procedure in which competences have been established and defined and employees are then requested to nominate up to six significant others who cover the range of suitable respondents. Those giving feedback are then asked to use a rating scale or comment on each of the dimensions. For example, Roberts (2001: 543) suggests managers might be assessed by their employees on 'softer' people issues such as communication and support, and their peers on issues such as teamwork. Indicators of both internal and external customer satisfaction may be used, and suppliers and subcontractors may also be asked to give feedback on the individual manager's performance and demonstration of competences.

Possible issues with performance appraisal

Whatever approach to performance appraisal is used, there will inevitably be issues and concerns. In essence, to assess an employee's performance necessarily involves some form of assessment against predetermined standards or behaviours. In both situations there will be an element of human judgement which, as we know, suffers from problems of reliability, validity and bias. Kinnie and Lowe (1990: 47) state that 'appraisers may find it difficult to identify and measure, the distinct contribution of each individual'; this can be because the appraiser does not really know the appraisee or because, as suggested by Howell and Cameron (1996: 28), employees are constantly moving from one project to another.

There may also be many external factors beyond the control of the individual employee which affect their performance, such as resources, processes, technology, corporate and HR strategy, working environment, external business context and management. Equally, the appraisal might be skewed because if there is a long time span between appraisals, managers may place greater importance on more recent performance, called the 'recency effect', thereby possibly ignoring incidents that had occurred earlier.

Role of line manager

Line managers/supervisors may lack the required technical skills and people management skills to be able to conduct an effective appraisal. In addition, a lack of time and resources may hinder line managers in providing comprehensive and effective performance reviews and objective-setting. Managers may perceive the appraisal process as a bureaucratic nuisance and form-filling exercise.

Demotivation consequences

An appraisal outcome that labels an employee as simply 'average', or determines that he or she is not a 'high flier', may lead to demotivation. To state the general principle: when one person begins to make a judgement on another, unless that judgement is favourable, reaction and resistance begin to set in (Margerison, 1976: 32).

Interpretation 'spin'

Roberts' (2001: 545) suggestion of the 'cascading' approach, of progressive levels of management setting objectives for the level below and consequently being assessed themselves by the attainment of these objectives can result in the manipulation and 'fudging' of standards. Further, there is a tendency to retain 'understanding' in the language rather than 'cascade' this to lower levels. Managers attempt to maintain their 'hierarchical' authority by using the interpretation of the 'spin' to reinforce relationships of power within the organisation; by so doing they lessen the effectiveness of the communication mechanisms and therefore of the process.

Conflicting roles

Newton and Findlay (2000: 129) make reference to the writings of McGregor, who draws attention to the issues of the conflicting roles of the appraiser as both disciplinary 'judge' and helpful 'counsellor', suggesting the modern emphasis of appraisal is on the manager as a leader who strives to assist employees achieve both their own and the company's objectives – acting as a sort of mentor or counsellor concerned with the personal growth and development of the employee. At the same time the manager is charged with identifying (and hopefully agreeing) strict targets for achievement and performance. This can involve identifying areas where previous performance has been less than satisfactory – leaving the manager in the role of judge. There are obvious tensions between the two roles.

Much of the literature suggests that this tension can, in part, be overcome by the employee taking an active role in the process. But that is assuming the employee wants to be involved and really wants to take responsibility for improving themselves by taking an 'active role' in the process – and they may not. For example, they may see the whole appraisal process as an attempt to control and manipulate them. Newton and Findlay (2000: 130) suggest employees may view this as a way of removing the responsibility for their development from the organisation, and placing it on their shoulders. In an era in which the notion of 'employability security' as distinct from 'job security' characterises the employment relationship, it is interesting to consider where the responsibility for investing in development lies – with the organisation, or increasingly as seems likely, directly with the employee. The interesting thing is that even as the appraisal process continues to be utilised as part of a spreading audit culture, some companies are already looking to cast it aside – or if they keep appraisals, making them, as Freeserve does, a process whereby employees solicit feedback rather than having it thrust upon them. It will be interesting to monitor how far this marks a turning of the tide against performance management appraisals.

Current trends

The interest in appraisals and other PBR systems draws on the long-standing tradition to divide reward packages between base and contingent elements. The changes in the mechanisms used to identify and quantify these contingent elements currently focus on the notion of rewarding the person rather than the role and links into the notion of 'new pay' which increases the emphasis on the motivational qualities of PBR systems. By linking pay to achievement, whether such achievement relates to production targets, attainment of competencies or objectives set within an appraisal meeting, organisations are seeking to quantify and reward individual contribution to the attainment of business goals or strategic aims. Individuals, whether pay is determined by position on a spine determined by job evaluation or otherwise, may receive increments based on length of service alongside performance elements; these 'service awards' reward experience and loyalty. However, such awards can be withheld where performance fails to meet the desired targets and are useful once 'poor' performance is identified as signals to other workers. Armstrong (2002) lists 15 features of performance management which were identified as being used by organisations in the 1998 CIPD survey. The results suggest that the most common of these (identified by over 60 per cent of the respondents) were objective-setting and review, annual appraisal and personal development plans (2002: 387). At the bottom of the ladder, despite all the discussion in various HR texts, with under 15 per cent acknowledgement were the balanced scorecard (5 per cent) peer appraisal (9 per cent), 360-degree feedback (11 per cent) and rolling appraisals (12 per cent). The results showed that organisations viewed performance management as integral to the employment relationship, thus an important part of managerial activity despite (as noted by 60 per cent of the respondents) being bureaucratic and time-consuming (2002: 388). In contrasting the results of the 1998 survey to those of the 1991 survey, Armstrong suggests a move from performance management 'systems' to a more holistic performance management 'process'. This process, it is suggested, focuses on inputs/outputs, development, flexibility and a shift of ownership towards the users and away from the HR function. Interestingly, taking the results into account, Armstrong suggests that the process also involves an increase in the application of 360-degree feedback (2002: 389).

The development of a process within which performance is related to both input and output is in part the result of the application of an objective-based approach located in the work of Kaplan and Norton (1992). The so-called balanced scorecard, although acknowledged as a feature by only 5 per cent of the respondents in the CIPD survey, underlies much of the discussion relating to the development of a strategic role for the HR function. In this approach there are four stages which start with a vision of the future, whether in the form of a vision statement *per se* or in terms of an answer to the question 'where do we want to be in *x* years?' From this we can identify how the organisation will be different if the targets are achieved in terms of four key areas (*Financial, Customer, Internal* and *Innovation/Learning*) which will determine the success of the organisation in a competitive environment. Reward strategies will impact on all of these areas to a greater or lesser extent by identifying as performance targets those elements which are critical to the successful acquisition of the vision for the future. The scorecard method can be used to identify specific instruments/measurements which can be used to set interim targets and therefore individual performance objectives. These may be competencies (can do), knowledge indicators (know-what) and/or commitment levels (know-why); critical elements in the attainment of these objectives are a strong psychological contract based on open communication, active participation and high-trust employment relationships. Research in 2003 (The Work Foundation, 2003) indicates that where employers are seeking to promote this type of performance management they will allow their employees to identify their own training needs (86 per cent), run regular team briefings (75 per cent), allow and encourage the development of transferable skills (73 per cent), tie reward to service by offering long-service awards (67 per cent) and operate a system of in-house brainstorming sessions or focus groups (66 per cent). The report suggests that employers are acknowledging that performance management ties broader HR policies into the attainment of the strategic goals of the organisation and that this objective can be achieved by the development of a strong psychological contract. Despite these moves, we can suggest that poor levels of goal attainment within organisations can be the fault of bad management of individual employee performance. A recent study by the consultants Mercer (2003) of 3500 employees concluded that a mere 20 per cent believe that their good performance will be rewarded while some 33 per cent feel their organisation operates in such a way that there is an inadequate link between pay and performance. From these results Gilbert notes that:

> Linking pay to performance requires a robust performance appraisal process and the active support of line managers . . . our results indicate that many managers lack either the training or the support to conduct the process.
> (Gilbert, P. on mercerhr.com, 2003)

The Mercer survey also noted that while firms may be good at appraising individuals, many are weak on providing effective feedback and offer this as a cause for their finding that performance management systems are rarely effective. We have suggested that in part their effectiveness rests on two foundation stones, high levels of motivation and a strong psychological contract; however, research by the CIPD (2003) notes that while most workers are 'happy in their work', fewer than 30 per cent trust their senior managers to look after their interests, indicating a psychological contract which is far from 'strong'. In order to address these problems and develop high-commitment management (HCM) policies, employers are introducing greater flexibility in terms of the employment relationship. These moves include the introduction of flexible benefits, competency-based pay, merit pay and broadbanding (IRS, 2002). The survey upon which these conclusions are based indicated that more than 60 per cent of the respondents used elements of merit-based pay, while over half operated market-related pay systems, suggesting some confusion and cross-over between internal (individual performance based) and external (market equity based) rationales for the development and implementation of reward strategies. This confusion brings into sharp focus the role of HR as a function in the development and implementation of strategic objectives. HR can measure the contribution it makes and/or impact it has against any number of measures; however, a recent IRS survey found that over half of their sample used business objectives or performance indicators, suggesting a continued link to performance management as a key role for HR practitioners (IRS, 2003). The same survey noted that 64 per cent stated that the HR department maintained sole responsibility for pay determination, with only 4 per cent suggesting this was the sole prerogative of line managers.

Stop & think

The report also notes that the typical week for an HR manager entails one day on strategy, two days on supporting line managers and two days on catching up on paperwork. Linked to the above relating to reward management, do you think the findings of the IRS survey indicate that in the area of reward management HRM is still a case of 'systems, figures and procedures'?

Taking the above results into account, how do you think organisations can convince their staff that performance will be rewarded?

Devise a mechanism by which an organisation you know could effectively get the message that 'performance equals higher rewards' across to their employees. What behaviours would they seek to encourage?

Performance management as a control mechanism

We started by noting that reward management systems can be seen as managerial attempts to gain control over the 'effort' side of the wage/effort bargain which mirrors their unilateral control of the wage side. A fundamental element of performance management is the development of control in relation to employee behaviours, motivation and loyalty. In modern parlance, performance management is a mechanism to control values rather than simply actions. With all the monitoring, discussion, measurement, evaluation and goal-setting, some performance management techniques give the impression that they are effective in controlling actions but often miss the target of securing control over effort levels because they do not develop powerful value systems. It is possible for these systems to have some effect on employee behaviours, to bring them into accord with organisation targets, while never really addressing the problem of underlying values. If, as Grint indicates, the traditional view is that 'good management is really concerned with good boundary management' (1997: 10), then performance management may offer a good traditional style in that it manages the boundary between acceptable and unacceptable performance; whether it moves beyond this to offer higher levels of commitment is debatable – we have suggested above that the process only secures that which it measures. There are more serious questions to be answered with regard to those items it cannot or does not attempt to measure. Without the link to the development and implementation of a system of organisational values it is arguable that performance management, whether seen as a process or a system, lacks the attainment of a self-generated goal. Linking performance, by the use of cafeteria reward systems, to individual choice may actually achieve the opposite by reducing the opportunity to link rewards to organisational values. However, by linking the attainment of performance levels which are sufficient to secure the desired reward the organisation could communicate to the employees that the organisation is changing by moving the goalposts to suit the new desirable set of values. In simple terms, we are suggesting that in order to achieve control over the effort side of the bargain, organisations need to acknowledge and apply management systems to the unarticulated links between:

Values – Behaviours – Performance – Growth

The argument here is that growth and performance are inextricably linked to behaviours which are founded upon personal and organisational values. Performance management is effective, therefore, only to the extent to which it can shape these values, irrespective of the measure to which it can change behaviours, as values are said to set the parameters within which people make decisions. Organisations must define, cascade and supervise their own values as they cannot be effectively imposed or imported; no amount of wall-mounted plaques, posters, credit-card-sized personal reminders or mugs can impose a set of values. Values must be lived and the performance management process should be designed to allow organisations to control the creation of the organisational language upon which values are based if it is to deliver control to the extent required within modern organisations.

Some difficulties

Do rewards work? At first sight this seems a simple, if not a simplistic question. The received wisdom has long been that the use of tools, variously described as incentive plans, bonus schemes, merit-based pay, or performance-related pay, is central to the development of improved performance. In part this is based on the accepted wisdom that 'the idea of dangling money and other goodies in front of people will "motivate" them to work harder' (Kohn, 1998: 27). Kohn (1998) goes on to argue that many compensation schemes assign more importance to money than is warranted and confuse compensation with reward. In an earlier argument, he went further to suggest that 'any incentive or pay-for-performance systems tends to make people less enthusiastic about their work' (Kohn, 1993a: 346). This, he suggests, is in part because people reason that if they need to be paid additional amounts to perform some task (or at some level) then what they are doing cannot be that interesting/valuable. Thus, such reward mechanisms merely encourage people to 'get the reward' and hence be less creative. Kohn sees the basic effect of contingency-based payment systems as 'destructive when tied to interesting or complicated task' (Kohn, 1993b: 348) in that they weaken intrinsic motivation. In an article responding to Kohn, Appelbaum (1993) notes most research indicates that 'Attempts to improve performance by manipulating compensation packages has proven to be counterproductive' (Kohn, 1993b: 369). In the same article Kozlowski offers an alternative view arguing that whilst 'elephants cannot fly and fish cannot walk, Kohn's argument that incentive plans cannot work defies the laws of nature' (Kohn 1993b: 371). He suggests that such plans encourage entrepreneurial spirit and focus minds on shareholder value. From this perspective therefore, incentive plans which include large elements of contingency-based pay, can be highly effective when employed in the appropriate circumstances. Alternatively Pfeffer (1998) includes as the fifth of his six 'myths about pay' that 'individual incentive pay improves performance' (1998: 125). This he links with the sixth myth which is that money is the primary reason people work. Pfeffer (1998) suggests that these myths undermine the ability of managers to recognise the real problem with performance and leads them to adopt ineffective solutions. In an era where productivity through effective labour management (including teamworking), customer focus (notably looking at the long term), strong decisive leadership, flatter hierarchies, and developing a cohesive culture have become central to HR thinking, contingency-based compensation, which encourages individualism, short-term focus, leaving leadership to the reward system, conflict-ridden hierarchies and cultural difference, is counterproductive. Pfeffer (1998) suggests that people work for meaning in their lives and indeed to have fun. He concludes that 'companies that ignore this fact are essentially bribing their employees and will pay the price in a lack of loyalty and commitment' (1998: 123). Perhaps we can see here a re-statement of the idea that 'A great deal of the ideology of work is directed at getting men [sic] to take work seriously when they know that it is a joke' (Anthony 1977: 5). As Pfeffer concludes 'Pay cannot substitute for a working environment high on trust, fun, and meaningful work' (1998: 128).

Conclusion

In this chapter we have discussed the notion of reward as an integral part of the managerial function which results from the definition of the employment relationship as a wage/effort bargain; as such, it was seen to operate in a contested relationship within which each party sought to determine the level of effort which constituted a 'fair day's work'. We argued that management have adopted various forms of reward system in order to communicate to the employees the required effort levels and to evaluate the levels of effort exerted. These have often been complex, confusing and ultimately failed to deliver the ultimate goal because they often restrict innovation and reward past achievements. It ought to be obvious that motivation occupies a central place in the rationale for the choices made by managers and hence attempts to understand the effectiveness of any particular reward system. In the application of this understanding of motivation, organisational policies have swayed between 'paying for numbers' and 'paying for skills', while always proving ineffective in the longer term because, we can suggest, they failed to convince people to take work seriously. However, it has also been argued that the idea that waving cash before people will motivate them, whilst an oft quoted 'wisdom' in modern society, is an oversimplification (see Kohn, 1998). Indeed, compensation managers need to take on board Slater's argument that 'The idea that everybody wants money is propaganda circulated by wealth addicts to make themselves feel better about their addiction' (1980: 25). Such an analysis would place the psychological contract in a more central position in the struggle for higher performance.

The issues surrounding the seriousness of work have recently been addressed by the development of the debates linked to the creation and maintenance of a contract in the mind. The psychological contract has been a rich source of ideas for the development of modern reward processes in that it goes beyond mere behaviours to consider the creation of values and understanding. Despite this attention, through which organisations have elaborated the existence of mutual obligations and duties, the psychological contract is seen to be a difficult tool to apply in the development of reward systems. Irrespective of these reservations, organisations have developed a performance management process which relies on the interaction between behaviours and values. These have included cafeteria pay systems, merit-based pay, team-based pay, management by objectives, 360-degree and other appraisal systems, designed to gain control of the effort side and return the levels of productivity purchased in the labour market.

HR practitioners have applied themselves to the development of systems of reward which are closely integrated with other organisational aims and reflect the strategic role played by reward in the achievement of these objectives. We argued that recent surveys suggest that all is not as it might appear from a glance at the literature. The employment relationship, and specifically the wage/effort or reward element, is still disputed territory within which neither side secures all their objectives. The Chartered Institute of Personnel and Development (CIPD) has a very useful website to refer to (www.cipd.co.uk).

Summary

- Reward strategies need to be viewed in the light of the employment relationship as an economic exchange. Employers need to exercise control over both sides of the wage/effort bargain to the greatest possible extent and in this light reward management attempts to enlarge the area of managerial control.

- These strategies have developed over the years since the industrial revolution through various phases and periods in response to the changing use and nature of technology. The basic nature of such schemes, however, continues to be that of payment by or for performance, whether such performance be pieces made, hours worked, merit achieved or compliance with organisational norms.

- Reward schemes attempt to generate a motivated workforce which is committed and loyal to the organisation.

- Motivation theory has evolved from a simple assumption based on notions of a rational economic perspective of employees – i.e. being motivated primarily by money – towards a more sophisticated human relations perspective which takes cognisance of the numerous and divergent 'needs' employees have. This more complex, though realistic assessment of what motivates employees requires managers to develop strategies which enable employees to realise an ever-greater sense of personal achievement and satisfaction in exchange for their contribution to the organisation.

- The psychological contract, seen in terms of transactional and relational elements, is increasingly being acknowledged as a significant aspect of the employment relationship. In the context of delayering, downsizing, limited career progression, the inability to offer a job for life, organisations need to change work patterns to ensure a sense of personal achievement, enhance employability security and engender relationship values in an effort to maintain a healthy psychological contract which will stimulate commitment and loyalty.

- Current debates surround the difficulties inherent in the motivation and management of knowledge workers, the control of emotional labour and the desire to secure additional profits via the application of reward strategies.

- The development of 'new pay' highlights an increased interest in the rules that are applied to the receipt of 'contingent' elements within reward packages.

QUESTIONS

1 Does the concept of employment relationships as economic exchange significantly add to our understanding of reward strategies?

2 To what extent is it possible for managers to convince workers 'to take work seriously when they know that it is a joke' (Anthony, 1977: 5) through the application of reward strategies?

3 How would you depict the evaluation of motivation theory?

4 Critically assess the extent to which money is the primary motivator for all employees.

5 In what way does the psychological contract influence the employment relationship?

1 Prepare a short report to the HR director in which you make three recommendations for improving performance using modern reward management techniques.

2 Write a short article for an in-house magazine which indicates the effects of poor performance on the attainment of organisational goals and how the use of a performance management system benefits all employees.

3 Prepare a short report to the HR director in which you make three recommendations for improving the morale among the workforce based on sound principles of motivational theory.

4 Debate with colleagues the proposition that 'the psychological contract is a confused and irrelevant concept in the context of the employment relationship'.

CASE STUDY

Widgets Are Us

Widgets Are Us is part of a major multinational company which located at a site in the UK in 1990. They manufacture widgets for the electronics industry which are then branded by their various customers. The company is non-union and in order to retain this status operates a 'workers' forum' for consultations; they do not negotiate in relation to reward packages or levels. The main site has three separate units each producing different sizes of widget for various markets.

Units One and Two consist of four production lines each of which runs a continuous assembly process operating seven days a week and 24 hours a day. The bulk of the workforce is female, part-time and/or agency temporary workers, the latter group comprising some 40 per cent of the staff in each Unit. Each line is divided into six 'areas' within which five workers comprise a 'team' with one designated a 'team leader'. They are paid a base rate with additions for each piece produced by the line during each shift; team leaders are paid at a rate which is 5 per cent above the rest of the team to reflect their responsibility for the team. The base rate is in line with the National Minimum Wage and the line is paid an additional 4p for each item passed by quality control as satisfactory. The quality control operatives are placed mid-way along the line to verify quality prior to the widgets being vacuum packed for dispatch and are paid on a monthly basis at a higher base rate with no incentive element. As staff members they enjoy a choice of additional benefits drawn from the company 'cafeteria' reward system which is not available to other line workers. The widgets are mass produced to agreed specifications for each customer and the line may make widgets with slightly different specifications during each shift (on occasions as many as three different specifications during any one shift). Each line has a line manager who has the responsibility of ensuring that the materials are available for each specification as and when necessary and there are two assistant production managers responsible for two lines each who direct the flow of work to ensure orders are met by priority rather than on a 'first come first served' basis. The team leaders are responsible for ensuring that their teams are up to numbers and report any deficiencies to the line manager. It is the line manager's role to secure authority from the assistant production manager to approach the 'in-house' agency in order to cover any shortfall in the required number of workers.

Each Unit has a goods in/out department which is staffed by a regular crew of 15 workers. These workers are predominately male, semi-skilled, higher earners who are employed on the same basis as the quality control workers. Their main role is to offload materials and transport them to the lines, as and when requested, to collect completed work and load it for distribution. The Units run a JIT system under which there is little or no storage of materials beyond a single day's requirements and vehicles are loaded during the shift for dispatch that evening; all distribution takes place on an overnight basis. The minimum number of drivers are directly employed, with any shortfall covered by contracts with local distribution organisations.

Case study continued

Each Unit therefore has a total three shift workforce of 200 production and distribution workers split into three shifts over a seven-day rota. No shift allowances are paid and overtime payments are not attracted for any hours below 40 whichever day they are worked; where over 40 hours are worked the overtime rate is time and a half whatever day worked. Production workers, excluding team leaders, are allowed 20 days' holiday a year, attract only statutory sick pay and are excluded from the company staff benefits. Temporary workers are treated as employees of the agency and their payment is left to the agency, which also deducts NI contributions and tax.

The third Unit is somewhat more specialised and produces bespoke widgets on a one-off basis primarily for export. It also includes an R&D section dedicated to advances in both widgets and their production. The Unit employs 20 semi-skilled production workers on the standard staff contracts and 10 specialist engineers paid an annual salary in line with local terms and conditions, which, as the area is depressed, are significantly below national averages.

Staff jobs are rewarded in a different manner in that they receive an annual salary with the additional option of picking benefits from the 'cafeteria' package based on the outcome of their appraisal. Only 'staff' are appraised and the merit element ranges between 1 and 5 per cent of their annual salary; they cannot take this value in cash and must select from the benefits cafeteria. These rules apply to team leaders, quality control operatives, warehouse operatives, line managers, assistant production managers, secretarial and administrative staff and office managers. Higher grades, including the engineers, negotiate their own packages on appointment and are then subject to the appraisal rules.

The organisation has a number of problems which the HR department need to address:

1. Units One and Two have high (up to 10 per cent per day) absence rates amongst the production workers.
2. They have a more serious problem with the weekends when the absence rate can be as high as 20 per cent.
3. Each has a turnover rate above the national average for the industry and they find temporary workers difficult to keep.
4. Unit Three has a higher than average turnover rate amongst the engineers.
5. Staff posts are fairly stable across the units but they find quality control workers are difficult to appoint from existing 'in-house' staff, possibly due to the lack of an incentive scheme which can result in their earnings being lower than those of the line operatives.

Questions

1 As an HR manager, how could you change the reward system to address each of these problems?

2 What measures would you take to strengthen the psychological contract?

References and further reading

Adams, J.S. (1963) 'Toward an understanding of inequality', *Journal of Abnormal and Social Psychology*, 67: 422–436.

Adams, J. (1965) 'Inequity in social exchange', in Berkowitz, L. (ed.) *Advances in Experimental Social Psychology*, 2. New York: Academic Press.

Adams, R.J. (1986) 'Two policy approaches to labour-management decision making at the level of the enterprise', in Craig Riddel, W.W. (ed.) *Labour–Management Cooperation in Canada*. Toronto: University of Toronto Press.

Anthony, P.D. (1977) *The Ideology of Work*. London: Tavistock Publications.

Appelbaum, E. (1993) 'Rethinking rewards', *Harvard Business Review*, Nov–Dec.

Armstrong, M. (1996) 'How group efforts can pay dividends', *People Management*, 25 January: 22–27.

Armstrong, M. (2002) *Employee Reward*. London: CIPD.

Arnold, J., Cooper, C. and Robertson, I. (1998) *Work Psychology: Understanding Human Behaviour in the Workplace*, 3rd edn. Harlow: Financial Times.

Austin, J. and Bobko, P. (1985) 'Goal setting theory', *Journal of Occupational Psychology*, 58: 289–308.

Bassett Jones, N. and Lloyd, G. (2004) 'Does Herzberg's Motivation theory have staying power?' *The Journal of Management Development*, 24, 10: 929–944.

Bean, R. (1994) *Comparative Industrial Relations*. London: Routledge.

Beer, M., Walton, R.E. and Spector, B.A. (1984) *Managing Human Assets*. New York: Free Press.

Blau, G. (1994) 'Testing the effect of level and importance of pay referents on pay level satisfaction', *Human Relations*, 47, 10: 1251–1268.

Blauner, R. (1964) *Alienation and Freedom: The Factory Worker and His Industry*. Chicago, Ill.: Chicago Press.

Bowey, A.M., Thorpe, R. and Hellier, P. (1986) *Payment Systems and Productivity*. Basingstoke: Macmillan.

Braverman, H. (1974) *Labour and Monopoly Capital: The Degradation of Work in the Twentieth Century*. London: Monthly Review Press.

Burawoy, M. (1985) *The Politics of Production*. London: Verso.

Callaghan, G. and Thompson, P. (2001) 'Edwards revisited: technical control and call centres', *Economic and Industrial Democracy*, 22, 1: 13–37.

Chadha Y. (2006) *Recognizing employees' efforts at Sara Lee Foods*. London: Melcrum Publishing Ltd.

CIPD (2003) *Pressure of Work and the Psychological Contract*. London: CIPD.

Conboy, B. (1976) *Pay at Work*. London: Arrow Books.

Cordery, J.L., Mueller, W.S. and Smith, L.M. (1991) 'Attitudinal and behavioral effects of autonomous group working: A longitudinal field study', *Academy of Management Journal*, 34: 464–476.

Cornelius, N. (2001) *Human Resource Management*, 2nd edn. London: Thomson Learning.

Crown, D.F. and Rosse, J.G. (1995) 'Yours, mine, and ours: Facilitating group productivity through the integration of individual and group goals', *Organizational Behavior and Human Decision Processes*, 64, 2: 138–150.

Daniels, K. (2006) *Employee Relations in an Organisational Context*. London: CIPD.

Dulebohn, J.H. and Martocchio, J.J. (1998) 'Employee perceptions of the fairness of work group incentive pay plans', *Journal of Management*, 24, 4: 469–488.

Earley, P., Connolly, T. and Ekergren, G. (1989) 'Goals, strategy development and task performance', *Journal of Applied Psychology*, 74: 24–33.

Etzioni, A. (1975) *A Comparative Analysis of Complex Organisations*. New York: Free Press.

Fisher, C. (1999) 'Performance management and performing management', in Leopold, J. *et al.* (eds) *Strategic Human Resourcing*. Harlow: FT/Pitman.

Folger, R., Konovsky, M.A. and Cropanzano, R. (1992) 'A due process metaphor for performance appraisal', in Straw, B.M. and Cummings, L.L. (eds) *Research on Organizational Behaviour*, pp. 129–177.

Freeman, R. (2001) 'Upping the stakes', *People Management*, February: 25–29.

Freeman, R.B. and Rogers, J. (1999) *What Workers Want*. Cornell, NY: Russell Sage Foundation.

Gooch, L. and Cornelius, N. (2001) 'Performance management: strategy, systems and rewards', in Cornelius, N. (ed.) *Human Resource Management*. London: Thomson Learning.

Gospel, H. (1992) *Markets, Firms, and the Management of Labour in Modern Britain*. Cambridge: Cambridge University Press.

Grayson, D. (1984) 'Shape of payment systems to come', *Employment Gazette*, April: 175–181.

Greenberg, J. (1987) 'A taxonomy of organizational justice theories', *Academy of Management Review*, 3, 3: 61–77.

Grint, K. (1997) *Fuzzy Management: Contemporary Ideas and Practices at Work*. Oxford: Oxford University Press.

Guest, D. (1998a) 'Is the psychological contract worth taking seriously?', *Journal of Organizational Behaviour*, 19: 649–664.

Guest, D. (1998b) 'On meaning, metaphor and the psychological contract: a response to Rousseau', *Journal of Organizational Behaviour*, 19: 673–677.

Guest, D. and Conway, N. (2002) 'Communicating the psychological contract: an employer perspective', *Human Resource Management Journal*, 12: 22–38.

Guzzo, R. and Noonan K.A. (1994) 'Human resources practices as communications and the psychological contract', *Human Resource Management*, 33, 3: 447–462.

Hackman, J. and Lawler, E. (1971) 'Employee reactions to job characteristics', *Journal of Applied Psychology Monograph*, 55: 259–286.

Hackman, J. and Oldman, G. (1980) *Work Redesign*. Reading, Mass: Addison-Wesley.

Hastings, S. and Dixon, L. (1995) *Competency: An Introduction*. Oxford: Trade Union Research Unit.

Herriot, P., Manning, W. and Kidd, J. (1997) 'The content of the psychological contract', *British Journal of Management*, 8, 2: 151–162.

Herriot, P. and Pemberton, C. (1995) *New Deals*. Chichester: John Wiley.

Herzberg, F. (1966) *Work and the Nature of Man*. Cleveland, Ohio: World Publishing.

Hill, S. (1981) *Competition and Control at Work*. London: Heinemann.

Howell, K. and Cameron, E. (1996) 'The benefits of an outsider's opinion', *People Management*, August: 28–30.

Huczynski, A. and Buchanan, D. (2001) *Organisational Behaviour: An Introductory Text*, 4th edn. Harlow: Prentice Hall.

IDS (1992) 'PRP grows as tax relief doubles', *IDS Study 520*, December.

IRS (2002) *IRS HR Essentials: Employment Facts, Research and Analysis*. Issue 02, December.

IRS (2003) *Employment Review 773*, May.

Jin, P. (1993) 'Work motivation and productivity in voluntary formed teams: A field study in China', *Organizational Behavior and Human Decision Processes*, 54: 133–135.

Kaplan, R.S and Norton, D.P. (1992) 'The balanced scorecard: measures that drive performance', *Harvard Business Review*, January–February: 71–79.

Kellaway, L.G. (1993) 'Nice little earner (profit-related pay)', *Financial Times*, 23 April, p. 14.

Kinnie, N. and Lowe, D. (1990) 'Performance related pay on the shopfloor', *People Management*, November: 45–49.

Klien, D.A. (1998) *The Strategic Management of Intellectual Capital*. Woburn: Butterworth-Heinemann.

Kohn, A. (1993a) 'Why Incentive Plans Cannot Work', *Harvard Business Review*, Sept–Oct.

Kohn, A. (1993b) 'Rethinking Rewards', *Harvard Business Review*, Nov–Dec.

Kohn, A. (1998) 'Challenging Behaviorist dogma: Myths about Money and Motivation', *Compensation and Benefits Review*, 30, 2: 27–33.

Kovach, K.A. (1987) 'What motivates employees? Workers and supervisors give different answers', *Business Horizons*, Sept–Oct: 58–65.

Kozlowski, A. (1993), in Kohn, A. 'Rethinking Rewards', *Harvard Business Review*, Nov–Dec.

Lawler, E.E. (1990) *Strategic Pay*. San Francisco, Calif.: Jossey Bass.

Lee, C., Law, K.S. and Bobko, P. (1999) 'The importance of justice perceptions on pay effectiveness', *Journal of Management*, 25, 6: 851–873.

Leventhal, G.S. (1976) 'Fairness in social relationships', in Thibaut, J. *et al. Contemporary Topics in Social Psychology*. Morristown, NJ: General Learning Press.

Lind, E.A. and Tyler, T. (1988) *The Social Psychology of Procedural Justice*. New York: Plenum.

Littler, C. (1982) *The Development of the Labour Process in Capitalist Societies*. London: Heinemann.

Littler, C. (ed.) (1985) *The Experience of Work*. Aldershot: Gower.

Locke, E. and Latham, G. (1984) *Goal Setting*. Englewood Cliffs, NJ: Prentice Hall.

Locke, E., Shaw, K., Saari, L. and Latham, G. (1981) 'Goal setting and task performance 1969–1980', *Psychological Bulletin*, 90: 125–152.

Lowry, D. (2002) 'Performance management', in Leopold, J. (ed.) *Human Resources in Organisations*. Harlow: FT/Prentice Hall.

Makin, J., Cooper, C. and Cox, J. (1996) *Organizations and the Psychological Contract*. Oxford: Blackwell.

Margerison, C. (1976) 'A constructive approach to appraisal', *Personnel Management*, July: 30–33.

McFarlin, D.B. and Sweeny, P.D. (1992) 'The psychological contract, organisational commitment and job satisfaction of temporary staff', *Leadership and Organisational Development Journal*, 21, 2: 84–91.

McGregor, D. (1957) 'An uneasy look at performance', *Harvard Business Review*, 35: 89–94.

Mercer Consultants (2003) 'Mind the productivity gap', in *IRS HR Essentials*, May.

Millward, N., Bryson, A. and Forth, J. (2000) *All Change at Work*. London: Routledge.

Miner, J.B. (2003) 'The rated importance, scientific validity, and practical usefulness of organizational behavior theories: a quantitative review', *Academy of Management Learning Education*, 9, 2: 250–268.

Mitrani, A., Dalziel, M. and Fitt, D. (1993) *Competency Based Human Resource Management*. London: Kogan Page.

Newton, T. and Findlay, P. (2000) 'Playing God? The performance appraisal', Chapter 8 in Mabey, C., Salaman, G. and Storey, J. (eds) *Strategic Human Resource Management: A Reader*. London: Sage in association with The Open University.

O'Doherty, D. (2001) 'Job design: signs, symbols and resignations', in Beardwell, I. and Holden, L. (eds) *Human Resource Management*, 3rd edn. Harlow: FT/Prentice Hall.

Orpen, C. (1997) 'The effects of formal mentoring on employee work motivation, organizational commitment and job performance', *The Learning Organization*, 4, 2. Research paper.

Pfeffer, J. (1998) 'Six dangerous myths about pay', *Harvard Business Review*, May–June.

Pinder, C. (1998) *Work Motivation in Organizational Behaviour*. Upper Saddle River, NJ: Prentice Hall.

Pritchard, D. and Murlis, H. (1992) *Jobs, Roles and People*. London: Nicholas Brealey.

Raub, S.P. (2001) 'Towards a knowledge-based framework of competence development', in Sanchez, R. *Knowledge Management and Organizational Competence*. Oxford: OUP.

Ritzer, G. (1997) *The McDonaldization Thesis*. London: Sage.

Ritzer, G. (2000) *The McDonaldization of Society*. London: Sage.

Robbins, S.P. (2002) *Organizational Behaviour*, New Delhi: Prentice Hall.

Roberts, I. (2001) 'Reward and performance management', in Beardwell, I. and Holden, L. (eds) *Human Resource Management*, 3rd edn. Harlow: FT/Prentice Hall.

Rollinson, D. (2002) *Organisational Behaviour and Analysis: An Integrated Approach*, 2nd edn. Harlow: Financial Times Prentice Hall.

Rosenfield, R. and Wilson, D. (1999) *Managing Organizational Behaviour: Text, Readings and Cases*, 2nd edn. London: McGraw-Hill.

Rousseau, D. (1995) *Psychological Contracts in Organizations*. Thousand Oaks, Calif.: Sage.

Rousseau, D. (1998) 'The problem of the psychological contract', *Journal of Organisational Behaviour*, 19: 665–671.

Rousseau, D. (2001) 'Schema, promise and mutuality: the building blocks of the psychological contract', *Journal of Occupational and Organisational Psychology*, 74: 511–541.

Rynes, L., Gerhart, B. and Minette, A. (2004) The importance of pay in employee motivation: Discrepancies between what people say and what they do. *Human Resource Management*, 43, 4: 381–394.

Schama, S. (1995) *Landscape and Memory*. London: HarperCollins.

Schuler, R.S. and Jackson, S.E. (1999) *Strategic Human Resource Management*. Oxford: Blackwell.

Schuster, J.R. and Zingheim, P. (1992) *The New Pay*. New York: Lexington Books.

Scott, H., Cheese, P. and Cantrell, S. (2006) 'Harley-Davidson', *Strategic HR Review*. Jan/Feb 5, 2: 28–31.

Shamir, B. (1991) 'Meaning, self and motivation in organizations', *Organizational Studies*, 12, 3: 405–424.

Slater, P. (1980) *Wealth Addiction*. New York: Dutton.

Sparrow, P. (1996) 'Transitions in the psychological contract', *Human Resource Management Journal*, 6, 4: 75–92.

Storey, J. (1992) *Developments in the Management of Human Resources*. Oxford: Blackwell.

Taylor, F.W. (1964) *Scientific Management*. New York: Harper & Row.

Taylor, P. and Bain, P. (1999) 'An assembly line in the head', *Industrial Relations Journal*, 30, 2: 101–117.

Taylor, P. and Bain, P. (2001) 'Trade unions, workers' rights and the frontier of control in UK call centres', *Economic and Industrial Democracy*, 22, 1: 39–66.

The Work Foundation (2003) 'Unwritten rules', in *IRS HR Essentials*. Issue 07, May.

Thompson, P. (1983) *The Nature of Work*. London: Macmillan.

Vroom, V.H. (1964) *Work and Motivation*. New York: John Wiley.

White, A. (2002) Interview with author at Jones the Bootmaker Ltd.

White, G. and Drucker, J. (2000) *Reward Management: A Critical Text*. London: Routledge.

Wiley, C. (1997) 'What motivates employees according to over 40 years of motivation surveys', *International Journal of Manpower*, 18, 3: 263–280.

Wilson, F. (1999) *Organisational Behaviour: A Critical Introduction*. Oxford: Oxford University Press.

Wood, A.W. (2000) 'Alienation', in *Concise Routledge Encyclopedia of Philosophy*. London: Routledge.

Wood, S. (ed.) (1982) *The Degradation of Work?* London: Hutchinson.

Woodruffe, C. (2006) 'Employee engagement', *British Journal of Administrative Manananagement*, Jan, 50: 28–29.

For multiple-choice questions, exercises and annotated weblinks specific to this chapter visit the book's website at **www.pearsoned.co.uk/beardwell**

Chapter 14

Employee participation and involvement

Peter Butler and Linda Glover

Objectives

- To provide definitions of employee involvement, participation and industrial democracy.
- To examine why the concept of employee involvement is closely allied to 'soft' HRM.
- To clarify the difference between 'cycles' and 'waves' of participation.
- To review evidence in respect of downwards communication, upwards problem solving, financial participation and representative participation.
- To examine recent developments in workplace consultation emanating from the EU.
- To critically evaluate the implications of selected new management initiatives for organisations and employees.

Introduction

This chapter focuses upon employee participation and involvement (EPI). Employee involvement is central to mainstream models of HRM and as such is an extremely important component of the contemporary study of HRM. However, as we shall see, EPI initiatives are characterised by ambiguity – both in terms of academic terminology, their application in the field and in terms of the outcomes for organisations and employees. Given the potential for confusion this chapter will at the outset seek to unpack the EPI construct. As will become clear, the subject matter is broad and actually comprises three distinct but related fields of study: employee involvement, employee participation and industrial democracy. The first section focuses upon definitions of each of these terms. Armed with some conceptual clarity the second section moves on to discuss the history of EPI. It will become evident that while managerially inspired employee involvement is currently ascendant, this is a relatively recent development – over the years the other components have occupied far more column inches, in the annals devoted to the topic. The third section focuses upon the managerial motives for EPI and shows that interpretations of managerial purpose range from those that view EPI interventions as positive for managers and employees (i.e. unitarist), to those who view managerial intent with suspicion and regard motives as primarily exploitative, to those who believe that mangerial goals are not so clear-cut and fall somewhere in-between these two extremes. The fourth section explores in more depth the precise nature of EPI practices and reviews some of the evidence relating to trends for the various mechanisms. The fifth section reviews contemporary developments at EU level. It will be argued that some of these are significant in heralding a potential renaissance for collective systems of employee participation. The chapter closes with a discussion of the highly topical area of the implications for organisations and employees of new management initiatives. Here we focus on the move from quality circles to quality management to high performance management.

Definitions

The topic of employee participation and involvement (EPI) has been a perennial feature of writings pertaining to the management of human resources. The resilience of the phenomenon and its capacity for reinvention over the last 100 years or so has been one of the more enduring features of studies of the employment relationship. Richardson (2003: 374) likens EPI to Cinderella in its ability to attract and enthral new audiences from one year to the next; a fixation that shows little sign of waning. A key problem facing students of EPI, however, is ambiguity in terminology, indeed Marchington and Wilkinson (2005) comment that 'employee participation and involvement are somewhat elastic terms and are amenable to a range of definitions'. EPI is often treated as a loosely specified concept within which a myriad of managerial interventions are collapsed.

Involvement and participation, while closely related, are conceptually and philosophically distinct and have similarly achieved prominence during differing historical periods. While writers in this field have long lamented the absence of universally accepted definitions (see Hespe and Little, 1971 and Pateman, 1970) we are today fortunate in that the terrain of EPI is far less theoretically impoverished than it was a generation or so ago. Indeed, following the emergence of the topic as discrete field of study it is possible to construct a reasonably precise set of conceptualisations, bringing some much needed order to the subject matter. Lewis *et al.* (2003: 248) have argued that 'important differences . . . exist between the concepts in relation to the exercise of power, the locus of control, the nature of employee influence, and the driving force behind each approach in practice'. More empirically, Marchington *et al.* (1992: 7–8) suggest that it is possible to draw distinctions in terms of the degree of employee involvement; the form which the involvement takes; the level in the organisational hierarchy at which individuals are involved; and the range of subject matter dealt with. In the final analysis these models suggest that the essence of any distinction centres on issues of power and influence.

Employee involvement

Employee involvement (EI) is central to most models of HRM. For example, employee involvement is seen as a central tenet of 'soft' HRM, where the focus is upon capturing the ideas of employees and securing their commitment. Storey (1992: 46) suggests that 'soft' HRM 'connotes a style of approach whose touchstones are the careful nurturing of, and investment in, the human stock'. Legge (2005: 105–106) comments that the soft 'developmental humanism' model involves 'treating employees as valued assets, a source of competitive advantage through their commitment, adaptability and high-quality (of skills, performance and so on) . . . the stress is therefore on generating commitment via "communication, motivation and leadership"'. As with HRM, the concept of employee involvement is strongly grounded in unitary theory – put simply it is assumed that managers and employees will 'march to the same tune'. Characteristically employee involvement initiatives are promoted by management with a view to mobilising the support and tacit knowledge of employees towards corporate goals. Marchington and Wilkinson (2005) observe that employee involvement has 'focused on direct participation of small groups and individuals, it is concerned with information sharing at work–group level, and it has excluded the opportunity for workers to have any inputs into high-level decision-making'. Mechanisms for employee involvement include suggestion schemes, quality circles and teamworking (we will return to discuss each of these in more detail later in the chapter). Marchington and Wilkinson (2005) draw a distinction between the *direct participation* that is typical of these schemes and *indirect participation* schemes such as consultative committees 'which are collectivist and representative in form'. They argue that direct participation is 'fundamentally different' from indirect participation as the roots of the latter tend to be found in notions of industrial democracy.

Critics have argued that employee involvement has management firmly in the driving seat and very limited real influence is relinquished or ceded to non-managerial actors. That is, employee involvement schemes 'extend little or no input into corporate or higher level decision making' and generally do not entail any significant sharing of power and authority (Hyman and Mason, 1995: 22). Simply put, employee involvement is 'soft on power' (Blyton and Turnbull, 2004: 272) the hallmark being that the 'range' (Marchington et al., 1992: 8) of subject matter dealt with is non-strategic in nature and of only localised operational importance. To the extent that there is any granting of influence to employees the locus is restricted to task or work group level (Lewis et al., 2003: 259). Any employee 'involvement' in higher order decisions is restricted to top-down information provision.

Box 14.1 Employee involvement

Practices and policies which emanate from management and sympathisers of free market commercial activity and which purport to provide employees with the opportunity to influence and where appropriate take part in the decision making on matters which affect them.

Source: Hyman and Mason, 1995: 21

Participation

Employee participation, as distinct to employee involvement, is grounded in pluralist thinking – a perspective that acknowledges the presence of divergent interests between different organisational stakeholders. Henceforth, when using the term 'participation', we refer to *indirect* forms such as consultative committees. Operationally speaking participation may be contrasted with employee involvement in that it derives invariably from employees, or their organisations (i.e. trade unions), as opposed to being employer led (Harley et al., 2005: 13). As Hyman and Mason (1995: 29) acknowledge, employee participation 'emerges from a collective employee interest to optimize the physical security and aspirational conditions under which employees are contracted to serve'. The motivation for participation therefore differs fundamentally from employee involvement in that it is borne of a desire to increase the influence of employees *vis-à-vis* the employer rather than being concerned with technical issues of corporate efficiency (see Box 14.2). Two outcomes follow. First, in contrast to the task-centred menu of practices that normally surround employee involvement, participation is more fundamentally power orientated – it is typically about joint decision making or co-determination (Blyton and Turnbull, 2004: 59). As such, conflict may occur, and could take the form of strikes, stoppages or working-to-rule. Recent examples include the firefighters dispute of 2002–3 which began over disagreements about pay and working conditions. Second, participation is likely to give employees (usually via the agency of their representatives) access to a relatively higher order 'range' of decisions (e.g. wage rates, introduction of new technology and training etc.) than that provided by the machinery of employee involvement. In Abrahamsson's (1977: 189) terminology, participation can be viewed as a political process contributing to high level decision making as opposed to the 'socio-technical nature' of employee involvement which restricts tangible employee influence to narrow production issues.

Because participatory schemes generally involve some dilution of managerial influence there is a long history of employers seeking to resist their encroachment. Consequently, the more enduring examples, such as the works council format found in many European countries, tend to have a strong statutory underpinning and have often been initiated by social democratic governments sensitive to the needs of labour (Payne and Keep, 2005).

> ### Box 14.2 Workers' participation
>
> Workers' participation is about the distribution and exercise of power, in all its manifestations, between the owners and managers of organisations and those employed by them. It refers to the direct involvement of individuals in decisions relating to their immediate work organisation and to indirect involvement in decision making, through representatives, in the wider socio-technical and political structures of the firm.
>
> *Source*: Brannen, 1983: 16

Within the UK participation has traditionally found expression through the medium of collective bargaining, rather than via mandated works councils. Collective bargaining is the mechanism through which trade unions and employers jointly regulate certain aspects of the employment relationship (for example, negotiating over pay and conditions such as leave entitlements, pensions and working hours). In terms of the level of influence exerted via this process the traditional trade union preoccupation with wage issues or 'economism' (Hyman, 1989: 45) has ensured that strategic matters, for example, decisions pertaining to capital investment, have rarely figured as substantive items on the bargaining agenda. Table 14.1 summarises some of the key differences between employee involvement and employee participation.

Industrial democracy

Industrial democracy is distinct from participation in that the goal is a more radical sharing of power within the employment relationship. Throughout the course of capitalist history various radical movements (e.g. the guild socialists, see below) have sought to greatly extend employee influence via calls for industrial democracy. The goal here is a more revolutionary reshaping of power within the employment relationship. Drawing on Marxian principles fundamentalist adherents to this approach argue that nothing less than the transfer of ownership and the means of production to workers is consistent with true workplace democracy (see Hyman and Mason, 1995: 9–12). The Israeli kibbutz, Yugoslavian experiments in self-management and the Mondragón corporation in the Basque region of Spain (see Cheney, 1999) have, at various times, been lauded as exemplars of this approach.

With one or two exceptions (e.g. The John Lewis Partnership (Flanders, 1968)) British experiments in industrial democracy have tended to be relatively modest affairs, for example,

Table 14.1 Employee involvement and participation compared

Employee involvement	Employee participation
Management inspired and controlled	Government or workforce inspired; some control delegated to workforce
Geared to stimulating individual employee contributions	Aims to harness collective employee input through market regulation
Employees often passive recipients	Employee representatives actively involved
Tends to be task based	Decision making at higher organisational levels
Assumes common interests between employer and employees	Plurality of interests recognised and machinery for their resolution provided

Source: Adapted from Hyman and Mason (1995).

Box 14.3 Industrial democracy

Adherents to this approach would argue that democratic procedures need to be 'injected at the highest organisational levels in order to restructure authority relations within industry and thereby make all aspects of industrial decision making available and accountable to the majority of the participants who are disenfranchised from existing structures'.

Source: Hyman and Mason, 1995: 18.

Figure 14.1 The escalator of participation

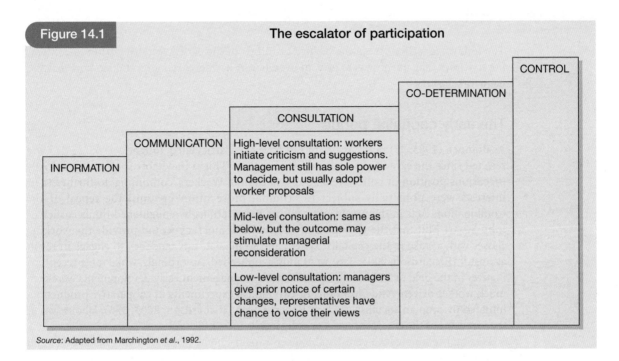

Source: Adapted from Marchington *et al.*, 1992.

the emergence of worker directors in some public sector enterprises in the 1960s and 1970s (see below). The goal has been to give employees some strategic influence via boardroom representation, not overturn the structure of corporate governance, i.e. working for rather than owning the company. In view of the traditional antipathy of employers towards any serious extension of employee influence the state or super state (in the form of the EU) has typically been the driver behind any change to the status quo.

The 'escalator of participation' (see Figure 14.1), as originally devised by Marchington *et al.* (1992), allows us to clarify visually the terrain of both participation and industrial democracy. The latter concept occupies the top step on the escalator. Participation conversely resides on the second step, possibly spreading onto the third depending on the precise nature of consultation. Consultation is itself a term that raises immense definitional problems; in part this is avoided by presenting the term as a continuum. Following Shuchman (cited in Poole, 1978: 26–27) and Bernstein (1976) the consultation 'step' contains three levels of consultation. Of these genuine participation only occupies the green shaded region. Following Pateman (1970) the other forms of consultation are best viewed as 'pseudo participation', i.e. it is only in high-level consultation that management take workers' views seriously and are likely to modify plans accordingly.

Stop & think

1 *Why is employee involvement described as 'unitarist'?*

2 *Why is employee involvement central to HRM?*

3 *What are the differences between direct participation via employee involvement and indirect participation?*

4 *Why might management resist moves towards greater industrial democracy?*

History of EPI

The following sections trace the history of EPI from the early capitalist period to contemporary times. The purpose is to give an overview of key developments and to show that EPI has a long history.

The early capitalist period

As Brannen (1983: 33) notes, issues of EPI have been 'articulated, fought over, conceded and rejected since the earliest years of industrial society'. This is inevitably so given the initially precarious position of collective labour *qua* capital. Workers 'combining' to further their interests were potentially subject to criminal prosecution up until the repeal of the Combinations Acts in the nineteenth century. Exhortations by enlightened thinkers such as John Stuart Mill that the provision of industrial democracy would provide the working classes with a stake in the capitalist system and so mediate any tendency to engage in revolt against it (Richardson, 2003: 376) went mostly unheeded. Accordingly, while most recent initiatives in the field of EPI have been brokered by management early developments were very much worker driven. Aside from one or two radical experiments in cooperative production, initiated by utopian socialists such as Robert Owen (Richardson, 2003: 376), labour was at the vanguard of the emergence of – or at least calls for – EPI.

During the nineteenth century the disenfranchisement of the working classes from all matters relating to workplace regulation gave rise to a radicalisation of employee demands in the form of syndicalism, i.e. demands for the means of production to be placed under worker control and later, guild socialism, i.e. a desire for the state ownership of industry. While philosophically distinct there was common ground in that both denied the legitimacy of the principles of ownership and control embodied within capitalism (Brannen, 1983: 46) and emphasised the necessity for workers' self-governance of industry (Brannen, 1983: 39) – that is a pure form of industrial democracy. Influenced by the Bolshevik revolution in Russia this period witnessed a considerable growth in left-wing ideology (Holden, 2001: 546). However, tangible employee influence only emerged through the growth of the pluralist practice of collective bargaining (i.e. indirect participation) – an institution that seeks *accommodation* with capital – not its overthrow. Interestingly, the growth in coverage of collective bargaining and the increased institutional strength of trade unions ushered in the first 'cycle' (Ramsay, 1977) of employee involvement. As far back as the 1860s firms were pioneering profit-share schemes as a means of 'detaching workers from their unions' (Ramsay, 1977: 483). Such practices, however, were not to gain widespread currency for a century or more.

The inter-war period: Whitleyism and joint consultation

The emergence of industrial syndicalism, while short lived, was not without legacy and it was indeed a factor motivating both politicians and employers to more thoughtfully review issues pertaining to EPI (Ramsay, 1977: 486). Set against a backdrop of widespread industrial conflict in the immediate aftermath of the First World War a government subcommittee of enquiry under J.H. Whitley, comprising both employers and trade union representatives, was established to consider how to achieve a permanent improvement in relations between employers and workers (Marchington *et al.*, 1992: 5). The key policy outcome was the suggestion that workers should be able to participate more fully in the regulation of employment conditions of most concern to them (Marchington *et al.*, 1992). The upshot was the creation of 73 joint industrial councils with over 1000 local committees, the aim being to discuss not only wages and conditions but also problems of industrial efficiency and management. Opinion regarding whether Whitleyism was ever intended to significantly impinge upon managerial prerogative has been a source of some controversy. Brannen (1983: 41) has argued that 'Whitleyism was the officially sponsored *compromise* with demands for worker control' (emphasis added) while for Ramsay the machinery was more about illusory worker control and union incorporation (see Ramsay, 1977: 487–488). Whatever the potential rationale, the initiative was short lived and by 1925 much of the Whitley infrastructure had fallen into disuse.

During the Second World War, EPI again witnessed something of a renaissance. Given the demands placed upon a vastly depleted labour force the government encouraged the creation of workplace Joint Production Committees (JPCs), both as a means of increasing production and efficiency and, according to Ramsay (1977: 490), neutralising militants. By 1943 there were over 4000 JPCs operating in private firms in engineering and related industries covering around 2.5 m workers (Brannen, 1983: 44). It has been estimated that around half of the committees succeeded in relation to their terms of reference (Ramsay, 1977: 490). Nevertheless, as with Whitleyism, enthusiasm for consultation proved ephemeral. Brannen (1983: 44) notes that by 1948 there were only 550 councils in existence. The reason for the brief longevity of such a major, and at times successful, EPI initiative has attracted significant academic comment. Ramsay (1977: 490) affords precedence to worker disillusion with the way in which the JPCs were used to bolster management power as disciplinary bodies and the like. That is, the original pluralist intent was subverted for an essentially unitary *raison d'être*, i.e. management trying to reorientate control. Brannen (1983: 44–45) argues, however, that such an interpretation sits uneasily with TUC exhortations made via its General Council in 1944 that consultation should be kept as a *permanent* feature of industrial organisations (Brannen, 1983). In any event, as with Whitleyism, widespread interest in EPI was again to move into another lengthy period of torpor as the consultation machinery was wound down.

Stop & think

1 Why was the Whitley committee convened?

2 What was its main contribution?

3 Why were JPCs discredited in the eyes of workers?

The 1970s 'High Noon' of industrial democracy

Much has been written about the 1970s revival of interest in industrial democracy. It warrants highlighting at the outset, however, that this version bore little resemblance to the syndicalism that enjoyed a brief but ultimately unfruitful vogue a century before. Where the syndicalism of the nineteenth century denied the legitimacy of capitalist ownership, the premise that management should wield ultimate authority was never seriously challenged in the 1970s.

Renewed interest in issues of workplace democracy arose because of a triple configuration of events. Firstly, the early 1970s marked Britain's accession to the then Common Market where there were already plans afoot for a 'Fifth Directive' on company law. Under these proposals companies with over 500 employees were to have supervisory boards, with one-third of their members representing employees (Clegg, 1979: 438). Powers were to be far reaching with a second-tier management board required to ask the approval of the supervisory board on major decisions such as closure and reorganisation (Brannen, 1983: 59). An opinion was formed within government circles that a considered response was needed if Britain was not to be 'swamped by alien policies' (Elliot, cited in Brannen, 1983). A second impetus was provided by the election of a Labour government in 1974. Six years earlier a Labour working party report, *Industrial Democracy*, had been adopted by the 1968 Party Conference (Ramsay, 1977: 494). In its election manifesto Labour pledged itself to implementing many of the report's recommendations via a specific industrial democracy Act (Brannen, 1983: 59). Thirdly, as Clegg (1979: 438) has noted, this period witnessed a 'remarkable reversal' in the attitude of the TUC. Previously the unions had never supported TU representation on company boards, the guiding philosophy being famously captured in Clegg's (1951) dictum that 'trade unions are an opposition which can never become a government'. As Lewis *et al.* (2003: 25) note, under this view, participation in decision making would have compromised the essentially oppositional role that unions had traditionally played. However, sensing a sea change TUC policy shifted to one of support for worker directors with prominent unionists, such as Jack Jones, calling for a real transfer of power and responsibility to workers (Ramsay, 1977: 494). This change of heart was significantly driven by the growing complexity of the financial structure of organisations: the emergence of multinational enterprise was making it difficult for unions to bargain knowledgably. As Crouch (1979: 109) noted at the time, union officials were increasingly coming to believe that they would need to gain more of an 'insiders' view to pursue matters satisfactorily.

These factors led to the setting up of the Bullock Committee of Inquiry charged with looking at ways of *achieving* boardroom participation (Brannen, 1983: 60). The terms of reference were an immediate source of controversy amongst the committee members comprising trade unionists, academics and employers. The latter argued that they had been forced to consider not *whether* but *how* employee directors should be appointed (Hyman and Mason, 1995: 143, emphasis in original). Reflecting this split, the output was actually two reports. The majority report (representing the views of the Chairperson and the trade unions and academic committee members) supported the creation of so called 'unitary boards' in private sector organisation. The formula $2x + y$ was devised, meaning parity representation of worker directors ($2x$) plus one or more neutral board member recommended by bodies such as ACAS (Hyman and Mason, 1995: 140). The minority report argued that any system should be based on a two-tier model as in Europe, with employee representatives sitting on a supervisory, i.e. policy, board (Hyman and Mason, 1995: 143).

Unsurprisingly British private sector management were 'vehemently opposed' (Brannen, 1983: 60) to the proposals. Indeed Cressey (cited in Lewis *et al.*, 2003: 251) has argued that the minority report was itself a 'pale reflection' of the rancour felt by British employers. Several ministers including the Secretary for Trade, Edmund Dell, shared the employers' views and pressed the government for the dilution of any legislation (Crouch, 1979: 111). The resultant White Paper in 1978 largely affirmed the latter position proposing the establishment of two-tier boards with employees being given a statutory right, if they wished, of representation on a supervisory board (Crouch, 1979: 60). Ultimately, however, some brief public sector experimentation with employee boardroom representation was the only tangible legacy of this sojourn. Hence, attempts were made to introduce worker director schemes into both British Steel and the Post Office (see Batstone *et al.*, 1983 and Brannen *et al.*, 1976). Even here, however, any involvement was mostly restricted to industrial relations issues. That is, the schemes did little to extend the 'range' of employee influence. Failure to make progress denoted that Britain remained one of the few Western European counties without a statutory framework for consultation or participation (Lewis *et al.*, 2003: 251). Political events ensured that any such change remained a generation away.

Stop & think

What factors sparked the renewed interest in workplace democracy? Why do you think private sector managers were 'vehemently opposed' to the proposals of the Bullock report?

Thatcherism and beyond

The 1980s represented a distinct watershed for EPI. The coming of Thatcherism and economic structural change provided a fertile climate for managerial experimentation with practices of employee involvement. The Conservatives were committed to the principles of voluntarism. That is, the premise that management should be allowed to introduce forms of involvement that they saw fit rather than having an external source imposed (Lewis *et al.*, 2003: 258). Thus, from the outset the incoming administration was opposed to Bullock recommendations. The Conservatives *were*, however, committed by their manifesto to encourage employee involvement through consultation, communication and financial involvement (Brannen, 1983: 60). The upshot was a legislative programme that *inter alia* sought to significantly diminish *collective* trade union power *and* encourage *individual* involvement, e.g. by granting tax relief for approved corporate employee share-ownership and profit-related pay schemes. As Blyton and Turnbull (2004: 263) acknowledge, 'in this the Conservative government sought to promote material rather than participative–democratic forms of employee involvement'.

That this period of Conservative rule saw levels of the trade union membership plunge to a post-war low needs no rehearsing. A variety of factors including the decline of the manufacturing sector and the rise of the service sector (much of which being historically non-union) contributed to the decline. Hyman and Mason (1995: 53) have argued that union weakness at political, industrial and organisational level provides employees with opportunities to contemplate alternative arrangements for employee relations. Perhaps unsurprisingly, therefore, the use of employee involvement increased substantially between 1984 and 1990. The overall form that employee involvement took was greater willingness to communicate directly with employees and an enhanced recognition of the potential contribution that employees could make to organisational performance (Marchington, *et al.*, 1992: 6). Employee involvement initiatives such as team briefings, quality circles, suggestion schemes, profit share and share ownership all grew after the late 1970s (Marchington *et al.*, 1992). The growth of employee involvement coincided with the rise of 'HRM' as a distinct approach to management.

While the Thatcherite era represented a permissive climate, the requirement for employee involvement was ultimately conditional on the move to a distinctive human resource management approach. Blyton and Turnbull (2004: 258) make the point well:

> For managers, support for 'involvement' stems largely from the principles of human relations management, which draws attention to the importance of the social aspects of organisation in general, and the connection between, on the one hand, communication and consultation between management and workforce, and on the other, increased worker commitment, higher job satisfaction and motivation, and reduced resistance to change.

As Holden (2001: 541) notes, under various influential HRM models, such as that proposed by the Harvard Business School, employee involvement was expounded as a key component of HRM strategies. In addition, the management gurus Tom Peters and Robert Waterman published their influential book, *In Search of Excellence*, in 1982, which very much expounded the managerial and organisational benefits of promoting employee involvement (and were openly dismissive of trade unions). Their books emphasised the value of employee involvement and echoed neo-human relations strictures in respect of their theories about motivation (i.e. make people feel valued and respected by management by walking around and encouraging bottom-up problem solving groups) – and higher commitment and motivation will necessarily follow because people feel valued and respected etc. In essence, HRM provided the philosophical compass for alterations to people management with employee involvement cast as a core component of the hardware and HRM's ascent was assisted by changes in the political and business environment and the influence of management gurus.

Surveying the scene in the late 1990s students of this field might have been forgiven for engaging in Fukuyamaesque 'end of history' pronouncements. The prospects for the rejuvenation of 'power centred participation' appeared bleak within the context of 'ascendant management, and individualistic and competitive values' (Harley *et al.*, 2005) wholly supportive of employee involvement. Indeed, as recently as 2000 Millward *et al.* (2000: 124) were able to confidently state: 'there has been a major shift from collective, representative, indirect and union based voice, to direct, non-union channels'. Broadly put, a shift from employee participation to employee involvement. However, the new millennium ushered in a renewal of interest in employee participation. Following the signing up of the New Labour government to the Social Chapter in 1999 the UK became increasingly touched by the EU's social agenda. More particularly, the consultation and participatory rights of British employees have been significantly enhanced by the European Works Council and Information and Consultation Directives. The workings of these institutions will be afforded critical coverage later in the chapter.

Stop & think

- *Why did the Thatcher government try to encourage employee share ownership via tax incentives?*
- *Why did trade union numbers fall in the Thatcher period?*
- *Why is employee involvement central to HRM?*

EPI: managerial motives

EPI and managerial motive

In the field of EPI the subject of managerial motive has long been a source of controversy. Reviewing the literature it is possible to posit a range of theoretical orientations as potentially driving managerial interest in the 'social technology' (Scholl, cited in Dachler and Wilpert, 1978: 2) that EPI represents. These theories, or 'vocabularies of participation' (Brannen *et al.*, 1976: 29), are derived from distinctly different value systems and may be bracketed under three headings: (i) a unitary approach which, following Delmotte (cited in Bolle De Bal, 1992: 614), may be termed *idyllic participation*, (ii) a *conflictual* model, and (iii) a *contingency* approach.

Idyllic participation

This essentially unitarist perspective is given the above title because EPI is treated as wholly benign and unproblematic from both a managerial and workforce stance. It is both a technique and an overarching managerial philosophy; positive-sum outcomes are envisaged as areas of common interest between employers and employee are highlighted. This position, to which many paragraphs have been devoted in both the academic and the more prescriptive management journals, draws its inspiration from the human relations school; the central postulate is that *both* management and worker interests are served through EPI. As Dachler and Wilpert (1978: 8) observe, 'increases in innovative behaviour and economic efficiency and productivity are seen as a correlate of individual and group development'. In a similar vein Argyris (1964) has argued that EPI leads to greater self-actualisation and higher levels of performance and hence the *integration* of individual and organisational needs. This intellectual tradition has spawned a mighty prescriptive literature, e.g., *The Human Side of Enterprise* (McGregor, 1960); *New Patterns of Management* (Likert, 1961); *Integrating the Individual and Organization* (Argyris, 1964) in which EPI is eulogised as a panacea capable of correcting a variety of corporate dilemmas and difficulties that arise from the 'debilitating effects of traditionally designed organisations' (Dachler and Wilpert, 1978: 7). Latterly, of course, these broad ideas have undergone a further renaissance and refinement due to the contemporary interest in HRM. Phrases such as 'job enrichment' and 'good communications' have become *de rigueur* amongst 'forward-looking' organisations.

In sum, all these subtle variations on a theme incorporate the common notion that the apparatus of EPI, in its broadest sense, including job enrichment, participative styles of management, work group re-organisation and improved communications have the potential to deliver a range of *both* individual and organisational benefits.

Notwithstanding the presence of a vast body of work derived from within this paradigm there are crucial theoretical shortcomings inherent within the position. A fundamental problem lies in the uncritical acceptance of unitary theoretical presuppositions that underpin the idyllic orthodoxy – a position that seems 'out of sync' with much of the empirical evidence. In recent years management has been the primary actor behind such initiatives. Within the idyllic rubric, however, EPI practices are treated implicitly as neutral interventions, the corollary being that participation is depicted as mutually advantageous, with attendant benefits accordingly accruing to both capital and labour. It is necessary merely to accept the truism that the employment relationship is at least partly distributive to expose the problems with such a position. By ignoring the potential for conflict within labour management relations, the idyllic position obscures the significant implications that participation schemes may have, not simply for efficiency and productivity *per se*, but for the pattern of intra-organisational social relations. This stance thus conceals the incorporative and manipulative functions that EPI may potentially serve when imposed as a managerial tool. Grenier and Hogler (1991: 314) make the point well:

> The structure and power underlying participative processes is complex, ambiguous, and manipulable and far from bestowing meaningful authority on workers, such techniques *may* enable managers to maintain a relationship of dominance and control (emphasis added).

This is not to suggest that EPI cannot give rise to attendant benefits to both capital and labour in certain settings, but rather that positive employee outcomes do not automatically flow from the very act of employee participation or involvement.

Stop & think

What are the key assumptions underpinning the idyllic view of EPI? What are the limitations of this approach?

The conflictual model

Over the last 25 years or so a body of more critical work emanating from an industrial sociology perspective has emerged questioning the underlying unitary and positive-sum assumptions of the idyllic position. Seminal to this was Harvie Ramsay's work whose 'cycles' thesis (Ramsay, 1977) was founded upon Marxist premises about the nature of production relations in capitalist societies. In contradistinction to the unitary assumptions underpinning 'idyllic' EPI, Ramsay takes as his point of departure the centrality of conflict and antagonism within the employment relationship.

Central to Ramsay's writings was the notion that management was most pre-disposed towards EPI when its authority was under threat from below – the aim being 'to nullify pressures to change the status quo' (Ramsay, 1977: 496). Managerial interest in EPI was seen to be a function of historical conjunctures in the ongoing conflict between capital and labour giving rise to 'clear waves or cycles of interest' (Ramsay, 1980: 50), in response to working class resistance; 'interest' was seen to ebb once the managerial crisis had passed. For example, a discrete wave or cycle identified by Ramsay in his original 1977 paper was the industrial democracy movement of that period (see earlier discussion). This and other initiatives of this era were dismissed by Ramsay as an incorporative means of countering the growth in shopfloor power. The thrust of Ramsay's critique was that systems of EPI were somewhat underhand creations, 'presented as concessions by superordinates . . . of some real degree of influence over decisions to those classed as subordinates' (Ramsay, 1980: 46), the ultimate purpose being to incorporate the workforce through a system of 'phantom participation', i.e. 'a skilful con-trick' (Ramsay, 1980: 49) – or more poetically – 'honeyed flypaper dangled out to capture the unwitting worker' (Ramsay, 1993: 79).

While highly influential, the cycles thesis is open to criticism. The tone of the original paper is of data being used to illustrate theory rather than test propositions. Ultimately managerial motivation cannot be assumed or rejected on philosophical grounds, but must be subjected to a rigorous analysis on a case-by-case basis. Ramsay's empirical reliance upon time series data to track the apparent 'cycles', and secondary qualitative accounts, of varying rigour and merit, to impute a causal relationship is strongly suggestive of the former illustrative approach, undermining the validity of the conclusions reached.

The most significant critique of Ramsay's work has come from members of the UMIST industrial relations team (Ackers *et al.*, 1992). Fundamentally Ramsay's focus on issues of workplace control is seen to be undermined by the renaissance of participation from the 1980s onwards, a period in which any 'threat from below' is broadly viewed as having dissipated. The 'cycles' thesis is seen to oversimplify the employment relationship reducing it to one of an overriding desire by management to control workers more effectively when increasingly management want employee commitment and motivation. This much having been said, it would be wrong to suggest that the essence of the cycles thesis is flawed in *all* cases. Indeed, there is much evidence that the introduction of EPI, or subsequent re-invigoration of EPI structures, may be stimulated by a perceived threat to managerial prerogatives (Marchington *et al.*, 1993). As Ackers *et al.* (1992: 274) argue, ultimately Ramsay's account is simply 'too narrow and partisan to serve as a useful *general* test for participation' (emphasis added).

Stop & think

What were the key elements of Ramsays 'cycles of control' thesis? How does this differ from the idyllic view? What were the criticisms of the 'cycles' thesis?

Contingency approach

The above literatures represent competing viewpoints on EPI. They are based upon highly partisan frames of reference invoking the notion that managerial intent is founded upon either progressive or reactive and defensive goals. A more subtle formulation has been afforded by the UMIST team, elements of which have been alluded to above (cf. Ackers *et al.*, 1992; Marchington *et al.*, 1992). In an in-depth study of 25 separate organisations the indeterminate nature of the functionality of EPI is stressed. From within their resultant 'explanatory matrix' (Ackers *et al.*, 1992: 268), it is possible to abstract two dominant drivers behind EPI. The first encapsulates elements of Ramsay's position, fulfilling his zero-sum expectations; participation is 'industrial relations' (Ackers *et al.*, 1992: 277) centred, aimed at incorporating or bypassing unions, the underlying rationale being concerned with control issues. Alternatively the importance of 'market participation' (Ackers *et al.*, 1992: 278) is stressed where 'economic pressures other than labour control and union avoidance considerations motivate participation' (Ackers *et al.*, 1992). In these settings influences such as the need for customer care in the service sector, or labour market problems (e.g. recruitment and retention), are viewed as pre-eminent. Here labour and product market pressures 'impact upon the human resource problem without having to pass through the distorting lens of industrial relations problems' (Ackers *et al.*, 1992: 278).

The UMIST team go on to describe specific scenarios in which participation is assumed by management to yield tangible benefits, shedding light on the logic of the latter approach. The environments depicted coalesce around areas in which the quality and efficiency of production is dependent markedly upon the constructive initiative, commitment and support of employees. This is captured, for example, in the above references to 'customer care' within the service sector. Ackers *et al.* (1992) likewise provide the example of the invocation of a quality culture within a broader TQM manufacturing environment. Similarly, in such settings participation is viewed as an adjunct to loyalty and hence employee retention, facets that are again viewed as contributing to effective production or service delivery.

The above position, implicitly drawing its analytical inspiration from contingency theory, represents a useful counter to the 'grand theory' catalogued earlier. It complements a growing body of literature suggesting that management is a strategic actor synchronising HR policies to wider business goals, although the extent to which such adjustments are genuinely strategic rather than tactical remains controversial.

Distinct to the Ramsay cycles metaphor, the UMIST team moved on to develop the notion of 'waves' (Marchington *et al.*, 1993). This marked a further important theoretical contribution because it allowed the ebb and flow of organisational EPI initiatives to be related not necessarily to corporate goals, but managers own career objectives. As Marchington (2005: 31–32) recollects, 'by treating each technique individually, it became possible to chart the dynamics of [employee] participation [and involvement] over time in relation to the growth and decline of different schemes rather than as a whole'. Via this route it was often possible to apportion specific techniques to 'internal champions' (Marchington *et al.*, 1993: 29) of EPI. That is, the waves were driven by a myriad of factors. Certainly sometimes these related to business contingencies but in other instances the driver was naked careerism or 'impression management' (Marchington *et al.*, 1993: 570). Hence, ultimately managerial intent in EPI is likely to be driven by a complex array of factors and as Marchington (2005) has recently argued, much work still needs to be done in examining the interplay between a mix of forces both within and outside the workplace.

Stop & think

- *What are the key elements associated with the contingency approach?*

- *What is meant by 'waves of participation'?*

- *Why is the notion of 'waves of participation' useful in terms of explaining the ebb and flow of EPI initiatives?*

EPI practices in the workplace

We will now examine a range of EPI practices used within contemporary organisations. Marchington *et al.* (1992) identify four categories of EPI initiatives:

- *Downwards communications.* This refers to top-down communication from management to employees. Typical practices include company newspapers, team briefing, communication meetings, video briefing, employee reports and the use of the intranet.

- *Upwards problem solving forms and teamworking.* Upwards problem solving refers to bottom-up communication and involvement structures that are generally designed with the aim of capturing ideas and solving production/service problems (either individually or in small groups). Typical mechanisms include suggestion schemes, and quality circles/problem solving groups. This category could also include attitude surveys which management may implement (or commission) to try to understand more about the general climate within the company and as a mechanism to allow employees to raise concerns and/or ideas for future changes that they would like to see. In addition to the typical forms of upwards problem solving already cited, Marchington and Wilkinson (2005) also identify the following forms, task-based participation and teamworking and self-management.

- *Financial participation.* This refers to schemes that allow employees a financial stake in the company. Typical mechanisms include employee share ownership schemes and profit related pay.

- *Representative participation.* This refers to mechanisms for indirect participation, for example, through trade unions, works councils and consultative committees. It means that employees are represented by elected representatives that have been drawn from their number.

Before we move on to discuss each of these categories in more detail, it is important to highlight once more points raised by Marchington *et al.* (1992) in respect of mechanisms for EPI. They argue that the mechanisms for EPI must be considered in respect of four dimensions:

1 The *degree* of involvement (the extent to which employees influence the final decision).
2 The *level* of involvement (whether at job, departmental or organisational level).
3 The *forms* of involvement (direct participation, indirect participation and financial).
4 The *range* of the subject matter being considered in the involvement scheme.

By considering each of these four dimensions, one can appreciate the relative levels of power and influence that the respective mechanisms allow. As we have already highlighted, a criticism of employee involvement initiatives (that are central to HRM) is that they afford very limited power and influence to employees. This is primarily because such mechanisms are essentially controlled by management and management have the final say as to what they will or will not accept. For example, in terms of *degree*, employees may have little influence over a final decision. In terms of *level* of involvement, employee involvement initiatives may essentially be dealing with locally based production issues (for example, problem solving activities). The *form* that employee involvement practices take will essentially be determined by management and the *range* of subject matter may, for example, revolve around work-based production problems rather than tackling higher-level issues of pay, conditions, redundancies etc.

In contrast, representative participation (here we refer especially to trade unions activities) are not primarily controlled by management and in the case of trade unions, their organisation and structure are not circumscribed by management. We can contrast employee involvement to representative participation by considering once more the four levels identified by Marchington *et al.* (1992). Taking trade unions as the example – trade unions are more likely to wield power and influence. They tend to have a higher *degree* of influence (if negotiations get tough, trade unions may coordinate industrial action), they may be negotiating at company or sector level (i.e. a high *level* of involvement), their *form* is not dictated by management, participation is indirect and they are likely to be involved in and negotiating on a wide *range* of subjects. Once the four dimensions are taken into account, one can understand why critics have argued that the employee involvement initiatives associated with HRM represent 'pseudo-participation'.

We will now discuss each of the four categories in more detail. As already highlighted, the terminology in this area is somewhat elastic (Marchington and Wilkinson, 2005) and the same issue applies to some of the practices, for example, the exact form and use of problem solving groups could vary both within and between organisations. However, the Workplace Employment Relations Surveys (WERS) give an indication of the general trends for each of the categories. The WERS surveys are particularly useful in that they are large scale. The initial survey was conducted in 1980 (when it was called the Workplace Industrial Relations Survey) and it was repeated in 1984, 1990, 1998 and again in 2004. This means that one can identify trends over a period of years. We will now discuss each of the categories in more detail.

Why do critics argue that employee involvement as part of a wider HRM approach represents 'pseudo-participation'?

Downwards communications

Downwards communications means top-down communication from management to employees. As indicated, this includes company newspapers, communication meetings, team briefings and the use of the intranet. Table 14.2 is taken from the first findings of the 2004 WERS survey.

An interesting observation is in the popularity of meetings with the entire workforce or briefings. Indeed, instances of these rose in both the private and the public sector. Holden (2004) explains that team briefing systems are normally used to cascade managerial messages down the organisation. Although team-briefing arrangements may vary, they are normally given to relatively small groups and (in terms of content) often focus on issues affecting production or service, targets etc. Team briefings are essentially top-down form of communication, but there is often some opportunity for employees to ask questions or perhaps even to lodge comments, queries or concerns. Evidence tends to show that team-briefing systems work better when the briefers are properly trained. Whilst evidence indicates that team-briefing sessions are generally welcomed, problems can also emerge. For example, some studies have shown a tendency for team briefing sessions to be cancelled when production pressures are high (Glover, 2001). Also, critics have noted that team-briefing sessions can be used to brief against existing trade unions or to try to dissuade employees from seeking union recognition in non-union firms.

Table 14.2 also shows that newsletters remain fairly widespread, especially in the public sector. Holden (2004) notes that newsletters can often be welcomed, but a potential limitation is that management retain editorial control – as such it is less likely that newsletters would be used as a forum to air employee grievances. The latest WERS survey also included questions about the use of noticeboards, e-mail, and intranet. Use of the e-mail and intranet was reported by more than 30 per cent of organisations. It is likely that the instances of usage

Table 14.2 Direct communication by sector of ownership

	Percentage of workplaces					
	1998			2004		
	Private sector	Public sector	All	Private sector	Public sector	All
Direct communication						
Meeting with entire workforce or team briefing	82	96	85	90	97	91
Systematic use of management chain	46	75	52	60	81	64
Regular newsletters	35	59	40	41	63	45
Noticeboards	–	–	–	72	86	74
E-mail	–	–	–	36	48	38
Intranet	–	–	–	31	48	34
Employee surveys	–	–	–	37	66	42

Source: Adapted from Kersley *et al.*, 2005: 18.

of e-mail and intranet will increase in years to come as more companies make use of these facilities. The use of employee surveys was captured by WERS 2004, and these were particularly popular in the public sector.

The rhetoric of HRM is that companies will focus on maintaining effective communication. Table 14.2 shows that many companies have the infrastructure in place for various forms of downwards communication, however, whether these mechanisms are always perceived as effective by employees is a different question (Glover, 2001).

Upwards problem solving and teamworking

Upwards problem solving mechanisms (such as suggestion schemes and problem solving groups) are generally designed for the purpose of capturing ideas and solving production and service problems. Task-based participation and teamworking and self-management can also be considered here. They are more substantive in nature as they are 'integral to the job and part of everyday working life' (Marchington and Wilkinson, 2005).

Suggestion schemes work on the principle that employees submit suggestions (for example, into a suggestion box), the suggestion is then reviewed by managers, a decision will be made as to whether to accept the suggestion or reject it. If the suggestion is accepted the employee will generally receive a direct financial reward. Such rewards may equate to a percentage of the overall saving that the suggestion will bring. Some companies may put a cap on the amount of cash that can be rewarded, but may 'top-up' with other products or services (for example, Ford had a suggestion scheme which had a cap on the amount of cash that would be awarded, but if the suggestion was particularly good and the value of the savings was particularly high, the 'top-up' could be a car). The WERS surveys of 1998 and 2004 indicated that around 30 per cent of organisations reported the use of suggestion schemes.

Upwards problem solving also includes problem solving groups (often referred to as quality circles in the 1990s). Problem solving groups are generally small in nature (for example, 6–8 people) and normally meet on a voluntary basis. The purpose of such groups is to identify quality or work-related problems and to produce a solution to the problem. Some organisations will offer problem solving groups administrative support, training and trained facilitators. Also, most groups will meet in worktime. However, in distinct contrast to suggestion schemes, there is not normally a direct financial reward for the solutions and ideas generated by such groups. Again, evidence shows that these initiatives can be welcomed, but problems can emerge if groups feel that their ideas are not listened to, or fail to be actioned. In terms of coverage, the WERS surveys showed an increase from 35 per cent of organisations reporting the existence of problem solving groups to 49 per cent in 1998 (Millward *et al.*, 2000).

In addition to these more traditional forms of upwards problem solving, Marchington and Wilkinson (2005) identify that task-based participation and teamworking and self-management are more distinctive in that they are integral to normal working life rather than a 'bolt-on' initiative. They explain that task-based participation can occur 'both horizontally and vertically'. The former means that employees engage in a wider variety of tasks, but these are at a similar skill level. Vertical participation means that employees, 'may be trained to undertake tasks at a higher skill level or they may be given some managerial and supervisory responsibilities'.

The concept of teamworking is very much linked and is now seen as a central feature of HRM (Mueller and Proctor, 2000). For example, the term 'multiskilling' is similar to horizontal task-based participation, essentially meaning that employees will move around tasks and will not be bound by strict job demarcation. Again, 'teamworking' can mean different things in different organisations. The WERS 1998 and 2004 surveys give an insight into what companies are reporting in terms of teamworking practices. Table 14.3 provides a summary of some of the findings.

Table 14.3 shows that over 70 per cent of organisations in 1998 and 2004 reported teamworking structures for core employees. The surveys also indicated that functional flexibility (multiskilling) was evident and that core employees had received some training for these

Table 14.3 Work organisation by sector of ownership

| | Percentage of workplaces | | | | | |
| | 1998 | | | 2004 | | |
	Private sector	Public sector	All	Private sector	Public sector	All
Some core employees in formally designated teams	72	85	74	68	88	72
Some core employees trained to be functionally flexible	69	67	69	67	64	66
Problem solving groups involving non-managerial employees	–	–	16	19	33	21
Some core employees trained in teamworking, communication or problem solving	35	65	41	45	65	48

Source: Adapted from Kersley *et al.*, 2005.

activities. The 2004 survey showed that only 21 per cent of organisations reported having problem solving groups that involved non-managerial employees – but that instances were higher in the public sector. Finally, training courses reported for general teamworking activities were for 48 per cent of organisations, but again instances were higher in the public sector.

The 1998 survey revealed an interesting finding in respect of teamworking. Again, whilst it found that a large percentage of organisations were reporting the use of teamworking, only 3 per cent of organisations seem to be allowing teams real autonomy – meaning that team members had responsibility for a specific product, had autonomy in terms of deciding how the job was done and had some authority to appoint their own team leaders. Therefore, whilst teamworking is widely reported in Britain, evidence still suggests that much of this is fairly low-level (for example, team members working together) and that instances of semi-autonomous teams and self-managing teams seem less apparent (Geary, 2003). Some would argue that self-managing teams are the ultimate in direct participation (and as such there is quite some way to go in the UK). Critics would argue that self-managing teams represent the ultimate in terms of management control in that they work on the basis of peer pressure and surveillance and are not genuinely liberating because they are always under the control of management (Garrahan and Stewart, 1992; Sewell and Wilkinson, 1992a; Taylor *et al.*, 2002). However, others have argued that teamworking tends to offer mixed consequences – and it is too stark to argue that the outcomes of it are either 'all good' or 'all bad'.

Financial participation

The third category is financial participation. This means that employees have a financial stake in the company. Given the constraints of space, we will now provide a brief review of mechanisms for financial participation.

Holden (2004) explains that 'the general aim of financial participation schemes is to enhance employee commitment to the organisation by linking the performance of the organisation to that of the employee'. He goes on to explain that various governments over the years have tried to encourage the growth of financial involvement schemes. For example, the Conservative government of 1979–1997 introduced a range of tax incentives for schemes including profit-related pay and employee share option schemes. The current Labour government have also introduced various schemes to try to stimulate financial involvement (Holden, 2004). One presumption is that if employees have a financial stake in the company, they are more likely to be committed to the success of the company and (perhaps) will be less likely to engage in forms of industrial action. Some would regard financial involvement as a 'win-win' scenario, i.e. that employees share some of the financial gains from success and that the employer will have a hard-working workforce that is interested in the overall performance of the company.

The three main forms of financial participation are profit-sharing, profit-related pay and employee share ownership schemes. Deferred profit-sharing schemes work on the basis that 'profits are put in a trust fund to acquire shares in the company for employees' (Gennard and Judge, 2005). The overall aim of such a scheme is to increase motivation and commitment, but Gennard and Judge (2005) observe that one of the problems can be creating a clear, identifiable link between effort and reward. For example, problems may emerge if individuals feel that they have worked hard, but that this effort is not adequately reflected in the profits that they share. Also, there will be an inevitable delay between the day-to-day behaviours of employees and the final calculation of profit and the rewards that flow back as a consequence. Again, this may mean that employees find it difficult to relate effort and reward.

Profit-related pay works on the basis that a proportion of an employee's pay is linked to the overall profits of the company. Again, the goal is to increase commitment and motivation and various governments have introduced tax breaks to try to encourage this type of scheme. In practice, profit-related pay can be difficult to calculate and some companies found that government tax-break schemes were not easy to administer.

The final form of financial participation is share ownership. This means that employees own shares in the company. Again, various governments have introduced incentives for share ownership schemes and these have sometimes been difficult to administer. For example, employee share ownership plans (ESOPs) were devised as a way of dealing with tax liability from share ownership schemes (Gennard and Judge, 2005).

Again, the WERS surveys are useful in that they give some indication into the relative spread of these schemes. There was a rise in profit sharing schemes from 19 per cent in 1984 to 46 per cent in 1998 (Millward *et al.*, 2000: 214). Millward *et al.* (2000) go on to suggest that this rise could probably be attributed to government intervention (certainly in the 1980s). They also observed that the UK multinationals were more likely to have a profit-related pay scheme, but the most influential factor appeared the size of the enterprise to which the workplaces belonged, and that profit-related pay was much more likely in enterprises that had 1000 or more employees. The survey also asked about why profit-related schemes had either been introduced or withdrawn and several reasons were noted:

- If a scheme had been withdrawn, the most common reason was a change of ownership.
- The second most common reason for withdrawal was that the scheme was too expensive to run (the costs of administration being a cited factor).
- The most common reason for the introduction of a profit-related pay scheme was that the workplace had undergone a change of ownership.
- The reason for implementing such a scheme varied. Some reported that a scheme had been implemented for tax relief reasons. Others reported that profit sharing was part of wider organisational changes where companies have been attempting to develop more sophisticated reward systems (Millward *et al.*, 2000).

The WERS surveys have also given an insight into the spread of share ownership schemes. They show, for example, that 13 per cent of workplaces had share ownership schemes in 1980, 22 per cent in 1984, 30 per cent in 1990 and a slight drop to 24 per cent in 1998 (Millward *et al.*, 2000: 216). Therefore, Millward *et al.* (2000) observed that the trend was different when compared to the trends in respect of profit sharing. However, they found that employee share ownership schemes were more likely in companies that had arrangements for employee voice (e.g. trade unions). The general conclusion was that increases in profit sharing and employee share ownership schemes were seen in the 1980s, but have tended to either tail off or reverse in the 1990s.

Representative participation

The final category is representative participation and this refers to mechanisms for indirect participation. Such mechanisms include works councils and trade unions. We discuss works councils in more detail elsewhere in this chapter, so will restrict ourselves to a brief review here. The main difference between representative participation and the other categories that we have discussed is that these structures are firmly based on the principles of pluralism. Early HRM models tended to be unitarist in nature and there was an assumption that unions and HRM 'don't mix'. However, recent evidence questions the early assumptions (Cully *et al.*, 1999; Glover, 2000) and trends towards partnership signal changing times (Guest and Peccei; 2001, Martinez Lucio and Stuart, 2002; Tailby *et al.*, 2004). Trade unions are clearly an important mechanism for representative participation and the field of industrial relations has historically been devoted to the study. In this section, we will reflect upon some general issues around the theme of trade unions and will introduce the concept of 'social partnership' that is becoming part of mainstream debate (Bacon, 2006; Martinez Lucio and Stuart, 2002; Tailby and Winchester, 2005). Again, the WERS surveys are very useful in terms of identifying general trends over a number of years and we will review some of the evidence.

One of the issues that we will raise here is the relative decline of forms of representative participation. In some ways, the climate for representative participation is more conducive when compared to the recent past. For example, the government passed the Employment Relations Act in 1999. The legislative programme included 'a statutory route for union recognition, an extension of rights for individual employees, a national minimum wage and closer engagement with the social policies of the European Union. A central aim of this legislative programme is to replace the notion of conflict between employers and employees with the promotion of partnership in the longer term (DTI, 1998)' (Bacon, 2006, p. 195). In addition legislation has come into force in respect of works councils (see below). However, despite these developments that appear to be more positive for trade unions, evidence continues to chart a decline and implications remain given that many employees are not covered by trade unions. We will return to this debate as the section unfolds.

Employee consultation has a long history, first coming to prominence as 'joint consultative committee' during the Second World War. There was a decline during the 1950s and 1960s followed by an increase in the 1970s. WERS has been able to capture trends in terms of the coverage of consultative committees since 1980. They are summarised in Table 14.4.

We can see that the percentage coverage of functioning consultative committees fell over the period from 1980–1998. The first findings of 2004 WERS indicated that JCCs were present in 14 per cent of organisations with 10 or more employees. Twenty-five per cent of workplaces did not have a workplace-level committee, but had 'a consultative forum that operated at a higher level in the organisation' (Kersley *et al.*, 2005: 14) and that JCCs were much more common in larger workplaces. The survey also gives insights into the operation of these committees. For example, 96 per cent had met at least twice in the previous year and 75 per cent had met at least four times. Topics discussed by such committees included: future plans (81 per cent), work organisation (81 per cent), employment issues (78 per cent), production issues (71 per cent) and financial issues (65 per cent) (Kersely *et al.*, 2005: 14). Interestingly, the survey found that financial issues and employment issues were more likely

Table 14.4 Percentage coverage of functioning consultative committees as shown by WIRS/WERS surveys

	All establishments (%)			
Survey date:	1980	1984	1990	1998
Functioning Consultative Committee	30	31	26	23

Source: Adapted from Millward *et al.*, 2000: 109.

to be discussed if the committee contained trade union representatives. Overall, the general trend in terms of consultative committees seems to have been marked by a slight decline.

The next form of representative participation that we will discuss is trade unions. As indicated, the field of industrial relations was traditionally devoted to the study of trade unions and we will necessarily have to restrict ourselves to discussing certain themes and will refer once more to WERS in order to give an indication of some of the trends in respect of trade union coverage.

In the early 1980s, 'HRM' tended to be viewed as unitarist. Indeed, one of the distinctions that Storey (1992) drew in his 'ideal types' continuum between personnel management/ industrial relations (PM/IR) on the one hand and HRM on the other was that the nature of relations in PM/IR was characterised as pluralist and HRM as unitarist. At the time there was much debate about the role of trade unions under HRM and Guest commented that 'the rising interest in HRM throughout the 1980s coincided with a steady decline in the significance of industrial relations as a central feature of economic performance and policy' (Guest in Storey, 1995: 110). During this period there was a wave of union derecognition by companies (Claydon, 1996). The climate of the 1980s was harsh for unions. In addition to the rise of anti-union legislation by the Thatcher government (for example, legislation covering balloting arrangements and secondary action – contravention of which could mean the courts could impose the sequestration of union assets) the same period saw the decline of manufacturing and the increase in the service sector. The manufacturing sector was a traditional stronghold for trade unions, whilst the service sector was viewed as more difficult to organise (given the fact that it often included small businesses, part-time (women) workers etc.). At the same time as structural, economic and political changes were taking place, HRM came into ascendancy. Some of its key tenets were direct participation, unitarism, the importance of customer orientation etc. and some felt that trade unions struggled to adjust to the changing context.

There have been some interesting changes more recently in terms of the relationship between trade unions and HRM. Traditionally, the relationship between trade unions and employers was often typified as 'them and us'. We can contrast this to some of the findings of WERS 1998 where Cully et al. (1999: 111) note that 'an active and strong trade union presence is compatible with the broad suite of high commitment management practices', i.e. the opposite that one would expect under previous stereotypes of 'them and us'. Indeed, WERS 1998 indicated positive links between high performance practices and trade union representation. There have been changes in the discourse about management and trade union relationships in recent years and now terms such as 'social partnership' and 'partnership' are widely referred to (Ackers and Payne, 1998; Guest and Peccei, 2001; Martinez Lucio and Stuart, 2002; Tailby et al., 2004). As the term implies, the overall meaning is that management and trade unions (or employee representatives) or management and employees will (try to) work cooperatively. However, 'partnership' is an ambiguous term and tends to be used differently by different stakeholder groups. For example, the CBI, TUC and IOD all interpret the term in different ways (Undy, 1999). Bacon (2006) observes that the CIPD adopted a rather unitarist perspective in 1997, emphasising partnership between employers and employees rather than advocating the role of trade unions, whilst the TUC emphasises the importance of trade union involvement in partnership arrangements.

Despite the ambiguity, the partnership debate does seem to signal that the unions have at least begun to (try to) reclaim the agenda, after the 'wilderness years' when numbers were declining and they were unsure of how to respond to HRM (Storey, 1995). The notion of partnership has offered some potential for unions to re-legitimise their role – not least because it is often linked to notions of increasing competitiveness. However, Bacon (2006) notes that the number of signed partnership agreements remains relatively low and that such agreements are only likely to be successful if managers are willing to work closely with the unions on a long-term basis and that managers refrain from making attacks on trade unions. He goes on to observe that it remains unclear as to whether such agreements deliver returns to managers and unions. For example, Guest and Peccei (2001) found that management enjoyed the main benefits from partnership, Martinez Lucio and Stuart (2002) found that concerns over employment security and the quality of working life remained problematic and that there was often a gap between the rhetoric of partnership and experiences of trade unionists on the ground and Suff and Williams (2004) concluded that 'the reality of market relations and the balance of power in the employment relationship imply that genuine mutuality is likely to be unobtainable in practice'. However, overall the partnership debate represents a shift in emphasis and the outcomes of such agreements for employers and employees will remain a key area of research.

We turn now to the empirical evidence on trade union coverage. Once again, WERS are especially useful because they offer insights into historical trends relating to trade union recognition. Table 14.5 summarises developments from 1980 to 1998 and shows quite clearly the extent of the decline in coverage of union recognition from 1980 to 1998. WERS 2004 indicates that recognition had fallen to 30 per cent for all workplaces and to 16 per cent in the private sector, but showed a slight rise to 90 per cent in the public sector (Kersley *et al.*, 2005: 12). One can see that whilst recognition remains high in the public sector, there were huge drops in recognition in the private sector and the final row shows that only 23 per cent of private service companies recognised unions in 1998. This trend is particularly significant given the overall increase in service sector employment in the UK. Indeed, union density fell from 39 per cent of employees in 1990 to 30 per cent by 1997 (Cully *et al.*, 1999: 293).

Reflecting on the first findings of WERS 2004, Kersley *et al.*, (2005: 35–36) observe that 'most striking of all, perhaps, was the continued decline of collective labour organisation. Employees were less likely to be union members than they were in 1998; workplaces were less likely to recognise unions for bargaining over pay and conditions; and collective bargaining was less prevalent'. Whilst the overall rate of decline seems to have slowed and 50 per cent of employees were employed in workplaces with a recognised trade union, approximately 33 per cent were union members and approximately 40 per cent had pay set via collective bargaining (Kersley *et al.*, 2005), there remain large sections of the British workforce that are not covered by trade union representation. Significantly, private services remain low in terms of unionisation, but tend to employ many women often on relatively low rates of pay – but such employees do not enjoy the backing of trade unions. Millward *et al.*, (2000: 236) reflect upon some of these themes and conclude that in future, the British economy is likely to generate more workplaces where, 'the nature of employment relationships is almost exclusively a matter for managerial choice'. Managerial choice could include approaches on a continuum from enlightened HRM to authoritarian regimes with few opportunities for the employee voice. The conclusion that they draw is that 'should the current reforms also prove insufficient, we see a yet more extensive floor of employee rights, rigorously enforced by state agencies, as the most feasible method of preventing the more extreme forms of exploitation that an unregulated labour market can produce in the increasingly competitive world in which Britain operates' (Millward *et al.*, 2000: 236).

Table 14.5 Trade union recognition by broad sector, 1980–1998

	Percentage			
Year of survey	1980	1984	1990	1998
All establishments	64	66	53	42
Public sector	94	99	87	87
Private sector	50	48	38	25
Private services	41	44	36	23

Source: Adapted from Millward *et al.*, 2000: 96.

- *What are the main trends in representative participation since 1980?*

- *What are the implications of these trends for organisations, managers and employees?*

- *Why do Millward et al. (2000) argue that a more extensive floor of employment rights may be needed to protect British employees?*

Works councils and consultation in the European Union

At this point we will pause to consider some of the more recent developments in respect of employee consultation. A recurrent theme within this chapter has been the ascendance of managerially inspired employee involvement. By and large, systems of indirect *participation*, that is mechanisms that seek to involve employees more fundamentally in the 'political structures of the firm' (Brannen, 1983: 16) fared less well throughout the seventeen-year period of Conservative government from 1979 to 1997. However, the decision of the incoming Labour government to sign up to the European Agreement on Social Policy (the Social Chapter) has put employee participation firmly back on the agenda.

There is a long history of a European level of interest in the theme of employee participation. As discussed, plans for a 'fifth directive' that sought to provide workers with boardroom representation were suspended inconclusively in 1982. A new framework for a European Company Statute was again launched in 1989 (Hyman and Mason, 1995: 33). This also called for workers to have board-level input. However, pressure form both employers and the British Conservative government ensured that the draft directive was never ratified (Hyman and Mason, 1995). As Leat (2003: 245) notes, ultimately such initiatives can be seen as running counter to the voluntarist tradition of the UK and even more so the *neo-laissez faire* approach adopted by British governments since 1979. The decision of the Blair government to bind Britain to the European Social Policy Protocol under the Treaty of Amsterdam (1999) consequently marked a fundamental change in policy. Following this move the directives agreed between 1994 and 1998, and all subsequent legislation under the social chapter, became applicable to British companies. In terms of EPI the most far reaching of these measures have been the directives on European Works Councils (1994) and Information and Consultation (2002).

The European Works Council directive

Background

The EWC directive, transposed into UK law in 1999, requires a EWC to be established in companies with at least 1000 employees within the EU and at least 150 employees in each of at least two member states. It is thus explicitly aimed at multinational enterprises (MNCs). It has been estimated that the directive covers around 1850 MNCs (Kerckhofs, 2002). By 2003, 639 MNCs had negotiated agreements (Waddington and Kerckhofs, cited in Hall and Marginson, 2005: 208). The directive is a response to the concerns of the European Commission with respect to the power of MNCs to take decisions in one member state that affect employees in others without these being involved in the decision-making process (Leat, 2003: 250). The legislation is thus intended to bridge the 'representation gap' between the growth of transnational decision making and employees' hitherto strictly nationally defined information and consultation rights (Marginson and Hall, 2005). The EWC directive is significant in that the requirement for mandated consultation (see Box 14.4) suggests some potential for the extension of employee influence.

Box 14.4 The competence of EWCs

EWCs have the right to meet with central management once a year. There must be information or consultation on:

- the structure, economic and financial situation of the business;
- developments in production and sales;
- the employment situation;
- investment trends; and
- substantial changes concerning the introduction of new working methods or production processes, transfers of production, mergers, cutbacks or closures of undertakings.

Impact of the directive

Over a decade after the directive's inception a reasonable amount of research has been conducted exploring the workings of these institutions. Reviewing the data Blyton and Turnbull (2004: 373–374) argue that EWCs overwelmingly tend to be management-led with restriction placed on the consultation procedure. These findings chime with Hall and Marginson's recent overview of the terrain where it is concluded that very few agreements depart from the formalised definition of consultation as set out in the directive, viz. 'the exchange of views and establishment of dialogue' between employee representatives and management (Hall and Marginson, 2005: 207). Only sporadically are firmer consultation rights provided such as the right of employee representatives to be allowed to respond formally to managerial proposals and receive a considered response *before* management acts (Hall and Marginson, 2005). The overall tenor of extant data is that limited headway has been made by these fora *vis-à-vis* of the extension of strategic employee influence (see, in particular, Stirling and Fitzgerald, 2000) with any impact restricted to the *implementation* of decisions rather than their actual substance.

A plausible interpretation of the current situation is that those organisations operating EWCs have been astute in shaping the workings of these institutions to organisational exigencies – rather than those of their employees. Hall and Marginson (2005) cite a study by Wills in which British managers generally had a positive view about the contribution of EWCs, seeing them as a means of reinforcing corporate communications, downplaying their consultative and representative role. Similarly, in Nakano's study of 14 Japanese MNCs (again cited in Hall and Marginson, 2005) managers perceived EWCs as providing benefits in terms of information provision; the fostering of cooperation between management and employee representatives; and the development of a wider corporate identity among employee representatives. Taken together these studies suggest that the EWC machinery is prone to be hijacked by management with these ostensibly pluralist structures reconstructed along unitary lines to form part of the organisational employee involvement apparatus. Arguably this stems from the original legislation that afforded organisations with considerable breadth in terms of how to operationalise the directive. In sum, to date the creation of EWCs appears to have done little to significantly improve the participation rights of British workers. Indeed, it is conceivable that, albeit unintentionally, mandated employee participation has significantly buttressed the employee involvement arrangements.

Stop & think

When did the EWC directive transpose into law and what were the main implications of this directive? Does the evidence suggest that the directive has significantly increased the degree of employee influence? If not, why not?

The Information and Consultation directive

Background

These new regulations make provision for employees to be consulted and given information on major developments in their organisation. They differ from the EWC directive as here coverage extends to *all* companies in the EU with over 50 employees – not just MNCs. Within a British context the directive has been portrayed as a useful corrective to the failure of voluntarism (Sisson, 2002: 2) allegedly giving rise to a 'representation gap' (Towers, 1997). The key significance of the legislation is that it potentially represents a vehicle for the extension of employee participation for employees without trade union representation.

The original proposals were strongly backed by the French amid objections from Germany, Ireland, Denmark and the UK. Although the directive was initiated under the social chapter, and hence subject to qualified majority voting, these four dissenters comprised a sufficient blocking minority to initially keep the proposals off the statute book. The UK's objection was based on the notion of 'subsidiarity': the doctrine that the EU should only legislate where the objectives cannot be reached by legislation at national level (www. eurofound.eu). The proposals were, however, accepted by the European Parliament in February 2002. Under a compromise position the UK (along with Ireland) has dispensation to phase in the legislation over a four-year period. Initially, only companies with 150 employees are covered.

Organisations with existing information and consultation arrangements, which have the support of employees, can continue operating them. In other circumstances employees must 'trigger' negotiations with their employer to agree new information arrangements. If the negotiations do not produce an agreement, statutory information and consultation arrangements become applicable (see Box 14.5).

Impact of the directive

It is too early to call upon empirical data to assess whether the directive will significantly extend employee participation. The operation of the directive is clearly not without difficulties, however. One potentially problematic area relates to the theme of training provision. Under the terms of the directive representatives will be required to comment on financial and strategically important data (see Box 14.5). Within this context Heller (1992: 153) has argued that managers have developed a range of theoretical schemas and vocabularies derived from economics and related disciplines with which representatives may not be familiar. Hence, the effectiveness of the consultation process will be steered at least in part by management's willingness to provide these bodies with the necessary resourcing. Bringing in trainers is expensive and in smaller organisations there can be problems in taking employees away from their core duties. Butler's (2004) study of non-union consultation furthermore suggests that it could conceivably be in management's best interests to eschew such training provision as a means of deliberately restricting the possibility of employee challenge to managerial decisions. It is far easier to argue that there is a convergence of interest over a particular course of action if representatives lack the skill to seriously challenge management's interpretation of events. Perhaps a

---

Box 14.5 **The right to information and consultation covers:**

- Information on the recent and probable development of the organisation's activities and economic situation;
- Information and consultation on the situation, structure and probable development of employment within the organisation;
- Information and consultation on decisions likely to lead to substantial changes in work organisation.

Source: www.eurofound.eu

more fundamental problem, however, is the nature of legislation which must be triggered by employees for it to apply. In unitary non-union settings the initiation of a participatory process by an employee grouping could be interpreted as an act of disloyalty. The potential costs and benefits will have to be closely weighed by aspiring employee delegates.

Stop & think

What are the key differences between the EWC directive and the Information and Consultation directive? Given the history of EPI initiatives reviewed in this chapter, what impact do you think the Information and Consultation directive will have on levels of employee influence?

New management initiatives: from quality circles, to quality management, to 'high performance management'?

We now bring this chapter to a close by reflecting upon a range of new management initiatives that have employee involvement as a central feature, i.e. our focus turns primarily to direct participation. By reference to WERS, we have laid out some of the contemporary trends in employee involvement (for example, in respect of downwards communication and upwards problem solving) and have catalogued a variety of employee involvement techniques routinely utilised by management. Over the last two decades, there have been a range of managerial initiatives that have incorporated employee involvement, primarily as a way of increasing organisational effectiveness by capturing ideas, eliciting commitment etc. Indeed Collins (2000) provides an extremely useful overview of a range of management 'fads and fashions', including TQM, Business Process Re-engineering and the Excellence phenomenon. He reflects upon the discourse associated with each of the chosen initiatives and upon empirical evidence (in particular, highlighting the gaps between the rhetoric of such initiatives and workplace 'reality'). Due to the confines of space, we focus on quality circles, quality management and one of the latest trends, high performance management (HPM). The reason for this choice is that one can see linkages between each of these developments. More importantly, quality management and high performance management are generally regarded as holistic interventions, rather than 'bolt on' practices.

Quality circles to quality management

We have already noted that quality circles (QC) are a form of upwards problem solving. Quality circles have a long history in the UK and Holden (2004) notes that they can be traced back to the period after the Second World War. The concept was originally developed in the USA, but were made popular by the Japanese. QCs became very popular in the 1980s, but evidence shows that activity declined towards the end of this decade. Some of the reasons for this decline included a lack of training, management failing to action ideas and (as a result) employees regarding them as a 'waste of time' (Heller *et al.*, 1998; Holden, 2004). One of the main limitations of the QC movement was that QCs tended to be a 'bolt-on' management initiative, rather than part of a wider management approach (Hill, 1995).

As intimated, the significance of QM was that it was conceptualised as an organisation-wide approach, i.e. a way of doing business rather than a particular set of techniques or practices (Hill, 1995). In common with HPM, the terminology is fluid and open to interpretation (Dawson, 1998) and the terms 'world-class manufacturing', 'lean production', 'just-in-time' are often subsumed under the QM banner, but in practice the outcomes of each (certainly for employees) could be quite different. In essence, Wilkinson *et al.*, (1998) suggest that QM tends to be characterised by three common principles: a customer orientation, a process orientation and an emphasis on continuous improvement. There are clear implications for HRM in that QM requires that employees actively engage in activities such as problem solving and that they orientate their behaviours and actions towards satisfying the customer (Alvesson and Willmott, 2002). As a result, employee involvement initiatives are generally regarded as central to QM, for example, continuous improvement can be facilitated by the activities of problem solving groups via upwards problem solving. Another outcome of QM was that it spurred on the move towards teamworking structures that have become so popular of late (Kersley *et al.*, 2005) and are now seen as part of a HPM approach.

The outcomes of QM for organisations and employees have been a matter of much debate (we will return to the latter in due course). In respect of the former, Jong and Wilkinson (1999) draw attention to the fact that whilst companies tended to report the use of QM, evidence shows that many adopted a 'pick and mix' approach and as a result, may not have enjoyed the full business benefits of QM. Studies suggest that whilst (T)QM became very fashionable in the late 1980s to mid-1990s, levels of 'successful' take-up and sustainability were quite low. However, there is some evidence that organisational benefits did accrue when companies were able to implement and sustain QM (Wilkinson *et al.*, 1998). Typical barriers to sustaining QM included; a lack of support and commitment from senior and middle management, business short termism, a lack of integration between QM and HR practices and a lack of contextual application (Redman and Grieves, 1998; Bradley and Hill, 1987; Dale and Cooper, 1994; Wilkinson *et al.*, 1997; Dawson, 1995). Pertinent observations are that QM tended to have a particular blind-spot in terms of industrial relations (Wilkinson *et al.*, 1998) and that it failed to 'model the political realities of organisation' (Collins, 2000: 212).

Despite the fact that the term 'QM' has fallen from fashion, Wilkinson *et al.*, (1998: 188) observe that many of the practices associated with QM such as teamworking, employee involvement, and continuous improvement have become embedded within the normal functioning of organisations. Dawson (1998) goes on to observe that 'institutional (for example, the European Foundation for Quality Management) and business market requirements' have created a climate within which QM will continue to exist. Essentially, the term 'QM' may have fallen from its height of popular usage, but has left the legacy of practices that continue to merit further study. Indeed, there is a relationship between QM thinking and HPM, to which we turn now.

High performance management

Despite HPM achieving increasing prominence over the last few years, there remains much confusion as to its precise nature. As Lloyd and Payne (2004: 13) observe 'not only is there no clear definition of the model, but there is also a fundamental lack of agreement about the specific practices it should and should not incorporate, as well as the meanings that are ascribed to those practices'. Developing this theme Butler *et al.* (2004) argue that academic accounts of the phenomenon use a wide range of terms, thereby heightening the uncertainty surrounding its underlying tenets. Thus, in addition to our chosen label of HPM, high performance work systems (Danford *et al.*, 2004); high involvement work systems (Harmon *et al.*, 2003); high commitment management (Baird, 2002) and similar formulations (see Figure 14.2) are all used. Butler *et al.* (2004) suggest that the significance of this observation extends beyond mere semantics. For example, a focus on high performance work systems suggests a mechanistic route to sales and revenue growth through quality management techniques such as statistical process control and conformity evaluation. This is the agenda popularised by quality gurus *including* Crosby, Deming, Feigenbaum, and Duran. Early models of QM often emphasised the important role of senior managers and quality professionals. Conversely high commitment management, given formal expression via the concept of (soft) human resource management (HRM), emphasises the importance of *all* organisational players (in rhetoric at least). From the perspective of resource-based HRM, competitive advantage is derived not from the formal organisation and shaping of work *per se*, but the constituent workforce (see Chapter 2 in this volume).

Figure 14.2	The lexicon of high performance management

Terminology	Studies	Dominant emphasis
High-performance work systems	Appelbaum *et al.* (2000) Danford *et al.* (2004) Farias *et al.* (1998) Harley (2002) Ramsay *et al.* (2000) Thompson (2003)	Production management
High-performance work practices	Handel and Gittelman (2004)	
High-performance work organisation	Ashton and Sung (2002) Lloyd and Payne (2004)	
High-involvement work systems	Edwards and Wright (2001) Felstead and Gallie (2002) Harmon *et al.* (2003)	Work organisation
High-involvement work practices	Fuertes and Sanchez (2004)	
High-performance practices	Goddard (2004)	
High-involvement management	Forth and Millward (2004)	
High-performance employment systems	Brown and Reich (1997)	
High-commitment management	Baird (2002) Whitfield and Poole (1997)	Employee relations

Source: Butler *et al.*, 2004.

Notwithstanding this apparent confusion, following the work of Bélanger *et al.* (2002) HPM may be viewed as combination of three elements. The first dimension, production management, is concerned with aspects of productive flexibility and process standardisation. A key facet here is *hard* quality management which characteristically involves the use of statistical tools to analyse variance from tolerance margins at each stage of the production process (Wilkinson *et al.*, 1998), which is subsumed within a wider TQM format. A quite distinct second dimension relates to work organisation. Here there has been a trend towards production activities based on knowledge, cognition and abstract labour. The centrepiece of the new approach is teamworking and again one can see the linkages between HPM and earlier models of QM. The practice of sharing skills across traditional demarcations 'is thus a fundamental feature of the emergent model' (Bélanger *et al.*, 2002: 39). The third sphere, 'employment relations', very much underpins the coherence of the former two components given the requirement for a committed, rather than merely compliant workforce (Bélanger *et al.*, 2002: 42–48). Two significant features emerge. Firstly, Bélanger *et al.* (2002) state there is a desire to align and support task flexibility via terms and conditions of employment. This is typically sought by making pay contingent on group performance (Appelbaum, 2002: 124). Secondly, HRM professionals are charged with the pursuit of social adhesion and commitment to the new production format and wider organisational goals. This involves 'efforts to fashion employment conditions and the modes of regulation of those conditions in such a way as to elicit the tacit skills of the workers and tie them more closely to the goals of the firm' (Bélanger *et al.*, 2002: 44). In other words, the central task becomes the inculcation of a unitary organisational culture, or in Guest's (2002: 338) terms, the creation of a social system in support of the technical system.

Controversy: the impact of HPM on organisational performance

The driving force behind the introduction of HPM is to enhance organisational perform-ance. In recent years the underlying assumption that HPM necessarily gives rise to positive improvements in performance has been subject to detailed investigation. That HPM has the *potential* to deliver organisationally benign outcomes appears to be well settled. Thus, Whitfield and Poole (1997: 755) have concluded that extant research is 'strongly supportive of the notion that firms adopting the high performance approach have better outcomes than those which do not'. These conclusions do, however, come with reservations. Firstly, these scholars argue that the perennial issue of causality needs to be considered (Truss, 2001). It is possible that the findings reflect that more successful firms use their competitive success as a basis to build more innovative practices.

A more significant second charge made by Whitfield and Poole (1997) concerns the narrow base on which the existing research has been undertaken. This is dominated by manufacturing, typically organisations competing on the basis of product quality and differ-entiation, as well as price. Building upon this theme, Ashton and Sung (2002: 165) have argued 'we still do not know the extent to which HPWP (high performance work practices) are only appropriate for certain types of industry or product market strategy'. Put simply, a more controversial area concerns not links to productivity *per se*, but whether HPM yields benefits in *all* settings. In Wood's (1999: 368) terms, the debate is whether high-performance systems will *universally* outperform all other systems or whether the optimal system is rela-tive to the circumstances of the firm. Pursuing this theme, Wood (1999) draws upon Porter's conceptual distinction between two generic approaches, cost minimisation and innovative/quality strategies, as a basis on which to differentiate contexts. Schuler and Jackson (cited in Wood, 1999) have highlighted the need to link, on the one hand, a Taylorist control approach with cost minimisation, and HPM to a quality-orientated strategy on the other. In other words, HPM is seen to be a suitable solution only in certain circumstances. Continuing research is needed that examines the relationship between HPM and organis-ational performance.

Controversy: the impact of new managerial practices on employees

In contrast to the increasing research on organisational outcomes there is far less systematic data regarding employee experiences new management initiatives (especially drawn from qualitative data). However, there have been attempts in recent years to 're-focus attention on the worker' Guest (2002: 335).

As explained, the direct intellectual antecedent of HPM was QM. Much of the sociological literature dealing with employee experiences of this production format can be allotted to one of four broad streams: optimistic perspectives (e.g. Piore and Sabel, 1984) exploitation per-spectives (e.g. Sewell and Wilkinson, 1992b), contingency perspectives (Hill, 1991) and the re-organisation of control (Rees, 1998). The optimistic perspective is that QM tends to be regarded as a 'win-win', i.e. that employees and employers both benefit and as such employee experiences are likely to be positive. For example, Peccei and Rosenthal (2001) identified pos-itive outcomes flowing from a service excellence initiative and that employees broadly welcomed the initiative. The exploitation perspective argues that QM is essentially typified by peer pressure, increased surveillance and management by stress. For example, in a classic article, Sewell and Wilkinson (1992b) use the metaphor of a panoptican to drive home the theme that QM increases surveillance within organisations. Wilkinson *et al.* (1997) argue that the early debate tended to cluster around the polar extremes of 'bouquets or brickbats' as summarised in Table 14.6:

Table 14.6 Employee involvement and TQM: contrasting perspectives

Bouquets	Brickbats
Education	Indoctrination
Empowerment	Emasculation
Liberating	Controlling
Delayering	Intensification
Peer group pressure	Surveillance
Responsibility	Surveillance
Post-Fordism	Neo-Fordism
Blame-free culture	Identification of errors
Commitment	Compliance

Source: Wilkinson *et al.*, 1997.

One can see the clear contrast between these two perspectives. More recently 'middle-ground' perspectives have emerged that tend to argue that QM is neither 'all good' nor 'all bad' and is likely to bring mixed consequences for employees. The contingency perspectives focuses mainly on the way that contextual factors (for example, management intransigence, lack of training etc.) affect QM and a central theme tends to be that QM often fails to live up to expectations. The re-organisation of control has links with a labour process perspective and 'the nature of production and the organisation of work tasks are considered to the crucial factors in determining the boundaries of employee autonomy and discretion. However, it stops short of concluding that the implications of QM for employees tend invariably to be negative. Rather, QM is here seen as one among the series of changes, which also embrace new technology and new payment systems, which re-organise the shop floor so that in some respects commitments is enhanced while in others control is also tightened' (Rees, 1998: 38). Evidence from studies from the contingency and re-organisation of control perspectives show that whilst aspects of QM are often welcomed, there is often a gap between rhetoric and the day-to-day reality in the workplace and the outcomes for employees are often ambiguous (Bacon and Blyton, 2000; Edwards *et al.*, 1998; Glover and Noon, 2005; Storey and Harrison, 1999). Overall, we can see that there is a diversity of perspectives about the implications of QM for employees ranging from the optimistic to exploitation at the extremes and with middle-ground emphasising mixed consequences. In many ways the debate about the impact of HPM on employees is following similar lines and it is to this that we now turn.

As explained, HPM has become increasingly popular both in terms of managerial rhetoric and as a focus for academic research and one angle has been to investigate the implications of HPM for employees. Butler *et al.* (2004) observe one can also see elements of the 'bouquets or brickbats' tradition in respect of the HPM debate (Wilkinson *et al.*, 1997). For example, proponents of HPM point to benefits for employees in terms of a rhetoric of empowerment and increased intrinsic rewards. Much, but not all, of this literature is contained within prescriptive accounts (see, for example, CIPD, 2004). We also find an exploitation perspective that centres upon the work intensification thesis and views HPM simply as a managerial ruse intended to extract greater effort from employees. Interestingly there is common ground between these competing claims. This is that techniques of HPM, mediated by worker outcomes, are likely to contribute to enhanced organisational performance. What *is* disputed, however, is the chain of causation.

As with QM, the optimistic perspective argues that the impact of HPM is mostly positive (for example, CIPD, 2004). Employees' experiences of work are enhanced and the outcomes are thus beneficial to both capital and labour. Increased task discretion and autonomy engender commitment, which, in turn, feeds into performance gains. The exploitation perspective also assumes a positive association between HPM and performance gains. However, the distinction is that any benefits take the form of minor gains in discretion, granted as a means of securing compliance with managerial aims. Such advances are far outweighed by work intensification, insecurity and stress (see Ramsay *et al.*, 2000: 505). Stress arises because of the added responsibility associated with the new production mode allied to increased pressure within the working environment due to the absence of buffers within lean production formats.

Unfortunately, there are only a handful of studies that have collected systematic data informing this debate. One of the most cited accounts in support of the optimistic thesis is that provided by Appelbaum *et al.* (2000). This study investigated *inter alia* the effects of HPM in three manufacturing sectors: steel, clothing and medical products with data collated from around 4000 workers. HPM was associated with positive performance gains and evidence was found linking various HPM practices to job satisfaction. This study provides support for David Guest's (2002: 354) assertion that 'there is consistent evidence that workers respond positively to practices associated with what is described as a high performance work system'. This much having been said, there is an emergent body of contrary case study evidence that does indeed point towards enhanced employee stress (see, for example, Danford *et al.* 2004; McKinlay and Taylor, 1996 and Brown, 1999).

As with the debate about the effect of QM for employees, some have adopted a more middle-ground position. Edwards and Wright (2000: 570) have argued that, 'polarizing the issue between critics and supporters is not helpful'. Such exhortation chimes with an increasing body of literature indicating that HPM is likely to give rise to more complex outcomes for employees than those suggested above. Utilising the 1998 Workplace Employee Relations Survey (WERS98), Ramsay *et al.* (2000) found that, on the one hand, the data pointed to some association between HPM and higher job discretion and commitment. However, on the other, job strain was also reported. This confirms Edwards and Wright's (2000: 569) assertion that the links between HPM and employee outcomes represent a 'shifting and variable complex whole', which cannot be reduced to employee enhancing or damaging effects. For Edwards (2001: 3) one key to explanation lies in understanding the balance between the need for creativity and control within the contemporary workplace under the new production system. Thus, 'the fundamental tension is between work design which provides responsibility and autonomy and that which calls for predictable work outcomes based on defined tasks and monitoring (Edwards, 2001).

One managerial solution to the above dilemma has been a shift away from command-and-control towards more indirect methods of tracking employee performance; that is, 'a change in the means of control' (Edwards, 2001) not a move away from all forms of control. Under new forms of work organisation the control system is based upon outcomes, not specific instructions to detail. Via the techniques of human resource management risks and responsibilities are internalised in the sense that employees are held responsible for their own actions (Edwards, 2001: 23). Thus, task discretion does not mean the lifting of organisational controls, rather the widespread use of HRM as opposed to more direct methods of control (i.e. the re-organisation of control). This is one means of reconciling the 'puzzle'. The contradictions are tapping into different aspects of a given worker's experiences arising from the multi-dimensional nature of HPM as identified by Bélanger and his colleagues. That is, increased responsibility (autonomy) arising from changes in work organisation, but also greater stress as risks are internalised via performance management and techniques of HRM. As with the debate about the implications of QM for employees, evidence remains contrasting and research will continue to uncover the complexities associated with this field of study.

Summary

- The terrain of EPI is broad and actually comprises three distinct but related concepts: employee involvement, employee participation and industrial democracy. The difference between these constructs is best understood in terms of variations in employee power and influence. Broadly speaking there is a continuum ranging from narrow task-based employee input (employee involvement (EI)) through to elements of co-determination or joint decision making (participation) extending to full-blown employee ownership (industrial democracy).

- The topic of EPI has a long history. Interestingly while employee involvement (EI) is nowadays ascendant this is a relatively recent phenomenon. In the past the field has been dominated by the themes of participation and industrial democracy. The current hegemony of employee involvement can be tracked to the 1980s and the emergence of neo-liberalism and various influential HRM models. While employee involvement is currently riding high developments at EU level have served to bolster the flagging fortunes of employee participation. The European Works Council and Information and Consultation directives provide employees with statutory rights to consultation hitherto denied to British workers. Academic commentators, however, have expressed reservations as regards whether the legislation has the potential to seriously compromise managerial prerogative.

- Direct participation is generally geared towards capturing the creativity of employees so that organisational performance improves.

- WERS shows a trend towards an increase in direct forms of participation and a decline in representative participation. An outcome of this trend is that large swathes of the British workforce are not covered by trade union representation. Often such employees are based in service sector organisations that offer minimal pay and conditions. There is a concern that the plight of these employees is largely determined by managerial choice and approaches can range from enlightened HRM to authoritarian management.

- In the field of EPI the topic of managerial motive has been a longstanding area of controversy. Ramsay's (1979) 'cycles of control' thesis is regarded as seminal. According to Ramsay management was only interested in employee involvement when there were threats to managerial power and hegemony. This stance has now been discredited. It is now widely acknowledged (e.g. Ackers *et al.*, 1992) that managerial goals are much more complex and cannot be reduced to issues of crude labour control. More creative goals that may be followed include the enhancement of customer care, employee recruitment and retention, and the invocation of a quality culture.

- The impact of a range of new management initiatives upon organisations and employees were reviewed. Evidence remains inconclusive as to the direct organisational benefits of the selected schemes. Evidence is also split as to the outcomes of these initiatives for employees.

CASE STUDY

Advanced Components

Advanced Components (AC) are a subsidiary of a large Anglo/French MNC called CarCo. AC produce specialist components for the car industry. AC are based in the north of England. CarCo went through a massive programme of rationalisation in the late 1970s, the mid-1980s and more recently in the late 1990s. They are beginning to explore opportunities for future growth and are in early talks about a potential joint venture in China. If this went ahead, the future of AC would be uncertain and the unions suspect that CarCo could close AC and relocate production in China.

The AC subsidiary has been on the same site since the industrial revolution, albeit under different names and different ownerships. AC employs 800 employees

Case study continued

on a single site. The site employed 8000 in 1970. Over the years it has reduced its headcount, via early retirement, voluntary redundancies and compulsory redundancies. The workforce are mainly male, the average age is 48 and the average length-of-service is 15 years. AC produces specialist products and the workforce comprises a mix of production and craft workers (such as electricians). Average pay is £28,000 and comprises a mix of basic salary, overtime and bonuses.

Advanced Components is strongly unionised and had a reputation for being one of CarCo's industrial relations blackspots of the 1960s and 1970s. During this period, relationships between management and unions were conflictual. However, trade union activity has been less militant in recent years. Indeed, many feel that AC adopted a 'bullying' and autocratic form of management in the 1980s when much of the downsizing took place. However, management now seem keen to promote more cooperative relationships for the future. Shop stewards realise that the long-term future is made more precarious by CarCo's negotiations within China. The trade unions have begun to express an interest in exploring the possibilities for a 'social partnership' agreement.

AC changed the name of their personnel department to the human resource department in 1995. The emphasis of the old personnel department had been very much upon industrial relations, health and safety and record keeping. There has been no system of appraisal or systematic training for the shopfloor or administrative staff. The apprenticeship system was the traditional training vehicle for shopfloor workers, but AC have not taken any new apprentices for 12 years. Any training that occurs tends to be on-the-job 'sitting with Nellie' but this approach is not formally managed. There is a corporate level, fasttrack management development scheme for identified high fliers, who are normally graduates. The high fliers are entered onto an MBA programme that is run by one of the UK's top business schools. The scheme has been very successful in terms of developing these individuals and tends to lead to accelerated careers for the individuals concerned and is still used today. There was no such formalised scheme for other white collar/managerial employees.

The change of label from the 'personnel department' to the 'human resources department' coincided with the implementation of quality management. The espoused strategy was QM would be supported by 'soft' HRM (including an emphasis on training and involvement). This signalled a change in management style (in rhetoric at least) and a more participative style was promised. However, many employees feel that this tends to be rather patchy and some managers

maintain an autocratic style. The company have been trying to improve direct participation for over a decade. They have a company newsletter, a suggestion scheme, a team briefing system and have tried to encourage problem-solving groups. However, the success of these has been mixed. The newsletter is read by about 30 per cent of employees. The suggestion scheme generated a lot of interest initially and one large award of £5000 was made. However, the number of suggestions has fallen and there is a perception that it is extremely difficult to win awards and that management are slow to process the paperwork and feedback on proposals. The team briefing system is mainly welcomed, but the satisfaction levels are very much affected by the quality of the team briefers. Some are naturally good, but others struggle and there is no training for team briefers. AC do have problem-solving groups, but in reality only a handful are active and productive. Levels of problem-solving group activity tends to ebb and flow according to how much encouragement individual managers offer.

AC now wish to implement a programme of changes to take them forward. They are calling the programme 'Towards 2010'. AC have analysed their current position and have identified key issues:

- Car components is an increasingly competitive market sector with threats from the Asia.
- AC must continue to decrease costs whilst increasing quality.
- AC believe that there is significantly more potential within their employee ranks than is currently being utilised.
- AC believe that they need to increase flexibility, particularly on the shopfloor.
- They will be investing in improved IT to improve the site operations. An IT system will be linked to the production lines and will track all aspects of the progress of raw stock to the point at which it leaves the site. The system will give all departments (e.g. sales, marketing, finance) access to information regarding the status of customer orders, stock levels etc. The implementation of the system will lead to a consequent reduction in white collar administrative staff. The system will be launched in January 2007.

AC wish to achieve the following in relation to its human resources:

- Increase productivity
- Improve the customer focus
- Increase quality
- Reduce labour costs
- Create a training and development strategy that covers all employees.

Case study continued

- Increase and broaden all employee skills at all levels.
- Encourage employee involvement.

The task

1 Advanced Components have asked you to summarise the EPI implications of 'Towards 2010'.
2 They have asked you to devise the following:
   (a) An EPI *strategy* that will guide all activities. You are required to write a briefing paper that will be distributed to all managers that summarises the key content of this strategy.

(b) Outline the *operational objectives* that describe what EPI practices should be implemented (or sustained) within the organisation by the year 2010.

3 You must explain the rationale for your strategy, indicating why it would be appropriate for implementation at AC.
4 AC recognise trade unions. What approach should AC take in respect of the unions?
5 What do you perceive to be the main barriers in terms of taking the EPI strategy forwards and how would you suggest that AC deal with these?

References and further reading

Abrahamsson, B. (1977) *Bureaucracy or Participation*, London: Sage Publications

Ackers, P., Marchington, M., Wilkinson, A. and Goodman, J. (1992) 'The use of Cycles: Explaining Employee Involvement in the 1990s', *Industrial Relations Journal*, 23, 4: 268–283.

Ackers, P. and Payne, J. (1998) 'British trade unions and social partnership: Rhetoric, reality and strategy' *International Journal of Human Resource Management*, 9, 1: 529–550.

Alvesson, M. and Willmott, H. (2002) 'Identity regulation as organizational control: Producing the appropriate individual', *Journal of Management Studies*, 39, 5: 619–644.

Applebaum, E. (2002) 'The Impact of New Forms of Work Organisations on Workers', in Murray, G., Bélanger, J., Giles, G. and Lapointe, P. *Work and Employment Relations in the High Performance Workplace*. London: Continuum.

Appelbaum, E., Bailey, T., Berg, G. and Kelberg, G. (2000) *Manufacturing Advantage*. Ithaca: Cornell University Press.

Argyris, C. (1964) *Integrating the Individual and Organization*. New York: Wiley.

Ashton, D. and Sung, J. (2002) *Supporting Workplace Learning for High Performance Working*. Geneva: International Labour Office.

Bacon, N. (2006) 'Industrial Relations' in T. Redman and A. Wilkinson (eds) *Contemporary human resource management*. Harlow: Prentice Hall:Financial Times.

Bacon, N. and Blyton, P. (2000) *Worker responses to workplace restructuring*. Paper presented at the BUIRA study group: What about the workers? Employee perspectives on HRM, Kings College, London.

Baird, M. (2002) 'Changes, Dangers, Choice and Voice: Understanding What High Commitment Management Means for Employees and Unions', *The Journal of Industrial Relations*, 44, 3: 359–375.

Batstone, E.. Ferner, A. and Terry, M. (1983) *Unions on the Board: An Experiment in Industrial Democracy*. Oxford: Blackwell.

Bélanger, P., Giles, A. and Murray, G. (2002) 'Workplace Innovation and the Role of Institutions', in Murray, G., Bélanger, J., Giles, A. and Lapointe, P. *Work and Employment in the High Performance Workplace*. London: Continuum.

Bernstein, P. (1976) *Workplace Democratization*. New Jersey: Transaction Books.

Blyton, P. and Turnbull, P. (2004) *The Dynamics of Employee Relations*, 3rd edn. Basingstoke: Palgrave.

Bolle De Bal, M. (1992) 'Participative Management', in Szell, G. (ed.) *Concise Encyclopaedia of Participation*. Berlin: Walter de Gruyter.

Bradley, K. and Hill, S. (1987) 'Quality Circles and Managerial Interests', *Industrial Relations*, 26, 1: 66–82.

Brannen, P. (1983) *Authority and Participation in Industry*. London: Batsford.

Brannen, P., Batstone, E., Fatchett, D. and White, P. (1976) *The Worker Directors: A Sociology of Participation*. London: Hutchinson.

Brown, C. and Reich, M. (1997) 'Micro-Macro Linkages in High Performance Employment Systems', *Organizational Studies*, 18, 5: 765–781.

Brown, T. (1999) 'Restructuring Teams and Learning: The Case of a Clothing Company', *Studies in Continuing Education*, 21, 2: 239–257.

Burchill, F. (1997) *Labour Relations*. Basingstoke: Macmillan.

Butler, P. (2004) Employee Representation in Non-Unions Firms: A Critical Evaluation of Managerial Motive and the Efficacy of the Voice Process. Unpublished PhD Thesis, University of Warwick.

Butler, P., Felstead, A., Ashton, D., Fuller, A., Lee, T., Unwin, L. and Walters, S. (2004) 'High Performance Management: A Literature Review', *Learning as Work Research Paper No. 1*, Centre for Labour Market Studies, University of Leicester.

Cheney, G. (1999) *Values at Work: Employee Participation Meets Market Pressure at Modragon*. Ithaca: ILR Press.

CIPD (2004) *Maximising Employee Potential and Business Performance*. London: CIPD.

Clegg, H.A. (1951) *Industrial democracy and nationalization: A study prepared for the Fabian Society*. Oxford: Blackwell.

Clegg, H. (1979) *The Changing system of Industrial Relations in Britain*. Oxford: Blackwell

Claydon, T. (1996) 'Union decognition: a re-examination', in Beardwell, I. (ed.) *Contemporary Industrial Relations: A critical analysis*. Oxford: Oxford University Press.

Collins, D. (2000) *Management Fads and Buzzwords: Critical Practical Perspectives.* London: Routledge.

Crouch, C. (1979) *The Political Economy of Industrial Relations.* Glasgow: Fontana.

Cully, M., Woodland, S., O'Reilly, A. and Dix, G. (1999) *Britain at Work: As Depicted by the 1998 Workplace Employee Relations Survey.* London: Routledge.

Dachler, P. and Wilpert, B. (1978) 'Conceptual Dimensions and Boundaries in Organizations', *Administrative Science Quarterly*, 23: 1–39.

Dale, B.G. and Cooper, C. (1994) 'Total Quality Management: Some Common Mistakes Made by Senior Management', *Quality World Technical Supplement*, March: 4–11.

Danford, A., Richardson, M., Stewart, P, Tailby, S., Upchurch, M. (2004) 'High Performance Work Systems and Workplace Partnership: A Case Study of Aerospace Workers', *New Technology, Work and Employment*, 19, 1: 14–29.

Dawson, P. (1995) 'Managing Quality in the Multi-Cultural Workplace', in Wilkinson, A. and Willmott, H. (eds) *Making Quality Critical: New Perspectives on Organisation Change*: 173–193. London: Routledge.

Dawson, P. (1998) 'The rhetoric and bureaucracy of quality management: A totally questionable method', *Personnel Review*, 27, 1: 5–14.

Edwards, P. (2001) 'The Puzzle of Work: Autonomy and Commitment plus Discipline and Insecurity', *SKOPE Research Paper No. 16*, University of Warwick.

Edwards, P. and Wright, M. (2000) 'High Involvement Work Systems and Performance Outcomes', *The International Journal of Human Resource Management*, 24, 4: 568–585.

Edwards, P., Collinson, M. and Rees, C. (1998) 'The determinants of employee responses to total quality management: Six case studies', *Organization Studies*, 19, 3: 449–475.

Farias, G.F. and Varma, A. (1998) 'High performance work systems: what we know and what we need to know', *Human Resource Planning*, 21, 2: 50–55.

Felstead, A. and Gallie, D. (2002) 'For better or worse? Non standard jobs and high involvement work systems', SKOPE Research Paper No. 28, University of Warwick.

Flanders, A. (1968) *Experiment in Industrial Democracy: A Study of the John Lewis Partnership.* London: Faber.

Forth, J. and Millward, N. (2004) 'High Involvement Management and Pay in Britain', *Industrial Relations*, 43, 1: 98–119.

Fuertes, M. and Sanchez, F. (2003) 'High involvement practices in human resource management: Concepts and factors that motivate their adoption', *International Journal of Human Resource Management*, 14, 4: 511–529.

Garrahan, P. and Stewart, P. (1992) *The Nissan Enigma: Flexibility at work in a local economy.* London: Mansell Publishing Limited.

Geary, J.F. (2003) 'New forms of work organisation: Still limited, still controlled, but still welcome?', in Edwards, P.K. (ed.) *Industrial relations: Theory and practice in Britain.* Oxford: Blackwell.

Gennard, J. and Judge, G. (2005) *Employee relations*, 4th edn. London: CIPD.

Glover, L. (2000) 'Neither poison nor panacea: Shop floor responses to TQM', *Employee Relations*, 22, 2: 121–141.

Glover, L. (2001) 'Communication and consultation in a green field site company', *Personnel Review*, 30, 3: 297–316.

Glover, L. and Noon, M. (2005) 'Shop-floor workers' responses to quality management initiatives: broadening the disciplined worker thesis', *Work, Employment and Society*, 19, 4: 727–745.

Goddard, J. (2004) 'A critical assessment of the high performance paradigm', *British Journal of Industrial Relations*, 42, 2: 349–378.

Grenier, D. and Hogler, R. (1991) 'Labour Law and Managerial Ideology: Employee Participation as a Control System', *Work and Occupations*, 16, 3: 313–333.

Guest, D. (2002) 'Human Resource Management, Corporate Performance and Employee Well-Being: Building the Worker into HRM', *The Journal of Industrial Relations*, 44, 4: 335–358.

Guest, D. and Peccei, R. (2001) 'Partnership at work: mutuality and the balance of advantage', *British Journal of Industrial Relations*, 39, 2: 207–263.

Hall, M. and Marginson, P. (2005) 'Trojan Horse or Paper Tiger? Assessing the Significance of European Works Councils' in Hyman, J. and Thompson, P. (eds) *Participation at Work: Essays in Honour of Harvie Ramsay.* Basingstoke: Macmillan.

Handel, J. and Gittleman, M. (2004) 'Is There a Wage Payoff to Innovative Work Practices?', *Industrial Relations*, 43, 1: 67–97.

Harley, B. (2002) 'Employee Responses to High Performance Work System Practices: An Analysis of the AWIRS95 Data', *The Journal of Industrial Relations*, 44, 3: 418–434

Harley, B., Hyman, J. and Thompson, P. (2005) 'The Paradoxes of Participation', in Harley, B. Hyman, J. and Thompson, P. (eds), *Participation and democracy at work: Essays in honour of Harvie Ramsay.* Basingstoke: Palgrave Macmillan.

Harmon, J., Scotti, D. and Behson, S. (2003) 'Effects of High Performance Work Systems Practices: An Analysis of the WIRS95 Data', *Journal of Industrial Relations*, 44, 3: 418–434.

Heller, F. (1992) 'Competence', in Szell, G. (ed.) *Concise Encyclopedia of Participation.* Berlin: Walter De Gruyter.

Heller, F., Pusic, E., Strauss, G. and Wilpert, B. (1998) *Organisational Participation: Myth and reality.* Oxford: Oxford University Press.

Hespe, G. and Little, S. (1971) 'Some Aspects of Employee Participation', in Warre, P. (ed.) *Psychology at Work.* Harmondsworth: Penguin.

Hill, S. (1991) 'Why quality circles failed but total quality might succeed', *British Journal of Industrial Relations*, 29, 4: 541–568.

Hill, S. (1995) 'From Quality Circles to Total Quality Management', in Wilkinson, A. and Willmott, H. (eds) *Making Quality Critical: New Perspectives on Organisational Change.* London: Routledge.

Holden, L. (2001) 'Employee Involvement and Empowerment', in Beardwell, I., Holden, L. and Claydon, T. *Human Resource Management: A Contemporary Approach.* Harlow: Prentice Hall.

Holden, L. (2004) 'Employee involvement and empowerment' in Beardwell, I. and Holden, L. (eds) *Human resource management: A contemporary approach*, 4th edn. Harlow: Prentice-Hall.

Hyman, R. (1989) *The Political Economy of Industrial Relations: Theory and Practice in a Cold Climate.* Basingstoke: Macmillan.

Hyman, J. and Mason, B. (1995) *Managing Employee Involvement and Participation.* London: Sage.

Jong, J. and Wilkinson, A. (1999) 'The state of Total Quality Management: A Review', *International Journal of Human Resource Management*, 10, 1: 137–150.

Kerckhofs, P. (2002) *European Works Councils; Facts and Figures.* Brussels: European Trade Union Institute.

Kersley, B., Alpin, C., Forth, J., Bryson, A., Bewley, H., Dix, G. and Oxenbridge, S. (2005). Inside the workplace: First findings from the 2004 Workplace Employment Relations Survey: ESRC, ACAS, PSI, DTI.

Leat, M. (2003) 'The European Union', in Hollinshead, G., Nicholls, P. and Tailby, S. (eds) *Employee Relations*. Harlow: Prentice Hall.

Legge, K. (2005) *Human resource management: Rhetorics and realities* (Anniversary ed.). Basingstoke: Palgrave Macmillan.

Lewis, P., Thornhill, A. and Saunders, M. (2003) *Employee Relations: Understanding the Employment Relationship*. Harlow: Prentice Hall.

Likert, R. (1961) *New Patterns of Management*. New York: McGraw Hill.

Lloyd, C. and Payne, J. (2004) 'The only Show in Town (if a pretty pathetic one at that) . . . Re-Evaluating the High Performance Workplace as a Vehicle for the UK High Skills Project', Paper presented to the International Labour Process Conference, Amsterdam.

Marchington, M. (2005) 'Employee involvement: Patterns and explanations', in Harley, B., Hyman, J. and Thompson, P. (eds) *Participation and democracy at work: Essays in honour of Harvie Ramsay*. Basingstoke: Palgrave Macmillan.

Marchington, M., Goodman, J., Wilkinson, A. and Ackers, P. (1992) *New Developments in Employee Involvement*. Department of Employment Research Series No. 2.

Marchington, M. and Wilkinson, A. (2005) 'Direct participation', in Bach, S. (ed.) *Personnel management: A comprehensive guide to theory and practice*. Oxford: Blackwell, pp. 382–404.

Marchington, M., Wikinson, A., Ackers, P. and Goodman, J. (1993) 'The Influence of Managerial Relations on Waves of Employee Involvement', *British Journal of Industrial Relations*, 31, 4: 553–576.

Martinez Lucio, M. and Stuart, M. (2002) 'Assessing the principles of partnership: Workplace trade unions representatives' attitudes and experiences', *Employee Relations*, 24, 3: 305–320.

McGregor, D. (1960) *The Human Side of Enterprise*. New York: McGraw-Hill.

McKinlay, A. and Taylor, P. (1996) 'Power Surveillance and Resistance: Inside the Factory of the Future', in Ackers, P., Smith, C. and Smith, P. (eds) *The New Workplace and Trade Unionism*. London: Routledge.

Millward, N., Bryson, A. and Forth, J. (2000) *All Change at Work?: British Employment Relations 1980–1998, as portrayed by the Workplace Industrial Relations Survey series*. London: Routledge.

Millward, N., Bryson, A. and Worth, J. (2000) *All Change at Work?* London: Routledge.

Mueller, F. and Proctor, S. (2000) *Teamworking*. Basingstoke: Macmillan Press.

Pateman, C. (1970) *Participation and Democratic Theory*. Cambridge: Cambridge University Press.

Payne, J. and Keep, E. (2005) 'Promoting workplace development: Lessons for UK policy from Nordic approaches to job redesign and the quality of working life', in Harley, B., Hyman, J. and Thompson, P. (eds) *Participation and democracy at work: Essays in honour of Harvie Ramsay*. Basingstoke: Palgrave Macmillan.

Peccei, R. and Rosenthal, P. (2001) 'Delivering customer-orientated behaviour through empowerment: An empirical test of HRM', *Journal of Management Studies*, 38, 6: 831–857.

Piore, M. and Sabel, C. (1984) *The Second Industrial Divide: Possibilities to Prosperity*. New York: Basic Books.

Poole, M. (1978) *Workers' Participation in Industry*. London: Routledge.

Ramsay, H. (1977) 'Cycles of Control', *Sociology*, 11, 3: 481–506.

Ramsay, H. (1980) 'Phantom Participation: Patterns of Power and Conflict', *Industrial Relations Journal*, 11, 3: 46–59.

Ramsay, H. (1993) 'Recycled Waste? Debating the Analysis of Worker Participation: A Response to Ackers *et al*.', *Industrial Relations Journal*, 24, 1: 76–80.

Ramsay, H., Scholarios, D. and Harley, B. (2000) 'Employees and High Performance Work Systems: Testing Inside the Black Box', *British Journal of Industrial Relations*, 38, 4: 501–531.

Redman, T. and Grieves, J. (1998) 'Managing strategic change through TQM: Learning from failure', *New Technology, Work and Employment*, 14, 1: 64–80.

Rees, C. (1998) 'Empowerment through quality management: Employee accounts from inside a bank, a hotel and two factories', in Mabey, C., Skinner, D. and Clark, T. (eds) *Experiencing Human Resource Management*. London: Sage Publications.

Richardson, M. (2003) 'Employee Involvement and Participation', in Hollinshead, G., Nicholls, P. and Tailby S. (eds) *Employee Relations*. Harlow: Prentice Hall.

Sewell, G. and Wilkinson, B. (1992a) 'Empowerment or Emasculation?: Shopfloor Surveillance in a Total Quality Organisation', in Blyton, P. and Turnbull, P. (eds) *Reassessing Human Resource Management*. London: Sage.

Sewell, G. and Wilkinson, B. (1992b) 'Someone to watch over me: surveillance, discipline and the just-in-time labour process', *Sociology*, 26, 2: 271–290.

Sisson, K. (2002) 'The Information and Consultation Directive: Unnecessary Regulation or an Opportunity to Promote Partnership', *Warwick Papers in Industrial Relations, Number 67*.

Stirling, J. and Fitzgerald, I. (2000) 'European Works Councils: Representing Workers on the Periphery', *Employee Relations*, 23, 1: 13–25.

Storey, J. (1992) *Developments in the Management of Human Resources: An Analytical Review*. London: Blackwell.

Storey, J. (1995) *Human Resource Management: A Critical Text*. London: Routledge.

Storey, J. and Harrison, A. (1999) 'Coping with world-class manufacturing', *Work, Employment and Society*, 13, 4: 643–664.

Suff, R. and Williams, S. (2004) 'The myth of mutuality?: Employee perceptions of partnership at Borg Warner', *Employee Relations*, 26, 1.

Tailby, S. and Winchester, D. (2005) 'Management and trade unions: Towards social partnership?', in Bach, S. (ed.) *Human resource managment: Personnel management in transition*. Oxford: Blackwell, pp. 365–388.

Tailby, S., Richardson, M., Danford, A. and Upchurch, M. (2004) 'Partnership at work and worker participation: an NHS case study', *Industrial Relations Journal*, 35, 5: 403–418.

Taylor, P., Mulvey, G., Hyman, J. and Bain, P. (2002) 'Work organization, control and the experience of work in call centres', *Work, Employment and Society*, 16, 1: 133–150.

Thompson, P. (2003) 'Disconnected capitalism: Or why employers can't keep their side of the bargain', *Work Employment and Society*, 17, 2: 359–378.

Towers, B. (1997) *The Representation Gap: Change and Reform in the British and American Workplace*. Oxford: Oxford University Press.

Truss, C. (2001) 'Complexities and controversies in linking HRM with organizational outcomes', *Journal of Management Studies*, 38, 8: 1121–1149.

Undy, R. (1999) 'Annual Review Article: New Labour's "Industrial Relations Settlement": The Third Way?', *British Journal of Industrial Relations*, 37, 2: 315–336.

Whitfield, K. and Poole, M. (1997) 'Organizing Employment for High Performance Theories, Evidence and Policy', *Organisational Studies*, 18, 5: 745–764.

Wilkinson, A., Godfrey, G. and Marchington, M. (1997) 'Bouquets, brickbats and blinkers: TQM and employee involvement in practice', *Organisation Studies*, 18, 5: 799–819.

Wilkinson, A., Redman, T., Snape, E. and Marchington, M. (1998) *Managing with Total Quality Management: Theory and Practice*. London: Macmillan.

Wood, S. (1999) Human Resource Management and Performance, *International Journal of Management Review*, 1, 4: 367–413.

For multiple-choice questions, exercises and annotated weblinks specific to this chapter visit the book's website at **www.pearsoned.co.uk/beardwell**

Malone Superbuy Ltd

Malone Superbuy is a large food retail company that has been established since the beginning of the twentieth century. Over the last 100 years the organisation has built a reputation for quality foods, and so depends on relatively discerning shoppers for its market; most of its outlets are in the South-West and South-East of Britain. The organisation is a large employer (more than 4000 employees); it is highly dependent upon part-time, female labour and casual student workers for shopfloor employees, with full-time management staff consigned to given stores. The firm does experience costly medium-to-high labour turnover, largely because of the unsocial hours to which all employees are rostered, and the transient nature of student labour. Wage rates are average for the sector, and were unaffected by the Minimum Wage Regulation. The organisation has never recognised trade unions, but has had a fairly informal system of local employee representation committees, many of which have fallen into disuse in recent years.

The food retail sector has recently experienced growing competition between the market leaders as attention has been drawn to the differentials between the price of food in the UK and in other European countries. British farmers have also been active in publicly denouncing the profiteering that has been evident in the retail food sector. Consequently, the big firms are engaged in 'price wars' and are actively increasing the quality and variety of goods on offer while also focusing on the level of service offered within their stores. Malone Superbuy is not in the top league, but nevertheless has been affected by increasing competition in the sector. To add to its troubles, the TGWU is actively recruiting employees, and it looks as if Malone's will be presented with a recognition claim for bargaining rights in the near future. To remain competitive in the market the firm must:

- improve the quality of service offered to customers throughout the organisation;
- find ways of cutting labour costs.

Further to developing a strategy for change to deal with market pressures, the firm must also decide whether it intends to:

- accept a trade union presence and attempt to build a partnership agreement;
- adopt a substitution or suppressionist approach to union recognition.

Activity

You are a member of an external team of HR consultants employed by the company to outline a strategy which will achieve employee support for increased competitiveness in an environment of change. The Managing Director has already decided that he wants a comprehensive report to indicate how the firm will move forward and this will be presented under the title, 'Superbuy Shapes Up For The Future!'. As a team your remit is to construct that report and your particular responsibility is to write the following sections:

1 Outline and discuss an appropriate HR Strategy (see also Chapter 2) for this organisation which will facilitate the coherent development of the firm within its particular context.

2 Suggest policy initiatives to address the labour turnover problems currently affecting the firm.

3 Develop a training programme which will enhance customer service skills amongst shopfloor staff.

4 Address the issue of employee representation with a reasoned consideration of whether to adopt substitution/exclusion approaches or to negotiate a recognition agreement with trade unions.

5 Consider how employee reward policies might be re-evaluated to encourage greater employee motivation and loyalty (without substantially affecting the wages bill!).

Part 5

INTERNATIONAL HUMAN RESOURCE MANAGEMENT

Introduction to Part 5

The considerable growth of interest in international human resource management stems from the rise of globalisation over the past half century, a phenomenon that has accelerated considerably over the last decade. This term describes the proliferation of international trading links, foreign direct investment, worldwide mergers and acquisitions and a burgeoning of telecommunications, faster and cheaper transport and rapid technological change. Globalisation has involved the integration of markets worldwide and on a regional level and is being stimulated further by the rise of new and potentially powerful markets in China, India and Eastern and Central Europe.

The rise of the multinational company (MNC) has been one of the most visible manifestations of globalisation. As companies and organisations expand their cross-border activities there has been a concomitant increase in business activity together with an increase in cross-border integration of their production processes. This in turn has created growing interest in the ways in which they achieve international management coordination and control and what effect such coordination has on HRM in the countries in which their operations are based.

The possible role of MNCs as forces for change in national HRM systems is just one element in a wider debate that is developing concerning the effects of globalisation on national economic and business systems. Are there varieties of capitalism that are each efficient in their own national contexts, or is globalisation creating new conditions in which some of those varieties cease to be sustainable, causing convergence towards a dominant global model?

The chapters that comprise this part cannot do justice to the complexity and scale of these issues. They merely serve to give you a flavour of some of the developments in the field and some of the debates that are now emerging. The part begins with a comparative perspective on HRM that takes up the question of international convergence by looking at pressures for change in Germany, Japan and the USA to see how far the highly institutionalised German and Japanese systems are being forced to move towards the more loosely regulated and managerially dominated American system.

The following chapter extends the comparative theme and the discussion of possible global convergence by examining the way HRM is developing in China and India. It uses cultural and institutional perspectives to explore how historically rooted national characteristics interact with international, globalising influences to shape HRM in these potentially huge global players.

The final chapter combines a range of academic perspectives to analyse and examine how human resources are managed in MNCs. It starts by showing how international operations offer firms advantages in terms of gaining access to human resources and knowledge. It then explores the different ways in which MNCs might choose to structure the international HR function and discusses how HR networks and expatriate managers are used to generate and transfer HR knowledge internally. Finally, it explores how their HRM practices are influenced by characteristics of their country of origin and of the countries in which they operate.

Chapter 15

HRM trends and prospects: a comparative perspective

Ian Clark and Tim Claydon

Objectives

- To demonstrate the nationally distinctive character of employment relations with reference to Germany, Japan and the United States.

- To show how patterns of employment regulation are embedded within wider features of societies, specifically their business systems.

- To identify and explain recent pressures for change in employment systems.

- To examine the nature and extent of change occurring in the German, Japanese and American employment systems.

- To examine the debate concerning whether national employment systems are converging towards the American model.

Introduction

There are great differences in how countries organise employment and manage the employment relationship. National employment systems vary in the extent to which workers are able to organise and act collectively to influence their terms and conditions of employment, how far they are involved in decision making within the enterprise, the level of protection they enjoy against job loss, the way jobs are designed and work is organised, and in many other ways. They also vary in terms of their outcomes for labour productivity, job creation, unemployment, the extent of equality or inequality of earnings and employment opportunity, the degree of employment security or insecurity experienced by workers, and overall economic performance.

National variations in employment systems reflect wider differences in national culture and institutions. They are the outcome of nationally distinctive histories of how national identity and statehood were forged, how industrialisation developed, and how the nature and outcomes of class conflicts shaped political institutions and relations between capital, labour and the state. For many analysts this means that national systems of employment regulation will always differ from each other in important respects, as will the employment relations practices of firms in different countries, since they embody nationally specific historical developments (Hall and Soskice, 2001; Maurice, Sellier and Silvestre, 1986; Whitley, 2000). Others, however, have argued that powerful socio-economic forces such as technological change, industrial development and more recently, globalisation force nation states along convergent paths, so that national differences in respect of economic and social organisation, including employment regulation, become less and less significant (Kerr *et al.*, 1960; Streeck, 1997). However, if this is the case, what are national systems converging towards?

In this chapter we look at three nationally based systems of employment regulation, those of Germany, Japan and the USA. In Germany, constitutional law has provided workers with rights to collective representation and participation in decision making as well as individual rights. Trade unions wield significant, albeit currently declining, influence and workers' representatives have a legal right to negotiate or to be consulted on a wide range of issues. This emphasis on joint regulation of the employment relationship has provided the basis for a high degree of worker–management cooperation in the workplace and has underpinned a production system based on high productivity and high quality output.

In Japan, management and unions have developed a cooperative relationship that is based on mutual commitment to the enterprise. Historically, leading Japanese employers have provided workers with wide-ranging welfare benefits, long-term employment security and internal training, and promotion prospects and salaries that reflect length of service as well as ability. The dependence of Japanese workers on their employers for so many aspects of their welfare has encouraged a high degree of cooperation with management. This in turn has supported a system of production that relies on workers supplying high levels of effort, taking responsibility for monitoring quality, solving production problems and identifying ways of improving the efficiency of the production process and the quality of the product.

In the USA, trade unions are weak, state intervention in employment matters is limited and management has a lot of freedom to determine most elements of the employment relationship; hiring and firing procedures, hours of work, wages and salaries, pay systems, work organisation and training. This has given rise to varied approaches to regulating the employment relationship.

There are two main reasons for focusing on the employment systems of these particular countries. First, at different points in recent history each has been seen as an example of excellence and a model to be emulated. Second, each of these models currently embodies a different paradigm of employment relations and HRM. The USA represents the liberal market model, Germany represents a model of social partnership and Japan is a model of enterprise-based partnership. Since the 1970s the US employment system has developed in ways that embody an outsider-based, shareholder model of capitalism; the German and Japanese employment systems reflect, albeit in different ways, insider-based, stakeholder models of capitalism (Dore, 2000). However, the German and Japanese systems have come under increasing strain during the last twenty years and there is debate about their sustainability in a globalised world economy currently dominated by the USA. This raises a fundamental question about the future viability of stakeholder forms of capitalism and the employment systems that have been associated with them. Is the US system so uniquely attuned to the conditions of a global economy that it will increasingly be emulated, not only by Germany, Japan and other modern capitalist societies, but also by the rapidly developing economies in Asia, notably China and India?

In the next sections of the chapter we shall:

● Describe the hitherto distinctive national characteristics of the German, Japanese and US employment systems;

● Explain how these national employment systems are supported by and in their turn support other social institutions as part of wider national business systems;

● Describe and explain the main currents of change in the German, Japanese and US employment systems;

● Review the debate over whether the changes that are taking place in national employment systems are leading to convergence towards a particular model.

National employment systems

In the next three sections of the chapter we describe what have come to be seen as the key features of the German, Japanese and American models of employment relations. Before we do so however, we need to issue a health warning. Any attempt to generalise about a country involves a degree of simplification. In reality there are considerable variations in the way work and employment are organised and employment relations are managed within individual countries. Descriptions of the American, German and Japanese models of employment and employment relations usually focus on formal institutions of employment regulation and on the employment practices that characterise the leading sectors of the economy. This does not give a complete picture of employment practice since the extent to which different types of organisation are subject to formal regulation differs and practices that are typical of leading sectors may be much less so of others in the same country. However, it does mean that we can identify the key features of national employment systems and compare them.

Germany: the social partnership model

In 1993 the German car manufacturer Volkswagen faced a crisis brought about by a sharp drop in sales.[1] The decline meant that 30,000 of the company's German workforce of just over 102,000 had become surplus to requirements. It was clear to VW management that they had to reduce labour costs but how could this be done in a way that was acceptable to employees? Traditional options of early retirement, voluntary redundancy and temporary reductions in working hours were unworkable because of the scale and immediacy of the problem. At the same time, the dismissal of 30,000 workers was unacceptable, particularly given that unemployment in the Lower Saxony region, where VW was located, was already running at 15 per cent. VW management therefore asked itself, how could VW reduce employment costs and improve productivity, competitiveness and financial performance while protecting jobs and conditions of employment?

Its response was to try to get employees and their representatives to agree to a new employment model for VW that involved a considerable element of shared sacrifice by workers in order to preserve jobs. Employees were asked to accept reductions in working hours to the equivalent of a four-day week with matching reductions in annual pay. They were asked to accept retraining and redeployment to different job grades where necessary. They were also asked to accept relocation to other VW factories in the region if required. The broad outline of the scheme was negotiated between VW senior management and the main trade union, IG-Metall. The details of the plan and how it would be implemented in VW's six German factories were decided in specially established negotiating committees and in discussions between management and Works Councils at company and factory level. The negotiation process was initially difficult as the unions and most employees were resistant to reductions in hours if they meant lower earnings. Therefore management put a lot of effort into meetings and seminars with employees to convince them of the necessity for this. Works Council representatives also met with employees to get their views and suggestions to form the basis of a negotiating agenda that they took to management.

The new employment model that was finally agreed involved the reduction from a five to a four-day week with a proportionate reduction in annual pay. To ease the impact of this on employees' monthly income, bonus payments that had previously been paid once a year, such as holiday pay, annual additional payments and Christmas bonus, were incorporated into

---

[1] This description of events at Volkswagen draws heavily on Kothen, G., McKinley, W. and Scherer, A.G. (1999) 'Alternatives to organisational downsizing: a German case study', M@n@gement, 2, 3 (special issue), pp. 263–86.

monthly pay. A second feature of the model was a block release system whereby employees could interrupt their employment to continue their education and training for a period of three to six months, although they would not be paid during that time. VW set up a 'coaching company' to provide further education and management development training to employees on block release. Finally the model included a scheme where newly trained workers would work for just 20 hours a week during their first year, thereafter increasing to 28.8 hours (the four-day week) over the next three and a half years. Older workers nearing retirement age would decrease their weekly hours in the same way.

As well as making changes to its employment pattern, VW management also introduced measures to increase productivity through a just-in-time production system that was linked to flexible hours working. This meant that employees could be required to work more than 28.8 hours in any one week. The extra hours worked would be counted as overtime hours that could be taken as time off at a later date. Employees were also organised into continuous improvement teams to find ways of improving productivity and efficiency.

VW's adjustment to the crisis experienced a number of difficulties in gaining initial acceptance and in the details of implementation. Nevertheless, VW was able to maintain the employment of over 100,000 workers and by 1996, 49 per cent of the workforce stated that they were satisfied with the new scheme while just 16 per cent said that they were dissatisfied, the remaining 35 per cent being neutral (Kothen, McKinley and Scherer 1999). Thus while the workforce in general was far from being in love with the new regime, there was a high level of acceptance based on the recognition that it was a jointly negotiated change that had protected employment.

VW is not typical of German companies. For one thing, it is part publicly owned. The state of Lower Saxony is a major shareholder and the governor of the region is a member of VW's supervisory management board. VW is also unusual, although becoming less so, in that it negotiates with unions at company level. Usually companies negotiate indirectly with the unions through their employers' associations at regional industry level to establish industry level collective agreements. Nevertheless this story about VW illustrates the key features of the German employment system and the German model of capitalism very well because it raises the questions of why VW management were so reluctant to implement mass sackings and how they were able to construct, through negotiation and consultation, a broad consensus in support of radical change. As we shall see, these issues can only be explained by looking at wider features of the German employment system and how it reflects broader features of the German model of capitalism.

The German employment system

Germany's system of employment relations was established in the aftermath of the Second World War but some of its features can be traced back to the Bismarck era of the late nineteenth century. The basic principle of the German system is one of collective self-regulation by employer and employee organisations within a framework of law. The German system has five key characteristics (Jacobi *et al.*, 1998). These are:

- *A framework of law*: This supports and regulates interest representation in employment relations. German employment relations law has established basic principles and institutional arrangements that allow employers and workers to regulate their own affairs with little direct interference from the state. Thus the 1949 Collective Agreement Act established collective bargaining rights for workers. The Works Constitution Act of 1952 and the Codetermination Acts of 1951 and 1976 give workers the right to elect works councils in workplaces employing 5 or more workers. They also provide for workers to be represented on the supervisory boards (see Glossary) of companies having more than 500 employees. In providing workers with legal rights to collective representation, the law made an important distinction between collective bargaining and co-determination, effectively creating the second key feature of the system, a dual structure of interest representation.

- *A dual structure of interest representation.* German employment relations law makes important distinctions between collective bargaining and co-determination in terms of their functions, institutions and the levels at which they operate. Collective bargaining establishes basic terms of employment such as wages and hours, what the Germans have called *issues of interest.* Co-determination deals with issues that arise from the application of industry-wide collective agreements to individual enterprises. These issues are known as *issues of rights.* Collective bargaining takes place at industry/regional level between trade unions and employers' associations. Co-determination is conducted between works councils and management at enterprise/workplace level. Trade unions and works councils are therefore separate legal entities, with distinct functions and separate arenas of action. Trade unions may call strikes in the event of disputes arising from a failure of collective bargaining negotiations to reach agreement on terms and conditions of employment. Works councils, on the other hand, have a legal obligation to work cooperatively with management for the good of the employees and the enterprise. In practice however, there has always been some overlap between the two. The majority of works councillors are trade union members and works councils have for a long time engaged in informal workplace bargaining with management over pay (Jacobi *et al.*, 1998). Since the 1980s the role of works councils in negotiating terms and conditions of employment has increased owing to decentralising tendencies in German industrial relations (see below, p. 587).

  The distinction between issues of interest and issues of rights and the differentiation between trade unions and works committees shape the law on industrial action in Germany. Strikes may be called when failure to agree terms and conditions in collective bargaining leads to a dispute (*a dispute over issues of interest*). Only trade unions, not works councils, have a legal right to call strikes. Once a collective bargaining agreement has been concluded there is a peace obligation on both sides for as long as the agreement lasts and strikes during the currency of a collective agreement are unlawful. Disputes that may arise over the interpretation or application of the agreement (*disputes over issues of rights*) must be dealt with through co-determination procedure or by arbitration in the labour courts.

- *Centralisation and coordination of collective bargaining at sectoral level.* This has been a third key feature of the German model. In the private sector collective bargaining has generally taken place in each region (*Lande*) between the trade union and the regional employers' association for the industry/sector concerned. In the public sector, collective bargaining is conducted at national level. The centralisation of collective bargaining is a crucial aspect of the dual system of representation since it means that collective bargaining operates at industry/sector level while co-determination operates at enterprise or workplace level. If collective bargaining took place at company or workplace level, as is the case in the USA or the UK, it would be much more difficult to differentiate between trade union activities and works committee activities. However, in recent years there has been a move towards decentralisation of bargaining in much of German industry (see below, p. 587).

- *Encompassing organisations of workers and employers.* Unions are legally required to represent all workers, not just their own members. Works councils represent all workers in a workplace. Also, although not legally required to do so, employers' associations have historically represented all employers in their industries. Collective agreements have therefore tended to cover all workers in each sector. This is recognised in law, so that workers effectively have a right to collective representation on basic terms and conditions of employment. Consequently, while the proportion of workers who are union members has always been relatively modest at around 35–37 per cent, 90 per cent have been covered by collective agreements (Jacobi *et al.*, 1998).

- *Social partnership.* While the German system recognises that there are legitimate differences of interest between capital and labour, there is also a strong emphasis on labour-management cooperation supported by the state. At the level of the economy the social partners, i.e. peak confederations of employers' associations and trade unions, participate in a three-way 'political exchange' with government on issues of national economic and social policy. At the sectoral level trade unions have developed a role as mediators between employer and employee interests rather than simply pursuing adversarial strategies against employers through collective bargaining (Jacobi *et al.*, 1998). At enterprise level, while works committees can constrain management actions on issues such as payments systems, work schedules, recruitment, transfer and dismissal, they are legally obliged to consider company aims and interests and not simply pursue immediate employee interests. This has supported the concept of the *professional enterprise community* (Lane, 1989). This term expresses a sense in which managers, employees and their representatives see themselves as the key stakeholders in the enterprise, acting as a coalition to guide its future.

These features of the German system of employment relations mean that employment issues are subject to a high degree of *institutional regulation*. In other words, the ability of management to exercise unilateral control over terms and conditions of employment is constrained by individual employment rights provided by state legislation and employees' rights to collective representation in decision making through collective bargaining and co-determination.

The employment system and the wider German business system

The German approach to employment regulation is an integral part of its broader approach to organising and regulating economic activity, i.e. its wider business system. In addition to the employment relations system, key elements of the wider business system in Germany are:

- *The nature of state regulation.* Since the 1960s *bargained corporatism* (Strinati, 1982) has been a guiding principle for state action in Germany. Compared with the United States, where market individualism exerts a powerful influence on government policies for the labour market, there is much greater direct state intervention to regulate aspects of employment. Germany's employment protection laws are noticeably stricter in the way they constrain employers' freedom to dismiss workers than those of the USA or the UK, although not as strict as those in Italy, Spain or France. The second crucial element of bargained corporatism in Germany is active state support for the collective organisation and representation of workers and employers. This support takes the form of statutory rights to collective organisation, collective bargaining and other forms of collective worker participation in decision making. Finally, as noted above, collective organisations of workers and employers have a role in negotiating with government over aspects of labour market regulation and wider issues of economic and social policy. Taken together, these three elements support a dense framework of institutional regulation of employment and in this way bargained corporatism supports and is in many ways synonymous with the concept of social partnership in Germany.

- *Corporate governance and finance.* German firms operate a 'stakeholder' model of governance in which management's obligation is not only or even primarily to shareholders but to the various needs of a range of stakeholders in the company, including employees. The stakeholder principle is supported by the German system of company finance. German companies obtain finance through long-term bank loans and cross-investments by other companies rather than share flotations. This pattern of company finance has meant that enterprises have not been subject to strong pressure to maximise short-term profits. As long-term creditors, banks have focused more on long-term growth and performance than on immediate profits. This in turn has meant that firms have been able to make significant long-term investments in research and development and employee training, leading to high productivity, which supports high wages and good working conditions. It has also meant that German employers have been willing to 'balance the pursuit of profit by a consideration of social justice' (Lane, 2000: 211). This has been manifested in co-determination rights, employee involvement in decision making on the shopfloor, commitment to long-term employment security, and generous welfare benefits financed through company payroll taxes. This particular version of the stakeholder model has been termed 'insider capitalism', reflecting the priority given to the interests of those working inside the firm, both management and employees, in good working conditions, long-term security and career prospects, relative to those of 'outside' interests such as the owners of the company. In this way the system of corporate governance underpins the ideologies of the professional workplace community and social partnership at enterprise level.

- *The vocational education and training system (VET).* Most school leavers who do not go on to higher education spend three years as apprentices in the vocational education system. The system provides classroom-based training in vocational schools with practical training in companies. This provides apprentices with broadly based training for a defined occupation, e.g. engineer, baker. The costs of training are shared between employers, who are legally obliged to provide funding and resources for training, government and apprentices themselves. Firms finance the provision of practical on-the-job training in the workplace, the state funds the vocational schools, and trainees accept relatively low wages. Trainees have to meet standards that are laid down by employers' organisations and trade unions and receive certificated qualifications that are universally recognised by employers.

The broad-based occupational nature of vocational training in Germany means that jobs are designed to match the range of occupational skills acquired by workers through formal training. Compared to the system of work organisation in the USA, where workers are fitted to jobs, under the German system jobs are designed to fit workers (Marsden, 1999). It also means that German workers are competent over a relatively wide range of tasks, some of which may include planning and coordination of production. The system also means that German workers are not tied to a single firm, as their skills are transferable across firms.

Germany's system of VET has not only resulted in a large supply of highly skilled workers. It has also helped to generate the high levels of worker-management cooperation that are characteristic of German industry. The apprenticeship system has historically enjoyed high regard in Germany and many German managers have been through apprenticeships, often in addition to taking higher education qualifications. Foremen, supervisors and many middle managers will have completed apprenticeships before obtaining further qualifications as a condition for promotion. This common grounding in technical education leads to workers, supervisors and managers sharing a common understanding of production issues and a common technical language. This in turn lays a basis for cooperation in the workplace that is founded on respect for superiors' technical expertise. In doing so it contributes to the concept of the professional enterprise community, which is part of the ideological basis for the high level of worker–management cooperation at workplace level (Lane, 1989).

> **Activity**
>
> Review the VW case at the start of the chapter and then make a list of the features of the German employment system and wider business system that help to explain why VW dealt with its crisis in the way that it did.

The German employment system and national competitiveness

The features of the German employment system and the wider business system described above have underpinned a distinctive strategy for competing in international markets.

- The high level of institutional regulation in Germany has made it difficult for employers to treat labour simply as a disposable commodity. Collective bargaining, co-determination and state legislation have resulted in high wages and restrictions on employers' freedom to dismiss workers. This means that employers have had to achieve competitiveness by ensuring that high wages are matched by high productivity and by competing on the basis of product quality rather than price. This has meant placing a relatively high emphasis on skill in the workforce and the production process.

- The consequences of the German system of VET are that German workers' broad skills mean that they are able to adapt to new technologies relatively easily and acquire additional skills within their occupational fields. They are also able to undertake aspects of production planning and problem solving to a higher degree than in many other countries. This, together with the high level of cooperation that is partly due to the training system, means that workers need relatively little supervision. Therefore firms employ fewer staff not directly engaged in production, which contributes to high productivity levels.

- The centralisation of collective bargaining and its formal separation from co-determination, together with the influence of social partnership ideology, have resulted in low levels of industrial conflict and have also kept inflationary wage pressures low. In this way the industrial relations system has contributed to quality of output in terms of reliability of supply and also to the control of wage costs.

The results have been high labour productivity and a competitive advantage in markets for sophisticated, innovative, high-value products based on high levels of research and development expenditure and sophisticated production techniques. This has allowed German firms to pay high wages without becoming uncompetitive and also to fund, through taxation, a comprehensive and generous welfare state.

Japan: the enterprise-based model

The extract displayed in Box 15.1 is taken from an article printed in *The Economist* in December 1995.

Box 15.1 Mitsubishi's company man

You could hardly find a better example of 'company man', that besuited creature who trades stolid loyalty for lifetime security, than Minoru Makihara, the president of Japan's Mitsubishi Corporation. Mr Makihara is a company man both by birth and marriage: his father spent his life with Mitsubishi; his wife is the great granddaughter of the firm's founder. He even grew up in the corporation's giant villa on what was then the outskirts of Tokyo, moving there after his father's death in 1942. He joined the company in 1956, aged 26, and happily admits that, for him, working in a large firm 'amounts to living life to the full'.

Never mind that company man may be on the way to extinction in Western firms, as they try to reinvent themselves as nimble, focused entrepreneurs. And never mind that even in Japan, after years of recession, lifetime employment is under unprecedented threat. At Mitsubishi Corporation, a huge, diversified trading house, company man still flourishes contentedly. The corporation gets the pick of Japan's best graduates. It offers them dormitories when they are young and single and social clubs throughout their lives; it even tries, informally, to find them a wife from within the corporate family.

Mitsubishi man has every reason to believe that, in his company at least, jobs for life will survive. After all, Mitsubishi is the world's biggest company, measured by sales . . . it is also the leading spirit in a *keiretsu* industrial group containing 29 companies (including Mitsubishi Bank and Mitsubishi Heavy Industries) which help each other to avert disaster. And, as a quintessential company man, Mr Makihara is an unqualified supporter of lifetime employment.

Source: The Economist, 9 December 1995, p. 65.

The Japanese employment system has been described as *welfare corporatism* or *corporate paternalism*. One way in which this has been expressed is in the diffuse nature of the relationship between the large Japanese company and its employees. As illustrated in Box 15.1, it has extended beyond the wage-effort bargain to include company responsibility for key areas of the employee's welfare. It has also extended beyond the employee to include family members. Thus Dore (1973) reported that at the Hitachi company during the 1950s and 1960s, all permanent employees were eligible for retirement bonuses, company pensions, social clubs and activities for retired workers, rented accommodation provided by the company, savings and loan schemes to aid house purchase, transport subsidies, sickness pay, educational loans for employees' children, gift payments made for weddings, births, marriages of children, and condolence gifts on an employees' death or the death of a family member.

The strength of welfare corporatism is largely due to the relative absence of a welfare state in post-Second World War Japan. In these circumstances the provision of extensive welfare benefits by large Japanese companies was a way of attracting the best employees during a time of labour shortage. The range and level of welfare benefits also rapidly became an important issue for trade unions in negotiations with employers as it did in the United States, where state welfare provision is also minimal.

Welfare corporatism has helped to foster what Sako (1997) described as *community consciousness* among Japanese workers and managers. This is expressed in high levels of employee commitment and cooperation with management and low levels of industrial conflict. Both managers and managed employees have come to see their personal futures as being inextricably intertwined with that of the company they work for. Thus it has been said that Japanese workers see their relationship with their company as a 'partnership of fate' that involves a strong element of personal loyalty to the company and feelings of responsibility to colleagues and superiors in return for long-term material security provided by the firm (Matanle, 2003).

Three key structural features of the employment system, often referred to as its 'three pillars', have underpinned welfare corporatism in Japan:

1 Lifetime employment.
2 Seniority-based pay and promotion.
3 Enterprise unionism.

Lifetime employment

Large Japanese corporations have filled the vast majority of their permanent vacancies by recruiting school-leavers and university graduates as trainees. Once hired, these workers have usually remained with the company until retirement. Essentially they have entered an internal labour market (see Chapter 4) that provides long-term employment security and fills vacancies by internal promotion rather than external recruitment. Historically Japanese employers have gone to great lengths to avoid dismissing workers during slack production periods. Depending on how long the slack period lasts, employers have used the time to provide workers with additional training or they have transferred workers internally or to other companies either temporarily or permanently rather than simply dismiss them. Some firms have even set up new subsidiary companies to absorb redundant employees. This reluctance among large firms to dismiss workers on grounds of redundancy has been attributed to three factors.

1 Fear that dismissals would damage their reputation and make it harder for them to recruit high quality university graduates in the future.
2 Legal restrictions that make dismissals difficult to defend in the courts.
3 Desire to avoid conflict with the union, which could lead to immediate disruption of production and weaken the basis for long-term cooperation (Rubery and Grimshaw, 2003).

Stop & think

Go back to the description of Mitsubishi in Box 15.1. How do you think Mitsubishi's keiretsu group helps it to avoid dismissing workers?

Seniority-based pay and promotion

The distinctive feature of the Japanese approach to pay is that instead of pay being job-related, i.e. determined by the nature of the job being performed, it is person-related. A key person-related criterion for determining pay is seniority as measured by age and length of service. Basic salaries are agreed for employees in different age bands, and annual salary increases also related to seniority, with longer-serving workers receiving larger increases. In addition to basic salary, workers receive merit bonuses based on evaluation by their superiors. However, while merit bonuses mean that workers with the same length of service are paid different amounts, merit payments still incorporate a seniority element. This is because of agreements between employers and unions that specify that workers with longer service receive higher average merit ratings. Seniority-based promotion from one grade to another does not mean that the workers' function changes, it just means 'more status and a higher level of annual salary increases' (Dore 1973: 99). In recent years employers have increased the weight attached to ability as opposed to age when determining pay, but how ability is determined is often vague (Matanle, 2003).

Enterprise unionism

While American trade unions are organised on an occupational or industrial basis and German trade unions on an industrial or sectoral basis, Japanese union organisation is based around individual enterprises. Thus corporations such as Nissan or Toyota have their own enterprise unions and enterprise union federations. Unions do coordinate their wage bargaining activity on a sectoral and national basis through the annual pay bargaining round – the 'spring wage offensive' (*shunto*). However, collective bargaining is essentially conducted at enterprise level. There is debate over the effectiveness of enterprise unions as representatives of employees' interests. Critics have argued that enterprise unionism means that trade union power is fragmented and thus weakened. They have also argued that enterprise-based unions identify too closely with the employing organisation and are too susceptible to interference from employers (Shirai, 1983). Supporters argue that enterprise-based unions make it easier for management and union to work together to resolve problems. It has also been argued that it has enabled Japanese unions to exert considerable influence on management decision-making, to the benefit of workers (Nakamura, 1997).

Dualism in Japan's employment system

The features discussed above have not applied equally to all enterprises and all workers in Japan. They are found in the large-firm corporate sector to a far greater extent than among small and medium-sized firms. Moreover, even within the corporate sector, not all employees enjoy lifetime employment and seniority-based pay and promotion. These conditions only apply to 'standard' employees, i.e. permanent, 'core' workers. A significant proportion of workers employed by large corporations in Japan are non-standard workers, i.e. seasonal, temporary and part-time workers. There is uncertainty as to what proportion of Japanese workers enjoy lifetime employment status. A common estimate during the 1980s was 35 per cent but some estimates were as low as 10 per cent (Oliver and Wilkinson, 1992). Inagami (1988) however, reported that long-term, if not lifetime, employment was becoming increasingly common among smaller firms as well as large ones. This was the result of the development of close, long-term relationships between large corporations and their smaller suppliers (see below), which gave the latter long-term commercial security and supported long-term employment contracts.

Stop & think

Why are lifetime employment and seniority wages less common in small firms than in the large corporations?

The employment system and the wider Japanese business system

As in Germany, Japan's employment system is embedded in a wider framework of institutionalised relationships, the most important of which are the role of the state, the principles of corporate governance and the system of vocational education and training.

State regulation

Japanese employment relations have sometimes been described as micro-corporatist. This refers to the close links between unions and management and the degree of union involvement in business decision making at enterprise level. There are also close links between employers and government and Japanese employers see their responsibilities as being not just, or even mainly, to their shareholders but also to their employees and the nation as a whole. However, the absence of an authoritative central trade union confederation and the decentralised nature of collective bargaining have prevented Japanese trade unions from engaging in political exchange with employers and the government. Therefore German-style bargained corporatism has not developed in Japan. This absence of trade unions from policy making has led to Japan being described as having 'corporatism without labour' (Shinoda, 1997). However, from the late 1980s some observers argued that this situation was beginning to change and that Japanese trade unions were developing a more coherent political voice at national level following the formation of a unified peak organisation, Rengo (Shinoda, 1997).

In Japan, as in Germany, government legislation supports workers' right to organise and act collectively although, unlike Germany, it has not laid out formal procedures for co-determination. Legislation also regulates labour market activity in Japan by establishing minimum standards with regard to wages, working time, dismissal and health and safety, although the operation of the law is nationally distinctive. For example, there is no statute that obliges employers to be able to give valid reasons for dismissing workers. This may well be because of leading employers' commitment to lifetime employment, which makes them extremely reluctant to resort to dismissal. Nevertheless, despite the absence of a specific statute, the courts have developed strict standards governing employers' conduct regarding dismissals on the basis of case law (Sugeno and Suwa, 1997). Here the law has developed so as to reinforce the practice of lifetime employment.

Corporate governance and finance

Japanese firms, like their German counterparts, operate on the stakeholder principle of governance. It can be argued that Japanese corporations operate a stronger version of the insider variant of this model than German firms, given their formal commitment to lifetime employment and to providing for the social welfare of their employees. As in Germany, Japanese corporations obtain most of their finance through bank loans and cross-investments (Oliver and Wilkinson, 1992). As in Germany, these financial links have led to employers developing a sense of collective identity that generates cooperation among firms and also provides a basis for them to negotiate collectively with government on policy issues. As in Germany, the reliance on bank finance and cross-investments rather than funds raised on the stock market reduces the pressure on Japanese managers to maximise short-run profits and encourages them to take a long-term view of company performance that places greater emphasis on the growth of market share. This has encouraged high rates of investment in capital equipment, research and development and the training of employees. It has also underpinned Japanese employers' commitment to providing long-term employment security for workers. Moreover, as was illustrated in Box 15.1, the tendency to prioritise insider interests that is fostered by the system of corporate finance is strengthened in Japanese firms by the fact that senior managers have themselves been part of the lifetime employment system, promoted from more junior positions within the company (Matanle, 2003).

The vocational education and training system

In contrast to German practice, new recruits are not selected on the basis of the occupational skills they possess but their ability to fit in to company values, work cooperatively with others and benefit from training in company-specific skills. The Japanese training system and the system of lifetime employment are closely interlinked. Unlike Germany, Japan does not have a well-developed national system of vocational training. Instead, training is enterprise-based. Employers take school leavers and college graduates and provide them with initial and continuing vocational training in sets of skills that are specific to the firm. Workers are trained using a mixture of formal training off the job and informal on the job training. A distinguishing feature of the enterprise-based system is its emphasis on continuing training over the employee's career in the firm. Permanent workers' careers typically involve gaining training and experience in a range of jobs within the company, updating and broadening their skills over time. Tasks are allocated on the basis of how workers are ranked in terms of their acquired firm-specific skills and experience rather than their formal occupational qualifications (Marsden, 1999). Workers who are more highly ranked by their supervisors in terms of length of service and ability are allocated the more demanding tasks, which may include the design and control of production processes and the management of quality (Lincoln and Kalleberg, 1992; Nakamura, 1997). The Japanese approach to training supports the seniority-based pay and promotion system as longer-serving workers are competent across a wider, more demanding range of tasks and therefore seen to warrant higher pay.

The Japanese employment system and national competitiveness

The key features of the Japanese employment system are widely seen as underpinning Japan's success in manufacturing, in particular the *lean production* system. Lean production is a method of mass production that achieves competitiveness by combining high quality with low costs of production. High quality is achieved through close attention to product and process design and continuous improvement of both the product and the production process (*Kaizen*). This involves teams of production workers taking responsibility for product quality, problem solving and making suggestions for quality improvements through quality circles and suggestion schemes. Low cost is achieved by making full use of equipment, minimising the amount of capital tied up in stocks of materials, parts, and finished products, and by intensive working. The use of low wage subcontractors from the non-corporate sector as suppliers is also an important source of cost competitiveness for Japanese corporations (Rubery and Grimshaw, 2003).

Lean production has been described as a fragile system of production (Rubery and Grimshaw, 2003). This is because the minimisation of stocks means so-called 'just-in-time' production, where raw materials, parts and components arrive as they are needed. Buffer stocks, which guard against interruptions to supply, are minimal. Therefore disruption at a supplier or at any stage in the actual production process within the firm has an almost immediate effect on production and output. Lean production is also fragile in the sense that it operates with minimum staffing levels. This makes attendance at work an important issue and requires that workers to cover for absent colleagues when necessary, something that contributes to the high levels of work intensity associated with lean production. It also relies on workers sharing their detailed job knowledge with management in order to achieve continuous quality improvement.

Because of all this the Japanese production system requires a highly disciplined and cooperative workforce that is functionally flexible and willing to accept considerable work intensification. The employment system enables these requirements to be met in the following ways:

- The lifetime employment system encourages workers to share their knowledge with management in the interests of continuous improvement. This is because long-term employment security means that workers are not afraid that sharing their detailed knowledge of production with management to improve efficiency will lead to job losses.

- More broadly, the lifetime employment system reinforces the workers' sense of being in a 'partnership of fate' (see above) in which their personal interests are inextricably intertwined with those of their company. This high level of personal identification with the firm means that workers have been willing to accept strict discipline and high work intensity, demonstrating what observers have called high commitment despite having limited autonomy and job satisfaction (Lincoln and Kalleberg, 1992).

- The enterprise-based union structure also contributes to worker–management cooperation. Inevitably unions identify closely with their companies because the union's organisation is limited to the company and dependent on it in the long run. More positively, the involvement of enterprise unions in management decision making helps to create a climate of mutual trust that underpins union and worker cooperation with management (Nakamura, 1997). It is also argued that the presence of a single union within the enterprise avoids demarcation disputes and makes it easier to deploy and redeploy labour so as to achieve functional flexibility of labour (Fujimura, 1997).

- Continuing training and job rotation mean that Japanese workers are functionally flexible, i.e. they can perform a range of tasks and thus cover for absent colleagues.

Activity

Germany and Japan are both noted for high levels of cooperation on the shopfloor between workers and management but this cooperation is achieved in different ways. Review the previous sections and try to identify the differences in the nature of workplace cooperation in Germany and Japan.

The American employment system: a managerial model

We can characterise the historical development of American capitalism and its subsequent patterns of institutional coordination as a competitive managerial capitalism where institutional actors (employers, employees, the state and customers) are coordinated by contractual and economic relations within comparatively free and open markets, (Chandler, 1977, 1990; Lazonick, 1991). So as a liberal market economy the United States exhibits arm's-length contractual relations within and between capital, labour and the state (Hall and Soskice, 2001).

The American employment system reflects the ideologies of individualism and egalitarianism, often summarised as 'getting ahead through individual effort and enterprise' that are central to the idea of America. As Hollingsworth (1997) observes, a significant feature of the American business system is the weakness of 'collective governance' in the private sector. Business associations that play a significant role in regulating markets and relations among firms in other national systems are not prominent in the USA and firms prefer to 'go it alone'. This is because American business never had to define itself collectively in opposition to aristocratic or feudal interests (other than the dispute over slavery) in the way European capitalists did.

As a result of this, individualism and more significantly, the ideology of egalitarian individualism is diffused throughout the American economy and civil society. Individual private property rights are seen to be the foundation of democracy, creating a strong presumption against state regulation. In the field of employment relations this has translated into a strong bias against external interference, whether by the state or trade unions, with the rights of management. The consequence is that compared with their counterparts in Germany and Japan, American managers are less constrained by legislation and social norms that restrict employers' rights to hire and fire and provide workers with rights to collective representation and participation in decision making.

This relative freedom has allowed American employers since the early part of the twentieth century to adopt a variety of managerially led approaches to workplace HRM and industrial relations. The stress on individualism and the rights of private property that characterised the development of the American business system resulted in a comparatively poorly developed labour movement in the USA. However, sustained periods of worker resistance combined with legislative interventions as part of the 'New Deal' programme in the 1930s witnessed the development of relatively sophisticated patterns of both unitarist and pluralist approaches to employment regulation in addition to traditional approaches based on 'hire and fire'. The remainder of this section summarises the three varieties of approach to HRM and industrial relations in the American business system.

Pluralism: the New Deal system

The late 1920s through to the early 1930s was a period of sustained economic collapse in the United States; often referred to as the 'Great Depression' this period witnessed the collapse of agriculture in the mid-west and California leading the emergence of 'dustbowls' and the collapse of employment in many elements of manufacturing industry. The latter saw the emergence of 'Hoovervilles' – shanty towns housing dispersed and unemployed workers named after the then President Herbert Hoover. In addition to unemployment in agriculture and manufacturing there were pockets of sustained resistance to some of the worst excesses of management control and de-skilling within the American model of management. Franklin Roosevelt was elected as President in 1933 on what has become termed a 'New Deal' ticket. Recognising the collapse and possible stagnation of American capitalism Roosevelt promised a series of government interventions to create jobs, provide a measure of social security and address the historic imbalance of power in the employment relationship.

New Deal legislation in the form of Section 7a of the 1933 National Industrial Recovery Act gave employees the right to organise and bargain collectively through representatives of their own choosing free from employer coercion and interference (practices that were common during the 1920s). In addition to this the legislation imposed a duty on employers to bargain with and cooperate with trade unions, banned company unions and also banned closed shop arrangements and secondary boycotts. The New Deal approach to workplace trade unionism and collective bargaining introduced truly independent trade unions into American workplaces for the first time, but provided no authoritative enforcement procedures. The effect of this was both to stiffen employer resistance to collective bargaining and stimulate militant worker resistance to management control.

Conflicts over unionisation were codified in 1935 by the National Labour Relations Act which re-affirmed employee rights to collective bargaining and proscribed employer interference with the process of bargaining or unionisation as an 'unfair labour practice'. However, unless compelled to do so by the courts many employers felt no compulsion to comply with rulings laid down by the National Labour Relations Act. The Supreme Court added further rights and obligations on employers and trade unions, in particular the right of an employer to replace economic strikers. More substantively the New Deal system and associated legislation led to the development of a form of employment regulation known as 'job control unionism'. This form of regulation is characterised by highly codified industrial relations practices such as:

- written contracts;
- detailed job descriptions;
- formalised grievance and disciplinary procedures;

- seniority rules to determine lay-offs and promotion between grades;
- provision for disputes arbitration and in some cases no-strike clauses (see Clark and Almond, 2006; Towers, 1997; Rupert, 1995).

In many respects the New Deal system created a constitutional framework for workplace industrial relations and HRM, yet employer resistance to the system saw the development of an employer led-managerially controlled alternative. A good number of large corporations never accepted New Deal collective bargaining and kept unions out of their plants through a combination of paternalism and authoritarianism that came to be known as Welfare Capitalism (see below). From the 1960s, increased international competition and the declining significance of domestic mass production led to shifts in the labour force away from blue-collar towards white-collar and professional occupations. These factors encouraged more employers to turn towards non-union strategies that involved relocating operations away from the traditional industrial regions of the north-east to greenfield sites in tax- and employer-friendly states in the south where New Deal industrial relations were much less entrenched (Kochan *et al.*, 1994).

Sophisticated unitarism: welfare capitalism

Welfare capitalism is a management approach to labour relations based on non-unionism and strong mutual commitment between employer and employees. Welfare capitalism is characterised by an ideological opposition to trade unions and collective bargaining in the workplace. Developed and extended during the 1930s, welfare capitalism co-existed with the New Deal model of labour relations. In many respects welfare capitalist employers in their espousal of sophisticated non-unionism laid the origins for what is now termed HRM in developing an authoritarian yet paternal approach to labour relations in which the firm rather than the state, trade unions or other third parties such as the courts or arbitration panels should provide for the security and welfare of employees.

To keep trade unions and collective bargaining out of their workplaces this type of employer devised and developed sophisticated union substitution strategies (Foulkes, 1980). Often under the auspices of 'founding family' control firms introduced innovative approaches to personnel management that included employment security provisions, provision of severance pay and unemployment insurance, pension provision, and health care insurance. More recently welfare capitalist firms have been associated with the deployment of team working, profit sharing and share ownership, workplace appraisals and employee rankings and performance related pay schemes for both teams and individuals, in other words with the techniques associated with HRM (Jacoby, 1997).

Lastly, welfare capitalist employers devised strong corporate cultures and branding techniques to pre-figure the company mission statement, company or brand strap lines and associated forms of scripted speech. Many successful welfare capitalist firms were protected by strong stable markets, for example, Kodak and as 'company town employers' engendered significant levels of employee loyalty. Examples of welfare capitalist employers that you might be familiar with include Kodak, Procter and Gamble, Standard Oil, Heinz and IBM. As paternalist employers welfare capitalists were and still are prepared to act in an authoritarian manner to suppress 'union drives' in the workplace and employment security, welfare capitalism and sophisticated HRM were the cornerstones of union substitution strategies designed to exclude trade unionism.

Traditional unitarism: 'lower road approaches'

American management has been influenced by the highly competitive nature of product markets and the attendant pressures for cost and price reduction. This, together with a scarcity of skilled labour, has encouraged the development of systems of management control over work organisation and product assembly that intensify and de-skill labour. In some sectors of employment, such as fast-food, apparel and food retailing, meat-packing, laundry services and delivery, cut-throat, cost and price-based competition has encouraged employers to minimise labour costs by taking 'low road' non-union approaches to HRM and industrial relations (Katz and Darbishire, 1999). Here management focuses on standardisation, strict job controls and de-skilling, provides low wages and limited fringe benefits and only limited access to employee development and training. Initially lower road approaches, sometimes summarised as 'hire and fire', pre-dominated in areas of employment not covered by New Deal and welfare capitalist employers. The retail giant Wal-Mart is often portrayed as an example of this approach.

In what ways might de-skilling and management control systems manifest themselves? For example, what role might information and communication technologies have in aiding management control and employee surveillance in lower road approaches to HR?

Varieties of employment regulation – and a dominant model

We have seen that the USA is characterised by a variety of systems of employment regulation. However, by the 1980s the typical large American corporation, whether unionised or not, had developed an employment system that featured the elements of an internal labour market. These were:

- tightly specified job descriptions and working methods;
- job security provisions;
- internal training and promotion for core workers;
- seniority rules to govern lay-offs and promotions;
- pay linked to the job rather than individual or company performance;
- company-financed pensions and health insurance.

Internalised systems developed partly in response to trade union pressure to provide secure jobs with predictable earnings, opportunities to increase earnings over the time spent in the company's employment, and social benefits in the absence of a developed welfare state. Some firms responded through New Deal collective bargaining. Others responded by developing internalised systems in the form of welfare capitalism as a substitute for unionisation (Cappelli, 1997). However, internalised systems also grew for reasons of managerial efficiency, i.e. they reduced supervision and turnover costs in ways that reflected wider features of the American business system that are outlined in the next section.

The internalised employment systems developed by large US companies differ in important respects from those in Germany and Japan. First, the commitment to providing long-term employment security is less strong than in Japan. Second, managed employees in American companies have far less influence over management decisions, even those affecting their own employment, than their counterparts in German and Japanese firms. Both of these differences reflect the relatively low level of institutionalised regulation of employment in the USA.

The employment system and wider aspects of the American business system

The nature of state regulation

American individualism is reflected in the reluctance of the state to play an active role in the regulation of business. The US economy is usually labelled a *liberal market economy*, that is one in which primacy is given to the market as the mechanism for coordinating economic activity and the influence of the state and collective organisations of employers and workers is small. Within this model government has undertaken minimal regulation of the labour market. It has supported the 'hire at will' doctrine, which means that workers have few statutory protections against dismissal other than on grounds of unfair discrimination. While the National Labor Relations Act provides workers with a legal right to vote for union representation, it leaves many avenues open to employers who wish to resist unionisation so the law is of limited effectiveness (Kochan *et al.*, 1986). The relative lack of statutory regulation of employment and the weakness of statutory support for collective bargaining results in a very flexible labour market that enables employers to make swift adjustments to the size of their labour force and also makes it easy for them to adopt 'low road' employment strategies.

The financial system and corporate governance

Relations between firms in the USA are market- and contract-based. Although some long-term inter-firm collaboration typical of more coordinated market economies is to be found in certain sectors such as defence, healthcare and electronics (Hollingsworth, 1997; Locke, 1996), for the most part relations between tend to be arm's length and contractual rather than long term and relational (Chandler, 1977, 1990; Lazonick, 1991; Hall and Soskice, 2001). The arm's length character of relations between firms in competitive demand-driven markets applies to the financial system too. Lacking the close, long-term links between banks and firms typical of the post-war German and Japanese business systems there is a correspondingly greater development of equity markets. Historically, share ownership has been much wider in the United States than elsewhere and as enterprises grew in size and complexity professional managers replaced owner-managers. This separation of ownership from control led to sophisticated hierarchies of professionalised management exercising considerable discretion in defining and achieving the goals of the firm and causing economists to develop new 'managerial theories' of the firm (Baumol, 1959; Williamson, 1964). These theories built and developed what O'Sullivan (2000) later termed the 'retain and reinvest' pattern of corporate governance in the American business system. Although heavily focused on short-term results managers nevertheless balanced the claims of shareholders against the need to retain profits to invest in product innovation. Professional managers also secured close control over labour through systematic mechanisation, labour de-skilling and bureaucratic forms of control (Braverman, 1974; Edwards, 1979; Littler, 1982).

Stop & think

Consider your workplace – is it an American-owned firm? If it is you should be able to identify examples of direct, technical and bureaucratic control systems. Even if your workplace is not American-owned it is likely to have direct, technical and bureaucratic control systems. In addition it could be the case that the presence of these types of controls in non-American firms demonstrates the wider impact of American management techniques.

The system of vocational education and training

The United States does not have a strongly developed system of vocational education and training. In particular there is little organised training provision for high-school leavers, who have to pick up skills through a mixture of informal and formal training once they enter employment (Cappelli, 1997). In the absence of a training system that produces workers with formal occupational qualifications, employers design jobs to their own specifications and then fit the workers to the jobs (Marsden, 1999). Company-provided training has therefore aimed at providing workers with narrow skills related to their particular job rather than the broad occupational skills produced by German apprenticeships or the combinations of firm-specific skills generated by in-company training in Japan. This is in line with the tendency to substitute capital equipment for skilled labour and rely on systematic technical and bureaucratic control over workers rather than providing for their involvement in decision making on the shopfloor. This in turn has reinforced the 'arm's length' relationship between management and labour.

The American employment system and national competitiveness

The wider impact of individualism on the American state, its financial institutions and patterns of industrial relations demonstrate that the central drivers of the American business system make it very dynamic. The institutional constraints on management are much weaker than in the German or Japanese business systems, so different models of company organisation, patterns of finance and employment relations can emerge alongside one another. The managerially led institutional features of the American employment system described above have underpinned a distinctive strategy for domestic and international competition.

● The low level of institutional regulation in the American employment system enables employers to treat labour as a disposable commodity and adjust wages and headcount in response to changes in labour and product market conditions. Also, workers work longer hours and have shorter holidays than in the UK and EU (although not Japan), which contributes to high labour productivity in the USA.

● The development of superior management capabilities, including systems for the management of people, meant that American firms developed a more systematic approach to work organisation and the control of labour than those in other countries in the twentieth century.

● An emphasis on investment in technological innovation. The competitive nature of domestic product markets in the USA forces management to introduce the latest technology as quickly as possible (Conference Board, McGuckin and van Ark, 2005). American management has also been more aggressive and quicker to deploy new technologies to control and monitor workers than management in other countries (ESRC, 2004; CIPD, 2006). This has been a further factor in the USA's productivity lead over other countries.

● Higher levels of capital per worker in the USA underpin high productivity levels (ESRC, 2004).

The visible hand of management has moulded a business system and employment system where management control and coordination of work organisation has combined with substitution of capital for labour to create sustained international competitive advantage in terms of productivity and unit labour costs.

Stop & think

How does the ability to treat labour as a disposable commodity shape US companies' competitive strategies? In the light of this why might some US companies decide to treat labour as a valued resource instead?

Three national systems: a summary

Our examination of American, German and Japanese employment systems has shown that while each is distinctive, the German and Japanese systems have more in common with each other than they do with the American system. In both Germany and Japan, albeit in different ways, there is a stronger emphasis on institutionalised regulation of the employment relationship as a basis for generating worker-management cooperation than there is in the USA, where the emphasis is much more on using the managerial prerogative to gain workers' compliance. This is explained by the more active role the state plays in Germany and Japan compared with the USA, particularly the stronger political and legislative support for employment protection and collective worker representation. Consequently, to a much greater extent than in the USA, workers are recognised as stakeholders whose interests have to be recognised alongside those of managers and owners. Analysts have argued that each of these systems has been successful in enabling the countries concerned to establish patterns of competitive advantage that have been the basis for their long-run economic growth and prosperity (Whitley, 2000; Hall and Soskice, 2001). Recently, however, each system has come under strain and this has created pressures for change.

Patterns of change in national systems

Since the 1970s national employment systems have come under pressures for change:

- The oil shocks and slowing down of economic growth in the 1970s;
- The return of mass unemployment in the 1980s and 1990s;
- The effects of radical technological change;
- The emergence of new organisational paradigms, e.g. lean production, HRM;
- The internationalisation of capital and investment and the rise of multinational companies;
- The spread of industrialisation and the emergence of new competitor nations challenging Western dominance;
- Intensification of international competition in markets for goods and, increasingly, services;
- Ideological challenges, e.g. the spread of free market ideology and individualism.

These forces have created pressures for change at the level of individual firms and at the level of national employment systems, focusing on:

- Flexibility;
- Decentralisation;
- Deregulation.

At firm level, management has sought functional, numerical and financial flexibility of labour. This has led to increased emphasis on training, skills development and team working (functional flexibility), greater use of non-standard employment contracts and out-sourcing (numerical) and increased use of contingent pay (financial).

Employers' search for labour flexibility has also been linked to government policies for the labour market. In order to encourage employers to create more new jobs and reduce unemployment, governments have, to varying degrees, legislated to:

- Make it easier for employers to make use of non-standard employment contracts;
- Make it easier for employers to dismiss workers for reasons of redundancy;
- Increase incentives to work and put more pressure on the unemployed to take work on offer or to retrain.

Changes at firm level and labour market level mean that changes are occurring in national employment systems.

Change in the USA: taking the low road?

We saw earlier that, despite the diverse approaches to employment regulation in the USA, internalised employment systems have been characteristic of the typical large US corporation. Since the 1980s, however, internalised employment systems have been eroded as many welfare capitalist and New Deal employers have implemented cost reduction strategies such as downsizing and concentration on core competencies. This re-structuring has reduced the size of core work groups, weakened internal labour markets and exposed more workers to lower road approaches to HRM. This is reflected in:

- withdrawal of commitments to job security;
- cut-backs in pension benefits;
- the increased use of *contingent labour* – part-time, fixed-term contract and temporary agency workers.

This has polarised experience of the employment relationship. A growing number of workers, particularly low-skilled workers, are subjected to lower road, commodity labour approaches to HRM. Meanwhile, higher road resourced-based approaches to HRM, currently labelled high performance work systems (see Chapter 2), have also become more widespread. However while these resource-based HRM systems provide employees with more rewarding work they also offer less security than the New Deal or welfare capitalist systems that they have replaced. To a great extent the commitment to providing long-term employment security has been replaced by provisions aimed at helping employees maintain their employability through training. One recent study noted that:

> … HRM firms have been distinguished from other non-union employers in the late 1980s and 1990s not by their employment security but rather by the extent to which they subsidise their employees' investments in skill development or job transfers.   (Katz and Darbishire, 1999: 23)

What this tells us is that even among those employers that value their employees more highly, there has been an erosion of commitment to internalised employment systems and a greater readiness to hire and fire as corporate circumstances change. Employers are requiring employees to bear more of the risks of employment. This has also been reflected in the spread of payment systems that link pay to company profits and in widespread cut-backs in company-financed pension schemes (Cappelli, 1997).

Reasons for shifts in the US employment system

The decline of internalised employment systems in the USA reflects the collapse of the conditions that supported them up to the 1970s, i.e. stable, steadily expanding mass markets that were relatively protected from overseas competition, and the way in which American capitalists responded to it.

Economic crisis

The American economy experienced a crisis in the 1970s and early 1980s. Economic growth slowed down, profits fell and inflation accelerated. At the same time foreign competition was intensifying. The Japanese in particular, secured a technological and productivity lead over the USA in the consumer electronics and automobile industries and began to penetrate deeply into the US market. This put pressure on US firms to cut costs, improve quality and become more responsive to changes in market demand. This meant that more and more managers came to believe that the benefits obtained from internal labour markets, i.e. stability and ease of management control, were outweighed by the costs, i.e. rigid job classifications that prevented the introduction of more efficient, productivity enhancing forms of work organisation, rigid wage structures that made it difficult to reward high performance, costly commitments to long-term employment and, in unionised companies, the length of time required to negotiate change (Kochan et al., 1986; Cappelli, 1997). The lack of political and legislative support for trade unions and collective bargaining meant that employers were able to take advantage of the recession and the threat of job losses arising from foreign competition to demand concessions from trade unions and, increasingly to move from unionised to non-unionised employment relations.

Shareholder value and changes in corporate governance

Since 1980 major changes have taken place in the financial system resulting from the intensity of foreign competition, a shift in shareholding from individuals to institutions, and sustained financial deregulation. Today institutional investors hold the majority of shares and they measure corporate success on the basis of quarterly and annual share price appreciation. These institutions have a preference to trade shares in order to realise capital appreciation and account for the majority of trading in large firm stocks. Together these factors, combined with the low transaction costs of the highly efficient US stock market, encourage rapid trading and since the 1980s have generated a sometimes aggressive 'hostile' market for takeovers or mergers and acquisitions. Expressed as the principle of 'shareholder value', these developments, rhetorically at least, aim to ensure that management works in the interests of the owners (shareholders) of the company (O'Sullivan, 2000).

We can trace the emergence of shareholder value to the crisis of American capitalism in the early 1980s. The recovery from the collapse of profits in the late 1970s and the aftermath of the Iranian oil shock of the early 1980s led American economists and management theorists to argue that stalled economic growth and declining productivity were not temporary but apparently permanent shocks to the American business system, (Hutton, 2002: 124). Together with institutional investors, economists and management theorists began to question and later reject many of the theoretical and institutional underpinnings of post-war economic success in the American business system. Economists rejected managerial theories of the firm that emphasised managerial discretion, the separation of ownership and control, shareholder deference to professional salaried managers and sales revenue maximisation (Means, 1930; Berle and Means, 1932; Chandler, 1977; Williamson, 1964, 1967; Baumol, 1959). Emphasising relatively new agency theories (Alchian and Demsetz, 1972; Jensen and Meckling, 1976) and transaction cost theories (Williamson, 1975), economists, consultants, investors and management theorists began to argue that the key characteristics of managerial capitalism were not efficiency and organisational capability but waste and inefficiency. This change in thinking gave birth to the idea of shareholder value. Formalised in 1986 via the formation of the Shareholders' Association, shareholder value became a kind of 'rank and file' movement and rescuer of American firms that were subject to what were perceived as incompetent, greedy, indulgent and lazy management (see Peters, 1992).

The growing dominance of shareholder value principles since the 1980s has led to a shift of management priorities. In order to ensure that managers are working in shareholders' interests, senior management performance is evaluated and rewarded through the use of stock options on the basis of the current share price. Consequently senior managers in the USA have become increasingly pre-occupied with maximising the short-term financial performance of their companies (Boyer, 2005; Jensen and Murphy, 1990). This represents a shift from the 'retain and invest' pattern of governance to what has been called the 'down-size and distribute' pattern, in which the workforce is cut back and work is intensified for those remaining in order to cut costs and boost profits, which are then distributed to shareholders in the form of higher dividends or capital gains realised as a result of an increase in the share price. The announcement of job cuts, which used to be seen as a sign of a company in trouble, is now more often taken as evidence of action to improve profitability through cost reduction and more effective work organisation. This has contributed to the extension of 'lower road' approaches to employment relations in firms that were once associated with New Deal or welfare capitalist approaches.

Where the USA leads the rest of the world follows?

The changes that have taken place in the USA are of particular significance since many analysts have argued that the USA is setting the pattern for the new century. They argue that the changes that took place in the USA during the 1980s led to the resurgence of the US economy and its current domination of the processes of political and economic globalisation. Meanwhile, the more institutionally regulated economies of Germany and Japan have experienced low economic growth and historically high levels of unemployment throughout the 1990s. Their productivity has also declined relative to the USA and they are also said to lag behind the USA in the development of new technologies. This has led many to argue that the problems of Germany and Japan are due to patterns of regulation that put too many constraints on business, raise the cost of employment, slow down decision making and deter new investment. This has made them uncompetitive in globalised markets, where they face competition from high quality, lower cost competitors. The recommended solution is to reform social welfare systems and labour market institutions so as to reduce employment costs, allow for greater wage flexibility and more flexible utilisation of labour and allow managers to initiate and implement change more quickly in response to market threats and opportunities.

Second, it has been argued that the emergence of global financial markets and the sustained growth of foreign direct investment by US-owned multinational companies are causing the shareholder value concept to take hold in countries such as Germany and Japan, which have hitherto operated a stakeholder form of corporate governance. Given the incompatibility of these two approaches and that key features of Germany and Japan's employment systems are embedded in the stakeholder model, the development of shareholder value pressures would undermine their existing patterns of institutional regulation and force them along the path of market liberalism.

In the American and British business systems debates over corporate governance now appear resolved in favour of shareholder value approaches. Recently the OECD has also argued for the primacy of shareholder interests, demonstrating the widening influence of the shareholder value principle (OECD, 2004). A key question is how far this Anglo-American transition to shareholder capitalism will be diffused to stakeholder systems such as those in Germany and Japan. Gulger *et al.* (2004) argue that 'American' measures of efficiency and competitiveness on the shareholder model are emerging as a growth regime for all western business systems and multinational companies irrespective of country of origin. Similarly, Carr (2005) argues that to compete globally German firms must develop 'professional management' on the Anglo-American business school model. Carr concludes that as German and Japanese firms globalise they become more similar in operations and strategies to British or American multinational firms.

Change in Germany: the erosion of social partnership?

Since the 1980s there has been growing criticism of key features of the German employment system. Once seen as underpinning German economic success, it has come to be viewed by many economic policy advisers and financial and business interests as a hindrance to renewed economic growth, competitiveness and job creation. The reasons for this disenchantment with the German model will now be discussed under the following headings.

Economic stagnation and unemployment

Over the last twenty years Germany has experienced slow economic growth and high, persistent unemployment. Unemployment in West Germany rose from 2.6 per cent in 1980 to 7.2 per cent in 1985 and did not drop below 5 per cent until the early 1990s, when there was a short economic boom following German reunification in 1990 (OECD, 2006). Since 1995 the unemployment rate in Germany as a whole has not fallen below 7 per cent and during 2005 it averaged 11.5 per cent (Federal Statistical Office Germany, 2006; OECD, 2006).

The underlying reasons for Germany's unemployment problem are much debated. There is a strong case for arguing that it stems from the problems of economic adjustment in the old East Germany, where unemployment reached an official level of 18 per cent in 1999, with observers suggesting that the true level was nearer 25 per cent (Tusselmann and Heise, 2000) and a monetary policy that has depressed levels of demand, rather than features of the labour market (Grahl and Teague, 2004). However, economic advisers and financial and business interests became increasingly critical of aspects of the employment system in general, particularly the level of employment protection and social welfare benefits for workers and the centralised system of collective bargaining, and demanded reforms to increase labour market flexibility.

The case against strong employment rights and social protection is that they raise the costs of employing labour and therefore discourage firms from creating more jobs. For example, because workers' strong employment rights make workforce reductions difficult and costly, employers prefer to achieve increases in output by raising the output of their existing workforce rather than hiring additional workers. Generous social welfare benefits are financed largely out of payroll taxes levied on employers. This means that non-wage costs of hiring workers are high as well as wage costs. This reinforces employers' reluctance to add to the size of their workforces and also deters new business start-ups. They also contribute to high unemployment among low-skilled workers by setting a 'floor' to wages that prevents them from falling to a level that would lead to more unskilled jobs being offered.

The criticism of centralised collective bargaining is that it sets too high a minimum wage, which together with the social welfare system prevents wages for unskilled workers adjusting to a level that would lead to more jobs being created. It is also argued that it prevents enterprises from addressing the need to develop more flexible ways of using labour in order to raise productivity and reduce costs. The reforms that have been demanded are that restrictions on the use of flexible forms of employment such as temporary and fixed-term employment should be eased, the level of social benefits should be cut back to ease the tax burden on employers and enable wages to be more flexible at the lower end of the market and that collective bargaining should be decentralised to allow for greater wage flexibility and permit negotiations on company-specific issues.

From stakeholder to shareholder principles?

Pressures for labour market reforms along American lines have been reinforced by the diffusion of the concept of shareholder value into the German business system. A number of developments have led some analysts to argue that strong pressures are developing to force Germany to converge towards the Anglo-American model of corporate governance based on shareholder value. Given the incompatibility of shareholder value with the existing stakeholder principle, its diffusion among German companies could lead to the eventual abandonment of the German employment system and convergence towards the liberal market model. Whether such a convergence is happening is under debate. A recent review of the literature by Edwards (2004) has identified three positions. The first argues that shareholder-value principles are taking hold in Germany as foreign ownership of German share capital increases, the proportion of firms' value-added distributed to shareholders rises and more senior managers are rewarded with stock options and profit-related bonuses. This is said to be undermining key institutions such as co-determination, with works councils becoming 'empty shells'. The second position stresses the limited extent of change in German corporate finance, with ownership still being highly concentrated, and the continued strength of co-determination as a 'central pillar' of corporate governance. The third view is that significant changes are occurring but there has been no transformation of the German system. Edwards' own case study of Volkswagen tends to support the argument for continuity. While VW has paid more attention to the interests of shareholders since the early 1990s and set higher target rates of return on capital, this has not led to US-style down-sizing or to attempts to weaken co-determination (Edwards, 2004).

After reading the material on the American business system and the German business system are you able to suggest why the German business system might be able to develop a more enlightened approach to shareholder value than that found in the UK or the USA? What role might the German employment relations model have in hindering or encouraging this development?

The main currents of change in German employment relations will now be discussed under the following headings.

Changes to employment law aimed at increasing labour market flexibility

As we noted above, the ongoing failure to create jobs and reduce unemployment has led to growing demands within Germany for measures to increase labour market flexibility to encourage job creation, attract foreign investment and stimulate economic growth (Grahl and Teague, 2004). The result has been a gradual and limited relaxation of restrictions on contingent forms of employment such as fixed term contracts and the use of temporary agency workers. The 1985 Employment Promotion Act and subsequent amendments have made it easier for employers to hire workers on fixed term contracts. The maximum length of time that an employer can keep a worker on a temporary agency contract has also been gradually extended from 3 months in 1972 to 6 months in 1985, 9 months in 1993 and 12 months in 1997. However, German employers have not rushed to hire contingent workers as a result. Fixed-term contract workers and agency temps together accounted for 7.8 per cent of employment in 1998 compared with 7.1 per cent in 1991. Moreover, permanent workers continue to enjoy strong employment protection rights, with dismissal still regarded as a last resort and employers are expected to explore all possible alternatives, including redeployment (Peuntner, 2003).

Weakening support for collective bargaining and co-determination

The proportion of workers who are trade union members has fallen in Germany. At the same time, a growing number of small and medium-size businesses do not have works councils, so that at the end of the 1990s an estimated 60 per cent of German workers were outside co-determination (Grahl and Teague, 2004). Among employers, the coverage of employers' associations is declining. Many companies in the East either did not join or else withdrew from employers' associations after unification in order to avoid centralised wage bargaining. In the West a number of small and medium enterprises have quit employers' associations in order to negotiate their own individual agreements with the trade unions and many new companies are not joining employers' associations. Nevertheless trade unions retain considerable influence and the percentage of workers covered by collective agreements in the West is still very high – around 90 per cent – although substantially lower in the East (Tuselmann and Heise, 2000).

Decentralisation of collective bargaining

More significant than any overall decline in collective bargaining coverage has been the trend towards decentralisation of collective bargaining. This has reflected the growing relative importance of 'qualitative issues' concerning changes in working practices, new technology and flexibility, which are specific to companies or workplaces, compared with wage bargaining. At the same time however, there have been examples of 'disorganised decentralisation' arising out of 'wildcat cooperation' between works councils and company management whereby they (illegally) agree to undercut or ignore the terms of collective agreements, usually on the grounds of preserving jobs. In an effort to eliminate wildcat cooperation and achieve a more coordinated and controlled decentralisation of bargaining, formal 'opening clauses' are being inserted into industry level agreements that allow enterprise managements and works committees to negotiate over more flexible working time arrangements or to undercut sectoral agreements on pay for limited time periods and in defined circumstances (Tuselmann and Heise, 2000). This controlled decentralisation not only reflects the interests of the unions in maintaining an over-arching structure of centralised bargaining. It also owes much to the fact that employers continue to value the way that centralised bargaining moderates wage pressure and acts as a force for stability in industrial relations.

Changes in co-determination

The role of co-determination has been strengthened by legislation that has provided stronger support for works council organisation and extended the influence of works councils over training and employment protection matters. Furthermore, decentralisation of collective bargaining has increased the role of works councils in establishing terms and conditions of employment. In particular they became closely involved in company modernisation programmes during the

1980s that focused on the introduction of new technologies, more flexible forms of working and new forms of employee involvement, such as quality circles and team working. While this evolution of the role of works councils can be seen as an extension of the social partnership model in the workplace it has been viewed by some as threatening to undermine their role as defenders of workers' employment rights. High unemployment and increasingly intense competition mean that works councils are under pressure to cooperate with management in 'building up an organisational consensus around corporate plans to succeed in global markets' that serves the interests of management, shareholders and the elite 'core' group of employees but exposes other workers to increasing insecurity (Grahl and Teague, 2004: 566).

Germany's economic difficulties have strengthened the critics and weakened the defenders of its employment system, most notably the German trade unions. High unemployment has created fear of job loss and, as we saw in the VW case, created a climate in which unions and works councils are under pressure to make concessions. At the same time German firms are becoming more open to the disciplines of the stock market and influenced by the principle of shareholder value. However, while significant changes are taking place, reform of the German system has been gradual, hesitant, and at times strongly resisted, particularly in the area of welfare reform, where there is strong continuing public support for Germany's excellent welfare state provision.

Stop & think

Why might German employers be wary of abandoning the German model of employment relations?

Change in Japan: the crumbling of the 'three pillars'?

Japan has experienced an even more marked slowing down in economic growth since 1990 than Germany, with an annual average growth rate of GDP of 1.6 per cent during the period 1991–1998. Unemployment in Japan also hit record levels of around 5 per cent (Inoue, 1999). While this appears low by European standards it has to be viewed in the context of the Japanese employment system and the extreme reluctance to dismiss workers. The unemployment figures mask a higher level of hidden unemployment and under-employment. The stagnation of Japan's economy, coupled with demographic and social changes, has put considerable strain on the employment system. As in Germany, this has led a growing number of observers, inside and outside of Japan, to argue that while the employment system may have underpinned Japan's economic success during the 1970s and 1980s, it is an obstacle to recovery in an increasingly globalised world economy. Thus in 1998 the Japanese Congress on Economic Strategy, an advisory body to the government, argued that the Japanese system attached too much importance to equality and fairness and that Japan needed to restructure itself as a 'more competitive society' (Inoue, 1999). Critics also argue that the lifetime employment system has become socially and economically divisive. While older workers continue to enjoy the benefits of lifetime employment, more and more young workers are denied them as job opportunities have become increasingly limited. The lifetime employment system is also based on an outdated male model of employment that is increasingly at odds with Japanese women's changing aspirations (Schoppa, 2006). Observers have also drawn attention to how the economic crisis has initiated or accelerated recent currents of change in Japan's employment system and questioned its long-term viability (Hattori and Maeda, 2000; Hanami, 2004).

The decline of enterprise unionism

The proportion of Japanese workers who are union members fell from 34.7 per cent in 1975 to 20.7 per cent in 2001. In addition, enterprise unions and their confederations have been subject to a growing criticism that they serve only the interests of the elite group of workers in the leading corporations (Hanami, 2004). In the past, enterprise unions have played an important role as a channel for employee voice in Japanese companies and as such have helped to create the basis for the high levels of worker–management cooperation that has been a characteristic of Japanese employment relations for most of the post-war period. Therefore the decline of enterprise unionism could threaten to weaken the system as a whole.

The decline of seniority-based pay and promotion

An ageing workforce and slow economic growth since 1990 have undermined the seniority pay system. This is because seniority-based pay depends on the balance in the workforce between younger, junior employees and older, more senior employees. Younger workers are paid less than is warranted by their productivity, while older workers are paid more. As long as the proportions of younger and older workers are balanced, the overall wage bill is in line with the productivity of the workforce. However it means that more young workers have to be hired each year to offset the effects of seniority-based wage increases for existing workers. But to be able to do this the company has to keep expanding to create new vacancies at entry level. The economic stagnation of the Japanese economy has meant that corporations have cut back on their recruitment of young workers. Therefore the overall age profile of the work-force has increased, causing company wage bills to be increasingly out of line with workers' productivity, thus increasing production costs and reducing profitability and competitiveness (Hattori and Maeda, 2000).

Reform of the wage and promotion system has also been encouraged by the increased pace of change in organisations. This means that skills and knowledge gained through seniority are at less of a premium. Therefore promotions are being linked more to individual perform-ance. Finally, it is claimed that moves to base pay on individual performance are in tune with changing social attitudes as younger generations of workers have developed more individu-alised sets of values and are less collectively oriented (Kusuda, 2000).

The outcome is that most Japanese corporations claim to be reducing the extent to which pay is determined by seniority and increasing the weight given to performance. A survey of large firms carried out by the Japan Productivity Centre for Socio-Economic Development in 1998 found that 76 per cent of respondents planned either to do away completely with seniority based pay or move to predominantly performance-based pay systems for their managerial employees (Hattori and Maeda, 2000). Regarding promotions, a survey carried out in 1999 for the Ministry of Labour found that over 80 per cent of companies said that they used ability and performance as criteria for promotions to managerial grades while 48 per cent used seniority. Also, more companies claim to have introduced 'fast track' promo-tion routes and are promoting people at a younger age (Matanle, 2003). However, Matanle has pointed out that these claims may exaggerate the true extent of change. For example, employees need to have spent specified periods of time acquiring prescribed skills and abili-ties in order to gain promotion to the next grade. This blurs the distinction between seniority and ability/performance and managers may continue to use age as a convenient proxy for performance. Moreover, the shift from seniority to performance-based pay has been concentrated on managerial staff (Inoue, 1999).

A retreat from lifetime employment?

The long period of economic stagnation throughout the 1990s has led companies to increase their use of fixed-term contracts and temporary agency workers. The number of workers on fixed-term contracts in Japan rose from under 1 million in 1992 to over 2 mil-lion in 2001, i.e. to just under 23 per cent of total employment. There was also a three-fold increase in the number of registered temporary agency workers from 0.5 million in 1992 to just under 1.5 million in 2001 (Hanami, 2004). This has been encouraged by legislation that has relaxed restrictions on the use of fixed-term contracts and made it easier to set up and run temporary employment agencies. At the same time, however, an amendment to the Labour Standards Law in 2003 tightened the restrictions on employers' right to dismiss workers (Hanami, 2004).

More spectacularly, household name companies have been forced to make major cuts in their workforces. In 1999 Nissan Motor Corporation, which had just been taken over by Renault, announced the closure of five sites in Japan with the loss of over 10,000 jobs. This, together with other job cuts in Japanese corporations, was widely interpreted as signalling the end of the lifetime employment system in Japan. However, what was not so widely reported was that Nissan promised to achieve the reductions through natural wastage, early retirement, increasing part-time employment and selling non-core subsidiaries (Symonds, 1999). More generally, research has found that large Japanese companies remain reluctant to lay off workers, even when there is a need to cut jobs. As at Nissan, natural wastage, early retirement and temporary or permanent transfer of workers to subsidiaries are still the preferred methods of reducing headcount (Watanabe, 2000; Kato, 2001; Matanle, 2003). A Ministry of Labour survey of large firms in 1999 found that roughly a third of respondents planned to maintain their existing lifetime employment systems while a little under half said that they planned to make partial revisions to their lifetime employment systems. Less than a fifth planned to make major changes (Hattori and Maeda, 2000). More recently, signs of a revival of the Japanese economy have given a further boost to confidence in the virtues of long-term employment (see Box 15.2).

Box 15.2 | ## Keidenran's Okuda lauds Japanese management for revival

'Japan was able to overcome the protracted recession because companies focused on long-term growth and did their best to avoid massive lay-offs even while grappling with the need to restructure', Japan Business Federation Chairman Hiroshi Okuda said . . .

He said, 'Japanese society has finally survived the long-standing economic slump because we, private firms, have stuck to the two bases of Japanese management: respect for people and long-term perspective'.

But Okuda's lecture was not an endorsement of the traditional management style. The corporate sector 'has been making necessary adjustments to accommodate the globalisation of the economy while giving consideration to job security', he said. Companies have 'tackled various reforms, for example, reviewing their seniority systems and introducing merit-based compensation'.

Source: The Nikkei Weekly, 6 March 2006.

Activity

Discuss why Japanese employers have been readier to reform the seniority wage system than retreat from lifetime employment.

We can see that some of the key principles that defined the Japanese employment system are being eroded. The principle of seniority in determining pay and promotion is being downgraded and companies have cut jobs and made more use of non-standard workers, i.e. temporary, fixed-term and part-time, when hiring. It may well be that these changes are having long-term effects on levels of trust and employee commitment, weakening the established basis for management–worker cooperation that has existed in Japan (Kwon, 2004). However, we can also see evidence of continuing commitment to the principle of lifetime employment and we have noted the limits to the shift from seniority to performance in determining pay and promotion. Even where changes are being made, they continue to be constrained by features of the existing system.

Change, convergence and divergence in employment systems

The employment systems of the USA, Germany and Japan have each undergone change in response to economic crises during the late twentieth century. In each case internalised employment systems have come under strain as a result of pressures to increase flexibility and reduce costs. America was the first country to adjust, prompted by deterioration in economic performance in the face of German and Japanese competition. The relative weakness of institutionalised regulation of the US business and employment system meant that the shift away from the bureaucratised internal labour market, which had in any case been gathering pace during the 1970s, was relatively rapid and complete. The story in Germany and Japan has been different, owing to the deeply embedded nature of institutionalised regulation of the employment relationship in those countries. In both cases change has been hesitant and uneven, with employers reluctant to abandon completely the systems that have yielded significant benefits in the past. As the extract in Box 15.2 shows, in Japan's case economic revival has led to the reaffirmation of a reformed lifetime employment model. Yet debate about the future direction of employment systems and, more fundamentally, the future direction of capitalist development, continues. The debate is framed round the question of whether, in an increasingly globalising world economy, diverse forms of capitalism that support nationally distinctive employment systems will continue to survive.

The debate concerning whether countries' business and employment relations systems are converging or not is not a new one. It has its origins in the 'industrialisation debate' of the 1960s. The convergence argument was advanced first by Clark Kerr and his colleagues (Kerr *et al.*, 1960). They argued that as countries became more industrially developed, their industrial relations systems would mature also. Specifically, they argued that industrial relations would become increasingly subject to institutional regulation through collective bargaining. Industrial conflict would wither away to be replaced by social consensus. Implicitly Kerr *et al.* assumed that nations would converge towards America's 'New Deal' industrial relations system.

Kerr's thesis came increasingly to be rejected during the 1970s as it was apparent that industrial relations systems remained widely diverse. The dominant view was that there were persistent national differences in:

- The strength and pattern of organisation among workers and employers;
- The level at which collective bargaining was conducted;
- The role of law in industrial relations;
- Ideological features of industrial relations.

These differences would remain because they were embedded in wider societal institutions so that change would follow nationally distinctive paths (Maurice, Sellier and Sylvestre, 1986).

Since the 1980s however, the debate over whether national employment and business systems are converging has been renewed in the light of the trend towards globalisation of the world economy. The argument is that first, increased international competition in markets for goods and services and also for capital investment is forcing firms to adopt the most efficient production methods in their sectors, e.g. lean production. This means that firms will increasingly tend to adopt the same approach to work organisation, training, pay, employee involvement etc. Where existing features of national systems of employment regulation are seen to prevent or hinder firms from adopting new techniques, they will come under growing pressure for reform. This tendency will be reinforced by the growing importance of multinational companies as they transfer practices developed in foreign subsidiaries back to their home country (see Chapter 17).

Second, international mergers and takeovers mean that companies are becoming increasingly international in their ownership, leading to the spread of arm's length relations between owners and managers and the consequent spread of shareholder value principles of governance. As we have seen, these principles are at odds with the stakeholder approach that has underpinned social partnership and welfare corporatist systems of employment regulation.

Third, the internationalisation of investment has meant that countries are in competition to attract and retain foreign direct investment. This means that there is pressure on governments to ensure that fiscal and monetary policies, industrial and labour market policies are 'business-friendly'. In particular it is argued that countries with high levels of regulation such as Germany and Japan are being forced to move towards the more lightly regulated liberal market model of the USA (Streeck, 1997).

Against this line of argument are those who argue that, despite the fact that national employment systems are subject to the same pressures arising from globalisation, their responses will be shaped by their historically developed patterns of institutional regulation. Smith and Meiskins (1995) identified three aspects of change that influence the possible extent of convergence:

- System imperatives – changes in the conditions of capitalist competition;
- Societal effects – how national institutional frameworks mediate system imperatives;
- Dominance effects – the influence of particular paradigms or countries in shaping production and employment systems.

System imperatives force change but change does not necessarily mean convergence. Societal effects imply divergence; dominance effects imply convergence. The question is whether societal effects outweigh or mediate dominance effects. If it is the case that the system imperative favours a particular type of employment system, this creates a strong dominance effect. Other systems become less competitive and under increasing pressure to move closer to the favoured model. Convergence advocates argue that today's system imperatives seem to favour the type of employment system associated with liberal market economies, creating a dominance effect that is putting pressure on other systems to converge on the US model. The question is how far dominance effects are counteracted or mediated by societal effects.

Stop & think

What are the main dominance effects operating on the German and Japanese employment systems? What societal effects that might limit the Americanisation of the German and Japanese employment systems?

Work by American scholars Katz and Darbishire (1999) suggests that it might be misleading to think in simple terms of convergence versus divergence. They found that in all of the countries they looked at – USA, UK, Australia, Italy, Japan and Sweden – employment systems were becoming more diverse. In each country four patterns of employment were spreading – a low wage pattern, i.e. the 'lower road' approach, a high performance-based HRM model, the Japanese lean production model, and a joint team-based model. As a result they claimed there was evidence of convergence but in the sense that employment systems in all countries were becoming more internally diverse. This may suggest that the frameworks of institutionalised regulation are weakening in countries where they have been strong, i.e. in Sweden, Italy, Japan and Germany, allowing managers more freedom to innovate as has been the case in the USA. However, the relative balance between each of the four patterns varied across countries and was influenced by national institutions – evidence of continued divergence.

This picture of 'converging divergences' (Katz and Darbishire, 1999) suggests that simple notions of convergence or divergence are inadequate to describe contemporary patterns of change across countries. A more useful concept might be hybridisation (Kwon, 2004). In terms of Smith and Meiskins' framework, hybridisation can be seen as the interplay of dominance effects and societal effects. Dominance effects mean that national employment systems come to share more common influences such as lean production, shareholder value and labour flexibility but societal effects mean that the way governments, employers and other actors use these influences to achieve change continues to reflect features of the existing system.

Conclusion

In looking at recent patterns of change in Germany and Japan, we have seen that there is some evidence that dominance effects are at work in the diffusion of shareholder value ideas and pressures to increase labour flexibility. However, we have also noted that limited and partial nature of the changes that have taken place. Societal effects mean that there is still support for the social partnership principle in Germany and for welfare corporatism in Japan. While we cannot rule out the possibility that Germany and Japan will move closer to the American model in the future, the fact that employment systems are deeply embedded in wider societal institutions suggests that while the German and Japanese systems are likely to evolve in response to new global pressures, this is not to say that they will come to replicate the US model. Indeed, the difficulty of predicting the future shape of employment systems is compounded when we consider the possible effects of the emergence of China and India as leading players in the new global economy.

Summary

- There are noticeable differences in the way the employment relationship is regulated in different countries such that we can identify different national employment systems.

- National employment systems can be compared on the basis of similarities and differences in the extent and patterns of institutionalised regulation of the employment relationship.

- Different countries' employment systems are embedded in and shaped by their wider business systems.

- Historically Germany, Japan and the USA have adopted different employment paradigms based on respectively social partnership, welfare corporatism and a managerially led model.

- Each of the three paradigms has been embedded in distinctive business systems that have in turn produced and supported distinctive strategies for achieving competitiveness in domestic and international markets.

- Since the 1980s each system has come under intense pressure to change in response to forces that many observers believe are encouraging the convergence of all employment systems towards the current US model.

QUESTIONS

1 Explain the terms 'social partnership', 'welfare corporatism' and 'managerial capitalism'. What is their significance for the regulation of the employment relationship?

2 How have the German, Japanese and American employment systems shaped the ways in which these countries compete in international markets?

3 Compare any two of the three systems discussed in this chapter to discuss how national differences in employment systems reflect wider institutional differences.

4 What have been the main pressures for change in the American, German and Japanese employment systems?

5 In what ways and how fundamentally are the German and Japanese systems changing?

6 In the light of the country studies in this chapter, consider the arguments for and against the likely convergence of national employment systems.

Chill enters cosy German boardrooms

David Gow

About 50 leading German business executives will this week draw up plans for radical changes to the system of co-determination which gives workers and unions seats in boardrooms. For decades the system has been seen as a boon for Europe's biggest economy but is now derided by Michael Rogowski, president of the Confederation of German Industry, as 'an error of history'. Mitbestimmung is increasingly seen as a baneful influence, preventing modernisation of a floundering economy, discouraging foreign investors, cementing a rigid labour market and forcing a flight of capital.

But the system, introduced in the British zone of occupation after the war ... has found staunch defenders in Chancellor Gerhard Schroder and Jurgen Schrempp, Daimler-Chrysler chief executive, as well as the unions.

Mr Schroder said last week he had always supported co-determination and that would remain the case. 'It has strengthened, not weakened, Germany', he said, echoing the words of his economics minister, Wolfgang Clement.

Mr Schrempp told *Stern* magazine he had 'very good experiences, all things considered' with the system, dealing over the past 20 years with very 'competent' labour representatives who were closely bound up with the firm and its success. 'In our case it works extraordinarily well.' Privately, British executives serving on German boards disagree.

The British originally imposed co-determination in the coal and steel industries, the industrial muscle behind Hitler's military power, in an effort to prevent the rebirth of Nazi-style aggression. Giving workers equal places in the boardroom with capital would act as a brake on over-ambitious expansion.

The nationwide system imposed by Willy Brandt's Social Democrat government gave workers and union representatives up to 10 seats on 20-strong supervisory boards which are designed to oversee the executive board in the development of company policy and strategy – including investment, rationalisation and closures. The chairman, normally representing investors, has the casting vote in the event of a deadlock.

Co-determination, its proponents say, has enabled German companies to manage change in an exemplary fashion through consensus. But critics argue that companies such as Opel, the carmaker shedding 10,000 jobs, and Karstadt, the retailer axing 5500 posts, have been plunged into financial crisis because the supervisory board postponed radical surgery or enjoyed too cosy a relationship with the executive board so that nothing ever happened.

Now Mr Rogowski and officials in the German Federation of Employers in effect want to hand all decision making powers to the executive board. Under the revised system being drawn up by their joint working group, all companies would be empowered to renegotiate co-determination arrangements.

If the 'social partners' fail to agree, a draft paper leaked to *Der Spiegel* last week says that only a third, rather than half, of all supervisory seats would be reserved for worker representatives. In Anglo-Saxon style firms with a single board, the worker representatives would be confined to a watered-down consultative council. In the coal and steel industries, co-determination (at board level) would cease altogether.

Worker representatives, often including union leaders active in a particular sector such as transport or chemicals, are delegated but Mr Rogowski's plans would force a ballot of the entire workforce.

Dennis Snower, head of Kiel's Institute for the World Economy, told a reporter from the *Suddeutsche Zeitung* last week that the system must be adapted to meet modern demands for entrepreneurial flexibility, especially among foreign investors.

The most telling business argument for change is that co-determination is an obstacle to cross-border mergers or, as in the case of Hoechst and Rhone-Poulenc (now Aventis) forces the transfer of the company headquarters outside Germany.

But EU company law reforms, in the making for 30 years, will enable transnational firms to become European plcs (or AGs in Germany), with little or no co-determination. So far, few British companies seem attracted by the idea, let alone by Mitbestimmung; their German rivals are much more interested.

Source: The Guardian, 25 October 2004.

Questions

1 Why have some employers such as Michael Rogowski sought to dismantle co-determination at board level?

Case study continued

2 In what ways does this report illustrate the pressures for change in the German employment system being generated by globalisation?

3 Why have so many German employers such as Jurgen Schrempp defended co-determination?

4 Consider the wider significance of this report for other employment systems that provide for worker involvement in strategic decision making such as Japan.

Activity

Using documentary and internet sources, do some research to find out whether the changes being proposed to the system of worker directors have actually been implemented. A good source is the European Industrial Relations Observatory On-line, which can be found at www.eiro.eurofound.ie. Go to 'browse by country' and click on Germany. The *European Industrial Relations Review* is another useful source.

References and further reading

Alchian, A. and Demsetz, H. (1972) 'Production, information costs and economic organization', *American Economic Review*, 62: 777–795.

Auerbach, J. (1964) 'The La Follete Committee', *Journal of American History*, 51, December: 435–459.

Bacon, N., Wright, M. and Demina, N. (2004) 'Management buyouts and human resource management' *British Journal of Industrial Relations*, 42, 2: 325–347.

Barjot, D. (ed.) (2002) *Catching Up with America: Productivity Missions and the Diffusion of American Economic and Technological Influence after The Second World War*. Paris: Sorbonne Press.

Baumol, W. (1959) *Business Behaviour, Value and Growth*. New York: Macmillan.

Berle, A. and Means, G. (1932) *The Modern Corporation and Private Property*. New York: Macmillan.

Bernstein, I. (1970) *The Turbulent Years*. Boston, USA: Houghton Mifflin.

Blair, M. (1995) *Ownership and Control: Rethinking Corporate Governance for the 21st Century*. Washington DC: Brookings Institute.

Bloom, N., Dowdy, J. and Dorgan, S. (2002) *Management Practices Across Firms and Nations*. London: McKinsey/LSE.

Boyer, R. (2000) 'Is a finance-led growth regime a viable alternative to Fordism? A preliminary analysis', *Economy and Society*, 29, 1.

Boyer, R. (2005) 'From shareholder value to CEO power: the paradox of the 1990s', *Competition and Change*, 9, 1: 7–47.

Braverman, H. (1974) *Labour and Monopoly Capital*. New York: Monthly Review Press.

Cappelli, P. (1997) *Change at Work: How American Industry and Workers are Coping with Corporate Restructuring and What Workers Must Do to Take Charge of their Own Careers*. Oxford: Oxford University Press.

Carr, C. (2005) 'Are German, Japanese and Anglo-Saxon strategic decision styles still divergent in the context of globalization?' *Journal of Management Studies* 42, 6: 1155–1188.

Chandler, A. (1977) *The Visible Hand: The Managerial Revolution in American Business*. Cambridge: CUP.

Chandler, A. (1990) *Scale and Scope: The Dynamics of Industrial Capitalism*. Cambridge: CUP.

Chartered Institute of Personnel and Development (2006) *People, Productivity and Performance – Smart Work*. London: CIPD. February.

Clark, I. (2000) *The State, Regulation and Industrial Relations*. London: Routledge.

Clark, I. (2006) 'Managing for shareholder value: theorising the evidence', Plenary Paper presented at the Advanced Institute of Management Research Workshop, London Business School, January. Forthcoming in the *Journal of Management Studies*, 2007, September.

Clark, I. (2007) 'An X factor – private equity firms, the market for corporate control and the management of human resources'. Unpublished working paper, Birmingham Business School.

Clark, I. and Almond, P. (2006) 'An introduction to the American business system' in Almond, P. and Ferner, A. (eds) *American Multinationals in Europe: Human Resource Policies and Practices*. Oxford: Oxford University Press.

Colling, T. (2001) 'In a state of bliss, there is no need for a ministry of bliss. Non-unionism, power and consent in the American business system', *Leicester Business School Occasional Paper Number 67*. Leicester Business School, De Montfort University.

Conference Board McGuckin, R. and van Ark, B. (2005) 'Performance 2005: productivity, employment and income in the world's economies'. New York: Conference Board. August.

Dore, R. (1973) *British Factory – Japanese Factory. The Origins of National Diversity in Industrial Relations*. London: Allen and Unwin.

Dore, R. (2000) *Stock Market Capitalism: Welfare Capitalism. Japan and Germany Versus the Anglo-Saxons*. Oxford: Oxford University Press.

Edwards, R. (1979) *Contested Terrain*. New York: Basic.

Edwards, T. (2004) 'Corporate governance, industrial relations and trends in company-level restructuring in Europe: convergence towards the Anglo-American model?' *Industrial Relations Journal*, 35, 6: 518–535.

ESRC (2004) *The UK's Productivity Gap – What Research Tells Us and What We Need To Know*. Swindon: ESRC.

Federal Statistical Office Germany (2006) www.destatis.de.

Foulkes, F. (1980) *Personnel Management in Large Non-Union Companies*. New Jersey: Prentice Hall.

Fujimura, H. (1997) 'New unionism: beyond enterprise unionism?', in Sako, M. and Sato, H. (eds) *Japanese Labour and Management in Transition: Diversity, Flexibility and Particpiation*. London: Routledge, pp. 296–314.

Gospel, H. and Pendleton, A. (2005) *Corporate Governance and Labour Management – An International Comparison*. Oxford: Oxford University Press.

Grahl, J. and Teague, P. (2000) 'The regulation school, the employment relation and financialisation', *Economy and Society*, 29, 1.

Grahl, J. and Teague, P. (2004) 'The German model in danger', *Industrial Relations Journal*, 35, 6: 557–573.

Gulger, K., Mueller, D. and Yurtoglu, B. (2004) 'Corporate Governance and Globalization', *Oxford Review of Economic Policy*, 20: 129–156.

Habakkuk, H.K, (1960) *American and British Technology in the 19th Century*. Cambridge: Cambridge University Press.

Hall, P. and Soskice, D. (2001) (eds) *Varieties of Capitalism: The Institutional Foundations of Comparative Advantage*. Oxford: Oxford University Press, opening chapter 'An introduction to varieties of capitalism' by the editors.

Hanami, T. (2004) 'The changing labour market, industrial relations and labour policy', *Japan Labor Review*, 1, 1: 4–16.

Hansmann, H. and Kraakman, R. (2001) 'The end of history for corporate law', *Georgetown Law Review*, 43, 9: 439–441.

Harris, H. (1982) *The Right to Manage*. Madison: University of Wisconsin Press.

Hattori, R. and Maeda, E. (2000) 'The Japanese employment system (summary)', *Bank of Japan Monthly Bulletin* (January), www.joy.or.jp/en/.

Hollingsworth, J.R. (1997) 'The institutional embeddedness of American capitalism' in Crouch, C. and Streeck, W. (eds) *The Political Economy of Modern Capitalism*. London: Sage.

Hounshell, D. (1984) *From the American System to Mass Production*. Baltimore: The Johns Hopkins University Press.

Hutton, W. (2002) *The World We're In*. London: Little Brown.

Inagami, T. (1988) *Japanese Workplace Industrial Relations*, Japanese Industrial relations Series 14. Tokyo: The Japan Institute of Labour.

Inoue, S. (1999) 'Japanese trade unions and their future: opportunities and challenges in an era of globalisation'. International Institute for Labor Studies, Discussion Paper 106. Geneva: ILO.

Jackson, G., Hopner, M. and Kurdelbusch, A. (2005) 'Corporate governance and employees in Germany: changing linkages, complementarities and tensions' in Gospel, H. and Pendleton, A. (eds) *Corporate Governance and Labour Management: An International Comparison*. Oxford: Oxford University Press.

Jacobi, O., Keller, B. and Muller-Jentsch, W. (1998) 'Germany: facing new challenges', in Ferner, A. and Hyman, R. (eds) *Changing Industrial Relations in Europe*. Oxford: Blackwell, pp. 190–238.

Jacoby, S. (1997) *Modern Manors: Welfare Capitalism since the New Deal*. New York: Princeton University Press.

Jensen, M. and Meckling, W. (1976) 'Theory of the firm: managerial behaviour, agency costs and ownership structure', *Journal of Financial Economics*, 3: 305–360.

Jensen, M. and Murphy, K. (1990) 'Performance pay and top-management incentives', *The Journal of Political Economy*, 98, 2: 225–264.

Kato, T. (2001) 'The end of lifetime employment in Japan? Evidence from national surveys and research', *Journal of the Japanese and International Economies*, 15: 489–514.

Katz, H. and Darbishire, O. (1999) *Converging Divergences: World Wide Changes in Employment Systems*. New York: Cornell University Press.

Kennedy, A. (2000) *The End of Shareholder Value: Corporations at the Crossroads*. New York: Perseus.

Kerr, C., Dunlop, J., Harbison, E. and Myers, C. (1960) *Industrialism and Industrial Man*. Cambridge, Mass.: Harvard University Press.

Kochan, T., Katz, H.C. and McKersie, R.B. (1986) *The Transformation of American Industrial Relations*. New York: Basic Books.

Kochan, T., Katz, H. and McKersie, R. (1994) *The Tranformation of American Industrial Relations*. New York: Cornell University Press.

Kothen, G., McKinley, W. and Scherer, G. (1999) 'Alternatives to organisational downsizing: a German case study', *M@n@gement*, 2, 3 (special issue): 263–286.

Kross, H. (1970) *Executive Opinion: What Business Leaders Said on Economic Issues*. New York: New York Press.

Kurdelbursch, A. (2002) 'Multinationals and the rise of variable pay in Germany', *European Journal of Industrial Relations*, 8, 3: 325–351.

Kusuda, K. (2000) 'Trends in wage systems in Japan', *Japanese Institute of Labor Bulletin*, April.

Kwon, Hyeong-ki (2004) 'Japanese employment relations in transition' *Economic and Industrial Democracy*, 25, 3: 325–345.

Landes, D. (1998) *The Wealth and Poverty of Nations*. London: Little Brown.

Lane, C. (1989) *Management and Labour in Europe*. Aldershot: Edward Elgar.

Lane, C. (2000) 'Globalization and the German model of capitalism – erosion or survival?' *British Journal of Sociology*, 51, 2: 207–234.

Lazonick, W. (1991) *Business Organization and the Myth of the Market Economy*. Cambridge: Cambridge University Press.

Littler, C. (1982) *The Development of the Labour Process in Capitalist Economies*. London: Heinemann.

Locke, D. (1996) *The Collapse of American Management Mystique*. Oxford: Oxford University Press.

Lincoln, J.R. and Kalleberg, A.L. (1992) *Culture, Control and Commitment: A Study of Work Organization and Attitudes in the United States and Japan*. Cambridge: Cambridge University Press.

Marsden, D. (1999) *A Theory of Employment Systems*. Oxford: Oxford University Press.

Matanle (2003) *Japanese Capitalism and Modernity in a Global Era: Refabricating Lifetime Employment Relations*. London: Routledge Curzon.

Maurice, M., Sellier, F. and Sylvestre, J-J. (1986) *The Social Foundations of Industrial Power*. Cambridge, Mass.: MIT Press.

Means, G. (1930) 'The Diffusion of stock-ownership in the United States', *Quarterly Journal of Economics*, 44, 4: 561–600.

Mishel, L., Bernstein, J. and Boushey, H. (2003) *The State of Working America*. New York: Cornell University Press.

Nakamura, K. (1997) 'Worker participation: collective bargaining and joint consultation', in Sako, M. and Sato, H. (eds) *Japanese Labour and Management in Transition: Diversity, Flexibility and Particpiation*. London: Routledge, pp. 280–295.

OECD (2004) *Principles of Corporate Governance*. Paris: OECD.

OECD (2006) *OECD Factbook*. www.sourceoecd.org.

Oliver, N. and Wilkinson, B. (1992) *The Japanization of British Industry: New Developments in the 1990s*, 2nd edn. Oxford: Blackwell.

O'Sullivan (2000) *Contests for Corporate Control and Economic Performance in the United States and Germany*. Oxford: Oxford University Press.

Peuntner, T. (2003) 'Contingent employment in Germany', in O. Bergstrom and D. Storrie (eds) *Contingent Employment in Europe and the United States*. Cheltenham: Edward Elgar, pp. 136–162.

Pendleton, A. and Gospel, H. (2005) 'Markets and relationships: finance, governance and labour in the UK' in Gospel, H. and Pendleton, A. (eds) *Corporate Governance and Labour Management – An International Comparison*. Oxford: Oxford University Press.

Peters, T. (1992) *Liberation Management*. New York: Macmillan.

Proudfoot Consulting (2005) *2005 Proudfoot Productivity Report – An International Study of Company Level Productivity*. London: Proudfoot/LSE.

Rappaport, A. (1998) *Creating Shareholder Value: A Guide to Managers and Investors*. New York: The Free Press. Revised edition of the 1986 original.

Rosenberg, N. (1976) *Spreading the American Dream: American Economic and Cultural Expansion, 1890–1945*. New York: Farrar, Strauss, Giroux.

Rubery, J. and Grimshaw, D. (2003) *The Organization of Employment: An International Perspective*. Basingstoke: Palgrave.

Rupert, M. (1995) *Producing Hegemony: The Politics of Mass Production and American Global Power*. Cambridge: Cambridge University Press.

Sako, M. (1997) 'Introduction: forces for homogeneity and diversity in the Japanese industrial relations system', in Sako, M. and Sato, H. (eds) *Japanese Labour and Management in Transition: Diversity, Flexibility and Particpiation*. London: Routledge, pp. 1–26.

Schoppa, L. (2006) 'Race to the bottom? Japanese multinational firms and the future of the lifetime employment system', *Japan Focus*, February. www.japanfocus.org.

Shinoda, T. (1997) 'Rengo and policy participation: Japanese-style neo-corporatism?', in Sako, M. and Sato, H. (eds) *Japanese Labour and Management in Transition: Diversity, Flexibility and Participation*. London: Routledge, pp. 187–214.

Shirai, T. (1983) *Contemporary Industrial Relations in Japan*. Madison, WI: Wisconsin University Press.

Smith, C. and Meiskins, P. (1995) 'System, societal and dominance effects on cross-national organisational analysis', *Work, Employment and Society*, 9, 2: 241–267.

Stewart, G. (1991) *The Quest for Value: The EVA Management Guide*. New York: Harper Collins.

Streeck, W. (1997) 'German capitalism: does it exist? Can it survive?' in Crouch, C. and Streeck, W. (eds) *Political Economy of Modern Capitalism*. London: Sage.

Strinati, D. (1982) *Capitalism, the State and Industrial Relations*. London: Croom Helm.

Sugeno, K. and Suwa, Y. (1997) 'Labour law issues in a changing labour market: in search of a new support system', in Sako, M. and Sato, H. (eds) *Japanese Labour and Management in Transition: Diversity, Flexibility and Participation*. London: Routledge, pp. 53–78.

Symonds, P. (1999) 'Nissan announces 21,000 jobs to go in Japan's first major downsizing', World Socialist Website, October. www.wsws.org.

Thompson, P. (2003) 'Disconnected capitalism: or why employers can't keep their side of the bargain', *Work, Employment and Society*, 17, 2: 359–378.

Towers, B. (1997) *The Representation Gap*. Oxford: Oxford University Press.

Tuselmann, H. and Heise, A. (2000) 'The German model at the crossroads: past, present and future' *Industrial Relations Journal*, 31, 3: 162–177.

Watanabe, S. (2000) 'The Japan model and the future of employment and wage systems', *International Labour Review*, 139, 3: 307–334.

Whitley, R. (2000) *Divergent Capitalisms: The Social Structuring and Change of Business Systems*. Oxford: Oxford University Press.

Williams, L. (2000) 'Shareholder value and financialisation: consultancy promises, management moves', *Economy and Society*, 29, 1.

Williamson, O. (1964) *The Economics of Discretionary Behaviour: Managerial Objectives in a Theory of the Firm*. New Jersey: Prentice Hall.

Williamson, O. (1967) 'Hierarchical control and optimum firm size', *Journal of Political Economy*, 75: 123–138.

Williamson, O. (1975) *Markets and Hierarchies: Analysis and Anti-Trust Implications*. New York: The Free Press.

For multiple-choice questions, exercises and annotated weblinks specific to this chapter visit the book's website at **www.pearsoned.co.uk/beardwell**

Chapter 16

Human resource management in China and India

Linda Glover and Anita Trivedi

Objectives

- To examine the convergence–divergence debate with respect to HRM in Asia.
- Application of cultural and institutional perspectives to understand HRM in China and India.
- To explore the developments in human resource management in the People's Republic of China.
- To explore the nature and development of human resource management in India.

Introduction

This chapter focuses upon China and India. It explores the general business context of each of these countries and reflects upon some of the human resource issues that are relevant to each. The chapter is designed to give readers an overview of the key issues for each country. Further reading is recommended if a detailed understanding of either/both countries is required and the reference list is offered as a useful starting point.

China and India are in the process of rapid development and together hold two-fifths of the world's population. China and India are becoming increasingly important in economic terms. As well as receiving inward foreign investment, developing countries are becoming important sources of foreign direct investment (UNCTAD, 2005). China has been called the 'factory of the world' as manufacturers increasingly locate operations there. India has become a popular base for call centre operations such as the HSBC bank. Chinese and Indian companies are becoming more established and some are buying well-known brands or forming strategic alliances in order to become global players. Examples include Lenovo's acquisition of IBM's PC division, Nanjing Automotive's acquisition of part of the Rover group and Tata Tea's acquisition of Tetley tea.

Some have argued that India and China face similar challenges in dealing with unemployment, regional disparities and the 'enduring poverty of farmers' (*The Economist*, 2005). China is often portrayed as more advanced in terms of economic development and India as 'big, lumbering and slow off the mark'. However, others have argued that India is emerging as a new 'Asian Tiger' (*The Economist*, 2005) and that whilst India could learn lessons from China in terms of economic growth, the Chinese model has been one of political authoritarianism and that India's tradition of democracy has much to commend it (*The Economist*, 2005).

The structure of the chapter is as follows. The first section considers the evidence as to whether there appears to be convergence or divergence in Asia. The second section moves on to discuss China and includes: an overview of the country, its economic growth and a brief history of the 'iron rice bowl' to 'socialism with Chinese characteristics'. The discussion then moves on to discuss HRM issues including: employment contracts, labour market concerns, recruitment selection and training, reward systems and employee relations, some cultural issues and problems around management skills, labour discipline and motivation. This is followed by a brief overview of Hong Kong, as it has a different history to mainland China.

The next major section focuses on India and includes: an overview of the country and its economic development, issues related to the national business system and the Indian business environment. It then moves on to consider HRM in India including; legal provisions, industrial relations, recruitment, reward and wages, training and skill development and finally the challenges, advantages and prospects for the future.

Convergence or divergence in Asia?

The assumption in the past was that management and employee relation practices could be transposed to any international context with requisite training and the implementation of proper systems of management, usually American. Another assumption by many Westerners was that Asian cultural influences on management could largely be ignored. This was a perspective strongly informed by imperialist attitudes that assumed that what was good for Western economies could automatically be transplanted into any socio-cultural context. As has already been noted in Chapter 15 on international HRM, these convergence assumptions have been rigorously challenged by divergence theorists from a cultural and institutional perspective, as well as by Whitley (1992) and his followers, who believe that each national context throws up its own unique business system. However, more recently there has been a return to the convergence view, much influenced by the phenomenon of 'globalisation' (a concept still largely ill defined and subject to much misunderstanding) and the relative decline of Japan in relation to the United States in the latter part of the 1990s.

Others have gone beyond the simplistic suppositions of convergence and divergence to capture the complexities that underpin HRM in a national context and as it interacts with global processes and practices. They have come to the general conclusion that divergence of HRM practices remains predominant. This is due to socio-cultural differences, varied investment patterns and financial institutional practices, and political and historical factors that have led to different stages of economic development (Warner, 1993; Easterby-Smith *et al.*, 1995; Leggett and Bamber, 1996; Paik *et al.*, 1996; Rowley, 1997; Sparrow and Wu, 1999; Warner, 2000).

Leggett and Bamber (1996) claim that despite enormous growth, high investment from foreign companies and closer cooperation through the Association of South East Asian Nations (ASEAN) and the Asia-Pacific Economic Cooperation (APEC) forum, Asia Pacific economies diverge into three tiers or levels of development.

- The top tier, led predominantly by Japan, also includes Australia, Hong Kong, New Zealand, Singapore, Taiwan and South Korea. The non-Anglo-Saxon countries are generally known as the *Asian tigers*, and are made up of what have come to be called *newly industrialised economies* (NIEs). These have witnessed impressive growth rates in their economies over the past 20 years, and are moving into a second phase of development where the reliance on cheap labour is being superseded by investment in high technology and service industries.

- The second tier is a second generation of tigers, comprising Malaysia, the Peoples Republic of China (PRC) and Thailand. They reflect the earlier experience of the older tigers, and are at present at the stage of being 'caught in a "sandwich trap" of cheap labour competition from below and exclusion from higher value-added markets from above' (Deyo, 1995: 23).

- The third tier, made up of Burma, India, Indonesia, the Philippines and Vietnam, comprises a diverse range of economies that have not reached the overall developmental stages of the first two tiers. What characterises this tier is the availability and abundance of cheap and unskilled labour.

However, as the case of India shows, the tier model does not accommodate varying levels, rates and nature of growth. Sections of the Indian economy have experienced enormous growth rate in the past 10 years. Some sectors like information technology, software, computing and the services sector are highly developed. Today, it is the fastest growing economy along with China and aiming to capitalise on its competitive advantage of a relatively young, English-speaking, skilled workforce to move up the value chain.

In sum, to put these economies into one all-embracing category does not do justice to the diversity of their cultures, nor the political and social structures that create their unique business systems. As Warner (2000: 177) states: 'There is hardly any evidence to support the classic convergence hypothesis . . . it is hard to argue that Asian HRM is fast converging to a common model'. In separating forms of convergence into 'hard' and 'soft' ('hard' being labour market and economic influences exemplified by deregulation and privatisation and institutional structures, and 'soft' being more concerned with sociocultural variables) Warner (2000: 181) concludes that:

> the Asia-Pacific model is far from homogeneous [and that there is] a vast range of geographical and demographic variation. The economic systems range from emerging from a communist planned economy to fully fledged liberalised market-based ones. The political systems also differ greatly, as do the social arrangements. There is probably less cultural variation but more variety than acknowledged by many writers in the field. There is in this sense a fair degree of residual cultural diversity in the Asia-Pacific region that is likely to continue into the new millennium. On the other hand, if there is a common direction in which the HR systems are moving, it is most likely to be towards business restructuring, deregulation and liberalisation vis-à-vis the challenges of globalisation.

Stop & think

What factors would prevent a true convergence of HRM practices in the Asia Pacific region?

China: economic growth and HRM

Introduction

The People's Republic of China (PRC) has an area of 9,561,000 square kilometres, and had an estimated population of 1.3 billion people in 2004. China contains 22 provinces, 5 autonomous regions and 4 municipalities. Its capital is Beijing, which has a population of 7,610,000 (*Financial Times*, 2005). It has borders with countries including India, Burma and Russia. China has one-party rule by the Chinese Communist Party (CCP). The National Peoples Congress (NPC) is the organ of supreme power and contains 2989 delegates selected by provinces, municipalities, autonomous regions and the armed forces. The main functions of the NPC include formulating and revising the constitution, approving members of the Standing Committee of the NPC, approving the president and the vice president and examining and approving plans for economic and social development. The Politburo of the CCP sets policy and controls administrative, legal and executive appointments. The nine-man standing committee of the Politburo is the focus of power (*Financial Times*, 2005).

China has experienced rapid economic, political and social development over more than two decades. The death of Mao Zedong in 1976 heralded the beginning of a period of economic reform led by Deng Xiaoping. During this period China adopted an 'open door' policy for encouraging trade and technology transfer. The management of the economy moved from a centrally planned *command economy* to a *socialist market economy* (CCCC, 1993). Annual economic growth has averaged 9 per cent since 1978. Domestic spending rose by five times in the 1990s. Total GDP was US$1.6 billion in 2004 and was expected to rise from US$1.9 billion to US$2.2 billion in 2005 and 2006 respectively (*Financial Times*, 2005).

There has been a rapid increase in the number of foreign-invested enterprises in China (Ding and Warner, 1999). Foreign investment in early 1996 was US$7.74 billion. This had risen to US$46.8 billion by 2001 and to US$55 billion in 2004 (Thornhill, 2002a; OECD, 2005). China was the largest recipient of foreign investment after the United States and received US$60 billion in FDI in 2004 (*The Economist*, 2005). The levels of China's foreign currency reserves were second only to those of Japan in 1999 (Kynge, 1999). In 2001, China's main trading partners were the United States, Japan and the EU to which it exported goods totalling 20.4, 16.9 and 15.4 per cent of its output respectively in 2001 (Thornhill, 2002a). Merchandise exports were US$593.4 billion in 2004 and were expected to rise from US$761.3 billion to US$889.6 billion in 2005 and 2006 respectively. Merchandise imports were $534.4 billion in 2004 and were expected to rise from US$653.4 billion to US$803.7 billion in 2005 and 2006 respectively (*Financial Times*, 2005).

Despite the success of the Chinese economy and the fact that it was not severely affected by the economic crisis in Asia during 1997–8 (Ding *et al.*, 2004), commentators have observed certain institutional weaknesses. The World Bank highlighted three main problems in its report 'China: weathering the storm and learning the lessons' (1999). These were:

- weaknesses in corporate governance, and a poor definition of ownership and accountability;
- government interference in investment decisions;
- slow progress in setting up satisfactory mechanisms by which to regulate the financial sector.

In conjunction with these institutional weaknesses, there were associated problems of corruption within the system. It was estimated that one-fifth (Rmb 117 bn) of central government revenues had been misused in the first eight months of 1999 (Kynge, 1999). The lack of legal regulation meant that foreign businesses often experienced problems when setting up businesses within China (Murray, 1994; Peng, 1994). These included dealing with broken contracts, incurring bad debts, and completing property developments. However, there is evidence that government is beginning to make progress with such issues, spurred by the need to implement rules and regulations in order to comply with its membership of the World Trade Organization (WTO). For example, Cody (2006) reports that the CCP disciplined more than 115,000 members for corruption and related violations in 2005 and that more than 15,000 were sent to court for prosecution. For example, a series of accidents in coal mines killed almost 6000 workers in 2005. Investigators found that local officials were not enforcing health and safety regulations due to the fact that they were either part-owners of the mines or were 'paid to look the other way' (Cody, 2006). Therefore, corruption remains a problem in China.

Accession to the WTO (in December 2001) has increased the pressure to deal with issues such as labour rights, trade union rights, employment conditions and human rights more generally. Zhu and Warner (2005) observe that China has received both praise and criticism from interest groups both within and outside of China. In respect of the latter, they observe that one of the critical areas of debate has centred upon employment relations. They argue that criticism has centred on issues such as, 'the implementation of international labour standards, the role of trade unions, working conditions, wage-price factors in relation to the cost of production and export competition in global market, social protection and social inequality, "efficiency" vs "fairness and justice" . . . "industrial democracy" vs "power, control and corruption"' (Zhu and Warner, 2005). China is a developing economy and labour is one of its key resources. Zhu and Warner (2005) explain that critics regard globalisation as part of a 'zero-sum game' which leads to an uneven distribution of benefits, where many employees work in poor conditions and exist on poverty wages. However, they also observe that accession to the WTO will bring increasing pressure from international governing bodies such as the ILO and organisations such as the International Confederation of Free Trade Unions (ICFTU) to improve employment rights and conditions (and the broader context of human rights).

China is now facing a changing climate of export opportunities and foreign investment on the one hand and industrial restructuring, downsizing and unemployment on the other. Some commentators have observed that the massive influx of foreign investment could 'undermine the viability of the country's remaining state-owned enterprises which still employ millions of workers' (Thornhill, 2002b: vi) and that membership of the WTO could accelerate the speed of redundancies in state-owned enterprises (SOEs). The industrial restructuring and related unemployment could be potentially critical given the lack of an adequate social security net at present (Mok *et al.*, 2002).

However, others have argued that membership of the WTO will lead to soaring export growth as restrictive quotas set by other countries are reduced or scrapped (Lardy, 2002). Other developing countries in Asia fear that foreign direct investment will centre upon China and that they will find it difficult to compete against Chinese exporters (Burton *et al.*, 2001). The question is whether the predicted 'export boom' will be sufficiently able to mediate the predicted levels of unemployment. Later in this section we provide an overview of some of the key business and HR issues that are impacting upon China today.

The 'iron rice-bowl' to 'socialism with Chinese characteristics'

An historical overview serves to provide a framework for understanding some of the contemporary human resource issues that are impacting upon China. The historical review begins by focusing upon the period during which Mao Zedong was in power. Child (1994: 36–38) suggests that one can categorise four main phases of industrial governance during this period. These are summarised below.

Phase 1: Central planning, 1953–56

Mao Zedong came to power in 1949. He advocated that China should move to an economy based upon socialist ownership. The Five Year Plan was launched in 1953. This included moves towards centralised planning and control from the state. Trade unions did exist, but their role was confined to dealing with welfare issues. Complicated piece-rate systems were used to reward many workers.

Phase 2: Decentralisation and the Great Leap Forward, 1957–61

The system of industrial governance that developed as part of the five-year plan was influenced by the Soviet system. Child argues that this tended to be very hierarchical, and as such was not in sympathy with a Chinese culture in which collectivism was a central feature. The Great Leap Forward was a period within which many of the collectivist values came to the fore. During 1957–61 control for much of industry passed from central to provincial government. However, a great emphasis was placed upon allegiance to the Communist Party, and factory directors had to report to party committees. The system of bonus payments was reduced.

Phase 3: The period of readjustment, 1962–65

The 1959–61 period saw a drop in agricultural output, followed by a famine. This was partly caused by an over-emphasis on expanding the manufacturing sector during the Great Leap Forward. The period of readjustment saw moves back towards more centralised planning; however, factory directors were given more control over day-to-day production issues.

Phase 4: The Cultural Revolution, 1966–76

The Cultural Revolution was a distinctive period, during which politics and ideology were the predominant concerns. There was a great emphasis upon allegiance to the Party. Factories moved away from hierarchical control towards using factory revolutionary committees as the management mechanism. In terms of rewards, 'competitive, individual and material incentive was rejected in favour of cooperative, collective and moral incentive' (Child, 1994: 37). Therefore, a context of collectivism and control developed. Child (1994: 39) comments that

> The Cultural Revolution was seen to have dissipated incentive and responsibility for economic performance through egalitarianism, the weakening of management, the general devaluation of expertise and the claim that ideological fervour and inspired leadership could substitute for technical knowledge . . . The xenophobia of the period had denied the country opportunities for inward investment and technology transfer.

Child's summary of the four phases of industrial governance gives an insight into the context that developed during the rule of Mao Zedong. The role of the state was central throughout. The state managed the economy, and increasingly enforced its ideology upon the citizens. China was relatively undisturbed by foreign influence during this period. Child notes that social and political discipline was used as an effective force for controlling the Chinese people.

One of the legacies of Mao's rule was the system that became known as the 'iron rice-bowl'. This related to the provision of lifetime employment and cradle-to-grave welfare structures (Ding *et al.*, 2000). The enterprise played both an economic and a social role, and would provide its employees with housing, medical support and education provision. Central to the enterprise were work units (*danwei*). The *danweis* formed the core of the community. Ding *et al.* (2000: 218) comment that a number of writers have suggested that the iron rice-bowl encouraged a high degree of 'organisational dependency'. They argue that organisational dependency is a deep-seated feature of the Chinese system, and that it has encouraged attitudes and behaviours that are difficult to change. The implications of organisational dependency interlinked with many of the HR issues that are discussed below.

China's industrial production was dominated by state-owned enterprises. These accounted for 80 per cent of industrial production in 1978 (Warner, 1997). Under the full employment system that emerged, the dismissal of workers was allowed only if a worker had committed 'gross negligence', but this term was open to interpretation, and the sanction was rarely used even if the individuals concerned were undisciplined. In order to avoid the problems that are associated with unemployment, a system of 'featherbedding' was used, which resulted in enterprises that were overstaffed, with low levels of productivity (Child, 1994). Wages were based on seniority, and there was no real incentive for employees to strive for promotion. There was no concept of a labour market, and individuals were not allowed to move within China to 'follow work'. Trade unions existed, but had a different role from their Western counterparts:

> The All China Federation of Trade Unions (ACFTU) were assigned two functions: by top-down transmission, mobilisation of workers for labour production on behalf of the State, and by bottom-up transmission, protection of workers' rights and interests.
>
> (Chan, quoted in Warner, 1997: 37)

Therefore the union role centred upon production and welfare issues. They would not be involved in negotiations on pay and conditions, as would be the norm in Western countries.

Stop & think

What are the key characteristics associated with the 'iron rice-bowl'? What behaviours did it encourage? Identify some of the key HR issues related to this period.

Post-1976: 'Socialism with Chinese characteristics'

After the death of Mao Zedong in 1976, Deng Xiaoping assumed power in China. Under his leadership China embarked on an economic reform programme. This included the commencement of an 'open door' policy in which international trade and the influx of foreign technology were encouraged. The term 'socialism with Chinese characteristics' was first used by Deng Xiaoping in 1982 to describe the approach to economic reform. China allowed joint ventures to operate from the early 1980s onwards. From this point, foreign invested enterprises (FIEs) became widespread. Foreign companies provided technology and managerial knowledge (Ding *et al.*, 2000).

In 1999 the government amended the constitution to formally recognise the concept of private ownership. Employment in the private sector rose from 150,000 to 32.3 million in the period from 1980 to 1999 (Montagnon, 1999a). FIEs were important in terms of providing employment, technology and modern management techniques.

However, the process of modernisation has not been painless. One of the key problems was that the State Owned Enterprises (SOEs) were overmanned and underinvested. Reports suggest that the number of bankruptcies in the PRC rose from 98 in 1989 to 8939 in 2001 and approximately 60 per cent of these were in SOEs (Thornhill, 2002a). In the period between 1998 and 2001, 25 million employees lost their jobs in SOEs. In 2002, 150,000 SOEs remained, employing 50 million workers and these numbers had fallen to 36 million by 2005. Workers in the SOEs had been socialised into the iron rice-bowl mentality, in which they expected that the organisation would provide cradle-to-grave employment and welfare. One of the aims of the modernisation programme was to move away from this. In 1992 personnel legislation was introduced that became known as the *three systems reforms*. The three key areas were: the introduction of labour contracts, performance-related rewards, and social insurance reforms. Warner (1996) provides a useful summary of the key differences between the traditional system and the emerging system of labour reforms within China (see Table 16.1).

The 1994 Labour Law provided a further spur to the modernisation. It aimed to provide regulation for 'a labour system compatible with a social market economy' (Warner, 1997: 33). The law covered a variety of issues, including the right for workers to choose jobs, equal opportunities, minimum wage levels, directives on working hours, and provisions for dispute handling and resolution. Warner comments that one of the implications of the 1994 Labour Law was that the distribution of power would be readjusted so that the trade unions could have more autonomy from the state.

The process of modernisation has meant that there is no longer a 'job for life'. Other aspects of the iron rice-bowl are also beginning to wane. From 1998 the *danweis* were no

Table 16.1 Summary of the differences in characteristics of the labour-management reforms

System characteristic	Status quo	Experimental
1 Strategy	Hard-line	Reformist
2 Employment	Iron rice-bowl	Labour market
3 Conditions	Job security	Labour contracts
4 Mobility	Job assignment	Job choice
5 Rewards	Egalitarian	Meritocratic
6 Wage system	Grade based	Performance based
7 Promotion	Seniority	Skill-related
8 Union role	Consultative	Coordinative
9 Management	Economic cadres	Professional managers
10 Factory party-role	Central	Ancillary
11 Work organisation	Taylorist	Flexible
12 Efficiency	Technical	Allocative

Source: Warner (1996: 33).

longer allowed to allocate subsidised housing, and allowances for education and medical support were slowly being reduced (Kynge, 1999). The modernisation programme led to SOEs being restructured and downsized. However, it is estimated that SOEs currently have 20 million employees excess to requirements (Montagnon, 1999a). Mok *et al.* (2002: 411) found that a 'strong sense of destitution and betrayal [was] experienced by most state workers who used to be the 'labour aristocracy' in China'. They go on to note that the sense of inequity has been fanned by the media attention that has focused upon successful millionaires. There is a concern that unemployed workers from the SOEs may not pass easily into the labour market. Evidence of worker unrest is emerging; for example, 216,750 strikes and demonstrations were recorded in 1998 which included 3.5 million workers. Within this number, there were some instances of violence and 78 deaths occurred (Mok *et al.*, 2002).

The government has set up a system of social security. The cost of the social security bill rose by 23 per cent in 1998, and unemployment rose from 3.1 per cent in 1998 to 5.5 per cent in 1999 (Montagnon, 1999a). Clearly, unemployment will remain as a key concern for some time to come, especially given the huge levels of surplus labour within the SOEs. Chinese officials are predicting that 10 million people may be affected by unemployment in urban areas in the period up to 2006 (Mok *et al.*, 2002). A process of modernisation is taking place, but the size and historical development of China mean that this is a slow process. We will return to some of these issues as the chapter progresses. Overall, the legacy of the iron rice-bowl is still apparent, and complete reform is still a long way off.

Stop & think

Identify key strengths and weaknesses in the Chinese economy. What human resource issues emerge from this context?

HRM with 'Chinese characteristics'?

Economic reforms in China have allowed the influx of foreign interests, and have set a new context in which both indigenous Chinese and foreign invested companies manage the employment relationship. There is a debate as to whether employment systems in the Asian bloc are converging towards common approaches to HRM or, alternatively, whether they are becoming more divergent as time goes by. Some have argued that an Asian model of HRM exists. The Asian model has been characterised by: non-adversarial relationships; low union density, or unions (as in China) that are closely controlled by the state; and low instances of overt industrial conflict. However, as we have already noted, academics are now beginning to appreciate that the Asian bloc is far from homogeneous, and differences in IR/HRM systems reflect different national histories and cultures (Leggett and Bamber, 1996; Rowley, 1997; Warner, 2000). Part of the remit of this section is to explore the extent to which employment systems in China are becoming more 'Westernised'. This seems possible for two main reasons: first, the high levels of foreign investment in the country, and second, the fact that the modernisation programme has increasingly subjected the SOEs in particular to the logic of the market.

The debate regarding the extent to which Chinese enterprises are adopting HRM is a problematic one. Academic perspectives on this issue relate back to the wider debate about the nature of HRM itself. Child (1994: 157) questions the extent to which one can utilise the term 'HRM' as a descriptor for the management of personnel in Chinese enterprises:

> Although definitions of personnel management and human resource management vary considerably, modern Western thinking tends to be predicated upon assumptions such as the primary contribution of competent and motivated people to a firm's success, the compatibility of individual and corporate interests, the importance of developing a corporate culture

which is in tune with top management's strategy for the firm, and the responsibility of senior management rather than employees' own representative bodies for determining personnel practices. It attaches importance to systematic recruitment and selection, training and development (including socialisation into corporate culture), close attention to motivation through personal involvement and participation in work and its organisation, appraisal and progression procedures and incentive schemes . . . This concept of human resource management is not found in Chinese enterprises.

Therefore authors such as Child believe that the term 'HRM' is unsuitable as a model for analysis to be used within the Chinese context. Others, however, are explicitly using mainstream HRM models in order to analyse human resource issues within China (Ahlstrom *et al.*, 2005; Zhu and Warner, 2004). For example, Benson and Zhu (1999) use Storey's model of HRM, which categorises four key elements of HRM (beliefs and assumptions, strategic aspects, management role, and key levers), in order to evaluate the extent to which six SOEs were adopting HRM practices. They refute Child's assertion that the concept of HRM is not found within Chinese enterprises. By reference to the Storey model, they conclude that there were three models of HRM within their sample. The first model was a minimalist approach, in which two of the SOEs had made few attempts to adopt an HRM approach. The second model was one in which two companies had attempted to adopt an HRM paradigm. Part of this was related to the fact that both of these companies were relatively small, and had strong connections with foreign companies via joint ventures or contracting arrangements. The third model represented a transitional stage between the old and the new. Benson and Zhu argue that there is evidence that some enterprises had developed the concept of and practices associated with HRM, and the extent to which this had happened depended upon factors such as market forces and changes in legislation. Their evidence does not, however, suggest that HRM is the dominant paradigm, and they acknowledge that factors such as China's historical development and cultural traditions can act as a barrier to the development of a Western model of HRM.

Clearly, the extent to which China is adopting an 'HRM' approach is a matter of some debate. The evidence seems to suggest that some enterprises may be adopting some of the practices that are associated with Western models of HRM, but it is unlikely that full-blown models are widespread. Some authors have focused upon the linkages between HRM and organisational performance within the Chinese context. Bjorkman and Xiucheng (2002), for example, found some support for the notion that organisational performance appeared to be positively influenced where companies had a strong integration between HRM and strategy. They also suggested positive relationships between performance-based rewards, individual performance appraisal and organisational performance. They do, however, acknowledge the relatively small size of their sample and the relative lack of understanding at present about the intervening variables that 'knit together' HRM and organisational performance. The following sections will review some of the evidence regarding different aspects of contemporary HR/personnel practice within China.

Employment contracts, surplus labour, social insurance and labour market concerns

Part of the modernisation process has included the shift to a more decentralised and flexible labour market. Indeed Zhu and Warner (2005: 360) comment that the Chinese labour-market is still in a 'nascent' state. The employment contract system was formally implemented in 1986, and it gave employers the ability to hire employees on contracts that specified the terms of employment. Under this system, enterprises were able to downsize and remove problematic employees (Ding and Warner, 1999). The drive to modernise the labour market was further progressed by the provision of subsequent legislation such as the personnel legislation of 1992 and the 1994 Labour Law. This meant that both individual and collective labour contracts could be set up. The collective contracts would cover employees belonging to an enterprise, and would be arranged via the trade union. Collective contracts would cover areas such as pay and conditions, working hours, holidays and welfare (Ding and Warner, 1999: 249).

New labour legislation is likely to come into effect in late 2006. Draft legislation entitled, *The Labor Contract Law of the Peoples Republic of China* was passed in October 2005 and could become law by late 2006. One of the key points is that the legislation emphasises the protection of employees' interests. For example, the draft legislation seeks to address, 'the existing common problems of infringing employees legitimate interests (especially in small to medium-sized firms), imposes penalties on employees who maliciously arrear the salaries of workers. It would also give employees the right to terminate the employment relationship if their employers fail to purchase social insurance for them in compliance with the law' (Li, 2006: 3). However, Li (2006: 3) points out that the draft legislation fails to give protection to certain groups of workers and 'is silent on employers' liability for their employees 'work-related injuries'.

Social insurance is emerging as a critical issue in China. As highlighted, one outcome of the reform programme has been that a substantial number of redundancies have been made. Seventeen million employees of SOEs had been laid off by the end of 1998 (Benson and Zhu, 1999). Prior to the economic reforms, the enterprise took responsibility for welfare issues such as pensions and medical cover. Since the reforms, the government has had to set up a system of social insurance. The funds for social insurance are contributed to by the state, the enterprise and individual employees (Ding and Warner, 1999). Social insurance is designed to act as a safety net, particularly for employees who are made redundant. One of the issues that China will have to deal with is the rising cost of social insurance (Montagnon, 1999a) and there is some concern that the social security fund will not be strong enough to support claims from it. The reasons for this include that: the system is fairly new and as a result, a mass of contributions has not built-up; many retirees did not make contributions into the scheme, but are now drawing from it; SOEs that have closed no longer make contributions for their employees and that the government did not make enough compensation for employees who were employed during the centrally-planned period (Zhu and Warner, 2005: 363). It has been estimated that the cost of moving towards a fully funded pension system by 2030 could reach Rmb 3000 billion (Thornhill, 2002a). Zhu and Warner (2005) comment that the problem is likely to be exacerbated in the future (by the ageing population) and that the government will have to consider injecting more money into the social security fund. As well as concerns about the levels of social security cover, there is a fear of further social unrest resulting from mass redundancies (Mok *et al.*, 2002).

In addition to concerns about social security, there are tensions in respect of general labour market issues. Overall, there is a shortage of skilled labour and an oversupply of unskilled labour in China. Zhu and Warner (2005) identify a number of key labour market concerns. First, that the imbalance in the labour market is likely to lead to increased competition for qualified workers between domestic private enterprises (DPEs), SOEs and foreign-owned enterprises. Second, that FDI has tended to flow into the coastal regions and large cities (and that this has been accelerated by WTO accession). This has led to regional disparities in terms of 'employment opportunity, income and engagements with a global economy' (2005: 360). They comment that whilst the government has a policy to develop the western regions, so far there has been limited foreign investment in these areas and that this is likely to lead to more domestic political tensions. Third, that there is a growing income gap between the top 20 per cent and bottom 20 per cent of the population. Fourth, that a large unregulated labour market of internal migrant workers exists and that this 'floating population' generally do not have proper registration or work permits and in this way have less protection against poor working conditions and exploitation. For example, it was estimated that there were 42 million migrant workers in Guangdong – larger than the population of Poland (Harney, 2005). Fifth, that the move from workers being regarded (in state rhetoric) as 'masters' of SOEs to 'employer and manager' relationships will require adjustment and 'that competition and insecurity among employees have become even more serious since China's WTO accession' (Zhu and Warner, 2005: 361).

Recruitment, selection and training

One of the impacts of the reforms has been that there is now greater mobility within the labour market. Prior to the reforms, workers were assigned to firms from labour bureaus. This often meant that workers were assigned even when they did not hold the requisite skill and knowledge for the job. There is greater labour mobility now, but some studies indicate that mobility remains lower for shopfloor workers (Tsang, 1994; Ding and Warner, 1999; Benson *et al.*, 2000). (A more recent phenomenon has been the surge in numbers of unregistered migrant workers, which is an issue to which we will return.) Table 16.2 demonstrates the continuing role of external agencies in the recruitment process.

There is contrasting evidence in respect of recruitment and selection practices in China. For example, Zhu and Dowling (2002) found that recruitment and selection practices were becoming less influenced by political bureaucracy and more influenced by economic and market concerns. For example, there was more emphasis upon personal competency as a criterion, rather than an individual's political background. This trend was more evident within foreign invested enterprises. In contrast, Ahlstrom *et al.* (2005) reveal fascinating insights into how personal networks and connections affected recruitment and selection practices in 16 foreign firms in China. They found, for example, that managers perceived potential benefits in strategic 'overstaffing'. The reason for this was to curry favour with local government officials by taking on workers from SOEs that were downsizing. In effect, if companies took on additional staff they could expect to 'negotiate some reciprocal benefits from the local government' (2005: 272), for example, a more helpful approach in respect of property deals. Managers also reported that recruiting members from retrenching SOEs could also bring useful industry contacts, for example, an SOE could be a customer of the foreign firm and deals could be lubricated by networks of personal contacts. This was particularly the case in respect of senior positions. The selection of well-connected individuals to management teams and boards of directors was seen as a paramount issue by some firms (not only to lubricate deals but also to impart knowledge about local rules and regulations so that the company could understand which rules had to be complied with). Finally, the study found that it was not unusual for companies to ask prospective employees for their list of connections with key officials and that, 'by hiring such connected individuals, firms ensure that they have a voice as

Table 16.2 Multiple recruitment methods in state-owned enterprises (SOEs) and joint ventures (JVs)

	SOEs *N* = 12	JVs *N* = 11
Sources for recruiting workers		
Secondary/technical school	11 (92%)	7 (64%)
Allocated by labour bureau	9 (75%)	2 (18%)
Labour market	7 (58%)	9 (82%)
Transferred from Chinese partner firm	NA	3 (27%)
Internal recruitment	2 (17%)	NA
Sources for recruiting managers		
Promoted from within the firm	12 (100%)	11 (100%)
Appointment by superior government body	7 (58%)	11 (100%)
Open recruitment	4 (33%)	7 (64%)
Appointed by parent firm	0	3 (27%)
University graduates	0	1 (9%)

Source: Ding and Warner (1999: 247).

officials at various levels and in different regions help to overcome difficulties' (2005: 277). This shows that 'guanxi' continues to affect the processes such as recruitment and selection and it is a   subject that we return to below.

One of the HR problems confronting China is the huge scale of training and development that is needed to ensure that industry and commerce can continue to develop. China has a large pool of unskilled and semi-skilled labour from which to draw, but there is a dearth of managerial employees and engineers with the skills and knowledge that modern industry and commerce require (Ding and Warner, 1999). Warner (1992) suggests that this relates back to two key factors. First, education and development were severely disrupted during the Cultural Revolution; for example, management development and training were banned during this period. The lack of effective training and development meant that there was a lack of educated managers and engineers, and the legacy of this still remains today. Second, the speed of economic development in China has meant that there is a great demand for educated, skilled staff. The state has responded by encouraging the development of an infrastructure for management development and training (Child, 1994). However, there remains a lack of systematic training within companies. Foreign investors in joint ventures (JVs) can find that Chinese partners often request an enormous amount of overseas training for indigenous employees. FIEs can also experience problems in retaining staff they have trained, especially given the tight labour market for skilled managerial and technical employees (Tsang, 1994). Training and development issues are likely to remain as continuing concerns for the future within China (Glover and Siu, 2000).

Reward systems and employee relations

The review above has highlighted some of the changes in relation to reward systems. The seniority-based flat rate system is now being replaced by systems that often have some link to performance. Wages were determined by legislation and regional agencies until the mid-1980s, and seniority was the most important factor in terms of employee earnings, but other aspects were entering the equation by the mid-1990s. Factors such as responsibility and qualifications have started to be taken into account (Benson et al., 2000). However, the evidence remains that SOEs are often unwilling to increase wage differentials. State enterprises have tended to pay equal bonuses to all employees regardless of the performance of individual employees. They have also retained a great degree of harmonisation of work conditions (Benson et al., 2000). This appears to be an example of the way in which the principle of equality has endured post-Mao.

Ding and Warner (1999) carried out a study that compared the average monthly wages of SOE and JV employees. Their evidence demonstrated that while SOEs and JVs tended to adopt the same basic wage structure -- a basic salary plus bonuses and allowances – the JVs tended to pay much more on average. The results are summarised in Table 16.3.

Therefore, while there have been overall moves to increase flexibility within reward systems and linkages between pay and performance, some aspects of the old system endure, including the reluctance of SOEs to penalise poor performers (Benson et al., 2000).

The discussion will now turn to employee relations. Trade unions have historically tended to play a different role within Chinese enterprises (compared with Western counterparts) and have tended to concentrate on welfare issues and assisting in production issues. Benson et al. (2000) comment that trade unions were traditionally 'relegated' to the role of 'watchdog' over issues such as health and safety and workers' rights. In addition, unions have historically been more 'pro-management' than 'pro-labour' in the private sector, partly due to management involvement in the leadership selection processes. However, there are some signs that changes are beginning to happen. Zhu and Warner (2005) observe that the role of trade unions seems to have been strengthened in some ways since the accession to the WTO. For example, the All China Federation of Trade Unions (ACFTU) has been involved in establishing a 'tripartite negotiation system' at national level, as such legitimising the role of trade unions in protect-

Table 16.3 Average monthly wages (RMB) 1994–96

Type of employee	SOEs (*N* = 12)	JVs (*N* = 12)
1994		
Workers	610	763
Section heads	745	933
Middle managers	758	1731
Senior managers	928	2479
1995		
Workers	722	933
Section heads	878	1103
Middle managers	894	1994
Senior managers	1048	2765
1996		
Workers	741	1098
Section heads	867	1294
Middle managers	930	2300
Senior managers	1150	3144

Source: Ding and Warner (1999: 251).

ing the economic interests of employees and representing them at state level. The first National Tripartite Committee was held in 2001 and contained representatives from the Ministry of Labour and Social Security, the China Enterprises Association and the ACFTU.

Zhu and Warner (2005) also observe that union activities are changing at enterprise level and that in addition to the traditional welfare role, trade unions are becoming involved in issues around lay-offs, re-employment and dispute settlement. However, downsizing in the SOEs has also affected union numbers and FOEs as DPEs tend to be less unionised. Indeed, they observe that management in the private sector enjoy 'extraordinary powers' over employment relations issues 'without being greatly concerned about workers rights in those non-union enterprises' (2005: 361). However, the draft of the '*Labor Contract Law of the Peoples Republic of China*' may offer more protection if it comes into law (in late 2006), given that one of its aims is to protect employees' interests.

Despite the fact that the state remains a powerful hegemonic force, Zhu and Warner (2004: 56) comment that

> . . . there are indications that the party/state also makes compromises from time to time in order to gain support from the masses, in particular through institutions such as ACFTU. The revision of trade union law in 2001, promoting tripartite negotiation system by recognising the legitimate role of the ACFTU, developing a national social security network (which has faced huge difficulties), and encouraging new investment and the creation of employment opportunities are some of the state initiatives.

If the draft legislation of 2005 passes into law, this could be added to the list. Lee Cooke (2002) observes that China is 'plagued by large-scale unemployment, low skills, low investment, management prerogatives and ineffective institutional intervention' and that the repercussions for workers are severe. Developments in respect of a tripartite system of control should help institutionalise industrial relations and legitimise the participation of groups such as trade unions, but overall it is likely that the state will seek to retain a high degree of control for the foreseeable future.

The preceding review has given an overview of the current situation in key areas such as employee resourcing, development and relations. It seems that China is beginning to use techniques that are derived from Western and Japanese practices. However, the full-scale adoption of Western-style techniques is unlikely, at least in the short term, as these would be incongruent with Chinese culture and the historical development of their business traditions. The following section will highlight some of the issues that impact upon the management of people in China.

Stop & think

- *Why has the number of redundancies increased in China in recent years?*
- *Why is training and development likely to be a key issue in years to come?*
- *What are some of the key trends in terms of rewarding employees in China?*

Some issues influencing HRM in China

Culture

This section will provide an overview of some of the issues that influence the management of people in China. These include the impact of culture, the lack of managerial skills, problems of labour discipline, and dealing with low motivation. Warner (2000) has noted that a great deal of divergence remains within the Asian bloc, and that one of the explanatory variables for this is the impact of national cultures upon human resource systems. Culture is a notoriously difficult concept to define, and it is hard to make broad generalisations that would fit all individuals and groups within a particular country. China, for example, comprises a huge land mass, and many argue that one can find differences in culture between people from the north compared with those of the south. For example, northern Chinese tend to speak Mandarin, while many southerners speak Cantonese. However, it is useful to outline some of the features that are associated with Chinese culture, in order to understand some of the HR issues that are affecting both SOEs and FIEs.

Child (1994: 28–32) provides an overview of some of the key aspects of Chinese culture. He points out that there is a degree of agreement that Confucianism is the basis for many Chinese traditions. An understanding of Confucianism does help one to understand certain values, attitudes and behaviours within the Chinese context. Fan (1995) suggests that Confucian ideologies are relevant to contemporary studies for four main reasons:

- Confucian ideology has become firmly rooted as an 'undeniable' system that governs many aspects of Chinese lives.
- Thousands of years of a feudalistic system have dominated the Chinese view of themselves and the world.
- To gain acceptance in China, new ideas have to be proved to be compatible with classics and tradition.
- The current economic reforms are not necessarily changing Chinese people's fundamental mentality or behaviour.

Kong Fu Ze (551–479 BC) was called Confucius by Jesuit missionaries. His philosophy on life became popular some 300 years later. The fifth Han Emperor, Wu, found that Confucian ideologies fitted well with the need to create a strong, centralised monarchy. Confucianism emphasised a respect for elders and the family, order, hierarchy, and a sense of duty. Confucius believed that individuals had a fixed position in society, and that social harmony could be achieved when individuals behaved according to rank (Jacobs *et al.*, 1995). There was an emphasis upon the 'correct and well-mannered conduct of one's duties, based upon a sound respect for the social conventions of a patrimonial society' (Child, 1994: 29). Age was respected, particularly in the case of male elders.

Child quotes Lockett (1988), who identified four values that are central to Chinese culture, and which are based upon Confucian ideologies:

- respect for age and hierarchy;
- orientation towards groups;
- the preservation of 'face';
- the importance of relationships.

'Face' is an important concept, and it relates to a person's social standing, position and moral character. Child (1994: 30) comments that the Chinese attach great importance to how they are viewed by others. 'Face' means that conflicts within a group would be kept private, as the group would be demeaned in the eyes of the wider community if conflict were overt. The importance of relationships is captured in the concept known as *guanxi*. Luo and Chen (1997: 1) note that '*guanxi* refers to the concept of drawing on connections or networks to secure favours in personal or business relations'. *Guanxi* relates to relationships that are outside the person's immediate family (Child, 1994: 30). The concepts of *guanxi* and 'face' are intertwined, and some have argued that they can act as inhibitors to the modernisation programme (Chen, 1995).

The preceding paragraphs have given a short overview of a complex subject. There is much evidence that FIEs often find it difficult to operate within China, and that some of the problems are caused by a lack of appreciation of Chinese culture (Chow, 2004). The examples quoted have highlighted some of the underlying tensions that have developed between foreign and Chinese partners. Peng (1994) has commented that foreign investors have complained that Chinese managers lack initiative, are unwilling to delegate, and are perceived to be unsystematic. Lockett (1988) argues that such behaviours reflect aspects of Chinese culture: for example, he reminds us that during the Cultural Revolution managers were promoted according to Party allegiance rather than on the basis of merit. He argues that this legacy has hampered the level of management skill in China. The tendency towards collective rather than individual orientation often leads to behaviours that clash with the behaviours expected by foreign counterparts. Chinese managers will often avoid taking individual responsibility, and Child (1994) argues that this is due to a combination of Chinese traditions and the Cultural Revolution.

Jacobs *et al.* (1995) argue, however, that there is too much emphasis upon the negative implications of Chinese culture. They argue that Confucian-based philosophies can lead to positive outcomes in the workplace, because of the emphasis upon 'diligence, responsibility, thrift, promptness, cooperation and learning' (p. 33). More research is needed in order to evaluate the impact of Chinese culture upon business performance.

Management skills, labour discipline and motivation

As highlighted, one of the issues affecting China today is a dearth of appropriate management skills. Tsang (1994) argues that the lack of skills relates to four main factors. First, the Cultural Revolution severely disrupted education, training and development. Second, central planning meant that managers had little autonomy. For example, all products were sold to the state at a predetermined price. Therefore managers did not have the scope to develop entrepreneurial skills. Third, mistakes were severely penalised, but achievements were not rewarded. Fourth, important decisions were made by collective consensus, managers saw themselves as an 'information conduit' and individuals were unwilling to take risky decisions (relating back to the danger of losing face). Again, these behaviours relate back to a combination of Confucian ideology and the legacy of the Cultural Revolution. The development of adequate levels of managerial skill is likely to remain as a key issue for the future.

Two linked issues are the problems of labour discipline and low motivation. Evidence suggests that Chinese managers are often unwilling to discipline staff, as they prefer to avoid overt conflict and maintain harmony (Tsang, 1994). While Chinese culture emphasises the importance of hard work and diligence, the system of featherbedding in SOEs meant that the enterprises were overstaffed and productivity was low. Tsang quotes from the *China Daily*:

> Labour discipline in our enterprises is very lax. Some workers don't work eight hours a day, a few are absent for a long time to engage in speculation and profiteering. Others even turn to street brawling and stealing of state property. There are also technically incompetent people who do not seek improvement, but just drift along, wasting their own and other people's time.
>
> (Tsang, 1994: 5)

This comment reflects the fact that China is going through the equivalent of an industrial revolution, in that many workers are being drawn from agricultural work to factory work. The problems highlighted above are reminiscent of those that faced nations such as the USA, Japan and the United Kingdom as they went through their own industrial revolutions and sought to find ways in which to control and motivate agricultural/migrant workers (Zuboff, 1988; Buchanan and Huczynski, 1997).

Glover and Siu (2000) have pointed out that foreign invested enterprises (FIEs) based in southern China often employ migrant workers from the north of China, indeed their numbers have grown dramatically (Harney, 2005). Their case study evidence suggested that the main aim of the migrant workers was to accumulate money and return home as quickly as possible. For this reason, they were not motivated by the prospect of career development, had a purely instrumental attachment to the company, and no real stake in the long-term prosperity of the firm. It is also important to point out that part of the attraction of the joint venture was that the company could take advantage of the low pay levels in China. In other words, the company was also operating in an instrumental way in respect of its use of manual labour in China. Glover and Siu identify a range of problems that were being encountered by the company, many of which were related to human resources issues rather than equipment failures. Burrell (1997) argues that although many of the world's workers are, in fact, peasants, traditional organisational theory has ignored this and has essentially led to a lack of knowledge and understanding about the motivations and aspirations of a numerically significant group of workers. More research is needed in this area.

Stop & think

How might an understanding of Chinese culture and traditions help FIEs when setting up new businesses in China?

Hong Kong: economic growth and HRM

It is relevant to refer to Hong Kong separately here, as it has a different history from that of mainland China. Hong Kong has a relatively small land mass of 1095 square kilometres. It has an estimated population of 6,687,200. It enjoyed rapid economic growth until the Asian crisis of 1997–98 when the economy dipped and unemployment rose. However, there is now evidence that Hong Kongs' economy is on the upturn. This section will give a short review of Hong Kong's historical development, and will highlight some of the issues that face the territory after its reunification with China.

Hong Kong became a British colony in 1843. The British wanted to secure a base from which to trade. Initially, one of the key exports to China was opium, which proved to be a lucrative business for the British. Drug taking was illegal, but there was a high demand for opium within China in the mid- to late 1800s. The Japanese invaded China and subsequently Hong Kong in the Second World War, and occupied Hong Kong between 1941 and 1945. They surrendered in 1945. The Communist Party came to power in China in 1949, and this provoked a wave of migration from China to Hong Kong. Many of the immigrants were traders and businessmen. Many had fought against the Communists during the civil wars in China, and tensions remained between the two factions. Hong Kong became wealthy in the period after the Second World War. Central to its success were the Asian 'tycoons', many of whom were immigrants who had left mainland China in 1949–50. The tycoons preferred to work with family members or close contacts, relating back to the Chinese concept of *guanxi*. However, there is an argument that Hong Kong will slowly move away from its patriarchal culture. Four main reasons have been highlighted. First, the first generation of Chinese businessmen are preparing to hand over to their children, many of whom have been educated in the West. Second, the financial crisis of 1997–98 made the businesses more reliant on Western capital. Third, the internet may pose a threat to more traditional ways of doing business in Hong Kong. Finally, Asia's maturing legal and financial framework may undermine the influence of Chinese networks overseas (Anon., 2000a).

Hong Kong was ruled under British sovereignty until 1997. As a result, it developed a capitalist business system that was influenced by Chinese culture and traditions. Sovereignty was handed back to mainland China in 1997 and China adopted a 'one country, two systems' approach in terms of Hong Kong. Hong Kong became a Special Administrative Region (SAR), and the agreement was that it would maintain its legal system and capitalist approach for at least 50 years. There were many concerns that the agreement would not protect the democratic rights of the people of Hong Kong, or that reunification would affect the economic progress of Hong Kong. In the event, the handover appeared to run smoothly. Hong Kong now has an executive-led, non-elected government and a legislative council (elected by universal suffrage). The system has not been without its problems, and Hong Kong must decide in 2008 whether or not it wishes to move to a fully elected government (*Financial Times*, 1999).

Hong Kong's economy was badly hit by the Asian economic crisis. GDP growth fell by 5.1 per cent in 1998 and by 1.5 per cent in 1999. Unemployment levels rose from 4.7 per cent in 1998 to 7 per cent in 1999 (*Financial Times*, 1999). Indeed, when South Korea, Singapore and the Philippines began to emerge from the Asian crisis, Hong Kong's GDP continued to fall. After 1997, Hong Kong began to be regarded as having an uncompetitive cost base. Several factors were cited as contributing to Hong Kong's problems, and four key issues emerged. First, property values were too high. Second, property rentals were too high. Third, service charges levied at ports and airports were too high (Lucas, 1999a). A fourth key problem related to wage levels within the territory. Prior to 1997, wage levels were spiralling without concomitant increases in productivity. After the onset of the Asian crisis, some large companies cut salaries and others moved operations abroad (Lucas, 1999a). Hong Kong had been used as a gateway to China, but China was increasingly shipping direct from its own ports (Lucas, 1999a).

Hong Kong's economy experienced two economic slowdowns in the five-year period from 1997/8 to 2002 (Leahy, 2002). During this period, property prices fell by 65 per cent and this contributed to a four-year period of deflation. In addition, unemployment rose and hit 7.8 per cent in 2002 (Leahy, 2002). Large companies, including Motorola, the Bank of Asia and Swire Pacific, continued to shed staff (Grammaticas, 2002). Hong Kong's ports continued to lose market share to mainland China by 2002, but air cargo exports rose and tourist arrivals increased in 2002.

There is evidence that the Hong Kong economy is now beginning to rebound. GDP rose by 8.6 per cent in 2004 and by 7.3 per cent in 2005. Unemployment hit a peak of almost 9 per cent in 2003, but fell back to 5.6 per cent in 2005. Exports grew by 11.4 per cent in 2005 and the major export markets were the Chinese mainland (45 per cent), the US (16 per cent), the EU (15 per cent) and Japan (5 per cent) (Hong Kong Trade Development Council, 2006). The UNCTAD World Investment Report indicated that Hong Kong was the second largest recipient of inward foreign direct investment (FDI) in Asia and the seventh in the world in 2004. If China's entry into the WTO leads to the predicted growth of exports, Hong Kong's small and medium-sized company sector could benefit in that they currently operate more than 6000 factories in mainland China (Jacob, 2002). Some believe that the future for Hong Kong's economy will lie in high technology. For example, it may be used as a base for developing China-relevant software (Lucas, 1999b). However, there are concerns that it is less advanced in this sphere than countries such as Singapore. In common with Hong Kong, Singapore has also been used as a small open economy that is a springboard to less developed economies. However, Singapore has been more aggressive in terms of offering incentives to attract preferred industries such as banking, technology and the media (Lucas, 1999b). Hong Kong has not offered the same degree of incentives to potential businesses. In terms of technology, in particular, there is also a concern that there could be a lack of skills to service the fast-growing technology sector within the local labour market (Lucas, 1999b). There is also a concern that only 25 per cent of school leavers go on to university within Hong Kong (Jacob, 2002).

Hong Kong has acted in recent years as 'a "half-way" house between a modern Western business society and the mainland China context' (Selmer *et al.*, 2000: 237). However, this role may diminish as the process of modernisation and openness in China continues to develop. Some of the specific HR issues include the fact that Hong Kong has strictly limited the importation of labour. Businesses are allowed to import construction workers and domestic help, but it has been more difficult to import potential managers (Fields *et al.*, 2000). Some studies have suggested that labour turnover among educated workers and managers tends to be high, and can pose a problem for Hong Kong businesses. Some companies are placing more emphasis upon internal development and promotion to try to alleviate this problem. Fields *et al.* (2000) have found that retention rates are higher in these cases. However, an adequate supply of skilled managers will be critical for Hong Kong's future, especially in the information technology sector.

Investment in training is a key issue. Fields *et al.* (2000) have found, for example, that some companies are reluctant to invest in training, and this is possibly linked to the problem of 'job-hopping' in Hong Kong. In addition, evidence suggests that training budgets have been cut in the light of economic slowdowns (Chu and Siu, 2001). The issue of wage rises has been dealt with above. Wage rises prior to 1997 tended to run ahead of productivity, so contributing to the fact that it was expensive to operate from Hong Kong. These were reigned in after 1997, and some employees had their salaries cut. This caused conflict in some industries. For example, Cathay Pacific cut the salaries of its pilots, and this led to 17 days of disruption in 1999, which cost the company between HK\$ 400 m and HK\$ 700 m.

This short review has highlighted some of the key differences in the historical and economic context of Hong Kong. It is clear that there are substantial differences between the system in Hong Kong and that of its mainland counterpart. It is also clear that Hong Kong's role of 'middle-man' between the West and the East may be further compromised as China continues to modernise.

Stop & think

What impact did the Asian crisis have on Hong Kong and why has the economy continued to suffer?

India

Introduction

As one of the largest democracies in the world with a strategic location in South Asia, India draws international attention. Today, it is the second fastest growing economy in the world with a GDP growth rate of 8.1 per cent at the end of first quarter of 2005–06. India is a founder member of the United Nations, Non-Aligned Movement, World Trade Organization and the Commonwealth. Post-colonial India has been crucial in voicing concerns of the developing countries of the South.

Spread over 3.3 million square kilometres with a population of over a billion, India is the second largest country in Asia and the seventh largest in the world. It shares international borders with eight countries: Pakistan and Afghanistan in the west; China, Nepal and Bhutan in the north; Myanmar and Bangladesh in the east and Sri Lanka in the south. It is a secular, sovereign, socialist, democratic republic with a parliamentary form of government. Comprising twenty-five states and seven Union territories, India is home to all main religions of the world in addition to numerous other sects and faiths. There are sixteen officially recognised languages, and over 150 other languages and more than 500 dialects. Hindi and English are the two official languages. The multi-ethnic, multi-lingual and multi-religious society of India is both its asset and its challenge.

In recent decades, especially since the 1990s, the focus on India has taken an economic dimension along with its continuing geopolitical significance. After liberalising its economy in the 1990s, India has increasingly moved towards external trade liberalisation and to attracting foreign direct investment by marketing itself as a rewarding destination with a large market and workforce potential. Its major trading partners are China, USA, UAE, UK, Japan and the European Union. The US, South Korea and Japan were major sources of foreign direct investment (FDI) inflow during the 1990s, increasingly joined by countries of Europe, with sectors such as automobiles, telecommunications and software attracting most FDI.

India is the second-most favoured destination for FDI in the world after China according to an AT Kearney's FDI Confidence Index that tracked investor confidence among global executives to determine their order of preferences among the 'dominant host countries' for FDI in Asia and the Pacific (UNCTAD). It has attracted more than three times as much foreign investment during the first half of 2005–06 fiscal, as during the corresponding period of 2004–05. That India has one of the largest English-speaking populations in the Asia-Pacific region with a high level of skill in engineering, computing and software is a significant reason for its attraction. It is also one of the largest exporters of skilled migrants in areas of software and financial services and software engineers. At the other end of the spectrum, it offers a mass pool of readily available cheap labour. Services are the major source of economic growth today.

Despite far-reaching changes to attract foreign investment, India has not become a favourite destination for foreign capital. Inward FDI flows, though consistently increasing from 1.9 per cent of Gross Domestic Product in 1995 to 3.4 per cent in 2004 are still modest compared to China (8.2 per cent in 2004), the other major destination of FDI in Asia (World Investment Report, 2005). The industrial and the services sector have registered growth of around 8 per cent in 2005, the highest after 1995–96, and an overall growth of about 7 per cent, which is good but below its potential. This is because of a number of challenges that India faces:

- The need for a more developed infrastructure, particularly in the energy sector.
- Increasing corruption in government and politics.
- Lack of adequate intellectual property protection.
- Unemployment, poverty and increasing inequality.
- Instability of output in agriculture and related areas.
- Low level of literacy rate; 51 per cent but unevenly distributed.
- Lack of national consensus on the extent, nature and role of FDI in the economy.

This section outlines the economic and political trajectory of India post independence (in 1947), the ongoing transformations since the 1980s and 1990s, and India's role in the global economy with an aim to understand the nature of its business system and practices.

Approach: culture, institutions and national business systems

Debates about business systems and practices progressively converging or the alternate view that national differences persist have continued since their first clear identification during the 1950s. In recent decades, 'globalisation' has renewed the debate with the increased connectivity among countries through communication, technology and internationalisation of trade, firms, work organisation, workers and trade unions. The trends towards liberalisation, deregulation and privatisation as also the rise and spread of multinational firms and the strategy and practices that they carry with them are ostensibly integrating and standardising economies, work and work practices worldwide.

Others question the simplistic assumptions behind the perceived uniformity. They argue that history, polity and culture of a country influence its institutions and the route that it takes to industrialisation. A number of studies have examined the influence of cultural assumptions that shape employer–employee relations, organisational culture and managers' actions in India. Hofstede (1991) found a high power distance society marked by low to moderate uncertainty avoidance, low individualism and a low masculinity culture. This is attributed to a tradition-bound society that values ties of family and extended family, inter-personal relations, age, seniority and status. It is a hierarchical society segmented by caste, religion and other group affiliations and a desire for proximity to sources of power.

For business, this translates into a paternalistic management style in largely family owned businesses and a preference for personalised relationships rather than a performance orientation. Management style and individuals display fatalistic tendencies, dependence, fear of power, obedience to superiors, tenacity, resilience, indiscipline, and a submissive, modest, unreserved and collectivist orientation. There is unwillingness to accept organisational change, a reluctance to take risks or bold decisions, lack of initiative in problem solving and disinclination to accept responsibility. A 'soft work culture' and a 'nurturant–task–leadership' style employ familial, cultural and moral means at the workplace. Recruitment, rewards and career progression is through family and social networks and based on loyalty, status and political connections for both the employer and the employee (Sharma, 1984; Singh, 1990; Sinha and Sinha, 1990; Tayeb, 1988; Budhwar and Debrah, 2001; Budhwar and Khatri, 2001).

While culture influences the business environment and management practices of a country and helps understand the differences between countries, it is difficult to measure and shows considerable variation within a country. A cultural approach does not accommodate change and tends towards stereotypes (McSweeney, 2002). National institutions on the other hand, are tangible and easier to study while accommodating the cultural as well as the politico-economic history of the country. Thus, each country has its own set of 'competitive advantage' in its politico-economic, legal, industrial relations, training and other provisions for firms and workers in their relations with the state and society. The resultant 'varieties of capitalism' in different countries mediate the influences of global economy and multinational practices (Lane, 1995; Whitley, 2000; Hall and Soskice, 2001).

Thus, a more contingent perspective that accommodates the influences of the global economy with continued significance of national institutions in an interactive process is adopted here to understand the Indian business system and human resource practices. There is a challenge of reconciling the diversity of workforce, industrial relation systems and legal provisions within India, on account of its vast landmass and federal nature of government, with the broad ambit of its 'national' institutions.

Activity

The preceding sections have provided an overview of India. Take a moment to think over the size and the nature of the Indian state and economy.

Questions

1 What does it tell us about its role and position in the global economy?
2 What role do culture and institutions play in understanding Indian business systems?

From a 'mixed' to an 'open' economy

India adopted the model of a planned and mixed economy after independence in 1947 that emphasised both public and private sector. Economic planning is carried out through five-year national plans. Currently, the tenth five-year plan is in progress. This section outlines the evolution of Indian economic policy in a historical perspective and its influence on the business and human resource environment.

Post-colonial India inherited gross inequality and imbalances in regional development. While encouraging private initiative, government used the public sector to develop, generate employment and provide access to basic facilities in the hitherto underdeveloped areas that might not be attractive to private investment. While it aimed at a faster rate of growth the emphasis was on regulation to protect domestic industry from foreign competition and to promote self-reliance through a policy of import substitution. This was evident in the first two five-year plans:

- First plan (1951–56). This plan focused on agriculture to ensure self-sufficiency in food-grains and to address poverty since a majority of population relied on agriculture for subsistence.

- Second plan (1956–61). Also known as the 'Mahalanobis' plan, the plan focused on industry and industrialisation. The main thrust of the plan was to install capacity in heavy industry. Initially successful in creating capacity and a move from a predominantly agrarian economy to one that produces a wide variety of consumer and industrial goods, reliance on regulatory mechanisms ultimately led to under-utilisation of capacities and the emergence of a licence-quota regime based on political patronage.

- In a number of successive plans from 1961–91, the performance progressively declined due to inflation, poverty and unemployment though there were some achievements in defence and agriculture (for details on five-year plans see Datt and Sundharam, 1999). According to Dreze and Sen (1995):

> Indian economic planning offered good illustration of horrendous over activity in controlling industries, restraining gains from trade, and blighting competitiveness; and, soporific under activity in expanding school education, public health care, social security, gender equity and land reform.

For the Indian economy the economic crisis of the 1980s spelt a decline in industrial production, high rate of inflation, fiscal indiscipline and a very low level of foreign exchange reserves by 1991. A turnaround in the Indian economy came with the economic reforms of 1991. These were engendered by a globalising world economy with trends towards liberalisation and privatisation that accompanied structural adjustment programmes proposed by the World Bank and the International Monetary Fund (for an assessment of industrial development post reform see Kaplinsky, 1997).

- Eighth Plan (1992–97); ninth plan (1997–2002). The outcomes were deregulation and introduction of a series of economic reforms that have carried on in successive plans. The currency was devalued and new industrial, fiscal and trade policies formulated. Reforms were undertaken in the public and the banking sectors. Foreign investment was liberalised (for details on reforms see the special issue of *Columbia Journal of World Business*, 1994).

  Aware of India's comparative advantage in information and communication technology and its export potential, barriers to the entry of foreign firms and technology transfer were removed, and finance for software development through equity and venture capital was provided along with institutional interventions. A number of software technology parks, including one in Silicon Valley, and training institutes have been set up to provide infrastructural and manpower support to the industry.

- Tenth plan (2002–07). Currently the tenth plan has carried on the spirit of reforms of the 1990s. The Indian economy was not adversely affected by the Asian crisis of 1997–98 because of control on capital flows, on disinvestments and on full convertibility as well as continued foreign exchanges remittances by migrant workers. The government has undertaken further reduction in state control and in addressing fiscal imbalance. The economy is being made more open to foreign direct investment in key sectors. Substantial reforms have been made in the financial, telecommunications and the shipping sector with increasing focus on energy infrastructure and supply. Some 51 per cent FDI is now allowed in single brand products in the retail sector and 100 per cent allowed in a number of new sectors (www.ibef.org).

To sum up, the historical experience of colonialism, the nature of Indian economy, the vision of constitution makers of independent India to create an equitable social democracy, and the influence of global economic changes, especially since the 1980s, all contribute to the way the Indian business system has evolved and continues to do so. The next section focuses on the nature of the Indian business system.

Indian business environment

In the light of an uneven and unequal development, it is not surprising that the public sector dominated the Indian business environment until quite recently. It continues to be significant as the largest employer of organised labour in India and in its envisaged role as harbinger of social and economic change. At the same time, it is also marked by excessive bureaucracy, under-utilised capacity, surplus labour, inefficient technology often associated with reduced productivity, quality and high costs – all leading to uncompetitive organisations. These factors influence recent efforts for downsizing and disinvestments in the sector.

Conversely, the private sector suffered. Though receiving some state support, excessive regulation and the licence-quota regime resulted in benefiting a few at the cost of stifling most private initiative. 'Protection' meant firms did not have the initiative to upgrade technology and training, mobilise resources or improve productivity and quality. Further, a policy of import substitution provided a captive market and removed the threat of competition for indigenous firms.

Liberalisation of policies has meant increased competition for both public and private firms from foreign ones. Privatisation has permitted entry of the private sector in areas that were hitherto reserved for the public sector, e.g. transport, telecom, banking, electricity among others. This requires them to change the infrastructure, technology, methods of production and work organisation to increase productivity, improve quality and reduce costs. For corporate management, it implies a shift from protective regulation to market-driven competition that has created opportunities for resource mobilisation from new sources, expansion, diversification and internationalisation (Venkata Ratnam, 1995; Krishna and Monappa, 1994; Rao et al., 1994). This is particularly evident in the large Indian conglomerates like Tatas, Reliance, Ranbaxy and the new computer giants like Infosys, Wipro and Satyam. At the same time labour law is being liberalised and the power of trade unions is declining.

Today, the services sector is the fastest growing, with a growth rate of 7.5 per cent in 1991–2000 that provides employment to 23 per cent of the workforce. A significant development has been that of the information communication technology, financial services, community services and the rise of software exports. Software exports have witnessed a growth rate of over 45 per cent during the decade 1989–2000, substantially higher than the global software industry. Indian software houses include TCS, Infosys, Wipro and Silicon Automation. Business Process Outsourcing from developed economies has also seen the rise of call centres. Microsoft, Dell, Ford, GE, Oracle, Compaq, Lucent and Nortel are scaling up their operations and American Express, IBM and foreign airlines like British Airways are offshoring their services to India. Some European and US firms are considering outsourcing their human resource and accounting departments to India as well (Bagchi, 1999; Joseph, 2001).

Accompanying above developments, the period (1980s–90s) has seen trends associated with the influence of Japanese and US styles of management on Indian business environment via the adoption of practices/terminologies of 'lean production', 'just-in-time', 'teamwork', 'total quality management' and 'performance based pay' among others. This stems in part from the training of many Indian managers abroad and adoption of Western management systems of teaching by institutes of management learning in India, and in part from the influx of MNCs into India (for an overview of government policy, structure and issues pertaining to MNCs see Venkata Ratnam, 1998; for the impact of reforms on different groups of companies see Vachani, 1997).

All the above developments have implications for the nature of human resource policies and practices in India that are discussed in the next section.

Activity

Take a moment to reflect on the nature of the Indian economic policy and business environment.

Question

In what ways have the historical evolution of the Indian economy and globalisation influenced its business environment?

Human resource management in India

HRM in India needs to be examined against the backdrop of differences in public and private sector management practices, the nature of its industrial relations systems, regional and sectoral differences in human resource practices and the impact of globalisation on business environment and practices.

Most of the HRM literature from academics in India and abroad emphasise the need for organisations to modernise, mechanise, introduce new technology and cope with workforce reduction, retention, skills and career development issues to become competitive. This entails human resource development in organisations in tandem with strategy development, develop an awareness of missions, appraise internal strengths, and improve compensation schemes and communication channels to develop better employee relations. Enhanced manpower planning, along with customer satisfaction, ranks high among the priorities of Indian managers (Venkata Ratnam, 1995; Sparrow and Budhwar, 1997; Budhwar and Sparrow, 1997).

Such developments in human resource management are visible in all sectors of economy, especially in traditional sectors like steel, pharmaceuticals and public sector organisations. At the same time, there are new sectors like software, information technology and Business Process Outsourcing (BPO) with their own specific patterns of human resource practices that are significantly different from other sectors. In view of the higher level of academic and other requirements specific to this sector, especially software, the tight labour market and rapid growth, salary and benefits are very high in this sector. Yet, so is the attrition rate. Software industry suffers 20–30 per cent attrition every year. The rapid growth of the industry also demands more skilled manpower that would help brand India as a quality destination rather than a low-cost one enabling it to counter threats of other cost effective destinations like China, Philippines and South Africa as well as a slowdown of demand.

While there are clear pressures towards convergence observable in trends towards liberalisation, changes in business environment and the influx of MNCs with their management practices, such developments are varied in their implementation and outcome and are continuously contested and negotiated by different actors. Thus, there are also visible limits to convergence. Organisations face the challenge of managing differences of region, religion, caste, language, age, gender, skills, nationality, sector and types of plants. Union influence remains strong. That 'labour' is a 'concurrent' subject, i.e. both central and provincial governments can legislate on it, is a significant reason for the observable heterogeneity. MNCs transform and standardise management practices but often modify and alter their policies and practices in response to the context (for examples, see Amba-Rao *et al.*, 2000 and Trivedi, 2006; for a comparative analysis of HRM practices in Indian public and private sector organisations see Budhwar and Boyne, 2004; between India and Britain see Budhwar and Khatri, 2001; between India and Thailand see Lawler *et al.*, 1995; within MNCs in India see Trivedi,

2006). These aspects are explored below with respect to legal provisions, industrial relations and specific practices of recruitment, rewards, training and skill development that exist in both indigenous and multinational firms.

Legal provisions

Labour being a concurrent subject, a plethora of laws that influence firms and workers exist but are weak on implementation (Harriss-White and Gooptu, 2001). From the 1920s to the 1940s a number of legal provisions for workers and trade unions were instituted:

- The Trade Union Act 1926.
- Royal Commission on Labour 1931 and appointment of labour officers in 1932.
- The Factories Act 1948.
- The Industrial Disputes Act 1948.
- Minimum Wages Act 1948.
- Employees State Insurance Act 1948.

Others followed these provisions like The Apprenticeship Act 1961, Maternity Benefit Act 1961, Payment of Bonus Act 1965 and the appointment of First National Commission on Labour 1969. It is considered that the pro-labour laws favour the workers and trade unions in India (Venkata Ratnam, 1995; Sparrow and Budhwar, 1997; for debate see Sengupta and Sett, 2000).

The situation has begun to change post economic reforms with increasing withdrawal of the state from the employment arena. There are pressures to reform labour laws to ensure flexibility and remove restrictions on firms' freedom to close sites and withdraw investment. The second National Commission on Labour (2002) was instituted to recommend comprehensive reforms in labour laws and provisions for labour in line with the requirements of economic liberalisation. Managerial rights are becoming more dominant in collective bargaining relationships and the power of unions is declining. These developments have accorded greater flexibility to the managers in their human resource policies with respect to adjustments of wages and benefits, suspension of trade union rights, and provided more freedom to modernise and increase productivity.

Increased flexibility and greater control over labour and trade unions are marketed as major attractions to foreign investors but they can also sometimes be used by firms to practice indiscriminate hiring and firing of employees, avoid payment of minimum wages and other benefits, and create an environment of fear by penalising any attempts at collective organisation by workers (for details, see Trivedi, 2006).

Accompanying such developments, globalisation of the economy has also put increasing pressure on firms to conform to international labour standards, occupational and health safety, and address child labour and human rights issues, environmental concerns, working conditions in Export Promotion Zones (EPZs) and social security mechanisms. This pressure has been exerted through international and national trade unions to a large extent and the latter are the focus of the next section.

Industrial relations

The influential role of the state in the Indian industrial relations system is attributed to the growth of trade union movement during the late colonial period and in conjunction with the freedom struggle which created common ground between political leaders and trade unions. The state has not only been the largest employer through the public sector but also a regulator, prosecutor and mediator in industrial relations (Ramaswamy, 1984; Bhattacharjee, 2001; Sengupta and Sett, 2000).

The following key features underpin Indian industrial relations. Tripartite consultations take place at the national level, reflecting the history of political support for trade uions by the state and the fact that most unions are affiliated to political parties. Works committees and joint management councils operate at the enterprise level. Dispute resolution machinery operates at four levels: bipartite negotiation, conciliation, arbitration and adjudication. Collective bargaining is conducted at different levels in different industries and is size specific. Large firms employing more than 300 persons have collective bargaining, including most MNCs, with the exception of those in electronics and a few in banking. At the managerial level, individual bargaining is more prevalent (for details about the evolution and assessment of industrial relations in an historical–structural context, see Bhattacharjee, 2001; Kuruvilla, 1996; Kuruvilla and Erickson, 2002; Kuruvilla *et al.*, 2002; Frenkel and Kuruvilla, 2002).

The extent and role of unions in India varies according to geography, sector and industry. While the state of West Bengal has a dominance of politically affiliated left-leaning trade unions, in Maharashtra enterprise-level unions, independent and unaffiliated, have a major presence. Gujarat has seen the rise of 'footpath unionism' and social-movement unions of unorganised workers, e.g. SEWA (Self-Employed Women's Association) whereas industrially and socially backward states of Andhra Pradesh and Bihar have radical and militant trade unions. Unionism is stronger in older industrial centres, in manufacturing units and in the chemical, pharmaceutical and automobile industries than in electronics units. Both public and private sector banks have entrenched unions but not so in foreign banks.

The great influence exercised by trade unions over the human resource policies of firms has begun to weaken with increasing withdrawal of state support and labour law reforms. Many unions are becoming more cooperative and less militant (Venkata Ratnam, 1995; 2001). There is a marked trend towards enterprise-based unions in response to the inability of central trade union organisations to address workers' everyday concerns (Ramaswamy, 1994). Different motives of unions underpin their varied responses to introduction of schemes of employee empowerment in Indian enterprises (Ramaswamy and Schiphorst, 2000).

Venkata Ratnam (2001) has identified multiple trends in industrial relations outcomes based on employer and trade union responses that are contextually dependent:

1 Conflictual industrial relations arising from limited resources, increasing costs and decreasing output.
2 An increase in managerial control over vulnerable trade unions.
3 Worker cooperatives taking over and managing bankrupt companies.
4 Cooperative unions making concessions in bankrupt firms.
5 Takeover of plants by workers.
6 Non-union workforce in new industries and new workplaces.

Another significant reason for the weakness of unions is the creation and development of new industrial areas – Export Promotion Zones and Special Economic Zones specifically to attract FDI – in areas free of union influence. It is common practice in such new industrial areas to circumvent the labour laws through the use of executive regulations. This limits unionisation in the firms located within it. Some firms allow enterprise-based unions but resist and restrict cross-industry or wider political alliances, i.e. in Japanese MNCs like Honda. In some cases, firms follow a vehement 'non-union' policy, i.e. in Korean MNCs like LG (for details, see Trivedi, 2006). Hindustan Lever and Philips have been hostile to any attempts to form federations of their company's unions (Venkata Ratnam, 1998).

In the climate of ongoing economic reforms, business demands centre around major structural changes such as reduction in the political influence of unions and inter-union rivalry, stopping multiple subscription of union membership and amendment of pro-labour laws such as the Trade Union Act 1926 (for details about the debate on reforms in industrial relations laws see Sengupta and Sett, 2000). Most of the above mentioned factors allow greater power and flexibility to managers to determine their human resource policies and practices that are helped by a situation of excess labour supply, high unemployment and increasing inequality and are discussed below.

Take a moment to review the legal and industrial relations system in India.

Question

1 Are they similar across the country or show differences?
2 Is the inflow of FDI and MNCs influencing labour laws and trade unions?

Recruitment

High population growth, uneven economic development, poverty and high unemployment prevalent in the country provide a readily available pool of labour to firms. At the same time, there is a growing number of educated and skilled personnel too. This allows firms flexibility in their recruitment patterns and variations in recruitment policies of firms are observable based on ownership, sector, industry, geographical location and skills.

The public sector has always had a formalised personnel system that uses standardised formal examinations and interviews to recruit its employees. The aim was to create a Weberian impersonal bureaucracy free of prejudice and discrimination based on a technical/rationalist approach. There are special provisions of quotas to recruit disadvantaged groups and communities and a specified percentage of local to broader population in recruitment. The personnel function has evolved from welfare and industrial relations to personnel development to human resource development during the 1980s.

In indigenous private firms, forms of recruitment vary though social networks have been predominant. In largely family-owned firms like the Birlas and the Singhanias, community and family networks played a major role in recruitment. Predominantly from traditional trading *Marwari* community, such firms were concentrated in particular industries like textile and cement, and in particular regions like Kanpur and Nagpur. At the same time, there were others like the Tatas, another family-based firm, which was among the earliest to adopt a more corporate style of management along with diversification in products and nature of its workforce and recruitment policies. Yet another is the chemical firm Asian Paints that recruits its permanent workers from other regions of India and temporary workers locally (for details, see Trivedi, 2006). At the managerial level, there is a move towards merit-based recruitment, particularly of junior managers, among private firms.

Greater variation in recruitment policies and practices is observable in the MNCs operating in India. It stems from a combination of economic-strategic approach of the firms towards cost-minimisation; institutional influences; societal expectations; the role of social networks and issues of power that operate within the organisation and its wider operating context.

Areas developed to attract FDI have a geographical concentration of workers, especially migrant workers, and are free from union influence. MNC policies vary from a simultaneous use of internal and external labour market for recruitment to reliance largely on external ones; from continuous labour turnover to segmenting the workforce by region (local/migrant), skill, age and gender. The segmentation often sees human resource managers travelling to recruit skilled workers from other regions of the country. On the other hand, recruitment of unskilled workers largely from local external labour market relies on the *strength of weak ties* (Granovetter, 1994) of region, community, friends and acquaintances among workers. Permanent workers are normally in the older age bracket as compared to young temporary workers. While production firms employ a predominantly male workforce, export units employ largely women.

Similar variation is observable in management too. Some MNCs, e.g. Korean firms, rely more on expatriates as senior managers with Indians in middle management, but the overwhelming majority employ and train Indian managers as senior executives (for details on MNC practices, see Trivedi, 2006). In high-tech industries like software and telecommunications, India has a comparative advantage in having highly skilled manpower and on-campus recruitment is the norm.

In the services sector, especially BPO, high rate of attrition of around 40 per cent poses a challenge for human resource management (for call centres, see Taylor and Bain, 2005). Some of the reasons are the age profile and expectations of employees and the working conditions at the workplace. The industry has concentrated on recruiting from the younger age group who join to make 'quick money' and leave for a better working environment and career development options than those provided in these 'internet sweatshops' that 'overlook talent'. To address these issues, BPO firms have begun to recruit mature talent, i.e. people over 35 years of age. Often these are outstation candidates (from small towns) and they are provided with shared accommodation. This also translates into changes in compensation and training policies to retain employees discussed in the following sections.

Rewards and wages

The theme of variation observed in industrial relations and recruitment practices above continues in remuneration and reward practices. It varies by the nationality of firms (indigenous/MNC), sector (public/private), industry (new/old; high-tech/low-tech) and skill and nature of employment contract of employees.

There is no uniform wage policy for all sectors of the economy. Although the Minimum Wages Act, 1948, is a centrally legislated act, minimum wages vary widely across states. However, the public sector is still largely characterised by standardised wages with other social benefits and security of employment but there is a greater move towards performance-related pay and promotion in private firms (Bordia and Blau, 1998). While public sector workers are much better off than private sector workers, the reverse is true in the case of senior managers (Venkata Ratnam, 2001). Some private firms also use labour laws to shift to temporary and contractual labour and often avoid payment of minimum wages or any other statutory benefits (Trivedi, 2006).

MNCs pay higher wages than their local counterparts and the working conditions are usually better in MNCs. This is true for employees at both ends of spectrum: cheap labour for cost-minimisation in manufacturing and call centres and the highly skilled manpower in computing and software. They also provide all the social security measures mandated by law like gratuity and provident fund to all workers, but pension funds are instituted only for their senior executives. This is evident both in manufacturing and the services sector.

Higher wages serve the twin purpose of employing better skilled personnel and at times as a means to curtail trade union developments. Young graduates are willing and happy to man the many call-centres for their comparatively higher remuneration packages. Workers are willing to work for higher wages and benefits even in the face of what they call an 'environment of fear and control' especially in manufacturing units while others prefer 'to earn less but be freer at the workplace' (Venkata Ratnam, 2001; Trivedi, 2006).

Variations in wages and benefits appear among firms and among different categories of workers within a firm. Ownership of the firm determines its remuneration policy. Korean firms are the highest paymasters followed by Japanese and then indigenous firms. Segmentation of the workforce into permanent, company casual, trainee and contract workers spells different packages for each group, thus reinforcing segmentation. Despite high wages, the differences in remuneration and rewards that exist between workers and managers is a major source of dissatisfaction (for details, see Trivedi, 2006).

In rapidly growing new industries such as information and communication technology where the supply of technical manpower is a constraint and employee mobility very high, salary and benefits are very high. There is a growing realisation that higher pay can not be enough to retain employees and schemes such as profit sharing, share option and other perks as well as a secure career and better communication are often offered to retain employees in such sectors.

Training and skill development

The nature of the training infrastructure and skill level varies in India on the basis of sector, industry and the type of skill. Training infrastructure is more extensive in the public sector but the quality is steadily declining whereas the emphasis on training is increasing in private firms. This is because high quality skills exist in the software industry and in business management but not in others.

In keeping with a welfare state and the social role of public sector, the state in India provided the training infrastructure, i.e. Industrial Training Institutes form the basis of organised industrial training in India. Apprenticeship systems are instituted in all public sector firms. For management, there has been a move from personnel administration to human resource development in the last decade. This is evident in provisions for systematic training schedules, identification of core competencies and multi-skilling in public sector firms.

Along with engineering and medical skills, recent decades have witnessed an increase in business and management institutes and courses in India as well as students obtaining business degrees from other countries like the US, UK, France and the Philippines. More organisations for providing technical skills required by the software and communications industry have been opened. More than 100,000 engineering graduates and 70,000 software professionals join the industry, both indigenous private and multinational firms, every year. According to Microsoft, India ranks second worldwide in the number of Microsoft Certified Engineers produced. These graduates represent the comparative advantage that India enjoys in terms of skilled professionals over other countries like China (Bagchi, 1999).

At the same time, low literacy, inadequate provision for health and education, a bias against vocational skills and an occupational preference for non-production jobs has created an uneven skill base. While the quality of skilled labour is good, it remains scarce in relation to the working population as a whole. Even in the information and communication technology industry where the highly skilled manpower is available, middle and lower level skilled personnel are in short supply. The training infrastructure is ageing and the technology obsolete. The emphasis on general education and insufficient interaction with industry has exacerbated these trends. More education of higher quality is provided to a few rather than a sound one for all. This leads to even greater inequality (Venkata Ratnam, 2001).

The literature on learning and development argues that for developing countries like India learning requires borrowing from industrially advanced countries with consequences for the distribution of skills. Following economic reforms and liberalisation of economy, it is envisaged that the role played hitherto by the public sector in employment creation and training will be supplemented and/or replaced by MNCs. It is assumed that skills upgrading will occur in response to the requirements of new, technologically sophisticated industries. Individual workplace-based learning will, over time, enhance the social stock of knowledge and skills, thereby promoting growth (Okada, 2004).

While this may be true at managerial level where Indian managers in MNCs are sent to the company's parent country for training, i.e. in Japanese MNCs or in the software industry, at junior management and worker level it is more doubtful, especially in manufacturing MNCs. Elger and Smith (1998) found that work processes in international firms are being simplified to minimise training requirements and facilitate the substitutability of labour. This reduces the dependence on experienced workers. Rationalisation and deskilling of jobs enhance the inter-changeability of workers, who do not need specific skills. Deskilling and multi-tasking rather than multi-skilling, and use of trainees for job completion rather than actual training, appear more the norm in most MNCs (for details, see Trivedi, 2006).

Even in new industries, like software and information technology, the comparative advantage has been based on labour cost advantage rather than innovation and quality. The focus has been mostly at the lowest end of the value chain, i.e. low-level design, on-site export of services and associated customised software development. There has been an increase in sales, exports and the number of firms but a decline in research and development intensity. A move up the value chain through enhanced skills is required here too to retain the comparative advantage. Wipro, India's second largest software services exporter, now recruits maths and science graduates and trains them for three years through on-the-job and classroom training at its Wipro Academy of Software Education. In the BPO firms, there is increasing focus on talent recognition and prospects for career development through offers of places on MBA courses and management diplomas (Bagchi, 1999; Joseph, 2001).

> **Activity**
>
> Foregoing sections have highlighted the variations in the recruitment, reward and training practices in Indian as well as multinational firms. Try to identify some of the factors responsible for such variations.

Challenges

The major challenges identified in the beginning of this section can be attributed to an imposition of reform policies without recognising the diversity of country circumstances; the one size fits all approach; the inability to address the social costs of reforms that have become more acute; and the consequent lack of national consensus on reforms.

Infrastructure

A combination of weak regulatory mechanisms and nature of FDI flow that is largely in non-core sectors has restricted the flow of investment in core sectors like infrastructure and energy. The government has demarcated additional investment of almost US$200 billion for energy infrastructure development and set up an Investment Commission to garner investments in the sector among others. It has prioritised power generation and distribution, telecommunications, national highway and ports development, rural electrification and higher education. One of the priority initiatives of the US–India CEO Forum Report (March 2006) is the setting up of a $5 billion infrastructure development fund. Wider skills upgrading is an imperative if India is to take advantage of the contemporary economic climate, e.g. more manpower for the information and communication technology industry, an area of comparative advantage, is urgently required.

Corruption

One of the reasons for greater flow of FDI to China has been the lower prevalence of corruption in its polity and executive compared with India. A study by Transparency International (2005) places India at the lower end of the table in terms of the ease of doing business and the average time taken to secure clearance for a start-up or to invoke bankruptcy. Corrupt practices are inherited from the licence-quota regime of earlier economic phases and a perception that reforms have been and continue to be introduced in India via covert rather than overt means. India seeks to address this through greater accountability and transparency in all its policies and measures related to privatisation and liberalisation and through open dialogue with all sections of society. The Rights to Information Act (2005) and setting up of vigilance commissions are a step in that direction.

Growth with equity

While jobs have been created, most of the new jobs are in the unorganised sector with low wages, poor working conditions, low job security and increased risk of safety and occupational health. Absence of adequate social security mechanisms have further increased and polarised inequalities. The government is instituting special programmes and fund allocation for addressing poverty, child development, mass education for the poor, the disadvantaged and women. However, more effort is required to increase employment opportunities, augment skill development, ensure rights of workers and trade unions, provision of education and health for all and the need for wider social dialogue among all actors and institutions.

Advantages

Despite the above-mentioned challenges that need to be addressed, India also enjoys certain advantages that, if built upon, would equip it to benefit from the ongoing economic changes.

Language

Advantages arising from knowledge of the English language, increasingly a lingua franca of globalisation, are evident in more than a million graduates that Indian universities produce regularly. Many of these work in the mushrooming call centres that have resulted from outsourcing of services to India from firms in Europe and the USA. There is also an ever-increasing percentage of senior executives from India in multinational firms and international organisations.

Skills

Higher-end spectrum training and skills, especially computing, software, heavy engineering and information technology is India's other comparative advantage. India, though a source of unskilled cheap labour, nevertheless produces a large number of graduates in mathematics and science as well as engineers and doctors from its vast network of engineering and medical colleges. Recent decades have seen a formidable rise in the number of graduates from management and business institutes and middle-level professionals for the software and communications industry. These form the Indian diasporas to the developed economies, e.g. software engineers in Silicon Valley; doctors in the UK; business managers; and researchers in universities.

Democracy

The democratic character of the Indian state provides a sustainable framework to manage diversity with an equitable distribution of resources and opportunities. Empowerment of the weak and the disadvantaged that a democratic process engenders, however slowly, would redress the imbalances created by a differentiated globalisation. The power of the electoral ballot restrains the excesses of global capitalism by exercising control over a national system that may favour it indiscriminately. This may help India address the challenges of poverty, inequality, low literacy and per capita incomes outlined earlier and strive towards a fairer society. It may also counter the corruption that is seeping into governance and polity.

Diversity

Diversity is the key to understanding the Indian context. It is diverse in its social makeup as well as the nature of its workforce, business practices, industrial relations and skill levels. This diversity, if harnessed properly, can yield good returns in the long run in terms of good business practices and a workforce with varied skills that will cater to different sectors and industry. Managers with an experience of diversity are often better equipped to adjust as well as respond to the increasingly diverse international workplace and to global competition.

Prospects

The ongoing transformations are overshadowing and often replacing the post-colonial identity of India, indeed of the developing world, though what the alternative may be remains uncertain. It could be that India on account of its comparative advantage continues to gain employment within the global division of labour between MNCs, nevertheless also growing its own MNCs and brands that will in turn seek global reach, e.g. Mittal Steels, Tatas, Reliance and Infosys. From this may emerge a new set of business practices and human resource policies. The probability of this happening is high with a projected growth of 9–10 per cent predicted by the World Bank. On the other hand, it might be that movement up the value chain is limited and India remains in a subordinate inter-dependent position within global capitalism. Continued analysis of the material issues and social struggles associated with global capitalism as it interacts with the Indian business system, keeping in mind that social processes are iterative and that the global economy continuously changing, would yield a clearer picture of the nature of human resource practices in firms in India.

Activity

Identify the major challenges and advantages facing the Indian business environment and practices in the globalising world economy.

Question

1 What do you think are the future prospects for India?

Summary

- The section on the People's Republic of China discussed key issues relating to human resource management, and outlined some of the key points in China's historical development under Mao. It illustrated the way the system known as the 'iron rice-bowl' continued to exert some degree of influence over contemporary practices. While China has enjoyed rapid economic growth, it is now confronting a number of problems, including restructuring, downsizing and unemployment. In response to this, it is having to develop a system of social insurance. There is a debate as to the extent to which HR practices within China are converging with Western approaches. This section concluded that while there is some degree of similarity, full-blown Westernised models of HRM are unlikely to take hold because of cultural and institutional differences. There are a number of issues that are impacting upon people management in China, including skills gaps, problems of labour discipline, and low motivation.

- The short review of Hong Kong highlighted the clear differences from the PRC, its mainland counterpart. It is also clear that Hong Kong's role of 'middleman' between the West and the East may be further compromised as the PRC continues to modernise.

- The section on India presented an overview of human resource management as it has evolved in the recent past, with special emphasis on the nature of changes in the Indian business environment and practices on account of current transformations in the global economy. Both cultural and institutional perspectives were employed to understand the similarities with standard global HR practices and many differences that persist in HR practices. The overarching theme was of variations in HR practices based on region, sector, industry, ownership and skill. Challenges and advantages arising out of national context and global influences were identified with some possible implications for India's role in the global economy.

Activity

China

As a member of the human resource development department of a large multinational corporation you have been given responsibility to devise a programme to prepare managers and other parent company employees who will be working in China.

Prepare a presentation that you might give to these employees, including general information on the country, history, culture, language and customs and work-related attitudes. Use anecdotes and solid examples to illustrate your presentation.

Questions

1 To what extent would you agree with the contention that existing models of HRM fail to recognise cultural differences, and that this is a weakness given the rapid rate of globalisation?

2 Outline the similarities and differences in terms of the approaches to the management of people in India and China.

3 To what extent would you agree with the view that there is an 'Asian model of HRM'?

Yummee Biscuits: Part 1

Yummee Biscuits is a large UK-based snack manufacturer that was set up in the nineteenth century. It is now one of the largest snack manufacturers in the UK. Over the past two decades it has been internationalising its operations, and has acquired companies in the USA and Australia. In 1995 it became involved in a joint venture in the south of the People's Republic of China (PRC). The Chinese partners were local businessmen who had no prior experience in biscuit-making. Yummee pumped in money and resources, and the Chinese partners set up the land deal. The biscuit factory was built on a greenfield site, and was equipped with state-of-the-art machinery. Work was organised on scientific management (Taylorist) lines, with strictly demarcated jobs and close supervision. Yummee took the view initially that it would be best to employ local Chinese managers to run the factory. However, in the following two years numerous problems occurred within the factory. These included problems of quality control, stock control, and failing to deliver orders to customers on time.

Yummee sent out a delegation of senior managers to investigate the problem. They found that many of the problems were related to a lack of managerial skill and poor coordination between different departments. They realised that it had been a mistake to assume that the indigenous Chinese managers could run the factory to British standards with little support or training. Yummee put all managers through management development training. This included topics such as leadership skills, communication skills, time management skills, and dealing with conflict. The training programmes were adapted from programmes that were delivered in the UK. Individual training needs were not assessed. The managers said that they had enjoyed the training, but the trainer felt that there could be an element of politeness involved. There was little improvement in the performance of the subsidiary one year later.

A senior executive from Yummee travelled to the subsidiary to inspect the plant. He sent a report outlining the key problems in the factory. These were the main points of his report.

Shopfloor problems

- There were low levels of motivation within the shopfloor ranks. Most of the shopfloor workers were from the north of China.
- Shopfloor workers seemed unwilling or unable to take on any level of responsibility.

- There seemed to be little interest in promotion or development opportunities.
- There was no appreciation of hygiene rules and regulations.

Management problems

- Many managers seemed unwilling to take responsibility.
- Managers would often prefer to hire members of their family rather than the best person for the job.
- Managers were often unwilling to discipline subordinates.
- Interdepartmental communication was poor.
- Managers seemed to spend a lot of time dealing with the personal problems of subordinates.

Questions

1 Does a knowledge of the historical and cultural development of China help you to understand the problems experienced in the PRC subsidiary? Give examples.

2 You have been asked to take over the running of the PRC subsidiary. What managerial initiatives would you implement to help resolve the above problems? What barriers would you face and how would you deal with them?

3 To what extent could a Western model of HRM be applied to the context of this factory? If not, why not? Give specific examples.

Yummee Biscuits: Part 2

Yummee Biscuits is now interested in opening a new biscuit factory in Shanghai. It is predicted that the factory will require 800 employees at all levels from senior management to shopfloor workers. The new factory will contain the following departments: human resource management, finance, sales and marketing, food production and distribution and quality control. Yummee will install new German biscuit-making machines, as it feels that these are the best on the market at the moment. The machines will be shipped in from Germany. The factory will produce a range of savoury and sweet biscuits.

Yummee has already purchased a site and expects the building to be complete by December 2007. It would like to put in place a skeleton staff in November and have full staffing in place by the end of December. It is especially keen to ensure that the factory produces quality products from the beginning and that production is brought online as smoothly as possible. The new factory will include a fully equipped training centre and the company will supply a learning resource centre as part of this development. It believes that training is crucial to the success of the venture. It is also keen to attract high-calibre staff, particularly at management levels. It expects to utilise some expatriate staff, but is keen to employ a high percentage of indigenous Chinese staff. It is also keen to avoid the problems that it experienced in its factory in the South of China.

Questions

Yummee has asked for guidance on the following issues:

1 How should it go about recruiting workers for the new factory? What recruitment channels would you recommend and why?

2 How would it organise the selection process for managers and shopfloor workers?

3 Provide guidance that focuses upon how it would develop a reward system for managers and shopfloor workers.

4 Produce a plan that focuses on meeting training and development needs. This should include the following details: timescale, resourcing requirements and staffing needs.

5 Are there any training programmes that would be compulsory for all?

6 What systems should be put in place to ensure that individual training needs are met?

7 Identify the critical success factors and barriers that would be related to each of these activities.

References and further reading

Those texts marked with an asterisk are particularly recommended for further reading. The issues covered in this chapter are also addressed in Chapters 8, 13 and 15.

There are also regular articles on Asian countries in the *International Journal of Human Resource Management* and the *Asia Pacific Business Review*. These two journals and the *Human Resource Management Journal* have had special editions on HRM in the Asian region in recent years. There are also occasional articles on Asian HRM in the many other journals that cover HRM subjects.

*Ahlstrom, D., Foley, S., Young, M.N. and Chan, E. (2005) 'Human resource strategies in post-WTO China', *Thunderbird International Business Review*, 47, 3: 263–385, May–June.

Amba-Rao, S.C., Petrick, J.A., Gupta, J.N.D. and Von der Embse, T.J. (2000) 'Comparative performance appraisal practices and management values among foreign and domestic firms in India', *The International Journal of Human Resource Management*, 11, 1: 60–89.

Anon. (2000a) 'The end of tycoons', *The Economist*, 29 April.

Anon. (2000b) 'Let the good times roll', *The Economist*, 18 April.

Ashton, D. and Sung, J. (1994) *The State Economic Development and Skill Formation: A New Asian Model?* Working Paper 3, Centre for Labour Market Studies, Leicester University, May.

Bagchi, S. (1999) 'India's software industry: the people dimension', *IEEE Software Magazine*, May/June.

Benson, J. (1996) 'Management strategy and labour flexibility in Japanese manufacturing enterprises', *Human Resource Management Journal*, 6, 2: 44–57.

Benson, J. and Zhu, Y. (1999) 'Markets, firms and workers in Chinese state-owned enterprises', *Human Resource Management Journal*, 9, 4: 58–74.

Benson, J., Debroux, P., Yuasa, M. and Zhu, Y. (2000) 'Flexibility and labour management: Chinese manufacturing enterprises in the 1990s', *International Journal of Human Resource Management*, 11, 2: 183–196.

Bhattacharjee (1999) 'Organized labour and economic liberalisation. India: past, present and future', Labour and Society programme, DP/105/1999. Geneva: IILS.

Bhattacharjee (2001) 'The evolution of Indian industrial relations: a comparative perspective', *Industrial Relations Journal*, 32, 3: 244–263.

Bjorkman, I. and Xiucheng, F. (2002) 'Human resource management and the performance of Western firms in China', *International Journal of Human Resource Management*, 13, 6: 853–864.

Bordia, P. and Blau, G. (1998) 'Pay referent comparison and pay level satisfaction in private versus public sector organisations in India', *International Journal of Human Resource Management*, 9, 1: 155–167.

Breman, J. (1996) *Footloose Labour: Working in India's informal economy.* Cambridge: Cambridge University Press.

Buchanan, D. and Huczynski, A. (1997) *Organisational Behaviour: An Introductory Text.* Hemel Hempstead: Prentice Hall.

Budhwar, P.S. and Boyne, G. (2004) 'Human resource management in the Indian public and private sector: an empirical comparison', *International Journal of Human Resource Management*, 15, 2: 346–370.

Budhwar, P.S. and Debrah Y.A. (eds) (2001) *Human resource management in developing countries.* London: Routledge.

Budhwar, P.S. and Khatri, N. (2001) 'A comparative study of HR practices in Britain and India', *International Journal of Human Resource management*, 12, 5: 800–826.

Budhwar, P.S. and Sparrow, P.R. (1997) 'Evaluating levels of strategic integration and development of human resource management in India', *The International Journal of Human Resource Management*, 8, 4: 476–494.

Burrell, G. (1997) *Pandemonium: Towards a Retro-Organisation Theory*. London: Sage.

Burton, J. (1999a) 'Economic squeeze calls for change', *Financial Times*, 20 October.

Burton, J. (1999b) 'The chaebol: the empire strikes back', *Financial Times*, 20 October.

Burton, J. (1999c) 'Banking: still reluctant to change', *Financial Times*, 20 October.

Burton, J., Jonquieres, G., Kazmin, A. and Mandel-Campbell, A. (2001) 'Enter the dragon: economic uncertainties raised by China's accession to the WTO are likely to put pressure on international trade relations for years to come', *Financial Times*, 10 December.

CCCC (1993) *The Work Report of the 14th Conference of the Central Communist Party*. Peoples Republic of China.

Chen, M. (1995) *Asian Management Systems: Chinese, Japanese and Korean Styles of Business*. London: Thunderbird/ Routledge Series in International Management.

Child, J. (1994) *Management in China in the Age of Reform*. Cambridge: Cambridge University Press.

Chow, I. Hau-siu (2004) 'The impact of institutional context on human resource management in three Chinese societies', *Employee Relations*, 26, 6: 626–642.

Chu, P. and Siu, W. (2001) 'Coping with the Asian economic crisis: the rightsizing of small and medium sized enterprises', *International Journal of Human Resource Management*, 12, 5: 845–858.

Cody, E. (2006) 'China cracks down on corruption', *Washington Post Foreign Service*, 15 February.

Datt, R. and Sundharam, K.P.H. (1999) *Indian Economy*. New Delhi: S. Chand and Company Ltd.

Deyo, F. (1995) 'Human resource strategies in Thailand', in Frenkel, S. and Harrold, J. (eds) *Industrialization and Labor Relations: Contemporary Research in Seven Countries*. Ithaca, NY: ILR Press, pp. 23–36.

Ding, D.Z., Ge, G.L. and Warner, M. (2004) 'HRM in China after the Asian financial crisis', *International Studies of Management and Organisation*, 34, 1: 10–31.

Ding, Z. and Warner, M. (1999) 'Re-inventing China's industrial relations at enterprise level: an empirical field study in four major cities', *Industrial Relations Journal*, 30, 3: 243–260.

* Ding, Z., Goodall, K. and Warner, M. (2000) 'The end of the "iron rice-bowl": whither Chinese human resource management?', *International Journal of Human Resource Management*, 11, 2: 217–236.

Dreze, J. and Sen, A. (1995) *India – economic development and social opportunity*. Delhi: Oxford University Press.

Easterby-Smith, M., Malina, D. and Yuan, L. (1995) 'How culture sensitive is HRM? A comparative analysis of practice in Chinese and UK companies', *International Journal of Human Resource Management*, 6, 1: 31–59.

Elger, T. and Smith, C. (1998) 'New Town, New Capital, New Workplace? The employment relations of Japanese inward investors in West Midlands New Town', *Economy and Society*, 27: 578–600.

Fan, X. (1995) 'The Chinese cultural system: implications for cross-cultural management', *SAM Advanced Management Journal*, 60, 1: 14–20.

Fields, D., Chan, A. and Akhtar, S. (2000) 'Organisational context and human resource management strategy: a structural equation analysis of Hong Kong firms', *International Journal of Human Resource Management*, 11, 2: 264–277.

Financial Times (1999) 'Country survey of Hong Kong', 30 June.

Financial Times (2005) 'World report: China' 7 November.

Frenkel, S. (1993) *Organized Labour in the Asia-Pacific Region: A Comparative Study of Trade Unions in Nine Countries*. Ithaca, New York: ILR Press.

Frenkel, S. and Harrod, J.A. (1995) *Industrialization and Labor Relations: Contemporary Research in Seven Countries*. Ithaca, New York: ILR Press.

Frenkel, S. and Kuruvilla, S. (2002) 'Logics of action, Globalisation and changing employment relations in China, India, Malaysia and the Philippines', *Industrial and Labor Relations Review*, 55, 3: 387–412.

Glover, L. and Siu, N. (2000) 'The Human Resource Barriers to the Management of Quality in China', *International Journal of Human Resource Management*, 11, 4: 867–882.

Government of India data from www.ibef.or; www.mea.nic.in and www.commerce.nic.in.

Grammaticus, D. (2002) 'Hong Kong unemployment surges', BBC News, 17 January.

Granovetter, M. (1994) *Getting a job: a study of contacts and careers*. Chicago: Chicago University Press.

Hall, P.A. and Soskice, D. (eds) (2001) *Varieties of capitalism: the institutional foundations of comparative advantage*. Oxford: OUP.

Harney, A. (2005) 'Guangdong: Paying the price of rapid development', *Financial Times*, 7 November.

Harriss-White, B. (ed.) (2002) *Globalisation and insecurity: political, economic and physical challenge*, Basingstoke, New York: Palgrave.

Harriss-White, B. and Gooptu, N. (2001) 'Mapping India's World of Unorganized Labour' in Panitch, L. and Leys, C. (eds) *Socialist Register 2001: Working Classes. Global Realities*, Canada: Merlin.

Heller, P. (1999) *The Labor of Development: workers and the transformation of capitalism in Kerala, India*. Ithaca, NY: Cornell University Press.

Hofstede, G. (1991) *Cultures and Organisations: software of the mind*. London: McGraw-Hill.

Hong Kong Trade Development Council (2006) 'Economic and trade information on Hong Kong', 22 February.

Jacob, R. (2002) 'From lavish parties to pessimism: businessmen say they feel "awful" but believe their prospects are good', *Financial Times*, 1 July.

Jacobs, L., Gao, G. and Herbig, P. (1995) 'Confucian roots in China: a force for today's business', *Management Decision*, 33, 9: 29–35.

Joseph, K.J. (2001) 'ICT, Economy and Labour', *Labour and Development*, 7, 2: 1–36.

Kaplinsky, R. (1997) 'India's industrial development: an interpretive survey', *World Development*, 25, 5: 681–694.

Krishna, A. and Monappa, A. (1994) 'Economic restructuring and human resource management', *Indian Journal of Industrial Relations*, 29, 4: 490–501.

Kuruvilla, S. (1996) 'Linkages between industrialisation strategies and industrial relations/Human Resource Policies: Singapore, Malaysia, The Philippines and India', *Industrial and Labor Relations Review*, 49, 4: 635–657.

Kuruvilla, S. and Erickson, C.L. (2002) 'Change and transformation in Asian industrial relations', *Industrial Relations*, 41, 2: 171–227.

Kuruvilla, S., Das, S., Hyunji, K. and Kwon, S. (2002) 'Trade union growth and decline in Asia', *British Journal of Industrial Relations*, 40, 3: 431–461.

Kynge, J. (1999) 'Reflections on half a century', *Financial Times*, 1 October.

Lane, C. (1995) *Industry and society in Europe*. Aldershot: Elgar.

Lardy, N. (2002) 'Problems on the road to liberalisation: China has joined the WTO on stricter terms than fellow members. If it is to succeed in opening its markets, the world should resist using protectionist provisions', *Financial Times*, 15 March.

Lawler, J.J., Jain, H.C., Venkataratnam, C.S. and Atmiyanandana, V. (1995) 'Human resource management in developing economies: a comparison of India and Thailand', *The International Journal of Human Resource Management*, 6, 2: 319–346.

Leahy, J. (2002) 'Still waiting for the correction: Hong Kong property prices have fallen 65% in the bubble years, but they remain expensive and could slide further', *Financial Times*, 30 November.

Lee Cooke, F. (2002) 'Ownership change and reshaping of employment relations in China: A study of two manufacturing companies', *The Journal of Industrial Relations*, 44, 1: 19–39.

Leggett, C. and Bamber, G. (1996) 'Asia Pacific tiers of change', *Human Resource Management Journal*, special issue: *HRM in the Asia Pacific Region*, 6, 2: 7–19.

Li, L. (2006) 'Labor contract law likely to pass this year', China Update, *Squire Sanders and Dempsey L.L.P.*, February 2006.

Lockett, M. (1988) 'Culture and the problems of Chinese management', *Organisation Studies*, 9, 4: 475–496.

Low, L. (1993) 'From entrepôt to a newly industrialising economy', in Low, L., Heng, T.M.H., Wong, T.W., Yam, T.K. and Hughes, H. (eds) *Challenge and Response: Thirty Years of the Economic Development Board*. Singapore: Times Academic Press.

Low, L., Toh, M.H. and Soon, T.W. (1991) *Economics of Education and Manpower Development: Issues and Policies in Singapore*. Singapore: McGraw-Hill.

Lucas, L. (1999a) 'Still lingering in negative territory', *Financial Times*, 30 June.

Lucas, L. (1999b) 'Tiger rivalry: jury still out on best methods', *Financial Times*, 15 September.

Luo, Y. and Chen, M. (1997) 'Does guanxi affect company performance?', *Asia Pacific Journal of Management*, 14, 1: 1–16.

Macroscan, Economic Research Foundation, Delhi.

Mamkoottam, K. (1982) *Trade Unionism: Myth and Reality: Unionism in the Tata Iron and Steel Company*. Delhi, Oxford: OUP.

McSweeney, B. (2002) 'Hofstede's model of national cultural differences and their consequences: A triumph of faith – a failure of analysis', *Human Relations*, 55, 1: 89–118.

Mok, K., Wong, L. and Lee, G. (2002) 'The challenges of global capitalism: unemployment and state workers reactions and responses in post-reform China', *International Journal of Human Resource Management*, 13, 3: 399–415.

Montagnon, P. (1999a) 'Agonising choices accompany change', *Financial Times*, 1 October.

Montagnon, P. (1999b) 'Banking: still reluctant to change', *Financial Times*, 20 October.

Morden, T. and Bowles, D. (1998) 'Management in South Korea: a review', *Management Decision*, 36, 5: 316–330.

Murray, G. (1994) *Doing Business in China*. Kent: China Library.

Noronha, E. (2000) 'Indian Trade Unions and Globalisation: Challenges and Opportunities for the Future', www.capstrans.edu.au/confpapers/Ernesto%252Noronha.pdf+INDIAN+INFORMAL+SECTOR+AND+UNIONS&hl=en&ie=UTF–8.

OECD (2005) Full details to be supplied at proof page.

Okada, A. (2004) 'Skills development and interfirm learning linkages under globalisation: lessons from the Indian automobile industry', *World Development*, 32, 7: 1265–1288.

Ouchi, W. (1981) *Theory Z*. New York: Avon.

Paik, Y., Vance, C. and Stage, D. (1996) 'The extent of divergence in human resource practice across three Chinese national cultures: Hong Kong, Taiwan and Singapore', *Human Resource Management Journal*, 6, 2: 7–19.

Park, W. and Yu, G. (2000) 'Transformation and new patterns of HRM in Korea', Conference paper at the International Conference on Transforming Korean Business and Management Culture, Michigan State University, 19–20 September.

Parry, J.P., Breman, J. and Kapadia, K. (eds) (1999) *The Worlds of Indian Industrial Labour*. New Delhi: Sage.

Peng, F.C. (1994) 'China: managers can learn from the methods of venture partners', *South China Morning Post*, April, 13, 15.

Ramaswamy, E.A. (1984) *Power and Justice: the state in industrial relations*. Delhi: OUP.

Ramaswamy, E.A. (1994) *The Rayon Spinners: The Strategic Management of Industrial Relations*. Delhi: OUP.

Ramaswamy, E.A. (1997) *A question of balance: labour, management and society*. Delhi, New York: OUP.

Ramaswamy, E.A. and Schiphorst, F.B. (2000) 'Human resource management, trade unions and empowerment: two cases from India', *The International Journal of Human Resource Management*, 11, 4: 664–680.

Rao, T.V., Silvera, D.M., Shrivastava, C.M. and Vidyasagar, R. (eds) (1994) *HRD in the New Economic Environment*. New Delhi: Tata McGraw-Hill.

Report of the First National Commission on Labour (1969), Ministry of Labour, Government of India, Delhi.

Report of the Second National Commission on Labour (2002), Ministry of Labour, Government of India, Delhi.

Rowley, C. (1997) 'Conclusion: reassessing HRM's convergence', *Asia Pacific Business Review*, special issue: *Human Resource Management in the Asia Pacific Region: Convergence Questioned*, 3, 4: 197–210.

Rowley, C. and Bae, J. (2002) 'Globalisation and transformation of human resource management in South Korea', *International Journal of Human Resource Management*, 13, 3: 522–549.

Selmer, J., Ebrahimi, P. and Mingtao, L. (2000) 'Personal characteristics and adjustment of Chinese mainland business expatriates in Hong Kong', *International Journal of Human Resource Management*, 11, 2: 237–250.

Sengupta, A.K. and Sett, P.K. (2000) 'Industrial relations law, employment security and collective bargaining in India: myths, realities and hopes', *Industrial Relations Journal*, 31, 2: 144–153.

Sharma, I.J. (1984) 'The culture context of Indian Managers', *Management of Labour Studies*, 9, 2: 72–80.

Siddique, S. A. (1989) 'Industrial relations in a third world setting: a possible model', *The Journal of Industrial Relations*, 31: 385–401.

Singh, J.P. (1990) 'Managerial culture and work-related values in India', *Organisation Studies*, 11, 1: 75–101.

Sinha, J.B.P. and Sinha, D. (1990) 'Role of social values in Indian organisations', *International Journal of Psychology*, 25: 705–714.

Sinha, P. (2001) 'Issues before the Indian Trade Union Movement' www.fesportal.fes.de/pls/portal30/docs/FOLDER/WORLDWIDE/GEWERKSCHAFTEN/BERICHTE/INDIA.PDF.

Sparrow, P.R. and Budhwar, P.S. (1997) 'Competition and Change: Mapping the Indian HRM recipe against worldwide patterns', *Journal of World Business*, 32: 224–242.

Sparrow, P. and Wu, P-C. (1999) 'How much do national value orientations really matter? Predicting HRM preferences of Taiwanese employees', in Lahteenmaki, S., Holden, L. and Roberts, I. (eds) *HRM and the Learning Organisation*. Turku, Finland: Turku School of Economics, pp. 239–284.

Tayeb, M. (1988) *Organisations and National Culture*, London: Sage.

Taylor, P. and Bain, P. (2005) 'India calling to the far away towns' the call centre labour process and globalisation', *Work, Employment and Society*, 19, 2: 261–282.

The Economist (2005) 'The insidious charms of foreign investment, The Tiger in front: A Survey of India and China' 5–11 March, p. 7.

Thornhill, J. (2002a) 'Private enterprise seen as way forward', *Financial Times*, 12 December.

Thornhill, J. (2002b) 'Companies rush in with the cash', *Financial Times*, 12 December.

Thornhill, J. (2002c) 'Asia's recovery "exposed to oil price volatility"', *Financial Times*, 10 April.

Thornhill, J. (2002d) 'Rebuilding the tiger: five years after East Asia suffered a devastating financial crisis, John Thornhill finds that the region has gone a long way towards improving corporate governance', *Financial Times*, 5 June.

Transparency International (2005) See Global Corruption Barometer: Corruption Perceptions Index; and Regional and national surveys and indices on www.transparency.org.

Trivedi, A. (2006) *Global factory, Indian worker*, unpublished PhD thesis, University of London.

Tsang, E.W.K. (1994) 'Human resource management problems in Sino-foreign joint ventures', *Employee Relations*, 15, 9: 1–14.

UNCTAD (2005) *World Investment Report 2005. Transnational Corporations and the Internationalisation of Research and Development*. Geneva: UNCTAD.

Vachani, S. (1997) 'Economic liberalisation's effect on sources of competitive advantage of different groups of companies: the case of India', *International Business Review*, 6, 2: 165–184.

Venkata Ratnam, C.S. (1995) 'Economic liberalisation and the transformation of industrial relations policies in India' in Verma, A., Kochan, T.A. and Lansbury, R. (1995) *Employment relations in the growing Asian economies*. London, New York: Routledge.

Venkata Ratnam, C.S. (1998) 'Multinational companies in India', *International Journal of Human Resource Management*, 9, 4: 567–589.

Venkata Ratnam, C.S. (1999) *The Case of India* in ILO (1999/3) *Trade unions in the informal sector: Finding their bearings: Nine country papers*. Geneva: ILO Bureau for Workers Activities.

Venkata Ratnam, C.S. (2001) *Globalisation and labour-management relations: dynamics of change*. New Delhi: Response Books.

Ward, A. (2002a) 'Hailed as an example to other Asian countries: economic transformation by Andrew Ward: But despite dramatic progress, economic weaknesses remain', *Financial Times*, 29 October.

Ward, A. (2002b) 'Country's largest company shifts upmarket and wins accolade: Samsung Electronics', *Financial Times*, 29 October.

Ward, A. (2002c) 'Benefits of restructuring are starting to filter through', *Financial Times*, 29 October.

Ward, A. (2002e) 'Strike hits Korean car makers', *Financial Times*, 6 November.

Ward, A. (2002f) 'South Korean unions set for privatisation protest', *Financial Times*, 25 February.

Warner, M. (1992) *How Chinese Managers Learn: Management and Industrial Training in China*. London: Macmillan.

Warner, M. (1993) 'Human resource management with Chinese characteristics', *International Journal of Human Resource Management*, 4, 1: 45–65.

Warner, M. (1996) 'Human resources in the People's Republic of China: the "three systems reforms"', *Human Resource Management Journal*, 6, 2: 32–43.

Warner, M. (1997) 'Management–labour relations in the new Chinese economy', *Human Resource Management Journal*, 7, 4: 3.

Warner, M. (2000) 'Introduction: the Asia-Pacific HRM model revisited', *International Journal of Human Resource Management*, 11, 2: 171–182.

Whitley, R. (1992) *Business Systems in East Asia*. London: Sage.

Whitley, R. (1999) *Divergent Capitalisms: The Social Structuring and Change of Business Systems*. Oxford: Oxford University Press.

Whitley, R. (ed.) (2000) *Divergent Capitalisms: the social structuring and change of business systems*. Oxford: Oxford University Press.

World Bank (1999) 'China: weathering the storm and learning the lessons', *Country Studies*, 8 January: 114.

World Investment Report (2005), UNCTAD; www.unctad.org/wir.

Zhu, C. and Dowling, P. J. (2002) 'Staffing practices in translation: some empirical evidence from China', *International Journal of Human Resource Management*, 13, 4: 569–597.

Zhu, Y. and Warner, M. (2004) 'Changing Chinese patterns of human resource management in contemporary China: WTO accession and enterprise responses', *Industrial Relations Journal*. 35, 4: 311–328.

Zhu, Y. and Warner, M. (2005) 'Changing Chinese employment relations since WTO accession', *Personnel Review*, 34, 3: 354–369.

Zuboff, S. (1988) *In the Age of the Smart Machine: The Future of Work and Power*. Oxford: Heinemann Publishing.

For multiple-choice questions, exercises and annotated weblinks specific to this chapter visit the book's website at **www.pearsoned.co.uk/beardwell**

Chapter 17

International HRM

Phil Almond and Olga Tregaskis

Objectives

- To examine factors that help explain the strategy and structure of MNCs.

- To examine the structure, role, and activities of international HRM functions in MNCs and the factors influencing these configurations.

- To consider the role of international HR networks and expatriates in generating and transferring HR knowledge in MNCs.

- To examine the influence of MNC country of origin and country of operation on HRM practice.

Introduction

This chapter deals with issues relating to the management of human resources within multinational corporations (MNCs), that is, firms that directly employ people in at least two countries. Such firms represent a substantial proportion of employment. In the UK, more than 25 per cent of manufacturing employment is in the subsidiaries of foreign multinationals, as well as 11.6 per cent of total employment in services (OECD, 2006). In addition, of course, many UK-owned firms also have international operations, and therefore have to engage in international human resource management, even if, as we will see, the issues faced by UK managers will be to some extent different in British-owned to foreign-owned MNCs. Finally, it is often argued that the management practices of foreign MNCs have a wider influence on HRM in domestic firms (cf. Dunning, 1958; Oliver and Wilkinson, 1992). This is particularly the case when firms are part of the supply chain to foreign MNCs. Overall, then, a large proportion of UK managers and workers are, directly or indirectly, affected by the human resource decisions of MNCs.

Of course, from an HR perspective, this only matters if the human resource issues facing managers in MNCs are somehow different to those in purely domestic firms. In other words, does the diverse group of firms that are MNCs have something in common, that is distinctive from other firms, which means we should analyse them together? This chapter will argue that MNCs should be considered as a distinct group of organisations, in a way that has some parallels with the way in which employment relations academics have long recognised that we need to treat, say, public sector organisations as a distinct group of employers.

The chapter will therefore explain what makes the process of human resource management distinctive in an MNC. It will, for instance, reflect the fact that managing the human resources of a firm becomes more complex when those human resources work in different national societies, for reasons which can be related back to the cross-national differences in employment relations systems introduced in the previous chapter. Differences in employment law and industrial relations systems between countries mean that some HR policies and practices may be legally and socially acceptable in a firm's operations in one country, but not in another. Equally, differences in national training and education systems are likely to mean that the skill and competence profile of the workers available on the labour market will differ from one country to another. Finally, differences in national management cultures may mean that some management styles are more appropriate in some national settings than others.

These national differences, though, are not just a 'problem' for the managers of MNCs to deal with; they can also be exploited to the advantage of the firm. Indeed, much of the literature on international HRM is dominated by a concern to identify and understand how MNCs manage their geographically dispersed workforces for both local and global competitive advantage. Questions typically asked in this literature concern the circumstances in which MNCs broadly attempt to pursue uniformity of HR policies across their international operations, and those in which there are advantages to having different policies in different countries. Such differentiation may in some cases be useful in order to meet the demands of local product markets, where national differences in customer demands mean that firms have to adapt their management of labour. In other cases, differentiation may take place in order to exploit most efficiently the local labour market; MNCs which originate in high cost, highly regulated economies may well choose not to transfer important elements of their HR systems to lower wage, lightly regulated economies, for example.

Despite the demands for and benefits that MNCs can accrue from differentiation there are strong competitive reasons for these organisations to want to coordinate and integrate their activities across geographical boundaries. To maximise economies of scale MNCs attempt to coordinate activities involving scarce critical and/or costly resources. Equally, it is argued that the more management processes and activities can be integrated across geographical boundaries the easier it is to share resources and knowledge. The HRM function in MNCs play a critical role in developing systems and process that promote internal consistency in how employees are treated. They also need to consider how they can identify and best use the skill and management talent that exists across the distributed MNC network. At the same time the desire for standardisation and integration in HRM needs to take account of the country differences that give rise to different employee expectations, perceptions and skills levels. This raises questions about how the international HR function can organise itself to address both the demands for integration and localisation. Which HRM activities should be coordinated or controlled by the corporate HR function and which activities should be localised? How can the HR function structure itself best address these competing demands for integration and localisation? And more recently the literature in the field has been concerned with how HR knowledge can be transferred across the MNC and whether global HR practices can be created from knowledge drawn from the subsidiaries as much as from that generated by the centre or corporate HR function.

These varying literatures and debates are considered in this chapter. We begin with the organisational focused literature by introducing the international strategic context MNCs operate within which then leads into the alternative models that have been proposed to explain how the international HR function is organised and its role. We then consider how HR knowledge is transferred focusing specifically on the role of international HR networks and expatriates. The chapter then shifts its focus to the national context literature and moves on to analyse the extent to which international HRM is affected by the national ownership of firms, and by the countries in which they operate. The role of managers in dealing with different national systems of employment relations (see Chapter 15) is highlighted here.

The international strategic context

The introduction to this chapter indicated that additional insights are necessary in order to understand HR management in MNCs, for the simple reason that one thing that all MNCs share is the challenge of coordinating managers and workers in more than one country. At the most basic level, this creates dilemmas for managers about the extent to which the firm should pursue consistent HR policies across its different national operations, or allow foreign subsidiaries to pursue the policies which are seen as appropriate for the specific national employment systems involved.

Clearly, however, all MNCs are not the same; they vary enormously along dimensions such as size, the number of foreign countries in which they have workforces, and in their degree of internationalisation (that is, the proportion of the firm's workforce, and of its sales, which are outside the original home country) and these differences impact greatly on the nature of management within such firms.

Differences in MNC structure

It is sometimes argued that some of the differences between international firms mean that, when discussing international management, we should distinguish between MNCs with different structural forms, and discuss the nature of management processes within each, rather than simply referring to 'multinational corporations' as if this group of firms were homogenous.

International business strategists have attempted to generate theory that makes it easier to interpret the complex world of international business. One of the best known is Prahalad and Doz's (1987) Integration–Responsiveness (IR) Grid. They argue that MNCs are faced with pressures to integrate and coordinate their activities on the one hand and on the other to respond to local (national) variations. The pressures driving integration and responsiveness faced by MNCs are summarised in Table 17.1.

These two pressures, namely integration and responsiveness, form the Integration–Responsiveness grid and MNCs adopt different strategies and structures depending on where they sit within this grid (see Harzing, 1999 for an in-depth review). So for example in a multi-domestic industry, such as utilities (e.g. water services) consumer demands and service provision are highly context specific. Thus the competitive strategy of a multinational's French subsidiary, for example, is largely independent of that of its UK counterpart. This is necessary because regulatory requirements, customer norms or government policy require a strategy that is responsive to local conditions. As such these subsidiaries compete in domestic markets and frequently with domestic companies. Equally, a decentralised organisational structure where subsidiaries are given a high degree of strategic and operational autonomy from its parent is the most efficient. However, often the parent retains some degree of control through setting performance targets. This type of organisation would be located in the bottom right-hand side of the grid (Figure 17.1). By contrast, in a global industry, such as consumer electronics, standardised product/service demands by customers and economies of scale dominate. The organisation's strategy prioritises efficiencies by producing standardised products, locating in the most cost effective economies and coordinating expensive resources such as equipment, or R&D. These organisations tend to centralise resources and responsibilities to the parent company, while the role of the subsidiaries tends to be sales and services. The strategic responsibility and operational freedom of subsidiaries is usually fairly tightly controlled by the parent. This type of organisation would be located in the top left-hand side of the grid.

There is a considerable degree of empirical evidence supporting the existence of multi-domestic and global organisational forms (Bartlett and Ghoshal, 1989; Harzing, 2000; Leong and Tan, 1993; Moenaert Caeldries, Commandeur and Peelen, 1994; Roth and Morrison, 1990). And the I–R grid is a simple and effective tool for explaining the key priorities shaping these organisations' strategies and structures. However, it is less effective at capturing the significance of the transfer of learning and innovation, which is an important strategic priority for the third type of international organisation, namely the transnational.

Table 17.1 Summary of the pressures making up the I–R grid

I–R grid	Pressures
Strategic coordination need is high where:	• Multinational customers are a large proportion of the customer base. For example, it is important to coordinate pricing, service and product support worldwide as the multinational customer has the ability to compare prices on this basis. • Global competition is likely. If companies operate in multiple markets global competition is highly likely. As such it is important to monitor and collect information on competitors' activities in the different countries in readiness for an appropriate and timely strategic response. • Investment in one or more parts of the business is high. For example, high-tech manufacturing or R&D are common high fixed costs. To maximise the benefits and yield the best return on capital investments global coordination is necessary.
Operational integration need is high where:	• Technological intensity is high. Technology intensive businesses often require a small number of manufacturing sites that enable quality and costs to be centrally controlled while serving wide geographically dispersed markets. • Cost reduction is a priority. This can be achieved through locating in low cost economies or building plants designed to maximise economies of scale. • The product is universal and requires minimal adaptation to local markets. This is typical in consumer electronics. • Manufacturing needs to be located close to essential raw materials or energy such as in the petrochemicals business.
Local responsiveness is high where:	• Customer demands vary across nations or regions. • Distribution channels need to be tailored to the characteristics of the country or region. For example, marketing of products may need to be nationally specific. • There are other similar products or where the product needs to be adapted to local needs. • Local competitors rather than multinational competitors define the market competition. • The host country places restrictions on the operating subsidiary.

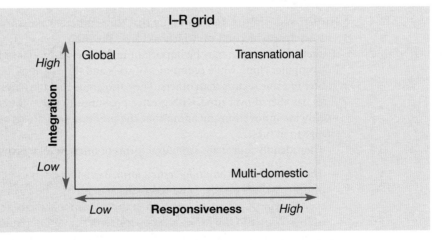

Figure 17.1 I–R grid

Stop
&
think

- *What sources of pressure are likely to demand strategic responsiveness by a multinational? Explain.*
- *What consequences does the pursuit of economic efficiencies have on local economies?*

Suggested reading: Ghoshal and Bartlett (1998) Managing Across Borders. *London: Random House: Part 1, pp. 1–81.*

Another prominent model in the international management literature is that developed by Bartlett and Ghoshal (1989). Their work elaborates on issues around innovation and knowledge transfer in MNCs. Like Prahalad and Doz (1987) they identify the different pressures facing firms, which push them towards different structural forms. Two of the pressures they identify share much in common with Prahalad and Doz's concepts of integration and responsiveness. However, they also identify a third pressure, namely, worldwide innovation. Each of these are discussed in more detail below.

- *Local differentiation.* This refers to pressures emanating from 'local' (which usually in this context means national) markets to offer distinctive products, or to offer services in a distinctive way. This can be caused by consumer tastes; for example, a supermarket chain seeking to operate in both the UK and Spain would have to take account of the fact that there is a much higher demand for fresh produce, and regional products, in Spain, and a higher demand for packaged meals in the UK. This might affect the necessary skills profile of the workforce in the two countries, and also would be likely to affect the way in which the national operations think about distribution and marketing. In other cases, pressures for local differentiation are brought about by national regulations; this is often the case in the utilities sector, for example.

- *Global integration.* Bartlett and Ghoshal argue that the technological developments of the last half-century mean that economies of scale became increasingly crucial to competitive success. In order to achieve the scale necessary to gain competitive advantage, firms may seek to create integrated production processes in different parts of the world. For example, in automobile production it is common for different parts of vehicles to be manufactured in different national subsidiaries of the major companies.

- *Worldwide innovation.* Here, the argument is that firms have come under increasing pressure to increase the pace of innovation, as markets and technologies evolve rapidly. In this context, Bartlett and Ghoshal argue that a logical response for many international firms is to encourage and support innovation in a coordinated way across their different international operations, rather than simply to rely on the innovative capacities of the original home country operations of the firm.

Bartlett and Ghoshal further argue that these different pressures exist to differing extents. This will partly depend on which sector(s) the MNC is operating in; national differences in markets, for example, may be important in food retail, but far less so (if at all) in the market for computer chips, while economies of scale and the extent of radical innovation will also be greater in some sectors than others. They also argue that the nature, and extent, of these pressures has altered over time, with greater pressures for global integration and particularly for worldwide innovation, meaning that the predominant structural forms of MNCs should change to fit these.

They identify four main structural forms of international firms. These are:

- *The multinational ('multidomestic') form.* Bartlett and Ghoshal, in common with a number of other writers on international management, use the term 'multinational' to refer to a specific type of structure, rather than to international firms in general. As we have chosen in this chapter to use MNC as a generic term for all international firms, to minimise terminological confusion we will refer to the type of firm Bartlett and Ghoshal mean here as 'multidomestic'. A multidomestic structure means that the headquarters of the MNC does not attempt to control strictly what happens in overseas subsidiaries, so these operate on a largely autonomous basis. Such firms are highly decentralised in HR, with little or no attempt to transfer practices across borders. Equally, few attempts are made at knowledge transfer. To a large extent, the relations between the HQ and foreign subsidiaries are confined to flows of finance. This structure is associated with circumstances in which customer tastes vary greatly from one nation to another, or where there are strong regulatory differences between countries, creating markets which are strongly national in nature.

Bartlett and Ghoshal associate this form with the first half of the twentieth century, but it should be noted that the multidomestic form of MNCs continues to exist in markets such as utility sectors, where national regulation makes extensive attempts at international coordination by HQ largely counterproductive.

- *The global form.* This is essentially a model in which HQ management takes home country management approaches, and tries to replicate them abroad in order to achieve economies of scale. In this model, there is a clear hierarchy, with HQ instructing foreign managers how to manage their operations, or using a high number of expatriate managers for the same reason. Strategic decisions will exclusively be taken at HQ level, with research and development also concentrated in the home country. This model of international management is most likely in markets where economies of scale are critical to competitive advantage. Bartlett and Ghoshal associate this model with the period between 1950 and 1980, although cases where HQ strongly directs policy abroad, and concentrates knowledge in the home base, continue to exist.

- *The international form.* In the global form, MNCs replicate a production technology worldwide, in order to produce an identical product in different national operations. The international firm goes one step beyond this, in that HQs become increasingly cognisant of cross-national differences in consumer demands. They export knowledge and expertise to foreign subsidiaries, but allow local management the ability to alter the nature of products and services to suit the nature of the local market. In these firms, control is somewhat less tight than in global firms, but the general tone of policy is still likely to flow from the HQ to subsidiaries.

- *The transnational firm.* In this final type of MNC, the firm moves away from being a hierarchy, with the HQ at the top and the various national subsidiaries below, and towards what is sometimes referred to as a 'heterarchy' (Nohria and Ghoshal, 1997), or network form of organisation. In such 'transnational' firms, then, management control is dispersed across the corporation, rather than being concentrated at HQ. Unlike in the previous three forms of international organisation, the various international units of the enterprise are highly interdependent. Because of this, there are extensive flows of people, knowledge and resources not just from HQ to foreign subsidiaries (as is frequent in the global and international forms), but also from foreign subsidiaries to HQ, and between different foreign subsidiaries. Such firms achieve coordination through shared decision making, aided by attempts to create a common managerial culture across the firm (sometimes referred to as 'normative integration', see Birkinshaw and Morrison, 1995: 737), rather than through rule-making from HQ. According to Bartlett and Ghoshal (1989), this network form of organisation allows international firms systematically to transfer learning and knowledge across their various international operations, while offering a more flexible, responsive form of coordination than the three previous models of organisation.

Stop & think

How do you think the role of a foreign subsidiary HR manager would differ between a multidomestic, global, international and transnational MNC?

As we mentioned above, Bartlett and Ghoshal argue that the most appropriate structure for MNCs has altered over time, with a broad movement from the multidomestic through to the transnational form. In the current context of internationalised markets, rapid transformations in production technology and product markets, and the need to combine global economies of scale with local or regional adaptability, they clearly argue that large MNCs, at least, should follow the transnational model.

In reality, though, many of even the larger MNCs do not follow the transnational model. There are several reasons for this. First, as Bartlett and Ghoshal would acknowledge, there remain product markets which are so nationally specific as to make the transnational structure an inappropriate organisational structure. Second, their models downplay the importance of organisational politics (Edwards and Rees, 2006: 77–81); the transnational structure is difficult to coordinate as, in reality, managers in different countries are liable to pursue their own objectives, with the result that the strategy of an international organisation which is not strongly hierarchical is more likely to be the result of continual negotiation rather than of rational planning. In other words, it is difficult for the senior executives of an organisation to create a rational network structure; how the network operates in reality will be affected by the range of managerial actors within the international organisation. Finally, Bartlett and Ghoshal largely ignore the extent to which MNC structures and strategies are affected both by the countries they originate from, and the countries they operate in. Such effects will be examined in a later section of this chapter.

Section summary

In summary, Prahalad and Doz provided an effective and simple model for appreciating the two competing pressures, integration and responsiveness, and their impact on MNC structures. However, their work underemphasised the importance of global innovation and knowledge transfer. This is addressed to a greater extent by Bartlett and Ghoshal who offer a fourfold typology of MNC structures; some of the effects of positioning along these dimensions on HRM and the international transfer of knowledge and learning will be explored below. They argue that pressures on such organisations to combine local differentiation, global integration and worldwide innovation mean that the transnational model is increasingly the most appropriate model to follow. However, it is increasingly argued (Ferner, 1997; Edwards and Rees, 2006) that Bartlett and Ghoshal's typology underestimates the roles of organisational politics and of national setting in determining how MNCs really operate. For this reason, many MNCs, even if they are seeking to achieve local differentiation, global integration and worldwide innovation, may not in reality operate according to the transnational model.

Configuration of the international HRM function

International HRM is defined as:

> The set of distinct activities, functions and processes that are directed at attracting, developing and maintaining an MNC's human resources. It is thus the aggregate of the various HRM systems used to manage people in the MNC, both at home and overseas.
>
> (Taylor, Beechler and Napier, 1996: 960)

Here we consider the models of international HRM that have been put forward to explain how the HR function is configured, the activities and roles undertaken and the factors affecting these. It is interesting to consider how external and institutional factors are treated within these models, an issue that will be explored in more detail in the latter part of this chapter. Since the early 1990s the international HRM literature has been dominated by models and typologies aimed at identifying the role and structure of international HRM functions aligned with organisational strategy. As a result of the attempt to 'explicitly link IHRM with the strategy of the MNC' (Taylor *et al.*, 1996: 960), this body of work is tightly tied to developments on multinational strategy-structure and is 'built on antecedents that are decades old' (p. 961). The human resource management systems at the international and national levels are seen as the mechanisms through which competitive demands are potentially realised. The key theoretical work in the field of international HRM thus draws heavily on the strategy-structure work of the international management researchers, most notably Bartlett and Ghoshal (1989), Hedlund (1986) and Prahalad and Doz (1987). The types of concerns that dominate this field are how such organisations can most efficiently structure their geographically dispersed operations to meet both global and local competitive demands? What is the nature of the control relationship between the parent and its subsidiaries? These questions in turn raise issues for international HRM in terms of what types of human resource management activity should be centralised to maximise integration and meet globalisation strategic imperatives, and what should be decentralised to allow localisation of policy and practice and to maximise local competitive advantage.

The five approaches reviewed here have each had a profound effect on the debates and theoretical development in this field. However, they each differ in the nature of the contribution they make. First, we will consider the Schuler *et al.* model which was developed as an analytical framework pulling together various conceptual and empirical work in the field providing researchers with a potential roadmap of the internal and external organisational factors influencing the issues, function, practices and impacts of international HRM. The importance of national context is recognised but not specified. Second, Taylor and colleagues (1996) focused on the conditions under which the parent was more likely to exercise control over its subsidiaries' activities. In particular the model emphasised the resource dependencies that existed between the parent and its subsidiaries. This says little about national contextual issues, but is important for unlike much previous writing in the field it recognises that subsidiaries of multinationals have much greater ability to control their own action and influence the degree of parent control over them by using resources that the parent needs as a means of trading or negotiating. The third model shifts its focus from the international HR function to the influence of management perceptions on multinational strategy. Perlmutter identifies variation in the mindsets or ways of thinking about the international environment, which he argues can affect the international nature of the organisation's management processes. This model has had a profound effect on international HRM debates for it underpins much of the theorising on the role of corporate HR functions in multinationals (e.g. Schuler, Dowling and De Cieri, 1993). The fourth and fifth models, by Adler and Ghadar (1990) and Milliman and Von Glinow (1990) respectively, are models of organisational change. They focus more on the relative influence of host and home country factors in shaping the role of the international HR function and in particular the role of expatriate managers in enabling international strategy. Both models adopt a similar perspective in terms of seeing the multinational progress through various stages of internationalisation, with each stage bringing into focus the importance of home and host country priorities. Here we see the potential for overlap between much of the comparative work and international HR theory, however as will be illustrated the discussion of home and host contextual issues is scant.

Schuler, Dowling and De Cieri (1993): integrative framework of international HRM

The Schuler *et al.* (1993) integrative framework of international HRM was, in essence, a conceptual framework that attempted to map HRM activity to the varying strategic requirements for integration and local responsiveness which define MNC strategy (Figure 17.2). Because of this it is extremely comprehensive in terms of the breadth of issues addressed although this is at the expense of depth in the explanation of these issues. This framework built upon the work of strategic HRM theorists researching HRM in domestic companies (Boam and Sparrow, 1992; Schuler, 1992; Lengnick-Hall and Lengnick-Hall, 1988; Wright and McMahan, 1992). As such, Schuler *et al.* define strategic international HRM as:

> Human resource management issues, functions, policies and practices that result from the strategic activities of multinational enterprises and that impact the international concerns and goals of those enterprises.

| Figure 17.2 | Integrative framework of strategic international HRM in MNEs |

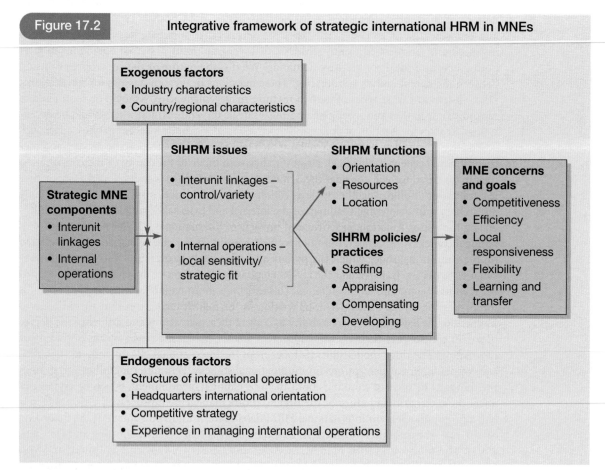

Source: Schuler et al. (1993: 722).

The overlap between the study of domestic and international HRM is discussed explicitly by Taylor *et al.* (1996: 960):

> Strategic Human Resource Management (SHRM) ..., is used to explicitly link with the strategic management processes of the organisation and to emphasise coordination or congruence among various human resource management practices. Thus, SIHRM is used to explicitly link IHRM with the strategy of the MNC.

This integrative framework of SIHRM identifies a series of strategic MNE (multinational enterprise) components, endogenous factors and exogenous factors that shape the issues, policy, practices and functions of HRM in international organisations. These determinants are explained, briefly:

1 Strategic MNE components include interunit linkages and internal operations. Interunit linkage is concerned with the need to differentiate or integrate several operations which are geographically dispersed (Ghoshal and Bartlett, 1998; Prahalad and Doz, 1987). Internal operations refer to how each unit operates within its local environment. The restrictions of national institutional or legislative frameworks are recognised along with the cultural diversity in attitudes towards work, management, authority and so forth (Hofstede, 1980; Laurent, 1983; Schein, 1984).

2 Exogenous factors relate to issues external to the organisation. For example, industry characteristics such as type of business and technology available, nature of competitors, degree

of change; and country/regional characteristics such as political conditions, economic conditions, legal requirements and socio-cultural context. They also argue that an extended version of this framework would include issues such as industry maturity, history, national industrial policy and level of unionisation. Here there is a clear overlap with the issues discussed by the comparative researchers.

3 Endogenous factors relate to internal organisational issues. For example, structure of the organisation, experience, or stage of internationalisation, competitive strategy and headquarter's international orientation.

Essentially the above three aspects of the framework bring together the work of the international management theorist and argue for their impingement on the management of human resources throughout the organisation. Specifically they argue that the strategic components, exogenous and endogenous factors affect the SIHRM function and associated policies and practices. The function can be affected in terms of its:

(a) orientation, i.e. the extent to which control of local activities are centralised or decentralised;

(b) the amount of financial and time resources committed to the development and management of international managers;

(c) where activities are located, i.e. in the local unit or at the corporate centre. Policies and practices are affected in terms of how they are developed and implemented to promote local autonomy, global coordination and integration.

Using agency theory (Jones, 1984) and resource dependency theory (Pfeffer and Salancik, 1978) Schuler *et al.* (1993) propose that an organisation's approach to HRM will vary between using a high level of parent country nationals and normative control measures to direct local behaviour versus high levels of local or third country nationals and normative control measures to enable the centre to guide policies while still allowing for local adaptation. HR philosophy will play a key role in providing local sites with general statements to guide their practices so they are in tune with the corporate approach but locally sensitive. There is also a need for local HR policy to fit with corporate policy if personnel are to be able to be selected, transferred and developed as an organisational resource as opposed to a subsidiary resource. As such they argue that in order for multinational companies to be flexible and adaptable to local circumstance, transfer learning and to retain strategic integration HR practices need to match strategic and cultural demands at the local level. A 'modus operandi' needs to be developed to enable HR practices to fit changing circumstances. While global HR policies need to be developed to be flexible enough to be applied to local HR practice. This perspective therefore not only focuses on HR policies and practices for the management of international managers but HR policies and practices for the management of local employees.

As indicated earlier, the role of national institutional factors is incorporated within the framework. Specifically, they argue uncertain political environments and high economic risk demand greater monitoring and control from the parent. While, high levels of heterogeneity, and complexity in legislative conditions affecting labour relations are likely to lead to the greater utilisation of local employees, rather than expatriates, in senior management positions at the subsidiary level. They also recognise that cultural diversity will demand greater attention by HR professionals in contexts where there is a business demand for integration and co-ordination. Thus the effects of the national institutional context are recognised in terms of the degree of control or autonomy given to the subsidiary by the parent and in terms of the centrality of expatriates.

The relationship between organisational structures and strategic international HRM policy and practice is discussed in relation to four organisational strategy–structures configurations, namely, the international divisional structure, the multinational structure, the global and the transnational. They state:

> Different structures of international operations create different requirements for autonomy, localisation and co-ordination, thus affecting the nature of and extent of SIHRM policies and practices; and the structures of the international operations of the MNE will impact the need for the units to develop mechanisms to respond to local conditions and to develop a flexible capability.
>
> (p. 446)

Given this, Schuler and colleagues propose that international divisional structures result in a strategic international HRM orientation that focuses on a single issue namely the selection of senior managers to head up local operations. The multinational structure focuses on selecting managers from anywhere in the company that can run local operations autonomously and with sensitivity to local conditions. The global structure requires a strategic international HRM orientation that selects managers who can operate under centralised control conditions. The transnational structure requires selecting and developing managers that can balance both local and global perspectives. Here again we see that the focus of the model is on explaining and matching the internal HR resources, via recruitment, selection or development, to meet the strategic needs of the organisations.

Schuler *et al.* (1993: 753) conclude that strategic international HRM is concerned with:

> Developing a fit between exogeneous and endogenous factors and balancing the competing demands of global versus local requirements as well as the needs of coordination, control and autonomy.

Whilst the model is comprehensive it has been criticised for failing to explain the micro-political processes that underpin parent–subsidiary relations (Quintanilla, 1999) and for being overly descriptive (Holden, 2000). In addition, whilst the model alludes to the impact of international HRM on both the international and local workforces, in reality the discussion tends to focus on management employees only (Ferner, 1994).

Using Schuler et al.'s framework of SIHRM:

(a) Identify the key concerns of the HRM function at the headquarters level.

(b) Identify the key concerns of the HRM function at the subsidiary level.

What is the role of the HR philosophy in MNCs?

Suggested reading: Schuler, R. Dowling, P. and De Cieri, H. (1993) 'An integrative framework of strategic international human resource management', Journal of Management, 19, 2, 419–459.

Taylor, Beechler and Napier (1996): exportive, integrative and adaptive model

Taylor *et al.* (1996) apply the resource-based theory of the firm to explain and predict why international organisations adopt different forms of strategic international HRM. Resource-based theory of the firm (Barney, 1991) applied to HR issues (Lado and Wilson, 1994) argues that HR can facilitate strategic goals by developing competencies within the organisation that are valuable, rare, hard to imitate and non-substitutable. Competencies are:

- *valuable* if they are differentiated and provide the company with something that they lack;
- *rare* if they are scarce or in short supply;

- *hard* to imitate where, for example, they are embedded within the firm's culture or history and thus based on collective values;
- *non-substitutable* where they cannot easily be replaced through recruitment, for example, in the case of tacit knowledge.

Applying this perspective, Taylor *et al.* suggested that the multinational could leverage resources at the national, firm and subsidiary level that could contribute to competitive advantage. Some of these resources would be context specific while others were context generalisable. This is illustrated by the exportative, integrative and adoptive strategic international HRM orientations towards corporate, subsidiary and employee group level HR issues, policies and practices. The concepts of these three SIHRM forms are based on previous work in international management and SIHRM (Hedlund, 1986; Perlmutter, 1969; Rosenzweig and Nohria, 1994; Rosenzweig and Singh, 1991). Each of these three orientations are explained below:

- *Adaptive*. HRM reflects subsidiary HRM systems designed to match the local environment. Differentiation is emphasised and HRM is concerned with the appointment of local senior managers but also with little transfer of HRM philosophies, policies, or practices from the parent to subsidiary or between subsidiaries. This approach focuses on attending to local differentiation needs and is polycentric in nature.
- *Exportive*. HRM focuses on replication of parent HR systems in subsidiaries. Integration is a key priority and all HRM functions are affected not just the international 'cadre' (managers). This approach focuses on maximising global integration and is ethnocentric in nature.
- *Integrative*. HRM is based on the notion of taking the best HRM systems from anywhere in the company and allowing for both global integration and local differentiation and is geocentric in nature.

At the level of the subsidiary the strategic international HRM orientation determines the level of transfer of parent HRM systems, which is based on the resource-dependency relationship between the parent and subsidiary. For example, exportive HRM leads to high control by the parent which promotes a high level of transfer of its HRM systems to achieve global integration. Under these conditions the subsidiary is highly dependent on the parent for HR systems and processes to enable integration. In contrast the adaptive HRM orientation demands little control and transfer of practices by the parent as differentiation is the priority. Under these conditions resource-dependency by both the parent and subsidiary is low. In the middle we have the integrative orientation which demands a balance between the transfer of some systems while maintaining the flexibility in the system to allow the subsidiary to adapt to the local context. Under these conditions, there is a parent–subsidiary inter-dependency. Finally, from the resource-dependence perspective they argue that parent control and standardisation of parent and subsidiary practice will be greater in those areas affecting employees 'most critical to the MNC's performance' (Taylor *et al.*, 1996: 978).

Taylor *et al.* also recognise that there are a number of factors that are likely to constrain the degree of parent control over subsidiary behaviour, namely method of subsidiary establishment, cultural and legal distance of host country from the parent or home country of the multinational. With respect to the first of these points the evidence suggests that subsidiaries that have been acquired have less in common with their parent HR systems than those that are greenfield sites, although this pattern may change over time. Equally, the greater the dissimilarity between the parent company's national culture and legal context, the less commonality between the parent and subsidiary's HR systems. This would follow from many of the institutional arguments outlined in Chapter 15.

Their work raises a number of implications. First, unlike much of the previous work Taylor *et al.* (1996) are more explicit about the impact of SIHRM on different occupational groups. They recognise that not all employees provide the same level of value to the company or provide the same level of critical resources. Traditionally broad distinctions have been made between white collar and blue collar workers. However, there is a need to refine this further by looking at other occupational groups that may be critical to competitive advantage, such as research staff or product designers. Second, their work raises a key question about the generalisability of HR practice beyond the context in which it was developed. What aspects of HRM practice are generalisable? Why? Third, and finally, their model lacks specificity with regard to what is transferred and how.

Activity

Now read the section below on Perlmutter's mindsets and consider the following question. Taylor *et al.* (1996) argued that the exportive, adaptive and integrative SIHRM orientations are linked to Perlmutter's ethnocentric, polycentric and geocentric mindsets respectively. Explain why and what this means for HRM practice in the case of each of the three orientations.

Suggested reading: Taylor, S, Beechler, S. and Napier, N. (1996) 'Toward an integrative model of strategic international human resource management', *Academy of Management Review*, 21, 4, 959–985.

Perlmutter (1969): mindsets

Perlmutter (1969) is widely recognised as one of the first theorists to propose a network-based model of how international companies organise globally. Perlmutter's classification has been applied primarily in the international human resource management literature rather than the international business field, from where it originated. Kobrin (1994) explains that Perlmutter's adoption by the international HRM theorists is largely because the classification is defined in terms of human resource management issues (e.g. training, recruiting, selecting people and resources). Perlmutter initially defined three organisational types based on senior management's cognitions or mindsets: the ethnocentric, polycentric and geocentric organisation. Later he defined a fourth mindset namely, the regiocentric. He argues that senior management mindsets reflect the extent to which home, host, global or regional values are perceived as important and in turn influence the international nature of management processes used in the company. These mindsets have been adopted by many in the international HRM field as a way of classifying different HRM approaches, for example:

- *The ethnocentric mindset* reflects a focus on home country values and ways of operating. As a consequence key positions in subsidiaries are filled by parent country nationals (i.e. expatriates). This gives the parent a high degree of direct control over the subsidiaries' operations.

- *The polycentric mindset* focuses on host country values and ways of operating. As a result key positions in the subsidiary are more likely to be filled by local employees and the parent company is less interested in controlling and homogenising the organisational culture.

- *The geocentric mindset* focuses on global values and ways of operating. These global values are not nationally specific but instead transcend national boundaries and become almost acultural. This approach looks to use the best people for the job selecting from all over the global organisation.

- *The regiocentric mindset* focuses on regional values and ways of operating. As a result the organisation is usually structured along regional geographical lines (e.g. Europe, America, and Asia Pacific Rim) and employees move around within these regions. This approach allows some degree of integration, but recognises regional diversity.

Schuler *et al.* incorporate Perlmutter's ideas into their framework arguing that these attitudes underpin a multinational's strategic international HRM orientation in terms of autonomy and standardisation of local HR practice (e.g. staffing, appraisal, compensation and training). The ethnocentric mindset promotes control and centralisation of HR activity, the polycentric mindset is aligned with local decentralisation, the geocentric mindset does not develop HR activity on the basis of nationality. We also saw how these mindsets were associated with

Taylor *et al.*'s integrative, adaptive and exportive orientations. While these relationships are somewhat scant in their detail they allude to the widening scope of the role of a corporate strategic international HRM function as organisational structures become more complex and network-like rather than hierarchical in nature. One of the primary problems with Perlmutter's approach is that it provides little explanation of how or why the organisation may move from one type of mindset orientation to another.

Adler and Ghadar (1990) and Milliman and Von Glinow (1990): organisational change models

Two models have been put forward that are based on organisational change models namely the product life cycle model of Adler and Ghadar (1990) and the organisational life cycle model of Milliman and Von Glinow (1990). These models have been designed to explain how and why the international HRM orientation of a multinational change over time in line with changes in its corporate strategy. Both approaches also recognise the variable importance of the parent or home country context and the host country context throughout each stage. In doing so they take a largely cultural approach.

The Adler and Ghadar (1990) model is based on the product life cycle (PLC) during internationalisation, first observed and described by Vernon (1966), and is a stage model of organisational change. In Adler and Ghadar's model they describe how the role of culture changes in salience and how HRM activities are modified at each stage in response to product strategic requirements and cultural requirements. These phases are described briefly in Table 17.2.

- *Phase I: Domestic.* Here the focus is on the home market. The products/services are unique, they have not been available before, therefore the price is high relative to cost and competition is minimal. As the products are unique there is no need for cultural sensitivity and if they are exported they are in a significantly strong position not to need adaptation. Indeed exportation of the product/service is based on the premise that 'foreigners' want the product/service unadapted. The HR needs are therefore not that demanding in international terms, i.e. expatriate assignments, internal business trips, cross-cultural training are not warranted for the export market. The international work is restricted to product or project specific technical competence (Mendenhall, Dunbar and Oddou, 1989). As domestic sales tend to dominate profits international aspects of management are not given to the best people nor seen as a valuable career move. International organisational development is not seen as relevant.

- *Phase II: International.* Here competition increases and international markets become more important for profit. There is a shift in focus from product development (R&D) to manufacturing and plants are set up locally and divisional structures emerge. Cultural sensitivity becomes critical to effective corporate strategies. However, decision making and control tend to remain with the parent. HR performs a vital role in attaining control of local operations. Home country personnel are used to transfer technology and management systems overseas where replication, rather than innovation, is the prime objective. Training in cultural sensitivity and adaptability is key at this stage.

- *Phase III: Multinational.* Here the product/service reaches maturity, competition is intense and the price has fallen. Coordination of resources becomes a vital tool in the reduction of costs. The role of culture becomes less important as the issue of reducing costs takes central position. As such the best people are usually chosen for international posts to increase profits and control costs. The management assumption at this phase is that organisational culture is more important than national culture therefore sensitivity to local cultures is seen to be less important and recruitment of international managers tends to be from those familiar with the parent culture.

- *Phase IV: Global.* The three prior phases were based on hierarchical structures. This phase is based on the assumption that the organisation will need to operate in all three phases simultaneously and therefore build 'complex networks of joint ventures, wholly owned subsidiaries and organisational and project defined alliances' (Adler and Ghadar, 1990: 240). Under such conditions the role of culture comes again to the fore. These organisations operate at a strategic level to combine responsive design and delivery quickly and cheaply. This negates the development of global R&D, production and marketing and therefore requires the management of culture and relationships external to the organisation. Success is based on international managers being able to communicate effectively in a culturally diverse environment. The delineation between expatriate and local managers disappears and the organisation needs to manage the dual demands of integration and local responsiveness (Doz and Prahalad, 1986).

Table 17.2 Globalisation and human resource management

	Phase I Domestic	Phase II International	Phase III Multinational	Phase IV Global
Primary orientation	Product or service	Market	Price	Strategy
Strategy	Domestic	Multidomestic	Multinational	Global
Worldwide strategy	Allow foreign clients to buy product/service	Increase market internationally, transfer technology abroad	Source, produce and market internationally	Gain global strategic competitive advantage
Staffing expatriates	None (few)	Many	Some	Many
Why sent	Junket	To sell control or transfer technology	Control	Coordination and integration
Whom sent		'OK' performers, salespeople	Very good performers	High-potential managers and top executives
Purpose	Reward	Project 'To get job done'	Project and career development	Career and organisational development
Career impact	Negative	Bad for domestic career	Important for global career	Essential for executive suite
Professional re-entry	Somewhat difficult	Extremely difficult	Less difficult	Professionally easy
Training and development	None	Limited	Longer	Continuous throughout career
For whom	No one	Expatriates	Expatriates	Managers
Performance appraisal	Corporate bottom line	Subsidiary bottom line	Corporate bottom line	Strategic positioning
Motivation assumption	Money motivates	Money and adventure	Challenge and opportunity	Challenge, opportunity, advancement
Rewarding	Extra money to compensate for foreign hardship		Less generous, global packages	
Career 'fast track'	Domestic	Domestic	Token international	Global
Executive passport	Home country	Home country	Home country, token foreigners	Multinational
Necessary skills	Technical and managerial	Plus cultural adaption	Plus recognising cultural differences	Plus cross-cultural interaction, influence and synergy

Source: Adler and Ghadar, 1990.

Drawing on your understanding of the PLC model consider the role of expatriates, local employees, host national culture and organisational training during each phase.

	Phase I	Phase II	Phase III	Phase IV
Expatriates	• Expatriates are from the parent company. • Focus on the transfer of technical competence to overseas operations; otherwise input is limited.			
Local employees				
Host national culture				
Organisational training				

Suggested reading: Adler, N. and Ghadar, F. (1990) 'Strategic human resource management: a global perspective', in R. Pieper *Human Resource Management: An International Comparison*. Berlin: Walter de Gruyter.

However, the Adler and Ghadar (1990) model is criticised for its emphasis on the role of the expatriate manager and management expertise, with little reference to other employee groups. Milliman and Von Glinow (1990) also argue that as it focuses on a product life cycle it is too narrow. International organisations often have multiple products and the stage of the cycle may vary across the strategic business units (SBU) changing the parent–SBU relationship. Therefore in response Milliman and Von Glinow (1990) apply the organisational life cycle (OLC) approach to provide a more general framework to understanding SIHRM at the parent and subsidiary level. This model was further refined in the paper by Milliman, Von Glinow and Nathan (1991). This approach is based on the premise that HRM responses will predictably vary in line with stages of organisational development. Their work highlights the importance of recognising the inter-relationships between the parent and subsidiary level in defining the nature of international HRM. They note that:

> The degree to which the corporate business and human resource strategies affect the SBU's strategic choices and practices depends on a number of fundamental characteristics of the MNC, such as its organisational culture, management style, and control systems.
>
> (Milliman and Von Glinow, 1990: 28)

The Milliman and Von Glinow (1990) model identifies four international HRM objectives, namely, timing, cost versus development, integration and differentiation:

● *Timing* refers to whether the organisation takes a short-term or long-term perspective in its business and international HRM strategy. The former requires quick responses the latter allows a longer period for implementation, which can mean longer international assignments and commitment to overseas operations.

- *Cost* refers to whether the organisation needs to focus on lowering costs or can focus on longer-term development issues in its overseas operations and the career paths of its expatriate managers.

- *Integration* relates to the use of expatriate managers in implementing informal control systems.

- *Differentiation* refers to the development of a network of home and host country managers to facilitate communication and control between the parent and subsidiary.

- These four objectives change over four OLC stages leading to a different pattern of international HRM. These stages are now explained in brief:

- *Stage 1.* As the firm starts out most of the international HRM is conducted on an ad hoc basis and international assignments focus on technical work skills with little emphasis on cultural training. The need for integration or differentiation is minimal.

- *Stage 2.* The number and extent of commitment in overseas operation increases. Short-term savings remain a priority and the need of integration is minimal. However, for successive growth of the overseas markets greater knowledge of the local environment is needed. Thus expatriate training in cultural sensitivity and languages becomes more important.

- *Stage 3.* As the business becomes well established, the organisation can take a longer-term perspective and integration becomes key, particularly for controlling costs. Home country expatriates provide control along with the transfer of home HRM systems and organisational culture. But as cultural sensitivity is less important training in this area for expatriates diminishes and career development for this group is not so long term. Sophisticated control systems such as socialisation, mentoring and succession planning are vital for promoting a unified organisational culture and integration.

- *Stage 4.* The demands for both integration and differentiation are evident. In response organisations need to invest in training and development to enhance the flexibility of the organisation to meet these demands. They also need to evolve a 'multicentric cultural perspective' (Milliman and Von Glinow, 1990: 32) which ensures awareness of the national cultures and subcultures at the subsidiary level.

The Milliman and Von Glinow (1990) model parallels closely the stages models proposed by Adler and Ghadar (1990). Both models provide prescriptions of international HRM types. While Stages 1 to 3 are themselves supported by empirical work the associated international HRM forms are theoretically extrapolated. Stage 4, like the work of the international management theorists is largely a theoretical concept. Mayrhofer and Brewster (1996) argue that in practice MNCs, irrespective of their need for integration or diversity, adopt an ethnocentric approach to IHRM with many relying heavily on the use of expatriate managers to control overseas operations. Another problem with the stages model is that it has become less relevant as MNCs adopt both domestic and international markets simultaneously (Taylor and Beechler, 1993) and with acquisitions, mergers and de-mergers there is less evidence that multinationals have to pass through each of these phases in order to internationalise.

Section summary

In this part we have looked at the organisational processes, policies and practices adopted by MNCs to address their international strategic goals. This has considered the question of the role of the international HR function, how it is organised and the activities undertaken. Furthermore complex relationships between the internal configuration of organisational strategies and structures have been considered in terms of how these meet variable external influences. The resource-dependent nature of parent–subsidiary relations as a mechanism of influence highlighted the multiple levels at which international HRM operate, and its differential impact on home and host country employees.

Knowledge and the transfer of HR policy and practice in international organisations

The models outlined in the section above emphasise the importance of integrating HRM and creating global HRM practices that transcend national boundaries. This presupposes that HR knowledge can be easily packaged and transferred across multinational units and across national borders. A recent survey conducted by Brewster, Harris and Sparrow (2002) for the CIPD found that 45 per cent of organisations in their study identified knowledge management as a central plank of their international HRM strategy. In this section we consider some of the difficulties associated with knowledge transfer and the role of international HR networks and expatriates in facilitating the transfer of HR policy and practice.

The nature of knowledge

Knowledge is most frequently defined in terms of its explicit and tacit qualities (Nonaka and Takeuchi, 1995). This classification is based on Polyani's (1962) expression of knowledge as having two complementary elements: the tacit which cannot be articulated and the explicit which can be articulated. Most of our knowledge is tacit in nature, particularly when we think of operational skills or know-how (Lam, 2000). This point is illustrated by Athanssiou and Nigh (2000: 474) when they suggest that while an individual may know how to ride a bike, he/she may not be able to explain how this is possible in relation to the laws of physics, thus, often, 'one knows more than one can tell'. In contrast, explicit knowledge, because it can be articulated, can be codified which makes it easier to transfer (Lam, 2000).

In terms of the transfer of knowledge it is argued that the transfer of tacit and explicit knowledge require different mechanisms. While the latter can be accumulated or stored at a central location or 'repositories' (Argote and Ingram, 2000), the former is dependent on close interaction. Tacit knowledge is personal and not subject independent. As such it is scattered throughout an organisation. Its transfer is highly dependent on the transferor's 'deeper awareness of the communicable details' (Athanassiou and Nigh, 2000: 474) and the transferee's ability to understand what is being communicated. Developing a shared understanding, or what Polanyi (1966: 61) refers as the 'same kind of indwelling', is fundamental to the effective transfer of tacit knowledge. Such shared understandings can best be generated through close interaction. There is a significant body of evidence that suggests developing a common understanding of the tacit dimension of knowledge is best achieved via face-to-face personal communications or strong social interaction (Nohria and Eccles, 1992).

Both modes of knowledge also demand differing methods for acquisition and accumulation purposes (Lam, 2000). It is argued that explicit knowledge can be generated through reasoning and deduction, and can be acquired from formal learning mechanisms such as reading, training, educational programmes. In contrast, tacit knowledge is dependent on practical context-specific experience. Thus in organisations tacit knowledge is acquired through personal experiences of different environments and face-to-face communications, close interactions are critical for the diffusion of this knowledge.

In sum, the tacit or explicit nature of knowledge requires alternative mechanisms for its effective transfer, accumulation and generation. Because explicit knowledge can be codified it becomes a public as opposed to an individual or private possession. In so doing this makes it easier to copy or replicate. As a result organisations are particularly interested in harnessing tacit knowledge for competitive purposes, which is by its nature much more difficult for competitors to replicate. However, the context-specific nature of tacit knowledge and its non-articulation places emphasis on personal interaction as a means of transferring and generating tacit knowledge. It is argued that the HR function is a source of a considerable degree of tacit HR knowledge (Lado and Wilson, 1994; Huselid, 1995).

The role of the social context in generating and transferring HR knowledge

Many of the models of international HRM discussed previously imply that explicit HR knowledge is contained within the policies and practices of the company but clearly overlook *how* this knowledge is transferred. Building on the earlier debates this section considers the importance of the social context for the generation and transfer of HR knowledge.

Taylor (2006) argues that HR functions play an important role in building social capital as a means of developing and transferring HR policies to achieve strategic integration. Social capital is defined as 'an asset embedded in relationships, communities, networks or societies (Leana and van Buren, 1999: 539). It potentially provides a means through which tacit knowledge can be transferred because it creates a conducive social or relational context (Tregaskis, Glover and Ferner, 2005). Nahapiet and Ghoshal (1998) identified three dimensions of social capital underpinning knowledge creation and diffusion in organisations: structural, cognitive and social dimensions (Box 17.1). This work emphasises the importance of personal interaction in networks for harnessing tacit knowledge.

Box 17.1 Dimensions of social capital

Structural dimension of social capital

This refers to the structure of the network, the nature of the ties in terms of being weak or strong, how they are combined to transfer knowledge and to combine knowledge. Evidence suggests that weak ties facilitate the search for information; however, they can hinder the transfer of knowledge particularly tacit knowledge. When the network is dealing with tacit knowledge strong ties have been found to be more effective (Hansen, 1999). The intensity of ties, their density, connectivity and hierarchy all influence the level of contact among network members and the ease with which information can be exchanged. The structural elements are also important in terms of the opportunity they offer to exchange knowledge more quickly than would be the case in the absence of such a network, and in facilitating flows of knowledge providing network members with opportunities to combine and exchange knowledge that would not arise if the network did not exist.

Cognitive dimension of social capital

This refers to the resources that foster the shared meanings and understanding among network members, such as common codes and language or share narratives that represent the way things are done. This cognitive dimension provides a shared context between group members that facilitates more effectively and efficiently the sharing of tacit knowledge and the potential to combine this knowledge in new and novel ways (Gulati, Nohria and Zaheer 2000).

A number of studies have found that network members that have worked together longer tend to work better together because they have developed shared routines and understandings that enable them to leverage the distinctiveness of group members for organisational purposes (Bantel and Jackson, 1989; Fisher and Pollock, 2004).

Relational dimension of social capital

This refers to the nature of the personal relationships that exist between network members in terms of, for example, the degree of trust, identification with others, a sense of obligation to others and the norms or expectations within the group regarding cooperation. These elements can affect access to knowledge, and the motivation to engage in knowledge exchange and combination activities.

Source: Tregaskis, Glover and Ferner, 2005: 10.

Implications for the generation and transfer of HR knowledge

The knowledge and social capital literature suggests that the generation and transfer of knowledge is socially embedded. As such one of the key mechanisms for the generation and diffusion of HR knowledge is the network. There has been an increasing body of work examining the role of transnational teams or networks in multinationals in knowledge creation and diffusion (Athanassiou and Nigh, 2000). However, less work has looked at networks involved in developing HR-related knowledge in international organisations. One of few studies to explore this issue in detail was conducted by Tregaskis, Glover and Ferner (2005) who examine the role of international HR networks in 13 multinational organisations. This research identified companies that had explicitly adopted formal international HR networks comprising headquarter-level (e.g. parent or regional) HR directors and senior-subsidiary-level HR managers. The case study evidence revealed that these forums had seven primary functions:

- global policy development;
- global HR policy implementation;
- best-practice creation and sharing;
- exploitation of the distributed HR expertise;
- creating buy-in to policy initiatives;
- information exchange;
- socialisation of the HR community.

These functions reflected the organisation's desire to achieve integration in certain areas of HR activity, such as performance management, succession planning, talent spotting, expatriate careers. They also reflected the ambition by some of the companies to generate new global HR knowledge by drawing together expertise and tacit knowledge of how HR issues operated in divergent national contexts. There was also evidence of two alternative decision making processes (i.e. top-down vs collaborative) at play in the performance of these functions. The collaborative decision-making process embraced national variation as part of the process toward integration. In contrast, the top-down decision making process tended to ignore or sideline national variation. The implication for the generation of new HR knowledge was stark. In the collaborative networks there was more opportunity for tacit knowledge to be exchanged among network members that had spent considerable time building the structural, relational and cognitive dimensions of the network. This tacit knowledge was used to create new global policies based, to a greater extent, on the joint experiences of the network members. The top-down model relied more heavily on HR knowledge that was generated at the centre, then codified and transferred through extensive implementation measures.

The value of networks for the rapid transfer of knowledge has also been explored by Brown and Duguid (1991) through what they refer to as 'communities of practice' (COP). Unlike the formal networks examined in the research by Tregaskis *et al.*, a COP may be informal in nature. Desouza (2003: 29) defines a COP as 'a group of people who have common tasks, interact and share knowledge with each other, either formally or informally'. These communities have a tacit and shared understanding of the group's identify and generate knowledge that is unique because the membership and the tacit knowledge of its membership is unique. Sparrow, Brewster and Harris (2004: 97) argue that the types of structures needed to support such communities include 'team processes for learning, reflection and appreciative enquiry, and co-enquiry, as opposed to simple expert–student relationships (headquarter-country operation)'. This suggests the generation of global HR practices within international HR communities of practice would require collaborative relations across subsidiary HR functions and between headquarters and subsidiary-level HR functions. It also challenges the nature of the parent–subsidiary control relationship that underpins many of the models explaining the configuration of the international HRM function.

You work in the UK HR function of a French owned chemical MNC. The headquarters HR function in France is keen for its subsidiary-level HR functions to exchange best practice ideas. However, you have found communication with HR functions in other countries very difficult. These difficulties are not due to language, instead there seems to be a reluctance on the part of your counterparts in the other countries to talk to each other and exchange ideas.

Questions

- How might the company move toward more network-based relations across the international HR community?
- How might the relational context of these networks be advanced?

Another significant mechanism for the generation and transfer of international HR knowledge is the expatriate manager. The role of the expatriate manager in knowledge diffusion in transnational organisations was recognised by Bartlett and Ghoshal (1995). However, work in this area is generally limited with a few exceptions (see Bonache and Brewster, 2001; Cerdin, 2003). Kostova and Roth (2003) suggest social capital is accumulated by international managers because of their boundary-spanning roles. Boundary-spanning roles refer to management roles that cross networks, functional or geographical boundaries. These individuals often act as the lynchpin between horizontal or vertical structures within the multinational network. As such international managers can act to help diffuse HR practices across these boundaries. But equally, there is a need for the HR function to consider utilising international HR professionals in boundary-spanning roles to facilitate the diffusion and generation of tacit HR knowledge (Tregaskis *et al.*, 2005).

Section summary

This section has considered how HR knowledge is generated and transferred across the international organisation. It is suggested that the tacit nature of knowledge and its context-specificity, demands organisational structures and processes that enable a social context for the generation and transfer of knowledge. In terms of the international HR function this raises possibilities for the role of formal networks, communities of practice and boundary spanning international HR roles. These are all issues relevant to the future direction of international HR research.

Country effects

This section considers influences on the international human resource management policies and practices of MNCs that are related to the country from which they originate, and the foreign countries in which they operate. As we will see, there is evidence that countries of ownership, and of subsidiary operation, have effects both on processes of international learning within MNCs, and on specific HRM practices such as the management of pay or collective industrial relations.

It should be noted that some writers on international management downplay the importance of such influences, or even, in some cases, virtually deny their existence. Particularly, some writers on globalisation often make the claim that current trends in the world economy militate against cross-national differences in management in general, driving a convergence of capitalisms generally towards a single model, heavily influenced by the currently dominant American model. At the extreme, the work of authors such as Kenneth Ohmae (1991) suggests a 'borderless world', or 'interlinked economy' in which the globalisation of production chains, product markets, corporate structures and financial flows makes national boundaries and the nation-state largely irrelevant. Following a similar logic, Reich (1991: 3) speculates about a future with 'no national products or technologies, no national corporations, no national industries'.

Against this, however, arguments are frequently made that the vast majority of MNCs retain a national identity. For example, the capital on which MNCs depend for investment remains predominantly based in the country of origin (Doremus, Keller, Pauly and Reich, 1998). Equally, in general, managerial control tends to be exerted by nationals of the original home country; for example, Ruigrok and van Tulder (1995) found that 25 of the 30 largest American-owned MNCs had no foreign nationals on their boards of directors. Additionally, it has often been argued that MNCs are often less 'transnational' than they may appear to be at first glance. Frequently, operations, particularly strategic functions such as research and development centres, remain disproportionately concentrated in the country of origin (Pauly and Reich, 1997; Hirst and Thompson, 1999).

Additionally, there are both economic and sociological reasons to expect that MNCs with their origins in different national systems of business and employment may operate in some-what distinctive ways, with effects on the nature of HR policies in their subsidiary operations across the world. From an economic perspective, it is commonly argued that the ways in which firms choose to internationalise, as well as their use of specific management practices, is a result of their embeddedness in specifically national institutional contexts which coincide with the firms' country of origin (c.f. Porter, 1990; Morgan, 2001; Whitley, 1999; Lane, 2001). The basic argument here is that firms' competitive advantage is rooted in their home country business systems, and that they will seek to replicate such advantages abroad. A good example of this can be found in the early development of the automobile industry. Faced with a lack of craft workers, but a plentiful supply of semi-skilled workers, and a large domestic market with relatively homogenous tastes due to (at the time) relatively small class distinctions com-pared with European countries, American firms such as Ford developed a mass production system which they later sought to internationalise. More recently, Japanese firms developed a competitive advantage in some areas of manufacturing, which can be related to elements of the Japanese business and employment systems such as the close links between companies within supply chains, enterprise unionism and employment security for core workers in large firms, permitting the development of the employee involvement and quality management programmes necessary to achieve more flexible forms of mass production (see Chapter 15). Again, in many cases, Japanese companies abroad have sought to replicate (or provide equiv-alents for) some of these policies.

In the international HRM literature, then, the term 'country of origin effects' (Ferner, 1997), sometimes referred to as 'home country effects', means those elements of the behav-iour of MNCs which can be traced back to the characteristics of the national business system from which the MNC originates. Country of origin business systems can influence HRM in many areas. For example, the preferred nature of industrial relations management may well be affected by senior executives' domestic experiences, affecting both how MNCs deal with trade unions in foreign subsidiaries, and policies in areas such as employee involvement and participation. Equally, the nature of training and education in the home country may affect managers' understandings of the appropriate competencies of workers and managers, and of work organisation. Employment-related policy may also be affected by business system effects outside the direct area of employment. For example, the nature of corporate finance in the country of origin may affect the extent to which senior executives adopt a short-termist 'shareholder value' mentality, which in turn may affect the extent to which they adopt a short-term or long-term approach to employment issues, with American or British firms per-haps, all other things being equal, being less willing to offer secure employment in subsidiaries than their Japanese counterparts, as managers in the latter group of firms have generally had less need to worry about short-term fluctuations in profitability (Whitley, 1999; Hall and Soskice, 2001).

Evidence on country of origin effects

Research into the HR and industrial relations practices and policies of foreign firms in the UK has revealed a number of ways in which subsidiary policy is often influenced by firms' embeddedness in their country of origin business system. Here, we review evidence on the influence of such 'country of origin effects' in foreign-owned firms in the UK. We particularly use evidence from a recent research project (Almond and Ferner, 2006), which examined employment relations and human resource management in the European subsidiaries of US MNCs. This identified that the 'Americanness' of US MNCs affected the nature of their management of human resources in a number of ways.

First, the management of the majority of the US MNCs is quite highly centralised (Ferner, Gunnigle, Wachter and Edwards, 2006). In contradiction to predictions that MNCs are evolving into devolved networks (cf. Nohria and Ghoshal, 1997), centralised rule-setting from the US headquarters of firms remained commonplace. Most of the firms involved in the research pursued uniformity of HR policies across countries, and subsidiary managers had to give strong arguments to global HQ when they wished to deviate from 'global' policy, which, as we argue below, was often fairly 'American' in nature. Control was achieved by measuring outcomes (such as the achievement of diversity targets, number of employees in each grade, etc.) at the HQ, rather than by high numbers of expatriate managers. This pattern of centralisation across international operations is an extension of the way American firms developed formalised, bureaucratic control systems in order to coordinate their varied activities across the USA, as analysed by Chandler (1976). Recently, the increased need for business units within US MNCs to be financially accountable in the short term, due to pressures for 'shareholder value' (O'Sullivan, 2000), has probably led to a tightening of central control in some US MNCs.

Given this pattern of centralisation, it is perhaps unsurprising that, for nearly all of the organisations studied, there was a considerable amount of 'forward' policy transfer of HR policy (that is, transfer of US policy to foreign subsidiary operations), but relatively little evidence of 'reverse' transfer from subsidiaries to the USA (Edwards, Collings, Quintanilla and Tempel, 2006). In this respect, most of the firms resembled Bartlett and Ghoshal's (1989) global, or international forms, more than the transnational form. Edwards and his co-authors argue that this pattern of organisational learning in the area of HR is influenced by the fact that US management theories and policies emanate from a liberal business and employment system, where there are relatively few 'constraints' on management decision making in the area of HR. This means that US managerial techniques are seen as relatively independent of the context in which they operate, when compared to HR policies developed in societies which are more actively regulated. For example, many German firms, and German subsidiaries of foreign MNCs, develop policies which allow them to develop high levels of functional flexibility, in response to their relative lack of freedom to compete on labour cost due to the nature of German collective bargaining, the need to consult with their workers through codetermination institutions, and the skills available to firms because of the nature of the co-determination system. However, such policies are difficult to export to countries such as the USA and UK which do not share these institutions, as the appropriate skills might not be so readily available, and the forms of cooperation between local workers and managers which are said to characterise large German firms might not be replicable in countries with substantially different industrial relations systems. Evidence from German MNCs suggests, for example, they make relatively little attempt to 'export' elements of the German system of employment to their UK operations (Ferner and Varul, 2000).

With regard to specific HR practices, the first area of policy on which US MNCs often exhibit country of origin effects is that of collective industrial relations. It is well known that employers in the USA are, on average, more resistant to trade union organisation than their counterparts in other developed industrial democracies (Colling, Gunnigle, Quintanilla and Tempel, 2006) and that the legal supports for trade union organisation and collective bargaining in the USA are weak in comparison to those in other countries. Both these facts reflect a variety of historical factors in the pattern of industrialisation in the United States (for more details, see Colling, 2000) which are distinct to those in Europe.

There have long been large subsidiaries of US MNCs in the UK which have operated non-union, human relations style policies (what would now be termed 'soft HRM'), even before the 1980s, when changes to the UK industrial relations climate made large non-union workplaces somewhat less unusual. The prototypical example here would be a firm such as IBM, which would historically offer relatively high pay and employment security to its workers, but would strongly resist efforts at trade union organisation. These firms generally were monopolistic firms in which the founding family retained substantial influence, under an ideology, often known as 'welfare capitalism' (Jacoby, 1997), that the firm, rather than trade unions or the state, should be responsible for the welfare of workers. Although changes to the American business system, and increased global competition, mean that firms from this group no longer offer 'jobs for life' there continue to be a substantial number of US MNCs that make the avoidance of trade unions abroad a central part of their HR strategy (see Colling *et al.*, 2006; Ferner, Almond, Colling and Edwards, 2005). In some cases, the American HQ of such firms makes explicit written guidelines, sometimes even published on corporate websites, that subsidiary managers should discourage trade union organisation. Additionally, as the above authors reflect, a number of firms which have not been able to avoid unionisation in the USA are anxious to do so abroad, perhaps due to their experience of highly conflictual industrial relations in their home country. Finally, of course, there are a number of 'low road' MNCs such as McDonald's which are strongly anti-union (cf. Royle, 2000). This is not to say, however, that all foreign subsidiaries of US firms operate non-union or anti-union policies. Some US MNCs, although seeking to avoid trade unions in the USA, make little effort to intervene in foreign industrial relations systems, providing that such systems do not impinge too heavily on their ability to pursue their desired HR policies (Ferner *et al.*, 2005).

Further effects can be seen in the management of pay and performance (Almond, Muller-Camen, Collings and Quintanilla, 2006). In particular, US MNCs were innovators in the area of formalised systems of performance-related pay in Europe (Muller, 1998), which can be seen as a reflection of the particularly market-oriented American employment system. This practice is now also diffused widely among large non-American firms (Faulkner, PitKethley and Child, 2004). It can still be argued, however, that the form the practice often takes in US MNCs, with forced distributions pushing given percentages of employees into high and low performing categories, and in some cases the threat of dismissal or reduced job security for lower performing groups, reflects specifically American managerial beliefs about employment. In particular, this type of practice can be related to the American notion of 'employment at will' meaning there is, for most US employees, little protection from unfair dismissal (cf. Almond *et al.*, 2006). Systems of performance management tend to be tightly controlled by US HQ, with relatively little freedom for national subsidiaries to adopt distinctive policies.

Stop & think

What are the advantages and disadvantages to a firm in attempting to pursue a uniform system of performance management across its international operations?

A number of US MNCs also export workforce 'diversity' policies from the USA. These are clearly linked to the social and legislative context of equal opportunity law, and to US firms' attempts to interpret equal opportunity law to their own advantage (Ferner, Muller-Camen, Morley and Susaeta, 2006). In many cases, US firms, having devised diversity policies for the USA, chose to export these abroad, thus imposing targets for the proportion of women, and sometimes other disadvantaged labour market groups, in management positions. This reflects how the nature of country of origin effects can change over time, as the home country institutional context changes. Political sensitivities to equality issues in the USA, prompted by the civil rights movement and reactions to it, have led to the development of a range of diversity policies, which have in many cases been internationalised through the formal management systems of US firms.

It has also frequently been argued that Japanese MNCs betray specifically 'Japanese' characteristics when operating abroad. Japanese economic success in the 1970s and 1980s sparked considerable academic interest in Japanese management methods, with a wave of interest both in the HR policies of Japanese subsidiaries themselves (cf., for example, Kenney and Florida (1993) and Milkman (1991) for US subsidiaries of Japanese MNCs; Morris, Wilkinson and Munday (2000) and Elger and Smith (1994) for their UK subsidiaries), and, in Britain, in 'Japanese' practices which were being imitated by UK firms (cf., for example, Oliver and Wilkinson, 1992).

It is difficult to compare the HR policies of the UK subsidiaries of Japanese MNCs directly with those of US MNCs. The main reason for this is that the overwhelming majority of Japanese Foreign Direct Investment in the UK has taken place in the last 25 years, into a UK industrial relations environment which had already been affected by Thatcherism and the economic crisis of the late 1970s/early 1980s. Much US investment is much older, going back in some cases to the Victorian era, meaning that many UK subsidiaries of US MNCs such as, say, Ford or General Motors, have a much more substantial 'British' heritage than Toyota or Nissan. Equally, much Japanese investment has involved so-called 'greenfield' sites, meaning that the Japanese MNCs involved had the opportunity to 'start from scratch' in terms of their management systems, and to recruit and select an entire, new workforce.

Indeed, one of the notable features of many Japanese subsidiaries investigated in this period was their very selective recruitment procedures, in many cases focusing on the recruitment of a young workforce with the ability to learn, rather than looking for experienced workers with substantial experience of other UK firms (Oliver and Wilkinson, 1992). This reflects practice among core workers in the largest Japanese firms, where workers are selected directly from school or university and expected to remain with the same employer for the majority of their career.

At least some of the larger Japanese inward investors also sought to replicate Japanese-type structures in their industrial relations policies. Rather than taking advantage of the 1980s industrial relations climate by seeking to exclude trade unions, some Japanese MNCs sought to reach single union agreements, whereby one trade union, usually the very moderate AEEU, represented all the different workforce groups within the firm. This differs from the more typical UK pattern in manufacturing, in which different occupational groups are represented by different trade unions, and replicates, to the extent that this is possible in a UK context, the company unionism present in the core Japanese firms at home. One 1990s survey of Japanese subsidiaries in South Wales found that 75 per cent had a single union deal (Innes and Morris, 1995). The extent to which these deals were favourable to the management of these firms is reflected in the fact that two thirds of such deals were single-union deals. The Japanese firms in the same survey tended to have fewer job grades, reflecting a lesser degree of job demarcation than in US firms, and were less likely to have performance-related pay (see above), but slightly more likely to have elements of single-status practices such as equal holiday leave, and the wearing of company uniforms by all employees. Perhaps surprisingly, however, in view of the 'Japanisation' literature, flexible work organisation arrangements such as teamworking were only slightly more prevalent, and employee involvement systems such as quality circles no more prevalent, than in US-owned firms. This is in spite of the fact that considerable case study evidence from the larger Japanese subsidiaries in the UK does suggest that these policies are used.

Part of the explanation for this could lie with the extent to which Japanese practices, then seen as a model to be emulated (Womack, Jones and Roos 1990), were being copied by rival firms. If this is the case, it remains possible that the nature of policies such as teamworking is qualitatively different in Japanese-owned and American-owned firms. At least equally importantly, however, as an important recent book, based on a long-term study of Japanese firms in Telford, argues (Elger and Smith, 2006), the portrait of Japanese management generally found in the English-language management literature is somewhat stereotypical. Specifically, the commonly understood Japanese HRM model only really applies to core workers in a small number of well-known firms. Elements of the model such as employment security and internal career structures do not extend to peripheral firms in supply chains, or to peripheral groups of the workforce, and very often Japanese MNCs used foreign workforces as part of this periphery. The picture Elger and Smith present of Japanese management in Telford, of union avoidance and intensified assembly line work and modest wages, is much more reminiscent of the less glorified peripheral work systems of Japan, than of the more paternalist HRM policies experienced by the core workers of core firms.

Finally, country of origin effects are likely to be stronger where the home country retains a substantial proportion of the MNC's operations. This is usually the case with US and Japanese firms, but, for obvious reasons, less common with large MNCs based in smaller countries. In these cases, internationalisation of the firm may mean a much greater degree of internationalisation of its management cadre, and often of its capital base (i.e. the larger continental European MNCs will tend, to raise, finance from the US stock market as well as from domestic sources), meaning that country of origin effects may tend, over time, to diminish. The work of Hayden and Edwards (2001) examines this process in the Swedish case.

Overall, one can say that the various effects of firms and their managers originating from one particularly national business system may lead them to be more likely to choose some policies than others. This is not an automatic process, however. One cannot simply say that firms will adopt a certain style of HRM just because they are from a given country, but they will predispose managers to certain choices over others in given contexts.

Host country effects

'Host country effects' is the term used to describe elements of MNC HR policy which are shaped by the context of the foreign countries that subsidiaries are located in. In other words, this concerns the way in which subsidiary HR policies and practices are shaped by a foreign MNC's interaction with employees, and host-country managers, working under different national rules and different national cultural and social systems. These rules and systems, along with levels of economic development and ease of access to markets, also provide countries with different competitive advantages. MNCs may sometimes choose to (or need to) deviate from their original, home country, policies, in order to exploit these advantages fully, while dealing with societal and cultural differences.

The broad term of 'host country effects' can perhaps be usefully split into a number of groups. First, there are effects which are imposed on the foreign MNC by host country constraints. These may arise directly from labour market regulation; as the previous chapter illustrates, host countries, even within European Union countries, still differ considerably in their regulation of core elements of the employment relationship such as wage protection, working time, employment security, worker participation and the trade union and collective bargaining rights of employees. In most European countries, for example, MNCs cannot simply choose to refuse to offer union recognition to employees. Equally, it is much harder, and more expensive, to dismiss permanent employees in some countries than in others. In other words, certain policies are either obligatory or prohibited in some societies, which has the effect of reducing the (legitimate) scope for strategic choice for foreign MNCs.

To this group of effects, one can also add elements of national cultural/societal understandings of the employment relationship which may not be written down in law, but which will affect the ways in which given HR practices will be interpreted by workers. For example, due to the nature of gender relations in Britain (see Chapter 4), employers in the UK, including foreign MNCs, benefit from a large workforce that is eager to take part-time employment with flexible working hours (i.e. working class women, and, increasingly, students) (Almond and Rubery, 2000). In France, while it is possible to recruit flexible part-timers due to the current high levels of unemployment in that country, most women in employment have historically tended to work full-time hours, meaning that part-time workers may be less content with their situation. While this does not, of course, stop a foreign MNC from employing a part-time workforce in France, managers should not be surprised if, as a result, their French employees display less 'commitment' than their British counterparts.

Second, host country effects are not only constraints on foreign MNCs. Indeed, if they were, there would be much less foreign direct investment. In fact, MNCs are constantly taking advantage of differences between different host countries (and other potential host countries). Much production, and, indeed, increasing proportions of service provision, takes place in global supply chains which seek to exploit national socio-economic differences. If the employment system of one country offers expensive, but skilled workers, with a high capacity for learning, while that of another offers largely untrained, but cheap labour, then many MNCs will locate the higher skilled work in the first, and the less skilled in the second. Similarly, the policies required to be seen as a 'good' or 'fair' employer in contemporary China, say, are clearly not as high as those in Germany, meaning that many firms will not choose to employ the same types of HR policies in these two very different environments. It should also be noted that MNCs' coordination of work extends beyond workplaces they directly own. As has been shown in recent years with regard to the sportswear industry, foreign MNCs can have fairly direct effects over working practices in the firms to which they increasingly contract out activities (Klein, 2000). While issues concerning subcontracted work in the developing world do not generally feature in the international HRM literature, it is necessary to recognise their importance in a fuller analysis of how MNCs manage human resources.

Finally, where an MNC locates a subsidiary in a country partly or mainly in order to exploit the national or regional product market, differences in consumer demand between nations may necessitate different ways of managing human resources. This was discussed briefly above in relation to the 'multi-domestic' form of MNC organisation, but will also apply to many firms which do not share that type of structure. While market differences may equally well be present in manufacturing as in the service sector, they are perhaps more likely to impact on HRM where there is direct contact between the employee and the customer.

The extent to which host country effects will cause differentiation in HR policies obviously depends on the nature of host country patterns of employment relations, and how different these are from those in the country of origin. This is sometimes referred to as 'institutional distance' (Kostova, 1999). For example, a US firm attempting to export a non-union system of HRM with a high performance-related element to pay would probably face far more difficulties in Germany than it would in the UK (for an example, see Almond *et al.*, 2005). By the same token, if the training system of one host country supplies the firm with a plentiful quantity of workers who have an otherwise scarce skill, it might well not choose to export all the elements of its corporate training programme to that country.

However, it should be noted that the strength of host country effects cannot simply be read off from a broad understanding of the nature of its institutions. In particular, the degree to which national economies depend on foreign MNCs for their success varies quite considerably from country to country. In countries such as Hungary or Ireland, where nearly half the manufacturing workforce works directly for foreign MNCs, one would expect this group of firms to have considerable lobbying power, and thus potentially a substantial collective impact on the nature of the overall business and employment systems (cf. Gunnigle, Collings, Morley and McAvinue 2003 for the Irish case).

At a more micro-level, the impact of 'constraining' host country effects may in practice be reduced if the MNC has a substantial choice about which countries it is located in. If the firm can produce credible threats that it may move part or all of its operations to more lightly regulated and/or lower cost countries, it is possible that some host country constraints can be 'negotiated' (particularly with local unions and local/regional governments), lessening their real impact. Less dramatically, the practice of 'coercive comparisons' (Marginson and Sisson, 2002), by which MNCs threaten (explicitly or implicitly) to withdraw investment in one subsidiary unless it matches the performance of another, is commonplace.

Another way of dealing with undesirable host country regulations, of course, is simply to disobey them. This is commonplace in the multinational fast food industry (Royle, 2000), but also happens in firms which do not follow 'hard', cost minimisation strategies quite so obviously (cf. Almond *et al.*, 2005; Colling *et al.*, 2006). The subsidiaries of MNCs, whose home country practices may challenge the assumptions behind host country employment relations systems, will frequently attempt to find ways of exploiting the 'malleability' of those systems (Muller-Camen *et al.*, 2001). When foreign MNCs succeed in avoiding the constraints of host country systems, they may begin to alter the nature of those systems, in that their practices may well be imitated by domestic firms. For instance, while some medium-large British non-union firms did exist in the post-war era, one might argue that US MNCs became a template for later attempts to create non-union 'soft HRM' workplaces in the UK. More recently, German employers have followed closely the attempts of German subsidiaries of US multi-nationals to create more flexible pay structures.

The negotiation of home and host country effects

Neither home or host country effects are automatic in their operation. It is important to take into account the fact that different organisational members, such as national and local managers, down to groups of shopfloor employees, have interests and goals of their own, which cannot simply be reduced to those of the 'Corporation'. In particular, it is important to take account of the ways in which host country socialisation affects the rationality of host country managers (Broad 1994). In other words, host country managers may, because of their own 'embeddedness' in their own society, have different ideas about what is 'good management', and what is 'fair' and 'just', than their foreign superiors. For example, in the recent study of US MNCs in Europe discussed above, German and British subsidiary managers, both coming from countries with much more pluralist industrial relations traditions than their American counterparts, often applied HQ industrial relations policy in a fairly pragmatic and accommodating way, allowing more role for collective labour than a strict reading of corporate policy might suggest (Colling *et al.*, 2006). Similar processes can be seen to operate in the UK subsidiaries of Japanese firms (Elger and Smith, 2006)

In other words, HR outcomes at subsidiary level result from different actors, at different levels of the organisation, with different power resources negotiating on the extent to which it is desirable to follow a 'global' policy, or to make allowances for local contingencies. In particular, local managers should have specific knowledge about the local situation and will have their own interpretations of the realities of what is likely to work in the local context. It may be difficult for an HQ manager to tell exactly how a foreign subsidiary workforce is likely to respond to a given HR initiative, or how strictly an element of employment law is enforced. Local managers therefore have a role in interpreting and negotiating precisely what the nature of 'host country effects' are in a given context. In other words, any analysis of policy transfer within MNCs needs to take account of organisational politics and the power resources of various actors (Edwards, 2004).

Summary

- This chapter has analysed international HRM by combining a range of academic perspectives in the area, from strategic approaches, to those focusing more on MNCs relations with their institutional environment. It highlights the fact that internationalised operations offer firms advantages in terms of access to human resources and to knowledge, while also dealing with the increasingly complicated nature of HRM when firms internationalise.

- The chapter highlights how HRM decisions in MNCs may be related to business strategy and structure, but with the added complication that global as well as national strategic factors would need to be taken into account by senior managers. It then examines the ways in which MNCs might choose to structure their international HR function in order to cope with the complexities of international management and the role of networks and expatriates in the generation and transfer of HR knowledge. The final section examines the potential effects on HRM strategies and structures of the country of ownership of MNCs, as well as of the countries in which they operate.

• As the chapter reflects, the coordination of human resources in MNCs is a socially complex affair. It should be emphasised that none of the models, or explanations, presented above to explain MNCs behaviour in HRM fully succeed in unwrapping this complexity. In examining the process of human resource management in the international firm, it is necessary to take account of strategies, internal structures and institutions together.

QUESTIONS

1 Explain what is meant by the terms integration and responsiveness in the context of MNCs. What effect can these have on how the MNC is structured, the nature of the parent–subsidiary control relationship and the flow of knowledge across the MNC?

2 Outline and explain, the key internal and external organisational factors that influence an MNC's approach to international strategic human resource management.

3 Explain why HR knowledge is difficult to transfer across an MNC.

4 How and why are the extent and direction of HR policy transfer likely to differ between multidomestic, international, global and transnational companies?

5 Examine the nature of HR policies in the UK subsidiaries of US and/or Japanese MNCs. What evidence is there of a 'country of origin' effect?

6 To what extent, and how, do you believe that British patterns of HRM have been affected by reports of the activities of foreign-owned MNCs in the UK?

CASE STUDY

All change at Linkz

Linkz is a German-owned transnational telecommunications company. It was established in 1935 as a domestic company. Since then the company has expanded internationally. It now operates in 140 countries, employs 104,000 people worldwide, including 22,000 in design centres spread across 25 countries. Approximately 40 per cent of the staff are employed within Germany, but expansion in employee numbers over the past 10 years has been greater outside of Germany.

Linkz began as a wireline telecomunications network supplier. In recent years it moved into wireless software design and it is in this, the area of mobile phones and networks that the business has expanded rapidly in the last 15 years. Linkz has 30 per cent of the global market share in mobile systems making it one of the leading mobile communications suppliers worldwide. Sales figures are largest for the Europe, Middle East, Africa region, followed by the Asia Pacific region, Latin America region and finally the North America region. Sales figures increased in 2006 by 10 per cent on the previous year. Japan is the company's largest market for third generation mobile phones. However, the European markets have showed some increase during 2005–06. In 2003 Linkz invested 20 per cent of its sales revenue in technical development.

The telecommunications industry has changed significantly in recent years. In the past Linkz sold telecommunications equipment to large monopolistic operators. Datacom and computer companies are venturing into traditional areas of the telecommunications market, as these voice and data industries converge a single multimedia industry is emerging. In addition, wireline and wireless phone technology has moved toward increasingly advanced digital technology and internet technology giving rise to 'third generation' technology and products, e.g. mobile phones with video and internet services. Worldwide deregulation has enabled the merging of wireline and wireless operators with global capabilities. As a result the market is becoming more transnational in nature. The number of global operators is shrinking, while at the regional or local level the number of operators is expanding. This means there is greater pressure for

Case study continued

global standards across the industry that enables compatibility between datacom and telecom systems. While at the local level the advances in technology have led to fierce competition between companies to deliver the latest innovations in products and services to customers. All this leaves Linkz with the demand for increased global efficiency and learning transfer to maximise on its investment in design capability. And the need to be highly sensitive to the demands of local customers given the nature of the competition.

Faced with these many pressures Linkz re-structured in a bid to move away from strong parent hierarchical control over its subsidiary operations, whilst still building on its global strengths and capability. It established four additional corporate headquarter offices, one for each of its regions (Europe, Middle East and Africa with a corporate office in London; North America with a corporate office in Texas; Asia Pacific with a corporate office in Hong Kong; Latin America with a corporate office in Miami) in addition to the home headquarters in Hamburg. The majority of the senior managers in these offices are German. The corporate offices hold responsibilities for finance, technology, supply and information technology, human resource management (HRM), marketing and strategic business development, corporate communications, and legal affairs.

The restructuring had notable implications for the design and HRM functions. In terms of design a corporate function was created with responsibility for coordinating R&D across the multinational network, particularly in relation to standardisation, patents, and strategic partnerships. In addition, a research centre was established in Hamburg responsible for advanced early 'blue sky' research. The role of design in the subsidiaries was reduced and shifted toward the development of highly specialised products for local customer markets.

The corporate HRM function had the responsibility of creating a global philosophy that enabled best-practice and policy from across the network to define the organisational culture. Diversity was seen as a feature of the organisation to be built upon rather than smoothed over. To facilitate this philosophy annual audits were carried out whereby HR teams from the regional corporate offices would visit subsidiaries to gain evidence of local best-practice that they deemed useful for global dissemination. In addition, HR professionals across the network would attend an annual internal HR conference where issues and experiences faced by the HR teams were discussed.

The HR intranet bulletin board and chat room provided additional mechanisms for the spread of innovation and networking among the internal HR community. The Linkz Management Academy (LMC) was established in Hamburg mandated to develop the managerial capability of its worldwide workforce. The LMC designed management development programmes for graduates and junior managers through to its senior managers. These involved academic and practitioner guest speakers from all over the world and usually combined off-site development with on-the-job learning, international transfers or secondments.

This restructuring created many challenges for how the corporate HR functions would achieve their mandate, and the competency requirements of these HR professionals to deliver in this changed context. The changes also created a trade-off between greater autonomy for the subsidiary in some areas versus the loss of control in others. For example, the subsidiary design functions now had almost total control over their activities relating to product design for local customers. However, they were no longer permitted to engage in long-term strategic R&D as this responsibility now lay with corporate R&D. For the design function the reorganisation also brought new challenges for local managers with regard to how to motivate and develop the necessary technical capability to cope with the changes in the industry and the organisation. While it also changed the career landscape for local senior managers in terms of their opportunity for local and international career advancement.

Given the reorganisation and changes in the market context faced by Linkz, consider the following:

1 What types of competencies do you feel the HR professionals in the corporate and regional headquarter offices would need to demonstrate to deliver against the international strategic demands of the organisation?

2 If you were tasked with designing a Linkz management development programme for middle managers what types of issues would it address and how would it be delivered?

3 Assess the nature of the motivational problems the design function's managers are likely to face, given the organisational changes and changes in the external context. As an HR manager working in partnership with design what solutions would you suggest?

4 What opportunities and threats might an international career structure bring to local managers?

References and further reading

Adler, N. and Ghadar, F. (1990) 'Strategic Human Resource Management: A Global Perspective', in Pieper, R. *Human Resource Management: An International Comparison.* Berlin: Walter de Gruyter.

Almond, P., Edwards, T., Colling, T., Ferner, A., Gunnigle, P., Muller-Camen, M., Quintanilla, J. and Wachter, H. (2005) 'Unraveling Home and Host Country Effects: An Investigation of the HR Policies of an American Multinational in Four European Countries', *Industrial Relations (Berkeley)*, 44, 2: 276–306.

Almond, P. and Ferner, A. (eds) (2006) *American Multinationals in Europe: Managing Employment Relations Across Borders.* Oxford: Oxford University Press.

Almond, P., Muller-Camen, M., Collings, T., and Quintanilla, J. (2006) 'Pay and Performance', in Almond, P. and Ferner, A. (eds) *American Multinationals in Europe: Managing Employment Relations Across Borders.* Oxford: Oxford University Press.

Almond, P. and Rubery, J. (2000) 'Deregulation and Societal Systems', in Maurice, M. and Sorge, A. (eds) *Embedding Organizations.* Amsterdam: John Benjamin.

Argote, L. and Ingram, P. (2000) 'Knowledge Transfer: A basis for competitive advantage in firms', *Organizational Behaviour and Human Decision Processes*, 82: 152–169.

Athanassiou, N. and Nigh, D. (2000) 'Internationalization, tacit knowledge and the top management teams of MNCs', *Journal of International Business Studies*, 31, 3: 471–488.

Bantel, K.A. and Jackson, S.E. (1980) 'Top management and innovations in banking: does the composition of the top team make a difference?', *Strategic Management Journal*, 13: 338–355.

Barney, J. (1991) 'Firm resources and sustained competitive advantage', *Journal of Management*, 17: 99–120.

Bartlett, C.A. and Ghoshal, S. (1989) *Managing Across Borders: The Transnational Solution.* Boston. MA: Harvard Business School Press.

Bartlett, C.A. and Ghoshal, S. (1990) 'The multinational corporation as an interorganizational network' *Academy of Management Review*, 15, 4: 603–625.

Bartlett, C.A. and Ghoshal, S. (1995) *Transnational Management*, 2nd edn. Boston, MA: Irwin.

Birkinshaw, J. and Morrison, A. (1995) 'Configurations of Strategy and Structure in Subsidiaries of Multinational Companies', *Journal of International Business Studies*, 26, 4: 729–754.

Boam, R. and Sparrow, P. (1992) *Designing and Achieving Competency.* London: McGraw-Hill.

Bonache, J. and Brewster, C. (2001) 'Knowledge transfer and the management of expatriation', *Thunderbird International Business Review*, 43, 1: 145–168.

Brewster, C., Harris, H. and Sparrow, P.R. (2002) *Globalizing HR: Executive Brief.* London: CIPD.

Broad, G. (1994) 'The managerial limits to Japanisation: a manufacturing case study', *Human Resource Management Journal*, 4, 3: 52–69.

Brown, J.S. and Duguid, P. (1991) 'Organizational learning and communities-of-practice: towards a unified view of working, learning and innovation', *Organization Science*, 2, 1: 40–57.

Cerdin, J-L. (2003) 'International diffusion of HRM practices: the role of expatriates', *Beta: Scandinavian Journal or Business Research*, 17, 1: 48–58.

Chandler, A. (1976) *The Visible Hand: The Managerial Revolution in America.* Cambridge, MA.: Belknap.

Colling. T. (2000) 'In a state of bliss there is no need for a ministry of bliss. Power, consent and the limits of innovation in American non-union companies'. Occasional paper, Leicester Business School, De Montfort University.

Colling, T. (2001) 'In a State of bliss, there is no need for a Ministry of Bliss: Some further thoughts on welfare capitalism', Occasional Paper, Leicester Business School, De Montfort University.

Colling, T., Gunnigle, P., Quintanilla, J. and Tempel, A. (2006) 'Collective representation and participation', in Almond, P. and Ferner, A. (eds) *American Multinationals in Europe: Managing Employment Relations Across Borders.* Oxford: Oxford University Press.

Desouza, K.C. (2003) 'Knowledge management barriers: why the technology imperative seldom works' *Business Horizons*, Jan–Feb: 25–29.

Doremus, P., Keller, W., Pauly, L. and Reich, S. (1998) *The Myth of the Global Corporation.* Princeton. NJ.: Princeton University Press.

Doz, Y.L. and Prahalad, C.K. (1986) 'Controlled variety: A Challenge for Human Resource Management in the MNC' *Human Resource Management*, 25, 1: 55–72.

Dunning, J. (1958) *American Investment in British Manufacturing.* London: Allen & Unwin.

Dunning, E. (1998) *American Investment in British Manufacturing Industry.* London: Routledge.

Edwards, T. (2004) 'The transfer of employment practices across borders in multinational companies', in Harzing, A.-W. and van Ruysseveldt, J. (eds) *International Human Resource Management*, 2nd edn. London: Sage.

Edwards, T., Collings, D., Quintanilla, J. and Tempel, A. (2006) 'Innovation and the transfer of organisational learning', in Almond, P. and Ferner, A. (eds) *American Multinationals in Europe: Managing Employment Relations Across Borders.* Oxford: Oxford University Press.

Edwards, T. and Rees, C. (eds) (2006) *International Human Resource Management: Globalization, National Systems and Multinational Companies.* London: FT Prentice Hall.

Elger, T. and Smith, C. (eds) (1994) *Global Japanization? The transnational transformation of the labour process.* Oxford: Oxford University Press.

Elger, T. and Smith, C. (2006) *Assembling Work. Remaking Factory Regimes in Japanese Multinationals in Britain.* Oxford: Oxford University Press.

Faulkner, D., PitKethley, R. and Child, J. (2004) 'International mergers and acquisitions in the UK 1985–1994: A comparison of national HRM practices', *International Journal of Human Resource Management*, 13, 1: 94–111.

Ferner, A. (1994) 'Multinational companies and human resource management: an overview of research issues', *Human Resource Management Journal*, 4, 2: 79–102.

Ferner, A. (1997) 'Country of Origin Effects and HRM in Multinational Enterprises', *Human Resource Management Journal*, 7, 1: 19–37.

Ferner, A., Almond, P., Colling, T. and Edwards, T. (2005) 'Policies on Union Representation in US Multinationals in the UK: Between micro-politics and macro-institutions', *British Journal of Industrial Relations*, 43, 4: 703–728.

Ferner, A., Gunnigle, P., Wachter, H. and Edwards, T. (2006) 'Centralization' in Almond, P. and Ferner, A. (eds) *American Multinationals in Europe: Managing Employment Relations Across Borders.* Oxford: Oxford University Press.

Ferner, A., Muller-Camen, M., Morley, M. and Susaeta, L. (2006) 'Workforce diversity policies', in Almond, P. and Ferner, A. (eds) *American Multinationals in Europe: Managing Employment Relations Across Borders.* Oxford: Oxford University Press.

Ferner, A. and Varul, M. (2000) '"Vanguard"' subsidiaries and the diffusion of new practices: a case study of German multinationals', *British Journal of Industrial Relations*, 38, 1: 115–140.

Fisher, H.M. and Pollock, T.G. (2004) 'Effects of social capital and power on surviving transformational change: the case of initial public offerings', *Academy of Management Journal*, 47, 4: 463–482.

Ghoshal, S. and Bartlett, C.A. (1998) *Managing Across Borders.* London: Random House, Part 1, pp. 1–81.

Ghoshal, S. and Westney, D.E. (1993) 'Introduction and Overview', in Ghoshal, S. Westney, D.E. (eds) *Organization Theory and the Multinational Corporation.* New York: St Martin's Press, pp. 1–23.

Gulati, T., Nohria, N. and Zaheer, A. (2000) 'Strategic Networks', *Strategic Management Journal*, 21: 203–215.

Gunnigle, P., Collings, D., Morley, M. and McAvinue, A.O. (2003) US multinationals and human resource management in Ireland: towards a qualitative research agenda, *Irish Journal of Management*, January: 7–25.

Hall, P. and Soskice D. (2001) *Varieties of Capitalism: The Institutional Foundations of Comparative Advantage.* Oxford: Oxford University Press.

Hansen, M.T. (1999) 'The search-transfer problem: the role of weak ties in sharing knowledge across organization subunits'. *Administrative Science Quarterly*, 44, 1: 82–111.

Harzing, A.-W. (1999) *Managing the Multinationals: an International Study of Control Mechanisms.* Cheltenham: Elgar Publishing.

Harzing, A.-W. (2000) 'An empirical analysis and extension of the Bartlett and Ghoshal Typology of Multinational Companies'. *Journal of International Business Studies*, 31, 1: 101–119.

Hayden, A. and Edwards, T. (2001) 'The erosion of the country of origin effect: a case study of a Swedish multinational company', *Relations Industrielles*, 56, 1: 116–140.

Hedlund, G. (1986) 'The Hypermodern MNC – A Heterarchy?' *Human Resource Management*, 25, 1: 9–35.

Hirst, P. and Thompson, G. (1999) Globalization in Question, 2nd edn. Cambridge: Polity Press.

Hofstede, G. (1980) *Culture's Consequences: International Differences in Work-Related Values.* Beverly Hills: Sage.

Holden L. (2000) 'International Human Resource Management', in Beardwell, I. and Holden, L. *Human Resource Management.* London: Prentice Hall, pp. 633–676.

Huselid, M. (1995) 'The impact of human resource management practices on turnover, productivity and corporate financial performance', *Academy of Management Journal*, 38, 3: 635–672.

Innes, E. and Morris, J. (1995) 'Multinational Corporations and Employee Relations: Continuity and Change in a Mature Industrial Region', *Employee Relations*, 17, 6: 25–42.

Jacoby, S. (1997) *Modern Manors: Welfare Capitalism since the New Deal.* Princeton, NJ: Princeton University Press.

Jones, G. (1984) 'Task visibility, free riding, and shirking: explaining the effect of structure and technology on employee behaviour', *Journal of Financial Economics*, 3: 305–360.

Kenney, M. and Florida, R. (1993) *Beyond mass production.* New York: Oxford University Press.

Klein, N. (2000) *No Logo.* London: Harper Collins.

Kobrin, S.J. (1994) 'Is there a relationship between a Geocentric mind-set and multinational strategy?' *Journal of International Business Studies*, third quarter: 493–511.

Kostova, T. (1999) 'Transnational Transfer of Strategic Organizational Practices: A Contextual Perspective', *Academy of Management Review*, 24, 2: 308–324.

Kostova, T. and Roth, K. (2003) 'Social capital in multinational corporations and a micro-macro model of its formation', *Academy of Management Review*, 28, 2: 297–317.

Lado, A. and Wilson, M. (1994) 'Human resource systems and sustained competitive advantage: a competency based perspective', *Academy of Management Review*, 19: 699–727.

Lam, A. (2000) 'Tacit knowledge, organizational learning and societal institutions: an integrated framework'. *Organization Studies*, 21, 3: 487–513.

Lane, C. (2001) 'Understanding the globalization strategies of German and British multinational companies: Is a "societal effects" approach still useful', in Maurice, M. and Sorge, A. (eds), *Embedding Organizations.* Amsterdam: John Benjamins.

Laurent, A. (1983) 'The cultural diversity of Western conceptions of management', *International Studies of Management and Organization*, 13, 1–2: 75–96.

Leana, C. and van Buren, H. (1999) 'Organizational social capital and employment practices', *Academy of Management Review*, 24, 3: 538–555.

Lengnick-Hall, C. and Lengnick-Hall, M. (1988) 'Strategic human resource management: A review of the literature and proposed typology', *Academy of Management Review*, 13: 454–470.

Leong, S.M. and Tan, C.T. (1993) 'Managing across borders: an empirical test of the Bartlett and Ghoshal [1989] organizational typology', *Journal of International Business Studies*, 24, 3: 449–464.

Marginson, P. and Sisson, K. (2002) 'Coordinated bargaining – a process for our times?', *British Journal of Industrial Relations*, 40, 2: 197–220.

Mayrhofer, W. and Brewster, C. (1996) 'In praise of ethnocentricity: expatriate policies in European multinationals', *International Executive*, 36, 6: 749–778.

Mendenhall, M., Dunbar, E. and Oddou, G. (1989) 'Expatriate selection, training and career pathing: a review and critique', *Human Resource Management*, 26, fall: 331–345.

Milkman. R. (1991) *Japan's California factories: Labor relations and economic globalization.* Berkeley, CA.: Institute Industrial Relations, UCLA.

Milliman, J.F. and Von Glinow, M.A. (1990). 'A life cycle approach to strategic international human resource management in MNCs', *Research in Personnel and Human Resources Management*, Supp. 2: 21–35.

Milliman, J.M., Von Glinow, A. and Nathan, M. (1991) 'Organizational life cycles and strategic international human resource management in multinational companies: Implications for congruence theory', *Academy of Management Review*, 16, 2: 318–339.

Mintzberg, H. and Waters, J.A. (1989) 'Of strategies, Deliberate and Emergent', in Asch, D. and Bowman, C. *Readings in Strategic Management.* Milton Keynes: Open University and Macmillan.

Moenaert, R.K., Caeldries, F., Commandeur, H.R. and Peelen, E. (1994) 'Managing Technology in the International Firm: an exploratory survey on organisational strategies'. Paper presented at the 20th Annual Conference of the EIBA (December), Warsaw.

665

Morgan, G. (2001) *The Multinational Firm*. Oxford: Oxford University Press.

Morris, J., Wilkinson, B. and Munday, M. (2000) 'Farewell to HRM? Personnel practices in Japanese manufacturing plants in the UK', *International Journal of Human Resource Management*, 11, 6: 1047–1060.

Muller, M. (1998) 'Human Resource and Industrial Relations Practices of UK and US Multinationals in Germany', *International Journal of Human Resource Management*, 9, 4: 732–749.

Muller-Camen, M., Almons, P., Gunnigle, P., Quintanilla, J. and Tempel, A. (2001) 'Between home and host country: multinationals and employment relations in Europe', *Industrial Relations Journal*, 32, 5: 435–448.

Nahapiet, J. and Ghoshal, S. (1998) 'Social capital, intellectual capital, and the organization advantage', *Academy of Management Review*, 23: 243–266.

Nohria, N. and Eccles, R.G. (1992) 'Face-to-face: making network organisations work', in Nohria, N. and Eccles, R.G. (eds) *Networks and Organizations: Structure, form and action*. Boston, MA: Harvard Business School Press.

Nohria, N. and Ghoshal, S. (1997) *The Differentiated Network: Organizing Multinational Companies For Value Creation*. London: Routledge.

Nonaka, I. and Takeuchi, H. (1995) *The knowledge creating company*. New York: Oxford University Press.

OECD (2006) *OECD Factbook 2006: Economic, Environmental and Social Statistics*. Paris: OECD.

Ohmae, K. (1991) *The Borderless World*. London: Macmillan.

Oliver, N. and Wilkinson, B. (1988) *The Japanization of British Industry*. Oxford: Blackwell.

Oliver, N. and Wilkinson, B. (1992) *The Japanization of British Industry*. Oxford: Blackwell.

O'Sullivan, M. (2000) *Contests for Corporate Control: Corporate Governance and Economic Performance in the United States and Germany*. Oxford: Oxford University Press.

Pauly, L. and Reich, S. (1997) 'National Structures and Multinational Corporate Behavior: Enduring Differences in the Age of Globalization', *International Organization*, 51, 1: 1–30.

Perlmutter, H.V. (1969) 'The tortuous evolution of the multinational corporation', *Columbia Journal of World Business*, 8–18.

Pfeffer, J. and Salancik, G.R. (1978) *The External Control of Organizations*. New York: Harper and Row.

Polanyi, M. (1962) *Personal Knowledge*. Chicago: University of Chicago Press.

Polanyi, M. (1966) *The Tacit Dimension*. Garden City, NY: Doubleday.

Porter, M. (1990) *The Competitive Advantage of Nations* (with a new introduction). Basingstoke: Macmillan.

Prahalad, C.K. and Doz, Y. (1987) *The Multinational Mission: Balancing Local Demands and Global Vision*. New York: The Free Press.

Quintanilla, J. (1999) 'The configuration of human resource management policies and practices in multinational subsidiaries: the case of European retail banks in Spain'. Unpublished PhD Thesis, University of Warwick.

Reich, R. (1991) *The Work of Nations: Preparing Ourselves for 21st Century Capitalism*. New York: Alfred A. Knopf.

Rosenzweig, P.M. and Nohria N. (1994) 'Influences on Human Resource Management practices in multinational corporations', *Journal of International Business Studies*, second quarter: 229–251.

Rosenzweig, P.M. and Singh, J.V. (1991) 'Organizational environments and the multinational enterprise', *Academy of Management Review*, 16, 2: 304–316.

Roth, K. and Morrison, A.J. (1990) 'An empirical analysis of the integration-responsiveness framework in global industries', *Journal of International Business Studies*, 22, 4: 541–561.

Royle, T. (2000) *Working for McDonald's in Europe*. London: Routledge.

Ruigrok, W. and van Tulder, R. (1995) *The Logic of International Restructuring*. London: Routledge.

Schein, E. (1984) 'The role of the founder in creating organizational culture', *Organizational Dynamics*, summer: 13–28.

Schuler, R. (1992) 'Strategic human resources management: linking the people with the strategic needs of the Business', *Organizational Dynamics*, summer: 18–32.

Schuler, R., Dowling P. and De Cieri, H. (1993) 'An integrative framework of strategic international human resource management', *Journal of Management*, 19, 2: 419–459.

Sparrow, P., Brewster, C. and Harris, H. (2004) *Globalising Human Resource Management*. Routledge: London.

Taylor, S. (2006) 'Emerging motivations for global HRM integration', in Ferner, A., Quintanilla, J. and Sanchez-Runde, C. (eds) *Multinational, Institutions and the Construction of Transnational Practices*. London: Palgrave.

Taylor, S. and Beechler, S. (1993) 'Human resource management integration and adaption in multinational firms', in Prasad, S. and Peterson, R. (eds) *Advances in International Comparative Management*, 8. Greenwich, CT: JAI Press, pp. 155–174.

Taylor, S., Beechler, S. and Napier, N. (1996) 'Toward an integrative model of strategic international human resource management', *Academy of Management Review*, 21, 4: 959–985.

Tregaskis, O., Glover, L. and Ferner, A. (2005) *International HR Networks*. London: CIPD.

Vernon, R. (1996) 'International investment and international trade in the product cycle'. *Quarterly Journal of Economics*, May.

Whitley, R. (1999) *Divergent Capitalisms*. Oxford: Oxford University Press.

Womack, J., Jones, D. and Roos, G. (1990) *The Machine that Changed the World*. New York: Rawson.

Wright, P. and McMahan G. (1992) 'Theoretical perspectives for strategic Human resource management'. *Journal of Management*, 18, 3: 295–320.

 For multiple-choice questions, exercises and annotated weblinks specific to this chapter visit the book's website at **www.pearsoned.co.uk/beardwell**

Global and local: the case of the inoperable HRM strategy

Medical Precision Systems (MPS) is a US-owned company based on the outskirts of Birmingham, Alabama, USA. It has been producing medical precision tools used in surgery since 1972, and has built up a well-respected business in the USA with a turnover of $150 million annually. Its Birmingham plant employs 2000 staff made up of skilled and semi-skilled workers. Most staff are employed in production process work, but a significant number work in research and development and other highly skilled and knowledge-based areas.

There are no unions and the Human Resources Department has consciously followed a policy of best-practice HRM to keep out union influence. There is a an excellent pensions scheme, a successful profit-sharing scheme, and a share options scheme whereby employees can choose to have bonuses in the form of company shares if they have worked at MPS for more than two years. Laying employees off is avoided as much as possible during slack periods in order to retain staff loyalty.

However, a performance management culture is strong at MPS, and there is an astringent appraisal system linked to remuneration and promotion. Target setting for groups and individuals has been strongly implemented for the past 20 years and refined over that time. A total quality management (TQM) programme has been in operation for the past 15 years, and work areas or cells are operated by teams. Under the TQM system groups of ten workers are allowed to elect a leader, who organises feedback sessions and reports to senior production managers. Annual staff opinion surveys are conducted on a range of employment and production issues. Training is taken seriously, and all employees attend sessions to train in teamworking and people skills, as well as sessions and courses of a more technical nature. MPS prides itself on its strong culture, and likes to communicate its values and vision clearly and frequently to the workforce. The mission statement 'MPS – working for the health of America' is printed on all pay packets and slips, and most communication bulletins.

There are excellent canteen and recreational facilities, the employees have a number of sports teams, and social events take place regularly.

Expanding overseas

Since the early 1990s MPS has decided to set up plants overseas, but in doing so is conscious that it needs a fairly educated workforce that can cope with the highly technical nature of the work. In addition, it has recognised that its major markets are in Europe, where it has been exporting since the early 1980s. The MPS board thus decided to open subsidiaries in the UK initially, followed by Sweden and later France.

The UK operation was acquired by taking over a medical engineering company in 1991 near Bath and initially employed 150 people rising to 350 by the end of the decade. The Swedish subsidiary was set up on a greenfield site in a business park on the outskirts of the university city of Uppsala in 1994, employing 50 and then 250 staff by the end of the decade. A new plant was set up in Lyons, France, in 1997 that employs fewer than 200 staff.

In 2001 the MPS HQ in Alabama was revamping its strategy in line with its global developments and commitments. The production and marketing side of the business were doing well, and there had been steady growth in the UK subsidiary in Bath and the Swedish subsidiary at Uppsala. Preliminary reports also indicated that the French subsidiary had enormous potential. However, the Director of Human Resources, Jim Grant, commissioned a full report on the overseas HRM operations as there had been difficulties experienced in HRM. Jim wanted to create an HRM strategy that would complement the new business strategy and at the same time solve the problems in the overseas subsidiaries.

The existing international HRM strategy

Using Perlmutter's typology, MPS's international HRM strategy can only be described as ethnocentric (see Chapter 17). It attempts to exert strong controls over its subsidiaries through the extensive use of expatriate managers in both technical and managerial areas of the business. Its goals in financial and production terms have been set by the parent company, and the local subsidiaries have little say. The feedback mechanisms have been implemented from the USA, backed with training programmes for all employees.

Expatriate managers have been told either to keep the unions out or to ensure that their influence is as minimal as possible. Loyalty schemes such as profit sharing have been introduced, and it is planned that the company share scheme will be introduced in 2002 across all subsidiaries. Annual staff opinion surveys have been implemented, and communication is emphasised as being fluid and as frequent as possible between expatriate managers, host country managers and employees.

TQM programmes have also been introduced, and are run with the teamworking systems and workplace feedback and improvement mechanisms. The strong MPS culture has been effectively reinforced through regular staff bulletins, and local company magazines in the language of the subsidiary company country. The mission statement is widely displayed, and a strong public relations image also supports the company culture.

While many of these initiatives have had success, there has been some reluctance and even opposition to others in the three European subsidiaries. In 2001 Jim Grant carried out a full review, and was able to make the following points in a report to the US HQ board.

HRM overseas in MPS: report by Jim Grant

One of the problems we have faced is the diversity of conditions in the subsidiaries, and the practices we follow in the USA do not always translate well in the local context. These problems concern expatriate managers, industrial relations, management style and the degree of control that subsidiaries believe is being exerted over them. Expatriate managers faced a considerable degree of difficulty when given assignments, particularly in the European subsidiaries. While all the senior managers in France and Sweden spoke excellent English, there were considerable communication barriers between the American expatriates and their subsidiary workforces. Common problems were incomprehension of each other's culture and working practices.

Expatriate manager feedback, Bath, UK

Joe Mendes, who runs the English operation, also commented that, despite the common language, he didn't always understand the British mentality. There was considerable resentment when it was suggested that weekend working be brought in to fulfil some emergency orders.

He also said the plant we inherited was highly unionised, with several technical and other unions operating. When he suggested having one union for negotiating purposes there was nearly a mass walk-out, and union officials became very obstructive. Another problem was the performance management system, which met with considerable initial difficulties in being set up. The unions and many employees felt the targets were too harsh and divisive, and they also felt that they had little control over them.

Expatriate manager feedback, Lyons, France

Andy Smith, who runs the French operation, had no problems in regard to the unions, as it was a greenfield site and it was relatively easy to exclude unions by recruiting new staff, although some of the technical staff had union membership. The major problem concerned management style. While there were some initial difficulties in setting up the performance management system, the main problem was with the feedback mechanisms. The French workforce could not see the point of the cellular feedback mechanisms, and preferred to have a line manager with an authoritative air, technically proficient and capable of directing the workforce towards work tasks.

Andy also had problems in getting the workforce to work extra hours, and he felt there were excessive holidays in France. 'Every time production seemed to be up running perfectly, another saint's day holiday would put out our schedule,' he said.

A works council was set up in accordance with French law, but in the eyes of most of the French workforce did not operate very effectively.

Expatriate manager feedback, Uppsala, Sweden

Gary Alder, head of the Swedish operation, reported that despite the subsidiary being a greenfield site start-up operation the workforce very soon joined unions, and by the end of the first year over 65 per cent of employees were union members. As in France and the UK, the Swedish workforce baulked at the targets set under the performance management scheme. However, there was considerable enthusiasm for the feedback mechanisms in the cellular manufacturing processes, and many interesting ideas and innovations emerged as a result of this.

The Swedes, like the French and the British, were not impressed by the attempts by American management to engender a 'gung ho' culture through culture training and attitudinal orientation sessions. Most employees in all three countries paid lip service to these sessions.

Under Swedish and EU law a works council had to be set up for management and employees, but the Americans, although having to conform to European and national laws, resented these meetings and tended to treat them with less than enthusiasm. They appeared in the eyes of one Swedish union organiser at times to be almost non-cooperative.

The general conclusion that Jim drew was that some HRM policies had been more successful than others.

Questions

1 Given the report, what would you advise Jim to recommend to the board in drawing up a new international HRM strategy?

2 How could this strategy be locally responsive and yet global in its scope?

Glossary of terms and abbreviations

Advisory, Conciliation and Arbitration Service (ACAS) Founded in 1975, aims to improve employment relations. It provides information, advice and training and will work with employers and employees to solve problems.

ACFTU The All China Federation of Trade Unions.

Added value Technically the difference between the value of a firm's inputs and its outputs; the additional value is added through the deployment and efforts of the firm's resources. Can be defined as FVA (financial value added), CVA (customer value added) and PVA (people value added).

AEL Accreditation of Experiential Learning.

Alienation Marx suggests it is a condition in which a worker loses power to control the performance, processes and product of his/her labour. Thus the very worker becomes a thing rather than a human being, in which state they experience powerlessness, meaninglessness, isolation and self-estrangement.

Androgogy 'The art and science of helping adults learn' (Knowles *et al.*, 1984: 60).

Annualised hours contract Relatively novel form of employment contract that offers management, and sometimes workers, a considerable degree of flexibility. The hours that an employee works can be altered within a very short time frame within a day, a week, or even a month. So long as the total hours worked do not exceed the contractually fixed annual amount an employee can be asked and expected to work from 0 up to anything in excess of 80 hours in any one week.

APL Accreditation of Prior Learning.

Appraisal The process through which an assessment is made of an employee by another person using quantitative and/or qualitative assessments.

Appraisal (360 degree) A system of appraisal which seeks feedback from 'all directions' – superiors, subordinates, peers and customers.

Attitude survey Survey, usually conducted by questionnaire, to elicit employees' opinions about issues to do with their work and the organisation.

Balanced scorecard An integrated framework for balancing shareholder and strategic goals, and extending these balanced performance measures down the organisation.

Best-fit Models of HRM that focus on alignment between HRM and business strategy and the external context of the firm. Tend to link or 'fit' generic type business strategies to generic HRM strategies.

Best-practice A 'set' or number of human resource practices that have the potential to enhance organisational performance when implemented. Usually categorised as 'high commitment', 'high involvement' or 'high performance'.

BMA British Medical Association.

Broadbanding Pay systems which have a wide range of possible pay levels within them. Unlike traditional narrow systems, there is normally a high degree of overlap across the grades.

BS 5750 British standard of quality, originally applied to the manufacture of products but now also being used to 'measure' quality of service. Often used in employee involvement (EI) as a way of getting employees to self-check their quality of work against a standardised norm.

BTEC Business and Technology Education Council.

Bundles A coherent combination of human resource practices that are horizontally integrated.

Bushido Japanese term meaning 'the way of the warrior'.

Business process re-engineering (BPR) System that aims to improve performance by redesigning the processes through which an organisation operates, maximising their value-added content and minimising everything else (Peppard and Rowland, 1995: 20).

Career 'The evolving sequence of a person's work experiences over time' (Arthur *et al.*, 1989: 8); 'the individual's development in learning and work throughout life' (Collin and Watts, 1996: 393).

CATS Credit Accumulation and Transfer Scheme.

Causal ambiguity The cause or source of an organisation's competitive advantage is ambiguous or unclear, particularly to the organisation's competitors.

CBI Confederation of British Industry. Powerful institution set up in 1965 to promote and represent the interests of British industry. Financed by subscription and made up of employers' associations, national business associations and over 10,000 affiliated companies. Works to advise and negotiate with the government and the Trades Union Congress.

CCT Compulsory competitive tendering.

CEE Central and Eastern European states formerly of the Soviet system including Russia, Bulgaria, Czech Republic, East Germany (GDR), Estonia, Hungary, Latvia, Lithuania, Poland, Romania, Slovakia, Slovenia.

CEEP European Centre of Public Enterprises.

Chaebols The large, family-owned conglomerates that dominate Korea's economy. The five leading *chaebols* prior to the collapse of Daewoo were Hyundai, Samsung, Daewoo, Lucky Goldstar and the SK group.

Chaos and complexity theories In contrast to traditional science, these more recent theories draw attention to the uncertainty, non-linearity and unpredictability that result from the interrelatedness and interdependence of the elements of the universe.

CIPD Chartered Institute of Personnel and Development – the professional organisation for human resource and personnel managers and those in related fields such as training and development. Website: www.cipd.org.uk.

Closed system System that does not interact with other subsystems or its environment.

COHSE Confederation of Health Service Employees.

Collective bargaining Process utilised by trade unions, as the representatives of employees, and management, as the representatives of employers, to establish the terms and conditions under which labour will be employed.

Competence 'The ability to perform the activities within an occupational area to the levels of performance expected in employment' (Training Commission, 1988).

Competences Behavioural repertoires that people input to a job, role or organisation context, and which employees need to bring to a role to perform to the required level (see also **Core competences**).

Competency-based pay An approach to reward based on the attainment of skills or talents by individuals in relation to a specific task at a certain standard.

Competitive advantage The ability of an organisation to add more value for its customers than its rivals, and therefore gain a position of advantage in the marketplace.

Configurational approach An approach that identified the benefits of identifying a set of horizontally integrated HR practices that were aligned to the business strategy, thus fitting the internal and external context of the business.

Constructivism Concerned with individual experience and emphasises the individual's cognitive processes.

Contingent pay Elements of the reward package which are contingent on other events (performance, merit, attendance) and are awarded at the discretion of the management.

Cooperatives Organisations and companies that are collectively owned either by their customers or by their employees.

Core competences Distinctive skills and knowledge, related to product, service or technology, that can be used to gain competitive advantage.

Cost minimisation This refers to a managerial approach that perceives human resources as costs to be controlled as tightly as possible. HR practices are likely to include low wages, minimal training, close supervision and no employee voice mechanisms.

CPSA Civil and Public Servants Association.

Culture The prevailing pattern of values, attitudes, beliefs, assumptions, norms and sentiments.

Danwei Central to the state-owned enterprises in China were work units or *danweis*.

DES Department of Education and Science, now renamed the Department for Education and Skills (DfES).

Deskilling The attempt by management to appropriate and monopolise workers' knowledge of production in an effort to control the labour process. To classify, tabulate, and reduce this knowledge to rules, laws and formulae, which are then allocated to workers on a daily basis.

DETR Department of the Environment, Transport and the Regions.

Development The process of becoming increasingly complex, more elaborate and differentiated, by virtue of learning and maturation, resulting in new ways of acting and responding to the environment.

Development centres Normally used for the selection of managers. They utilise a range of intensive psychological tests and simulations to assess management potential.

DfEE Department for Education and Employment, now renamed the Department for Education and Skills (DfES).

Discourse The shared language, metaphors, stories that give members of a group their particular way of interpreting reality.

Downsizing Possibly the simplest explanation is given by Heery and Noon (2001: 90) as 'getting rid of employees'. A modern 'buzzword' used to indicate the reduction of employment within organisations.

Double-loop learning *See* single-loop learning.

Dual system German system of vocational training for apprentices, which combines off-the-job training at vocational colleges with on-the-job training under the tutelage of *meister* (skilled craft) workers.

EC European Community. The term superseded the EEC after the SEM, as describing more than purely economic union. Since 1992 has been renamed European Union (see below).

ECSC European Coal and Steel Community, founded in 1952.

EEC European Economic Community. A term used to describe the Common Market after the Treaty of Rome 1957.

Efficiency The sound management of resources within a business in order to *maximise* the return on investment.

Efficiency wages Wages paid above the market rate to attract better workers, induce more effort and reduce turnover and training costs.

Effectiveness The ability of an organisation to meet the demands and expectations of its various stakeholders, albeit some more than others.

EI Employee involvement; a term to describe the wide variety of schemes in which employees can be involved in their work situation.

e-Learning Use of new technology such as e-mail, the internet, intranets and computer software packages to facilitate learning for employees.

Emergent Strategies which emerge over time, sometimes with an element of trial and error. Some emergent strategies are incremental changes with embedded learning, others may be adaptive in response to external environmental changes.

Employability The acquisition and updating of skills, experience, reputation – the investment in human capital – to ensure that the individual remains employable, and not dependent upon a particular organisation.

Empowerment Recent term that encompasses EI (employee involvement) initiatives to encourage the workforce to have direct individual and collective control over their work processes, taking responsibility for improved customer service to both internal and external customers. Generally confined to workplace-level issues and concerns.

EMU European Monetary Union.

Enterprise unions Japanese concept of employee unions associated with only one enterprise and the only one recognised by the company. One of the 'three pillars' of the Japanese employment system.

Epistemology The assumptions made about the world which form the basis for knowledge.

EPU European political union.

ESOPS Employee share option scheme, whereby employees are allowed to purchase company shares or are given them as part of a bonus.

ET Employment Training.

ETUC European Trade Union Confederation.

EU European Union, so named in 1992 (formerly EC).

Exit policy Policy/procedures that facilitate prompt and orderly recovery or removal of failing institutions through timely and corrective action. There were restrictions placed on closure and retrenchment in view of the social costs and their political ramifications that are now being eased.

Factor of production An input into the production process. Factors of production were traditionally classified as *land* (raw materials), *capital* (buildings, equipment, machinery) and *labour*. Labour is usually seen as a variable factor of production because labour inputs can be varied quite easily at short notice, unlike capital, the amount of which cannot be varied easily in the short run. Internalising the employment relationship transforms labour into a *quasi-fixed factor of production* because it restricts the employer's freedom to cut jobs at short notice.

FIEs Foreign invested enterprises.

Firm-specific skills Skills that can be used in only one or a few particular organisations.

Fit The level of integration between an organisation's business strategy and its human resource policies and practices. 'Fit' tends to imply a top-down relationship between the strategy makers and the strategy implementers.

FKTU Federation of Korean Trade Unions.

Forked lightning, the Mae West Language and concepts used by city financiers working on the international currency and commodity markets. Used to describe the patterns formed by fluctuating price movements as they get represented on dealers' screens.

Functional flexibility The ability of management to redeploy workers across tasks. Functional flexibility can be horizontal – redeployment across tasks at the same level of skill, and/or vertical – the ability to perform tasks at different (higher) levels of skill.

GDP Gross domestic product.

GNVQs General National Vocational Qualifications.

Guanxi Chinese term that refers to the concept of drawing on connections or networks to secure favours in personal or business relations.

Hard HRM A view of HRM that identifies employees as a cost to be minimised, and tends to focus on 'flexibility techniques' and limited investment in learning and development (see also **Soft HRM**).

Hegemony The imposition upon others of a powerful group's interpretation of reality.

High-commitment management Used to describe a set of HR practices aimed at enhancing the commitment, quality and flexibility of employees.

High-performance work practices A term that gained currency in the 1990s that sought to link bundles of HR practices with outcomes in terms of increased employee commitment and performance which in turn enhances the firm's sustained competitive advantage, efficiency and profitability.

HMSO Her Majesty's Stationery Office. Publishers of parliamentary proceedings, official government documents and reports. Privatised in 1996 and now known as The Stationery Office (TSO).

Holistic Treatment of organisations, situations, problems as totalities or wholes as opposed to a specific, reductionist approach.

Horizontal integration Level of alignment across and within functions, such that all functional policies and practices are integrated and congruent with one another.

HRD Human resource development.

Human capital The knowledge, skill and attitudes, the intangible contributions to high performance, that make employees assets to the organisation.

Human relations Associated with the pioneering work of Roethlisberger and Dickson, Elton Mayo and others, who studied the importance of community and collective values in work organisations. These studies first identified that management needed to attend to the 'social needs' of employees.

Ideology The set of ideas and beliefs that underpins interpretations of reality.

IIP Investors in People.

ILO International Labour Organization.

IMS The Institute of Manpower Studies. Located at the University of Sussex.

Institutional vacuum/representation gap Situation in which collective bargaining is no longer the dominant form of establishing terms and conditions of employment, but no recognisable or regulated channel of employee representation or employee voice has emerged to replace it.

Intellectual capital The hidden value, and capital, tied up in an organisation's people (knowledge, skills and competencies), which can be a key source of competitive advantage and differentiate it from its competitors.

IPD Institute of Personnel and Development; see also **CIPD**.

IRDAC Industrial Research and Development Advisory Committee of the Commission of the European Communities.

IRS Industrial Relations Services. A data gathering and publications bureau that collects and analyses movement in key variables of importance to the study and practice of industrial relations.

ITBs Industrial Training Boards. Set up in 1964 to monitor training in various sectors of the economy. Most were abolished in 1981, but a few still survive.

JCC Joint consultative committee; body made up of employee representatives and management, which meets regularly to discuss issues of common interest.

Job enlargement Related to job rotation, whereby a job is made bigger by the introduction of new tasks. This gives greater variety in job content and thereby helps to relieve monotony in repetitive jobs such as assembly line working.

Job enrichment Adds to a cycle of work not only a variety of tasks but increased responsibility to workers. Most associated with autonomous work groups introduced into Volvo's Kalmar plant in Sweden in the 1970s.

Job rotation Originally introduced in the 1970s for members of a team to exchange jobs to enliven work interest, but also used recently to promote wider skills experience and flexibility among employees.

JV Joint venture.

KCTU Korean Confederation of Trade Unions.

Knowledge-based age Reflects the move to a global environment, where tacit and explicit knowledge becomes a key source of competitive advantage for organisations.

Knowledge-based organisation One that manages the generation of new knowledge through learning, capturing knowledge and experience, sharing, collaborating and communicating, organising information and using and building on what is known.

Labour process The application of human labour to raw materials in the production of goods and services that are later sold on the free market. Labour is paid a wage for its contribution, but capital must ensure that it secures value added over and above what it is paying for. Some call this efficiency. Others prefer the term 'exploitation'.

Learning Complex cognitive, physical, and affective process that results in the capacity for changed performance.

Learning cycle Learning seen as a process having different identifiable phases. Effective learning may be facilitated if methods appropriate to the various phases are used.

Learning style Individuals differ in their approaches to learning, and prefer one mode of learning, or phase of the learning cycle, to others.

Learning organisation (LO) 'A Learning Company is an organisation that facilitates the learning of all its members and consciously transforms itself and its context' (Pedler *et al.*, 1997: 3).

LECs Local Enterprise Companies. Scottish equivalent of TECs. There are 22 in existence. (*See* TECs.)

Leverage The exploitation by an organisation of its resources to their full extent. Often linked to the notion of stretching resources.

Licence-quota regime The practice in a state regulated economy where a business has to obtain permission to manufacture (licence) as well as the quantity to produce (quota) from the licensing authority (state) before commencing production.

Lifetime employment Japanese concept whereby in large corporations employees are guaranteed a job for life in exchange for loyalty to the organisation. One of the 'three pillars' of the Japanese employment system.

LMS Local management of schools.

LSC Learning and Skills Council.

Maastricht Protocol Part of the Maastricht Treaty dealing with the Social Chapter (Social Charter), allowing Britain to sign the treaty without signing the Maastricht Protocol or Social Chapter.

Maastricht Treaty The content was agreed at a meeting at Maastricht in the Netherlands and signed in a watered-down form in Edinburgh in 1992. It was rejected and then accepted by the voters of Denmark in two referendums. It concerns extending aspects of European political union (EPU) and European and Monetary Union (EMU).

Management gurus Phenomenon of the 1980s, when academics, consultants and business practitioners began to enjoy celebrity status as specialists on the diagnosis of management problems and the development of 'business solutions'. Includes people such as Tom Peters, Rosabeth Moss Kanter, John Harvey Jones and M.C. Robert Beeston.

McDonaldisation The reduction of organisation to simple, repetitive, and predictable work processes that make the labour process more amenable to standardised calculation and control.

MCI (Management Charter Initiative) Employer-led initiative with the aim of developing recognised standards in management practice.

Measured day work MDW is a system within which pay is fixed against specific levels of performance during the 'day' rather than by the hourly performance or piece-rates.

Mentor More experienced person who guides, encourages and supports a younger or less experienced person.

MSC Manpower Services Commission. Previously had responsibility for training but was abolished in 1988.

Mission statement A statement setting out the main purpose of the business.

NACETT National Advisory Council for Education and Training Targets now incorporated into the Learning and Skills Councils.

NALGO National and Local Government Officers Association.

NASUWT National Association of School Masters/ Union of Women Teachers.

National curriculum Obligatory subjects of the UK's school system, introduced via the Education Reform Act 1989.

National minimum wage Introduced by the National Minimum Wage Act 1998, this sets the minimum rate of reward any worker can receive on an hourly basis. The scale is age related and linked to inflation through an annual upgrade.

NATO North Atlantic Treaty Organization. Western defensive alliance set up originally in 1949 to promote economic and military cooperation among its members. The original members were Belgium, Britain, Canada, France, Italy, Norway, Portugal and the Netherlands. Greece and Turkey joined in 1952, and the former West Germany in 1955.

NCU National Communications Union.

NCVQ (National Council for Vocational Qualifications) Government-backed initiative to establish a national system for the recognition of vocational qualifications.

Nemawashi Japanese term for consensus.

NHS National Health Service.

Nenko Japanese term meaning seniority and ability. One of the 'three pillars' of the Japanese employment system.

Networking Interacting for mutual benefit, usually on an informal basis, with individuals and groups internal and external to the organisation.

New Deal Government initiative that provides training for 18–24-year-olds who have been out of work for more than six months, and 25-year-olds and over who have been unemployed for longer than two years.

New Deal in America Programme of economic and social reconstruction initiated by President F.D. Roosevelt in 1933 that aimed to lift the USA out of the Great Depression that hit the country in 1929.

Non-union firms Organisations which do not recognise trade unions for collective bargaining purposes; this may be throughout the organisation or at plant or business unit level. So, for example, IBM, frequently quoted as an example of a soft-HRM non-union firm, does, in fact, recognise unions in Germany, as does McDonald's, another organisation strongly associated with an anti-union stance.

NSTF National Skills Task Force.

NUCPS National Union of Civil and Public Servants.

Numerical flexibility The ability of management to vary headcount in response to changes in demand.

NUPE National Union of Public Employees.

NUT National Union of Teachers.

NVQs National Vocational Qualifications. An attempt to harmonise all VET qualifications within the UK by attributing five levels to all qualifications, from level 1, the lowest, to level 5, the highest.

OMC Open Method of Coordination is an alternative to previous attempts at harmonising legislative forms and procedures within the European Union. In place of substantive legislation on specific issues, strategic objectives and operational guidelines are set for member states and monitoring procedures put in place to assess their performance.

Open system System that is connected to and interacts with other subsystems and its environment.

OSC Occupational Standards Council.

Paired comparisons A system of appraisal which seeks to assess the performance of pairs of individuals, until each employee has been judged in relation to each other.

Paradigm A well-developed, and often widely held, set of associated assumptions that frames the interpretation of reality. When these assumptions are undermined by new knowledge or events, a 'paradigm shift' occurs as the old gives way (often gradually and painfully) to a new paradigm.

Payment by results Reward systems under which worker output or performance determines elements of the package.

Performance-related pay Payment systems which in some way relate reward to either organisational or individual performance. Often used as a way to motivate white-collar workers, usually based on a developed appraisal system.

PFI Private Finance Initiative.

Phenomenology Concerned with understanding the individual's conscious experience. It takes a holistic approach and acknowledges the significance of subjectivity.

Pluralism Theoretical analysis of the employment relationship that recognises inequality between capital and labour where each of the interest groups has some conflicting and some common aims. To address these issues, pluralists argue that employees should be facilitated to act collectively, usually as a trade union, to redress such imbalances. Management, as the representatives of employers, should engage in collective bargaining with trade unions to establish consensual agreements on issues of conflict and commonality.

Positivism The orthodox approach to the understanding of reality, and the basis for scientific method.

Post-Fordism A claimed epochal shift in manufacturing that sees a move away from mass production assembly lines and the development of flexible systems that empower and reskill line workers. Associated with the move towards niche products and volatile consumer demand.

Postmodernism A term used (often loosely) to denote various disjunctions from, fragmentations in, or challenges to previously common understandings of knowledge and social life.

PRB Pay review body.

Predetermined motion time systems A member of the time-rate pay systems family under which rewards are calculated based on time and piece. As a standard form of incentive bonus scheme, PDMT schemes rewards are set using the pseudo-scientific measurement of activity.

Profit sharing Scheme whereby employees are given a bonus or payment based on a company's profits.

Private Finance Initiative Where the government contracts out projects such as prison management, hospital building, road construction etc. to the private sector, then leases back the service over an extended period of time.

Psychological contract The notion that an individual has a range of expectations about their employing organisation and the organisation has expectations of them.

Psychological (psychometric) testing Specialised tests used for selection or assessing potential. Usually in the form of questionnaires. They construct a personality profile of the candidate.

Quality circle (QC) Group made up of 6–10 employees, with regular meetings held weekly or fortnightly during working time. The principal aim is to identify problems from their own area.

Ranking A method of assessing and ordering individual performance using a predetermined scale.

Rating A determined measure or scale against which an individual's performance is measured.

Reification The conceptualisation and treatment of a person or abstraction as though they were things.

Resource-based view Strategy creation built around the further exploitation of core competencies and strategic capabilities.

RCN Royal College of Nursing.

Rhetoric The often subtle and unacknowledged use of language to 'persuade, influence or manipulate'.

Rightsizing See Downsizing.

Ringi Japanese form of employee involvement.

SCOTVEC Scottish Vocational Education Council.

SEA Single European Act 1987. Proposed the creation of a single European market for trade on 31 December 1992.

SEDB Singapore Economic Development Board.

SEM Single European market, also known as '1992' owing to the date it was set up. See SEA.

Single-loop learning Detection and correction of deviances in performance from established (organisational or other) norms. Double-loop learning is the questioning of those very norms that define effective performance. (Compare efficiency and effectiveness.)

Single-table bargaining Arrangement under which unions on a multi-union site develop a mutually agreed bargaining agenda, which is then negotiated jointly with management.

Single-union deal Arrangement under which one trade union operates to represent all employees within an organisation; this is usually a preferred union sponsored by management.

Social Chapter Another name for the Social Charter, which emerged from the Maastricht meeting in 1989.

Social Charter A programme to implement the 'social dimension' of the single market, affording rights and protection to employees.

Social complexity The complex interpersonal relationships that exist within organisations, within and between teams and individuals.

Social constructionism Holds that an objective reality is not directly knowable. The reality we do know is socially constructed through language, discourse and social interaction.

Social partnership Process whereby employers and employees establish a framework of rights based upon minimum standards in employment, flexibility, security, information sharing and cooperation between management and employees' representatives.

Social relations in production The patterns and dynamics produced and reproduced in action by individuals and collectives employed in the labour process.

Sociotechnical The structuring or integration of human activities and subsystems with technological subsystems.

SOE State-owned enterprise.

Soft HRM A view of HRM that recognises employees as a resource worth investing in, and tends to focus on high-commitment/high-involvement human resource practices. See also **Hard HRM**.

Stakeholders Any individual or group capable of affecting or being affected by the performance and actions of the organisation.

Stakeholder society One in which individuals recognise that only by making a positive contribution to contemporary society can they expect a positive outcome from society.

Stakeholders in social partnership Those groups with an interest in promoting strong social partnerships at work, i.e. the state, employers and their organisations, employees and their organisations.

Strategic management The process by which an organisation establishes its objectives, formulates strategies to meet these objectives, implements actions and measures and monitors performance.

Suggestion scheme (box) Arrangement whereby employees are encouraged to put forward their ideas for improving efficiency, safety or working conditions. Payment or reward is often given related to the value of the suggestion.

Supervisory boards Part of the dual management board structure required by law in all German enterprises listed on the German stock exchange. Day-to-day management is the responsibility of the management board, which is accountable to the supervisory board. The supervisory board appoints, overseas and advises the management board. It also participates directly in key strategic decisions. Supervisory boards are elected by shareholders and where firms employ more than 500 employees in Germany, membership of the board must also include employee representatives. Employee representatives make up one-third of the supervisory board membership in companies having 500–2000 employees and half of the membership in companies having over 2000 employees.

Sustainable competitive advantage The ability of an organisation to add more value than its rivals in order to gain advantage and maintain that advantage over time.

SVQs Scottish Vocational Qualifications.

Synergy Added value or additional benefit that accrues from cooperation between team members, or departments, such that the results are greater than the sum of all the individual parts.

System Assembly of parts, objects or attributes interrelating and interacting in an organised way.

Systemic Thinking about and perceiving situations, problems and difficulties as systems.

Tacit knowledge Knowledge that is never explicitly taught, often not verbalised, but is acquired through doing and expressed in know-how.

Team briefing Regular meeting of groups of between 4 and 15 people based round a common production or service area. Meetings are usually led by a manager or supervisor and last for no more than 30 minutes, during which information is imparted, often with time left for questions from employees.

TECs Training and Enterprise Councils. These operated in England and Wales and were made up of local employers and elected local people, to create local training initiatives in response to local skill needs. Their function was taken over in 2002 by Learning and Skills Councils.

Theory 'X' & 'Y' Based on McGregor's thesis on managerial change. Two contrasting views of people and work. Theory X sees people as inherently lazy, unambitious and avoiding of responsibility. Theory Y sees work as natural as rest or play and being capable of providing self-fulfilment and a sense of achievement for those involved.

Thinking performer A set of competencies that should guide CIPD members (Chartered Institute of Personnel and Development) through their careers.

TQM Total quality management, an all-pervasive system of management-controlled EI based on the concept of quality throughout the organisation in terms of product and service, whereby groups of workers are each encouraged to perceive each other (and other departments) as internal customers. This ensures the provision of quality products and services to external customers.

Transferable skills Skills that can be used anywhere in the economy.

Tripartitism Systems of industrial relations whereby the state, employers associations and trade unions oversee and govern labour market initiatives and related policies, e.g. wage levels and increases.

TUC Trades Union Congress.

TUPE Transfer of Undertakings (Protection of Employment) Regulations.

UNICE Union of Industrial and Employers Confederations of Europe.

Unison Public service union formed following merger of COHSE, NALGO and NUPE.

Unitarism Theoretical analysis of the employment relationship based on managerial prerogative, valuing labour individually according to market assessments, and which views organised resistance to management authority as pathological.

Value chain A framework, for identifying where value is added and where costs are incurred.

VDU Visual display unit – a computer screen, for example. That component of a computer that transmits often dangerous levels of radiation.

VET Vocational education and training.

Vertical Integration In terms of SHRM, the level of alignment between an organisation's business strategy and its HR strategy, policies and practices.

Vision (statement) A desired future state, or an attempt by an organisation to articulate that desired future state.

VQs Vocational qualifications.

Wa Japanese term for harmony.

Wage drift A gradual and uneven increase in wages in certain sectors of the economy resulting from variable, informal bargaining activities reflecting areas of localised union strength. Such increases are supplementary to any formally agreed wages formula. If allowed to grow unchecked, this practice can lead to inflationary measures.

Weberian bureaucracy Associated with the research and writing of the sociologist Max Weber (1864–1920), who observed and studied the growth of vast organisational bureaucracies. Notable for the extreme degree of functional specialisation, formal rules and procedures, and long lines of command and authority. Staffed by professional, full-time, salaried employees who do not own the resources and facilities with which they work.

Works councils Committees made up either solely of workers or of joint representatives of workers, management and shareholders, which meet, usually at company level, to discuss a variety of issues relating to workforce matters and sometimes general, wider-ranging organisational issues. Usually supported by legislation, which compels organisations to set them up.

YOP Youth Opportunities Programme. A programme initially set up in 1978 and revived in 1983 to help unemployed youth to gain employment skills.

YT Youth Training (formerly Youth Training Service, YTS).

Zaibatsu Large, diversified Japanese business groups, which rose to prominence in the early twentieth century, such as Mitsubishi, Mitsui and Sumitomo.

References

Arthur, M.B., Hall, D.T. and Lawrence, B.S. (eds) (1989) *Handbook of Career Theory*. Cambridge: Cambridge University Press.

Collin, A. and Watts, A.G. (1996) 'The death and transfiguration of career: and of career guidance?', *British Journal of Guidance and Counselling*, 24, 3: 385–398.

Heery, A. and Noon, M. (2001) *Dictionary of Human Resource Management*. Oxford: Oxford University Press.

Knowles, M.S. and Associates (1984) *Androgogy in Action*. San Francisco, Calif.: Jossey-Bass.

Pedler, M., Burgoyne, J. and Boydell, T. (1997) *The Learning Company: A Strategy for Sustainable Development*. London: McGraw-Hill.

Peppard, J. and Rowland, P. (1995) *The Essence of Business Process Re-engineering*. Hemel Hempstead: Prentice Hall.

Training Commission (1988) *Classifying the Components of Managing Competencies*. Sheffield: Training Commission.

Index